Nineteenth-Century Literature Criticism

Topics Volume

Guide to Gale Literary Criticism Series

For criticism on	Consult these Gale series
Authors now living or who died after December 31, 1999	*CONTEMPORARY LITERARY CRITICISM (CLC)*
Authors who died between 1900 and 1999	*TWENTIETH-CENTURY LITERARY CRITICISM (TCLC)*
Authors who died between 1800 and 1899	*NINETEENTH-CENTURY LITERATURE CRITICISM (NCLC)*
Authors who died between 1400 and 1799	*LITERATURE CRITICISM FROM 1400 TO 1800 (LC)* *SHAKESPEAREAN CRITICISM (SC)*
Authors who died before 1400	*CLASSICAL AND MEDIEVAL LITERATURE CRITICISM (CMLC)*
Authors of books for children and young adults	*CHILDREN'S LITERATURE REVIEW (CLR)*
Dramatists	*DRAMA CRITICISM (DC)*
Poets	*POETRY CRITICISM (PC)*
Short story writers	*SHORT STORY CRITICISM (SSC)*
Literary topics and movements	*HARLEM RENAISSANCE: A GALE CRITICAL COMPANION (HR)* *THE BEAT GENERATION: A GALE CRITICAL COMPANION (BG)* *FEMINISM IN LITERATURE: A GALE CRITICAL COMPANION (FL)* *GOTHIC LITERATURE: A GALE CRITICAL COMPANION (GL)*
Asian American writers of the last two hundred years	*ASIAN AMERICAN LITERATURE (AAL)*
Black writers of the past two hundred years	*BLACK LITERATURE CRITICISM (BLC)* *BLACK LITERATURE CRITICISM SUPPLEMENT (BLCS)* *BLACK LITERATURE CRITICISM: CLASSIC AND EMERGING AUTHORS SINCE 1950 (BLC-2)*
Hispanic writers of the late nineteenth and twentieth centuries	*HISPANIC LITERATURE CRITICISM (HLC)* *HISPANIC LITERATURE CRITICISM SUPPLEMENT (HLCS)*
Native North American writers and orators of the eighteenth, nineteenth, and twentieth centuries	*NATIVE NORTH AMERICAN LITERATURE (NNAL)*
Major authors from the Renaissance to the present	*WORLD LITERATURE CRITICISM, 1500 TO THE PRESENT (WLC)* *WORLD LITERATURE CRITICISM SUPPLEMENT (WLCS)*

ISSN 0732-1864

Volume 220

Nineteenth-Century Literature Criticism

Topics Volume

Criticism of Various
Topics in Nineteenth-Century Literature,
including Literary and Critical Movements,
Prominent Themes and Genres, Anniversary
Celebrations, and Surveys of National Literatures

Kathy D. Darrow
Project Editor

GALE
CENGAGE Learning

Detroit • New York • San Francisco • New Haven, Conn • Waterville, Maine • London

Nineteenth-Century Literature Criticism, Vol. 220

Project Editor: Kathy Darrow

Editorial: Dana Barnes, Elizabeth Cranston, Kristen Dorsch, Jeffrey W. Hunter, Jelena O. Krstović, Michelle Lee, Thomas J. Schoenberg, Lawrence J. Trudeau

Content Conversion: Katrina D. Coach, Gwen Tucker

Rights and Acquisitions: Sara Crane, Barb McNeil, Mardell Glinski Schultz

Composition and Electronic Capture: Gary Oudersluys

Manufacturing: Cynde Lentz

Product Manager: Janet Witalec

For product information and technology assistance, contact us at
Gale Customer Support, 1-800-877-4253.
For permission to use material from this text or product,
submit all requests online at **www.cengage.com/permissions.**
Further permissions questions can be emailed to
permissionrequest@cengage.com

Gale
27500 Drake Rd.
Farmington Hills, MI, 48331-3535

LIBRARY OF CONGRESS CATALOG CARD NUMBER 84-643008

ISBN-13: 978-1-4144-3854-2
ISBN-10: 1-4144-3854-0

ISSN 0732-1864

Printed in the United States of America
1 2 3 4 5 6 7 13 12 11 10 09

Contents

Preface vii

Acknowledgments xi

Literary Criticism Series Advisory Board xiii

Preface

Since its inception in 1981, *Nineteenth-Century Literature Criticism* (*NCLC*) has been a valuable resource for students and librarians seeking critical commentary on writers of this transitional period in world history. Designated an "Outstanding Reference Source" by the American Library Association with the publication of is first volume, *NCLC* has since been purchased by over 6,000 school, public, and university libraries. The series has covered more than 500 authors representing 38 nationalities and over 28,000 titles. No other reference source has surveyed the critical reaction to nineteenth-century authors and literature as thoroughly as *NCLC*.

Scope of the Series

NCLC is designed to introduce students and advanced readers to the authors of the nineteenth century and to the most significant interpretations of these authors' works. The great poets, novelists, short story writers, playwrights, and philosophers of this period are frequently studied in high school and college literature courses. By organizing and reprinting commentary written on these authors, *NCLC* helps students develop valuable insight into literary history, promotes a better understanding of the texts, and sparks ideas for papers and assignments. Each entry in *NCLC* presents a comprehensive survey of an author's career or an individual work of literature and provides the user with a multiplicity of interpretations and assessments. Such variety allows students to pursue their own interests; furthermore, it fosters an awareness that literature is dynamic and responsive to many different opinions.

Every fourth volume of *NCLC* is devoted to literary topics that cannot be covered under the author approach used in the rest of the series. Such topics include literary movements, prominent themes in nineteenth-century literature, literary reaction to political and historical events, significant eras in literary history, prominent literary anniversaries, and the literatures of cultures that are often overlooked by English-speaking readers.

NCLC continues the survey of criticism of world literature begun by Gale's *Contemporary Literary Criticism* (*CLC*) and *Twentieth-Century Literary Criticism* (*TCLC*).

Organization of the Book

An *NCLC* entry consists of the following elements:

- The **Author Heading** cites the name under which the author most commonly wrote, followed by birth and death dates. Also located here are any name variations under which an author wrote, including transliterated forms for authors whose native languages use nonroman alphabets. If the author wrote consistently under a pseudonym, the pseudonym will be listed in the author heading and the author's actual name given in parenthesis on the first line of the biographical and critical information. Uncertain birth or death dates are indicated by question marks. Single-work entries are preceded by a heading that consists of the most common form of the title in English translation (if applicable) and the original date of composition.

- The **Introduction** contains background information that introduces the reader to the author, work, or topic that is the subject of the entry.

- The list of **Principal Works** is ordered chronologically by date of first publication and lists the most important works by the author. The genre and publication date of each work is given. In the case of foreign authors whose works have been translated into English, the list will focus primarily on twentieth-century translations, selecting those works most commonly considered the best by critics. Unless otherwise indicated, dramas are dated by first performance, not first publication. Lists of **Representative Works** by different authors appear with topic entries.

- Reprinted **Criticism** is arranged chronologically in each entry to provide a useful perspective on changes in critical evaluation over time. The critic's name and the date of composition or publication of the critical work are given at the beginning of each piece of criticism. Unsigned criticism is preceded by the title of the source in which it appeared. All titles by the author featured in the text are printed in boldface type. Footnotes are reprinted at the end of each essay or excerpt. In the case of excerpted criticism, only those footnotes that pertain to the excerpted texts are included. Criticism in topic entries is arranged chronologically under a variety of subheadings to facilitate the study of different aspects of the topic.

- A complete **Bibliographical Citation** of the original essay or book precedes each piece of criticism.

- Critical essays are prefaced by brief **Annotations** explicating each piece.

- An annotated bibliography of **Further Reading** appears at the end of each entry and suggests resources for additional study. In some cases, significant essays for which the editors could not obtain reprint rights are included here. Boxed material following the further reading list provides references to other biographical and critical sources on the author in series published by Gale.

Indexes

Each volume of *NCLC* contains a **Cumulative Author Index** listing all authors who have appeared in a wide variety of reference sources published by Gale, including *NCLC*. A complete list of these sources is found facing the first page of the Author Index. The index also includes birth and death dates and cross references between pseudonyms and actual names.

A **Cumulative Nationality Index** lists all authors featured in *NCLC* by nationality, followed by the number of the *NCLC* volume in which their entry appears.

A **Cumulative Topic Index** lists the literary themes and topics treated in the series as well as in *Classical and Medieval Literature Criticism, Literature Criticism from 1400 to 1800, Twentieth-Century Literary Criticism,* and the *Contemporary Literary Criticism* Yearbook, which was discontinued in 1998.

An alphabetical **Title Index** accompanies each volume of *NCLC*, with the exception of the Topics volumes. Listings of titles by authors covered in the given volume are followed by the author's name and the corresponding page numbers where the titles are discussed. English translations of foreign titles and variations of titles are cross-referenced to the title under which a work was originally published. Titles of novels, dramas, nonfiction books, and poetry, short story, or essay collections are printed in italics, while individual poems, short stories, and essays are printed in roman type within quotation marks.

In response to numerous suggestions from librarians, Gale also produces an annual paperbound edition of the *NCLC* cumulative title index. This annual cumulation, which alphabetically lists all titles reviewed in the series, is available to all customers. Additional copies of this index are available upon request. Librarians and patrons will welcome this separate index; it saves shelf space, is easy to use, and is recyclable upon receipt of the next edition.

Citing *Nineteenth-Century Literature Criticism*

When citing criticism reprinted in the Literary Criticism Series, students should provide complete bibliographic information so that the cited essay can be located in the original print or electronic source. Students who quote directly from reprinted criticism may use any accepted bibliographic format, such as University of Chicago Press style or Modern Language Association style.

The examples below follow recommendations for preparing a bibliography set forth in *The Chicago Manual of Style,* 14th ed. (Chicago: The University of Chicago Press, 1993); the first example pertains to material drawn from periodicals, the second to material reprinted from books:

Franklin, J. Jeffrey. "The Victorian Discourse of Gambling: Speculations on *Middlemarch* and *The Duke's Children*." *ELH* 61, no. 4 (winter 1994): 899-921. Reprinted in *Nineteenth-Century Literature Criticism*. Vol. 168, edited by Jessica Bomarito and Russel Whitaker, 39-51. Detroit: Thomson Gale, 2006.

Frank, Joseph. "*The Gambler*: A Study in Ethnopsychology." In *Freedom and Responsibility in Russian Literature: Essays in Honor of Robert Louis Jackson,* edited by Elizabeth Cheresh Allen and Gary Saul Morson, 69-85. Evanston, Ill.: Northwestern University Press, 1995. Reprinted in *Nineteenth-Century Literature Criticism*. Vol. 168, edited by Jessica Bomarito and Russel Whitaker, 75-84. Detroit: Thomson Gale, 2006.

The examples below follow recommendations for preparing a works cited list set forth in the *MLA Handbook for Writers of Research Papers,* 6th ed. (New York: The Modern Language Association of America, 2003); the first example pertains to material drawn from periodicals, the second to material reprinted from books:

Franklin, J. Jeffrey. "The Victorian Discourse of Gambling: Speculations on *Middlemarch* and *The Duke's Children.*" *ELH* 61.4 (Winter 1994): 899-921. Reprinted in *Nineteenth-Century Literature Criticism*. Eds. Jessica Bomarito and Russel Whitaker. Vol. 168. Detroit: Thomson Gale, 2006. 39-51.

Frank, Joseph. "*The Gambler*: A Study in Ethnopsychology." *Freedom and Responsibility in Russian Literature: Essays in Honor of Robert Louis Jackson.* Eds. Elizabeth Cheresh Allen and Gary Saul Morson. Evanston, Ill.: Northwestern University Press, 1995. 69-85. Reprinted in *Nineteenth-Century Literature Criticism*. Eds. Jessica Bomarito and Russel Whitaker. Vol. 168. Detroit: Thomson Gale, 2006. 75-84.

Suggestions are Welcome

Readers who wish to suggest new features, topics, or authors to appear in future volumes, or who have other suggestions or comments are cordially invited to call, write, or fax the Product Manager:

Product Manager, Literary Criticism Series
Gale
27500 Drake Road
Farmington Hills, MI 48331-3535
1-800-347-4253 (GALE)
Fax: 248-699-8884

Acknowledgments

The editors wish to thank the copyright holders of the criticism included in this volume and the permissions managers of many book and magazine publishing companies for assisting us in securing reproduction rights. Following is a list of the copyright holders who have granted us permission to reproduce material in this volume of *NCLC*. Every effort has been made to trace copyright, but if omissions have been made, please let us know.

COPYRIGHTED MATERIAL IN *NCLC*, VOLUME 220, WAS REPRODUCED FROM THE FOLLOWING PERIODICALS:

Early American Literature, v. 22, fall, 1987. Copyright © 1987 by the University of North Carolina Press. Used by permission.—*French Review,* v. 62, April, 1989. Copyright © 1989 by The American Association of Teachers of French. Reproduced by permission.—*German Quarterly,* v. 80, spring, 2007. Copyright © 2007 by the American Association of Teachers of German. Reproduced by permission.—*Literature and Medicine,* v. 26, fall, 2007. Copyright © 2007 The Johns Hopkins University Press. Reproduced by permission.—*Mosaic,* v. 35, March, 2002. Copyright © 2002 *Mosaic.* Acknowledgment of previous publication is herewith made.—*Nineteenth-Century Fiction,* v. 27, June, 1972 for "The Doctors in 'Rappaccini's Daughter'" by M. D. Uroff. Copyright © 1972 by the Regents of the University of California. Reproduced by permission of the publisher.—*Nineteenth-Century French Studies,* v. 20, fall-winter, 1991-92. Copyright © 1991 by *Nineteenth-Century French Studies.* Reproduced by permission.—*Romanticism,* v. 13, 2007. Copyright © 2007 Edinburgh University Press Ltd. Reproduced by permission.—*South Atlantic Review,* v. 64, spring, 1999. Reproduced by permission.—*Studies in American Fiction,* v. 24, spring 1996. Copyright © 1997 Northeastern University. Reproduced by permission.—*Studies in Romanticism,* v. 45, fall, 2006. Copyright © 2006 by the Trustees of Boston University. Reproduced by permission.—*Victorian Studies,* v. 50, autumn, 2007. Copyright © 2007 Indiana University Press. Reproduced by permission.—*Women in German Yearbook,* v. 18, 2002. Copyright © 2002 by the University of Nebraska Press. All rights reserved. Reproduced by permission of the University of Nebraska Press.

COPYRIGHTED MATERIAL IN *NCLC*, VOLUME 220, WAS REPRODUCED FROM THE FOLLOWING BOOKS:

Bailey, Dale. From *American Nightmares: The Haunted House Formula in American Popular Fiction.* Bowling Green State University Popular Press, 1999. Copyright © 1999 Bowling Green State University Popular Press. Reproduced by permission.—de Oliveira, Teresa Martins. From "Fontane's *Effi Briest* and Eça de Queirós's *O Primo Bazílio*: Two Novels of Adultery in the Context of European Realism," in *Theodor Fontane and the European Context: Literature, Culture and Society in Prussia and Europe.* Edited by Patricia Howe and Helen Chambers. Rodopi, 2001. Copyright © 2001 Editions Rodopi B.V., Amsterdam. Reproduced by permission.—Dickerson, Vanessa D. From *Victorian Ghosts in the Noontide: Women Writers and the Supernatural.* University of Missouri Press, 1996. Copyright © 1996 by The Curators of the University of Missouri. All rights reserved. Reprinted by permission the University of Missouri Press.—Furst, Lilian R. From "Halfway Up the Hill: Doctresses in Late Nineteenth-Century American Fiction," in *Women Healers and Physicians: Climbing a Long Hill.* Edited by Lilian R. Furst. University Press of Kentucky, 1997. Copyright © 1997 by The University Press of Kentucky. Reproduced by permission of the University Press of Kentucky.—Herndl, Diane Price. From *Invalid Women: Figuring Female Illness in American Fiction and Culture, 1840-1940.* University of North Carolina Press, 1993. Copyright © 1993 The University of North Carolina Press. All rights reserved. Used by permission of the publisher.—Hodges, Elizabeth Perry. From "The Letter of the Law: Reading Hawthorne and the Law of Adultery," in *Law and Literature Perspectives.* Edited by Bruce L. Rockwood. Peter Lang, 1996. Copyright © 1996 Peter Lang Publishing, Inc., New York. All rights reserved. Reproduced by permission.—Keith, Lois. From *Take Up Thy Bed and Walk: Death, Disability and Cure in Classic Fiction for Girls.* Women's Press Ltd., 2001. Copyright © 2001 Louis Keith. Reproduced by permission.—Matlock, Jann. From "The Limits of Reformism: The Novel, Censorship, and the Politics of Adultery in Nineteenth-Century France," in *Cultural Institutions of the Novel.* Edited by Deidre Lynch and William B. Warner. Duke University Press, 1996. Copyright © 1996 Duke University Press. All rights reserved. Used by permission of the publisher.—Rothfield, Lawrence. From *Vital Signs: Medical Realism in Nineteenth-Century Fiction.* Princeton University Press, 1992. Copyright © 1992 Princeton University Press. All rights reserved. Reprinted by permission of Princeton University Press.—Swenson, Kristine. From *Medical Women and Victorian Fiction.* University of Missouri Press, 2005.

Gale Literature Product Advisory Board

The members of the Gale Literature Product Advisory Board—reference librarians from public and academic library systems—represent a cross-section of our customer base and offer a variety of informed perspectives on both the presentation and content of our literature products. Advisory board members assess and define such quality issues as the relevance, currency, and usefulness of the author coverage, critical content, and literary topics included in our series; evaluate the layout, presentation, and general quality of our printed volumes; provide feedback on the criteria used for selecting authors and topics covered in our series; provide suggestions for potential enhancements to our series; identify any gaps in our coverage of authors or literary topics, recommending authors or topics for inclusion; analyze the appropriateness of our content and presentation for various user audiences, such as high school students, undergraduates, graduate students, librarians, and educators; and offer feedback on any proposed changes/enhancements to our series. We wish to thank the following advisors for their advice throughout the year.

Adultery in 19th-Century Literature

The following entry provides criticism on the treatment of adultery in nineteenth-century literature.

INTRODUCTION

The societal shifts of the nineteenth century—particularly the examination of religious beliefs, the expansion of women's roles, greater amounts of free time among the middle classes, and the novel-reading phenomenon among women of leisure—prompted a mass cultural anxiety about the state of the family and especially the state of marriage. Although romantic sensationalism remained a force in fiction-writing of this time, a new school developed—realism—in which writers sought to portray life not as it should be but rather as it actually was. Generally, authors depicted the individual's struggles against forces that were beyond his or her control, whether natural, political, social, or psychological, and focused on the realities of daily life. Realism's focus on the middle classes made it the ideal medium in which to explore family matters, including marriage and the prospect of adultery.

Although adultery had been a subject in oral and written literature for centuries, it was not until the development of the realist novel that the experience and its ramifications could be fully explored. With middle-class women in the precarious situation of having neither independent wealth nor practical working skills, the belief among writers such as Gustave Flaubert, Leo Tolstoy, and Kate Chopin was that marriage, often regarded as a means of negotiating a difficult social and economic landscape, was in fact stultifying to women who might have preferred to explore their sexuality and independence. Consequently, authors sought to engage readers in a political discussion about the role of the state in dictating morality, both in the domestic realm, with debates over marriage, adultery, and divorce, and in the literary sphere, with the government censoring novels that were considered scandalous. The publication of Flaubert's *Madame Bovary* in a French periodical in 1856, along with Flaubert's subsequent publication of text that had been cut by the periodical's editors because they feared censorship, drew the ire of government prosecutors, who put Flaubert on trial for obscenity. Likewise, an earlier novel by Auguste Luchet, *Le Nom de famille* (1841), was the subject of censorship, and Luchet was similarly tried. But while Luchet was convicted on obscenity charges for his novel in which

adulteresses escape punishment, Flaubert was acquitted; the protagonist in *Madame Bovary* suffers a miserable decline and death. Emma Bovary is a woman enamored of the Romantic ideal who soon tires of her marriage to a dull country doctor and engages in flagrant affairs, first with a wealthy neighbor and later with a lawyer. Flaubert's highly detailed explication of Emma's daily life, including its many outward signs of bourgeois success, is set in stark contrast to her dramatic love affairs, substantial indebtedness, and eventual suicide. A harsh critic of the middle classes, Flaubert essentially maintains that it is her grasping pursuit of the bourgeois lifestyle that causes Emma's downfall. *Madame Bovary* was published in novel form in 1857 and went on to become one of the most celebrated European novels and the quintessential novel of adultery.

Furthering their depiction as women with serious character flaws, adulteresses are commonly portrayed in nineteenth-century literature as inept or disinterested mothers. Emma Bovary is abusive to her daughter, while Anna Karenin in Tolstoy's *Anna Karenina* (1875-77) and Edna Pontellier in Chopin's *The Awakening* (1899) both treat their children fondly but keep them at a distance and ultimately feel overwhelmed by their care. Money is another common symbol in these stories: Emma Bovary obsessively pursues the financial resources she lacks; Anna Karenin, a member of St. Petersburg's highest social echelon, loses her status and wealth as a result of her affair with Vronsky, who is an officer in the military and thus beneath her socially. Adulterous women tend to meet unfortunate ends in the literature of this period. Emma Bovary, Anna Karenin, and Edna Pontellier all commit suicide, while the title character of Theodor Fontane's *Effi Briest* (1895)—considered by many critics to be the greatest realist novel in German literature—dies of tuberculosis after her affair is discovered.

Of the major novels about female adultery published during the nineteenth century, Nathaniel Hawthorne's *The Scarlet Letter* (1850) has been said to feature the least accusatory tone against its protagonist, Hester Prynne. She is depicted as a victim of ruthless Puritanical judgment who suffers the death of her lover and the loss of her daughter but is permitted to live out her natural lifespan. While Anna Karenin is treated with sympathy because she is an intelligent and sensitive woman who suffers deep regret over her actions and Effi Briest is presented as childlike and incapable of making moral decisions, Emma Bovary is considered a deliberately unlikeable character. In the case of Edna

Pontellier, it is she who is the realistic one in her affair with Robert. As critic Cynthia Griffin Wolff has noted, Edna's "awakening" means she is no longer bound by social conventions; when Robert expresses his desire to marry her, in Wolff's words, "She wants a new paradigm; he merely wants to rearrange the actors of the old one, and Edna firmly rejects his falsifying, custombound notions." Ultimately, Edna drowns herself not out of shame or guilt but as a final means of escape from her situation.

REPRESENTATIVE WORKS

Leopoldo Alas
La regenta [as Clarín] (novel) 1884

Charlotte Brontë
Jane Eyre: An Autobiography. 3 vols. [as Jane Eyre, edited as Currer Bell] (novel) 1847

Champfleury
Les Bourgeois de Molinchart (novel) 1855

Kate Chopin
The Awakening (novel) 1899

Gustave Flaubert
Madame Bovary, mours de province. 2 vols. [*Madame Bovary: A Tale of Provincial Life*] (novel) 1857

Theodor Fontane
L'Adultera [*The Woman Taken in Adultery*] (novel) 1882
Cécile (novel) 1887
Effi Briest (novel) 1895

Benito Pérez Galdós
Fortunata y Jacinta (dos historias de casadas). 4 vols. [*Fortunata and Jacinta: Two Stories of Married Women*] (novel) 1886-87

Johann Wolfgang von Goethe
Die Wahlverwandtschaften. 2 vols. [*Elective Affinities*] (novel) 1809

Nathaniel Hawthorne
The Scarlet Letter: A Romance (novel) 1850

Auguste Luchet
Le Nom de famille. 2 vols. (novel) 1841

Edgar Allan Poe
"The Purloined Letter" (short story) 1845; published in journal *Gift*

Eça de Queiróz
O crime do Padre Amaro [*The Sin of Father Amaro*] (novel) 1876
O Primo Basílio [*Cousin Basilio*] (novel) 1878

Mary Robinson
Memoirs of the Late Mrs. Robinson, Written by Herself. With Some Posthumous Pieces. 4 vols. (memoirs) 1801

George Sand
Indiana. 2 vols. (novel) 1832

Eugène Sue
Les Mystères de Paris [*The Mysteries of Paris*] (novel) 1842-43; published in *Journal des débats*

Leo Tolstoy
Anna Karenina (novel) 1875-77; published in journal *Russkii vestnik*

Mason Locke Weems
God's Revenge Against Adultery (essay) 1815

Émile Zola
La Faute de l'abbé Mouret [*The Abbé's Temptation*] (novel) 1875

BACKGROUND: TRANSGRESSION AND MORAL RHETORIC

Shirley Samuels (essay date fall 1987)

SOURCE: Samuels, Shirley. "Infidelity and Contagion: The Rhetoric of Revolution." *Early American Literature* 22, no. 2 (fall 1987): 183-91.

[*In the following essay, Samuels explores American postrevolutionary literature that links sexual transgression and "religious and political excesses" with dissolution of the family and rebellious activity.*]

An eighteenth-century New England minister who wrote a history of the American Revolution once described the need to "dress" his history modestly: "laboured elegance and extravagant colouring only brings her into suspicion, hides her beauty, and makes the cautious reader afraid lest he is in company with a painted harlot" (Gordon 393). While it seems understandable that a minister would not want his reader to keep "company with a painted harlot," the conjunction of history and harlotry here appears rather striking. This nervousness about licentious sexuality in language—explicitly linked to apparently very different political and social topics—extended to other writers, ministers, orators, and politicians in the young republic. They protected themselves by claiming to use a conservative rhetoric in their efforts to extradite the "alien" dangers of both deism and radical democracy. However, they proceeded by emphasizing the dangers of the loose woman and attempting to educate the American people about the contagion of her infidelity, paradoxically enhancing the sexual associations they claimed to be protecting themselves against.

One of the most famous of these educators, known today for his fulsome *Life of Washington,* was "Parson" Weems, who spent thirty years peddling books and tracts with titles like *The Bad Wife's Looking Glass* and *God's Revenge Against Adultery.* Presented as moral lessons, rooted in an idealized concept of sexuality and the family, these tracts also discussed political issues, a mixture common in eighteenth- and early nineteenth-century writings to the point that the rhetoric of sexuality and the family became nearly interchangeable with that of religion and politics. This interchangeability is a direct concern of the early American novel. Apparently centered on gothic sensationalism and sentimental seduction, the novel in this period reveals itself finally as a major locus for contemporary anxiety about the stability of the family and its freedom from unfaithfulness and the contamination of the outside world.

In *God's Revenge Against Adultery,* published in 1815, Weems presents two exemplary cases of the dangers of infidelity: the "accomplished Dr. Theodore Wilson, (*Delaware*) who for seducing Mrs. Nancy Wiley, had his brains blown out by her husband," and the "elegant Mr. James O'Neale, Esq. (*North Carolina*) who for seducing the beautiful Miss Matilda d'Estrange, was killed by her brother" (143). At first glance, the moral for adulterers seems to be to stay clear of family members; at second, to beware of women with disturbing names. But, as Weems unfolds them, the crucial problem with these scenes is that neither seducer has been educated to control his excessive desires. One professes himself a deist, and the other joins in religious revivals; both transgress the controlled confines of religious thought while violating the confines of the family. And despite the specifics of geography in Weems's account, it also becomes clear that this problem of uncontrolled desire is a national one, that this pamphlet is finally as much about political and religious education in the new republic as about adultery.

Dr. Theodore Wilson deceives his wife because "He was infected with that most shameful and uneasy of all diseases, an incurable lust or itching after strange women." His "disease" is not from natural causes, however: "this elegant young man owed his early downfal

to reading 'PAINE'S AGE OF REASON'" (146). This "libertine publication" sets loose Wilson's "boundless ardor for animal pleasures" and encourages him with "bold slanders of the bible" so that Wilson "threw aside his father's good old family bible, and for a surer guide to pleasure took up the AGE OF REASON!" Paine's incitement to deism has not been uniformly treated as a "guide to pleasure," but religious infidelity becomes more than metaphorical as Wilson's disease spreads.

Wilson begins a liaison with the wife of a tavern-keeper. Nancy Wiley has been poorly educated; she over-values her own beauty and "neglect[s] those immortal beauties of the mind WISDOM and PIETY" (150). Briefly, her husband catches them together and kills Wilson, whereupon Wilson's wife dies of grief. The only beneficiary in Weems's account is Wilson's younger brother, who forsakes the "strenuous idleness" of a study of the law to study divinity "and is now the pastor of the first Presbyterian church in Philadelphia" (166).

The moral here appears to be that religion provides surety against Paine's dangerous excesses, but "Case the Second" provides a countering example. Here, a "rich old gentleman, whose name was L'Estrange" has found wealth but not happiness: "In spite of my money, I find I am growing old and crazy . . . I'll go to the BIBLE and see if I can find happiness there." He learns, curiously enough, that "religion, properly defined, is only the ART OF HAPPINESS," and therefore opens his home to religious revivalists, especially embracing young Mr. O'Neale, who "professed himself a CONVERT!" (169). Unfortunately, young O'Neale's education, like that of Nancy Wiley, has been "worldly minded," and he has sought "his happiness in the concupiscences of the FLESH, the chief among which is the appetite for SEX" (170).

Looking for this happiness, in spite of his "conversion," O'Neale attempts to seduce Miss Matilda L'Estrange, "but her natural modesty, strengthened by education," helps her resist him until she, too, experiences a religious conversion. She reaches a "transport" of "convulsive joy, her breasts heaving and panting—her color alternately coming and going, now crimsoned with joy and delight and now pale and exhausted as if near overcome with fatigue" (172). In this sexual "holy extacy," Matilda seeks out O'Neale and throws "her arms around his neck," "fondly pressing him to her swelling breasts." These "virgin caresses" "served to kindle higher the fever of brutal passion"; O'Neale takes advantage of the moment, and "Miss L'Estrange was ruined . . . by a villain under the sacred garb of religion" (173). Of course she becomes pregnant and her family casts her out. Her brother shoots O'Neale, who laments, "Oh had I been but early brought up to religion and some good trade, I had never come to this miserable end!" (187).

O'Neale's lame regrets, and these case histories generally, emphasize the importance of a careful upbringing, safe from the introduction of false texts and the introduction of desires that exceed the bounds of marriage and the family. Purportedly a pamphlet about the dangers of adulterous sex, this turns out to be a tract that insists on a concept of education conservatively cordoned off from either deism or revivalism. Why are both of these extremes of religious discourse linked with illicit sexual desire? Put another way, why did post-Revolutionary writers see both religious and political excesses as threats to the family?

The best-known deist was Thomas Paine, whose *Age of Reason* was vilified for making religious infidelity accessible to the masses. In other words, the language was straightforward and anyone could afford to buy it, since Paine subsidized its publication.[1] Thirty-five replies to Paine's *Age of Reason* were published within a decade of its appearance (1794-1796), suggesting the alarm with which it was received.[2] Even more than the document itself, these replies link an "infidelity" of religious thought with infidelity within the family and, by implication, the state. Timothy Dwight, the conservative New England minister and Yale president, mounted several prominent attacks on Paine and other deists with his satirical "The Triumph of Infidelity" and sermons like "A Discourse on Some Events of the Last Century" (1801). In the latter, Dwight attacks infidelity as a composite of *opposition to Christianity, devotion to sin and lust,* and a *pompous profession of love to Liberty*" (265). Clearly, deism as a threat to institutionalized Christianity has become inseparable from a sexuality that erodes the boundaries of the family and a version of democracy that endangers the state.

If the exponents of this deistic creed had presented a "candid and logical opposition to Christianity," Dwight claims, "no reasonable objection [could] be made." But they insist on insidious rhetoric: the "Infidels have neither labored, nor wished, to convince the understanding, but have bent all their efforts to engross the heart." The reader, "engaged by the ingenuity of the writer, is lost in a mist of doubtful expressions and unsettled sentiments. His faith is constantly solicited to gravely described dreams; and his eye is required to fix on the form of a cloud." Like Weems, Dwight appears to be describing a process of seduction. The "ingenuity of the writer" is focused on the method rather than on the matter of persuasion, so that "From the highway of common sense [the reader] is invited into bypaths" (265-67). Implicitly, Dwight suggests that if Paine had stuck with the *Common Sense* writings, he would find no fault with his "ingenuity." But Paine, and other deists, have strayed "into bypaths," and the former efficacy of attempts to "convince the understanding" is now channeled into "engrossing the heart."

Indeed, infidels seem to be dangerous by virtue of their talents and the diversity of their application: "Their writings have assumed every form, and treated every subject of thought." From "lofty philosophical discourse," they have "descended . . . to the newspaper paragraph; from regular history to the anecdote; from the epic poem to the song." The influence of deism is everywhere: "in a note subjoined to a paper on criticism or politics; in a hint in a book of travels" (268). What is most insidious about deism, then, is its omnipresence and the hapless plight of the reader who must assent despite himself. Since infidelity may be at work in the most innocuous writing, all forms of writing become suspect.

The nervousness that Dwight displays about the omnipresence and diversity of deistic writings may help explain why he finds infidelity a political as well as a sexual and a religious threat. Besides separating the faithful from the infidel in matters of religion, the notion of infidelity penetrated political disputes in several ways. The concept of religious boundaries was fostered by the politically and professionally dominant Federalists who claimed to hold a monopoly on religion (against democratic deism). In fact, as the historian Griffin has shown, many of the so-called benevolent associations that appeared during the early nineteenth century (like the Bible Society or the American Tract Society, which distributed almost two million pamphlets in the first half of the century) were Federalist-inspired attempts to maintain social order. These associations saw the Bible as a "moral police" that kept "guard over property and life" and was "better than every measure of secret espionage to which a Napoleon or a Nicholas might resort." Finally, claimed the Home Missionary Society, *"The Gospel is the most economical police on earth."*[3]

The kind of policing that was carried out in the name of the Bible extended from the benevolent societies to other institutions such as schools, and particularly to the relatively new American institution of literature. At the heart of these gestures of containment was a model of social control that took the form of a clearly defined hierarchical family order. Since the French Revolution had introduced a model of revolution that seemed to undermine this order, writers of the period frequently worked to keep the notion of Revolution contained politically and metaphorically as a "family affair," a process that became linked with the desire to confine and institutionalize the family.

Even such apparently innocuous terms as the "sacred honor" of the nation point to the conjunction of religious and sexual beliefs at the heart of national and familial identity. They may also shed a new light on the literature of the early Republic. Novels like Brockden Brown's *Wieland,* in many ways *because* of their gothic concern with incest, repressed desires, and lurid crimes, successfully "make the picture of a single family a model from which to sketch the condition of a nation"

(33-34). That is, by so luridly depicting the threat posed to the family by the outside world, these novels encouraged and promoted a conservative, closed model of the family, though at the same time, in *Wieland*'s closed circle of incestuous violence we can see that concentration on the family produces its own threats. The representative family-as-nation that was portrayed in numerous political pamphlets of the Revolutionary War found a fictional form, then, in novels of the early Republic. National concerns were portrayed as domestic dilemmas, since to preserve the nation it was conceived necessary to preserve the family as a carefully constituted supporting unit. Therefore the sexual infidelity that represented the greatest threat to the family was presented as a national threat, especially after the French Revolution when women were popularly understood to be the instigators of the dread mob that came to stand for democratic rule, and Liberty came to be depicted as a whore.

As Timothy Dwight, among others, saw it, the French Revolution had unleashed Infidelity as the loose woman of the barricades:

> Emboldened beyond every fear by this astonishing event, Infidelity . . . walked forth in open day, and displayed her genuine features to the sun. Without a blush she now denied the existence of moral obligation, annihilated the distinction between virtue and vice, challenged and authorized the indulgence of every lust, trod down the barriers of truth . . . lifted up her front in the face of heaven.
>
> (269)

In other words, Democracy appears as a brazen whore. Dwight again conflates the abhorrent possibilities of allowing infidelity to have a recognized place in religious discourse, allowing "democracy" to control the affairs of state, and allowing the "genuine features" of prostitutes to be exposed "to the sun." Each act again involves the others; each spells out destruction to church, state, and family. What Dwight seemed to fear most was that the loose morals introduced by this loose woman might be accompanied by a dread contagion, perhaps venereal, and he preached against whatever would "spread the disease," suggesting that Jacobin democracy was a form of the yellow fever plague that had so terrorized Americans at the time of the Terror in France.

"The cursed foul contagion of French principles has infected us," wrote Secretary of the Navy George Cabot in 1798. "They are more to be dreaded . . . than a thousand yellow fevers" (160, 78). The fear of the French during the period of the "undeclared war" with France was so strong that the Sedition Act of 1798 seems to have been enacted as a cure for the "infernal French disease," spread through the newspapers, but also through contact with the French themselves (hence the accompanying Alien Acts). This emerging American tendency to see the principles imported from France as a contagious disease was supported by an odd conjunction of events: "Jacobinism had first appeared in the United States," as Miller has noted, "at almost the same time the country suffered its worst outbreak of yellow fever—the great epidemic of 1793" (40).[4] Proponents of the Alien and Sedition Acts feared that French immigrants would "contaminate" the American character; their "loose morals and irreligion threatened to infect Americans" caught in their "vile and loathsome embrace" (Miller 52). America's alliance with France, which Paine had called "open, noble and generous," had turned into the whining of "a weak dupe, who find[s] himself compelled to turn an unfaithful wench out of doors" (Paine 132; Gibbs 118).

The American novel that most nearly confronts this conflation of plague, politics, and sexual anxieties is Charles Brockden Brown's *Arthur Mervyn, or Memoirs of the Year 1793* (1798). Because that weak dupe, Arthur Mervyn's father, fails to turn his unfaithful wench out of doors and instead marries her, Arthur feels an "alien and an enemy to the roof under which I was born" (19). Driven to find a new family and a new roof, Arthur ends up in Philadelphia, which was in 1793 the center of both revolution and plague. Refugees from the French Revolution crowded the streets, and the French privateer Sans Coulottes was popularly understood to be the source of the plague that infested the city. Both, as we have seen, were blamed for the dissolution of families. Arthur's search for a family in the midst of this chaos is more than the typical picaresque depiction of a country boy who comes to the city to have adventures. Rather, the novel educates Arthur about families, until he can construct one of his own with his "mamma" and bride-to-be, Achsa Fielding.

Even in this projected marriage, however, safe with the "rights of the relation" the family confers, Arthur fears the intrusion of what is presented at once as sexual competition and a political threat. He dreams that Achsa's former husband, who joined the French Revolution and was killed in the Reign of Terror, returns to claim Achsa and to stab Arthur. This dream affects him to the point that he feels compelled to put aside his pen "till all is settled with my love." He announces that the last words of the book, "THE END," will be his pen's "last office, till Mervyn has been made the happiest of men" (446). The apparent optimism of this ending is profoundly undercut by Arthur's repeated "till," a qualification that causes us to look for an epilogue that is not forthcoming and to become subject to the same "ominous misgiving" that has "infected" Arthur's anticipation of his marriage: "That time—may nothing happen to prevent it—but nothing can happen" (445). The nervous interjection is not reassuring. Instead, we are reminded that, although Arthur has protested that his "happiness depended not on . . . revolutions," the disruptive effects of revolutions must be continually guarded against. One of the more unrecognized aspects of Brown, as "father of the American novel," is that underlying his more radical gothic sensibilities is a rather conservative concentration on education and the family—a concentration which anticipates the focus on the family in succeeding American novels. *Arthur Mervyn* is a prime example of this dual concentration: what Arthur's adventures teach him to desire is home and family, while the uncertainty of the novel's ending promotes a similar desire in the reader.

Brown's novel, then, reflects this contemporary conjunction of a fear of sexuality and a fear of contagion. Uncontrolled sexuality was threatening because it involved the downfall of the family. This threat proved rhetorically effective in describing the threat to the institution of church and state perceived in deism and in Jacobin democracy. The threat to the contiguous and mutually dependent institutions of family, church, and state was further seen as a contagious "disease" imported from France. The coincidence of a virulent yellow fever epidemic in Philadelphia the same year that the Terror ruled in Paris reinforced this metaphor in a politically convenient way, bringing home the Jacobin threat. And the response of early American novels was to domesticate the threat even more thoroughly. Brought into households as an educational tool, the novel taught Americans what to fear. Arthur's adventures teach him to desire home and family, while the uncertain threat of the novel's ending at once promotes a similar desire in the reader and reinvokes the threat presented to him by the outside world, an uncertainty and threat that itself, in the terms that the novel insists upon, produces a desire for ongoing narrative "treatment," calling, in effect, for the institution of the novel.

Notes

1. Paine's work cost threepence, while Godwin's *Political Justice* was prohibitively expensive at three guineas. Reported in Grylls (16).

2. Mason Weems even peddled a version of Paine's *Complete Works* that contained a reply instead of the *Age of Reason*. Reported in Skeel (296).

3. The first phrases are from a speech by Emory Washburn on the Bible Society in 1847; the last from the publications of the Home Missionary Society in 1837. Cited by Griffin (95, 91, 94).

4. See Hedges, both Levine essays, and Samuels for further discussions of the conflation of the dangers of yellow fever and radical democracy in this period. For further primary documents, see Davis.

Works Cited

Brown, Charles Brockden. *Arthur Mervyn, or Memoirs of the Year 1793.* Bicentennial ed. Ed. Sydney Krause. Kent, Ohio: Kent State Univ. Press, 1980.

———. *Wieland, or The Transformation; an American Tale.* Bicentennial ed. Eds. Sydney Krause, S. W. Reid and Alexander Cowie. Kent, Ohio: Kent State Univ. Press, 1977.

Davis, David Brion, ed. *The Fear of Conspiracy: Images of Un-American Subversion from the Revolution to the Present.* Ithaca: Cornell Univ. Press, 1971.

Dwight, Timothy. *A Discourse on Some Events of the Last Century.* New Haven: 1801. Rpt. in *American Thought and Writing,* eds. Russel Nye and Norman Grabo. Boston: Houghton Mifflin, 1965. 265-67.

Gordon, William. *The Letters of William Gordon.* Rpt. in Massachusetts Historical Society, *Proceedings* 62 (1929-1930): 393.

Griffin, Clifford. "Religious Benevolence as Social Control, 1815-1860." *Ante-Bellum Reform.* Ed. David Brion Davis. New York: Harper & Row, 1967.

Grylls, Rosalie. *William Godwin and His World.* London: Odham's, 1953.

Hedges, William L. "Benjamin Rush, Charles Brockden Brown, and the American Plague Year." *Early American Literature* 7 (1973): 295-311.

Levine, Robert. "Arthur Mervyn's Revolutions." *Studies in American Fiction* 12 (1984): 145-60.

———. "Villainy and the Fear of Conspiracy in Charles Brockden Brown's *Ormond.*" *Early American Literature* 15 (1980): 124-40.

Miller, John. *Crisis in Freedom: The Alien and Sedition Acts.* Boston: Little, Brown, 1952.

Paine, Thomas. *The Life and Major Writings of Thomas Paine.* Ed. Philip Foner. Secaucus, N.J.: Citadel, 1974.

Samuels, Shirley. "Plague and Politics in 1793: *Arthur Mervyn.*" *Criticism* (1985): 1-23.

Skeel, E. E., ed. *Mason Locke Weems, His Works and Ways.* New York: privately printed, 1929.

Weems, Mason. "God's Revenge Against Adultery." 1815. Rpt. in *Three Discourses.* New York: Random House, 1929.

ADULTERY AND CENSURE

Jann Matlock (essay date 1996)

SOURCE: Matlock, Jann. "The Limits of Reformism: The Novel, Censorship, and the Politics of Adultery in Nineteenth-Century France." In *Cultural Institutions of the Novel,* edited by Deidre Lynch and William B. Warner, pp. 335-68. Durham, N.C.: Duke University Press, 1996.

[In the following essay, Matlock examines the novel's role as a vehicle for political and social protest during France's July Monarchy—the constitutional monarchy

of Louis-Philippe from 1830 to 1848—focusing on Auguste Luchet's censorship trial for his novel Le Nom de famille, *in which adulteresses go unpunished.*]

> People of France! Great and generous people! . . .
> They insult your name, what does it matter to you!
> They spit in the face of your repudiated history and
> you laugh! They take away your children to send them
> to die from the plague and the Saharan winds, so you
> have other children! They imprison your writers, they
> ruin your press, so you stop reading. They close your
> theaters, so you do without and go drinking. They con-
> fiscate your liberties along with your honor, so you say
> that you had too many liberties and that honor is only a
> word!
>
> —Auguste Luchet, preface to *Le Nom de famille*

As his fourth novel went to press in December 1841, Auguste Luchet could hardly have predicted that he would soon become one of those writers to whom he alluded in his preface, condemned to imprisonment by the July Monarchy government.[1] In March 1842, nevertheless, in an unprecedented move on the part of the state, Luchet was tried for every offense available to the censors—for "exciting hatred and contempt against the government, troubling public peace by exciting contempt and hatred of citizens against various classes of people, offending public morality, and deriding the religious values held by the majority of the French people."[2] In a trial that lasted only one day, Luchet was found guilty and condemned to the radical penalty of two years in prison and a one-thousand-franc fine. His novel was ordered destroyed. Hounded into exile, the novelist would be made an example for others who attempted to use the genre of the novel as an instrument of political protest.

The trial of Luchet's *Nom de famille* is remarkable for the way it cut across a series of battles—over adultery, divorce, class, national identity, and especially, the state's power to regulate morality—at a key moment in the transformation of the novel in France. Although we have traditionally looked to the 1857 trial of *Madame Bovary* as the watershed moment in state intervention in the novel, many of the problematics thematized in ironic ways by Flaubert's Second Empire novel were in fact articulated by novels of the July Monarchy, and in particularly trenchant ways by *Le Nom de famille* and its trial. As this essay will argue, the battle over Luchet's work not only fixed the stakes for the participation of the novel in politics and social reform for decades to come but also set new boundaries for literary and press transgressions that long fueled disputes among critics, novelists, and the state.

The trial of *Le Nom de famille* was a radical new departure for the July Monarchy state. Though Louis-Philippe's regime had years before betrayed the promises of free speech guaranteed by its Charter—as the

preface to Luchet's censored novel lamented—pursuing the press with increasing rapacity, preventing the performance of plays, and policing visual imagery before its distribution, prior to 1842 the novel had escaped political prosecution.[3] And although some twenty works with explicit sexual content were censored annually—many of them reprints of eighteenth-century works like those of Sade and Mirabeau[4]—only three novels seem to have been seized for political reasons by the July Monarchy state. Luchet's was the first, followed almost immediately by the confiscation of an autobiographical novel by a youthful first-time author. Another "literary trial" would occur in 1847, this time of a *roman-feuilleton* in a Fourierist newspaper, with serious reprisals for the government.[5] While these later episodes of censorship seemed to assault a kind of novel and, in the later case, the kind of newspaper that published it, Luchet's unusually severe punishment spotlighted him as the kind of writer the state would no longer tolerate. As the author of three previous novels, former editor of *Le Temps* in 1830, and coauthor of several widely discussed plays, Luchet had a public presence that ensured that the prosecution of his work would not escape notice.[6] Most surprising given his harsh sentence, Luchet's contemporaries in the press did not rise up in vigorous protest as they had in previous cases of censorship. *Le Nom de famille* had touched a nerve, and even those living the daily threat of the censors were hesitant to condone its tactics.

Because Luchet's novel, like those of many of his contemporaries, took as themes several of the most disputed issues of his era, the trial must be read in the context of an ever-spiraling fear that literary texts could elicit resistance, revolt, and social change. Like the trial of Flaubert's *Madame Bovary* in 1857, the trial of *Le Nom de famille* turned on perceptions of private life and the possibility of literature to promote change in the most intimate spheres of society.[7] Also like Flaubert's trial, that of Luchet exposed the stakes of the battles in which the novel had come to participate and the fragility of the institutions it was seen to threaten. This essay explores the politics of both this novel and its condemnation in the context of mid-nineteenth-century debates about the novel. It seeks to explain the investments of the state of 1842 in censoring this text and the terms through which the novel as an increasingly legitimized cultural institution had come to threaten state interests. I look first, therefore, at this novel's position amid debates about the genre in July Monarchy France. I then turn to the specific social battle to which this novel lent its reformist plots, over the possible reinstitution of divorce after the Revolution of 1830. The social novel of adultery—of which Luchet's work is an exemplary manifestation—waged its own literary war in a battle particularly destabilizing to the July Monarchy regime. And yet, as I show in the third section of this essay, nothing about the content of Luchet's novel marks it as extreme enough to have warranted either the censorship of the state or the silence of the author's contemporaries. One must, I argue, look beyond its content at the aesthetic and political battles in which this novel set new boundaries. This essay argues, ultimately, that the trial of Luchet's novel is the culmination of a battle waged by and against the literary itself. If Luchet ultimately lost that battle, his censorship trial demonstrates how high the stakes had become. Read today, both for its literary criminality and for its participation in a network of battles over the novel as a cultural institution, Luchet's text has a curious way of refiguring the debates in which it became the scapegoat, and of illuminating the forces at work in the new novel itself.

MONARCHY PLOTS

Luchet's 1841 work turned on a central dilemma of the nineteenth-century European novel: what is a woman to do whose marriage does not satisfy her desires? Like dozens of July Monarchy novelists before him, including Honoré de Balzac, George Sand, and Eugène Sue, Luchet positioned his characters amid moral dilemmas that seemed inevitably to lead to transgression of the accepted moral values of his era. If, as Tony Tanner (1979) has suggested, the nineteenth-century novel's preoccupation with adultery articulates in thematic terms the genre's very transgressive mode,[8] nothing could be more exemplary in this domain than the plot line of Luchet's *Nom de famille*. The Marquise de Tancarville, happily married to a man of similar interests and standing, finds herself unable to have a child. Although divorce, still legal in the Empire of the novel's opening moments, might have freed her to gratify her maternal desires in a new alliance, the Marquise instead throws herself into the river. She is saved by the novel's hero, Georges Maurice, who is referred to as *le républicain* by the narrator of a work that stolidly opposes Maurice's values to those of the aristocrats whose life he comes to transform. Believing himself loved, Maurice spends an idyllic period with the Marquise during her husband's absence from Rouen, only to find himself dropped flat when she becomes pregnant. Disconsolate, the Republican, who has never told his lover that his own father condemned hers to the guillotine during the previous revolution, turns to warfare against the aristocracy that has betrayed him. Appearing at the child's christening to announce his paternity, he is turned out as a madman. Years later, by a turn of events as typical of the July Monarchy novel as of the theatrical melodrama on which it drew, Maurice finds himself convalescing in the very chateau in which the Marquise lies dying. Summoned to her bedside, he witnesses her confession to her husband that the man driven from their home a decade before had indeed spoken the truth: the child they have been raising is not only the fruit of adultery but the result of the Marquise's desperate manipulations of her husband's legal responsibilities of pa-

ternity. Forgiven in her dying moments by the benevolent Marquis, she confides her son Ernest to the care of both "fathers." Maurice is to raise the boy, posing as his tutor, while the Marquis continues to confer his name, rank, and fortune upon his wife's adulterous offspring.

Unlike the forlorn children of aristocrats in other novels of this era, of which Sue's Fleur-de-Marie is a stunning example, who demonstrate their high birth through noble actions despite their fall into the most debasing of circumstances, Ernest de Tancarville is rotten to the core. Unable to appreciate his tutor's loving upbringing and contemptuous of social conventions, he refuses to bow to any moral code, whether that of his biological father or that of the man whose name he bears. Although Maurice's imprisonment for republican activities prevents him from blocking Ernest's marriage to a woman he believes his son does not deserve, the father miraculously escapes prison to discover the misery of the young woman, herself the adulterous progeny of his best friend, republican journalist Lagrange. No sooner do we learn Marie's true parentage than Ernest has embroiled himself in a newspaper scandal that leads him to kill the aging Lagrange in a duel. Horrified by her husband's murder of her father, Marie resists her husband's socially endorsed marital rights and refuses to return to his household. Overwhelmed by the corruption of his adopted son, the Marquis finally disavows Ernest publicly, naming for the first time his son's true parentage. But before the Marquis has finished the speech that would forever limit Ernest's political aspirations, the son runs Maurice through with a sword, leaving the stunned Marquis languishing from shock. At the end of the novel that, in the words of Luchet's prosecutor, has involved a triple patricide ("Justice Criminelle" 1842, 1), the name of the family borne by Ernest remains intact. The last two paragraphs of *Le Nom de famille* leave doubt that this now murderous character is ever prosecuted. After the death of the Marquis we are told, "There was no will: Ernest was the Marquis de Tancarville and master of two hundred fifty thousand pounds of income" (Luchet [1841], 2:196).[9]

Innumerable works contain political allusions "keener than those we find in Luchet's book," argued defense attorney Jacques Favre in the trial of 10 March 1842 ("Justice Criminelle" 1842, 2). Reading from the works of Théophile Gautier and Jacques Peuchet, Favre sought to demonstrate that any number of other novels contained "obscenities or political ideas contrary to the established order," none of which had led to censorship despite their potential offensiveness ("Justice Criminelle" 1842, 2).[10] His client's work, he argued, had been unfairly scapegoated. What, indeed, differentiated Luchet's novel from dozens of others published in the previous decade that waged frontal assaults on the family, marriage, the aristocracy, and the government?

To listen to the critics of the July Monarchy novel, any number of works might have been targeted for the same offenses as *Le Nom de famille*. Seen as heirs to the revolutionary demands of 1830 and precursors of those of 1848, the novels of this period were targeted for every imaginable social ill by conservative critics bent on salvaging what they called religious, family, and moral values. For prize-winning essayist Jules Jolly, "insurrection" had been forced to retreat after 1830, but it had found a home in literature (1851, 10). Speaking to everyone and comprehensible by all, the novel gave free berth to dogmatism and combative theories, wrote critic Eugène Poitou in 1857: "everywhere we . . . see the same idea, . . . the same falsifying of truth, the same slander against society" (1857, 9, 82). Writing in 1841 in the very month of publication of Luchet's novel, G. de Molènes of the influential *Revue des deux mondes* condemned popular novelists like Sue and Frédéric Soulié, whom he saw as tailoring their works to the taste of an ever more avid public in what he called an "equally disastrous double effect" of the public on writers and of writers on the public (1841, 1018).

The explosion of the *roman-feuilleton* into the daily press in 1836 had, as de Molènes suggested, radically transformed the ways novels were read. Appearing several times weekly in newspapers of all political persuasions, novels like those of Sue, Soulié, Balzac, and Sand alternated their episodes with reviews of the Salon, theater, and other novels, often authored by those, like Luchet, who continued to publish in volume form alone. The July Monarchy interest in the novel, fostered by its increasing visibility, was further spurred along by its very vitality. Some fifty to a hundred new novels were published in volume form annually, made affordable to a bourgeois public by cheaper paper and printing methods.[11] Reading rooms, rising in numbers from the late Restoration throughout the 1840s, permitted men and women of all classes to rent newspapers and books for a minuscule fee. Literacy rates rose sharply, especially for women and the working classes.[12] More important—possibly due to these transformed conditions for reading—the novel had begun to delve into new subjects, becoming ever more concerned with the present, the social world, and the potentially marginal individuals in the midst of polite society. The new novel of the July Monarchy, in both its serialized and bound forms, had gained a much greater public and with it a new legitimacy, even as conservatives complained that it compromised all that society ought to hold dear.[13]

The novel's critics above all attacked its novelty, its insistence on treating the contemporary world and the socially relevant, its concern with much debated issues like divorce, adultery, bastardy, the plight of workers, and paternal, marital, and women's rights. Sue was condemned for inciting the working class to revolution. Soulié was assaulted for tempting women to duplicity

and crime. Balzac was criticized for seducing women into adultery. Sand was imagined to be the source of marital trauma in bourgeois households.[14] Few contemporary novelists were immune to criticism, yet few seemed to suffer much in popularity for all the attacks. Even as conservative critics like Charles Nisard and Alfred Nettement waged war against this new literature,[15] novelists prolifically produced chapter after chapter of melodrama and social commentary. By the middle years of the July Monarchy, the novel had become, like the press itself, a major instrument of social criticism, hardly univocal in its goals but caught up in exchanges that questioned the institutions on which the French state had hitherto been seen to rely.

The censorship of Luchet's novel came on the heels of a series of major press scandals and amid an increasingly violent discussion of the role of the novel in challenging social institutions. More important, it came dead center into debates about marriage and the family that the novel of the previous decade had avidly promoted. Luchet's work was, as we shall see, part of a more generalized trend in the novel toward a specific kind of social criticism that particularly targeted the institutions of the family and marriage. One could say that Luchet was censored both for pushing the limits of the possibilities for the new novel and for engaging in that novel's most typical moves. In the following two sections, I would like to examine the context for the July Monarchy novel's social criticism and to consider how Luchet's contemporaries involved themselves in its demands for reform.

DIVORCE PLOTS

"Marriage is *the* central subject for the bourgeois novel," Tony Tanner has argued. Because, for Tanner, marriage is "the all-subsuming, all-organizing, all-containing contract for bourgeois society," the bourgeois novelist cannot avoid somehow engaging the subject of marriage (1979, 15). Adultery, Tanner has contended, represents the main topic for the bourgeois novel because it provides a new ("novel") plot for the lives it transforms (377). Threatening the contract of marriage, it enables the novel generically to rehearse potential breakdowns in the contract between reader and text, and to represent the risks of refusing or evading either structure (17). Tanner's account of the "narrational urges" of adultery in the novel is persuasive for the examples he reads at length (Rousseau's *Julie*, Goethe's *Wahlverwandschaften,* and *Madame Bovary*), but it interprets the transgressions of adultery as existing in an ahistorical time warp. Tanner believes divorce, which he calls "the main way in which society came to cope with adultery," was rejected as a solution by the novels he considers because "the novelist realized that divorce was a piece of surface temporizing, a forensic palliative to cloak and muffle the profoundly disjunctive reverberations and implications of adultery" (18). Since for most of the nineteenth century, divorce was not even a *possible solution* for disrupted marital contracts, one might need to rethink its position in relation to the novel of adultery. Since divorce was not legal either in the *ancien régime* or between 1816 and 1884, it is hardly surprising that neither Julie nor Emma Bovary imagined it as an alternative. For the novel of the July Monarchy, and for the novel of the 1830s in particular, divorce was not only a central demand of characters but also a specific political goal of many authors. And if adultery turns out to be the topic par excellence of these novels, the breakdown in contracts it implies targets a much greater breakdown in contracts, between the July Monarchy state and the bourgeois supporters who believed they would be rewarded with a relaxing of the laws enforcing indissoluble marriages. The July Monarchy novel staged adultery as part of a political gesture, and when it was thwarted, as in the case of Luchet's *Nom de famille,* this seems to have occurred because adultery and divorce alike were imagined as deeply destabilizing to an already unstable regime.

Opponents of divorce in the July Monarchy made repeated appeals to three stories, each with a novelistic quality of its own. The first involved the social anarchy and libertinism they evoked as resulting from the 1789 revolutionaries' loosening of marital ties. The second story told by the *anti-divorciaires* revolved around the dangers of adulterous desire encouraged by the possibility of marital dissolution. The third story—relayed and reinterpreted by Luchet's novel—centered on the potential havoc created in families by transformations in the contractual obligations of marriages.

Those who believed the family had been radically transformed by the revolutionary freedom to divorce found ample statistical evidence to make their case. One marriage out of four was dissolved in Paris between the revolutionary legalization of divorce in September 1792 and 1803, when the first Napoleonic restrictions on divorce took effect. Approximately twenty thousand marriages were terminated in the nine largest cities in France in this same period. One might have concluded from statistics that French citizens had been looking for ways to rid themselves of unwanted spouses as eagerly as they had sought voting rights and a republican government (Phillips 1988, 257-60). Perhaps most striking was the number of women petitioning for divorce: 74 percent of the petitions filed in Paris were those of women.[16] Though no statistics tell how many of these women, whose average age was thirty-six (Phillips, 1988, 274), married again and had children by a second marriage, such decisions were more than plausible. In the twenty-four years during which divorce was possible, women were able to assert a power over their private lives that had hitherto been imaginable only through widowhood or marital infidelity fraught with

scandal. From the stories told by statistics and echoed in the hysteria surrounding July Monarchy attempts to relegalize divorce, women were both imagining changes in the institutions of the family and demanding that those changes respond to their desires.

What Margaret Cohen has called, in relation to the feminine social novel of the July Monarchy, "a second chance at sex" (1995, 106)[17] haunted divorce legislation throughout the nineteenth century. If legislators balked, after the Restoration's abolition of divorce in 1816, at liberalizing marital laws, they appear to have done so precisely to thwart the desires of women and men who sought something more than their marriages offered. It is hard to say whether this recurring concern in divorce debates was religious puritanism or simply blind allegiance to marriage in whatever form it took—arranged by parents, imposed by families, or initiated by lovesick teenagers. Whatever their motives, the opponents of divorce were as dead set against offering individuals a second chance at sex as they were against the potential results of such unions, progeny from a second marriage.[18] With a coldhearted fatalism, hard-liners urged the unhappy woman to turn her heart to God, as if she deserved neither love nor sex, and as if a childless marriage—especially agonizing in an era when motherhood was elevated as the supreme fulfillment of a woman's nature—was either her fault or her just punishment for wanting more.

"Must we obliterate marriage from our institutions and our morals?" asked Antoine Hennequin in one of the many antidivorce pamphlets published during the July Monarchy. "Must we give weapons to seduction and encouragement and rewards to adultery?" (1832, 1). For Hennequin, who saw divorce as a source of ruses and lies and as the validation of extramarital license, changed laws would assure the adulterer, "tomorrow you won't have to blush anymore" (8-9), and thus foster the most dangerous urges in spouses. Divorce would not, he pointed out fervently, "make the dagger fall from the hands of the patricidal wife or turn her away from her plots to serve poison to her husband" (71).[19] Hennequin's depiction of violent women, desperately plotting the end of their marriages, is part of an argument that equated desire with criminality:

> The possibility of divorce by mutual consent, considered a way to reconcile the security of the victim with the impunity of his executioner, seems to say to spouses fit to hear such advice: Go ahead! Strike! If the scheme fails, divorce by mutual consent will enable you to achieve the goal to which crime failed to bring you. It's no longer the scaffold, it's the hope of a new marriage that will come to present itself to the thoughts of the guilty spouse. Thus divorce by mutual consent abets crime and does not prevent it.
>
> (76)

Hennequin's pamphlet offered few recourses to women (or men) whose sufferings in loveless marriages had not driven them to adultery and crime. His novelistic rendering of the plots encouraged by divorce suggested that he imagined no middle ground between desperation and resignation. If unhappy marriages had already hatched transgressive plots, Hennequin wanted the partners to such plots to answer to their crimes. If not, then certainly the partners of indissoluble marriages could find some reasonable means to honor their contracts.

The specter of marital breakdown haunted July Monarchy France in part owing to a series of highly public episodes that shed light on the problematic ways in which marriages were arranged, families constructed, and, especially, women asked to bear the burden of contractual obligations in which they had given no consent. Flora Tristan's separation from her husband and subsequent adulterous liaisons drew attention when he attempted to murder her on a Paris street in 1838. Marie Cappelle-Lafarge's disastrous marriage, arranged by a marriage broker in 1839, was imagined to have ended in murder in part because she lacked the options to extract herself from a contract with a man who wed her for a dowry to save himself from bankruptcy. Feminist journalist Poutret de Mauchamps, editor of *La Gazette des femmes* and author of a petition for the reestablishment of divorce (1837), was tried for moral corruption along with her lover in 1838 and sentenced to prison. George Sand's liaisons with de Musset and Chopin were read as evidence of her contempt for the institution of marriage and correlated to the political ideology of her novels in ways that inevitably made her a partner to adultery and marital breakdown.[20] Public expectations that the bourgeois monarchy would gratify its supporters with a liberalization of divorce laws were dashed annually from 1831 to 1834 as legislation zipped almost unanimously through the Chambre des Députés only to be quashed in the Chambre des Pairs.[21] By 1835, when the September Laws narrowed press options for protest of the regime, complaints over the corruption rooted in the very heart of the bourgeois family remained a prickly though acceptable way to take jabs at the monarchy. Caricatures of Louis-Philippe as a pearhead could no longer make it past the censors, but the monarch's henchmen could find few excuses to block the publication of images, like Gavarni's *Fourberies des femmes,* that hinted at the cuckolding of the bourgeoisie who upheld his regime.[22]

The discourse of adultery, especially when accompanied by explicit demands for divorce rights, became a powerful way of indicting the July Monarchy government for its failure to respond to the desires of its original supporters. It also emerged as a subtle tool for demonstrating the corruption of the bourgeoisie depicted as blind to the intrigues of its own interiors. In its propagandistic forms, in pamphlets, petitions, and press editorials, that discourse spun tales of woe around the plight of unhappy spouses, especially neglected wives.

In its novelistic versions, including Luchet's *Nom de famille* and dozens of July Monarchy social novels, unhappy spouses began to demand and procure solutions in ways that spurned traditional marriage plots, putting in place—as we shall see in the following section—a literary aesthetic of didacticism and utilitarianism as much debated as the institution of marriage itself. The possibility of social change tendered by the July Revolution had unleashed social demands that altered the very forms in which those demands might be asserted. Marital breakdown haunted Louis-Philippe's regime, and the possible plots it took—adultery, bastardy, and especially divorce—gave shape to tools for political protest hitherto unimaginable as wielding such power. The political goals appropriated by the novel thus emerged as a logical extension of social reformism, and the genre's growing didacticism seemed a logical answer to state attempts to muzzle voices demanding an overhaul of social institutions.

"When you forged our chains, powerful legislators, you did not foresee all our opposition, and it's too bad for you," rails Luchet's Marquise de Tancarville on her deathbed.

> Women's honor! Women's duty! Words that echo because they are empty. When Napoleon saw a pregnant woman go by, he greeted her, they say, and did not ask her how she got that way. A woman's honor, a woman's duty, is to be a mother. It's her glory. It's her life! . . . For us, marriage is an institution as despicable as it is fierce; if we are faithful, it brings us scorn; if we are guilty, it destroys us.
>
> (Luchet [1841], 1:98, 101; "Justice Criminelle" 1842, 2)

This passage, indicting not only marriage as an institution but women's responsibilities within marriage, emerged in the trial of Luchet's novel as the prosecutor's evidence of its "offense to public morals." The Marquise's rationale for her adultery, here confessed as her desire to become a mother, provides no potentially redeeming features for the state. Hers is no elevation of maternal instincts, no confession of repentant passion, but rather an indictment of the social institutions that she saw as leaving her no choice but lies, manipulation, and adultery. Strangely enough, though her speech begins with an appeal to the ignorance of state legislators, her "crime" transpired in an era during which divorce was logistically possible, though neither she nor her husband chose to exercise that right. Distraught over their failure to produce an heir, the Tancarvilles entertain every option, the novel tells us:

> How many times the thought of appealing to divorce came to seduce them and shine like a beacon amidst the wreck of their life! But divorce was a revolutionary resource, an incentive to debauchery, voted by men full of crime and blood, and it could not be permitted that a

Tancarville or a Croixmare seek salvation in a law representing treason against God.

                                                                            (1:27)

Ernest, heir to the "name of the family," is born into the Tancarville household on Christmas day 1809. By the time the Marquise lies dying, divorce has been definitively outlawed by the Restoration government. Her deathbed protest, nevertheless, seems directed at the very government that has, since 1830, failed to loosen the "chains" she imagines emptying out the meaning of "women's honor." Small wonder, perhaps, that her remorseless adultery was presented during the trial as an assault on the morality promoted by that government.

According to the prosecutor, Nouguier, the goal of Luchet's novel was to "dump insults and contempt on what makes up the family, from birth to death." In its very title, Nouguier saw its overall view, that "the name given by the family is only a lie." Its epigraph, "*Is pater ist quem nuptiae demonstrant,*" borrowed from Roman law, which held that a child born into a marriage was that of the husband, was read by the prosecution as further evidence that Luchet wanted nothing better than to destroy the very foundations on which society rested ("Justice Criminelle" 1842, 1). Interestingly, this very maxim had turned up a decade earlier as part of Hennequin's argument against liberalizing marital dissolutions. For Hennequin, "the interest of morals and the dignity of marriage" made it essential that if proof existed that "the child born during a marriage cannot belong to the husband," then no man should have to honor the child as his own: "an adulterous wife must not be able to award to the fruit of her licentiousness the advantages of legitimacy; marriage would be debased if it was condemned by laws to protect with its shield children who manifestly do not belong to it" (1832, 65-66). It is precisely this "debasement" which Luchet's novel, both in its epigraph and its plot line, is read by the state prosecutor as embracing. Both the children of adultery in this novel have been raised ignorant of their true paternity, their origins veiled by the lies of wives and the complicity or blindness of husbands. Into the Tancarvilles' aristocratic household, into the Wilds' bourgeois home, children have innocently come bearing names of families to which they do not, according to social norms, rightfully belong.

The failure of these family names to properly mask adulterous liaisons is, however, precisely what gives a plot to this and many other contemporary novels. The didactic urges of Luchet's novel can be fulfilled only through a narrative that dislocates the socially acceptable from its complacent foundations and plummets its characters into the disorders of intrigues that conventions disallow. The new plots provided for lives by adultery in the July Monarchy novel promoted a challenge to social institutions and demanded marital reform but simultaneously destabilized novelistic institutions in ways that endangered both reformist goals and literary aesthetics.

"Marriage is perjury," argues protagonist Léonie in an 1837 novel depicting three extramarital relationships (Auger 1837, 2:28). Given lengthy speeches opposing both marriage and society's particularly heinous treatment of married women, artist Léonie refuses the marriage arranged by her family in order to pledge her heart to a young man she has met painting alongside her in the Louvre: "I will defy the opinions of the hypocrite and vicious throng. What does its view matter to me? I have made myself a man. I want to be free. I am an artist!" (Auger 1837, 1:246). Called exemplary of the social novels of this era (Evans 1936, 144), Hippolyte Auger's *La Femme du monde et la femme artiste* uses scandalous plot lines and vociferous polemics to demonstrate didactically the failure of social institutions to serve the interests of women caught in their contracts. Michel de Masson's *Vierge et martyre* (1836) depicts the trials of the child of an adulterous union between a woman whose life is ruled by her abusive pimping husband and the man of noble heart who had once sought to marry her. Begging him on her deathbed to protect their child from her husband, the adulterous woman hopes to extract the girl from the physical and emotional battery that has precipitated her own untimely death. In order to prevent Clémentine's marriage to a corrupt, aging baron, Montlieu winds up forced to marry the girl himself, effectively entering into an incestuous relationship with his own daughter. Tormented by her husband's sexual rejection, Clémentine grows increasingly drawn toward adultery with a young man Montlieu pushes in her direction. Unable to break her marriage vows, however, she commits suicide, leaving her husband/father suspected of her murder.

Similarly, a series of novels from the 1830s pointedly demand the re-institution of divorce. Madame Monborne's *Une Victime* (1834) depicts the torments of a young orphan married against her will to a profligate who spends his time either gaming or in prison. Unable to divorce him, she attempts to support herself to no avail, ultimately losing her child and sinking into ever greater poverty and desperation. She is saved by the man she had once hoped to marry and lives happily with him until her criminal husband has her imprisoned and tried for adultery. She poisons herself in court, begging only that her "death inspire toward [her] sex the indulgence of laws" (Monborne 1834, 366). Jenny Bastide's *Elise and Marie* (1838) likewise demands the legalization of divorce by showing the unfortunate results of an arranged marriage between an aging marquis and a girl who had hoped to marry another. Driven to violent jealousy when Elise draws happiness from intriguing with the young viscount, her husband kills his rival in a duel—only to discover he has murdered his own son from a previous adulterous liaison.[23]

The social novel of adultery and divorce has a striking tendency to depict women's suffering in terms that doom even their most heroic efforts to discover alternatives. The attempt of Auger's Léonie to "say an eternal goodbye to what is 'done' and to social tyranny" fails to bring her the happiness she expected. When social opprobrium finally drives her to ask her beloved to marry her, he rebuffs her in a scene that seems to warn others who might try to live so freely. Every love affair in Auger's novel ultimately ends disastrously for the woman. Every woman is betrayed, either by her lover or by social conventions that entrap her in a loveless marriage. Each woman is forced to admit, as one character portentously insists, that "society has its laws and we must respect them" (Auger 1837, 1:256). The power of such a novel's polemic lies, however, in its poignant account of the constraints on women's lives that, in Léonie's words, offer them only a choice between "guilty joys or sorrow" (2:275).

At the forefront of the literary maneuvers that transformed the July Monarchy novel into a political statement were two overlapping generic trends that seemingly culminated in Luchet's novelistic moves and his subsequent embattlement with the press and state. The first, a trend as much in the press and theater as in the novel, was a clarion call for the usefulness of art. The second emerged in what Margaret Cohen has called the "feminine social novel" (1995, 2). The former, its novelistic versions best exemplified by Sue's *Mystères de Paris,* explicitly called for social change, through either the ideas elaborated in its narration or plot lines that made characters the mouthpieces for specific political visions. The latter, emphasizing that these works had as goals "to demonstrate, to move, and to improve" (Cohen 1995, 98), engaged in a didacticism that almost inevitably resulted in the destruction of the female protagonist herself.

The heroine's demise—or at least the demise of her desires—enunciated the fullest demonstration of the imagined truth that women's lives fail to meet their needs.[24] Regardless of the politics of these novels, characters and their desires were sacrificed to plot lines that infallibly demonstrated the private sufferings of women. When the plots of the feminine social novel were allied with the reformist projects of the social novel—as was the case with the work of Luchet, Masson, and Auger— women's tragic plights were staged to demonstrate the need for social change. Female characters were made to suffer as part of a plot for the greater good, and with increasing fervency, as a justification for legislative reform.

The July Monarchy social novel seemed to have a peculiarly forceful need for the stories of women's entrapment in social institutions beyond their control. Whether these stories are told from the women's points of view, whether the works are penned by women or by men, and whether the women represented ultimately find some salvation, the novels that questioned the family and marriage repeatedly depended on women's transgressions to illuminate the limitations of current laws and practices. Whether the novel depicted such transgressions as inevitable, as did *Une Victime,* or as manipulative and duplicitous, as did *Le Nom de famille,* its representation of what Cohen calls the "socio-moral truth" of women's failure to live either inside or outside their own society (1995, 95) evoked demands for social and moral reform in a world beyond the novel. Like the antidivorce pamphlets that, as we have seen, turn on the dangers of women whom marital contracts cannot restrain, the social novels of marital reform need women out of line in order to articulate political positions. Only by projecting into the most intimate spheres of women's lives can legislators, courts, and novels imagine the disorders to be found there destabilizing enough to warrant change. As novels and divorce pamphlets alike suggest, men may suspect that women are intriguing according to their own laws, but only women know the real terms for the plots they have been breeding.

Luchet's novel, borrowing from the reformist urges of the utopian social novel and from the intimate visions of the feminine social novel, had a curious way of confirming the worst fears of the *anti-divorciaires.* Not only do its female adulteresses go unpunished, but their children are never exposed for usurping the names and positions of families to which they do not belong. Luchet's novel's depiction of adultery without reprisal is not, however, a singular one for its era. A comparison with a feminine social novel with a similar plot line suggests, in fact, that something beyond the content of Luchet's novel may have been at stake in the censorship it encountered.

Like *Le Nom de famille,* the short novel published in 1837 under the pseudonym "la Baronne de T . . ." revolves around the desires of a woman to become a mother outside the constraints of marriage. Unlike the Marquise de Tancarville, however, this novel's female protagonist is not herself married prior to the intrigue she engineers with a man she has courted over a winter of balls. Always hidden behind a mask, refusing to reveal her identity or explain her rejection of his marriage offers, she finally gives way to her desires and has him transported to her house where, under the cover of darkness, she commits the adulterous act that lets her bear his child. Her letter explaining her refusal of marriage and her desire to have his child only further convinces Pèdre of his desire to marry her, but despite valiant searches, he cannot find her. Pèdre at last grows bitter toward this woman whom he believes wanted nothing from him but a baby. When he is reunited with her at her château after being wounded in battle, he refuses all contact, contemptuous of her manipulations, until his daughter wins him over. He finally agrees to marry Lady Marie Dudley, whose name has at last been revealed to him, but only in order to have a claim over the child to whom he will now give his name. He plans to depart as soon as they are wed, in a ceremony during which he assumes that his bride will again remain veiled, expecting to return only when their daughter comes of age. But Marie reveals her face in the church and rides back to the château with her husband and child. Softened at last by her beauty, but especially by their daughter's pleadings, Pèdre cannot bear to leave. Instead, he falls into his wife's arms, at last becoming the husband she might have wanted so long ago had the plights of her own mother and aunt not hardened her against marriage.

One might ask why *Mystère* escaped the censors when some four years later a novel with such a similar content did not. Unlike Luchet's Marquise, Marie Dudley passionately loves the man she seduces. But also unlike the Marquise, this woman manages to have her cake and eat it too. Never obliged to renounce her original understanding of the limitations of marriage, even when she reconciles with Pèdre, she winds up using the mechanisms of masquerade to achieve a dream marriage with a man who understands her needs for independence, love, and respect. And though the child is represented as the goal to which she aspired, maternity is finally made irrelevant to love when the newlyweds set off for Paris on a honeymoon at the novel's conclusion, leaving the child with Marie's confidante. The novel's indictment of traditional views of marriage not only remains intact but is therefore validated by the results of the woman's plots. Unlike Luchet's novel, where the adulterous child wreaks havoc on the life of every parent in sight, this work uses the adorable child to procure the best of unions and suggests the creation of a nuclear family that will resemble any other despite the child's original bastardy and the mother's illicit sexual intrigues.

Mystère is in some ways more revolutionary than Luchet's *Nom de famille,* for it offers the protection of appearances to a woman who follows her own desires, acts according to her own code of conduct, and rejects social norms. Luchet's female protagonist winds up not only dead but the mother of a monster. Yet by embracing, in its conclusion, the appearances of the socially acceptable nuclear family, *Mystère* contracts the guise of the most happily ending bourgeois novel: everyone is in place according to the institutions of marriage and the family; what matter how they got there? Luchet's novel, as the censors pointed out, did its best to demonstrate the breakdown of the institutions it represented—

the family, marriage, fatherhood, and the state—even as it rejected the solutions of its characters to the problems they confronted. If, in the words of the prosecutor, this novel showed the "name of the family" to be nothing more than a lie ("Justice Criminelle" 1842, 1), it failed to provide palliative fictions to replace it. One was left, instead, with the name of the family intact, but emptied of its meaning. Small wonder, perhaps, that the censors sought to put in its place the name of the state as a warning to any who would so devalue the institutions invested by it.

Such a conclusion is a risky one, however, for it has an uncanny way of reproducing the conclusions of Luchet's trial. Any comparisons we might make between Luchet's censored novel and its uncensored counterparts inevitably restage the interpretive gestures of the censors, placing his work again on trial and reading it under surveillance. The danger of such comparisons is that one can argue, like the state prosecutor, that Luchet's novel elicited the censors' acts, but one cannot prove with any certainty that it was unjustly attacked. One can hypothesize how it offended the state, but one cannot be sure of the reasons its leftist contemporaries left it all but undefended.

Nevertheless, one might imagine ways in which this novel failed the reformist and Republican goals it claimed to serve. By transforming the adulterous son into an agent of vengeance against society, Luchet ultimately undermined whatever influence, either genetic or environmental, the saintly Republican Maurice might have had upon his son. Despite the goodness of the adulterous man, the transgression of marital boundaries proves disastrous for all parties. It is as if the blood of the Marquise, an agent of duplicity and betrayal, has poisoned whatever nobility the Republican might have brought to their progeny. The sins of mothers are here visited upon both Ernest and his wife Marie. The novel was therefore unlikely to win fans among female readers used to the plot devices of the feminine social novel. Despite its apparent justification of adultery and demands for the reinstitution of divorce, this novel portrays both women who seek sex outside their marriages as manipulative, neglectful of duty, and hardhearted. The only female character spared by Luchet's novel, ultimately, is the gentle Marie, who emerges as a pawn in a broader social attack rather than as a novelistic personality in her own right. She exists, it would seem, more to provide Ernest with another father to destroy, and to allow the novelist another mother to indict, than to demonstrate any possibility of social reform. Like the children imagined by the antidivorce pamphleteers, children caught up in struggles over family names and inheritance thanks to their parents' dissolution of social contracts, Marie is a victim for whom no solutions can be found. And although, in her married state, chained to the abusive Ernest, she serves as evidence of the need for divorce in July Monarchy society, she remains only a tormented victim. Unable to divorce her husband—even after his murder of their fathers—she serves only as a painful reminder that the very kind of adultery that has poisoned all their lives has become an inevitability. She can become at best a lure for readers of Luchet's promise, in the last paragraph of his novel, that he will write her love story as an alternative to the broken contracts in which this novel has engaged. But even that imagined story will remain—as long as the social novel fails in its reformist goals of forcing the government to legalize divorce—only another account of adultery and transgression like the one that set this novel in motion.

One might imagine that there is another story to tell about the censorship of Luchet's *Nom de famille* that goes beyond its Republican and antistate rhetoric, the subversive nature of its characters' acts, the narrator's attitude toward its impenitent women and ineffectual men, and the novel's failure to offer alternatives to the social institutions it attacks. That story, of Luchet's participation in the remaking of the role of the novel, is inevitably related to the novel's transgressive content. But it is even more so a story of the attempt of literature to move beyond the spheres of fiction into the realm of public life. As we shall see in the following section, the tensions wracking the novel of adultery and divorce became particularly visible in the battles around Luchet's novel because this text transgressed imagined contracts of what the novel might do, and incited terror over what might be done with novels.

THE LIMITATIONS OF FORM

The year prior to Luchet's trial was an explosive one, both for Louis-Philippe's government and for the press that opposed it. In August 1841, eight newspapers had been seized for publishing "false news." Late that fall, the Chambre des Pairs condemned the editor of the leftist *Journal du peuple* to five years imprisonment for complicity in an antigovernment plot, the assassination attempt of Quénisset against the Duc d'Aumale in September 1841. The lack of proof of Dupoty's guilt left the press reeling: that newspapers could now be condemned as complicitous in plots against the regime simply on the basis of their views suggested a level of repression yet more ferocious than any previously seen during the July Monarchy.[25] More press trials and more scandals would follow in swift succession. Forty-eight days into the new year, *Le Temps* would claim that since 1 January, press trials in Paris and the provinces had witnessed condemnations amounting to sixty-eight thousand francs and eight years, eight months of prison time.[26] In January 1842, the director of *Le Charivari* was sentenced to two years in prison and a one-thousand-franc fine. Its publisher was also fined in a trial that condemned presses for agreeing to print material that might later be viewed as offensive to the state.

In the course of the winter and spring, *Le Siècle, Le National, La Gazette de France, La Mode,* and *Le Temps* would find themselves hauled before the courts of France and subjected to heavy fines and imprisonment, almost always for protests technically allowed by the July Monarchy Charter.[27] One thing had become certain: the July Monarchy government was no longer willing to take risks with the opposition, from either the press or other agents demanding reform.

The press scandals of the July Monarchy in general, and of 1841-42 in particular, set the stage for a showdown with the reformist novel in three ways. First, because voices of protest in the press were increasingly under siege, individuals who might otherwise have opted to speak out in newspapers seem to have chosen increasingly to use the hitherto safe space of the novel for social commentary. Second, because the leftist press was running scared, embattled by several years of confiscated papers, heavy fines, and prison sentences, the government could expect editors to act cautiously in leaping to the defense of those it targeted for excessive indiscretions. Third, because the government was increasingly eager to shut down voices of dissent, it had begun targeting not only newspapers but their publishers, some of whom were simultaneously involved in the publication of novels.

Read as the trial of a novel, Luchet's heavy condemnation makes little sense. Other novels were launching boisterous attacks on the state and its institutions. Other authors were telling similar stories, often with similarly revolutionary outcomes. Even if other novelists masked their critiques by placing them in the mouths of characters, any number of Luchet's contemporaries challenged the government, the family, and women's roles in ways that could have been construed as immoral or subversive.

Read in the context of struggles over the press, Luchet's censorship has an altogether different valence. The battle over divorce and marital rights had given a political dimension to the novel of ideas that brought the genre in new ways into the cultural sphere. Its authors' desires for legislative change caused the divorce novel to take up explicitly questions previously articulated by the Chambres des Députés and Pairs, the press, and pamphlet literature. The result was not just a call for the utility of art and for social reform but a pretense to veracity that allied the novel with press goals and made it subject to similar kinds of scrutiny.[28] "Ambitious well beyond its powers," wrote Louandre of the didactic novel in 1847, "instead of confining itself wisely to the study of the human heart, it has set itself up as a reformer, as a political preacher; it has tried to intervene in all public affairs and to govern the world" (1847, 682). In order to achieve this mission, deplored by Louandre but held up as exemplary by critics like Emile

Souvestre, the novel became increasingly "carried toward the true": "For the true in everything has its importance: it clings by a link more or less free to the useful, which is nothing other than the true in practice, and to the virtuous, which is nothing other than the true in the order of morality" (Souvestre 1836, 123).

Such a notion of the importance of veracity to the reformist novel was embraced by Luchet with even more vehemence than by most of his contemporaries. His preface to *Frère et soeur* claimed, for example, that "all the facts" making up this text "are real; with one exception, all the characters appearing in it are living" (Luchet 1838, 1:1). *Le Nom de famille* voiced a similar refusal of fictionality:

> *Le Nom de famille* is no more a novel than *Frère et soeur.* The characters who come into play in the action of this second work are living and contemporary like those who populated the first. The imagination of the author had nothing to do with the production of scenes or with the catastrophe that follows.
>
> (Luchet [1841], 2:72)

For Luchet to claim the reality of his works inscribed the novelistic within a generic mode that was as journalistic as it was politically subversive. And as soon as the novel answered to Souvestre's mission of becoming "journalism with art and reflection as well" (Souvestre 1836, 123), it found itself caught in new binds. Drawing on traditional novelistic devices, authors may have hoped to use literary machinations to mollify critics and avoid the condemnation of political views that in the press would surely have met with censorship. By allying themselves with the embattled press to convey demands for social change, and insisting on the contemporary realism and truth of their representations, novels could not continue to pass for inconsequential fictions.

Luchet's appropriation of the goals of political propaganda, pamphlets, or newspaper editorials may have heightened the novel's chances of achieving political change, but it also bound him to new codes. Walking the fence between journalism and fiction, he was pinioned simultaneously by the formal strategies of the narrative modes the social novel had infused with new life and by anxieties over what truth in a novel might imply. His novel's cross-class adultery, condemnations of the aristocracy, complaints over women's imprisonment in loveless marriages, snipes at religious values, and, especially, its bleak picture of the corruptions of the family offered few palliatives for state readers on guard against challenges to authority. Its plays on real names and potentially real corruption within ostensibly real French institutions engaged it more fully in the debates of its era but, as we shall see, also threatened its very survival. We could say that Luchet was tried, not just for depicting the subversion of cultural institutions, but for subverting cultural expectations of the novel.

"We can consider Mr. Luchet's novel from three very different points of view, as an argument about society, as a political pamphlet, and as a mere narrative," wrote the literary critic "Old Nick" in the republican newspaper *Le National* in November 1841. For this critic, whose paper's political views aligned most closely with those of the author of *Le Nom de famille,* Luchet's novel had gone too far:

> The argument about society calls for the abolition of the family—the primary basis of Fourierist theories; the pamphlet, which takes up the most room and holds the most important position in this new work, is an energetic, sincere, and virulent attack against certain men and certain principles; the novel, often sacrificed, is made up of a few scenes in which the dramatic effect is once in a while procured rather violently.

What *Le National*'s critic called an "impartial reading" culminated in an assessment of "this slightly bizarre whole" that assaulted the novel for attempting to answer difficult social questions with a generic form "Old Nick" believed inappropriate for "serious dialectic" (1841, 1).

Luchet was not new to such accusations. His previous novel, *Frère et soeur,* had been called a "political pamphlet in two volumes" by *La Revue française* (Review of *Frère et soeur* 1838, 389). As in 1842, his earlier novel had been used by the anonymous critic to articulate a more generalized attack on the genre's involvement in social questions:

> In the moral anarchy that is the brilliant side of our era, all true and false principles, good or bad, have their literary representation. The novel especially, that work so facile in the way it is treated over the passage of time, is like a tribune, familiar and accessible to all, from which all doctrines are professed, and all social and humanitarian questions are debated.
>
> (392)

Despite the critic's certainty that the novel lacked either charm or interest, he nevertheless accorded *Frère et soeur* a lengthy review that sought to oppose both its social commentary and the form it used to attack "religion, science, politics, morality, social bonds and the family, and individual and professional relationships" (389). In *Frère et soeur* he saw "a plan for revolt or, if one wants to soften the term, a plan for general reform, beginning with the family and ending with politics and religion" (390). The novel, one might have inferred from criticism on both the right and the left, had no business engaging in social reform, let alone social revolt.

Critical hostility toward Luchet's writings was sufficiently pronounced that the state action against *Le Nom de famille* had been all but tacitly authorized in advance. Despite vehement protests in 1842 over the various episodes of press censorship, most Parisian newspapers responded to Luchet's penalty with a few restrained lines announcing the results of his trial. The lone exceptions, a newspaper on the right—*La France*—and one on the left—*Le National*—ended up using Luchet's conviction as a way of lambasting each other rather than opposing the state's newest means of encroaching on freedom of speech. If press trials had promoted the solidarity of newspapers with the most furiously opposed views,[29] Luchet's trial had the curious result of dividing not only the left of which he was a part but the opposition press in general.[30]

Despite their ambivalence about the novel condemned by the state, the editors of *Le National* expressed outrage at this further attack on authorial freedoms. But their editorial expressed yet another worry, one that, in light of their harsh critique of November 1841, seemed decidedly justified: that the state had viewed the left's rejection of Luchet's new novel as permission to censor it. "What will serious criticism become, when it believes itself nothing more than the predecessor of public prosecution?" asked *Le National*'s editors two days after Luchet's condemnation. "What will happen to the writer who would dare to judge a book he fears that his arguments may be but the precursors of a prosecutorial indictment?" The failure of *Le National* to ask what might happen to *writers* who express their opinions in *novels* seemed oddly masked by another rhetorical appeal: what would happen to criticism if writers feared being allied with the censorship of novels? Why so much concern about critics? Why so little concern with novelists? Or why, at least, so little concern about this novelist?

Possibly, we could hypothesize, because this novelist was himself so little concerned with the press and its critics. Hell-bent on presenting the truth of his society in the interest of reforming it, Luchet's novel had declared its mission all the more necessary because of the failures of the contemporary press. "What we call the periodical press represents two quite separate kinds of men, those who write and those who pay," declared the narrator of *Le Nom de famille* in a diatribe that implicated far more than the corrupt Ernest de Tancarville who used his father's name to become editor of a nameless Parisian daily. Although the narrator attributed the corruption of the press to "those cunning wretches to whom we owe the penal and social organization of the press," he nevertheless imagined state constraints as having created writers and editors who were "almost all [forced] to bow down before capital." What Luchet's narrator called "that degradation of thought by money" (Luchet [1841], 2:138) had, he claimed, contaminated other means of expression as well, such as the pamphlet and the bookstore. Sooner or later, he promised, if the king's men had their way, "the novelist, the historian, and the poet will also be obliged to mutilate themselves

in order to live" (2:139). Though such a pronouncement may have seemed farfetched in late 1841, its presence in a novel that those very king's men ordered destroyed seems more than prophetic. The very real censorship of this novel performed an all too real indictment of the press that was willing to look the other way.

But Luchet's adhesion to veracity went even further in its needling of the press and in its transgressions subversion of traditional novelistic codes. Luchet's narrator's depiction of corruption at every level of the press had a provocative way of pointing a finger at newspapers on both the right and the left without actually naming names. The novel's insistence on its truth value left readers trying to identify not only the potentially adulterous progeny of aristocratic families to whom Luchet had given recognizable, existing names but the corrupt newsmen embroiled in scandals like those detailed in the last sections of the novel.[31] Not surprisingly, *Le National*'s November 1841 review focused heavily on its discomfort with the climate of suspicion with which Luchet surrounded his characters and their potential models: "The personal attack, when mixed with a work of the imagination, is as a general principle, the most perfidious and the most dangerous of all," fulminated *Le National*'s critic, safely avoiding references to anyone in particular he saw this novel as attacking. "The liberty of the novel must not be confused with that of the newspaper: they are two very separate things" ("Old Nick" 1841, 2). The newspaper, explained "Old Nick," laid out all the facts at its disposition, not seeking to cover anything over with ambiguities. The individuals attacked therefore had the right to respond in their own defense, or even to take the writer before the courts. Similar attacks in a novel play havoc, he argued, for no one could prove that this supposedly fictional work had anything more than a circumstantial relationship to reality.

Cloaking his attacks on the aristocracy and press with potential fictionality, Luchet had nevertheless appropriated a language of realism and contemporary truth to launch his critiques beyond the range of the novelistic. As soon as we believe the narrator who condemns the state and its supporters for their preparedness to act against the novel, we find ourselves struggling to read this work against the grain of the generic category to which it only seems to belong. If, in the words of the state prosecutor, this is a novel according to which "family names are only lies," it is equally a literary work that makes use of the name of the novel to diffuse truths its form might belie. Through its author's attempts to stretch the social reformism of the genre, the name of the novel is strained into a fiction.

Luchet's violation of the implicit contract of the novel's fictionality had a significant role to play in each of the accusations leveled against *Le Nom de famille* by the state prosecutor in 1842. As evidence of the novel's "excitement of hatred and contempt against the government," state censors cited passages from its account of the cholera epidemic and the riots of 1832, which read more like a piece of editorial journalism than a chapter in a literary work. As proof of the novel's attempt to disturb public peace by inciting hatred against a class of people, the prosecutor read indictments of the nobility, and particularly of the existing Croixmare family of Normandy: "old nobility, pure line of descendants, arrogant race." Although the state censors made no explicit reference to the offense the novel may have represented for the aristocratic families whose names it borrowed, the fact that such families had a history that stretched back to the Middle Ages nevertheless inscribed the novel's accusations within a register of truth that its defenders had difficulty disavowing. "I have never heard those families mentioned in our history," declared Favre during the trial, suggesting that Luchet's choice of names was purely serendipitous. Like any author, claimed Favre, Luchet had to use some name: "If we refuse him the right to borrow names of famous families, why would we authorize him to give plebeian names to the actors of his drama?"

Such pleas, though logical out of context, nevertheless failed to move a jury that had been reminded, not only by the critics of *Le National* but by Luchet himself, that "the characters who come into play in the action of this work are living and contemporary." Luchet could not have it both ways: either his characters were real people, named with real aristocratic names, positioned in a landscape of contemporary events, surrounded by corruptions the narrator wished to depict as terrifyingly real, and therefore adulterous, corrupt, and debased, or they were pure fictions and therefore unable to make good on his promises of truth. Luchet was either guilty of pushing his fiction too far into the realm of truth, or a literary prevaricator whose claims of truth had no substance. Either way, Luchet's revision of the novel's contract of fictionality had a powerful way of provoking questions about the role of art in society, about the boundaries between fiction and journalism, and about the limits of both form and reformism.

THE TRIALS OF THE SOCIAL NOVEL

"They'll bring a lawsuit against you," author Aloïse de Carlowitz is warned by her neighbor, who has just read the novel she is about to publish. "A lawsuit! Against me!" she retorts, insisting that her characters—even the republicans—ask only for "the triumph of their opinions by means of debate" (Carlowitz 1835, 1:31). Not only has Carlowitz, in her *Le Pair de France ou le Divorce,* rejected violence as a means for social change, but she has studiously avoided providing her own political opinions in any explicit form anywhere in her novel. This woman's novel "of no importance" simply

repeats, she argues, what one "hears every day in meetings of petit bourgeois families and in the brilliant salons of high society" (1:37). Her novel's veracity lies in an attentiveness to what people already believe and desire: "I hope that people will be grateful to me for having tried to call the attention of the public to an important social question"—her society's need for a law allowing divorce (1:34-35).

If adultery in the novel signals a breakdown in the contracts of society and of literature, the July Monarchy social novel's appeals for divorce legislation require an appropriation of verisimilitude that might necessitate new contracts. For the characters of these loveless marriages of convenience to acquire the rights to make new alliances, the novel must assume a form that inserts it into the most fervent debates of real-life society. "For a quarter of a century," wrote critic Eugène Poitou in 1857 of the literature of the July Monarchy and early Second Empire,

> there has been no shortage of attacks, whether open or roundabout, insidious or violent; there has been no shortage of abuse, of slander, and of insults, of which marriage has not been the butt. It seems that all *false systems* and all immoderate passions have united in order to deliver an attack on marriage. It has been the common enemy; it once served as the living symbol of moral law, and at the same time as the Ark of the Covenant that guarded the trust of private and public morals.
>
> (67-68; my emphasis)

The novel, "false system" par excellence, had moved during the July Monarchy into a realm of truth that found it, in Poitou's words, putting the family—and marriage—on trial (179). The new contract of truth it pledged could not preserve the appearances on which the novel had so long depended to shield it from accusations of sedition and subversion. Like the adulterous liaisons it depicted in order to call for marital reform and divorce legislation, the new social novel of veracity had radically disrupted the terms on which society depended for order. The trial of words it elicited had revealed fears running far deeper than novelists or social critics might have imagined. "What is then that thing which they bring back into fashion again, all the while remaining afraid to name it?" asked Luchet at his trial. "Is the word more terrible than the deed?" ("Justice Criminelle" 1842, 2). *Le Nom de famille* had installed a grammar of aesthetics and social reform that left the state struggling to put its own version of truth in the place of what it claimed were egregious falsities. Refusing to authorize the new relationships, new contracts, and new terms for society that novelists like Luchet demanded, the July Monarchy government saw itself with no choice but to try to stem the flow of these novels with a mission of truth. Luchet was found guilty as tried.

"Literature reproduces the system that makes it what it is," argues Mary Poovey. Literature does not resist ideology but reproduces it, exposing the "system of social and institutional relations" that nourishes it. "Because literary texts mobilize fantasies without legislating action, they provide the site at which shared anxieties and tensions can surface as well as be symbolically addressed" (1988, 123-24). When the literary text presumes to move into the realm of legislative authority, demanding change, appropriating power, it may well expose more than shared anxieties and tensions.

Luchet's novel pledged to demonstrate the failings of the social institutions of his era, to name the meaninglessness of the family ties authorized by the state, and to articulate the very real catastrophes it imagined emanating from relationships reduced to empty fictions. Inscribed into the melodramatic causality of the novel tradition, however, Luchet could not entirely achieve either his own political goals or those attributed to him by the censors. Despite its narrator's claims that he would seek reform for women trapped, like the Marquise and Marie, in marriages that do not satisfy their needs, this novel has a peculiar way of entrapping its female characters even more firmly in the interstices of fiction and truth on which it rhetorically depends.

The novel of adultery serves in powerful ways to indict the governments of nineteenth-century France for their blindness to the desires of citizens, but it can do little more with the plots of marital breakdown than replicate the social mores that place women's desires under surveillance. Invading the private lives of families and the private thoughts of women, the adultery novel puts women's behavior under surveillance to stage it as transgressive. Demonstrating the dangers to women who want more, the social novel would call for social change, as it were, over their dead bodies. Despite its reformist goals, it institutionalizes a circumspect gaze that puts the private lives of women and men on trial and justifies increased state intervention into the private sphere. The censorship of novels—long imagined as works read privately in the closed spaces of the home—could be seen as a pendant of that intervention. But Luchet's novel was not penalized because of the dangerous desires it was imagined to breed in youthful readers. It was censored instead for making a public spectacle of the private sphere, and for using that spectacle to indict the most public of institutions, the state, for its abuses of private rights. Though its author would be only barely remembered among those who challenged, with literature and words, the social institutions of nineteenth-century France, the severity of his penalty was adequate proof that his challenge had been read as not only one of words but somehow, also, one of deeds.

"May the warrant of the Assize Court put a brake on all those works of scandal that multiply in swarms around us!" demanded the Monarchist *La France* the week af-

ter Luchet's trial. Inviting the state to seek out other novelists and journalists who engaged in similar forms of blasphemy, the conservative newspaper reveled in the example made of this "republican work . . . of immorality and irreligiosity." Strangely uncritical of the politics of censorship to which other right-wing newspapers were regularly subject, *La France* applauded the widening of the net of repression around voices in opposition to its views. Literary criticism, it argued, was unable to meet society's need to silence authors like these. The state's intervention, it hoped, would be only the beginning of a repression that might end the "explosion of bad books that, beneath frivolous titles, deprave imaginations and trouble consciences."[32]

La France's wish was not gratified. With increasing furor, the French people and their press rose up to protest that, contrary to the words of Luchet's preface, they did not have "too many liberties." Though the July Monarchy state continued to pursue the press with venom throughout its remaining six years of power, the novel was only once more subject to censorship after March 1842.[33] And when the censors' next blow fell on a literary text, with the confiscation of *La Démocratie pacifique* for its roman-feuilleton, *La Part des femmes,* the press would rise up furiously to defend the small newspaper and its novelist. Only months later, the battles in which these novels engaged—over marital rights for women, improved conditions for the working class, and freedom of speech and press—would be played out on the barricades of February 1848. Though divorce would not be made legal, even amid the new dreams of the Second Republic, and freedoms of speech and press would flicker only briefly before the conservative crackdowns of the Second Empire, the reformist novel would be imagined for decades as having fueled the dreams of revolutionaries and as forming the political goals of a generation of republicans. That Luchet would return to Paris, in the wake of the Revolution, to help edit *La Réforme,* one of the most powerful leftist papers of 1848, was only further proof that the institutions of July Monarchy censorship had failed to meet their mark.

Read a century and a half later for its position in the battles of culture, the work of Auguste Luchet reminds us of the desires and anxieties trafficked through the novel form. *Le Nom de famille* may represent the failures of literature to achieve the reformist goals it touted so loudly. But at the same time, the censored text does not allow us to forget the powers the novel sought to appropriate, which for readers, writers, and the state of July Monarchy France, could not remain purely fictional.

Notes

I am grateful to Margaret Cohen and Frédéric Cousinié for stimulating discussions and research advice.

1. The monarchy of French Orleanist king Louis-Philippe came to power as a result of the Revolution of 1830, which brought an end to the restored Bourbon monarchy of Charles X. Promising greater liberties than either Napoleon Bonaparte's Empire or the Restoration, Louis-Philippe's "bourgeois monarchy," which gained its power through the support of bankers and landholders, found itself caught up in constant corruption scandals, including those involving the abridgment of liberties of speech and press, and ended in the fighting of the Revolution of 1848, which mobilized worker demands in explicit ways for the first time in the century.

2. A slightly abbreviated transcript of Luchet's trial of 10 March 1842 was published in the "Cour d'Assises de la Seine" section of *La Gazette des tribunaux,* 11 March 1842, 1-3. The accusations levied against his novel were detailed by the state prosecutor, Nouguier (see p. 1).

3. On the September Laws of 1835 and their repercussions for censorship, see Krakovitch 1985, 62-78; Collins 1959, 82-99; and Matlock 1994, chap. 6. Luchet had already felt the weight of those betrayals when *Ango,* the play he coauthored with Félix Pyat in 1835, was closed down by the ministry for ostensibly alluding to other scandals brewing in the government. On the censorship of *Ango,* see the authors' preface to the play (Luchet and Pyat 1835, vi); its censorship file in the Archives Nationales, F-21, 1134; Krakovitch 1985, 56; and Hallays-Dabot 1862, 307-8.

4. Virtually none of these works were discussed by critics or the press in the context of state limitations on liberties. For a substantive list of works censored in the July Monarchy, see Drujon 1879. According to James Smith Allen, 19.4 publications, including, I assume, books, journals, and illustrations, were censored annually during this period. Relatively few newly published books seem to have been censored (Allen 1991, 90). One example of a nonpornographic book censored for political reasons was Alphonse Esquiros's *Les Vierges folles* (1840), a socialist manifesto on prostitution and working-class women.

5. Both of the other novels that met with political prosecution, Marcellin de Bonnal's *Lamentations, ou la Renaissance sociale,* censored just after Luchet's in 1842, and Antony Méray's *La Part des femmes,* censored for two episodes of its *feuilleton* in 1847, were first novels by unknowns. Although the censorship of both works met with substantial press discussion, neither author was sufficiently well known to be a state target. I have discussed the censorship of *La Part des femmes* in Matlock 1994, chap. 7.

6. On Luchet's political and literary career, see Maitron 1965, 2:34-35; Hébert 1913; and Green 1990. His previous novels were *Henri le prétendant* (1832); with Michel de Masson, *Thaddéus le ressuscité* (1836); and *Frère et soeur* (1838). He also participated in the collections *Paris révolutionnaire* and *Le Livre de cent et un* and had published a work on Paris (*Paris, esquisses dédiées au peuple parisien* [1830]). He was considered sufficiently important to be asked to write prefaces for two other social novelists of his era, Elisa Billotey (*L'Agent de change* [1837]) and Ferdinand Vaucher (*Les Grisettes vengées* [1838]). He returned from exile to become editor of the leftist newspaper *La Réforme* and an active republican in 1848. Luchet's publisher, Hippolyte Souverain, was also placed on trial by the government, suggesting that the state was trying to use this trial to target other writers published by him: Balzac, Soulié, Sand, and Léon Gozlan. Defended furiously by Luchet, who claimed Souverain had never read the book he published, the house was acquitted of complicity in the 1842 trial.

7. On Flaubert's trial see La Capra 1982; Wing 1987; Leclerc 1991, 129-222; and Matlock 1995.

8. "The novel, in its origin, might almost be said to be a transgressive mode, inasmuch as it seemed to break, or mix, or adulterate the existing genre-expectations of the time" (Tanner 1979, 3).

9. In a final word, the narrator proposes that if he lives long enough he will "tell those who like the heroic story of Auguste and Marie" (Luchet [1841] 2:196). No such novel was ever published. All translations, unless otherwise noted, are my own.

10. Jacques Peuchet was the author of a number of works of scandalous "history," including the 1834 *Mémoires tirés des archives de la police.* Critic and novelist Théophile Gautier was best known for *Mademoiselle de Maupin* (1834).

11. Louandre claims there are an average of 210 new novels per year, with a high of 284 in 1833 and a low of 185 in 1841, excluding reprints of French novels from the previous two centuries and foreign novels (1847, 681). My estimates from an examination of the *Bibliographie de France* in these years are much lower. In 1841, for example, the rubric "Romans et contes" lists 234 works, of which fewer than sixty were novels printed for the first time in that year. See also Wood 1960.

12. On reading rooms and their transformation of the reading public of the Restoration and July Monarchy, see Parent-Lardeur 1982. On literacy rates and the transformation of the reading public, see Hébrard 1985; Allen 1991; and Furet and Ozouf 1982.

13. On the growing prestige of the novel in the July Monarchy, see Iknayan 1961, 50-84.

14. I analyze these attacks in Matlock 1994, chaps. 1 and 3 (Sue), chap. 5 (Balzac), chap. 8 (Soulié and Sand).

15. Nisard's attacks on the novel were published in the *Revue de Paris* (1833) and greeted by vigorous counterattacks by novelist and critic Jules Janin in the following year (1834). Nettement's attacks, especially on the *roman-feuilleton,* were published in the Monarchist, Catholic *La Gazette de France* and republished as *Études critiques sur le feuilleton roman* (1845).

16. Between two-thirds and three-quarters of the petitioners in other French towns were women, and 40 percent of those women in at least one town had been married before the age of twenty-one (Phillips 1988, 261, 271).

17. The best introduction to the nineteenth-century social novel remains Evans 1936.

18. In a divorce pamphlet appealing to the legislators of 1831, Jean Journel underlined the dangers of second unions in which children are produced. The "horrible disorder" of such arrangements, in which education, morality, and especially inheritance might be compromised led Journel to demand that the current legislation be soundly rejected (1831, 10).

19. Debates over divorce continued to turn on depictions of the homicidal wife up through the 1880s, though her crimes were often used as a plea for divorce, as in the case of Naquet's arguments ("Let the civil code liberate the wife. She will seek the protection of the law instead of taking vengeance with arsenic, sulphuric acid, or a revolver"), *Journal officiel,* Sénat, 1er trimestre 1884, 962 (26 May 1884), cited in Phillips 1988, 427. Emile Barrault, author of the novelistic plea for divorce, *Eugène,* published a further argument in 1847, entitled *La Pathologie du mariage,* claiming that had divorce been legal, the Duc de Choiseul-Praslin might not have needed to murder his wife in 1847. I have discussed the Choiseul-Praslin case in Matlock 1993.

20. On Flora Tristan, see Desanti 1972; Michaud 1984; and Strumingher 1988. On Cappelle-Lefarge, see Matlock 1994, chap. 8. On Poutret de Mauchamps, see Moses 1984, 98-107, and the *Gazette des femmes,* 1 May 1837, 6. For indictments of Sand, see Poitou 1857, 74-82. Louis Maigron, writing in the early twentieth century, still eagerly attacked Sand for the destruction of a generation of marriages (1910).

21. On July Monarchy attempts to reinstitutionalize divorce, see Ronsin 1992, 27-110.

22. On the censorship of caricature during the July Monarchy, see Cuno 1985 and Goldstein 1989, 119-68. I have discussed Gavarni's equivocal position in the politics of censored caricature in a chapter of my book in progress, *Desires to Censor: Spectacles of the Body, Aesthetics, and Vision in Nineteenth-Century France,* a version of which will appear as Matlock 1996. I am grateful to my research assistant Sharon Haimov for sharing her observations on the *Fourberies des femmes* and divorce debates in the July Monarchy in her honors thesis (1993).

23. Unable to tolerate her fate, Elise commits suicide. Hortense Allart's *Settimia* (1836) calls for moral reform in both its preface and its plot line, which explicitly seek to demonstrate the need for divorce in order to liberate women's full potential. Likewise, Barrault's *Eugène* (1839) elaborates a series of intrigues in which an unhappily married woman increasingly turns her hopes to the passage of a law permitting divorce but is satisfied only upon the death of her husband. Despite the *Revue de Paris*'s ambivalence toward the social novel, Barrault's novel received a very positive review in that publication (B., A. 1839).

24. The feminine social novel, unlike classic narrative, does not present disorder that can be made into order or an enigma awaiting solution but rather, in Cohen's description, "an event instantiating the opening kernel of socio-moral truth" that will be borne out by the emphatic repetitions of its plot line (1995, 95-96).

25. See Ledré 1960, 179, and Collingham 1988, 294-95.

26. *Le Temps,* 18 February 1842, 3, col. 2.

27. By June, the centrist *Temps* had been forced to fold on a technicality of publication that may have been intended as much to warn other papers as to undo this upholder of Louis-Philippe's government. See *Le Temps,* 15-17 June 1842, as well as a particularly forceful critique of press censorship in *La Revue indépendante,* June 1842, 804-5.

28. In her study of the English novel between 1832 and 1867, Catherine Gallagher has argued that "narrative fiction, especially the novel, underwent basic changes whenever it became part of the discourse over industrialism" (1985, xi). The discourse of industrialism, Gallagher contends, "led novelists to examine the assumptions of their literary form." At the same time, "the formal structures and ruptures of these novels" revealed "paradoxes at the heart of the Condition of England Debate." Just as English industrial novelists transformed the "unsettled assumptions of the novel"

into objects of scrutiny, the French social novelists of the same era found themselves making similar mimetic claims for the novel and questioning its form in new ways—particularly when they turned to considerations of marriage and the family and the plight of women in society.

29. See especially the joint press declaration of 27 December 1841, printed in all of the papers that opposed the government's heavy censorship, among them *Le National, La Gazette de France, La Phalange, Le Siècle,* etc.

30. This result was further underscored by debates over Bonnal's censorship the following week. See Janin 1842 and Forest 1842.

31. The duel that ends in the death of Marie's newspaperman father undoubtedly resonated for July Monarchy readers with a veracity that recalled Emile de Girardin's killing, in a duel in 1836, of the leftist journalist Armand Carrel.

32. *La France,* 12 March 1842, 1, col. 3; 14 March 1842, 1, col. 1-2.

33. After Luchet's conviction, however, critics continued to call for increases in censorship of novels, as much of the fervor over Eugène Sue's 1842 *Mystères de Paris* attests: "As we wait for justice to be done," wrote Paulin Limayrac in the *Revue des deux mondes,* "this novel, which has caused much harm, is still dangerous" (1844, 96).

Works Cited

Allart, Hortense. 1836. *Settimia.* 2 vols. Paris: Arthus Bertrand.

Allen, James Smith. 1991. *In the Public Eye: A History of Reading in Modern France.* Princeton: Princeton University Press.

Armstrong, Nancy. 1987. *Desire and Domestic Fiction: A Political History of the Novel.* New York: Oxford University Press.

Auger, Hippolyte. 1837. *La Femme du monde et la femme artiste.* 2 vols. Paris: Ambroise Dupont.

Bakhtin, M. M. 1981. *The Dialogic Imagination.* Ed. Michael Holquist. Trans. Caryl Emerson and Michael Holquist. Austin: University of Texas Press.

Ballaster, Ros. 1992. *Seductive Forms: Women's Amatory Fiction from 1684 to 1740.* Oxford: Clarendon.

Barrault, Emile. 1839. *Eugène.* Paris: Delessert.

———[Mme de Casamajor, pseud.]. 1847. *La Pathologie du mariage.* Paris: Comon.

Bastide, Jenny (Madame Camille Bodin). 1838. *Elise et Marie.* 2 vols. Paris: Dumon.

Billotey, Elisa. 1837. *L'Agent de change.* Preface by Auguste Luchet. Dieppe: Delevoye-Barrier.

Bonnal, Marcellin de. 1841. *Lamentations de Marcellin de Bonnal, ou la Renaissance sociale.* Paris: published by author.

Brodhead, Richard H. 1993. *Cultures of Letters: Scenes of Reading and Writing in Nineteenth-Century America.* Chicago: University of Chicago Press.

Carlowitz, Aloïse de. 1835. *Le Pair de France ou le Divorce.* 3 vols. Paris: Charles Lachapelle.

Cohen, Margaret. 1995. "In Lieu of a Chapter on Some French Women Realist Novelists." In *Spectacles of Realism: Gender, Body, Genre,* ed. Margaret Cohen and Christopher Prendergast. Minneapolis: University of Minnesota Press. 90-119.

Collingham, H. A. C. 1988. *The July Monarchy: A Political History of France 1830-1848.* London: Longman.

Collins, Irene. 1959. *The Government and the Newspaper Press in France, 1814-1881.* Oxford: Oxford University Press.

Cuno, James B. 1985. "Charles Philipon and La Maison Aubert: The Business, Politics, and Public of Caricature in Paris, 1820-1840." Ph.D. diss., Harvard University.

Desanti, Dominique. 1972. *Flora Tristan: La Femme révoltée.* Paris: Hachette.

Drujon, Fernand. 1879. *Catalogue des ouvrages, écrits, et dessins de toute nature poursuivis, supprimés, ou condamnés depuis le 21 octobre 1814 jusqu'au 31 juillet 1877.* Paris: Rouveyre.

Evans, David-Owen. 1936. *Le Roman social sous la monarchie de juillet.* Paris: Presses Universitaires de France.

Forest, P. 1842. "Un Feuilleton de M. Jules Janin." *La Phalange,* 20 Mar., 2-4.

Furet, François, and Jacques Ozouf. 1982. *Reading and Writing: Literacy in France from Calvin to Jules Ferry.* Cambridge: Cambridge University Press.

Gallagher, Catherine. 1985. *The Industrial Reformation of English Fiction: Social Discourse and Narrative Form, 1832-67.* Chicago: University of Chicago Press.

———. 1994. *Nobody's Story: The Vanishing Acts of Women Writers in the Marketplace.* Berkeley: University of California Press.

Goldstein, Robert J. 1989. *The Censorship of Political Caricature in Nineteenth-Century France.* Kent, Ohio: Kent State University Press.

Green, Nicholas. 1990. *The Spectacle of Nature: Landscape and Bourgeois Culture in Nineteenth-Century France.* Manchester: Manchester University Press.

Haimov, Sharon. 1993. "The Personal Becomes Political: Divorce Debates in July Monarchy France, 1830-1848." Honors thesis, Harvard University.

Hallays-Dabot, Victor. 1862. *Histoire de la censure théâtrale en France.* Paris: Dentu.

Hébert, Félix. 1913. "Auguste Luchet (1805-1872)." *L'Abeille de Fontainebleau,* Jan.-Aug.

Hébrard, Jean. 1985. "Les Nouveaux lecteurs." In *Histoire de l'édition française,* vol. 3, ed. Henri-Jean Martin and Roger Chartier. Paris: Promodis. 470-509.

Hennequin, Antoine-Louis-Marie. 1832. *Du Divorce.* Paris: Gabriel Warée.

Iknayan, Marguerite. 1961. *The Idea of the Novel in France: The Critical Reaction, 1815-1848.* Geneva: Droz.

Janin, Jules. 1834. "Manifeste de la jeune littérature: Réponse à M. Nisard." *Revue de Paris,* Jan., 5-30.

———. 1842. "La Littérature et la Cour d'Assises." *Journal des débats,* 14 Mar., 1-3.

Jolly, Jules. 1851. *De l'influence de la littérature et du théâtre sur l'esprit public et les moeurs pendant les vingt dernières années.* Paris: Amyot.

Journel, Jean. 1831. *Considérations sur le divorce.* Lyon: Sauvignet; Paris: Dentu.

"Justice Criminelle: Cour d'Assises de la Seine, Audience du 10 mars, 'Affaire de Presse.—Roman intitulé *Le Nom de famille.*'" 1842. *Gazette des tribunaux,* 11 Mar., 1-3.

Krakovitch, Odile. 1985. *Hugo censuré.* Paris: Calmann-Lévy.

La Capra, Dominick. 1982. *The Trial of Madame Bovary.* Ithaca: Cornell University Press.

———. 1985. *History and Criticism.* Ithaca: Cornell University Press.

Leclerc, Yvan. 1991. *Crimes écrits: La Littérature en procès au XIXe siècle.* Paris: Plon.

Ledré, Charles. 1960. *La Presse à l'assaut de la monarchie (1815-48).* Paris: Armand Colin.

Limayrac, Paulin. 1844. "Simples essais d'histoire littéraire, IV: Le Roman philanthrope et moraliste. *Les Mystères de Paris.*" *Revue des deux mondes,* Jan., 75-97.

Louandre, Charles. 1847. "Statistique littéraire: De la production intellectuelle en France depuis quinze ans: Littérature ancienne et étrangère, poésie, roman, théâtre." *Revue des deux mondes,* Nov., 671-703.

Luchet, Auguste. 1830. *Paris, esquisses dédiées au peuple parisien.* Paris: Barbezat.

———. 1832. *Henri le prétendant.* Paris: Canel.

———. 1838. *Frère et soeur.* 2 vols. Paris: Souverain.

———. [1841.] *Le Nom de famille.* 2 vols. N.p.: n.p., n.d.

———. 1842. *Le Nom de famille.* 2d (unmarked) ed. 2 vols. Paris: Souverain.

Luchet, Auguste, and Félix Pyat. 1835. *Ango.* Paris: Dupont.

Luchet, Auguste, and Michel de Masson. 1836. *Thaddéus le ressuscité.* 4th ed. Paris: Dupont.

Maigron, Louis. 1910. *Le Romantisme et les moeurs.* Paris: Champion.

Maitron, Jean. 1965. *Dictionnaire biographique du mouvement ouvrier français, 1789-1864.* Vol. 2. 1836. Reprint, Paris: Editions Ouvrières.

Masson, Michel de. 1836. *Vierge et martyre.* Paris: Werdet.

Matlock, Jann. 1993. "The Dead Duchess, the Dead Duke, and Bette Davis: The Scandalous Histories of the 1847 Choiseul-Praslin Affair." Paper presented at the Berkshires Conference on Women's History.

———. 1994. *Scenes of Seduction: Prostitution, Hysteria, and Reading Difference in Nineteenth-Century France.* New York: Columbia University Press.

———. 1996. "Blagues Lithographiques et spectacles féminins: Les Rires de Gavarni et Baudelaire, et les regards de la modernité en France au dixneuvième siècle." *Les Annales, E.S.C.* Forthcoming.

Mauchamps, Poutret de. 1837. "Pétition." *Gazette des femmes,* 1 May, 6.

Méray, Antony. 1847. *La Part des femmes.* In *La Démocratie pacifique,* 27 May-1 July; 21 July-14 Aug.

Michaud, Stéphane, ed. 1984. *Un Fabuleux Destin: Flora Tristan.* Dijon: Presses Universitaires de Dijon.

Molènes, G. de. 1841. "Revue littéraire: Le Roman actuel." *Revue des deux mondes,* Dec., 1002-22.

Monborne, Madame B. 1834. *Une Victime: Esquisse littéraire.* Paris: Mouillefarine.

Moses, Claire Goldberg. 1984. *French Feminism in the Nineteenth Century.* Albany: State University of New York Press.

Nettement, Alfred. 1845. *Etudes critiques sur le feuilleton roman.* 2 vols. Paris: Perrodil.

———. 1854. *La Littérature française sous le gouvernement de juillet.* 2 vols. Paris: Lecoffre.

Nisard, Charles. 1833. "D'un commencement de réaction contre la littérature facile à l'occasion de la Bibliothèque latine-française de M. Panckoucke." *Revue de Paris,* Dec., 211-28, 268-87.

"Old Nick." 1841. "Critique: I. *Le Nom de famille,* par A. Luchet; II. *La Pension bourgeoise—La Marquise de Contades,* par A. de Lavergne." *Le National,* 19 Nov., 1-3.

Parent-Lardeur, Françoise. 1982. *Les Cabinets de lecture: La Lecture publique à Paris sous la Restauration.* Paris: Payot.

Phillips, Roderick. 1988. *Putting Asunder: A History of Divorce in Western Society.* Cambridge: Cambridge University Press.

Poitou, Eugène. 1857. *Du Roman et du théâtre contemporains et de leur influence sur les moeurs.* Paris: Auguste Durand.

Poovey, Mary. 1988. *Uneven Developments: The Ideological Work of Gender in Mid-Victorian England.* Chicago: University of Chicago Press.

Reid, Roddey. 1993. *Families in Jeopardy: Regulating the Social Body in France, 1750-1910.* Stanford: Stanford University Press.

Review of *Frère et soeur,* by Auguste Luchet. *Revue française,* 7-8 Sept., 389-92.

Ronsin, Francis. 1992. *Les Divorciaires: Affrontements politiques et conceptions du mariage dans la France du XIXe siècle.* Paris: Aubier.

Souvestre, Emile. 1836. "Du Roman." *Revue de Paris,* Oct., 116-28.

Strumingher, Laura. 1988. *The Odyssey of Flora Tristan.* New York: Peter Lang.

T . . . , Baronne de [pseud.]. 1837. *Mystère.* Paris: Desforgues.

Tanner, Tony. 1979. *Adultery in the Novel: Contract and Transgression.* Baltimore: Johns Hopkins University Press.

Vaucher, Ferdinand. 1838. *Les Grisettes vengées.* Preface by Auguste Luchet. Paris: Souverain.

Wing, Nathaniel. 1987. *The Limits of Narrative.* Cambridge: Cambridge University Press.

Wood, John S. 1960. *Sondages.* Toronto: University of Toronto Press.

Elizabeth Fay (essay date fall 2006)

SOURCE: Fay, Elizabeth. "Mary Robinson: On Trial in the Public Court." *Studies in Romanticism* 45, no. 3 (fall 2006): 397-423.

[*In the following essay, Fay explores the notoriety of the English poet, novelist, and memoirist Mary Robinson, the wider implications of which affected "the production of narrative intersections in legal, popular culture, and literary discourses."*]

Trials for Adultery: or, the History of Divorces. Being Select Trials at Doctors Commons for Adultery, Fornication, Cruelty, Impotence, & c. From the Year 1760, to the present Time. Including the whole of the Evidence in each Cause. Together with the Letters, & c. that have been intercepted between the amorous Parties. The whole forming a complete History of the Private Life, Intrigues, and Amours of many Characters in the most elevated Sphere: every Scene and Transaction, however ridiculous, whimsical, or extraordinary, being fairly represented, as becomes a faithful Historian, who is fully determined not to sacrifice Truth *at the Shrine of* Guilt *and* Folly. *Taken in Short-Hand, by a Civilian.*[1]

During the Romantic period, the ways in which narrative strategies of a variety of discourses influenced and helped construct each other's worlds in relation to the tensions produced by the socio-political stresses of the French Revolution were intensely focused on the family and its networks. These bi-directional influences were so successful that they have become normalized, the literary reflections of these influences being read as indelible textual strategies. This essay considers the production of narrative intersections in legal, popular culture, and literary discourses through the case of Mary Robinson (1758-1800) to examine how a woman celebrity, known for her sexual liaisons and acting career as much as for her copious literary production, and most famous for belonging to the pre-Regency constellation of the demi-monde, responded in nuanced ways to public representations of her—both *ad hominem* or scandal mongering publications, and politicized or critical public images—in her autobiographical poetry and fiction. These representations participated in the shifting relations between the public sphere and its irascible advocate, publicity. Robinson's literary responses were indirect, often deflecting attention away from her own story and sense of victimization toward the general cultural fate of women. I am particularly interested in Robinson's use of images of the stressed, fractured, or threatened family to expose a variety of gender inequalities that heightened men's political and social flexibility at the expense of women's. In Robinson's texts the family becomes denaturalized, its presumptive structure put in question, not because of female behavior but because of legal codes that safeguarded a cultural double standard in which manliness expends domestic ties. In order to flesh out the relation between legal and cultural standards in Robinson's textual bodies, I will be less concerned with the more obvious choices of her (seemingly) domesticating narratives—her *Lyrical Tales* for instance, or her novels depicting families in threat—and more concerned with those autobiographical texts that allow her to stage publicly the manly attacks of others on her person as an exploration of the gendered implications of such attacks, and to put forward a self-defense that redresses their legal sanctioning.[2]

I. PROPER DISCOURSES

To speak of propriety in relation to one of the more celebrated members of London's late eighteenth-century demi-monde may seem an odd beginning, except that Mary Robinson's literary career was in many ways a quest for respectability, and "proper" was not always a term applicable to the social elite. Neither the Prince of Wales nor any of the women sexually associated with him, including his wife, were able to muster this trait with any frequency, the exception being the mistress to which he repeatedly returned, Maria Fitzherbert. Discursive propriety must itself be held in relation to the fictional quality of any text; even in proper or defensible discourses disinterestedness vies with public interest. As the volume title I have taken for my epigraph reveals despite its disclaimer, the historical fact of legal transcriptions is self-interested: narratively framed as the exposure of private acts for public good, the title titillates even as it screens authorial scandal mongering. The same dynamic was at work in political cartoons of the day, whose immense popularity and often daily publication spread reputed or reported scandal faster than any verbal text could do.[3]

Facts must be balanced against images of the ideal woman and the ideal family that the press simultaneously used to rebuke and slander public figures whether they were "fairly represented, as becomes a faithful Historian" or misreported as becomes the partisan press. Mary Robinson was well aware of this truism as she struggled throughout her life to maintain a reputable character despite what must have seemed at times continuous onslaught in the press, with its vicious political caricatures. The exposure of public sphere assaults on individuals depended on assigning morally questionable intentions to individual or private acts, a dependence also necessary to the trade in criminal conversation or adultery narratives. ("Crim con" trials were suits for damages against the wife's lover, often preliminary to a Parliamentary divorce trial, but also occasionally used by husbands to lucratively pimp their wives. Narratives of these trials were usually anonymous scripts by law students and clerks, cheaply published.)[4] However, the press exposés were amplified by partisan conflict, character slander, and the substitution of proper character for caricature. These elements of public warfare, often amounting to publicity stunts, could take on the group quality of armies battling—Tories, Whigs and radicals fought each other by singling out individuals to stand for the whole—but for the individuals in question, public attack could feel like a dueling match to which they must respond in counterfeits or self-defense. Such an experience was fraught, however, for once individuals speak for themselves they step out of the synecdochal position publicly assigned them, and implicitly accept the charge of impropriety. Their published defense can now be publicly evaluated

as a proper discourse or, to use the term for civil cases attempting monetary damages for adultery, as a criminal conversation. The analogy is helpful in understanding the tensions to which women were particularly vulnerable. By the mid-eighteenth century, monetary claims had largely replaced dueling to settle male disputes of honor, and by the 1780s and '90s the courts were virtually flooded with crim con cases.[5] Just as money had symbolically replaced the lawful exchange of sword thrusts or pistol shots, so discourse entered the symbolic realm of repute and character assassination as words became an acceptable vehicle for duels of honor, to be judged thereby. Improper characterization, whether unfounded press attacks or anti-republican, anti-social, or sexually titillating texts, might appeal to the public's love of partisan politicking and scandal, but personal defenses needed to abide by the public-sphere laws of warfare: one may be judged innocent or guilty, but he will be judged by men's laws. Women must know beforehand that these laws privilege idealized femininity, the erasure of real women, and a presumption of female guilt if a woman attempts to defend herself.

For a woman, the figurative charge of criminal conversation was whatever would single her out for publicized attack, whether in the law court, the press, or political cartoons, tarnishing her forever. In "Congreve's Way of the World and Popular Criminal Literature," John E. Loftis explores the relation between actual published accounts of trials and a dramatic scene in which crim con trials are used to leverage behavior in a play that may have influenced Robinson's self-interpretation as legally disenfranchised.[6] Loftis reads the concise dialogue of Congreve's scene to indicate the audience's familiarity with the "events and artifacts and the attitudes associated with them" as well as the way in which the threat of such a trial "embodies values and cultural attitudes in action" (562). Any woman who lived in the public eye needed to emphasize propriety and proper family relations to escape such charges; any woman who inhabited the "ton" as Mary Robinson did, dancing along the edge separating the demi-monde from polite society, was a chargeable target. And yet Robinson could not accept this fact of manly culture, and attempted throughout her career to assert her right to speak out in the public forum.

Although Mary Robinson was born to a respectable middle-class family, her American father's seafaring career and financial disasters eventually led to his desertion of the family, leaving wife and children to manage on their own. Despite this, Robinson received an intermittent formal education, including time at a finishing school north of Westminster where David Garrick saw her. Although she chose to marry rather than act with Garrick in *King Lear* (he offered to train her as Cordelia, giving her the confidence later to try acting), both options provided similar outcomes in her case. Her law clerk husband Thomas Robinson, an illegitimate son, had married her in an unsuccessful attempt to secure recognition and an inheritance from his father, and after the couple moved to London he sought to use her sexually to gain loans from aristocratic friends.[7] However, escaping marital disaster by taking up the stage at this juncture would also have placed Mary, not born to a thespian family as was Sarah Siddons, in a less than respectable career. In any case, the Robinsons soon landed in debtor's prison where Mary launched her literary career with a subscription volume of poetry, and from there the stage represented a different kind of respectability.[8]

Thus Mary Robinson began her career in an interesting subject-position regarding both the ideal nuclear and extended family model, for her father abandoned their family during her adolescence, and her mother encouraged her to marry—without evidence of his finances—a man who turned out to be a "counterfeit," the illegitimate product of adultery. Within this already improper situation, her husband Thomas Robinson encouraged his friends to consider her sexual favors a token of economic exchange (the same exchange on trial in crim con disputes). When she and her husband separated in 1780 after the birth of two daughters, her acting career, her brief but highly public reign as mistress of the Prince of Wales, and her long-term liaison with the war hero Colonel Tarleton situated Robinson as a demimondaine. If all her life she struggled to resist the character of a demi-rep, a woman of tarnished reputation, she nevertheless also labored to retain the status accorded the demi-monde as supplement to le beau monde. Demi-mondaine hostesses and courtesans could wield considerable power, and were sometimes difficult to distinguish from social elites like Lady Jersey and Lady Conyngham, later mistresses to the Prince of Wales (more tarnished now than when Robinson was his intimate). Such power was worth preserving, as Robinson knew.

Herself no icon of domesticity, it may then seem odd that Robinson's poems and novels continually focus on the roles of mothers and daughters, women in love and those deserted by their lovers, in terms of family models in their ideal and exploded forms. But in fact, familial terms are brought to trial in her works, tyrannical relations pitted against companionate marriages, and marital codes compared to the expressive liberation of Rousseau's emotionalism and espousal of sincere love. Robinson also walked the other side of the line: as much as she attempts to think through in literary works the critical nexus of family relations in a radicalized time moving inexorably towards a reactionary conservatism, and as much as her memoir, her Wollstonecraftian feminist pamphlet, and her novels attempt to establish authorial and personal propriety, Robinson also wrote much verse, from her Della Cruscan odes to her

autobiographical *Sappho and Phaon* (1796), that countered a proper self with a Rousseauistic one, playing out her passions publicly for all to see. This emotionalism served to give depth to a character continually at the mercy of public rumor regarding her less than circumspect liaisons, public chastisement in print caricatures, and public opinion regarding adultery and divorce. But such texts did not help Robinson defend herself as did the more proper discourse of her novels and discrete verse. In reflecting on chaste marriage versus Rousseau's assertion of emotional and physical imperatives (leading to the promulgation of "free love" as well as the public fascination with criminal conversation), Robinson's novels could argue against legalistic definitions of the family that made familial irresponsibility possible. Her emotion-based texts, by contrast, draw on an affiliate sensibility to that which fed the desire for lascivious cartoonage and the soft porn of crim con narratives. Why, we should ask, would she engage in both kinds of textual strategies, and why in particular would she indulge in sensualist texts when she was so often herself targeted by misogynist and pornographic caricatures depicting her sexual relations with the Prince of Wales and charged with the partisan politics of those relations? Indeed, long after that one-year affair was over she would have been sensitive to the anonymous moralizing or sensationalizing pamphlets of divorce trial narratives, and I believe would have responded to implicit comparisons between her own story and the scandal-mongering of publicized adultery cases in her most autobiographical works.

The answer to questions about Robinson's flirtation with public reputation must lie in the line drawn for dueling matches, a line similar in nature to the one women must observe in all their choices over proper and improper acts. Robinson derived power from dancing along this line rather than observing its strict demarcation, flirting with impropriety while posing as a proper lady. Her poems and novels, whether tuned to a domestic femininity or a Rousseauistic indiscretion, similarly play with discursive propriety, dwelling not only on the problem of the family's integrity in the face of women's socio-political and legally restricted subject position, but also on the problems of the sexually suspect woman. These texts thus set up the field for verbal duels with public-sphere voices. Her prose revisiting of Mary Wollstonecraft's *Vindication*, the *Letter to the Women of England* (1799), for instance, is a plea for women's need for social and legal self-defense against character slander, especially sexual slander. In thinking through Robinson's choice of textual strategies, it is helpful to consider a third option for women writers to the opposition between discursive propriety and criminal conversation; it is one for which Robinson manfully strove, self assertion. As she herself acknowledges, this is a male option, but in a woman's hands one that challenges the assumptions of gendered roles within the ideal family, that unit of integrity so necessary to the ideal republic.

Ideal families, however, are fictional not historical constructs. In them, servants do not spy on their employers as in real life, where if called for a servant's testimony is required by law. As older versions of ideal family units were being revised into a new tale of Rousseauistic affection, women writers seized on domestic fiction as an ideal way to reassess the prescriptive against the experience of everyday life. Historians of the family describe its physical lineaments in the West as temporally and geographically variable; however two main types dominate through the ages: stable families, which follow the primogeniture model of "patriarchal" and "stem" families, and unstable families, whose size rises and shrinks as children are produced and then leave the household, and which cease to exist on the death of its spousal partners.[9] But novelists like Fanny Burney and Jane Austen after her were considering how supposedly stable families were made unstable when practice did not follow the ideal plan of inheritance laws, wards were cheated or tricked by their guardians, and eldest brothers neglected sisters and female relatives. Robinson, like the radicals Wollstonecraft and Mary Hays, went further in asking what happens when children are conceived outside the marital unit so that different configurations of the ideal family are necessary. For conservative and radical novelists alike, the domestic is the political, the private is a matter for public reevaluation.[10] The crucible for this evaluation is the companionate marriage, in which affection rather than property is the reason for the family's birth, and disaffection the reason for its dissolution.[11] Although disaffection may be the root cause of divorce and crim con trials, however, the law judges marital conflict based on the marriage contract, which follows from patriarchal family structure: the provision by the husband of bed, board and clothing, and the provision by the wife of her "conversation" or care, and stainless reputation.[12] For Robinson these barebones of contracts that, like lovers' promises, can be broken by husbands with impunity (as does Thomas Robinson, the Prince of Wales, and eventually Bonastre Tarleton after him), make the exploded family an appropriate subject for her social critique, and make her argue ceaselessly for a relational rather than family model, one based on emotional and not legal contract. Thus her "family," consisting of herself and her surviving daughter, is a viable alternative to the ideal family, while even her long-term liaison with Tarleton is a better "marriage" than what she had experienced with her legal husband. From this perspective, crim con and divorce trials provide the context for Robinson's public face as well as for her social critiques.

2. FACING THE PUBLIC

Mary Robinson had two public faces—chaste authorial propriety (which she argues for in her *Memoirs*) and the demi-mondaine (which she exhibited in public outings to Vauxhall and St. James Park as the Prince's mistress)—both of which are stereotypes born of patriarchal conceptions of womanhood. It is on the basis of these stereotypes that the textual and visual attacks on her were launched, and so it is perhaps for very good reasons that she came to find even her dramatic ability to inhabit either of them at will confining (in her writing she is the virtuous mother, but her affairs make clear how at ease she was playing the mistress). Instead, she begins to argue for a third option, that of the vocally assertive woman whose self-respect is more valuable than society's opinion. This is an option that allows her to walk between categories of womanhood, for it is a presumptively male right. It is important, then, to consider the gender inflections of Robinson's public face (maternal femininity, demi-mondaine, or masculinely assertive) as she considers the problem of honor and character assassination.

Robinson's public face can be hard to pin down. Also known as Perdita, Tabitha Bramble, Bridget, Julia, Horace Juvenal, Laura Maria, Lesbia, Oberon, Portia, Anne Francis Randall, and Sappho, one has to ask, who is the private woman? How can we know her? What the political caricatures of her make clear is that wanting to know her privately can be done only as a public venture, as an inquiry into her private, that is sexual, life—and that to make this inquiry in a public way is to politicize it. As the crim con narratives make clear, any publicizing of sexuality makes it public domain, available for political and legal uses and abuses. It is this aspect of publicity that Robinson's *Letter to the Women of England,* which I will discuss more fully later, brings into the open, analyzes, and argues against. By publishing a pamphlet concerning the abusive gendering of public *action,* Robinson counters publicity with *publi*cation, a conscious offensive against legal duplicity. The *Letter,* its title emphasizing the publicizing of private texts, creates a parallel text to Robinson's literary and consciously autobiographical *Sappho and Phaon,* in which the private life becomes the argument for the public wrong of defamation. Defamation has two senses here, for the poem is intended to refute scandal mongering about Robinson's private life, but its historical reference is the de-fame-ing suffered by women poets who value love over art, emotion over production, private acts over public deeds, and are thus forgotten as artists. The comparative to both of Robinson's texts in this sense is indeed that staple of turn-of-the-century popular culture, the crim con narrative, in which women's private acts are displayed as unretractable, legally criminal products, bodies over which two men may duel not for love but for money and property.[13]

A common claim of the usually anonymous crim con narratives is that their publication is corrective: "This publication may perhaps effect what the law cannot: the transactions of the adulterer and the adulteress will, by being thus *publickly circulated,* preserve others from the like crimes, from the fear of shame, when the fear of punishment may have but little force."[14] I want to compare the nature of adultery narratives with how Robinson's literary works reflect her vulnerability to the kind of public denuding characteristic of these highly sensationalistic pamphlets, to see how her textual defensiveness and the revisionism tangible in her most autobiographical works reflect a response to the discursive maneuvers such sensationalist narratives employed. Because divorce was nearly impossible and necessitated proving criminal conversation, it was metaphorically an immoral discourse. To be read in terms of the crim con and divorce pamphlets would have turned Robinson, who supported herself and others through her writing, into an unpublishable author. Her response in some of her most important texts, especially her autobiographical sonnet sequence *Sappho and Phaon,* its prefatory essay, and her *Letter to the Women of England,* specifically respond to the discursive tactics used by divorce pamphleteers. In giving voice to the sexual or adulterous woman, Robinson reclaims the woman whose sexual favors are the lost property of the crim con trial, but who, in having given away these favors, may now not defend herself either in her own voice or through legal counsel. She is effectively absent, legally less valid than her maid-servants testifying against her.

Significantly, Robinson's *Memoirs,* composed during the last two years of her life (1798-1800) and finished posthumously by her surviving daughter, Maria Elizabeth, provide a revisionist and defensive depiction of a highly moral woman influenced by her emotional loyalties to important men, and characterized by her deeply maternal feelings for this daughter. If *Sappho and Phaon* (1796-97) and *Letter to the Women of England on the Injustice of Mental Subordination* (1799, signed "Anne Frances Randall") treat the problem of the deserted woman and the undefended woman respectively, her *Memoirs* treat the problem of family relations as they fail to protect the woman. Of course, readers bought her *Memoirs* to read it as a tell-all of her affair with the Prince of Wales; *Sappho and Phaon* traded on her public affair with the war hero Tarleton; and her *Letter to the Women of England* singles out character attacks against women as the representative corrective for female "mental subordination," but highlights the sensational news story of a woman literally defending her honor. Her autobiographical sonnet sequence and feminist pamphlet can be read together with her memoir, then, as a nexus of texts that use scandal mongering and improper discourse to refocus public regard away from disreputable discourses pervading the literary marketplace, and to contest their authority. Yet, in speaking out, Robinson takes on a masculine edge through this literary dueling with her detractors in the press. Using her reputation for beauty and popularity on the stage,

and suppressing her sexual attractiveness to men (which she does in her *Memoirs,* where she plays the ingénue throughout, and in *Sappho and Phaon* where she plays the aggressively loving and thus masculine partner to her lover), she combats lewd ploys to objectify her as a mere sexual toy by portraying herself as a victim of male inattention and carelessness. Loss of care (from the wife, however) is, of course, what crim con suits based monetary damages on. The contrast in gendered losses is telling, and by pressing her advantage Robinson highlights the absurdity of women's subject position under the law and under the marital conditions that obtain.

3. CRIMINAL CONVERSATIONS

Trial narratives about adultery and divorce were necessarily scandalous, given their subject, but they ranged from providing moralizing prefaces that put a good face on the unsuppressed details provided by witnesses, to undisguised titillation enhanced by lascivious frontispieces or first page illustrations of the lady alone or of the lady and her lover. They were typically short octavo pamphlets unbound and without boards, and costing a shilling. Consumers would bind a collection of them, but when resold these volumes were often missing their illustrations, sometimes still discernible however from the transfer of the frontispiece onto the title page.[15] The vanished frontispieces speak loudly of such portraits' fetishistic purpose but not of the lady's person or her own story.

While early crim con trials were often of aristocratic and wealthy families, by the 1790s when Robinson was writing her most defensive works they were largely of middle-class families. Although Robinson was allied through her sexual affairs with the highest classes, she was a merchant's daughter, vulnerable to the sexual economy of crim con narratives with their profiteering from women's secrets. Indeed, the market strategy of these pamphlets is not far from Mary Robinson's account of her husband's own attempts to barter his new wife's sexual favors for loans from his wealthy friends. A typical middle-class trial of this period was *Adultery. The Trial of Mr. William Atkinson, Linendraper, of Cheapside for Criminal Conversation with Mrs. Connor, Wife of Mr. Connor, Late of the Mitre, at Barnet: which was tried in Hilary Term, 1789, in the Court of King's Bench, Before Lord Kenyon.*[16] The moralizing advertisement of this trial narrative, designed to attract those perusing a bookshop, begins by intoning,

> The frequency of trials for *Adultery,* by which the parties become so much exposed, would alone, it might be thought, be a sufficient reason in some measure to stop some of the many instances that have been exhibited to public view, by a legal investigation of the charges brought by the offended party; or at least have made them more cautious in the commitment of a crime

strictly prohibited by the Almighty, and of the most fatal consequence to families . . .

(*Advertisement* v)

The *Advertisement* goes on to explain the criminality of adultery and a cursory history of its punishments, the implicit comparison rendering the mere compensation of financial award a civilized solution. Although the two thousand pounds the former innkeeper, Mr. Connors, is suing for damages will be reduced by half by the jury, the *Advertisement* makes this enormous amount seem natural compensation for wrongful conversation. This civilizing tone continues into the text itself, in which the anonymous author explains to the lay reader the plea, and justifies his novelized and dramatized version of the trial by commenting that, "The *substance,* instead of the *literal form* of the pleadings is thus concisely stated, with a view of conveying at once the real meaning of the action, without perplexing the reader with dry formal cant and professional jargon" (6, emphasis in original). Literal is exchanged for literary, yet salacious details are rendered literally, rewriting the ideolect of the witnesses (all servants at the inn) through dramatic dialogue. The reader effectively reads a narrative that, when not rendering the defending and accusing counsels' statements to the jury, turns to staged drama.

Q. How did Mrs. Connor appear with respect to her cloaths?

A. Her handkerchief was ruffled very much.

(13)

The dialogues between barrister and witness not only aid in visualizing the trial, but they efface the reality that an actual play would have revealed: that neither of the accused parties, nor the accuser, play any part in the drama. Their stories are entirely told by others within the restrictions set by legal practice, and guided by the conventions of legal discourse. Thus we discover that the two lovers were seen several times in the bar in a state of rumpled or semi-undress, and one morning Mrs. Connor was discovered in Mr. Atkinson's room at the inn, which he took when visiting Barnet on business, while he was still in bed in his shirt. The maid-servant attested that there was an impression of two bodies in the bed, and that there was "something on the sheets" (15), while the waiter attested that he had seen something on the floor another time, and a third servant that the lovers' hands were often in each others' bosoms.

The defense, however, declared that Mr. Connor had to have known about the affair, since it took place at "a public inn upon a road, where all the transactions passing in the house must be, in a certain degree, public" (22). As private affairs become the currency of public knowledge, the public nature of this liaison justifies the pamphleteer's publicizing of its story, while his use of novel and dramatic technique render the "dry cant" of legalese into bedtime reading. Mary Robinson, novelist, actress, dramatist, and celebrated mistress, would have had a hard time not reading herself into this form of public discourse. Significantly, when she published her sonnet sequence *Sappho and Phaon* in order to substitute an allegorical account of her long-term affair with the famed Colonel Tarleton of the Green Dragoons 1st Regiment, she borrows from the kind of legalized discourse available in crim con narratives for her defensive preface.[17] Like the anonymous author of the Atkinson trial narrative, Robinson also provides a cursory history of precedents for her role as poet; like him, she too finds in ancient history the grounds for her current undertaking, with its civilizing attention to women's experience in the face of faithless lovers—yet this experience is entirely left out of the Atkinson pamphlet. Robinson's most salient point in the preface is that she will practice the Petrarchan or "legitimate sonnet" in *Sappho and Phaon,* rescuing this now debased because unregulated—we might say adulterous—form from its criminal practitioners. Poets of 'illegitimate' sonnets "profess the art of poetry" yet compose sonnets of "more than thirty lines," attend to little rule, and follow their own amorous inclinations.[18] Their excesses produce a "heterogeneous mass of insipid and laboured efforts," and Robinson emphasizes the salaciousness of their enterprise when "trembl[ing], lest that chaos of dissipated pursuits which has too long been growing like an overwhelming shadow . . . menac[es] the luster of intellectual light." She worries that their "profligacy" will "reduce the dignity of talents to the lowest degradation" (146). Like the author of the Atkinson pamphlet, Robinson uses moralizing terms to root out damaging acts, but unlike him she does so to reduce the transgressive love of others to a dry cant. Her literary efforts to re-establish the purity of the Petrarchan love sonnet, with its strains of true love, are made in the face of the inevitable fate of poetic genius, to be "assailed by envy, stung by malice, and wounded by the fastidious comments of concealed assassins" (148). Wrongful discourse, criminal conversation, intercourse, and narrative all interweave here to produce a strong defense against those who have used her relations with the Prince and Tarleton against her. In *Sappho and Phaon,* she is announcing, she will retell the story from her own perspective through a dramatization of heroically poetical love, a move that masks the audacity of her role as active lover—the male position—rather than passive beloved, and readers will see Tarleton's betrayal of her as indefensible and (terrible for a war hero) disloyal. This is a strategic move, one resonant with the para-legalese of crim con narratives and the discourses of publicity.

In another published crim con case, *The Trial of the Hon. Charles Wyndham* (1791), Mr. Hodges brought charges against Wyndham, although the defense showed he was only the last of many of Mrs. Hodges' lovers. One of these lovers was the Prince of Wales himself, the revelation of which led the court to dismiss serious consideration of Hodges' claim for damages. Witnesses testified that the Prince came frequently to visit Mrs. Hodges at night, and that he would ask Hodges to leave them together, and once had Hodges attend a Parliamentary debate for him while he comforted himself in Mrs. Hodges' bed. Such evidence classified Mrs. Hodges with the lower ranks of the Prince's circle of mistresses, among which Mary Robinson must ever reside in genteel and popular judgments.[19] Lord Kenyon ends the Wyndham trial by comparing the behavior of Mr. Hodges and the Prince to another piece of high drama: "I remember a case once, not quite so scandalous as this, where Theophilus Cibber carried a pillow to a gentleman for the express purpose of committing adultery with his wife—His action was afterwards scouted with indignation" (22). As Lord Kenyon notes, Hodges' behavior is that of "prostitut[ing] his wife," a common defense for alleged adulterers to leverage against their accusers, and one which goes back to the historical precedent of Lord Audley, who despite his abusive behavior (in later divorce trials the wife had to prove extreme spouse abuse as well) was tried on moral charges (among them, forcibly prostituting his wife), similar to crim con cases which are retributive rather than vindicative.

The Earl of Castlehaven, Mervyn Lord Audley, was convicted and executed "for carosing and Ravishm't to his wife and comittings of sodomy" in 1631.[20] When a case is ruled through analogy with the Audley principle, the wife's illicit behavior becomes her husband's fault and damages are disallowed.[21] In Audley's trial, Walter Bigges explains to the court that the Countess of Castlehaven's page was given gifts of money and deeds to lands and possessions by Lord Audley: "He let this Henry Skipwith who was called his favorit spend of his estate 500th p[er] anno and if his wife and daughter did want any thing though necessary they must lye first with Skipwith and hee must be their paymaster and not otherwise" (7). According to the Countess' testimony, "He would make Skipwith come naked into hir chamber and bed and delighted in calling up his servants to shew their privityss and make hir looke on and comend those that had the largest," and moreover, Skipwith "lay with hir whilst she made resistance and my Lo[rd] held hir hands and one of hir feete."[22] Audley was also accused of "telling Skipwith and his daughter they being in bed he sitting on the bedside that he had rather have a boy of his getting then by any other in the world" (ms 7). As the prosecuting attorney comments, "But I fynd things beyond imagination for I fynd his ill intentions bent to have his wife prostitute hireselfe to his base groomes which the wickedest man that ever I heard of before would have to be vertous and good, how bad so-

ever himselfe were. But for him he was Baude to his owne wife nay let y[ou]r grace suffer mee to speake a more homely word, he was both pander and bawde to his owne wife, most sordid base and inhumane" (ms 6). However, Lady Audley did have a son, and the oddest fact of the trial is how late it took place: Audley's defense was that this son, now 21 years old, had plotted with his wife because "the one desyred lands the other a younger husband and therefore they plotted his death" (ms 11). Sounding eerily like Count Cenci's claims against his family in Shelley's *The Cenci* (1819), Audley's trial appears to have been the result of a family dissolution that finally caught up with him. Certainly this is his historical reputation, as the father of marital pandering. But Lord Kenyon clearly sees the stage dramatics of the Wyndham case in addition to its family dynamic. In relating the claimant, by Audley precedent to Theophilus Cibber, son of Colley and briefly the husband of Susannah Cibber, to Hodges, Kenyon puts pandering in its place as an illicit staging of private matters. The theatrical world had long been associated with free sex, but here Kenyon draws what is for Robinson a darker connection: acting and prostitution are yoked like a chiasmus as illicit goods. For Robinson there might be an even tighter circle drawn between her husband's attempts to pander her and Theophilus Cibber's attempt to rid himself of his wife, as well as between the well-respected Susannah Cibber and Robinson's own claims of virtue defended. Such cases may well have been at the back of her mind when she wrote, with appropriate pseudo-legalese, her *Letter to the Women of England*.

4. DUELING

What is interesting about the configuration of honor, publicity, and criminal conversation is how mutable the boundaries between these are for men. Crim con trial narratives focus on witnesses, most frequently domestic servants (the most resorted to sources of information in the Prince of Wales' various attempts to spy on his wife). Servants' reports of affectionate conversation in non-public rooms and hands in the wrong private places provide "facts," verifiable or not, to be pirated for public consumption. When dueling was no longer the legally sanctioned ritual for disputes of honor, men turned to monetary compensation as a civilized alternative for those quarrels involving cuckoldry. The public dishonor transferred to the husband from his wife's defaced body is translated into a symbolic coinage of public repute. While she remains disreputable, the husband has reduced his enemy's pockets, symbolically draining the adulterer's seed to restore his own pockets. When crim con suits are revealed to be cons for husbands who, having pimped their wives, now want to fleece the johns, they also reveal how the legal circulation of women's bodies, honor, and currency in adultery trials is the same as that of marriages. Thomas Robinson's attempt to pimp his new wife for gambling loans is merely a variant on the hypocrisy of the marriage contract's double standard. The substitution of property damages for dishonor does not negate the fact that the honorable currency between two men is still metonymically a duel, and that the tainted woman remains silenced and defaced. Now a property of no value, she may be publicly ridiculed, her private affairs bared to prurient eyes as her revealing portrait fronts the narrative of the affair in question. As the editor of *Trials for Adultery* notes, "It requires little or no apology for the publication of these trials. It may, perhaps . . . deter the wavering wanton from the completion of her wishes" but "When a woman (especially of the superior class) has lost that inestimable jewel, virtue; alas! How is she fallen! . . . she is indeed become the object of the scorn, pity, and derision of her relations, her former associates, and the public" (iv).

An adulterous woman engages the public eye in ways similar to that of the stage actress, men of honor haunting the green room just as they purchased crim con narratives and political cartoons, for women's sexual bodies were up for sale. The sexual discourse of theatricality was echoed in the semi-pornography of the hugely popular political caricatures. In one of James Gillray's political cartoons during the Prince's infatuation with Robinson, she is depicted as a tavern whirligig.[23] Staked through the cervix, woman's other "mouth" or sex-text orifice, Gillray uses Robinson iconically to illustrate the Prince's party flipflops as breezy revolutions or mere words. Caricaturists' and journalists' fears that Robinson had undue influence on the Prince would recur for each of his mistresses, and in the cases of Maria Fitzherbert and the ambitious Lady Jersey these fears were realized. But Robinson was singled out for singularly vicious attacks in the press, her Whig and feminist leanings not yet in full bloom but her political body already a magnet for public scrutiny and judgment.

The attacks on Robinson's reputation may have been merely generic in nature; after all, political cartoons of Princess Caroline several decades later similarly depicted her as sexually voracious, politically meddlesome, and with her hand in other people's pockets or national treasuries despite her lack of access to the Prince's ear. Robinson could not fail to have noticed a generic assault on female reputation similar to the political caricature: the frontispiece or accompanying illustrations to crim con trial narratives. The frontispiece for the Wyndham Trial for example is set as an oval portrait of "Mrs. Hodges" in revolutionary-style dress (kerchief over chest, short jacket with collar and lapels open wide, button on cuffs at wrist, bustle and overskirt with skirt revealed in front, adaptation of man's top hat on head, frizzed wig). But her kerchief is opened to expose her left breast and nipple as she poses her head away from the viewer but looks out of the left corners

of her eyes (orienting her pupils with her exposed breast) so that she flirts with the viewer. The courtesan that Robinson became as the Prince's Perdita was merely a version of a more common type.

Such types were boundary usurpers, women who used sex to translate the private into public, conversation into destructive acts, and to undo the natural order. Trials concerning sexuality played on these transgressions while balancing them with the observance that man's legal power in the private sphere could easily turn to tyrannical abuse. Thus many crim con narratives begin with prefatory comment on tyranny, not as a politicized reference but as a kind of popular historiography. As the prosecution declares in the Audley Trial, "the prisoner is hon[ora]ble the crymes diplor[a]ble of which he is inditd, which if they fall out to be true and which is to be Left to traill [trail] I dare be bould to say never poet ffaigned [feigned] nor Histriographers writt of any soe fowle [foul] though Suetonius hath curiously set forth the vices of some of the Emperours, whoe had absolute power and all manner of Liberty thus might make them carelesse of all manner of punishment" (ms 4). This reference to Suetonius is echoed in Romantic-era crim con trials as a set-piece commentary on despotic abuses that can occur in the domestic sphere.[24] Robinson, following Wollstonecraft's lead, takes the tyranny argument as a given in her *Letter to the Women of England,* citing "the tyranny of man" as part and parcel of "the tyranny of custom," condensing Suetonius' history into a single fact: "the yoke of sexual tyranny."[25] This is not a strong link to the trial narratives, but the use in her *Letter* of an allusively legalized discourse to promote her view of women's present subjugation is: "Let WOMAN once assert her proper sphere, unshackled by prejudice, and unsophisticated by vanity; and pride, (the noblest species of pride,) will establish her claims to the participation of power, both mentally and corporeally" (2). Referring to "philosophical sensualists" like Jean-Jacques Rousseau (1), Robinson builds her case that women's real debility in society is not their mental inferiority to men, but their inability to defend themselves under the current sexual economy. Arguing on the grounds of natural law that the sexual double standard is indefensible, Robinson defends herself and her fellow women through a strategic male metonymy: the duel. Literally and figuratively dueling was still the most effective riposte to assaults on a man's honor, and to refuse to challenge one's abuser was unnatural. But neither a woman's reputation, if attacked by vicious rumor and scandal-mongering or even a man's false word, nor a woman's rights under the legal code, could be repudiated or upheld by the defenses available to men. As Robinson points out, when women attempt to defend their honor they are viewed as aberrant aggressors. Robinson's appropriation of the male strategy of dueling for rhetorical purposes rebalances the double standard; using a defense lawyer's argumentation, she indicates that being on trial is woman's condition and that speaking out—an illicit act in courts of law, and by extension in the public sphere—is her natural recourse. In the court of public opinion she fights for the respect she deserves.

> The barbarity of custom's law in this *enlightened* country, has long been exercised to the prejudice of woman:—and even the laws of honour have been perverted to oppress her. If a man receive an insult, he is justified in seeking retribution; and his courage rises in estimation, in proportion as it exemplifies his revenge. But were a WOMAN to attempt such an expedient, however strong her sense of injury, however invincible her fortitude, or important the preservation of character, she would be deemed a murdress. Thus, custom says, you must be free from error; you must possess an unsullied fame: yet, if a slanderer, or a libertine, even by the most unpardonable falshoods [sic], deprive you of either reputation or repose, you have no remedy. He is received in the most fastidious societies, in the cabinets of nobles, at the toilettes of coquets and prudes, while you must bear your load of obloquy, and sink beneath the uniting efforts of calumny, ridicule, and malevolence.
>
> (4-6)

Her point about what is "denominated the *defenceless sex*" is clearly argued, but it also seems clearly oriented toward the slanderous discourse of the crim con pamphlets. The "nature" in natural rights becomes disarticulated in the female case: a natural daughter, as one of Robinson's novel titles clarifies, is an illicit being produced by criminal conversation.[26] Legally detyped, she can have no proper voice and thus becomes the most egregious case of woman's condition. A husband may accuse his wife of adultery, of illicit conversation, but she is undefended: the plaintiff's lawyer argues the husband's case, the defending lawyer argues the lover's, and she, one of the principals, is relegated to the status of innuendo as servants and other gossips of the publicly private home gain ascendancy over their mistress by publishing their suspicions abroad in court.

Moreover, if crim con trials were the attempts by cuckolded husbands to recover damages to their property, that is, their wife's bodily and emotional company—her conversation—and the crim con pamphlets were an attempt to sell this conversation for profit, Robinson discovered that after publishing her *Letter* under a pseudonym she would have to recover her property or, like the lascivious body, it would belong to someone else. In her advertisement to the second edition, retitled *Thoughts on the Condition of Women, and on the Injustice of Mental Subordination* (1799), she is unequivocal: "Finding that a Work on a subject similar to the following, has lately been published at Paris, Mrs. Robinson is induced to avow herself the Author of this Pamphlet." Self-assertion or avowal becomes synonymous with swordplay as the woman writer fends off claimants to her textual body.

Finally, Robinson's revisionist *Memoirs,* which purchasers supposed would be a titillating revelation of her affair with the Prince of Wales, but which was instead an effort to bleach all stain from the fabric of her life, supported her contentions in the *Letter to the Women of England* by sharing her own account of her relations with libertines, slanderers, and deserting fathers, husbands and lovers. Repeatedly she emphasizes her attempts to keep a family home together and to care for her mother and her daughter, the *Memoirs* serving to reknit the interstices of a family undermined by masculine resorts to social and political power. As she declaims in her *Letter,*

> Man is able to bear the temptations of human existence better than woman, because he is more liberally educated, and more universally acquainted with society. Yet, if he has the temerity to annihilate the bonds of moral and domestic life, he is acquitted; and his enormities are placed to the account of *human frailty.* Such partial discriminations seem to violate all laws, divine and human! If WOMAN be the weaker creature, her frailty should be the more readily forgiven. She is exposed by her personal attractions, to more perils, and yet she is not permitted to bear that shield, which man assumes; she is not allowed the exercise of *courage* to repulse the enemies of her fame and happiness; though, if she is wounded,—she is *lost for ever!*
>
> (6-7)

Being lost forever was a fate Robinson very much feared, both in social reputation and in literary fame. But her authorial behavior replicated her at times audacious dance with propriety in public spaces. In this she much resembled a higher placed and more public figure who also had much to do with the Prince of Wales, his demi-monde lifestyle, and the problem of wounded reputation and its legal redress: the Princess of Wales. Like Robinson, Princess Caroline played with and exploited the boundaries between mistress and wife, criminal and proper conversation, propriety and rebellious display, and like Robinson she suffered under legal codes drawn by men.

5. COURTLY PUBLICITY

Princess Caroline's divorce hearing before Parliament in 1820, two decades after Robinson's demise, allows us to see how Robinson's fears about women's publicly sexual status could play out on a political stage. As a self-dramatizing woman who manipulated the fine line between the proper and the improper as assiduously as had Robinson, but who was also extremely careless at times about its implications for her public face, Princess Caroline offers a good example of what even the most privileged woman might expect in Robinson's world. And although she is best contrasted to the Prince's natural wife Maria Fitzherbert, Caroline is best compared to Robinson as the Prince's mistress, for the Prince fell for both Robinson and Caroline visually, in staged images (Robinson as Perdita, Caroline as a portrait miniature) of an ideal woman: proper, silent, and still. Clearly neither Wollstonecraft's arguments nor Robinson's works had been efficacious in changing the rules of the game by the time Caroline needed them. Anything but an ideal public persona for female royals was not permitted; moreover, Caroline's body was the property disputed between Whig and Tory politicians. In her divorce "trial," the private sphere would be not only made public, but turned into political warfare, a dueling match become a royal battlefield.[27]

However, like Robinson, Caroline attempted to assert her person and her voice. The Prince's determination to divorce his wife led to the initial "Delicate Investigation" (George's attempt to have Caroline's adopted son proven to be her own), and continual spying on her interactions with others. She retaliated by keeping a diary that exaggerated discordant family events, mentioning her entries to others to consciously exploit scandal. Intended to harm the Prince and Queen Charlotte, and to avenge herself on any who had crossed her (including the Prince's mistresses) "the red book" was, as Caroline hinted numerous times, somewhat fanciful. Eventually her version of George's politicizing of family relations, events drawn from her yearly diaries, and uncomplimentary character sketches of the royal family became public enough within her own and radical circles that at least one variation on the published ripostes to the "Delicate Investigation" reflected her own perspective rather than that of Whig politicians using her marital difficulties to gain sway with the public. But if Caroline's textual play between fact and fiction resembled Robinson's use of autobiography to flesh out positions for verbal dueling matches, in intention it differed greatly, for its indiscretions were scandalous, and it aimed to wound rather than defend.

The Book of the Princess, containing the proceedings of the "Delicate Investigation," was printed in 1807 by her Whig supporters, but its copies were burnt when political winds shifted. However, one or more copies survived in addition to her manuscript diary (to which she continued to add new revelations), and Spencer Perceval serialized and then republished the entire account as *The Book!* in 1813[28] to reveal the already unpopular Prince's role in instigating the affair, thus embarrassing both him and the Tory party, and to attack the unsupportive and vengeful Queen.[29] This was to counter Thomas Ashe's 1811 *Spirit of the Book,* a confessional supposedly by Caroline and possibly at the commission of Carlton House, intended to counter Caroline's threatened and actual publication of various letters to and from the Prince and of her diary.[30] Grub Street had a field day publishing variants of Ashe's *Spirit of the Book* and Perceval's *The Book!,* but when one such publication *The Book Itself! Private Memoirs . . . being a complete answer to the Spirit of the Book*[31] ap-

peared (probably ghostwritten using Caroline's freely spread intimations on the royal family), it had been revised into an allegory differing from that of Ashe's gothic romance, its overt fiction calling into question the truth value of Ashe's fabrication. *The Book Itself!* gives voice to Caroline's perspective in a way oddly aligned with her "red book." The Prince of Cumaria, encouraged to marry by his father, King of the Albs, in order to discharge his debts, gives up "the charms of the fat, yet beauteous and fascinating, Fitzhar, known by the surname of 'the fat witch'" (Maria Fitzherbert) in order to marry Augusta Princess of Bornburck. The Prince is subsequently tricked by courtiers into believing his newborn baby is the product of the Princess' affair with "Scarecrow" in their own house, "Coralton Hall." Reading like a cross between a sentimental novel and a gothic, the *Private Memoirs* not only depicts the Princess as the ideal woman and victimized heroine, but reveals a familiarity with adultery trial narratives, their use of (not always reliable) servants as witnesses, and their reliance on the dramatic questioning of witnesses to gain information (unlike the letters, documents and depositions that crowd the pages of Perceval's *Book!*). Like Robinson, Caroline also used trial discourse in her letters and self-narratives to plot her feints and counters against all-powerful men who threatened to undo her. Epistolary dueling, whether the publication of Caroline's letters to the Prince and King that she provided for Perceval's edition of *The Book!,* or the belles lettres of her "red book" (uncannily resurfacing in *The Book Itself!* with its pro-Caroline view of her marital mistreatment), could—as in Robinson's *Letter to the Women of England*—form an effective strategy for self-assertion. But Caroline's motives were much more personal than Robinson's—she was fighting for property rights over her annual income and her daughter—rather than for women's legal and civil rights, or for textual rights. Nevertheless, the crossover between autobiography and imaginative literature, correspondence and belles lettres, provides an interesting comparison between the princess and the mistress as they battled the man who each had romantically idealized to their detriment.

Robinson's texts may have been more rigorously truthful, more assertively voiced, and more defensively aimed than were Caroline's, but they achieved the same blurring of biographical verity. Not only was Ashe's *Spirit of the Book* only somewhat factual, Caroline's damning diary somewhat fictional and the *Private Memoirs* of *The Book Itself!* almost entirely so (indeed, this was the titillating tell-all concerning Royal misbehavior the public was waiting for rather than Robinson's *Memoirs*), but the public read them all as versions of one another, just as they read Robinson's texts through the lens of scandalous gossip. In both cases, the woman only aided the dis-reputation caused by the kind of untruths Robinson complains of in her *Letter.* When first

Henry Brougham and then Samuel Whitbread wrote letters for Caroline to send to the Prince in her own name to use as leverage against his restrictions on her, their ghostwriting was just one more version of Ashe's *Spirit of the Book,* itself simply another in the genre of verbal satiric cartoons of public women like those also penned against Robinson.[32] Claiming one's own voice as a woman could be difficult whether the male impersonator was attempting to help or hinder public reputation. One of these letters, which the Prince repeatedly refused to read, was published in the *Morning Chronicle,* probably without Caroline's aid, and became known as "The Regent's Valentine" (Fraser 231). It did create more public support for her, and in fact she was continually threatening such public outings, but generally Caroline's belief in the inherent privacy of (her own) letters created more trouble for her than her publicizing of letters could remedy.[33] While the final effect of these quasi-documents was the culminating divorce trial of Caroline, their intermediate effect was sensation. The populace almost consistently supported the genial Caroline over her spendthrift and moody husband, and when she left to roam the Continent during Napoleon's captivity she was greeted everywhere by courts where her story was known, and "her" book—actually Ashe's—was being avidly read. Despite the gossip mongering, and unlike Robinson, Caroline was nearly always considered the victim of an abusive and neglectful husband by the public even when newspapers reported daily on the three-month Parliamentary debate over George's divorce bill (with witnesses and cross-examinations, this was effectively her divorce trial).[34]

In this, her story considerably resembles that of Mary Robinson, even down to the legal argumentation of Brougham's letters that he wrote for her to the Prince. But Brougham ups the ante staked by Robinson, noting that a "guiltless woman," such as the Princess claimed to be, has no choice but to engage the enemy: "If her honour is invaded, the defence of her reputation is no longer a matter of choice . . . these ought to be the feelings of every woman in England" (quoted in Fraser 232). Brougham seems to have Robinson's *Letter to the Women of England* in front of him as well as Wollstonecraft's *Vindication,* using the fencing motif Robinson deploys to take the man's strategic posture of aggression through self-assertion. Yet these are Brougham's words, not Caroline's; she herself would defeat Brougham's and Robinson's stratagem by playing the coquette, and embodying the masculinist view of women as the flirter with propriety so detested by Wollstonecraft. Even if her *Book Itself!* takes a legal stab when the heroine's letter to her Prince begins, "condemned without knowing my accuser or my crime . . ." (16), in her actual letter-duels with her husband Princess Caroline resorted to male intervention either through the King or through courtiers and politicians such as Brougham, and her battles were considered even by her supporters to be aggressive and unfeminine. This is apparent from the feints and counterfeints involved in telling her own story—from her diary to Ashe's *Spirit of the Book,* from *Spirit of the Spirit* (a pirated abridgement) to Perceval's *The Book* and the Caroline-influenced *The Book Itself!,* from the publication of the "King's Case" and her trial minutes to Robert Huish's sympathetic, flowery and enormous two-volume *Memoirs of Caroline* published the year of her death to capitalize on public interest.[35] As men attacked, exploited and defended her, Caroline herself publicly played both sides of the gender game. In this she abused social proprieties even though common opinion supported her throughout, and—shut out of George's coronation, even having a door slammed in her face as she tried to enter Westminster (a superlative metaphor of her marital experience)—she finally left her public nowhere to place her and, literalizing Sappho's solution, died soon after.

In attempting to defend herself to her public, Robinson was constantly aware of—and in contrast to Caroline, far more observant of—the fine line between feminine and masculine behavior. Sappho's self-silencing leap of suicide at the end of her tale is determined by the female artist's strategic maneuvering between masculinist self-assertion and self-defense, and feminine subservience. But in creating multiple ways to portray herself as being on trial, Robinson has pushed the borders for understanding the cultural definitions of women's roles: mistresses or courtesans versus wives, public women versus private women, criminal conversation versus women's proper discourse. "What," Robinson's most aggressively defining texts seem to ask, "may a woman say for herself?" Caroline's divorce hearing seems to suggest that nothing at all is best. In the end, her "trial" came down not to textual offenses—the sending of improper letters, a deed she was much given to and which constituted one of the mainstays of crim con trials—but bodily defenses. Her case was decided on the same improprieties that were often decisive factors in adultery cases: whether or not others, especially domestic servants, witnessed her placing her hands in the wrong man's pockets. Signally, this was never the charge brought against Robinson in political caricatures. If Caroline's story meant improper penning (indeed, her penmanship and spelling were always suspect for she was badly educated), Robinson's hands accomplished a rather different task in using discursive proprieties as cultural weapons. In inhabiting bodily rather than discursive positions in such public ways, however, Caroline re-normalized the gender divisions Robinson (like Wollstonecraft) had so manfully striven against.

In effect, there have been four ways of being on trial organizing this essay: criminal conversation cases, Robinson's verse defense of her emotional "marriage" to Tarleton, Robinson's legal arguments which position women as perpetual trial defendants in her *Letter to the Women of England,* and Princess Caroline's divorce hearing. All of these ways of being tried are extremely public ones in which the domestic and private spheres women supposedly inhabit are transformed into publicity venues. In each, whether it is an actual court of law or a published document, women are unable to defend attacks on their honor and reputation either through legal recourse with its masculinist prerogatives or through the private act of dueling. In each case others' words are weapons used against women, whether it is the domestic servant testifying (reliably or capriciously) in court about spied activities, or a lover's desertion that silences the woman's words. Each of these break apart the home even as they dispute the woman's bodily intention, and in destroying her social place they wreck the woman's public face. Legally speaking, not to caricature Robinson's physical disability but to verify it, the woman is left without a leg to stand on.

Notes

1. *Trials for Adultery: or, the History of Divorces . . .* 2 vols. London: Printed for S. Bladon, No. 13, Pater-noster Row; 1779 (vol 1), 1780 (vol 2).

2. I want to thank Margaret Hunt for her perceptive reading of a short version of this essay. Scholarship on Robinson that informs this essay includes Ashley Cross, "From Lyrical Ballads to Lyrical Tales: Mary Robinson's Reputation and the Problem of Literary Debt" *SiR* [*Studies in Romanticism*] 40.4 (2001): 571-605; Judith Pascoe's "Mary Robinson and the Literary Marketplace," *Romantic Women Writers: Voices and Countervoices,* ed. Paula R. Feldman and Theresa M. Kelley (Hanover: UP of New England, 1995), 252-315; Pascoe's *Romantic Theatricality: Gender, Poetry and Spectatorship* (Ithaca: Cornell UP, 1997); Sharon M. Setzer, "Romancing the Reign of Terror: Sexual Politics in Mary Robinson's *The Natural Daughter,*" *Criticism* 39 (1997): 531-55; and Eleanor Ty, *Empowering the Feminine: The Narratives of Mary Robinson, Jane West, and Amelia Opie, 1796-1812* (Toronto: U of Toronto P, 1998).

3. For scholarship on political caricature, see Diana Donald's *The Age of Caricature: Satirical Prints in the Reign of George III* (New Haven: Yale UP, 1996); Katharine Kittredge, ed., *Lewd and Notorious: Female Transgression in the Eighteenth Century* (Ann Arbor: U of Michigan P, 2003); M. Dorothy George, *Hogarth to Cruikshank: Social Change in Graphic Satire* (London: Penguin, 1957); and Kevin Gilmartin, *Print Politics: The Press and Radical Opposition in Early Nineteenth-Century England* (Cambridge: Cambridge UP, 1996).

4. The claim in crim con trials was for property damages against the wife's body and the husband's loss of her companionship. However, here companionship is defined in terms of wife's duties (caretaking) rather than affection as in a companionate marriage. See Susan Staves, "Money for Honor: Damages for Criminal Conversation," *Studies in Eighteenth-Century Culture* 11 (1982): 279-98. Laura Hanft Korobkin's *Criminal Conversations: Sentimentality and Nineteenth-Century Legal Stories of Adultery* (NY: Columbia UP, 1998) usefully fleshes out the relation between crim con narratives and sentimental fiction, but focuses on American 19th-century law and literature. See also Elaine Jordan, "Criminal Conversation: Mary Wollstonecraft's *The Wrongs of Woman,*" *Women's Writing* 4.2 (1997): 221-34.

5. In the mid-17th century, with the collapse of ecclesiastical authority, common law courts began to try adultery cases as civil rather than criminal offenses. Lawrence Stone notes that adultery trials increased dramatically between 1740 and the 1790s (*The Road to Divorce* [Oxford: Oxford UP, 1990] 247).

6. *Studies in English Literature* 36.3 (Summer, 1996): 561-78. Loftis, however, is more interested in the public's familiarity with published criminal trials available in what is now referred to as the *Old Bailey Sessions Papers,* whereas I am concerned with the much less available and much more scurrilous published accounts of crim con trials.

7. *Memoirs of the Late Mrs. Robinson, Written by Herself* (London: Printed by Wilkes and Taylor, 1801).

8. The Robinsons marry in April 1773 and visit Mr. Harris at his estate where Mary is disabused of her husband's falsehoods concerning his family; their first daughter is born 18 months later. The following year Mary's first volume of poems appears and the family spends Thomas' prison term at Fleet Prison (3 May to 3 August, 1776). Mary debuts at Drury Lane under Sheridan's direction on 10 December 1776. Three years later nearly to the day she wins the heart of the Prince of Wales as Perdita in *The Winter's Tale.*

9. Lawrence Stone discerns three models of family organization: the early Open Lineage Family, the Restricted Patriarchal Nuclear Family (dominant in the upper classes from the Renaissance to 1700), and the Closed Domesticated Nuclear Family (rising with Enlightenment culture), in *The Family, Sex and Marriage in England 1500-1800* (NY: Harper Colophon, 1979 [1977]). Rosemary O'Day's history of the family in England, France

and New England helpfully argues against these restrictive definitions, showing that actual families deviated from these models according to temporal and regional pressures and needs. Her work helps us see that families depicted in women's novels may have been typical rather than idiosyncratic representations: *The Family and Family Relationships, 1500-1900: England, France, and the United States of America* (New York: St. Martin's P, 1994). Josef Ehmer shows that historians' attempts to establish historical, regional or class distinctions between types of families in Britain and Europe, and between the relative affection in or outside of marriage between partners cannot be done categorically: "Marriage," in *Family Life in the Long Nineteenth Century 1789-1913,* ed. by David I. Kertzer and Marzio Barbagli (New Haven: Yale UP, 2002) 282-321. Thus women's attempts to reconfigure the family either imaginatively or literally were enabled by knowledge of other models for the family unit available elsewhere in Britain or in Europe.

10. Nancy Armstrong has most carefully worked out the politics of domestic fiction for historical argumentation in *Desire and Domestic Fiction: A Political History of the Novel* (NY: Oxford UP, 1987).

11. Stone defines companionate marriages as the affectionate alternative to the traditional arranged marriage, arising in the late 17th century and increasing in the 18th century. See "The Companionate Marriage" in *The Family, Sex and Marriage in England* 217-53. Rosemary O'Day cites evidence from this period in New England to show loss of marital affection as an increasing reason for divorce petitions (155).

12. See O'Day 156. In addition, my survey of crim con trial narratives shows that they often contain comments to the jury by judge or barrister concerning the expectation of the wife's conversation. Divorce trials, by contrast, are argued on grounds of undue cruelty reflecting the basic tenets of bed, board and clothing rather than disaffection.

13. Unlike the triangulation of desire analyzed by Eve Sedgwick, in which a homosocial bond between two men is articulated as mutual desire for a woman, here the two men's desires for a woman spell out their opposition to each other. Nevertheless, it is again the woman who loses, for the husband's goal is to gain damages from the lover while divesting himself of his wife, while the lover's goal is to prove that either the wife has had lovers previous to himself or that the husband has purposely set him up or "pimped" his wife. However the court decides, her character is lost. For Sedgwick's essential account, see *Between Men:*

English Literature and Male Homosocial Desire (NY: Columbia UP, 1985) 1-5, 18-20.

14. Editor's Preface to *Trials for Adultery: or, the History of Divorces,* Vol 1: iv.

15. I am grateful for this information to David Ferris, Curator of Rare Books and Manuscripts, Harvard Law School Library.

16. London: printed for Couch and Lakin, Curzon-street, Mary-Fair; and sold at no. 55, Fleet-street; and at the Royal Exchange.

17. See Robert D. Bass, *The Green Dragoon: The Lives of Banastre Tarleton and Mary Robinson* (NY: Holt, 1957).

18. *Mary Robinson: Selected Poems,* ed. Judith Pascoe (Peterborough: Broadview, 2000) 145.

19. "Gentlemen, it will be enough for you, if I can prove to you, that other persons than her husband had access to her, with the knowledge of her husband; and although I do not stand up to state to you, that there was any express consent on the part of Mr. Hodges that Mr. Waltier should enjoy his wife, yet, if I prove, that long previous to that time, there were others, several others, I might say many others, yet, Gentlemen, I shall satisfy you with regard to this, that it was perfectly well known to Mr. Hodges, (he never complained); there was that fort of silence and acquiescence which amounted to consent: This was the case of Mrs. Hodges and the Flemish banker. This was the case of another person, whose name I shall endeavour to conceal: the circumstances of this case I must shortly state, because they are so very striking."

This lady had lodgings in Pall-Mall; she was perfectly easy of access, and her husband was so little desirous of barring the door, that I shall prove to you, an application was made when Mr. Hodges was in bed with his wife; that he came out of that bed—opened the door, went out of the house, and permitted the gentleman, who rapped at the door, to go into the room. I shall prove to you, that the person to whom I allude, walked into the house; asked whether Mr. Hodges was at home; was told that he was, but had gone to bed. 'Bed,! Bed!—it does not signify, I'll go up stairs.' He accordingly went up stairs to the door, rapped at it, and thus addressed Mr. Hodges.

'My dear Hodges—do get up; there is a debate in the House of Commons going forward, and I am desirous to know the result—get up, and give me an account of that debate—I'll stay here, and do you come and give me the result of it.'

"Mr. Hodges immediately put on his cloaths, and went to the House of Commons; and no doubt his friend did not remain until his return, for people can debate longer than they can—Mr. Hodges came back at his leisure. I shall prove this simple fact, which I have stated to you: I shall forbear stating some other parts of the case, respecting Mrs. Hodges character, which is not necessary to the cause. It is with compunction that I stand up to call this kind of evidence: I have too much of it. If I can prove this, shall I not be intitled to a verdict?" (*Trial of the Hon. Charles Wyndham* 11-12).

20. The Audley Trial, 1631, Harvard Law Library MS 1241: "The Arraignm't of Mervyn Lord Audley, Earle of Castlehaven at Westminster hall the 25th day of Aprill 1631 for Carosing [sic] and Ravishm't to his wife and comittings of sodomy as it was tried before Thomas Lord Coventry, Lord Keeper of the great seale of England and Lord high steward for that day with the Judges and 26 of the Nobility—" (hereafter cited by ms page number).

21. That is, the Audley trial would provide the historical precedent for reasoning by analogy. If Lady Castlehaven's husband could force her to commit adultery (she claimed he arranged and abetted her rape), which was the verdict of his peers, then other husbands could behave as egregiously; or if a husband simply encouraged or consented to adultery, again he shouldn't be able to collect damages from the lover. My thanks to Margaret Hunt for clarifying this point. In *A House in Gross Disorder: Sex, Law, and the 2nd Earl of Castlehaven* (Oxford: Oxford UP, 1999), Cynthia B. Herrup argues that although the charge against Audley was rape and sodomy, the real crime committed by Audley in a sexually unregulated age, and for which he was beheaded, was his "failure as a head of household which affected the image of every male head of household; his failure to be honorable spoke more specifically to his fellow peers" (77), this dishonor including encouraging cross-class sexual liaisons, which threatened to drain the aristocracy through potentially polluted lineage, a fear exacerbated by his gifts of land and money to favored servants that deprived his legitimate son of a full inheritance. See esp. 77-88.

22. ms 8. Skipwith also testified that "The Lord made him lye with him at Fountayne and at Salisbury and once in the bed and spent his seede but did not penetrate his body, and that he heard he did not soe with others; that Skypwith lay with the yong Lady often, and that the Lord desyred a boy by him" (ms 9). The sexual relations were convoluted in this household: Skipwith claimed "that the Earle used his body as a woman, but never peirced it, only spent his seede betweene his thighs," and that Audley had "stood by and in-

couraged him to get hir with child" (ms 10); Lady Audley also slept with several servants with or without Audley's orders, and her daughter was prostituted to Audley's lovers as well. However, despite equivocations on spousal testimony, rape of a defamed woman (that is, Lady Audley after she had consorted with Skipwith), and the definition of buggery, the court found Audley's religious philandering more egregious in the end (he was accused of being a papist in the morning, an Anglican in the afternoon, and an atheist at night), and the women's participation in this nightmare scenario comprehensible in light of the husband's despotism.

23. See Anne K. Mellor's discussion of portraits and print representations of Robinson in "Making an Exhibition of Her Self: Mary 'Perdita' Robinson and Nineteenth-Century Scripts of Female Sexuality" *Nineteenth-Century Contexts* 22 (2000): 271-304. For Gillray's style, see *Fashionable Contrasts: Caricatures by James Gillray,* intro. and annotations by Draper Hill (London: Phaidon, 1966), and Thomas Wright and R. H. Evans, *Historical and Descriptive Account of the Caricatures of James Gillray* (NY: B. Blom, 1968).

24. The advertisement to *The Trial of Mr. William Atkinson* offers the following: "There were several modes of punishing *Adultery* among the Grecians, among that of putting out the eyes. And the Locrians observed this custom in latter ages, being compelled to the observance of it by Zaleucus, their law-giver, whose rigour in executing this law is very remarkable; for having caught his son in *Adultery,* he resolved to deprive him of his sight, and remained a long time inexorable . . ." (v).

25. First Edition (London: Printed for T. N. Longman, and O. Rees, No. 39, Paternoster Row, 1799) 55, 84, 60.

26. *The Natural Daughter* (1799). Another title, *Walsingham; or, The Pupil of Nature. A Domestic Story* (1797) similarly hints at entanglements of a domestic schema gone awry.

27. Flora Fraser gives a strong sense of this in her biography, referring to the Regent's "campaign" against Caroline, likening Caroline's response to a "general on the move," and the hearing itself as a "royal battle" complete with its "challenge" and "champion." *The Unruly Queen: The Life of Queen Caroline* (London: Macmillan, 1996) 321, 355, 361.

28. *Edwards' Genuine Edition. "The Book!" or, The Proceedings and Correspondence upon the Subject of The Inquiry into the Conduct of her Royal Highness The Princess of Wales, under a commis-*

sion appointed by the King, in the year 1806. Faithfully copied from Authentic Documents. To which is prefixed A Narrative of the Recent Events, That have led to the publication of the Original Documents: with a Statement of Facts relative to The Child, Now under the Protection of Her Royal Highness [by Spencer Perceval] (London: Printed by and for Richard Edwards, 1813/New York: Reprinted for Eastburn, Kirk, and Co, No 86 Broadway).

29. Radical pressmen such as William Mason, William Hone, and William Benbow also promoted Caroline's cause through both fictional and iconic interpretive codes, producing a barrage of pamphlets and caricatures to counter the viciously anti-Caroline literature and caricatures of the loyalist press concerning her extra-marital sexual relations, particularly with Bartolomeo Pergami while she was in self-exile on the Continent. See Iain McCalman's study of this street warfare in *Radical Underworld: Prophets, Revolutionaries, and Pornographers in London, 1795-1840* (Oxford: Clarendon, 1988).

30. McCalman claims that Perceval himself hired Grub Street hacker Ashe to write *Spirit of the Book,* although if so, its Tory tone and negative portrayal of Caroline is difficult to understand, especially when Perceval republished the investigation documents two years later in *The Book!*

31. *The Book Itself! Private Memoirs* [*of Queen Caroline*—added in pencil], *interspersed with Curious Anecdotes of several Distinguished Characters, being a complete answer to the Spirit of the Book* (London: printed for, and published by J. Bushnell, No. 7, Hatton-Wall, Hatton-Garden). Price Six-Pence. This book, cheaply printed with a poorly done color plate illustrating a young woman begging on bended knee to a gentleman, while another gentleman tries to restrain her, reveals all the hallmarks of Caroline's imagination. The many spelling errors for more sophisticated words are likewise indicative of her writing style, although the frequent typos are the result of a cheap and hurried edition. Undated, it must have been written between 1806-7 and George III's final collapse in December of 1810, since it ends with the conclusion to the "Delicate Investigation" (1806-7) and the King of Cumaria's apology to the heroine for the Prince's behavior, a letter whose assertions reveal that the King is still in control and the Regency has not yet begun.

32. Such as the pornographic *Memoirs of Perdita,* portraying her supposed affair with Lord Malden (London: G. Lister, 1784), cited in Judith Pascoe, Introduction, *Mary Robinson: Selected Poems* 29.

33. Both she and the Prince published letters by or to members of the royal family, including her own letters in *The Book!* and the Prince's publication of his father's letters regarding Caroline, the latter act greatly distressing the King. Lord Eldon, Lord Chancellor at the time of their publication, believed, and it was publicly rumored, that it was the Prince's disloyal act of publishing his father's letters that led to the second lengthy recurrence of his illness (Fraser 141).

34. In "Cobbett, Coleridge and the Queen Caroline Affair," Tim Fulford shows how entangled Caroline's adultery was in national affairs; public sympathy was swayed not only by political and Grub Street hacks, but by well known literary participants in the public sphere such as Cobbett and Coleridge (*SiR* 37.4 [Winter 1998]: 523-44).

35. *Spirit of the Spirit, abridgement of Spirit of the Book, comprising particulars of delicate enquiry and memoir of life of that most virtuous and illustrious princess* (London, 1812); *King's Case Stated; appeal to House of Parliament on proceedings pending against the Queen,* by J. Webster Wedderburn (London, 1820); *Minutes of evidence on second reading of bill intituled [sic] "Act to deprive Her Majesty Queen Caroline Amelia Elizabeth of title, prerogatives, rights, privileges, and exemptions of Queen Consort of this realm, and to dissolve marriage between His Majesty and said Caroline Amelia Elizabeth"* (N.P., 1820); Robert Huish, *Memoirs of Caroline, Queen of Great Britain, with letters and other documents,* 2 vols. (London, 1821). At over 600 pages per volume, Huish (who also authored biographies of George III and Princess Charlotte prior to that of Caroline) makes the most capital out of Caroline's extraordinary life: not only did this biography come out in the year of her death, but it is highly stylized, written as if to be excerpted in large chunks for the literary reviews.

MAJOR AUTHORS AND SIGNIFICANT WORKS

Bruce E. Fleming (essay date April 1989)

SOURCE: Fleming, Bruce E. "An Essay in Seduction; or, The Trouble with *Bovary*." In *Emma Bovary,* edited by Harold Bloom, pp. 165-73. New York: Chelsea House Publishers, 1994.

[*In the following essay, originally published in* French Review *in April 1989, Fleming presents a metatheoretical examination of absence and inevitability in* Madame Bovary.]

Madame Bovary is surely one of the most troubling of the members in good standing of the pantheon of World Literature. Even when we have put it down, it continues to itch: what, we wonder, is this book really about?—surely not (we think) this wretched woman and her melodramatic end. And this sense that neither the characters nor the plot can, in fact, really be the point of this work feeds our impulse to grasp after meta-theories. Perhaps, we suggest, the work is about the relation of art to life (and is thus the story of a female Don Quixote), or is about inaction (and is thus the story of a Mrs. Hamlet), or mirrors the modern world or bourgeois society, or expresses a state of boredom or ennui, or—remembering Flaubert's desire to write a book about "nothing"—is only about words. Our impulse with such theories, at any rate, is certainly to talk more in terms of negatives than positives: what is absent, what is not done, what cannot ever have been. Yet none of these suggestions, I think, does justice to our experience of reading the work. For I would characterize this as being one of extraordinary passivity coupled with a sense of overwhelming inevitability: we must, that is, wait at every moment for the author to tell us what comes next—though when we have it, that something seems almost frustratingly logical.

My suggestion is that we can best explain such a perception by considering the work as an essay in seduction. By essay I mean seeing it not so much as the arrangement of particular people and events but as an illustration of logically possible permutations on a given state, a kind of thesis novel without a thesis. And seduction is like desire (a concept more common in contemporary analysis) in that both imply the lack of something; yet unlike desire, seduction is nothing more than a pattern of forces of which we ourselves are part, not a relationship with a defined other. And it is precisely the lack of a definition of people as substantial entities that characterizes *Madame Bovary*. (For an analysis of the novel in terms of desire see René Girard's work on deceit and desire in the novel, 63f.)

A number of other commentators, including Erich Auerbach and Tony Tanner—whom I will be considering here—have offered theories that take as their point of departure this sense of there somehow being a hole at the center of this book. Yet it seems the unavoidable tendency of such theories that begin with the perception of something missing in *Madame Bovary*, to find the meaning of the novel in precisely the fact of lack, to make coherence of incoherence. And this, it seems to me, is to deny away the perception of centerlessness or absence that produced these theories in the first place. It is just this reader experience that *Madame Bovary* does not, at the level of character and plot, "make sense" that I am concerned with preserving; my hope is to offer a meta-theory that explains our sense of what is missing in the work without at the same time explaining it away.

In terms of character, moreover, the presupposition of such theories is that the second Mrs. Charles can be analyzed exactly as if she possessed the same coherence that we ascribe to living human beings as a presupposition of their comprehensibility. The incoherence and absence that these theories perceive in Emma is, as a result, taken as a quality of personality—as Aristotelean analysis allows us to understand a character whose very lack of consistency constitutes his consistency, or the way Lacanian analysis makes "sense" of the lack in a character such as Hamlet. The one thing that such analysis forbids us to conclude is that Madame Bovary simply doesn't make sense. And this is precisely what I am claiming here.

Nonetheless the impulse of these commentators to speak in terms of character and plot with regard to the novel is, I think, perfectly understandable. For the book produces what I will be calling here a "character-effect" and a "plot-effect," the illusion of character and plot without their substance. These effects are characterized by, respectively, the pasting together of opposing qualities of character, and the alternation of actions between diametrically opposite poles of action. All of these, in turn, are strung together by the most tenuous chain of all, what I call mere temporality—the structure of "and then, and then, and then."

These notions can be clarified by an appeal to E. M. Forster's discussion in *Aspects of the Novel* (86). Emma is not, to be sure, what Forster would call a "flat" character (one characterized by a recurring tag action)—but this does not mean she is a "round" one either. Instead, she is the easiest and most simplistic development on a flat character—someone who is a pasting together, front to back, of diametrically opposed character traits. And Forster arrives at a concept similar to what I call "mere temporality" by making a distinction between story—that is, succession—and plot, which involves causality. An example of the first for Forster is: "The king died and then the queen died." An example of the second would be: "The king died; and then the queen died of grief." And it is in this first category that, I believe, *Bovary* falls. (Seymour Chatman suggests that the mind has a natural tendency to see the first as the second, 45-46.)

Yet I think we arrive most ineluctably at the conclusion that neither Emma nor the world she lives in "make sense" by avoiding it as long as possible: by asking repeatedly of Emma and the actions that mark turning points in her life the one question we may legitimately ask both of real people and of characters in novels that aspire to the same status of coherence: "why?" It is the consistently disappointing results of doing so that drive us to the conclusion that the question itself is illegitimate.

The first major change in her life was the move from the convent (on which the period at her father's farm may be taken as an added post-script) to married life.

Why, we ask, did she marry Charles? And to this question I do not believe we have an answer. To be sure, we are told that she had tired of the adolescent fantasies of romantic novels and visceral religion. Clearly she was (so to say) fallow ground, ripe for the next logical step of a relation with another person. Yet we never have any indication that marriage in general, or her marriage with Charles in particular, was the result either of rational choice or of pressure from either her father or her situation. The conversation between father and daughter regarding it is, after all, as unseen by us as it is by Charles, and the bride remains impassive at the wedding and the morning after. Of Emma's motivation here, that is, we know only that she has no other pressing interests. And this means only that the subsequent event *could* follow upon the first—not that it was in any sense probable. The events of convent, farm, and marriage are related only by the link of temporal succession: first one thing happens, then the next. (Charles' reactions here, as always, are a lack of reactions—all based on the fact that he understands nothing, sees nothing. And this should no more be confused with insensitivity than Emma's lack of a motivation for acting should be confused with boredom—for it represents the absence of an entire faculty, not a defect in an extant one.)

Since Emma was never in love with Charles, she is in no position to fall out of love with him; her relation with another man is not (causally) produced by her married life—instead, once again, it merely follows upon it. She falls in love with Léon because, so to say, he is there in the novel to fall in love with. For this is the first swing of her pendulum of passions that is the pattern of her life. It is followed by a swing in the opposite direction: she becomes domestic, virtuous. (The oscillations are not so wide now as they later become, the extremes of her behavior less extreme.) At this point Léon grows discouraged, and leaves; Rodolphe reaps what Léon, as well as the guest at the ball, have sown. And when Léon returns to Emma's life it is only to carry out the pattern of this same oscillation which Emma had in the meantime already lived out with Rodolphe.

At no point, however, do we have a sense of *why* things happen. We can, to be sure, always identify that which—using Aristotelean terms—we may call the efficient cause, but never the final one. That is, given that things do happen, we can give the reasons why they have done so. What we cannot do, however, is explain why they *should* do so, or predict for the future. And this substitution by Flaubert of a series of efficient causes for a final one contributes to the production of what I am calling the "plot-effect." If, for example, we ask why it was that Emma was seduced by Rodolphe, we may give the efficient causes: his position, the smell of his haircream, the fact that he is an attractive male. What we cannot answer is the question of why Emma

is susceptible to *this* seduction, at *this* time. Why does she retreat into virtue at the end of the affair? The efficient cause is surely her disgust with Charles' bungling of the club-foot operation. But why should exasperation with Charles produce *this* result, *this* swing back of the pendulum? It is this question which is never posed and never answered. The same is true of the affair with Léon: after the carriage ride, she regrets and becomes virtuous. Why? We cannot say. For she hasn't hesitated to compromise herself with Rodolphe, and not for a moment did she feel guilty about it. The answer seems to be merely: because the choices at any one time are limited to the two extremes of virtue and vice, and we have not had the latter in a while.

The character-effect with respect to Emma's two lovers is produced by a similar combination of opposites. Clearly Rodolphe is somewhat brutal—made so, Flaubert suggests, by his contacts with the demi-monde. Yet he is clearly involved emotionally with Emma, and he too has a capacity for tenderness—both of which are suggested by the scene in the moonlight before their projected flight. But his drops of water for tears on the final letter, as well as this letter's ruthlessly rational composition, represent the opposite trait of brutality. So too for Léon, who also seems simply a combination of admirable and despicable (or at least pitiable) traits. Playing a role, happy to have "une vraie maîtresse" yet also involved emotionally, he is at once both exploiter and exploited. The equivalent for Léon of Rodolphe's letter is his engagement to another woman, which takes place off stage, and enters the action only in the form of the printed announcement.

In effect, Emma has the same affair twice. To be sure, Flaubert manages to give this repetition what seems to be the overall connection of a logic tighter than that of mere temporality by limiting the affairs to two (so that the second "re-writes" the first to an appreciable degree, as a third or subsequent ones would not), by the trick of framing one around the other, and by suggesting that she has begun to tire of the second as she had not done of the first. Yet though Flaubert may tell us that she is tiring (just as he tells us earlier that she is bored with her life)—this does not mean that we need believe it; no character in fiction forgets sooner than Emma, or learns less from more experiences. And through this relatively slight formal re-arrangement of material the pendulum of involvement and withdrawal ticks back and forth. We can, in fact, imagine it ticking through a third affair, a fourth, a hundredth. For if Emma is capable of forgetting the first affair enough to have a second one, why is she not capable of a hundred and first? It seems that she dies simply because she has had affairs with all the available men that Flaubert has introduced, and because she has nowhere else to borrow money—given that her relations with the outside world are defined in terms of these two means of contact. The logical possibilities are exhausted, so the heroine must disappear.

There is yet another phenomenon in the book that contributes to the sense that we are, in fact, dealing with a coherent human being in Emma: the alteration of divergent narrative points of view offered in the text with no attempt at reconciliation. For this bundling together of points of view encourages us further to fill in the vacant areas between them, to ascribe knowledge to characters who have none and logic to situations that lack it. An example of this is the passage where Flaubert describes Emma's reading in the convent as a child (35-36). First we are made conscious of the book as an object by a reference to it in physical relation to Emma's body, as if from a point in the air not far from her face: "Elle frémissait, en soulevant de son haleine le papier de soie des gravures." We then move to the objects portrayed in the picture: "C'était, derrière la balustrade d'un balcon, un jeune homme" and so on; upon this follows a summarizing, non-physical description passage where we have a précis of both the portrayed world and the fact of its portrayal in Emma's: "ou bien les portraits anonymes des ladies anglaises à boucles blondes". At this point the sentence takes on the air of being mere objective fact, offered in present tense and in the second person: "qui vous regardent avec leurs grands yeux clairs" and so on. We then find ourselves once again on the level of perception, but one offered in a grammatical impersonal: "On en voyait d'etalées dans des voitures, glissant au milieu des parcs" etc. And the passage which follows continues in this constant alteration of pictured world and the manner of picturing—fingers that are turned up like pointed slippers, the virgin forest that is (an ironic aside) "bien nettoyée"—and the subsequent paragraph ends up back in Emma's room where the dormitory is silent and the light falls from the lamp over her head.

The most important result of this flickering point of view is that by following it we acquire a great deal of knowledge about Emma's situation. Moreover we get this knowledge, so to say, on the sly—so that we are encouraged to forget that Emma does not know as much as we. And it is this that contributes to the illusion of a substantial character. This is perhaps clearest during the moment when Emma, realizing that Léon is growing weary of her, sits by the convent wall and regrets her childhood (263-64): "Elle n'était pas heureuse, ne l'avait jamais été. D'où venait donc cette insuffisance de la vie, cette pourriture instantanée des choses où elle s'appuyait?" Up to this point in the text we can imagine that these sentences are an indirect discourse rendering of her thoughts, taking over from the direct quote ("se disait-elle") of the preceding paragraph. But finally the paragraph arrives at the following sentence: "Chaque sourire cachait un bâillement d'ennui, chaque joie une malédiction, tout plaisir son dégoût, et les meilleurs

baisers ne vous laissaient sur la levre qu'une irréalisible envie d'une volupté plus haute." And by this time it is clear that we have left Madame Bovary's head and are in another world entirely—though, because of the progression of the paragraph from direct discourse, to indirect, to an abstract level, we are unlikely to be aware of having done so. The result is that we half-attribute these reflections to Emma, almost believe her to be a creature that can change from within rather than being subject to (because defined by) the merciless force of chance.

Jean Rousset has analysed this phenomenon; some of his observations are similar to my own. For example, he points out that in the processes of shifting the point of view "Flaubert at times fills out Charles's usual perceptions, just as he sometimes puts in Emma's mind reflections or shades of irony that couldn't possibly be hers" (444). Yet Rousset explains this mixing of points of view as the effect of Flaubert's alternations between the structure of, on one hand, the traditional novel and, on the other, the anti-novel that it seems he wanted to write—his discovery during the act of writing that he was "the greatest novelist of inaction, of ennui, of stagnation" (457). From my point of view, however, it seems unlikely that this can be the almost accidental result of something that crept up on the author unawares, given its major role in the production of the so rigorously produced character-effect in the work. This effect seems far too calculated and, under the circumstances, logical, to be merely the result of misjudgement on Flaubert's part.

Erich Auerbach makes a similar point about what Emma knows and does not know, though also with different conclusions from mine. He is considering the scene where Emma sits with Charles at table and is overwhelmed with disgust. He quotes Flaubert, then comments: "*Toute l'amertume de l'existence lui semblait servie sur son assiette*—she doubtless has such feelings, but if she wanted to express it, it would not come out like that; she has neither the intelligence nor the cold candor of self-accounting necessary for such a formulation" (484). Auerbach, that is, agrees that the expression of these things is beyond Emma, that it represents a point of view out of her reach. Yet his argument, as I suggested above, is that this very fact characterizes Emma's life, and her character. His commentary on this passage continues as follows: "The way in which language here lays bare the . . . very wretchedness of [her] life . . . excludes the idea of true tragedy . . . she is always being tried, judged, and . . . condemned" (490). Yet I think Auerbach is being too forgiving, too ready to explain. Flaubert does in fact clearly say *it seemed to Madame Bovary* that all the bitterness of existence, and so on. It will not do to have so ready as justification, for the fact that it can seem nothing of the kind, that Flaubert is condemning Mme Bovary for not doing what he says she is in fact doing.

It is the loyalty of these commentators to the notion that Mme Bovary is the simulacrum of a coherent human being that I perceive to be the greatest flaw in their analyses. Commentators influenced by Lacan, such as Tony Tanner, take the same point of departure (unsurprisingly: Lacan was, after all, a psychologist). This seems most easily shown in one of Tanner's parenthetical asides: "If we may speak in Sartrean terms for a moment we may say that Emma yearns towards a dream of Being engendered by the Nothingness of her existence and experience—the vagueness of the terms is itself a part and symptom of her plight" (338). *Emma yearns, her plight*: we are still in the realm of an analysis of character and situation that presupposes a coherence, on the personal level, in Emma's incoherence. Moreover, Tanner's treatment of the oscillation between extremes of Emma's actions, which I have been considering here, is in psychological terms as well (308).

Our experience in reading this book is one of passivity: if at any point we put our finger in the novel and look up, we stop the action utterly. This, I proposed, was the result of the fact that the characters are merely a bundling together of opposite qualities, their actions merely an alternation between extremes. The best way to take account of these facts is by considering the book as an essay in seduction. For in the situation of seduction, neither the object nor the originator (subject) of the relation need be defined off from the other—cannot, in fact, be so defined if the relation is to continue—and neither of these, in turn, can be defined off from the sentiment that links them. (In a Lacanian analysis of language of desire we at least have a clear notion of what it is we lack.) Certainly no particular action towards the attainment of the goal is implied, for action requires both separating out the goal and conceptualizing the distance between ourselves and it—a distance which we may then set about removing. The distance itself, however, must remain, ill-defined though the components may be; when there is no longer any distance between the poles of a situation of seduction the relation is at an end.

In my consideration above I repeatedly asked "why?" If we continue using "wh-" words in questions we may compile a list of some of the principal sorts of seduction—all of which are to be found in *Madame Bovary*. First, there is seduction of place—which answers the question *where*?—produced when we imagine inherently other a place, a country, or a way of life linked to these. Secondly, we may find seductive a time other than that in which we are situated (answering the question *when*?), thus fixating either on the future as a time inherently better or more beautiful than the present, or losing ourselves in the past as a never-to-be-repeated idyll. Third, there is seduction by *what* we are not, as adolescents and children have crushes on people simply because they are adults, or dress well, or have a posi-

tion they admire—or as we imagine certain situations, positions in life to be inherently more attractive than our own. Last—though not of course least—there is sexual seduction, which I view as seduction by *whom* we are not. For sex (I avoid a lengthy consideration of the psychology and philosophy of sex) is at least to some extent based on our narrowing of the distance between ourselves and a being which is at once complementary to ourselves and irrevocably Other, a being that defines us, limits us—and at the same time completes us.

Now, all of these are situations where the half-attained, the half-ourselves-and-half-other, is held (for greater or lesser periods) in a state of tension. And this, from the point of view of the person in the relation of seduction, means: held from us by constraints as various as our age and sex, the geography of our position on the globe, the strictures of our society, or the ineluctable nature of time itself which moves in one direction only. Thus we may proceed to a consideration of the relevance of these types of seduction in the case of Emma Bovary by considering the things which constrain her. To these we will find corresponding a list of things (as best they can be differentiated from their situations) which seduce her. (This correspondence will hardly be on a one-to-one basis, since it is her situation as a whole that ultimately constrains her in all its aspects.) In no particular order, then, I suggest the following list of those factors which constrain, confine, and render unhappy that most unhappy of modern heroines.

First, Emma is out of place physically. In a word, she is far too pretty for her surroundings, not as much the *paysanne* as would be appropriate in a world still defined by a correspondence between rank (and the freedom from manual labor it implied) and physical beauty. This fact is remarked by Rodolphe as well as by the marquis who invites the Bovarys to the ball. Second, she is out of place with her tastes and refinements. These tastes were partly acquired at the convent; partly, it seems, they are her natural inclination. (It is, after all, her flourishes with house and table that Charles finds so devastating.) Third, she does not love her husband, and feels both his presence in the house and her role as his wife to be a constraint. (We may legitimately ask if she could have loved any husband—but the answer to this is the same as that given repeatedly above: we do not know.) Fourth, she hates small towns, and is forced to live in one. Fifth, there is the suggestion that Emma may find monogamy itself constraining—which in turn is linked to the sixth sort of constraint, namely, that Emma finds being a woman in itself limiting. Both of these last find expression in her thoughts concerning the birth of her daughter: a man, she reflects, is free; when she is displeased with Léon she thinks that he is "mou comme une femme". And her fascination with the act of breaking marital bonds is evident ("J'ai un amant! J'ai un amant!").

Thus with these constraints in mind, we can list some of the seduction to which Emma is prey. Clearly she is seduced by place. She dreams constantly of the two paradigmatic dream-lands of the Romantics, Scotland and Italy, and fantasizes her life with Rodolfe in a haze of crags and fountains, fruit and fishermen worthy of the worst of Byron. Nor need she look so far: Paris seems heaven itself, even Rouen possesses at first an air of the mystical and mythical. And if we are interested in co-ordinating constraints with seductions, we may see here elements of four and five from the list above, as well as possible traces of two.

Second, she is seduced by time: she (like all Romantics) is taken by the Age of Chivalry; she dreams of her own childhood, or she dreams of the future with Rodolphe, of a second ball, of something, anything, that is to happen—like Prufrock, waiting for a knock upon the door. Time past and time future—both seem desirable. Third, she is seduced by position, by the (asexual) sense of what people are. This is clear in her reaction to the drooling old duke at the ball, as well as (to a large extent) to the tenor Lagardy—which kind of seduction, moreover, plays a role at least conceptually separable from the sexual one in her two affairs. She gives in to Rodolphe because his hair has the same smell as that of the guests at the ball, and gives in to Léon as a partial transference of her feelings for the tenor. Thus each of the two sexual affairs (and we may call sexual seduction the fourth sort of seduction) is mediated by a seduction of position.

The fifth sort of seduction operative here is that of art itself—or at least, of its romantic, dreamy variety. This is one of the most critically remarked varieties of seduction at work here, to the point where we frequently forget that by the time Emma agrees to marry Charles, she has voluntarily put away the books to which she was addicted, finding them tiring. To be sure, the subsequent opera and ball each have about them some of the elements of this seduction by art and artifice—but at some point this dissolves into other sorts of seduction relations: we recall that Emma has already become bored with the second act of *Lucia* in the presence of Léon. Thus this sort of seduction does play a role in the work, but it is just as clearly only one sort of seduction among many. And lastly, it is clear that for a time in her childhood Emma was seduced by the crystalline perfection of the world of religion—or at least by its visual and tangible manifestations. This too has received more than its fair share of attention, undoubtedly because of the ironic contrast between crude piety and the intellectual pretensions of religion found more strongly in other works of Flaubert (for example "Un Cœur Simple").

Thus my claim is that Emma is not a character with a personality at all, but rather a walking textbook of seductions. It is this fact which, I suggest, is the source of our problems in conceptualizing as discrete entities either the character or her actions—for the first takes definition from the second; neither can be separated from the other. On the other hand, I think it is undeniable that if we feel nothing else for Emma, we feel at least sympathy—and that this is the source of what is after all our great willingness to follow the exploits of a creature otherwise so vacuous. But this is as it should be. For seductions imply constraints, and it is with the *constraints* limiting Emma that we sympathize, not with the character so limited. In fact, I would suggest that we feel these constraints the more acutely precisely because of the vacuity of that which they constrain.

The work gives us, thus, the outlines of actions, the skeletons of persons, and a game of connect-the-dots for actions; it is an airy world of girders and armatures rather than even the constructions of people. Yet this too is as it should be, precisely because it is a world defined by seduction—the book an essay upon it. Commentators like Auerbach and Tanner see Emma as a fly caught in a spider's web of society and the world around her. Instead, I think she is herself the diaphanous threads, her motions merely tremblings in the wind as of the web itself, her life its own prison: that force field of locked longing and frozen wants, that purgatory of desire unenunciated which constitutes seduction.

Works Cited

Auerbach, Erich. *Mimesis: The Representation of Reality in Western Literature.* Princeton: Princeton UP, 1953.

Chatman, Seymour. *Story and Discourse: Narrative Structure in Fiction and Film.* Ithaca: Cornell UP, 1978.

Flaubert, Gustave. *Madame Bovary.* Paris: Garnier, 1961.

Forster, E. M. *Aspects of the Novel.* New York: Harcourt, Brace, and World, 1927.

Girard, René. *Deceit, Desire, and the Novel: Self and Other in Literary Structure.* Baltimore: Johns Hopkins UP, 1965.

Lacan, Jacques. "Desire and the Interpretation of Desire in *Hamlet.*" *Yale French Studies* 55/56 (1977): 11-52.

Rousset, Jean. "*Madame Bovary*: Flaubert's Anti-Novel; An Aspect of Flaubert's Technique: Point of View." *Madame Bovary: Backgrounds and Sources, Essays in Criticism.* Paul de Man, ed. New York: Norton, 1965. 439-457.

Tanner, Tony. *Adultery in the Novel: Contract and Transgression.* Baltimore: Johns Hopkins UP, 1979.

Tony Williams (essay date fall-winter 1991-92)

SOURCE: Williams, Tony. "Champfleury, Flaubert and the Novel of Adultery." *Nineteenth-Century French Studies* 20, nos. 1-2 (fall-winter 1991-92): 145-57.

[*In the following essay, Williams analyzes the development of the "novel of adultery" in Champfleury's* Les Bourgeois de Molinchart *and Flaubert's later* Madame Bovary, *noting Flaubert's anxiety about the earlier novel's subject matter being too close to his own, but ultimately finding that comparing the two works highlights Flaubert's great achievement.*]

One of the most dramatic ways of demonstrating the complexity of the treatment of the problematics of love and marriage in *Madame Bovary* is to compare Flaubert's novel with Champfleury's *Les Bourgeois de Molinchart,* which was published a few years earlier and touches upon similar themes. Flaubert read Champfleury's novel when it first began to appear in instalments in *La Presse* in 1854.[1] By this time, he had almost reached the end of Part II of *Madame Bovary* and there is no question of his having been directly influenced by Champfleury.[2] Flaubert did, however, express a degree of alarm at the appearance of a novel, which in intention at least was similar to his own: "Il y a parité d'intentions plutôt que de sujet et de caractères."[3] Both novelists, it could be said, set out to explore the problematics of love and marriage in a provincial setting but whereas Flaubert produced what has been described as "the most important and far-reaching novel of adultery in Western Literature,"[4] Champfleury completely failed to tackle the fundamental issues. If Champfleury taught Flaubert anything, it was a lesson in how *not* to write a novel of adultery.

Any novelist setting out in the 1850s to explore the predicament of the unhappily married woman could not but be aware of the powerful precedent set by Balzac in novels such as *La Femme de trente ans.* Balzac had dramatized the conflict between the wife's need for independence and the husband's attempts, backed by the legal system, to impose his authority over her. Flaubert and Champfleury give a new slant to this conflict by reducing the husband's insistence upon his authority. Both novelists create husbands who are far from tyrannical. The patriarchal assumption that the wife is a possession belonging to the husband is, however, still held. Recounting his own unfortunate experience of having been shot at by an irate husband, one of the minor characters in *Les Bourgeois de Molinchart,* Joncquières, reflects "cet homme est dans son droit; je lui ai pris son bien, il a le droit de se venger" (64).[5] Similarly, Charles delights in the thought that "à présent, il possédait pour la vie cette jolie femme qu'il adorait" (35).[6] Adultery in both novels, therefore, represents the *dispossession* of the husband, with the impact this has depending on the

perspective from which it is viewed. Champfleury most frequently adopts the idealizing viewpoint of the lover, constructing the plot around his attempts to rescue the heroine from the clutches of her boorish husband and failing to give adequate expression to either the wife's or the husband's experience. Although Louise is described as "dévorée bientôt par les ennuis du mariage" (23), Champfleury does not dwell on her frustration or make it the motive force for adultery. If Louise finally commits adultery, it is more by accident than design. More preoccupied by his archaeological and antiquarian interests, Creton du Coche does not value his wife; we are told virtually nothing about his reactions when he discovers her with Julien. In contrast, although Flaubert gives a full picture of Emma's frustrations and disillusionment, endowing them with propulsive force, he begins and ends the novel by adopting the viewpoint of the pathetically wronged husband and at crucial junctures in the main body of the novel switches to the lover's point of view in order to convey excitement or satiety.

The differences in focus are linked with each novelist's choice of main participants in the triangular configuration of the novel of adultery. Flaubert was struck by significant differences between his characters and Champfleury's: "Ceux du mari, de sa femme et de l'amant me semblent être très différents des miens. La femme m'a l'air d'un *ange*."[7] The biggest and most crucial difference—one which determines the shape of the novel—is between the two heroines. Louise is presented by Champfleury as a saintly figure of resignation. For ten years she has put up uncomplainingly with the repetitious conversation and offhand treatment of her husband. Emma, on the other hand, may be the victim of a society that offers inadequate opportunities for women, but she is too restive and demanding to show the same toleration of what she perceives as her husband's doltishness. Louise devotes much of her limited energy to resisting the advances of her aristocratic admirer—even before the main action begins she has adopted a repressive posture: "elle avait valsé avec lui, et aux sensations particulières qui la troublèrent, elle se promit de ne plus danser avec le comte" (31). This contrasts with Emma's ready surrender to the "licensed vertigo" of the waltz at La Vaubyessard (54-5). The fundamental difference is that, although Champfleury presents her husband as a boorish buffoon, Louise can find no fault in him and hence, according to the logic of the novel of adultery, never thinks she is entitled to seek solace outside marriage: "Louise se trouvait coupable parce qu'elle ne voyait pas son mari coupable: l'égoïsme de M. Creton du Coche, la parfaite indifférence qu'il témoignait à sa femme ne semblaient pas des motifs absolus de condamnation" (261-2). In making Louise so undemanding, Champfleury prevents the build-up of the exasperation with marriage which would have become the dynamic force propelling the heroine into adultery. Flaubert, on the other hand, emphasizes the way in which Emma's hostility to her husband helps to drive her towards adultery. The conditions of married life are such as to generate feelings which belie the virtuous exterior she maintains in her relationship with Léon: "la médiocrité domestique la poussait à des fantaisies luxueuses, la tendresse matrimoniale en des désirs adultères" (111). The same perverse logic is at work even when he has left Yonville: "Dans l'assoupissement de sa conscience, elle prit même les répugnances du mari pour des aspirations vers l'amant" (127). But the way in which the energy that leads Emma to hurl herself recklessly into adultery is generated from within marriage is illustrated most dramatically in her feelings for Rodolphe after the clubfoot operation: "cette tendresse, en effet, chaque jour s'accroissait davantage sous la répulsion du mari" (192). The image that most aptly encapsulates Louise's fundamental attitude in her marriage is that of the helpless animal: "vous recevez tranquillement des insultes comme un boeuf à l'abattoir" (279). She goes through the novel ineffectually flapping her angel's wings, unable to generate an active desire or response, in no way responsible for the fate that befalls her. In contrast, the image with which Emma is most frequently associated is that of the bird, attempting to soar above the plane of mundane marital life into some ideal realm of romantic bliss and erotic fulfillment. In accordance with this image, Flaubert has created a heroine who, harboring desires and longings that find no expression within marriage, feels entitled to and goes in active pursuit of personal fulfillment, even if this takes her outside marriage. It is difficult to see how such a passive figure as Louise could ever become an unfaithful wife. In order to achieve this end, Champfleury resorts to making her the passive victim of the machinations of various people around her. She is tricked into meeting Julien (256) and into running away (280). The result is that adultery is never anything more than an accident, the outcome of a plot against her. Apart from Julien, the impetus for her to commit adultery comes from her sister-in-law, who stands to gain financially if her brother's marriage breaks up. Even when she finally commits adultery Louise remains totally passive. Emma Bovary is also to some extent manipulated by others—by Rodolphe in particular. Broadly speaking, however, she seeks strenuously to impose her own wishes on those around her, attempting to make both her husband and her lovers dance to a romantic tune. What happens to her is presented primarily as a consequence of her wish to control her own destiny. One of the most significant mythological substructures in *Madame Bovary* relates to the story of Arachne, who challenged the goddess Minerva at weaving: "Emma, Arachne-like, is setting herself up in rivalry to the goddess, that is, presumptuously assuming her capacity to compose the pattern of her own life."[8]

Much of what is to come is implicit in the opening portrait each novelist gives of the heroine. In both cases the hands are described in some detail:

> Quoique le comte fût du meilleur monde, il ne se rappelait pas avoir jamais touché de mains si douces, si souples et montrant un peu leurs veines; car malgré que la peau en fût un peu brunie, comme la figure et tout le corps, mille petites veines bleues s'y jouaient et s'y entremêlaient capricieusesment.
>
> (30)

> Sa main pourtant n'était pas belle, point assez pâle peut-être, et un peu sèche aux phalanges; elle était trop longue aussi, et sans molles inflexions de lignes sur les contours.
>
> (16)

Emma's hands fall well short of the ideal of aristocratic delicacy that Louise's come close to attaining. Champfleury chooses to describe Louise for the first time after she has fainted. Inevitably this renders the heroine somewhat lackluster and expressionless: "les grands yeux noirs de Louise formaient la partie la plus appelante de sa fibre; cependant, étant fermés, ils offraient le charme particulier d'un or plus bruni qui colorait les paupières" (30). This contrasts strikingly with the first mention of Emma's eyes: "Ce qu'elle avait de beau, c'étaient les yeux; quoiqu'ils fussent bruns, ils semblaient noirs à cause des cils, et son regard arrivaient franchement à vous avec une hardiesse candide" (16). Champfleury completes his portrait with a description of the mouth suggesting an innocuous purity: "la bouche entr'ouverte montrait un évanouissement sans douleur et laissait passer un souffle aussi pur qu'un petit vent qui aurait traversé un rosier" (31).[9] Emma's mouth, in contrast, is much more active. She is shown sucking her fingers ("tout en cousant, elle se piquait les doigts, qu'elle portait ensuite à sa bouche pour les sucer", 16) and a little later licking drops of liqueur from her glass ("le bout de sa langue, passant entre ses dents fines, léchait à petits coups le fond du verre", 23). The components of each description are similar but in the one case they are idealized and motionless, evoking a mental image of the heroine that is as dull as ditchwater, whilst in the other, they are consistent with the domestic world in which the heroine is placed and mobile, producing a very different impression of repressed vitality and sensuality. Champfleury's way of dealing with the female form is to render it inert, draining not just blood but all energy and desire from the heroines body. Flaubert, on the other hand, divides Emma up into appetizing morsels,[10] which taken together suggest a sensuous and resolute presence.

Champfleury, Baudelaire, insisted, was a joker under the skin.[11] Louise is viewed seriously but her husband, Creton du Coche is a bourgeois buffoon and is presented in an unremittingly comic light. He resembles

Homais in his interest in the local environment and respect for science. Although he no longer works, he likes to be referred to as "maître" and generally behaves in a pompous manner. Essentially a passive figure, he falls readily under his sister's thumb: "l'avoué avait un de ces caractères faibles qui trouvent un certain bien-être à se courber sous l'autorité" (89). His predominant attitude to his wife is one of indifference shading into offensiveness, as Jonquières points out: "tu as été le témoin de la manière dont l'avoué traite sa femme, avec quel sansfaçon il lui répond, et les moindres occasions qu'il saisit pour l'humilier" (122). However, he allows Louise to please herself: "il n'insiste pas quand je manifeste le moindre désir" (79). Nothing lightens the picture of unrelieved dullness: "Depuis dix ans il n'avait jamais changé de conversation" (23). Charles Bovary, in contrast, is devoted if inarticulate in his admiration, a decent if doltish husband. The reader is invited to register Emma's view of him as distorted and, unlike Creton du Coche, he provokes a good deal of sympathy. His concern for Emma is genuine and her death brings about a dramatic transformation in him, allowing the reader to gauge how Emma has consistently underestimated and undervalued the depth of his devotion to her. In this way Flaubert is able to make the real consequences of adultery in terms of human suffering impinge upon the reader.

Julien de Vorges is a conventionally idealized hero—aristocratic, romantic-minded and totally different from both the rabble of Molinchart and Creton du Coche, as Louise insists: "M. de Vorges est d'une grande noblesse et d'une grande fortune; vous ne pouvez l'égaler en rien" (36). His first entrance in the novel—masterfully cracking his whip to disperse the butchers of Molinchart hot on the trail of the roe-deer—conforms to the pattern of the hero rescuing the damsel in distress. The image of the dashing hero of romance, who might have stepped out of one of the sentimental novels Emma reads in the convent-school, is undercut by the image of the frustrated lover, moodily and palely loitering with uncertain intent in the streets of Molinchart. Champfleury's conception of Julien is shallow; he is an incoherent blend of Rodolphe-like forcefulness and Léon-like ineffectiveness. Flaubert, in comparison, invents figures who subvert both the bogus image of the attentive lover found in the sentimental novel and the conventional image of the male sex as the strong sex.[12]

Champfleury's limited conception of the heroine as angelic martyr leaves him with little scope beyond showing her suffering in silence. The basic course of the narrative of *Les Bourgeois de Molinchart is* not dictated by Louise but by those around her. She becomes the victim of a highly melodramatic scheme of persecution rather than of the conditions of marriage itself. The prime mover is Ursule Creton du Coche, bent upon discrediting Louise, and at almost every stage Louise fails to

make an active contribution to the course of events. Flaubert, one can infer from the following extract from a letter from Bouilhet, was critical of the way the plot peters out as Champfleury comes to rely increasingly on the exceptional persecution of Louise by Ursule in order to motivate her adulterous relationship:

> Je savais, du reste que le roman de Champfleury finisssait en queue de poisson. C'est une chose qui arrivera toujours. Je ne le crois pas complet, ni carré par la base.
>
> Ce que tu me dis pour les délires *motivés* me paraît juste. Oui, c'est rococo, toutes réflexions faites; c'est trop dramatique, dans le mauvais sens du mot, et tu as bien fait d'y regarder à deux fois.[13]

Champfleury does not explore the relationship between Louise and her husband in any depth. To start with he gives an extremely perfunctory account of courtship: "Vers quarante ans, l'avoué s'était senti porté vers les ordres du mariage, et il épousa mademoiselle Louise Tilly, jeune fille dont la beauté faisait grand bruit dans le monde de Molinchart, mais qui n'avait pour don que sa beauté" (23). The adoption of Charles's point of view in the opening chapters of *Madame Bovary* precludes a full presentation of Emma's feelings but Flaubert manages, nonetheless, to suggest some of the motives for Emma's acceptance of a state that is destined to bring her much unhappiness in a key retrospective paragraph:

> Mais l'anxiété d'un état nouveau, ou peut-être l'irritation causée par la présence de cet homme, avait suffi à lui faire croire qu'elle possédait enfin cette passion merveilleuse qui jusqu'alors s'était tenue comme un grand oiseau au plumage rose planant dans la splendeur des ciels poétiques;—et elle ne pouvait s'imaginer à présent que ce calme où elle vivait fût le bonheur qu'elle avait rêvé.
>
> (41)

As the main action of the novel begins with the pursuit of the roe-deer, which occurs ten years after her marriage, Champfleury gives an equally perfunctory account of the early stages of marriage, compressing the first ten years into a couple of pages: "Cette jeune femme, dévorée bientôt par les ennuis du mariage, allait aux soirées de la sous-préfecture [. . .]; mais elle se trouvait isolée depuis la mort de son père" (23). These "ennuis du mariage" and "ennuis secrets" (25), which are left largely unspecified by Champfleury, form the main focus of the final chapter of Part I of *Madame Bovary* in which full expression is given to Emma's growing dissatisfaction with married life. Both heroines find the conversation of their husband limited:

> Depuis dix ans il n'avait changé de conversation. La femme de l'avoué, pendant ces dix ans, se condamna à un dévouement absolu, elle écoutait ou feignait d'écouter son mari.
>
> (23)

La conversation de Charles était plate comme un trot-
toir de rue, et les idées de tout le monde y défilaient
dans leur costume ordinaire, sans exciter d'émotion, de
rire ou de rêverie.

(42)

The flat narratorial statement in the first of these ex-
tracts sounds too sweeping and Louise's resigned response is lacking in variation. The focalized assertion in
the second extract is an emotional reaction and the
slightly strained image of the pavement gives it subjective coloring and conveys the heroine's mounting frustration. Where Champfleury, relying on bald statement
and imprecise overview of her position, keeps the reader
at a distance from the heroine's experience, Flaubert by
giving the fullest and most concrete expression to Emma's marital misery, invites the reader to participate in
her warped emotional life.

The moment at which the limitations of marriage become apparent is of crucial importance. Both novels
contain scenes where the heroine leaves her normal surroundings and reflects on her situation. Whereas Emma's mind, when she goes out to Bannevilie, finally focuses on a specific thought ("Pourquoi, mon Dieu, me
suis-je mariée?", 46), Louise is made to forget the limitations of her existence ("Louise oubliait qu'elle était
prisonnière dans la petite ville de Molinchart," 27).
Whilst Emma's dissatisfaction is expressed through the
elaborate image of her life being like a North-facing attic ("Mais elle, sa vie était froide comme un grenier
dont la lucarne est au nord, et l'ennui, araignée silen-
cieuse, filait sa toile dans l'ombre à tous les coins de
son coeur", 46), Louise's vague longings are dissipated:
"perdue dans des rêveries aussi vagues que la forme des
nuages, la jeune femme oubliait momentanément sa vie
rapetissée" (28). Flaubert uses the natural world to reflect and intensify Emma's melancholy state, whilst
Champfleury is carried away by his desire to present
the local caves, used as human habitations, as interesting and the countryside as attractive. In both scenes
there is a dynamic element that contrasts with the heroine's marital torpor. Emma's greyhound offers an image
of restlessness as it circles round and Emma compares
herself to it: "Puis, considérant la mine mélancolique
du svelte animal qui bâillait avec lenteur, elle
s'attendrissait, et, le comparant à elle-même, lui parlait
tout haut, comme à quelqu'un d'affligé que l'on con-
sole" (46). The coach seen by Louise, on the other hand,
offers an image of effective escape as it "s'élance joy-
eusement dans la vallée qui mène à Paris" (27). It affords Louise, however, no more than a brief respite in
which she forgets "sa vie rapetissée" before returning to
Molinchart.

The circumstances of the first meeting with the man
who is to become her lover differ significantly. The
opening scene of *Les Bourgeois de Molinchart* relies on

the out of the ordinary: a roe-deer, pursued by a band
of bloodthirsty butchers, obligingly takes refuge in the
house of Louise, who tries to save its life, aided by the
Comte de Vorges, whose hunting instincts are curbed in
order to meet her request. In this initial encounter Julien
claims—in all sincerity—that providence has brought
them together ("je vous ai rencontré par hasard, ou
plutôt la Providence l'a voulu", 33) and his dominant
response to Louise is pity rather than desire (42 and
70). The meeting of Emma and Rodolphe in the Doctor's surgery, in contrast, is perfectly plausible. Rodolphe cynically uses "the fate brought us together" cliché,
assesses Emma's position realistically, and formulates
his intentions clearly and coarsely ("'Oh!, je l'aurai!'",
134)

Subsequently much of Louise's behavior consists in resisting Julien. She is reluctant to have dinner with him
in her own home (but forced in the end to eat humble
venison pie), refuses to visit him in his mother's château or to meet him in Molinchart. At one point a dinner is held in the château and there is a certain amount
of foot contact under the table. This turns out, however,
to be between Julien and Madame Chappe, whose feet
have been mistaken for Louise's, with the result that
Louise is effectively being bypassed by the main course
of events. A very different effect is created by the description of Léon's placing of his foot on the chair on
which Emma is sitting (86) and rapid withdrawal of his
foot when he happens to stand on Emma's dress (101).
Such details, which depend upon the erotic charge carried by Emma's dress and objects close to her, suggest
unconscious sexual attraction.

The stone-walling that Louise's fundamental attitude
leads to is finally undermined by jealousy ("en un clin
d'oeil, les serpents de la jalousie mordirent le coeur de
Louise", 161), but a jealousy that rests upon the mistaken belief that Julien is in love with a circus per-
former, La Carolina. But even jealousy can produce
only a modest change in attitude: "Alors, Louise se ré-
volta contre elle-même et résolut de lutter contre sa
passion avec plus d'énergie" (179). In comparison
Emma offers no real resistence. In Part II Léon is too
inexperienced to constitute a real threat and she enjoys
playing the part of the virtuous wife and mother. With
Rodolphe she is an easy prey, impelled as she is by the
build-up of suppressed libidinal desire, suggested in the
following image: "l'amour, si longtemps contenu, jail-
lissait tout entier avec des bouillonnements joyeux"
(167).

If he were relying simply upon the heroine's desire,
Champfleury would not have been able to push the
novel towards the desired conclusion. Therefore he is
forced to resort to the machinations of Ursule and Madame Chappe, taking all the initiative away from Louise. Since she is unaware of their scheming to create an

appearance of guilt on her part, Louise is repeatedly surprised to find herself in Julien's company ("Vous ici, monsieur, dit la jeune femme stupéfaite; on me trompe donc!", 256). In contrast, Emma's entry into adultery is amply motivated by the accumulated frustrations of married life. With Rodolphe there is still a vestige of virtuous resolution, leading her initially to reject his advances (164), but this is rapidly followed by her yielding. With Léon, Emma is more swayed by "le charme de la séduction" than by "la nécessité de s'en défendre" (242).

The chapter entitled "misères d' intérieur" deals with Louise's virtual imprisonment and persecution, when she is falsely accused of betraying her husband. The person responsible for her suffering is not her husband but Ursule and the Dames Jérusalem and their treatment of Louise is conveyed in luridly melodramatic terms ("Une joie cruelle était peinte sur les traits de la vieille fille," 263; "mais à chaque instant les ongles de la vieille fille reparaissaient et déchiraient le coeur de Louise," 271). Champfleury has not confronted the "problem" of marriage as such. If one were to take Ursule away there would be no problem, Louise would be content, or at least resigned to her lot. The misery endured by Louise is not seen as stemming from marriage itself. At one stage, Emma feels persecuted by Charles's mother, who wants her to be more economical, but her plea, made ironically to her lover, is felt to be exaggerated: "Ils sont à me torturer. Je n'y tiens plus. Sauve-moi" (198). Throughout the novel Emma's suffering arises directly out of the conditions of her marriage, as perceived by someone who harbors high expectations. The imagery of constriction, associated with marriage, suggests that Emma's hardship stems from a sense of being hemmed in, although Charles, as we have seen is not tyrannical. At the apex of the novel Flaubert places a bungled clubfoot operation involving Hippolyte's leg being put into a wooden box that has the effect of making it turn gangrenous. This complicated contraption and the effects it has could be seen as a miniaturized version of what happens in the novel as a whole, the complex system of marriage producing in a different sphere the same painful results.

The *locus classicus* for seduction in nineteenth-century fiction is the carriage or hired cab.[14] Although other novelists may not be explicit in their treatment, little doubt is left in the reader's mind about what has taken place in the conveyance. In Champfleury's novel, however, it is not possible for inferences to be made, suggesting that the physical dimension of the angelic heroine's experience can never he properly realized. The idealising tendencies at work in the presentation of both Louise and Julien produce some curious results at the final moment of physical encounter. We are told that as they travel to Paris in the carriage "ils n'étaient même plus des humains, des êtres vivants; c'étaient des âmes

qui se rencontraient dans des étreintes célestes" (281). As befits such disembodied angels, "ils n'avaient plus consience de leurs corps" and the incongruous impression is created of bodies, like unsupervised machines, going haywire: "La voiture roulait toujours; au dedans, c'étaient des étreintes poignantes et fiévreuses à briser des barres d'acier. Leurs âmes s'étaient fondues en une seule et faisaient sentinelle autour d'eux" (281). Champfleury resorts to "points de suspension" to designate what he is simply incapable of visualizing. It would seem, in fact, from what follows that Louise has not succumbed to Julien's advances. The "pourpre pudique" of her face in the inn where they stop and her "doux abattement" (283) suggest that she has still to go like the proverbial lamb to slaughter. Flaubert on the surface might be thought to be equally evasive since virtually nothing is said about the behavior of the occupants in the hired cab. But the very indirection of the writing, going perversely against the grain of the reader's interest, contains a wealth of suggestion. The way in which the cab careers around Rouen, the demoralization of the cabbie, the sweating horses constitute an oblique commentary on the behavior of the occupants, in the throes of the same, and by implication equally futile, "fureur de la locomotion" (250).[15]

Louise's experience of adultery is dealt with in an extremely cursory fashion, a whole year of life in Paris being compressed into the last few pages of the last chapter. The central element revolves around her shame at being akin to the prostitutes she sees around La Madaleine: "à partir de ce jour-là, elle ne voulait plus continuer à vivre de la vie luxueuse des femmes entretenues" (291). Flaubert, in contrast gives a full account of the way Emma's adulterous relationships take on a kind of conjugal regularity: Emma and Rodolphe are compared to "deux mariés qui entretiennent tranquillement une flamme domestique" (175) and Emma and Léon: "se connaissaient trop pour avoir ces ébahissements de la possession qui en centuplent la joie" (296). Given Champfleury's lack of insight into the progression of human relationships it is not surprising that the final separation of the lovers in *Les Bourgeois de Molinchart* is unpersuasive. Julien's interest wanes not because he is tired of Louise but because he fears she will one day tire of him ("je craignais la satiété de sa part", 304). The final separation is brought about by the intervention of the law leading to Julien's incarceration (308). Flaubert's account of the deterioration is much more extended. Finally, the opposition between marriage and adultery is collapsed in the famous sentence, "Emma retrouvait dans l'adultère toutes les platitudes du mariage" (296). Such an insight, subversive of both marriage and adultery, lies well beyond the limits of Champfleury's grasp of the problem.

Champfleury's novel, Flaubert and Bouilhet agreed, peters out. We are not told what happens to Louise when she returns home after Julien's imprisonment. This is partly because the novel ends with a long letter from Julien to his friend, Jonquières, but the result is that Louise is completely eclipsed. There is no decisive re-action to the experience of adultery such as leads Emma to take her own life. Equally we are told nothing of Creton du Coche's reaction to her return, whereas Flaubert gives an extended and moving account of Charles's collapse after Emma's death. Champfleury has painted a picture in which whole sections have been left blank, highlighting the comprehensive nature of Flaubert's treatment.

One of the main reasons why Champfleury's account is so unsatisfactory is that he has little idea of how to combine the account of his heroine's development with the description of provincial life. There are several chapters dealing with aspects of life in Molinchart in which the heroine does not figure at all. Flaubert, in contrast, ensures that Emma is never eclipsed in this way. A dramatic difference can be seen in two scenes of provincial life selected for detailed treatment. Champfleury gives a full description of a prize-giving,[16] which Louise attends with Julien's mother. Nothing of any significance happens to the heroine on this occasion, which degenerates into a series of ridiculous flops. What drama there is relates to the Countess's daughter, Elisa de Vorges, who is terrified by the leathery skin of Ursule Creton du Coche. In the Comices agricoles chapter Flaubert, by means of skilful orchestration, manages to combine a full-scale presentation of the multiple activities with the development of Emma's relationship with Rodolphe. Flaubert is able to keep the narrative focus on Emma for some of the time because she is going through what is meant to be seen as an important stage in her relationship with Rodolphe but he also sets up a series of parallels between the speechifying and rhetorical manipulation of the crowd by the provincial dignitaries and Rodolphe's claptrap and rhetorical manipulation of Emma. The "demisiècle de servitude" (155) of Catherine Leroux, is part of a telling social comment but also bears a suggestive resemblance to Emma's underlying position in a man's world.

Flaubert may have at first regretted, when he read *Les Bourgeois de Molinchart,* that he was unable to publish *Madame Bovary* sooner,[17] but there was no real danger of Champfleury stealing his thunder and he subsequently came to think that nobody would be likely to see any connection between the two works.[18] If a comparison *is* made, however, it turns out to be wholly in Flaubert's favor and makes the nature of his achievement in addressing the central issues associated with the novel of adultery even more apparent.

Notes

1. See letter dated 2 August 1854 in which he writes "J'ai lu les cinq feuilletons du roman de Champfl-

eury", Flaubert, *Correspondance,* ed. J. Bruneau, 2 vols. (Paris: Bibliothèque de la pléiade, 1980) 2: 562. The reference, as Jean Bruneau points out in the notes, is not to *Madame d'Aigrizelles,* as previous editors of the *Correspondance* had thought, but to *Les Bourgeois de Molinchart,* which was written between January and November 1853, appeared in instalments in *La Presse* in 1854 and was published in book-form in 1855. Having noted the similarity between Champfleury's novel and *Madame Bovary,* Jean Bruneau observes that "les deux romans mériteraient d'être attentivement comparés, d'autant plus que Flaubert a pu tenir compte du roman de Champfleury en terminant et en revoyant son oeuvre" (*Correspondance* 2: 1261). The only detailed study of the two novels to have been made so far is Pier Luigi Pinelli, "Une Emma Bovary à Laon: Louise Creton du Coche", *Letterature,* 10 (1987): 63-100.

2. Flaubert was generally dismissive about the Realist school, with which Champfleury was closely associated, claiming to have written *Madame Bovary* "en haine du réalisme." The following, probably apocryphal, claim has been attributed to Flaubert: "J'ai fait *Madame Bovary* pour embêter Champfleury. J'ai voulu montrer que les tristesses bourgeoises et les sentiments médiocres peuvent supporter la belle langue", A. Albalat, *Flaubert et ses amis* (Paris: Plon, 1927) 68. It is also worth noting that a number of quotations from *Les Bourgeois de Molinchart* are included in the *Album de la Marquise,* which was to form part of the projected second volume of *Bouvard et Pécuchet.* See *Bouvard et Pécuchet,* ed. C. Gothot-Mersch (Paris: Folio, 1979) 479 and 482.

3. *Correspondance* 2: 562. Flaubert went on, however, to express a degree of concern about one similarity he perceived: "La seule chose embêtante, c'est un caractère de vieille fille dévote, ennemie de l'heroïne (sa belle-soeur), comme, dans la *Bovary,* Mme B[ovary] mère ennemie de sa bru, et ce caractère s'annonce très bien.—Là est pour moi jusqu'à présent la plus grande ressemblance et ce caractère de vieille fille est bien mieux fait que celui de ma bonne femme, personnage fort secondaire, du reste, dans mon livre." When he had read more instalments Flaubert became convinced that the two novels did not have too much in common: "Cela me rassure de plus en plus; la conception et le ton sont fort différents" (*Correspondance* 2: 566).

4. Tony Tanner, *Adultery in the Novel* (Princeton: Princeton University Press, 1979) 235.

5. All page references are to the Librarie Nouvelle edition of the novel (Paris: 1855) 1-310.

6. All references are to C. Gothot-Mersch's edition, (Paris: Garnier, 1971). See also "Charles finissait par s'estimer davantage de ce qu'il possédait une pareille femme," 43.

7. *Correspondance* 2: 562.

8. M. Lowe, *Towards the Real Flaubert. A Study of "Madame Bovary"* (Oxford: Clarendon Press, 1984) 70.

9. This description is one of the passages from the novel selected for inclusion in the *Album de la Marquise* (*Bouvard et Pécuchet* 479). Flaubert clearly felt that this kind of idealization constituted a form of "bêtise."

10. For a discussion of this process of morcelization see Tony Tanner, *Adultery in the Novel* 249-65.

11. "Champfleury, le poète a un fond de farceur," C. Baudelaire, "Puisque Réalisme il y a," in *L'Art Romantique,* ed L. J. Austin (Paris: Garnier-Flammarion, 1968) 102.

12. For the subversion of the traditional image of the male sex see the unfocalized analysis of Rodolphe's avoidance of Emma: "il l'avait soigneusement évitée par suite de cette lâcheté qui caractérise le sexe fort" (316).

13. *Correspondance* 2: 968.

14. See Jean Pommier, "*La Muse du Département* et le thème de la femme mal mariée chez Balzac, Mérimée et Flaubert," *L'Année Balzacienne,* (Paris: Garnier, 1961) 191-221.

15. For a full and persuasive analysis of this scene see Sartre, *Flaubert: L'Idiot de la famille 3 vols.* (Paris: Gallimard, 1971) 2: 1278-85. Sartre suggests, in particular, that "C'est la transcendance humaine que l'auteur veut écraser contre la terre; c'est le projet humain qu'il prétend abolir; ce sont les fins humaines qu'il veut réduire à un ensorcellement de corps inanimés."

16. Flaubert also intended to include such a scene at one stage. See the reference to "une distribution de prix de petites filles qui serait suivie d'un dîner" in a scénario published in *Madame Bovary. Nouvelle version,* ed. J. Pommier and G. Leleu (Paris: J. Corti, 1947) 17.

17. See *Correspondance* 2: 563: "N'importe, il est fâcheux que la *B[ovary]* ne puisse se publier maintenant! enfin! qu'y faire?"

18. *Correspondance* 2: 366: "Personne autre que toi ou moi ne fera, je crois, le rapprochement. La seule chose pareille dans les deux livres, c'est *le milieu,* et encore!"

Cynthia Griffin Wolff (essay date spring 1996)

SOURCE: Wolff, Cynthia Griffin. "Un-Utterable Longing: The Discourse of Feminine Sexuality in Kate Chopin's *The Awakening*." In *The Calvinist Roots of the Modern Era,* edited by Aliki Barnstone, Michael Tomasek Manson, and Carol J. Singley, pp. 181-97. Hanover, N.H.: University Press of New England, 1997.

[*In the following essay, originally published in* Studies in American Fiction *in spring 1996, Wolff explains changing notions about female sexuality in nineteenth-century American medical discourse and the ways in which Kate Chopin addressed and subverted them in* The Awakening.]

Because novelists are particular about beginnings, we should notice that *The Awakening* opens with two things: sumptuous sensory images and an outpouring of babble—words that resemble ordinary speech but that really have meaning for no one, not even the speaker:

> A green and yellow parrot, which hung in a cage outside the door, kept repeating over and over:
>
> "*Allez vous-en! Allez vous-en! Sapristi!* That's all right!"
>
> He could speak a little Spanish, and also a language which nobody understood.
>
> (19)

Although an onlooker is able to enjoy this vivid scene, the parrot cannot; moreover, there is a sense of enigma (or fraud) about this bird who seems able to communicate but is not. Indeed, the absolute discontinuity between the bird's "discourse," its exotic plumage, and its feelings (whatever they may be) is even more significant to the larger themes of the novel than the fact that he is caged. Or perhaps this very disconnectedness (and the bird's consequent isolation) defines the cage.

Critics admire the "modernism" of Chopin's work, the strong spareness of the prose and the "minimalism" of a narrative whose absences are at least as important as its action and whose narrator maintains strict emotional and moral neutrality. What we may not fully appreciate is the relationship between these elements and Edna Pontellier's personal tragedy, a relationship whose terms are announced by the apparent disarray of the novel's brilliant beginning. This is a tale about *not* speaking, about disjunction—about denials, oversights, prohibitions, exclusions, and absences. It is not merely about things that are never named, but most significantly about stories that cannot be told and things that can be neither thought nor spoken because they *do not have a name.*

After about 1850, the notion of a "woman's sexual awakening" became, by definition, an impossibility—a contradiction in terms—because the medical establishment in America began to promulgate the view that normal females possessed no erotic inclinations whatsoever (and one cannot awaken something that does not exist). William Acton, the acknowledged expert on the nature of women's sexuality and author of "one of the most widely quoted books on sexual problems and diseases in the English-speaking world," wrote: "The majority of women (happily for society) are not very much troubled with sexual feeling of any kind. What men are habitually women are only exceptionally. It is too true, I admit, as the divorce courts show, that there are some few women who have sexual desires so strong that they surpass those of men, and shock public feeling by their consequences."[1] Acton's work elaborated a comprehensive system of women's "inequality" to men; and it was so universally respected that his sentiments can be taken to represent opinions that were held throughout much of America during the second half of the nineteenth century. Certainly they defined the stern attitudes of the society in which Edna Pontellier had been reared, Calvinistic Presbyterianism, a latter-day bastion of Puritan thought.[2]

American Puritanism had always preached that although the woman was to be "regarded as equal to man in her title to grace," she was nonetheless "the weaker vessel" and thus was obliged to pursue all endeavors as a "subordinate to the husband" (Haller 121). From the beginning, this definition of the feminine role had created tensions and conflict: it had often produced instances of strong, passionately outspoken women; however, the assessment of these women's behavior had varied greatly. Nonetheless, until the nineteenth century, English and American Puritanical beliefs about woman's nature were relatively consistent: women were wanting in neither emotional energy (in general) or sexual energy (in particular); indeed, the second was thought to be a concomitant of "innate depravity," which was often associated with other forms of aggressive behavior that were inappropriate for women. In America, Puritanical communities gave considerable attention to the various means that could be employed to *control* a woman's sexual behavior, and early novels that were popular on both continents—*Pamela, Clarissa, Charlotte Temple,* and *The Coquette*—focused explicitly on the dilemmas that attended feminine sexual drive.[3]

When Anne Hutchinson "stepped out of the role the community defined for her," a special sort of "woman-problem" was defined in America—in part sexual, but more generally political—for "if a woman could instruct men, then all legitimate authority was in jeopardy" (Lang 42-43). The prototypical response had been formulated in Hutchinson's day: require women to assume their divinely ordained, subordinate position. Her failure to do so would result (so the argument ran) not merely in civil misrule but in grotesque sexual misconduct. Thus in the Hutchinson case, the phantoms of

both social turmoil and sexual license haunted the trial: "everywhere in the court examination, one finds the insinuation that Hutchinson is, like Jezebel, guilty of fornication" (43).[4]

Although Puritanism in America had begun to lose its vitality as a unifying cultural force by the end of the eighteenth century, and the clearly defined vision of human nature that had characterized its earliest days was gradually eroded, the fear of a woman's transgressing the boundaries that circumscribed her role lingered and seemed to justify a potentially lethal form of repression. Even at the time of Hawthorne's great work—and certainly by the beginning of the Civil War—Americans had displaced the reality and complexity of Puritanism with a trope; and the *trope,* "Puritanical," was used generally (and rather carelessly) to denote *conservatism* and *repression,* especially sexual repression. Paradoxically, although in loose usage repressive "Puritanism" had generally come to have negative connotations where women were concerned, repressive modes of defining women's "appropriate" role persisted and were generally applauded. Such a response may well have been the conservative reaction to the first Woman's Movement—with its outspoken leaders and its demands for female empowerment. Thus it is not surprising that during the flowering of late-nineteenth-century American Victorianism, major changes further constricted these widely disseminated notions of a woman's innate nature.

The superficial attitudes and norms seemed the same: it was deemed inappropriate for a woman to enact aggressive behavior, and it was deemed scandalous for a woman to indulge in passionately sexual conduct. Yet whereas seventeenth-century Puritans had presumed that women (like men) were innately passionate, late-nineteenth-century Americans presumed that women (*unlike men*) had a certain innate "passivity" and "purity": "appropriate" female behavior—silence and a revulsion from sexual activity—was therefore also considered to be *"natural"* female behavior. The deep, persistent Puritan heritage in American culture imparted a virulent force to such attitudes, and a number of Protestant sects actively promoted them.[5]

In the 1870s and continuing through the end of the century, the Presbyterian Church in America suffered a crisis over the role of women that might well be defined by the question, "Shall Women *Speak?*"[6] The embroglio began when a Newark clergyman invited two women into his pulpit to speak in favor of the Temperance Movement. Seeing an opportunity to reaffirm the precedent of women's "naturally" subordinate role, the Presbytery of Newark brought formal charges against the minister. In the minds of the accusers, the issue was far from narrow: "the subject involves the honor of my God. . . . My argument is subordination of sex. . . .

There exists a created subordination; a divinely arranged and appointed subordination of woman as woman to man as man. Woman was made for man. . . . The proper condition of the adult female is marriage; the general rule for ladies is marriage. . . . Man's place is on the platform. It is positively base for a woman to speak in the pulpit. . . . The whole question is one of subordination" (qtd. in Boyd 287). For both the Puritan Fathers and their late-nineteenth-century Calvinist descendants, the specter of a woman speaking out was portentous: at best, it was unsettling to the male hierarchy; at worst, it augured chaos. Suffragists could also discern the importance of this case, and the dispute among Newark Presbyterians became a notorious part of "the record of their struggle" and was widely publicized (Boyd 291).

Confronted with what they feared might become a similar provocation, the Presbyterian clergymen of Edna Pontellier's youth demanded that women keep to their "natural sphere" of home, hearth, and motherhood. As for women's sexuality, William Acton was their more than sufficient spokesman.

All of Acton's formulations are sweepingly comprehensive and inescapably normative, and in this respect he resembled the Puritans. He does not admit of gradations among women; nor does he entertain the possibility that additional data—testimony from women themselves, perhaps—might contradict or even emend his pronouncements. Instead, he presents his ideas as nothing less than a description of both a divinely ordained condition and a condition for middle-class respectability. He clearly considers the absence of passion in "normal women" to be a good thing (for its presence in a decent female would "shock public feeling"); and he refers dismissively to "prostitutes" and "loose, or, at least, low and vulgar women" whose strong libidinous drives "give a very false idea of the condition of female sexual feelings in general." In short, the innate frigidity of women signified a form of refinement and could be used as a touchstone for respectability.

The official "scientific" and "medical" view can be stated quite simply: an average woman (a "decent" woman) possesses no sexual feelings whatsoever. Thus it is not enough to say that *The Awakening* is a novel about repression (that is, about a situation in which a woman possesses sexual feelings, but is prohibited from acting upon them). It is, instead, a novel about a woman whose shaping culture has, in general, refused her the right to speak out freely; this is, moreover, a culture that construes a woman's self-expression as a violation of sexual "purity" and a culture that has denied the existence of women's libidinous potential altogether—has eliminated the very *concept* of sexual passion for "normal" women.

The consequences are emotionally mutilating (in the extreme case, some form of mental breakdown would result).[7] In such a culture, if a "respectable" woman supposes herself to feel "something," some powerful ardor in her relationship with a man, she can draw only two possible inferences. Either her feelings are not sexual (and should not be enacted in a genital relationship), or she is in some (disgraceful) way "abnormal." Moreover, because there is presumed to be no such entity as sexual feelings in the typical woman, a typical (i.e. "normal") woman will literally have no words for her (nonexistent) feelings, will have access to no discourse within which these (nonexistent) passions can be examined or discussed, will be able to make no coherent connection between the (unintelligible) inner world of her affective life and the external, social world in which she must live.[8] Finally, if she feels confusion and emotional pain, her culture's general prohibition against speaking out will make it difficult, perhaps impossible, to discuss or even reveal her discomfort.

Of course there was an escape hatch (infinitesimal, and insufficient). After all, men and women did marry, did have sexual intercourse, doubtless did (sometimes) enjoy their love-making, and did (occasionally) find ways to discuss the intimate elements of their relationship.[9] The range and resourcefulness of their individual solutions must remain a mystery. However, the publicly approved forms of discourse for female desire are a matter of record. Medical and psychological experts concluded that although women had no sexual drives per se, they often possessed a passionate desire to bear children: such ardor was both "normal" and (inevitably) sexual. On these terms, then, sexual activity—even moderate sexual "desire"—was appropriate in "normal" women. However, a profound displacement or confusion was introduced by this accommodation: the language of feminine sexuality became inextricably intertwined with discourse that had to do with childbearing and motherhood.

According to Acton (and to others who followed his lead), nature itself had made the longing to have children the essential, causative force of a woman's sexual "appetite." Thus men and women were essentially different: men have sexual impulses and needs (and these are quite independent of any wish to sire offspring); women crave children (and consequently they might be said—very indirectly—to "want" sexual activity). "Virility" and "maternity" were defined as parallel instincts that were nonetheless fundamentally dissimilar; and a woman's possessing sexual ardor *independent of her yearning for babies* became a defining symptom of abnormality or immorality or both:

> If the married female conceives every second year, we usually notice that during the nine months following conception she experiences no great sexual excitement. . . .

Love of home, of children, and of domestic duties are
the only passions [women] feel.

As a general rule, a modest woman seldom desires any
sexual gratification for herself. She submits to her husband's embraces, but principally to gratify him; and
were it not for the desire of maternity, would far rather
be relieved from his attentions.

(Acton 138, 164; my emphasis)[10]

Scholars have accepted almost as cliché the fact that in
late-Victorian America "motherhood" was exalted as an
all-but-divine state. However, if we do not also understand the oblique (and contradictory) sexual implications of this cultural ideal, we may be unaware of the
confusion and conflict it engendered.

This definition of feminine sexuality radically displaced
a woman's passionate desires: unlike males, who were
permitted to "possess" their sexuality and were consequently allowed to experience passion directly and *as a
part of the "self,"* females were allowed access to sexuality only indirectly—as a subsidiary component of
their desire for children. It was literally unimaginable
that any "decent" woman would experience sexual appetite as an immediate and urgent drive, distinct from
all other desires and duties. Men "owned" their libido;
women's libido was "owned" by their prospective children.[11]

Any woman would find this concatenation of denials
and demands unbalancing; however, in *The Awakening,*
Chopin renders these cultural regulations of women's
role in ways that are designed to demonstrate their potentially lethal consequences, for in Edna's case, the already vexed situation is brought to crisis by a superad-
ded disjunction: a conflict of "religions" and "cultures."
The summer at Grand Isle marks the moment when catastrophe begins.

Reared as a Presbyterian in Kentucky, Edna has been
married to a Creole for many years. Nonetheless, she
has never become "thoroughly at home in the society of
Creoles; [and] never before had she been thrown so intimately among them" (27-28). It is not that Creoles do
not have a rigorous sexual code: their customs follow
the boundary conditions that Acton and his fellow theorists have postulated. However, far from being Bible-
bound, sober and staid, so long as they remain within
the rules of this code, they permit themselves an extraordinary freedom of sensual expression. Thus a lusty
carnal appetite in *men* is taken for granted. (Robert has
his affair with the Mexican girl, everyone knows about
it, and no one thinks to disapprove.) However, the case
of Creole *women* is different, for their sexuality may
exist only as a component of "motherhood." Nevertheless, so long as they accept this model, women, too,
may engage in a sumptuous sexual life. Mme Ratignolle, the "sensuous Madonna," embodies the essence
of ardor and voluptuous appetite thus construed.

Such a system imposes penalties (Adèle's accouche-
ment is one specific marker for the price to be paid);
however, within these limiting conditions, the Creole
world is more densely erotic than any community Edna
has encountered. It revels frankly and happily in the
pleasures of the flesh—not merely enjoying these delights with undisguised zest but discussing them in public with no shame at all. Edna can recognize the inherent "chastity" of such people, but their habits
nonetheless embarrass her profoundly:

Madame Ratignolle had been married seven years.
About every two years she had a baby. At that time she
had three babies, and was beginning to think of a fourth
one. She was always talking about her "condition." Her
"condition" was in no way apparent, and no one would
have known a thing about it but for her persistence in
making it the subject of conversation.

(27)

A late-twentieth-century reader may innocently suppose
that Adèle's preoccupation is purely maternal. The full
truth is quite otherwise: in the discourse of the day,
Adèle has elected to flaunt her sexuality—to celebrate
both her ardor and her physical enjoyment. Robert enters the festive, flirtatious moment by recalling the "lady
who had subsisted upon nougat during the entire—,"
and is checked only by Edna's blushing discomfort.

All such instances of candor unsettle Mrs. Pontellier,
for example, when she responds with shock to Mme
Ratignolle's "harrowing story of one of her *accouche-
ments*" (28). This strange world, with its languorous climate and frankly sensuous habits, is a world where
"normal," "respectable" women openly vaunt pleasures
that are unfamiliar to her. She is fascinated and eventually profoundly aroused. And although she is bewildered by these new sensations, once having been
touched by them, she becomes unwilling to pull away.
Much of the novel, then, is concerned with Edna's quest
for a viable and acceptable mode of owning and expressing her sexuality: first by locating the defining
boundaries for these feelings and thus being able to define and name what she feels inside herself; second by
finding some acceptable social construct which will permit her to enact them in the outside world and to make
an appropriate, vital, and affirming connection between
the "me" and the "not-me" (Laing, *Self* 17-53).

Edna's easiest option is "collusion," to become a
"mother-woman"; however, she rejects this role violently because of the displacements and forfeitures that
it would impose. If, like Adèle, she were willing to disguise her erotic drives in the mantle of "motherhood,"
she might indulge the many delights of the body as
Adele patently does. However, such a capitulation
would not allow her really to possess her own feelings—nor even to talk about them directly or explicitly.

It would maim the "self," not unify and affirm it: like Adèle, Edna would be obliged to displace all of her sexual discourse into prattle about "the children" or her [pregnant] "condition," fettering her carnal desires to the production of babies; and part of what was really *inside* (that is, her sexual drive) would be displaced on to something *outside* (society's construction of female appetite as essentially "maternal"). In the process, the authority and integrity of her identity would be compromised, and instead of making contact with the outside world, she would be merged into it and controlled by it. Edna loves her children and is happy to be a mother; however, she refuses to define her sexuality in terms of them.[12]

Thus Edna's rejection of this emotional mutilation lies behind the many tortured examinations of her relationship to the children and informs such assertions as: "I would give up the unessential; I would give my money, I would give my life for my children; but I wouldn't give myself" (67). Renouncing what she can clearly recognize as an unacceptable violation of her emotional integrity is Edna's most confident step toward freedom.[13]

She shrugs away from marriage for many of the same reasons, declaring that she will "never again belong to another than herself" (100). The problem is neither immediate nor personal: it is not Léonce, per se, that Edna repudiates, but the warped forms of intimacy that he represents. Like Adèle, Léonce is acquainted with no discourse of feminine sexuality other than some variant on the language of "motherhood." This conflation is revealed in the couple's first intimate scene. Léonce has returned from an evening of card-playing, jolly at having won a little money—"in excellent humor . . . high spirits, and very talkative" (23). To be sure, he does not "court" his wife; yet he is scarcely brutal or coarse, and his gossipy, somewhat preoccupied manner as he empties his pockets might be that of any long-married man. Indeed, it is *Edna's* unapproachable manner that disrupts the potential harmony of the moment. There is nothing peculiar about the "action" of this scenario, nor is it difficult to read the subtext: Léonce would like to conclude his pleasant evening with a sexual encounter; his wife is not interested.

The real oddity has to do with language. Although the couple falls into a kind of argument over their differing inclinations, sex itself is never mentioned. Instead, when Léonce chooses to rebuke his wife (presumably for her passional indifference to him), he employs a vernacular of "motherhood" to do so. "He reproached his wife with her inattention, her habitual neglect of the children. If it was not a mother's place to look after children, whose on earth was it?" (24). With this alienated discourse, neither party can talk about the real source of unhappiness; however, Léonce at least has "acceptable"

alternatives (for example, we should probably not suppose that he is celibate during his long absences from home). Edna has none—not even the satisfaction of being able to define the exact nature of her despondency.[14]

She generally shuns the effort to assert herself, and to a remarkable degree she has detached herself from language altogether. As Urgo has observed, "For the first six chapters of the novel, she says all of four sentences" (23). Moreover, although she has lived among the Creoles for many years, "she understood French imperfectly unless directly addressed" (56). On this occasion, then, it is not surprising that she "said nothing and refused to answer her husband when he questioned her" (24). This is her customary reaction. Although Chopin's narrator refrains from moralizing about Edna's predicament, she does give the reader information from which it is possible to extrapolate Mrs. Pontellier's reasons for avoiding speech.

After her minor disagreement with Léonce, Edna begins to weep: "She could not have *told* why she was crying. . . . An *indescribable* oppression, which seemed to generate in some *unfamiliar* part of her consciousness, filled her whole being with a *vague* anguish" (24-25; my emphasis). At the most literal level, Edna is absolutely unable to "tell" why she is crying: her deepest passions have no "true" name. Society has given them only false names, like "maternity"; and such a discourse of feminine sexuality both distorts a woman's feelings and compromises her authority over them.

Thus Edna's recoil from language—her refusal to comply with this misrepresentation—is a primitive effort to retain control over her "self":

> She had all her life long been accustomed to harbor thought and emotions which *never voiced themselves*. They had never taken the form of struggles. They belonged to her and were *her own*, and she entertained the conviction that she had a right to them and that they concerned no one but herself.
>
> (66-67; my emphasis)

Nor is it surprising that Edna has always been deeply susceptible to fantasies—to her inward "dreams" of the cavalry officer, of the engaged young man from a neighboring plantation, of the "great tragedian." A person can and does entirely possess the products of his or her own imagination because (like the passions that infuse them) they are a part of the self. Thus, falling into fantasy becomes another way by which Edna seeks to maintain the integrity of self.

In some primitive way, silence also is Edna's only appropriate reaction to society's way of defining female sexuality: for if women were imagined to have no sexual feelings, *not to speak* would (ironically) be the way to "communicate" this absence. Yet not to speak has an annihilating consequence: it is, in the end, not to *be*—not to have social reality. One can never *affirm* "self" merely through silence and fantasy—can never forge that vital connection between the "me" and the "not-me" that validates identity. A "self" can mature only if one strives to articulate emotions; learning to name one's feelings is an integral component of learning the extent and nature of one's feelings, and what is undescribed may remain always "indescribable"—even to oneself—"vague" and even "unfamiliar." Moreover, without some authentic, responsive reaction from another, no one can escape the kind of solitude that increasingly oppresses Edna during the summer of her twenty-ninth year.[15]

Indeed, the dispassionate tone of Chopin's novel may be related to the complexity of Edna's quest, for Edna cannot "solve" her problem without an extraordinary feat of creativity. She must discover not merely a new vernacular with which to name her feelings—not merely a new form of plot that is capable of containing them—but also an "audience" that both comprehends and esteems the story she might ultimately tell. Thus the true subject of *The Awakening* may be less the particular dilemma of Mrs. Pontellier than the larger problems of female narrative that it reflects; and if Edna's poignant fate is in part a reflection of her own habits, it is also, in equal part, a measure of society's failure to allow its women a language of their own.

Most immediately personal is Edna's enchantment with forms of "communication" that do not require words. She is entranced by the ocean because its "language" neither compromises nor distorts her most intimate passions. Yet it cannot allow her to assert and confirm "self"; for ironically, like society, the sea requires an immersion of "self" (and this is, perhaps, the reason Edna has feared the water for so long):

> Seductive; never ceasing, whispering, clamoring, murmuring, inviting the soul to wander for a spell in abysses of solitude; to lose itself in mazes of inward contemplation.
>
> The voice of the sea speaks to the soul. The touch of the sea is sensuous, enfolding the body in its soft, close embrace.
>
> (32)

Music also seems to have "spoken" to Edna, most often conjuring primly conventional emotional "pictures" in her mind. However, as soon as she stirs from her sensual torpor and discards the prim and the conventional, music begins to conjure something more violently demanding: "no pictures of solitude, of hope, of longing, or of despair. But the very passions themselves were aroused with her soul, swaying it, lashing it, as the waves daily beat upon her splendid body" (45). Without the customary "pictures" to contain them, these emotions clamor for expression with an intensity that is all but unbearable.

It is troubling that the narrative conventions to which Edna is habitually drawn are so formulaic, that they decline to attempt some model of feminine initiative or some assertion of explicitly feminine passion. She configures her outing with Robert as "Sleeping Beauty" ("'How many years have I slept?' she inquired" [57]). Her dinner-table story is passive—the romance of a woman who was carried off "by her lover one night in a pirogue and never came back" (90). And if, as Sandra Gilbert has argued, Edna presides over a "Swinburnian Last Supper" just before her death (44), this moment when the "old ennui" and "hopelessness" overtake her once again must be read not as a new birth of Venus but as a poignant prefiguration of her return to that sea whence she came (Chopin 109).[16]

Yet troubling as Edna's habits of mind may be, Chopin also makes it clear that it would have taken more than daring ingenuity to alter her situation. The demand for women's rights alarmed sexual theorists, who construed all changes in the accepted paradigm as portents of anarchy. Their response was to reaffirm the conventional life story by insisting that women's dissatisfactions could be readily dismissed as nothing but an evidence of their innate inferiority: "In medical colleges, in medical books, in medical practice, woman is recognized as having a peculiar organization, requiring the most careful and gentle treatment. . . . Her bodily powers are not able to endure like those of the other sex" (qtd. in Barker-Benfield 200). When Léonce begins to discern the differences in Edna's manner and takes his concerns to Dr. Mandelet, their conversation recapitulates these nineteenth-century discussions of woman's nature:

> "She's odd, she's not like herself. I can't make her out. . . . She's got some sort of notion in her head concerning the eternal rights of women.". . .
>
> "Woman, my dear friend," [the Doctor responded,] "is a very peculiar and delicate organism—a sensitive and highly organized woman, such as I know Mrs. Pontellier to be, is especially peculiar. . . . Most women are moody and whimsical."
>
> (85-86)

It would take invention and resolution indeed to counter such a confident weight of received opinion—more than most women (most people) possess.

If the power of Edna's narrative ability is insufficient to retaliate against such fettering force, her primary choice of "audience" merely recapitulates her other problems. Instead of discerning Robert's true nature, she fancies him to be the lover of her dreams. She does not heed the conventions within which their flirtation begins; instead (as Adèle observes), she makes "the unfortunate blunder of taking [him] seriously" (35). Nor does she very much attend to Robert's conversation; for although he has spoken enthusiastically of going to Mexico, his untimely departure catches her entirely by surprise. Thus the exact nature of their intimacy is always best for Edna when it must be inferred (because it has not been put into words):

> [Robert] seated himself again and rolled a cigarette, which he smoked in silence. Neither did Mrs. Pontellier speak. No multitude of words could have been more significant than those moments of silence, or more pregnant with the first-felt throbbings of desire.
>
> (49)

Neither the reader nor Edna herself can know whose "desire" has been felt nor precisely what the object of this "desire" might be. However, the (almost overtly ironic) use of "pregnant" suggests that it is Edna, and not Robert, who has suffused this moment with unique intensity—and, most important, that she has not yet escaped all of those conventional constructions of female sexuality that bind it to maternity.[17]

Mademoiselle Reisz and Alcée Arobin (characters in and audiences for Edna's nascent narratives) both hold out the possibility that Edna might resolve her dilemma by usurping the prerogatives of men. Yet each offers a "solution" that would constrain Edna to relinquish some significant and valued portion of herself.

Ivy Schweitzer has observed that Mademoiselle Reisz, "a musician and composer, represents one extreme possibility; she exemplifies the artist with . . . 'the soul that dares and defies' conventionality, transgresses boundaries, and transcends gender" ("Maternal" 172). Mademoiselle Reisz also holds out the independence that men can achieve in a career. Yet Edna chooses not to follow this avenue; and Mademoiselle Reisz's admonition that the artist "must possess the courageous soul" (Chopin 83) may have been less of a deterrent than the example of that lady's own life. Fulfillment through aesthetic creativity appears to offer authentic expression to only one portion of the self. Mademoiselle Reisz "had quarreled with almost everyone, owing to a temper which was self-assertive and a disposition to trample upon the rights of others"; having no sensuous charm or aesthetic allure ("a homely woman with a small weazened face and body and eyes that glowed" [44]), she presents a sad and sorry prospect of some future Edna-as-successful-artist. What woman seeking sexual fulfillment would willingly follow the pathway to such a forfeiture of feminine sensuous pleasure as this?

Arobin offers the opposite. Something simpler but equally wounding. Lust. Sex divorced from all other feelings. The expression of that raw libido that was presumed to be part of men's nature (as "virility") but was categorically denied as a component of the normal female. Yet Edna finds that limiting sexuality to this form of expression imposes a distortion fully as destructive as society's construction of "maternity."

Arobin pursues Edna by pretending that casual sexuality is some fuller, more "sincere" emotion (he is careful never to mention love). And although his practiced style invites "easy confidence," it is also filled with "effrontery" (96)—with the desire to treat her as no more than a "beautiful, sleek animal waking up in the sun" (90). His manner could seem "so genuine that it often deceived even himself"; yet "in a cooler, quieter moment," Edna recognizes that it would be "absurd" to take him seriously (98). This form of eroticism explicitly excludes the integral complexity of Edna's unique "self": she might be anyone, any "sleek animal waking up in the sun," any woman whose "latent sensuality [would unfold] under his delicate sense of her nature's requirements like a torpid, torrid sensitive blossom" (126). Thus the aftermath of their consummation is not an affirmation of identity for Edna but another form of maiming—a cascade of simple sentences in largely parallel form to configure alienation and disintegration—the novel's shortest, most mutilated chapter, less than half a page. These lay bare the harsh realities of existence, "beauty and brutality," and conclude with nothing but a "dull pang of regret because it was not the kiss of love which had inflamed her" (104).

By the time Robert returns, Edna has all but exhausted the limited possibilities of her world; and if her first preference is once again to construe him dreamlike— "for he had seemed nearer to her off there in Mexico" (124)—she has gained the courage to speak forbidden discourse in the hope of inventing a new kind of narrative. "I suppose this is what you would call unwomanly," she begins, "but I have got into a habit of expressing myself. It doesn't matter to me, and you may think me unwomanly if you like" (127). They return to her little house, and when Robert seems to doze in a chair, she rewrites the sleeping beauty story by reversing their roles and awakening *him* with a kiss, "a soft, cool, delicate kiss, whose voluptuous sting penetrated his whole being. . . . She put her hand up to his face and pressed his cheek against her own. The action was full of love and tenderness" (128-29).

Reality is the realm into which Edna would lead Robert: a complex kingdom of sensuous freedom commingled with "love and tenderness," a place where man and woman awaken each other to share the "beauty and brutality" of life together in mutual affirmation. Each owning sexual appetite; both sharing the stern burdens of brute passion.

Edna is shocked, then, to discover Robert speaking a language of "dreams": "I lost my senses. I forgot everything but a wild dream of your some way becoming my wife." Even worse, Robert's "dream" retains the confining accouterments of the narrative Edna has journeyed so far to escape. She wants a new paradigm; he merely wants to rearrange the actors of the old one, and

Edna firmly rejects his falsifying, custom-bound notions. "You have been a very, very foolish boy, wasting your time dreaming of impossible things. . . . I give myself where I choose" (129). When Robert responds with perplexity to this new assertion of autonomy, Edna is offered the opportunity to show him what fortitude might mean.

Female sexuality had been falsified by the construct of "maternity"; however, there was one barbarous component of femininity, one consequence of feminine sexuality, that even the mother-woman could never evade. As Carroll Smith-Rosenberg explains:

> In the nineteenth century, with its still-primitive obstetrical practices and its high child-mortality rates, she was expected to face severe bodily pain, disease, and death—and still serve as the emotional support and strength of her family. As the eminent Philadelphia neurologist S. Weir Mitchell wrote in the 1880s, "We may be sure that our daughters will be more likely to have to face at some time the grim question of pain than the lads who grow up beside them. . . . To most women . . . there comes a time when pain is a grim presence in their lives."
>
> *(Disorderly* 199)

Having confronted the harsh "masculine" fact of unmitigated sexual desire, Edna entreats Robert to comprehend the inescapable pain and danger of the "feminine" by acknowledging the reality of childbirth. Having risked the scorn of being judged "unwomanly" by speaking her feelings and by awakening Robert with an act of love and passion conjoined, she asks him to demonstrate comparable courage. He, too, must leave dreams and half-truths behind, must comprehend the full complexity of *her* experience—both the brutality and the beauty—if he is to share in the creation of this new narrative of ardent devotion. "Wait," she implores, as she leaves to attend Adèle; "I shall come back" (130).

After the delivery, Edna's still-fragile, emergent self is shaken. In response to Dr. Mandelet's queries, she shrugs away from language: "I don't feel moved to speak of things that trouble me." Her desires continue to trail a fairy-tale hope of absolute happiness: "I don't want anything but my own way" (132). Still her anticipated reunion with Robert fortifies her. She foresees the opportunity to resume their love-making; and she believes there will be a "time to think of everything" (133) on the morning to follow, a chance to fashion the story of their life together. However, she has refused to consider his weakness and his fondness for illusions. Thus she is unprepared for the letter she finds: "I love you. Good-by—because I love you" (134). In the end, Edna has discovered no partner/audience with whom to construct her new narrative, and she cannot concoct one in solitude.

Nonetheless, she concludes with a narrative gesture of sorts—a concatenation of the parlance of "maternity."

Perhaps it is a tale of the son, Icarus, defeated by overweening ambition: "A bird with a broken wing was beating the air above, reeling, fluttering, circling disabled down, down to the water." Perhaps a tale of babies: "Naked in the open air. . . . She felt like some new-born creature, opening its eyes in a familiar world that it had never known." Most likely, it is a tragic inversion of the birth of Venus: "The touch of the sea is sensuous, enfolding the body in its soft, close embrace" (136).

So Edna has failed. Or rather, being a woman with some weaknesses and no extraordinary strengths, Edna has chosen the only alternative she could imagine to the ravaging social arrangements of her day. (Only seven years earlier, "The Yellow Wallpaper" had attracted wide attention to the same stifling, potentially annihilating constructions of "femininity.") However, we cannot forget that, if her heroine faltered, Kate Chopin fashioned a splendid success. *The Awakening* is the new narrative that Mrs. Pontellier was unable to create: not (it is true) a story of female affirmation, but rather an excruciatingly exact dissection of the ways in which society distorts a woman's true nature. The ruthless contemporary reviews leave no doubt that Kate Chopin had invented a powerful (and thus threatening) discourse for feminine sexuality. And although the novel was forced to languish (like yet another "sleeping beauty") largely unread for three quarters of a century, the current respect it enjoys is a belated affirmation of Kate Chopin's success.

Notes

1. We might be tempted to suppose that this attitude was in some essential way "Puritanical." However, Degler makes it clear that these explicit notions of women as totally devoid of passion entered American culture rather late (251-52). Quoted material within the text is from Degler 250 and Acton 162-63.

2. Chopin makes it clear (though unobtrusive) that Edna's background was repressive in many ways and that Edna was profoundly shaped by it. She writes of Sunday with its "Presbyterian service, read in a spirit of gloom by [Edna's] father" (35). It is significant that the age Edna mentions is both the age at which girls enter adolescence (and might under other circumstances begin to contemplate a sexual awakening) and the age at which Gilligan has found that many women "lose their voice" (12).

3. As early as 1563, the Englishman John Foxe recorded accounts of exemplary strong women in his *Book of Martyrs*; yet in America not many decades later, Anne Hutchinson's "strength" was heartily condemned. The intense mid-nineteenth-

century climate of Amherst Puritanism produced probably the most "uppity" feminist voice of all—Emily Dickinson. For an extended examination of this phenomenon see my studies *Samuel Richardson,* "Literary Reflections," and *Emily Dickinson.*

4. One interesting difference between the seventeenth-century Puritans and their nineteenth-century inheritors is in their estimation of women's capacity for sexual passion. In Anne Hutchinson's day, few doubted that the average woman was possessed of sexual appetite (such an appetite was part and parcel of the shared human inheritance: "innate depravity"); the emphasis, then, was upon control of that appetite. However, by the later nineteenth century, the forcible disempowerment of women had advanced to the point where (in Acton's formulation, for instance) the "natural capacity" for sexual passion was missing in women. All serious Christians—perhaps especially the Puritans—would have discerned that the supposed compliment in this construction of the feminine was in reality a grotesque mutilation: she is rendered somewhat *less* than fully human.

5. Acton was an Englishman whose work found wide acceptance in America. Clearly, therefore, the attitudes about a woman's "normally" asexual nature were a feature of high Victorianism in England. The fact that my discussion is limited to America does not mean to imply that our English cousins were more sexually "liberated" with regard to a woman's nature.

6. Penfield suggests that "only the Lutherans, Southern Presbyterians, United Presbyterians . . . and Episcopalians among Protestants are more conservative on issues relating to women in the mainstream of church life" (119). The Congregationalists had been thrown into disarray almost a half-century earlier by a similar issue concerning women (the Grimke sisters) who had been permitted to speak in churches against slavery. As Boyd and Brackenridge suggest, even "during the last two decades of the nineteenth century, the inherent conservatism of the Presbyterian church caused social customs and traditions to be modified only slowly and not without tension and turmoil" (108).

7. Laing discusses difficulties that result from a failure to relate the "inside-me-here-now-good-real-pleasant" to some "outside" and "recognized" (or acknowledged) self. "The attempt to find a satisfactory stable combination between good-bad, empty-full, inside-outside, me-not-me, may take up a great deal of energy—so [an individual] may feel exhausted, empty, inside *and* outside" (*Politics* 91, 93-94). This analysis allows us to understand

Edna's profound ennui throughout the novel—her sense of lassitude—for little in her lifetime (either before or after her marriage) has very much facilitated the development of an authentic and socially confirmed sense of self.

8. For a description of the treatment of "hysteria" in women see Smith-Rosenberg, *Disorderly* 206-207, 211.

9. See Rothman, throughout, for some insight into these solutions.

10. For a critique of perspectives like Acton's, see Chodorow, who argues that women's unhappiness stems in part from being forced to "live through their children" (44).

11. Laing's discussion of false naming sheds light on Edna's predicament (*Self,* chaps. 8, 9). See also Yaeger, who ties the linguistic problems of the novel to notions of property and ownership.

12. Almost twenty years ago, I wrote an essay on this novel, "Thanatos and Eros: Kate Chopin's *The Awakening,*" reprinted in complete form (Chopin) and in abridged form (Culley). What I am attempting here is not a fundamentally different reading of this novel (which still seems to me to present the tragic plight of a woman whose "identity" is never forged into a coherent, viable "self"), but a reading that traces the *social or cultural origins* of Edna's problem. See also Edna's reading of Emerson and her and Kouidis's discussion of her determination to achieve a "unified self."

13. Since Edna's children make very few actual demands upon her time or energy (she has all the "childcare" one might wish for and a mother-in-law who is apparently quite happy to bestow attention and affection upon her grandchildren), the emphatic quality of her renunciation—the almost obsessive way she returns to the problem—may seem odd unless a reader understands the tortured connection between female sexuality and "motherhood" decreed by American society in the late nineteenth century. Urgo insightfully examines Edna's habit of silence at the beginning of the novel. However, I cannot agree with his conclusion that Edna's story "about the woman who paddled away with her lover one night" represents the "discovery of a narrative voice" (28). This fairy-tale ending does not constitute much of a narrative advance over Edna's adolescent fantasies.

14. Chopin focuses on Edna, but she allows the reader to see that Léonce is injured by this system, too. One supposes that he understands at least *some* of

what he wants (more enthusiastic sexual receptivity from his wife); however, he can't *say* such a thing bluntly—because no "decent" or "sensitive" husband would make such a demand of his wife (who presumably only tolerated his advances because she had an interest in bearing children!). Hence he, too, cannot define the sources of his unhappiness:

> It would have been a difficult matter for Mr. Pontellier to define to his own satisfaction or any one else's wherein his wife failed *in her duty toward their children.* It was something which he felt rather than perceived, and he never voiced the feeling without subsequent regret and ample atonement.
>
> (26; my emphasis)

The problem really has nothing at all to do *with the children,* of course. Yet the discourse of "mothering" is all Léonce has been allowed if he wants to voice his disappointment.

15. See Bauer and Lakritz's excellent discussion of the social and cultural dialogues that inform this novel. They note but do not trace the origins of the quasimedical terminology that lies at the root of Edna's problem. See also George.

16. Showalter has observed that "the New Women writers of the 1890s no longer grieved for the female bonds and sanctuaries of the past . . . [but] demanded freedom and innovation" (175). Clearly, Edna does not have the creative power to fashion these new narratives.

17. Chopin gives us many clues concerning Edna's inability to see Robert as anything other than an extension of her own desires. Thus, when he cannot be with her, "She wondered why Robert had gone away and left her. It did not occur to her to think he might have grown tired of being with her the livelong day. She was not tired, and she felt that he was not" (59).

Works Cited

Acton, William. *The Functions and Disorders of the Reproductive Organs in Childhood, Youth, Adult Age, and Advanced Life.* 4th Am. ed. Philadelphia: Lindsay and Blackiston, 1875.

Barker-Benfield, G. J. *The Horrors of the Half-Known Life: Male Attitudes Toward Women and Sexuality in Nineteenth-Century America.* New York: Harper, 1976.

Bauer, Dale Marie, and Andrew M. Lakritz. "*The Awakening* and the Woman Question." Koloski 47-52.

Boyd, Lois A. "Shall Women Speak?" *The Journal of Presbyterian History* 56.4 (Winter 1978): 281-94.

Boyd, Lois A., and Douglas Brackenridge. *Presbyterian Women in America: Two Centuries of a Quest for Status.* Westport, Conn.: Greenwood, 1983.

Chodorow, Nancy. *Feminism and Psychoanalytic Theory.* New Haven: Yale UP, 1989.

Chopin, Kate. *The Awakening: Case Studies in Contemporary Criticism.* Ed. Nancy A. Walker. New York: St. Martin's, 1993.

Culley, Margo, ed. *The Awakening.* 2nd ed. New York: Norton, 1994.

Degler, Carl N. *At Odds: Women and the Family in America from the Revolution to the Present.* New York: Oxford UP, 1980.

George, E. Laurie. "Women's Language in *The Awakening.*" Koloski 53-59.

Haller, William. *The Rise of Puritanism.* New York: Harper, 1957.

Koloski, Bernard, ed. *Approaches to Teaching Chopin's* The Awakening. New York: Modern Language Association, 1988.

Laing, R. D. *The Politics of the Family and Other Essays.* New York: Pantheon, 1969.

———. *Self and Others.* Harmondsworth, England: Penguin, 1971.

Lang, Amy Schrager. *Prophetic Woman: Anne Hutchinson and the Problem of Dissent in the Literature of New England.* Berkeley: U of California P, 1987.

Penfield, Janet Harbinson. "Women in the Presbyterian Church—an Historical Overview." *Journal of Presbyterian History* 55 (Summer 1977): 107-24.

Rothman, Ellen K. *Hands and Hearts: A History of Courtship in America.* New York: Basic, 1984.

Schweitzer, Ivy. "Maternal Discourse and the Romance of Self-Possession in Kate Chopin's *The Awakening.*" *Boundary* 2.17 (Spring 1990): 158-86.

Showalter, Elaine. "Tradition and the Female Talent: *The Awakening* as a Solitary Book." Chopin 169-89.

Smith-Rosenberg, Carroll. *Disorderly Conduct: Visions of Gender in Victorian America.* New York: Knopf, 1985.

Urgo, Joseph R. "A Prologue to Rebellion: *The Awakening* and the Habit of Self-Expression." *SLJ* [*Southern Literary Journal*] 20 (1987/88): 22-32.

Woolf, Cynthia Griffin. *Emily Dickinson.* New York: Knopf, 1986.

———. "Literary Reflections of the Puritan Character." *Journal of the History of Ideas* 19.1 (Jan.-Mar. 1968): 13-32.

———. *Samuel Richardson and the Eighteenth-Century Puritan Character.* Camden, Conn.: Archon, 1972.

Elizabeth Perry Hodges (essay date 1996)

SOURCE: Hodges, Elizabeth Perry. "The Letter of the Law: Reading Hawthorne and the Law of Adultery." In *Law and Literature Perspectives*, edited by Bruce L. Rockwood, pp. 133-68. New York: Peter Lang, 1996.

[*In the following essay, Hodges discusses Nathaniel Hawthorne's interpretation of Puritan imagination in* The Scarlet Letter, *finding that the author's emphasis on ambiguity and resisting reductive interpretation creates "tension between the demands of structure and the force of experience," a tension that can also exist in the formation of legal structures.*]

The short first chapter of *The Scarlet Letter* ends with talk of a wild rose-bush, covered with gem-like flowers, growing on one side of the door to the ugly, weather-stained prison—"the black flower of civilized society."[1] This door, with its rusty, "ponderous" ironwork, "looked more antique than anything else in the new world . . . it seemed never to have known a youthful era" (75). The rose-bush beside it, "by a strange chance," had been "kept alive in history," but how or why we are never told. Hawthorne will do no more than pluck one of its flowers and present it to the reader, as a symbol of "some sweet moral blossom" found along the way, or as relief to the dark tale of human sorrow.

We might wonder why Hawthorne roots his rose at the threshold of his story, merely to pluck it, to let its inexplicable force fade into a moral lesson. The rose-bush, like other central images in the novel—the letter "A" and the forest, for example—holds the potential for ambiguity. It not only grows next to the prison, the "black flower of society"; it grows out of the same soil. By linking these two different flowers, the prison and the rose-bush, Hawthorne is alerting us to the complexity of his fable. To "read" the rose as an emblem of youth or of love and its passing would be a kind of reduction, analogous to the moralistic or narrowly allegorical readings of fiction which Hawthorne's opening invites us to resist.

The figure of the rose introduces us to one of Hawthorne's essential concerns: the danger of reductive reading, or of judging too quickly. Most of the major and minor characters in the novel—the tormented lover and guilty minister, Arthur Dimmesdale; the cold, vengeful husband, Roger Chillingworth; the town gossips and magistrates—are guilty at one time or another of reducing the complex humanity of Hester Prynne to the fixed meaning associated with the letter she must wear on her breast for life, the "A" that identifies her, simply, with the single fact of adultery. In opposition to the culture-bound, formalizing impulse of the Puritan community, Hester and her spritely daughter Pearl appear to be in touch with the imaginative forces that re-

sist reductive readings. Hester, in Hawthorne's words, "assume[s] a freedom of speculation . . . our forefathers . . . would have held to be a deadlier crime than that stigmatized by the scarlet letter" (183). Pearl, inheriting her mother's passionate nature and defying, as a "demon child," the very definition of the human, sports about with the "waywardness of an April breeze" (197). For Hawthorne, the speculative, the natural, and the demonic, perceived by the Puritans as transgressive, are essential elements of the human imagination which, subject to the shaping hand of art, challenges the traditional boundaries and cliches established by collective institutions.

Hawthorne's fiction thus presents us with a dilemma recognized by lawyer and poet alike; for in both legal and imaginative writing, some reduction is inevitable. If poems, in Marianne Moore's phrase, are "imaginary gardens with real toads in them," it is because the imagination has been disciplined into giving them shape. Likewise, when Oliver Wendell Holmes in one of his most quoted lines claims that "the life of the law has not been logic: it has been experience," he recognizes, like Moore, the tension between the demands of structure and the force of experience, or the real.[2] The law for Holmes provides a form for channeling society's uncontrollable passions and putting an end to the interminable cycle of revenge. But boundaries, necessary as they are to the survival and the creation of forms, can at times inhibit or distort their growth. How to balance the conflicts inherent in this drama is the story of both law and literature, and of Hawthorne's *Scarlet Letter.*

HAWTHORNE AS BRICOLEUR

Before turning to the workings of the Puritan imagination in Massachusetts in the 1640's, let us look at Hawthorne's method to illustrate the psychological and technical complexity that accompanies the act of reading and writing. His method is not unlike a lawyer's when he builds a case—juxtaposing past and present, precedent and context—but he is perhaps more wary than the lawyer of plucking the rose too quickly and effacing the signs of paradox and ambiguity.

In the prelude to *The Scarlet Letter,* Hawthorne takes an autobiographical detour to describe his experience working as a functionary at the Custom-House in Salem. Meditating on his own professional life, he dips back into his past, calling up images of two notorious ancestors: one a stern soldier, legislator, and judge; the other, the judge's son, Hawthorne's great-great grandfather, who "inherited the persecuting spirit" (41) and participated in the witchcraft trials of 1692. These "stern and black-browed Puritans" would have scorned as "worthless if not positively disgraceful" his work as a "writer of storybooks" (41-42).

As part of this meditation Hawthorne provides portraits of his fellow workers, devoting special attention to one old General, once strong and massive, "not yet crumbled to a ruin," a man who offered Hawthorne a "rare instance . . . of a person thoroughly adapted [unlike Hawthorne] to the situation which he held" (55). Hawthorne describes this man in a way that anticipates the strategy he will use in telling the tale of Hester Prynne:

> To observe and define his character . . . was as difficult a task as to trace out and build up anew, in imagination, an old fortress, like Ticonderoga, from a view of its gray and broken ruins.
>
> (51-52)

His job, as a writer, has been to reconstruct from the broken ruins—the remaining wall, the "shapeless mound . . . overgrown with grass and alien weeds"—a portrait of the brave old General. *The Scarlet Letter* has been similarly reconstructed from a pile of "heaped up rubbish" (59) discovered "one idle and rainy day" in a deserted corner of the attic of the Custom-House. Within this rubbish Hawthorne has chanced upon a curious small package wrapped in ancient yellow parchment and tied with faded red tape. Within the packet he has discovered a "rag of scarlet cloth," moth-eaten, which, after some fiddling, takes on the shape of a capital "A"; and some "half dozen sheets of foolscap" containing various particulars of Hester Prynne's life as written down by a Mr. Surveyor Pue in the 1750's from the oral testimony of aged persons who in their youth had known Hester as a "very old, but not decrepit woman." These material relics and the testimonies and ghostly voice of Mr. Pue emerging from them provide the "groundwork" (65) from which Hawthorne builds and "dresses up" his tale.

Responding to his own professional crisis and uncertainty about his future as a writer (he was about to lose his job at the Custom-House, his only stable source of income), Hawthorne imagines that it is the ghost of Mr. Pue that serves as his "official ancestor," in place of his great-great grandfather, exhorting him to seize upon this occasion and "bring his mouldy and motheaten lucubrations before the public" (64). The passage reflects both the author's personal anxieties and his strategy as a writer, and suggests that the two are related. Unpacking layer after layer of potential meaning, the author discovers no final clarity but, rather, a solitary, ambiguous letter which tempts him to tackle the awesome task of imaginative reconstruction. At the same time the storyteller fears he has lost his power over "the tribe of unrealities" that now confront him (65). Anxiety about the source of that power is figured by his evocation of ancestors, both real and "official," neither of whom is simply discarded or displaced. His witch-hanging ancestor, whose profession and perspective he will ultimately renounce, gives voice, strident though it may be,

to the formalizing impulse which has its part to play in structuring the material fragments of the past. Surveyor Pue invites him to exploit the full potential of his narrative gift.

It is striking that the stories his ancestral voices tell him have at their center a matter of law. The fragmented testimonies of Mr. Pue bring to life the old figures of the judge and his son, whose own efforts to structure the particulars of human behavior had such a different goal and followed such a different logic. For while the law pursues coherence with the aim of bringing structure and homogeneity to the community (by hanging witches, for instance), Hawthorne's fiction, by contrast, reminds us that such coherence is purchased at a cost. But it does more; it questions whether such coherence is even possible. Thus, if at the beginning of the novel Hester's "A," here preserved in the rag of cloth, seems to testify to the law's univocal efficacy, no one at the end of the novel, even after the dying Dimmesdale confesses his guilt, will be able to agree on what they actually saw on the minister's chest.

MYTH, HISTORY, AND LAW

The Scarlet Letter dramatizes the struggle between form and experience by exposing the limitations of such seemingly definable categories as history and myth. Hawthorne's quarrel with his own past is played out in his novel among characters struggling to adapt their lives to a new context. He situates their story in a particular moment in real history—the decade of the 1640's in the Massachusetts Bay Colony in which first generation Puritans are building their community in the New World. Their town stands at the edge of the wilderness, a tiny rough-hewn settlement planted between a savage unknown and the civilization of an Old World, "a paternal home" all had left behind (85). Just as Hawthorne struggles to shape his story, so too will the characters of the novel struggle to piece and hold together the meaning of their lives.

What strikes one about this historical context is its instability. The story takes place at a transitional moment, between old and new. The settlers brought with them a rigid legal and moral code based on Mosaic law. They hoped to plant in this wilderness a new Eden, free from the political conflict and religious persecution experienced in England during the sixteenth and seventeenth centuries. Sustained by a strict, typological reading of the Old Testament, they sought to establish a new theocracy in which the covenant between God and his people demanded strict performance of his laws. As John Winthrop suggested in the spring of 1630 in a sermon delivered from the deck of the flagship *Arbella,* survival in the new land would depend on their keeping God's commandments:

> . . . we are commanded this day . . . to keep His commandments and His ordinances and His laws and the

articles of our covenant with Him, that we may live and be multiplied, and that the Lord our God may bless us in the land whither we go to possess it: but if our hearts shall turn away so that we will not obey, but shall be seduced and worship . . . other gods, our pleasures and profits, and serve them, it is propounded unto us this day, we shall surely perish out of the good land whither we pass over this vast sea to possess it.[3]

Winthrop's terms, which echo God's warning to the people of Israel, would have resonated on a literal as well as a spiritual level for settlers threatened not only with a perilous sea voyage but with cold, hunger, disease, and hostile attacks on land. The Puritans' belief in the covenant permeated every aspect of their physical and spiritual lives, binding the two spheres together. In Hawthorne's story Governor Bellingham and his fellow magistrates used this vision not only to unite the community but to control, by humiliation, banishment, or death, any wayward member. Hester's case forced them to test the ground of that vision. In violating one of God's original commandments, her act of adultery challenged the community's vision of itself, its past and its future.

Although we speak here as if history referred to a stable, definable reality, we must also understand the Puritan community as a rhetorical construct precariously bound together by myth and desire. Winthrop's theocratic vision relies on ancient and sacred myths which come, after years, to behave like history. This sacred tradition legitimates his argument in the ears of his listeners; it provides the unchallenged framework through which the Puritans understand their history and the future that will flow from it. But it does so partly by denying or effacing other aspects of that history—collective as well as personal, objective as well as fictive or unconscious.

In his essay *Nomos and Narrative* Robert Cover makes a similar point about the law, suggesting that law, like history, has an inevitable entanglement with myth, or, as he calls it, narrative: "no set of legal institutions or prescriptions exists apart from the narratives that locate it and give it meaning. For every constitution there is an epic, for each decalogue a scripture. Once understood in the context of the narratives that give it meaning, law becomes not merely a system of rules to be observed, but a world in which we live."[4] Cover is suggesting that although the law desires to stake out a claim about its fairness, objectivity, or neutrality, such a claim is misguided because laws originate, not in an all-knowing, clairvoyant mind, like that of God or of Plato's philosopher king, but rather in the contextual narratives of a given society—in its particular language, history, and myth. The law, in other words, does not speak clearly and univocally, as God is supposed to have done on Mt. Sinai. It grows out of and is constructed from multiple voices within a particular community. One wants, in Cover's view, to base one's in-

terpretation of law on an understanding of those voices rather than to impose what may appear from one's own perspective to be a more correct, more universal principle of justice: "each 'community of interpretation' that has achieved 'law' has its own *nomos*—narratives, experiences, and visions to which the norm articulated is the right response . . . different interpretive communities will almost certainly exist and will generate distinctive responses to any normative problem of substantial complexity."[5] For Cover the laws of each community should be read in light of the norms of its particular culture. Ideally, lawyers and judges would provide the "right response," "right" that is, not in terms of some universal or objective sense of right, but "right" from the community's perspective.

The communitarian response to the limits of legal formalism allows us to recognize, if we have failed to before, that the rhetoric of precedent, handed down for generations, can, like history, deafen our ears to other voices, most often of those who are powerless or who are discriminated against. But determining how and if Cover's "right" and particular response is in fact right remains the constant burden of legal interpretation. Lawyers and judges repeatedly ask whether it is best for a cobbler to fit a shoe to each foot or for a factory to mass produce the shoe, knowing that it will fit most feet well enough to wear. In inviting us to think about the perspective of a cobbler's world, Cover is asking us to recognize the extent to which all law is constituted by the complex mythology of particular people and thus to resist picking the rose too soon.[6] The history of the laws against adultery illustrates the extent to which law can grow out of the particular narratives or communal *nomos* of its society. Both the laws and the narratives underlying them vary so that an historical summary is impossible, but they seem to fall into two principal categories. Looking at old Babylonian, Hebraic, or Hindu law, for instance, or at later laws influenced by the Church, we find a tendency to consider adultery a moral transgression. Looking at early English and Germanic law, however, we see adultery treated rather as a threat to the family line or as a violation of property rights. To complicate matters, the laws within any given community may evolve over time to reflect some combination of these two approaches.[7] Moreover, supporting the various social arguments there is often a psychological argument implying that adultery is "a blow to a man's pride" which he has a need—and so a right—to avenge.[8] If the specific reasons for the laws are, as one writer put it, "as numerous and ancient as the races of man," so too are the remedies.[9] An aggrieved husband may kill the rival or a member of the latter's kinship group, or he may call for a regulated fight or public humiliation of the interloper. Alternatively, the adulterer himself may voluntarily submit to physical punishment, or offer some form of payment, including a new wife for the husband.

The literary fortunes of adultery are as various as its historical description. Indeed among legal themes it is unquestionably the most prominent, providing the principal motivation for narrative fiction from Homer's *Iliad* down to the latest best seller. In *Adultery in the Novel* Tony Tanner goes so far as to see sexual transgression as the key to the development of the novel. We have the *Iliad,* he says, because Paris—the guest and outsider—broke the taboo against sleeping with his host's wife. After citing further instances (*Tristan, Lancelot, La Nouvelle Heloise, Madame Bovary,* and many others) he goes on to argue that adultery becomes the obsession of the bourgeois novel because of the central importance of marriage in bourgeois society.[10] The breaking of one bond (by adultery) portends the dissolution of all bonds; individual transgression leads to social disintegration. Tanner's point here is that the force that disrupts the social order is the force that drives on the narrative.

This figurative extension of the notion of adultery attests to the breadth and depth of society's vulnerability: sexual transgression touches on the deepest questions of self definition and social stability. The final act of Shakespeare's *Merchant of Venice,* a play concerned ostensibly with questions of legal and social justice, shows us how pervasive the anxiety about sexual transgression can be.[11] Following the trial and banishment of Shylock, the reunited lovers slide into mutual accusations of infidelity, even as they recall the night of their betrothal (V.1.17-22). The fantasy of a perfect harmony between lovers and citizens ("a concord of sweet sounds"), spun out in Portia's moonlit garden, is undermined by Jessica's repudiation of music (V.1.69) and by the subsequent arguments over lost rings and broken oaths that end the play. Shylock may have been judged, social harmony inaugurated, but a pervasive worry over transgression and betrayal nonetheless remains. The fear of sexual infidelity can no more be banished than a pound of flesh can be cut from a living body. Infidelity and oath-breaking are too close to the social heart.[12]

What is at stake in the breaking of marital bonds is ultimately the integrity of society itself. Infidelity and oath-breaking in the private sphere anticipate treason in the public sphere so that, as Lorenzo warns, "The man that hath no music in himself . . . [i]s fit for treasons, stratagems, and spoils" (V.1.83-85). The transgressions at the core of festive comedy thus reflect a fear, which finds expression in the laws a society develops to preserve its integrity. These laws, Cover has suggested, arise from the particular *nomos* of a community, but the argument also works in reverse. The laws can, over time, become part of that *nomos,* helping to structure the myths and language by which the society defines itself. The history of the laws against adultery illustrates this reciprocal work of self definition.

ADULTERY: PRIVATE OR PUBLIC WRONG?

From earliest times adultery, like homicide, was considered a private wrong against the victim and his kingship group, and most primitive societies left the punishment of adultery in the hands of the injured person and his kin. The retaliation against the person who had committed the offense gave rise to long-lasting blood feuds between different clans or tribes. Belief in the principle of retaliation seems to lie at the source of the earliest law codes and, as we shall see, plays a prominent role in the laws prohibiting adultery. Steeped in the epics that document these feuds, Holmes has argued that "the early forms of legal procedure were grounded in vengeance."[13] Thus if a beast kills a man, the beast is slain and cast out; if a slave kills a man, the slave is given up to the relatives to use him as they please; if an inanimate thing causes death, it is cast out beyond the borders. The liability in early times, in Holmes's view, "seems to have been regarded as attached to the body doing the damage, in an almost physical sense. . . . [T]he hatred for anything giving us pain . . . leads civilized man to kick a door when it pinches his finger."[14]

We find this principle at work in the earliest laws that seek to redress the violation associated with adultery. The Code of Hammurabi, dating from about 2250 B.C., punishes both adulterer and adulteress (unless the husband or king decides otherwise):

> If the wife of a seignior has been caught while lying with another man, they shall bind them and throw them into the water. If the husband [lit., "owner," "master"] of the woman wishes to spare his wife, then the king in turn may spare his subject [lit., "his slave"].[15]

Permission to kill an adulterer or adulteress was actually contained in the written codes of many ancient societies. This sort of redress—directed against the actual body of the aggressor—gradually gave way to various legal substitutions which, by averting the blood feud, sought to maintain social order. Regulated fights or public humiliation of the offender would sometimes satisfy the victim's thirst for revenge. In certain societies the offender might agree to allow the victim to throw spears at him or hack his body with knives.[16]

Building on Holmes's view, Jeremy Weinstein argues that the most significant change in the development of primitive law occurred when the responsibility for righting a wrong shifted from the individual to the state. To insure social control the state sought to "assert a monopoly of force prohibiting its use by any other than itself."[17] What were once considered private wrongs against an individual "came to be seen as a public wrong against the domestic order and therefore against the state."[18] The system of private settlement between warring parties was gradually suppressed as the state increasingly asserted its own right to punish wrongs.[19] By taking responsibility for punishing the crime, the state hoped to co-opt private vengeance; rather than allow the husband to kill his wife or her lover, and thus initiate a blood feud, the state attempted to settle the dispute according to its own laws. This plan, however, did not always work. It often failed to satisfy the victim's psychological need for revenge. And rather than force its point, the state would often look the other way when an aggrieved husband exercised his vengeance on his own.

We find this curious tug of war between state and individual over the punishment of adultery vividly played out in the records of the earliest English kings. In their laws sexual offenses occupy a prominent place among other private wrongs—homicide, severe personal injury, theft, and the abduction of women and children—wrongs affecting a person's body or property. Aethelberht's *Dooms* (ca. 600 A.D.), the oldest surviving literary document in any Teutonic tongue and arguably the first in the "grand traditions of English law and English literature,"[20] provides an unusually complete set of laws detailing the compensation a man would pay for violating any part of the body, from head to toe: for seizing the hair, breaking the outer cover of the skull, disabling a shoulder, destroying the hearing, striking off an ear, piercing an ear, lacerating an ear, knocking out an eye, piercing a nose, knocking out a tooth (a different price for each tooth), destroying a nail on the finger, or on the toe (a different price for each finger or toe), for destroying the generative organs, to name only a few; for each offense a man paid a fixed compensation.[21]

The adultery laws (and laws against illicit sex in general) were equally comprehensive. Underlying these laws was the institution of the bride-price marriage, the gift to the bride's father or next of kin to secure consent for the marriage. Any illicit sex upset the husband's and father's expectations regarding the bride-price and was felt as a wrong to the kinship group in which she lived.[22] For lying with a king's maiden a man would pay 50 shillings (equal to about 50 cows); one would pay a different price for lying with a nobleman's serving maid, a commoner's serving maid, or a slave (and there were slaves of different classes).[23] The compensation depended on the severity of the crime and on the social class of the person violated. Section 31 provides an interesting alternative for the freeman:

> If [one] freeman lies with the wife of [another] freeman, he shall pay [the husband] his [or her] wergeld,[24] and procure a second wife with his own money, and bring her to the other man's home.

The *Dooms* also tacitly allowed a husband to kill the man he found with his wife. The Code thus permitted several options for the offended husband. He could ex-

act his vengeance, accept compensation, or accept a new wife. These options suggest a certain ambivalence, and perhaps a certain pragmatism, on the part of the lawmakers about just how to handle adultery and the feelings it aroused. Even though the Code sought to diffuse resentments arising from private wrongs—by setting a price on every conceivable wrong to the body—it also seemed to recognize the real difficulty in successfully containing the force of resentment. At some level compensation could never repair the loss or injury felt to one's sense of self.

This small section of English law concerning adultery shows that even within a single "culture" the law is not particularly stable.[25] But despite the fact that various options were left open to the offended husband, the idea of protecting one's own integrity and pride remained constant. Alfred's Code, issued between 871 and 893, codified this principle, providing the first English example of a rule that explicitly permitted a husband to exercise his vengeance:

> A man may fight, without becoming liable to vendetta, if he finds another [man] with his wedded wife, behind closed doors or under the same blanket; or [if he finds another man] with his daughter [or sister]; or with his mother, if she has been given in lawful wedlock to his father.[26]

This law points both to the distant past—to the code of Hammurabi, Mosaic law, and Roman law, which gave the husband the option of killing the man he had discovered lying with his wife—and to our own time—to state statutes which explicitly permitted the husband to exercise his vengeance well into the twentieth century. In Texas, for example, as recently as 1973, murder was permitted if the husband had discovered the parties in the act of adultery, before they had separated.[27] And Georgia permitted a husband or father to kill the lover of his wife or child under limited circumstances until 1977.[28] Such statutes reflect a psychological no less than a social motive. In taking over the punishment of the offense, the state could never fully succeed in suppressing the powerful resentment aroused by adultery. Thus, in certain clearly defined situations, the law endorsed murder, sometimes tacitly, sometimes explicitly.

What effect did Christianity have on the laws against adultery? Although England's conversion began with the mission of Augustine in 597, Christian ethical precepts did not begin to make themselves felt in the written laws until the tenth and eleventh centuries. With the spread of Christianity in the eighth and ninth centuries adultery had come to be seen as a sin, but this attitude did not noticeably affect the laws. Earlier law—Aethelberth's *Dooms* and its successors—had generally focused on the specific compensation required for particular offenses. Alfred's Code, issued between 871 and 893, continued to reflect the effort of these earlier codes both to regulate blood feuds by requiring payment to offended husbands[29] and, at the same time, to allow the husband (or father) to exercise his vengeance without fear of retribution from the victim's family.[30] By and large, adultery was treated during this period as a private wrong despite the presence of Christianity.

Beginning with the Central Codes, issued between 900 and 1100, adultery, prostitution, and other forms of illicit union were classified as sins and explicitly forbidden.[31] This shift had an important ideological component: sexual offenses became moral wrongs against the state rather than private wrongs against the individual and, as a result, punishments sometimes assumed a new severity. The laws of Cnut, for example, sought to enforce monogamy, by mutilation if necessary.[32] It remained true, however, that the main thrust of English law into the early twelfth century was to control the blood feud. Thus while new laws arose reflecting Biblical influence, the kings also retained the two approaches of older laws, the one urging compensation, the other regulating (which often meant permitting) revenge.[33]

The complex legal picture which emerges by the twelfth century reflects both the socio-political realities behind these earlier codes and, increasingly, the state's growing interest in consolidating political power. Adultery was now subject to severe punishment by the state, but the laws were not uniformly enforced. It could be regulated by compensation, but it remained the only wrong for which compensation had not become obligatory.[34] During the rule of the Normans adultery continued to be a crime whose punishment escaped the full force of the state. Eager to solidify their authority, the Normans made extensive reforms in the law by repealing the death penalty for most crimes and instituting the *lex talionis,* or "eye for an eye" (Exodus 21:2-22:17, and Leviticus 24:20). Rather than be hung or flayed for a crime, an offender might have his eyes put out, or have his feet or his hands cut off, or be castrated, "so that the trunk remains alive as a sign of his treachery and wickedness; for the penalty inflicted on malefactors should be in proportion to the crime committed."[35] Despite such efforts to take responsibility for all punishment, the state continued, however, to permit an exception in the case of adultery; under the Laws of William I, an aggrieved husband was permitted to slay the adulterer.[36] Rather than transforming the legal codes, Christianity simply imposed its own ideology on pre-existing layers of older law.

Weinstein claims that it was in the twelfth century, that adultery was reclassified as a matter related to marriage and turned over to the ecclesiastical courts.[37] Pollock and Maitland, in *The History of English Law,* have suggested that had the church "left the matter to laymen," state sanctions in matters of sexual morality would have been far sterner.[38] But history does not show, in the case

of adultery, a clear development from the ethos of revenge to the ethic of law. Husbands continued to act against their rivals; the state, in not punishing the retaliation, often granted tacit permission for it; the church, with the gradual decline of its authority, was ineffective; and personal, silently sanctioned, retribution persisted.[39]

Puritan law is a product of this complex past and brings together its dominant motifs: Christian morality, which labels adultery as a moral offense; Mosaic law, which punishes adultery with death; and early English law, which, as we have seen, never resolves its ambivalence over whether the punishment of adultery should be carried out by the state or left to the individual. Reflecting this ambivalence, *The Scarlet Letter* stands on a precarious line between primitive law, where private wrongs are righted by an individual act of revenge, and modern state law, where the state takes over the job of punishing the wrong. Hawthorne's tale invites us to look more closely at the interdependence of myth and law proposed by Robert Cover. Its narrative relies on bits and pieces drawn from the mythical, historical, legal, and theological past, and evokes the complexity of this legacy, from both a technical and a psychological point of view. It seems, in fact, to bring together the darker, more sinister aspects of both state and private law. The magistrates of the state, who are also the guardians of the soul, fall victim to the rigid formalism of its laws. The wronged husband, Roger Chillingworth, gives in to his insatiable desire for vengeance and subjects Dimmesdale to psychological torture. Only Hester and Pearl offer imaginative alternatives to both Puritan formalism and the excesses of personal vindictiveness.

THE LETTER OF THE LAW

Turning directly to the Puritan laws of colonial Massachusetts, we find that lawmakers in October 1631, soon after their arrival on American soil, passed the first law punishing by death both parties guilty of adultery.[40] For technical reasons this law was abrogated and a new version substituted in 1637/38. In December 1641 the Court adopted the Body of Liberties. Section 94, entitled "The Capitall Lawes of New-England," lists fifteen capital offenses, all of them taken directly from Mosaic law.[41] These fifteen laws seem to give shape to the Puritan vision, especially if we consider their order. The first law forbids worshipping false gods, and the third protects God's name from blasphemy. Between them, in second place, is the prohibition against witchcraft.[42] Together these three laws concern commerce with the supernatural. The fifteenth law, by contrast, prohibits conspiracy and any form of rebellion against or subversion of the Commonwealth. God and the state thus provide the frame for the body of social regulations which prohibit, in order, premeditated murder, flaying another in passion or through guile, bestiality, sodomy, adultery, copulation with a woman-child under ten, rape, theft, and bearing false witness. Hester's act of adultery belongs to a group of crimes which defy social norms and threaten to defile what the community holds sacred—on the one hand God's name, and, on the other, the security of the commonwealth.[43]

The 1641 law remained the same for the 1660 and 1672 editions of the law, and on May 20, 1694 the General Court in Boston passed an Act against Adultery and Polygamy, in which adultery was no longer a capital offense.[44] The new law introduced the letter penalty, partly in response to the fact that the death penalty was rarely enforced.[45] The Colonial Laws of Massachusetts report that in March 1644 a couple was condemned to death.[46] The Massachusetts Colony Records report only five cases of adultery between 1636 and 1654, and no one was sentenced to death.[47] The Plymouth Colony Records are not clear about whether adultery was a capital offense, but they do provide what appears to be the earliest evidence of the use of the letter penalty. In 1639 and 1641 adulterers were carted through the street or whipped and required to wear the letter "A" or "A D" cut out in cloth and sewn upon the arm or upper back.[48] In 1658 the Court passed a law codifying the practice of whipping and wearing letters sewn on the upper garment.[49]

Although death was the legal punishment for adultery, courts hesitated to act with such harshness, often relying on, and applying at their discretion, traditional English punishments for non-capital offenses, including the stocks, the whipping post, the pillory, and the cleft stick.[50] Such public displays served to keep before the community's eyes the constant image of human error and its consequences. Thus citizens guilty of such theoretically capital offenses as adultery, incest, and blasphemy might have found themselves standing on the pillory or by the whipping post, or sitting in the gallows with a halter around their neck. And last but not least, they could have been wearing a label stuck in their hats or a letter pinned on their sleeve. Letters, badges, or labels existed for scores of offenses in the seventeenth-century colonies, including whoredom, incest, drunkenness, profane swearing, unclean and lascivious behavior, and thieving. Temporary exposure of an offender with a label or letter indicating the nature of the offense was common, and was incorporated in several of the penal statutes.[51] The letters were cut from cloth or written on paper, and were worn around the neck, on the hat, or on the garment. Occasionally an offender accepted a placard "in pride and pleasure" as a protest against ecclesiastical tyranny—"A WANTON GOSPELLER," for example.[52]

The letter penalty is related not only to the general tradition of public humiliation but to such intimate forms of bodily punishment as branding, stigmatizing, and mutilation which were common in the early-modern period. In her discussion of scolding and other crimes uniquely associated with women in sixteenth-and seventeenth-century England, Lynda Boose shows how shaming rituals were used against women in order to limit the perceived challenge to patriarchal authority. She notes, in particular, an "upsurge in witchcraft trials and other court accusations against women," including scolding, brawling, and dominating one's husband.[53] The scold, defined legally as a "troublesome and angry woman, who by her brawling and wrangling amongst her Neighbors, doth break the publick Peace and beget, cherish, and increase publick Discord,"[54] was punished publicly by being placed in a pillory or submerged in water on a cucking stool. This ritual form of disgrace was designed to shame the scold into forsaking the devil and giving up her "devilish tongue."[55] Paraded through town in a cart to the accompaniment of carnivalesque music and indecent gestures and sounds, she was subject to physical as well as moral humiliation.[56] The harsh public exposure degraded, at the same time as it disoriented and discomforted, the malefactor. Woman was dethroned and reduced to a joke—for having been too outspoken.

Scolding may be linked to blasphemy and even to adultery by way of the figure of the "devilish tongue." As Boose and others have pointed out, a talkative woman was frequently associated with a sexually available woman; excess in either area was perceived as a threat to social stability.[57] Mosaic Law implies a similar relation: speaking against God, committing adultery, and practicing witchcraft are all presented as "defilements," "abominations," and "perversions." In other words, they are all understood as negations of God's authority or profanations of his holy name. Leviticus 20, for example, illustrates the close connection between sexual, verbal, and political misconduct on the one hand and witchcraft on the other. In the opening verses, child sacrifice is described as "giving one's seed to Molech," and worship of foreign gods is condemned under the familiar figure of "whoredom." This condemnation provides the introduction to a long list of sexual offenses, beginning with adultery: "And the man that committeth adultery with another man's wife, even he that committeth adultery with his neighbour's wife, the adulterer and the adulteress shall surely be put to death" (20.10).[58] The law against witchcraft occurs only in the last verse of the chapter (20.27): "A man also or woman that hath a familiar spirit, or that is a wizard, shall surely be put to death."[59] It seems tagged on to the list of sexual offenses, but the fact that it appears in this context at all suggests an intuition about the link between different orders of transgression—a link that becomes fully conscious in seventeenth-century New England.[60] In the new theocratic community, sexual offenses, together with other "defilements," were likewise transformed from private into public wrongs. Disobeying any one of the commandments was evidence of a "devilish tongue" and became tantamount to an act of treason against God and State—an example of linguistic and legal transference which Hawthorne so masterfully recreates in *The Scarlet Letter.*

Underlying the textual force of the Puritan laws against illicit sexuality are deep-seated myths that link sexuality with defilement. These would explain not only the content of God's capital laws, but his repeated references to words and acts that profane or defile. In his major study on the relationship between sexuality, violence, and ritual sacrifice, René Girard suggests that this association is fueled by sexuality's connection to menstrual blood and by men's fear of it.[61] Most primitive people, Girard argues, sought to avoid contact with blood; their experience suggested that whenever violence was unleashed, blood flowed, stained, and contaminated whatever it touched. Once unleashed it became contagious, like a disease, and one act of violence bred another. This is the old story of the blood feud, and when a sexual violation is at the core of the violence—like Paris's abduction of Helen, which launches the Trojan war, or Jason's betrayal of Medea, which triggers her unspeakable rage against her children—the psychological link between sexuality and violence is reaffirmed. Once a community feels threatened with contamination, it seeks to purify itself—by banishing or killing the source of pollution.

The alternative, and this is Girard's main point, is for the community to rid itself of impurity by ritual sacrifice. A sacrificial victim (animal or human) is chosen and serves to absorb the internal tensions, feuds, and rivalries pent up within the society. When the victim is sacrificed, the elements of dissension, and thus the social violence, are, for a time, eliminated. The purpose of the sacrifice, Girard explains, is "to restore harmony to the community, to reinforce the social fabric."[62] One could argue that the kinds of punishment we have been looking at serve a similar function. The community, by branding a person, either literally or with a letter, inscribes on that person his or her status as victim. And even though that victim may not be literally sacrificed, he or she becomes the repository of the community's ills. Thus Hester Prynne bears her society's displaced fears of sexuality, demons, and witches—in short, of its own impurity and potential violence.

THE SCARLET LETTER

When Hester stands on the scaffold, with the scarlet letter on her breast, and Pearl in her arms, she becomes the target of society's desire to purify itself and in so doing to reconfirm its social and moral boundaries. As an adulteress, she could have been legally condemned to death, but in the magistrates' "great mercy and tenderness of heart" (89) she is spared and allowed to

stand three hours on the platform of the pillory and to wear, for life, "a mark of shame upon her bosom" (89). Some in the community lament this "great mercy." The gossips standing close by, reminiscent of a Greek chorus, respond variously to Hester's plight, but the harshest suggests that Hester has contaminated them all: "This woman has brought shame upon us all, and ought to die. Is there not law for it? Truly there is, both in the Scripture and the statute-book" (79). Even though adultery was rarely punished by death, the voice of this pitiless dame resonates in a community whose members pride themselves on the fact that their "godly New England" is a place where "iniquity is searched out, and punished in the sight of rulers and people" (88). The stranger in town, the as yet unnamed Roger Chillingworth, comments that "she will be a living sermon against sin, until the ignominious letter be engraved upon her tombstone" (90). And the narrator, reflecting on the inner trials that Hester would undergo day after day, summarizes the social view of Hester:

> Giving up her individuality, she would become the general symbol at which the preacher and moralist might point, and in which they might vivify and embody their images of woman's frailty and sinful passion. Thus the young and pure would be taught to look at her, with the scarlet letter flaming on her breast,—at her, the child of honorable parents,—at her, the mother of a babe, that would hereafter be a woman,—at her, who had once been innocent,—as the figure, the body, the reality of sin. And over her grave, the infamy that she must carry thither would be her only monument.
>
> (104)

To reassert its own innocence the community banishes Hester, allowing her to live in an abandoned cottage, on the outskirts of the town, on the shore, away from any other habitation, "shut out" from the sphere of social activity. Like its new inhabitant, this remote spot draws to itself the fantasies associated with the symbol Hester herself has become: "a mystic shadow of suspicion immediately attached itself to the spot" (106). Children would creep to the window and upon "discerning the scarlet letter on her breast, would scamper off, with a strange contagious fear" (106).

Hester's isolation is brought on and intensified by the mark society places upon her, a mark "more intolerable to a woman's heart than that which branded the brow of Cain" (108). For a while everyone reviles her—rich and poor, men and women, children and nature: "Every gesture, every word, and even the silence of those with whom she came in contact, implied, and often expressed, that she was banished and as much alone as if she inhabited another sphere . . ." (108). Children shun her and throw stones; clergymen stop in the street to warn others against her sin; in their sermons they point to her as an example. The extreme literalists (the "vulgar" Hawthorne calls them) see the letter not as mere cloth, but rather, as a "terrific legend": "red-hot with infernal fire [which] . . . could be seen glowing all alight, whenever Hester Prynne walked abroad in the night-time" (112).

All these different facets of the community read and understand Hester only in terms of the letter on her breast. Literally and figuratively, the letter becomes a simple badge of exclusion: "Man had marked this woman's sin by a scarlet letter, which had such potent and disastrous efficacy that no human sympathy could reach her, save it were sinful like herself" (113). Marked off from society by this univocal sign, Hester becomes an object of aversion and fascination, in which the community can contemplate without danger the evil that it fears. The letter functions like another instrument of discipline, the pillory, which so graphically announces its purpose: "to confine the human head in its tight grasp, and thus hold it up to the public gaze" (83). Hester's complex humanity—her beauty, her imagination, her sexuality, her intelligence—is reduced to a "badge of shame," a label whose message is easy for readers to seize—a plucked rose.

To restrict imagination and limit the possibilities of narrative—to create, in other words, a formal structure through which society could define and shape itself—was a principal aim of the Puritan codes. The power of this ideal, and its danger, are best depicted in the character of Dimmesdale, who is as revered by society as Hester is reviled. Learned, eloquent, handsome, and childlike, he displays a "freshness and fragrance, and dewy purity of thought, which . . . affected people like the speech of an angel" (93). They perceive him as a paragon of holiness, a saint on earth. Hawthorne goes behind this adulation, however, and describes his limitations in terms that recall his own Puritan ancestors: Dimmesdale has "an order of mind that impelled itself powerfully along the track of a creed, and wore its passage continually deeper with the lapse of time. In no state of society would he have been what is called a man of liberal views; it would always be essential to his peace to feel the pressure of a faith about him, supporting, while it confined him within its iron framework" (145). Reliance on this framework ultimately prevents Dimmesdale from reading or stepping beyond the literalism that is, in its own way, as firmly inscribed in his heart as the letter "A" is on Hester's breast. To escape with Hester, Hawthorne notes, would have been to "escap[e] from the dungeon of his own heart—[to] breath[e] the wild, free atmosphere of an unredeemed, an unchristianized, lawless region" (245).

In the eyes of the community, Dimmesdale's limitation is a major source of strength. His eloquent and rational articulations reaffirm the creed his listeners want to hear and sustain the myths on which they depend for a sense of security. Two scenes effectively illustrate the exact

parameters of his thought. In the first, the magistrates have threatened to remove Pearl from Hester's care, "for her temporal and eternal welfare" (133), after her childish response to a theological question—that she had not been made at all but had been "plucked by her mother off the bush of wild roses, that grew by the prison door" (134)—revealed the depravity of her three-year-old soul. Dimmesdale, rather than challenging the magistrates' logic, reconfigures it, suggesting that God has sent the child to Hester to work upon her heart. Intended as a blessing, a retribution, a torture, a pang, a sting, an ever recurring agony in the midst of joy, the child, he argues, would remind Hester of her fall and save her from further sin. "Let us leave them," he concludes, "as Providence hath seen fit to place them" (137).

In the second scene Chillingworth has responded to Dimmesdale's query about the origins of the black leafy herbs he has collected from the top of a grave, suggesting that they have "sprung out of a buried heart, to make manifest an unspoken crime" (152). Parrying the allusion to his secret guilt and shrinking from the invitation to reveal his soul, Dimmesdale counters that one can only know the secrets of the heart at the end of judgment day. Dimmesdale retreats, as before, to the abstractions of his "stifled study," evading the different, more complex truth of the here and now.

Dimmesdale passes on to his parishioners the same logic, the same defenses, and the same fears that characterize the community at large and allow them to judge and condemn Hester. But Dimmesdale also reveals the personal torment of a man who knows that the system is vulnerable. In his case, the personal conviction and the body politic which he represents as minister are threatened not from the outside but from within—by his own unorthodox urgings. Insofar as he hearkens to those urgings, Dimmesdale also hears the terrifying voice of the law. And rather than admit his own failure before the law, he, like the members of his community, projects that failure onto something outside the self—the witch Mistress Hibbins, who seems to materialize in response to his internal anxiety. Dimmesdale gives voice to this extreme anxiety after the meeting in the forest where Hester convinces him to leave with her. On his way back to town he wonders if, in fact, he has contracted with the Devil, feeling at one and the same time tempted by dreams of happiness and fearful of the "infectious poison" (237) of sin that has been "rapidly diffused throughout his moral system." In his moment of psychological crisis, he actually encounters Mistress Hibbins, the shadowy presence who haunts the entire community and serves as the repository of fears which it knows but will not acknowledge. Dimmesdale rushes to take refuge in his study, with the letter of God's word—with his Bible and its "rich old Hebrew, with Moses and the Prophets speaking to him, and God's voice through all" (238). Dimmesdale may return from the forest a less naive and wiser man, but he never gives up the structure of his orthodoxy. He is, finally, as committed to the letter of the law as are the magistrates and town gossips.

Hester, Pearl, and Mistress Hibbins are figures onto which society projects its own inner fears. Like words, like penalty letters even, these women becomes signs which gather to themselves extrinsic meanings. Thus to Hester are transferred the community's fears of its own transgression and violence. As the polluted enemy who will contaminate the rest, she must be isolated. By banishing her to its borders rather than destroying her as it would a sacrificial victim, the community hides from itself the knowledge of its own inherent violence. Each member's belief in the purity of the community, sustained by his faith in its system of law and morality, provides the security necessary to point his finger in accusation at the guilty one; but the reverse is also true—accusation sustains one's faith in the integrity of the system. Once one discovers, as young Goodman Brown does, that transgression no less than accusation is integral to the community, the sustaining structure of faith begins to crumble, and one has to come to terms with a different sort of self-knowledge. Rather than take this step, however, society tends to fix on its scapegoats to save the structure. One marks the Hester Prynnes of the world, and their children, like Pearl, grow up in the shadow of the letter, imagining that one day they will inherit the "A" themselves. The symbol that Hester is compelled to wear on her outer garment risks being internalized by the next generation and experienced as natural.

COUNTER-SPIRITS OF THE LAW

Every judicial reading of the law is grounded, as Hawthorne's fiction illustrates, in a community's circumstances—in its myths, history, laws, and hopes for the future. The law, however, tends to conceal that fact, as Portia does in the *Merchant of Venice,* when she disguises herself in legal robes to decide Shylock's fate. Rather than reveal the individuality or bias of the judge who dons the robe, the law seeks to create an image of an impersonal, objective, principled arbiter, immune to personal preferences. The sign of the robe helps sustain the illusion of professional neutrality. To keep this image intact the Court also relies, as Dimmesdale does, on rhetorical forms which, like the robes that conceal the person, function as a rational and principled cover for the complex origins—both rational and irrational—of the law. Once constituted on the basis of past myths that have found their way into legal discourse, these forms can assume in time a mythic power which society uses to bolster its political and moral order.

Traces of this kind of mythic genesis are particularly evident in debates over constitutional interpretation.

Criticizing the way the 1985 Supreme Court read the Constitution, Edwin Meese, for example, argued that the opinions of the Court were, "on the whole, more policy choices than articulations of constitutional principle."[63] Rather than defer to the text and intention of the Constitution, the Court, he claimed, "inaccurate[ly] read the text of the Constitution" and "disregarded . . . the Framers' intention that the state and local governments be a buffer against the centralizing tendencies of the national Leviathan" (Meese, 3). He argued for a return to principled reading which "could avoid . . . the charge of incoherence" and "would not be tainted by ideological predilection" (Meese, 9). Through certain word choices Meese also evoked the sanctity of the Constitution: "We will endeavor to resurrect the original meaning of constitutional provisions and statutes as the only reliable guide for judgement . . . Our guide will be the sanctity of the rule of law . . . Only the sense in which the laws were drafted and passed provide a solid foundation for adjudication."

What is at stake here is a dream of continuity that relies on the rhetoric of first causes, forefathers, roots, foundations, and the sacred. Meese imagines an ongoing tradition traceable back to an original seed—a kind of textual Eden whose boundaries are clearly set: no "pouring of new meaning into old words" where the activist reader mutilates the integrity of the text. To speak of interpreting the Constitution "without departing from the literal import of the words" (Meese quoting Joseph Story) is to envision a world in which words have fixed beginnings and meanings that remain stable over time (10). The questionable premise is that there is such a thing as a complete, coherent text whose intentions we have access to.

This dream of coherence, continuity, and stability informs in different ways the thinking of many judges and operates on the reader in much the same way that the letter "A" operates on members of the Puritan community. To refer to the sanctity of law, to roots, to Judeo-Christian principles, to "liberties deeply rooted," "fundamental rights embedded," or "bedrock principle underlying" is to call up traces of a national and moral past which appears to lend impersonal force to partisan convictions.[64] Consciously or unconsciously minds are opened or closed by such references.

Both law and fiction, however, give strong voice to the impulses that resist reification. Judges like Blackmun, Douglas, and Brennan rely on "principle" and "history" to support their readings of the Constitution, but they tend to ask, as Brennan does, what do the words mean in our time? In his opinion in *Griswold v. Connecticut* Justice Douglas justifies a reading that extends the reach of the first amendment to include rights (relating to birth control) not expressly stated in the Constitution. The Bill of Rights, he argues, includes "penumbral" or "peripheral" rights which create a "zone of privacy"—a "sacred" area protected from invasion by the government.[65] In his dissent in *Bowers v. Hardwick* Justice Blackmun resists blind imitation of the past, arguing that "it is revolting to have no better reason for a rule than that it was laid down in the time of Henry IV."[66] He invests "principles" and "underlying values" with a cultural and legal history that allows him to shift the issue away from homosexuality to privacy, thus creating a new conceptual framework for subsequent thinking about this issue. The "principle" that his Constitution embodies, he explains, is a "promise," that "a certain private sphere of individual liberty will be kept beyond the reach of government."[67] Brennan's dissents often describe the Constitution as a living, evolving entity whose full meaning cannot be revealed either by doctrinal precedent or by evidence of original intent: "The Constitution is not a static document whose meaning on every detail is fixed for all time by the life experience of the Framers."[68] Douglas, Blackmun, and Brennan, unlike Meese, see the Constitution as an open rather than a closed text and emphasize its transformative purpose.

Activist and non-activist judges often rely on the same rhetoric, but the activist's view of language, skeptical of first causes and responsive to change, leads to very different conclusions. In Hawthorne's world, Brennan's opponents might have argued that his readings were diabolical, contrary to revealed law and threatening to the fabric of society. In *The Scarlet Letter* itself, the vitalizing, transformative threat to orthodoxy is embodied in the figure of Pearl, who recalls Hawthorne's initial inspiration: the rose growing by the prison door. The fruit of a paradoxical love, Pearl is the flower that refuses to be plucked and reified. For some she is the thorn who, in Chillingworth's disparaging words, knows "no law, nor reverence for authority, no regard for human ordinances or opinions, right or wrong . . ." (154). What Chillingworth cannot, or will not, see in Pearl is what the reader comes to admire most: her wild, native imagination which, like Hawthorne's, "communicated itself to a thousand objects, as a torch kindles a flame" (118). Without playmates she creates her own "visionary throng"; every object—sticks, rags, flowers—is transformed; solemn pine trees become Puritan elders, ugly weeds their children whom Pearl would smite and uproot. But the letter on her mother's breast, elaborately embroidered with flourishes of gold thread, is a particular source of fascination. Like all curious readers confronted with an enigmatic sign, she incessantly questions the letter. Untutored in the "correct" social reading of the letter, she weaves her own fantasy of meaning: "As the last touch to her mermaid's garb, Pearl took some eel grass, and imitated, as best she could, on her bosom the decoration with which she was so familiar on her mother's. A letter,—the letter A,—but freshly green, instead of scarlet" (195). For Pearl the letter is a

kind of hieroglyphic, subject to her revisionary imagination. Hester allows the child to read on her own rather than impose on her daughter what society had imposed on her—a predigested formula for behavior. And Pearl's own behavior—the wild, capricious forms into which she throws herself—is a mystery to those around her—a "living hieroglyphic" (223) of the secret her parents sought to hide.

For judges too the law is a letter, a hieroglyphic, subject to revision and manipulation. A plain meaning theory functions to reduce the play of meaning for purposes of social control. A notion like Douglas's zone of privacy enlarges the frame for the play of meaning. The frame is still there, but subject to transformation (even as Pearl's "A" is still there, though woven with green leaves). When that frame threatens to disintegrate, readers can become anxious. When Hester removes her letter from her breast, Pearl is disconcerted. How far can one push the edges of the frame without dismantling something essential? How far can one protect private identity and keep in tact a sense of social order? These questions, if they can be answered at all, cannot be answered in the abstract. They can only be broached within the cultural contexts in which they occur. Fiction allows us to see multiple aspects of that context; the law compels us to see in it bits and pieces.

No one, however, has complete control over this process. Fictional narrators make us amply aware of this fact. Melville, in *Billy Budd,* for example, tells us explicitly that the story has no real end. Budd dies, but that is not the end. There are the "ragged edges"—the brief news report giving us the party line, and then the poem, and our own re-readings. In Hawthorne there is no single rose to be plucked. The reader is left to choose among various theories. The tale ends with Dimmesdale's final confession, the image of his body sinking down on the scaffold, his head held against Hester's breast. A multitude witnesses this deposition, watches Pearl kiss her father's lips and weep, hears Hester's final hope and Arthur's confirmation of the painful redemptive process, and his last farewell. "That final word came forth with the minister's expiring breath. The multitude, silent till then, broke out in a strange, deep voice of awe and wonder, which could not as yet find utterance, save in this murmur that rolled so heavily after the departed spirit" (269). The deep voice which could not yet find words points to the impossibility of a single message. The spectators can reach no agreement about what they have seen on Dimmesdale's breast. Those who claim to have seen a scarlet letter argue that the stigma was self-inflicted, or that it was produced by Chillingworth through the use of magic and poisonous drugs, or that it was an organic effect of the "ever active tooth of remorse gnawing from the inmost heart outward" (270). Others swear there was no mark at all and that he never acknowledged in his last words any connection with Hester's guilt.

Despite the sense of an ending, the reader is left, like the characters at the end, seeking answers or choosing among possible accounts of what had been seen on the scaffold. The tale gathers itself for a moment into a coherent image of Dimmesdale dying on the scaffold, in Hester's arms, a multitude standing by in awe. But this picture dissolves into fragments, ambiguities, discrete letters, waiting to be discovered in the dark corner of the attic. And we might argue that this disintegration is motivated by the force of violation which constantly threatens to destabilize any myth. Fiction is constantly dissolving its frames so that we do not become too comfortable with the plucked rose. The law needs to keep the frame in tact. And how it does so is the burden of all constitutional interpretation.

Notes

1. Nathaniel Hawthorne, *The Scarlet Letter* (New York: Penguin Books, 1983), 76. All subsequent citations are taken from this edition.

2. Oliver Wendell Holmes, *The Common Law* (Boston: Little Brown and Company, 1946), 1.

3. John Winthrop, "A Model of Christian Charity," in *The American Puritans: Their Prose and Poetry,* ed. Perry Miller (New York: Anchor Books, 1956) p. 84.

4. Robert Cover, "Nomos and Narrative," *Harvard Law Review* 97 (1983): 4-5.

5. Ibid., p. 42.

6. See also Robert Cover, "Folktales of Justice: Tales of Jurisdiction," *Capital University Law Review,* 14 (1985): 179.

7. In addition to the legal codes from individual societies, two studies are particularly useful: Daniel Murray, "Ancient Laws on Adultery—A Synopsis," *Journal of Family Law,* 1 (1961). Murray's summary includes a brief look at the early laws in the Middle East, the Far East, Greece, Rome, the British Isles, and Germany. Jeremy D. Weinstein, "Adultery, Law, and the State: A History" *Hastings Law Journal,* 38 (1986) focuses primarily on English and American law, beginning with early English law just before 600 A.D. and continuing through early common law in the thirteenth century to developments that have influenced current treatment of adultery statutes in the United States.

8. Murray, "Ancient Laws on Adultery," 89; Weinstein, "Adultery, Law, and the State," 195-96.

9. Ibid, 89.

10. Tony Tanner, *Adultery in the Novel* (1979), 16.

11. As Richard Weisberg points out in *Poethics And Other Strategies of Law and Literature* (New York: Columbia University Press, 1992), manipulation of bonds is at the center of the judicial and social plot: all bonds in the play are implicitly on trial, including those between young lovers, man and wife, parent and child, lenders and borrowers, master and servant, man and his religion. One might also argue that violation of certain bonds is a necessary component of psychological growth; that Portia and Jessica, for instance, have to learn how to violate their fathers in order to remake themselves in a new union with their prospective bridegrooms; that in the final act Shakespeare brings together the new generation to establish a new society in which marriages are celebrated and the festival spirit of comedy reigns. But Shakespeare's text is haunted by a sense of love's fragility and the dangers of transgression. I would agree in part with Weisberg's view that Portia "reinvigorates Shylock's Jewish ethics" by standing firm on commitments and promises (94); that Bassanio and his friends are equivocal towards verbal obligations; that Shylock remains unequivocally committed to his race, his marriage, and his bond. But I would hesitate to draw so stark a line between oath keepers and oath breakers. Verbal wit and slippage of language are the essence of comedy and one might argue that rather than "replace" comedy on the island of Belmont (102), commitment operates through it.

12. In suggesting that "Shylock is gone but not forgotten" (Weisberg, 104)—that his legalistic mode lives on—Weisberg invites us to ponder "whether his values are not somehow better, more direct, more forceful" than those looser and easier values of the Venetians. This legalistic mode, present throughout the play, is, as we know, the one Portia uses against Shylock in the trial. One might also argue that it is just this sort of exaggerated formalism—together with its rhetorical limitations so ironically dramatized, for example, by Aragon's and Morocco's suit to Portia—that Shakespeare and Portia turn against the character who epitomizes it.

13. Oliver Wendell Holmes, *The Common Law* (Cambridge: Belknap Press of Harvard University Press, 1963), 6.

14. Ibid., 13.

15. Hammurabi, *The Code of Hammurabi, Section 129,* trans. Theophile J. Meek. In James B. Pritchard, ed., *Ancient Near Eastern Texts Relating to the Old Testament,* 3d ed., (Princeton: Princeton University Press, 1969), 171.

16. See Weinstein, 198. This sort of "peaceful solution," called "composition," flourished, according to Weinstein, in primitive and later archaic law. The wrongdoer voluntarily offered himself up or agreed to accept some form of public humiliation.

17. Weinstein, 195. Weinstein is building on an argument put forth by E. Adamson Hoebel in *The Law of Primitive Man: A Study in Comparative Legal Dynamics* (Cambridge: Harvard University Press, 1954): "The really significant shift . . . in the development of primitive law is [that] . . . [p]rivilege-rights and responsibility for the maintenance of the legal norms are transferred from the individual and his kinship group to the agents of the body politic as a social entity" (329).

18. Weinstein, 199.

19. In *The Law of Primitive Man* Hoebel warns against setting up too stark a contrast between a primitive society, supposedly marked by retaliation and blood revenge, and modern societies which have substituted damages for vengeance: "there is an error in the conventional evolutionary idea. It lies in the notion that there ever was a time when torts were not emendable or a time when blood feud prevailed unchecked . . . the societies of man have from the outset wrestled with the problem of maintaining internal peace and harmony" (329).

20. See A. S. Diamond, *Primitive Law Past and Present* (1971), 57.

21. These laws can be found in F. L. Attenborough, *The Laws of the Earliest English Kings* (New York: Russell & Russell, Inc., 1922). See especially sections 33ff.

22. Weinstein, 203-5.

23. See sections 10-16 in the *Dooms.*

24. "Wergeld" means the value set on a freeman's life. It literally means "man's price." See Weinstein, footnote 71, and F. Pollock & F. Maitland, *The History of English Law* (2d ed. 1898), 47.

25. I can only suggest a few reasons here. The culture itself may not have been particularly stable. In 597 Augustine, under a mission from Pope Gregory the Great, arrived in England and converted the country to Christianity. It is not clear whether the *Dooms,* which codified pre-existing law and added fresh legislation, were promulgated by a pagan or a Christian king. Some argue that they were written after Aethelberht converted to Christianity in the first years of the seventh century, others that they were written over several years, beginning as early as 565 when Aethelberht became king. (See Weinstein, 204 and accompanying notes.)

Looking at the laws of different cultures as well as those of England, we find extraordinary variety in both the concept and treatment of adultery. With the Ashanti, for example, adultery with any of the wives of a chief was considered an offense against the royal ancestors. The offender was tampering with women sacred to the ancestors, and the penalty was death, in a hideous form: a dance of death in which the victim was dissected into small bits (see Hoebel, 240). The Eskimos, by contrast, were reputed to lend and exchange their wives with good will. But if a man had intercourse with a married woman without her husband's consent, it was viewed as a challenge to his position as a man. Outright appropriation of another man's wife could result in homicide (see Hoebel, 83).

26. See Attenborough, 62-93, for the text of Alfred's Code. The quoted passage is from cap. 42, section 7. See also Weinstein, 207-208, and Murray, 98-99. Murray notes that the Code of Hammurabi, Mosaic law, and Roman law also emphasized the importance of the husband's discovering the woman "within closed doors and under the same blanket."

27. Texas Penal Code, art. 1220 (Vernon 1925).

28. See Weinstein, 229ff., for a more extensive discussion of the scattered statutes that permitted husbands and fathers, in a variety of circumstances, to slay marital interlopers. A section of one opinion handed down in Georgia by J. Lumpkin in 1860 (Biggs v. State, 29 Ga. 723), is worth quoting: "Is it not their [the jury's] right to determine whether, in reason or justice, it is not as justifiable in the sight of Heaven and earth, to slay the murderer of the peace and respectability of a family, as one who forcibly attacks habitation and property? What is the annihilation of houses or chattels by fire and faggot, compared with the destruction of female innocence; robbing woman of that priceless jewel, which leaves her a blasted ruin, with the mournful motto inscribed upon its frontals, 'thy glory is departed'? Our sacked habitations may be rebuilt, but who shall repair this moral desolation?"

29. Alfred's Code, cap. 10.

30. Alfred's Code, cap. 42, section 7.

31. The Central Codes of Edward and Aethelstan can be found in F. L. Attenborough, *The Laws of the Earliest English Kings,* 114-17, 126-43. The Codes of Edgar, Aethelred, and Cnut may be found in A. Robertson, *The Laws of the Kings of England From Edmund To Henry I* [1925], 16-19, 24-29, 52-71, 174-219.

32. II Cnut, cap. 53.

33. Thus the laws of William I and of Henry I in the late eleventh and early twelfth centuries echo the laws of Anglo-Saxon kings, which permitted a husband to kill his rival if the latter is found alone with his wife behind closed doors. See Leis Willelme, cap. 35 and Leges Henrici Primi, 82, section 8, in Robertson, *The Laws of the Kings of England From Edmund to Henry I.*

34. Weinstein, 210.

35. Willelmi Articuli Retracti, Sec. 17, found in Robertson, *The Laws of the Kings of England,* 251.

36. Murray, 100. See also the Laws of William I, Sec. 35, in Robertson, 269.

37. Weinstein, 211.

38. F. Pollock & F. Maitland, *The History of English Law,* 2d ed. (1898), 367.

39. Common law remedies gradually developed under the umbrella of such categories as trespassing, theft, breach of the king's peace, loss of consortium, criminal conversation, enticement, and alienation of affections. See Weinstein, 212-25.

40. The law punishing adultery with death was passed by the Court of Assistants in October 1631 (*Massachusetts Colony Records,* I., 91). The question of enforcement came up in Boston on June 6, 1637 (Ibid., 197): two men and one woman were jailed and in March 1638 they were sentenced to be whipped and banished (Ibid., 225).

41. "The Capitall Lawes of New-England, as they stand now in force in the Common-Wealth, 1641, 1642," in *The Laws and Liberties of Massachusetts, 1641-1691,* Vol. I, comp. John D. Cushing (Wilmington: Scholarly Resources Inc., 1976).

42. It is interesting to note that the Puritans have altered the order in the Decalogue by working in witchcraft between the first commandment, which forbids false gods, and the second, which forbids blasphemy. Compare Exodus 20.

43. In England before 1650 adultery was a violation of Mosaic Code but was not punished as a crime. This posed a problem for the colonists who based their civil and criminal code on the laws of England. Offenses easily recognized as violations of English law were relatively easy to deal with. Those, like adultery, which were violations of Mosaic law but not ranked as penal offenses in England were more troublesome. Despite its statutory silence on the question of adultery, however, Parliament, from Henry VIII to Charles I, continued to worry about it and, after a century of debate, passed the Act of 1650 classing adultery and incest as felonies. (This unpopular law was not

renewed.) The same spirit which moved Parliament to pass the 1650 Act pushed colonial lawmakers to pass their own law against adultery in October 1631. In *The Colonial Laws of Massachusetts* (1672; repr., Boston, 1890), 4ff. William Whitmore gives an account of the tension between the people, who pressed for clear articulation of the laws, and the magistrates who resisted the passage of a law repugnant to the laws of England.

44. The second section of the Act of 1694 reads as follows: "And if any man shall commit adultery, the man and woman that shall be convicted of such crime before their Majesties' justices of assize and general gaol delivery, shall be set upon the gallows by the space of an hour, with a rope about their neck, and the other end cast over the gallows; and in the way from thence to the common gaol shall be severely whipped, not exceeding forty stripes each. Also every person and persons so offending shall forever after wear a capital A, of two inches long, and proportionate bigness, cut out in cloth of a contrary color to their clothes, and sewed upon their upper garments, on the outside of their arm, or on their back, in open view. And if any person or persons, having been convicted and sentenced for such offense, shall at any time be found without their letter so worn, during their abode in this province, they shall, by warrant from a justice of the peace, be forthwith apprehended, and ordered to be publicly whipped, not exceeding fifteen stripes, and so from time to time, *toties quoties.*" Reproduced in the *Ancient Charters,* 1815.

45. Andrew McFarland Davis, *The Law of Adultery and Ignominious Punishments* (Worcester, Mass.: Press of Charles Hamilton, 1895). After coming across "certain papers connected with a criminal case, in which the culprit was, in 1743, sentenced to wear a letter sewed upon his outer garment," and taking account of "the great popularity of Hawthorne's *Scarlet Letter.*" Davis became interested in finding out "how early in the history of the Colony, or how late in the days of the Province, sentences of this character were imposed" (2). His paper, delivered to the American Antiquarian Society on April 24, 1895, provides the best account I have found of the letter penalty in the colonies. It traces legislation in the Massachusetts Bay Colony relative to adultery, describes various kinds of letter penalties, and looks briefly at related forms of punishment in seventeenth century England. Davis was unable to confirm the origins of letter penalty, finding no mention of it in the statutes, in the form books used by Justices, in ecclesiastical law, or in books devoted to "curious punishments." He did find evidence, however,

of the use of labels which were often placed in the hat of the offender (22-26).

46. See *The Colonial Laws of Massachusetts* (1672; repr., Boston, 1890): on March 5, 1644 a man and woman guilty of adultery were sentenced to death. In his *Journal of 1644* Winthrop mentions the death of Mary Latham who had committed adultery with several young men.

47. On March 12, 1638, in Newton, two men and one woman were sentenced to be whipped and banished for adultery (*Massachusetts Colony Records*, I, 225); on September 7, 1641, a Quarter Court sentenced an adulterous man to be set on the gallows with a rope about his neck and then sent to prison (Ibid., I, 335); on September 8, 1642, in Boston, the Court received a message requesting that an Indian be punished for attempting to ravish a man's wife (Ibid., II, 23); in 1648 a woman was acquitted on two charges of adultery but whipped for "evil adulterous behavior and swearing" (Ibid., II, 243); in 1654 a woman was accused of adultery but not found guilty (Ibid., IV, pt. I, 193). See Davis, 8-9 and 14-15.

48. In 1639 a woman found guilty of adultery was sentenced to be whipped and to wear a badge on her left sleeve. If she was found abroad without it, she was to be burned in the face with a hot iron. See *Plymouth Colony Records, Laws, 1623-1682*, 132. In 1641 a man and a woman were sentenced to be whipped at the public post and to wear two letters, "A D," on the outside of their uppermost garment. Ibid., II, 28.

49. *Plymouth Colony Records, Laws, 1623-1682*, 95.

50. G. Harrison Orians in "Hawthorne and Puritan Punishments" (*College English*, 13 (May 1952): 424-32) provides a summary of these and other punishments, focusing on the ones Hawthorne refers to in his tales ("Endicott and the Red Cross," "Main Street," "The Maypole of Merrymount," "The Gentle Boy," *The Scarlet Letter*). The two most common forms of punishment in the colonies were the stocks and the whipping post. Loiterers, tipplers, disorderly soldiers, and persons guilty of profane swearing, for example, were placed in the stocks; drunkards, fornicators, vagabonds, defamers of magistrates, blasphemers, and disobedient children were whipped; the pillory could be substituted for some of these offenses, including forgery and blasphemy, the cleft-stick for calumny, blasphemy, defamation of magistrates, railing and reviling. For more detailed information on the use of these punishments in the colonies one may consult the *Massachusetts Colony Records*; Colony Records for individual towns, including Boston, Plymouth, and Salem;

Felt's *Annals of Salem* [1827]; Cotton Mather's *Magnalia Christi Americana* and *The Faithful Monitor* (1704); Thomas Hutchinson's *History of Massachusetts Bay* (1764); John Winthrop's *Journals*; William Sewell's *History of the Quakers* [1728]; and *Ancient Charters and Colony Laws* (1815). Hawthorne is known to have read widely in these and other sources, particularly during the period biographers call "the solitary years"—1835-47. In addition, he received from two friends, James T. Fields and W. D. Ticknor, a set of the *State Trials* which he acknowledged "held him spellbound" since 1832. Edmond Cahn, Professor of Law at New York University, reported in a letter to *The Times Literary Supplement* 7 (London: October 1955, 589) that he was the current owner of Hawthorne's set of the *State Trials*.

51. The *Massachusetts Colony Records*, I, Felt's *Annals*, Josselyn's *Account of Two Voyages to New England* [1674], and the *Plymouth Colony Records*, III, provide numerous examples of the use of letters and placards in the colonies during the mid-seventeenth century. A selective list follows: on September 3, 1633, a man was sentenced to pay a fine and wear for a year a white sheet of paper on his back denouncing him as a "DRUNKARD" (*Massachusetts Colony Records*, I, 107); on March 4, 1634, Robert Coles was sentenced to wear around his neck the letter "D," cut from red cloth and set on white (Ibid., I, 112); on April 5, 1636, William Perkins was sentenced to wear for an hour a white sheet of paper marked with the letter "D" (Ibid., I, 172); on March 5, 1639, a man was whipped and required to wear the letter "V" on his garment, for lewdness (Ibid., I, 248); on September 3, 1639, a thief was sentenced to wear the letter "T" on his garment (Ibid., I, 268); on December 3, 1639, two women were sentenced to wear a paper indicating their offense (light behavior) (Ibid., I, 284); on March 29, 1681, two women were to be imprisoned a night for incest, whipped or fined, and sentenced to stand in the Salem Meeting House with a paper on their head indicating the crime (Felt's *Annals*, 270); in his *Two Voyages* Josselyn reports that an English woman, guilty of fornication with an Indian, was required to wear an Indian, cut out of red cloth, sewn on her right arm for a year (178). See also Davis, 18-21, who lists these and other instances. And see note 48 above for the account of the three adulterers sentenced in Plymouth Colony in 1639 and 1641 to wear letters for their offense; and note 45 for Davis's reference to Andrew Flemming who was convicted of incest in 1743 in Groton and sentenced to stand one hour on the gallows with a rope around his neck, to be whipped 40 stripes, and to wear the letter "I" for life.

52. Davis, 22.

53. Lynda E. Boose, "Scolding Brides and Bridling Scolds: Taming the Woman's Unruly Member," *Shakespeare Quarterly* 41 (1991): 184.

54. Ibid., 186, quoting from William Sheppard (or Shepherd), *A Grand Abridgment of the Common and Statute Law of England* (London, 1675).

55. Ibid., 186, quoting from Church of England, *Certain Sermons or Homilies* (London: Society for Promoting Christian Knowledge, 1908), 154.

56. Ibid., 189.

57. Drawing on recent historical scholarship, Boose notes a dramatic rise during the years 1560-1640 in those crimes labelled "interpersonal disputes," particularly in those involving sexual misconduct, scolding, slander, physical assault, defamation, and marital relations. An increased concern about social order gave rise, she suggests, to harsher criminal statutes "directed primarily against vagrants and female disorder" (195). She points out that during these years "an obsessive energy was invested in exerting control over the unruly woman—the woman who was exercising either her sexuality or her tongue under her own control rather than under the rule of a man. As illogical as it may initially seem, the two crimes—being a scold and being a so-called whore—were frequently conflated" (195). See also Patricia Parker, *Literary Fat Ladies: Rhetoric, Gender, Property* (London and New York: Methuen, 1987).

58. Compare the law forbidding a man to sleep with a married woman in Deuteronomy 22:22: "If a man be found lying with a woman married to an husband, then they shall both of them die, both the man that lay with the woman, and the woman: so shalt thou put away evil from Israel." Verses 23-29 enumerate additional laws governing sexual behavior between men and woman.

59. The law against witchcraft, which figures so prominently among the capital laws of New England, is listed in the Old Testament among "divers laws" rather than among the offenses presented in the Decalogue. We find it mentioned for example in Exodus 22:18 ("Thou shalt not suffer a witch to live") and in Deuteronomy 18:10-11 among the abominations that God will drive out ("There shall not be found among you any one that maketh his son or his daughter to pass through the fire, or that useth divination, or an observer of times, or an enchanter, or a witch. Or a charmer, or a consulter with familiar spirits, or a wizard, or a necromancer").

60. It is not within the scope of this paper to explore evidence of these links in England, France, and Germany. Limiting ourselves to early New England, we find that the devil was more often, though not exclusively, associated with women, and that trials against witches ended up reinforcing existing social boundaries and traditional morals. See Carol F. Karlson, *The Devil in the Shape of a Woman: Witchcraft in Colonial New England* (New York: W. W. Norton & Company, 1987), which examines the rise and fall of witchcraft in seventeenth-century New England and includes a chapter on the role of witchcraft in shaping and maintaining the structure of Puritan society. For another study of witchcraft in New England at this time see also John Putnam Demos, *Entertaining Satan: Witchcraft and the Culture of Early New England* (New York: Oxford University Press, 1982).

61. Rene Girard, *Violence and the Sacred,* trans. Patrick Gregory (Baltimore and London: The Johns Hopkins University Press, 1977), 33-36.

62. Ibid . . . 8. See also the chapter entitled "Oedipus and the Surrogate Victim," 68-88, for Girard's discussion of how the Thebans displaced their own violent impulses onto the person of Oedipus, who becomes the repository of the community's ills and, once sacrificed, the prime example of the human scapegoat.

63. Edwin Meese III, Speech to D.C. Chapter of the Federalist Society July 9, 1985, Washington D.C., reprinted in *The Great Debate: Interpreting Our Written Constitution* (Washington, D.C.: Federalist Soc., 1986), 9; Edwin Meese, "Address," in Sanford Levinson and Steven Mailloux, eds., *Interpreting Law and Literature: A Hermeneutic Reader* (Evanston, Ill.: Northwestern Univ. Press, 1988), 25.

64. For example, in Texas v. Johnson, Chief Justice Rehnquist defines the symbolic nature of the flag with reference to its role in particular moments in American history. He argues that the flag, because it has embodied more than 200 years of our history, "is not simply another 'idea' or 'point of view' competing for recognition in the market place of ideas." It is a unique symbol "embodying our nation," "a uniqueness that justifies a governmental prohibition against flagburning"; it is regarded "by millions and millions . . . with an almost mystical reverence." The flag is to be revered as vigorously as Hester's letter is to be reviled, and Rehnquist's conclusion could apply to both: "Surely one of the high purposes of a democratic society is to legislate against conduct that is regarded as evil and profoundly offensive to the majority of people—whether it be murder, embezzlement, pollution, or flag burning." See Texas v. Johnson, 491 U.S. 397, 109 S.Ct. 2533 (1989).

Justice White in Bowers v. Hardwick argues that the liberties "deeply rooted in this nation's history" do not extend a fundamental right to homosexuals to engage in acts of consensual sodomy. "Proscriptions against that conduct have ancient roots." In his concurring opinion Chief Justice Burger expands this argument and, citing Roman, English, and American law, claims that homosexual conduct has been subject to state intervention "throughout the history of Western civilization. Condemnation of those practices is firmly rooted in Judeo-Christian moral and ethical standards." In his short one-paragraph statement he takes time to quote Blackstone's description of "the infamous *crime against nature*" as an offense of "deeper malignity" than rape, a heinous act "the very mention of which is a disgrace to human nature," and a "crime not fit to be named" (4 W. Blackstone, *Commentaries* [1765-69], 215). Burger concludes: "To hold that the act of homosexual sodomy is somehow protected as a fundamental right would be to cast aside millennia of moral teaching." See Bowers v. Hardwick, 478 U.S. 186, 106 S.Ct. 2841 (1986).

Burger, like Hawthorne's Puritan magistrates, is relying on the notion that sodomy represents a coherent, identifiable, and stable category of behavior which can be traced back to the beginnings of Western civilization. The Court refused to see beyond the letter "S" and to address Hardwick's larger concern that the statute violated his rights, not as a gay man, but as a person (See "Brief for Respondent in Bowers v. Hardwick," in *Landmark Briefs and Arguments of the Supreme Court of the United States: Constitutional Law: 1985 Term Supplement,* Philip B. Kurland and Gerhard Casper, eds. (Frederick, Md.: University Publications of America, 1987), 404, 411. A "person" cannot be defined in terms of a particular act; for as Michael Foucault has argued, every act implies "a past, a case history, a childhood, . . . a type of life, a life form, . . . a morphology, . . . a species." (See Foucault, *I The History of Sexuality,* trans. Robert Hurley (New York: Vintage Books, 1980), 43.)

65. Griswold v. Connecticut, 381 U.S. 479 (1965), at 484.

66. Bowers v. Hardwick, 478 U.S. at 199. Blackmun was joined by Justices Brennan, Marshall, and Stevens.

67. Ibid., at 203.

68. Marsh v. Chambers, 463 U.S. 783 (1983) at 816. See also Brennan's speech at The Text and Teaching Symposium, held at Georgetown University, October 12, 1985, Washington, D.C. (reprinted in *The Great Debate,* and in Levinson and Mailloux): "[T]he genius of the Constitution rests not in any static meaning it might have had in a world that is dead and gone, but in the adaptability of its great principles to cope with current problems and current needs." p. 17.

Teresa Martins de Oliveira (essay date 2001)

SOURCE: de Oliveira, Teresa Martins. "Fontane's *Effi Briest* and Eça de Queirós's *O Primo Bazílio*: Two Novels of Adultery in the Context of European Realism." In *Theodor Fontane and the European Context: Literature, Culture and Society in Prussia and Europe; Proceedings of the Interdisciplinary Symposium at the Institute of Germanic Studies, University of London, in March 1999,* edited by Patricia Howe and Helen Chambers, pp. 207-15. Amsterdam: Rodopi, 2001.

[*In the following essay, de Oliveira offers a comparison between Theodor Fontane's 1895 novel* Effi Briest *and Eça de Queirós's 1878* O Primo Bazílio, *arguing that the two novelists diverge in the standards upon which they judge their respective tragic heroines and their societies.*]

The two novels which I am going to compare, *O Primo Bazílio (Cousin Basilio)*[1] and *Effi Briest,*[2] belong to a series of realist novels on the theme of adultery which appeared in various European countries in the nineteenth century.[3] The first major novel in this series was Flaubert's *Madame Bovary,* published in 1857. Other works in this group are Tolstoy's *Anna Karenina,* 1875-76, *La Regenta* by Clarín, published between 1884-85 and Theodor Fontane's novels of adultery, *L'Adultera (The Woman taken in Adultery)* (1880) and *Cécile* (1887). It is important to note that the Portuguese novel, *O Primo Bazílio,* appeared in 1878, almost twenty years before *Effi Briest,* which is a very late example of this type of novel.[4]

The Portuguese writer, José Maria de Eça de Queirós, was born in 1845 in a small village in the north of Portugal and graduated in Law from Coimbra in 1866. His first writings date from the end of this period spent in Coimbra; *feuilletons* in which the influence of Victor Hugo and Michelet can be seen together with that of Baudelaire, Nerval and Heine. The strange nature of Eça's writings caused surprise among the literary circles of the time. In Coimbra, Eça came into contact with young academics, who were fascinated by the happenings in Europe and by thinkers such as Darwin, Michelet, Hegel, Comte and above all, Proudhon.

After graduating, Eça settled down in his parents' house in Lisbon and began his professional life; after a short period spent working as a lawyer, he took up administrative posts and finally opted for a diplomatic career. As Portuguese consul he lived first in Havana and later in Newcastle-on-Tyne, where he wrote *O Primo Bazílio,* which he finished in 1876. He was later transferred to Bristol, and then to Paris, where he died in 1900. He had a brilliant career as a journalist, social critic and novelist, which is why he is the best known Portuguese writer of the 1800s, and along with Antero de Quental, the most prominent figure of the *Generation of 70,* a group whose aim was to reform Portuguese society and to introduce a new realist type of writing. Their philosophical models were mainly Taine and Proudhon and their literary models were above all Flaubert, but also Baudelaire and Zola. Later, Eça de Queirós went through another stage in his writing, a *fin-de-siècle* style in which he concentrated more on the development of characters and less on their socio-economic background, which had been such a strong trait in his earlier works.[5]

Just as Fontane is considered the chronicler of Berlin society at the end of the last century, so Eça de Queirós can be considered the chronicler of the Lisbon of his time, painting a true and all-encompassing picture of this society. He studies the effect of the clergy on the middle class in *O crime de Padre Amaro,*[6] and adultery committed by a woman in *O Primo Bazílio*; the decadence of the upper-middle-class and the aristocracy is the main theme of *Os Maias*;[7] he also studies other character types, such as the politician, the man of letters, the Don Juan, the pious woman and the woman corrupted by romantic art. While Fontane gives prominence to the aristocracy in his writing, Eça's main focus in his novels is on the bourgeoisie, of which he is highly critical.

O Primo Bazílio, published in Lisbon in 1878, belongs to a school of writing that the author himself describes as realist-naturalist and its trademark is a caustic irony which is typical of Eça's style.[8] As in the other novels on the theme of adultery which appeared in Europe in the second half of the nineteenth century, the analysis of the situation of women allows us clear insight into the society of the time which it chronicles.

In theme and structure, semiotics and narrative, the work is very similar to *Effi Briest*. Luíza de Brito is a twenty-five-year-old middle-class woman from Lisbon. When the novel opens she has been married for three years to a placid young engineer who works for the Ministry of Public Works. She lives an idle and contented existence, devoting her time to reading romantic literature and household tasks, in a state of happiness that is not overshadowed by the absence of children. This idyllic situation is threatened by two journeys in opposite directions; her husband leaves Lisbon for the provinces on business, and her cousin, and ex-fiancé, arrives from Brazil, where he has lived for some years.

The main themes of the first part of the novel are infidelity and death and these are referred to in conversation, in musical and literary references, as well as on a symbolic level. If we note that the incompatibility between the mistress and her maid is made apparent from the start, we can see that the plot which is the basis of the novel is present *in nuce* from the first chapters. The second part of the narrative deals with Bazílio's wooing of his cousin, her seduction and the adultery, which will rapidly lead Luíza to a feeling of disillusionment. Bazílio turns out to be disrespectful, demanding, and less attractive than her own husband. A new phase of the narrative begins when Juliana, the maid, reveals that she has in her possession letters which Luíza had written to her lover; Juliana is bitter, spiteful and suffers from a serious heart condition; she makes ever-increasing blackmail demands on her mistress, subjecting her to humiliation after humiliation. On hearing of the blackmail demands, Bazílio flees to Paris and the heroine's despair increases, particularly when her husband returns and is surprised and angered at the special treatment the maid is given in the house. Juliana holds the upper hand in the duel with her mistress and increases her blackmail demands until she becomes her own victim. Her death is greeted with relief by the reader and the heroine alike, but does not lead to the happy ending the reader may have expected or even hoped for. Worn out by her troubles, Luíza becomes seriously ill with a "brain fever" and after a short period of convalescence, her condition deteriorates; she dies after two days of agony, which is described in great detail by the narrator.

Both this novel and *Effi Briest* relate the tragic fate of a young woman at the end of the last century, who allows herself to be seduced—in a more or less classic way—by a Don Juan figure who promises distraction from a tedious and idle life. Another similarity between the novels is the fact that both heroines are discovered and punished, and die as a result of this punishment. The main difference between the novels, and the point that I wish to analyse in more detail, lies in the attitude of the authors to what they are writing about, namely in the way each judges his heroine and her adulterous behaviour.

We cannot forget that we are dealing with an age in which the question of women's position in society was in vogue.[9] In Germany the works of positivist and determinist thinkers were popular, as were those of Schopenhauer and Nietzsche. They all saw women as inferior and subordinate to men. At the same time other thinkers such as August Bebel and the emancipation movement put forward a positive image of women, which led to frequent discussion of the situation of women in philosophical, legal and socio-political circles.[10] In Portugal, where women's movements were not yet organised, only a few writers dealt with this subject from a cultural point of view. Among the *Generation of 70* in particular,—under the influence of Michelet and Proudhon—we can find images of women which range from a euphoric and romanticised picture to a critical view which saw women as lesser beings, in need of protection.

Eça de Queirós's critical attitude towards women, and in particular towards urban middle-class women, a subject he wrote a lot about in non-fiction texts, is very different from that of Fontane.[11] In the few non-fiction texts that the German author wrote on the subject he shows a benevolent attitude to women, whom he appreciates because of their imperfections.[12] In the novels that I am comparing we can see that Fontane does not condemn his heroine, whereas Eça de Queirós censures not only his heroine but also the society in which she lives. These different attitudes affect the diegetic development of the novel and also the narrative techniques used.

We must first look at the different choice of events to be related and the effect that the textual economy has on the different stages of the narrative. To illustrate Elsbeth Hamann's comment on the symmetrical nature of Fontane's novel, I would like to note that Effi's seduction as she returns from a journey to the forester's house occurs almost in the middle of the novel, in the third of six narrative sequences, in the nineteenth chapter out of a total of thirty-six.[13] In the first two parts, the author presents the main character and the circumstances that have made her what she is, and by describing her evolution in detail gains the sympathy and the understanding of the reader for her behaviour. This kind of preparation does not exist in *O Primo Bazílio*, where we meet the heroine during the short seduction and then during the adultery itself and the process of blackmail. As we feel we do not know her well, we empathise less with her. In this connection it should be said that the initial description of the heroine in *O Primo Bazílio*, which is clearly disphoric, leads to a feeling of distance between the writer and Luíza, in contrast to what happens in *Effi Briest*, in which the initial description of the heroine is very positive.

To return to the structure of the novels, we can see that the Portuguese novel, like the German one, is practically symmetrical; however, its central point is not the seduction scene, but the scene in which Juliana begins to blackmail her mistress. Thus, in *O Primo Bazílio* the adultery and the blackmail are given equal weight and importance in the text. The structure of the novel leads the reader to see Luíza's punishment after the adultery as redressing the balance which had been disturbed by her mistake and, in this way, the punishment appears as a natural result of her previous behaviour.

An analysis of the narrative voice makes it clear that Fontane sympathises with his heroine, whereas Eça is harshly critical. In both novels a heterodiegetic narrator is present. In *Effi Briest* the narrator's presence is scarcely noticeable and dialogue is given a prime position, which allows the reader to see the action from various points of view. What is more, Fontane carefully selects the characters who are to be put in a focal position, giving a special place to the figure of the heroine, who thus gains the empathy of the reader. In *O Primo Bazílio*, which belongs to an earlier phase of narrative writing, the narrator's judgmental perspective is superimposed on the dialogue of the characters and the narrator can be interpreted as the voice of the author himself.[14] In the Portuguese novel, the narrator adopts the point of view of a number of characters, which may be Eça's way of giving us a rounded view of society; a special place is given to the heroine, although the effects are different from those in Fontane's text: Luíza is placed at a distance from the reader and unmasked by the author's strong, critical and ironic presence.[15]

To turn now to the external circumstances of the two heroines, we note that as well as the obvious difference in nationality, there are also great differences with regard to age and social position. Eça's heroine, Luíza, had come of age before marrying, whereas, at sixteen, Fontane's heroine typifies careless youth, which immediately reveals the position of the authors with regard to blame. Another important factor has to do with the marriages of these two girls; in neither case was it a marriage of love but rather a case of the heroine doing what society expected of her. In order for this to happen, girls were socialised and guided by their mothers, who were mainly responsible for their upbringing. In the German novel it is noteworthy that it is the mother who receives the marriage proposal and who communicates it to her daughter, producing a reaction for which Effi had long been prepared. In *O Primo Bazílio*, the proposal is made directly to the daughter, whose age and social class justify a greater autonomy; her first thought is, however, that her mother will be pleased and relieved by her acceptance of the proposal.

Although Effi is from a rural aristocratic background and is married to a Prussian civil servant and Luíza is only a middle-class woman from Lisbon, there are surprising social parallels between the two novels. In Portugal industrial development happened late, flooding the towns with cheap female labour, which allowed middle-class women to lead an idle life, leaving the work to maids.[16] In Germany this type of life was more typical of the aristocracy. In *Effi Briest*, in contrast to *O Primo Bazílio*, the woman is not denigrated for her idleness. Her ties with nature and open spaces, and her ambitions to project herself and to attain social brilliance, as well as her inability to adapt to closed and restricted spaces, are factors which do not lead us to see her in a negative light. In spite of the apparent similarity, there are differences in the way in which Luíza and Effi spend their time. They both play the piano, embroider and read. However Luíza's pastimes like those of Emma Bovary, are ultra-romantic;[17] if romanticism exists for Effi, it is the fantasy and mythology associated with being "a child of nature" and is not associated with the harmful influence that excessive romanticism has on the heroine in the Portuguese novel.

The most important trait that the two protagonists share is, however, a lack of strength of character. Effi's inner conflict, her attraction to opposites, to gambling and to danger, which is underlined by various symbols and allusions, is referred to not only by many characters in the novel, but also by Effi herself. Worried about her inconstant nature, and comparing herself to her future husband, Effi declares not long before her wedding:

> "And I think Niemeyer went on to say he's a man of principle. And that, I imagine, is a bit more. Oh, and I . . . I haven't any."[18]

Luíza de Brito's potential inconstancy is discussed at the beginning by her husband, Jorge, on the eve of his departure for the Alentejo, when he asks a friend to watch over his wife. In his absence he does not want Luíza to entertain at home a female friend from her childhood, whom he considers to be a libertine:

> "Luíza is an angel, poor thing" . . . "In some ways she is still a child! She can see no evil. She's so good, she just let's things happen. Just look at what happens with Leopoldina: they were brought up together, they were friends, so she doesn't have the courage to ask her to leave. She feels awkward about it, she's too kind. It's understandable! But you can't go through life like that!" [. . .]
>
> "So Sebastian, if you see her here while I'm away, if you find out that Leopoldina is coming here, say something to Luíza! Because that's the way she is, she doesn't stop to think: she puts things out of her mind and doesn't stop to think about them. She needs someone to warn her, someone to say to her: 'Come on, madam, this cannot be!' And then she is the first to agree! You come round and keep her company, play some music for her, and if you see any sign of Leopoldina, you say to her: 'Madam, this is not right.' She can be firm if she feels she's supported. Otherwise she's intimidated and lets her come. She's unhappy about it, but she simply does not have the courage to say to Leopoldina: 'I don't want you here, go away!' She doesn't have the courage for anything: her hands begin to shake, her mouth becomes dry . . . She's a woman, she's very much a woman!"[19]

In fact it is this tendency to "let things happen" which rules Luíza's life.[20] Before marrying, she has gone from the arms of Bazílio to those of Jorge in a theatrical but, at the same time practical, gesture and has got used to happiness. Once her husband has gone and Bazílio has returned, the latter has no difficulty in conquering her affections. The opinion that Frau Briest has of her

daughter "She likes to be carried along"[21] is also applicable to Luíza. They both allow themselves to be guided by others and they are both attracted to the unknown. The attitude of the authors towards their heroines is, however, very different. Eça describes his heroine in positivist terms, explaining her behaviour by her background and the circle in which she lives; the society that formed and nurtured Luíza has turned her into an empty vessel, who reacts with her emotions to external events and who is ready to conform to what is expected of her. She is incapable of a moral thought, for which she substitutes mystical musings and in her trance-like state her degradation increases. Alongside this causal determinism, Eça de Queirós adopts a highly critical position; his criticism is aimed not only at his heroine but also at the society she belongs to, whose behaviour and interaction he unmasks.

In *Effi Briest,* on the other hand, the opposition between the aspirations of the heroine and society, lead to a positive view of the protagonist and the condemnation of society. Effi's volubility is seen not as a sign of emptiness, but rather as an indication of her inner wealth which is shown by her difficulty in adapting. Fontane's heroine is portrayed as a multi-faceted human being with a complex psyche, which justifies the contradictions that exist within her; she is at the same time a child of nature (*Naturkind*) and a member of society (*Gesellschaftsmensch*), Eve, Mary and Melusine.[22] Effi's inability to feel remorse is, more than anything a criticism of a society which imposes its own norms as moral norms. The opposition between "being" and "seeming to be", which is mainly analysed in the novel through the conscience of the character, reveals Effi's honest nature. This honesty does not signify total lucidity and freedom. Although these characteristics are not entirely absent, as they are in *O Primo Bazílio,* they are relativised. Although they do not lead to total justification of Effi's behaviour—she cannot be said to be blameless—they do lead the reader to be kindly disposed towards her.

In the same way, the main difference in the treatment of the theme of adultery is the way in which the heroine herself is evaluated. In *Effi Briest,* the differences between the couple, the disappointment which Effi feels concerning her marriage, the absence of explicit references to the meetings between the lovers and the adultery itself, the importance given to the heroine's inner thoughts, the fact that the relationship comes to an end because of external factors and the way in which the lovers' flight is described, all make the adultery itself appear less significant and help to preserve the dignity of the female character.

On the other hand, in *O Primo Bazílio* the reader knows from the start that the married couple have a good relationship, which makes the adultery appear more shocking and the adultery itself is described in lengthy, almost sordid detail. Added to this, the ease with which Luíza allows herself to be seduced by her cousin, and her moral alienation, increase Luíza's guilt, though she is seen as a product of her education and environment.

The way in which the two main characters behave after the discovery of the adultery shows better than anything else Fontane's forgiving attitude towards his heroine, quite unlike Eça's attitude to Luíza. Effi is banished, but her transfiguration before her death is quite unlike Luíza's acceptance of her shameful and shaming punishment, and her physical decline and death. The veiled tone of Fontane's criticism, which is both typical of poetic realism and of a certain *fin-de-siècle* type of fatalism present in the German novel, differs greatly from the radical tone of the Portuguese novel, in which the satirical narrator places himself at a distance from the events narrated.

To conclude we can say that a common feature of the two novels is the careful study of women and their situation in a society that does not permit them to develop in an independent and responsible way. The indictment of Prussian social norms in *Effi Briest* corresponds in *O Primo Bazílio* to the criticism of the heroine and of the society in which she lives—Lisbon society towards the end of the last century, a society marked by ultra romanticism, by hollow politics and *petit-bourgeois* moralising. Eça de Queirós paints a clear, but sharply ironic picture of this society, which makes this novel, like *Effi Briest,* compulsory reading for anyone who wishes to learn more about the late nineteenth-century European realist novel.

Notes

1. The edition of the text used is *Eça de Queirós: O Primo Bazílio,* ed. by Luiz Fagundes Duarte. Lisbon: Publicações D. Quixote 1990. The novel appeared in English as Cousin Basilio, transl. by Roy Campbell. London: Max Reinhardt 1953.

2. The edition used is *Theodor Fontane: Effi Briest,* transl. by Hugh Rorrison and Helen Chambers, London: Penguin Books 2000.

3. I have compared these two novels in my thesis 'A Mulher e o Adultério nos romances *Effi Briest* de Theodor Fontane e *O Primo Bazílio* de Eça de Queirós', University of Oporto, Ph.D., 1998. The critical bibliography on this theme is very limited. Only the four following articles deal with the comparison of the two novels, and it is interesting to note that all of the articles appeared in the 80s and 90s, which demonstrates the increasing interest in comparative literature in the literature of non-central-european countries: Helmut Hatzfeld: 'Die

religiöse Diskussion in *O Primo Bazílio* (1877) und *Effi Briest*'. *Aufsätze zur portugiesischen Kulturgeschichte,* vol. 16 (1980), pp. 66-74; Christoph Rodiek: 'Probleme der vergleichenden Rangbestimung literarischer Werke (*Effi Briest, La Regenta, O Primo Basílio*)'. In: *Neohelicon. Acta comparationis Literarum Universarum,* 15, 1 (1988), pp. 275-300; Heinz L. Kretzenbacher: 'Das Kulturthema Ehre. Über Ehre, Ironie und kulturelle Interferenz: Ehebruch und Ehrenkonflikt bei Theodor Fontane und Eça de Queirós'. In: *Jahrbuch Deutsch als Fremdsprache,* vol. 16 (1990), pp. 32-75; Teresa Martins de Oliveira: 'Dienstmädchengestalten in den Romanen *O Primo Bazílio* von Eça de Queirós und *Effi Briest* von Theodor Fontane'. In: *Runa—Revista Portuguesa de Estudos Gemanísticos,* 26, 2 (1996), pp. 553-561. Some approaches on this theme also appear in Orlando Grossegesse: *Konversation und Roman. Untersuchungen zum Werk Eça de Queirós.* Stuttgart: Franz Steiner 1991.

4. Cf. Alexander Coleman: *Eça de Queirós and European Realism.* New York: New York University Press 1980. Other articles on the theme of women and adultery in the work of Eça de Queirós in English are: Elizabeth Lowe: 'Love as liturgy and liturgy as love: The satirical subversion of worship and courtship in Eça de Queiroz'. In: *Hispania,* 61, 4, December (1978), pp. 912-918; and Peggy Sharpe-Valadares: 'The heavenly and the earthly cities: the female paradigm in the work of Eça de Queirós'. In: *Luzo-Brazilian Review,* 24, 2 (1989), pp. 117-130.

5. About the different stages on Eça de Queirós' writing, cf., among others, Óscar Lopes e Arnaldo Saraiva: *História da Literatura Portuguesa.* Oporto: Porto Editora 1996, p. 925 ff . . .

6. English translation: Eça de Queirós: *The Sin of Father Amaro,* transl. by Nan Flanagan. London: Max Reinhardt 1962; reprinted London: Transworld Publisher 1964.

7. The novel is translated into English as Eça de Queirós: *The Maias,* transl. by Patricia McGowan and Ann Stevens. London: Bodley Head 1965.

8. Cf. among others, Da Cal, Ernesto Guerra: *Língua e Estilo de Eça de Queiroz.* Coimbra: Livraria Almedina 1981.

9. Cf. Claudia Honegger: *Die Ordnung der Geschlechter. Die Wissenschaften vom Menschen und das Weib: 1750-1850.* Frankfurt a. M.: Campus 1991.

10. Cf. August Bebel: *Die Frau und der Sozialismus.* Stuttgart: Jubiläumsausgabe, 25th ed. 1895.

11. Eça de Queirós's opinions about women at this time are documented in the letters he wrote to Teófilo Braga, 12 March 1878, and Rodrigues de Freitas 30 March 1878, in which he comments on the ethical and aesthetic ideals in *O Primo Bazílio*. On this theme see also the review *As Farpas,* in particular the numbers of May 1871, March 1872 and September-October 1872.

12. As an example of the benevolent attitude of Fontane towards women, see his letter of 10 October 1895 to Colmar Grünhagen. In: Theodor Fontane: *Fontanes Briefe in zwei Bänden,* ed. by Gotthard Erler. Berlin, Weimar 1986, p. 382.

13. Cf. Elsbeth Hamann: *Theodor Fontanes Effi Briest aus erzähltheoretischer Sicht.* Bonn: Bouvier 1984, pp. 78-87.

14. On the evolution of perspectivisation in narrative writing, cf. Franz K. Stanzel: *Theorie des Erzählens.* Göttingen: Vandenhoeck & Ruprecht 1974, pp. 177-182.

15. Cf. Óscar Lopes: 'Efeitos de Queirosianos de polifonia vocal n' *O Primo Basílio.'* In: *Eça de Queirós "Os Maias". Actas do 1° Encontro Internacional de Queirosianos,* ed. by Isabel Pires de Lima. Porto: Edições Asa 1990, pp. 109-115.

16. Cf. Teresa Martins de Oliveira: *Dienstmädchengestalten in den Romanen O Primo Bazílio von Eça de Queirós und Effi Briest.*

17. On the affinities of the figures of Luiza de Brito and Emma Bovary, cf. among others, João Medina: 'O Bovarismo (Da Emma Bovary de Flaubert à Luíza de Eça) and Luíza ou a triste condição (feminina) portuguesa. (N'o Centenário de *O Primo Bazílio*)'. In: *Eça de Queiroz e a Geração de 70,* ed. by João Medina. Lisbon: Moraes Editores 1980, pp. 105-111 and 117.

18. Rorrison and Chambers: *Theodor Fontane: Effi Briest,* p. 25.

19. Translations into English are my own unless otherwise indicated.

"—A Luíza é um anjo, coitada—mas tem coisas em que é criança! Não vê o mal. É muito boa, deixa-se ir. Como este caso da Leopoldina, por exemplo; foram criadas do pequenas, eram amigas, não tem coragem agora para a pôr fora. É acanhamento, é bondade. Ele compreende-se! Mas enfim as leis da vida têm as suas exigências!. . . ."

"—Por isso, Sebastião, enquanto eu estiver fora, se te constar que a Leopoldina vem por cá, avisa a Luíza! Porque ela é assim: esquece-se, não reflex-iona. É necessario alguém que a advirta, que lhe diga:—Alto lá, isso não pode ser! Que então cai logo em si, e é a primeira! . . . Vens por aí, fazes-lhe companhia, fazes-lhe música, e se vires que a Leopoldina aparece ao largo, tu logo:—Minha rica senhora, cuidado, olhe que isso não! Que ela, sentindo-se apoiada, tem decisão. Senão, acanha-se, deixa-a vir. Sofre com isso, mas não tem coragem de lhe dizer: Não te quero ver, vai-te! Não tem coragem para nada: começam as mãos a tremer-lhe, a secar-se lhe a boca . . . É mulher, é muito mulher! . . ." Eça de Queirós: *O Primo Bazílio,* p. 51.

20. Cf. Eduardo Lourenço de Faria: '*O Primo Bazílio*: Structure vide ou structure remplie?' In: *Sillages,* 4 (1974), pp. 57-68.

21. Rorrison and Chambers: *Theodor Fontane: Effi Briest,* p. 158.

22. The importance and the meaning to be given to the mythological and to the mythical elements in the characterisation of Effi Briest on the one hand and to the sociological and psychological elements on the other, vary according to the tendencies of the period and to the critical view of the analyst. Besides the sociological and psychological interpretation, of which the works of Müller-Seidel (cf. Walter Müller-Seidel: *Theodor Fontane, Soziale Romankunst in Deutschland.* Stuttgart: Metzler 1975, pp. 332-377, and of Hans-Heinrich Reuter: *Fontane,* vol. 2. Munich: Nymphenburg, 1968, pp. 640-647, are paradigmatic, we find interpretations that tend to accept a double motivation, that is both sociological and mythological (cf. Donald C. Riechel: '*Effi Briest* and the Calendar of Fate'. In: *Germanic Review,* 48, (1973), pp. 189-211; and Peter Paul Schwarz: '"Tragische Analysis" und Schicksalsdeutungen in Fontanes Roman *Effi Briest*'. In: *Sprachkunst. Beiträge zur Literaturwissenschaft,* 7, 2 (1976), pp. 247-260. It is commonly noted that the mythological and mythical elements, allied to a complex web of motifs, contribute to creating a deeper social and psychological dimension in the heroine (cf. Reinhart Thum: 'Symbol, motif and »Leitmotiv« in Fontanes »Effi Briest«'. In: *Germanic Review* 54 (1979), pp. 115-124; on the motif of Melusine in *Effi Briest,* cf., among others, Renate Schäfer: 'Fontanes Melusine-Motiv'. In: *Euphorion,* 56 (1962), pp. 69-104; Diethelm Brüggemann: 'Fontanes Allegorien'. In: *Neue Rundschau,* 82, 2-3 (1971), pp. 290-310 and pp. 486-505; and Hubert Ohl: 'Melusine als Mythos bei Theodor Fontane'. In: *Mythos und Mythologie in der Literatur des 19 Jahrhunderts,* ed. by Helmut Koopmann. Frankfurt a. M.: Klostermann 1979, pp. 289-305.

Brian Tucker (essay date spring 2007)

SOURCE: Tucker, Brian. "Performing Boredom in *Effi Briest*: On the Effects of Narrative Speed." *German Quarterly* 80, no. 2 (spring 2007): 185-200.

[*In the following essay, Tucker examines the German concept of* Langeweile, *boredom and the dragging on of time, in* Effi Briest, *arguing that Fontane's use of this notion serves as a fundamental narrative function.*]

Effi Briest is a "boring" book. This is not the kind of critical judgment one normally makes, and for two reasons. First, "boring" comes across as negative and banal, and academic criticism's task is generally not to disparage its object but rather to unfold that object's complexity. Second, and more important, it is an emotionally laden appraisal that ventures away from the work itself and into the realm of affective response. For both these reasons, declaring a work boring is bad critical form.

But what if one could develop a concept of boredom that is both positive and based on textual evidence? What if one could show that boredom is precisely the point of a book like *Effi Briest*? Boredom, in this sense, would denote not a narrative defect but a narrative strategy; it would become an object of interest. In what follows, I attempt to locate just this notion of boredom in *Effi Briest,* one based on *Langeweile,* the German equivalent of boredom. *Langeweile* literally means a "long while," and it describes a particular relationship to time in which time seems to stretch and drag on. This specific sense of boredom permeates all levels of *Effi Briest.*

My argument for the centrality of boredom in Fontane's novel has three stages. First, it expounds in more detail this specifically German sense of boredom and shows how Effi suffers not only from a lack of distraction but also and primarily from a time that has grown long. Second, it treats the performative dimension of boredom in the novel. By analyzing the relationship of narrative time to narrated time, it demonstrates how the novel effects the very boredom that it describes in its eponymous heroine. While the novel casts boredom as a problem of time becoming long, it also calibrates the act of narration such that the time of reading becomes longer when Effi is bored. Finally, on the basis of these findings, I return to the frequently discussed gaps, or lacunae, in Fontane's narrative style. Scholars have noted that the novel never describes its most important events directly. It prefers merely to hint at the intimate affair that remains obscure until Innstetten discovers the compromising letters. These gaps and ambiguities have often been studied as interesting aberrations within a novelistic practice that is supposedly realistic. Only once their function is located within a narrative calculus of boredom, however, does it become clear how they push the reader toward a particular ethical judgment. The variations in narrative speed lead the reader to condemn the life of boredom and isolation to which Effi is consigned, rather than her attempt to escape her unhappiness.

Narrated Boredom in *Effi Briest*

Boredom is the point of departure for the main nineteenth-century novels of adultery. Gustave Flaubert's Emma Bovary, for example, is trapped in the web of an interminable *ennui*.[1] And, more pertinent to the present case, there exists another literary reworking of the Ardenne affair, the publicly reported affair and duel upon which Fontane modeled his story. It is entitled *Zum Zeitvertreib,* a way of "passing the time." In a more literal sense, though, "Zeitvertreib" indicates that one must forcefully drive away a time that has become stagnant, so that this novel, too, portrays the affair as a problem of boredom. In fact, in a letter to Friedrich Spielhagen, Fontane commented on the title and expressed his approval: "Meine Frage, 'ob der Titel glücklich gewählt sei', ließ ich gleich nach der Lektüre fallen, weil ich empfand, daß das, was dem Leser seinen Standpunkt anweisen soll, nicht besser ausgedrückt werden kann" (*Briefe* 4:585). In Fontane's reading, it is the excess of time that properly positions the reader vis-à-vis the novel's events.

Effi Briest continues this thematic tradition when it casts boredom as a constant danger for Innstetten's young bride and as the impetus for her adultery. Effi confesses her pre-marital anxieties to her mother, saying, "Was ich nicht aushalten kann, ist Langeweile" (193).[2] When Frau von Briest recounts these conversations to her husband, she worries too: "Für die stündliche kleine Zerstreuung und Anregung, für alles, was die Langeweile bekämpft, diese Todfeindin einer geistreichen kleinen Person, dafür wird Innstetten sehr schlecht sorgen" (200). Effi, through the course of her short marriage and life, fights to the death against boredom, a fight that she ultimately loses.

Zum Zeitvertreib, Spielhagen's counterpart to *Effi Briest,* enriches the common notion of boredom as negative affect, as a discontentment that goes along with having no distractions and nothing to do. Although this lack of occupation plays a role in boredom—as well as in Effi's particular predicament—Spielhagen's title underscores the temporal element of boredom that one must combat when "killing time." Ludwig Völker, reflecting on the semantic differences among the various terms for boredom, notes that, while other languages' terms begin "von einem Affektmoment," the German develops "aus einem Länge-Empfinden." It denotes "ein Bewußtsein der—aus welchen Gründen auch immer—sich dehnenden und stillstehenden Zeit" (13). Boredom, then, is a condition under which one perceives time as passing more slowly than it normally should, so that its length seems to increase. It naturally stands in antonymic relation to *Kurzweil,* an outdated word for amusement, for whatever makes time seem to pass more quickly.

In his analysis of boredom as a fundamental attunement, Martin Heidegger draws out this temporal relation within the concrete sense of *Langeweile.* "*Langeweile* [. . .] zeigt fast handgreiflich, und besonders in unserem deutschen Wort, ein *Verhältnis zur Zeit,* eine Art, wie wir zur Zeit stehen, ein *Zeitgefühl*" (120). The temporal experience of boredom is one of time dragging, slowing almost to a standstill. We combat this feeling, Heidegger notes, through *Zeitvertreib,* "ein Zeit antreibendes Verkürzen der Zeit, die lang werden will" (145). Boredom thus comprises not only a lack of distraction but also an excess of time. And in "passing" or "killing time," one seeks to drive time along in order to drive its oppressive length (i.e., boredom) away.

We need not follow Heidegger's analysis into the abysses of *Dasein* to see that *Effi Briest* operates with a similar concept of boredom. Fontane's characters perceive time in its slowness and length. Effi, for example, complains to her husband during her first winter in Kessin that "ich vergehe vor Langerweile" (255). What is striking here is not so much Effi's complaint but its context. The narrative voice prefaces the conversation between the Innstettens with this remark: "Im übrigen blieb aüch nach dem Silvesterball alles beim alten [. . .], und so kam es denn, daß der Winter als recht lange dauernd empfunden wurde" (254). The narrative binds Effi's boredom to a specific sensation of time passing more slowly, and thus lasting longer than it should. Although Heidegger questions the notion of a fixed, objective pace for time's passage, Fontane's novel consistently measures boredom (as a subjective relationship to time) against the objective rate of its passage. On the one hand, there is an hour, a day, or in this case, winter, which lasts a certain amount of time that can be measured with the clock or the calendar. On the other hand, there is the subject's relationship to this interval of time, and it can seem to the subject as if it traverses this interval either quickly or slowly, so that the interval seems either to rush by or to linger indefinitely. In the boredom that oppresses Effi in Kessin, time continually lingers and drags, so that these intervals of time expand beyond their normal bounds.

The condition of possibility for this sense of boredom is a subjective apprehension of time, and *Effi Briest* underscores this subjective relationship to time from the very outset. The novel opens with the following sentence:

> In Front des schon seit Kurfürst Georg Wilhelm von der Familie von Briest bewohnten Herrenhauses zu Hohen-Cremen fiel heller Sonnenschein auf die mit-

> tagsstille Dorfstraße, während nach der Park- und Gartenseite hin ein rechtwinklig angebauter Seitenflügel einen breiten Schatten erst auf einen weiß und grün quadrierten Fliesengang und dann über diesen hinaus auf ein großes in seiner Mitte mit einer Sonnenuhr und an seinem Rande mit Canna indica und Rhabarberstauden besetztes Rondell warf.

(171)

We can distill the initial action as follows: a wing of the Briest house blocks the sunlight and casts a shadow on the sundial located in the flower bed. The sundial registers the passage of time, so that the novel's very first sentence obscures the possibility of measuring time objectively. Without light, the sundial is useless, and time can only be gauged subjectively. Lacking this instrument of temporal measurement, the story increasingly places Effi's perceptions at the center of time's passage. Indeed, the novel's ending again reflects this development from objective to subjective time. On the final page, the epitaphic words "Effi Briest" replace the sundial depicted on the very first page. The narrative even draws attention to this succession: "Auf dem Rondell hatte sich eine kleine Veränderung vollzogen, die Sonnenuhr war fort, und an der Stelle, wo sie gestanden hatte, lag seit gestern eine weiße Marmorplatte, darauf stand nichts als 'Effi Briest' [. . .]" (426). Through the course of the story, the subject and its relationship to time supplant the objective measure of time.[3]

The novel's opening scenes offer a second image of the discrepancy that arises between the steady progression of the clock and Effi's apprehension of time. The family is expecting the visit of Baron von Innstetten promptly at one o'clock, and Frau von Briest wants to ensure that her daughter looks presentable upon his arrival. Here, Effi's mother and friends represent strict adherence to the clock—in opposition to Effi's more malleable notion of time. Her friend Hulda tries to curtail their play, saying, "Nun aber ist es höchste Zeit, Effi" (178). Effi, however, counters the admonition—with its unconscious allusion to an impending wedding, or *Hochzeit*—by saying that she still has plenty of time. Many readers have noted how much foreshadowing Fontane packs into this opening: for example, Effi's reckless, playful antics; her stories of renunciation and infidelity. In this respect, the temporal allegory (of whether Effi still has time—to spend with her friends, to be a child) plays an important role. While Effi is accused of running late, she accuses the Baron of being early, of arriving *before she is ready*—both in the more immediate sense of not having changed clothes and, as we later learn, in the broader sense of not being prepared to bear the burden of adult social obligations.

All this bickering over minutes and quarters of an hour concludes with the mother's exasperated remark: "Nie hältst du Zeit" (179). One would probably translate this statement as "You're never on time," or "You never keep track of time." But, taken at its word, the passage accuses Effi of not *holding on* to time, not holding time in her grasp. Although Effi believes she has a firm grip on time, this becomes the predicament of the novel: time constantly slips her grasp, becomes stagnant, and drags on. In both these respects, the novel begins by opening the possibility of boredom as *Lange-weile*, as a subjective relationship to time in which time becomes long.[4]

Scholars often describe boredom along gender lines, as a problem inherent in women's restricted social roles. Patricia Meyer Spacks, for example, argues that boredom is a social construction that coincides with the emergence of industrial capitalism, the bourgeoisie, and the notion of leisure in the late-eighteenth and nineteenth centuries.[5] Women of this period, especially those of the upper classes, were doubly excluded: they were allowed to participate neither in the professional world (reserved for men) nor in the world of domestic labor (reserved for servants). Spacks describes the situation in nineteenth-century England: "No longer needed for household tasks, young women have no clear responsibilities and no meaningful occupation" (174).

Such restrictive gender roles certainly contribute to Effi's boredom in Kessin. While her husband attends important political functions, Effi stays at home. While the servants attend to all the household tasks, Effi must find some distraction to pass the time. Boredom in *Effi Briest* maps onto these gender roles, and the novel reinforces the conventions of gender through contrasts in age (old husband—young wife) and in disposition (pedantic, strict husband—impulsive, passionate wife). These contrasts pertain directly to the form of boredom outlined above—not only as paralyzing tedium but also as time grown long. While Effi is the character who cannot hold time in her grasp, Innstetten is characterized as follows: "es entsprach seinem Charakter und seinen Gewohnheiten, genau Zeit und Stunde zu halten" (202). Innstetten, in contradistinction to Effi, holds on to time precisely. He is associated with order and conforming to the rule of law, and he deals with time in the same way. He insists that its passage adhere to the rule of the clock and the calendar. Because he never lets time stretch beyond its bounds, he never experiences the "long while" of boredom.[6] In other words, it is not simply that Innstetten has a career and obligations whereas Effi does not, although this difference clearly factors in her boredom. The decisive contrast between Effi and her husband is that they relate to time differently, and that Effi allows time to slip out of order and to become long. In short, the order that Innstetten relishes (and upon which his bureaucratic career depends) is incompatible with Effi's more flexible relationship to time.

Narrative Boredom in *Effi Briest*

As we move from the engagement in Hohen-Cremmen to marital life in Kessin, I want to shift the focus from a depiction of boredom through narrative to its performance in and by narrative. Boredom may be a theme that underlies most novels of adultery, but *Effi Briest* distinguishes itself from other works in this tradition in that it enacts the same form of boredom it describes. Spacks asserts that "Boredom defies narration" (61). She explains that a novel cannot narrate emptiness and monotony because, in order to succeed, it must hold the reader's interest. Here one should keep in mind the different connotations contained in the words "boredom" and *Langeweile*. If one's notion of boredom rests solely upon an affect, and a negative one at that, such as discontentment, then conveying boredom to a reader in a way that sustains interest poses difficulties. Fontane, however, works with another aspect of boredom—the perception of temporal length. This understanding opens new possibilities for the novel both to depict boredom and to produce it for the reader at the level of narrative, as a consequence of narrative.

Effi Briest "bores" the reader—it lets time grow long—by adjusting narrative time in its relation to narrated time. By narrative time, I mean the amount of time—usually measured in terms of printed space—devoted to the representation of a scene, and by narrated time, the time that passes within the diegetic scene.[7] These two measures determine the narrative's speed. In *Narrative Discourse*, Gérard Genette defines the speed of a narrative as "the relationship between a duration (that of the story, measured in seconds, minutes, hours, days, months, and years) and a length (that of the text, measured in lines and in pages)" (87f.). When the story depicts Effi as particularly bored, the narrative time swells in relation to narrated time (which is to say, the narrative speed slows), and that same narrative time shrinks drastically when something interesting happens. In other words, the narrative adheres to the logic of *Langeweile* and *Kurzweil*: boredom lasts a long time, whereas distraction is what passes the time quickly and makes it shorter. In so doing, the narrative approximates Effi's point of view in her subjective relationship to time and invites the reader to participate in her boredom.

So how does the novel enact boredom? Despite introducing categories of speed and duration, Genette admits that the detailed analysis of narrative speed is virtually impossible: "diegetic time is almost never indicated (or inferable) with the precision that would be necessary [to analyze effects of rhythm]" (88). Not so in *Effi Briest*, whose frequent temporal signposts make it well suited to the study of narrative speed. One should note, first, how often the reader receives precise statements of narrated time: almost every chapter and subsection begins by indicating the time of its events. "Ende August war da" (187), "Innstetten war erst sechs Uhr früh von Varzin zurückgekommen" (233), "Es schlug zwei Uhr" (283), "Drei Tage danach" (345), and so on. These are but a few examples of the narrative's pervasive concern with conveying the time and duration of events. In fact, it is so meticulous in this regard that Christian Grawe has tried to ascertain the exact historical dates of the novel's major occurrences.[8] Second, one should note that the novel is far less precise in its control of narrative time, the amount of time that a reader takes to traverse a particular interval of narrated time. The two registers of narrated time and narrative time thus replicate the two temporal components of boredom: the objective rate of time's passage and the subject's perception of time. In this way, the narrative voice synthesizes the contrast between Effi and Innstetten in their relations to time: it ostensibly holds time firmly in its grasp and yet quietly lets time slip out of its grasp. It holds one register of time to a strict *Ordnung* as it allows another to stretch out of proportion.

The novel's calculus of boredom thus includes two complementary aspects: the expansion of narrative time in boredom, and its contraction for events of interest. First, narrative time expands while Effi is in Kessin, that is, when she is most bored. One might object to this detail as evidence of a narrative strategy, even if one accepts it as fact. One could argue, that is, that Kessin is the centerpiece of the entire story. Everything turns on the events that transpire there, so it receives the most narrative attention and hence the most space. That would be a strong counterargument, were it true that those events upon which the story turns—such as the rendezvous with Crampas—receive the most attention. However, as many have noted, and I shall return to this point later, they do not receive much attention. And this constitutes the second aspect of the calculus of boredom: those events that break the monotony in Kessin and provide a welcome distraction are given either short *Schrift* or are omitted altogether.

One can best observe the fluctuation of narrative speed when scenes of extreme boredom are juxtaposed with those events that Effi looks forward to when she is bored, such as a visit to Hohen-Cremmen. Take, as a first example, the evening in Kessin during which Effi must pass the time by herself while Innstetten attends a political dinner (Chapter 9). The narrator signals her lack of occupation by asking, "Arme Effi. Wie sollte sie den Abend verbringen?" (226), a question posed in the third-person that nonetheless invites the reader to share in her predicament. The reader then follows her in great detail through a series of aimless activities that she performs with indifference. It seems to Effi that it takes a great deal of time to cross the interval of this evening, an interval that the narrative measures exactly: "fast auf zwölf Stunden" (226). As a result of the narrative lens's

tight focus on this scene, it also takes the reader a long time to cross the span of the evening—about six pages for six hours of waking narrated time. The next morning's conversation requires almost another ten pages, so the speed of narrative has slowed considerably. As Effi suffers from *Langeweile,* the time of reading becomes long.

Of course, one might wonder how fast narrative is supposed to move. What is a "normal," orderly pace for time, for narrative? It is true that, lacking a normative standard for narrative speed, an isolated example says little about a narrative technique designed to enact boredom. After all, it could be that the entire novel moves at a rate of about one page per hour and that there is no observable fluctuation in the ratio of narrative to narrated time. But that is not the case here. The previous example becomes more telling when contrasted with the visit to Hohen-Cremmen that Effi has been yearning for, imagining, and planning for some time. She writes to her mother in anticipation of her daughter's birth in July, seven months in advance: "sobald ich einigermaßen wieder bei Wege bin, komme *ich,* nehme hier Urlaub und mache mich auf nach Hohen-Cremmen. Ach, wie ich mich darauf freue [. . .]" (252). By her own account, Effi has been looking forward to the trip home as a break from boring Kessin for the better part of a year. The trip finally takes place after the child's baptism in mid-August, and the narrative portrays it thus: "Mitte August war Effi abgereist, Ende September war sie wieder in Kessin" (269). After the novel announces how intensely Effi desires a change of scenery, the trip is over as soon as it begins. It is telling that the novel indicates the length of narrated time precisely (Effi spends six weeks at home), while the narrative time shrinks to the briefest mention. The effect is that these small excitements and distractions—even when they last six weeks—rush by so quickly that we seem never to have left the monotony of Kessin.

Now I have slightly misrepresented the depiction of Effi's trip home, for the narrative does devote a couple of pages to its retrospective description. Nevertheless, there are two important points to consider: first, even this description is given under the shadow of her already having returned to Kessin, i.e., as a memory and, second, the six *weeks* of her absence still occupy less than half the space of her six *hours* of boredom in the previous example. The unfortunate side effect of *Kurzweil* is that it never lasts as long as *Langeweile.*

A similar contraction of narrative time occurs when Effi leaves Kessin for Berlin and enjoys the company of her mother and cousin Dagobert. The narrative voice interrupts their fun to report, "So waren schon beinah vierzehn Tage vergangen" (339), and the "schon" in this passage indicates a measure of surprise at how quickly time is passing. The reader, too, might be surprised by how quickly time is passing, for Effi's five weeks in Berlin rush by in just under ten pages. And in the novel's only direct mention of physical intimacy with Crampas—he covers her hand with kisses—time again seems to pass at an accelerated rate. "Effi blickte sich um, und im nächsten Augenblicke hielt der Schlitten vor dem landrätlichen Hause" (308). This encounter is not boring by anyone's standards, and indeed time seems here to move quickly and get very short. The scene ends before Effi can even look around; it is over, literally, in the blink of an eye.

What one observes in these examples is that, by varying its degree of focus and attention to detail, the narrative determines the rate at which the reader experiences narrated time. That rate fluctuates from about two weeks per page for matters that interest Effi to about one hour per page when she is bored. All narratives dictate their audience's experience of time to some extent, but *Effi Briest* is distinctive in that the fluctuation in discourse corresponds to a fluctuation within the story. By calibrating the relationship between narrated and narrative time, the novel subtly makes Effi the temporal focalizer for the events in Kessin: things that transpire there are colored by her perception of the passage of time.

There are some exceptions to this narrative pattern. It would overstate the case to claim that a slow narrative pace always corresponds to boredom, whereas a fast pace always corresponds to entertainment or distraction. *Effi Briest* is not a monochromatic novel, and it has other motivations for choosing a tight narrative focus and going into greater detail. It also lingers over descriptions when it introduces new characters and places, for example, or when it conveys conversations that advance the plot.[9] The pattern works best for the time in Kessin, and it works best as a general principle: all in all, one finds that when the novel draws attention to a scene as particularly boring or particularly exciting, it uses narrative speed to shape the reader's experience of time and create an identificatory effect.

To describe Fontane's novel as performing boredom naturally calls to mind the type of utterances that J. L. Austin classifies as "performatives." Nevertheless, even though *Effi Briest* effects a kind of boredom through its language, this does not qualify as an explicit performative (e.g., "I bet," "I promise") in Austin's sense of the term: an utterance that does not describe but rather *does* what it says in the act of saying it. For one thing, narrative does describe. Moreover, even if the narrative did include explicit performatives in its description, these utterances would lack the appropriate circumstances to qualify as effective performatives. One should therefore understand the performance of boredom in this novel as a "perlocutionary" speech act, one that produces certain effects as a consequence of what it says, even though the words themselves are not acts. Although Austin is

far more enthusiastic about illocutionary speech acts (those like "I bet" that do something in the very moment of utterance), literary language constitutes for him a special case in which illocutionary acts do not apply.[10] Focusing on variations in narrative speed allows one to interpret large sections of the novel as a perlocutionary speech act, and it presents an opportunity to locate in fictional writing—in narrative itself—a performative dimension with extradiegetic force.

For the reader, the drama of *Effi Briest* consists in the conflict it stages between the perlocutionary force of narrative time and the archetypal illocutionary act of "I do" that unites couples in wedding ceremonies. That force becomes acute once the novel takes up questions of fault, punishment, and social duty: by aligning the reader with Effi's temporal perspective and by involving the reader in her boredom, the novel makes it more difficult to judge her actions harshly. This argument follows James Phelan's conception of narrative, in which "texts are designed by authors in order to affect readers in particular ways," and in which "those designs are conveyed through language, techniques, structures, forms, and dialogic relations of texts [. . .]" (18). The narrative voice signals its sympathy for the protagonist in several ways, through privileged access to Effi's thoughts and emotions, for instance, or through glowing descriptions of her character. It thus distances itself and the reader from the ethical condemnation that, according to moral dictates within the story, follows reflexively upon her affair. The calibration of narrative time, the focalization of time through Effi's character, is yet another way in which the novel encourages an identificatory, sympathetic response in the reader.

In letters written shortly after *Effi Briest*'s publication, Fontane alludes to the ethical judgments that its readers must make. He summarizes the response of the many readers who sympathize with the protagonist:

> "ja, Effi; aber Innstetten ist ein 'Ekel.'" Und ähnlich urtheilen alle. Für den Schriftsteller in mir kann es gleichgültig sein, ob Innstetten [. . .] als famoser Kerl oder als "Ekel" empfunden wird, als Mensch aber macht mich die Sache stutzig.
>
> (*Briefe* 4:506)[11]

Fontane admits to being taken aback by his audience's response. While he thought he had crafted an ethical conundrum that pitted sympathy and circumstance against duty and principle, his readers saw it differently. Instead, they saw a clear-cut case of right and wrong, sided with Effi, and dismissed Innstetten's position (connected to the revenge code and social ostracism) in the harshest terms. In other words, it seems that Fontane (the person, at least, if not the writer) underestimated the persuasive force of his narrative and its effect on the reader. Seen from a distance, Innstetten has been

wronged at least as much as Effi, and he seeks in retribution nothing more than what the prevailing social
code entitles him to. The difficulty, however, is that the
narrative does not allow one to see the events from a
neutral and disinterested distance. While the story asks
the reader to judge its events, the discourse asks the
reader to judge in a particular way, for Effi and against
her husband's principles, a fact to which Fontane's contemporary readers richly attested.[12]

EMPTY SPACES IN *EFFI BRIEST*

This characterization of *Effi Briest* runs the risk of un-
derreading as long as it fails to take the Chinaman into
account. The novel cannot be construed as boring, one
might argue, because it contains a ghost story that keeps
its readers on tenterhooks. Even the evening of extreme
boredom cited above ends with the excitement and anxiety of a haunting (although, in that instance, the anxiety
is actually what makes boredom inevitable because it
prevents Effi from simply going to bed early). Moreover, one cannot ignore the ghost story, because Fontane stresses its importance in a letter of November 19,
1895. He writes in response to a review, "wie Sie her-
vorgehoben haben, steht die Sache [the ghost story]
nicht zum Spaß da, sondern ist ein Drehpunkt für die
ganze Geschichte" (*Briefe* 4:506). The letter leaves open
the question of *how* the ghost story constitutes a pivotal
point in the story, and it will be instructive in this context to consider Effi's remarks on the ghost. She writes
to her mother:

> Kannst Du Dir denken, Mama, dass ich mich mit un-
> srem Spuk beinah ausgesöhnt habe? [. . .] immer das
> Alleinsein und so gar nichts erleben, das hat doch auch
> sein Schweres, und wenn ich dann in der Nacht auf-
> wache, dann horche ich mitunter hinauf, ob ich nicht
> die Schuhe schleifen höre, und wenn alles still bleibt,
> so bin ich fast enttäuscht und sage mir: wenn es doch
> nur wiederkäme [. . .].
>
> (256f)

Effi is certainly frightened of the ghost, but her primary
complaint—even in the face of the supernatural—remains her boredom. This boredom has become so extreme that she has reconciled herself to the ghost. Indeed, she is disappointed when it does not appear
because its appearance would suspend her boredom. On
this view, the ghost is a pivotal point because the story
turns on the alternation of *Langeweile* and *Kurzweil* and
the ghost represents a momentary respite from boredom.

It is telling that the ghost is an apparition, an ersatz for
an absent human being. Frances Subiotto's insightful
reading of the ghost story connects this figure to "the
sleight-of-hand that Fontane perpetrates so that in fact
nothing really happens" (137). The ghost stands in for
the affair with Crampas and (dis)embodies the absence

at the center of the story. It is, after all, the ghost of a
man who died of star-crossed love, so that it reflects,
for Effi, the danger of any attempt to escape the root
causes of her boredom—her marriage to an older Prussian bureaucrat, as well as the expectations placed upon
her by class and gender. In terms of the larger narrative
design, the ghost reinforces the novel's "absence of
event" and thereby contributes to the pattern of narrative boredom. It represents the trace of what never
shows itself directly, and in this sense it provides a figure for the narrative at large, which is riddled with the
traces and the haunting presence of what is absent.[13]

Subiotto's reading has the advantage of connecting the
ghost story to another interpretive crux, namely, the
gaps, incompletions, and indeterminacies in Fontane's
prose. These empty spaces are a recurrent topic in the
scholarship on *Effi Briest*. Valerie Greenberg, for instance, finds the novel gripped by "an undertow of incomplete stories" (776). Sofia Källström has continued
the discussion more recently with her study of such ambiguities as "ein konstitutives Textmerkmal" in *Effi Briest* (9). Källström finds in the novel a pervasive narrative reticence: it rarely states things important to the
plot directly, though their presence is felt throughout.

Although such gaps are widely recognized phenomena
in Fontane's prose, they are seldom connected to a
larger narrative strategy or poetological ground. The focus on narrative gaps in their own right can lead, for
example, to discussions of "the discretion of the German Realist novelist as regards sexual matters," so that
one cannot determine precisely the beginning and extent of Effi's seduction (Ritchie 566). Yet such piquant
indeterminacies are not the only consequence of a novel
that never bothers to narrate its juiciest details. Other,
more theoretically informed studies appeal to a modern-
ist aversion to closure and thus locate Fontane among
the seeds of a pullulating narrative ambiguity in literary
modernism.[14] Källström takes a slightly different tack
and connects Fontane's narrative style to reception theories in which gaps engage the reader in the construction
of meaning.[15] Both approaches attempt to rescue Fontane from his position at the rear-guard of a fading realism by demonstrating that these gaps deviate from a
purely realistic representation.

The present analysis of boredom in *Effi Briest* opens a
new perspective on these narrative gaps by examining
them not only in their existence but in their function.
Empty spaces in Fontane's narrative tend to coincide
with events of great feeling or interest. That a novel
should skip over some of its most crucial events is,
from the perspective of narrative boredom, no longer
paradoxical: it skips over them precisely because they
are crucial and interesting. Such gaps hold an important
place in the novel's design in that they represent the extreme pole of variations in narrative speed. For crucial

events—such as Effi's affair with Crampas—the narrative time contracts to a vanishing point. The events disappear altogether and the reader only learns of them retrospectively. If a much-anticipated visit home received but a cursory mention, it is only fitting that the most anticipated events of all receive no direct mention. One can speculate that, if the story described in titillating detail the meetings between Effi and Crampas, the reader would find it more difficult to believe that Kessin had bored Effi oppressively. By focusing instead on monotonous intervals and by passing over potentially interesting events, the novel executes that "sleight-of-hand" in which nothing really happens.

It is only once one examines the novel as a generator of boredom that its empty spaces gather together to form an overarching emptiness, or as Kant writes in his anthropological treatise "Von der langen Weile und dem Kurzweil," a horrible vacuum. "Die in sich wahrgenommene Leere an Empfindungen erregt ein Grauen (*horror vacui*) und gleichsam das Vorgefuehl eines langsamen Todes" (7:233). The horror of this emptiness is such that one must fill it, and the oppressive task of filling a void, of passing time, bears on Effi throughout the story. In Berlin, Effi's cousin Dagobert hopes for a chance to go to war because, "Unsereins möchte doch auch mal an die Reihe kommen und hier diese schreckliche Leere [. . .] endlich los werden," a gesture that connotes both a sartorial and an existential void (337). The characters are willing to subject themselves to terror, danger, and any number of other unpleasant situations, if only for a chance to escape the time that has grown excruciatingly long and empty. At the base of their boredom lies an encounter with temporality, with what Heidegger would call the temporality of Dasein.[16] Their attempts to escape from a temporal vacuum fuel the suspicion that perhaps being itself comprises an emptiness that cannot be filled, regardless of the distractions—love, career, war, etc.—that one tries to employ. In Fontane's novel, this confrontation with temporality shapes the lives of Effi and those around her, and only Rollo, the loyal dog, remains immune to its effects since he possesses "kein Organ für Zeitmaß" (422).

In trying to explicate the correspondence between narrative speed and Effi's perception of time, I have used terms such as "design" and "strategy," which imply a certain degree of intention. While there is, to my knowledge, no direct evidence that Fontane construed boredom in its concrete sense as a "long while," there is evidence that he intentionally designed the novel to focus precisely on monotonous intervals. A note from an early manuscript draft indicates how he sought to capture his characters' boredom in language:

> Diesen *zweiten* Winter in Krotoschin [later to become Kessin] muß ich ziemlich genau schildern, sie sind viel zu Haus, haben wenig Verkehr, [. . .] *sie* würde sich

> mit den kl. Leuten amüsieren, aber ihm ist es zu langweilig und so sind sie viel allein und sie wird halb gemüthskrank [. . .].[17]

What Fontane wants to portray exactly—and hence at length—are those periods in which boredom sets in. Such detailed attention brings with it the side effect that these monotonous stretches grow longer and take more time to read. The effects of narrative speed thus derive naturally from the choices Fontane makes as a writer. He wants the reader to spend time with the protagonist, even to sympathize with her. He wants to give a lyric rendering of her situation, and that situation frequently involves boredom. In other words, this paper might make the correspondence between story and discourse appear more directly intentional than it actually is, but I believe it arrives analytically at what Fontane produces intuitively.

The attempt to enact boredom (rather than just depict it) ultimately provides an opportunity to reassess Fontane's status as a realist writer and his work's relationship to other nineteenth-century novels of adultery. While the narrative project detailed here sounds like a decidedly modern device, it actually accords with Fontane's notion of realism, which to him never implied the direct reproduction of reality.[18] The writer, he believed, must transform reality through the medium of art in order to make it as plausible and vivid as possible. In a review of Gustav Freytag's *Die Ahnen*, Fontane describes the novel's task: "er soll uns eine Welt der Fiktion auf Augenblicke als eine Welt der Wirklichkeit erscheinen [. . .]" (239). With this goal in mind, it makes sense that the novel would use all the means available—including narrative structure—to convey its fiction to the reader as reality, to create for the reader a reality that corresponds to its fictional world. In *Effi Briest,* narrative speed fulfills this function. Fontane adds another element to the novel's task: "Der moderne Roman soll ein Zeitbild sein, ein Bild *seiner* Zeit" (242). He means that the novel should draw from and reflect its own age and historical context. But when connected to the narrative strategy of *Effi Briest,* the passage acquires an unintended connotation. *Effi Briest* accomplishes its novelistic task—in Fontane's terms, it overcomes the gap between fiction and reality—precisely by being a *Zeitbild,* an image of time, not only an image of the novel's time but also an image of Effi's relationship to time. At certain moments, the fiction of Effi's time becomes reality, in that the novel makes it the reader's time as well.[19]

The attention to narrative speed furthermore helps situate *Effi Briest* in relation to other adultery narratives of the same period. Flaubert, whose *Madame Bovary* critics regularly cite with regard to *Effi Briest,* famously declared that he wanted to write "un livre sur rien," a book about nothing that would cohere through the internal force of its style (2:31). While the two novels are often mentioned together for their obvious thematic affinities, my examination of how *Effi Briest* enacts boredom suggests another way to link these two novels. They also share an aesthetic goal: Fontane works toward a similar end when he employs narrative speed as an internal force to constitute meaning and to convey to the reader an experience of emptiness.

Notes

1. On the difference between *ennui* and boredom, namely, that *ennui* is often understood as more profound and universal, see Martina Kessel's *Langeweile,* especially 21f. For more on Flaubert in this context, see Richard Kuhn's literary history of ennui, *The Demon of Noontide.*

2. All citations from *Effi Briest* are taken from the Nymphenburger edition.

3. Russell Berman also interprets the opening and closing scenes in terms of temporality, although differently than I do. He finds in the novel two conflicting temporalities, one historical and political, the other cosmic and natural. He writes that the sundial "will be removed to make room for the gravestone, pointing to the temporality of eternity that challenges the secular calendar of state" (344).

4. Edith Krause finds numerous symbols of sexual desire in the opening scenes. She asserts that Effi's boredom stems from a depression based on her problematic relationship with her mother (119). Our readings of the introduction diverge in that, while Krause focuses on conflicting familial relations, I am more concerned with conflicting temporal relations.

5. Cf. Spacks, 6-31. For more on boredom as a quintessentially modern experience, see Elizabeth Goodstein's excellent study *Experience without Qualities: Boredom and Modernity.*

6. Jeffrey Schneider points out that too many critics oversimplify Innstetten through "a false opposition of seemingly immutable gender differences" (266). In fact, Innstetten's relationship to time and to boredom changes over the course of the novel, and to do it justice, one would have to consider carefully his reaction to Effi's affair, especially when he perceives the emptiness of his bureaucratic life. Such considerations lie beyond the scope of my argument, though, which focuses on Effi because she serves as the novel's temporal focalizer.

7. The terms "narrative time" and "narrated time" mean to approximate the German "Erzählzeit" and "erzählte Zeit," respectively. In his *Dictionary of Narratology,* Gerald Prince suggests the terms "discourse time" and "story time" as English equivalents. I use the pair based on the verb "to narrate" because it captures the relationship of process and product present in the German. Prince elsewhere describes the relationship of these two times as "narrative speed." See his *Narratology,* 54-59.

8. According to Grawe, the ghost appears on December 14, 1877; Innstetten discovers Crampas's letters on June 30, 1885; and the duel takes place on the first day of the following August. See Grawe 51-53.

9. Effi's first winter in Kessin constitutes another exception to the pattern. The narrative voice notes that "vor allem waren sie [die Monate] so monoton gewesen" (256) and then proceeds to skip over most of the winter. Perhaps Spacks is correct insofar as this type of boredom—with its long stretches of tedium and monotony—really does defy narration. This could be why the narrative chooses, instead, to focus on intense scenes of boredom as symptomatic of the longer spans it leaves aside.

10. On the difference between illocutionary and perlocutionary acts, see J. L. Austin, *How to Do Things With Words,* especially Lecture IX.

11. See also the letter to Clara Kühnast (27 October 1895), *Briefe* 4:493, where Fontane expresses similar sentiments.

12. In his analysis of the honor code's role in *Effi Briest,* Jeffrey Schneider cautions against blaming individual characters for the marriage's failure. He finds, instead, that the novel exposes the entire institution of marriage as fragile. As my reading has tried to show, the tendency to blame Innstetten derives from the rhetorical force of Fontane's narrative. See Schneider 265f.

13. Subiotto describes the ghost as "a good objective correlative of the whole" (141).

14. As an example, see Greenberg's conclusion, 778.

15. See Källström, especially chapter 2.3, "Unbestimmtheit in der Literatur-wissenschaft" 27-40.

16. "Die Langeweile," Heidegger writes, "entspringt aus der Zeitlichkeit des Daseins" (191).

17. I cite here from the materials to *Effi Briest* in the *Grosse Brandenburger Ausgabe,* 397. It is remarkable that Fontane connects boredom in this case to Innstetten. What would amuse Effi would only bore him, and vice versa. The passage thus returns to the connection between boredom and gender expectations: Effi's role as a wife requires her to do things with Innstetten that she finds stultifying

and simultaneously prevents her from pursuing her own amusement.

18. Cf. his essay "Unsere Lyrische und Epische Poesie seit 1848," in which he states that true realism subjects its object to a process of purification and transfiguration (12f).

19. Thomas Mann makes this connotative register of "Zeitbild" explicit when he describes *Der Zauberberg* as "ein Zeitroman im doppelten Sinn," a novel that paints a portrait of an epoch and simultaneously makes times itself an object of representation (611). Given Mann's remarks about time in the novel, it is likely that the structural analysis carried out here could also yield insights into the *Zauberberg*'s composition. Though this is not the place to embark on a detailed consideration of Mann's novel, I note in passing that, as Hans Castorp is drawn further into the *Zauberberg*'s timeless world, the chapters become progressively longer. Mann describes the intended correspondence between story and discourse succinctly: "Das Buch ist selbst das, wovon es erzählt" (612).

Works Cited

Austin, J. L. *How to Do Things With Words.* Ed. J. O. Urmson and Marina Sbisà. Cambridge: Harvard UP, 1962.

Berman, Russell. "*Effi Briest* and the End of Realism." *A Companion to German Realism 1848-1900.* Ed. Todd Kontje. Rochester: Camden House, 2002. 339-64.

Flaubert, Gustave. *Correspondance.* Ed. Jean Bruneau. 4 vols. Paris: Gallimard, 1973.

Fontane, Theodor. *Effi Briest. Grosse Brandenburger Ausgabe,* Bd. XV. Ed. Christine Hehle. Berlin: Aufbau-Verlag, 1997-.

———. *Effi Briest. Sämtliche Werke,* Bd. VII. Ed. Edgar Gross. Munich: Nymphenburger Verlagshandlung, 1959. 169-427.

———. "Gustav Freytag. *Die Ahnen.*" *Sämtliche Werke,* Bd. XXI/1. Ed. Kurt Schreinert. Munich: Nymphenburger Verlagshandlung, 1963. 231-48.

———. "Unsere Lyrische und Epische Poesie seit 1848." *Sämtliche Werke,* Bd. XXI/1. Ed. Kurt Schreinert. Munich: Nymphenburger Verlagshandlung, 1963. 7-33.

———. *Werke, Schriften, Briefe,* Abteilung IV, *Briefe.* Ed. Otto Drude et al. Munich: Hanser, 1976-1982.

Genette, Gérard. *Narrative Discourse.* Trans. Jane Lewin. Ithaca: Cornell UP, 1980.

Goodstein, Elizabeth. *Experience without Qualities: Boredom and Modernity.* Stanford: Stanford UP, 2005.

Grawe, Christian. *Theodor Fontane: Effi Briest.* Frankfurt a.M.: Verlag Moritz Diesterweg, 1985.

Greenberg, Valerie. "The Resistance of *Effi Briest*: An (Un)told Tale." *PMLA* 103.5 (1988): 770-82.

Heidegger, Martin. *Die Grundbegriffe der Metaphysik. Gesamtausgabe,* Bd. 29-30. Ed. Friedrich Wilhelm von Herrmann. Frankfurt a.M.: Klostermann, 1983.

Källström, Sofia. *"Das Eigentliche bleibt doch zurück." Zum Problem der semantischen Unbestimmtheit am Beispiel von Theodor Fontanes* Effi Briest. Uppsala: Uppsala UP, 2002.

Kant, Immanuel. *Gesammelte Schriften.* Berlin: Koeniglich-Preussische Akademie der Wissenschaften zu Berlin, 1902-.

Kessel, Martina. *Langeweile.* Göttingen: Wallstein, 2001.

Krause, Edith. "Desire and Denial: Fontane's *Effi Briest.*" *The Germanic Review* 74.2 (1999): 117-29.

Kuhn, Richard. *The Demon of Noontide.* Princeton: Princeton UP, 1976.

Mann, Thomas. "Einführung in *Den Zauberberg.*" *Gesammelte Werke in zwölf Bänden,* Bd. XI. Ed. Hans Bürgin. Frankfurt a.M.: S. Fischer, 1960. 602-17.

Phelan, James. *Living to Tell About It: A Rhetoric and Ethics of Character Narration.* Ithaca: Cornell UP, 2005.

Prince, Gerald. *A Dictionary of Narratology.* Lincoln: U of Nebraska P, 1987.

———. *Narratology: The Form and Functioning of Narrative.* New York: Mouton, 1982.

Ritchie, J. M. "Embarrassment, Ambiguity and Ambivalence in Fontane's *Effi Briest.*" *Formen Realistischer Erzählkunst. Festschrift for Charlotte Jolles.* Ed. Joerg Thunecke. Nottingham: Sherwood Press, 1979. 563-69.

Schneider, Jeffrey. "Masculinity, Male Friendship, and the Paranoid Logic of Honor in Theodor Fontane's *Effi Briest.*" *The German Quarterly* 75.3 (2002): 265-81.

Spacks, Patricia Meyer. *Boredom.* Chicago: U of Chicago P, 1995.

Subiotto, Frances. "The Ghost in *Effi Briest.*" *Forum for Modern Language Studies* 21.2 (1985): 137-50.

Völker, Ludwig. *Langeweile.* Munich: Fink, 1975.

Dana Medoro (essay date fall 2007)

SOURCE: Medoro, Dana. "So Very Self-Evident: Adultery and Abortion in 'The Purloined Letter.'" *Literature and Medicine* 26, no. 2 (fall 2007): 342-63.

[*In the following essay, Medoro places Edgar Allan Poe's short story "The Purloined Letter" in the context of the mid-nineteenth century proliferation of informa-*

tion on contraception, abortion, and sexuality in the United States, contending that the events alluded to in the letter are couched in common euphemisms of the time.]

> The cushions we probed with the fine long needles you
> have seen me employ.
>
> Edgar Allan Poe, "The Purloined Letter," 1845

In 1846, the sixteenth edition of William A. Alcott's *The Young Man's Guide* hit the American streets, maintaining its cautionary message that the world was an awfully smutty place, "abound[ing] in impure publications [and] licentious paintings and engravings, which circulate in various ways."[1] According to Alcott, not only was it crucial for a young man's moral development to avoid such objects, but it was also necessary for him to know their subtle traps: the obscene picture "under cover of a watch case," the seemingly innocuous book steeped in double entendres (334). To make sure that his readership understood what he meant by "double entendres," Alcott included both a phonetic key to it—"pronounced *entaunders*"—and a definition:

> By this is meant *decent speeches, with double meanings.* I mention these because they prevail, in some parts of the country, to a most alarming degree. . . . Now no serious observer of human life and conduct can doubt that by every species of impure language, whether in the form of hints, innuendos, double entendres, or plainer speech, impure thoughts are awakened, a licentious imagination inflamed, and licentious purposes formed, which would otherwise never have existed.
>
> (311)

For Alcott, as for many of his concerned medical and moral contemporaries, the lure of these vices ("not only *social* but also *solitary*") dangerously illuminated the way "to disease and premature death" (314). Such pronouncements formed, of course, an increasingly common refrain of nineteenth-century sexual advice literature directed at both men and women; to take up Michel Foucault's paradigmatic formulation, they were part of the social mechanisms that turned sex into *"the* secret" in an "endlessly proliferating economy" of biopolitical discourses and regulations.[2] But what is so interesting about Alcott's account here lies less with its anxieties about human erotic activity than it does with Alcott's sense of having to wage an almost losing battle against a kind of print culture that promoted, in increasingly cunning and indefatigable ways, the very activity he sought to restrict. If, as historian Ronald Walters shows, we can trace an intensification of concern with the sexual behavior of the young American population to the proliferation of advice literature in the 1830s and 40s, then we must also see this concern as a motivated response, at least in part, to the creative flair of a certain kind of text passing itself off as something very

different from its surface appearance—as something that slips across a guarded threshold, narrowly eluding the vigilant eyes of America's reputable establishment, rather like a purloined letter, the secret contents of which threaten to bring down the entire house.[3]

This is how the nineteenth-century market in reproductive control and sexual education operated. Although Alcott does not directly mention it, perhaps for fear of appearing lewd, the publishers of pamphlets, advertisements, and tracts publicly disseminating racy information drew upon a vibrant realm of double entendres and euphemisms, particularly in the wake of state laws passed against the sale of contraceptives and the practice of abortion in the two decades before the Civil War.[4] According to Janet Farrell Brodie in her extraordinary *Contraception and Abortion in Nineteenth-Century America,* antebellum Americans quickly learned that "[d]omestic manuals" and "private medical guides for ladies" carried contraceptive advice and ways of incurring miscarriage and that condoms and douching syringes could be purchased where "voluntary-motherhood" products were sold.[5] Throughout the 1840s, gynecological surgeons couched surgical abortions in terms of "unblocking" uterine obstructions; regular physicians sometimes added tiny postscripts to advertisements noting that their wives served female patients for "ailments" related to "suppressed" or arrested menstruation.[6] And like many of their colleagues in the medical profession, popular lecturers on health and physiology imparted details about reproduction in, as Brodie puts it, a "far from unique . . . mix of information and innuendo" (109). Moreover, printed warnings about such insidious materials, by critics like Alcott for instance, inadvertently effected a broader awareness of the availability of birth-control information and erotic materials; in the process of denouncing fornication or abortion, they often disseminated crucial information about it. In some cases, the denouncement itself was just a cover for an announcement, a kind of deft double entendre governing the appearance of outrage. For example, the July 21, 1839, edition of New York's *Sunday Morning News* carried an article proclaiming that the famous abortionist Mrs. Restell "persevered in her nefarious traffic" of pills for "married women who had been indiscreet." Following a statement about New York City's "wise statute" against abortion, as well as a warning that Mrs. Restell euphemistically called herself a "midwife and professor of diseases of women," the author of the article astonishingly reproduces Mrs. Restell's ad in its entirety: "Mme Restell's Sure Remedies—Price $5 and $10; can only be procured at her office, No 1 East 52nd Street." Within this mixture of admonition and exposition, the extent to which the article actually opposed the distribution of Mrs. Restell's product is sufficiently obscured.[7]

Such diverse and circuitous routes around genteel morality and state laws did not proceed entirely unnoticed, however, and several states went so far as to draft legislation against the use of any ambiguous language in reports, pamphlets, and advertisements concerning ailments particular to women. Yet, throughout the 19th century, the laws against it notwithstanding, ambiguous, euphemistic wording continued to frame the sale of products and procedures: the "Female Regulator," the "Woman's Friend," the "Samaritan's Gift for Females." In the words of one New York gynecologist, "every schoolgirl knows the meaning of these terms."[8] According to Helen Lekfkowitz Horowitz, many purveyors of abortion and contraception also figured out how to blur "the boundary between commerce in contraceptives and works of physiology. . . . Given the way that many works of physiology were advertised, it seemed possible that some authors were using the cover of science to print racy material" (284). In fact, in a fairly early American printing of *Artistotle's Masterpiece* (1817), the publisher seems to have attempted to head off exactly this accusation, avowing in the preface that the book was not intended to "stir up bestial appetites" of "unclean" readers but that it was made for women whose "modesty" precluded them from asking for help "in matters of the womb."[9]

In the medical schools themselves, the number of publications on the anatomy of female fertility—particularly the mysteries of ovulation and menstruation—also grew at an extraordinary rate. As historian of gynecology, James Ricci, puts it: "The gynaecological literature of the first half of the nineteenth century is immense; of the latter half, gigantic."[10] By mid-century, American gynecologists were divided in their support of abortion, and those who opposed it began actively seeking the support of church and state. With the promotion of the theory that life began at conception, abortion became linked to the "characteristic privilege of sovereign power . . . the right to decide life and death" (to quote Foucault on the state's surveillance of sex), and as an increasing number of gynecologists began to equate it with infanticide, abortion came under a new slate of statutory regulations.[11] Abortion also became tied to fears of adultery and promiscuity, to a prevailing belief that the procedure literally erased evidence of sexual misconduct and therefore licensed it. For one mid-century gynecologist, anxious about the direction of American civilization, it seemed that "the old-fashioned womb [would] cease to exist, except in history."[12]

It is within this remarkably public world of advertisements, books, newspaper articles, and laws on the subject of reproductive control that I wish to place "The Purloined Letter." Published in 1845, at the high point of what Walters calls the "public discourse about sex and related matters" in nineteenth-century America, Poe's tale engages with the controversies these dis-

courses generated and revealed, and it does so by means of the very same indirection and innuendo that suffuse many of them.[13] As a result, it illuminates, even as it attempts to screen, the secrets contained within the purloined letter, pushing us to ask what exactly is so pressing about the "affair" of a letter stolen from a woman's "boudoir":

> 'Perhaps it is the very simplicity of the thing which puts you at fault,' said [Dupin].
>
> 'What nonsense you *do* talk!' replied the Prefect, laughing heartily.
>
> 'Perhaps the mystery is a little *too* plain,' said Dupin.
>
> 'Oh, good heavens! who ever heard of such an idea?'
>
> 'A little *too* self-evident.'
>
> 'Ha! ha! ha!—ha! ha! ha!—ho! ho! ho!'—roared our visiter, profoundly amused.
>
> (331)

If we're the kind of readers who are in the know, those familiar with the trials of famous abortionists (such as Madame Restell) printed throughout the New England papers in the 1840s, with the trade in erotic materials (as well as with the arrests of the tradesmen), and with the contraception ads that seemed to have been slipped into every possible magazine, then we can begin to hear the subject of reproductive control being spoken in "The Purloined Letter." As Jacques Lacan notes about Poe's tale, the "dialogue may be more fertile than it seems."[14] It is only by inferring the matter and magnitude of the letter's contents, moreover, that we can then fathom both the depth of the urgency it repeatedly communicates and the questions the letter raises about adultery and abortion in mid-nineteenth-century America.

In this essay, I argue that Poe's "The Purloined Letter" is immersed in the kind of double entendres that Alcott discerns in every corner of his mid-nineteenth-century world—from euphemistic advertisements for abortions to slyly erotic medical guidebooks—and that the tale's "decent speeches with double meanings" underscore its exploration of the decoys surrounding sex in 1840s America. Through its layers of innuendo and its metaphors, "The Purloined Letter" also explores the theme of passing (as white, as faithful, as legitimate, as something other than what you are), binding the notion of a counterfeit self or appearance to cultural tensions about the sexual freedom of white women. It is this particular anxiety about women, captured in the maneuvers of Poe's "exalted royal personage," that the tale's most famous critics, Jacques Lacan, Jacques Derrida, and Barbara Johnson, at once detect and overlook in their discussions of its hidden and surface narratives. Contrary to their shared conviction that the contents of the letter are never revealed, that the letter's significance does not lie with this revelation but with the actions its absence precipitates, I will demonstrate that the contents of the letter are almost entirely divulged and necessarily so; we just have to identify the context within which the tale's innuendo resonates. Like the light-fingered and "lynx-eye[d]" Minister, who assembles a series of interconnected hints, manages to decipher the over-turned letter and thus "fathom[s] [the woman's] secret," Poe's reader can follow the same trail toward the peculiar and perilous nature of an open secret.[15]

A key hint arises in the tale's attention to the cleverness of the characters who can decode what another character's body tries to disguise or suppress. Thus, although the Minister cannot read an "unexposed" letter, he discerns its significance by tracing its appearance on the table first to the "confusion of the personage" and then to her sudden composure in relation to the "personage who stood at her below" (332-333). Dupin adopts the same strategy, reading the Minister's body language—his "yawning, lounging, and dawdling"—as an elaborate performance designed to mask an intensity of energy at the same time that Dupin himself conceals the movement of his own eyes behind dark glasses (346). If two can play at that game, then so can three. Because the woman in the tale, who also uses the strategy, does not overtly react when the Minister steals her letter, she quickly obscures her despair, splitting her bodily appearance from what she hides beneath its surface or within it. To the man at her elbow, nothing changes. He sees her for what she is: completely visible and above suspicion, like the letter on the table. He does not presume any contradictory meaning to her composure, nor the fact that something on display might also be out of sight.

In such ways, Poe's narrative immediately connects the physical existence of the woman with the letter, placing their shared and material manifestations into a framework of congruency. In fact, the kinetic shift through which the Minister "perceives the paper" and then "fathoms her secret" effectively merges the woman with the letter, as the one entity encloses the secret of the other. The word "fathom" is telling, too, because its etymological affinity with nautical exploration suggests the sense of literally plumbing something deep and dark. What I want to stress in this discussion, or to return to the surface of the tale, is the contextual legibility not only of the letter but also of the woman's body. She may never directly appear to the narrator, may never come forward for a complete description, but she sets all of the events in motion; she contacts the police, devises a reward, and describes the letter to the Prefect, whose own detailed description of it to Dupin and the narrator is not duplicated, only recounted. This sly, second-hand representation on the part of Poe's narrator once again aligns the woman's body with her letter, generating the idea that what she wants back is precisely that alignment, that ability to decide how to rep-

resent—and perhaps whether to deliver—something in her keeping. As she works behind the scenes to regain this control, Poe indicates that the potential danger to her body is very real, for his narrator opens "The Purloined Letter" with reference to "the affair of the Rue Morgue, and the mystery attending the murder of Marie Rogêt," and therefore casts "The Purloined Letter" as part of a trilogy in which the women compelling the other two investigations are mutilated cadavers (330). Their wretched fate frames her story, and she seems to know it.

The tale abruptly shifts from the narrator's recollection of the murdered women to the intrusion into his study of the Prefect, an action he casts as a coincidence in light of his present musings.

> [T]o any casual observer, [Dupin and the narrator] might have seemed intently and exclusively occupied with the curling eddies of smoke that oppressed the atmosphere of the chamber. For myself, however, I was mentally discussing certain topics which had formed matter for conversation between us at an earlier period of the evening; I mean the affair of the Rue Morgue, and the mystery attending the murder of Marie Rogêt. I looked upon it, therefore, as something of a coincidence, when the door of our apartment was thrown open and admitted our old acquaintance, Monsieur G—, the Prefect of the Parisian police.
>
> (330)

This is a significant narrative move because it indicates another behind-the-scenes design: a prompting to bear in mind that the narrator is not omniscient but present in the tale, making decisions about what to include and suppress, about what to cast as coincidental or interconnected. As an ally and admirer of Dupin, who is himself a "partisan of the lady concerned," the narrator finds himself treading carefully around the particulars of the purloined letter (348). Too much is at stake. But he is also a story-teller, and his impulse is to urge his reader through artful suggestions and juxtapositions toward the secrets opening up around him. His hinting is rich, and things are laid out with a seeming innocence and frankness—and the double entendres and sexual innuendo cover their own tracks. Thus, if he had to, he could protest that his inclusion of the description of the musket that shoots blanks is just a description of an empty musket and not an allusion to anyone's penis (347-348); that the reference to an "unusual gaping in the joints" or to a "secret drawer" simply describes furniture and not a woman's pelvis (335, 336); that Paris is Paris and America, America.

No discussion of Poe's tale can proceed without taking into account the fact that Poe's cagey language compelled extended deliberations from, as Barbara Johnson puts it, "two eminent French thinkers whose readings emit their own . . . call-to-analysis."[16] For it seems that the debate between Jacques Lacan and Jacques Derrida over "The Purloined Letter," coupled with Johnson's own dazzling intervention into it, has come to frame Poe's text with a definitive, if not final, word on it. Getting past this circumference in order to offer anything new necessitates, I think, keeping in clear view the levels of complexity and the textual detail that each of these thinkers brings to bear upon and unearths from "The Purloined Letter." We cannot, in other words, simply acknowledge the Lacan-Derrida-Johnson context for reading "The Purloined Letter" and then set it aside. Again in Johnson's words: "The urgency of these undertakings [Derrida's, Lacan's] cannot . . . be overestimated, since the logic of metaphysics, of politics, of belief, and of knowledge itself is based on the imposition of definable objective frontiers and outlines whose possibility and/or justifiability are here [in "The Purloined Letter"] being put into question" (231). Between them, Lacan and Derrida entirely overturn the impression that "much is made of nothing" in Poe's tale, as an early reviewer described it in 1845.[17] And, following them, Johnson elucidates the link Poe forges between language and power, clarifying what it means for subjectivity to be formed within a structure and "by a letter" (248).

Because all three analyses take up questions surrounding being, legitimacy, and femininity, all three inadvertently point to the same issues surrounding abortion in the 1840s, issues that become legible in "The Purloined Letter" once a historical frame of reference is set around it. When this frame is set, the lines of inquiry in Lacan and Derrida through Poe's text to questions concerning why "the law holds the woman in position as a signifier," as Lacan puts it, can then be directed to concerns that reproductive control liberated women in unpredictable social and symbolic ways.[18] To clarify: if Lacan sees at work in "The Purloined Letter" the law of language as it forces the subject into a system of sexual difference, a law he understands as a paternal claim to and redirection of maternal production and identification, then the question of the subject's origin within the maternal body becomes another level of that claim. The phallus (understood as patriarchal discourse and injunction) shores up the immense anxiety of nonexistence and of existence's contingency upon the mother's prerogative, bringing the physiological origin of an embryo in line with the symbolic origin of an embryonic subject. The vulnerability of the entire system rests on the possibility that the mother can violate the law and suspend this teleological narrative of subjectivity; if careful and quiet, only she knows if a fetus truly exists and what its name really might be—bastard or heir—regardless of paternal entitlement. The criminalization of abortion in Poe's time developed out of that existential vulnerability and through a medical-philosophical narrative that pulled the fetus into view and obscured

the woman attached to it. Thus, it is at precisely the places where Lacan and Derrida work out such concepts as sign and origin in Poe's tale that the allusive themes of pregnancy and termination also unfold, and "The Purloined Letter" aligns the question of a woman's reproductive choice with the broader questions of framing and truth, contingencies and contracts.[19] The medical archives of nineteenth-century gynecology permit us to recognize what Poe's innuendo intimates on a very specific level: "a personage of most exalted station" is pregnant by a man other than her husband, "the other exalted personage," and she possesses the option of abortion, a procedure by which she can erase the only material evidence, apart from the letter, of her affair (332).

Given the presence of arguments in 1840s America that abortion and adultery went hand in hand—that reproductive control could license women to cuckold men—it is significant that Lacan calls the woman in Poe's tale the guardian of legitimacy and notes that "we are assured of but one thing: the Queen cannot bring [the letter] to the knowledge of her lord and master" (42). In fact, it's as though Lacan assumes "The Purloined Letter" is about an affair, that it is of course a love letter connected in some way to betrayal and to "the ceremony of returning letters [at] the extinction of the fires of love's feasts" activating the plot (40). For Lacan, that people in high places commit adultery is a matter not really worth discussing; the exalted rank of the protagonists in "The Purloined Letter" simply saves their escapades "from vaudeville" (33). Yet, the more pressing issue in his analysis involves the way in which the tale functions as an allegory of psychoanalysis and the letter a signifier that possesses its subjects. As a result, he at once raises and evades the very questions he poses about legitimacy and about the role that a woman (or "woman") plays as its "guardian" within a structure of paternal inheritance and naming. What, for instance, is indicated about this structure if the words of a woman function as the only confirmation of both the presence of a fetus and the identity of its father? Lacan traces instead the path by which the letter, associated as it is with absence and femininity, arrives at the place of sexual difference. In a way, my argument follows his route, back to the female body and to a scene of symbolic castration in which the phallus is cut off from the certainty of paternity.[20]

According to Lacan, even if Dupin were to rip up the letter, we would still have a kind of metaphysical language, still be subjected to it; Dupin's guarantee of the letter's return to its protector demonstrates the fulfillment of his duty to communicate the sign's conflict with being: its split nature in relation to, as Derrida puts it, the symbolic absence "between the legs of woman," "the place of castration."[21] But the woman is more than the letter's guardian or protector; she is also its source, and the condition of its theft points to an identifiable relocation and not necessarily to a timeless law. For Derrida, Lacan's interpretation not only establishes the phallus as a privileged signifier "depend[ing] neither on the signified, nor on the subject," but also erects a kind of "authentic life" for it, one that somehow persists in a realm beyond its material contingencies (423). "Materiality," says Derrida, "the sensory and repetitive side of the recording, the paper letter, drawings in ink, can be divided or multiplied, destroyed or set adrift. . . . If by some misfortune the phallus were divisible or reduced to the status of a part object, the entire edifice would collapse, and this must be [he adds with irony] avoided at all costs" (472-73, 478-79). The system of the symbolic, as Lacan thus formulates it, keeps the phallus in its proper place as, Derrida says, a "symbol only of an absence" and in the custody of (though not represented by) the woman (424). Derrida argues that, as a consequence, Lacan invests his interpretation in the "truth" of castration and in a theory of the signifier's "destiny as destination" (436). "What is called man and what is called woman might be subject to [phallogocentrism]," Derrida concedes, but "[a]ll of phallogocentrism is articulated on the basis of a determined *situation*, . . . An (individual, perceptual, local, cultural, historical, etc.) situation on the basis of which what is called a 'sexual theory' is elaborated . . ." (480-481).

From Derrida's perspective, the woman in "The Purloined Letter" is a figure who both sustains and threatens the system which contains her; everything about her leaks its divisions. The power of her letter resides in the writing itself, not in some original essence, for as Poe's tale indicates, the contracts, cast as both fiat and blackmail, bind one figure to another within a structure of fiction and narration. Poe's narrator is deeply invested in writing, Derrida reminds us, and how it transmits history and inheritance through a network of narrated frames.[22] In this network, and in the absence of any other proof, one could add that a child is the King's if the Queen says it is. Derrida's insistence upon the importance of the *parergon*, or the narrative frames, in fact creates an analogy with the woman's corporeal existence: like the story's enclosure within other stories, which gets repeatedly overlooked, her pregnant body becomes rendered as similarly supplemental, derivative, and ornamental material in relation to the paternal narrative of birthright that is generated through it. Yet, like Lacan, Derrida does not elaborate upon this analogy, nor upon the pun repeatedly produced around the issue of the woman "delivering" the letter. Though similarly rich in double entendres that open up the structure of sexual difference to the problem of its reproduction, Derrida's essay stops short of exploring how the threat of femininity, as Poe's tale indicates, is located between her words and her body—a body that threatens to split not in half but into two (438).

In her essay on the dizzying triptych of Poe, Lacan, and Derrida, Barbara Johnson draws attention to the rivalry between Dupin and the Minister within "The Purloined Letter" and to the rivalry between Derrida and Lacan over it. Pointing out where their theories tend to overlap and illuminate each other, Johnson notes Derrida's failure to acknowledge his debt to Lacan's *Écrits* and Lacan's refusal to credit Derrida's grammatology. In her own reading of Poe's tale, she folds their points together in order to address a third rivalry: that of Atreus and Thyestes, the story Dupin refers to in the letter he leaves for the Minister in place of the stolen one. Thus, enclosed within "The Purloined Letter" is an allusion to a tale involving adultery, infanticide, and debts recovered by ruthless violence. In fact, the Atreus-Thyestes reference functions as much more than a literary allusion and becomes a powerful echo, sounding a message down through Poe's tale and into the letters (Dupin's, the woman's) themselves. In Johnson's words, the "story is framed by its own content" (236). Moreover, in the version of the myth to which Dupin refers, it's a purloined letter that informs King Atreus of his wife's betrayal with his brother Thyestes; the Queen's own handwriting names Thyestes, not Atreus, as the father of her child. Brilliantly taking all of these debts and rivalries together, Johnson asserts that "the questions [raised by these texts] are legion: What is a man? Who is the child's father? What is the relation between incest, murder, and the death of a child? What is a king? How can we read the letter of our destiny? What is seeing?" (236).

Although Johnson does not track these questions back into "The Purloined Letter," preferring to leave them as latent implications about the contingent nature of power, the tale itself follows them through to prospective answers. It binds the mythological account of adultery to the events at hand and artfully implies that, like Atreus's wife, this "exalted personage" is also pregnant. And although Johnson contends that the "letter's message is never revealed" (113), we are permitted to read all of the other words in "The Purloined Letter" and to consider what we select for detection—to go wide instead of deep. Without disputing the far-reaching, philosophical ideas that Johnson uncovers in or addresses through the tale, I remain unsure about her point that Poe offers "no possibility of a position of analytic mastery" (214). For, as a potential victim of the fierce retribution steadily referenced across the tale, the woman must assume this position and influence the interpretative direction of her letter. It is she who must master the events in an attempt to secure the letter's return to her, and her perspective exists in relation to the narrator's dispersed and repeated references to death and mutilation. She not only faces the prospect of being killed but of being killed in the kind of frenzy of violence that engulfs the women in the Rue Morgue and Marie Rogêt, as well as the cadavers served up for dinner in the myth of Atreus and Thyestes.

Ostensibly describing a "game of puzzles," Dupin's words here hint at the text's method of disclosing how the woman's hidden letter reflects her "excessively obvious" embodied perspective:

> A novice in the game generally seeks to embarrass his opponents by giving them the most minutely lettered names; but the adept selects such words as stretch, in large characters, from one end of the chart to the other. These, like the over-largely lettered signs and placards in the street, escape observation by dint of being excessively obvious; and here the physical oversight is precisely analogous with the moral inapprehension by which the intellect suffers to pass unnoticed those considerations which are too obtrusively and too palpably self-evident.
>
> (345)

The letter's content may not be directly presented to us but its message is disseminated throughout (or "stretched" across) the tale and beyond it, in the Atreus-Thyestes myth and in the texts circulating in Poe's 19th-century America. These signifiers indicate a signified and even a referent: a fetus, one that the "exalted royal personage" may or may not bring to term.

We are told at the outset, for example, that the woman's urgent concern rests on 'the non-appearance of certain results'—evasive wording that slyly imparts how the suspicion of pregnancy begins with the nonappearance of a certain monthly event (332). The Prefect later divulges that "[t]he personage robbed is more thoroughly convinced, every day, of the necessity of reclaiming her letter" (333). And again later: "[t]he fact is, it is becoming of more and more importance every day; and the reward has been lately doubled" (337). The passage of time, a pivotal element in the woman's distress, becomes bound up with the growing size of the reward, and because the latter does not remain fixed as the former progresses, this implication follows: that as the days and months pass, the reward is not the only thing growing in size. Mirroring or duplicating (in financial terms) another expanding entity in the woman's keeping, the reward has both a metaphorical and literal purpose in the text. This purpose becomes especially legible when it is considered in relation to the words "conceal" and "concealment," which occur no fewer than seven times in the tale and which resonate with a lengthy (at least two-centuries) legal and public perception of hidden, clandestine pregnancies and suspicious infant deaths. Poe's nineteenth-century audience would have known that the word "concealment," accompanied by any hint of a missing newborn, denoted a very serious crime. In Dupin's words, "in all cases of concealment, a disposal of the article concealed—a disposal of it in this *recherché* manner—is in the very first instance, presumable and presumed" (341).

If a child is in fact born in the eighteen-month time frame of the tale, then he or she bears only the appearance of legitimacy and presents a surface behind which something else is hidden, a surface the letter threatens to break, a lineage it can set off course. "'Well, I may venture so far as to say,' the Prefect hints, 'that the paper gives its holder a certain power in a certain quarter where such power is immensely valuable'" (332). The implicit question as to why lineage is traced through paternity thus also resonates throughout the tale, for paternal naming and inheritance involve the sovereignty of the conceptual over the material and a severing of the link to the mother's body. In the tale's "economy of justice," to borrow Johnson's terminology—"The Purloined Letter" is after all a *"crime* story," she emphatically reminds us (214)—the redirection (or theft) of legitimacy from a maternal connection to a paternal claim underscores all of the male rivalries over the letter. The purloining of what belongs to a woman, moreover, takes place in front of her eyes: "Its rightful owner saw, but, of course, dared not call attention to the act, in the presence of the third personage who stood at her elbow" (Poe 333). That is, she comprehends the system of which she is a part, she perfectly sees how it works, and she maneuvers for latitude within it. As John Muller and William Richardson suggest in their interpretation of Lacan's essay on the tale, "The position of woman as signifier recalls Lévi-Strauss's thesis . . .: that the origin of language and culture involved establishing pacts by means of the exchange of women between groups (for whom the women then symbolized the pacts)."[23] A suggestive pun quickly emerges in the word "letter": if we consider that a woman's body lets blood monthly, makes her a blood letter, then this letter's circulation within a male system founds her value upon a process of exchange. The patrilineal direction of kinship, in other words, equates the meaning of the female body with a sealed envelope, one that contains a contract formulated in relation to a restricted economy. As Derrida muses, what if the letter were the property of no one, if its writing were set "adrift," "graft[ed] onto other writings" (484)? Or, in the words of one of the 1840s' most popular physicians and lecturers on sex and reproduction, Frederick Hollick, "No mater how obtained, by purchase, force, or strategem, a woman, as a wife, has always been considered . . . as a mere possession, like an animal. [The idea] crops up in many of our laws, customs, and ways of thinking and speaking. The term, 'my wife,' is still used by many with the same intent and meaning as my dog, or my horse."[24]

In "The Purloined Letter," we are told that the Minister who takes the letter fixes a "large black" seal on it, a seal bearing the D— cipher or the Minister's initial. The seal, originally "small and red, with the ducal arms of the S— family," is obscured and the woman's "diminutive and feminine" handwriting is marked over in a "bold and decided" way (346). These seals determine the worth and authenticity of the letter and its contents, a letter that, now protruding from a cheap card-rack, gives the appearance of "worthlessness" (347). By virtue of the tale's metaphorical dexterity, the image of the letter's placement (the careless thrusting of it, no less) among "five or six visiting cards" insinuates the idea of promiscuity and illuminates the idea that the Minister can take the same entity (the woman, her letter, her fetus) and cast it within an entirely different frame (346). He possesses the story that can turn something pure into something prostituted. Suspended in this narrative, the woman risks the loss of her whiteness; the "soiled and torn condition of the letter" reflects back upon her and her offspring. Should the letter's contents be revealed, the possible child would be written off as worthless and illegitimate, a dead-end in the line of descent. He or she may look like the real thing, but would fall into the same category as a "trumpery fillagree card-rack of pasteboard," hanging from an umbilical-like "dirty blue ribbon." (346).

The play of color, of black against blue and red, furthermore, draws definitions of race and blood quantum into the crisis. Given that antebellum white women, especially the "exalted" or blueblood ones, were invested with the safekeeping of blood purity against any kind of amalgamation, it is possible that the tale's resolutely unnamed matter of blackmail generates the homophonic double of "black male" and thus adds another level of possible transgression to the secrets of the letter.[25] Although any kind of promiscuity threatened to sidetrack a line of descent from its so-called uncorrupted origin, it was the potential for contamination of white by black that lent the threat such urgency. As Joan Dayan writes in "Poe, Persons, and Property":

> Poe moves us back to a time when a myth of blood conferred an unpolluted, legitimate pedigree ("The Fall of the House of Usher" or "William Wilson," both 1839) and forward to an analytics of blood that ushered in a complex of color: the ineradicable stain, the drop that could not be seen but must be feared ("Ligeia," "The Masque of the Red Death," or *The Narrative of Arthur Gordon Pryn* [1838]). . . . An innate quality (the unseen blood stain) could result in the conversion of a person into property. . . .[26]

The transformation through blood did not work the other way around, of course, for a white man's seal on a black woman's body conferred nothing in antebellum America, and descent remained traced through her.

Like the tales mentioned by Dayan, "The Purloined Letter" captures, in similarly allusive language, the possibility of an imperceptible stain upon a family of a "most exalted station" (Poe 332). And, at the same time that it explores the ways in which adultery in the 1840s was not just a matter of infidelity but a crime against the blood, an opening up of blood-lines to uncontrolled

circulation, it gestures toward the accompanying development of proto-eugenic gynecological treatises on racial degeneration through bad breeding.[27] As physician Thomas Burgeland rhetorically asks in his 1837 study *Physiological Observations,* "would [the abolitionist] feel any objection for his daughter to enter into a matrimonial connexion with one of those beings whose cause he so impetuously advocated?" (35). Or as Hester Pendleton exclaims in a similar vein, a woman must choose her mate wisely; it is not by chance that "one child is born a fool, another a prodigy."[28] In an oblique reference to Madame Restell, the "infamous lady physician," Pendleton warns her readers to avoid the services she advertises "in the daily papers;" a woman should not do what she wants and then allow herself to "be probed with a whalebone." All of these kinds of perils crowd upon and into the purloined letter, a document that is, as we are told, "much soiled and crumpled" as it passes from the woman's boudoir to the Minister's apartment (Poe 346).

In such a degraded condition, the letter's description yields a subtle pattern of double entendres, especially when it is combined with that of the Minister's apartment. Noting these echoes, Derrida raises the possibility that "'the purloined letter, like an immense female body, stretch[es] out across the Minister's office when Dupin enters,'" adding that Dupin ultimately locates it "between the 'legs' of the fireplace" (440). In the context of nineteenth-century gynecology, the letter's position on the fireplace becomes a tongue-in-cheek reference to popular theories of a wayward woman's overheated womb, the *furor uterinus,* resulting from thwarted and illicit love.[29] Moreover, if we can read the woman's body as metaphorically "stretched across" the room, then the very medical-like instruments used to probe it should not be tossed aside as irrelevant information, even if they're considered ineffective procedure on the tale's literal level of narration. Because these instruments tend only to be noted in the tale's scholarship as evidence of the police's failed detective work, the woman's body once more recedes to the background and the obvious "protrusion" of her letter fails to designate what is happening with her belly. Putting this stretched and splayed body back in the picture brings into focus the subject of nineteenth-century reproductive control, spotlighting in particular the trademark utensils of gynecology's abortion procedures: the uterine sound and curette, two long and needle-like utensils used to probe the uterus for different types of growths.

In *One Hundred Years of Gynaecology, 1800-1900,* James Ricci discusses how the development of gynecology into the nineteenth century's largest field of medical specialization was accompanied by countless new procedures and instruments. As he puts it, "The female genital organs were subjected to minute analysis and [different] areas were described in detail" (5). Gynecologists created four-hundred different kinds of specula and used them, along with the sound and the curette, to boldly "explore the cavity of the uterus" (25). Although Ricci does not mention it, the spectacular expansion of gynecology in the 1830s and 40s—as well as the controversies he notes over women's submission to hazardous treatments involving sounds and curettes—must be understood in terms of women's quest for reproductive control. A curette, for instance, was not in all cases used to tap benign uterine cysts. Many nineteenth-century American women would have learned how to read the secondary meanings of gynecological procedures and advertisements. Making something illegal or illicit does not repress it, as Foucault reminds us, but rather multiplies ways of saying and not saying it:

> 'Suppose you detail,' said [the narrator of "The Purloined Letter"], 'the particulars of your search.'
>
> 'Why the fact is,' [replied the Prefect] . . . 'we searched *every where*. . . . We opened every possible drawer; and I presume you know that, to a properly trained police agent, such a thing as a *secret* drawer is impossible. Any man is a dolt who permits a "secret" drawer to escape him in a search of this kind. The thing is *so* plain. There is a certain amount of bulk—of space—to be accounted for in every cabinet. . . . After the cabinets we took the chairs. The cushions we probed with the fine long needles you have seen me employ. From the tables we removed the tops.'
>
> 'Why so?' [asked the narrator] . . . 'Couldn't the cavity be detected by sounding?' . . .
>
> 'By no means, if, when the article is deposited, a sufficient wadding of cotton be placed around it.'
>
> 'But you could not have removed—you could not have taken to pieces *all* the articles of furniture in which it would have been possible to make a deposit in the manner you mention. A letter may be compressed into a thin spiral roll, not differing much in shape or bulk from a large knitting-needle, and in this form it might be inserted into the rung of a chair, for example. . . . I presume . . . you probed the beds and bed-clothes'
>
> 'Certainly: we opened every package and parcel. . . . We also measured the thickness of every book-*cover,* with the most accurate admeasurement, and applied to each the most jealous scrutiny of the microscope. Had any of the bindings been recently meddled with it would have been utterly impossible that the fact should have escaped observation. Some five or six volumes, just from the hands of the binder, we carefully probed, longitudinally, with the needles.'
>
> 'You looked into the cellars?'
>
> 'We did.'
>
> (335-337)

With trenchant echoes of gynecological instruments and procedures, and through droll metaphors for the dark interiority of the female anatomy (cabinets, cavities, cellars), this dialogue represents the unrepresentable:

the secret of abortion contained within the purloined letter.[30] "What is all this boring, and probing, and sounding, and scrutinizing with the microscope . . . ?," asks Dupin in both a condensed recapitulation of the telling verbs and an almost verbatim duplication of the language of surgical gynecology (341). Like everything else in the tale, that which is private, secret, and unspoken is at the same time public, clear, and apparent—at least when approached through a particular frame of reference.

As a result, gestures and words meant to disguise information may in fact divulge it. This is Dupin's advantage. Behind his dark glasses and ironic statements, he reads both linguistic and corporeal signs: the Minister's sham laziness, the Prefect's vocal hesitations. The question of the body's production of signs also occurs in the tale's attention to handwriting; it seems that handwriting is something unique, inherently recognizable, something that ties, like an umbilical cord, the production of the words to the producer of them. It's because the letter is in the woman's distinctive handwriting that she is in such trouble. Furthermore, Dupin remarks that the Minister will know who fooled him with a new letter because Dupin's own handwriting will be familiar to him. We also observe the Prefect write and sign the reward check for Dupin. In each case, the handwriting at once materializes a source and a destination.

But, twice the word "*fac-simile*" occurs in the tale, thus collapsing any guarantee or endorsement of authenticity (347, 348). "The Purloined Letter" here opens onto the issue of passing that follows from its exploration of adultery and abortion. In other words, if bodies give something away or express something authentic, it is because a conceptual framework of surface and depth, of the feigned and the *bona fide,* is already in place. What is counterfeit in one context is sterling in another. Though the body may be a source of signifying innovations, there is nothing inherent in the blood, nothing that yields a timeless secret or value. Even a maternal body, with its pronounced dilation, can be concealed or circumvented, and the question of paternity can certainly be covered up.

Dupin returns exactly this possibility to the woman in "The Purloined Letter." If there is a child born (after all that probing), then Dupin permits it to pass as legitimate, realizing that passing is all there is. If an abortion took place, he leaves it out of his scheme's equation; his goal is not to see the woman punished as an adulteress who tried to get rid of the evidence.[31] Though motivated by his own desire to outwit the Minister and to cash in on the reward, Dupin's remarks about the success of his reasoning resonate with significance about blood quantum, legitimacy, and morality. He states:

> [M]athematical reasoning is merely logic applied to observation upon form and quantity. The great error lies in supposing that even the truths of what is called *pure*

algebra, are abstract or general truths. . . . What is true of relation—of form and quantity—is often grossly false in regard to morals, for example. . . . There are numerous other mathematical truths which are only truths within the limits of *relation*. . . . [O]ccasions may occur where x^2+px is *not* altogether equal to q.

(342-43)

His words here seem to directly quote and disparage the kind of racial "science" circulating in early nineteenth-century America and evident in this 1815 algebraist's theorem:

. . . [T]he algebraical notation is the most convenient and intelligible. Let us express the pure blood of the white in the capital letters of the printed alphabet, the pure blood of the negro in the small letters of the printed alphabet, and any given mixture of either, by way of abridgment in MS. letters.

Let the first crossing be of *a*, a pure negro, with A, pure white. The unit of blood of the issue being composed of the half of that of each parent, will be *a*/2 + *A*/2. Call it, for abbreviation *b* (half-blood).

Let the second crossing be that of *b* and B, the blood of the issue will be *b*/2 + *B*/2, or substituting *b*/2 its equivalent, it will be *a*/4 + *A*/4 + *B*/2, call it *q* (quarteroon) being 1/4 negro blood.[32]

The algebraist then continues through several more mathematical formulas, concluding with "*e*": "But if *e* be emancipated, he becomes a free white man, and a citizen of the United States to all intents and purposes" (114). For Dupin, the world cannot be so neatly ordered; it is a place of metaphors and combinations and not of rigid categories. Repudiating the kind of black-and-white notions which dictate, for instance, that no one man can be both "mathematician and . . . poet," he refuses to allow the purloined letter to be put in the service of taxonomies of blood and legitimacy (Poe 344). In the end, his thinking averts the kind of fratricidal violence implied in the myth of Atreus and Thyestes, which, in 1845, amounts to a foreboding message about the escalating rhetoric surrounding racial identity, white motherhood, and the future of the nation.

Notes

1. 330. Alcott's italics.

2. *The History of Sexuality*, 35, 48. Foucault's italics.

3. See Walters' Introduction to *Primers for Prudery: Sexual Advice To Victorian Americans*, in which he analyzes the market for the literature in terms of a complex "web of personal and social considerations" (15).

4. In the 1830s and 1840s, every major New England newspaper carried advertisements for abortion drugs, condoms, and surgical abortion procedures; in some cities, advertisements for these products and procedures were also left in hotel lobbies and in railroad depots. In response to the emerging legislation, the number of ads remained high, but their wording became increasingly veiled. See also Horowitz, *Rereading Sex*, 70-122.

5. See Janet Farrell Brodie's chapter titled "The Antebellum Public Audience," 136-80. See also Nancy Theriot's *Mothers and Daughters in Nineteenth-Century America*, in which she demonstrates that the term "voluntary motherhood" was in circulation well before the late nineteenth-century feminist movement of the same name came into being (Theriot, 41-2).

6. For example, the January 7, 1843, issue of *The New York Lancet*, which carried an advertisement by a Mr. J. H. Ross, "Cupper and Leecher," who publicized in barely readable text that "Mrs. R. applies Leeches to the Os Uteri"—one way to cure the problem of a woman's so-called arrested monthly bleeding.

7. New York *Sunday Morning News*, July 21, 1835.

8. Quoted in Brodie, *Contraception and Abortion*, 225. See also her chapter titled "Criminalizing Reproductive Control" for the progression of state laws against contraception and abortion in the second half of the nineteenth century.

9. Pseudo-Aristotle, v.

10. *One Hundred Years*, vii.

11. Foucault, 147. See the last chapter of *The History of Sexuality, Vol. I*, in which Foucault analyzes how definitions of sex and life came under state power. The "thorough medicalization of women's bodies," Foucault asserts, was carried out "in the name of the responsibility [women] owed to the health of their children, the solidity of the family institution, and the safeguarding of society" (146). See also Brodie on the rise of restrictive legislation in her chapter "Criminalizing Reproductive Control," which opens with her argument that the second half of the nineteenth century saw a new effort to "restore American 'social purity'" through the restriction of sexuality and the "control of reproduction" (254).

12. Quoted in Ricci, *One Hundred Years*, 37.

13. Walters, *Primers for Prudery*, 2.

14. "Seminar," 34.

15. Edgar Allan Poe. "The Purloined Letter." *The Fall of the House of Usher and Other Writings*. (London: Penguin, 1986), 332. All quotations from the tale are from this text. All italics are Poe's.

16. "The Frame of Reference," 213.

17. "There is much made of nothing in 'The Purloined Letter,'" writes the reviewer in 1845, "the story of which is simple . . ." Quoted in Mabbott, "The Text," 5.

18. "Seminar," 81.

19. If anything breaks the contract binding women to a notion of instinctive motherhood, it's abortion. According to Helen Lefkowitz Horowitz's findings, any news in the 1840s that a married woman had paid a visit to Madame Restell threatened the foundations of "male control" (206).

20. For example, on the front page of *Madame Restell, by a physician of New York,* the author included the epigraph, "Thou shalt not commit adultery."

21. *The Post Card,* 444, 439. Derrida's italics.

22. The Dupin trilogy repeatedly calls our attention to written material: the reward check, the letter, and the Prefect's notes in "The Purloined Letter"; the books, newspaper articles, and the reward notice for the orangutan in "The Murders in the Rue Morgue"; the quoted newspaper articles that make up the majority of "The Mystery of Marie Rogêt."

23. *The Purloined Poe,* 95.

24. *The Origin of Life,* 723.

25. The word "blackmail" had entered the language about a half-century before Poe's time. For a great discussion of blackmail and its link to the policing of sexual standards, see McLaren, *Sexual Blackmail.*

26. 119.

27. To offer just three examples here: Burgeland, *Physiological Observations,* which asserts that "*the Negro Race nearly approaches the monkey*" (36, Burgeland's italics); Walker, *Intermarriage; or the Mode in Which, and the Causes Why, Beauty, Health and Intellect Result from Certain Unions, and Deformity, Disease and Insanity, from Others,* which establishes criteria for mate selection; and Lugol, *Why Will You Die, or Researches on Scrofula,* with reference to the propagation of disease by inheritance and intermarriage, which imagines great families becoming "extinct" because of "defects" produced by "cross[ing] the races" (106, 233).

28. *The Parents Guide,* 1, 209.

29. See Dixon, *Perilous Chastity: Women and Illness in Pre-Enlightenment Art and Medicine* for an in-depth discussion of this condition. Dixon's study of numerous paintings of seventeenth- and eighteenth-century lovesick women highlights the repeated depiction of a woman with open legs before a firepot or a fireplace. See, in particular, her chapter titled "The Womb Occupied, Restored, and Satiated: Corporeal Cures" for the references to *furor uterinus* in medical treatises, proverbs, emblem books, and dictionaries of the time. Though Dixon does not mention it, many of the paintings she reproduces for discussion also depict the spread-legged woman holding a letter, the contents of which we cannot see, as she swoons before a doctor.

30. This notion of the obscured representation of abortion is also asserted by Laura Saltz in her essay on "The Mystery of Marie Rogêt." Demonstrating that Poe knew that a botched abortion was the probable cause of Mary Rogêt's death and drawing on the newspaper accounts of Madame Restell's trials, Saltz argues that "The Mystery" is a tale that buries an abortion within its elliptical, layered narrative. Saltz also discusses "The Murders in the Rue Morgue," the other tale in the trilogy that includes "The Purloined Letter," but she only once refers to "The Purloined Letter." In a provocative assertion, she states: "Like the purloined letter, her [Marie's] corpse is visible, but the undisclosed crime against her is held in sufferance" (242).

31. I don't necessarily mean to turn Dupin into a reproductive-rights hero here; it's implied, for instance, that he holds onto the letter until the reward exponentially increases. In other words, by waiting for things to get bigger and bigger, he prolongs the woman's anxiety and possibly waylays her option of seeking an abortion. What Dupin seems most invested in—other than the money—is the permission for something or someone to be two things at once.

32. Quoted in Sellers, *Neither Black Nor White,* 113-14.

Bibliography

Alcott, William A. *The Young Man's Guide.* 16th ed. Boston: T. R. Marvin, 1846.

Brodie, Janet F. *Contraception and Abortion in Nineteenth-Century America.* Ithaca: Cornell University Press, 1994.

Burgeland, Thomas. *Physiological Observations.* London: W. Day, 1837.

Dayan, Joan. "Poe, Persons, and Property." In *Romancing the Shadow: Poe and Race.* Edited by J. Gerald Kennedy and Liliane Weissberg, 106-26. Oxford: Oxford University Press, 2001.

Derrida, Jacques. *The Post Card: From Socrates to Freud and Beyond.* Translated by Alan Bass. Chicago: University of Chicago Press, 1987.

Dixon, Laurinda. *Perilous Chastity: Women and Illness in Pre-Enlightenment Art and Medicine.* Ithaca: Cornell University Press, 1995.

Foucault, Michel. *The History of Sexuality: An Introduction.* Vol. 1, *The History of Sexuality.* New York: Vintage, 1990.

Hollick, Frederick. *The Origin of Life.* New York: The American News Company, 1845.

Johnson, Barbara. "The Frame of Reference: Poe, Lacan, Derrida." In *The Purloined Poe: Lacan, Derrida, and Psychoanalytic Reading.* Edited by John P. Muller and William J. Richardson, 213-51. Baltimore: Johns Hopkins University Press, 1988.

Lacan, Jacques. "Seminar on 'The Purloined Letter.'" *The Purloined Poe: Lacan, Derrida, and Psychoanalytic Reading.* Edited by John P. Muller and William J. Richardson, 28-54. Baltimore: Johns Hopkins University Press, 1988.

Lefkowitz, Helen H. *Rereading Sex: Battles Over Sexual Knowledge and Suppression in Nineteenth-Century America.* New York: Alfred A. Knopf, 2002.

Lugol, J. G. *Why Will You Die, or Researches of Scrofula.* New York: Fowler and Wells, 1847.

Mabbott, Thomas O. "The Text of 'The Purloined Letter,' with Notes." In *The Purloined Poe: Lacan, Derrida, and Psychoanalytic Reading.* Edited by John P. Muller and William J. Richardson, 3-27. Baltimore: Johns Hopkins University Press, 1988.

McLaren, Angus. *Sexual Blackmail: A Modern History.* Cambridge: Harvard University Press, 2002.

Muller, John and William Richardson, ed. *The Purloined Poe: Lacan, Derrida, and Psychoanalytic Reading.* Baltimore: Johns Hopkins University Press, 1988.

New York *Sunday Morning News.* July 21, 1835.

Pendleton, Hester. *The Parents Guide for the Transmission of Desired Qualities to Offspring.* New York: Fowler and Wells, 1848.

Physician of New York. *Madame Restell: An Account of Her Life and Horrible Practices.* New York: 1847.

Poe, Edgar Allan. "The Purloined Letter." In *The Fall of the House of Usher and Other Writings.* London: Penguin, 1986.

Pseudo-Aristotle. *Aristotle's Master-piece.* New York: 1817.

Ricci, James. *One Hundred Years of Gynaecology, 1800-1900.* Philadelphia: Blakiston, 1945.

Ross, J. H. "Cupper and Leecher." *The New York Lancet.* January 7, 1843.

Saltz, Laura. "(Horrible to Relate!) Recovering the Body of Marie Rogêt." In *The American Face of Edgar Allan Poe.* Edited by Shawn Rosenheim and Stephen Rachman, 237-70. Baltimore: Johns Hopkins University Press, 1995.

Sellers, Werner. *Neither Black Nor White Yet Both: Thematic Explorations of Interracial Literature.* Oxford: Oxford University Press, 1997.

Theriot, Nancy. *Mothers and Daughters in Nineteenth-Century America: The Biosocial Construction of Femininity.* Lexington: University Press of Kentucky, 1996.

Walker, Alexander. *Intermarriage; or the Mode in Which, and the Causes Why, Beauty, Health and Intellect Result from Certain Unions, and Deformity, Disease and Insanity, from Others.* London: John Churchill, 1838.

Walters, Ronald. *Primers for Prudery: Sexual Advice to Victorian Americans.* Baltimore: Johns Hopkins University Press, 2000.

FURTHER READING

Criticism

Amann, Elizabeth. *Importing* Madame Bovary: *The Politics of Adultery.* New York: Palgrave Macmillan, 2006, 276 p.

> Examines European novels of the late nineteenth century that drew heavily from *Madame Bovary* and provided a new way of looking at Flaubert's iconic novel of adultery.

Armstrong, Judith. *The Novel of Adultery.* London: Macmillan, 1976, 182 p.

> Evaluates the novel of adultery in the context of the social norms and mores that led to the institution of marriage as a fundamental element in the order of society.

Bensick, Carol. "His Folly, Her Weakness: Demystified Adultery in *The Scarlet Letter.*" In *New Essays on* The Scarlet Letter, edited by Michael J. Colacurcio, pp. 137-59. Cambridge: Cambridge University Press, 1985.

> Argues that Hawthorne addressed adultery as a social problem requiring pragmatic solutions in *The Scarlet Letter.*

Egan, Ken, Jr. "The Adulteress in the Market-Place: Hawthorne and *The Scarlet Letter.*" *Studies in the Novel* 27, no. 1 (spring 1995): 26-41.

> Likens Nathaniel Hawthorne, as a male writer in the artistic marketplace, to Hester Prynne, arguing

that "for Hawthorne, to be a male writer in his culture was necessarily to be an 'adulteress,' that is, a feminized adulterer of the 'truth.'"

Eliason, Lynn R. Introduction to *L'Adultera,* translated by Lynn R. Eliason, pp. 1-10. New York: Peter Lang, 1990.
    Provides a biographical and critical overview of Theodor Fontane, the author of *L'Adultera* and *Effi Briest.*

Goscilo, Helena. "Motif-Mesh as Matrix: Body, Sexuality, Adultery, and the Woman Question." In *Approaches to Teaching Tolstoy's* Anna Karenina, edited by Liza Knapp and Amy Mandelker, pp. 83-9. New York: Modern Language Association of America, 2003.
    Examines the structural unity Tolstoy imposed on *Anna Karenina* with motif-meshes, most significantly, Goscilo argues, the "body-appetite-sex-marriage-adultery" mesh.

Hess-Lüttich, Ernest W. B. "Negotiating Social Relationships: Fontane's Gossip; The Rhetoric of Discreet Indiscretion in *L'Adultera.*" In *Negotiation and Power in Dialogic Interaction,* edited by Edda Weigand and Marcelo Dascal, pp. 267-88. Amsterdam: John Benjamins Publishing Company, 2001.
    Analyzes the presence and function of gossip as a narrative device that provides information on social interaction in *L'Adultera.*

Meyer, Priscilla. "*Anna Karenina,* Rousseau, and the Gospels." *Russian Review* 66, no. 2 (April 2007): 204-19.
    Traces the ways in which Tolstoy drew from both French adultery novels and his understanding of the New Testament Gospels to develop an adulterous heroine who is both sympathetic and destructive to the family ideal.

Osborne, John. "Vision, Supervision, and Resistance: Power Relationships in Theodor Fontane's *L'Adultera.*" *Deutsche Vierteljahrs Schrift für Literaturwissenschaft und Geistesgeschichte* 70, no. 1 (March 1996): 67-79.
    Examines the presence of the "male gaze" in *L'Adultera.*

Overton, Bill. *The Novel of Female Adultery: Love and Gender in Continental European Fiction, 1830-1900.* London: Macmillan, 1996, 284 p.
    Comprehensive analysis of female adultery in nineteenth-century novels from France, Russia, Denmark, Germany, Portugal and Spain; includes a primary and secondary bibliography.

Rancour-Laferriere, Daniel. "Anna's Adultery: Distal Sociobiology vs. Proximate Psychoanalysis." *Tolstoy Studies Journal* 6 (1993): 33-46.
    Provides a social and biological Darwinian reading of Anna's adultery in *Anna Karenina.*

Reis, Levilson C. "Artifacts of Adultery: Flaubert's Use of Kitsch in *Madame Bovary.*" *French Studies Bulletin,* no. 85 (winter 2002): 10-13.
    Examines the ways in which Flaubert's household objects in *Madame Bovary* serve as clues to Emma's character.

Rippon, Maria R. "Stained-Glass Windows." In *Judgment and Justification in the Nineteenth-Century Novel of Adultery,* pp. 21-55. Westport, Conn.: Greenwood Press, 2002.
    Explains the common nineteenth-century literary trope of windows, particularly stained-glass windows, used to illuminate an adulteress's motivations.

Segal, Naomi. *The Adulteress's Child: Authorship and Desire in the Nineteenth-Century Novel.* Cambridge, England: Polity Press, 1992, 257 p.
    Examines the subjectivity of the mother as represented by the mother-child dyad in the nineteenth-century novel.

Sinclair, Alison. "Models of Deception: Charles Bovary, Trevelyan, Innstetten." In *The Deceived Husband: A Kleinian Approach to the Literature of Infidelity,* pp. 175-98. Oxford: Clarendon Press, 1993.
    Analyzes cuckolded husbands in *Madame Bovary* and *Effi Briest.*

Tanner, Tony. *Adultery in the Novel: Contract and Transgression.* Baltimore: Johns Hopkins University Press, 1979, 383 p.
    Seminal work on the subject of adultery in fiction, concentrating on three "bourgeois" novels: Rousseau's *La nouvelle Héloïse,* Goethe's *Die Wahlverwandtschaften,* and Flaubert's *Madame Bovary.*

Thickstun, Margaret Olofson. "Adultery versus Idolatry: The Hierarchy of Sin in *The Scarlet Letter.*" In *Fictions of the Feminine: Puritan Doctrine and the Representation of Women,* pp. 132-56. Ithaca, N.Y.: Cornell University Press, 1988.
    Traces the ways in which Nathaniel Hawthorne addressed the Puritan placement of crimes of the spirit over crimes of the flesh in *The Scarlet Letter.*

White, Nicholas. "Painting, Politics and Architecture." In *The Family in Crisis in Late Nineteenth-Century French Fiction,* pp. 150-75. Cambridge: Cambridge University Press, 1999.
    Considers the "sexual and political polarities" of French Realist novels of the nineteenth century.

Victorian Ghost Stories

The following entry provides criticism on nineteenth-century ghost stories, particularly those of the Victorian era.

INTRODUCTION

The Victorian era, a period associated with the reign of Queen Victoria from 1837-1901 (although it arguably began several years prior, upon passage of the Reform Act in 1832) was a time of unprecedented scientific and medical exploration and intense interest in the paranormal. Although adherence to conventional religion was fading and science was becoming preeminent in explaining the natural world, particularly theories about nature and evolution (which the young naturalist Charles Darwin had started to formulate on the second voyage of the *HMS Beagle* from 1831 to 1836), occultism became a fad. This paradox was not lost on some of the era's most prominent thinkers, including Thomas Carlyle and T. H. Huxley, who commented on the apparent oddity of the phenomenon. Carlyle, in particular, expressed awareness in his writings of the deep longing for mystery and immortality. Many of the investigations into the paranormal during this period took place under the guise of quasi-scientific study, particularly in the practices of mesmerism, which had first been promoted by the Viennese Dr. Franz Anton Mesmer in the late eighteenth and early nineteenth centuries, and phrenology, the belief that particular propensities of the human brain affected the shape of the skull, thus permitting personality traits to be indentified through an examination of a person's head. In the 1850s, a belief in spiritualism took hold, resulting in a boom in séances and "mediums" who could allegedly communicate with the dead. Popular especially with the middle and upper classes and creative individuals, including writers such as Elizabeth Barrett Browning and William Butler Yeats, spiritualism traced its roots to the work of the Swedish scientist and philosopher Emanuel Swedenborg (1688-1772), who believed the brain held the connection between the soul and body and who claimed to have experienced visions of Christ. After Swedenborg's death, sects based on his beliefs sprung up in England.

In the literature of the time, the supernatural was used regularly as a device to examine any number of social and cultural trends in both Great Britain and the United States. In works that exemplify the ghost story genre, there is much overlap with the older genre of Gothic fiction, which is believed to have been established in 1764 with the publication of Horace Walpole's novel *The Castle of Otranto*. Gothic fiction is characterized by a move away from eighteenth-century Enlightenment values toward the intellectual and aesthetic values of Romanticism, in particular a series of stock characters that includes nefarious villains, helpless maidens, ghostly apparitions, and various monsters such as vampires and werewolves. A century later, the American writers Edgar Allan Poe and Nathaniel Hawthorne were among the earliest to successfully integrate the Romantic elements of the Gothic with the unique concerns of the rising middle class in the United States. Poe's "The Fall of the House of Usher" (1839) and Hawthorne's *The House of the Seven Gables* (1851) fall into the category of haunted house stories, wherein it is not a ghost that threatens the natural order but rather a house with an evil sensibility. Hawthorne's setting of his haunted house in the United States rather than in an exotic foreign land is considered a significant literary development in that it allowed him to address questions of the wisdom of establishing an American aristocracy, the evolution from a rural to an urban economy, and the consequences of materialism. Unlike Poe, however, Hawthorne's supernaturalism was not pessimistic; his haunted-house novel ends with the heroine and her lover marrying and moving to the country.

Gradually the genre of supernatural fiction that sprang from the Gothic romance was applied to mundane, middle-class settings, thus giving rise to the ghost story proper, whose settings typically were ordinary houses in which the inhabitants required a ghostly fright to set them back on the right path. Social issues also came to the fore in these stories, particularly in those that took place in suburban settings. Critic Lara Baker Whelan noted that Charlotte Riddell's 1875 story "The Uninhabited House" explores middle-class Victorians' anxieties about the entrance of the lower classes into their newly developed suburban strongholds. Fears of industrialization and even pollution similarly crop up in Margaret Oliphant's "The Open Door" (1882) and the anonymously published "A Tale of a Gas-Light Ghost" (1867). Unlike the domiciles in earlier Gothic tales, the houses in these suburban ghost stories are not yet in ruins but rather are in a state of decline, not just because of their hauntedness but also because they are likely to be inhabited by the lower classes. Ghost stories also provided a medium in which women writers could explore the changing role of their sex, both in regard to images of angelic purity and self-sacrifice and the rise

103

of early feminism, by using the figure of the ghost as a metaphor for, according to critic Thomas H. Fick, "negotiations of the physical and metaphysical" and the true nature of womanhood. In this sense, ghost stories allowed women to variously challenge and reinforce the Victorian notion that they were primarily spiritual beings, and, in the case of stories by such writers as Alice Cary and Catherine Sedgwick, exact revenge on the men who betrayed and abandoned them. Other women writers of ghost stories used the genre in a more radical way, exploring race and gender. With Charles Dickens, Henry James, and other major literary figures publishing ghost stories, the genre held an appeal for readers of both high- and low-brow periodicals, and women writers easily adapted their works to the popular press. Caroline H. Butler's "Love and Ghosts" (1846) and Charlotte Perkins Gilman's "The Giant Wisteria" (1891) were both popular pieces that drew from but also subverted the Gothic tradition for the sake of social criticism. A common interpretation of stories like these is that the ghosts are meant to symbolize women's entrapment in the domestic sphere and overall historical oppression. Similarly, the Irish writer Joseph Sheridan Le Fanu drew from Swedenborgian spiritualism and early Freudian psychoanalysis to produce ghost stories suffused with psychological insight and political depth. As with Poe and Hawthorne, Le Fanu used the ghost story to examine the dangers and inevitable decline of the aristocracy, but he also included the victimization of the Irish at the hands of imperial England, questioning, like his female counterparts, power and enforced submission throughout history.

REPRESENTATIVE WORKS

Anonymous
"A Tale of a Gas-Light Ghost" (short story) 1867; published in journal *New Christmas Annual*

Matthew Arnold
"Stanzas from the Grand Chartreuse" (poetry) 1855; published in journal *Fraser's Magazine*

David Brewster
Letters on Natural Magic (nonfiction) 1832

Emily Brontë
Wuthering Heights. 2 vols. [as Ellis Bell] (novel) 1847

Caroline H. Butler
"Love and Ghosts" (short story) 1846; published in journal *Graham's American Monthly Magazine*

Alice Cary
"Ghost Story, Number I" (short story) 1855; published in journal *Ladies' Repository*

"Ghost Story, Number II" (short story) 1855; published in journal *Ladies' Repository*

Catherine Crowe
The Night-Side of Nature; or, Ghosts and Ghost-Seers. 2 vols. (short stories) 1848

Charles Dickens
A Christmas Carol, in Prose: Being a Ghost Story of Christmas (novella) 1843
The Haunted Man and the Ghost's Bargain: A Fancy for Christmas-time (novella) 1848
"To Be Taken with a Grain of Salt" (short story) 1865; published in journal *All the Year Round*
"The Signal-Man" (short story) 1866; published in journal *All the Year Round*

Charlotte Perkins Gilman
"The Giant Wisteria" (short story) 1891; published in journal *New England Magazine*

Nathaniel Hawthorne
The House of the Seven Gables: A Romance (novel) 1851

Henry James
The Turn of the Screw (novella) 1898

Andrew Lang
Cock Lane and Common Sense (nonfiction) 1894

Joseph Sheridan Le Fanu
"A Strange Event in the Life of Schalken the Painter" (short story) 1839; published in journal *Dublin University Magazine*
Ghost Stories and Tales of Mystery (short stories) 1851
The House by the Churchyard. 3 vols. (novel) 1863
Uncle Silas: A Tale of Bartram-Haugh. 3 vols. (novel) 1864
A Lost Name. 3 vols. (novel) 1868
"Green Tea" (short story) 1869; published in journal *All the Year Round*
The Chronicles of Golden Friars. 3 vols. (short stories) 1871
In a Glass Darkly. 3 vols. (short stories) 1872
The Purcell Papers. 3 vols. (short stories) 1880
The Watcher and Other Weird Stories (short stories) 1894

Edward Bulwer Lytton
"The Haunted and the Haunters; or, The House and the Brain" (short story) 1859; published in journal *Blackwood's Edinburgh Magazine*

Harriet Martineau
"The Ghost That Appeared to Mrs. Wharton" (short story) 1850; published in journal *Household Words*

Margaret Oliphant

"Earthbound" (short story) 1880; published in journal *Fraser's Magazine*

"The Open Door" (short story) 1882; published in journal *Blackwood's Edinburgh Magazine*

"The Portrait" (short story) 1885; published in journal *Blackwood's Edinburgh Magazine*

John Henry Pepper

The True History of the Ghost; and All About Metempsychosis (essay) 1890

Edgar Allan Poe

"Berenice" (short story) 1835; published in journal *Southern Literary Messenger*

"Morella" (short story) 1835; published in journal *Southern Literary Messenger*

"Ligeia" (short story) 1838; published in journal *American Museum*

"The Fall of the House of Usher" (short story) 1839; published in journal *Burton's Gentleman's Magazine*

"The Tell-Tale Heart" (short story) 1843; published in journal *Pioneer*

Charlotte Riddell

Frank Sinclair's Wife: And Other Stories. 3 vols. (short stories) 1874

The Uninhabited House (short story) 1875

The Haunted River: A Christmas Story (short story) 1877

Weird Stories (short stories) 1884

Harriet Prescott Spofford

Sir Rohan's Ghost: A Romance (novel) 1860

Harriet Beecher Stowe

Uncle Tom's Cabin; or, Life Among the Lowly. 2 vols. (novel) 1852

OVERVIEWS

Vanessa D. Dickerson (essay date 1996)

SOURCE: Dickerson, Vanessa D. "Ghosts of the Victorians." In *Victorian Ghosts in the Noontide: Women Writers and the Supernatural,* pp. 12-26. Columbia: University of Missouri Press, 1996.

[*In the following essay, Dickerson addresses the dichotomous Victorian devotion to science and facts alongside a preoccupation with ghosts and the supernatural.*]

That preeminent man of science and letters, T. H. Huxley, shook the supernatural dust from his feet on January 29, 1869, when he curtly declined the London Dialectical Society's invitation to consider the subject of spiritual manifestations. "I take no interest in the subject," he wrote. "But supposing the phenomena to be genuine—they do not interest me. . . . If any body would endow me with the faculty of listening to the chatter of old women and curates in the nearest cathedral town, I should decline the privilege, having better things to do." Huxley's peremptory if not combative missive belies the age's unique hauntedness. As Ronald Pearsall wrote in *The Table-Rappers,* "The Victorian period was not only a haunted age; it was also, in every sense of the word, a hallucinatory age, lending itself to every type of illusion, even at the level of bricks and mortar. . . . [There were] money boxes disguised as books, substantial looking doors that on examination was [*sic*] merely cunning paintwork, solid-looking chairs that were, in fact, featherlight, being manufactured from papier maché." Such furnishings, calling into question the very results of the mechanical accomplishments of the age, set the stage for the specters and ghosts whose place in and impact on the times proved just as substantial as any technological creation or advancement the age could boast. For one of the most interesting, if little appreciated, paradoxes of the Victorian period is that while it was the age of Darwin and Mill—an age that called for and prided itself on "Facts, sir; nothing but Facts!"—this same age was preoccupied with the supernatural, especially with the idea of ghosts.[1]

This is not to say that the Victorians had a monopoly on ghosts. As Gillian Bennett reminds us in *Traditions of Belief,* "Belief in occult forces is both endemic and ancient, one of the most enduring matters of interest." Yet the fact that the belief in ghosts is a primal and longstanding one does not controvert its special significance for the period. For in nineteenth-century England, the ghost figured as one of the cornerstones of what Alfred Russel Wallace—biologist, naturalist, and co-originator with Charles Darwin of the theory of evolution—in 1878 identified as "this revival of so-called supernaturalism," an acknowledgment of supernatural phenomena unparalleled "in the history of human thought; because there never before existed so strong, and apparently so well-founded a conviction that phenomena of this kind never have happened and never can happen." In *Cock Lane and Common Sense,* Andrew Lang, the Victorian man of letters best known for his work with fairy tales, also notes the nineteenth century's investment in ghosts. "In the Middle Ages—the 'dark ages'—modern opinion would expect to find an inordinate quantity of ghostly material," wrote Lang, "but modern opinion would be disappointed. Setting aside saintly miracles, and accusations of witchcraft, the minor phenomena [ghosts, clairvoyance, noises, and so on] are very sparsely recorded." Lang went on to observe with no little disdain that "the dark ages do *not,* as might have been expected, provide us with most of this material. The last forty enlightened years give us more bogles than all the ages between St. Augustine and the Restoration." A particularly compelling focus for the energy, ambivalence, and anxiety that typified the period, the ghost became, if not, in M. H. Abrams's words, a "period-metaphor," then, in Carlyle's even more appropriate coinage, one of the "signs of the times," a marker of social, historical, and philosophical positionality, an emblem of "the perplexed scene where we stand."[2]

The ghost was after all a provocative, in some cases provoking, image not just for fiction writers such as Bulwer Lytton, Charles Dickens, and Robert Louis Stevenson, but also for other eminent Victorians who wrote to and about the times.[3] Thus, Matthew Arnold conjures up one of the most evocative nineteenth-century ghosts in the resounding and oft-quoted lines from "Stanzas from the Grande Chartreuse," a Victorian zeitgeist: "Wandering between two worlds, one dead, / The other powerless to be born."[4] This spectrally announced betweenness, a condition with which Victorians could identify, since they found themselves between medieval god and modern machine, monarchy and democracy, religion and science, spirituality and materiality, faith and doubt, authority and liberalism—this condition of betweenness familiar to men would prove practically synonymous with the lives of Victorian women.

The dualities, tensions, and anxieties of a people so ambiguously situated have been documented by scholars including Walter E. Houghton, who, noting the age to be a transitional one, determined that "never before had men thought of their own time as an era of change *from the past to the future.*" Although the telling and apt designation of the age as a period of change, transition, and progress is no misconception, it proves imprecise if not problematic when applied to Victorian spirituality, for in this arena the Victorians did not necessarily have a sense of moving on. They were caught between belief in the old order and faith in the new one evidenced in science and technology. Aware of this inertia, Houghton cites Carlyle, "The Old has passed away . . . but, alas, the New appears not in its stead; the Time is still in pangs of travail with the New."[5] At the intersection of a world dying if not dead and one all alive with potential though not yet born, the wonderings and wanderings of Victorians describe a condition of Arnoldian suspension and ambiguous animation that constitutes ghosthood. The figure of the ghost can represent very well the paradox of the Victorian frame of mind, touted for its utility and rationality, yet tenacious of its spirituality.

When Charles Darwin published in 1859 one of the most definitive texts of the age of intellect, *The Origin*

of Species, he strengthened the hand of science, which had been chiseling away at the concepts of miracle, creation, and supernaturalism. Ultimately, the onslaught of science, materiality, fact, and reason, which in the nineteenth century culminated in such works as Robert Chambers's *Vestiges of the Natural History of Creation,* Darwin's *Origin,* Huxley's "On a Piece of Chalk," and the Higher Criticism of the Bible, shook the church but only stirred up the ghosts (the gain in knowledge and understanding was great, but the loss in spiritual security was vexatious) as Darwin and other thinkers deprived the age of one of life's greatest miracles and exchanged the wondrous and purposeful workings of the universe for a law of natural selection that finally, as J. A. V. Chapple has commented, "seemed far more uncontrollable and random" than the scientific insistence on "law" indicated.[6]

As early as the 1830s, the Victorian prophet Thomas Carlyle would consider "with some half-visible wrinkle of a bitter sardonic humour" the scientific debunking of life's mysteries:

> Our Theory of Gravitation is as good as perfect: Lagrange, it is well known, has proved that the Planetary System, on this scheme, will endure for ever; Laplace, still more cunningly, even guesses that it could not have been made on any other scheme. Whereby, at least, our nautical Logbooks can be better kept; and water-transport of all kinds has grown more commodious. Of Geology and Geognosy we know enough: what with the labours of our Werners and Huttons, what with the ardent genius of their disciples, it has come about that now, to many a Royal Society, the Creation of a World is little more mysterious than the cooking of a Dumpling; concerning which last, indeed, there have been minds to whom the question, *How the apples were got in,* presented difficulties.

As Carlyle, posing as editor of *Sartor Resartus,* takes stock of the advances science has made in accounting for the workings of the universe, he disparages the self-congratulatory tone and the complacency, if not indeed the offensive confidence, underlying the scientific pronouncements about the nature of things. Yet, for all science's certainty about the "good as perfect" theory of gravitation, about a planetary scheme that "will endure for ever," and its confident guess that the planetary system "could not have been made on any other scheme"—for all its vaunted command of the facts and knowledge of the universe it cannot address the simple but profound question of how "*the apples* [the spark, the soul, the spirit of the universe] *were got in.*" While the efforts, discoveries, and inventions of scientists and men such as Darwin, Lyell, Huxley, Davies, Faraday, Watt, Arkwright, and Stephenson continued to demystify and mechanize the world with finitude, empiricism, and materialism that rendered life "little more mysterious than the cooking of a Dumpling," the apples to which Carlyle satirically refers were the Victorians' spiritual longing for the infinite, the inexplicable, the immortal, a longing that remained constant though now troubled.[7]

Carlyle, whose prose writings earned for him the holy status of prophet-seer, was keenly aware of and wrote aggressively about the relations between the old and the new, about the living miracle of the spiritual and the dead fact of the material. In one of his typically windy and passionate deliveries as *Sartor Resartus*'s Teufels-dröckh, Carlyle bridges the gaping chasm between spirit and fact with the figure of the ghost:

> Again, could anything be more miraculous than an actual authentic Ghost? The English Johnson longed, all his life, to see one; but could not, though he went to Cock Lane, and thence to the church-vaults, and tapped on coffins. Foolish Doctor! Did he never, with the mind's eye as well as with the body's, look round him into that full tide of human Life he so loved. . . . Are we not Spirits, shaped into a body, into an Appearance; and that fade away again into air, and Invisibility? This is no metaphor, it is a simple scientific *fact*: we start out of Nothingness, take figure, and are Apparitions; round us, as round the veriest spectre, is Eternity. . . .—Ghosts! There are nigh a thousand million walking the earth openly at noontide; some half-hundred have vanished from it, some half-hundred have arisen in it, ere thy watch ticks once.
>
> O Heaven, it is mysterious, it is awful to consider that we . . . are, in very deed, Ghosts!

In this passage Carlyle argues, in the words of George Eliot's Ladislaw, that "the true seeing is within." But blinded by the "shows of things," humankind must perforce live in "the very fact of things": human beings stop at the "Appearance" or "*vesture*" of things and so thereby miss the reality of the "divine mystery"—the ghost.[8] Carlyle reminds his readers of the realness of the unseen, averring that spirituality is a fact. He thus extends the bounds of reality with his use of the word *ghost,* a literalization of spirit.

While Carlyle appropriated the ghost as an emblem or avatar of an eternal reality, others tried to dispel or exorcise it as a figure of trespass. Some scientists were especially annoyed when, oddly enough, science itself became haunted. Through the quasi-scientific explanations that undergirded such phenomena as mesmerism and spiritualism, supernatural beliefs and old a priori truths were provided with an unlikely vehicle. Mesmerism, a phenomenon in which a controller made passes over some bodily part of a subject, rendering that subject liable to a trancelike and restorative sleep—this mesmerism, or animal magnetism, as it was called by its discoverer, "the founding father of modern hypnosis," Viennese doctor Franz Anton Mesmer (1734-1815), was based on the scientific concept of a magnetic field or Newtonian fluid surrounding all things in the universe.[9] This field could be tapped by magnetic individuals who then controlled certain responsive subjects. Mesmerism

would in turn pave the way for the midcentury advent of spiritualism, as the same fluid that enabled one body to communicate energy and currents to another body also facilitated human communication with dead spirits.

Mesmerism itself had earlier in the nineteenth century been allied with another so-called science that preceded it: phrenology. During the early part of the nineteenth century, this quasi science, the basic theories of which were expounded by Franz Joseph Gall, identified in the brain over thirty propensities (including amativeness, acquisitiveness, secretiveness), sentiments (self-esteem, veneration, ideality), and intellectual faculties (individuality, language, causality) that could serve as the basis for the "analysis of mental character." Phrenology asserted that the brain was the center of both thought and feeling and that the size of different organs of the brain determined human behavior. Dr. John Elliotson, who sacrificed a medical chair at London University for his work with these fringe sciences, would be one of a number of adherents who tried to connect phrenology to mesmerism. But as Karen Chase points out in *Eros and Psyche,* her study of personality in three Victorian writers, the two "sciences" were an unlikely pair, "sharing little more than their hostility to established psychological theories."[10]

As a science, phrenology was more contained and centered in the physical than was mesmerism. Phrenologists had instruments they used to measure the head, providing among other things "the measure of an organ's power." The organs of the brain were intricately mapped and numbered. There was a comforting and more solid empirical dimension to this science than to that of mesmerism, whose main "instruments" were the touch or pass of a hand, the voice, the will, and an invisible magnetic field and fluids. On the one hand, the mesmeric "treatment necessary to restore the patient to harmony, with himself and with nature," as Janet Oppenheim observes, "had far more in common with the stroking, or laying-on of hands, practiced by faith healers and village wizards than with the standard eighteenth-century doctor's bag of frequently murderous medical tricks." On the other hand, as John D. Davies has pointed out in his text on phrenology in nineteenth-century America, *Phrenology: Fad and Science,* phrenology had a utilitarian dimension that members of society in Britain as well as in America must have found appealing:

> Phrenologists told their age how to be happy, how to choose a profession, how to select a wife, how to raise children; not only did they maintain that education was of supreme importance but they offered detailed curricula and pedagogical techniques. Other sociological and psychological applications were the diagnosis and cure of insanity, the conduct of penology, and the reform of the criminal. . . . Finally, for the common man, who did not understand philosophy, psychology,

or physiology, phrenology afforded a "scientific" method of character analysis, aptitude testing, and vocational guidance. This young, experimental, and somewhat protean science was of interest to scientists, doctors, social thinkers, and reformers of every description; and for those persuaded by its optimistic and utilitarian interpretation of life it offered hope for all and a vision of ultimate perfection.

It is not that mesmerism and spiritualism did not also proffer utopian ideas of perfectibility, but whereas phrenology provided detailed answers for daily living, mesmerism's and spiritualism's more spiritual provisions and promises were neither so immediate nor so concrete; they were supernatural. Phrenology, however, appeared to be, as John Purkis has observed, "the conclusion of a chain of reasoning which seemed unassailable. If there are no supernatural forces or spirits which could account for mental phenomena, then the mind must be the brain and nothing else." As a result of this or a similar mode of reasoning, phrenology was adopted, championed, or seriously considered at various points not only by Elliotson, who founded the Phrenological Society in 1824, but also by Charles Bray, the author of *The Philosophy of Necessity* and a friend of both George Combe, a dedicated phrenologist, and novelist George Eliot, who had a phrenological cast made of her head. While Charles Dickens set greater store by mesmerism, he too considered phrenology, while Charlotte Brontë, who consented to a phrenological examination, occasionally peppered her novels with allusions to phrenology and physiognomy that, according to Chase, provided among other things "terse assessments of character." Phrenology, "less flamboyant," to borrow Oppenheim's words, than mesmerism, especially during the early nineteenth century, certainly achieved a level of respectability not vouchsafed kindred enthusiasms.[11]

Although the phrenologist, mesmerist, and spiritualist all aimed, as Oppenheim puts it, to explain their "accomplishments in physical terms," there remained a "nonmaterial strain." These fringe sciences made the medical and scientific establishment uneasy, as it felt itself visited by the specters of magic and supernaturalism from which it was trying to free itself. "The subject of Animal Magnetism," wrote distinguished nineteenth-century naturalist Alfred Russel Wallace, who was both president of the Anthropological Society of London and a champion of spiritualism, "is still so much a disputed one among scientific men, and many of its alleged phenomena so closely border on, if they do not actually reach what is classed as supernatural, that I wish to give a few illustrations of the kind of facts by which it is supported." The business of doctors and scientists, men such as Michael Faraday, John Tyndall, and T. H. Huxley, would be ultimately to controvert these illustrations of the purported facts. "In the Victorian period," Oppenheim explains, "science and medicine were seeking to anchor themselves firmly in the physical world,

distinctly divorced from all disreputable thought systems whose insubstantial foundations could cast doubt on the weightiness of the scientific endeavor. Mesmerism, spiritualism and even phrenology as well, had roots in a magical, occult past, where divination, humors, and conjured apparitions abounded." Like the figure of the ghost, the pseudosciences partook of two worlds, hovering somewhere between science and the supernatural, between the reality of the head and the mystery of the spirit.[12]

Interestingly enough, it was not only the pseudo but also the hard or legitimate sciences that opened a portal for the supernatural. Across the Atlantic, where spiritualism had got its start, literary man and advocate of spiritualism Epes Sargent wrote in *Planchette,* published in 1869,

> The further science carries its analysis, the more does the material world lose that character of rigidity which our external senses attach to it; and the more does it seem plastic under spiritual laws. Modern chemistry has shown us that all solid bodies may exist as aeriform; that even iron may be converted into an invisible gas; and the diamond which to our senses is inert, ponderable matter, may be volatilized in the fire of the burning mirror so as to develop neither smoke nor cinders. On the other hand, fire, essentially volatile, can be condensed in the calcination of metals, so as to become ponderable.

Science, then, according to Sargent and others such as De Montlosier, the French nobleman, statesman, and author of *Des Mystère de la vie humaine,* whom Sargent cites, was demonstrating how "all the bodies of the universe might be volatilized and made to disappear in those spaces which our ignorance calls *the void.*"[13] In other words, science gave palpable proof of how the solid or concrete could be transformed into the impalpable, the invisible, the ghostly. In this instance, chemistry created a twilight space that made the eerie phenomenal claims of the fringe sciences seem possible if not probable.

As much as the supernaturalism of mesmerism and spiritualism was the despair of science it was also the proverbial thorn in the episcopal side of the religious establishment, which found itself during the nineteenth century in some disarray. In a letter to her friend Ottilie von Goethe, art historian and social critic Anna Jameson in 1851 wrote that "between our Ultra-religionists, puseyites and non-believers we are in a charming state of confusion." In this condition, the church faced a powerful resurgence of supernaturalism. With its traditional and biblical ties to the otherworldly ideas of heaven and hell, of spirit possession and ghosts, the church ought logically to have had no difficulty with mesmerism, spiritualism, and ghosts. Certainly some spiritualists were quick to point out scripturally sanctioned precedents, and some members of the church as eagerly welcomed spiritualism. Thus, as late as 1900, one clergyman argued, "Indeed, Spiritualism fitted very nicely into Christianity. . . . In the first place, Spiritualism had rehabilitated the Bible." According to this clergyman, people "were asked to believe in Bible miracles, and at the same time taught that, outside the Bible records, nothing supernatural ever happened. But now the whole thing had been reversed. People now believed in the Bible because of Spiritualism; they did not believe in Spiritualism because of the Bible."[14] Despite the fact that mesmerism and spiritualism seemed to resurrect sacred miracles, the church did not necessarily or eagerly embrace either the new science or the new movement; on the whole, it was as distrustful of these phenomena as was science.

In his history of spiritualism, novelist Arthur Conan Doyle, who had a great interest in the subject, observed, "No class has shown itself so sceptical and incredulous of modern Spiritual manifestations as those very clergy who profess complete belief in similar occurrences in bygone ages, and their utter refusal to accept them now is a measure of the sincerity of their professions." The church's refusal to recognize the phenomena of spiritualism was also a measure of ecclesiastical intimidation, for the religious establishment no doubt felt its authority threatened by the secularization and democratization of church affairs that occurred as both men and women began to claim more power over spiritual matters at the séance tables. As Howard Kerr, in his study of American spiritualism, observed, "The religious implication of this millennial impulse was that men no longer needed to depend on church and clergy and scripture for proof of the soul's immortality." While the church called for patience that would by and by net good Christians the Kingdom of God and a reunion with loved ones, séances where individuals could supposedly communicate through mediums with the dead offered more direct and immediately gratifying contact with the other side. The church stood on tradition, while spiritualism tried to stand on science: "Faith has been abused until it has become impossible to many earnest minds, and there is a call for proof and for knowledge. It is this which Spiritualism supplies. It founds our belief in life after death and in the existence of invisible worlds, not upon ancient tradition or upon vague intuitions, but upon proven facts, so that a science of religion may be built up, and man given a sure pathway amid the quagmire of the creeds."[15]

The resulting relations between scientific and ecclesiastical systems and supernaturalism were complex. Generally speaking, science had at some point undermined or refuted the claims of both the clergy and the supernaturalists. Yet clergymen who either denied the reality of spirits communicating with the living or denounced raps, taps, and spirits as demonology became by default

the bedfellows of science, which would, one scholar has argued, supplant religion: "Science as it has become institutionalized has tended to make the same overriding claims as were previously made by religion, to be the 'Truth', and the only correct method of studying the universe. When science takes this step it changes from being an empirical study into a faith or 'religion'. . . . Science has become a faith for western man in the nineteenth and twentieth centuries." For those in the nineteenth century who were unsatisfied with the defunct supernaturalism of the church or with what William Johnston in 1851 called "the general faith in science as a wonder-worker," there was the vital supernaturalism of spiritualism. "An attempt to use scientific methods . . . to establish the existence of the supernatural,"[16] spiritualism sought to embrace both the religion and the science that repelled it.

Disavow it as they would, the priest, the scientist, the eminently practical man were all hard put to lay the supernatural to rest, especially because in England as well as in America spiritualism was "repeatedly bringing ghosts to public attention." Florence Marryat enthusiastically reported that she herself had converted hundreds of educated people, while William Howitt declared that spiritualism had "received the assent of about twenty millions of people in all countries." In 1881, Epes Sargent similarly maintained, "In less than forty years it [spiritualism] has gained at least twenty millions of adherents in all parts of the world. Adapting itself, through its eclectic affinity with all forms of truth, to all nationalities and classes, and repeating its peculiar manifestations everywhere."[17]

Exaggerated or not, these numbers attest to the significance of the ghosts that graced the séance tables. They figured so prominently in Victorian life that they got the attention of the illustrator and caricaturist George Cruikshank, whose business it was to identify and magnify issues endemic to his society. Intending to deliver a lighthearted but well-aimed blow to the pates of the spiritually gullible, Cruikshank in 1863 rapped the spirit-rappers:

> Now it will be as well here to inquire what good has ever resulted from this belief in what is commonly understood to be a ghost? None that I have ever heard of, and I have been familiar with all the popular ghost stories from boyhood, and have of late waded through almost all the works produced in support of this spiritual visiting theory, but in *no one instance* have I discovered where any beneficial result has followed from the supernatural or rather unnatural supposed appearances.

Exasperated by all the concern about ghosts, the eminently practical Cruikshank responded with a question, "Wherein lies the utility of ghosts?" Having "waded" through a sea of "works produced in support of this spiritual visiting theory," Cruikshank could not discern the metaphorical or metaphysical charge spirits gave to corporeality, if not to corpses.[18]

According to Nina Auerbach, ghosts did offer certain "gifts" to Victorian men and women who sought to keep their faith from "disappear[ing] into the void of science." Having "nothing left to believe in but their lives," these men and women could "find spiritual authority in the revelations of a life" or a self, the "extraordinariness" of which was most intensely realized in death. "In the nineteenth-century imagination, death [that] gain[ed] stunning power," to vivify the self and to "crystallize . . . identities," would be realized in "the Victorian ghost, that spectacular epitome of the own self." Holding out "the vibrancy, the momentary transformations, the heightened, crystallized energy, of the stage," the ghost "embodi[ed] those intimations of potency the living dream of and fear." Ghosts concretized not just the afterlife but also being. Affirming as they did the staying power of life, ghosts figuratively if not literally filled the air of a people who both enjoyed the material prosperity that science and technology had brought about and yet reluctantly relinquished the idea of God or at least the transcendental feeling of "living on."[19]

The Victorians lived lives energized, perhaps sometimes enervated, by the contradiction inherent in this conflict. Nowhere did this energy, born of the complex relations among science, religion, and the supernatural, manifest itself more publicly, earnestly, or officially than in the establishment of the Psychical Society. Although the society was not the first of its kind, it was more widely recognized than its prototypes, for one thing because it, along with its sister branch in America, gathered, studied, and published the greatest wealth of material on occult phenomena.[20] The Society for Psychical Research may in fact be seen as an epistemological culmination of the Victorians' passion for assurances on the question of ghosts and thereby the meaning of life.

Victorians had in essence clamored for some resolution about the supernatural. No doubt, the failure of other agencies like the Dialectical Society to determine conclusively whether the supernatural was real, the remonstrances of such writers as Cruikshank, and the promptings of writers such as Catherine Crowe, who maintained "that whether these manifestations be from heaven or hell, or whether they exist at all or not, is a question that we have every right to ask of those who, having qualified themselves for investigations, are bound to answer"—these precipitated the birth of the society. For the question of ghosts proved so very pressing that the Victorians, led by a professor of physics, Sir William Barrett, finally organized on February 20, 1882, a learned society to employ rigorous scientific methods to settle, if possible, but certainly to investigate, the supernatural. In *Spiritualism and Nineteenth-Century Letters,* Russell and Clare Goldfarb give a role call of the Society for Psychical Research that impresses one with a sense of the age's ambivalent fascination with mystery and spirits and its commitment to science and factual inquiry:

> The Society for Psychical Research was founded by scientists and by spiritualists, by sons of clergymen and by graduates of Cambridge and Oxford; the founders were Barrett, Henry Sidgwick, the first president of the Society, Frederic W. H. Myers, Edmund Gurney, and Frank Podmore, a civil servant among academics and natural philosophers; the spiritualist members were the Reverend W. Stainton Moses, Morell Theobald, Dr. George Wild, and Dawson Rogers. A distinguished physicist, Oliver Lodge, joined the group in the 1890s, but by this time the Society had a number of eminent members: W. E. Gladstone and Arthur Balfour, Prime Ministers; eight Fellows of the Royal Society, including Alfred Russel Wallace, Lord Rayleigh, and Balfour Stewart; the poet laureate of England, Alfred Tennyson; and other literary figures such as John Ruskin, "Lewis Carroll," and John Addington Symonds. Nearly one thousand people joined the Society for Psychical Research in its first decade of existence.

That only women are missing from this list of the founding assembly, which constituted a mix of skeptics, believers, and the undecided, of those from academic, scientific, political, and religious communities, is indicative of Victorian determination to get at the heart of the supernatural fuss by pooling as many male perspectives as possible.[21]

While "psychical researchers were interested in all types of inexplicable phenomena," those that called the question most insistently were ghosts.[22] "We may defy the supporters of this apparition doctrine to bring forward one circumstance in connection with these ghosts, which corresponds in any way with the real character of the CREATOR, where any real benefit has been known to result from such sounds and such appearances—none, none, none," Cruikshank insisted, then continued,

> whereas we know that there has been a large amount of human suffering, illness, folly, and mischief, and in former times, we know, to a large and serious extent, but even now, in this "age of intellect," when we come to investigate the causes of some of the most painful diseases amongst children and young persons, particularly young females, we find, on the authority of the first medical men, that they are occasioned by being frightened by mischievous, thoughtless, or cruel persons, mainly in consequence of being *taught in their childhood to believe in ghosts.*[23]

The fact of the matter is that although Cruikshank and other skeptics like Huxley, who finally equated the folly of spiritual manifestations with the twaddle of curates and women, would have liked very much to relegate ghosts to the domains of old women's chatter, children's boogie bears, and young girls' prepubescent anxiety, spirits there were abroad in Victorian England, which found itself in the anomalous position of being the most haunted age of intellect.

Notes

1. Huxley, "Letter," in *Report on Spiritualism,* 229; Pearsall, *The Table-Rappers,* 139; Charles Dickens, *Hard Times,* 47.

2. Bennett, *Traditions of Belief,* 23; Wallace, *Miracles and Modern Spiritualism: Three Essays,* 54, 149; Lang, *Cock Lane and Common Sense,* 28, 30; Abrams uses the expression "period-metaphor" in *Natural Supernaturalism: Tradition and Revolution in Romantic Literature,* 31; see Carlyle's "Signs of the Times" in *A Carlyle Reader,* ed. G. B. Tennyson, 34.

3. More recently Nina Auerbach has noted the ghost's relation to the theatrics of Victorian lives in *Private Theatricals: The Lives of the Victorians.*

4. *Poetry and Criticism of Matthew Arnold,* 187.

5. *The Victorian Frame of Mind, 1830-1870,* 1, 9.

6. *Science and Literature in the Nineteenth Century,* 82.

7. *Sartor Resartus,* 25, 3. In *The Victorian Frame of Mind,* 110, Houghton, who writes about, among other things, the anti-intellectualism that was also afoot during the Victorian period, makes an important distinction between the scientific and intellectual mind versus the practical and mechanical mind that helps account for the complex relations of apparently antagonistic ideas of science and the supernatural.

8. Carlyle, *Sartor Resartus,* 200-201; Eliot, *Middlemarch,* 142; Carlyle, "The Hero as Poet. Dante; Shakespeare," 115.

9. E. R. Hilgard, introduction to *Mesmerism: A Translation of the Original Scientific and Medical Writings of F. A. Mesmer,* xi. For his ideas about fluids and fields, Mesmer relied largely on Newton's theory of the tides; he also relied on Volta and Galvini's work with magnets.

10. George Combe, *Notes on the United States of North America during a Phrenological Visit in 1838-9-40,* 1:xviii; Chase, *Eros and Psyche,* 105-6.

11. Chase, *Eros and Psyche,* 56; Oppenheim, *The Other World: Spiritualism and Psychical Research in England, 1850-1914,* 211; Davies, *Phrenology: Fad and Science; a Nineteenth-Century American Crusade,* 5; Purkis, *A Preface to George Eliot,* 34-36; Chase, *Eros and Psyche,* 54; Oppenheim, *The Other World,* 210.

12. Oppenheim, *The Other World,* 210; Wallace, *Miracles and Modern Spiritualism,* 64 (for information about Wallace's part in the spiritualist movement and for an examination of how Wallace, a co-discoverer of natural selection, reconciled his scientific findings with his spiritualistic faith, see Oppenheim, *The Other World,* 297-325); Oppenheim, *The Other World,* 223. See also Fred Kaplan's *Dickens and Mesmerism: The Hidden Springs of Fiction,* in which he rightly notes the "utopian" aspects of mesmerism that "appealed to the heart as well as to the head," a mesmerism that "had not only a strand of scientific but also an elaborate weave of Romantic and revolutionary utopianism that contained threads from western society's inheritance of religion and magic" (7).

13. *Planchette; or, The Despair of Science. Being a Full Account of Modern Spiritualism, Its Phenomena, and the Various Theories Regarding It. With a Survey of French Spiritism,* 374.

14. Jameson, "Letter 142"; Arthur Conan Doyle, *The History of Spiritualism,* 2:263.

15. Doyle, *History of Spiritualism,* 2:248; Kerr, *Mediums, and Spirit-Rappers, and Roaring Radicals,* 11; Doyle, *History of Spiritualism,* 2:248.

16. Geoffrey K. Nelson, *Spiritualism and Society,* 140; Johnston, *England as It Is: Political, Social, and Industrial in the Middle of the Nineteenth Century,* 1:245; Nelson, *Spiritualism and Society,* 140.

17. Kerr, *Mediums, and Spirit-Rappers, and Roaring Radicals,* 55; Howitt, "Letter," in *Report on Spiritualism,* 236; Sargent, *The Scientific Basis of Spiritualism,* 7.

18. George Cruikshank, *A Discovery Concerning Ghosts: With a Rap at the Spirit-Rappers,* 2.

19. Auerbach, *Private Theatricals,* 107, 4, 3, 12, 89, 100, 93, 89, 107, 101. For an in-depth study of Victorians and death, see Garrett Stewart's *Death Sentences: Styles of Dying in British Fiction.* For recent critical and feminist explorations of death see Regina Barreca, ed., *Sex and Death in Victorian Literature;* Elisabeth Bronfen, *Over Her Dead Body: Death, Femininity, and the Aesthetic;* and Elisabeth Bronfen and Sarah Webster Goodwin, eds., *Death and Representation.* I borrow the expression *living on* from George Eliot's *The Lifted Veil,* 2.

20. See Oppenheim's section on "The Forerunners of the SPR" in *The Other World,* 123-35.

21. Crowe, *Spiritualism and the Age We Live In,* 141; Goldfarb and Goldfarb, *Spiritualism and Nineteenth-Century Letters,* 128. In all fairness, women would become a part of the Society, which eventually had a woman president in Eleanor Balfour Sidgwick.

22. Mary Walker, "Between Fiction and Madness: The Relationship of Women to the Supernatural in Late Victorian Britain," 231.

23. Cruikshank, *A Discovery*, 20.

Bibliography

Abrams, M. H. *Natural Supernaturalism: Tradition and Revolution in Romantic Literature.* New York: Norton, 1971.

Adorno, Theodor W. "The Essay as Form." In *Notes to Literature,* edited by Rolf Tiedemann, 1:3-36. New York: Columbia University Press, 1991.

Alaya, Flavia. "Victorian Science and the 'Genius' of Woman." *Journal of the History of Ideas* 38 (1977): 261-80.

Allott, Miriam. *Elizabeth Gaskell.* London: Longman, Green, and Co., 1960.

Armstrong, Nancy. *Desire and Domestic Fiction: A Political History of the Novel.* New York: Oxford University Press, 1987.

Arnold, Matthew. *Poetry and Criticism of Matthew Arnold.* Edited by Dwight Culler. Boston: Houghton Mifflin, 1961.

Ashley, Michael, ed. *Mrs Gaskell's Tales of Mystery and Horror.* London: Victor Gollancz, 1978.

Auerbach, Nina. *Private Theatricals: The Lives of the Victorians.* Cambridge: Harvard University Press, 1990.

———. *Woman and the Demon: The Life of a Victorian Myth.* Cambridge: Harvard University Press, 1982.

Baker, Augusta, and Ellin Greene. *Storytelling: Art and Technique.* New York: R. R. Bowker, 1977.

Barreca, Regina, ed. *Sex and Death in Victorian Literature.* Bloomington: Indiana University Press, 1990.

———. "Writing as Voodoo: Sorcery, Hysteria, and Art." In *Death and Representation,* edited by Elisabeth Bronfen and Sarah Webster Goodwin, 174-91. Baltimore: Johns Hopkins University Press, 1993.

Basham, Diana. *The Trial of Woman: Feminism and the Occult Sciences in Victorian Literature and Society.* Washington Square: New York University Press, 1992.

Bellringer, Alan W. *George Eliot.* New York: St. Martin's Press, 1993.

Bennett, Gillian. *Traditions of Belief: Women and the Supernatural.* London: Penguin, 1987.

Black, Helen. *Notable Women Authors of the Day.* London: Maclaren, 1906.

Bloom, Harold, ed. *The Brontës.* New York: Chelsea House, 1987.

Bonaparte, Felicia. *The Gypsy-Bachelor of Manchester: The Life of Mrs. Gaskell's Demon.* Charlottesville: University Press of Virginia, 1992.

———. *The Triptych and the Cross: The Central Myths of George Eliot's Poetic Imagination.* New York: New York University Press, 1979.

Boumelha, Penny. *Charlotte Brontë.* Bloomington: Indiana University Press, 1990.

Brantlinger, Patrick. *The Spirit of Reform: British Literature and Politics, 1832-1867.* Cambridge: Harvard University Press, 1977.

Braude, Ann. *Radical Spirits: Spiritualism and Women's Rights in Nineteenth-Century America.* Boston: Beacon Press, 1989.

Bray, Charles. *Phases of Opinion and Experience during a Long Life: An Autobiography.* London: Longmans, Green and Co., 1884.

———. *The Philosophy of Necessity.* 2 vols. London: Longman, Orme, Brown, Green, and Longmans, 1841.

Briggs, Julia. *Night Visitors: The Rise and Fall of the English Ghost Story.* London: Faber, 1977.

Bronfen, Elisabeth. *Over Her Dead Body: Death, Femininity, and the Aesthetic.* New York: Routledge, 1992.

Bronfen, Elisabeth, and Sarah Webster Goodwin, eds. *Death and Representation.* Baltimore: Johns Hopkins University Press, 1993.

Brontë, Charlotte. *Jane Eyre: An Authoritative Text, Backgrounds, Criticism.* Edited by Richard J. Dunn. New York: Norton, 1971.

———. "Editor's Preface." In *Wuthering Heights: Revised, an Authoritative Text with Essays in Criticism,* by Emily Brontë, edited by William M. Sale Jr., 9-12. New York: Norton, 1972.

———. *The Professor: A Tale.* New York: Harper, 1857.

———. *Villette.* Edited by Mark Lilly with an introduction by Tony Tanner. New York: Penguin, 1979.

Brontë, Emily. *Wuthering Heights: Revised, an Authoritative Text with Essays in Criticism.* Edited by William M. Sale Jr. New York: Norton, 1972.

Carlyle, Jane Welsh. *Letters and Memorials of Jane Welsh Carlyle.* Prepared for publication by Thomas Carlyle. Edited by James Anthony Froude. 3 vols. London: Longmans, Green, and Co., 1883.

———. *New Letters and Memorials of Jane Welsh Carlyle.* Annotated by Thomas Carlyle and edited by Alexander Carlyle with an introduction by Sir James Chrichton-Browne. London: John Lane, The Bodley Head, 1903.

Carlyle, Thomas. *A Carlyle Reader.* Edited by G. B. Tennyson. Cambridge: Cambridge University Press, 1984.

———. "The Hero as Poet. Dante; Shakespeare." In *Prose of the Victorian Period,* edited by William E. Buckler, 113-29. Boston: Houghton Mifflin, 1958.

———. "Labour." In *Past and Present,* edited by Richard Altick, 196-200. New York: New York University Press, 1977.

———. *Sartor Resartus.* Edited by Kerry McSweeney and Peter Sabor. New York: Oxford University Press, 1987.

Carpenter, Lynette, and Wendy K. Kolmar, eds. *Haunting the House of Fiction: Feminist Perspectives on Ghost Stories by American Women.* Knoxville: University of Tennessee Press, 1991.

Cecil, David. *Early Victorian Novelists: Essays in Revaluation.* London: Constable and Co., 1934.

Chambers, Robert. *Vestiges of the Natural History of Creation.* New York: Humanities Press, 1970.

Chapple, J. A. V. *Science and Literature in the Nineteenth Century.* London: Macmillan, 1986.

Chapple, J. A. V., and Arthur Pollard, eds. *The Letters of Mrs Gaskell.* Manchester: Manchester University Press, 1966.

Chase, Karen. *Eros and Psyche: The Representation of Personality in Charlotte Brontë, Charles Dickens, and George Eliot.* New York: Methuen, 1984.

Chitham, Edward. *A Life of Emily Brontë.* Oxford: Basil Blackwell, 1987.

Combe, George. *Notes on the United States of North America during a Phrenological Visit in 1838-9-40.* 2 vols. Philadelphia: Carey and Hart, 1841.

Cosslett, Tess. *Woman to Woman: Female Friendship in Victorian Fiction.* Atlantic Highlands, N.J.: Humanities Press International, 1988.

Cott, Nancy. *The Bonds of Womanhood: "Woman's Sphere" in New England, 1780-1835.* New Haven: Yale University Press, 1977.

Cottom, Daniel. *Abyss of Reason: Cultural Movements, Revelations, and Betrayals.* New York: Oxford University Press, 1991.

Cox, Michael, and R. A. Gilbert, eds. *Victorian Ghost Stories: An Oxford Anthology.* Oxford: Oxford University Press, 1991.

Craik, W. A. *Elizabeth Gaskell and the English Provincial Novel.* London: Methuen, 1975.

Crowe, Catherine. *Ghosts and Family Legends: A Volume for Christmas.* London: Newby, 1859.

———. *The Night Side of Nature; or, Ghosts and Ghost Seers.* 2 vols. Folcroft, Pa.: Folcroft Library Edition, 1976.

———. *Spiritualism and the Age We Live In.* London: Newby, 1859.

Cruikshank, George. *A Discovery Concerning Ghosts: With a Rap at the Spirit-Rappers.* London: Frederick Arnold, 1863.

Daly, Mary. *Pure Lust: Elemental Feminist Philosophy.* Boston: Beacon Press, 1984.

Darwin, Charles. *The Origin of Species: A Variorum Text.* Edited by Morse Peckham. Philadelphia: University of Pennsylvania, 1959.

Davies, John D. *Phrenology: Fad and Science; a Nineteenth-Century American Crusade.* New Haven: Yale University Press, 1955.

Davis, Christina. "Interview with Toni Morrison." In *Toni Morrison: Critical Perspectives Past and Present,* edited by Henry Louis Gates Jr. and K. A. Appiah, 412-21. New York: Amistad, 1993.

De Beauvoir, Simone. *The Second Sex.* Translated by H. M. Parshley. New York: Random House, 1974.

De Montlosier, François Dominique de Reynaud. *Des Mystère de la vie humaine.* 2 vols. in one. Brussels: Dumont et Compagnie, 1829.

De Morgan, Sophia. *From Matter to Spirit: The Result of Ten Years' Experience in Spirit Manifestations. Intended as a Guide to Enquirers.* London: Longman, Green, Longman, Roberts, and Green, 1863.

Dickens, Charles. *Hard Times.* New York: Penguin, 1969.

———. "The Signalman." In *The Signalman and Other Ghost Stories,* 1-13. Chicago: Academy Chicago Publishers, 1988.

Dickerson, Vanessa D. "The Ghost of a Self: Female Identity in Mary Shelley's *Frankenstein.*" *Journal of Popular Culture* 27, no. 3 (winter 1993): 79-91.

Doyle, Arthur Conan. *The History of Spiritualism.* 2 vols. in one. New York: Arno Press, 1975.

Easson, Angus. *Elizabeth Gaskell.* London: Routledge and Kegan Paul, 1979.

Eliot, George. *Adam Bede.* Edited by Stephen Gill. New York: Penguin, 1980.

———. *Daniel Deronda.* Edited by Barbara Hardy. New York: Penguin, 1967.

———. *The Lifted Veil.* New York: Penguin, 1985.

———. *Middlemarch.* Edited by Gordon S. Haight. Boston: Houghton Mifflin, 1956.

————. *The Mill on the Floss.* Edited by A. S. Byatt. New York: Penguin, 1979.

————. "Prospectus of the *Westminster and Foreign Quarterly Review.*" In *George Eliot: Selected Essays, Poems, and Other Writings,* edited by A. S. Byatt and Nicholas Warren, 3-7. New York: Penguin, 1990.

————. *Romola.* Edited by Andrew Sanders. New York: Penguin, 1980.

————. *Scenes of Clerical Life.* Edited by David Lodge. New York: Penguin, 1973.

————. "Worldliness and Other-Worldliness: The Poet Young." In *Essays of George Eliot,* edited by Thomas Pinney, 335-85. New York: Columbia University Press, 1963.

Felman, Shoshana. *What Does a Woman Want? Reading and Sexual Difference.* Baltimore: Johns Hopkins University Press, 1993.

Feltes, N. N. "Phrenology: From Lewes to George Eliot." *Studies in the Literary Imagination* 1 (1968): 13-22.

Ffrench, Yvonne. *Mrs. Gaskell.* Denver: Alan Swallow, 1949.

Fuller [Ossoli], Margaret. *Woman in the Nineteenth Century, and Kindred Papers Relating to the Sphere, Condition, and Duties of Woman.* Edited by Arthur B. Fuller. Boston: Jewett, 1855.

Ganz, Margaret. *Elizabeth Gaskell: The Artist in Conflict.* New York: Twayne, 1969.

Gaskell, Elizabeth. *Cranford and Cousin Phillis.* Edited by Peter Keating. New York: Penguin, 1976.

————. *The Letters of Mrs Gaskell.* Edited by J. A. V. Chapple and Arthur Pollard. Manchester: Manchester University Press, 1966.

————. *The Life of Charlotte Brontë.* London: Dent, 1971.

————. *The Works of Mrs. Gaskell.* Edited and introduced by A. W. Ward. 8 vols. New York: AMS Press, 1972.

Gilbert, Sandra M., and Susan Gubar. *The Madwoman in the Attic: The Woman Writer and the Nineteenth-Century Literary Imagination.* New Haven: Yale University Press, 1979.

Gilmour, Robin. *The Victorian Period: The Intellectual and Cultural Context of English Literature, 1830-1890.* London: Longman, 1993.

Gissing, George. *New Grub Street.* Edited by Bernard Bergonzi. New York: Penguin, 1968.

Goldfarb, Russell M., and Clare R. Goldfarb. *Spiritualism and Nineteenth-Century Letters.* Cranbury, N.J.: Associated University Presses, 1978.

Gray, Beryl. Afterword to *The Lifted Veil,* by George Eliot. New York: Penguin, 1985.

Gray, B. M. "Pseudoscience and George Eliot's 'The Lifted Veil.'" *Nineteenth-Century Fiction* 36 (1982): 407-23.

Haight, Gordon S. *George Eliot: A Biography.* Oxford: Oxford University Press, 1968.

————, ed. *A Century of George Eliot Criticism.* Boston: Houghton Mifflin, 1965.

————, ed. *The George Eliot Letters.* 9 vols. New Haven: Yale University Press, 1954.

Haining, Peter, ed. *A Circle of Witches: An Anthology of Victorian Witchcraft Stories.* New York: Taplinger, 1971.

Hardinge [Britten], Emma. *Modern American Spiritualism: A Twenty Years' Record of the Communion between Earth and the World of Spirits.* New Hyde Park, N.Y.: University Books, 1970.

Hellerstein, Erna Olafson, Leslie Parker Hume, and Karen M. Offen, eds. *Victorian Women: A Documentary Account of Women's Lives in Nineteenth-Century England, France, and the United States.* Stanford: Stanford University Press, 1981.

Helsinger, Elizabeth K., Robin Lauterbach Sheets, and William Veeder. *The Woman Question: Society and Literature in Britain and America, 1837-1883.* 2 vols. Chicago: University of Chicago Press, 1983.

Hilgard, E. R. Introduction to *Mesmerism: A Translation of the Original Scientific and Medical Writings of F. A. Mesmer,* edited and translated by George Bloch. Los Altos, Calif.: William Kaufmann, 1980.

Holcombe, Lee. *Wives and Property: Reform of the Married Women's Property Law in Nineteenth-Century England.* Toronto: University of Toronto Press, 1983.

Houghton, Walter E. *The Victorian Frame of Mind, 1830-1870.* New Haven: Yale University Press, 1957.

Howitt, Mary. *Mary Howitt, an Autobiography.* Edited by Margaret Howitt. 2 vols. Boston: Houghton, Mifflin and Co., 1889.

Howitt, William. *The History of the Supernatural.* 2 vols. London: Longman, Green, Longman, Roberts, and Green, 1863.

Hughes, Winifred. *The Maniac in the Cellar: Sensation Novels of the 1860's.* Princeton: Princeton University Press, 1980.

Huxley, Thomas H. *On a Piece of Chalk.* Edited by Loren Eiseley. New York: Scribner, [1967].

Irigaray, Luce. *This Sex Which Is Not One.* Translated by Catherine Porter. Ithaca: Cornell University Press, 1985.

Jacobus, Mary. *Reading Woman: Essays in Feminist Criticism.* New York: Columbia University Press, 1986.

James, Henry. *The Turn of the Screw: An Authoritative Text, Backgrounds and Sources, Essays in Criticism.* Edited by Robert Kimbrough. New York: Norton, 1966.

Jameson, Anna. "Letter 142." In *Letters of Anna Jameson to Ottilie Von Goethe,* edited by G. H. Needler, 175. London: Oxford University Press, 1939.

Janouch, Gustav. *Franz Kafka und seine Welt.* Stuttgart: Hans Deutsch Verlag Wien, 1965.

Johnston, William. *England as It Is: Political, Social, and Industrial in the Middle of the Nineteenth Century.* 2 vols. Shannon, Ireland: Irish University Press, 1971.

Kaplan, Fred. *Dickens and Mesmerism: The Hidden Springs of Fiction.* Princeton: Princeton University Press, 1975.

———. "'The Mesmeric Mania': The Early Victorians and Animal Magnetism." *Journal of the History of Ideas* 35 (1974): 691-702.

Kerner, Justinus. *The Seeress of Prevorst, Being Revelations Concerning the Inner-Life of Man, and the Interfusion of a World of Spirits in the One We Inhabit.* Translated by Catherine Crowe. London: Moore, 1845.

Kerr, Howard. *Mediums, and Spirit-Rappers, and Roaring Radicals: Spiritualism in American Literature, 1850-1900.* Urbana: University of Illinois Press, 1972.

Knoepflmacher, U. C. *George Eliot's Early Novels: The Limits of Realism.* Berkeley: University of California Press, 1968.

———. "Thoughts on the Aggression of Daughters." In *The Endurance of "Frankenstein": Essays on Mary Shelley's Novel,* edited by George Levine and U. C. Knoepflmacher, 88-119. Berkeley: University of California Press, 1979.

La Belle, Jenijoy. *Herself Beheld: The Literature of the Looking Glass.* Ithaca: Cornell University Press, 1988.

Lang, Andrew. *Cock Lane and Common Sense.* New York: AMS Press, 1970.

Lansbury, Coral. *Elizabeth Gaskell: The Novel of Social Crisis.* New York: Harper and Row, 1975.

Laski, Marghanita. *George Eliot and Her World.* London: Thames and Hudson, 1973.

Leadbeater, C. W. *Clairvoyance.* Adyar, India: Theosophical Publishing House, 1903.

Le Fanu, Sheridan. "Green Tea." In *In a Glass Darkly,* edited by Robert Tracy, 5-40. Oxford: Oxford University Press, 1993.

Levy, Anita. *Other Women: The Writing of Class, Race, and Gender, 1832-1898.* Princeton: Princeton University Press, 1991.

Linton, Eliza Lynn. *Ourselves.* London: Chatto and Windus, 1884.

———, ed. *Witch Stories.* London: Chapman and Hall, 1861.

Marks, Patricia. *Bicycles, Bangs, and Bloomers: The New Woman in the Popular Press.* Lexington: University Press of Kentucky, 1990.

Marryat, Florence. *The Ghost of Charlotte Cray and Other Stories.* New York: Munro, 1884.

———. *The Spirit World.* Leipzig: Tauchnitz, 1894.

———. *The Strange Transfiguration of Hannah Stubbs.* Leipzig: Tauchnitz, 1896.

———. *There Is No Death.* New York: Lovell, Coryell and Co., 1891.

Martin, Emily. *The Woman in the Body: A Cultural Analysis of Reproduction.* Boston: Beacon Press, 1987.

Martineau, Harriet. *Miscellanies.* 2 vols. Boston: Hilliard, Gray, and Co., 1836.

———. *Miss Martineau's Letters on Mesmerism.* New York: Harper, 1845.

———. *Society in America.* New York: Saunders and Otley, 1837.

Martineau, Harriet, and Henry George Atkinson. *Letters on the Laws of Man's Nature and Development.* Boston: Mendum, 1851.

McVeagh, John. *Elizabeth Gaskell.* New York: Humanities Press, 1970.

McWhirter, David. "In the 'Other House' of Fiction: Writing, Authority, and Femininity in *The Turn of the Screw.*" In *New Essays on "Daisy Miller" and "The Turn of the Screw,"* edited by Vivian R. Pollak, 121-48. Cambridge: Cambridge University Press, 1993.

"Mesmeric Deceptions—The Whipton Prophetess." *Lancet* 1 (1847): 178-79.

Mill, John Stuart. *The Subjection of Women.* Cambridge: MIT Press, 1970.

———. "What Is Poetry?" In *Victorian Prose and Poetry,* edited by Lionel Trilling and Harold Bloom, 76-83. Oxford: Oxford University Press, 1973.

Mitchell, Sally, ed. *Victorian Britain: An Encyclopedia.* New York: Garland, 1988.

Moers, Ellen. *Literary Women.* Garden City, N.Y.: Anchor Books, 1977.

Moore, Katharine. *Victorian Wives.* London: Allison and Busby, 1974.

Morrison, Toni. *Beloved.* New York: Alfred A. Knopf, 1987.

————. *Song of Solomon.* New York: Alfred A. Knopf, 1977.

Myers, William. *The Teaching of George Eliot.* Totowa, N.J.: Barnes and Noble, 1984.

Nelson, Geoffrey K. *Spiritualism and Society.* New York: Schocken Books, 1969.

Oliphant, Margaret. *Autobiography and Letters of Mrs. Margaret Oliphant.* Edited by Mrs. Harry Coghill. Leicester: Leicester University Press, 1974.

————. *A Beleaguered City.* 1900; Westport, Conn.: Greenwood, 1970.

————. "Sensation Novels." *Blackwood's* 91 (1862): 564-84.

————. *Two Stories of the Seen and the Unseen.* Edinburgh: Blackwood, 1885.

Oppenheim, Janet. *The Other World: Spiritualism and Psychical Research in England, 1850-1914.* Cambridge: Cambridge University Press, 1985.

Orel, Harold. *The Victorian Short Story: Development and Triumph of a Literary Genre.* Cambridge: Cambridge University Press, 1986.

Owen, Alex. *The Darkened Room: Women, Power and Spiritualism in Late Victorian England.* Philadelphia: University of Pennsylvania Press, 1990.

Pater, Walter. *The Renaissance: Studies in Art and Poetry.* Introduction by Lawrence Evans. Chicago: Academy Press, 1977.

Patmore, Coventry. *The Angel in the House.* 4th ed. London: Macmillan, 1866.

Pearsall, Ronald. *The Table-Rappers.* London: Joseph, 1972.

Penzoldt, Peter. *The Supernatural in Fiction.* London: Peter Nevil, 1952.

Purkis, John. *A Preface to George Eliot.* London: Longman, 1985.

Pykett, Lyn. *Emily Brontë.* Savage, Md.: Barnes and Noble, 1989.

————. *The "Improper" Feminine: The Women's Sensation Novel and the New Woman Writing.* New York: Routledge, 1992.

Redinger, Ruby V. *George Eliot: The Emergent Self.* New York: Alfred A. Knopf, 1975.

Report on Spiritualism of the Committee of the London Dialectical Society, Together with the Evidence Oral and Written, and a Selection from the Correspondence. London: Longman, Green, Reader and Dyer, 1871.

Riddell, Charlotte. *The Collected Ghost Stories of Mrs. J. H. Riddell.* Edited by E. F. Bleiler. New York: Dover Press, 1977.

————. *The Uninhabited House.* In *Five Victorian Ghost Novels,* edited by E. F. Bleiler, 3-112. New York: Dover Press, 1971.

Roth, Ernest. *A Tale of Three Cities.* London: Cassell, 1971.

Russett, Cynthia Eagle. *Sexual Science: The Victorian Construction of Womanhood.* Cambridge: Harvard University Press, 1989.

Sargent, Epes. *Planchette; or, The Despair of Science. Being a Full Account of Modern Spiritualism, Its Phenomena, and the Various Theories Regarding It. With a Survey of French Spiritism.* Boston: Roberts Brothers, 1869.

————. *The Proof of Immortality.* Boston: Colby and Rich, 1875.

————. *The Scientific Basis of Spiritualism.* Boston: Colby and Rich, 1881.

Sawyer, Ruth. *The Way of Storytellers.* New York: Viking, 1953.

Schor, Hilary M. *Scheherezade in the Marketplace: Elizabeth Gaskell and the Victorian Novel.* New York: Oxford University Press, 1992.

Schor, Naomi. "This Essentialism Which Is Not One: Coming to Grips with Irigaray." In *Engaging with Irigaray: Feminist Philosophy and Modern European Thought,* edited by Carolyn Burke, Naomi Schor, and Margaret Whitford, 57-78. New York: Columbia University Press, 1994.

Schreiner, Olive. *The Story of an African Farm.* Edited by Joseph Bristow. Oxford: Oxford University Press, 1992.

————. *Woman and Labour.* Toronto: Henry Frowde, 1911.

Shelley, Mary. *Frankenstein, or the Modern Prometheus.* Edited by M. K. Joseph. London: Oxford University Press, 1969.

Shorter, Clement. *The Brontës: Life and Letters; Being an Attempt to Present a Full and Final Record of the Lives of the Three Sisters. . . .* 2 vols. New York: Haskell, 1969.

Showalter, Elaine. *A Literature of Their Own: British Women Novelists from Brontë to Lessing.* Princeton: Princeton University Press, 1977.

Shuttleworth, Sally. *George Eliot and Nineteenth-Century Science: The Make-Believe of a Beginning.* Cambridge: Cambridge University Press, 1984.

Sinclair, Marie, Countess of Caithness. *A Midnight Visit to Holyrood.* London: C. L. H. Wallace, 1887.

Spretnak, Charlene, ed. *The Politics of Women's Spirituality: Essays on the Rise of Spiritual Power within the Feminist Movement.* New York: Anchor Books, 1982.

Stevenson, Robert Louis. *Dr. Jekyll and Mr. Hyde.* New York: Bantam Books, 1981.

Stewart, Garrett. *Death Sentences: Styles of Dying in British Fiction.* Cambridge: Harvard University Press, 1984.

Stimpson, Catharine R. Foreword to *Independent Women: Work and Community for Single Women, 1850-1920,* edited by Martha Vicinus, ix-x. Chicago: University of Chicago Press, 1985.

Stockton, Kathryn Bond. *God between Their Lips: Desire between Women in Irigaray, Brontë, and Eliot.* Stanford: Stanford University Press, 1994.

Stoneman, Patsy. *Elizabeth Gaskell.* Bloomington: Indiana University Press, 1987.

Sullivan, Jack. *Elegant Nightmares: The English Ghost Story from Le Fanu to Blackwood.* Athens: Ohio University Press, 1978.

Summers, Montague. *The Geography of Witchcraft.* 1927. Reprint. London: Routledge and Kegan Paul, 1978.

Tayler, Irene. *Holy Ghosts: The Male Muses of Emily and Charlotte Brontë.* New York: Columbia University Press, 1990.

Tennyson, Alfred, Lord. *In Memoriam.* Edited by Robert H. Ross. New York: Norton, 1973.

Tuana, Nancy, ed. *Feminism and Science.* Bloomington: Indiana University Press, 1989.

Uglow, Jennifer. *Elizabeth Gaskell: A Habit of Stories.* New York: Farrar Straus Giroux, 1993.

————. Introduction to *Victorian Ghost Stories by Eminent Women Writers,* edited by Richard Dalby, ix-xvii. New York: Carroll and Graf, 1988.

Vogler, Thomas A., ed. *Twentieth Century Interpretations of "Wuthering Heights": A Collection of Critical Essays.* Englewood Cliffs, N.J.: Prentice-Hall, 1968.

Walker, Mary. "Between Fiction and Madness: The Relationship of Women to the Supernatural in Late Victorian Britain." In *That Gentle Strength: Historical Perspectives on Women in Christianity,* edited by Lynda L. Coon, Katherine J. Haldane, and Elisabeth Sommer, 230-42. Charlottesville: University Press of Virginia, 1990.

Wallace, Alfred Russel. *Miracles and Modern Spiritualism: Three Essays.* London: Spiritualist Press, 1878.

Wechsberg, Joseph. *Prague: The Mystical City.* New York: Macmillan, 1971.

Whitehill, Jane, ed. *Letters of Mrs. Gaskell and Charles Eliot Norton, 1855-1865.* London: Oxford University Press, 1932.

Wickwar, J. W. *Witchcraft and the Black Art.* London: Herbert Jenkins, 1973.

Winsbro, Bonnie. *Supernatural Forces: Belief, Difference, and Power in Contemporary Works by Ethnic Women.* Amherst: University of Massachusetts Press, 1993.

Woolf, Virginia. *A Room of One's Own.* New York: Harcourt Brace, 1929.

Wright, Edgar. *Mrs. Gaskell: The Basis for Reassessment.* London: Oxford University Press, 1965.

Lara Baker Whelan (essay date March 2002)

SOURCE: Whelan, Lara Baker. "Between Worlds: Class Identity and Suburban Ghost Stories, 1850 to 1880." *Mosaic* 35, no. 1 (March 2002): 133-48.

[*In the following essay, Whelan analyzes nineteenth-century ghost stories as metaphors for Victorian class anxiety.*]

The emergence of the Victorian suburb was a middle-class phenomenon, born of two competing desires: to escape contact with the urban lower classes, and to remain in close and necessary contact with the cash nexus located in urban centres. The suburb was further shaped throughout mid-century by an aesthetic sensibility borrowed from the upper-class country-house ideal and modified to the smaller living spaces of villas and semi-detached homes. This aesthetic grew out of the middle class's concern with reinforcing precarious class boundaries by physically marking suburban space as "classed." That this aesthetic was borrowed and replicated in new working-class and lower-middle-class suburban estates was a source of great anxiety to other middle-class suburbanites, particularly those who had just recently risen from the lower segments of Victorian society. This diffusion of an aesthetic meant to signify class membership made it increasingly difficult to determine the class of the inhabitants of a home or neighbourhood simply by looking at it. And yet, because of the suburban emphasis on privacy, expressed both in architecture and in ideology, looking from the outside was often all that was possible. Despite its problematic nature (from a middle-class perspective), this adaptation continued virtually unabated throughout the greatest period of British suburban growth (1850-1880) and beyond, destabilizing class boundaries by allowing more and more newcomers to take on the trappings of middle-class living and irrevocably blurring what was intended to be a visible line between the working and middle classes.

As suburban building boomed and rents came down, more and more of the various strata of Victorian society were able to move out of rank and crowded city centres into homes that approximated middle-class villadom. This resulted in an increasing middle-class concern with the extent to which appearances and "reality" came together at any given social or cultural site, including the suburbs, and led to the great middle-class concern with "normality." As Michel Foucault points out in *Discipline and Punish: The Birth of the Prison,* "normalization [became] one of the great instruments of power at the end of the classical age" (184), and throughout the nineteenth century, "normality," as defined by middle-class values, was the mark of social identification. As part of this process of "normalizing" class behaviours, Nancy Armstrong argues that fiction in general "helped to formulate the ordered space we now recognise as the household [. . .] and used it as the context for representing normal behaviour" (23). According to her, domestic fiction took on the task of taming "new domains of aberrance," which were beyond or above the law (163). Yet domestic fiction was not the only genre to take on this cultural task. A related and relatively unexamined genre, the suburban ghost story of the mid- to late-Victorian period, fulfills a similar function; its narrative structure is also concerned with ordering and "normalizing" domestic space. Unlike domestic fiction, however, where female agency is emphasized, the Victorian suburban ghost narrative provides a middle-class male hero the opportunity to order the space of a haunted house that has been disrupted by a specter, and, through a fantasy of excluding this specter, to reassert (the readers') middle-class values.

For many readers, the ghost story genre is partially or wholly synonymous with the Gothic tradition established earlier in the century by Ann Radcliffe and Horace Walpole in novels like *The Mysteries of Udolpho* and *The Castle of Otranto* (respectively). The defining elements of such supernatural narratives, where disembodied spirits haunt crumbling castle ruins, seems strangely at odds with the "modernity" of the Victorian suburb and the spirit of the nineteenth century in general. However, much as the earlier Gothic novels addressed contemporary cultural concerns of nationhood, civilization, and nature (see Anne Janowitz's *England's Ruins: Poetic Purpose and the National Landscape*), the suburban ghost story of this period, of which there were many examples published in popular periodicals, addresses anxieties about the instability of suburban space during the time of the most uncontrolled and rampant suburban growth. The anxiety inherent in the instability of suburban space resonated with the anxiety traditionally provoked by supernatural elements of ghost stories. In this essay, I analyze four main themes of suburban ghost literature in the middle third of the nineteenth century: the use of suburban setting to highlight class instability; the ghost figure as threat to middle-class suburban culture; the upwardly mobile middle-class male hero who nullifies the threat of both the supernatural and the undomesticated; and, the use of the ghost as a disciplinary force that can go where the middle-class eye could not. Whether it is the location or the inhabitants of the haunted house that contribute to its borderline status within the suburb, that liminality seems essential to the appeal of the suburban ghost story.

Understanding the context of Victorian suburbanization may help ground the discussion of "suburban" literature. The Victorians defined *suburb* quite broadly. In the case of London, some sources, such as Percy Fitzgerald's *London City Suburbs as They Are Today* (published in 1893), begin with Westminster and Chelsea, defining *suburb* as anything outside the City proper but within the limits of what came to be known as the London County Council. Others, such as James Thorne's *Handbook to the Environs of London* (published in 1876), ranged as far afield as Brighton and Cambridge, taking dormitory suburbs into consideration. Because there was no real consensus at the time about what exactly constituted a suburb, my working definition of *suburb* as the areas outside the City and Westminster, where recent building had been primarily residential rather than industrial or commercial, seems to be as accurate and useful as any contemporary definition.

The suburbs of London were the fastest growing areas in all of England in the 1870s (Briggs 324). In contrast to northern cities, the London suburbs grew 50 percent *per decade* between 1861 and 1891 (Dyos 19), with the greatest growth occurring in two separate "spikes" in the 1860s and 1870s (Jones 324; Thompson 13). This explosive growth meant that the "limits" of what was urban and what was ex-urban were constantly shifting around London, more than around any other city in Great Britain, making London "ground zero" for developing cultural concerns about class and space in the suburbs.

We know that the nineteenth century was a time of coalescence and alliance-building for the British middle classes, but very little has been written about the suburbs as a site of this struggle. In the 1970s, several geographers and sociologists, led by H. J. Dyos, became interested in the Victorian suburb as a historical artifact and studied exactly who moved into and out of the suburbs, what kinds of businesses were established, what rents were charged, how many families lived in each house, how long houses remained unlet, and other minutiae of Victorian suburban life. Rather than a vast band of quiet middle-class households, what these scholars found was a constantly shifting, economically unstable, socially heterogeneous space where once respectable middle-class neighbourhoods could become working-class refuges within ten years, and full-blown slums within forty.

Ideally, the Victorian suburb engendered domesticity, provided privacy and protection from the gaping masses, promoted respectability, and simulated the country-house lifestyle on a scale that was less grand, less wasteful, and altogether more in line with middle-class values of prudence, propriety, and comfort than *actual* country-house living. Charles Dickens's description of Oliver Twist's recovery at the Maylies's cottage retreat, written about 1837, is an example of this ideal:

> It was a happy time. The days were peaceful and se-rene; the nights brought with them neither fear nor care; [. . .] [Oliver] would walk with Mrs. Maylie and Rose, and hear them talk of books; [. . .] he would work hard, in a little room which looked into the gar-den. [. . .] And when Sunday came, [. . .] there was the little church, in the morning, with the [. . .] sweet-smelling air stealing in at the low porch. [. . .] The poor people were so neat and clean. [. . .] Then there were the walks, as usual, and many calls at the clean houses of the labouring men. [. . .] There was fresh grounsel, too, for Miss Maylie's birds; [. . .] there was rare cricket-playing, sometimes on the green; or failing that, there was always something to do in the garden, or about the plants. [. . .] It is no wonder that, by the end of that short time, Oliver Twist had become com-pletely domesticated.
>
> (239-41)

The domesticating atmosphere of a lifestyle that in-cluded gardening, fresh air, exercise, and time for intel-lectual improvement was a great enticement to those families who had, or thought they had, achieved middle-class status.

As membership in the middle class grew throughout the century, and as members of that class tried to find ways both to define themselves in contrast to other classes and to solidify their power base, the suburb and its at-tendant lifestyle came to represent everything that was vital to the middle class's perception of itself. As social historian John Burnett points out, the Victorian middle class was still insecure in its position at mid-century, even though it seemed to have taken control of Victo-rian social structure. It needed a code that could "define status: [that] would serve as a unifying force to combat the enemies without and protect the members within, affording a private retreat behind which the strains and stresses of business life could be washed away" (99). This code, with its basis in security and privacy, was enmeshed with the middle-class suburban ideal. The suburb, as middle-class property, came to stand for middle-class propriety.

The suburb was imagined as a space that enabled its in-habitants to walk the narrow line between constant and uncontrolled contact with the urban "residuum" and ru-ral isolation from the sources of capital. Based on the purported success of this balancing act, the middle class invested heavily in suburban building and in the social ideology of the suburbs. Presumably, only those in the middle class, as defined by salary and occupation, could

afford to live there and, as there was almost nothing there *but* street upon street of houses, no one but those in the middle class would want to go there. This was the theory; the reality turned out to be quite different.

The problem was that the suburban ideal of privacy, quiet, respectability, and social homogeneity was, in fact, only a figure in most cases. Suburban environ-ments were often dismal, if not downright unhealthy. Public sanitation codes were rarely enforced; drains and sewers were poorly built and sometimes backed up into areas and gardens. The homes themselves were shod-dily constructed and poorly planned. The privacy of-fered by the suburban estate, and built into the subur-ban villa, was constantly violated by a variety of "interlopers" who threatened the security and stability of what was constructed, both literally and figuratively, as *solely* middle-class space. Thus, more often than not, the suburban ideals for the structural and social envi-ronment failed to materialize, leaving suburbanites frus-trated, disappointed, and sometimes fearful.

A significant proportion of popular fiction written pri-marily for the middle classes appealed to these emo-tions in ghost stories set in suburban environments. In many ways, the epitome of this genre is Mrs. J. H. Rid-dell's 1875 novella *The Uninhabited House,* because, in it, Riddell plays on several strands of suburban anxi-eties that would have been recognizable to her readers. By making the ghost character a rich speculative builder, Riddell gives a nod to the real financial benefits that could accrue from suburban building. At the same time, however, Riddell evokes social stereotypes about the type of person involved in the actual building of the suburbs—the speculative builder. The ghost figure, al-though rich, has working-class Irish roots and is firmly connected (as were most speculative builders) with the grade of craftsman below artisan (jobbing carpenters, for instance). This *nouveau riche* figure of unsavoury origin haunts his suburban home, making this house lit-erally uninhabitable. Uninhabited suburban houses rep-resented a failure both in real-money investment and in social control. When houses went uninhabited for too long (representing a loss for the landlord and/or build-ers with mortgages on the property), desperation on the part of the leaseholder was likely to lead to a division of a house meant for a single middle-class family into several "rooms" that were more suitable for lower-class inhabitants. Thus, the uninhabited house also figures as a sign of the mutability of suburban space. In order to "rescue" this space from the brink of social and finan-cial disaster, Riddell introduces a male hero who figures out how to expel the specter and return the property to its "rightful" place (both as a site for middle-class do-mesticity and as a site for earned income). These themes—liminal spaces, uninhabited or uninhabitable houses, misplaced lower-class figures, and middle-class male heroes—are the major tropes of suburban ghost stories of the period. Each element has something to tell us about how the middle class imagined and experienced the suburban ideal.

The suburban ghost story often introduces the abandoned and uninhabitable suburban house before any ghosts are brought into the narrative. The suburb of Riddell's *The Uninhabited House* is an area west of London on the banks of the Thames. Dismal and grey, the neighbourhood has seen better days; its tendency to flood seasonally has driven many of the original residents to seek higher ground. The area still has enough "tone" to be considered "suitable in every respect for a family of position" (3) owing to the division it marks between isolation from urban concerns and reasonable proximity to London's financial district, yet the status of this borderline space is indeterminate. If "good" tenants can be found for it, the area may remain "suitable" for the future; if not, an abandoned home will signal to potential residents that the neighbourhood is no longer a good place in which to invest one's salary or, more importantly, one's reputation. Since the heroine of the story depends on the rental of the house for her income, any threat to the neighbourhood is a threat to her survival as a respectable woman. Thus, in Riddell's story, the setting works to evoke anxious feelings in empathetic readers and sets the stage for the appearance of the ghost.

For Victorian ghost stories set in suburban space, the "borderline" status of a particular neighbourhood or home takes the place of the more conventional ruined castle or dark forest in setting an appropriately "scary" stage. Take, for example, the suburb of Margaret Oliphant's "The Open Door," published about 1860. In this story, a recently built villa on the outskirts of Edinburgh is disturbed by a disembodied moaning near the ruins of an older estate. Due to its isolation and its connection with the older and more "aristocratic" structure, the newer house at first seems to be more country estate than suburban villa. But telling narrative details, such as the industrially polluted river running through the property and the convenient number of trains into town, indicate the villa's suburban status and its precarious position on that margin between urban and rural. "A Tale of a Gas-light Ghost," published anonymously in the same decade as Oliphant's "The Open Door," also incorporates quintessentially liminal suburban space as the primary setting. Events in this story take place in a town near London that is about to become suburban thanks to the imminent arrival of the railroad. Located on the outskirts of this village, the haunted house in "A Tale of a Gas-Light Ghost" thus becomes doubly liminal—a suburb of a suburb.

In all three of these stories, the haunted houses are ones that leasing agents find difficult to rent, an element typical of suburban ghost stories. Two other examples, "Old Mrs. Jones" and "The Old House in Vauxhall Walk," published by Riddell in her 1882 collection entitled *Weird Stories,* are set in neighbourhoods on the decline. In "Old Mrs. Jones," the haunted house is in a suburban area south of the Thames that had been respectable in the recent past but which is slowly slipping into working-class hands, as evidenced by the current inhabitants, a cabman's family. "The Old House in Vauxhall Walk," on the other hand, is set in a neighbourhood clearly unreclaimable for the middle classes. The haunted house in this story is in Lambeth, a "dreary district" where "the fumes of the gas works seemed to fall with the rain" (85). The state of the house mirrors the state of the neighbourhood in general, which, "once inhabited by well-to-do citizens, [is] now let out for the most part in floors to weekly tenants" (86). Note the shift here from "citizens" to "tenants"; this is all the more significant given that the residents of this particular haunted house are servants.

These settings are evocative of the precarious nature of suburban living. Most suburban developments were not planned as coherent neighbourhoods; land was bought piecemeal by individuals or small building companies and developed according to whatever fancy took the builder. Sometimes, a builder might buy only one lot; very rarely did one builder buy large numbers of lots at one time. Stylistically, suburban streets were a hodgepodge of Gothic, post-Gothic, and Georgian, or anything in between. Many builders, knowing their market, incorporated external features of the more expensive villas and country houses into their plans in order to mark their houses as suitable middle-class residences from the street (Burnett 115, 25). These decorations often took up materials and costs that should have been devoted to the structures themselves. Often suburban houses did not last more than forty years before falling down or becoming uninhabitable due to drafts, bad drainage, and rising damp (156). Because a particular development could deteriorate rapidly into a physically uncomfortable mess, suburbanites were usually on the lookout for a "better" situation, while those looking to make their way into the middle class often moved into "deteriorating" neighbourhoods as the rents became more affordable. In a way, then, *all* suburban space of this era could be considered on the margin between one state of being and another; suburban ghost stories play up transitional anxieties by focussing on the kinds of suburban environments that were most obviously problematic.

The suburban house in supernatural fiction becomes the locus of a struggle for dominance between the lower class or class-less and a middle class interested in solidifying its position within the Victorian social structure. In the suburban ghost story, a ghost is rarely just a ghost. Instead, the ghost is figured as a specter that haunts the middle-class conceptions of order, either as criminal or as an unstable element in suburban space. Deborah Epstein Nord points out that "middle-class observers recorded the descent into the netherworld of poverty not as a journey into unknown territory [. . .] but as a fall into a gaping hole at the edge of society" (321). In the same way, it might be argued, middle-class writers figured what emerged from that hole as spectral creatures of the netherworld. Often, dirt and disease were associated in the middle-class mind with both the urban *under*world and the supernatural *other*world. Nord further argues that "the disconcerting *invisibility,* the *undetectability,* of this process of *invasion and infiltration* might inspire the reformer's audience to attack social problems at hand before they *overran the boundaries* of the netherworld" (84, emph. mine). In the metaphor of the ghost-invader, both the ghost and the underclass invader are invisible, undetectable, and transgressive of every boundary the suburbanite tried so carefully to erect between himself and the Other.

In "The Ghost That Appeared to Mrs. Wharton," published in *Household Words* in 1850, Harriet Martineau describes the unfortunate situation of Mrs. Wharton, an eminently respectable matron living in a suburb of a Northern manufacturing town. Mrs. Wharton is troubled by the appearance of "a most hideous—a most detestable face—gibbering and making mouths" at the foot of her bed in the middle of the night (140). The spectral figure even goes as far as to occasionally intone, "I come to see you whenever I please" (142). As the hauntings continue, Mrs. Wharton actually learns to live with her specter, eventually able to sleep right through its visits. Then, after several years, she is invited to tour the local glass works with the vicar, where she recognizes the specter in the face of one of the workers, a "half-wit" glass blower. The man confesses that he had discovered a secret passage from one of the lower rooms of the glass works to Mrs. Wharton's cellar, and he visited her whenever her supply of coals was low enough to enable him to get through the opening.

If his appearance and demeanour were not frightening enough, the intruder "posing" as a ghost evokes several of the themes regarding intruders in suburban space. First, the anxiety surrounding the man's spectral appearances is intensified by his vaguely threatening "I come to see you whenever I please," which implies the failure of middle-class domestic space to keep working-class populations at bay. Second, that Mrs. Wharton could become so accustomed to these invasions that she no longer took notice of them has disturbing ramifications for the middle-class suburbanite striving for social homogeneity. After all, if Mrs. Wharton can become inured to a working-class man having unlimited access to her very bedroom, then what might be the future of neighbourhoods where middle class and working class mix freely?

Other ghost stories of the period have similar social implications that might be seen to threaten the fabric of Victorian (or at least middle-class) social order. In Riddell's *The Uninhabited House,* for example, both the ghost figure and his murderer are, in a sense, social impostors. Despite his grand home built with the profit from shoddy speculative suburban building, the murdered-man-turned-ghost is of decidedly "inferior" origins. The son of a small builder, he was, according to the narrator, unable to pronounce his H's correctly and had a less-than-imposing physical presence. The narrator describes him as "bluff in manner, short in person, red in the face, cumbersome in figure, addicted to naughty words, not nice about driving fearfully hard bargains; [he was] a man whom men hated, not undeservedly" (11).

The key to his social position could also be determined from his occupation; middle-class readers knew that "most [builders] lived an almost hand-to-mouth existence, [. . .] the usual practice being to raise a mortgage on one floor of a house to finance the next stage" (Burnett 24). Indeed, as Dyos points out, "speculating builder [. . .] [was] frequently used as [a term] of abuse" (89). However, the man who turned this undesirable figure into a ghost—the murderer—is not figured as a hero in the narrative, as one might expect. Not only is he, too, a speculative builder, but he is "by day" a low-level clerk unable to live within his means.

Neither the murderer nor the murdered in *The Uninhabited House* ideally belongs in a suburban setting because of their problematic relationship to the cash nexus, a relationship which to a great extent defined who "belonged" in the middle class. The ghost, in life, was not only *nouveau riche* but had made his new riches off the middle class, which invested in suburban building more than any other industry (Sheppard 101; Rodger 24). The murderer, on the other hand, is carefully characterized by Mrs. Riddell as the type of person without the middle-class values of self-help and hard work who tries to leapfrog into the middle class by a shortcut (speculation) that ultimately fails. When the ghost succeeds in confronting and "eliminating" his murderer, both pretenders to the middle class are removed from suburban space. This allows the heiress to the property to destroy the house, which represents misappropriated social worth, and replace it with a suburban estate that is, presumably, responsibly planned and represents a good middle-class investment opportunity.

Apart from being problematic in themselves, the ghosts in suburban ghost stories are often connected with attracting unsavoury elements to middle-class space. In "A Tale of a Gas-Light Ghost," the security of a new and potentially prosperous suburb is threatened by the arrival of a murderer as tenant of a new but abandoned villa. This wealthy and reclusive man goes there to escape a ghost that haunts his person rather than his home. The neighbours are agape with curiosity about the man, and he eventually accepts an invitation to a local dinner given by the respectable members of the local society. When, during the dinner party, a corpse is discovered by navvies digging an embankment for the nearby railway line, the haunted man dies suddenly. The implication that a crime has been committed in this emerging border between the new economy and the old emphasizes the ultimate unknowability of suburban existence; one cannot depend on the physical space to provide the measure of the people living within it. In this story, readers can make out the seemingly close connections between the failure of suburban development (figured in the abandoned villas), the arrival of the Other within a supposedly closed border (murderers were not supposed to be able to live "among us"), and violent death on the margin that divides Britain's past and future. Stories like these alternately agitate and relieve their middle-class readers; at the end of the stories the ghosts are laid to rest or removed from suburban space, and the threat, although frighteningly evoked, is nullified.

Because the ghosts in these stories seem to emphasize the rogue elements of middle-class suburban culture that most suburbanites did not want to face, it might be possible to read these stories as subversive of the middle-class quest for homogeneity and privacy in the suburbs, were it not for one feature—the rising middle-class male hero who, in almost all these stories, nullifies the threat of the invasive ghost. These men are generally either clerks who have fallen on hard times or members of the middle class who have otherwise been displaced. Yet all the men intend to make their own fortunes, and the solution to a ghostly suburban mystery tends to secure them a foothold in the middle or upper middle classes. The appearance of a specter enables the middle-class male to defend his space, to say, "I belong here and you don't—get out!" The specter, once avenged, disappears and leaves the male in possession of the house; the boundaries are again defined and closed; and the male is rewarded with money, a wife, or both.

In *The Uninhabited House,* for example, the hero is a clerk in a law office who undertakes the eviction of the ghost for money and the possibility of marriage to the daughter of the speculative builder. The perceived danger of his task does indeed win the notice and eventual admiration of the daughter, and when the ghost has been removed and justice has been done, the hero marries the young woman. The implications for the middle class are complex; as a clerk, the hero is technically a member of the lower levels of the middle class, and, as the daughter of a speculative builder, the heroine's class status is also problematic because of her "low" origins. However, the clerk's victory wins him not only the sub-

stantial reward of twenty-five pounds but also a raise in position, with the potential for continued success. The daughter, now dissociated from her father by a long period of suffering while his ghost haunted "her" house, has an inherited income that is embellished by her profit on the new estate; thus, as an heiress and landlord she is firmly established in the middle class as well.

In Riddell's "The Open Door," the hero is also a clerk who undertakes the job of "evicting" the ghost for a reward and the admiration of his paramour, Patty, who has a little too much of the housemaid about her to qualify as genteel middle class. However, the text implies that she is the proper wife for a lower-level clerk with few prospects of rising in the world: she is "the blithest, prettiest, most useful, most sensible girl that ever made sunshine in a poor man's house" (43). Here propriety is emphasized over property. The clerk is rewarded when he clears the house of its ghostly problem, and he promptly takes a job as the manager of a farm far away from London. He feels that this work is more suited to his inclinations and cannot deny that it is also a great rise in position and prospects; as he says, "I [. . .] make both ends meet comfortably" (67), something his own family never managed, which reflects in their case a low level of both propriety *and* property. Thus, the hero aligns himself with middle-class values both by choosing a wife who will help him "make ends meet" and by taking a position both "properly" suited to his class and representative of property.

"The Old House in Vauxhall Walk," another story by Riddell, also concerns itself with the trope of the rising middle-class male. The underlying disturbing element in this story is the displacement, however temporary, of the middle class. After a dreadful row with his father, the young hero is "houseless—homeless—hopeless!" (85) when he discovers one of his former servants living in a very large (and haunted) house in a slightly seedy suburb. In this case, two young middle-class men profit by bringing about an end to the ghostly activities in the suburban house. The proper heir to the ghost's fortune is restored to his position when the ghost is eliminated (he can "reclaim" the house), while the young hero, previously in disgrace with his father, receives a handsome reward that enables him to get his own start in life. The narrative further implies that in seeing the misery resulting from the ghost-woman's pride and greed, the young hero is more amenable to reconciliation with his father, ensuring a further domestication or normalization of family relations. As he himself tells his father, "I mean to strive to make a better thing of my life than I should ever have done had I not gone to the Old House in Vauxhall Walk" (101).

The suburban ghost story, then, reassures its middle-class readers on a number of fronts by giving the hero a chance to reinforce middle-class codes of behaviour and values. Armstrong argues that domestic fiction provides representations that reject the "carnival" element and thus shore up middle-class control (17). The suburban ghost story allows the middle class to fantasize about the restoration of order and control in their homes and neighbourhoods at a time when they felt under attack from many directions.

Suburban ghost stories not only reassure middle-class readers that suburban space can be defended from lower-class invaders but also serve as a reassurance about the middle class's ability to police *itself*. If privacy was to be so vital to middle-class life, then it was crucial that those with a middle-class position be trusted to behave at all times in a way that upheld middle-class morality. Yet, as everyone knew, some members of the middle class did commit crimes and/or live disreputable lifestyles. Thomas Boyle records that, after about 1850, "barbarous behaviour among the buttoned-up and respectable was generally reported" in the newspapers (35). These newspaper reports "tend[ed] more and more to suggest that deterioration in the social fibre often occurs where things have the greatest appearance of propriety" (40). Suburban ghost narratives further work to reassert moral boundaries by revealing those seemingly respectable middle-class characters who have "let the side down" by committing some outrageous crime. Without the ghost, every single murderer or wrongdoer in these stories stands a fair chance of getting away with it, and, therefore, of letting the "disease" of moral depravity hide out in the suburbs. The ghost, with the help of the middle-class male hero, exposes the criminal and expels him or her from a previously safe social position. This is the case even when the ghost, in life, was a "bad" character. Armstrong points out that in *Oliver Twist,* Nancy's ghost comes back to "work on the side of legitimate authority" (184), no matter how much she resisted its hold on her in life. The same can be said for suburban ghosts; the apparition always appears to reinforce cultural codes and provide a moral lesson for the living, even while it represents an invasion of middle-class space. A ghost story may offer further assurance that middle-class standards can be instituted universally and enforced—crime and all manner of disreputable goings-on will eventually be revealed and exorcized.

Foucault argues that, "in a society in which the principal elements are no longer the community and public life, [. . .] relations can be regulated only in a form that is the exact reverse of spectacle" (216). A specter, invisible, watching, accomplishes this "new" form of regulation because it can know what goes on inside the private home and reveal it (with help from the middle-class male hero) to a select group, for it and it alone knows the "true" story of whatever happens inside the house. It can watch, and through it, the subject can be

seen and disciplined. In these ways, the suburban ghost story can be seen to play an important role in buttressing the middle-class code and reassuring nervous suburbanites that intruders of any sort are, in fact, subject to regulation.

Take, for example, the subplot of Riddell's "Old Mrs. Jones." After Mrs. Jones and her husband disappear, a cabman and his family take the Jones's now slightly seedy suburban house on a three-year lease with the intention of renting out most of the rooms to lodgers. However, the family is bothered by the presence of the ghost of Old Mrs. Jones, who knocks into people and drags things about until no tenants will stay in their rented rooms more than two weeks, resulting in the imminent ruin of the cabman's family. As the narrator makes clear, the working class are misplaced in this neighbourhood and are ruining themselves in attempting to acquire a comfortable middle-class lifestyle. The narrator of this story comes down very hard upon Dick Tippens, the cabman, who "was not laying by a farthing but spending such of his superfluous cash as did not go in the best of good eating [. . .] in the purchase of useless articles of various kinds [. . .] each and all destined eventually to find their way to the pawnbroker as surely and infallibly as the sparks fly upwards" (175). Of Mrs. Tippens the narrator remarks, "I do not think she was a good manager, for she spent up to the hilt of her income. [. . .] She was always considering how to increase her 'gettings,' but she never gave a thought as to how she might save them" (178). Throughout the narrative, the omniscient voice of the narrator makes dreadful predictions about the fate of the Tippens family: "No-one [. . .] could possibly have thought evil days were looming in the distance for both husband and wife" (179); "she had only to say what she wanted, and he would be quite at her service—a promise he found it convenient to forget when evil days fell upon Dick and his wife" (184). What's worse, Tippens brings an old drunkard, an ex-stableboy, into the house to make repairs, but "Old Mickey" manages to install himself as a permanent fixture at the local pub, bringing the tone of the neighbourhood even lower. Finally, when Mrs. Jones's ghost is avenged by the discovery of her husband as murderer, the house mysteriously catches fire and the cabman-landlord and his family are forced to move to another, more "suitable" neighbourhood.

In this story, then, the ghost is at first the catalyst for a situation by which more people who are unsuited to the suburban lifestyle "invade" the neighbourhood. However, in drawing attention to the crime committed in the house, and the subsequent fire that both eradicates all traces of itself and precludes any further misplaced residents, Mrs. Jones's ghost makes amends for her intrusion by warding off the prospect of suburban degeneration.

Popular fiction was not the only genre to address suburban anxieties, but these ghost narratives do so, for the most part, in an uncritical way, not questioning the validity of middle-class fears but rather playing on them in order to appeal to as wide a readership as possible. Sensation fiction of the same period, on the other hand, takes up the issue of the suburb as a means, very often, to subverting middle-class claims on suburbia and questioning the use of suburban space as a reliable means of control by "surveillance." The fiction of Wilkie Collins and Charles Dickens after 1850, in particular, examines the suburbs in ways that echo but also question the tropes found so often in contemporaneous short fiction. In their works, the suburb has a significant role in the "abnormal" or "undomesticated" aspects of Victorian culture. I would hesitate to suggest that one genre borrowed from or grew out of the other. Instead, I would argue that all the representations of the suburb as eerie or grotesque in some way arose from a kind of cultural *zeitgeist* as Victorians struggled to make sense of a phenomenon about which they were deeply conflicted. What is significant about the suburb's appearance in fiction is not that authors should choose it as a subject—after all, it was impossible to ignore suburban growth in this period—but that when chosen it should so often be a site of fear at the same time that, in other works, the suburb was being heralded as a way for the middle class to acquire all the benefits of the *rus in urbe* ideal. What catches our attention as readers, and very likely caught the attention of Victorian readers as well, is that a space assumed to be safe and wholesome should so often be portrayed as dark and sinister. Suburban ghost stories were an attempt to bring some light to the darker aspects of suburban living, with perhaps only marginal success.

Works Cited

Armstrong, Nancy. *Desire and Domestic Fiction: A Political History of the Novel.* New York: Oxford UP, 1987.

Boyle, Thomas. *Black Swine in the Sewers of Hampstead: Beneath the Sewers of Victorian Sensationalism.* New York: Viking, 1989.

Briggs, Asa. *Victorian Cities.* London: Odhams Books, 1963.

Burnett, John. *A Social History of Housing, 1815-1985.* 2nd ed. London: Methuen, 1986.

Dickens, Charles. *Oliver Twist.* 1837. New York: Bantam, 1982.

Dyos, H. J. *Victorian Suburb: A Study of the Growth of Camberwell.* Leicester: Leicester UP, 1973.

Fitzgerald, Percy. *London City Suburbs as They are Today.* London: Leadenhall, 1893.

Foucault, Michel. *Discipline and Punish: The Birth of the Prison.* Trans. Alan Sheridan. New York: Vintage, 1979.

Janowitz, Anne. *England's Ruins: Poetic Purpose and the National Landscape.* Cambridge, MA: Basil Blackwell, 1990.

Jones, Gareth Stedman. *Outcast London: A Study in the Relationship between Classes in Victorian Society.* Oxford: Clarendon, 1971.

Martineau, Harriet. "The Ghost that Appeared to Mrs. Wharton." *Household Words* 2 (November 1850): 139-43.

Nord, Deborah Epstein. *Walking the Victorian Streets: Women, Representation and the City.* Ithaca, NY: Cornell UP, 1995.

Oliphant, Margaret. "The Open Door." c. 1860. *The Gentlewoman of Evil.* Ed. Peter Haining. New York: Taplinger, 1967. 32-71.

Radcliffe, Ann. *The Mysteries of Udolpho: A Romance.* London: Penguin, 2001.

Riddell, Mrs. J. H. *Weird Stories.* London: J. Hogg, 1882.

———. *The Uninhabited House.* 1875. *Five Victorian Ghost Stories.* Ed. E. F. Bleiler. New York: Dover, 1971. 1-112.

———. "Old Mrs. Jones." *The Collected Ghost Stories of Mrs. J. H. Riddell.* Ed. E. F. Bleiler. New York: Dover, 1977. 173-215.

———. "The Old House in Vauxhall Walk." *The Collected Ghost Stories of Mrs. J. H. Riddell.* Ed. E. F. Bleiler. New York: Dover, 1977. 85-101.

———. "The Open Door." *The Collected Ghost Stories of Mrs. J. H. Riddell.* Ed. E. F. Bleiler. New York: Dover, 1977. 38-67.

Rodger, Richard. *Housing in Urban Britain, 1780-1914.* London: Macmillan, 1989.

Sheppard, Francis. *London, 1808-1870: The Infernal Wen.* London: Secker & Warburg, 1971.

"A Tale of a Gas-Light Ghost." *The Gentlewomen of Evil.* Ed. Peter Haining. New York: Taplinger, 1967. 202-12.

Thompson, F. M. L. "Introduction: The Rise of Suburbia." *The Rise of Suburbia.* Ed. F. M. L. Thompson. Leicester: Leicester UP, 1982.

Thorne, James. *Handbook to the Environs of London.* 1876. London: Godfrey Cave, 1983.

Walpole, Horace. *The Castle of Otranto.* London: Penguin, 2001.

BACKGROUND: GHOST STORIES OF THE EARLY NINETEENTH CENTURY

G. R. Thompson (essay date 1983)

SOURCE: Thompson, G. R. "Washington Irving and the American Ghost Story." In *The Haunted Dusk: American Supernatural Fiction, 1820-1920,* edited by Howard Kerr, John W. Crowley, and Charles L. Crow, pp. 11-36. Athens: University of Georgia Press, 1983.

[*In the following essay, Thompson argues against the prevailing notion that the psychological ghost story was born in the mid- to late nineteenth century, finding instead that it was the early nineteenth-century American writer Washington Irving who introduced psychological elements to the ghost story.*]

In the introduction to her well-known anthology *The Supernatural in the English Short Story* Pamela Search attempts to categorize the types and modes of supernatural agency in the tale of terror, the ghost story, and the Gothic tale.[1] While she tries to keep her distinctions clear, she ends up blurring Gothic, horror, ghostly, and supernatural tales into one. Perhaps this loose classification is adequate for her purposes (and perhaps instinctively right), but along the way she makes a discovery. The "horror tale had its heyday in the earlier years" of the twentieth century, she writes; but "since then another kind of weird fiction has come into its own—the psychological ghost story" (p. 13). What she means by psychological ghost story, however, is not a tale in which apparently supernatural events turn out to be the misperceptions of a nervous narrator or distraught character. As Search defines it, the psychological ghost story is "the *inconclusive* tale of the supernatural" (p. 13), exemplified by the tales of Walter De La Mare. In fact, she implies that De La Mare invented the type.

In stories like his, a *possible* supernatural agency is balanced off against a *possible* psychological "explanation," with more or less ambiguous results. We are unsure whether the events narrated are real or misperceived; we are not concerned, however, with psychological misperception in itself but with the inconclusive character of the story. This kind of tale, Search claims, is more effective than the old-fashioned ghost story because "when the horror is left undefined it becomes all the more real to us in our imagination, and the inconclusive ending of the tale leaves us with our doubts and fears unresolved, and therefore more terrible."[2]

Now everyone knows that Henry James, not Walter De La Mare, invented the psychological ghost story. Search knows the conventional wisdom on the history of the

type too. Therefore she defends her claim by suggesting that although in *The Turn of the Screw* (1898) James anticipated the technique, he did not combine "the supernatural with the psychological" nearly "so compellingly as De La Mare." At this point, Search's opinion about the quality of James's effects as compared with De La Mare's may be called into question, but we might not challenge her historical accuracy regarding the ghost story proper—even if the names of Bierce, Poe, Hawthorne, and Irving come momentarily to mind. But then we are brought up short by her comment that "there have been stories of this type ever since Le Fanu wrote his famous *Green Tea.*"

Joseph Sheridan Le Fanu (1814-73) may have been the greatest British ghost-story writer of the nineteenth century, but "Green Tea" is only vaguely about a "ghost" and it came late in his career (1869). "Green Tea" tells the story of a mild-mannered and morally upright minister, Mr. Jennings, who is bedevilled by a sinister monkey with glowing red eyes. Information is filtered through the papers of one Dr. Hesselius, who has "treated" Jennings for his apparently hallucinatory demon: the monkey is visible to no one but Jennings. At times it even sits on his Bible during sermons, so that he seems to his hearers nervous and distracted, frequently breaking off in the middle of a text. Jennings tries various means of warding off the demon, and it disappears from time to time, but always returns. Jennings finally consults Hesselius, who has treated many weird cases. Hesselius concludes after Jennings's suicide that a chemical reaction, the result of recurrent overdoses of strong green tea, must have opened up some "inner eye" in the man's mind. A rift in the tissue or interface between an occult world and the ordinary, everyday world allowed Jennings a glimpse of an alien realm of being. On the other hand, we are reminded, Jennings had a family history of suicidal mania.[3] "Green Tea," Julia Briggs observes in her recent study *Night Visitors: The Rise and Fall of the English Ghost Story,* is "poised, somewhat mystifyingly, between these two explanations."[4]

"Green Tea" is the focal point of another new study of the ghost story as well. Jack Sullivan, in *Elegant Nightmares: The English Ghost Story from Le Fanu to Blackwood,* devotes to the tale a chapter entitled "The Archetypal Ghost Story."[5] Even if we grant for the sake of argument that "Green Tea" actually is an inconclusive story about a "ghost," it is still puzzling to discover that this new type is the archetype. What happened to the prototypes, where ghosts were either actual supernatural presences or were satisfactorily explained away? And how is it that the archetype is the new "variant" or a "development"? Sullivan writes that in 1839 "a new kind" of "ghost appeared in English fiction" (p. 11) with the publication of Le Fanu's "Schalken the Painter," a macabre tale about a demonic or ghostly lover who claims a living bride and transforms her into a ghost. The technique of narration, Sullivan claims, was "revolutionary"; there is a double point of view involving the perspective of the victimized young girl's befuddled uncle and that of her horrified fiancé. The plot moves toward a dream sequence, where a coffin is transformed into a Victorian four-poster. "Schalken the Painter" is, according to Sullivan, the "promising start" of a development in ghostly fiction that culminates thirty years later in "Green Tea," which represents the new ghost story in "its most uncompromising form" (p. 12).

Sullivan seems to sense that he is on shaky ground in his claims for Le Fanu, for he is quick to disqualify Edgar Allan Poe as a ghost-story writer. He observes that 1839 was not only the publication date of "Schalken the Painter," but also of Poe's "The Fall of the House of Usher." But in Le Fanu the ghost seems simultaneously "to emerge from within as well as invade from without" (p. 11). His concern with "Usher" implies that something similar happens in Poe. But Poe's story, he says, is an "exercise in cosmic paranoia rather than a tale of the supernatural" (p. 11). Sullivan has a point, but the same might be said of Le Fanu's "Green Tea," if it is to be read as the inconclusive tale he claims it is. Sullivan attempts to cover himself on another point as well: "As the less than reliable narrator of a horror tale, Hesselius is part of a tradition which begins with Poe's narrator in 'The Tell-Tale Heart' and culminates in the governess's account in *The Turn of the Screw*," but the "narrative problems are more complex than those in Poe" (p. 29). One wonders in what ways Poe's narrators before 1843—those of "MS. Found in a Bottle" (1833), "Berenice" (1835), "Morella" (1835), "Ligeia" (1838), and "William Wilson" (1839)—are so clearly reliable, or in what ways the double point of view of "Usher" is less complex than the editorial siftings of "Green Tea."

Sullivan, like most critics of the ghost story, admits that he uses the phrase "ghost story" as a "catch-all term." But since all the stories he deals with are, he says, "apparitional, in one sense or another . . . 'ghost story' is as good a term as any" (p. 9). If so, how then are the apparitions of Poe's tales "of a different order" from Le Fanu's in "Green Tea"? Although "horror story" is "not quite as all-inclusive" a term, Sullivan writes, "most English tales fall into the class of *both* ghost and horror story, so that the terms are almost interchangeable" (p. 9). He observes that "Lovecraft's 'supernatural horror' neatly fuses both terms," *ghost* suggesting the supernatural realm and *horror* apparently suggesting "physical mayhem and revulsion" (p. 9). Such comment echoes standard thumbnail definitions of one effect of the Gothic. Is the Gothic, then, different from the ghost story only in its wider applicability to fear-driven narrative, so that the ghost story is limited in its effect to an "apparition"? Sullivan tells us that there "is little to be gained . . . by attempting to determine precisely" what the limits are between "ghost and horror tales" (p. 9). This allows him to denigrate the Gothic tradition and claim as a novelty in the ghost story something that has already reached an apogee in the American Gothic tale as practiced by Irving, Hawthorne, and Poe.

In his eagerness to separate the ghost story from the Gothic, Sullivan claims that "the modern ghostly tale is as much a reaction against the Gothic as an outgrowth of it," for Gothic ghosts were largely "decorative," lacking the "more actively loathesome, menacing quality of modern ghosts" (pp. 5-6). Part of this menacing quality comes from the centrally inconclusive nature of the Le Fanu "archetype." Sullivan attacks "theory-obsessed critics" who would read such a work as "Green Tea" as Freudian or Christian allegory and thus miss the teasing, elusive, enigmatic quality of the tale. As the archetypal ghost story, he says, "Green Tea" is representative of a fundamentally disordered universe, incapable of rational codification. This point, Sullivan claims, is not noted by other writers on the ghost story (p. 5). If so, it must be the result of their inattention to the basic modes of the Gothic tale, for the disordered universe of the Gothic is the matrix from which the ghost story issues in its various forms.

Although it is conventional to divide the Gothic romance into two types—the supernatural and the explained supernatural—actually four modes may be usefully distinguished.[6] Historical Gothic is ontologically undifferentiated. The presence of an occasional demon or ghost is not necessarily significant for either the ontology *or* the epistemology of a text. In supernatural Gothic, the occult is in fact a central assumption. In the explained Gothic, the final assumption is that the supernatural does not, finally, interpenetrate the everyday world: all seemingly occult phenomena are the result of misinformation or misperception. But in ambiguous Gothic, it is the *tension* between the supernatural and the everyday that generates dread. Briggs does a somewhat better job than Sullivan in setting forth the development of the psychological ghost story within the Gothic tradition. Although she too sees "Green Tea" as a prime example, she traces the inconclusive tale back to the German writer, Hoffmann, a contemporary of Irving: "If any one writer can be credited with the invention of this twist it is E. T. A. Hoffmann," who, she observes, had greater impact on French and American writers than on any English writer (pp. 144-45). She mentions "The Golden Flower-Pot" (1814, rev. 1819) and "A New Year's Eve Adventure" (1814-16), neither of which is strictly a ghost story, though supernatural realms do intrude on the everyday world. But she does not mention Hoffmann's predecessors in the inconclusive supernatural, notably Ludwig Tieck and J. A. K. Musaeus, who enjoyed a certain vogue in both Britain and America. Nor does she speak of Hoffmann's contemporaries, like Clemens Brentano, "Bonaventura," Achim von Arnim, Jean Paul Friedrich Richter, and other explorers of the supernatural and psychic realms in fiction.[7] Similarly, she fails to mention key French writers, like Théophile Gautier and Prosper Mérimée, who were early concerned with the wavering line between the supernatural and the natural. She does acknowledge a later nineteenth-century writer, Maupassant, noting that "The Horla" (1887), a tale about an invisible creature haunting a possibly deranged narrator, antedates *The Turn of the Screw*. Other important omissions include major American writers: Brown, Irving, Hawthorne. Presumably this is because there are so few out-and-out ghost stories among the Americans, though the British examples cited are frequently not strict ghost stories either.

Like Sullivan, Briggs does deal with Poe, who, she says, "created the prototypes of a number of variations on the psychological ghost story" (p. 145). Why Poe is singled out as having written more ghost stories than Irving or Hawthorne is unclear; certainly those of his tales that could be said to deal with ghosts per se are as few as those of the other two American writers. Nevertheless, she identifies three prototypes of Poe's psychological ghost tales: one is the description of grotesque events in such a way as to throw doubt on the narrator's sanity; a second is the dramatization of the narrator's urge to self-destruction; a third is the indication of a particular form of mental disturbance, such as the schizophrenia of William Wilson. The only other historical commentary she offers is the observation that the psychological ghost story uses the Radcliffe method of rational explanation of seeming marvels, but with "a more open-ended effect" (p. 143). Apparently, then, the originator of the psychological ghost story in English is Poe, about whom Sullivan is so concerned. But I would like to press the matter back a generation further, to Washington Irving, a writer who was not only deeply influenced by German romantic fiction, but who also did in fact write *ghost* stories.

II

Some of Irving's best known tales represent the range of modes for the ghost story, complicated, however, by his sportive humor.[8] A straight supernatural tale is found in "Dolph Heyliger" (1822). What seems to be an actual ghost in a haunted house leads Dolph into a series of adventures that eventually uncovers treasure, while during the course of the narrative the ghost-ship of the Hudson makes its appearance and disappearance. In "The Spectre Bridegroom" (1820), a story with a skillful blend of humor and ominous mystery, there is a central, horripilated scene where a mysterious guest at a wedding feast seems to rise up to a gigantic height to cry out that he is late for his appointment with the worms. It is all explained at the end. The bride and her

family have never seen the intended groom, whose party has been ambushed on the way to the bride's castle. A survivor comes with the melancholy news of the slain bridegroom, is mistaken for the intended groom, and, before he can explain, is smitten with the beauty of the bride to be. He assumes the groom's identity, and exits with the portentous cry that he is dead so that he can later return to carry off the bride without protest from her father. "The Legend of Sleepy Hollow" (1819) exhibits what is on the surface a legitimate ghost, but it too is written in the explained mode. After the headless horseman has chased Ichabod Crane through the night and has hurled his "head" at him by the bridge, we are offered a sly innuendo that Brom Bones, the competing suitor for the beautiful Katrina, has staged the whole thing, though the remains of a shattered pumpkin are by no means conclusive evidence for the narrator—despite Bones's knowing smile. There is no particular mystery about the events of the tale, but the explanation is less overt and the effect somewhat more open-ended than that of "The Spectre Bridegroom." Whether or not the strange figures in the mountains in "Rip Van Winkle" (1819) qualify as ghosts, the story overtly presents an encounter with the supernatural, except that there is again the wink of innuendo regarding the timing of Rip's return to his village, which comes after the death of his shrewish wife. The theme of revolution becomes personal as well as political, suggesting that Rip's legendary sleep may have been the useful contrivance of a henpecked husband. Still, we are not sure but what the ghosts from the past that Rip reports seeing do in fact exist, despite all the consumption of alcohol. It is an interconnected series of lesser-known tales, however, that is Irving's main contribution to the psychological ghost story.

Although *Tales of a Traveller* (1824) is generally regarded as Irving's least successful work, its opening section, "Strange Stories by a Nervous Gentleman," undergoes a surprisingly complex progression from supernatural to explained to ambiguous ghost stories, and thence to psychological Gothic.[9] Moreover, the entire series is unified by a progressive development of an erotic theme, a central concern of the Gothic tradition. The Nervous Gentleman, we are told by the narrator-author (Geoffrey Crayon), is the very same gentleman that tells the tale of "The Stout Gentleman" in *Bracebridge Hall* (1822). After a playful introduction (in which it is suggested, though not confirmed, that the "Great Unknown" personage of that tale who so puzzles the Nervous Gentleman may be no less than Sir Walter Scott), the basic frame of the sequence of tales is established.[10] A baronet hosts a hunting dinner for an indeterminate number of guests, but it includes the second narrator (that is, the Nervous Gentleman) and several other odd persons. Among them are an Irish captain of dragoons; the Gentleman with the Haunted Head, one side of whose face does not match the other; a thin, hatchet-faced gentleman with protruding lobsterlike eyes; the Inquisitive Gentleman, who is never satisfied with a story as given; the old Gentleman with the Flexible Nose; a country clergyman; a beetlebrowed barrister with a hawk's nose. The night is windy and rainy, perfect for ghost stories. The Gentleman with the Haunted Head is first to answer the call for ghost stories by relating "The Adventure of My Uncle," which is followed by accounts from the others of experiences that relatives have had (an aunt, a grandfather) until the Gentleman with the Haunted Head tells a second tale, the "Adventure of the German Student." His second tale, as we shall see, returns to and extends the Gothic ambiguity of his first.

The Gentleman with the Haunted Head sets the scene of "The Adventure of My Uncle" in an ancient château in Normandy. The uncle is given a room in the tower of the oldest part of the château, which in ancient times had been the donjon. The chamber has a "wild, crazy look," with high narrow windows in which the casements rattle with every breeze (p. 27). The door stands ajar, opening on a long, dark corridor that "seemed just made for ghosts to air themselves in, when they turned out of their graves at midnight" (p. 28). The wind springs up to a hoarse murmur through the passage. Unable to force the door completely shut against the damp, chilly breeze, the uncle piles up the bedclothes and falls asleep. He is awakened by the old clock of the château and thinks he counts thirteen strokes. He begins to fall asleep again, but then he hears the sound of footsteps approaching the doorway. The door opens ("whether of its own accord, or whether pushed open, my uncle could not distinguish") and a "figure all in white" glides in (p. 29). It is the apparition of a tall and stately woman dressed in an ancient fashion. She walks to the fireplace, where the bluish light of the flames reveals a beautiful but ghastly, pale face "saddened by care and anxiety" (p. 30). The figure casts a "glassy look about the apartment, which, as it passed over my uncle, made his blood run cold, and chilled the very marrow of his bones. It then stretched its arms toward heaven, clasped its hands, and wringing them in a supplicating manner, glided slowly out of the room" (p. 30). Since the uncle is a "man of reflection," he does not "reject a thing because it was out of the regular course of events" (pp. 30-31). But because he is also a man of firmness and is "accustomed to strange adventures" (a point that will prove important later), he goes gradually back to sleep.

The next morning, walking with the Marquis de—, owner of the château, the uncle sees in the picture gallery "a full-length portrait," which strikes him as being "the very counterpart of his visitor of the preceding night." He remarks to the marquis, "Methinks . . . I have seen the original of this portrait." The marquis replies that "that can hardly be, as the lady has been dead

for more than a hundred years" (p. 32). The marquis then tells him the long story of the Duchess de Longueville, who played a part in the civil wars in the youth of Louis XIV. Imprisoned in the château of Dieppe, she escaped through an unguarded postern gate of the castle and made her way to the sea. She nearly drowned in an attempt to board a ship through the storm-tossed surf and finally had to return to the countryside on horseback, arriving at the very château where the uncle has been spending the night. She stayed in the same apartment the uncle has just occupied. The marquis tells him he remembers the precise date because "there is a tradition—that a strange occurrence took place that night.—A strange, mysterious, inexplicable occurrence—" (p. 36). But the marquis refuses to tell more, to the great exasperation of the uncle, who finally blurts out, "I saw that lady last night." The marquis listens attentively to the details of the uncle's story and then takes a pinch of snuff and says "Bah!" (p. 37).

Here the uncle's story also breaks off, and the exasperated hearers ask the Gentleman with the Haunted Head for more details.

> ". . . and what did your uncle say then?"
>
> "Nothing," . . .
>
> "And what did the Marquis say farther?"
>
> "Nothing."
>
> "And is that all?"
>
> "That is all."

At this, the "shrewd old gentleman with the waggish nose" offers an "explanation"; he surmises that "it was the old housekeeper, walking her rounds to see that all was right." To which the *narrator* now abruptly says "Bah!" (p. 37).

A subtheme of the tale is concerned with tale-telling itself, a cumulative major theme of the entire sequence of tales. During the marquis's long, digressive history of the duchess, the uncle is repeatedly exasperated with his inability to get to the point. The irony that the point is not to be revealed further underscores the metafictional concern. Moreover, each of the group brings to the *event* of the *tale* his own preconceptions. With artful symmetry, the narrator has the marquis say "Bah!" to the uncle's supernatural tale of the ghost, just as the narrator says "Bah!" to the rational explanation offered by one of the hearers.

This playful little frame has more importance for the whole series of tales than may be immediately evident. As a narrator aware of his audience, the Gentleman with the Haunted Head has a character in his uncle's narrative scoff at part of the uncle's narrative (the ghost story) in a way that will provoke dissatisfaction with the Gentleman with the Haunted Head's entire narrative. This sets up an opportunity for him to scoff at his hearers in a direct parallel with that of a character in the narrative, the marquis, who is himself also a narrator. From the point of view of the entire frame narrative, the Nervous Gentleman, as narrator of "Strange Stories" within Geoffrey Crayon's narrative *Tales of a Traveller,* has the Gentleman with the Haunted Head scoff at the response of a hearer (the Gentleman with the Flexible Nose) as a parallel with the response of the marquis as narrator-hearer in the uncle's narrative as narrated by the Gentleman with the Haunted Head, to whom the uncle had narrated the two tales and their frame. One of the ironies this structure generates is that the Gentleman with the Haunted Head hereby aligns himself, as hearer, with the skeptic of his uncle's narrative, which he himself has just narrated, while simultaneously aligning himself, as narrator of an actual ghost story, with its narrator (his uncle). As the distinction blurs between apparent fact (the series of narratives the group tells, at the baron's château) and the apparent fiction (the double narrative and the denial of the facts of one, at the marquis's château), an infinite regression almost (but not quite) opens up. He contends that the supernatural fact of the tale is proved by the fact that his uncle was so accustomed to strange sights that he would have no trouble distinguishing a ghost from a housekeeper. The conclusion does not settle anything, of course; it merely blurs subjectivity and objectivity absurdly together. As the tale dissolves into its humorous frame of teller and hearers, it becomes poised abruptly, mystifyingly pointless, between the two poles of the supernatural and the explained.

The hearer who asks the questions is the Inquisitive Gentleman, described in the opening frame narrative as one who "never seemed satisfied with the whole of a story; never laughed when others laughed; but always put the joke to the question. He could never enjoy the kernel of the nut, but pestered himself to get more out of the shell" (p. 20). Of course, this is precisely the ironic position to which the reader of the interlinked series of "Strange Stories" is forced. The Nervous Gentleman, recounting the whole sequence to Geoffrey Crayon, then concludes that he is inclined to think the Gentleman with the Haunted Head really does have an "after-part of his story in reserve." But when he refuses to say anything more, there begins to appear something in his "dilapidated countenance that left me in doubt whether he were in drollery or earnest" (p. 38). This complicates the problem of subjectivity and objectivity even further, paralleling the ironic narrative tone of the whole set of tales and frames.

If one compares Irving's version of this tale with the anonymously published "Story of an Apparition" (1818) in *Blackwood's Edinburgh Magazine* or with Scott's "The Tapestried Chamber; or, The Lady in the Sacque"

(1828), the differences between the British and the American handling of the same story are striking. Irving had visited Scott at Abbottsford in 1817, where he heard from him a story told to Scott in 1807 by Miss Anna Seward of Lichfield. Irving encouraged Scott to construct a tale from it, and perhaps the appearance of the *Blackwood's* tale the next year (though Scott's authorship is uncertain) is the result. In any case, the suggestion in Irving's opening frame narrative that the "Great Unknown" is Scott (whose protruding backside was all the Nervous Gentleman ever got to see in *Bracebridge Hall*) seems to be an oblique allusion to the challenge of constructing a ghost story from the legend. Both the Scott version and the *Blackwood's* version are straight supernatural stories about the "ghost of an unfortunate ancestress," to whom Scott attributes murder, incest, and suicide, whereas Irving's figure is more heroic and her fate totally uncertain.[11] Coleman Parsons observes that although the owner of the castle in Scott's story is a "complete skeptic on the subject of supernatural appearances" just the day before, he "does not try to explain his guest's experience as a dream, a vagary of the imagination, or an optical illusion. Instead, he believes and immediately sets about closing up the tapestried chamber."[12] In neither of the British versions is there much narrative framing, much less thematic or ontological ambiguity, and neither evidences metafictional concern for the narrative effect (serious or otherwise) on the auditors or readers of the tale.

The abrupt inconclusiveness of this first tale leads the Gentleman with the Flexible Nose to tell a more "satisfying" story, or at least what initially seems to the listeners more satisfying, "The Adventure of My Aunt." Although a brief anecdote, it is repeatedly intruded upon by the hearers. A strong-willed widow moves to a lonely house in Derbyshire. One evening while looking at herself in the mirror to see if she is still attractive enough to interest a "roistering squire" in the neighborhood, "she thought she heard something move behind her" (p. 41). But all she sees is a newly installed portrait of her dead husband. She gives a heavy sigh to his memory, whereupon her sigh is "re-echoed, or answered by a long-drawn breath" (p. 41). Momentarily, she thinks she sees one of the portrait's eyes move. But instead of being frightened, she goes downstairs and has her servants arm themselves with whatever is at a hand and leads them back to her room, herself brandishing a red-hot poker, saying, "Ghosts! . . . I'll singe their whiskers for them!" (p. 42). She orders the portrait taken down, and there in what was once a clock-niche stands a former servant of the house, armed with a knife, but trembling before the widow's ferocity. He had cut an eyehole in the portrait to watch for a chance to steal her money.

At this point, the relatively undeveloped story seems to the hearers well "concluded." But the Inquisitive

Gentleman wants to know more. What did they do with the intruder—hang him? The narrator, the Gentleman with the Flexible Nose, says that the widow merely ordered him to be "drawn through the horsepond, to cleanse away all offences, and then to be well rubbed down with an oaken towel" (p. 44). Still unsatisfied, the Inquisitive Gentleman asks, "And what became of him afterwards?" The narrator suggests that perhaps he was sent to Botany Bay as a criminal. But now the Inquisitive Gentleman wants to know if the aunt had her maid sleep in the room with her afterward. No, she married the roistering squire. These questions pick up a motif introduced earlier in the telling of the tale, when the Gentleman with the Haunted Head first interrupts the narrative to comment (with a knowing look) on the aunt's being able to see the portrait's eye with the back of her head toward it. To this the narrator had replied that she saw it reflected in the mirror (p. 41). Now, despite the first consensus that this "last narrator had brought his tale to the most satisfactory conclusion," the very genre of the tale is under question. The Inquisitive Gentleman is not at all satisfied with the ontology of the tale: "But I don't see, after all . . . that there was any ghost in this last story" (p. 44). The implication, in the frame narrative, is that the explained mode is ultimately as unsatisfactory as the unexplained first tale.

The newly dominant dissatisfaction with explained ghosts leads, ironically, to "The Bold Dragoon; or, The Adventure of My Grandfather," told by the Irish captain, who says, "If it's ghosts you want, you shall have a whole regiment of them" (p. 44). The irony, of course, is that the ghosts in his tale—pieces of furniture that dance—are not necessarily any more "real" than the "ghost" behind the aunt's portrait of her husband, though the explanation is more covert. The Irish narrator's grandfather was himself a dragoon, a bold, "saucy, sunshiny fellow," who "always had a knack of making himself understood among the women" (p. 43). This last bit of information, later elaborated, at first seems digressive but is actually central to the ghostly adventure. Moreover, it also makes clearer the underlying erotic motif of the entire sequence of "Strange Stories." The grandfather stops at an "old rackety inn" with a sign "that promised good liquor." The landlord does not like his "saucy eye." Told that there are no rooms available, the Bold Dragoon determinedly slaps his thigh (in an earlier version his tight buckskins are mentioned), and the "slap went to the landlady's heart" (p. 48). He likewise charms all the ladies of the household, who hatch a plan "to accommodate him" with "an old chamber, that had for some time been shut up." The landlady's daughter remarks to him in apparent admiration, "I dare say you don't fear ghosts" (p. 49).

That night "not a female head in the inn was laid on a pillow . . . without dreaming of the Bold Dragoon" (p.

51). He himself finds "the blood in his veins . . . in fever heat," supposedly, according to the narrator, because he is "a warm-complexioned man" and the "great bags of down" both on top of him in the cover and below in the mattress begin to "melt" him (pp. 51-52). The Inquisitive Gentleman here wants to know if the maid had warmed the bed too much. "I rather think the contrary," replies the narrator, adding that for whatever the reason, his grandfather "jumped out of bed and went strolling about the house." "What for?" the Inquisitive Gentleman asks. "Why, to cool himself . . . or perhaps to find a more comfortable bed—or perhaps—But no matter what he went for—he never mentioned—and there's no use taking up our time in conjecturing" (p. 52). Having warded off this attack on his story, the narrator continues. His grandfather "had been for some time absent from his room, and was returning, perfectly cool, when just as he reached the door, he heard a strange noise within." Remembering the story of the room's being haunted, he peeps in to see "a pale weazen-face fellow, in a long flannel gown and a tall white night-cap with a tassel to it, who sat by the fire with a bellows under his arm by way of bagpipe, from which he forced . . . asthmatical music" (p. 53). Suddenly a long-backed, leather-covered chair, "studded all over in a coxcombical fashion," slides up to "an easy chair, of tarnished brocade, with a hole in its bottom, and led it gallantly in a ghostly minuet about the floor" (p. 53). Except for a great clothes-press, the rest of the furniture and other items join in the dance. To the Bold Dragoon the clothes-press seems like a female, a corpulent dowager, at a loss for a partner. Therefore, he bounces into the room and seizes the clothes-press "upon the two handles to lead her out," for he is "a true Irishman, devoted to the sex, and at all times ready for a frolic." But as soon as he does this, "whirr! the whole revel was at an end," the pieces of furniture shrink in an instant quietly into their places, and he finds himself "seated in the middle of the floor with the clothes-press sprawling before him, and the two handles jerked off, and in his hands" (p. 54).

The Inquisitive Gentleman here suggests that this is not a ghostly experience either. "This was a mere dream!" he says, explaining away the ghosts. But the Irish narrator will have none of it. "The divil a bit of a dream!" he says. "There was never a truer fact in this world" (p. 54). He continues, telling how the noise from the crash of the clothes-press brings the landlady and landlord and their daughter, along with the barmaid and all the chambermaids, up to see what is the matter. By way of explanation, the grandfather "related the marvellous scene he had witnessed." Moreover, the broken clothes-press "bore testimony to the fact." The landlady, however, "did not seem half pleased with the explanation." But her daughter "corroborates" it by recollecting that a famous juggler who died of St. Vitus's dance had been the last occupant of the chamber and must have infected the furniture (p. 55).

So the dream explanation is countered by the pseudoghostly explanation. But the tale finally comes down on the side of psychological explanation rather than remaining poised ambiguously between the two. For the tale is actually a sly account of the Bold Dragoon's sexual exploits during the night; and his vision, or drunken dream, or concocted explanation is appropriately erotic, from the bellows (traditionally a phallic symbol from the Middle Ages on), to the "coxcombical" leather-backed chair leading out the "tarnished" "easy-chair" with a hole in her bottom, to the dowager clothes-press in need of a partner. The other pieces include "a three-legged stool . . . horribly puzzled by its supernumerary leg" and a pair of "amourous tongs" which seize "the shovel round the waist" (p. 53).

The chambermaids come forward to "corroborate" the Bold Dragoon's story. They had "all witnessed strange carryings on in that room," and "declared this 'upon their honors,'" the quotation marks giving the sly wink (p. 55). Here the Inquisitive Gentleman asks if the grandfather had gone to bed again in the room. The Irish narrator says, "That's more than I can tell. Where he passed the rest of the night was a secret he never disclosed." Apparently, he had several options among the daughter, the barmaid, and the chambermaids. The narrator adds at this point that his grandfather was "apt to make blunders in his travels about inns at night," which "it would have puzzled him greatly to account for in the morning" (p. 55). Apparently missing the point, or possibly indulging further the ironic hoax, the Knowing Old Gentleman asks: "Was he ever apt to walk in his sleep?" On the surface, such a question reverts to the dream interpretation, but the amorous point is concluded when the narrator, whatever his perception of his grandfather's story, replies with finality: "Never that I heard of" (p. 56).

III

The old Gentleman with the Haunted Head now objects that the first stories have been of a burlesque turn, and he proposes to tell a real ghost story, the "Adventure of the German Student." Its place in the sequence of "Strange Stories" is significant. The first story, also told by this narrator, is an unconcluded tale of seeing a ghost that is the image of a portrait; the abrupt end and refusal to go further exasperate the hearers' desire for a more or less rational conclusion. Whether supernatural or not, the story requires for them some sort of framing in the normative world. But the Gentleman with the Haunted Head silently features a face that leaves the Nervous Gentleman in doubt as to whether there is a serious tale there or only a hoax. The second tale, "Adventure of My Aunt," is a fully explained piece that is initially satisfactory to the hearers because of the rational explanation, but subsequently unsatisfactory because the listeners want real ghosts. The third tale has both a rational psychological explanation and a supernatural explanation, but with a satiric undercurrent that finally, though somewhat subtly, makes the ghost-dance more probably the half-drunken dream, half-shrewd cover story of the amorous Bold Dragoon.

"Adventure of the German Student," the next logical step in tale-telling in the sequence of stories, is equidistantly poised between psychological explanation and the demonic. The three tales that follow the "German Student" continue the theme of the mysterious portrait in a series of Chinese-box narratives, each one seemingly explained by the next narrative, but actually finding only a partial resolution. The "German Student" is the pivotal tale of the "Strange Stories," dividing the sequence in half, fully developing the ambiguous technique, and changing the tone of the series from humorous to somber, though maintaining the irony.

Young Wolfgang, a German student in Paris during the Reign of Terror, is initially presented as someone whose imagination has been "diseased" by his studies in "spiritual essences." He becomes obsessed by the idea that "there was an evil influence hanging over him," an "evil genius or spirit seeking to ensnare him and ensure his perdition" (p. 57). This characterization is background to a recurrent dream of a woman's face that "haunts" him both in sleeping and waking moments. This "shadow of a dream" becomes "one of those fixed ideas which haunt the minds of melancholy men, and are at times mistaken for madness" (p. 59). Thus contradictory suggestions are set up: he is mad and he is not. One stormy night he crosses the square where public executions are held and in the flashing lightning sees the guillotine. At the foot of the steps of the scaffold, revealed in a "succession of vivid flashes of lightning," is a "female figure, dressed in black," sitting on one of the steps, leaning forward (p. 59). She looks up and in "the bright glare of the lightning" reveals to Wolfgang "the very face which had haunted him in his dreams," pale and disconsolate, though beautiful (p. 60). He takes her to his apartment, where, after some soothing conversation, he suddenly asks her to pledge herself to him. He says to her:

> "I pledge myself to you for ever."
>
> "For ever?" said the stranger, solemnly.
>
> "For ever!" repeated Wolfgang.
>
> The stranger clasped the hand extended to her: "Then I am yours, murmured she."
>
> (p. 63)

Having spent the next morning looking for more spacious apartments, he returns to find her lying dead on the bed. When the police arrive, they inform him that "she was guillotined yesterday." Wolfgang undoes a black collar around her neck, and "the head rolled on the floor!" (p. 64). At this point the reader is confronted with two possibilities: either Wolfgang is mad and has hallucinated the experience, or he has spent the night with a ghost. On the surface, the tale seems to be in the explained mode, and critics have generally read it that way: the mad young German has carried away a corpse and made love to it. But the introductory characterization presents opposing possibilities, each equally viable. Somehow, though his imagination is diseased, he is not mad. His own response does not resolve either possibility. He returns to the obsession mentioned in the second paragraph of the tale: "The fiend! the fiend has gained possession of me! . . . I am lost for ever." The narrator then remarks: "He was possessed with the frightful belief that an evil spirit had reanimated the dead body to ensnare him" (p. 64). This observation neither confirms nor denies the actuality of supernatural manifestation. Certainly, if she were in fact a ghost, Wolfgang's pledge "for ever" insures his damnation, and her response, "I am yours," also means "you are mine." Traditionally, a demonic pact drives one insane. From the moment of the pact—whatever the actuality of subsequent events—Wolfgang is damned. His "madness," whether at the scaffold or at the end, may be the sign of the pact. The story is poised, like Le Fanu's "Green Tea" thirty-five years later, between these two possibilities for a final ambiguous twist.

The wry conclusion of the narrative frame for this story underscores the essential ambiguity. The Inquisitive Gentleman asks the narrator (the old Gentleman with the Haunted Head) if all this is "really a fact." "'A fact not to be doubted,' replied the other. 'I had it from the best authority. The student told it me himself. I saw him in a mad-house in Pairs'" (p. 64). The "madness" confirms the "fact." What fact? That the story was told? That a ghost possessed the student? That the student was mad? The ambiguous structure of the tale within a tale, providing thereby "witnesses" who testify to the central "fact" of the narrative, serves only to emphasize the essential epistemological ambiguity of the tale, thereby also underscoring its ontological ambiguity.

The German Student's adventure is followed by the "Adventure of the Mysterious Picture," told by the overall frame narrator, the Nervous Gentleman (as filtered through the "author"). After the tale of the German Student, the guests retire, and the host, the baronet, says that one of them will sleep in a haunted room, but none shall know which it is "until circumstances reveal it" (p. 66). The Nervous Gentleman is shown to a room resembling in general style and furnishings those "described in the tales of the supper-table" (p. 66). He becomes uneasy in the presence of a portrait of a young man's face "that appeared to be staring full upon me, with an expression that was startling." The "emotions it

caused were strange and indefinite . . . something like what I have heard ascribed to the eyes of the basilisk, or like that mysterious influence in reptiles termed fascination." Every time he shields his eyes in an effort to "brush away this illusion . . . they instantly reverted to the picture, and its chilling, creeping influence over my flesh and blood was redoubled" (p. 67). The expression on the face of the young man is of the "agony of intense bodily pain" combined with a scowling "menace." The total effect is of "some horror of the mind," by which the picture awakens in the narrator an "inscrutable antipathy" (p. 68).

The next morning the Nervous Gentleman remarks on the "most singular and incomprehensible" effect the picture had on him (p. 74). The parallel with the opening story highlights important differences. Although the first story is not truly concluded, the protagonist sees or thinks he sees the ghost of the image in a portrait; this frame sequence develops a vague, amorphous unease. The other guests, being in a bantering mood, laugh at the Nervous Gentleman's apprehensiveness, whereupon the baronet reveals that the picture is well known for "the odd and uncomfortable sensations it produces in every one that beholds it" (pp. 74-75). Tantalizingly, he informs them that with this effect "there is connected a very curious story" (p. 74). The guests of course wish to hear it, and unlike the Gentleman with the Haunted Head, who refused to tell more after the first tale, the baronet obliges them. The final two tales, "The Adventure of the Mysterious Stranger" (a brief account of how the baronet met the personage in the portrait) and "The Adventure of the Young Italian" (the manuscript tale of his own life left by the Italian in the baronet's possession), do not deal with ghosts and so need not receive much discussion here. But it should be noted that the sequence moves from psychological uneasiness in the presence of the young Italian, who was afraid to be alone and kept glancing fearfully over his shoulder, to the Italian's story of his own psychological anxiety over uncertain filial affection, betrayed friendship, and romantic love. Each tale is to be explained by the next; after the young Italian's murder of a former friend, the themes of shame and guilt intertwine with the need for moral and psychological expiation.

The tales of the second half of the "Strange Stories" series gradually darken. Except for a final twist in the frame narrative, they are not humorous. But the last frame sequence does humorously or ironically extend the theme of psychological misperception. After the baronet reads the Italian's manuscript, the guests are most curious to see the mysterious portrait. Afterward, all comment that "there was a certain something about the painting that had a very odd effect upon the feelings" (p. 120). Later the host reveals to the Nervous Gentleman that actually "not one of them has seen it." For seeing that "some of them were in a bantering vein" he "did not choose that the memento of the poor Italian should be made a jest of. So I gave the housekeeper a hint to show them all to a different chamber" (p. 120). The humor of the final frame incident, which concludes the stories of the Nervous Gentleman, returns us to the tone of the opening while apparently underscoring the theme of the dominance of the subjective over the objective. Actually, however, subjective and objective are balanced off against each other. The impact of the real portrait upon the Nervous Gentleman is not necessarily explained or diminished, though, at the same time, it may be surmised that the baronet's mentioning that one of them would sleep in a haunted chamber predisposed the "nervous" gentleman to further nervousness. This possibility is given further support by his noting correspondences between his room and those of the ghost stories, and by the portrait theme of the first tales (including the dream-portrait of the face of the woman in the German's tale), which the Nervous Gentleman may have subconsciously recalled.

"Strange Stories by a Nervous Gentleman" is thus a remarkable early experiment with point of view, narrative frames, and Gothic modes, representing the range of supernatural, explained, and ambiguous techniques, while effecting a complex intertwining of epistemological and ontological ironies within a metafictional structure. The "Adventure of the German Student" is perhaps the earliest well-crafted example in English of the inconclusive psychological ghost story, strategically placed within a complicated series of ghost stories of varying modes, with thematic interruptions, frames, and shifting points of view far more complex than those of Le Fanu's "Green Tea."

IV

From the foregoing discussion it is clear that British-oriented studies of the ghost story make a historical error in attributing the origin of the inconclusive psychological ghost story to Le Fanu's "Green Tea" or "Schalken the Painter," or to Richard Barham's "Henry Harris." The experimental fiction and drama of German Romanticists at the end of the eighteenth century antedate such techniques, and the American psychological ghost story precedes British examples by a generation or more. It is, however, apparently accurate to claim that the ambiguous mode of the Gothic, with its intricate manipulations of frames, its metafictional implications of point of view, its intrusions of humor, and its general polyphony of tone, was not much in evidence in Britain until after the publication of Le Fanu's later tales. *Wuthering Heights* (1848) perhaps presents a special case, but the major exception would seem to be James Hogg's *Private Memoirs and Confessions of a Justified Sinner* (1824), along with a handful of his tales about dream-selves. In America, however, the ambiguous mode is dominant. The early American ghost

story is one manifestation of the Gothic impulse of American dark Romanticism. After Irving, the ambiguous Gothic tale reaches an apex with Hawthorne and Poe, who tend to work within the larger Gothic tradition rather than focusing on the ghost story. A reader searching for straight ghost stories in the writings of Hawthorne and Poe will in fact turn up fewer than a dozen that might qualify.

In part, this unghostly aspect of the development of American Romantic fiction may be explained by our major writers' immersion in the philosophical complexities of the Romantic movement. The conventional observation on the supposed preponderance of explained Gothicism in American Romantic fiction results from a partial misreading of such stories as Irving's "German Student." Such a reading posits the influence of the Radcliffe method of explained Gothic, without much substantiation of Radcliffe's appeal to the American mind or influence on American writers other than Charles Brockden Brown; it is related to the general proposition that a pragmatic American materialism is a national characteristic.[13] While suggestive, the assertion is finally simplistic. For one thing, such a view ignores not only the ecclesiastical history of America, but also the later influence of Scottish Common Sense School philosophy and of British empiricism, as represented by Hume and Berkeley, whose philosophical inquiries seemed to cast doubt on the existence of materiality.[14]

Just as for European writers, for Americans the human mind becomes the key element in the matter-spirit dilemma. Their speculation is marked by a recurrent apprehension that all matter may be a mental construct, just as all dreams of the spiritual world may be a delusion. Americans become obsessed with the subject-object dialectic in Kant, who is reinterpreted by German writers like Fichte, interpreted again by Coleridge, and once more reinterpreted by Carlyle—not to mention the numerous lesser translations and explications of German philosophy by Frederic Henry Hedge and other Americans.[15] The transcendentalist writers in America—especially the later Emerson and Thoreau, but also even Whitman—grapple with the same matter-spirit-mind paradox as do the dark Romanticists, though the point of view is diametrically opposite. There is hardly any such thing as a simple American materialism discoverable in the Romantic era, and the philosophy of mind derived from Germany and Britain has a major influence on the form of American Gothic fiction.

Although a complete history of the Gothic tradition in America requires a meticulous survey of stories by minor popular writers, it seems safe to say of the major American writers that the ambiguous tale reaches another high point later in the century simultaneously with renewed interest in the ghost story as a genre. That the psychological ghost story, as defined here, does not reflect the concerns merely of the last half of the nineteenth century but those of the first half as well is a point especially pertinent to American fiction. The continuum between the earlier nineteenth century and the later as suggested by the related subgenres of the Gothic tradition deserves further examination, both for developments in literary form and for the implications for the *Zeitgeist* of a century. The century between the beginnings of Romantic fiction and the outpouring of fantastic and occult fiction in the 1880s and 90s through the 1920s suggests a continuity of aesthetic and philosophical concerns for the writer in America.

I would suggest that the development of the major modes of Gothic tale-telling by the American Romantics leads directly to the inconclusive psychological ghost story associated with later nineteenth-century writers like Bierce, Howells, and James. Their ghost stories represent the continuation of the ontological and epistemological themes of the Gothic strand of American Romanticism. If one wanted to argue for a break in a continuous line of development, I should hazard, tentatively, the suggestion that it occurs not so much in the later nineteenth century as in the obsessively "realist" fiction of the first half of the twentieth, where the Gothic seems separate from the "mainstream" in a way that it is not in the nineteenth. For even southern "Gothic" writers, like Faulkner, Welty, or O'Connor, seem to have less connection with the ghost-story writers of the popular magazines, or with writers of "weird" tales like Lovecraft, than did their predecessors two generations earlier. The later nineteenth-century writers, I would argue, continue an unbroken line. Irving, Poe, and Hawthorne are the direct ancestors of Howells's formulation of the "vague shapes of the borderland between experience and illusion" in *Shapes that Haunt the Dusk* (1907), of James's deliberate ambiguity in "The Jolly Corner" (1908), "The Friends of the Friends" (1896), and *The Turn of the Screw* (1898), of Bierce's mystification in "The Damned Thing" (1893), "The Eyes of the Panther" (1891), and especially "The Death of Halpin Frayser" (1893).

In British writing of the second half of the century, we find an exaggerated interest and belief in psychic experience transcending normal perception and cognition, and a concomitant renewed belief in scientific verifiability of an occult realm. But in America, in tension with the persisting Romanticism generated by the transcendental movement, and in the midst of the popularity of spiritualism, writers associated with the rise of realism inherit the legacy of an unresolved dilemma from the Romantic age. Perplexity persists about the fusion (or even relation) of material and spiritual worlds, of essence and perception. To see the development of the "supernatural" tale in nineteenth-century America divorced from its Romantic naturalist context (especially from the paradoxical materialist-spiritualist doctrines of

transcendentalism) is to do violence to the historical record and distort our understanding of both the history of genres and the interconnection between world view and aesthetics in historical eras. For the mental apprehension of the body-spirit fusion persists as a problematic construct shaping by acceptance or denial—or by an indeterminacy in between—the world view of major nineteenth-century American writers. As a sub-genre of the Gothic tale of the "supernatural," the form of the development of the ghost story in America reveals the intellectual crises of an entire century. Unexpectedly, it reaches early full exposition in the seemingly slight, sportive sequence "Strange Stories by a Nervous Gentleman," by Washington Irving, who stands near the fountainhead of a major stream of American literary history.

Notes

1. Pamela Search, *The Supernatural in the English Short Story* (London: Bernard Hanison Limited, 1959), pp. 7-20.

2. Ibid. Cf. Tzvetan Todorov, *The Fantastic: A Structural Approach to a Literary Genre,* trans. Richard Howard from the 1970 French ed. (Cleveland: Case Western Reserve University Press, 1973), wherein the term *fantastic* is used to indicate a "reader hesitation" principle; the reader is unsure whether the "events" of the text are to be taken as "real" or not. This narrowed use of the term *fantastic* and Search's "inconclusive" tale parallel somewhat my formulation of the "ambiguous mode" of Gothic literature, introduced below.

3. *Best Ghost Stories of J. S. Le Fanu,* ed. E. F. Bleiler (New York: Dover, 1964), pp. 178-207.

4. Julia Briggs, *Night Visitors: The Rise and Fall of the English Ghost Story* (London: Faber, 1977), p. 144; cf. p. 51.

5. Jack Sullivan, *Elegant Nightmares: The English Ghost Story from Le Fanu to Blackwood* (Athens: Ohio University Press, 1978), pp. 11-31.

6. For fuller discussion, see "Gothic Fiction of the Romantic Age: Context and Mode," the introduction to *Romantic Gothic Tales 1790-1840,* ed. G. R. Thompson (New York: Harper and Row, 1979), pp. 13-38. Like Sullivan, Briggs makes the usual bifurcation of Gothic into "two distinct types": supernatural and explained (p. 143).

7. For a fuller overview, see my discussions of "romantic irony," the "grotesque and arabesque," and the "nightside" in *Poe's Fiction: Romantic Irony in the Gothic Tales* (Madison: University of Wisconsin Press, 1973), pp. 19-38, 105-16, 139-41, 160-64, and notes. A recent article on German, British, and American Gothic is Pamela J. Sheldon and Kurt Paul's "Daylight Nightmares,"

Gothic 1 (1979): 1-6. Also see Henry A. Poch-mann, *German Culture in America: Philosophical and Literary Influences 1600-1900* (Madison: University of Wisconsin Press, 1957), *passim.*

8. Little has been written about Irving and the ghost story, but there are a few useful works on Irving and the Gothic. See esp. John Clendenning, "Irving and the Gothic Tradition," *Bucknell Review* 12 (1964): 90-98; Donald A. Ringe, "Irving's Use of the Gothic Mode," *Studies in the Literary Imagination* 7 (1974): 51-65; and William L. Hedges, *Washington Irving: An American Study 1802-1832* (Baltimore: Johns Hopkins Press, 1965).

9. Edward Wagenknecht in *Washington Irving: Moderation Displayed* (New York: Oxford University Press, 1962) writes: "Irving himself thought *Tales of a Traveller* his best book. . . . He was developing a new theory of narrative form . . . which might have come to more than it did if further experiments had not been discouraged by the savage press the book received. . . . It is true of course that the book lacks unity" (p. 177). For a different view and for a fine, insightful discussion of the structure and effect of "Strange Stories," and of the blending of the absurd, the humorous, and the macabre in the sequence, see Hedges's chapter, "The Way the Story Is Told," in *Washington Irving,* pp. 191-212; he and I study the material from different perspectives, but with parallel conclusions regarding unity, though he tends to hedge, somewhat nervously, about the quality of the "German Student."

10. My text for *Tales of a Traveller* is vol. 9 of *Works of Washington Irving* (New York: G. P. Putnam's Sons, 1881). This is the "Author's Revised Edition," and in it *The Sketch Book* and *Tales of a Traveller* are bound together without repagination.

11. "Story of an Apparition" appeared in *Blackwood's* in 1818 and is reprinted in *Romantic Gothic Tales.* "The Tapestried Chamber" has been widely reprinted and is conveniently found in *Short Stories by Sir Walter Scott,* with an introduction by Lord David Cecil (rpt. London: Humphrey Milsford, 1970). "The Great Unknown" was the appellation given to the then-anonymous author of *Waverly* (1814), whose identity was the subject of much speculation in Britain.

12. Coleman Parsons, *Witchcraft and Demonology in Scott's Fiction* (Edinburgh: Oliver and Boyd, 1964), p. 129; see also pp. 130-31.

13. The presumption of an "American" materialism is still widespread, especially among European critics; for a useful argument for the dominance of the explained mode in America, see Oral Sumner

Coad, "The Gothic Element in American Literature before 1835," *Journal of English and Germanic Philology* 24 (1925): 72-93.

14. For a recent, concise survey of theories of the mind in America, see Rita K. Gollin's "Available Traditions," chap. 2 of *Nathaniel Hawthorne and the Truth of Dreams* (Baton Rouge: Louisiana State University Press, 1979), pp. 19-40. The present essay is part of a longer work; the concluding speculations about subject and object are elaborated in "The Apparition of This World: Transcendentalism and the American Ghost Story," in *Bridges to Fantasy: Essays from the Second Eaton Conference,* ed. Robert Scholes, Eric S. Rabkin, and George Slusser (Carbondale: Southern Illinois University Press, 1982), pp. 90-107, 207-9.

15. See Pochmann, *German Culture in America,* for a detailed survey.

Kelly Grovier (essay date 2007)

SOURCE: Grovier, Kelly. "Dream Walker: A Wordsworth Mystery Solved."[1] *Romanticism* 13, no. 2 (2007): 156-63.

[*In the following essay, Grovier assesses the identity of the ghostly "dream-walker" in Book Five of William Wordsworth's Romantic-era philosophical poem* The Prelude.]

Among the many mysteries surrounding the writing and imagination of William Wordsworth is the inspiration for the figure of the phantom drifter who haunts the apocalyptic beginning of Book Five of *The Prelude.*[2] In the so-called 'Arab dream' passage, Wordsworth describes encountering a wraith-like wanderer crossing the desert sands on a dromedary. The traveller, who is carrying a stone and a shell (bizarrely referred to as 'books' in 'the language of the dream'), explains that he is on a mission to bury his 'twofold treasure' before 'the fleet waters of the drowning world' destroy them. The surreal stranger seems a product of pure invention—unlikely to have been based on any actual person Wordsworth knew or knew about—who shifts spectrally from being 'the very knight / Whose tale Cervantes tells, yet not the knight' to 'an arab of the desert too'; of these, Wordsworth says, he 'was neither, and was both at once'.[3]

Like 'The Rime of the Ancient Mariner', Wordsworth's and Coleridge's co-invention of some seven years earlier, the 'Arab dream', first drafted in February 1804, has attracted endless critical speculation about the possible cultural and psychological forces that might have provoked it. A dizzying array of antecedents for the dream has been posited, each pointing to a possible philosophical, religious, literary or scientific source. Part of the difficulty has had to do with confusion surrounding just who is doing the dreaming in the first place. In its original version, the vision is said to have been related to Wordsworth by a 'listless' friend (thought by many commentators to be Coleridge),[4] who is described as mischievously 'going far to seek disquietude'. But revising *The Prelude* in 1838, four years after Coleridge's death, Wordsworth took credit for the dream himself, rewriting the episode in the first person with himself as the dreamer.

In unravelling the passage, attention has focused in particular on the nature of the phantom's accessories—the stone and shell—and their curious rendering in the poem as volumes of writing: 'one that held acquaintance with the stars', and 'the other', more perplexing still, 'that was a god, yea many gods, / Had voices more than all the winds, and was / A joy, a consolation, and a hope'.[5] In 1956, Jane Worthington Smyser made an important breakthrough when she uncovered Wordsworth's debt to Adrien Baillet's *Life of Descartes,* published in 1691, which describes a series of dreams that troubled the seventeenth-century philosopher, one of which occurs in a library and features two books—a dictionary and a volume of poetry.[6] As for the flood, everyone from Josephus to Robert Southey has been credited with supplying Wordsworth with literary examples.[7]

But what has escaped speculation almost entirely are prototypes for the rambler himself; critics have been content to accept Wordsworth's own acknowledgement in the poem that he is a kind of 'semi-Quixote',[8] tinged perhaps with a shade of Romantic orientalism, in the manner of 'Kubla Khan'. I believe, though, that the passage is a coded tribute to a friend from Wordsworth's days as a young radical in Revolutionary France: a figure who, however improbable it may seem, was an authentic traveller across the Arabian wastes—one who not only claimed to be on an endless mission to bury his own books, but whose identity, according to his contemporaries, shifted ceaselessly before their very eyes. That individual was John 'Walking' Stewart.

Walking Stewart is one of those forgotten cultural barometers by which the intellectual climate of an entire age may be measured. His unusual nickname derives from his reputation for having crossed, on foot, a greater portion of the known world than any person before him—a thirty-year peregrination, beginning in Madras in 1765, which took him across the divided principalities of India, through Persia and Turkey, across the deserts of Abyssinia and Arabia, through northern Africa, into every European country as far east as Russia, as well as over to the new United States and into the upper reaches of Canada. Though Stewart subsequently published nearly thirty works expounding the personal

philosophy of life he developed during his extended excursion, he refused to elaborate on his actual adventures. He insisted to anyone who pressed him for anecdotes regarding, for example, his captivity in Mysore, or his narrow escape from being sacrificed to an alien god while crossing the Persian Gulf, or the cause of the deep indentation on the left side of his skull, that his 'were travels of the mind'.[9] This was a remarkable abstention, given the period's obsession with travelogues and picturesque tours. What little we know of Stewart's life comes chiefly from fragments of reminiscences of those who crossed his winding path and, especially, from the obituaries written in the months after he was found dead in his rooms just off Trafalgar Square on 20 February 1822 (the morning after his seventy-fifth birthday), an empty bottle of laudanum lying beside him.

Two affectionate tributes by one of Stewart's closest acquaintances, Thomas De Quincey who considered Stewart not only 'a sublime visionary' and 'a true philosopher', but 'the most interesting person by far of all [his] friends' in London—are the most vivid of the surviving records of his elusive existence.[10] It is from De Quincey that we know not only about Wordsworth's friendship with Stewart in the fevered weeks following the September Massacres in Paris in 1792, but also Wordsworth's opinion that Stewart was 'the most eloquent man' on the subject of nature he ever met. And it is De Quincey who gives us the first uncanny link between the shape-shifting figure in the 'Arab dream' and Walking Stewart, whose own material presence seemed to defy the laws of physics. 'There must have been,' De Quincey attests in one of two obituaries that he wrote, 'three Walking Stewarts in London.'

> I met him and shook hands with him under Somerset House. . . . Thence I went, by the very shortest road (i.e., through Moor Street, Soho—for I am learned in many quarters of London), towards a point which necessarily led me through Tottenham Court Road: I stopped nowhere, and walked fast; yet so it was that in Tottenham Court Road I was not overtaken by (that was comprehensible), but overtook, Walking Stewart.[11]

One is initially inclined to dismiss De Quincey's recollection as little more than the fancy of an affectionate friend—an early indication, perhaps, of just how much De Quincey missed his extraordinary companion. It is, after all, a cliché to say that one sees someone whom one misses 'everywhere'. Remarkably, though, Stewart's ubiquity is corroborated by independent testimony. A death notice in the London Magazine for 1822 echoes the exceptional terms of De Quincey's tribute:

> There are several kinds of pedestrians, all celebrated and interesting in their way. . . . The Walkers, indeed, like the lichens, are a vast genus, with an endless variety of species; but alas! the best and most singular of the tribe is gone! . . . You saw him on Westminster

Bridge, acting his own monument; you went into the Park,—he was there, fixed as the gentleman at [Westminster Bridge]; you met him, however, at Charing Cross, creeping on like the hour-hand upon a dial, getting rid of his rounds and his time at once! Indeed, his ubiquity appeared enormous,—and yet not so enormous as the profundity of his sitting habits! He was a profound sitter. Could the Pythagorean system be embalmed, what a hen would now be tenanted by Walking Stewart! Truly, he seemed always to be going, like a lot at an auction, and yet always at a stand, like hackney-coach! Oh! What a walk was his to christen a man by,—a slow, lazy, scraping, creeping, gazing pace,—a shuffle,—a walk in its dotage, a walk at a standstill! . . . Well!—Walking Stewart is dead!—He will no more be seen enniched in Westminster Bridge;—or keeping his terms as one of the Benchers of St James's Park; or haunting the pavement with moving but unlifted feet. In vain we look for him 'at the hour when he was wont to walk'. The niche in the bridge is empty of its amiable statue—and he is gone from this spot, he is—gone from all—for he was ever all in all!—Three persons seemed departed in him.—In him there seems to have been a triple death!—He was Mrs. Malaprop's 'Cerberus—three gentlemen at once!'[12]

The legend of Stewart's omnipresence survived at least until the end of the nineteenth century, when, in 1891, a short sketch of Stewart by H. S. Salt appeared in the popular miscellany *Temple Bar*. Recalling Stewart's 'mysterious ubiquity' matter of factly as 'one of his characteristics', Salt rehearsed what was by then the accepted phenomenon: 'When you knew you had just left him plunged in profound reverie in the Park or on the Bridge, you would be amazed to meet him a few minutes later in a different quarter of London, perhaps travelling steadily towards the very point where you believed him to be comfortably ensconced.' So indelible a presence on the London psyche had Stewart become that his eventual death and disappearance, according to Salt, was widely felt to be 'deserving of a triple lamentation'.[13] The cumulative accounts surrounding Stewart are baffling to any would-be biographer, and indeed begin to bleed blurrily into 'the language of the dream' as Wordsworth's encounter with the quixotic phantom amid the wasteland of his imagination. 'Where really was he?' The picture does not become much clearer when one sets aside the disparate testimonies of perhaps imaginatively over-heated individuals such as De Quincey or the obituary writer for the *Annual Bibliography and Obituary*,[14] and attempts to establish Stewart's whereabouts at any given time. For every educated stab one takes at pinning Stewart's existence down to a particular time or place, the chronological atlas of this singularly elusive life seems to spin defiantly beneath the effort. Take, for example, a single month: November 1792. De Quincey insists that Wordsworth and Stewart were acquainted with one another 'during the early storms' of the French Revolution in Paris, during Wordsworth's short sojourn there in the anxious weeks before he returned to England in early December 1792.[15]

But an obituary for the *Gentleman's Magazine,* appearing the year before De Quincey's article, claims that in November 1792 Walking Stewart was in dire straits thousands of miles from France, being held as a captive of the notorious Tippoo Sultan of Mysore in Seringapatam, southern India, and that Stewart's release was only then being negotiated by a Sir James Sibbald, who had been delegated by the East India Company to settle terms of peace with the opportunistic Tippoo.[16] Neither De Quincey's nor the *Gentleman's Magazine* account is compatible with a third version of events, pieced together from forgotten playbills from Drury Lane for 1792. It seems that in November of that year, Walking Stewart was the subject—the affectionate target, as it were—of a theatrical send-up at the Theatre Royal: a commercially successful 'operatic farce' by the playwright William Pearce, entitled *Hartford-bridge; or, The Skirts of a Camp,*[17] starring the popular singer Elizabeth Clendening[18] and the leading comedy actor of the day, Joseph Munden, in the role of Peregrine Forester, caricaturing Stewart.[19] The success of the production relied entirely on the audience's familiarity with the legend, persona, and purported habits of Stewart—on his being, in other words, a celebrated fixture of London life around that time. Each of these three versions authoritatively and credibly places Stewart in three different parts of the world at the same moment: Paris, Seringapatam, and London. 'Three Walking Stewarts' indeed.

Oddly, the twenty-odd published works by Stewart that have survived are preoccupied chiefly with expounding the notion that human identity, as conventionally conceived, is an illusion. The 'self', Stewart asserted again and again, is a mirage, a temporary modality of material being in a state of ceaseless dissolution through time and space: 'The mode of being called man', he explained,

> can have no positive or absolute identity; it resembles the river whose mode of existence is the form of its channel. The flux of water in the river, like the flux of the matter in the body, can have no identity or sameness, but is incessantly on the movement, caused by evacuation and repletion.[20]

Stewart was certain that he had hit on a fundamental, though previously unappreciated human truth about human identity—a truth that was, he said, 'so simple, so familiar to sense, so irresistible to reason', that 'I think I shall have no difficulty in gaining assent of every mind that has the least spark of sense, candour or liberation, from prejudice in his nature. The fact of analogy that I allude to is that all composition is decomposition'.[21]

Components of what Stewart called 'the great integer of nature',[22] every material body whether sentient or inert, active or passive, living or dead participates in a process of continual material interchange with every other body—composing and decomposing into and out of everything in endless self-regulation. Stewart would have argued that the reason why he had been identified in more than one place at a given moment was that he was in more than one place at any given moment, as indeed everyone and everything else is. The extreme form of atomism *ad infinitum* to which Stewart subscribed participated in, yet was far more radical in its existential implications than, contemporary eighteenth-century French and English trends in materialist thinking as expounded by Lord Shaftesbury, David Hartley, Joseph Priestley, Denis Diderot or Baron d'Holbach. In the strange light of Stewart's reasoning, Louis XVI, for instance, was enjoined to be merciful to his subjects not because of any abstract moral imperative or intellectual appeal to inalienable rights of man as advocated by Thomas Paine or Priestley, but because the King was (literally, physically) the very subject whom he subjected: 'the matter that at any given moment constitutes the King upon the throne', Stewart insisted, 'that same indestructible matter in a few moments disperses . . . into millions of ruptured peasants'.[23] The world, in Stewart's singular vision, is, as it were, a great lava lamp of mutating forms, a phantom dream of shapes and semi-shapes; to attribute static identity, let alone power and authority, to any one mode or momentary convergence of material substance would be, in such a system of belief, naive and arbitrary, as pointless as anointing a passing cloud 'the King of Clouds'.

Given the frustrating dearth of surviving documentation—no diaries or journals, no death certificate or grave, no estate or heirs, and only two letters—it is perhaps not surprising that no comprehensive biography of Stewart has ever been undertaken. In 1943, Bertrand Harris Bronson published a spirited article-length sketch, in which he skilfully reconciled many of the contemporary obituaries, the tributes by De Quincey, and a handful of breathless sightings in which Stewart's existence seems to dissolve almost before it is recorded.[24]

In 1786, the celebrated tenor and friend of Mozart, Michael Kelly, remembered being all but whiplashed by a brief encounter with Stewart when the two were introduced in Vienna. Kelly recalled Stewart—'whose pedestrian exploits', he said, 'were universally spoken of'—as 'a great oddity', 'a well-informed, accomplished man' with 'a most retentive memory'; 'a great enthusiast about music, but not about beef-steaks'. 'The last little walk he had taken was from Calais, through France, Italy and the Tyrol, to Vienna, and in a few days,' Kelly recalled, 'he was going to extend it as far as Constantinople.'[25] Five years later, the astonishment recorded by Kelly was amplified by a small notice in a newspaper in Albany, New York:

> On Thursday last, arrived in this city from London, via New York, and the same evening set off for Canada,

Mr Stewart, the noted pedestrian—who, we are told, has travelled over the greater part of Europe, Asia, and Africa on foot; and has come to this country for the purpose of completing his travels, by making the tour of the American world. Mr Stewart is a middle-aged man, about six feet high—and what is particularly remarkable, he is said to eat no animal food, and but one meal a day.[26]

Born in Bond Street in 1747, Stewart seems to have been from the first an unruly rapscallion whose refusal to buckle down at school resulted in rustications from both Harrow and the Charterhouse. In 1763, Stewart's father, in a vain attempt to discipline his incorrigible son, secured him a position as scribe with the East India Company on the farthest fringes of the burgeoning Empire—Madras. It wasn't long, though, before Stewart was writing contemptuous letters to the Company's Board of Directors insisting that he was 'born for nobler pursuits, and higher attainments, than to be a copier of invoices and bills of lading to a company of grocers, haberdashers, and cheesemongers'.[27] This was in 1765, and Stewart's attitude to authority was fuelled not by adolescent rebelliousness, but by a principled belief that the East India Company was exploiting the native resources and good will of its host—as exemplified by the institution's refusal to learn the native languages of the Indian people.[28]

Indignantly idealistic, Stewart resisted all temptation to secure for himself the kind of private fortune many of his young colleagues were amassing in Madras in the second half of the eighteenth century, and abruptly left the Company. Evicted from his family home two years earlier and now unable to countenance what he felt was the moral turpitude of his powerful employer, Stewart was left with little choice other than to reinvent himself from scratch. From the faint vestiges of Stewart's itinerary that survive, there is little wonder that he would eventually distil from his experiences a philosophical system based on the immutable mutation of human identity. Not long after leaving Madras, he found himself among the hundreds of Europeans held captive in Mysore by the fearsome ruler Haidar Ali, whose appetite for torturing prisoners reputedly included branding, the chopping off of noses and upper lips, and forced circumcision.[29] Eventually satisfied that Stewart's trespassing on his territory was inadvertent, Haidar Ali pressed Stewart into military service as a commander of a column of soldiers fighting for control of southern India. After a hair-raising escape from captivity, which resulted in his skull being dented by a bullet or sword, Stewart found himself next in the neighbouring principality of Arcot, where in due course he rose from being a translator for the mischievous Nawab, Muhammad Ali Khan, to the position of Prime Minister. In this capacity, Stewart set himself the goal of raising sufficient funds for his return to England. In due course, though not before leaving the Nawab's accounts in disarray, Stewart was ready to head for home.

His path lay through Persia and Persepolis. The British Library preserves a letter posted from the grand ancient town of Esfahan, in modern-day Iran, addressed to Warren Hastings, in which Stewart offers his services as a political look-out.[30] Later, attempting to cross the Persian Gulf when a savage squall arose, Stewart suddenly found himself, the 'only Giaour on board', accused of having brought misfortune on the vessel. After he had talked the superstitious crew out of sacrificing him, a compromise was reached whereby for the remainder of the journey he would be hoisted in a hencoop, dangling over the ship's side.[31] There, suspended between wave and wind, sea and sky, life and death, Stewart, according to a pamphlet published by a relative after his death, experienced a moment of preternatural insight out of which he would create the system of philosophy which would have such a profound impact on the imagination of Wordsworth.

By the time he met the twenty-two-year-old poet in a panic-stricken Paris in late 1792, Stewart was a living legend throughout Europe and America—a courageous adventurer who had survived everything from enslavement and war to the eviscerating sands of Arabia. Before arriving in France, Stewart had arranged to publish with James Ridgway, the radical publisher of Thomas Paine's contraband treatise *The Rights of Man,* a tract entitled *The Apocalypse of Nature,*[32] which contains in embryo the essence of the atomistic philosophy that Stewart gradually refined over the next thirty years. Among the ideas expressed in the work is the belief that every particle in nature, however minute or inert, possesses not only a level of consciousness (such ideas were already being accommodated by the eighteenth-century associationist David Hartley in his philosophy of vibrating matter) but an inviolable moral dimension as well. It is only in the context of Stewart's singular strain of extreme materialism that one can find philosophical authority for Wordsworth's formulation that 'to every natural form, rock, fruit, and flower, / Even the loose stones that cover the highway, / I gave a moral life'.

Stewart believed his ideas to be so radical, he was convinced that the works which contained them would be hunted down and destroyed by the repressive powers of the age. De Quincey recalls having to promise Stewart he would preserve his work against the onslaught that it would inevitably face. Stewart was sure, De Quincey says,

> that all the kings and rulers of the earth would confederate in every age against his works, and would hunt them out for extermination as keenly as Herod did the

innocents of Bethlehem. On this consideration, fearing that they might be intercepted by the long arms of these wicked princes . . . he recommended to all those who might be impressed with a sense of their importance to bury a copy or copies of each work, properly secured from damp & c., at a depth of seven or eight feet below the surface of the earth, and on their death-beds to communicate the knowledge of this fact to some confidential friends.[33]

Many of Stewart's works are embossed with a version of this paranoid enjoinder and there is every reason to suppose that the young Wordsworth would have been called upon to grab a spade as well. Whether De Quincey kept his word and translated Stewart's works into Latin before burying them at the foot of Helvellyn, no one now knows. Only Wordsworth seems to have taken the task to heart, secreting below the surface of his masterpiece, *The Prelude,* a hypnotic memorial to the bizarre books of the philosophical wanderer time forgot.

Notes

1. A version of this article first appeared in *The Times Literary Supplement* (16 February 2007), 14-15.

2. All quotations from the 'Arab dream' refer to *The Prelude: The Four Texts (1798, 1799, 1805, 1850),* ed. Jonathan Wordsworth (London, 1995).

3. Ibid., lines 120, 136, 123-4, 125, and 126.

4. Ibid., lines 62 and 52.

5. Ibid., lines 103, 104, 107, 107-9.

6. Jane Worthington Smyser, 'Wordsworth's Dream of Poetry and Science: *The Prelude, V*', *PMLA,* 71 (1956), 271-2: 'in a dream, Descartes, like the dreamer in *The Prelude,* beheld two books, one of which contained all scientific knowledge, while the other, which he valued more highly, contained all the inspired wisdom of poetry, the basic similarity between Descartes' dream and the dream in Book V of *The Prelude* is both obvious and striking'. Smyser also nominates Wordsworth's French mentor in 1792, Michel Beaupuy, as the listless friend who recounted the dream to him, a proposal which Jonathan Wordsworth says '[t]here is little to support' [*The Four Texts,* 579, note 49].

7. Cf. Theresa M. Kelley, 'Deluge and Buried Treasure in Wordsworth's Arab Dream', *Notes and Queries,* 225 (February, 1980), 70-1: 'one source that links Wordsworth's allusion to the Deluge with the treasures [is] the Deluge account that appears in Josephus' *A History of the Jews*; Wordsworth owned this work, in William Whitson's translation, and the third edition of the *Encyclopaedia Britannica* which repeats Josephus' account of the Deluge'. David Chandler, 'Robert

Southey and *The Prelude*'s "Arab Dream"', *Review of English Studies,* 54 (May 2003), 203-19.

8. *The Prelude,* Book V, line 142.

9. *The Times* (Friday, 22 February, 1822), 4; col. c: 'His journies would have been highly interesting if had published an account of them, but he disdained the usual pursuits of travellers, constantly answering inquiries as to the manners, customs, & c., of the various countries he had visited, by stating that *his* were *travels of the mind,* in order to ascertain and develop the polarity of moral truth.'

10. *The Works of Thomas De Quincey,* ed. Grevel Lindop et al. (21 vols, London, 2000-3), iii. 141 and xi. 247.

11. Ibid., iii. 135.

12. [Reynolds, J. H.], 'Walking Stewart', *London Magazine,* 6 (1822), 410-11.

13. H. S. Salt, 'Walking Stewart', *Temple Bar,* 93 (September-December, 1891), 573.

14. 'John Stewart, Esquire: Better Known By the Name of "Walking Stewart"', *The Annual Biography and Obituary, For the Year 1823,* 7 (London: Longman, Hurst, Rees, Orme, and Brown, 1823), 101-9.

15. De Quincey, iii. 134.

16. *The Gentleman's Magazine,* 92 (March 1822), 279.

17. William Pearce, *Hartford-bridge: or, The Skirts of the Cam An Operatic Farce* (London, 1793). '[Stewart's] character has been attempted', according to Reverend Bray, 'to be introduced on the stage, in the afterpiece of *Hartford Bridge*'. [Anna Eliza Bray (Mrs), *A Description of the Part of Devonshire Bordering on the Tamar and the Tavy: its Natural History, Manners, Customs, Superstitions, Scenery, Antiquities, Biography of Eminent Persons, & c. & c. in a Series of Letters to Robert Southey, Esq.* (London, 1836), 331.]

18. Elizabeth Clendining (b. 1767, d. 1799), played the role of Clara—a part specially composed for her by William Shield. Her first song was encored, and 'the depth and fullness of her middle and lower tones, and the sweetness of the upper ones were acknowledged and admired'. Haslewood, ii. 384.

19. The magnetism of Munden's portrayal attracted the attention of the portrait painter Samuel De Wilde, who executed a portrait of Munden as Peregrine Forester which was exhibited at the Royal Academy in 1795 and is thought to be among De Wilde's best works. The vicarious visage of Stewart, outrageously kitted in 'high brown boots, black breeches, a long, bright green coat edged in black fur with gold braid, black decorations and large leopard skin cuffs, a short black fur coat, a waistcoat that appears to be made of layers of feathers, a black stock with a big white frill at the front, and a large tricorn hat', is now in the Garrick Club's collection. (See Geoffrey Ashton, *Pictures in the Garrick Club: A Catalogue* (London, 1997), 326-7; illustration no. 622.) A notice for *Hartford-bridge* appeared in *The Times* (5 November 1792) 2, col. a.

20. John Stewart, *The Revolution of Reason; or, the Establishment of the Constitution of Things in Nature* (London, 1794), 7.

21. John Stewart, *The Sophiometer; or, Regulator of Mental Power; Forming the Nucleus of the Moral world, to Convert Talent, Abilities, Literature, and Science, into Thought, Sense, Wisdom, and Prudence, the God of Man; to Form those Intermodifications* (London, 1812), 292.

22. John Stewart, *Scripture of Reason and Nature* (London, 1813), xix.

23. John Stewart, *The Book of Intellectual Life* (London, 1818), 157 and 149.

24. Bertrand Harris Bronson, 'Walking Stewart', in *Essays and Studies,* 14 (Los Angeles, 1943), 123-55.

25. *Reminiscences of Michael Kelly of the King's Theatre, and Theatre Royal, Drury Lane* (2 edn, 2 vols, London, 1826), i. 246-8.

26. Uneda, *Notes and Queries,* 2nd series, 8 (24 September, 1859), 247.

27. *Gentleman's Magazine,* 92 (March 1822), 279-80.

28. John Stewart, *Travels over the Most Interesting Parts of the Globe, to Discover the Source of Moral Motion; Communicated to Lead Mankind through the Conviction of the Senses to Intellectual Existence, and an Enlightened State of Nature* (London, [1790]), 219-21: 'Why are not the writers sent to the manufacturing towns to learn the state of the investments, to relieve the poor weaver from an oppression, which destroys industry in its source, and is the cause of all debasement in the quality, and deficiency in the quantity? Why are they not sent into the country to learn the languages, customs, and tempers of the natives—to see how the collection of the revenue is formed—to remove the baneful hand of oppression, which destroys and depopulates the farms?'

29. Cromwell Massey's prison journal, by permission of the India Office Library and Records, British

Library, MSS. Eur. B392, discussed in Linda Colley, *Captives: Britain, Empire and the World, 1600-1850* (London, 2002), 285-91.

30. British Library, Warren Hastings MSS, Add. MS 29167, folios 259-60.

31. *Annual Biography*, 105. Accounts differ as to just how long Stewart was left dangling. Where this account suggests that the ordeal lasted only 'some hours', others describe something far more gruelling: 'He was exposed to the spray of the sea for a fortnight, but was provided with food every day, and suffered no other inconvenience than that of being in such an uncomfortable situation.' John Taylor, *Records of My Life* (2 vols, London, 1832), i. 286-7.]

32. John Stewart, *The Apocalypse of Nature, wherein the Source of Moral Motion is Discovered and a Moral System Established* (London, [1790]). A self-contained work, *The Apocalypse of Nature* was considered by Stewart himself to be volume two of the above-mentioned *Travels over the Most Interesting Parts of the Globe*.

33. De Quincey, iii. 138.

MAJOR AUTHORS AND SIGNIFICANT WORKS

Thomas H. Fick (essay date spring 1999)

SOURCE: Fick, Thomas H. "Authentic Ghosts and Real Bodies: Negotiating Power in Nineteenth-Century Women's Ghost Stories." *South Atlantic Review* 64, no. 2 (spring 1999): 81-97.

[*In the following essay, Fick analyzes the way women writers of ghost stories in the nineteenth century both subverted and upheld the tenets of male hegemony.*]

Toward the end of *Uncle Tom's Cabin* Harriet Beecher Stowe relates what she titles "An Authentic Ghost Story." The ghost is Cassy, Simon Legree's mistress and the self-elected savior of Emmeline, the young woman whom Legree has bought to be Cassy's successor. Cassy feigns an escape to the swamp and then, draping herself in a sheet, issues nightly from her attic hiding place to haunt the mansion with her groans, screams, and spectral appearances. And as Legree drinks himself to death "a stern, white, inexorable figure" appears intoning "'Come! come! come!'" (492).

This story is clearly "authentic" in an unusual sense: not because the ghost is a real spirit but because it is a living and vengeful woman. Everything Cassy does—from placing a bottle neck in an attic knothole to generate ghostly wailings to draping herself in sheets—serves to evoke and parody the "ghostly legends, and supernatural visitations" (467) in which Legree believes so strongly. Yet at the same time, when she dons her sheets she is giving physical existence to past wrongs: her "spirit" is presumed to be that of the slave woman who died in the attic, probably from Legree's abuse. Cassy's theatrics thus interpret the "ghost" as the living body of social sin, which can secure freedom for the victim and exact revenge on the sinner.[1] Legree, on the other hand, refuses to read beyond the supernatural to the social text: for him ghosts are just ghosts. It is in keeping, therefore, that his drinking should bring on what the narrator calls "that frightful disease that seems to throw the lurid shadows of a coming retribution back into the present life" (492)—should bring on, that is, a deadly serious version of the physical/metaphysical confusion that Cassy's masquerade enacts. The sufferings of the afterlife are literally enacted in Legree's present body, and this retributive transformation of the supernatural into the natural mirrors Cassy's enactment of metaphysical terrors in physical forms. Stowe's evangelical Christian narrative acknowledges in this way that justice may be physical and immediate as well as spiritual and deferred.

Recent critics and anthologists have documented the significant social dimensions of women's ghost stories (Carpenter and Kolmar, Bendixen, Salmonson)—a genre-specific version of what Jane Tompkins calls the "cultural work" of American fiction. But as Stowe's chapter suggests, not all nineteenth-century ghost stories concerned the supernatural. Tompkins oversimplifies Stowe's views when she argues that for Stowe "Reality . . . cannot be changed by manipulating the physical environment; it can only be changed by conversion in the spirit because it is the spirit alone that is finally real" (133). On the contrary, in a substantial body of women's writing (including *Uncle Tom's Cabin*) the supernatural is frequently the natural in masquerade. I mean this quite literally: as Stowe's sardonic introductory commentary to "An Authentic Ghost Story" makes clear, spirits are sometimes no more than low-tech physical effects dressed up by ignorance. Thus, when Cassy dons a sheet to "walk, at the most approved ghostly hours, around the Legree premises" (491), she is taken as a spirit because no one dares to look closely: "as everybody knows, when the bodily eyes are thus out of the lists, the spiritual eyes are uncommonly vivacious and perspicuous" (490). In short, the body, abetted by ignorance, often subtends "spirit." This imposture, I want to argue, allowed women writers to acknowledge the higher spiritual nature of women without proscribing worldly action. In this it mirrored the real-life function of mediumship which, as Ann Braude notes, "gave women a public leadership role that allowed them to remain compliant with the complex of values of the period that have come to be known as the cult of true womanhood" (82).[2] The social dimension of what Stowe called "an authentic ghost story," that is, depended upon eliding the difference between the physical and the spiritual in the interests of defending a woman's higher nature against the depredations of men on the one hand, and of claiming space for action in the world of human relations on the other.

Cassy's impersonation exemplifies this tactic in particularly stark terms because her "ghost" uses the spiritual to give the slave woman's body (triply present in herself, Emmeline, and the dead slave) a power and effectiveness it could have in no other way. As a black woman, Cassy could not in life claim the spiritual, disembodied status of the mid-nineteenth-century white woman (Legree's or Augustine St. Clare's mothers, for example), which operates to constrain masculine aggression. As Hazel Carby has argued in *Reconstructing Womanhood,* race restricts the prerogatives of "true womanhood" by making chastity impracticable for slave women. Cassy's body is literally the possession of another. But her return disguised as pure postmortem spirit appropriates the spiritual status of true white womanhood while suggesting that white women's spirituality could be more firmly grounded in the physical world. For white women, the authentic ghost similarly marked out an emotional territory beyond the thematics of victimization, a thematics that finds its origin in the seduction and betrayal plot of popular novels like Susanna Rowson's *Charlotte Temple* and Hannah Foster's *The Coquette.* As Nina Baym remarks, women authors "objected to the sexual center of these novels of sensibility, and not merely on prudish grounds. They were unwilling to accept, and unwilling to permit their readers to accept, a concept of woman as inevitable sexual prey" (26).

In a broader sense Stowe's "authentic ghost story" is also paradigmatic of a number of nineteenth-century women's ghost stories because it points to the problematic relationship between body and soul for nineteenth-century women writers, and to significant tensions in Victorian American thinking about gender relations and social action. Most women and many feminists (including Margaret Fuller, Catharine Beecher, and Harriet Beecher Stowe) accepted a fundamental distinction between men and women, assigning women the higher—that is, more spiritual—station. Yet this distinction also posed problems because threats to women's independence were often physical (rape or seduction), and effective remedial action was physical as well. In its purely supernatural modes, the woman-authored ghost story could "critique mainstream male culture, values, and tradition" (Carpenter and Kolmar 1), but it

could also be implicated in the problem: the assumption of differing natures and the relegation of ameliorative action to the afterlife (or the afterlife's representatives in this world) left women at something of an impasse— the body as a site of repression and agent of reform could be easily overlooked.[3] Richard Brodhead indirectly explores this possibility in his discussion of the Veiled Lady—"a figure for the disembodiment of women in nineteenth-century domesticity, that is, for the construction of 'woman' as something separate from or opposed to bodily life and force" (50). For Brodhead the Veiled Lady, who like the authentic ghost appears habitually draped in white, registers the simultaneous creation of a "newly publicized world of popular entertainment" and "a newly privatized world of woman's domestic life" (53). Like the Veiled Lady, the authentic ghost registers a similar clash between public and private, bodily force and disembodied domesticity, self-assertion and victimization. But unlike the prototypical Priscilla in Hawthorne's *Blithedale Romance,* the veiled ladies of the authentic ghost story are their own exhibitors, playing bodily force as if it were disembodied. In what follows I want to look at how women's authentic ghost stories respond to cultural disincorporation through their negotiations of the physical and metaphysical.

* * *

I will begin with Catherine Sedgwick's "The Country Cousin" (1830) because it reveals so many of the authentic ghost story's conventions and because its representative quality is no chance circumstance: throughout her career Sedgwick demonstrated a remarkably acute sensitivity to literary modes and practices.[4] "Country Cousin" begins with a lament for the passing of the "dark empire of superstition" (67) and the promise of some good spectral action, yet it signally fails to follow through with this promise: the English-born Mrs. Reginald Tudor tells a ghost story whose purpose is to cure one of her two granddaughters of snobbish urban contempt for her unsophisticated country cousin and whose ghost turns out to be, like Cassy, an abandoned woman draped in a sheet.

The setting for Mrs. Tudor's ghost story suggests how it should be understood. The story is told "near the witching time of night" (73) but there is no sense of dread. The three young women draw chairs around the "matronly rocking-chair" (73) of Mrs. Tudor who, in the "intimate, and endearing" (73) space of her own apartment, becomes "the true grandmother, easy, communicative, and loving" (73). As the setting suggests, the tale she will tell is not intended to frighten but to reassure, to confirm the bonds of affection and community evoked in the story's frame and threatened by Isabel's attitude toward her cousin. Mrs. Tudor's character complements the setting: she is "in all acts of kindness, condescension, and humanity, a Christian; and is not Christianity the foundation, the essence of republicanism?" (69). The story will go on to answer this rhetorical question in the affirmative by merging Christianity, republicanism, sentiment, and morality through the medium of a supposed ghost. And the threat to republican virtue is a version of Susanna Rowson's Montraville in *Charlotte Temple*. He is a British soldier who abandons his pregnant wife but is finally brought securely into the fold: Americanized, Christianized, and republicanized.

The story is simple in outline: it chronicles the lives of two sisters, daughters of an authoritarian, rabidly anti-British father during and after the Revolutionary War. M'Arthur, a wounded British soldier, is nursed by the sisters and falls in love first with Emma (the more timid and obedient), and then with Anna (the more rebellious), who weds him against her father's will. Anna is disowned by her father and abandoned by her husband, whose child—a blind son—she bears. For five years M'Arthur forgets his wife, until "at last came that monitor, so friendly, so necessary to human virtue, that messenger of Heaven—sickness" (90). After recovering, he returns to find his wife. As he approaches the village the surrounding woods seem threatening, and when he passes the family burial plot M'Arthur sees a ghostly figure resembling his wife and enveloped in what appears to be a winding-sheet approach a grave and rest her head on it. M'Arthur himself approaches, prostrates himself on the ground, and at this moment the figure becomes instinct with life: "Anna, his living Anna, stood before him" (94). (We learn that she had come to mourn at the grave of her recently deceased son.) M'Arthur falls senseless in her arms and is a faithful and kind husband for the rest of his life.

And that's the ghost—really no ghost at all. What's important, however, is the authentic ghost's effect on the living—in both Mrs. Tudor's story and the frame narrative. As does Cassy's somewhat different ghost, the "ghost" of Anna belongs to and acts in the natural realm of love, fidelity, sympathy, commitment. This is most immediately apparent in M'Arthur's response to the ghost. We are told that all M'Arthur's habits of mind and life are opposed to superstition, and that he suspects he's being tricked by "a mere phantasm of the brain" (93). Yet finally "his reason assented to the convictions of his senses, and yielding himself to the power of this awful visitation from the dead" (93), he breathes a prayer. It's at this point that the spiritual reveals itself as physical, the ghost of Anna as his living wife. Note that once M'Arthur surrenders his reason to emotion, the supernatural is no longer needed. What's important is the act of submission to proper feeling: by praying and swooning M'Arthur does what Legree can't or won't. The "ghost" completes the reform that sickness had begun and at that moment her metaphysical garb becomes unnecessary.

M'Arthur is the literary (and cultural) descendent of Montraville in Rowson's vastly popular seduction novel *Charlotte Temple* (1791)—a work whose concerns are reflected in most of the "authentic ghost stories." Montraville, as Cathy N. Davidson notes, is a problematic villain who "sees himself as an honorable suitor anticipating wedlock" and whose "villainy is so sanctioned by his society that it can pass as virtue" (136). Like Montraville, M'Arthur is an honorable military man who acts badly; like Montraville he abandons his pregnant lover (here also his legal wife). Even his encounter with Anna's apparent ghost parallels Montraville's with Charlotte's real corpse. In a chapter titled "Retribution," Montraville, who has "some remains of compassionate tenderness for the woman whom he regarded as brought to shame by himself" (116), seeks a living Charlotte but stumbles instead upon her funeral, learns her story, and tries to right the wrongs. However his sickness, unlike M'Arthur's, comes too late for moral reform; wounded in a fight with the perfidious Belcour, he is "overcome with the agitation of his mind and loss of blood" (118) and spends the rest of his life subject to fits of melancholy.[5]

The basic scenario of seduction, abandonment, and retribution in "Country Cousin" is clearly a version (though less sensational) of the one we find in *Charlotte Temple* or in Stowe's "Authentic Ghost Story," where Legree—no problematic villain like M'Arthur/Montraville—is pointedly not allowed to survive his agitation. In each narrative the "ghost" is a living woman who acts retributively or correctively upon a living man. The natural-supernatural exorcises the specter of seduction; in Sedgwick's tale the abandoned woman weeping at the grave of her child is taken again as a respected wife. While still maintaining—indeed exaggerating—her passive and spiritual nature, the story shows how Anna enforces moral justice and brings together those wrongly kept apart. And the ghost story has a similar effect in the frame narrative. Just as the ghost makes M'Arthur a faithful and loving husband, so the ghost story teaches Isabel to be a faithful and loving cousin. Isabel and Lucy recognize their mothers (and Isabel's father, M'Arthur) in Mrs. Tudor's ghost story and Isabel gives up her pride to welcome her cousin wholeheartedly.

In the way her rebellious sexuality is punished with five years of suffering and the death of her first born before Anna joyously enters into successful motherhood, we might see a version of what Linda Kerber calls the "republican mother." According to Kerber, the figure of the republican mother, who cheerfully gives herself to the rearing of patriotic children, is a displacement of the politically and sexually active woman who figured in revolutionary texts (269-88). Though Anna is not politically active, her explicit rebellion against paternal authority shows itself in sexual terms and in a historical context saturated by national politics. But Anna is unlike the republican mother because her rebellious tendencies ultimately are not brought under control but rewarded: she gets true love, wealth, a high-spirited daughter. It is M'Arthur who needs to be corrected. Anna's story is in effect the story of how rebellion and even violence against male authority can be literally bodied forth under protection of the spirit—as Cassy does much more explicitly in "An Authentic Ghost Story." "Country Cousin" can be seen as reworking the ideas of Mercy Otis Warren's verse play *The Ladies of Castile* (1790) within the context of domestic ideology in the 1830s. Warren's play follows two women: the yielding and submissive Louisa is destroyed by revolutionary turmoil (the false report of her lover's death sparks her suicide) while her bolder counterpart, Maria, survives and grows stronger (Kerber 269-70). Similarly, the "celestial spirit" (87) for which Emma is overtly praised in "Country Cousin" leads directly to post-Revolutionary misfortunes. At her father's behest she marries a man she does not love, goes to live a life of poverty in the west, and dies an early death leaving a "meek, timid" (70), and penniless daughter. Emma's story illustrates what happens when rebellion bows to "the straight line of filial duty" (77), when body is sacrificed to, rather than authenticated by, the spirit.

The cultural function of Stowe's and Sedgwick's ghost stories can be clarified by comparing them with one of the most famous male-authored tales of woman's revenge—an authentic ghost story conceived in terror rather than hope and narrated to justify rather than expiate a crime. Like "Country Cousin" and "An Authentic Ghost Story," Edgar Allan Poe's "Ligeia" explores the relationship between body and spirit in the nineteenth-century construction of womanhood. But in Poe's nightmare version of the authentic ghost story the woman's body is itself the object of dread and repulsion, the spirit an object of veneration that must be sustained even at the expense of the woman's life. (It is perhaps for this reason that "Ligeia" has enjoyed such long and continued success: like many of Poe's stories it speaks shrewdly to deep-seated anxieties about boundary violations.) In the first part of the story Poe's narrator constructs an ideal woman, one who "came and departed as a shadow" and whose "low sweet voice" and "marble hand" (249) are an index of his investment in the spiritual as a way of policing the body. Ligeia is the "celestial spirit" that Sedgwick subverts in "Country Cousin," but unlike Emma she will not bow to the straight line of filial (or spousal) duty; she will not be defined wholly as spirit. She is "violently a prey to the tumultuous vultures of stern passion" (253), a quality which, as the narrator's anxious language makes clear, links her with a repugnant and intolerable physicality.

When he says, "I saw that she must die" (255), he is therefore marking himself not as the passive witness of her demise, but as an active agent—in desire if not in fact.

And Ligeia does die. But even after death she fights not to be wholly spirit, and this rebellion constitutes the horror of the story. Ligeia appropriates the body of the narrator's abused second wife in order to accomplish her revenge on the one who first denied, and then did away with, her physical presence. When she returns in (or through) Rowena's body it is not because the narrator wills her return, even though he seems to license this post hoc fallacy by juxtaposing his indulgent "waking visions" (265) of Ligeia with the revivification of the corpse he is gazing upon. But visions are ontologically identical with the spirit to which Ligeia has been reduced in death: they forbid rather than demand presence. When Ligeia comes back it is through her will to bodily presence. The woman's refusal to remain a "vision" explains the story's at first puzzling conclusion. If the "apparition" (267), now no longer so visionary, is the narrator's lost love returning from the dead, why then does he say it "paralyzed—. . . chilled me into stone" (267)? And why is the woman whose "passionate devotion amounted to idolatry" (255) now described as "shrinking from his touch" (268)? And why does he shriek aloud as if she is not his lost love but Medusa or a vampire? I think it matters little whether one reads the story as a tale of the supernatural or of the natural; what is important are the values it encodes. Poe's story is told from the viewpoint of an unrepentant M'Arthur, or a Legree driven to the madhouse rather than the grave—a man for whom the worst possible ghost is one of flesh and blood. This is the ghost that Fanny Fern evokes at the end of "Fashionable Invalidism," her attack on the culturally imposed ideal of sickness and physical mortification as woman's proper estate:

> I like a nice bit of beefsteak and a glass of ale, and anybody else who wants it may eat pap. I go to bed at ten, and get up at six. I dash out in the rain, because it feels good on my face. I don't care for my clothes, but I *will* be well; and after I am buried, I warn you, don't let any fresh air or sunlight down on my coffin, if you don't want me to get up.
>
> (342)

Fern redefines the ring-tailed-roarer of male southwestern humor as the irrepressible sign of woman's healthy physical presence—a ghost that packs a punch and offers an alternative to what Price Herndl terms the "(super) 'natural' invalidism" of Poe's, Irving's, and Hawthorne's female characters, in whom the union of mind and body is possible only through unnatural or supernatural means (81).

Like Fanny Fern, the women in women's authentic ghost stories have the (un)canny ability to come back from the grave, sometimes inhabiting another woman's body as Cassy metaphorically inhabits the dead slave woman's, sometimes taking full possession of their own bodies as the white-shrouded Anna does when she weeps on her son's grave. The ostensible victims' resilience reminds us of Nina Auerbach's "woman and the demon," the "cultural myth of a slain and self-restoring heroine" that centers on "the self-transforming power surging beneath apparent victimization" (15, 34). These "ghosts" give the powerful and self-transforming heroine a physical presence that still accommodates Victorian assumptions about women's higher (that is spiritual) nature: the spiritual is indispensable cultural window dressing for the body's subversive power.

Alice Cary's ghost stories, and particularly the four published in the *Ladies' Repository* in 1855, are among the most complex explorations of the body/spirit nexus I am concerned with here. The best of these is "Ghost Story, Number II," an explicit rewriting of the seduction narrative and, like Stowe's "authentic ghost story," a rescripting of woman's spirituality as a triumph of the body. Cary turns from tragedy and melodrama to comedy, from a concern with what has gone wrong to what can go right—though not without a few contretemps. Specifically, "Number II" is structured to give the man a place not just as seducer, repentant sinner, or madman, but as active participant in the reconstruction of woman as body and soul, and the narrative technique reflects this process. The tale of seduction, abandonment, and comic recapitulation is told equally by Aunt Jenny (the authentic ghost) and her husband, Uncle Nat; it is an act of social reconstruction and narrative completion. At the story's conclusion the ghost is exorcised and the community strengthened because both husband and wife—potential predator and victim—construct together an alternative narrative. In this it provides one answer to "Ligeia," which is not only narrated by a single obsessive speaker from no place and to no one, but is only a beginning, concluding as it does with Ligeia's return, an event that should be the story's climax rather than end. But the series as a whole goes beyond this foundation narrative to raise questions about the gendered relations between body and spirit. While Cary keeps to the identification of women with the authentic or corporeal ghost and men with the literal specter, she also suggests that these oppositions are not absolute, and particularly that men are not excluded by nature from emotion and commitment—that, like Montraville and M'Arthur, their actions are determined by social pressures and expectations and so may be reshaped. Considered as a series, Cary's ghost stories show that men and women can help to take back the night.

"Number II" is typical of Cary's stories because the apparently casual narrative structure conceals tight thematic relationships. The narrator begins with her recollections of the life and death of Amos, the practical joker who also figures in "Ghost Story Number I." Though no seducer (he's too much the ageless bad boy), in both stories Amos is a nightmare combination of Rip Van Winkle and Tom Sawyer and his wake is accompanied by ghostly phenomena of the hackneyed chain-rattling sort. Amos provides an oppositional context for the primary ghost story, which is told to a convivial mid-winter gathering of friends and neighbors that mirrors the intimate and loving group at Mrs. Tudor's. Jenny begins the common story: orphaned at fifteen, she has recently taken work at a lonely inn, one room of which remains mysteriously locked. On the night of her future husband's arrival a superstitious co-worker tells her why. Ten years before, a beautiful young woman and older gentleman arrived together, the man offering "no support or soothing words to the wife, if so she were" (161). The man leaves the next morning and does not return. After waiting several days, the young woman walks six miles to the post office, but finds no message and dies shortly thereafter sitting upright at the window of her room. After she is placed in her coffin her father arrives, insisting he saw her sitting at the window. He takes her body away, but the inn's owner and staff now say that her spirit haunts the room, sometimes sitting at the window or walking up and down, but at other times "taking possession of the bed and sometimes groaning aloud"; they even insist that "one or two persons had been nearly strangled by her" (173). But these gestures are easily contained by locking the room, from which the spirit is apparently unable to pass. The woman is not only powerless when alive, but powerless as a ghost as well, adrift in death as well as in life.

Any nineteenth-century reader would be familiar with the basic outline of the mystery woman's story: it is the standard seduction and betrayal scenario to which woman's fiction, as defined by Nina Baym, habitually responds (26, 51).[6] This is how things stand when Uncle Nat arrives at the inn on a "black and stormy night" (161) similar to the one on which the abandoned woman and her consort arrived years earlier. All rooms except the haunted one are taken, and rather than sleep uncomfortably on the floor Nat decides to brave the spirit's presence. And Jenny, who has laughed at the ghost story, agrees "to answer for any harm that should happen [to] the guest who slept there that night" (160) and goes to sleep. Yet despite this casual response Jenny clearly feels a deep—though in this case probably unconscious—sympathy with the abused woman's plight. She is an orphan, working a hundred miles from home, and has just met an older man from whom, as she delicately phrases it, she has received "more than the share of civilities which I was accustomed to receive" (160). This gentleman will now be the first person in ten years to occupy the ghost's room. His decision not only places him in the physical space of the seducer, but since Nat pooh-poohs any such thing as a ghost it emphasizes the powerlessness of the ghost to redress her grievance through spirit.

What the wronged woman's spirit needs and gets is an authentic ghost, but—and this is where Cary alters both the meaning and narrative structure of the typical authentic ghost story—neither Jenny nor the narrator tells this part. Instead, after explaining how she fell into uneasy sleep, Jenny turns smiling to her husband and says, "'you may as well tell the rest'" (163): "the old gentleman drew himself up, and looking proudly on his wife took up the thread of the story" (163). (This is somewhat as if Ligeia had politely requested Poe's narrator to tell her side of the story, and he obliged.) Nat explains how he is awakened when the door, which he has secured with chairs, is forced open and a figure clothed in white glides silently into the room. After a moment of fright Nat discovers it's no ghost but the attractive housekeeper he had flirted with at dinner. He puts his arms around her neck and wakes her with a kiss. Like Cassy or Ligeia, then, Jenny appears to be a sort of avenging spirit. But she does not seek the terrible revenge exacted in Stowe's tale and narrowly averted in Poe's, but engineers instead a sort of fairy-tale ending to her own isolation and fear, converting the seducer into husband, the vulnerable orphan into happy wife, and—apparently—helping to free the ghost, who is never mentioned again. The specter of seduction has been exorcised as much by a good man's occupation of the haunted room as by Jenny's appropriation of a sister's distress.

And yet we can legitimately ask if things are as simple as the fairy-tale ending of this co-narrative suggests. Has the subversive physical presence of the "authentic ghost" been enrolled in the service of some master narrative of domestic bliss and happy subordination? There is some support for this speculation. Although we are told that Aunt Jenny has "a smiling, rosy face, . . . and a smooth, white brow, that had never seen a wrinkle of care or sorrow" (155), this confident assertion seems untenable in light of her experiences: orphaned at fifteen and with no money and not many friends, she is forced to go out to service in "'a lonesome neighborhood'" (159) a hundred miles from home. Little wonder, then, that the community is interested in "why so pretty a young woman [had] married an old widower" (155). In short, even though Jenny seems happy, she has married, at not much more than sixteen, an older widower, some of whose six children were most likely not much younger than she. This is a burden, however one twists it, as post-bellum women's literature makes clear. In Rose Terry Cooke's "How Celia Changed Her Mind" (1892), for example, the title character receives a proposal from an "old farmer with five uproarious boys," who "had considered it a good idea to marry someone who would make a home for him and earn his living" (134). And although Cary never

married she was obliged to entertain a similar proposal when she was 15: her father remarried and moved into a new house, leaving her in the old one to take care of four younger siblings. It is perhaps understandable, then, that when Jenny begins her tale she twists her wedding ring on her finger, a gesture that in works like Cooke's "The Ring Fetter" (1859) and Chopin's *The Awakening* (1899) suggests confinement rather than freedom. The specter of powerlessness is therefore not an easy one to exorcise and lingers at the edges of Jenny and Nat's story. Nat is no Simon Legree, of course, but the dangers that Jenny's experiences rescript as comedy linger as an important part of the narrative, reminding the reader that cultural circumstances are as real as authentic ghosts.

Marjorie Pryse draws a similar conclusion in her essay on Sarah Orne Jewett's ghost story "The Foreigner" when she notes that the final appearance of the specter is anticlimactic, and that "the story dramatizes not the appearance of the ghost but rather Mrs. Todd's attempt to translate the experience of being 'foreign' for her listener, our narrator." The impulse to "'translate' or to 'interpret' life for listeners and readers," Pryse continues, "explains the realist's intention" (246). In this sense "Ghost Story Number II" is realistic because it attempts to make sense of and to improve the conditions of life—a version of what Robyn Warhol terms "interventive" realism. In its narrative strategy, that is, the authentic ghost story mirrors the authentic ghost that is its subject; it appropriates the trappings of spirituality while directing its energy toward the recovery of power in the larger social body. For this reason, "Ghost Story Number II" (like Sedgwick's "Country Cousin") ends by calling attention to the ghost story's healing effect on its audience: when everyone parts "it was with kindly feeling stirred up, and hearts strengthened and steadied for the work and the warfare of life" (164). The cheery conclusion to Cary's authentic ghost story is the consequence of interpreting the actual conditions of life for its listeners, which in turn is made possible by the cautious but potentially subversive reworking of expectations about women's place in the body/soul hierarchy, a bit of literary sleight-of-hand that endorses the body by appealing to the soul. We can find this subversive strategy recast as philosophy by Eliza Farnham in *Woman and Her Era* (1864). Farnham adapts the tenets of Transcendentalism to argue that:

> we must not lose sight of the fundamental truth that the human being is to be studied, not only in his lower, but in his higher nature, primarily through the material organization which first makes him known. This is not materialism. . . . It is simply asserting that organization is the visible hand-writing of God in the world of Life.
>
> (20)

Farnham's preemptive philosophy keeps the imprimatur of spirit while authorizing a social agenda grounded in and for the body—a philosophy that also underlies the subversive quality of the authentic ghost story.

Julie Bates Dock has recently observed about "The Yellow Wallpaper"—another celebrated ghost story whose narrator gives her spectral double a body—that modern critics assume early readers saw the story's horror but not its sexual politics, and that this assumption misinterprets early readers' "efforts to read politically in their own times" (60). Modern critics have generally been silent on the subject of early readers' responses to the ghost story, content with unravelling the political texts and subtexts for a modern critical audience. Considering the scarcity of recorded responses to the works discussed here I can do little more than that myself. But like Dock I argue for the early audience's ability to read politically: the authentic ghost story renders in dramatic terms the nineteenth-century woman reader's desire—if not always her ability—to act forcefully in the realm of the body politic. If the ghost is authentic because it is a woman acting bodily in this world, then the ghost story is authentic because it affects the world outside the narrative—it has cultural substance. The "authentic ghost story" is not metaphysical fluff or spine-tingling amusement but offers a scheme for using nineteenth-century assumptions about woman's spiritual nature to argue for women's action in the physical world.

Notes

1. Sandra Gilbert and Susan Gubar see Cassy "exploiting the story of the madwoman in the attic" (534) in her search for justice. Diane Roberts maintains that "Stowe denies the reality of the supernatural to give further strength to Cassy's agency: she moves in and out of Gothic discourse, evoking and parodying it to stress Cassy's central role in Legree's growing madness" (83).

2. Braude borrows this influential term from Barbara Welter.

3. Writers acknowledged this problem in various ways. Stowe, the evangelical Christian, assigns the highest spiritual status to the feminized Christ figure Uncle Tom, but makes sure that after his death George Shelby gives Simon Legree a good thrashing. And the angelic Eva St. Clare dispenses wisdom and goes to heaven, but Cassy dispenses earthly justice while temporarily assuming the spiritual mantle.

4. Sedgwick authored the earliest examples of what Nina Baym terms "woman's fiction" (53) and in other works creatively employed existing narrative formulae. As Michael D. Bell notes, for example, in her historical romance *Hope Leslie* (1827) Sedgwick uses romantic conventions "not as meaningless stereotypes, but as effective ways of communicating a message that literate contemporaries would understand" (213-4).

5. In *Invalid Women* Diane Price Herndl discusses the representation of women's illness, focusing on patriarchal culture as the source of women's illness, on the way illness is used to characterize women's efforts at artistic expression, and on the real effects of illness and its representations. In the ghost stories I discuss here, however, the women are usually well—often threateningly so (see the discussion of Fanny Fern's "Fashionable Invalidism"). The men, on the other hand, get sick and even if they do not die like Legree, they recover only to accept the women they have wronged. This inverts the culture of illness that Price Herndl is most concerned with.

6. Baym also remarks that *Charlotte Temple, The Coquette,* and *The Power of Sympathy* "present an unqualified picture of woman as man's inevitable dupe and prey. . . . From a woman's point of view, this is a demoralized literature" (51).

Works Cited

Auerbach, Nina. *Women and the Demon: The Life of a Victorian Myth.* Cambridge: Harvard UP, 1982.

Baym, Nina. *Woman's Fiction: A Guide to Novels by and about Women in America, 1820-1870.* Ithaca: Cornell UP, 1978.

Bell, Michael D. "History and Romance Convention in Catharine Sedgwick's *Hope Leslie.*" *American Quarterly* 22 (1970): 213-21.

Bendixen, Alfred. *Haunted Women: The Best Supernatural Tales by American Women Writers.* New York: Ungar, 1985.

Braude, Ann. *Radical Spirits: Spiritualism and Women's Rights in Nineteenth-Century America.* Boston: Beacon, 1989.

Brodhead, Richard H. *Cultures of Letters: Scenes of Reading and Writing in Nineteenth-Century America.* Chicago: U of Chicago P, 1993.

Carby, Hazel V. *Reconstructing Womanhood: The Emergence of the Afro-American Woman Novelist.* New York: Oxford UP, 1987.

Carpenter, Lynette and Wendy K. Kolmar. *Haunting the House of Fiction: Feminist Perspectives on Ghost Stories by American Women.* Knoxville: U of Tennessee P, 1991.

Cary, Alice. "Ghost Story, Number I." *Ladies Repository* 15 (1855): 17-22.

———. "Ghost Story, Number II." *Clovernook Sketches and Other Stories.* Ed. Judith Fetterley. New Brunswick: Rutgers UP, 1987. 151-64.

Cooke, Rose Terry. "How Celia Changed Her Mind." *"How Celia Changed Her Mind" and Selected Stories.* Ed. Elizabeth Ammons. New Brunswick: Rutgers UP, 1986. 131-50.

Davidson, Cathy N. *Revolution and the Word: The Rise of the Novel in America.* New York: Oxford UP, 1986.

Dock, Julie Bates. "'But One Expects That': Charlotte Perkins Gilman's 'The Yellow Wallpaper' and the Shifting Light of Scholarship." *PMLA* 111:1 (1996): 52-65.

Farham, Eliza. *Woman and Her Era.* New York: A. J. Davis and Co., 1864.

Fern, Fanny. "Fashionable Invalidism." *Ruth Hall and Other Writings.* Ed. Joyce W. Warren. New Brunswick: Rutgers UP, 1986. 341-2.

Gilbert, Sandra and Susan Gubar. *The Madwoman in the Attic: The Woman Writer and the Nineteenth-Century Literary Imagination.* New Haven: Yale UP, 1979.

Kaplan, Anne E. *Motherhood and Representation: The Mother in Popular Culture and Melodrama.* New York: Routledge, 1992.

Kerber, Linda K. *Women of the Republic: Intellect and Ideology in Revolutionary America.* Chapel Hill: U of North Carolina P, 1980.

Poe, Edgar Allan. "Ligeia." *The Complete Works of Edgar Allan Poe. Prose Tales, Vol. I.* Ed. James A. Harrison. New York: AMS P, 1965. 248-68.

Price Herndl, Diane. *Invalid Women: Figuring Illness in American Fiction and Culture, 1840-1940.* Chapel Hill: U of North Carolina P, 1993.

Pryse, Marjorie. "Women 'at sea': Feminist Realism in Sarah Orne Jewett's 'The Foreigner.'" *American Literary Realism* 15 (1982): 244-52.

Roberts, Diane. *The Myth of Aunt Jemima: Representation of Race and Region.* New York: Routledge, 1994.

Rowson, Susanna Haswell. *Charlotte Temple.* Ed. Cathy N. Davidson. New York: Oxford UP, 1986.

Salmonson, Jessica Amanda, ed. *What did Miss Darlington See? An Anthology of Feminist Supernatural Fiction.* New York: Feminist P, 1989.

Sedgwick, Catharine Maria. "Country Cousin." *Tales and Sketches.* Philadelphia: Carey, Lea, and Blanchard, 1835. 67-96.

Stowe, Harriet Beecher. *Uncle Tom's Cabin, or, Life Among the Lowly.* New York: Library of America, 1982.

Tompkins, Jane. *Sensational Designs: The Cultural Work of American Fiction 1790-1860.* New York: Oxford UP, 1985.

Warhol, Robyn R. "Poetics and Persuasion: *Uncle Tom's Cabin* as a Realist Novel." *Essays in Literature* 13 (1986): 283-98.

———. *Gendered Interventions: Narrative Discourse in the Victorian Novel.* New Brunswick: Rutgers UP, 1989.

Welter, Barbara. "The Cult of True Womanhood, 1820-1860." *Dimity Convictions: The American Woman in the Nineteenth Century.* Columbus: U of Ohio P, 1976. 21-44.

Dale Bailey (essay date 1999)

SOURCE: Bailey, Dale. "The Sentient House and the Ghostly Tradition: The Legacy of Poe and Hawthorne." In *American Nightmares: The Haunted House Formula in American Popular Fiction*, pp. 15-24. Bowling Green, Ohio: Bowling Green State University Popular Press, 1999.

[*In the following essay, Bailey argues that the haunted house stories of Edgar Allan Poe and Nathaniel Hawthorne served as departures from the more straightforward ghost story, even as it was taking shape in England in the nineteenth century, and strongly influenced the development of the subgenre to the present day.*]

1.

In *Men, Women, and Chainsaws: Gender in the Modern Horror Film* [1992], Carol Clover describes a process by which the mainstream cinema of the nineties gradually absorbed the materials and formulae of the early eighties slasher film. The process was not without its ironies, among them the 1991 Best Picture Oscar win for Jonathan Demme's *Silence of the Lambs* (based upon Thomas Harris's novel), which reworked themes and conventions established by John Carpenter in his 1978 drive-in classic, *Halloween.* Unfortunately, the process of assimilation involved significant trade-offs; whatever the slasher film gained in artistry, it lost—at least from the cultural critic's perspective—in clarity of theme. The anxieties and tensions so lucidly exposed in movies like *Friday the Thirteenth* and *Texas Chainsaw Massacre* are in slicker (more expensive) films disguised by the subterfuge and misdirection necessary to make them amenable to a more sophisticated (adult) audience. As Clover points out, such sophisticated movies, whatever their individual merit, are

> low-risk films. They are in any case not films that take the kind of brazen tack into the psychosexual wilderness that made horror in the seventies and eighties such a marvelously transparent object of study. Unless and until the direction changes again, I suspect we will

soon be back to the dominant fiction in its dominant forms, out of which we must dig meanings rather than have them displayed so obviously and so spectacularly before us.

(236)

The reverse of this process—and the consequences Clover describes—occurs with the haunted house formula. If many of the themes the American haunted house tale invokes are rooted in a tradition of social criticism, the formula itself finds its origin in the complex and subtle literature of the American Renaissance, which borrowed a series of conventions already extant in the European gothic and cast them into uniquely American form. The gradual assimilation of those conventions into the popular literature of today led to simplification and standardization; as a result, contemporary popular fiction distills the resonances of the haunted house tale into their rawest and most powerful elements. The structure we glimpse through shrouds of ambiguity in the romances of Hawthorne and Poe stands clearly exposed in paperbacks such as *The Amityville Horror* [1977]. For these reasons, it would be a mistake to examine the permutations of the haunted house formula ahistorically. Moreover, a brief look back at those nineteenth-century tales—especially as they compare to the ghostly tales of James and Wharton—will enable us to bring a problem of definition into sharper focus: How does the haunted house tale, at least in its contemporary form, differ from the traditional ghost story?

2.

Ironically, it is unlikely that Hawthorne or Poe would even have thought to ask such a question. While, as Stephen King points out, the gothic archetype of the Bad Place has been around since "the caveman who had to move out of his hole in the rock because he heard . . . voices back there in the shadows" (266), there is little evidence that Hawthorne or Poe consciously intended to revolutionize that archetype.

Not that they didn't see themselves as genre innovators. Poe rightly thought of himself as both a theorist and practitioner of literature, and, we might argue, he did more than any other writer to lay out the conventions which govern the modern short story. His pronouncements on the form anticipated the formalist emphasis on unity by almost a century, just as his notions of abnormal psychology, especially the operation of guilt and repression, antedated Freud. Similarly, in the preface to *The House of the Seven Gables,* Hawthorne consciously rejects the novel's "minute fidelity" to reality in favor of the creative latitude of the romance (1).

It's hardly surprising, then, that most readers have viewed the issue of genre in "The Fall of the House of Usher" and *The House of the Seven Gables* in the context of Poe and Hawthorne's comments on the matter. Frequently anatomized as an example of Poe's theory of short fiction, "Usher" is more often seen as an expression of the gothic tradition than a revision of it.[1] Similarly, on the question of genre in *Seven Gables,* critics have focused on Hawthorne's concept of the romance.[2] Such readings are entirely legitimate, of course, but they shed little light on the influence Poe and Hawthorne exercised over the contemporary paperback formula of the haunted house. And as we shall see, that influence, while perhaps indirect, is significant.

In both works, of course, we can discern the inchoate outlines of the formula we touched upon in Chapter 1. Both present us with an interloper in an ancient house with an ill history—the perhaps unreliable narrator of "Usher," who alone escapes to tell the tale; young Phoebe Pyncheon, the innocent country cousin of the corrupt urban Pyncheons in *Seven Gables.* A series of perhaps supernatural events forms the bulk of both narratives. And both end with one of the accepted variations of the formula. In "Usher," the narrator escapes with his life as the house crumbles into the leaden tarn behind him. In *Seven Gables,* Phoebe and Holgrave, her young daguerreotypist love interest, leave the house intact when they move to the country.

And yet, a skeptic might object, almost *any* gothic novel, European or American, could be so synopsized. Take, as an obvious example, Horace Walpole's urgothic, *The Castle of Otranto*; here, the beautiful Isabella, damsel in distress, is rescued by the heroic Theodore, stranger to the mysterious castle. Otranto itself serves as setting for all manner of bizarre and supernatural events—from bleeding statues to giant helmets falling out of the blue. And the novel ends with the castle's destruction as a ghostly image of Duke Alfonso, avatar of long-unpunished crimes, rises majestically into the heavens. The haunted house formula existed for years previous to our arbitrary point of origin in the American Renaissance, such a skeptic might argue—correctly.

But, of course, he would be wrong as well. For if we concede that Poe and Hawthorne adapted a formula long extant in European gothic fiction and previously employed in America by writers such as Charles Brockden Brown, then we must also recognize their significant contributions to that formula. Those contributions substantially alter Walpole's gothic model, enriching it with uniquely American resonances which would eventually provide impetus for the thriving (dare we say) cottage industry of paperback haunted house novels, and establishing a small but significant set of conventions which would serve to distinguish the American haunted house tale from the genteel ghost story simultaneously being developed by Sheridan Le Fanu on the other side of the Atlantic.

3.

"Elegant nightmares," critic Jack Sullivan calls those tales, and it is worth turning aside for a moment to consider the connotations of that term, especially as it applies to Edith Wharton and Henry James, nineteenth-century American masters of the ghost story. No doubt, the subgenres share a number of cosmetic similarities; however, as a comparison of Wharton and James to Poe and Hawthorne will show, the ghost story is finally distinct from the haunted house tale as it exists in contemporary fiction.

They make an interesting group, our quartet of supernatural writers, not least because of the reputations we grant them. All of them have found a place in the academic canon, and yet we don't accord them all the same respect. On one hand, we have Hawthorne and Poe—Hawthorne, dour moralist of the nineteenth century, casting a cold eye over the sins of his Puritan fathers, and worse yet, Poe, three-fifths genius and two-fifths sheer fudge, that raving lunatic of American letters, that drunken pedophile dying in his Baltimore ditch. He's the literary equivalent of the girl you knew in high school—a date or two is fine, but you wouldn't want to take him home to mother. "That Poe had a powerful intellect is undeniable," T. S. Eliot once remarked, "but it seems to me the intellect of a highly gifted young person before puberty. The forms which his lively curiosity takes are those in which a pre-adolescent mentality delights" ["From Poe to Valéry." *Hudson Review* 2 (1949): 327-43,] (335).

Weigh against them James and Wharton, high priest and priestess of the cult of complexity. Moralists, yes, but they operate not with Hawthorne's leaden symbolism; their method is all subtlety and psychological acuity, substituting for the shrill madness of Madeline Usher's oubliette the delicate savagery of the dinner table, the rapier irony of the lady's chamber. Wharton and James are all waltz to the rollicking beat of Poe's manic reel. And Hawthorne doesn't dance.

Broad clichés? Of course. Painting in primary colors? Absolutely.

But here, as in most clichés, we find a core of truth.

Primary colors show up the clearest.

Hawthorne presents us with Maule's curse—"God hath given him blood to drink" (16)—and a corpse "saturated" with crimson (15). Poe's narrator flees screaming into the night as Madeline Usher's corpse totters across the threshold of her brother's chamber. Such vulgarity is beneath James—after all, as he once noted, to take Poe "with more than a certain degree of seriousness is to lack seriousness one's self" (280), and whatever virtues James may have lacked, seriousness did not number among them. So it is that people rarely die in the ghostly fiction of James, and when they do, as in *The Turn of the Screw,* they do it politely, with a minimum of fuss. The method in the ghost stories of Wharton, his greatest disciple, is much the same. In "Afterward," as we shall see, she perfects it. No one dies at all. He simply disappears.

Partially, then, the elegance of such nightmares—the elegance of the genteel ghost story as practiced by James and Wharton—is a matter of tone, a reluctance, quite literally, to go for the throat. In horror fiction of any kind, tone is of pivotal importance. But in the ghost story, more than the haunted house tale, tone gives rise to a central thematic ambiguity. How should a ghost story be told? At second hand, through shrouds of uncertainty, preferably around a fireplace on a chill winter night. This is precisely how *The Turn of the Screw* begins: the authority of the governess's tale is called into question by the larger narrative in which it is embedded, that of the unnamed narrator who introduces the tale and to whom the story is first briefly synopsized and then read aloud, by firelight (on Christmas Eve, no less), by yet a third narrator, Douglas. The story is like a stone cast into a pool of placid water. The stone—the "truth" of the events that occurred at the country estate of Bly during the governess's tenure—is irrevocably lost. Our only indication that the water was ever disturbed is the series of concentric rings rippling outward from the point of impact, rings of interpretation—the governess's, Douglas's, the narrator's, even our own—growing progressively vaguer in proportion to their distance from the center.

The ambiguity inherent in this structure has given rise to the crux in academic criticism on *The Turn of the Screw*: are the ghostly events at Bly supernatural in origin or are they the product of the governess's imagination? Edmund Wilson's 1934 argument that the malign apparitions of Peter Quint and Miss Jessel are hallucinatory symptoms of the governess's suppressed sexual desire marked a turning point in James criticism.[3] If the resulting debate has become tedious, it has at least emphasized the essential ambiguity of the tale. As David Cook and Timothy Corrigan argue, *The Turn of the Screw* defies resolution: "By constantly undermining and restoring his narrator's credibility, James transforms a narrative which is potentially a ghost story or a mystery tale about a demented governess into a very subtle fiction about the process of fiction itself" (65).[4] In short, whatever we decide about the reality of Peter Quint and Miss Jessel must at last be only that—a decision, in some respects wholly arbitrary. In the end, the story highlights the indeterminacy of knowledge.

Even tales that dispense with the tired machinery of the ghost story—the fireplace, the winter night—depend upon the essential ambiguity of the ghostly experience.

Wharton's "Afterward" presents Lyng, an English estate said to be haunted by a ghost who can be identified only long after the haunting occurs. When Americans Ned and Mary Boyne purchase Lyng, Mary discovers the truth of the legend: her husband disappears with a mysterious visitor—"a slightly built man" later identified as Bob Elwell (62), a victim of her husband's unscrupulous business practices. Elwell committed suicide sometime after the Boynes purchased Lyng; apparently he has returned to exact his revenge.

Those few critics who have commented on "Afterward" have read it in social or psycho-sexual contexts.[5] Richard Kaye, Janet Ruth Heller, and Dale Bachman Flynn see the story as a metaphor for a crumbling marriage. Jenni Dyman places the story in the context of marital conventions endemic in upper-class nineteenth-century America, especially the Cult of True Womanhood, which isolates the wife from the morally corrupt sphere of capitalism.[6] All such readings, however, depend upon the element of ambiguity inherent in the tale. For example, Ned Boyne can be seen as a closeted homosexual abducted by his "male paramour," as Kaye suggests (12), only because the tale ends in indeterminacy. It is not clear that Boyne is dead; he may have merely abandoned his wife. Though the story strongly implies that the "ghost" and Bob Elwell are one and the same, Mary's belief that the ghost of Lyng can be recognized only "afterwards" suggests an alternative reading: that her identification of the "slightly built man" and Elwell, which is confirmed by no other character, is a subconscious palliative for the pain of her broken marriage.

Because "Afterward" is typical of Wharton's method, Dyman has convincingly argued that Wharton's horror, like that of James, is "always psychological . . . not physical" (6)—in short, the ghost story's tendency to eschew physical mayhem produces the overriding ambiguity which distinguishes it from the haunted house tale.[7] The contemporary formula of the haunted house tale, on the other hand, typically exploits such ambiguity only early in the text, later resolving it in favor of a clearly supernatural explanation. As we shall see, this tendency derives from the embryonic haunted house tales of Hawthorne and Poe.

And yet, here too a skeptic might reasonably object. After all, the psychological/supernatural crux has also been a focus of modern criticism on Poe and Hawthorne. Michael Dunne, for example, argues that Hawthorne's manipulation of historical authority in *Seven Gables* simultaneously qualifies and confirms the reality of the apparitions who parade through the parlor of the Pyncheon mansion every midnight (124).[8] Similarly, countless critics have questioned the reliability of Poe's narrator in "The Fall of the House of Usher": is his apparently supernatural description of Madeline Usher's return from the grave, with its absurd echoes of the in-terpolated "Mad Trist" of Sir Lancelot Canning, the self-serving product of guilt or terror?[9]

Certainly it might be. The fascination of "Usher"—indeed of many supernatural tales—is that it is enigmatic enough to support any number of readings, even mutually exclusive ones. "Usher" is a mirror, reflecting the bent of our particular genius. But we should not let this malleability disguise the tale's centrality to the tradition of the haunted house. After all, as Jerry Palmer points out, genres develop "diachronically" (127), across time; what is germinal in "Usher" and *Seven Gables* will only later come to fruition. The fact is, there is nothing genteel about either tale. The visceral physicality of their supernatural imagery outweighs mere psychological ambiguity. All the arguments about unreliable narrators in an entire university library can't outweigh the persuasive authority of Madeline Usher's animate husk as it lurches across the threshold into her shrieking brother's arms or the horror of Judge Pyncheon's bloody onlooking corpse as the shades of his ancestors progress in silent judgment through the parlor of Hawthorne's many-gabled house.

4.

Of course, our skeptic could object, countless gothic works, from Walpole's *Castle of Otranto* to Louisa May Alcott's *A Long Fatal Love Chase,* have sacrificed psychological complexity for colorful action. And indeed, the skeptic is right: their tendency to reduce ambiguity in favor of the clearly supernatural implications of physical mayhem does not alone qualify Poe and Hawthorne as formula-innovators. Rather, they graft a number of new characteristics to Walpole's gothic template. The nature of these innovations differs in each case—neither Poe nor Hawthorne produced a mature example of the haunted house tale—but taken together they produce the formula we see in mature manifestations in so many of their paperback descendants.

Most obviously, and perhaps most significantly, both Poe and Hawthorne displace the supernatural focus of the text from the figure of the ghost—the revenant spirit of a human being—to the house. This isn't the case in *The Turn of the Screw.* Bly—however important it may be to critics who read the tale in terms of class conflict[10]—is of secondary importance. Though large and old, it poses no threat to the governess. The problem is the human spirits of Peter Quint and Miss Jessel, the former servants. Similarly, Wharton's Lyng, though supposedly haunted, is not itself malign; indeed, the Boynes find the idea of sharing their home with a ghost rather charming. The human spirit of Bob Elwell is the story's principal antagonist. Moreover, Elwell's ghost is not intrinsically connected with Lyng, which acquired its reputation for being haunted long before Elwell's death. (Wharton never addresses the incoherence of this plot point: is there another ghost at Lyng?)

As their titles frequently suggest, however, the house it-self—the physical structure—serves as antagonist in the haunted house tale. In "The Fall of the House of Usher," despite the famous ambiguity of Poe's phrase (does the "House of Usher" refer to the family or their home?), we are introduced to the cracked facade of the mansion long before the neurasthenic figures of Roderick and Madeline Usher make their appearance. And while the House of Usher is in many respects typical of the tradi-tional gothic setting—a vast, ancient, aristocratic man-sion in a vaguely European landscape—Poe attributes to it at least one revolutionary quality which will be-come central to the haunted house formula: the house is alive. It possesses its own malign will.

Roderick Usher is "enchained by certain superstitious impressions in regard to the dwelling which he ten-anted," our unnamed narrator tells us (403). The nature of this superstition later becomes clear. Roderick Usher believes that the "home of his forefathers" is self-aware:

> The condition of the sentience had been here, he imag-ined, fulfilled in the method of collocation of these stones—in the order of their arrangement, as well as in that of the many fungi which overspread them, and of the decayed trees which stood around—above all in the long undisturbed endurance of this arrangement.
>
> (408)

An obscure conjunction of architecture and geometry has endowed the house with a malign will and intelli-gence utterly distinct from any merely human revenant. Contemporary writers of haunted house tales almost in-variably echo Poe's statement.

"No human eye can isolate the unhappy coincidence of line and place which suggests evil in the face of a house," Shirley Jackson writes in *The Haunting of Hill House,*

> and yet somehow a manic juxtaposition, a badly turned angle, some chance meeting of roof and sky turned Hill House into a place of despair, more frightening because the face of Hill House seemed awake, with a watchful-ness from the blank windows and a touch of glee in the eyebrow of a cornice.
>
> (34)

Moreover, because such sentience does not possess the house, but derives from its very structure, the house cannot be redeemed; instead it must be destroyed. "Ex-orcism cannot alter the countenance of a house," Jack-son informs us. "Hill House would stay as it was until it was destroyed" (35). The protagonists of haunted house tales take Jackson's injunction to heart. We wit-ness few exorcisms in such stories, but we see plenty of wreckage: the House of Usher collapses into its tarn, King's Overlook Hotel is destroyed by an exploding boiler, and Jack Cady's Tracker House, like Lisa Cantrell's Manse, is torn down to make way for new construction.[11]

Even when the house survives, the characters acknowl-edge the need for its destruction. Anne Rivers Siddons's *The House Next Door* ends as Walter and Colquitt Kennedy wait for dark, when they will creep across the lawn and burn the eponymous house. A former tenant of Jackson's Hill House warns Dr. Montague that "the house ought to be burned down and the ground sowed with salt" (71). Hawthorne himself, though he doesn't attribute any supernatural prescience to the House of Seven Gables, depicts that house—and not the ghosts who may or may not exist there—as the external mani-festation of Pyncheon moral corruption. "Under that roof," comments Holgrave, Hawthorne's hero and spokesman,

> through a portion of three centuries, there has been per-petual remorse of conscience, a constantly defeated hope, strife amongst kindred, various misery, a strange form of death, dark suspicion, unspeakable disgrace.
>
> (185)

Nor does Holgrave fail to anticipate the heroes of later haunted tales in his conclusions: "The house ought to be purified with fire—purified until only its ashes re-main" (184).

The House of the Seven Gables also foreshadows the development of the haunted house tale in at least two other significant ways. First, Hawthorne dispenses with much of the traditional gothic machinery which seems so ludicrous to modern readers. *The House of the Seven Gables* is set not on some windswept alpine height but in Hawthorne's contemporary Salem. More important still, this American setting forces him to reduce the tra-ditional gothic castle to a house—a magnificent house with a storied history, to be sure—but a mere house nonetheless. And, as we will see, this reduction of scale has profound thematic consequences.

In retrospect, Hawthorne's decision to dislocate the conventions of the gothic novel in this fashion may seem obvious, even pre-ordained; in reality, it was a stroke of genius.[12] For the first time, the haunted house became a natural device for exploiting particularly American themes; indeed, *The House of the Seven Gables* has often been read in this fashion. Marcus Cun-liffe, for example, argues that the novel highlights the danger of establishing an American aristocracy based upon inherited wealth. Other critics have focused on the problem of the American past, the moral consequences of American materialism, the rising tide of technology and the resulting sense of cultural impermanence, and the question of ethics and American capitalism.[13] Haw-thorne, like Poe before him, helped to establish the flexibility of the haunted house not merely as a plot de-vice but as a symbol with profound resonance for American writers.

While this reduction of physical scale from castle to house broadened the haunted house formula's thematic horizon, it also served to narrow the tale's focus—and herein we find Hawthorne's second innovation. As in Walpole's *Castle of Otranto,* the gothic castle functioned as a symbol of corrupt political authority. Hawthorne retains this conceit in the authority of Colonel Pyncheon and his sinister descendant, Judge Pyncheon. However, while the machinations of these figures drive the novel's plot, Hawthorne shifts the focus of the narrative to the family gradually developing within the House of Seven Gables. If only because they are so rarely on stage, neither Colonel nor Judge Pyncheon dominates the reader's imagination as do traditionally Byronic heroes such as Monk Lewis's Ambrosio or Emily Brontë's Heathcliff.

Critics have generally concurred with Hawthorne's belief that *The House of the Seven Gables* is "less gloomy" than *The Scarlet Letter* (Wagenknecht [*Nathaniel Hawthorne: The Man, His Tales and Romances* (1989)] 95). This lightening of mood can be attributed to Hawthorne's focus on the psychically wounded residents of the House—the child-like Clifford, the grim Hepzibah, the overly serious Holgrave—as they gradually thaw in the sunlit presence of Phoebe. Significantly, Phoebe is a Pyncheon in name only: she grew up in the country, free of the moral fog that envelops her urban cousins, and her values are thoroughly middle class.[14] Though she cannot entirely renovate the House of Seven Gables, she serves at least to brighten its darker corners. Indeed, she becomes something of a maternal figure in the novel, lifting Clifford out of his prison-induced gloom, brightening the absurd shop Hepzibah has established to meet expenses, and leavening the chill intellectualism of Holgrave with sanguine emotion. In this core of wounded figures, bound together by their love for Phoebe and their opposition to the rapacious material appetites of Judge Pyncheon, we can trace the dim outlines of the contemporary haunted house tale's central figures: the imperiled nuclear family. In the conclusion of the novel, Phoebe and her symbolic children escape the House of Seven Gables, bound for a new home and a new life, free of the blight of history.

In the contemporary haunted house tale, as we shall see, the imperiled family also usually escapes, though sometimes at terrible—indeed fatal—cost. The characters who pay that ultimate price, as they vary from text to text, betray the secret of the haunted house tale's longevity. In the hands of the best paperback novelists, the haunted house becomes a strikingly versatile metaphor; transcending the glossy clichés of formula, it drags into light the nightmarish tensions of gender, class, and culture hidden at the heart of American life.

Notes

1. See Minoru Hirota's articles "A Comparative Study of *Wuthering Heights* and 'The Fall of the House of Usher'" [*Studies in English Language and Literature* 27 (1977): 115-36] and "The Elements of American Romance in *Wuthering Heights*: Concurrent Origin and Themes found in *Wuthering Heights* and 'The Fall of the House of Usher'" [*Studies in English Language and Literature* 30 (1980): 57-75], Frederick S. Frank's "Poe's House of the Seven Gothics: The Fall of the Narrator in 'The Fall of the House of Usher'" [*Orbis Litterarum* 34 (1979): 331-51], Peter Obuchowski's "Unity of Effect in Poe's 'The Fall of the House of Usher'" [*Studies in Short Fiction* 12 (1975): 407-12], and Walter Evans's "'The Fall of the House of Usher' and Poe's Theory of the Tale" [*Studies in Short Fiction* 14 (1977): 137-44]. Also of interest on the relationship between "Usher" and the European gothic tradition are Marianne Juhl and Bo-Hakon Jorgenson's "Why Gothic Fiction?" [*Isak Dineson: Critical Views,* ed. Olga Anastasia Pelensky (1993)] and G. R. Thompson's "Locke, Kant, and Gothic Fiction: A Further Word on the Indeterminism of Poe's 'Usher'" [*Studies in Short Fiction* 26 (1989): 547-60]. Craig Howes comments on "Usher" as short fiction in "Teaching 'Usher' and Genre: Poe and the Introductory Literature Class" [*Journal of the Midwest Modern Language Association* 19 (1986): 29-42].

2. While almost every commentator on the book touches upon Hawthorne's definition of the romance, it is the focus of a number of studies, most obviously John C. Stubbs's *The Pursuit of Form: A Study of Hawthorne and the Romance* [1970]. John Engell focuses on defining the romance in the context of gothicism in "Hawthorne and Two Types of Early American Romance" [*South Atlantic Review* 57 (1992): 33-51]. Also of direct interest is Brook Thomas's "*The House of the Seven Gables*: Reading the Romance of America" [*PMLA* 97 (1982): 195-211].

3. Permutations of Wilson's reading abound, including Thomas Cranfill and Robert L. Clark's exhaustive analysis, *An Anatomy of The Turn of the Screw* [1965], Robert W. Hill Jr.'s "A Counterclockwise Turn in James's *The Turn of the Screw*" [*Twentieth-Century Literature* 27 (1981): 53-71], Dennis Chase's "The Ambiguity of Innocence: *The Turn of the Screw*" [*Extrapolation* 27 (1986): 197-202], and Stanley Renner's "'Red hair, very red, close curling': Sexual Hysteria, Physiognomical Bogeymen, and the 'Ghosts' in *The Turn of the Screw*" [*Henry James, The Turn of the Screw,* ed. Peter G. Beidler (1995)]. Defenses of the supernatural interpretation include Nathan Bryllion Fagin's "Another Reading of *The Turn of the Screw*" [*Modern Language Notes* 56 (1941): 196-202], Alexander E. Jones's "Point of View in *The Turn of the Screw*" [*PMLA* 74 (1959): 112-22],

John J. Allen's "The Governess and the Ghosts in *The Turn of the Screw*" [*Henry James Review* 1 (1979): 73-80], and Charles K. Wolfe's "Victorian Ghost Story Technique: The Case of Henry James" [*Romantist* 3 (1979): 67-72].

4. Christine Brooke-Rose may have been the first to propose such a reading in a sequentially published article called "The Squirm of the True" [*PTL: A Journal for Descriptive Poetics and Theory of Literature* 1 (1976): 265-94; 513-46; 2 (1977): 517-62]. See also Shlomith Rimmon's chapter on the novel in *The Concept of Ambiguity: The Example of James* [1977], Shoshona Felman's "Turning the Screw of Interpretation" [*Yale French Studies* 55-56 (1977): 94-207], William R. Goetz's "The Frame of *The Turn of the Screw*: Framing the Reader In" [*Studies in Short Fiction* 18 (1981): 71-74], and Terry Heller's *The Turn of the Screw: Bewildered Vision* [1989].

5. Criticism on Wharton's ghostly tales is limited. In "Edith Wharton's Ghost Stories" [*Criticism* 12 (1970): 133-52], Margaret McDowell devotes only a sentence to "Afterward." In "Powers of Darkness" [*Times Literary Supplement* 13 June 1975: 644-45], an overview of Wharton's ghostly fiction, R. W. B. Lewis doesn't even mention the story. Allan Gardner Smith contributes a cursory examination of the ghostly tales to *Edith Wharton: Modern Critical Views* [ed. Harold Bloom (1986)].

6. For a detailed analysis of the Cult of True Womanhood, see Barbara Welter's *Dimity Convictions: The American Woman in the Nineteenth Century* [1976].

7. In *The Supernatural in the English Short Story* [1959], Pamela Search also defines such tales as a distinct type, "the psychological ghost story" (13), offering as a primary example the work of Walter De La Mare.

8. In "Maule's Curse, or Hawthorne and the Problem of Allegory" [*In Defense of Reason* (1938)], Yvor Winters describes Hawthorne's technique of providing both natural and supernatural explanations as the "formula of alternative possibilities" (170). See also Marcus Cunliffe's "*The House of Seven Gables*" in *Hawthorne Centenary Essays* [ed. Roy Harvey Pearce (1964)].

9. The question of Poe's narrator—and the related issue of whether the events at the House of Usher should be seen as supernatural—has been endlessly debated. G. R. Thompson makes an especially cogent argument that the narrator is deranged by terror in *Poe's Fiction: Romantic Irony in the Gothic Tales* [1973]. For an alternative view,

see Patrick F. Quinn's "A Misreading of Poe's 'The Fall of the House of Usher'" [*Ruined Eden of the Present: Hawthorne, Melville, and Poe*, ed. G. R. Thompson and Virgil L. Locke (1981)].

10. Such readings tend to see the governess as a woman who wishes to rise above her station through marriage to the aristocratic owner of Bly. Variations on this theme include Edwin Fussel's "The Ontology of *The Turn of the Screw*" [*Journal of Modern Literature* 8 (1980): 118-28], Heath Moon's "More Royalist Than the King: The Governess, the Telegraphist, and Mrs. Gracedew" [*Criticism* 24 (1982): 16-35], Graham McMaster's "Henry James and India: A Historical Reading of *The Turn of the Screw*" [*Clio* 18 (1988): 23-40], and Bruce Robbins's "Shooting Off James's Blanks: Theory, Politics, and *The Turn of the Screw*" [*Henry James Review* 5 (1984): 192-99].

11. Richard Matheson's 1971 novel *Hell House* is the exception that proves the rule. The book ends with the successful exorcism of Belasco House.

12. Though Charles Brockden Brown anticipated Hawthorne's Americanization of the gothic, he did not establish the motif of the house as Hawthorne and Poe did. Like Anne Radcliffe, Brown provided unambiguously rational explanations for apparently supernatural events; in this sense, his work runs counter to the prevailing formula of the haunted house novel.

13. On the question of the past, see Richard Harter Fogle's *Hawthorne's Fiction: Light and Dark* [1952] and Mildred K. Travis's "Past vs. Present in *The House of the Seven Gables*" [*ESQ: A Journal of the American Renaissance* 58 (1970): 109-11]. Charles Swann's *Nathaniel Hawthorne: Tradition and Revolution* [1991] concentrates on issues of technology and modernity, as does Richard F. Fleck's "Industrial Imagery in *The House of the Seven Gables*" [*Nathaniel Hawthorne Journal* 1974: 273-76]. Michael T. Gilmore explores the tension between art and commerce in "The Artist and the Marketplace in *The House of the Seven Gables*" [*ELH* 48 (1981): 172-89], while Henry N. Smith's "The Morals of Power: Business Enterprise as a Theme in Mid-Nineteenth-Century American Fiction" [*Essays on American Literature in Honor of Jay B. Hubbell*, ed. Clarence Ghodes (1967)] focuses on the ethics of capitalism.

14. In "A Domestic Reading of *The House of the Seven Gables*" [*Studies in the Novel* 21 (1989): 1-13], Susan Van Zanten Gallagher also suggests that Phoebe represents traditional values. She argues that Phoebe is modeled on the domestic heroine of contemporary sentimental novels. In *Haw-

thorne's *Narrative Strategies* [1995], Michael Dunne concurs, noting that Phoebe is the literal angel in the house to Hepzibah's ironic version of that ideal (172-74).

Helen Groth (essay date autumn 2007)

SOURCE: Groth, Helen. "Reading Victorian Illusions: Dickens's *Haunted Man* and Dr. Pepper's 'Ghost.'" *Victorian Studies* 50, no. 1 (autumn 2007): 43-65.

[*In the following essay, Groth discusses the foregrounding of the visual experience among Victorian readers and audiences in John Henry Pepper's stage interpretation of Charles Dickens's novella* The Haunted Man and the Ghost's Bargain, *noting that both Pepper and Dickens were fascinated with the effects of vision on memory and illusion.*]

In December of 1862, John Henry Pepper's spectacular adaptation of Charles Dickens's *The Haunted Man and The Ghost's Bargain* (1848) at the Royal Polytechnic Institution on Regent Street transfixed London audiences. In its initial incarnation, Pepper's "Ghost" combined a novel form of optical illusion with Dickens's uncanny tale of a man called Redlaw who is forced to confront the horrific consequences of his desire to be free of his past. The illusion focused on the moment in Dickens's *Haunted Man* when Redlaw's spectral double appears to grant his wish that his memory be erased, a wish accompanied by a curse that condemns all those who come in contact with him to the same fate. Confronted with the brutal consequences of his desire, Redlaw ultimately repents, and his punitive ghost lifts the curse.

Dickens's tale, which was itself indebted to mid-century debates about the nature of memory and illusion, provided Pepper with a stock of ready-made images and ideas, including illustrations by John Tenniel, John Leech, and others. Dickens's insistence on the civilizing power of memory, its ability to suppress the chaos of individual desire and to foster social responsibility, nicely complemented Pepper's own didactic use of illusion to promote rational responses to seemingly inexplicable supernatural phenomena. Underlying this mutual emphasis on order and continuity, however, was a fundamental anxiety about the fallibility of perception and memory in organizing stimuli into patterns that reinforced normalizing historical continuities. This concern was not unique to Pepper and Dickens, and it indicates the immersion of both men in mid-century debates about the eye and the mind—Pepper, through his converging interests in optics and natural magic; and Dickens, through a number of literary and scientific sources and a close network of friendships with prominent medical

figures like John Connolly and John Elliotson.[1] This article examines Dickens's and Pepper's shared preoccupation with memory and illusion in the context of the evolving visual vernacular of the Victorian period, a vernacular characterized by active skepticism toward visual and psychological phenomena. Analyzing the ways in which Dickens's tale encourages readers to interrogate the epistemological bases of memory and perception, I track Pepper's translation of the text into a popular theatrical event designed to exploit the recollective powers of an increasingly visually literate mid-century audience.

HAUNTED MEN

The first illustrated edition of *The Haunted Man and The Ghost's Bargain* introduced the central character Redlaw, a reclusive chemist plagued by his past, through a sequence of visual frames.[2] These begin with John Tenniel's double frontispiece depicting Redlaw sitting and gazing into a fire while his spectral double mirrors his posture unseen to all but the reader. . . . On the facing page, the paths to heaven and perdition are intimated by an angel and an enshrouded figure holding an innocent child between them. . . . Pointing toward darkness, the child augurs of the corruption of innocence that will follow in the wake of Redlaw's surrender to the dark forces that haunt his mind. Tenniel's third plate, which illustrates the first page of the first chapter, portrays a child reading in the foreground of another fireside scene, holding his book up to capture the illumination of the flames. . . .This plate inaugurates the text's self-reflexive study of representation: while the child reads, smoky shadows take shape, combining fantastic oriental and supernatural figures with the distorted forms of familiar domestic bodies and objects.

Accompanying these images is the narrative frame Dickens provides in his first description of Redlaw. Visually self-conscious, this portrait derives from the privileged perspective that narrative form allows:

> Who that had seen him in his inner chamber, part library and part laboratory,—for he was, as the world knew, far and wide, a learned man in chemistry, and a teacher on whose lips and hands a crowd of aspiring ears and eyes hung daily,—who that had seen him there, upon a winter night, alone, surrounded by his drugs and instruments and books; the shadow of his shaded lamp a monstrous beetle on the wall, motionless among a crowd of spectral shapes raised there by the flickering of the fire upon the quaint objects around him; some of these phantoms (the reflection of glass vessels that held liquids), trembling at heart like things that knew his power to uncombine them, and to give back their component parts to fire and vapour;—who that had seen him then, his work done, and he pondering in his chair before the rusted grate and red flame, moving his thin mouth as if in speech, but silent as the dead,

would not have said that the man seemed haunted and the chamber too?

(328)

Redlaw is portrayed in this static passage as a scientist whose considerable intellectual powers to illuminate and inspire have turned inward, taking the form of a self-destructive melancholia that threatens to "uncombine" his own psyche just as the chemical elements may be induced to uncombine, "to give back their component parts to fire and vapour." Alienated from social responsibility, he exists in a delusional state where everyday objects take on uncanny forms, dark doubles of their prosaic functions as tools of his trade. In this state, Redlaw does not recognize the humanizing function of memory that the tale insists upon. While the story "gives voice to one of the central tenets of mid-Victorian social, psychological, and fictional discourse," namely, that "memory, with its assurance of a continuous identity through time, functions as the grounding for social and personal morality" (Shuttleworth 47), here memory is precisely what has plunged Redlaw into despair. Dickens's association of memory with melancholy reflects a growing awareness on the part of the author and Victorians more generally that the continuous self might be an illusion produced by a fallible memory's creative reinvention of the past. What the respected physician Henry Holland termed "double-consciousness" (9) and later materialist psychologists such as G. H. Lewes and William Carpenter would speak of as "streams of consciousness" (Lewes 2: 62-65) and "unconscious cerebration" (Carpenter 541) suggested that memories of which one was normally aware might conceal a chaos of unconscious thoughts, dreams, and desires. This obscured knowledge, having carved deep grooves into the individual psyche, could make itself manifest in the right context.

According to Carpenter, the conditions of authorship were capable of providing just such a context for the emergence of buried memories. In *Principles of Mental Physiology* (1874), Carpenter describes the "storing up of ideas in the Memory" as

> the psychological expression of physical changes in the Cerebrum by which ideational states are permanently registered or recorded; so that any trace left of them, although remaining so long outside the "sphere of consciousness" as to have *seemed* non-existent, may be revived again in the full vividness under special conditions.

(436)

Later in the same discussion of the "Consciousness of Personal Identity," Carpenter illustrates his explanation by citing Dickens's accounts of the uncanny symptoms that arise from the intense concentration required by the process of writing. The act of writing, he claims, inscribes the memory with images so vivid that when recollected, they seem to emerge from lived experience:

> when the Imagination has been exercised in a sustained and determinate manner,—as in the composition of a work of fiction,—its ideal creations may be reproduced with the force of actual experiences; and the sense of personal identity may be projected backwards (so to speak) into the characters which the Author has "evolved out of the depths of his own consciousness,"—as Dickens states to have continually been the case with himself.

(455)

Carpenter likens this to the reproduction of ideas or events in dreams so real that they inspire the dreamer to ask, "Did this really happen to me, or did I dream it?" (455-56).

The sense of psychic disturbance and temporal discontinuity evoked by such false memories similarly emerges from Dickens's literary use of illusion, which captures both the affective impact and the unconscious registration of atmosphere on the mind of the reader. Like many of his contemporaries, Dickens regarded these kinds of spectral appearances as evidence of the often-irreconcilable disjunction between physical perception and mental association—transient yet recurrent perceptual and mnemonic lapses. As Fred Kaplan has explained, Dickens's interest in the therapeutic powers of mesmerism might have provided a useful source for this evocation of the dissociative hypnotic state induced by intense reverie. David Brewster, a man who would later become one of Dr. Pepper's mentors, attempted to offer a physiological explanation for the fantastic images that occasionally arise from these lapses. In his popular *Letters on Natural Magic* (1832), he writes:

> Effects still more remarkable are produced in the eye when it views objects that are difficult to be seen from the small degree of light in which they happen to be illuminated. The imperfect view which we obtain of such objects forces us to fix the eye more steadily upon them; but the more exertion we make to ascertain what they are, the greater difficulties do we encounter to accomplish our object. The eye is actually thrown into a state of painful agitation, the object will swell and contract, and partly disappear, and it will again become visible when the eye has recovered from the delirium into which it has been thrown. This phenomenon may be most distinctly seen when the objects in a room are illuminated with the feeble gleam of a fire almost extinguished.

(101)

Straining to distinguish between truth and illusion, the eye quivers and swells into delirium as if possessed of a mind of its own. Like Dickens, Brewster stresses the way visual distortions make the observer conscious of the imperfect interaction of mind and eye in the act of perception. Faced with an everyday occurrence—the distorting effects of firelight—the mind tries unsuccessfully to coordinate perception and recollection.

Brewster's instructive tone encourages readers to reproduce for themselves the visual effects he describes—just as Pepper's audiences at the Royal Polytechnic were encouraged to demystify optical phenomena through a proactive process of recollective association. Not surprisingly, Dickens also demystifies optical metaphors to create a sense of collective memory in the scenes that follow his initial description of Redlaw's fire-lit study in *The Haunted Man*. Here the narrator describes similar twilight scenes taking place everywhere, as if to emphasize that optical illusion, visual distortion, and fantasy are everyday phenomena:

> When twilight everywhere released the shadows, prisoned up all day, that now closed in and gathered swarms of ghosts. When they stood lowering, in corners of rooms, and frowned out from behind half-opened doors. When they had full possession of unoccupied apartments. When they danced upon the floors, and walls, and ceilings of inhabited chambers, while the fire was low, and withdrew like ebbing waters when it sprung into a blaze. When they fantastically mocked the shapes of household objects, making the nurse an ogress, the rocking horse a monster, the wondering child, half-scared and half-amused, a stranger to itself. . . . When he sat, as already mentioned gazing at the fire. When, as it rose and fell, the shadows went and came. When he took no heed of them, with his bodily eyes; but let them come or let them go, looked fixedly at the fire. You should have seen him then.
>
> (*Christmas* 331)

Recalling the phantasmagoric effects of a child's magic lantern, the shadows come to life on the fire-lit walls of countless homes across England and beyond. "Everyone," as Freud would later say of "The Uncanny" (1919), seems possessed by the same "dread and creeping horror" (222), yet nothing is clearly visible. Familiar "household objects" inhabit a liminal space where the eye strains to hold onto what it should be seeing. But all this is lost on Redlaw: unseen by "his bodily eyes," these distorted impressions pass unregistered into his fevered reverie rather than fostering a civilizing sense of identification and sociability, further intensifying his dissociative tendencies.

It is this profound alienation from the present that summons the ghost:

> As the gloom and shadow thickened behind him, in that place where it had been gathering so darkly, it took by slow degrees,—or out of it there came, by some unreal, unsubstantial process—not to be traced by any human sense,—an awful likeness of himself! Ghastly and cold, colourless in its leaden face and hands, but with his features, and his bright eyes, and his grizzled hair, and dressed in the gloomy shadow of his dress, it came into his terrible appearance of existence, motionless, without sound.
>
> This, then, was the Something that had passed and gone already. This was the dread companion of the haunted man!
>
> (341-42)

The specter is an externalization of what are later described as the "banished recollections" underlying the "inter-twisted chain of feelings and associations" haunting Redlaw's conscious thought (346). Emanating from the darkest recesses of his mind, the specter materializes, by an "unreal, unsubstantial process," that part of Redlaw's psyche that eludes the reach of his will. Redlaw's ghost is thus a terrifying embodiment of the fragmentation of his psyche—a figure that ultimately forces him to recognize the distortive moral effects of his narcissistic dwelling on past wrongs.

This potentially therapeutic application of illusion again echoes contemporary writing about double consciousness, especially when a dream-like state is induced by recurring memories. John Addington Symonds describes the unhealthy conditions that can result in instances of ghostly double consciousness in two public lectures, *Sleep and Dreams* (1851), delivered three years after the publication of *The Haunted Man*:

> A friend present to our sight produces an image more vivid than any we can at any time call up by an act of memory. Just think what confusion would arise if remembered sensations and present sensations were of equal vividness. The real and the unreal would be intermingled. . . . One person is really present, and the light reflected from his body produces a certain impression on the retina. Which again excites in our brain, and through it, in our mind, an image which is so vivid as to make us believe instinctively, what is really the case, that he stands before us. But the analogous sensation which the person of another individual, who may be no longer living, once excited in our minds, is at the same time revived; and yet we do not think the latter individual present, though he is perceived by what is called the mental eye. The image is distinct, but is far less vivid than the former, and indeed than any other object of present sensation, so that the living and the dead are kept separate. This is the state of the case in the healthy condition of the mind and its organ. But the occurrence of disease may alter this relation between present and remembered sensations. The latter may become equally vivid with the former. The person subject to such disorder believes persons to be before him who are not really so, because the images in his mind have, under morbid action, become unnaturally vivid, have acquired the same liveliness as present perceptions, and though revived only in his mind, are projected into the sphere of vision. This is the rationale of apparitions, ghosts and spectral illusions.
>
> (10-11)

A healthy memory distinguishes between present external objects and illusory manifestations of the past. But in its very vividness, an unhealthy memory like Redlaw's allows the real and the unreal, the present and the past, the internal and the external, to blur. Although Symonds, like Dickens, transforms this interplay into a salutary lesson for his audience, its dangers can easily be imagined.

John Leech's illustration of the appearance of Redlaw's specter (which echoes but varies slightly from Tenniel's frontispiece) reinforces the phenomenon of double consciousness that Dickens's text describes. . . . The specter behind the chair rests his head on his hand and gazes into the fire, mirroring Redlaw's melancholic reverie. The only difference between them is the specter's bemused expression, the signal that he is what Symonds calls "non ego," a separate consciousness beyond the will of the mind he haunts (10). Dickens reveals the meaning of this smile on the facing page, where he describes Redlaw and his ghost struggling over the same memories, the former alternating between resistance and mesmerized submission as the ghost repeats the history of Redlaw's treacherous betrayal by a friend who stole the woman he loved and, in the process, broke the heart of his now-dead sister. This traumatic dialogue culminates in Redlaw's unraveling as past and present are radically severed by the "bloodless hand" of his double (343). Unsurprisingly, this dramatic scene is one that Pepper would also choose to recreate on stage, revealing not only an entrepreneurial dramatic sense but a shared fascination with questions of perception and the mind. Not the least of these remains unanswered by Pepper throughout his theatrical rendition of *The Haunted Man*: what ontological status does the ghost have? "Some people have said since, that [Redlaw] only thought what has been herein set down; others, that he read it in the fire, one winter night about twilight time; others, that the Ghost was but the representation of his own gloomy thoughts" (*Christmas* 411).

RECOLLECTED ILLUSIONS

Dr. Pepper's "Ghost" is one of the most famous precinematic adaptations of Dickens's work; histories of early cinema frequently note that it inspired the Lumière Brothers to choose the Polytechnic for the first English exhibition of their cinematography (Mannoni 264-88). Initially inspired by *The Haunted Man*, Pepper and his collaborator Henry Dircks possessed, as Dickens did, an archive of natural magical and scientific literature: Samuel Hibbert's widely read *Sketches of the Philosophy of Apparitions* (1824), Samuel Warren's *Diary of a Late Physician* (1832-38), and David Brewster's *Letters on Natural Magic,* all of which explored the relationship between illusion and "the recollected images of the mind" (Hibbert iii).[3] Pepper and Dircks were pragmatic readers who combined fanlike admiration of Dickens's ghost stories with savvy technological entrepreneurialism. They also shared Dickens's assessment of earlier, worthy (but dull) Polytechnic programs:

> The Polytechnic Institution in Regent Street, where an infinite variety of ingenious models are exhibited and explained . . . is a great public benefit and a wonderful place, but we think a people formed *entirely* in their hours of leisure by Polytechnic institutions would be an uncomfortable community.

("Amusements" 14-15)

By the late 1850s, however, the Polytechnic had become a far more entertaining and imaginative place (During 145). Orchestrated primarily by Pepper, this change—which roused the criticism of the Polytechnic's more high-minded supporters—was primarily a pragmatic response to market pressures when the Institution was in danger of financial ruin. Pepper encouraged patrons to linger in the exhibition hall after paying their shilling entry fee to marvel at the mechanical devices and models that filled the room, including the legendary diving bell and optical gadgetry ranging from the more traditional cosmorama to kaleidoscopes, stereoscopes, and photographic cameras. But the main attraction took place in the lecture hall beyond, where increasingly fantastic magic lantern spectaculars were performed by Pepper, Henry Langdon Childe, George Buckland, and others three times a day.[4] The program in the hall was ever-changing and included adaptations of *A Christmas Carol,* the "Gabriel Grubb" sequence from *Pickwick Papers, The Cricket on the Hearth,* as well as *Alice in Wonderland,* Thackeray's *The Rose and the Ring,* Tennyson's *Elaine,* and many others. The highlight of the annual program was the spectacular Christmas season, during which Pepper's "Ghost" made its first appearance in 1862 ("Polytechnic"). In that show, Pepper and Dircks resurrected *The Haunted Man,* extending Dickens's preoccupation with memory and illusion by making his text a spectral presence behind their own performance and relying upon the collective memory of their audiences.

Inspired by Dickens and by Tenniel's and Leech's illustrations, Pepper used a combination of painted backdrops, lighting effects, and mirrors to construct his theatrical magic. The lecture script wove an anti-spiritualist message through Dickens's story, at the same time instructing the audience about optical effects more generally. Pepper and Dircks were keen to maintain the visual dynamic of Dickens's text and did so by dramatically enlarging its most spectacular aspects. In all of this, however, they never obscured the questions Dickens's tale raised about the mutually reinforcing fallibility of memory and perception. These were made immediate by the show's central illusion: a simple but spectacular three-dimensional specter that appeared to walk through solid objects before fading away . . . (Wilkie 72). It was produced by a specially designed magic lantern concealed beneath the stage that projected a strong light onto an actor positioned before a sheet of glass that extended from pit to ceiling between the audience and the stage. A moving image of the concealed actor would then appear superimposed on a second actor onstage above, so that when the latter enacted Redlaw's feverish desire for amnesia, his spectral double came to life. . . .

Dircks's account in *The Ghost!* (1863) of his role in reworking Dickens's tale to suit the demands of the magic lantern lecture format provides the clearest contemporary description of what audiences would have seen:

> A student is seen sitting at a table spread over with books, papers and instruments. After a while he rises and *walks about* the chamber. In this there is nothing remarkable. But the audience is perplexed by a different circumstance: they see a man rising from his seat and see him walking about, but they also see that *he still sits immovably in his chair*—so that evidently there are two persons instead of one, for, although alike in dress, stature, and person, their actions are different. They cross and recross; they alternately take the same seat; while one reads, the other is perhaps walking; and yet they appear very sullen and sulky, for they take no notice of each other, until one, after pushing down a pile of books, passes off by walking through the furniture and walls.
>
> (65)

This vignette distils Dickens's whole tale into a single illusionistic scenario. Like Tenniel and Leech, Pepper and Dircks present the illusion as a symptom of Redlaw's dissociative reverie. Surrounded by scholarly paraphernalia, he remains mesmerized *"immovably in his chair,"* while his ghostly double wanders the stage. Dircks's mention of the "sullen and sulky" demeanor of both man and ghost also suggests that the staged illusion drew inspiration from Leech's depiction of Redlaw's misanthropic pose as well as that illustrator's portrayal of the specter, who stands slightly removed, his lip curled. The ambiguity surrounding the mutual awareness of man and ghost indicates that Pepper understood Redlaw's specter to be a perceptual aberration induced by a diseased memory. This would account for the anti-spiritualist emphasis of Pepper's lecture, and calls to mind Dickens's recurring refrain throughout the tale: to "keep one's memory green" (411), vivid and enlivened by healthy social interaction, rather than distorted by melancholic narcissism.

In his account of the illusion, *The True History of the Ghost; and all About Metempsychosis* (1890), Pepper compares his lecture to George Cruikshank's skeptical pamphlet, *A Discovery Concerning Ghosts; with a rap at the "spirit-rappers"* (1863). In typical self-aggrandizing style, Pepper overstates his performance's impact, claiming that he needed to be escorted home after the show, so sensational was it. He describes the first scene of the illusion as particularly popular:

> The ghost illusion was first shown in what was called the small theatre of the Royal Polytechnic, but as the audience increased so rapidly it was removed by the following Easter and shown on a grander scale in the large theatre of the Institution, and where the dissolving views were usually exhibited.
>
> The late Mr. O'Connor, of the Haymarket, painted the first scene used, representing the laboratory of "The Haunted Man," which Christmas Story the late Charles

Dickens, by his special written permission, allowed me to use for the illustration of the Ghost illusion. The ghost scene ran for fifteen months, and helped realise, in a very short time, the sum of twelve thousand pounds, not counting what I received for granting licenses to use the Ghost, and also the sums realised during many successive years as new ghost stories were brought out.

> (12)[5]

Pepper's description of O'Connor's painted backdrop suggests that he was inspired both by Dickens's phantasmagoric account of Redlaw's "drugs and instruments and books" and by Leech's more detailed illustration of the crowded bookshelves that line the walls of the study, filled with skulls, books, various scientific instruments, and bottles containing mysterious artifacts. As Pepper notes, the ghost illusion had a long afterlife in various theatrical and later fairground attractions, but none had the same impact as his own adaptation.[6]

Both accounts by Pepper and Dircks indicate their desire to confront audiences with an illusion that required active deciphering. Their intentions were successfully realized, according to contemporary accounts: the *Illustrated London News* enthusiastically reported that Pepper's "Strange Lecture" caused "phantoms to appear at will, such as to produce the fullest impression of their reality [while] at the same time a real body will pass through them" ("Polytechnic"). Pepper's lecture undoubtedly compounded the thrill of this initial visual impact. Like many other Polytechnic Lecturers, Pepper was somewhat of a celebrity in the 1860s, and his obituarist Edmund H. Wilkie reports that his lectures were an engaging mixture of conversational fluency and carefully scripted erudition (72).

Dircks confirms the public notoriety of the illusion in his version of events, even though he resented it becoming synonymous with Pepper's name. He claims that the illusion resonated with "the public mind" by summoning associations with a shared archive of dreams, "fancies," specter dramas, and ghost stories:

> An invention of so large a scale [as Pepper's "Ghost"] being expensive to adopt, could have no success unless it captivated the public mind. And, in this respect, considering its imperfections to the present time of its exhibition, "The Ghost" has never failed to draw crowded, admiring audiences. It was the absolute realization of all that ever had been dreamt, or ever had occupied frenzied fancies, or formed the staple conceits of dramatists and romancers.
>
> (23)

Dircks then goes on to explain the manner in which viewers of the illusion seemed to draw on recollections of their past experiences to process the spectacle. He continues:

We first see and then exercise our mental faculties. In forming judgments we bring to bear on the subject all our experience, reading, study, and power of investigation. If the offered mystery has its equal in some jugglery we have seen, then doubt steps in; or, if we have seen a scientific experiment closely allied to alleged mystery, doubt again interposes; and so on, step by step, we compare the unknown subject with what is known bearing any collateral quality.

(23)

According to this logic, an illusion, no matter how elaborately conceived and executed, will only succeed if it can be consciously related to a previous experience stored in the memory. Dircks makes a distinction here between illusions that form part of an avowed narrative sequence and those designed to produce cognitive or perceptual aberrations. In the case of the latter, the spectator must bring to bear associative and analytical powers to demystify and contextualize the unknown. This inductive approach echoes John F. W. Herschel's ascription of illusion to a flaw in the mind or memory, an error in logic rather than perception: "though we are never deceived in the sensible impression made by external objects on us, yet in forming our judgments of them we are greatly at the mercy of circumstances, which either modify the impression actually received, or combine them with adjuncts which have become habitually associated with different judgments" (83). Thus, memory is profoundly unreliable and subjective, much like Dickens's portrayal of Redlaw's selective recall and the distortions of present perceptions that it produces. Hermann von Helmholtz called the sequencing of events that Herschel's explanation implies the "grammatical relations" or syntax into which the mind translates a series of images or visual events (3: 23). It is this perceptual syntax that enabled individuals like the viewers of Pepper's illusion to train their minds to recognize and normalize mysterious anomalous visual stimuli.

In framing the cognitive interplay between memory and illusion, Dircks acknowledges Brewster's *Letters on Natural Magic,* which insistently extolled the therapeutic virtues of systematic, logical demystification—the principle means by which viewers might bring specters and other ghostly apparitions back under the rationalizing control of the healthy mind:

When a spectre haunts the couch of the sick, or follows the susceptible vision of the invalid, a consciousness of indisposition divests the apparition of much of its terror, while its invisibility to surrounding friends soon stamps it with the impress of a false perception. The spectres of the conjurer, too, however skilfully they may be raised, quickly lose their supernatural character, and even the most ignorant beholder regards the modern magician as but an ordinary man, who borrows from the sciences the best working implements of his art. But when, in the midst of solitude, and in situa-

tions where the mind is undisturbed by sublunary cares, we see our own image delineated in the air, and mimicking in gigantic perspective the tiny movements of humanity;—when we see troops in military array performing their evolutions on the very face of an almost inaccessible precipice, . . . when distant objects, concealed by the roundness of the earth, and beyond the cognizance of the telescope, are actually transferred over the intervening convexity and presented in distinct and magnified outline to our accurate examination;— when such varied and striking phantasms are seen also by all around us, and therefore appear in the character of real phenomena of nature, our impressions of supernatural agency can only be removed by a distinct and satisfactory knowledge of the causes which gave them birth.

(215-16)

This passage resonates strongly with Dickens's tale, both in its emphasis on the contingency of illusion and in the obvious relish Brewster takes in describing the various causes and effects of visual phenomena. Brewster never doubts that illusions, no matter how extraordinary, have rational causes. And yet underlying this confidence, there is a persistent anxiety about the fragility of the mind, its susceptibility, especially in moments of intense isolation, to see its "own image delineated in the air" in the manner of Redlaw's ghost, "mimicking in gigantic perspective the tiny movements of humanity."

Pepper, even more than Dircks, was influenced by Brewster's demystifying ethos—a fact that seems contrary to his career as an avowed illusionist but reveals all the more pointedly the role memory was thought to play in making sense of illusions. Like Brewster, Pepper published many popular books addressing the growing interest in "useful knowledge," including *The Boy's Playbook of Science* (1860) and *Popular Lectures for Young People and Half Hours with Alchemists* (1855). In the former, he reveals the mysteries of the technology behind the Polytechnic illusions in a discussion of "Light, Optics and Optical Instruments" which is illustrated by an engraving of "The Interior of the Optical Box at the Polytechnic—looking towards the screen" (255). This helpful behind-the-scenes glimpse allowed Polytechnic audiences to rationalize the mystery of Pepper's Ghost via the lens of past knowledge in the manner Dircks describes above. More generally, Pepper's explanation of his own spectacular illusion suggests that an emerging and rapidly expanding visual vernacular fostered skeptical curiosity which worked profitably in concert with, rather than against, visual and textual illusions.[7] It is in this spirit that Pepper also turned to Dickens, whose public readings provided a powerful example of the performative translation of familiar literary texts into spectacular events of collective identification and recollection. To quote the contemporary eyewitness account of Dickens's admiring friend Charles Kent,

Densely packed from floor to ceiling, these audiences were habitually wont to hang in breathless expectation upon every inflection of the author-reader's voice, upon every glance of his eye,—the words he was about to speak being so thoroughly well remembered by the majority before their utterance that, often, the rippling of a smile over a thousand faces simultaneously anticipated the laughter which an instant afterwards greeted the words themselves when they were articulated.

(20)

Kent provides a vivid image of an audience who knew their Dickens by heart, who were so familiar with the twists and turns of plot, character, and description that they preemptively responded with knowing pleasure. Pepper and Dircks attempted to replicate this dynamic by weaving their illusions into one of Dickens's familiar narratives. Doing so was undoubtedly astute. As the early filmmaker Cecil Hepworth (a habitué of the Polytechnic during Pepper's heyday) remarked, most pre-cinematic spectacles failed because they did not integrate their visual effects into a compelling narrative their audiences knew from memory and did not, as a result, keep viewers engaged beyond the first moment of wonder and delight (205).

As if aware of and eager to avoid this possibility, Pepper reworked his original script in 1863 to include more extensive readings from *The Haunted Man,* and the run of the show was extended well beyond the Christmas season. In the initial Christmas program for December of 1862, the performance was divided into three main segments. The first segment showcased a version of Cinderella, performed with dissolving views and dioramic and shadow effects. This was followed by "the remarkable illustration of Mr. Charles Dickens's idea of 'THE HAUNTED MAN,' in a new and curious illusion, devised by Henry Dircks, Esq., and other singular Experiments [which] will be included in the new Philosophical Entertainment by Professor J. H. PEPPER entitled A STRANGE LECTURE" (*London*). Finally, Valentine Vox, the "Celebrated Ventriloquist," closed the show. This format, however, was substantially altered after 1 June 1863, during the Whitsun Holiday Entertainments. From this point on, the program and advertising bills began with Pepper's illusion, which included an extended reading from Dickens's tale, promoted thus: "Great Additions to and New Experiments in Professor Pepper's Lecture on Optical Illusions. Professor Pepper will (by the kind permission of the Author) read and illustrate a portion of Mr. Charles Dickens's Tale of THE HAUNTED MAN AND THE GHOST will actually appear to walk across the New Platform arranged in the Large theatre" (*London*).[8] Perhaps Pepper hoped to create his own illusionistic version of Dickens's extraordinarily popular public readings.[9] If this was his intention, he met with more success than Dickens himself, who tried and failed to adapt *The Haunted Man* into a reading script (Collins 103).

Early reviews of "Pepper's Ghost" suggest that the association with Dickens was always powerful. Claiming enthusiastically that Pepper's show was the most wonderful series of "optical illusions ever placed before the public," a critic in *The Times* in December of 1862 remarked that

The spectres and illusions are thrown upon the stage in such a perfect embodiment of real substance, that it is not till the *Haunted Man* walks through their apparently solid forms that the audience can believe in their being optical illusions at all. Even then it is almost difficult to imagine that the whole is not a wonderful trick, for people cling to the old saying, that seeing is believing, and if ever mere optical delusions assumed a perfect and tangible form they do so in this strange lecture. Why did not the medium and spirit rappers get hold of this invention before it was made public? The illusions might fail to convince, but at least they would have left all seekers after spiritual revelations in a sore state of puzzle and uncertainty, as they most certainly do now at the Polytechnic.

(qtd. in Dircks 6)

This review captures the excitement inspired by the revelatory powers of Pepper and Dircks's invention. The reviewer playfully considers the broader cultural implications of new technology with the power to give uncanny visual form to a perennial epistemological question—the role the eye plays in the psychology of belief. A clear picture of the Polytechnic audience, puzzled and uncertain, also emerges. Unlike the dupes of spiritualist charlatans, their eyes have been trained according to the Polytechnic ethos, which, conforming to Henry Brougham's principles for the diffusion of useful knowledge, privileged logic over belief (1-10). An early Polytechnic publication outlined the Institute's foundational vision for the education of eye and mind:

The education of the eye is, undeniably, the most important object in elementary instruction. A child will pass many years before he can be made thoroughly to understand, by *unassisted* description, the cause of motion in a Steam Engine. . . . In like manner, the powers of Galvanism, the properties of Electricity, the mysteries of Chemistry, the laws of Mechanics, the theory of Light, the developments of the microscope, the wonders of Optics, the construction of Ships, with various other matters in Science and Art, are made palpable by exhibition; and thus instruction is rapidly and pleasurably communicated in awakening curiosity, excitement, and attention, and by such means leaving a durable impression.

(*Royal* 5-6)

Read in this context, the "sore state of puzzle and uncertainty" suffered by Pepper's audiences suggests the novelty of the illusion itself, which challenges "the durable impression" of how things usually work, forcing viewers into the laboring assimilation of present anomalies with familiar logical and narrative sequences. Dickens's tale was primary among those familiar sequences. Dircks remarks that the Polytechnic audiences knew "more about optics than some very clever men even 100 years ago," but they also knew their Dickens (31). To quote Dircks's account of his initial pitch to the Polytechnic managers, "Among a long list of pieces which I had arranged in 1858, I usually directed attention to one which I proposed, calling it 'Charles Dickens, Esq.'s Haunted Man,' from his well-known Christmas piece of that name, conceiving that it would command a double interest" (65).

Reincarnated as Pepper's Ghost, Dickens's haunted man thus becomes a catalyst for active epistemological speculation, technological curiosity, and literary nostalgia. Dickens's psychological framing of the illusions produced by a diseased memory unmoored from social responsibility haunts Pepper and Dircks's synecdochic adaptation, serving as a familiar basis for the creation of a new form of visual entertainment and narrative temporality. In their mutual preoccupation with time and the psychological effects of the self-consciously staged production of illusion, both Dickens and Pepper foreshadow what Mary Ann Doane evocatively describes as early cinema's "hyperbolic recourse to the figures of life, death, immortality and infinity" (3).

Notes

I would like to thank the Australian Research Council for funding this research. A range of archives have also provided access to research material and much needed assistance: the University of Westminster archive, the Bill Douglas Centre, the University of Exeter, and the British Library. For advice and assistance in preparing this article, I wish to thank the Department of English, Macquarie University, Michele Pierson, David Ellison, and the *Victorian Studies* referees.

1. Shuttleworth recounts the influence of Connolly on Dickens's writing, and particularly on *The Haunted Man,* in "'The Malady of Thought'" 46-59.

2. The first edition of the tale, illustrated by John Tenniel and John Leech, was published as *The Haunted Man and the Ghost's Bargain. A Fancy for Christmas Time.* References in this article are to Dickens, *Christmas Books* 323-412.

3. Warren's three-volume collection of diary passages includes an account of a haunted student like Redlaw, albeit with a very different set of neuroses. In this case, the law student becomes consumed by the idea that he has seen a specter with flaming eyes after returning from a particularly stressful day at court. Warren struggles to convince his patient of the meaning of this spectral visitant, in part by encouraging him to re-

member and reinterpret his homoerotic dreams of the specter running into his arms and holding him in a prolonged embrace (1-48).

4. Humphries outlines the central role of the Polytechnic in the further popularizing of the magic lantern at the nexus of popular education and entertainment at this time (21-23).

5. Pepper's claim that he received Dickens's permission to use the Christmas story seems to be inaccurate; nothing in the latter's correspondence substantiates this.

6. Randall Williams's popular walk-up version of the ghost show in the 1890s did lead to his "Grand Phantascopical Exhibition" at the World's Fair in Islington in 1896, which included the first fairground cinema show (Heard 3).

7. These observations are indebted to Pierson's analysis in *Special Effects: Still in Search of Wonder* (1-51).

8. By 31 August 1863, the whole performance was more of a hybrid of earlier and later versions but still included a reading from Dickens: "Professor Pepper's adaptation of Mr. Dircks's Original and most startling GHOST ILLUSION! In three scenes. First scene: Reading from Dickens's 'HAUNTED MAN' and appearance of the GHOST and SPECTRE of the sister. Second scene: THE ARTIST'S STUDIO. The Ghostly visitor in the form of a Rival Artist. THE GHOST DRINKING A GLASS OF WATER!! (*This Illusion must be seen to be believed.*) The reading of the *LOVE LETTER,* and mysterious arrival of the Little Postman 'CUPID'" (*London*). This format continues into the next year's Christmas program as well.

9. For an insightful analysis of the politics of affect in Dickens's public readings, see Small.

Works Cited

Brewster, David. *Letters on Natural Magic. Addressed to Sir Walter Scott, Bart.* 1832. London: William Trigg, 1868.

Brougham, Henry. *Practical Observations upon the Education of the People, Addressed to the Working Class and Their Employers.* London: Longmans, 1825.

Carpenter, William. *Principles of Mental Physiology.* London: Henry S. King, 1874.

Collins, Philip. *Charles Dickens: The Public Readings.* Oxford: Oxford UP, 1975.

Cruikshank, George. *A Discovery Concerning Ghosts; with a rap at the "spirit-rappers".* London: Frederick Arnold, 1863.

Dickens, Charles. "The Amusements of the People." *Household Words* 1 (30 Mar. 1850): 13-15.

———. *Christmas Books. A Reprint of the First Editions, with illustrations, and an introduction, biographical and bibliographical, by Charles Dickens the younger.* London: Macmillan, 1892. 323-412.

———. *The Haunted Man and the Ghost's Bargain. A Fancy for Christmas Time.* London: Bradbury and Evans, 1848.

Dircks, Henry. *The Ghost! As Produced in the Spectre Drama, popularly illustrating the marvellous optical illusions obtained by the apparatus called the Dircksian Phantasmagoria.* London: E. and F. N. Spon, 1863.

Doane, Mary Ann. *The Emergence of Cinematic Time: Modernity, Contingency, the Archive.* Cambridge: Harvard UP, 2002.

During, Simon. *Modern Enchantments: The Cultural Power of Secular Magic.* Cambridge: Harvard UP, 2002.

Freud, Sigmund. "The Uncanny." *Complete Psychological Works of Sigmund Freud.* Ed. James Strachey. 22 vols. London: Hogarth, 1959. 17: 218-52.

Heard, Mervyn. Introduction. *The True History of Pepper's Ghost.* By John Henry Pepper. 1890. Facsimile ed. London: Projection Box, 1996. I-VI.

Helmholtz, Hermann von. *Treatise on Physiological Optics.* 1856. Ed. James P. C. Southall. 3 vols. New York: Dover, 1962.

Hepworth, Cecil. *Came the Dawn: Memories of a Film Director.* London: Phoenix House, 1951.

Herschel, John F. W. *A Preliminary Discourse on the Study of Natural Philosophy.* 1831. Chicago: U of Chicago P, 1987.

Hibbert, Samuel. *Sketches of the Philosophy of Apparitions; or, an Attempt to Trace such Illusions to the Physical Causes.* London: Whittaker, 1824.

Holland, Henry. *Chapters on Mental Physiology.* London: Longman, Brown, Green and Longmans, 1852.

Humphries, Steve. *Victorian Britain through the Magic Lantern.* London: Sidgwick and Jackson, 1989.

Kaplan, Fred. *Dickens and Mesmerism: The Hidden Springs of Fiction.* Princeton: Princeton UP, 1975.

Kent, Charles. *Charles Dickens as a Reader.* London: Chapman & Hall, 1872.

Lewes, George Henry. *The Physiology of Common Life.* 2 vols. Edinburgh: Blackwood and Sons, 1860.

The London Polytechnic Institution Programmes of Entertainments, etc. Sep. 1861-Dec. 1878. London, 1861-1878. British Library Collection. N. pag.

Mannoni, Laurent. *The Great Art of Light and Shadow. Archaeology of the Cinema.* Trans. Richard Crangle. Exeter: U of Exeter P, 2000.

Noakes, Richard. "Spiritualism, Science and the Supernatural in Mid-Victorian Britain." *The Victorian Supernatural.* Ed. Nicola Bown, Carolyn Burdett, and Pamela Thurschwell. Cambridge: Cambridge UP, 2002. 23-43.

Pepper, John Henry. *The Boy's Playbook of Science, including the various manipulations and arrangements of chemical and philosophical apparatus required for the successful performance of scientific experiments.* London: Routledge, 1860.

———. *Popular Lectures for Young People and Half Hours with Alchemists.* London: Sampson & Low, 1855.

———. *The True History of the Ghost; and all About Metempsychosis.* London: Cassell & Co., 1890.

Pierson, Michele. *Special Effects: Still in Search of Wonder.* New York: Columbia UP, 2002.

"The Polytechnic." *Illustrated London News* 42.1 (3 Jan. 1863): 19.

The Royal Polytechnic Institution, for the advancement of the arts and practical science; Catalogue for 1845. New ed. London: Reynell and White at the Royal Polytechnic Institution, 1845.

Shuttleworth, Sally. "'The Malady of Thought': Embodied Memory in Victorian Psychology and the Novel." *Memory and Memorials, 1789-1914.* Ed. Matthew Campbell, Jacqueline M. Labbe, and Sally Shuttleworth. London: Routledge, 2000. 46-59.

Small, Helen. "A Pulse of 124: Charles Dickens and a Pathology of the Mid-Victorian Reading Public." *The Practice and Representation of Reading in England.* Ed. James Raven, Helen Small, and Naomi Tadmor. Cambridge: Cambridge UP, 1996. 263-90.

Symonds, John Addington. *Sleep and Dreams; Two Lectures.* London: John Murray, 1851.

Warren, Samuel. *Diary of a Late Physician with notes and illustrations by the editor.* 3 vols. Edinburgh: Blackwood, 1832-38.

Wilkie, Edmund H. "Professor Pepper—A Memoir." *The Optical Magic Lantern Journal and Photographic Enlarger* 2 (June 1900): 72-74.

James Walton (essay date 2007)

SOURCE: Walton, James. "Natural Supernaturalism." In *Vision and Vacancy: The Fictions of J. S. Le Fanu,* pp. 73-97. Dublin: University College Dublin Press, 2007.

[*In the following essay, Walton explores major recurring themes and imagery in Le Fanu's supernatural fiction, focusing on the author's attempts to expose the "demonic" in everyday life.*]

Are we not Spirits, that are shaped into a body, into an Appearance; and that fade-away again into air and Invisibility? This is no metaphor, it is a simple scientific fact: we start out of Nothingness, take figure, and are Apparitions.

Carlyle, *Sartor Resartus*

'It's very hard, you see, to meet with a genuine ghost . . . ; they generally turn out impostors.'

Le Fanu, *Guy Deverell*

Where does spirit live? Inside or outside
Things remembered, made things, things unmade?

Seamus Heaney, *Squarings* 2, 'Settings', xxii

Le Fanu's novels, in keeping with the conventions of sentimental or romantic, or sensational, or melodramatic 'realism', transpose their ghosts and demons into the metaphoric key. As in actual life, characters in the nineteenth-century novel are 'haunted' by others, by a personal or historical past, by the dead. They are 'possessed' by a desire or an ambition that lends itself to personification as a demonic tempter. Like everyday speech, the discourse of the novel affirms the uncanniness of the ordinary. The paranormal attaches itself to the figure of common life as vehicle to tenor, or as 'strange', 'sinister', and 'secret' attach themselves to the definition of *heimlich* (Freud, 'The Uncanny' 220-6). In certain cases the vehicle of the supernatural metaphor is raised to the magnitude of a story-*within*-the-story, acting as a dark mirror of the novel's principal action, as a *figural* plot.

The clearest case of such doubling occurs in 'A Strange Adventure in the History of Miss Laura Mildmay' (1871). Thanks to M. R. James, the interpolated 'Madam Crowl's Ghost' is far better known than the novella that contains it. The heroine's history casts its shadow as a tale of infanticide; the 'resurrection' of Captain Torquil as Mr Burton in the outer tale is doubled by the posthumous reappearance of a murderous hag in the inner one.

Much less clear is the pertinence to *The House by the Churchyard* of a two-chapter digression on the serial hauntings of a Tiled House on the outskirts of Chapelizod. The stories in Chapter XI belong to local tradition and are told, like 'Madame Crowl's Ghost', to the ingénue by an old nurse, but have no bearing on the younger woman's life. The first recounts a series of sightings on the house's grounds of the ghosts of a woman and child. The second, presented as a collage of testimony, relates how the house's former proprietor, an earl whose return to his home after an absence manifested itself only as a 'frightful rattle' at the window and a voice pleading 'Let me in' (his words echoing those of Catherine Earnshaw's ghost in *Wuthering Heights*). When he finally gains entry, his presence is felt but not seen until he appears, to lethal effect, before a servant's daughter: 'a fine man' in 'silk morning-dress' and a 'velvet cap' and 'his throat . . . cut across, and wide open' (60-1). Chapter XII consists in an 'authentic' account (documented as evidence in a lawsuit) of the harassment of a family of tenants of the Tiled House by a ghost visible at first only as a fat but aristocratic-looking hand trying, at last successfully (like the spectral earl in the nurse's story), to enter the house. In the end, like the earl, the spectre reveals itself to a terrified child in the figure of a 'gentleman, fat and pale, every curl of whose wig, every button and fold of whose laced clothes, and every feature and line of whose sensual, benignant [*sic*], and unwholesome face, was . . . minutely engraven upon his memory' (67-8).

In short, the history of the Tiled House, drawn from oral tradition and public records, is made up of a series of ghost stories that contribute to the aura surrounding the house's current occupant who calls himself Arthur Mervyn, newly arrived and yet already regarded as the 'genius of that haunted place' (69). The ghostly, and haunted, stranger is the son of an attainted nobleman, Lord Dunoran, who committed suicide after being wrongfully convicted of murder. Mervyn's purpose in returning to Chapelizod is to bury his father, exonerate him, and recover his forfeited title and estate. His lordship's title recalls one of the author's early tales of a fallen family, 'Some Account of the Latter Days of the Hon. Richard Marston of Dunoran', and the account of his character links him and his deserted wife and child to the house's spectral visitants: 'He used the Tiled House for a hunting-lodge, and kept his dogs and horses there—a fine gentleman, but vicious, always, I fear, and a gamester; an overbearing man, with a dangerous cast of pride in his eye' (311). The link between the dead father and the ghostly earl is reinforced when Mervyn hears a 'knocking on the window-pane' accompanied by the words 'let me in' and remembers 'the old story of the supernatural hand' (320). The hand in this instance is a natural one (though its owner is compared to a 'phantom'), for the action occurs within the natural order of the novel. The merging of ghost story with supernatural metaphor makes the Tiled House a model of Le Fanu's House of Fiction, haunted, or 'haunted', by figures from an undead, a persistently resurrected, past.

The plots of Le Fanu's novels depend almost without exception upon a series of metaphorical, that is, profane or naturalised, resurrections, of apparent returns from the dead. The hero of *Guy Deverell* (1865) seems the reincarnation of his murdered father. Under the management of his uncle/mentor (disguised as a sinister Frenchman), he arrives (also incognito) at the murderer's estate on a mission (of which he is unaware) to avenge his father's death and claim his birthright. In a scene with his grandmother, who has been unnerved by his resemblance to her dead son, Deverell obliquely reveals his identity by translating from the Old French a supernatural tale 'Concerning a Remarkable Revenge After Sepulture'. The tale, however, reverses the moral economy of the novel. Its young hero, avatar of the murder victim, is 'brought back' to life through the 'infernal arts' of his mentor (figured as a Hungarian magician) who has taken the form of a vampire— 'among the most malignant and awful of the manifestations of the Evil One' (232). As dark analogue to the novel's romantic plot, the vampire story repeats an abiding theme of Le Fanu's that survives his 'translations' of Anglo-Irish history into English fiction. Deverell's supernatural fable draws attention to something *un*natural in a received idea of rightful succession (an idea, as Burke himself and Lord Clare recognised, that could not bear much looking into).¹ A legacy lost to a murderer is regained in the novel's main plot by imposture, in its shadow-plot by vampirism and black magic. Like the doubling of Austin and Silas Ruthyn, Knowl and Bartram-Haugh, like the disclosure of Carmilla's *blood*-relationship to her victim, Guy Deverell's 'dreadful, dreadful story' (233) identifies the protagonist's birthright, however justly recovered, as an inheritance of evil.

* * *

'The *present* is the inheritance of evil.' This aphoristic version of Le Fanu's secular typology appears in *A Lost Name* (1868; 1: 243), his second (and much the longest) retelling of 'Some Account of the Latter Days of the Hon. Richard Marston of Dunoran' (1848). In the first revision, 'The Evil Guest' (1851), the setting is shifted from Ireland to England. The second is also set in England but the blighted name of the original title character (a different Richard Marston from the one in *Willing to Die*) is changed to Mark Shadwell. All three versions of the murder mystery treat the crime itself as one of the fatal consequences of an evil inheritance, prompting speculation about the *origin* of the family curse, an historicised version of original sin. Like Burke's enquiry into origins, Le Fanu's takes him to a place of indeterminacy, a region where the 'imagination is finally lost' (*Enquiry* 64). At its supposititious 'origin' Burke's divine unites with the demonic, his Beautiful with the Sublime, a 'deceitful maze, through which the unsteady eye slides giddily, without knowing where to fix, or whither it is carried' (105): 'If we could advance a step farther', he adds, 'we should be still equally distant from the first cause' (117).

Like the griffins on their coat of arms, the 'origin' of the Shadwells of Raby 'goes back into mystery' (2: 72). Their British lineage, like that of the accursed family in *Checkmate,* can be traced from the Conquest. If Le Fanu intends attributing the family's outlaw strain to that event, he is of Thomas Paine's party without knowing it: 'A French bastard landing with an armed ban-

ditti, and establishing himself king of England against the consent of the natives, is in plain terms a very paltry rascally original' (*Common Sense* 13). Rather than lose himself, however, in the maze of history, Le Fanu provides a *terminus a quo* for the Shadwell curse in the form of a local legend, a ghost story dating from the sixteenth century and founded on an actual crime and suicide. Haunting becomes shorthand for history. '*A spectre is haunting Europe . . .*'.

Known as the 'gaze-lady', the agent or 'spiritual minister' of the Shadwells' destruction is the ghost of a woman who, having been wronged by the family patriarch, leaped to her death from the top of the ancestral manor house, now a vacant ruin. At intervals of 110 years she returns to Raby, under different identities, as a beautiful, 'fiendish' seductress, to 'entangle and beguile' its proprietor and bring the family name closer to extinction (1: 258-61).

At first the ghost story in *A Lost Name* appears to serve, like the Ghost's Walk in *Bleak House,* like the phantom lady and the link-man in *Uncle Silas,* as a kind of *leitmotif* or poetic analogue to the history of the decline of an aristocratic family. The legend of the gaze-lady, however, exceeds the limits of analogy by merging with the principal action, to which it contributes an irreducible element of the supernatural. The vengeful ghost's last scheduled appearance at Raby coincides with the arrival, as companion/governess to the Shadwell daughter, of Agnes Marlyn, a callous, Frenchified opportunist of the Becky Sharp school, but one adapted to the darker purposes of melodrama. Her hatred is directed against a whole class rather than a family, and her design on Mark Shadwell is one of exploitation rather than punishment. Her presence at Raby brings on the prophesied end to the Shadwell name, and on her palm she bears the star-shaped scar of the gaze-lady.

An occult explanation of the Shadwell catastrophe gains further support from the testimony of Mark's bookkeeper, a visionary madman named Carmel Sherlock who sees the end of the intrigue from the beginning. Emerging as he does from the shadows (the '*chiar*' oscuro') as if 'called away from a task that still occupies his brain' (1:5), a keeper of accounts and student of 'old books', a professed 'fatalist' (1: 16), gifted with second sight and foreknowledge and disqualified from normal relations with the other characters, Sherlock might be regarded as a distorted reflection of the author in the text. Amid the general disorder of his mystical utterances, there are echoes of Swedenborg:

> 'The act of death, you know, is the labour of man in the flesh, and the bringing forth of the intermediate man, who in turn evolves the man immutable.'
>
> (1: 288-9)

> 'Which is more spiritual? You call all the immortal sights and voices that are about us, fancies proceeding

from our own perishable brains; but I perceive, and consider them, as belonging to God's outer household of immortal spirits.'

(3: 81)

'Haven't you seen celestial faces that changed when you came near? Every one knows what horror is— these transformations. Therefore, sir, it is better to wait for the spiritual world, when the essence of things will appear, and into that world I go smiling, bidding my eternal farewell to the illusions of mortality.'

(3: 85)

Like Le Fanu, Sherlock stresses the dark or demonic side of the Swedenborgian system. The above passage on horrid transformations, signifying privileged access to another's inner spirit, has its counterpart in the *omniscient* narrator's observation on Agnes Marlyn:

In fairy lore we read of wondrous transmutations and disguises. How evil spirits have come in the fairest and saddest forms; how fell and shrewd-eyed witches have waited in forest glades by night, in shapes of the loveliest nymphs. So, for a dream-like moment, one might see, under the wondrous beauty of the girl, in that spell of momentary joy, a face that was apathetic and wicked.

(1: 41)

The madman's vision derives authority from the interventions of the narrator himself. They echo each other:

NARRATOR.

In an evil world the evil is the more potent spirit, and overawes the good.

(1: 243)

God is good, you say. . . . Alas! most certainly He is also the God of every evil thing—the God of pain, of madness, and of death. Look around on the gloom of this transitory world. If here and there is a broken light of heaven, are there no glimmerings and shadows of hell?

(2: 21)

CARMEL SHERLOCK.

'Dreams are not sent from God, nor caused by him, but must be demoniacal, since nature is demoniacal, not divine.'

(2: 133)

[After quoting Dante's description of the Seventh Circle of Hell]: 'There it is—the forest—an infernal metamorphosis. The same thing only worse; not the tap roots only, but stems, boughs, foliage, all in hell. Dante's forest of suicides—. . . damned spirits.'

(2: 124)

Although an authentic supernatural presence in *A Lost Name* tends to substantiate Sherlock's visions, his status as figure of authorial omniscience is compromised by an inability to recognise Agnes Marlyn as the last incar-

nation of the gaze-lady and agent of the Shadwells' ruin. For him the evil agent is Mark Shadwell's wealthy cousin, Sir Roke Wycherly, an overripe rake and infidel like Mark himself, who holds a mortgage on the Shadwell property and has invited himself to Raby for an ulterior purpose. On the theme of Roke's hidden motive, Sherlock's prescience again proves incomplete. He misses the baronet's chief intention in imposing himself on Raby, which consists in renewing an old liaison with Agnes Marlyn. His less fixed plan is to make an offer of marriage to Shadwell's daughter, Rachel. To the abject father, the prospect of such a union would be welcome. To Sherlock, hopelessly, silently in love with Rachel, it supplies the occasion for a prevision of horror: he knows that he would kill the expected guest to prevent the defilement of his beloved.

Even before Roke's arrival, Sherlock seeks to avoid the catastrophe by asking to be released from Shadwell's service. From this point his career runs parallel with that of his *un*visionary counterpart in the earlier 'Richard Marston' stories. In 'Some Account of the Latter Days . . .' and 'The Evil Guest' a colourless servant named Merton, having learned that the visiting baronet (Sir Wynston Berkley) carries with him a fortune in banknotes, feels an irresistible impulse to murder him for his money. The impulse resembles demonic possession: 'something muttered the infernal suggestion in his ear. . . . He contended against it in vain; he dreaded and abhorred it; but still it possessed him. . . . This horrible stranger which had stolen into his heart, waxed in power and importunity, and tormented him day and night' ('The Evil Guest' 294-5). Sherlock, for his part, feels that he has caught the infection of evil from the intended victim: 'Something came into the house with him' (1: 297). Both servants enter the guest's room with murderous intent only to find that he has already been murdered.[2] In all three versions of the story the servant remains guilt-ridden, though the true killer is his employer, and in each case the murder is witnessed by the governess (in the 'Marston' tales a Mlle De Barras, Agnes Marlyn in *A Lost Name*) who blackmails the murderer into a marriage that ends with his madness and suicide.

The squire's devoted, neglected, and at last deserted and dying wife conforms to the type of the innocent victim in Le Fanu's accounts of a family fatality. Also typical, apart from the doomed squire himself, are an unwelcome guest and a daughter who in the end escapes the curse. Missing from the 'Marston' stories are the explanatory legend whose supernatural ingredient leaks into the 'realistic' narrative and a second-sighted character who takes the legend for revealed truth.

In 'The Evil Guest', Richard Marston's servant is 'possessed', but by an impulse to larceny and murder. Marston himself is 'haunted', first by the 'phantoms of ruined time and opportunity' (250) and at last, his 'eyes burning with the preterhuman fires of insanity' (323), by the 'grotesque and infernal chimera' of his dead victim (319). Among Le Fanu's novels, the touch of *un*naturalised supernaturalism in *A Lost Name* has no counterpart, the nearest approach to such intervention coming perhaps in the final paragraph of *Uncle Silas* where the heroine, in the voice of her dead father, redefines her autobiography as an occult spiritual allegory.

The esoteric 'vision' in *Uncle Silas* strikes one nevertheless as an afterthought. In *A Lost Name* it is fragmentary, incoherent, and compromised throughout by the Swedenborgian seer's mental state. The hesitant admission into these novels, through a distorting medium, of a recondite version of the supernatural, might best be understood as a metonym for the 'spiritual' predicament faced by those members of Le Fanu's class who concerned themselves with such things. In Edmund Burke's Ireland, 'Protestant ascendancy' had already reduced 'Protestant' to nothing more than 'the name of a persecuting faction, with a relation of some sort of theological hostility to others, but without any sort of ascertained tenets of its own, . . . for the patrons of this Protestant ascendancy neither do nor can, by any thing positive, define or describe what they mean by the word Protestant' ('Letter to Richard Burke' 66). Words like 'occult' and 'hermetic' can apply to a discrete mind to which the established order, spiritual and temporal, has revealed itself as a 'sinister vacancy from which authority has withdrawn'.[3]

All in the Dark (1866), which appeared between *Guy Deverell* and *A Lost Name,* affirms vacancy in its own way by assuming a deflationary comic attitude towards all manifestations of the spirit. The visionary universe is shrunk to the dimensions of a provincial séance conducted by a dotty spinster under the influence of an American quack named Elihu Bung.[4]

The Bung system satirises itself. Its votary, Dinah Perfect, is humoured in her spiritualism, from motives of affection and financial dependence, by a physician, a clergyman, a nephew, and a female protégé. The latter pair are diffident lovers, and the power of Aunt Dinah's otherworldliness resides in its capacity to keep them apart. On the authority of her familiar daimon, and in anticipation of her death, she forbids her nephew, William Maubray, to marry until five years have passed:

> 'Depend upon it, if you disobey you are a ruined man all your days; and if I die before the time, I'll watch you as an old grey cat watches a mouse—ha, ha, ha! And if you so much as think of it, I'll plague you—I will. Yes, William, I'll save you in spite of yourself, and mortal was never haunted and tormented as you'll be, till you give it up.'
>
> (2: 133)

Her threat expresses the rage of a dying generation to impose its will upon the future. (The rage will achieve powerful embodiment in the matriarchal Lady Vernon of *The Rose and the Key*.)

A passive hero, William has so far proved susceptible to the effect of 'well-authenticated' horror stories and to a brand of 'pleasing terror' and 'delightful melancholy' associated with the Gothic heroine (1: 62, 2: 209). Only once has his aesthetic distance from the supernatural been violated by an actual, unexplained visitation, and for this occasion the narrator draws on the devices of the old, non-fictional ghost story: 'I am now going to relate a very extraordinary incident; but upon my honour the narrative is true' (1: 63). In the midst of a hypnagogic sleep, William becomes aware of a 'gigantic' presence that seizes his wrist with a 'tremendous gripe', then disappears. The visitation is followed by a familiar Le Fanuian vacancy: 'no figure but his own was there' (1: 64-5). But the mark of the intruder's grip remains on his wrist, and the episode serves as the basis for a series of dream/hauntings related to Aunt Dinah's threat.

Prematurely resigned to losing his beloved Violet Darkwell to a rival, William responds to his aunt's demand by renouncing a prospect already lost, but summons the pluck to refuse the vow of celibacy. In consequence of his disobedience, he dreams again. This time his visitant is the apparition of Dinah, declaring herself dead, begging 'don't let me go!' and clasping his wrist with a cold hand that leaves its impression after he wakes (2: 126-7).

Still alive, in her room, reading about the Woman (or Witch) of Endor (1 Samuel 28: 7-25), Dinah interprets William's vision as a warning and the seizure of his wrist as evidence of his link to the spirit world. Impressed at least by the *physical* evidence of a nocturnal assault, the hero seeks counsel from the local clergyman, whose response epitomises a Protestant tradition of uneasy conjecture about spiritualism and the source of apparitions:[5]

> 'I don't say there's *nothing* in it, . . . there *may* be a great deal—in fact, a great deal too much—but take it what way we may, to my mind, it is too like what Scripture deals with as witchcraft to be tampered with. If there be no familiar spirit, it's *nothing,* and if there be, *what* is it?. . . . I hope you don't practise it . . . ; nothing would induce *me* to sit at a seance, I should as soon think of praying to the devil. I don't say, of course, that every one who does is as bad as I should be; it depends in some measure on the view you take. The spirit world is veiled from us, no doubt in mercy—in mercy, sir, and we have no right to lift that veil.'
>
> (2: 172-3)

Dr Wagget's expression of theological uncertainty (or equivocation) joins a medley of responses to the problem of spiritual intervention in this slight novel. Before the crisis with Aunt Dinah, William has settled for the effects of late hours, terror fiction, and 'strong coffee' (1: 58). Bung's visions depend on furniture, ouija-like divination, and 'spirit-rapping'. But Dinah's personal creed, in her simplest account of it, owes less to a Yankee charlatan than to a Swedish mystic: 'I know perfectly well we are surrounded by spirits—disprove it if you can—and unequivocally have they declared themselves to me' (2: 109). When the haunting of the hero resumes, Le Fanu's narrator reverts to the claims of circumstantial 'proof' made by the old 'true relation' and the modern ghost story:

> I come now to some incidents, the relation of which partakes, I can't deny, of the marvellous. I can, however, vouch for the literal truth of the narrative; so can William Maubray; so can my excellent friend Doctor Wagget; so also can my friend Doctor Drake, a shrewd and sceptical physician, all thoroughly cognisant of the facts.
>
> (2: 204)

The purpose of the present history, we are redundantly told, is the ghost-genre's oldest and simplest one: the conversion of the Sadducee:

> Again, my reader's incredulity compels me to aver in the most solemn manner that the particulars I now relate of William Maubray's history are strictly true. He is living to depose to all. My excellent friend Doctor Drake can certify to others, and . . . the Rector of the parish, to some of the oddest. Upon this evidence, not doubting, I found my narrative.
>
> (2: 218)

In this novel the redundant claim of the old 'true relation' proves a feint. After Dinah's death, William reviews her warning letters and continues to be haunted, but not by a ghost. On four occasions he wakes from a dreamless sleep to find objects in the room rearranged to form, as in Freud's dream-narratives, a picture puzzle or rebus signifying the stages of his transgression and punishment (see *The Interpretation of Dreams* 277). In the first instance his aunt's letters have been placed under the heel of his boot (2: 219); in the second his cane has been affixed to the bed curtains, 'an image, as it seemed to him, of suspended castigation' (2: 226); in the next his love poems to Violet have been torn to pieces (230-1); at last, a print of Dinah's, showing a cat stalking a mouse (in fulfilment of her prophecy), is nailed to his door (232). When this mute allegory has run its course he is awakened as before by the grip of a hand around his wrist.

To William the personal application of these events is painfully evident. For a solution to the mystery of their origin he (and the reader) must await the result of a night-watch conducted by the clergyman and the physician. Their report is that the hero, a sleepwalker, has

been haunting himself—a literal truth that would apply, of course, in a figurative sense to the rest of Le Fanu's haunted heroes and heroines. The present novel's pastiche of the 'true relation' has provided a demonstration rather of the illusoriness than of the reality of the 'spirit'.[6] The *un*haunting of the hero strikes the first note in the chorus of benign disenchantment with which the story ends:

> From Aunt Dinah's last letters we learn that she gave up her occult convictions (and with them her grandiosity) in favour of a mild orthodoxy, a renunciation that coincided significantly with her loss of power over language: 'I make for future the Bible my only guide, and you are not to mind what I said about waiting five—only do all things—things—with prayer, and marry whenever you see goo, seeking first God's blessing by pra—.' (2: 257)

As for Wagget the clergyman, on the evidence of William's case he has undertaken a treatise that naturalises all supernatural claims not included in the Apostle's Creed and enforced by the Act of Uniformity (whose '*ipso facto*' it solemnly echoes):

> 'If apparitions *be* permitted, they are no more supernatural than water-spouts and other phenomena of rare occurrence, but also, *ipso facto, natural*. In any case a Christian man, in presence of a disembodied spirit should be no more disquieted than in that of an embodied one, *i.e.*, a human being under its mortal conditions.'
>
> (2: 261)

The last act of the romantic comedy consists, appropriately, in marriage between hero and heroine, a ceremony which the narrator places in the sequence of events sanctified in the *Book of Common Prayer*:

> As we walk to the village church, through the churchyard, among the gray, discoloured headstones that seem to troop slowly by us as we pass, the lesson of change and mortality is hardly told so sublimely as in the simple order of our services. The pages that follow the 'Communion' open on the view like the stations in a pilgrimage, The 'Baptism of Infants'—'A Catechism'—'The Order of Confirmation'—'The Solemnisation of Matrimony'—'The Visitation of the Sick'—'The Burial of the Dead.' So, the spiritual events of life are noted and provided for, and the journey marked from the first question—'Hath this child been already baptised or no?' down to the summing up of life's story—'Man that is born of a woman, hath but a short time to live, and is full of misery. He cometh up and is cut down as a flower, he fleeth as it were a shadow, and never continueth in one stay.'
>
> (2: 288-9)

The citation stops just short of a passage that might have served as epigraph to *All in the Dark*, whose clear 'lesson' is rather one of 'change and mortality' than of eternal life: 'In the midst of life we be in death'. The story ends happily—'while the sun is shining'—in the middle of a journey from darkness to darkness.

In light of this conclusion, and in partial mitigation of its flimsiness, *All in the Dark* might be regarded as one of Le Fanu's Prospero-like speeches. By presenting a phenomenalist view of the order of nature (one that will achieve lyric expression in *Chronicles of Golden Friars*), he may be seen to join a long procession of nineteenth-century writers. What (if anything) distinguishes *All in the Dark* is its critical coverage of ways in which custom has defined the supernatural—romantic, realistic, occult and orthodox—and its assigning all of them to the order of the imagination. It serves as a lucid illustration of the *poetics* of the supernatural that William Maubray's 'ghost' should be domesticated, brought *home* to the dreams of a troubled conscience, with no loss of symbolic value. In this respect Le Fanu's comic novel belongs to a line of descent from the Clara Reeve-Ann Radcliffe school of Gothic naturalism.

* * *

Terry Castle has shown how Radcliffe's 'explained' or naturalised apparitions anticipated the later novel's displacement of the supernatural from its literal to a figurative sense—'into the realm of the everyday'. Such displacement, or 'rerout[ing]' would become idiomatic to the genre, indispensable to its representation of experience, from Scott to Henry James and beyond. *The Mysteries of Udolpho,* says Castle, 'encapsulated new structures of feeling, a new model of human relations, a new phenomenology of self and other':

> a crucial feature of the new sensibility of the late eighteenth century was, quite literally, a growing sense of the ghostliness of other people. In the moment of romantic self-absorption, the other was indeed reduced to a phantom—a purely mental effect, as it were, on the screen of consciousness itself. The corporeality of the other . . . became strangely insubstantial and indistinct: what mattered was the mental picture, the ghost, the haunting image.
>
> ('The Spectralization of the Other' 124-5)

Castle acknowledges that this effect of 'romantic' self-consciousness was grounded in empirical psychology. Her citation of Locke allows us to regard the 'haunting' of Robinson Crusoe and Pamela (discussed in Chapter Two) as examples of the modern 'spectralisation of the other'. But it is rather a lyric flight of Hume's (again) that captures most precisely the spirit of the 'new phenomenology':

> The mind is a kind of theatre, where several perceptions successively make their appearance; pass, re-pass, glide away, and mingle in an infinite variety of postures and situations. . . . [But the] comparison of the theatre must not mislead us. They are the successive perceptions only, that constitute the mind; nor have we the most distant notion of the place, where these scenes are represented, or of the materials, of which it is composed.
>
> (*Treatise* 253)

Variants of this image of an insubstantial theatre would recur as the predominant figure for the *un*real city or 'phantasmagoria' of Balzac, Dickens, Thackeray, Baudelaire, Dostoevsky, Mann, Joyce, Eliot, and, for a more specialised purpose, Walter Benjamin. No *flâneur* in his own right, Le Fanu evokes the city metonymically in the form of the empty, therefore haunted, streets of 'The Familiar' and 'Mr Justice Harbottle', the Vanity Fair of London high life in *Loved and Lost* and *Willing to Die,* the devils' paradise of *Haunted Lives* (2:174), and the dreamlike masquerade of continental society in 'Spalatro' and 'The Room in the Dragon Volant'. 'Phantasmagoria' is the word he uses most often for the spectacle that the material world presents to its bewildered captives.

In theory and practice, Ann Radcliffe's poetics of 'terror' provided a demonstration of the haunted scepticism that complicates most varieties of 'realism' in narrative art from the Age of Richardson and Fielding to the present. In her posthumously published dialogue 'On the Supernatural in Poetry' (1826) Radcliffe's theme is no less phenomenological than aesthetic. She identifies as a source of the sublime the endless deferrals to which mind is subjected in its approach to external reality. Aesthetic terror consists in an intensification of that uncertainty which is the mind's necessary element, 'awaken[ing] . . . to a high degree of life' those faculties that are merely disabled, paralysed, by the shock of horror, terror's *un*aesthetic 'opposite' (168).

A too familiar illustration of Radcliffe's theory is the episode of the veiled picture in *Udolpho.* Unveiled, the thing seems 'no picture', but an object of horror that causes the heroine to fall 'senseless' to the floor (294). Thirty-six chapters later the object is revealed as a picture after all—the *trompe l'œil* representation, in wax, of a worm-infested corpse. Arriving as it does near the end of the novel, this revelation completes Radcliffe's model of the phenomenology of her fictive world, whose 'depths' all exist on the surface, whose approach to reality cannot take us beyond representation.

'Horror', for Radcliffe, names something fraudulent in art. It pretends to confront the audience with an unmediated reality, saying to its object, like Lear to Tom o' Bedlam, 'Thou art the thing itself.'' The audience to Radcliffe's essay was probably acquainted with detailed accounts of the slow decomposition or violent disintegration of the human body not only in *The Monk* but in *Melmoth the Wanderer.* A horrid mutilation and murder in Maturin's novel is the work of a Spanish mob, brutalised by the Inquisition. The victim, a 'parricide', is reduced to a 'a mangled lump of flesh' that still 'howled . . . for life—mercy' until being 'trodden . . . into sanguine and discoloured mud by a thousand feet' (255-6). The episode seems indebted to a scene in *The Monk* where a cruel Prioress, persecutor of the martyred Agnes, is pelted with 'mud and filth' by a mob that 'stifled with howls and execrations her shrill cries for mercy', then 'beat' and 'trod upon' her corpse 'till it became no more than a mass of flesh, unsightly, shapeless, and disgusting' (356).

The violence in Lewis and Maturin arises in an atmosphere toxic with religion. In their scenes of horror, ideas of soul and body, self and other, dissolve into a 'formless mass' (*Melmoth* 256), revealing in both authors' treatment of a hyper-religious milieu a subtext of materialism. In *Melmoth,* prisoners of the Inquisition are reduced by fire to a quantity of cinders sufficient to fill a single coffin. Maturin's narrator finds a moral in the spectacle that would apply as well to Le Fanu's use of horror in an early attempt at historical fiction: 'Certainly a lump of cinders was no longer an object even of religious hostility' (251).

In *The Fortunes of Colonel Torlogh O'Brien: A Tale of the Wars of King James* (1847), the burning of a Protestant house by rapparees produces the only sort of spectre that haunts Le Fanu's vision of Jacobean Ireland:

> Through the bars of a window . . . were thrust the knee and the head of a figure, whose escape had been rendered impracticably by two transverse bars which, deeply sunk in the side walls, secured the rest. The head, and one arm and shoulder, as well as one knee, were thrust through the iron stanchions, and all was black and shrunk, the clothes burned entirely away, and the body roasted and shrivelled to a horrible tenuity; the lips dried up and drawn, so that the white teeth grinned and glittered in hideous mockery, and thus the whole form, arrested in the very attitude of frenzied and desperate exertion, showed more like the hideous, blackened effigy of some grinning ape, than anything human.

(114)[8]

In Le Fanu's novel the fate of Maturin's parricide is matched by that of a faithless character, loyal to neither side but captured by Williamite troopers and reduced by repeated applications of the strappado to a 'senseless and mutilated mass of humanity', his skull at last mercifully smashed 'to pieces' by the blow of a musket (280-1).

The function of such images of horror in a historical novel is to bring home to the reader, from a temporal distance, the abject materiality that underlies all doctrinal and temporal differences. In the opening pages of *Torlogh O'Brien* Le Fanu's historian mediates the distance by means of a 'magic mirror' that reflects an old plot in the sense both of conspiracy and of a contrived structure of events. Plot in the second sense is resolved conventionally by a merger, through marriage, of Protestant and Catholic. As a device of Art this conclusion proves fragile by comparison with the merger achieved by Nature in obliterating the marks of identity and humanity itself.

In *Melmoth the Wanderer* Maturin used footnotes as a means of bringing home, of reeling in (as in Freud's *fort-da* game)[9] the actual source of his Spanish horrors from their (for him) origin in Georgian Ireland. Dropping the mask, he declares that the incineration of the Spanish prisoners was based on an event that he witnessed (just four years before his novel's publication) in St Stephen's Green (251) and the reduction to bloody pulp of the parricide on two political murders in Dublin that occurred within his lifetime (256-7). This (literally) subliminal information gives away a secret of the Gothic mode, and draws attention to meanings that are hidden in it so that the reader can find them. It dissolves the alterity of the fiction's fantastic content, retrieves from foreign parts—Spanish or Italian, redolent of Dark Age Catholicism—that is, assimilates to the meaning of *heimlich,* the bigotry, hypocrisy, and cruelty of a regime founded on tyranny and superstition.

For the use of such a distancing or defamiliarising techniques, together with touches of horror, narrative discontinuity, identification with the outlaw, and hostility towards established (represented as Catholic) authority, 'Spalatro' (1843) is Le Fanu's most Maturinesque fiction.[10] Represented as a translation and framed as the 'Notes' of Fra Giacomo, the title character's father-confessor, 'Spalatro' belongs to the genre of criminal autobiography.[11] It might be described more specifically, like 'The Tale of the Spaniard' in *Melmoth,* as a *Bildungsroman* from Hell. Unlike Maturin's Spaniard, however, Spalatro is a notorious outlaw (and therefore a popular hero) whose story, instead of confining itself to the horrors of life under a system of domestic and political despotisms, recounts the stages in the development of a lawless sensibility. Although he has less in common with Monçada than with Melmoth, Spalatro has been led to this condition by a series of demonic tempters (or the shapes of one such figure) wearing the mask of legitimate authority. The first of these (or their first incarnation) is the tutor assigned to him by his cold, aloof stepfather. A Carmelite monk, Brother (also called 'Father') Anthony presents a white-haired, venerable appearance that makes him, like Uncle Silas and like Captain Torquil in the character of Mr Burton, a 'picturesque impersonation of reverend old age' (340). In his 'spiritual' teaching he is a follower of Melmoth and a forerunner of the Mysterious Lodger:

> He had . . . a strange pleasure in unsettling all the most established convictions of my mind, and in thus

plunging me into an abyss of fearful uncertainty and scepticism from which I have never quite escaped. This kind of metaphysical conversation he not unfrequently seasoned with indirect and artful ridicule of religion. . . . He had . . . in a remarkable degree, the Satanic art of clothing vice in the fairest disguise.

(340-1)

The 'Father's' effect on Spalatro is repeated by Spalatro's on Fra Giacomo, whose words seem to echo Catherine Le Fanu's more than any that the author uttered in his own voice: 'My mind is full of doubts and fears. I have no more certainty, no more *knowledge*; mystery and illusion are above, and below, and around me. May God sustain me else my mind will be lost, irrevocably lost, in the abyss of horror' (339). In each case the speaker, like Melmoth, has the power to 'fascinate' his auditor while committing an assault on moral and religious convention. Le Fanu has here greatly simplified an effect of Maturin's nested narratives by constructing an analogy between the subversive voice and the hidden author, the fascinated listener and the reader. Maturin's chain of analogies also connects authorship with aggression but brings us much closer to the ambivalent heart of the horror-aesthetic. An exemplary *mise en abîme* in *Melmoth* begins with an internal narrator affronting the sensibilities of his silent, passive audience (the protagonist, the reader) with his eye-witness account of the parricide's savage mutilation. At first, paralysed by the spectacle, he identifies himself with the aggressors, echoing their 'wild cries'. Then, sensing that the awful power of the scene resides in the victim, he begins to echo 'the screams of the thing that seemed no longer to live, but still could scream . . . for life—life' (256). To this point the novel has given us at least two examples of *aestheticised* violence: a Spanish tapestry depicting 'beautifully tortured' Moors (32); a naked young monk among his persecutors, making 'a groupe worthy of Murillo' (108). Much later, the spectacle of nature struggling to become art is reprised in the moonlit figure of a youth who has sold his blood to feed his family, his 'snow-white limbs . . . extended as if for the inspection of a sculptor, and moveless, as if they were indeed what they resembled, in hue and symmetry, those of a marble statue' (422). In the midst of this sequence, the scene of the parricide's reversion to a 'formless mass' seems to represent the retaliation of nature against art, or matter against mind.[12] Yet the narrator-as-artist has managed to retrieve from the event a defining moment (however degraded) of heroic myth or tragedy in which the victim's immortality is assured by his communal dismemberment. In the passage of *Monk*-like horror, the victim appears, like Orpheus, to have been survived by his voice, and it is *his* voice that has remained with the present narrator as the teller of a tale of lovers horribly transformed by starvation in a monastic dungeon for the diversion of an audience of impotent voyeurs (204-15). Narrator and reader, witness and spectator, perpetrator and victim, are entangled together in the web of Maturin's narrative.

In his Preface to *The Secret Agent*, Joseph Conrad disclaims an intention of 'elaborating mere ugliness in order to shock' (38) or of committing 'a gratuitous outrage on the feelings of mankind' (43). The passage most at issue would be his callously detailed account of the fragments to which a retarded youth is reduced by a bomb planted on him by an *agent provocateur*. The author admits only to the application 'an ironic method to a subject of that kind' (41). The outrage was the work of opposed ideologies—revolutionary and reactionary—that acted as one: 'a brazen cheat exploiting the poignant miseries and passionate credulities of a mankind always so tragically eager for self-destruction' (39). The description would serve as well for *Melmoth the Wanderer*. Together with the impersonalising devices of irony and melodrama, Maturin uses a series of narrative masks and, as secret agent, or *agent provocateur*, engages the participation of an audience-within-the-text to expose by 'outrage' the *real* 'feelings of mankind'.

In the footnote to the episode of the parricide's death, Maturin recounts in his own person an event that 'was related to me by an eye-witness'; that is, like the narrators within the body of the text, he occupies both sides of the narrative transaction.[13] His setting is Ireland, his genre history, and his theme, as in the Spanish fiction, the transformation of spectator into victim, and, by extension, the power of author over audience. Maturin's history-as-metafiction concerns the assassination in 1803 of the Lord Chief Justice of Ireland: 'Pike after pike was thrust through his body, till at last he was *nailed to a door*, and called out to his murderers to "put him out of his pain"'. Drawn to his window by the 'horrible cries,' a citizen in nearby lodgings stands 'gasping with horror, his wife attempting vainly to drag him away. He saw the last blow struck—he heard the last groan uttered, as the sufferer cried, "put me out of pain", while sixty pikes were thrusting at him. The man stood at his window as if nailed to it; and when dragged from it, became—*an idiot for life*' (257).

That italicised phrase presents an extravagant illustration of the transformative power of 'outrage'. The point that Maturin stresses repeatedly in text and footnote is that, in the words of his Spanish narrator, 'The drama of terror [Radcliffe's "horror"] has the irresistible power of converting its audience into its victims' (257). The redundant image of transfixion—literal in the case of the Chief Justice's murder, metaphoric in its application to the spectator's response—merely repeats the Spaniard's account of his own fixation in the presence of horror: 'offering worlds in imagination to be able to remove from the window, yet feeling as if every shriek I uttered was as a nail that fastened me to it' (256).

In both scenes, of course, spectacle has been transposed into printed text. Victim and spectator, like character and reader, are subject to the power of the author who identifies himself as such in the footnote, turning the sequence of horror-scenes into a parable of art as a form of aggression, a 'gratuitous outrage on the feelings of mankind'. In *The Secret Agent,* the artist-as-anarchist is figured in the stunted, dingy character of the Professor, who compensates for his impotence by the manufacture of terrorist bombs (one of which he always carries, ready for detonation, under his coat). Itinerant like Melmoth and Spalatro and their Satanic prototype—but on a pedestrian scale and within the city limits—he is classed by Conrad among those 'whose ambition aims at a direct grasp upon humanity—. . . artists, politicians, thinkers, reformers, or saints' (103): 'He was a force. His thoughts caressed the images of ruin and destruction. He walked frail, insignificant, shabby, miserable—and terrible in the simplicity of his idea calling madness and despair to the regeneration of the world' (269).

Conrad's shrunken megalomaniac might have been regarded as the last metamorphosis of a Romantic outlaw whose line of descent extends from Milton's 'sublime' Anarch—'far superior', said Shelley, 'to his God' ('Defence' 526)—and includes the Richardsonian rake, Schiller's 'majestic monster', the Gothic villain, the Byronic hero. In Conrad's novel the figure is reduced to the dimensions of a *Punch* caricature; in Le Fanu's 'Spalatro', as Father Anthony, he merely shows his age: 'a few locks of snow-white hair, venerably covered his temples, and a long and singularly handsome beard of the same pure white, fell upon his bosom'. But the lineaments of the rebel remain visible beneath the patriarchal disguise. He is Ann Radcliffe's Schedoni, a half-century later:

The Italian

> His figure was striking . . . it was tall, and, though extremely thin, his limbs were large and uncouth, and as he stalked along, wrapt in the black garments of his order, there was something terrible in its air. . . . An habitual gloom and severity prevailed over the deep lines of his countenance; and his eyes were so piercing that they seemed to penetrate, at a single glance, into the hearts of men, and to read their most secret thoughts.

(34-5)

'Spalatro'

> His figure was rather tall, though slight, and might once have been athletic, but now it was bowed under the weight of years. . . . One relic of departed youth alone remained to this venerable man, it was the fiery vivacity of an eye, which seemed as though it had never rested or grown dim—an eye under whose glance the buried secrets of the heart arose and showed themselves, which nothing could baffle or escape.

(340)

Although Spalatro himself is billed as 'the most powerful [robber] of any age', the story is not about his criminal history but about his visionary education under the tutelage of Father Anthony. Thanks to the apostate-monk's influence he has become resigned to his own damnation, having embraced a doctrine of occult fatalism that defines him as 'one' with Satan, destined to 'merge for ever into that dark mind' (458), and that paradoxically resembles the *supra*lapsarian delusions of Browning's Johannes Agricola and James Hogg's 'Justified Sinner':

> 'Were I to tell you why I believe in [God and the devil] you would think me mad. I have seen things, these eyes have seen them, which my lips shall never tell. Were I to speak them, you and all other men would laugh at me, and you would pronounce the TRUTH, because it is unlike what you are in the habit of seeing every day, an impossibility and a lie; but of this be assured, that I know better than any other man can what is in store for me.'

(339)

As a gratuitous illustration of his 'spiritual' precepts, Father Anthony rapes Spalatro's beloved stepsister, repelling with preternatural force the hero's attempt to restrain him. The incident prompts the monk's protégé to leave the cold security of his stepfather's castle and to 'throw' himself upon the chances of the world (341).

In an episode that Le Fanu will repeat with substantial modifications in *The Cock and Anchor* (1845), the hero loses himself in a wood, picks up a servile companion, receives from a stranger directions to an isolated inn that proves to be a den of thieves. (In *The Cock and Anchor* they are Jacobite conspirators.) The inn's proprietor presents a grossly enlarged, grizzled, and fanged image of age and authority, and the building itself, with its 'mixed character of a house and a castle', partly 'decayed' and 'even ruinous', seems a Gothicised version of the step-paternal estate. A human link between the two places is provided by the surprising appearance of a kitchen-maid who has fled the stepfather's service and who warns the hero of the inn-crew's murderous intentions (345).

The tapestried (and barred) chamber in which Spalatro is installed supports one's sense of the inn's incongruously palatial size. 'Vast and dim', its 'vacancy' illuminated by a solitary candle, big enough to accommodate a recess (familiar frame for Le Fanuian horrors) which in itself is described as a 'huge and solitary chasm', the room is separated from the inhabited part of the house by 'a long succession of passages, and chambers, and staircases' (347). From a place of concealment within this maze, Spalatro watches helplessly as the murderers, gathered in the kitchen, behead his drugged companion, catching the torrent of blood in a bucket (350). The criminal beheading will be doubled by the legal one that ends the hero's life.

Thanks to his stepfather's former servant, Spalatro escapes the fatal inn. The transition from Grand Guignol to Roman carnival is marked only by the end of Part I. The abruptness of this change of setting is consistent with the treatment of the hero's Roman adventures as a series of transformation scenes. He immerses himself in the vices of a city which carnival has transformed into 'the fantastic mazes of a bewildering and gorgeous dream' (446). The genius of the place, or of the shifting spectacle, emerges from the crowd of revellers dressed as a harlequin who leads Spalatro by magical powers of compulsion on a wild chase through town and country. When they come to a stop the antic figure performs an act of 'extraordinary ventriloquism', spellbinding the hero with an enigmatic song that seems to invoke Satanic intervention. At this point he reveals himself as Father Anthony.

If it is one of the Italian Comedy character's traditional functions to act as a reflexive figure, a mirror of the audience's motley passions, then Spalatro's Harlequin-Priest plays his role with rare precision:

> Suddenly he stopped short before me, and by an unearthly sympathy I was constrained to do the same: he sate down upon the earth; by an irresistible impulse I did so likewise. We were opposite to one another—face to face, and scarcely a yard asunder. He tossed his arms wildly in the air—I could not choose but do the same: he writhed his features into contortions such as delirium never portrayed, each one of which, with frenzied exaggeration, I felt forced to imitate. Into these hideous grimaces he threw, at times, expressions of demoniac passion so fearfully intense, that hell itself could not have exceeded them: these too, I was forced to follow, and the dreadful passions themselves possessed me in succession, while all the time, independently of these malignant inspirations, there remained within me, as it were looking on, a terrified self-consciousness. He yelled forth blasphemies the most awful, while my very brain sickened with horror—the unearthly power constrained me to echo them all, tone for tone, and word for word. He advanced his face, I did the same—our features almost touched. He burst into a peal of laughter like that of lunacy, I joined howling in horrible mirth. Every word *he* spoke, *I* spoke—every movement *he* made, *I* made too. My motions all corresponded with his, with the simultaneousness and accuracy with which shadow follows substance; I felt as if my identity was merging into his.

(448)

At last, as the evil mime holds a dagger to his throat, a passer-by prevents Spalatro from doing the same, and his familiar demon vanishes after undergoing Hoffmannesque metamorphoses into a quaking bush and a slithering otter.

Delivered from suicide but not from demonic possession, Spalatro falls ill, then resumes his course of exploratory self-indulgence before losing himself, as at the beginning, but in an *urban* wilderness, under the spell of a charming old man in antique dress who leads him to the door of a decayed 'mansion' or 'palace' in a strange and utterly desolate district. This time his guide, though not (apparently) another incarnation of Father Anthony, is linked to the tempter by his power of fascination and by a 'venerable' growth of 'snow-white hair' (449). The tour on which he takes the hero is through time rather than space, to a metaphysical rather than a physical location. Its destination is an underworld inhabited by an extinct aristocracy, and the old man's introductory speech concisely sets forth the fate of Le Fanu's patrician families from 'The Fortunes of Sir Robert Ardagh' (1838) to 'Sir Dominick's Bargain' (1872):

> '—in almost every house this street contains, you see the monument of some noble family gone to ruin, wasted by prodigality, or struck down into the dust by the heavy arm of power. Those who dwell here seldom seek to look into the staring, noisy world; they think not of the present, but ever upon the past. . . . Silence here holds her eternal court . . . yet, amid all this lonely silence, is there any quiet for heart or brain? Oh, eternal, unforgiving spirit! is there any rest—is there any unconsciousness?'

(450)

The great house contains, like Le Fanu's other great houses, a gallery of family portraits, including an exact likeness of Spalatro's host, who identifies its subject as his ancestor. A second portrait depicts a beautiful young woman, his daughter, through whom he will work his power of enchantment, enthralling the hero to an undead past.

The building proves a kind of mausoleum, its inhabitants vampires. The host leads Spalatro into a vast chamber (tapestried again, like his room in the bloody inn) whose dimensions are obscured by a translucent vapour, forming a 'veil between human vision and sights, perhaps, unsuited to its ken' (452). Having offered his unwitting guest a blood-feast, the proprietor-turned-magus conjures out of the mist a delirious vision of the beauty and horror of an obsolete civilisation:

> strange lights and shadows flitted over it; sometimes tracing in the eddying vapours wild ghastly features, which vanished almost as soon as they appeared, and sometimes dimly showing monstrous shapes, and now and then more faintly-traced forms of surpassing grace—all gliding and wheeling, appearing and melting away, separating and mingling like the endless shiftings of a wondrous dream.

'At length', the visual imagery turns auditory: 'there came a low and marvellously sweet sound of far-off music', the signal in Maturin's novel of an appearance by the Wanderer, but here raised to the magnitude of 'holy choirs singing a requiem over the dead':

the sound stole floating along, sometimes broken and disordered, as though the untutored wind swept at random through the chords of a thousand-stringed instrument, then again, coming with perfect harmony and unspeakable melody over the senses, until once more the music would lose itself in the wild burst of the wailing wind.

(452-3)

From this mingling of art and nature, like Pope's 'Emblem of Music caus'd by Emptiness' (*Dunciad* I, 36), emerges the figure, from the portrait gallery, of Spalatro's unearthly enchantress, 'a model of preternatural loveliness'. At first she seems no more than a copy of Hoffmann's Olympia: 'The beautiful form moved lightly over the floor, but seemingly without more volition or purpose of its own than belongs to a mere automaton; the lips pale as marble, the eyes fixed and glittering, and every muscle of the perfect face still as death' (453). Upon restoring herself with blood, she surpasses the orders of art and nature alike, becoming 'a divinity, clothed in the eternal majesty of ideal beauty', an object of worship to the Outlaw-as-Artist until all vision has deserted him except that of his own damnation.

After the spectral palace and its inhabitants have disappeared into darkness, Spalatro searches obsessively for his *belle inconnue*. In his dreams her image mingles with that of the 'abhorred monk', whom he detects slithering like a snake from his bed in the midst of an amorous reverie. This merger, or collision, between the 'ideal' object and unlawful passion precisely (and bombastically) anticipates Laura's ambivalence toward the Carmilla-wraith, but the suggestion of mere *auto-erotic* fantasy (with its attendant fears) is more apparent:

> Beautiful betrayer—passionately-beloved phantom—unearthly lover—what have I done? I am a fear and wonder to myself. . . . Sweet terrible illusion, I will not curse thee: 'twas I—*I* and not thou who wooed these strange horrors. . . . Still night after night thy footsteps are my guide, thy smiles my life, thy bosom my pillow: the vital taper burns away—down, down, wasting in the fierce glare of fever. Where, where will end this agony of love and despair? . . . Cruel, beautiful destroyer! Thou wilt drink my life away sweetly, slowly. . . . I am all thine own. . . . All men move around me strangers, and as far away from my world of existence as from the dimmest star. . . . I have but one companion, one interest, one object; ever within me dread and loathing wrestle against passionate love in eternal agony.

(456)

The Gothic monk and the undead patriarch, if not identical in fact, are, like other elements in the separate episodes of Spalatro's history, associatively linked. Both have designs on the hero's soul. Despite the warnings

of his 'unearthly lover', a mere 'vainly resisting' instrument of her father's will, the hero once again follows the old man into the occult mansion and encounters again an infernal vision of the cultural past, here expanded to the dimensions of a disintegrating patriarchal universe:

> A vast chamber, lighted dazzlingly with a thousand lamps, or rather stars, for they were not supported nor suspended by any thing, but glowed, flickered, and sported, separate and self-sustained, rolling and eddying high in air—expanding, and contracting, and yielding in glorious succession all the most splendid colours which imagination can conceive. Beneath this gorgeous and ever-shifting illumination a vast throng of shapes were moving—all enacting, but with a repulsive and hideous exaggeration, the courteous observances and jollity of a festive meeting. Some glided to and fro with courtly ease, but bearing upon their lifeless faces the fearful stamp of sin and eternal anguish; others sate looking on, their fixed features writhed into smiles which, but to dream of, would appal the fancy for days; others, with ghastly idiotic grimaces, made hideous music from strange instruments, which panted and quivered, and writhed like living things in agony; others leaped, and danced, and howled, and glared like the very fiends of madness; and all formed a crowd of such terrific and ghastly horror as words cannot even faintly shadow forth.

In the midst of this phantasmagoria, or microchaos, 'I feared nothing', Spalatro declares, but 'revelled in the horrors', and from among these appears once again 'the beautiful form of the mysterious being who had won my very soul'. Having assured him that both she and his soul are lost to him, the enchantress together with her orgiastic company dissolves into darkness despite his protest: 'Stay, stay, beautiful, beloved illusion . . .—I can love no other' (457).

Like Schalken the painter, Spalatro faints before the fading vision and is awakened by the sexton of an empty church. Before committing the first of the crimes for which he will be executed, he has accepted the sentence of eternal damnation. His sin belongs rather to Le Fanu's time, place, and class than to his own. It has consisted in a solitary, habitual, estranging, debilitating indulgence in erotic fantasy (figured as the serial approach and withdrawal of an incorporeal lover). The 'artisan' of this 'fatal rage', quoth the eighteenth-century moralist, is *'imagination'* (Bennett and Rosario 7). The faculty, it seems, to which Spalatro loses his 'soul' also makes him a type of the Romantic artist. His prowess as visionary *and* outlaw gives him a claim to the title assumed by Balzac's—and the nineteenth-century novel's—greatest master criminal, the protean Vautrin, who styles himself 'un grand poète' of 'actions' and 'sentiments' (*Père Goriot* 112).

The art of 'Spalatro,' moreover, reveals how the faculty that isolates and distinguishes the hero, his source of delight and torment, is in itself the product of an *exter-*

nal order, a set of cultural traditions, spiritual and temporal, that have been so drained of authority as to be represented by an empty church, a blasphemous monk, an orgy of the dead, a bloodsucking patriarch. Le Fanu's first vampire story has supplied a critical metaphor for a treatment of the relationship between age and youth, tradition and modernity, that runs throughout his work. 'Vampirism', says Mc Cormack, 'is seen as the survival of the past at the expense of the present' (*Sheridan Le Fanu* 190). Victor Sage has observed the same phenomenon in Le Fanu's atavistic use of eighteenth-century comedy, calling it 'a form of cultural memory, in which the nightmares of the past are explicitly, but subtly, revived, often revealing the bankrupt heritage of an aristocracy that has lost its capacity to resist its own history and is willing to prey on its own young in order to retain power' ('Resurrecting the Regency' 29).

As *confessional* narrator, Le Fanu's outlaw illustrates a Foucauldian principle by proving himself no less subjected than subjective. For subjectivity itself is imposed from without as well as produced from within. Spalatro's apostasy has spared, from the ruins of traditional belief, God, the devil, and predestination, and he has submitted his destiny to these ineluctable forces, condemning himself on their authority before his condemnation by a court of law. Foucault, having traced the rise of confessional narrative from the middle ages, speaks of a 'metamorphosis in literature' concurrent with a revolution in epistemology:

> we have passed from a pleasure to be recounted and heard, centering on the heroic or marvellous narration of 'trials' of bravery or sainthood, to a literature ordered according to the infinite task of extracting from the depths of oneself, in between the words, a *truth* which the very form of the confession holds out like a *shimmering mirage*. Whence too this new way of philosophising: seeking the fundamental relation to the true, not simply in oneself—in some forgotten knowledge, or in a certain primal trace—but in the self-examination that yields, through a multitude of fleeting impressions, the basic certainties of consciousness.
>
> (59-60; emphasis added)

'Consciousness', of course, places 'certainty' at a distance from any transcendent or even verifiable reality. As a certainty of consciousness, the 'TRUTH' that Spalatro claims for his narrative—a truth that 'other men . . . would pronounce . . . an impossibility and a lie'— can be reconciled with solipsism. His criminal career (we are assured) is history, his memoir is vision, a 'shimmering mirage'. It follows that the 'translator,' should concede a measure of authority to the claims of the Sadducee. In an afterword addressed to a friend, or reader-surrogate, he questions whether even Fra Giacomo, faithful transcriber of the outlaw's tale, believed it to be true. For his own part he tries to naturalise Spalatro's visions by attributing them to *delirium tre-*

mens, then proceeds to reduce the hero's macabre romance, or amorous delusion, to a kind of comic pantomime.

Yet ('joke as we may') Spalatro's words, as intended, commit an assault on received attitudes. They have shaken the faith of his father-confessor ('I have no more certainty') and have led the facetious 'translator' to adopt a more radically sceptical position than mere naturalist beseems:

> Philosophy does but teach us the extent of our ignorance (I think I saw that somewhere or other before, but no matter). Do the dead return from the grave? Do strange influences reveal to mortal eye the shadowy vistas of futurity? Can demoniac agencies possess the body as of old, and blast the mind? What are these things that we call spectral illusions, dreams, madness? All around us is darkness and uncertainty. To what thing shall we say I understand thee? All is doubt—all is mystery.
>
> (458)

This conclusion has less to do with admitting the possibility of spiritual intervention than with establishing, for critical purposes, the equivalence of external and internal, literal and metaphorical hauntings, demons, cases of 'possession'. The Art of the supernatural or uncanny has for its object of imitation a sceptic's model of Nature, a 'universe of the imagination, nor have we any idea but what is there produc'd'. Moral philosophy from Hume forward refuses the licence offered by this subjective idealism. In fiction it provides the material for a most important modern character, the shadow of the author in the text. Le Fanu, in 'The Mysterious Lodger', identified Humeian scepticism specifically (as if it were Milton's 'The Mind is its own Place') with free-thinking, and free-thinking with the Satanic, which gets full play in that tale's eponymous demon.

Father Anthony is the first such devil's advocate in Le Fanu's fiction; Spalatro's life of crime is the result of his teaching. Beginning with *The House by the Churchyard* (1863) Le Fanu produced a series of novels in which the attributes of master and protégé, mastermind and outlaw, are embodied in separate characters or united in one without recourse (except metaphoric) to the supernatural. This character is an impostor (or forger), a plotter *within* Le Fanu's plot, a demonic agent whose schemes, for good or ill, disrupt the inertia of the little world in which he is placed and demonstrate the fragility of the structures of belief and practice upon which that world is founded. In response to the fictions of historical continuity and moral community, he offers an *opposing* fiction.

To Georg Lukács, such a 'demonic' presence was essential to the 'psychology' of the novel, or 'epic of a world that has been abandoned by God' (*Theory of the*

Novel 88). The opposing, or demonic, version of reality rather supplements than repudiates the communal one, for 'the world', says Lukács,

> has a coherence of meaning, a causality, which is incomprehensible to the vital effective force of a god-become-demon [from whose] viewpoint the affairs of such a world appear purely senseless. The demon's power remains effective because it cannot be overthrown; the passing of the old god supports the being of the new; and for this reason the one possesses the same valency . . . as the other.
>
> (86-7)

This version of the demonic-in-the-world fits Le Fanu's case precisely, and places him in a tradition of poets in prose and verse who have engaged with a second self in dubious battle for the determination of the real. For the purposes of the present study, the lines of this tradition converge on the demiurgic figure of Balzac.

Notes

1. In a speech before the Grattan parliament (1789), Lord Clare reminded 'the gentlemen of Ireland' that 'The Act [of Settlement] by which most of us hold our estates was an Act of violence—an Act subverting the first principles of the Common Law of England and Ireland.' Cited by Foster 257; see also E. M. Johnston, *Ireland in the Eighteenth Century* 161.

2. The predicament shared by the would-be murderers in 'Richard Marston', 'The Evil Guest', and *A Lost Name* seems itself the product of serial borrowings. It first occurs in Balzac's 'L'Auberge rouge' (1831), which appeared in translation, unattributed and partly disguised, as 'The Red Inn of Andernach' in *Dublin University Magazine* (June-July, 1834). In all five narratives the character who has been forestalled in his murderous intention bears the guilt of the crime. Balzac's fatalism and mysticism (with its touches of Swedenborg and Mesmer) are at last rehearsed in disordered form by Carmel Sherlock. 'L'Auberge rouge' is a framed narrative. 'The Red Mill of Andernach' (signed 'Iota') adds a frame, removing the initial setting from Paris to Bruges. Its narrator in the end identifies his story as destined for the *DUM* and issues at the beginning the following disclaimer, as if challenging Balzac to assert his rightful claim: 'at this distance of time, I cannot venture to arrange my knowledge according to the various channels through which it has flowed in upon me, or say which is truth, which is fiction. If I have plagiarised from any man, let him come and take his own' (634).

3. As Seamus Deane observes, 'Any world that was lost had occultism as its friend—whether that of

the Irish peasantry, of the old Gaelic, or of the recent Anglo-Irish civilisation' (*Strange Country* 111).

4. *All in the Dark* was written in the same spirit of ridicule as an article that appeared in *DUM* two years earlier (1862). The anonymous author of 'Spiritualism' called the practice of 'spirit-rapping' a 'vile compound of hysteric charlatanism and barefaced imposture' and observed that 'this new outburst of modern superstition found its way hither from [the United States], whose doings so often sound like a wild caricature of our own English ways' (4-5). The tone seems incongruous in a journal that treated seriously such topics as 'The State of Sleep-Waking', 'The Occult Sciences' and 'Animal Magnetism'.

5. For a brief account of the mixed opinions of Protestant theologians towards apparitions and specifically towards the powers attributed to the Woman of Endor, see Keith Thomas 587-95.

6. In 'Maître Cornélius', a second work by Balzac to appear in translation in *DUM*, the title character commits, on a far greater scale than William Maubray, acts of self-punishment in his sleep. A fabulously wealthy miser, paranoid, banker to royalty, Cornélius becomes victim of a series of robberies for which his apprentices are condemned to death. When he's revealed as the unconscious thief, exposure and the failure to find his hidden treasure drive him to suicide. Like *All in the Dark*, 'Maître Cornélius' prepares the reader for a supernatural event before supplying a psychological explanation. But in scope the two stories are as unequal as *Melmoth the Wanderer* and *Willing to Die*. 'Maître Cornélius', set in the France of Louis XI, can be taken as a fable on the venality at the core of state power. *All in the Dark* concerns itself with the moral inhibitions of a diffident lover.

7. Anne Williams interprets Radcliffe's 'horror' in light of Julia Kristeva's 'abject': 'According to Kristeva, the things we experience as "horrible" evoke that early ["pre-Oedipal"] anxiety about materiality and the borders of the self, between "me" and the "improper/unclean"':

> Horror marks a threat to the bodily integrity of the 'I'—its very existence in the Symbolic. It stirs dim anxieties about our inexorable materiality, a fact that, according to Kristeva, must be repressed so that we may enter the Symbolic, establishing the boundaries between 'I' and 'not-I', our 'insides' and 'outside.' . . . Radcliffe's statement that horror 'freezes' or 'contracts' the perceiver is therefore apt, for these terms imply both a feeling of repulsion and that reassertion

of selfhood, the necessary securing of bound-aries that the horrible has obscurely disturbed.

(*Art of Darkness* 75-6; *Kristeva, Powers of Horror* 2 and passim)

8. This account of the charred victim is confronted on the facing page by 'Phiz's' stark illustration.

9. See *Beyond the Pleasure Principle* 10-17. Freud's famous anecdote of the child who symbolically casts off, then reels in his connection with the mother (contingent, material existence) is preceded by the 'dark and dismal' subject of patients who relive in dreams the horrors of war. In *The Monk, Melmoth* and *Torlogh O'Brien* the recurrence of horror can be taken as the acknowledgement of a familiar yet hidden, or displaced, fact of mere organic existence. Maturin's footnotes indicate a recognition that his wide-ranging, fantastic horror-fiction served as the displacement of national and personal nightmare.

10. Wayne E. Hall has seen a connection between 'Spalatro' and an atypical tale by Charles Lever that appeared in *DUM* eight months earlier. 'Carl Stelling—The Painter of Dresden' (1842) is a framed narrative that includes a passive hero and the uncanny portrait of an undead *femme fatale* who acts under the control of a demonic old man. Observing similarities between Le Fanu's work for the magazine and specific contributions by Lever and Isaac Butt (see p. 201, n. 8 above), Hall suggests that the author of 'Spalatro' consciously accommodated himself to 'the tastes of [*DUM*'s] editors' (*Dialogues in the Margin* 113). Butt served as editor from 1834 to 1838, Lever from 1842 to 1845. The similarities to which Hall refers appear as early in Le Fanu's work as 'Schalken the Painter' (1839) and as late as 'The Room in the Dragon Volant' (1872), three years after his own connection with the magazine had come to an end.

11. In Radcliffe's *The Italian* (1797) Spalatro is the name of an assassin hired by the demonic Schedoni to kill the heroine. Haunted by his former crimes in the shape of a beckoning bloody hand, Spalatro demurs, leaving the task to Schedoni, but resumes his part as a threat to Ellena after Schedoni spares her upon discovering that she's his daughter. In Vol. 111, Chapter 2, fragments of Spalatro's criminal history are delivered to Schedoni by one of Radcliffe's Shakespearean clowns. To Schedoni, the narrative 'resembles a delirious dream, more than a reality', 'the vision of a distempered brain' (284), a description that fits Le Fanu's narrative far better than the clown's.

The Spalatro of Le Fanu's verse drama *Beatrice* (1865), a devil in monkish disguise, bears a closer resemblance to Father Anthony than to the Spalatro of the 1843 tale. His 'cold eyes'

> . . . ever seem to search and smile
> And find in all things something vile.

(36)

Commissioned by a powerful, jealous *femme fatale* to dispose of the heroine, he causes his servant to murder her.

12. The metamorphoses of aestheticised violence in *Melmoth* might have affected the thinking of Maturin's grand-nephew, Oscar Wilde, on the precariousness of art. First there is Dorian Gray's final view of his portrait: 'The thing was still loathsome—more loathsome, if possible, than before—and the scarlet dew that spotted the hand seemed brighter, and more like blood newly spilt' (168); then the following reference to a struggle in 'The Critic as Artist', Part II: 'just as Nature is matter struggling into mind, so Art is mind expressing itself under the conditions of matter' (317).

13. The present reading of the relationship between text and footnotes in *Melmoth* has been substantially lifted from Mc Cormack, *Dissolute Characters* 4-6; see also his 'Irish Gothic and After', *The Field Day Anthology of Irish Writing,* Vol. 2, 833-4.

Works Cited

ABBREVIATIONS

BGS: *Best Ghost Stories of J. S. Le Fanu.* Ed. E. F. Bleiler. New York: Dover, 1964.

CW: *The Collected Works of Joseph Sheridan Le Fanu.* Ed. Devendra P. Varma. New York: Arno, 1977.

DUM: *Dublin University Magazine.*

GSM: Le Fanu, *Ghost Stories and Mysteries.* Ed. E. F. Bleiler. New York: Dover, 1975.

IGD: Le Fanu, *In a Glass Darkly.* Ed. Robert Tracy. Oxford: Oxford UP, 1993.

I WRITINGS BY LE FANU

'An Account of Some Strange Disturbances in Aungier Street.' *BGS*: 361-79.

'An Adventure of Hardress Fitzgerald, a Royalist Captain.' *CW. The Purcell Papers.* Vol. 3: 136-224.

All in the Dark. 2 vols. *CW.*

'An Authentic Narrative of a Haunted House.' *BGS*: 419-30.

'Beatrice. A Verse Drama in Two Acts.' *The Poems of Joseph Sheridan Le Fanu.* Ed. Alfred Perceval Graves. *CW*: 1-86.

'Borrhomeo the Astrologer: a Monkish Tale.' *DUM* 59 (Jan.-June 1862): 55-61.

'Carmilla.' *IGD*: 243-319.

'A Chapter in the History of a Tyrone Family.' *GSM*: 189-215.

Checkmate. Stroud: Sutton, 1997.

The Cock and Anchor. 3 vols. *CW.*

'The Evil Guest.' *GSM*: 241-331.

'The Familiar.' *IGD*: 41-82.

The Fortunes of Colonel Torlogh O'Brien: A Tale of the Wars of King James. CW.

'The Fortunes of Sir Robert Ardagh.' *BGS*: 340-60.

'Green Tea.' *IGD*: 5-40.

Guy Deverell. New York: Dover, 1984.

'The Haunted Baronet.' *BGS*: 61-77.

Haunted Lives. 3 vols. *CW.*

The House by the Churchyard. London: Anthony Blond, 1968.

'The Last Heir of Castle Connor.' *The Purcell Papers.* Vol. 1. *CW*: 98-200.

A Lost Name. 3 vols. *CW.*

Loved and Lost. See *My Own Story; or, Loved and Lost.*

'Madam Crowl's Ghost.' *BGS*: 47-60.

'Mr. Justice Harbottle.' *IGD*: 83-118.

My Own Story; or, Loved and Lost. DUM 72 (July-Dec. 1868): 254-67, 381-94, 500-18, 617-32; 73 (Jan.-May 1869): 19-33, 142-54, 259-70, 381-95, 505-11.

'The Mysterious Lodger.' *GSM*: 332-72.

'Passage in the Secret History of an Irish Countess.' *The Purcell Papers.* Vol. 2. *CW*: 1-102.

'Phaudrig Crohoore.' *The Poems of Joseph Sheridan Le Fanu. CW*: 127-34.

'The Room in the Dragon Volant.' *IGD.* 119-242.

The Rose and the Key. Stroud: Sutton, 1994.

'Schalken the Painter.' *Ghost Stories and Tales of Mystery. CW*: 106-35. (See 'Strange Event . . .').

'Shamus O'Brien.' *The Poems of Joseph Sheridan Le Fanu. CW*: 113-26.

'Sir Dominick's Bargain: A Legend of Dunoran.' *BGS*: 431-43.

'Some Account of the Latter Days of the Hon. Richard Marston of Dunoran.' *DUM* 31 (Jan.-June 1848): 473-97, 586-607, 728-56.

'Spalatro, from the Notes of Friar Giacomo.' *DUM* 21 (Jan.-June 1843): 338-51, 446-58.

'The Spectre Lovers,' in 'Ghost Stories of Chapelizod.' *GSM*: 126-35.

'A Strange Adventure in the History of Miss Laura Mildmay.' *Chronicles of Golden Friars.* Vol. 1. *CW*: 3-278.

'Strange Event in the Life of Schalken the Painter. Being a Seventh Extract from the Legacy of the Late Francis Purcell, P. P. of Drumcoolagh.' *DUM* 13 (May, 1839): 579-91.

The Tenants of Malory. 3 vols. *CW.*

'Ultor de Lacy: A Legend of Cappercullen.' *BGS*: 444-66.

Uncle Silas. Ed. Victor Sage. London: Penguin, 2000.

'Wicked Captain Walshawe, of Wauling.' *GSM*: 105-15.

Willing to Die. 3 vols. *CW.*

Wylder's Hand. New York: Dover, 1978.

The Wyvern Mystery. Stroud: Sutton, 2000.

II OTHER

Abrams, M. H. *Natural Supernaturalism: Tradition and Revolution in Romantic Literature.* New York: Norton, 1973.

Altick, Richard D. *The Shows of London.* Cambridge, Mass.: Harvard UP, 1978.

Andriano, Joseph. *Our Ladies of Darkness: Feminine Dæmonology in Male Gothic Fiction.* University Park: Pennsylvania State UP, 1993: 98-105.

'Animal Magnetism.' *DUM* 38 (Oct. 1851): 687-707.

Ashton, Dore. *A Fable of Modern Art.* Berkeley: U of California P, 1991.

Backscheider, Paula K. *Spectacular Politics: Theatrical Power and Mass Culture in Early Modern England.* Baltimore: The Johns Hopkins UP, 1993.

Backus, Margot Gayle. *The Gothic Family Romance: Heterosexuality, Child Sacrifice, and the Anglo-Irish Colonial Order.* Durham, NC: Duke UP.

Bakhtin, Mikhail. *Rabelais and His World.* Trans. Hélène Iswolsky. Bloomington: Indiana UP, 1984.

Balzac, Honoré de. 'L'Auberge rouge.' *La Comédie humaine.* Ed. Marcel Bouteron. Paris: Bibliothèque de la Pléiade, 1949-65. Vol. 9: 954-88. See 'Iota.'

————. 'Avant-Propos.' *La Comédie humaine*. Vol. 1: 3-16.

————. 'Le Chef-d'œuvre inconnu.' *La Comédie humaine*. Vol. 9: 389-414.

————. *La Cousine Bette*. *La Comédie humaine*. Vol. 6: 135-524.

————. 'La Duchesse de Langeais.' *La Comédie humaine*. Vol. 5: 125-254.

————. 'La Fille aux yeux d'or.' *La Comédie humaine*. Vol. 5: 255-323.

————. *Histoire des Treize*. See 'La Duchesse de Langeais' and 'La Fille aux yeux d'or.'

————. *Illusions Perdues*. *La Comédie humaine*. Vol. 4: 464-1056.

————. 'Louis Lambert', 'Les proscrits', 'Jésus-Christ en Flandre'. Ed. Samuel S. de Sacy. Paris: Gallimard, 1980.

————. 'Maître Cornelius' [*sic*]. Trans. of 'Maître Cornélius.' *DUM* 3 (February-March, 1834): 129-48, 265-84.

————. 'Melmoth réconcilié.' *La Comédie humaine*. Vol. 9: 267-310.

————. *Le Peau de chagrin*. *La Comédie humaine*. Vol. 9: 11-249.

————. *Le Père Goriot*. Ed. Pierre Citron. Paris: Garnier-Flammarion, 1966.

————. *Séraphita*. *La Comédie humaine*. Vol. 10: 457-589.

————. *Splendeurs et misères des courtisanes*. *La Comédie humaine*. Vol. 5: 654-1148.

'Balzac—His Life and Career.' *DUM* 70 (1867): 363-76.

'Balzac—His Literary Labours.' *DUM* 70 (1867): 510-29.

Barthes, Roland. 'The Reality Effect.' *The Rustle of Language*. Trans Richard Howard. Berkeley: U of California P, 1989: 141-48.

Baudelaire, Charles. *Les Fleurs du mal*. Trans. Richard Howard. Boston: Godine, 1982.

Baudrillard, Jean. 'The Trompe-l'Oeil.' *Calligram: Essays on New Art History From France*. Ed. Norman Bryson. Cambridge: Cambridge UP, 1988: 53-62.

Bennett, Paula, and Vernon A. Rosario II. 'Introduction: The Politics of Solitary Pleasures.' *Solitary Pleasures: The Historical, Literary, and Aesthetic Discourses of Autoeroticism*. Ed. Bennett and Rosario. New York: Routledge, 1995: 1-17.

Berkeley, George. 'On the Roman Controversy, to Sir John James, Bart.' *The Works of George Berkeley, Bishop of Cloyne*. Ed. A. A. Luce and T. E. Jessop. London: Nelson, 1955. Vol. 7: 143-55.

Blake, William. *The Complete Poems*. Ed. W. H. Stevenson. London: Longman, 1989.

Böhme [Boehme], Jakob. *Mysterium Magnum; or, An exposition of the first book of Moses called Genesis. . . .* Trans. J. Ellistone and J. Sparrow. London, 1654. Repr. Ann Arbor: University Microfilms, 1964.

Bowen, Elizabeth, 'Introduction.' *Uncle Silas: A Tale of Bartram-Haugh*. London: Cresset, 1947: 7-23.

Brewster, Sir David. *Letters on Natural Magic: Addressed to Sir Walter Scott, Bart*. London: Murray, 1832.

Brontë, Charlotte. *Jane Eyre*. Ed. Michael Mason. London: Penguin, 1996.

————. *Villette*. Ed. Mark Lilly. Harmondsworth: Penguin, 1979.

Browne, Nelson. *Sheridan Le Fanu*. London: Arthur Barker, 1951.

Bryson, Norman. *Looking at the Overlooked: Four Essays on Still Life Painting*. Cambridge: Harvard UP, 1990.

Bunyan, John. *The Pilgrim's Progress*. Ed. N. H. Keeble. Oxford: Oxford UP, 1998.

Bürger, Gottfried August. 'Leonora.' Trans. J[ames] C[larence] M[angan]. *DUM* 28 (December, 1846): 656-63; also 'The Ballad of Leonore.' Trans J. C. Mangan. *DUM* 4 (October, 1834): 509-13.

Burke, Edmund. 'Letter to Richard Burke, Esq.' *The Works of the Right Honourable Edmund Burke*. Vol. 6. London: Bohn, 1856: 61-80.

————. 'Letter to Sir Hercules Langrishe, Bart., M. P. on the Subject of the Roman Catholics of Ireland, and the Propriety of Admitting Them to the Elective Franchise, Consistently with the Principles of the Constitution, as Established at the Revolution.' *The Works of the Right Honourable Edmund Burke*. Vol 3: 298-344.

————. *A Philosophical Enquiry into the Origin of Our Ideas of the Sublime and the Beautiful*. Ed. Adam Phillips. Oxford: Oxford UP, 1990.

————. *Reflections on the Revolution in France*. Ed. Conor Cruise O'Brien. London: Penguin, 1986.

Butt, Isaac ('Edward. S. O'Brien'). 'The Murdered Fellow.' Chapter 11 of *Chapters of College Romance*. *DUM* 5 (March, 1835): 332-52.

Carlyle, Thomas. 'Characteristics.' *Critical and Miscellaneous Essays*. Boston: Houghton Mifflin, 1881. Vol. 3: 5-48.

————. 'E. T. W. Hoffmann.' *German Romances: Translations From the German.* Vol. 2. New York: Scribners, 1898: 3-21.

————. *The French Revolution: A History.* Vol. 2. London: Dent, 1929.

————. *Sartor Resartus [and] On Heroes and Hero-Worship and the Heroic in History.* London: Dent, 1908.

Carroll, Lewis. *Alice in Wonderland* and *Through the Looking-Glass.* Ed. Roger Lancelyn Green. Oxford: Oxford UP, 1971.

Castle, Terry. *Masquerade and Civilization: The Carnivalesque in Eighteenth-Century English Culture and Fiction.* Stanford: Stanford UP, 1986.

————. 'Phantasmagoria and the Metaphorics of Modern Reverie.' *The Female Thermometer: Eighteenth-Century Culture and the Invention of the Uncanny.* New York: Oxford UP, 1995: 140-67.

————. 'The Spectralization of the Other in *The Mysteries of Udolpho*.' *The Female Thermometer*: 120-39.

Cavell, Stanley. 'The Uncanniness of the Ordinary.' *In Quest of the Ordinary: Lines of Skepticism and Romanticism.* Chicago: U of Chicago P, 1988: 153-78.

Clery, E. J. *The Rise of Supernatural Fiction, 1762-1800.* Cambridge: Cambridge UP, 1995.

Coleridge, Samuel Taylor. *Biographia Literaria.* Ed. James Engell and Walter Jackson Bate. Princeton: Princeton UP, 1983.

————. *The Complete Poems.* Ed. William Keach. London: Penguin, 1997.

Collins, Wilkie. 'The Lady of Glenwith Grange.' *Mad Monkton and Other Stories.* Ed. Norman Page. Oxford: Oxford UP, 1994: 165-94.

Conrad, Joseph. *The Collected Letters of Joseph Conrad.* Ed. Frederick R. Karl and Laurence Davies. Vol. 3. Cambridge: Cambridge UP, 1988.

————. *Heart of Darkness: An Authoritative Text, Backgrounds and Sources, Criticism.* Ed. Robert Kimbrough. Third Edition. New York: Norton, 1988.

————. *A Personal Record. The Mirror of the Sea* and *A Personal Record.* Ed. Morton Dauwen Zabel. Garden City: Anchor, 1960: 175-304.

————. *The Secret Agent: A Simple Tale.* Ed. Martin Seymour-Smith. Harmondsworth: Penguin, 1984.

Cornwell, Neil. *The Literary Fantastic: From Gothic to Postmodernism.* Hemel Hempstead: Harvester Wheatsheaf, 1990.

Coughlan, Patricia. 'Doubles, Shadows, Sedan-Chairs and the Past: The "Ghost Stories" of J. S. Le Fanu.'

Critical Approaches to Anglo-Irish Literature. Ed. Michael Allen and Angela Wilcox. Totowa: Barnes & Noble, 1989: 17-39, 171-2.

Crary, Jonathan. *Techniques of the Observer: On Vision and Modernity in the Nineteenth Century.* Cambridge, Mass.: MIT Press, 1990.

Deane, Seamus. *Strange Country: Modernity and Nationhood in Irish Writing Since 1790.* Oxford: Clarendon, 1997.

Defoe, Daniel. *Colonel Jack. [The History and Remarkable Life of the Truly Honourable Col. Jacque].* Ed. Samuel Holt Monk. Oxford: Oxford UP, 1989.

————. *Robinson Crusoe: Authoritative Text, Contexts, Criticism.* Ed. Michael Shinagel. New York: Norton, 1994.

————. 'A True Relation of the Apparition of One Mrs Veal.' *Romances and Narratives By Daniel Defoe.* Ed. George A. Aitken. London: Dent, 1895. Repr. New York: AMS, 1974. Vol. 15: 223-38.

De Quincey, Thomas. *Confessions of an English Opium Eater* in *Confessions of an English Opium-Eater and Other Writings.* Ed. Barry Milligan. London: Penguin, 2003: 3-88.

————. 'Suspiria de Profundis.' *Confessions of an English Opium-Eater and Other Writings*: 89-190.

Dickens, Charles. *David Copperfield: Authoritative Text, Backgrounds, Criticism.* Ed. Jerome H. Buckley. New York: Norton, 1990.

————. *Little Dorrit.* Ed. John Holloway. Harmondsworth: Penguin, 1967.

————. 'Nurse's Stories.' *The Uncommercial Traveller and Reprinted Pieces.* London: Oxford UP, 1958: 148-58.

————. *Oliver Twist.* Ed. Peter Fairclough. London: Penguin, 1985.

Dostoyevsky, Fyodor. *Crime and Punishment.* Trans. David Magarshack. New York: Penguin, n. d.

Eliot, T. S. *The Complete Poems and Plays, 1909-1950.* New York: Harcourt, Brace, 1952.

————. 'In Memoriam.' *Selected Essays.* London: Faber, 1951: 328-38.

Ellis, S. M. *Wilkie Collins, Le Fanu and Others.* New York: R. R. Smith, 1931.

Fanger, Donald. *Dostoevsky and Romantic Realism: A Study of Dostoevsky in Relation to Balzac, Dickens, and Gogol.* Chicago: U of Chicago P, 1967.

Ferris, Henry. See 'Herfner, Irys.'

Fielding, Henry. *Tom Jones: The Authoritative Text, Contemporary Reactions, Criticism.* Ed. Sheridan Baker. New York: Norton, 1995.

Fletcher, Angus. *Allegory: The Theory of a Symbolic Mode.* Ithaca: Cornell UP, 1964.

Foster, R. F. *Modern Ireland, 1600-1972.* New York: Penguin, 1989.

Foucault, Michel. *The History of Sexuality.* Vol. 1. *An Introduction.* Trans. Robert Hurley. New York: Vintage, 1990.

'French Novels and Novelists.' *DUM* 36 (1850): 349-57.

Freud, Sigmund. *Beyond the Pleasure Principle.* Ed. and trans. James Strachey. New York: Norton, 1989.

———. *The Interpretation of Dreams. The Standard Edition of the Complete Psychological Works of Sigmund Freud.* Trans. James Strachey. Vol. 4. London: The Hogarth Press, 1981.

———. 'The Uncanny.' *The Standard Edition of the Complete Psychological Works of Sigmund Freud,* Vol. 17: 217-56.

Furst, Lilian. *All is True: The Claims and Strategies of Realist Fiction.* Durham, NC: Duke UP, 1995.

Gallup, Jane. *Reading Lacan.* Ithaca: Cornell UP, 1985.

'Die Geistertodenglocke. The Ghost-Dead-Bell.' *DUM* 59 (1862): 473-79.

'Ghosts.' *DUM* 23 (1844): 264-65.

'A Glimpse of the Supernatural in the Nineteenth Century.' *DUM* 58 (1861): 620-29.

Gill, Richard. *Happy Rural Seat: The English Country House and the Literary Imagination.* New Haven: Yale UP, 1972.

Godwin, William. *Things As They Are, or, The Adventures of Caleb Williams.* Ed. Maurice Hindle. London: Penguin, 1988.

Goethe, Johann Wolfgang von. *Italian Journey.* Ed. Thomas P. Saine and Jeffrey L. Sammon. Trans. Robert R. Heitner. New York: Suhrkamp, 1989.

———. *Poems of Goethe.* Trans E. A. Bowring *et al.* Boston: Estes and Lauriat, 1883; repr. New York: Gordon Press, 1974.

'Goethe's Posthumous Works—No. 1. *Faust.*' *DUM* 2 (1833): 361-85.

Gombrich, E. H. *Art and Illusion: A Study in the Psychology of Visual Perception.* New York: Princeton UP, 1969.

Grootenboer, Hanneke. *The Rhetoric of Perspective: Realism and Illusionism in Seventeenth-Century Dutch Still-Life Painting.* Chicago: U of Chicago P, 2005.

Hall, Wayne E. *Dialogues in the Margin: A Study of the 'Dublin University Magazine'.* Washington, D. C.: The Catholic University of America P, 1999.

Heilman, Robert B. 'Charlotte Brontë's 'New' Gothic,' *From Jane Austen to Joseph Conrad.* Ed. Robert Rathburn and Martin Steinmann, Jr. Minneapolis: U of Minnesota P, 1958: 118-32.

Heller, Tamar. 'The Vampire in the House: Hysteria, Female Sexuality, and Female Knowledge in Le Fanu's "Carmilla".' *The New Nineteenth Century: Feminist Readings of Underread Victorian Fiction.* Wellesley Studies in Critical Theory, Literary History, and Culture, Vol. 10. New York: Garland, 1996: 77-95.

'Herfner, Irys' [Henry Ferris]. 'A Few More Words About Mesmerism—The State of Sleep-Waking.' *DUM* 24 (1844): 78-90.

———. 'German Ghosts and Ghost-Seers.' *DUM* 17 (1841): 32-51, 217-32.

———. 'Mesmerism.' *DUM* 23 (1844): 37-53, 286-301.

Hibbard, G. R. 'The Country House Poem of the Seventeenth Century.' *Journal of the Warburg and Courtauld Institutes* 109 (1956): 159-74.

Hoffmann, E. T. A. 'Automata.' Trans. Alexander Ewing. *Best Tales of Hoffmann.* Ed. E. F. Bleiler. New York: Dover, 1967: 71-103.

———. 'The Datura Fastuosa.—A Botanical Tale.' *DUM* 13 (1839): 707-27.

———. 'The Golden Pot.' Trans. Thomas Carlyle. *The Works of Thomas* Carlyle. Vol. 22. *German Romances.* New York: Scribner's, 1898: 23-114.

———. *'Princess Brambilla', 'The Golden Pot' and Other Tales.* Trans. Ritchie Robertson. Oxford: Oxford UP, 1992: 119-238.

———. 'The Sand-Man.' Trans. J. T. Bealby. *Best Tales of Hoffmann*: 183-214.

Hofstede de Groot, Cornelis. *A Catalogue Raisonné of the Most Eminent Dutch Painters of the Seventeenth Century.* Cambridge: Chadwick-Healy, 1976. Vol. 5: 309-418.

Hogarth, William. *Engravings By Hogarth.* Ed. Sean Shesgreen. New York: Dover, 1973.

Howe, Irving. *Politics and the Novel.* New York: Meridian, 1957.

Hugo, Victor, 'Préface.' *Cromwell.* Paris: Garnier-Flammarion, 1968: 61-109.

Hume, David. *A Treatise of Human Nature.* Ed. L. A. Selby-Bigge. Oxford: Clarendon Press, 1978.

Huxley, Thomas Henry. 'On the Physical Basis of Life.' *Methods and Results: Collected Essays.* Vol. 1. London: Macmillan, 1894: 130-65.

'Iota.' 'The Red Inn of Andernach: A Tale Within a Tale.' *DUM* 3 (June, 1834): 632-46; 4 (July, 1834): 79-98.

Iser, Wolfgang. 'The Reading Process: A Phenomenological Approach.' *Modern Criticism and Theory: A Reader.* Ed. David Lodge. London: Longman, 1988: 212-28.

James, Henry. *The Complete Notebooks of Henry James.* Ed. Leon Edel and Lyall H. Powers. New York: Oxford UP, 1987.

———. 'The Beast in the Jungle.' *Henry James: Complete Stories, 1898-1910.* New York: Library of America, 1996: 496-541.

———. 'The Liar.' *Henry James: Complete Stories, 1884-1891.* New York: Library of America, 1999: 321-71.

———. 'The Middle Years.' *Autobiography.* Ed. Frederick W. Dupee. New York: Criterion, 1956: 547-600.

———. *The Sacred Fount.* New York: Grove Press, 1979.

———. *The Turn of the Screw: An Authoritative Text, Backgrounds, and Criticism.* Ed. Robert Kimbrough. New York: Norton, 1966.

James, M. R. (ed.). *Madam Crowl's Ghost and Other Tales of Mystery by Joseph Sheridan Le Fanu.* London: G. Bell, 1924.

Jansen, G. 'Gottfried Schalcken.' *From Rembrandt to Vermeer: Seventeenth-Century Dutch Artists.* Ed. Jane Turner. Grove Dictionary of Art. New York: St. Martin's, 2000: 328-9.

Johnston, E. M. *Ireland in the Eighteenth Century.* Dublin: Macmillan, 1964.

Jonson, Ben. *The Complete Poems.* Ed. George Parfitt. New Haven: Yale UP, 1982.

Joyce, James. *A Portrait of the Artist as a Young Man.* Ed. Chester A. Anderson. New York: Viking, 1968.

———. *Ulysses.* Ed. Hans Walter Gabler. New York: Vintage, 1986.

Kelsall, Malcolm. *Literary Representations of the Irish Country House: Civilization and Savagery Under the Union.* New York: Palgrave Macmillan, 2003.

Kreilkamp, Vera. *The Anglo-Irish Novel and the Big House.* Syracuse: Syracuse UP, 1998.

Kristeva, Julia. *Powers of Horror: An Essay on Abjection.* Trans. Leon S. Roudiez. New York: Columbia UP, 1982.

Lacan, Jacques. *Écrits: A Selection.* Trans. Alan Sheridan. New York: Norton, 1977.

Lanyer, Aemilia. *The Poems of Aemilia Lanyer: Salve Deus Rex Judaeorum.* Ed. Susanne Woods. New York: Oxford UP, 1993.

Le Fanu Papers. National Library of Ireland. Microfilm P. 2594.

Lever, Charles ('the Editor'). 'Carl Stelling-the Painter of Dresden.' *DUM* 20 (July, 1842): 59-74.

Levin, Harry. *The Gates of Horn: A Study of Five French Realists.* New York: Oxford UP, 1966.

Lewis, Matthew G. (trans.). *The Bravo of Venice: A Romance.* New York: Arno, 1972.

———. *The Monk: A Romance.* Ed. Howard Anderson. Oxford: UP, 1973.

Locke, John. *An Essay Concerning Human Understanding.* Ed. Peter H. Nidditch. Oxford: Clarendon Press, 1975.

Lukács, Georg. *The Historical Novel.* Trans. Hannah and Stanley Mitchell. Boston: Beacon, 1963.

———. *Studies in European Realism.* New York: Grosset & Dunlap, 1964.

———. *The Theory of the Novel: A Historico-Philosophical Essay on the Forms of Great Epic Literature.* Cambridge, Mass.: M. I. T. Press, 1971.

Mc Cormack, W. J. *Dissolute Characters: Irish Literary History Through Balzac, Sheridan Le Fanu, Yeats and Bowen.* Manchester: Manchester UP, 1993.

———. *From Burke to Beckett: Ascendancy, Tradition and Betrayal in Literary History.* Cork: Cork UP, 1994.

———. Introduction. 'The Intellectual Revival.' *The Field Day Anthology of Irish Writing.* Ed. Seamus Deane *et al.* Derry: Field Day, 1991. Vol. 1: 1173-7.

———. Introduction. 'Irish Gothic and After.' *The Field Day Anthology of Irish Writing.* Vol. 2: 831-54.

———. 'Setting and Ideology: with Reference to the Fiction of Maria Edgeworth.' *Ancestral Voices: The Big House in Anglo-Irish Literature.* Ed. Otto Rauchbauer. Dublin: Lilliput Press, 1992: 33-60.

———. *Sheridan Le Fanu and Victorian Ireland.* Oxford: Oxford UP, 1980. Repr. as *Sheridan Le Fanu.* Stroud: Sutton, 1997.

McKeon, Michael. *The Origins of the English Novel, 1600-1740.* Baltimore: The Johns Hopkins UP, 1987.

Mangan, James Clarence ('The Out and Outer'). 'Chapters on Ghostcraft: Comprising some account of the life and Revelations of Madame Hauffe, the celebrated Wurtemberg Ghost-seeress.' *DUM* 19 (1842): 1-17

———. 'The Man in the Cloak: A Very German Story.' *The Collected Works of James Clarence Mangan: Prose.*

Ed. Jacques Chuto *et al.* Dublin: Irish Academic Press, 2002. Vol. 1, 1832-1839: 239-66.

————. 'The Thirty Flasks.' *The Collected Works of James Clarence Mangan: Prose.* Vol. 1, 1832-1839: 178-238.

Mann, Thomas. *Death in Venice: A New Translation, Backgrounds and Contexts, Criticism.* Ed., trans. Clayton Koelb. New York: Norton, 1994.

Marcus, Steven. *The Other Victorians: A Study of Sexuality and Pornography in Mid-Nineteenth-Century England.* New York: Basic Books, 1966.

Marvell, Andrew. *The Complete English Poems.* Ed. Elizabeth Story Donno. New York: St. Martin's, 1974.

Mastai. M. L. d'Otrange. *Illusion in Art: Trompe l'Œil: A History of Pictorial Illusionism.* New York: Abaris, 1975.

Matthiessen, F. O. *The James Family.* New York: Knopf, 1947.

Maturin, Charles. *Melmoth the Wanderer.* Ed. Douglas Grant. Oxford: Oxford UP, 1989.

Mayer, David III. *Harlequin in His Element: The English Pantomime, 1806-1836.* Cambridge, Mass.: Harvard UP, 1969.

Meisel, Martin. *Realizations: Narrative, Pictorial, and Theatrical Arts in Nineteenth-Century England.* Princeton, Princeton UP, 1983.

Melada, Ivan. *Sheridan Le Fanu.* Boston: Twayne, 1987.

Mellard, James M. *Using Lacan, Reading Fiction.* Urbana: U of Illinois P, 1991.

Milbank, Alison, *Daughters of the House: Modes of the Gothic in Victorian Fiction.* New York: St Martin's, 1992.

————. 'From the Sublime to the Uncanny: Victorian Gothic and Sensation Fiction.' *Gothic Origins and Innovations.* Spec. issue of *Costerus.* n. s. 91 (1994): 169-79.

Mill, John Stuart. *Autobiography.* London: Oxford UP, 1940.

————. 'Coleridge.' *Mill on Bentham and Coleridge.* Cambridge: Cambridge UP, 1980: 99-168.

————. *The Letters of John Stuart Mill.* Ed. Hugh S. R. Elliott. London: Longman, Green, 1910. Vol. 2.

Milman, Miriam. *Trompe-l'Œil Painting: The Illusions of Reality.* New York: Skira/Rizzoli, 1982.

Milton, John. *Paradise Lost: A Poem in Twelve Books.* Ed. Merritt Y. Hughes. Indianapolis: Odyssey, 1962.

'Miscellanea Mystica.' *DUM* 26 (1845): 175-86.

'More Ghosts; Old and New.' *DUM* 72 (1869): 395-407.

Molière, [Jean-Baptiste Poquelin]. *Molière's 'Tartuffe' or 'The Impostor.'* Trans. Christopher Hampton. London: Faber, 1984.

Moynahan, Julian. *The Anglo-Irish: The Literary Imagination in a Hyphenated Culture.* Princeton, Princeton UP, 1995.

'O'Brien, Edward S.' See Butt, Isaac.

'The Occult Sciences—Magic.' *DUM* 29 (1847): 28-42.

O'Donoghue, D. J. *The Life and Writings of James Clarence Mangan.* Dublin: Gill, 1897.

O'Neill, Patrick J. 'German Literature and the *Dublin University Magazine,* 1833-50: A Checklist and Commentary.' *Long Room* 14-15 (Autumn 1976-Spring 1977): 20-31.

'Out and Outer, The.' See Mangan, James Clarence.

Ovid, *Metamorphoses.* Trans Rolfe Humphries. Bloomington: Indiana UP, 1958.

Paine, Thomas. 'Common Sense.' *Political Writings.* Ed. Bruce Kuklick. Cambridge: Cambridge UP, 1-45.

Parsons, Coleman O. 'Ghost-Stories Before Defoe.' *Notes and Queries* 201 (July, 1956): 293-98.

Peterson, M. Jeanne. 'The Victorian Governess: Status Incongruence in Family and Society.' *Suffer and Be Still: Women in the Victorian Age.* Ed. Martha Vicinus. Bloomington: Indiana UP, 1972: 3-19.

Pope, Alexander. *The Poems of Alexander Pope.* Ed. John Butt. New Haven: Yale UP, 1963.

Praz, Mario, *Mnemosyne: A Parallel Between Literature and the Visual Arts.* Princeton: Princeton UP, 1970.

Pritchett, V. S. 'An Irish Ghost.' *The Living Novel.* New York: Reynal & Hitchcock, 1947: 104-8.

Radcliffe, Ann. *The Italian.* Ed. Frederick Garber. Oxford: Oxford UP, 1968.

————. *The Mysteries of Udolpho.* Ed. Bonamy Dobrée. Oxford: Oxford UP, 1970.

————. 'On the Supernatural in Poetry.' *Gothic Documents: A Sourcebook, 1700-1820.* Ed. E. J. Clery and Robert Miles. Manchester: Manchester UP, 2000: 163-72.

————*The Romance of the Forest.* Ed. Chloe Chard. Oxford: Oxford UP, 1999.

Reade, Charles. *Hard Cash.* New York: Thomas Crowell, n. d. 2 vols.

Richardson, Samuel. *Clarissa, or, The History of a Young Lady.* Ed. Angus Ross. Harmondsworth: Penguin, 1985.

———. *Pamela, or, Virtue Rewarded.* Ed. T. C. Duncan-Eaves and Ben D. Kimpel. Boston: Houghton Mifflin, 1971.

Richetti, John J. *Popular Fiction Before Richardson: Narrative Patterns, 1700-1739.* Oxford: Clarendon, 1992.

Riddell, [Charlotte Elizabeth], 'Nut Bush Farm.' *The Collected Ghost Stories of Mrs. J. H. Riddell.* New York: Dover, 1977: 1-31.

Roop, Kel. 'Making Light in the Shadow Box: The Artistry of Le Fanu.' *Papers on Language and Literature* 21 (1985): 359-69.

S. F. 'Divination, Witchcraft, and Mesmerism.' *DUM* 38 (1851): 687-707.

Sadleir, Michael. *Dublin University Magazine: Its History, Contents and Bibliography.* Dublin, 1938.

Sage, Victor. *Horror Fiction in the Protestant Tradition.* New York: St. Martin's, 1988.

———. *Le Fanu's Gothic: The Rhetoric of Darkness.* Houndmills: Palgrave, 2004.

———. 'Resurrecting the Regency: Horror and Eighteenth-Century Comedy in Le Fanu's Fiction.' *Victorian Gothic: Literary and Cultural Manifestations in the Nineteenth Century.* Ed. Ruth Robbins and Julian Wolfreys. Houndmills: Palgrave, 2000: 12-30.

Scott, Sir Walter, *Old Mortality.* Ed. Angus Calder. Harmondsworth: Penguin, 1982.

———. 'The Tapestried Chamber.' *The Two Drovers and Other Stories.* Ed. Graham Tulloch. Oxford: Oxford UP, 1987: 310-31.

Sedgwick, Eve Kosofsky. *The Coherance of Gothic Conventions.* New York: Methuen, 1986.

Shelley, Mary. *Frankenstein, or, The Modern Prometheus.* Ed. M. K. Joseph. London: Oxford UP, 1969.

Shelley, Percy Bysshe. 'A Defence of Poetry.' *Shelley's Poetry and Prose: Authoritative Texts, Criticism.* Second Edition. Ed. Donald H. Reiman and Neil Fraistat. New York: Norton, 2002: 509-35.

Sidney, Philip. *An Apology for Poetry, or, The Defence of Poesy.* Ed. Geoffrey Shepherd. London: Nelson, 1965.

'Spiritualism.' *DUM* 60 (July 1862): 1-13.

Stafford, Barbara Maria, and Frances Terpak. *Devices of Wonder: From the World in a Box to Images on a Screen.* Los Angeles: Getty Publications, 2002.

Stallknecht, Newton P. *Strange Seas of Thought: Studies in William Wordsworth's Philosophy of Man and Nature.* Bloomington: U of Indiana P, 1958.

Starr, George. 'Why Defoe Probably Did Not Write *The Apparition of Mrs Veal*'. *Eighteenth-Century Fiction* 15 (April-July, 2003): 421-50.

Stephen, Leslie. 'De Foe's Novels.' *Hours in a Library.* London: Smith, Elder, 1892. Vol. 1: 1-46.

Sterne, Laurence. *Tristram Shandy: An Authoritative Text, The Author on the Novel, Criticism.* Ed. Howard Anderson. New York: Norton, 1980.

Stoichita, Victor I. *The Self-Aware Image: An Insight into Early Modern Meta-Painting.* Trans. Anne-Marie Glasheen. Cambridge: Cambridge UP, 1997.

Stoker, Bram. *Dracula: Authoritative Text, Contexts, Reviews and Reactions, Dramatic and Film Variations.* Ed. Nina Auerbach and David J. Skal. New York: Norton, 1997.

'Stories of Second Sight and Apparition.' *DUM* 3 (1834): 547-59.

'The Style of Balzac and Thackeray.' *DUM* 64 (1864): 620-27.

Swedenborg, Emanuel. *Arcana Cœlestia.* 12 Vols. Trans. John Faulkner Potts. New York: Swedenborg Foundation, 1951-56.

———. *Heaven and its Wonders and Hell From Things Seen and Heard* [*Heaven and Hell*]. Trans. J. C. Ager. New York: Swedenborg Foundation, 1952.

Tanner, Tony, 'Introduction.' *Villette.* Harmondsworth: Penguin, 1979: 7-51.

Thackeray, William Makepeace. *Vanity Fair: A Novel Without a Hero.* Ed. Geoffrey and Kathleen Tillotson. Boston: Houghton Mifflin, 1963.

Thomas, Keith. *Religion and the Decline of Magic.* New York: Oxford UP, 1997.

Thomas, Tammis Elise. 'Masquerade Liberties and Female Power.' *The Haunted Mind: The Supernatural in Victorian Literature.* Ed. Elton E. Smith and Robert Haas. Lanham, Md.: Scarecrow Press, 1999.

Tracy, Robert. 'Loving You All Ways: Vamps, Vampires, Necrophiles and Necrofilles in Nineteenth-Century Fiction.' *Sex and Death in Victorian Literature.* Ed. Regina Barreca. Bloomington: Indiana UP, 1990: 32-59.

Veeder, William. '"Carmilla": The Arts of Repression.' *Texas Studies in Literature and Language* 22 (1980): 197-223

Walton, James. '"The Liar" and Le Fanu.' *Short Story* 12: 2 (Fall, 2004): 97-104.

———. 'The Romance of Gentility: Defoe's Heroes and Heroines.' *Literary Monographs* 4. Ed. Eric Rothstein. Madison: U of Wisconsin P, 1971: 89-135.

Watt, Ian. *The Rise of the Novel: Studies in Defoe, Richardson and Fielding.* Berkeley: U of California P, 1959.

Wilde, Oscar. 'The Critic as Artist.' See *The Picture of Dorian Gray.*

———. *The Picture of Dorian Gray: Authoritative Texts, Backgrounds, Reviews and Reactions, Criticism.* Ed. Donald L. Lawler. New York: Norton, 1988. This collection includes an excerpt from 'The Critic as Artist': 313-19.

Wilkinson, Robin. '"Schalken the Painter"/Le Fanu the Writer.' *Études Anglaises* 56: 3 (July-September 2003): 275-84.

Williams, Anne. *Art of Darkness: A Poetics of Gothic.* Chicago: U of Chicago P, 1995.

Yeats, W. B. *The Collected Poems of W. B. Yeats.* New York: Macmillan, 1959.

Zschokke, Heinrich. *The Bravo of Venice: A Romance.* See Lewis, Matthew G. (trans.).

FURTHER READING

Criticism

Bown, Nicola, Carolyn Burdett, and Pamela Thurschwell, eds. *The Victorian Supernatural.* Cambridge: Cambridge University Press, 2004, 305 p.

Collection of essays that explore various aspects of literary supernaturalism in mid- to late nineteenth-century English writing, including that of Charles Dickens, George Eliot, and Robert Browning.

Briggs, Julia. *Night Visitors: The Rise and Fall of the English Ghost Story.* London: Faber, 1977, 238 p.

Traces the literary and cultural history of the ghost story from its beginnings in the writings of Lucian to its apex during the Victorian era and the eventual loss of interest among readers.

———. "The Ghost Story." In *A Companion to the Gothic,* edited by David Punter, pp. 122-31. Oxford: Blackwell, 2000.

Discusses the ghost story within the broader context of the Gothic.

Downey, Dara. "'The Dead Woman in the Wallpaper': Interior Decorating and Domestic Disturbance in the American Ghost Story." In *Death Becomes Her: Cultural Narratives of Femininity and Death in Nineteenth-*

Century America, edited by Elizabeth Dill and Sheri Weinstein, pp. 37-56. Cambridge, England: Cambridge Scholars Publishing, 2008.

Explores the significance of domestic objects in ghost stories written by nineteenth-century American women.

Frank, Michael C. "Photographing Ghosts: Ancestral Reproduction and Daguerreotypic Mimesis in Nathaniel Hawthorne's *The House of the Seven Gables.*" *Litteraria Pragensia* 17, no. 34 (December 2007): 40-57.

Discusses Hawthorne's use of daguerreotypes in *The House of the Seven Gables* as a device to "reveal hidden aspects of reality."

Gentile, Kathy Justice. "Supernatural Transmissions: Turn-of-the-Century Ghosts in American Women's Fiction: Jewett, Freeman, Wharton, and Gilman." In *Approaches to Teaching Gothic Fiction: The British and American Traditions,* edited by Diane Long Hoeveler and Tamar Heller, pp. 208-14. New York: Modern Language Association of America, 2003.

Explores the question of why the ghost story genre experienced a surge in popularity among prominent American women writers in the 1890s.

Harris, Sally. "Spiritual Warnings: The Ghost Stories of Joseph Sheridan Le Fanu." *Victorians Institute Journal* 31 (2003): 9-39.

Explains Le Fanu's interest in spiritualism and the ways in which it manifested itself in his short stories.

Knight, Mark. "'The Haunted and the Haunters': Bulwer Lytton's Philosophical Ghost Story." *Nineteenth-Century Contexts* 28, no. 3 (September 2006): 245-55.

Finds that Edward Bulwer Lytton's short story "The Haunted and the Haunters; or, The House and the Brain" explored many of the most pressing scientific and philosophical questions of the Victorian era.

Lustig, T. J. *Henry James and the Ghostly.* Cambridge: Cambridge University Press, 1994, 317 p.

Argues that ghosts and ghostliness were significant not just as plot devices in James's stories in the genre but also served to inform the "great dynamic forces" that run through the entire body of his work.

Martin, Carol A. "Gaskell's Ghosts: Truths in Disguise." *Studies in the Novel* 21, no. 1 (spring 1989): 27-40.

Analyzes the similarities between realist and supernatural fictions of Elizabeth Gaskell.

Miall, David S. "Designed Horror: James's Vision of Evil in *The Turn of the Screw.*" *Nineteenth-Century Fiction* 39, no. 3 (December 1984): 305-27.

Contends that James intended the apparitions in *The Turn of the Screw* to be taken literally as actual ghosts, and that this literal reading does not contradict his ambivalence toward the existence of the supernatural.

Nałęcz-Wojtczak, Jolanta. "Joseph Sheridan Le Fanu and New Dimensions for the English Ghost Story." In *Literary Interrelations: Ireland, England and the World,* edited by Wolfgang Zach and Heinz Kosok, pp. 193-98. Tübingen, Germany: Gunter Narr Verlag, 1987.

Contends that Le Fanu's uniquely Irish ghost stories were precursors to the Freudian-influenced psychological ghost stories of the later nineteenth and early twentieth centuries.

Schaper, Susan E. "Victorian Ghostbusting: Gendered Authority in the Middle-Class Home." *Victorian Newsletter,* no. 100 (fall 2001): 6-13.

Finds that Victorian haunted house stories have much to reveal about gender dynamics and "gendered constructions of cultural power" that existed at the time.

Smajic, Srdjan. "The Trouble with Ghost-Seeing: Vision, Ideology, and Genre in the Victorian Ghost Story." *ELH* 70, no. 4 (winter 2003): 1107-35.

Relates the proliferation of ghost stories in the nineteenth century to the Victorian fixation on sight and the visual.

Smith, Elton E., and Robert Haas, eds. *The Haunted Mind: The Supernatural in Victorian Literature.* Lanham, Md.: Scarecrow Press, 1999, 139 p.

Anthology of essays that address Victorian supernatural literature from a variety of disciplines and theoretical viewpoints, including Marxist, feminist, and poststructuralist.

Stiffler, Muriel W. *The German Ghost Story as Genre.* New York: Peter Lang, 1993, 166 p.

Defines the characteristics of the ghost story as it appears in the German literary tradition and questions whether it exists as an independent literary genre.

Weinstock, Jeffrey Andrew. "Female-Authored Gothic Tales in the Nineteenth-Century Popular Press." In *Popular Nineteenth-Century American Women Writers and the Literary Marketplace,* edited by Earl Yarington and Mary De Jong, pp. 74-96. Newcastle: Cambridge Scholars Publishing, 2007.

Examines the ways in which American women writers of the nineteenth century appropriated aspects of the Victorian Gothic sensibility to created a new type of popular protest literature.

———. *Scare Tactics: Supernatural Fiction by American Women.* New York: Fordham University Press, 2008, 228 p.

Examines the various metaphorical meanings lent by supernatural plot elements to fiction by American women writers, including works by Edith Wharton, Harriet Beecher Stowe, Mary E. Wilkins Freeman, and Charlotte Perkins Gilman.

Women and Medicine

The following entry provides criticism on subjects pertaining to women and medicine in nineteenth-century literature.

INTRODUCTION

Prior to the nineteenth century, day-to-day medical issues were traditionally handled in the domestic sphere by women. With most physicians residing a great distance from their largely rural patients, even wealthy households typically relied on the knowledge of either the female head or servant to address matters of health unless the illness was deemed serious enough to summon the doctor. Professional nurses also served communities in the absence of physicians, and midwives presided over the majority of births. Recipes for home remedies were passed down through generations of women and, because so many treatments and cures were herbal or food-based, medical advice naturally became featured, alongside recipes and cleaning tips, in the popular household manuals published and widely read by women, such as *The Compleat Housewife,* written by Mrs. E. Smith in 1742, and *The Maternal Physician,* written by an anonymous "American Matron" (now known to have been Mary Palmer Tyler) in 1818. However, beginning around the 1830s—coinciding roughly with the Victorian era in Great Britain, a strong influence upon the culture of the United States at the time—the official practice of medicine began to evolve from a mostly homeopathic enterprise learned through apprenticeship to a professional vocation that demanded a formal university education. Women doctors were already a rarity, primarily because girls were not, for the most part, groomed for college entrance. In the early years of the Victorian period, the professionalization of medicine took an even more pronounced turn against women, in large part because of the growing notion that medical practice, or even medical study, ran counter to the fundamental norms of womanly behavior and psychology. These norms were outlined in and popularized by an 1854 poem by Coventry Patmore, "The Angel in the House," which posited that women were by nature passive, self-sacrificing, and possessed of physical, emotional, and spiritual purity. Likewise, "conduct books," some written by women, began to appear, which purported to teach women how to attain the angel ideal. Maintaining that the study and practice of medicine required a strong stomach and level head, advocates of the "Angel in the House" model of womanhood insisted

that females would be damaged—and even "unsexed"—by such activities. Later, the American physician Dr. Edward H. Clarke argued in his 1873 treatise *Sex in Education* that any kind of formal schooling was inappropriate for girls after they entered puberty, because intellectual activity, especially during menstruation, caused atrophy of the uterus and ovaries, sterilization, masculinization, and insanity. British observers agreed that women were unfit for medical practice, with one male physician writing in the noted medical journal *Lancet* that women who hoped to become doctors were guilty of a "horrible and vicious attempt deliberately to unsex themselves." Women's role was as wife and mother, not doctor.

In response to this line of thought, proponents of a newly strengthened women's movement demanded not only education but suffrage. In the United States, women began to establish their own medical schools, beginning with the New England Female Medical College in 1848. The English-born Elizabeth Blackwell was the first woman to earn a medical degree in the United States, from New York's Geneva College, in 1849. In 1857 Blackwell, along with her sister Emily and Dr. Maria Zakrzewska, a Polish-born German physician, opened the New York Infirmary for Indigent Women and Children. Zakrzewska went on to found, in 1862, the New England Hospital for Women and Children, which was the first hospital in Boston, Massachusetts. Women like Blackwell and Zakrzewska, however, performed much of their work with little support from the male medical establishment. Florence Nightingale, on the other hand, was possibly the best-known and most-admired exception to the widely held notion that medical practice was adverse to women's health and wellness. A Victorian-era nurse, educator, and statistician, Nightingale was held up as an example of the purity and selflessness of women despite her practice of medicine in part because she never married and instead devoted her entire life to caring for others. Becoming outraged over the lack of medical services available to British soldiers during the Crimean War (1853-56), Nightingale took a staff of volunteer nurses to Turkey to set up better facilities. Later, she helped train American women to work as nurses during the Civil War (1861-65). Nightingale and Blackwell opened the Women's Medical College in London in 1869. Unlike many of the women in her time who aspired to become physicians, Nightingale was not, at least in extant sources, excoriated or accused of "unsexing" herself for the sake of her job. Some of the women who did become physicians in the Victorian era found a dearth of information on gynecology, sexuality, and pregnancy available to women and took it upon themselves to publish educational pamphlets and books. The perceived delicacy of these topics meant that their authors straddled a difficult line between presenting information accurately and authoritatively and maintaining an air of propriety in a highly restrictive society. Some fiction writers of the time did, nevertheless, take up the cause of women in medicine. In 1877 Charles Reade fictionalized the attempts of Sophia Jex-Blake, one of Britain's first female physicians, to enter medical school and earn a degree in his sensationalized popular novel *A Woman-Hater*. In the United States a number of well-known writers published novels with female protagonists who were doctors, including *Dr. Breen's Practice* (1881) by William Dean Howells, *A Country Doctor* (1884) by Sarah Orne Jewett, and *The Bostonians* (1886) by Henry James.

The changing nature of medicine in the nineteenth century coincided with both the perception of women as naturally fragile and with a spate of illnesses that would come to define the century medically, socially, and aesthetically, especially for women—most notably tuberculosis and a variety of mental illnesses both real and imagined. A deadly airborne disease that attacks the lungs, tuberculosis was known during the nineteenth century as consumption and was closely associated with writers and artists because it was believed to produce bursts of creativity in its victims. It also came to be associated in the later part of the century with ideals of female beauty, as sufferers were marked by extremely pale skin and enlarged eyes. Additionally, the majority of tuberculosis victims were women of childbearing age, making it the most common killer of women at the time. But it was the mental condition generally categorized as "neurasthenia" from which women, both real and fictional, would suffer most particularly. Unable to fulfill the Angel in the House expectation or to escape the notion that they were ruled by their biology, some women did simply collapse into depression, while others may have been pushed into it by well-meaning but misguided male physicians who prescribed a regimen of complete cessation of physical and intellectual activity known as the "rest cure." Because intellectual stimulation, and especially the act of novel-reading, was believed to account for a wide variety of female illnesses, women frequently were denied access to reading—or writing, if they were creatively inclined—materials under doctors' orders. The best-known literary work detailing the negative effects of the rest cure is Charlotte Perkins Gilman's 1892 short story "The Yellow Wallpaper," in which a woman's physician husband confines her to a bedroom after diagnosing her with depression and hysteria. Unable even to walk freely around the house, she gradually becomes obsessed with the patterns in the yellow wallpaper in her room and goes

mad. Invalidism became the catch-all condition of undefined illness among middle- and upper-class women who were essentially incapacitated by boredom and lack of activity. Further, cultural and medical rhetoric considered women to be "natural invalids"—frail, overly excitable beings who were, contradictorily, at their best and most natural when they were in a state of chronic illness doing nothing at all. Both Nathaniel Hawthorne and Edgar Allan Poe were ambivalent about this notion of womanhood, and both attempted to address the figure of the woman invalid in their works, notably *The Blithedale Romance* (1852) and "Rappaccini's Daughter" (1844) by Hawthorne, and "Ligeia" (1838) by Poe. The confluence of feminine perfection and illness was particularly striking in writings about children. In *Jane Eyre* (1847), Charlotte Brontë contrasts the illness and death of the saintly Helen Burns with the robustness of the title character, who is rebellious and difficult, while the death of Beth March in Louisa May Alcott's *Little Women* (1868-69) likewise teaches her sister Jo to be more patient, gentle, and feminine. Washington Irving's *Biography and Poetical Remains of the Late Margaret Miller Davidson* (1841) tells the life story of the American child poet Margaret Miller Davidson, who died of tuberculosis shortly before her sixteenth birthday. Always a sickly child, Davidson was discouraged from reading and writing despite her talents because doctors believed the effort brought on episodes of illness. Margaret, like her fictional counterparts Helen and Beth, is portrayed by Irving as exemplifying the tenets of angelic womanhood, suffering, like so many other Victorian women, for her goodness and purity.

REPRESENTATIVE WORKS

Louisa May Alcott
Hospital Sketches (sketches) 1863
Little Women; or, Meg, Jo, Beth and Amy. 2 vols. (novel) 1868-69

George Gardiner Alexander
Dr. Victoria: A Picture from the Period. 3 vols. (novel) 1881

Charlotte Brontë
Jane Eyre: An Autobiography. 3 vols. [as Jane Eyre, edited as Currer Bell] (novel) 1847
Shirley: A Tale. 3 vols. [as Currer Bell] (novel) 1849

Emily Brontë
Wuthering Heights. 2 vols. [as Ellis Bell] (novel) 1847

Fanny Burney
The Wanderer, or Female Difficulties. 3 vols. (novel) 1814

Memoirs of Dr. Burney, Arranged from His Own Manuscripts, from Family Papers, and from Personal Recollections. 3 vols. (nonfiction) 1832

Lydia Maria Child
The Mother's Book (nonfiction) 1831

Edward H. Clarke
Sex in Education: A Fair Chance for Girls (essay) 1873

Wilkie Collins
The Dead Secret. 2 vols. (novel) 1857

Henry Curwen
Dr. Hermione (novel) 1890

Arthur Conan Doyle
"The Doctors of Hoyland" (short story) 1894; published in journal *Idler*

Maria Edgeworth
Belinda. 3 vols. (novel) 1801

Anne Elliot
Dr. Edith Romney. 3 vols. [anonymous] (novel) 1883

Gustave Flaubert
Madame Bovary, mours de province. 2 vols. [*Madame Bovary: A Tale of Provincial Life*] (novel) 1857

Elizabeth Gaskell
Cousin Phillis: A Tale (novella) 1864

Charlotte Perkins Gilman
"The Yellow Wallpaper" (short story) 1892; published in journal *New England Magazine*

Nathaniel Hawthorne
"The Birth-mark" (short story) 1843; published in journal *Pioneer*
"Rappaccini's Daughter" (short story) 1844; published in journal *United States Magazine and Democratic Review*
The Blithedale Romance (novel) 1852

William Dean Howells
Dr. Breen's Practice (novel) 1881

Therese Huber
Luise: Ein Beitrag zur Geschichte der Konvenienz [as Ludwig Ferdinand Huber] (novel) 1796

Washington Irving
Biography and Poetical Remains of the Late Margaret Miller Davidson (biography) 1841

Henry James
The Bostonians. 3 vols. (novel) 1886

Sarah Orne Jewett
A Country Doctor (novel) 1884

Sophia Jex-Blake
"Medicine as a Profession for Women" (speech) 1869

Harriet Martineau
Deerbrook. 2 vols. (novel) 1839

Henry Maudsley
The Physiology and Pathology of Mind (nonfiction) 1867

Annie Nathan Meyer
Helen Brent, M.D. (novel) 1891

Florence Nightingale
Notes on Nursing: What It Is and What It Is Not (nonfiction) 1860

Elizabeth Stuart Phelps
Doctor Zay (novel) 1882

Edgar Allan Poe
"Ligeia" (short story) 1838; published in journal *American Museum*
"Life in Death" (short story) 1842; published in journal *Graham's Magazine*; revised as "The Oval Portrait," 1845
"The Philosophy of Composition" (essay) 1846; published in journal *Graham's Magazine*

Charles Reade
A Woman-Hater (novel) 1877

Johanna Schopenhauer
Gabriele. 3 vols. (novel) 1819-20
Die Tante. 2 vols. (novel) 1823

Herbert Spencer
The Principles of Biology. 2 vols. (nonfiction) 1864-67
The Study of Sociology (nonfiction) 1873

Margaret Todd
Mona Maclean: Medical Student [as Graham Travers] (novel) 1894

Thomas Trotter
View of the Nervous Temperament (essay) 1807

Mary Palmer Tyler
The Maternal Physician [anonymous] (nonfiction) 1818

Ellen Wood
East Lynne [as Mrs. Henry Wood] (novel) 1861

OVERVIEWS

Diane Price Herndl (essay date 1993)

SOURCE: Herndl, Diane Price. "(Super)'Natural' Invalidism: Male Writers and the Mind/Body Problem." In *Invalid Women: Figuring Feminine Illness in American Fiction and Culture, 1840-1940,* pp. 75-109. Chapel Hill: University of North Carolina Press, 1993.

[*In the following essay, Herndl explores the response of nineteenth-century American male writers to the changing view of women by the medical establishment, notably the belief that activities of the mind necessarily—and generally negatively—affected the health of the body.*]

> Now, never losing sight of the object of supremeness, or perfection, at all points, I asked myself—"Of all melancholy topics, what, according to the *universal* understanding of mankind, is the *most* melancholy?" . . . The death . . . of a beautiful woman is, unquestionably, the most poetical topic in the world.
>
> —Edgar Allan Poe, "The Philosophy of Composition" (1846)

> But Nature's got rules and Nature's got laws
>
> —Laurie Anderson, "Monkey's Paw" (1990)

Few texts so relentlessly celebrate the feminine invalid as Washington Irving's *Biography and Poetical Remains of the Late Margaret Miller Davidson* (1841). Margaret, a tubercular child poet, died just a few months short of her sixteenth birthday, a victim of the same disease that had, fourteen years earlier, claimed her older sister Lucretia (who was, herself, a famous poet). The biography is usually ignored in the Irving corpus. When it is noticed, the criticism is usually derisive. Stanley T. Williams, Irving's 1935 biographer, one of the few critics to even mention the *Biography,* calls it a "sweet confection" that is "the ultimate of the sentimental tendency in him and probably his worst piece of writing" (*The Life of Washington Irving,* 108). Expressing his incredulity over a passage of the biography, Williams considers whether "such idiocies [are] a devastating proof that Irving had gone quite to seed" but concludes that "Irving was not a mawkish donkey; it is rather that he understood certain emotional criteria of the age" (110). But Irving's contemporaries reacted to it quite positively: Edgar Allan Poe, reviewing it in *Graham's*

Magazine, heaped great praise on the biography (despite his doubts about Margaret's poetical abilities), writing, "Few books have interested us more profoundly" (93).

The biography may be too sentimental for the cynical tastes of late twentieth-century readers, but it was extremely popular in its time; it went through eleven editions between 1841 and 1857. The biography is actually a collaborative text, written by Irving who borrowed heavily from the notes given him by Margaret's mother, herself an invalid (Irving describes his meeting with her: "She was feeble and emaciated, and supported by pillows in an easy chair, but there were the lingerings of grace and beauty in her form and features" [10]). It represents an interesting blend of the sentimental and the romantic. Margaret's mother describes her as what we would recognize as a Little Eva figure, sent as a Christian exemplar to the world, and Irving describes her as a type of the doomed artist. In the intersection between these two voices we can read the struggle between these two discourses.

THE DOMESTIC AND THE ROMANTIC (SUPER)NATURAL

The struggle between discourses is staged in the question of what Margaret's life had meant; that is, whether the world was better off for her poetry or would have been a better place had she lived—for, within the medical model of closed energy, her health and her writing are considered completely inimical. On his first meeting with Margaret, Irving had cautioned her mother "against fostering her poetic vein" after he had seen that she was "prone to the same feverish excitement of the mind" as her sister had been (10). The next time he sees Margaret, three years later, he notices that the interval had "rapidly developed the powers of her mind, and heightened the loveliness of her person, but [his] apprehensions had been verified. The soul was wearing out the body" (11). The whole biography is dedicated to tracing the battles between Margaret's mind and her body, documenting the alterations in her health and her intellect. When she is writing poetry, she is happy but her body wastes away; when she agrees to stop her diligent studies (she teaches herself the classical languages and French and reads world history as well as world literature voraciously) and her writing, her health improves but she becomes despondent.

Irving turns the narration of Margaret's death entirely over to her mother, Mrs. Davidson, quoting at great length a letter she wrote to Catharine M. Sedgwick when Margaret had died. (Sedgwick had befriended the family years earlier when she wrote Lucretia's biography.) In the course of this letter, the sentimental vision becomes the clearest. Mrs. Davidson sets the scene and outlines the powerful lesson to be learned from Margaret's example:

Oh, my dear madam, the whole course of her decline was so unlike any other deathbed scene I ever witnessed; there was nothing of the gloom of a sick chamber; a charm was in and around her; a holy light seemed to pervade every thing belonging to her. There was a sacredness, if I may so express it, which seemed to tell the presence of the Divinity. . . . My dear Miss Sedgwick, how I have felt my own littleness, my total unworthiness, when compared with this pure, this high-souled, intellectual, yet timid, humble child; bending at the altar of her God, and pleading for pardon and acceptance in his sight, and grace to assist her in preparing for eternity.

(144)

At the end of the letter, Mrs. Davidson refers to Margaret as her "angel child" and describes a packet of papers she had found, sewn together (like Emily Dickinson's "fascicles" would be), which contained Margaret's religious self-examinations. Although they are "of too sacred a nature to meet the public eye," we are told that they are evidence of "a heart chastened and subdued by the power of divine grace" (151).

Mrs. Davidson's narrative concentrates on Margaret's holiness, her bravery, and her dedication to making her family happy. When she mentions Margaret's poetry, it is always a kind of domestic poetry that she celebrates—a poem dedicated to Mrs. Davidson herself about the powers of motherhood, or a poem that contrasts worldly fame (as a poet) and heavenly happiness, finding the former greatly lacking. For Mrs. Davidson, Margaret's poetry makes her different, but it is her piety, her kindness, and her bravery that make her exceptional and notable. Her implicit argument is that Margaret's death is linked to her holiness, a visible sign of it and a means to its propagation in the world.

Irving's interest in Margaret is poetical. He is by no means antithetical to Mrs. Davidson's position, but when the narrative shifts to the domestic or the sentimental, he leaves the text in her words.[1] But when he turns to Margaret's work or her poetry, he resumes control of the narration. When Irving narrates, his attention is focused on her reading, her relationship to nature, and her writing. He dwells on her precocious storytelling, her quickness to learn, the diversity of her reading. Throughout, however, he evinces the worry that such efforts were making her more interesting and attractive at the same time that they were killing her: "Her highest pleasures were intellectual," he writes, but he notes that "it was necessary to keep her in check, lest a too intense pursuit of knowledge should impair her delicate constitution" (20-21).

For Irving, Margaret represents the romantic, tubercular artist, a kind of female John Keats whose intellectual and poetical brilliance literally *consumes* her body.[2] While Mrs. Davidson concentrates on Margaret's pos-

session by the Holy Spirit, Irving concentrates on her possession by a poetic spirit. He writes of the "almost unearthly lustre of her eye" (11) and her "premature blossomings of poetic fancy" (18).

Periodically, Margaret is told to halt her studies and her writing (she is "especially warned" about the "exciting exercise of the pen" [65]), and she does, to the apparent benefit of her physical condition, but she finally cannot restrain her need to write and in every case ends up back at work. And in every case, this return to work is accompanied by a worsening of her physical condition: "A few weeks of this intellectual excitement was followed by another rupture of a blood-vessel in the lungs, and a long interval of extreme debility" (69). What is striking about Irving's contribution to the *Biography* is his absolute wonder at the intimate connection between mind and body. He completely accepts the medical model of closed energy and the need to maintain balance but without the medical sense of the girl's guilt for exciting "bad natural tendencies." He seems to accept Margaret's death as her tragic destiny as a poet and even sees it as evidence that she was a poet.

Irving's attitude toward the female child-poet offers us a way into an exploration of Poe's and Hawthorne's representations of invalid women and is suggestive of a mid-nineteenth-century belief system in which questions of mind and body, agency and subjectivity, gender roles and "separate spheres," come into complex interaction. The doubled discourse of the *Biography*—with its narration by both Mrs. Davidson and Washington Irving—is more obviously contradictory than that we will see in Poe's and Hawthorne's work but is indicative of a doubleness we will encounter in all of their writings about female invalids.

Despite the rigid distinction that has been made in American literary criticism between "domestic" or "sentimental" and "romantic" writers, American authors during the mid-nineteenth century were all responding to the same cultural situation, and often in very similar ways, as the example of Washington Irving's and Mrs. Davidson's collaboration demonstrates. But while chapter 2 focused on women writers, this chapter takes up the male response to the changing discourses on medicine and women. The women in Edgar Allan Poe's and Nathaniel Hawthorne's fiction are a particularly sickly lot. These male writers adopted the cultural and medical figure of the invalid woman and, as Poe reveals in "The Philosophy of Composition," elevated her death to the status of the "most poetical" subject. Nowhere does she appear more often than in Poe's stories, and nowhere is she as consistently placed in the context of science and art than in Nathaniel Hawthorne's tales. Scrutinizing the shape of her figure in several short texts—"Ligeia" and "The Oval Portrait" (Poe), "The Birthmark" and "Rappaccini's Daughter" (Hawthorne)—and in a longer work by Hawthorne—*The Blithedale Romance*—will illuminate why the invalid woman became so firmly established in the fiction of male writers at mid-century.[3]

I have separated Stowe, Southworth, and Bullard from male writers here not because I have chosen to privilege either set of writers or because I agree with the critical segregation that has occurred in the past but because the male and female authors in the mid-nineteenth century had different ideological agendas. While women writers were trying to set out a place in the culture where their worth could be established and their value(s) upheld, male writers found themselves with the need to reassess their own roles in the culture and their relationships to women, to women's work, and to their own work. The fundamental reorganization of culture suggested by both domesticity and feminism made the question of what men were to do problematic. For example, as Jane Tompkins argues in *Sensational Designs,* Stowe's *Uncle Tom's Cabin* leaves "groom[ing] themselves contentedly in a corner" as the only viable male role in human history (146). For male writers who wanted to do more than groom, then, domesticity, not to mention feminism, could have been perceived as being as much of a threat to men as was medical discourse to women. Their writing would have had to reject certain tenets of domesticity and feminism; the medical model of invalid women would certainly have been an appealing alternative for men who questioned the ideology of the female-dominated discourses.

In a culture as dramatically segregated by gender as was mid-nineteenth-century American society, it is to be expected that male and female concerns were separate and, at times, antithetical. G. J. Barker-Benfield argues in *The Horrors of the Half-Known Life* that men experienced a very different kind of pressure than did women. These pressures—which he describes as the need to suppress emotion, to develop themselves as individuals without reference to a family or the larger community, and to prove themselves capable within the harsh public sphere of competition—amounted to a continual need for strict self-control that was often translated into a need to control women and to resist their civilizing influence.[4] The need to interpret and understand gender roles, for men and women, was strong.

Both male and female writers, therefore, were writing literature that was, as Kenneth Burke in *The Philosophy of Literary Form* argues literature always is, "equipment for living . . . [that] would *protect*" them against some threat (61). But male and female writers sensed different threats: women were responding to the threat that they perceived medical science offered (as I explain in chapter 2), while men were responding to the possible threat of women's growing social power as well as to the increasingly straitened roles prescribed for men, including medical restrictions on male roles.

Despite these distinctions, it is important to keep in mind that "women's fiction" (written by and for women) and "men's fiction" (written by and for men) appeared side by side in the same popular magazines and periodicals. The easy differentiation of the "quality" of these stories by such earlier critics as J. T. Frederick, who writes in "Hawthorne's Scribbling Women" that the female editors of these periodicals "took in each other's wash, so to speak" (236), cannot bear up under close scrutiny. The difference between them is more a matter of the questions they seek to resolve than of quality.

That ideological difference gives shape to the figure of the invalid woman in Poe's and Hawthorne's tales, an ideology that questions the claims made by women for feminine moral power and for the importance of women's role in the household at the same time that it seems to resist the medical discourse on which "separate spheres" ideology rests. In "The Oval Portrait," "Ligeia," "The Birthmark," "Rappaccini's Daughter," and *The Blithedale Romance,* Poe and Hawthorne directly address the problematic relation between mind and body as it appears in medical discourse. Whereas the medical man asserted that the body could be exercised only at the expense of the mind, and vice versa, Poe and Hawthorne search for a new union of mind and body in which the two do not compete for primacy. Eventually they cannot resist the power of the medical definition, though; however desirable the union appears, the stories make it finally impossible, unless through unnatural or supernatural means. The woman's death, then, besides being an aesthetic moment, allows for the transcendence of certain natural laws (as understood by nineteenth-century science). The dead woman's "supernatural" power is not, as it is in women writers' texts, a result of her legacy of faith and good works but a result of some diabolical, unnatural force, tinged with gothic horror. That horror in turn questions the aestheticism of her death and reinscribes it with a different kind of power.

Running alongside their questions about nature are also questions of responsibility. At moments, Poe and Hawthorne seem to follow E. H. Dixon's lead and blame the woman for her own death, or they blame at least a specifically female nature, but at others, they seem to follow Stowe and blame their male protagonists for insensitivity and outright cruelty. In every case, the question of responsibility for a woman's invalidism and death becomes a central question of the text and one that both authors refuse to settle. Like Washington Irving, then, they leave the question of the meaning of the woman's life and her death open.

The remainder of this chapter will trace this interaction of the natural, the unnatural, and the supernatural aspects of women's illnesses in Poe's and Hawthorne's fiction against the background of the same discourses on women's health that were examined in chapters 1 and 2—definitions of women as invalids, as civilizing forces, as the equals of men. Here my focus will be on the particular problem for the nineteenth-century male writer of defining the relationship between man and woman as the relationship between mind and body.

THE MIND/BODY PROBLEM

Poe and Hawthorne were influenced by European romantic thought, as were most American writers in the mid-nineteenth century. But, as Americans steeped in the Puritan and expansionist traditions of the new country, they could not import European theories of mind and art without some conflict and confusion. The romantic faith in the primacy and natural goodness of the individual mind, confidence in the wonderful and supernatural, rejection of empirical scientific thought, and belief in the power of the artist came to America through a filter of ethical and religious thought that stressed seriousness, held to a doctrine of natural sinfulness, and expressed faith in the "divine light" of individual spiritual direction. The romantic celebration of the primitive and the natural was complicated in America by expansionist and bourgeois faith in the goodness of progress, the value of wealth, and the importance of material possessions.

For the European romanticist, the power of an individual man's mind was exactly that—a male power. In the romanticism of such writers as Jean-Jacques Rousseau, William Wordsworth, and even Mary Wollstonecraft, it was the male who was associated with the mind and culture; woman was associated with the body and nature.[5] This association was never without its discontents in European thought, but in a country that in its early days granted enormous freedom to women and that had a history of strong and independent females in its religious and prairie life (if not elsewhere), such an association would have been especially uncomfortable. Nevertheless, woman as nature is a frequent trope in American writing,[6] as is the dissociation of woman and mind. This dissociation stands behind Poe's images of women who are terrifying to the degree that they are intellectual (especially Morella and Ligeia) and behind Hawthorne's problematic representations of women writers and artists (his comments on the "damn'd mob of scribbling women" and his portrayal of a female intellectual in *The Blithedale Romance* and of women artists in *The Marble Faun* can easily be read as condemnations of female artistic and intellectual work).[7]

This envisioning of intellectual women as anomalous is common, according to anthropologist Michelle Zimbalist Rosaldo in "Women, Culture, and Society," whenever women "defy the ideals of male order" (32). She argues that "whatever violates a society's sense of order will be seen as threatening, nasty, disorderly or wrong"

(31) or, we might add, sick. But at the same time that romanticism equated woman with nature and the principles of nonrationality, its emphasis on self-determination and individuality established an intellectual atmosphere in which the debate on women's rights could be opened.[8] As Sherry Ortner explains in "Is Female to Male as Nature Is to Culture?," "Woman cannot be consigned fully to the category of nature, for it is perfectly obvious that she is a full-fledged human being endowed with human consciousness just as a man is" (75-76). The result of this contradiction is that women are "seen to occupy an intermediate position between culture and nature" (84).[9]

This intermediacy, this existing in both nature and culture, results in the confusingly doubled representation of women in so many cultural texts: "We can begin to understand then how a single system of cultural thought can often assign to women completely polarized and apparently contradictory meanings, since extremes, as we say, meet. That she often represents both life and death is only the simplest example one could mention" (Ortner, 85). Woman can be represented as not only both life and death but, as we shall see in Beatrice Rappaccini and Zenobia, both abundant health and tragic illness.

This contradictory representation of women is borne out in other ways in Poe's and Hawthorne's fiction. Alongside the ambivalent relation between women and nature is the equally ambivalent relation between women and culture. The tales ask: what if women were removed from their roles as arbiters of culture? They reveal the fear that "if you [change] woman's position by removing her from her moral superiority, her pedestal, by blurring the lines between the spheres, she would threaten order" (G. J. Barker-Benfield, *The Horrors of the Half-Known Life*, 48). But there is also a recognition in the fiction that the real threats to order "were men, craving autonomy, tempted to repudiate political authority as well as the ties of heterosexual obligations. Men were projecting onto women what they feared from themselves" (ibid.). The contradictions in the fiction result from the confrontation between these two views. In these texts, men attempt, but cannot fully succeed, to make women entirely body. Women try to assert their powers of mind but cannot, finally, assert their own intellectual strength.[10]

This contradiction returns us to a central problem in the medical discourse on women—the relation of mind and body to the establishment of separate spheres. For while the female discourses of domesticity and feminism were threatened by the medical discourse (as we saw in the previous chapter), it is equally true that the whole medical understanding of the body was threatened by those female discourses. If woman could develop her mind without ruining her body, then not only were the medical men wrong about women, but the whole basis for maintaining separate gender spheres was wrong, too. If body and mind could coexist without draining each other, then their relation to each other would become troubled.[11] And while this new relation would seem to offer remarkable potential, it also offers an enormous threat to a worldview that had been developing for centuries, a threat to the very fabric of society.

Women's role would not be the only role in this society that would change with a new understanding of the mind/body relation. The correlative, that man could likewise develop his body without risk to his mind, was equally threatening in that it would require a complete rethinking of male roles.[12] The dissolving of the comfortable divisions among men, into laborers and thinkers, for example, would be as problematic as would that of divisions between the sexes. But, again, the potential must have been tantalizing to men for whom the status quo meant a devotion to either thought or body but not both. Men faced different medical strictures than did women, but they were strictures nonetheless.

In short, the conflicts between medical, domestic, feminist, and romantic discourses are played out in the shifting relations between sets of paired terms—mind/body, culture/nature, health/sickness, man/woman. Those conflicts appear in texts by Poe and Hawthorne as contradictions, as impossibilities within the tales, and as doubts about male roles as well as female, about male as well as female illness.

The figure of the invalid woman in Poe's and Hawthorne's fiction is shaped by these contradictions in the cultural representations of woman. On the one hand, she is nature, to be worshipped and admired in her native state, as well as an object to be possessed, exploited, and developed.[13] So the invalid woman also represents an imperfect and even threatening nature. On the other hand, she is an individual, with human powers of mind and responsibility for her own self-determination. In fictions concerned with the individual and the difficulties and necessities of maintaining a sense of individuality, the figure of woman as nature represents several dilemmas. How can woman be both representative of nature and a self-determining individual? How can she be both mind and body? Can she?

One "solution" to the problem of woman's representation was to figure her into the one place accepted and expected by the culture: that of the invalid. As invalid, woman takes her place on the side of the body and nature—since these are "naturally" the defining features of the invalid. In this figuration, woman specifically symbolizes a nature that is in keeping with expansionist belief; that is, she needs man's intervention. Representing women as "natural invalids" creates its own problems, however. As nature, woman becomes inhuman.

As the *object* of man's (medical) intervention, she loses her standing as *subject* to a large degree. Treated as natural invalid, woman stands as a challenge to the faith in the validity and self-determination of the individual and, in being defined almost exclusively as body, as a threat to the hope for a unity of mind and body. If she is understood as only a representative of nature, as something other than a being with the power to direct her own fate, then she must either be discounted as human or stand as a threat to the notions of individuality and freedom.

Further, the cultural climate at mid-century would not easily allow such an equation. Women like Margaret Fuller and Elizabeth Cady Stanton were speaking out openly against such definitions; an entire feminist movement was beginning to assert female equality. The domestic writers who published in the same periodicals as Poe and Hawthorne were redefining the culture/nature distinction in such a way that women's moral guidance in the home came to represent the civilizing force of culture, while the male world of competition came to represent a kind of reversion to nature.[14] It would not be possible (or, perhaps, even desirable) to represent woman as equal to nature. But what would be entailed in an acceptance of women as intellectual equals? There were almost daily claims to both the feminine power of mind *and* the civilizing power of women in the home. Such claims complicated the representation and understanding not just of women's roles but also of men's roles.

The power of this conflict for male writers becomes apparent when we include in it the issue of reproduction. Sherry Ortner in "Is Female to Male as Nature Is to Culture?" explains, using Simone de Beauvoir's *Second Sex,* that one basis for the association of men with culture and women with nature is woman's ability to bear children. Men, to assert their creativity, must reproduce "'artificially' through the medium of technology and symbols . . . [creating] relatively lasting, eternal, transcendent objects, while the woman creates only perishables—human beings" (75). In other words, men reproduce intellectually, while women are restricted to physical reproduction. For men to accept women's abilities to reproduce culture as well as nature would be, therefore, tantamount to admitting their own inferiority in being able to reproduce only culture, only mind, while women have access to both means. What we will see in "The Oval Portrait," "Ligeia," "The Birthmark," "Rappaccini's Daughter," and *The Blithedale Romance* is the desperate questioning of the mind/body relation. The texts take several tacks on the problem: they represent masculine attempts to redefine women as natural invalids (to deny women's association with culture), to imagine a male ability to reproduce nature, and to deny outright the power of the female mind and body. Poe and Hawthorne illustrate that such strategies for dealing with the contradictory, intermediate position of women are only partially successful, at best.

While other male writers avoid this contradiction by largely ignoring women—Ralph Waldo Emerson, Henry David Thoreau, and Herman Melville are the most obvious examples—Hawthorne and Poe "resolve" it with the woman's death. But this death itself "solves" the problem of female figuration in contradictory ways. In death, the woman becomes no longer human, so she can be nature as well as something more than human; she becomes perfect or supernatural. Granting the woman this measure of power and transcendence compensates her for the power and individuality that she is denied. At the same time, the fiction of self-determination is preserved by making the woman responsible for her own sickness; her death then becomes a punishment for her inability to overcome nature's inadequacy. In agreement with the contradictory position held by E. H. Dixon and other medical authorities, here woman is condemned to suffering, illness, and death both by nature and by her own willful misbehavior. But this male discourse is disrupted in Poe's and Hawthorne's fiction by the domestic and feminist claim that women are really made to suffer by the misbehavior of men. There is ample evidence in all five texts that women are the victims of male abuse. Their deaths end the question of responsibility in the texts but not for the reader (nor, perhaps, for the writers). The "resolutions," then, offer no solution to the dilemma. The figure of the invalid woman in Poe's and Hawthorne's fiction compounds the contradictions already found in the culture, especially in medicine and popular fiction. Woman is the principle of nonrationality—nature—and is therefore good, but she also needs improvement; further, she both is and is not personally responsible for her "inadequacies." The male characters fare no better—their own troubled and doubled relation to mind and body, to culture and nature, often leaves them sick, or alone, or both.

MAKING NATURAL ART OF WOMEN

Two tales reveal much about the contradictions of woman's representation. In Edgar Allan Poe's "The Oval Portrait" (1842) the narrator, who is wounded and ill, sees a fascinating portrait of a beautiful young woman and reads a brief story of its painting: she had obediently acquiesced to her husband's desire to paint her portrait and had fallen ill while sitting for it; he did not notice her rapid fading and, at the moment of his completing the portrait, she died. Hawthorne's "The Birthmark" (1846) is the model for the old doctor joke, "The operation was a brilliant success, but, unfortunately, the patient died." In that tale, a talented scientist becomes obsessed by a birthmark on his beautiful wife's cheek and, in the process of removing it, kills her.

The similarities between these tales are remarkable; it seems likely that Poe's tale was an inspiration for Hawthorne's.[15] Both husbands are devoted to their professions and find that the only way to maintain passion for their wives is to combine it with passion for their professions. Both wives are strikingly beautiful. Both husbands are explicitly trying to equal the feats of nature in order to "reproduce" nature: Poe's artist cries, "This is indeed *Life* itself!," at the moment he finishes his portrait (and his wife's life); Hawthorne's scientist openly pits himself against the power of nature in trying to "perfect" Georgiana. Finally, both tales center on the question of whether the wife was merely the price that had to be paid for the husband's exceptional accomplishment or whether the husband is guilty of monomania and murder.

Hawthorne's tale has often been interpreted as being about the dilemmas facing the artist. These readings focus on Aylmer as "tragic hero," to use Robert Heilman's phrase, rather than as villain. Aylmer's fault lies not with his treatment of his wife but with his failure to recognize soon enough that perfection is not attainable in this world. This view is endorsed by the entry in Hawthorne's notebook that was the origin of the story: "A person to be the death of his beloved in trying to raise her to more than mortal perfection; yet this should be a comfort to him for having aimed so highly and holily" (*The American Notebooks of Nathaniel Hawthorne*, 624). Poe's story, too, can be read as an artist's tragedy, losing a "beloved" in trying to achieve a high and holy art.[16] Such readings make woman the symbol either of the price nature exacts for such knowledge and achievement or of nature itself, receding always into unreachable distances as the heroic artist nears her.

In contrast, Judith Fetterley in *The Resisting Reader* describes "The Birthmark" as a story not of failure but of success. Her description of it as "the demonstration of how to murder your wife and get away with it" (22) seems as appropriate to Poe's tale as to Hawthorne's. Fetterley argues that the criticism of the tale as a story of misguided idealism misleads readers. Instead of a story about "the unhappy consequences of man's nevertheless worthy passion for perfecting and transcending nature," it is actually "a brilliant analysis of the sexual politics of idealization and a brilliant exposure of the mechanisms whereby hatred can be disguised as love, neurosis can be disguised as science, murder can be disguised as idealization, and success can be disguised as failure" (22-23). She argues that it is really a story about "the sickness of men" and their diseased relation to feminine sexuality and woman's power to reproduce (27-28). Furthermore, it destroys the image of science as an objective and rational endeavor that exists outside of morality, values, and emotions (30). Leland Person, in his reading of the story in *Aesthetic Headaches*, agrees with Fetterley, but he credits Hawthorne with anticipating her critique: "Hawthorne explicitly criticizes his protagonist and indicts his sadistic treatment of his wife" (109).

These two tales are about both the tragedy of the noble artist and wife abuse. In the same way that Aylmer and the painter in Poe's story cannot maintain passion for their wives without recourse to art and a challenge to nature, Poe and Hawthorne cannot work out their complicated relationship to art and nature without recourse to woman. At the heart of both stories is the conflict that I outlined earlier: woman both is and is not a symbol of nature, is and is not a self-determining individual. Her death "resolves" this contradiction.

Both tales are stories of exploitation and a kind of failure. The husband is not able to have his wife and make art of her, too. In each story, as Fetterley notes of "The Birthmark," the husband displays much hostility toward his wife, but it is clear that he nonetheless recognizes the woman's value as possession, since he wishes, in one case, to duplicate it and, in the other, to increase it. The tragedy of the stories, then, becomes the failure to recognize the woman's "true worth," which is, as the "value" of women has been for centuries, her ability to reproduce, to act for her husband in creating "life itself." Luce Irigaray explains in "Women on the Market" that in the patriarchal system in which men exchange women and in which, therefore, women are treated as objects, women have one of two kinds of value. They can have commodity value as objects that can be traded or, once traded, utility value as objects with the ability to produce heirs. Women in this system never have value in and of themselves, then, but only in relation to male needs. "When women are exchanged, woman's body must be treated as an abstraction. . . . The exchange operation cannot take place in terms of some intrinsic, immanent value of the commodity. . . . They are exchanged . . . as women reduced to some common feature. . . . *Woman has value on the market by virtue of one single quality: that of being a product of man's labor*" (175, emphasis in original).

Poe and Hawthorne represent the man's failure as a failure to recognize his own value as the creator/reproducer of culture and his wife's value as the reproducer of nature. In both stories, the man is armed with the necessary technology and art to create "relatively lasting, eternal, transcendental objects" but wastes his energies trying to "merely" reproduce nature. The husband fails to see his wife's utilitarian value as a producer of babies because he is overwhelmed by her commodity value as a beautiful object, and thereby he loses the opportunity to produce heirs through her.

In both tales, therefore, the husband is ultimately a loser. He not only loses his original "capital" (his wife), he also misses out on the reward of his labor, his cre-

ation of culture—the painter's lifelike work is hidden away in a dark recess in a tiny room of an abandoned chateau, and Aylmer can hardly exhibit a dead Georgiana's cheek to the scientific community. These failures of art and science mirror Poe's and Hawthorne's contradictory representations of woman and nature. The authors share the European romanticist's view that nature cannot be bettered, that man is subject to nature, but they also share the capitalist, expansionist, patriarchal notion of nature as that which is to be subjected to man's control. Women, who here represent the "natural" ability to (re)produce "life itself," must die in these tales because of the ultimately impossible resolution of these two forces.

The wives' deaths here also apparently resolve another ideological problem: that raised by women's insistence on their own power in the home. Here, neither wife can assert her power, first, because the husband in each story has relegated her to the status of material for his work and, finally, because he kills her. In so doing, he unequivocally returns her to a state of nature, for she has ceased being human—ashes to ashes, dust to dust. But just as the women in Stowe's and Southworth's novels gain moral power at their deaths, so, too, do these women. Just as the woman's death fails to resolve her intermediate position between nature and culture, so, too, does it fail to resolve her ambiguous relation to power. Poe's narrator leads us to believe that the woman in "The Oval Portrait" endows the painting with her life, achieving a gothically supernatural effect over viewers, and even though Georgiana tells Aylmer not to repent, hers is the moral voice at the end of the story explaining to him that he had "rejected the best the earth could offer" (*The Complete Novels and Selected Tales of Nathaniel Hawthorne*, 1032). These women do not leave the legacy of faith and good works that female characters in women's fiction so often do, but they do leave behind men who are finally defeated by woman's ultimate supernatural power.

The tales illustrate the impossibility of maintaining a consistent symbolic equivalence between woman and nature in a narrative system that emphasizes individuality and autonomy. The invalid is both innocent victim and, because she willingly acquiesces to her husband's will, conspirator in her own demise. She is both beautiful and in need of perfecting. She represents nature as well as culture. Finally, she accedes to the role we have seen established by nineteenth-century society and medicine: she is both subject to nature's whim and guilty of aggravating bad natural tendencies.

The scene in "The Oval Portrait" could well represent a more personal dilemma for Poe. The artist in the narrative enacts what Poe himself might have felt he was doing: making art out of the deaths of women. As Marie Bonapart argues in her early ground-breaking *The Life and Works of Edgar Allan Poe: A Psychoanalytic Interpretation,* Poe's tales about women have their origins in his mother or wife, both of whom died from tuberculosis.[17] Given Poe's unrelenting motif of sickly women, Bonapart's biographical reading is persuasive. Still, writers do not produce texts exclusively out of their own private experiences. The particular economic, intellectual, and political milieu in which a writer works also shapes the text. Poe, as an active editor of a number of magazines and journals, was intimately involved with contemporary culture. That culture is as much a part of his fiction as are his own psychological idiosyncracies. Cultural constructions of gender and illness played as important a part in his portraiture of women's illness as did his personal experience.

Edgar Allan Poe's female characters stand out in American fiction as the most unrelentingly sickly. They are, almost to a woman, beautiful, mysterious, and fated to die. Poe's narrators, usually mad or ill themselves, frequently concede that the women's deaths are a result of their having been too good for this world. Like Stowe's Eva and Southworth's Hester Grey, they are too perfect for its corruption. Like the title character in "Eleonora," they are often "made perfect in loveliness only to die" (*The Complete Tales and Poems of Edgar Allan Poe,* 651). And like the women in domestic fiction, their deaths do not necessarily end their stories. Poe's women, sickly and weak in life, gain power at their deaths—power over the narrator or their near relations—through supernatural means. Whether it is Madeline Usher breaking free of her tomb, Berenice being found alive after burial,[18] Eleonora speaking in the wind, or Morella taking over her daughter's body, Poe's female characters show even more energy and power in death than in life. Poe's stories thus share much common ground with the women's fiction of the decade and, like those stories and novels, invite a reading in the context of the discourses on medicine and woman's power in the home.

One story in particular encapsulates Poe's problematic figure of the powerful female invalid—"Ligeia" (1839), the tale that Poe himself in 1846 called "undoubtedly the best story I have written" (quoted in Joan Dayan, *Fables of Mind,* 172). This story hinges on an understanding of the mind/body relation as well as the man/woman relation. It sets out the difficulties of understanding what man's relation to the "new woman" could be and uses the conventions of gothic horror to explore the woman's new power. This story also dramatically reveals the troublesome doubleness we encounter in the representation of the invalid, leaving the question of exactly what happens in the story finally unanswered.

Poe sets out the question of a kind of mind/body relation in the epigraph to the story, from Joseph Glanvill, which states that "the will therein lieth, which dieth not.

Who knoweth the mysteries of the will with its vigor? . . . Man doth not yield himself to the angels, nor unto death utterly, save only through the weakness of his feeble will" (654). The tale is, indeed, a question of will, of whether a woman can will herself to resist death, of whether a man can will himself to see her return to life. The opening of the story, too, dwells on questions of mind and body. The narrator describes himself only in terms of mind; the opening lines are about his memory: "I cannot, for my soul, remember. . . . My memory is feeble" (654). But Ligeia, despite "her rare learning," which was "immense," is described almost entirely in terms of body, the one thing our feeble-memoried narrator has not forgotten: "There is one dear topic, however, on which my memory fails me not. It is the *person* of Ligeia" (654, emphasis in original). He dwells for two pages on the wonders of her body, looking for classical analogies and finding her to exceed even these.

When he finally gets to her mind and intellectual abilities, he does it through Glanvill again and notes that she had "an *intensity* in thought, action or speech . . . [and a] gigantic volition" (657, emphasis in original). In fact, all of his descriptions of Ligeia's mind, character, and emotions cast her in the mold of "too muchness"; he uses adjectives of size ("immense," "gigantic") and quantity (the "overflowing of her heart" is "more than passionate"; her devotion to the narrator is "more than womanly" [657-58]). But it is her body that takes precedence, her body that he remembers, despite his sense that it was her will, her powers of mind, that made her exceptional. As we will see with Zenobia in *The Blithedale Romance,* it is this too-muchness of mind, this superabundance, that kills Ligeia. As did Margaret Miller Davidson's, Ligeia's "soul was wearing out the body" (Washington Irving, *Biography and Poetical Remains of the Late Margaret Miller Davidson,* 11); "Ligeia grew ill. The wild eyes blazed with a too—too glorious effulgence; the pale fingers became of the transparent waxen hue of the grave; and the blue veins upon the lofty forehead swelled and sank impetuously with the tides of the most gentle emotion" (657-58). Ligeia's illness, in other words, intensifies her too-muchness. But where Margaret's supernatural powers were holy, Ligeia's become horrific when, after her death and her husband's remarriage to the Lady Rowena, she possesses the dead body of Rowena.

As are the deathbed scenes in domestic fictions, Ligeia's death is full of pathos, but it is a very different kind of pathos. Rather than accepting her death as a transition to a holier plane, Ligeia struggles against it and resists. Our narrator confesses his surprise at this: "There had been much in her stern nature to impress me with the belief that, to her, death would have come without its terrors; but not so. Words are impotent to convey any just idea of the fierceness of resistance with which she wrestled with the Shadow. I groaned in anguish at the pitiable spectacle" (658). This struggle outlines the problem with Ligeia. Against the backdrop of sentimental heroines who accept their deaths, her resistance to death must seem a fear of the afterlife, a fear of some kind of retribution. Is Ligeia guilty of some crime? Our narrator cannot discount this possibility, since he confesses to the fact that he never even knew her patronymic. Has she some guilty past? We can, of course, only speculate, but it would have been precisely the kind of speculation a nineteenth-century reader, accustomed to the conventions of representing guilty women, would have engaged in. Like Juliette Summers, Ligeia's abundance makes her questionable; her "wild desire for life—for life—*but* for life" (658, emphasis in original) makes her suspicious. If there is a contrast drawn between women in this tale, it is not really between Rowena (who likewise fears death) and Ligeia, but between Ligeia and the female figures in domestic fiction.

The division in this story is not really between the two women; despite the fact that one is "dark" and the other "light," one intellectual and strong (even as she fights death), the other a feeble and weak-willed invalid, they are, finally, interchangeable. Both sicken and die, and Rowena's body, on its bier, becomes Ligeia's body, too. The real division in this story is between the genders: the narrator is all mind (if weak minded) and the women are all body (despite Ligeia's great will and mind). In fact, the use to which Ligeia puts her mind (if we are to believe the narrator's story that she wills herself to kill Rowena and then assume her body, a question to which I will return) is to become, again, a body. And as Cynthia Jordan has pointed out in *Second Stories*, despite the fact that the narrator repeatedly mentions the "almost magical melody, modulation, distinctness, and placidity of her very low voice" (657), he never actually records anything she says.[19] She remains, in his version of the story, at least, always all body.[20]

Whether we are to trust this version of the story, though, remains an open question. Over and over Poe casts doubt on his narrator; the narrator tells us about his opium habit, claiming to have married Rowena during a "mental alienation" caused by that habit.[21] He admits the uncertainty of his vision when he describes the moment that he believes Ligeia has poisoned Rowena ("I saw, or may have dreamed that I saw" [663]) and when he describes his "visions of Ligeia" while watching the "hideous drama of revivification" going on in Rowena's body. If our narrator is all-mind to Ligeia's all-body, he remains a pitiful excuse for mind. Poe leaves us with an insoluble dilemma: either Ligeia returns from the dead to inhabit the dead body of her successor, or an opium addict believes that he has seen his dead second wife return to life as his dead first wife.[22]

Early in the story, our narrator admits his inferiority to Ligeia: "I was sufficiently aware of her infinite supremacy to resign myself, with a child-like confidence, to her guidance through the chaotic world of metaphysical investigation" (657). We are left to decide whether it is because he is without her continued guidance that he turns to opium, or whether it is because of the guidance he *had* received from her. A tale that so prominently features questions of will leaves open the central question of the man's power of will. Does Ligeia's power drive him to drugs? Are all men to become "child-like" in the presence of powerful women and profligate when that influence is gone? Poe leaves open the question of whether we are to read the story as one about the horrors of a woman with a will of her own or as a tale of the horrors of the divisions between mind and body, men and women.

THE NATURAL *PHARMAKON* IN THE GARDEN

Woman's complicity in her own illness and death and her relation to science become the central questions in "Rappaccini's Daughter." This tale would seem, at first glance, to remove the question of the woman's blame for her own illness. Beatrice, like many of the other invalid women we have seen so far (and will yet see), is the victim of abuse: without her consent, or apparent foreknowledge, her father has tainted her with his poisons. She is, symbolically, a victim of sexual abuse; it is a liquid produced by her father that "taints" her and makes her an unsuitable love object for a young man.[23] Nonetheless, her father lures a young man, Giovanni Guasconti, to his garden and, to provide a mate for Beatrice, imbues him with poisons, too. As soon as Beatrice realizes her part in the tainting of Giovanni, she proclaims her despair at the turn of events, claims her innocence, and takes her own life by drinking an "antidote" to the poisons that permeate her system, an antidote that has been given to Giovanni by Rappaccini's rival, Baglioni.[24]

The clarity of Beatrice's innocence, though, is clouded. Returning to the entries in Hawthorne's *American Notebooks* that provided the basis for the tale, one finds that Hawthorne's model for Beatrice was a legend of a woman fed on poisons who was sent to Alexander's court to murder him (623).[25] Hawthorne's attitude toward the symbol of physical disease is ambiguous in that he writes that he would like to "symbolize moral or spiritual disease by disease of the body" (625).[26] Closer to the tale, however, is the most damning indictment of Beatrice: Hawthorne's playful preface to the story. Attributing the story to M. de l'Aubepine (French for "hawthorn") and professing to discuss de l'Aubepine's works, Hawthorne discusses instead his own tales, offering French titles that are literal translations of his English titles, with one glaring exception. "Rappaccini's Daughter" becomes "Beatrice; ou la Belle Empoisonneuse," that is, "Beatrice, or the Beautiful Poisoner." The change in this title is significant because it gives Beatrice her own name rather than introducing her by her father's. In so doing, it emphasizes her autonomy and, by describing her as a "Beautiful Poisoner," suggests that her role is an active one—she is not the poisoned but the poisoner.[27] Furthermore, it is a specifically feminine role (*empoisonneuse* rather than *empoisonneur*), one which allows her to use her beauty to accomplish the poisoning.[28]

The suggestions of Beatrice's guilt leave open the crucial question of the story: is she the innocent victim or the guilty one caught in her own trap? Hawthorne manages to have it both ways. Like women in the medical and cultural discourses of the time, like Georgiana, Ligeia, and the woman in Poe's "Oval Portrait," she is both innocent and guilty, beautiful and horrible. Like Ligeia, she is made attractive by that which also makes her horrible. Beatrice is nature that has been "improved" by science—she is the most beautiful woman in Padua (a city where many have died of love)—but she is also nature that has been made unnatural. The poison in her system makes her alluring and more attractive, but it also makes her unapproachable. She is pure but tainted at the center of her being. Her representation is polarized in the same way that Sherry Ortner describes cultural representations of women generally: she is pure, but polluted ("Is Female to Male as Nature Is to Culture?," 72).

Reading "Rappaccini's Daughter" as "Beatrice, or the Beautiful Poisoner" emphasizes her role as not the innocent victim of male abuse but the active, if misled, temptress and destroyer of men, a fallen Eve. The poison in her system, though instilled in her by her father, is the essence of what she is and of what gives her enormous power to tempt men and to lead them astray. Although Beatrice represents an altered nature that is evil, perverted, and cruel—her breath kills animals and wilts flowers—she also embodies the innate danger of a femininity that is corrupt and tainted. Her father's evil is represented outwardly by his "sickly and sallow" appearance (1052) and by an "infirm voice" that signals that he is "affected with inward disease" (1046), but hers is hidden by a mask of beauty and "a bloom so deep and vivid that one shade more would have been too much. She looked redundant with life, health and energy" (1046). Beatrice represents extremes: she is "redundant" with health, but she is also diseased. Beatrice's surface beauty hides the underlying menace of femininity from men. In this respect, Beatrice resembles two other figures of feminine illness from the 1840s. In a New England schoolbook, children were introduced to two women, Dissipation and Housewifery; Dissipation, like Beatrice, has a pretty mask and a pleasing appearance that hide "a countenance wan and ghastly with sickness" (quoted in Barbara Epstein, *The Politics of*

Domesticity, 75). An illustration from 1840 represents syphilis as existing under the guise of beauty; the drawing features a fashionably dressed woman holding a mask of beauty over a skeletal face of corrupt flesh (Sander Gilman, *Difference and Pathology,* 106). As in these representations of feminine illness, Beatrice's "abundant health" is but a mask for her true invalidism.

As Aylmer does Georgiana, Giovanni and Baglioni diagnose Beatrice, deciding that she is ill and in need of Baglioni's medicine. Her disease is even worse than Georgiana's because hers is contagious. Giovanni, like the lover Socrates describes in Plato's *Phaedrus,* is infected by a disease that is transmitted through the eyes: "He is in love. . . . He does not understand his own condition and cannot explain it; like one who has caught a disease of the eyes from another, he can give no reason for it; he sees himself in his lover as in a mirror, but is not conscious of the fact" (255d). After watching Beatrice from the window of his room, he no longer can concentrate on work; "She had at least instilled a fierce and subtle poison into his system" (1051). She transforms his previous "remarkable beauty of person" (1044) to the point that when he meets Baglioni in the street, the professor comments on the change in his appearance (1052). Beatrice leaves her lover corrupted and cut off from normal human relations. Read in this way, Beatrice's death is less a tragedy than was her perverted life. The end of the story represents the proper end of all evil things, however beautiful and tempting.

We should note that one of the things that makes Beatrice so frightening is her supposed unnatural development of mind. Baglioni, despite his ignorance of Beatrice's real nature, suggests this possibility to Giovanni: "I know little of the Signora Beatrice save that Rappaccini is said to have instructed her deeply in his science, and that, young and beautiful as fame reports her, she is already qualified to fill a professor's chair" (1049). Beatrice denies that she has this knowledge, but the suggestion of it lingers. Like Ligeia's immense learning, Beatrice's supposed combination of great powers of mind with great youth and beauty leave her questionable; her unnaturalness tinges her with the gothic supernatural.

Persuasive as this interpretation is, Hawthorne did not entitle the story "Beatrice." Instead, his title calls attention to familial relations, to Beatrice's subjection to a tyrannical and abusive father, and to her passive position in the social system. Beatrice becomes the innocent victim of male abuse and misuse of power.[29] She retains the power of allure and temptation, but these are unwitting and, to the extent that they corrupt Giovanni and herself, unwanted gifts. She is just another of her father's possessions—imprisoned and tainted by him, kept from normal society and from normal pursuits. Like her "sister"—the large violet flower she resembles, embraces, and wears as an ornament—she is the innocent but perverted creation of a man who would use science to tamper with nature.

Read as "Rappaccini's Daughter," the story becomes not one of a misguided, star-crossed love affair between a young man and a beautiful but tainted young woman; it becomes instead a story about the struggle between two older men for control over a beautiful and intelligent young man, a story of homosocial desire.[30] Professor Rappaccini uses Beatrice's altered nature to lure Giovanni away from Baglioni, a rival professor. Baglioni, in turn, questions Beatrice's purity in hopes of defeating Rappaccini's hold over Giovanni. At one significant point, Baglioni thinks to himself, "It is too insufferable an impertinence of Rappaccini, thus to snatch the lad out of my own hands" (1053). In this arrangement, Beatrice becomes merely the object of exchange that establishes a relation between men. She is forced into a position that, according to feminist theorists Gayle Rubin and Luce Irigaray, negates woman's existence as a subject:

> The circulation of women among men establishes the operations of society, at least of patriarchal society. Whose presuppositions include the following: the appropriation of nature by man; the transformation of nature according to "human" criteria, defined by men alone; the submission of nature to labor and technology; the reduction of its material, corporeal, perceptible qualities to man's practical concrete activity; the equality of women among themselves, but in terms of laws of equivalence that remain external to them; the constitution of women as "objects" that emblematize the materialization of relations among men, and so on.
>
> (Irigaray, "Women on the Market," 184-85)

Thus, the end of the story takes on a feminist cast; Beatrice recognizes her function in the contest between her father and Baglioni and, refusing to be an object of exchange, disqualifies herself for that role. In a symbolically significant move, she drinks the "antidote" that will remove the flowers' poisons from her system; that is, she "de-flowers" herself.[31] A deflowered woman, of course, has no value as an object of exchange. "Once deflowered, woman is relegated to the status of use value, to her entrapment in private property; she is removed from the exchange among men" (ibid., 186). Beatrice's final act is explicitly that of a subject; she moves to cure herself of the poison in their (patriarchal) system. Her taking of her own life is meant to teach Giovanni and Rappaccini a lesson. Her last words are, "Oh, was there not, from the first, more poison in thy nature than in mine?" (1065). But this one act as an independent subject leads to her death, that is, to the end of her subjectivity, as she becomes an object whose only power is to edify men.

Neither reading of the tale, as "Beatrice, or the Beautiful Poisoner" or as "Rappaccini's Daughter," entirely accounts for every aspect of the figure of the invalid woman as Hawthorne draws it. As Nina Baym notes of this story, it "may be too rich, in the sense that it is susceptible to a number of partial explanations, but seems to evade any single wholly satisfactory reading" (*The Shape of Hawthorne's Career,* 107).[32] Beatrice is the unnatural, artificial, and dangerous creation of a perverted science as well as the innocent natural child untouched by civilization, the "noble savage" that Rousseau envisioned. In Beatrice, the conflicted attitude of the male writer toward woman and nature is dramatized; man's "improvements" on nature make it, in fact, more attractive and alluring, but they also contaminate it. There is, however, no way to approach nature without altering it. In this system, woman is made both more alluring and more unapproachable by man's intervention. The figure of the invalid drawn here is not simply natural or unnatural, good or bad, innocent or guilty. Nor is it altogether clear who in the story is sick or well. Baglioni and Giovanni decide that Beatrice is ill and therefore needs to be "cured" by the antidote. But throughout the story, it has been Rappaccini and Giovanni who have been described as ill. Beatrice, even as she accepts the antidote, questions whether she is more ill than the men around her. Like the Greek word for poison, *pharmakon,* which means both remedy and poison, Beatrice is both the cause of and the cure to Giovanni's illness. As Jacques Derrida explains in "Plato's Pharmacy," *pharmakon* is a sign that represents mutually exclusive properties: it is both poison and remedy; both natural, since it comes from herbs and plants, and unnatural, since it is distilled and blended; and it is that which, even though "exterior" to the subject, nevertheless enacts a profound change within the "interior" of the subject. Like the *pharmakon,* Beatrice represents mutually exclusive properties. In Rappaccini's inside-out garden, antidotes are poisons, improvements are corruptions, evil is innocence. Beatrice's "illness" makes her, as her father explains, invulnerable to the ordinary "condition of a weak woman" (1064), but it makes her vulnerable to the charms of the first man she meets. Beatrice is the *pharmakon* in Hawthorne's garden.

"Rappaccini's Daughter" is ultimately a tale centered on the question of who has the power to define illness, to define what is natural and unnatural. Beatrice asserts her right to decide her own fate, but this assumption of power kills her and leaves all three men still alive. The tale may question the propriety of masculine definitions of femininity, but one cannot take it outside the context of nineteenth-century aesthetics, in which woman's weakness is "poetic" and "beautiful." Any "lessons" from such stories are therefore subsumed into aesthetic evaluation. Questions of the woman's power to shape culture are elided in the definition of women as "unnatural nature" and "supernatural invalids."

A Return to the Garden: The Healthy
Invalid

Beatrice Rappaccini is not Hawthorne's only super-abundantly healthy heroine who ends up dead; Zenobia, in *The Blithedale Romance* (1852), fits this pattern as well. Coverdale, the narrator, describes her in terms that make her a type of "able-bodied womanhood" (to use Martha Verbrugge's phrase):

> It did one good to see a fine intellect (as hers really was, although its natural tendency lay in another direction than towards literature) so fitly cased. She was, indeed, an admirable figure of a woman, just on the hither verge of her richest maturity, with a combination of features which it is safe to call remarkably beautiful, even if some fastidious persons might pronounce them a little deficient in softness and delicacy. But we find enough of those attributes everywhere. Preferable—by way of variety, at least—was Zenobia's bloom, health, and vigor, which she possessed in such overflow that a man might well have fallen in love with her for their sake only.
>
> (447)

It is all the more striking that this model of healthy womanhood ends up drowning herself and becoming, by novel's end, *just* body, and a horrible one at that. It is tempting to argue that Hawthorne resolved the doubleness of Beatrice Rappaccini's characterization by splitting the female figure in this work into two women, Zenobia and Priscilla—the famous dark and light ladies of his later romances.[33] But what we see in *The Blithedale Romance* is that Zenobia refigures the same doubleness, that she even reenacts Beatrice's own suicidal "resolution," and that Hawthorne still manages to have it both ways by disclaiming the narrative (through his troublesome narrator).

I do not want to offer a full-fledged reading of *The Blithedale Romance* here; I intend to examine the repetition in that text of the earlier figures from "Rappaccini's Daughter" and to place them within the mid-century debate over women, medicine, and gender roles. What we see in the romance are specific repetitions of the scene from the earlier tale: a marked identification between women and flowers; a setting that is specifically pastoral, gardenlike, and isolated; strong homosocial desire between men;[34] the interaction between an innocent-in-love and a beloved who is ambiguously represented as both ideal and tainted (Priscilla and Zenobia);[35] and a narrative that establishes its own "plausible deniability." The significant change from Beatrice to Zenobia is that while Beatrice's intellectual abilities are suggested in the tale but denied by her, there is never any doubt that Zenobia represents the absolute union of mind and body. As we saw above, Coverdale describes her as a "fine intellect . . . fitly cased."[36] Even in his praise of her, Coverdale notes that

"fastidious persons" would find her body too much but states that he finds her "preferable." Of course, by novel's end, in his "confession," he admits that he has come around to the "fastidious" point of view, preferring the "softness and delicacy" of Priscilla. Much has been made in the criticism of the threat Zenobia offers to Coverdale, but the real threat Zenobia poses is to the whole foundation of medical and social thought: she is a fully sexual woman with a fully active mind, suffering from no obvious medical ill effects of this super-abundance. This is the threat that has to be contained within the novel.

Leland Person argues in *Aesthetic Headaches* that "Zenobia resists containment by type or by language; her presence always implies more than Coverdale or Hawthorne can denote" (148), but what we see in Zenobia's suicide is precisely the containment of the threat she offers to the sociomedical definition of the female. This is not to deny the power of Zenobia's voice within the text or the potential disruptive force she represents. Several recent critics have recognized the dialogism of *The Blithedale Romance*.[37] Leland Person contends that "like Beatrice Rappaccini, Zenobia effectively demands that Coverdale encounter a woman in her fully human nature; she subverts his inclination to idealize." He goes on to suggest that, in incorporating Zenobia's pronouncements on the oppression of women, Hawthorne allows the revolutionary potential of her voice into his text (152). Dale Bauer, in *Feminist Dialogics,* argues that Zenobia's language "cannot be fully appropriated and, therefore, is a constant threat" (48) but that she is finally violently silenced to maintain the social order.

The threat that Zenobia offers to the system represented by the de facto patriarch of Blithedale, Hollingsworth, and Coverdale is precisely the same threat that the Blithedale experiment offers to American culture at large, as is the promise that she offers—the utopian ideal of the perfect union of mind and body, intellect and sexuality. From the first, the Blithedalers anticipate the rewards of developing both their minds and bodies, but the reality casts doubt on the possibility. Coverdale describes both the hope and the reality they confront:

> The peril of our new way of life was not lest we should fail in becoming practical agriculturists, but that we should probably cease to be anything else. While our enterprise lay all in theory, we had pleased ourselves with delectable visions of the spiritualization of labor. It was to be our form of prayer, and ceremonial of worship. Each stroke of the hoe was to uncover some aromatic root of wisdom, heretofore hidden from the sun. . . . Our thoughts, on the contrary, were fast becoming cloddish. Our labor symbolized nothing, and left us mentally sluggish in the evening. *Intellectual activity is incompatible with any large amount of bodily exercise.* The yeoman and the scholar . . . are two distinct individuals and can never be melted or welded into one substance.
>
> (477, emphasis added)

The ideal of becoming farmer-poets, of uniting intense intellectual work with hard physical labor, is never realized at Blithedale. Zenobia teases Coverdale with being no Robert Burns and tells him that her vision of him in the future is modeled on Silas Foster, with the *Farmer's Almanac* for his literature and nothing on his mind but the farm. Hollingsworth defends Coverdale's abandonment of poetry because it is unfitting to his new physique: "Coverdale has given up making verses now. . . . Just think of him penning a sonnet, with a fist like that!" (478).

In "The Birthmark" and "Rappaccini's Daughter," Hawthorne had represented intellectual men as not at all physical. Both Aylmer and Rappaccini are pale, sallow, and sickly looking men, defined by their great intellectual powers to the same extent that the women in the texts are defined by their physicality. When a man is physical—as with Aylmer's assistant, Aminadab, or Silas Foster—he is correspondingly nonintellectual. Such division is, as we have seen, in harmony with nineteenth-century models of health and gender roles. What the Blithedalers propose to do violates not just *social* restrictions but the restrictions of *nature,* as they were defined in the nineteenth century. As the character who is most clearly defined as both intellectual and physical from the outset, Zenobia *embodies* this violation of natural laws.[38]

As with Beatrice Rappaccini, it is this very unnaturalness that makes Zenobia so attractive. A man "might well have fallen in love with her" for the sake of her "overflow" of health and intellect. Throughout the romance, until his "confession" of his love for Priscilla (and perhaps even afterward), we suspect Coverdale of having done just that. Her attraction, though, is the same attraction that Blithedale holds—a violation of the rules of nature and society. There are a lot of reasons why the utopian experiment fails, as Coverdale indicates, but the central reason is that its attempt to unite mind and body, to combine the production of culture with the natural production of agriculture, to question the differences between men and women, dooms it to failure not just by violating social norms but by violating the laws of nature.[39] Just as Blithedale must cease to exist to maintain the social order, Zenobia must cease to exist to maintain the natural order on which society is based.

That maintaining of order is not accomplished by the murder of Zenobia, as some critics tend to suggest, but by illness.[40] For during the mid-nineteenth century, suicide was explicitly understood as a disease. In his study of American suicide, *Self-Destruction in the Promised Land,* Howard Kushner traces the changes in attitude toward suicide from Puritan times to the present and writes, "By the 1830s melancholy and suicide, no longer religious or legal issues, had become almost exclusively the concern of medical men. And if melancholy were a disease, a melancholic individual was no more responsible for committing suicide than for contracting smallpox. This transformation of consciousness signalled the medicalization of suicide that had emerged unchallenged by the 1840s" (34). The association between suicide and illness was so strong that witnesses and juries at suicide inquests in Victorian England "sometimes seem to have been puzzled when they could remember" no examples of past instances of insanity, nerves, or depression, "and yet death did indeed seem to be self-inflicted" (Olive Anderson, *Suicide in Victorian and Edwardian England,* 227).[41]

It is neither Hollingsworth nor Coverdale nor guilt over her treatment of Priscilla that does Zenobia in but the very condition that had at first appeared to Coverdale as an "overflow" of "bloom, health, and vigor." The cost of such overdevelopment of mind and body, intellect and sexuality, medical convention held, would have to be a complete physical or mental collapse, just as the social experiment of Blithedale would necessarily have had to collapse. What we see in Zenobia's final scene is her final mental breakdown.

The last time we see Zenobia alive is in chapter 26, "Coverdale and Zenobia." There, we finally witness her collapse, the impossibility of "bloom, health, and vigor" to "fitly case" such an intellect. After Hollingsworth's judgment of her and his choice of Priscilla, Zenobia "began slowly to sink down" (569). The chapter describes her "woman's affliction" in terms that are clear indications of a suicidal melancholy, or that would have been to the reader in 1852. When Zenobia's sobs finally abate, Coverdale describes her appearance: "[She] stared about her with a bewildered aspect, as if not distinctly recollecting the scene through which she had passed, nor cognizant of the situation in which it left her. Her face and brow were almost purple with the rush of blood. They whitened, however, by-and-by, and, for some time, retained this deathlike hue. She put her hand to her forehead, with a gesture that made me forcibly conscious of an intense and living pain there" (570). Such a description could almost be (and would have been recognized as) testimony at an inquest; the "intense and living pain" in Zenobia's head would have been a clear indication of the "incipient brain illness" or "derangement of mind" that Anderson and Kushner describe as typical of testimony at such hearings. Later in the chapter, Coverdale remarks on the "strange way in which her mind seemed to vibrate from the deepest earnest to mere levity" (572), and Zenobia herself claims to be "sick to death" (573). Certainly, Hollingsworth's judgment of her triggers this descent, but Zenobia's own assertion, that "the whole universe, [the female] sex and yours, and Providence, or Destiny, to boot, make common cause against the woman who swerves one hair's breadth out of the beaten track" (571), finally holds. The "whole universe . . . and Providence, or Destiny" cannot allow the divergence from the "beaten track" that Zenobia's intellectual physicality represents. It is nature's law that decrees that she must collapse, not Hollingsworth's.[42]

Her final appearance in the novel, as a horribly mis-shapen "spectacle," completes Zenobia's transformation to all body. As with Georgiana, she becomes a thing to be looked at, an almost-art *object*: "She [is] the marble image of a death agony" (578). Despite his recognition that he should not describe the scene ("Were I to describe the perfect horror of the spectacle, the reader might justly reckon it to me for a sin and a shame" [578]), Coverdale dwells on the scene at length, not just on its horror but on the display of Zenobia's body ("Her knees . . . her arms . . . her hands . . . her lips . . . the poor thing's breast"). He is convinced that, had she known how she would look, Zenobia would never have committed this act: "Being the woman that she was, could Zenobia have foreseen all these ugly circumstances of death . . . she would no more have committed the dreadful act than have exhibited herself to a public assembly in a badly fitting garment" (579). The body that Coverdale had once believed a "fit" casing for her great intellect is now no more than body and is, to that degree, horrible.

We can read in this final scene some of the same doubleness of Georgiana's and Beatrice's deaths: it is a death of the woman's own choosing, yes, but it is also not her fault but the fault of nature. Here is a death caused by the cruelty of men, by their insensitivity and refusal to recognize her as a sentient being in her own right, but, again, it is not really their fault either. Zenobia even re-enacts the "de-flowering" of self that we saw in Beatrice's death, when she removed the flower that had been her symbol throughout the romance. Like Beatrice, Zenobia signals that she is no longer "on the market" and available to men. But are we to finally understand the unfairness of that market, or is this a symbolic suggestion that Zenobia's cover (her mask of innocence) has finally been blown?

At mid-century, a woman's death by drowning carried with it cultural connotations that defy a simple reading of Zenobia's death. Coverdale, trying to understand why a woman of Zenobia's great beauty would have chosen a mode of death he finds "the ugliest," reasons, "She had seen pictures, I suppose, of drowned persons in lithe and graceful attitudes" (578-79). Such pictures and sculptures were abundant in the nineteenth century. Joy Kasson discusses the impact of Edward A. Brackett's very popular sculpture, *Shipwrecked Mother and Child* (1850), in *Marble Queens and Captives* and traces its origins to a 1788 engraving of Jacques-Henri Bernardin de Saint-Pierre's *Paul et Virginie* (by T. Johannot and E. Isabey), depicting the graceful dead body of

a drowned woman. Olive Anderson shows that in London in the 1840s the stereotype of female suicide was deeply romantic and usually featured "a distraught girl flinging herself from a high bridge, or a beautiful woman's damply draped body 'Found Drowned' and lying by moonlight." She cites example after example in popular novels, paintings, prints, ballads, songs, and melodramas. (*Found Drowned* is, in fact, a painting by G. F. Watts, based on Thomas Hood's poem, "The Bridge of Sighs," which Anderson reproduces [202].)

But while the victim of shipwreck was undeniably a victim, the female suicide, Anderson argues, was more ambiguous: "For the middle class, the female suicide was essentially a sinner; for the working class, she was a victim. For the former, suicide was the inevitable final retribution for fornication or adultery. . . . By contrast, the unchanging message conveyed by the songs and melodramas which working-class people favoured was that 'the woman always pays' and 'the poor get all the kicks'" (199). But by the 1840s, she shows, even middle-class people were beginning to see female suicides as "the result of cruel wrongs" (202). The children of criminals and drunkards, in particular, were depicted as victimized, and we learn in the course of the novel that Zenobia's father had been a criminal.

How, then, do we read Zenobia's suicide? As a result of disease brought on by the unnatural exercise of both mind and body? As a sign of "fornication or adultery," the possibility of which tantalizes Coverdale throughout the romance? As a sign of her victimization at the hands of men throughout the text (her father, Westervelt, Hollingsworth, Coverdale)? The medical explanation of her death is certainly persuasive, but it does not overrule the other explanations or even exclude them all. And the fact that we have only Coverdale's version of the events, which is surely of only dubious reliability, means that again, as with the doubled titles of "Rappaccini's Daughter," Hawthorne refuses to give an answer. Is it a feminist romance? A medical parable? He finally has it both ways.

THE "FEVERISH POET"

During the illness that initiates him into Blithedale society, Coverdale whispers to Hollingsworth that Zenobia is a witch, that she would vanish if he were to take her secret talisman, her exotic flower. When Hollingsworth reports Coverdale's accusations to Zenobia, she responds, "It is an idea worthy of a feverish poet" (465). One aspect of "The Oval Portrait," "Ligeia," "The Birthmark," "Rappaccini's Daughter," and *The Blithedale Romance* that I have left, as yet, unexplored is the sickness of the men. Poe's narrators are almost always sick: the narrator of "The Oval Portrait" is in a "desperately wounded condition"; the narrator of "Berenice" is "ill of health, and buried in gloom"; the narrator of "Eleonora" admits, "Men have called me mad." Both of Hawthorne's scientists, too, are of questionable health: Aylmer and Rappaccini are both pale and look unhealthy, even though nothing is ever noted explicitly to define them as ill. *The Blithedale Romance* makes the illnesses of men a little clearer: Coverdale confides, "It is my private opinion, that, at this period of his life, Hollingsworth was fast going mad" (471), and Coverdale is the only one in the romance to define himself as "an invalid" (which he does twice in the chapter describing his recovery from the flu [468, 469]).

Leland Person argues that these sickly men signify Poe's and Hawthorne's understanding of the unhealthy separation of character traits by gender:

> In projecting women into art objects in order to contain their creative energy, male characters repress those aspects of their own minds—especially their own creative power—with which women are identified; they thus run the risk of committing themselves to a creative process that is not only destructive of women but self-destructive as well. Most important, these male writers seem aware of the problem. The objectification of women which feminist critics have decried, in other words, should be understood as an extreme that male authors themselves recognized to be destructive both to the male self and to a masculine poetics.
>
> *(Aesthetic Headaches, 6)*

Such an explanation works beautifully within the framework of Laingian psychology that Person uses, but it is not very persuasive within the historical frame of a nineteenth-century understanding of mind and body. Poe's and Hawthorne's men are certainly understood to be self-destructive to the extent that they indulge in their monomanias[43] and to the extent that they develop their minds at great cost to their bodies, but such self-destruction would not have been understood as part of the oppression of women.

If we follow the argument made by G. J. Barker-Benfield in *The Horrors of the Half-Known Life,* it would have been the pressure exerted on the nineteenth-century man to succeed—to develop his mind and earning potential at the expense of his body and feelings—that would have *caused* the representations of women as objects and contributed to the oppression of women. Barker-Benfield argues that nineteenth-century theories held that male insanity was caused by both the harsh "realities of the world" of business and the greater sexual appetite of men. Since the business world and male sexuality were considered part of the "restless, insatiable, vicissitudinous, and essential nature of male society . . . the male tendency to insanity was [therefore regarded as] ineluctable." He contends that this had a deleterious effect on men's attitudes toward women:

> The effect of this was first to register the enormous pressure on men, intensified by their feeling that it was a given of their society (the instability of which was

accordingly and necessarily a given too), and of their sexual role within it. The characteristic disorder of boom and slump was, as Tocqueville put it, an "endemic disease" of the democratic "temperament." The corollary of accepting such conclusions about men was to direct social/medical/psychological expertise at that area of society that was not a given, that was not held by men to be so inalienable as the nature of their own existences, and consequently was more controllable, that is, to direct it at women.

(57)

To make claims that Poe or Hawthorne were mid-nineteenth-century feminists who saw the dangers of the objectification of women even more clearly than did women authors of the time is, probably, to engage in too much wishful thinking. It does seem likely, however, that in the same way that female authors like Stowe, Southworth, and Bullard chafed against the medical definitions and restrictions on women, Poe and Hawthorne chafed against medical definitions of men that promised them insanity if they tried to combine "too much" exercise of the intellect with "too much" exercise of their bodies and their sexuality. That such medical pronouncements were uncomfortable seems clear. That they could develop a twentieth-century understanding of the role of these definitions in oppressing women and restricting men seems unlikely.

Ultimately, whether one believes that Poe and Hawthorne joined their male artist/scientist figures in the objectification and destruction of female figures or that they represent those artist/scientist figures as horrors who oppress women and bring on their own destruction depends on one's reading of their attitudes toward those sickly male narrators and characters. Is *their* illness the illness that Hawthorne in his notebooks meant to use to "symbolize moral or spiritual disease by disease of the body"? Or does that illness remain the province of women? Finally, it is both—a critique of the patriarchal medical language that would define woman as always (an) invalid by projecting the "sickness of men" onto her and an embodiment of that patriarchal language. At best, the texts enact the invalidization of women they criticize. Like the female-authored texts we saw earlier, however much these tales resist the power of the medical discourse, they are finally incorporated by or into it.

Later in the century, as medical theory became increasingly powerful, much of this kind of uncertainty would disappear in novels like Oliver Wendell Holmes's *Elsie Venner* (1861). In this physician-authored novel about a young doctor's encounter with a snake-woman, there are questions of whether the woman is evil or just misguided, whether she is natural or supernatural, but there is no question of the need for a physician's intervention and no question of any male guilt. The townspeople in the story are divided not by religious differences but by their physician preference (the town has two), but everyone defers to the medical men. Questions about medicine, like those raised by Laura Curtis Bullard, Poe, and Hawthorne, would have to take on new forms to combat an increasingly solidified medical profession at the end of the nineteenth century.

In the first half of the nineteenth century, the invalid woman was established permanently as a literary figure in the conventions of American fiction. Aspects of the figure determined by the social conditions of the mid-nineteenth century have remained part of her representation long after those conditions changed. The contradictory shape of the figure—simultaneously representing power and weakness, innocence and guilt, blamelessness and fault, subservience and independence—carries on into later works. The invalid woman not only shapes literary conventions of how illness is represented but also helps determine how our culture defines illness, femininity, and normality.

Notes

1. Irving, in fact, writes that he has "digested and arranged the following particulars [from Mrs. Davidson's notes], adopting in many places the original manuscript, without alteration." He goes on to note that the biography is, in fact, "almost as illustrative of the character of the mother as of the child" (*Biography,* 11).

2. Sontag has written extensively on the damage done by the metaphors associated with tuberculosis in *Illness as Metaphor.* My argument in this book will follow a different track from Sontag's. While I agree that the figures of illness are often detrimental to the real human beings who suffer from the illness, I do not believe, as Sontag seems to, that one can ever stop that metaphorizing process. It seems more fruitful to explore and examine the metaphors than to urge a halt to metaphoricity.

3. Since I cannot deal with all of Poe's and Hawthorne's fiction in this chapter, there are some significant omissions here. I do not, for example, deal directly with the much healthier Hester Prynne or Phoebe Pyncheon. My argument is not meant to apply to all of Hawthorne's women but to those particular instances in which narrative dilemmas are settled by or at the woman's death. For discussions that do deal more exhaustively with Hawthorne's depiction of women, see Baym, *The Shape of Hawthorne's Career* and "Thwarted Nature: Nathaniel Hawthorne as Feminist," and Person, *Aesthetic Headaches.*

4. These assertions are explained at length in Barker-Benfield, *The Horrors of the Half-Known Life* (3-61). He points out that by the end of the century, this resistance would be crystallized by Huck

Finn's unwillingness to be adopted and "civilized" by Aunt Sally.

5. For a theoretical fleshing out of the place of mind and body in romanticism, see Kaplan, "Pandora's Box." For the history and two views of this association of woman with nature and the body rather than culture and the mind, see Griffin, *Woman and Nature,* and Irigaray, *Speculum of the Other Woman.* For two excellent anthropological discussions of the relation between the trope of woman as nature and the oppression of women, see Ortner, "Is Female to Male as Nature Is to Culture?," and Ardener, "Belief and the Problem of Woman."

6. In *The Lay of the Land,* Kolodny discusses how American attitudes toward landscape and physical nature were shaped by notions of gender; she points to the repeated trope of nature as a woman. Jehlen discusses other American attitudes toward nature and the land in *American Incarnation.* For a thorough discussion of the trope of woman as nature, see Griffin, *Woman and Nature.*

7. See Hull's "'Scribbling Females' and Serious Males" for a discussion of Hawthorne's private attitude toward women writers and artists. Both Baym in *The Shape of Hawthorne's Career* and "Thwarted Nature" and Person in *Aesthetic Headaches* offer a rereading of Hawthorne's relation to women, arguing that he was much more sympathetic than has been suggested up to this point.

8. Early and important feminist theorists like Mary Wollstonecraft and Margaret Fuller attest to the connection between romantic thought and the woman's rights movement. Romanticism was, at least in its earliest stages, ideologically connected to the idea of revolution and equality for all, an idea traced by Bartlett in "Liberty, Equality, Sorority," by Donovan in *Feminist Theory,* and by Tims in *Mary Wollstonecraft.* That notable romanticists did not agree with women's equality does not negate the influence romanticism may have had on early feminist thinking.

9. Ardener, in "Belief and the Problem of Woman," describes this same intermediacy as ambiguity, because women are subsumed under the title "mankind" (defined against its opposite, "the wild") but also opposed to "man" (14).

10. Baym makes a similar point: women, "though made to suffer as bodies, . . . are denied existence as mind." She uses this observation as the basis for arguing that Hawthorne "is suggesting . . . that the male inability to deal with woman's body is the *source* of all the abstract formulations that function as so many defenses against, and diversions from, the truth" ("Thwarted Nature," 66).

11. Chapter 5 takes up the problem of how the mind/body relation was addressed when the closed energy model finally crumbled at the end of the century.

12. See Barker-Benfield, *The Horrors of the Half-Known Life,* chapter 3, for more information on the nineteenth-century conception of "man's work."

13. This doubled attitude toward nature is explored in detail by Kolodny in chapter 4 of *The Lay of the Land.*

14. Ortner argues that the polarization common to feminine symbolism makes inversions of polar equations like woman = nature, man = culture, easy ("Is Female to Male as Nature Is to Culture?," 86). She cites several other historical instances in which woman have been equated with culture and men with nature.

15. Person points out that Poe "anticipates the artist-scientists" of Hawthorne in the narrator's refusal to see what effect his art is having on his bride and in his preference for the "aesthetic version of woman" (*Aesthetic Headaches,* 44).

16. Bonapart argues that "The Oval Portrait" expresses Poe's feelings of guilt that two women's deaths had been the models for so much of his own art (*Life and Works of Edgar Allan Poe,* 259).

17. Poe's confidence in the sickly woman's absolute power was probably due in large part to episodes from his life. Bonapart draws detailed analogies between Poe's portraits of powerful, though dying or dead, women and the characteristics of both his sickly mother and his dying wife to argue that all these women represent an infantile confidence in maternal omniscience and a childish wish/fear that his all-powerful mother could return to life (ibid., 218).

18. Poe's tale of Madeline's breaking free of her tomb and Berenice's being buried alive may be more realistic than has been previously thought. Dixon, in his discussion of hysteria, cites "numerous cases" of hysterics being buried only to reveal, upon exhumation of the body, "indubitable appearances of resuscitation." He chides the American public for the "rapidity with which we hurry our dead to the grave," arguing that to foreign visitors, "it looks like, and too often is, evidence of a want of affection" (*Woman and Her Diseases,* 141).

19. Jordan, in *Second Stories,* reads "Ligeia" in sequence with "The Fall of the House of Usher" and the three Dupin detective tales to conclude that "Poe saw the danger—to art and to culture—of the androcentric tradition . . . and he was indeed experimenting with the idea of a radically different consciousness, one that would be capable of imaginative revision" (150). Jordan's argument is persuasive; however, I am not trying to make any final conclusions about all of Poe's tales in this chapter.

20. Dayan, in *Fables of Mind,* reads Ligeia's reembodiment as resurrection: "Poe thus takes on the idea of resurrection and defines it expressly as a resurrection of the *body*" (177). This suggests a different way to read Ligeia as a Christ figure against domestic heroines who function, though very differently, as Christlike.

21. Since the mid-nineteenth-century word for psychiatrist was "alienist," we are to understand that our narrator also suffers from temporary bouts of insanity, which is yet more reason to doubt him.

22. See Dayan's reading of this story, "The Intelligibility of Ligeia," in *Fables of Mind* for a different point of view. She argues that "The point, of course, is not whether 'Ligeia' is a story of 'real magic' or one 'of remorse and hallucination' by a psychopathic killer or bookish dreamer, nor to entertain other super-naturalist explanations, but to look at the transaction between Ligeia and Rowena as an epistemological problem to be solved" (178).

23. The name "Beatrice" also suggests sexual abuse. It is usually understood, as Hawthorne hints in the tale, to refer to Dante's Beatrice, but several years later, in *The Marble Faun,* Hawthorne repeatedly calls attention to Beatrice Cenci, who was raped by her father. The "Beatrice" of this story likely has her origin in both of these earlier figures.

24. The question of why Baglioni's "antidote" kills Beatrice has been addressed by Uroff in "The Doctors in 'Rappaccini's Daughter'" as an allusion to the nineteenth-century conflict between allopathic and homeopathic medicine. No one in the nineteenth century, no matter their medical philosophy, had much understanding of why medicines worked as they did; allopathy and homeopathy represented two different theories of how drugs operated in the system. Uroff maintains that the Hawthorne story is an antidoctor allegory, upholding neither the allopathic nor the homeopathic theory; he argues that it illustrates the devastating effects of both medicines. In "'Rappaccini's Daughter' and the Nineteenth-Century Physician," Gross agrees and argues further that the story exemplifies the deep distrust of doctors among the nineteenth-century public. Hallissy, on the other hand, maintains in "Hawthorne's Venomous Beatrice" that Baglioni, an allopath, does not understand that

Rappaccini, a homeopath, has created Beatrice not as a poison but as an antidote to poison. While these are very interesting theories about the intersection of literature and medicine, they do not solve the metaphysical question of Beatrice's innocence or guilt or why the antidote kills her.

25. Had Hawthorne's story been written a few decades later, it could almost have been considered realism. Arsenic became an important cosmetic in the late nineteenth century, and there were reports (perhaps apocryphal) that women who regularly used it had killed their husbands with kisses (Haller and Haller, *Physician and Sexuality*, 144).

26. This second entry also describes Dr. Rappaccini himself and "The Bosom Serpent."

27. According to the *Oxford English Dictionary*, "poisoner" can mean either one who or that which poisons, so "poisoner" is not always an active role. It is, however, most commonly used to refer to one who poisons, while noxious substances are most often described as "the poison" or "poisonous." In any case, this reading of "the Beautiful Poisoner" does not depend on Beatrice's intent but on the fact that it is she who poisons Giovanni. Hawthorne writes, in the active voice, that it is she who "instilled a fierce and subtle poison into his system" (1051).

28. The term *empoisonneuse* also refers, in colloquial usage, to a woman who is in the way, who obstructs desires, who is a nuisance.

29. This is more or less in line with Person's reading of the story. He reads it as the challenge that the acceptance of a woman's right "to define herself in her own words" brings; he argues that when Giovanni finally refuses to allow Beatrice her own self-definition, "Beatrice is vicitmized by a male imagination that cannot overcome its own fear of woman" (*Aesthetic Headaches*, 117-18).

30. I am borrowing the term "homosocial desire" from Sedgwick's *Between Men*.

31. In *The Interpretation of Dreams*, Freud notes that flowers can frequently symbolize female sexuality, specifically with reference to defloration. "The dream had made use of the great chance similarity between the words 'violet' and 'violate'—the difference in their pronunciation lies merely in the different stress upon their final syllables—in order to express 'in the language of flowers' the dreamer's thoughts on the violence of defloration" (*Complete Psychological Works*, 5:376). (One notes the coincidence that Beatrice's favorite flower is purple.)

Freud explains with reference to a different dream that flowers can serve as a double symbol of sexual purity and corruption: "[Dreams] show a particular preference for combining contraries into a unity or for representing them as one and the same thing. . . . The same blossoming branch (cf. '*des Madchen's Bluten*' ['the maiden's blossoms'] in Goethe's poem '*Der Mullerin Verrat*') represented both sexual innocence and its contrary" (4:318-19).

32. Baym herself reads the story as a troubling allegory of faith—troubling because it is antithetical to Hawthorne's usual critique of "visionary delusion." She concludes that it is also an "allegory of sex," in which "Giovanni is a type of the sexually confused Victorian male, struggling between his wish to accept sex as a beneficent part of life and his strong conviction that it is unnatural and evil" (*The Shape of Hawthorne's Career*, 109). This is largely the same conclusion to which Person comes in *Aesthetic Headaches*.

33. For examples of the criticism that does read Hawthorne's women within the light-dark symbolism, see Carpenter, "Puritans Preferred Blondes"; Rahv, "The Dark Lady of Salem"; and Birdsall, "Hawthorne's Fair-Haired Maidens."

34. For a good discussion of the homoerotic element of *The Blithedale Romance*, see Lauren Berlant, "Fantasies of Utopia," 36-37.

35. Hawthorne interestingly shifts the gender of the innocent here and adds an element of homosocial desire between women, too; this is, perhaps, part of the overall suggestiveness about free love (see Lauren Berlant, "Fantasies of Utopia," for a discussion of the role of love in *The Blithedale Romance*). There is also a critical question of Priscilla's innocence; she, too, seems to embody the ambiguity of innocent/guilty. For a reading of Priscilla as a sexually experienced, reformed prostitute, see Lefcowitz and Lefcowitz, "Some Rents in the Veil."

36. Baym argues that Zenobia's "Legend of the Silvery Veil" illustrates the problem of the mind/body imbalance; she suggests that Zenobia's tale points to the contrast between Zenobia's physicality and Priscilla's spirituality as evidence that "a crude equation has been made between spirit and lack of body" that finally results in "an abnormal sex indeed, in which young, frail, immature girls become objects of sexual interest while fully sexed adult women are experienced as frightening, corrupt, or repellent. The ideal is diabolic" (*The Shape of Hawthorne's Career*, 197).

37. Jordan does not address *The Blithedale Romance* in *Second Stories*, but she argues that in other Hawthorne fictions he represents the eruption of the female voice.

38. Baym argues that Zenobia "unites sex, art and nature in one symbol" (*The Shape of Hawthorne's Career,* 190).

39. Lauren Berlant argues that the failure of love and the language of love finally destroys the utopian experiment of Blithedale: "Love acts as a thread that travels through the various elements that constitute the manifest and buried historical sites on which individuals negotiate their lives in this narrative: ultimately the novel questions the language of love itself, exposing love's inability truly to mediate, to merge, to illuminate, to provide a clarifying model of anything, whether utopian or tragic" ("Fantasies of Utopia," 33).

40. Schriber argues in "Justice to Zenobia" that Zenobia is murdered. Bauer also comes close to this position: "Hollingsworth has effectively willed Zenobia to death, for he has insisted that she either succumb to his patriarchal system of reform or lose her place to her rival Priscilla" (*Feminist Dialogics,* 45).

41. The history of attitudes toward and laws about suicide seems to coincide between England and America at this time. Anderson in *Suicide in Victorian and Edwardian England,* Kushner in *Self-Destruction in the Promised Land,* and Gates in *Victorian Suicide* all cite different evidence but come to much the same conclusions.

42. The notebook entry on which Zenobia's death is based also cites melancholy as the cause for suicide: "On the night of July 9th, a search for the dead body of a drowned girl. She was a Miss Hunt, about nineteen years old; a girl of education and refinement, but depressed and miserable for want of sympathy—her family being an affectionate one, but uncultivated. . . . She was of a melancholic temperament" (Hawthorne, *American Notebooks,* 112).

43. Hawthorne's mad men—Aylmer, Rappaccini, and Hollingsworth—all suffer from the nineteenth-century mental disease monomania, defined as a morbid fixation on one particular thing. For an extended argument on male madness in mid-century American fiction, in particular in Herman Melville's "Bartleby the Scrivener" (1853), and the harshness of mercantile life, see Gillian Brown's "The Empire of Agoraphobia" in *Domestic Individualism.*

Bibliography

Agnew, Jean-Christophe. "The Consuming Vision of Henry James." In *The Culture of Consumption,* edited by Richard Fox and T. J. Jackson Lears, 65-100. New York: Pantheon, 1983.

Alcott, Louisa May. *Little Women.* 1868. Reprint. New York: New American Library, 1983.

Allen, Elizabeth. *A Woman's Place in the Novels of Henry James.* New York: St. Martin's Press, 1984.

Anderson, Olive. *Suicide in Victorian and Edwardian England.* Oxford: Clarendon Press, 1987.

Ardener, Edwin. "Belief and the Problem of Woman." In *Perceiving Women,* edited by Shirley Ardener, 1-28. New York: Wiley, 1975.

Armstrong, Nancy. *Desire and Domestic Fiction: A Political History of the Novel.* New York: Oxford University Press, 1987.

Bakhtin, M. M. *The Dialogic Imagination: Four Essays.* Edited by Michael Holquist; translated by Caryl Emerson and Michael Holquist. Austin: University of Texas Press, 1981.

Bannister, Robert. *Social Darwinism: Science and Myth in Anglo-American Thought.* Philadelphia: Temple University Press, 1979.

Banta, Martha. *Imaging American Women: Idea and Ideals in Cultural History.* New York: Columbia University Press, 1987.

Bardes, Barbara, and Suzanne Gossett. *Declarations of Independence: Women and Political Power in Nineteenth-Century American Fiction.* New Brunswick, N.J.: Rutgers University Press, 1990.

Barker-Benfield, G. J. *The Horrors of the Half-Known Life: Male Attitudes toward Women and Sexuality in Nineteenth-Century America.* New York: Harper and Row, 1976.

Barrett, Michèle. "Ideology and the Cultural Production of Gender." In *Feminist Criticism and Social Change,* edited by Judith Newton and Deborah Rosenfelt, 65-85. New York: Methuen, 1985.

Bartlett, Elizabeth Ann. "Liberty, Equality, Sorority: Origins and Interpretations of American Feminist Thought—Frances Wright, Margaret Fuller, and Sarah Grimké." Ph.D. dissertation, University of Minnesota, 1981.

Bauer, Dale. *Feminist Dialogics: A Theory of Failed Community.* Albany: State University of New York Press, 1988.

Baym, Nina. "Hawthorne's Women: The Tyranny of Social Myths." *Centennial Review* 15 (1971): 250-72.

———. *Novels, Readers, and Reviewers: Responses to Fiction in Antebellum America.* Ithaca, N.Y.: Cornell University Press, 1984.

———. *The Shape of Hawthorne's Career.* Ithaca, N.Y.: Cornell University Press, 1976.

————. "Thwarted Nature: Nathaniel Hawthorne as Feminist." In *American Novelists Revisited: Essays in Feminist Criticism,* edited by Fritz Fleischmann, 58-77. Boston: G. K. Hall and Company, 1982.

————. *Woman's Fiction: A Guide to Novels by and about Women in America, 1820-1870.* Ithaca, N.Y.: Cornell University Press, 1978.

Beecher, Catharine. *Letters to the People on Health and Happiness.* New York: Harper and Brothers, 1855.

Bell, Millicent. "The Dream of Being Possessed and Possessing: Henry James's *The Wings of the Dove.*" *Massachusetts Review* 10 (1969): 97-114.

Belsey, Catherine. "Constructing the Subject, Deconstructing the Text." In *Feminist Criticism and Social Change,* edited by Judith Newton and Deborah Rosenfelt, 43-64. New York: Methuen, 1985.

Berlant, Jeffrey L. *Profession and Monopoly: A Study of Medicine in the United States and Great Britain.* Berkeley: University of California Press, 1975.

Berlant, Lauren. "Fantasies of Utopia in *The Blithedale Romance.*" *American Literary History* 1.1 (1989): 30-62.

Berman, Jeffrey. *The Talking Cure: Literary Representations of Psychoanalysis.* New York: New York University Press, 1985.

Biasin, Gian-Paolo. *Literary Diseases: Theme and Metaphor in the Italian Novel.* Austin: University of Texas Press, 1975.

Birdsall, Virginia Ogden. "Hawthorne's Fair-Haired Maidens: The Fading Light." *PMLA* 75 (1960): 250-56.

Bonapart, Marie. *The Life and Works of Edgar Allan Poe: A Psychoanalytic Interpretation.* Translated by John Rodken. London: Imago Publishing Company, 1949.

Boone, Joseph Allen. *Tradition Counter Tradition: Love and the Form of Fiction.* Chicago: University of Chicago Press, 1987.

Boston Women's Health Book Collective. *Our Bodies, Ourselves.* New York: Simon and Schuster, 1984.

Boydston, Jeanne, Mary Kelley, and Anne Margolis. *The Limits of Sisterhood: The Beecher Sisters on Women's Rights and Woman's Sphere.* Chapel Hill: University of North Carolina Press, 1988.

Braden, Charles S. *Spirits in Rebellion: The Rise and Development of New Thought.* Dallas: Southern Methodist University Press, 1963.

Brooks, Cleanth, R. W. B. Lewis, and Robert Penn Warren. *American Literature: The Makers and the Making.* Vol. 1. New York: St. Martin's Press, 1973.

Brown, Gillian. *Domestic Individualism: Imagining Self in Nineteenth-Century America.* Berkeley: University of California Press, 1990.

Brown, Herbert R. *The Sentimental Novel in America, 1789-1860.* Durham, N.C.: Duke University Press, 1940.

Brown, Joanne. "'Take Me to the River': The Water-Cure in America." *Medical Humanities Review* 1.2 (1987): 29-34.

Brownstein, Rachel. *Becoming a Heroine: Reading about Women in Novels.* New York: Viking Press, 1982.

Bullard, Laura Curtis. *Christine: A Woman's Trials and Triumphs.* New York: De Witt and Davenport, 1856.

Bullough, Vern, and Martha Voght. "Women, Menstruation, and Nineteenth-Century Medicine." In *Women and Health in America,* edited by Judith Walzer Leavitt, 28-38. Madison: University of Wisconsin Press, 1984.

Burke, Kenneth. *The Philosophy of Literary Form.* Berkeley: University of California Press, 1973.

Cady Stanton, Elizabeth, Susan B. Anthony, and Matilda Joslyn Gage, eds. *History of Woman Suffrage.* Vol. 1. Rochester, N.Y.: Charles Mann, 1881.

Carpenter, Frederic I. "Puritans Preferred Blondes: The Heroines of Melville and Hawthorne." *New England Quarterly* 9 (1936): 262-64.

Cayleff, Susan E. *Wash and Be Healed: The Water-Cure Movement and Women's Health.* Philadelphia: Temple University Press, 1987.

Chesler, Phyllis. *Women and Madness.* Garden City, N.Y.: Doubleday, 1972.

Clinton, Catherine. *The Other Civil War: American Women in the Nineteenth Century.* New York: Hill and Wang, 1984.

Cogan, Frances B. *All-American Girl: The Ideal of Real Womanhood in Mid-Nineteenth-Century America.* Athens: University of Georgia Press, 1989.

Coward, R., and J. Ellis. *Language and Materialism.* London: Routledge and Kegan Paul, 1977.

Crews, Frederick. *The Sins of the Fathers.* New York: Oxford University Press, 1968.

Culler, Jonathan. *On Deconstruction.* Ithaca, N.Y.: Cornell University Press, 1982.

————. "Story and Discourse in the Analysis of Narrative." In *Pursuit of Signs,* 167-87. Ithaca, N.Y.: Cornell University Press, 1981.

David, Deirdre. *Intellectual Women and Victorian Patriarchy: Harriet Martineau, Elizabeth Barrett Browning, and George Eliot.* Ithaca, N.Y.: Cornell University Press, 1987.

Davidson, Cathy N. *Revolution and the Word: The Rise of the Novel in America.* New York: Oxford University Press, 1986.

Dayan, Joan. *Fables of Mind: An Inquiry into Poe's Fiction.* New York: Oxford University Press, 1987.

Degler, Carl N. "What Ought to Be and What Was: Women's Sexuality in the Nineteenth Century." *American Historical Review* 89 (1974): 1467-90.

Delmar, Rosalind. "What Is Feminism?" In *What Is Feminism?,* edited by Juliet Mitchell and Ann Oakley, 8-33. New York: Pantheon, 1986.

Derrida, Jacques. "Freud and the Scene of Writing." In *Writing and Difference,* 196-231. Chicago: University of Chicago Press, 1979.

———. *Of Grammatology.* Translated by Gayatri Spivak. Baltimore: Johns Hopkins University Press, 1976.

———. "Plato's Pharmacy." In *Dissemination,* translated by Barbara Johnson, 61-172. Chicago: University of Chicago Press, 1982.

Dijkstra, Bram. *Idols of Perversity: Fantasies of Feminine Evil in Fin-de-Siècle Culture.* New York: Oxford University Press, 1986.

Dixon, E. H. *Woman and Her Diseases, from the Cradle to the Grave: Adapted Exclusively to Her Instruction in the Physiology of her System, and All the Diseases of Her Critical Periods.* 10th ed. New York: A. Ranney, 1855.

Doane, Mary Ann. "The Clinical Eye." In *The Female Body in Western Culture,* edited by Susan Suleiman, 152-73. Cambridge: Harvard University Press, 1985.

Donegan, Jane. *"Hydropathic Highway to Health": Women and Water-Cure in Antebellum America.* New York: Greenwood Press, 1986.

———. "'Safe Delivered' but by Whom?" In *Women and Health in America,* edited by Judith Walzer Leavitt, 302-17. Madison: University of Wisconsin Press, 1984.

Donovan, Josephine. *Feminist Theory: The Intellectual Traditions of American Feminism.* New York: Continuum, 1988.

———. "The Silence Is Broken." In *Women and Language in Literature and Society,* edited by Sally McConnel-Ginet, Ruth Borker, and Nelly Furman, 205-18. New York: Praeger, 1980.

Douglas, Ann. *The Feminization of American Culture.* New York: Alfred A. Knopf, 1977.

Douglas Wood, Ann. "'The Fashionable Diseases': Women's Complaints and Their Treatment in Nineteenth-Century America." *Journal of Interdisciplinary History* 4.1 (1973): 25-52.

DuBois, Ellen Carol, ed. *Elizabeth Cady Stanton, Susan B. Anthony: Correspondence, Writings, Speeches.* New York: Schocken Books, 1981.

———. *Feminism and Suffrage: The Emergence of an Independent Women's Movement in America, 1848-1869.* Ithaca, N.Y.: Cornell University Press, 1978.

Duffin, Lorna. "The Conspicuous Consumptive: Woman as Invalid." In *The Nineteenth-Century Woman: Her Culture and Physical World,* edited by Sara Delamont and Lorna Duffin, 26-56. New York: Barnes and Noble Books, 1978.

Ecob, Helen Gilbert. *The Well-Dressed Woman: A Study in the Practical Application to Dress of the Laws of Health, Art, and Morals.* New York: Fowler and Wells Company, 1892.

Edel, Leon. *Henry James: A Life.* New York: Harper and Row, 1985.

Ehrenreich, Barbara, and Deirdre English. *Complaints and Disorders: The Sexual Politics of Sickness.* Old Westbury, N.Y.: Feminist Press, 1973.

———. *For Her Own Good: 150 Years of the Experts' Advice to Women.* New York: Anchor Press, 1978.

Emerson, Ralph Waldo. "The Transcendentalist." In *Selections from Ralph Waldo Emerson,* edited by Stephen E. Whicher, 192-206. Boston: Houghton Mifflin, 1957.

Epstein, Barbara L. *The Politics of Domesticity: Women, Evangelism, and Temperance in Nineteenth-Century America.* Middletown, Conn.: Wesleyan University Press, 1981.

Faust, Langdon Lynne. *American Women Writers: A Critical Reference Guide from Colonial Times to the Present.* New York: Frederick Ungar, 1983.

Felman, Shoshana. "The Critical Phallacy." *Diacritics* 5.4 (1975): 2-10.

Fetterley, Judith. *The Resisting Reader: A Feminist Approach to American Fiction.* Bloomington: Indiana University Press, 1977.

Flexner, Eleanor. *Century of Struggle: The Woman's Rights Movement in the United States.* Rev. ed. Cambridge: Harvard University Press, 1975.

Foucault, Michel. *The Birth of the Clinic: An Archaeology of Medical Perception.* Translated by A. M. Sheridan. New York: Vintage Books, 1975.

———. *Discipline and Punish.* Translated by Alan Sheridan. New York: Vintage Books, 1979.

———. *History of Sexuality.* Vol. 1, *An Introduction.* Translated by Robert Hurley. New York: Pantheon, 1978.

———. *Madness and Civilization.* Translated by Richard Howard. New York: Vintage Books, 1973.

―――. *Power/Knowledge: Selected Interviews and Other Writings, 1972-77.* Edited and translated by Colin Gordon. New York: Pantheon, 1980.

―――. "What Is an Author?" In *Textual Strategies,* edited by Josué V. Harari, 141-60. Ithaca, N.Y.: Cornell University Press, 1979.

Fowler, Virginia C. *Henry James's American Girl: The Embroidery on the Canvas.* Madison: University of Wisconsin Press, 1984.

Frederick, J. T. "Hawthorne's Scribbling Women." *New England Quarterly* 48 (1975): 231-40.

Freud, Sigmund. *Complete Psychological Works.* 24 vols. Translated by James Strachey. London: Hogarth, 1953-74.

Fryer, Judith. *The Faces of Eve: Women in the Nineteenth-Century American Novel.* New York: Oxford University Press, 1976.

Gallop, Jane. *The Daughter's Seduction: Feminism and Psychoanalysis.* Ithaca, N.Y.: Cornell University Press, 1982.

―――. "Snatches of Conversation." In *Women and Language in Literature and Society,* edited by Sally McConnell-Ginet, Ruth Borker, and Nelly Furman, 274-83. New York: Praeger, 1980.

Gates, Barbara. *Victorian Suicide: Mad Crimes and Sad Histories.* Princeton, N.J.: Princeton University Press, 1988.

Gay, Peter. *The Education of the Senses.* New York: Oxford University Press, 1984.

Geertz, Clifford. *The Interpretation of Cultures.* New York: Basic Books, 1973.

Genette, Gerard. *Figures of Literary Discourse.* Translated by Alan Sheridan. New York: Columbia University Press, 1982.

Gilbert, Sandra, and Susan Gubar. *The Madwoman in the Attic: The Woman Writer and the Nineteenth-Century Literary Imagination.* New Haven: Yale University Press, 1979.

Gilman, Charlotte Perkins. *The Living of Charlotte Perkins Gilman: An Autobiography.* New York: D. Appleton-Century Compnay, 1935.

―――. "Why I Wrote 'The Yellow Wallpaper'?" In *The Charlotte Perkins Gilman Reader,* edited by Ann J. Lane, 19-20. New York: Pantheon Books, 1980.

―――. *Women and Economics.* Boston: Small, Maynard, and Company, 1899.

―――. "The Yellow Wallpaper." 1891. Reprinted in *The Charlotte Perkins Gilman Reader,* edited by Ann J. Lane, 1-19. New York: Pantheon Books, 1980.

Gilman, Sander. *Difference and Pathology: Stereotypes of Race, Gender, and Madness.* Ithaca, N.Y.: Cornell University Press, 1985.

―――. *Disease and Representation: Images of Illness from Madness to AIDS.* Ithaca, N.Y.: Cornell University Press, 1988.

―――. *Seeing the Insane.* New York: John Wiley and Sons, 1982.

Gordon, Linda. "Voluntary Motherhood: The Beginnings of Feminist Birth Control Ideas in the United States." In *Women and Health in America,* edited by Judith Walzer Leavitt, 104-16. Madison: University of Wisconsin Press, 1984.

Greene, Gayle. "Feminist and Marxist Criticism: An Argument for Alliances." *Women's Studies: An Interdisciplinary Journal* 9 (1981): 29-45.

Greene, Gayle, and Coppélia Kahn. *Making a Difference: Feminist Literary Criticism.* New York: Methuen, 1985.

Greene, Theodore P. *America's Heroes: The Changing Models of Success in American Magazines.* New York: Oxford University Press, 1970.

Griffin, Susan. *Woman and Nature.* New York: Harper Colophon Books, 1978.

Griffith, Elisabeth. *In Her Own Right: The Life of Elizabeth Cady Stanton.* New York: Oxford University Press, 1984.

Gross, Seymour. "'Rappaccini's Daughter' and the Nineteenth-Century Physician." In *Ruined Eden of the Present: Hawthorne, Melville, and Poe,* edited by G. R. Thompson and Virgil Lokke, 129-42. West Lafayette, Ind.: Purdue University Press, 1981.

Gubar, Susan. "'The Blank Page' and the Issues of Female Creativity." *Critical Inquiry* 9 (1981): 243-63.

Hale, Nathan G., Jr. *Freud and the Americans: The Beginnings of Psychoanalysis in the United States, 1876-1917.* New York: Oxford University Press, 1971.

Hale, Sarah Josepha. *The Lecturess, or Woman's Sphere.* Boston: Whipple and Damrell, 1839.

Hall, Stuart. "Cultural Studies: Two Paradigms." *Media, Culture, and Society* 2 (1980): 57-72.

Haller, John S., and Robin M. Haller. *The Physician and Sexuality in Victorian America.* New York: W. W. Norton, 1974.

Hallissy, Margaret. "Hawthorne's Venomous Beatrice." *Studies in Short Fiction* 19.3 (1982): 231-39.

Harris, Barbara J. *Beyond Her Sphere: Women and the Professions in American History.* Westport, Conn.: Greenwood Press, 1978.

Harris, Susan K. *Nineteenth-Century American Women's Novels: Interpretive Strategies.* Cambridge: Cambridge University Press, 1990.

Hawthorne, Nathaniel. *The American Notebooks of Nathaniel Hawthorne.* Edited by Randall Stewart. New Haven: Yale University Press, 1932.

———. *The Complete Novels and Selected Tales of Nathaniel Hawthorne.* New York: Modern Library, 1937.

Heilman, Robert. "Hawthorne's 'The Birthmark': Science as Religion." *South Atlantic Quarterly* 48 (1949): 575-83.

Helsinger, Elizabeth K. *The Woman Question: Society and Literature in Britain and America, 1837-83.* New York: Garland, 1983.

Holmes, Oliver Wendell. *Elsie Venner: A Romance of Destiny.* Boston: Ticknor and Fields, 1861.

Holmes, Stewart W. "Phineas Parkhurst Quimby: Scientist of Transcendentalism." *New England Quarterly* 17 (1944): 356-80.

Homans, Margaret. *Bearing the Word: Language and Female Experience in Nineteenth-Century Women's Writing.* Chicago: University of Chicago Press, 1986.

Hull, Ramona E. "'Scribbling Females' and Serious Males." *Nathaniel Hawthorne Journal* 5 (1975): 35-59.

Hunter, Dianne. "Hysteria, Psychoanalysis, and Feminism: The Case of Anna O." *Feminist Studies* 9.3 (1983): 464-88.

Irigaray, Luce. *Speculum of the Other Woman.* Translated by Gillian C. Gill. Ithaca, N.Y.: Cornell University Press, 1985.

———. "This Sex Which Is Not One." In *This Sex Which Is Not One,* translated by Catherine Porter and Carolyn Burke, 23-33. Ithaca, N.Y.: Cornell University Press, 1985.

———. "Women on the Market." In *This Sex Which Is Not One,* translated by Catherine Porter and Carolyn Burke, 170-91. Ithaca, N.Y.: Cornell University Press, 1985.

Irving, Washington. *Biography and Poetical Remains of the Late Margaret Miller Davidson.* 2d ed. Philadelphia: Lea and Blanchard, 1841.

Irwin, John T. *American Hieroglyphics.* New Haven: Yale University Press, 1980.

Jacobus, Mary, ed. *Women Writing and Writing about Women.* London: Croom and Helm, 1979.

James, Alice. *The Diary of Alice James.* Edited by Leon Edel. 1934. Reprint. New York: Penguin American Library, 1982.

James, Henry. *The Aspern Papers.* 1888. Reprinted in *The Turn of the Screw and Other Short Novels,* edited by Willard Thorp, 153-251. New York: New American Library, 1962.

———. "The Beast in the Jungle." 1903. Reprinted in *The Turn of the Screw and Other Short Novels,* edited by Willard Thorp, 404-51. New York: New American Library, 1962.

———. *Daisy Miller.* 1878. Reprinted in *The Turn of the Screw and Other Short Novels,* edited by Willard Thorp, 93-152. New York: New American Library, 1962.

———. *The Letters of Henry James.* Vol. 1. Edited by Leon Edel. Cambridge: Harvard University Press, 1974.

———. *The Notebooks of Henry James.* Edited by F. O. Matthiessen and Kenneth B. Murdock. New York: Oxford University Press, 1947.

———. *The Wings of the Dove.* Edited by J. Donald Crowley and Richard Hocks. 1902. Reprint. New York: W. W. Norton, 1978.

Jameson, Fredric. *The Political Unconscious: Narrative as Socially Symbolic Act.* Ithaca, N.Y.: Cornell University Press, 1980.

Janeway, Elizabeth. *The Powers of the Weak.* New York: Alfred A. Knopf, 1980.

Jehlen, Myra. *American Incarnation: The Individual, the Nation, and the Continent.* Cambridge: Harvard University Press, 1986.

———. "Archimedes and the Paradox of Feminist Criticism." *Signs* 6.4 (1981): 575-601.

———. "The Family Militant: Domesticity versus Slavery in *Uncle Tom's Cabin.*" *Criticism* 31 (1989): 383-400.

Jewett, Sarah Orne. *A Country Doctor.* 1884. Reprint. New York: New American Library, 1986.

Johnson, Barbara. *The Critical Difference: Essays in the Contemporary Rhetoric of Reading.* Baltimore: Johns Hopkins University Press, 1980.

———. *A World of Difference.* Baltimore: Johns Hopkins University Press, 1987.

Johnson, Richard. "What Is Cultural Studies Anyway?" *Social Text* 6.1 (1987): 38-80.

Jones, Edgar R. *Those Were the Good Old Days: A Happy Look at American Advertising, 1880-1930.* New York: Simon and Schuster, 1959.

Jordan, Cynthia. *Second Stories: The Politics of Language, Form, and Gender in Early American Fictions.* Chapel Hill: University of North Carolina Press, 1989.

Kamuf, Peggy. "Writing Like a Woman." In *Women and Language in Literature and Society,* edited by Sally McConnell-Ginet, Ruth Borker, and Nelly Furman, 284-99. New York: Praeger, 1980.

Kaplan, Cora. "Pandora's Box: Subjectivity, Class, and Sexuality in Socialist Feminist Criticism." In *Making a Difference: Feminist Literary Criticism,* edited by Gayle Greene and Coppélia Kahn, 146-76. New York: Methuen, 1985.

Kasson, Joy. *Marble Queens and Captives: Women in Nineteenth-Century American Sculpture.* New Haven: Yale University Press, 1990.

———. "Power and Powerlessness in Nineteenth-Century Sculpture." Lecture, University of North Carolina, Chapel Hill, 1987.

Kaston, Carren. *Imagination and Desire in the Novels of Henry James.* New Brunswick, N.J.: Rutgers University Press, 1984.

Kelley, Mary. *Private Woman, Public Stage: Literary Domesticity in Nineteenth-Century America.* New York: Oxford University Press, 1984.

———. "The Sentimentalists: Promise and Betrayal in the Home." *Signs* 4.3 (1979): 434-46.

Kelly, Howard, and Walter L. Barrage. "E. H. Dixon." In *Dictionary of American Medical Biography.* New York: D. Appleton and Company, 1928.

Kleinman, Arthur. *Patients and Healers in the Context of Culture.* Berkeley: University of California Press, 1980.

Kolodny, Annette. *The Lay of the Land: Metaphor as Experience and History in American Life and Letters.* Chapel Hill: University of North Carolina Press, 1975.

———. "A Map for Rereading: Or, Gender and the Interpretation of Literary Texts." *New Literary History* 11 (1980): 451-67.

———. "Reply to Commentaries: Women Writers, Literary History, and Martian Readers." *New Literary History* 11 (1980): 587-92.

Kristeva, Julia. "Women's Time." *Signs* 7.1 (1981): 13-35.

Kushner, Howard. *Self-Destruction in the Promised Land: A Psychocultural Biology of American Suicide.* New Brunswick, N.J.: Rutgers University Press, 1989.

Lacan, Jacques. *Ecrits: A Selection.* Translated by Alan Sheridan. New York: W. W. Norton, 1977.

Lamphere, Louise, and Michelle Zimbalist Rosaldo, eds. *Women, Culture, and Society.* Stanford: Stanford University Press, 1974.

Leavitt, Judith Walzer. *Brought to Bed: Childbearing in America, 1750-1950.* New York: Oxford University Press, 1986.

———. "'Science' Enters the Birthing Room: Obstetrics in America since the Eighteenth Century." *Journal of American History* 70 (1983): 281-304.

———, ed. *Women and Health in America.* Madison: University of Wisconsin Press, 1984.

Lefcowitz, Barbara F., and Allan B. Lefcowitz. "Some Rents in the Veil: New Light on Priscilla and Zenobia." *Nineteenth-Century Fiction* 21 (1966): 263-75.

Lentricchia, Frank. *Criticism and Social Change.* Chicago: University of Chicago Press, 1985.

———. "Patriarchy Against Itself: The Young Manhood of Wallace Stevens." *Critical Inquiry* 13.4 (1987): 742-86.

Lesage, Julia. "Women's Rage." In *Marxism and the Interpretation of Culture,* edited by Cary Nelson and Lawrence Grossberg, 419-28. Urbana: University of Illinois Press, 1988.

Lewis, Sinclair. *Arrowsmith.* New York: Harcourt, Brace and Company, 1925.

McCormack, Peggy. "The Semiotic of Economic Language in James's Fiction." *American Literature* 58.4 (1986): 540-56.

Macherey, Pierre. *A Theory of Literary Production.* Translated by Geoffrey Wall. London: Routledge and Kegan Paul, 1978.

MacKinnon, Catherine. "Desire and Power: A Feminist Perspective." In *Marxism and the Interpretation of Culture,* edited by Cary Nelson and Lawrence Grossberg, 117-36. Urbana: University of Illinois Press, 1988.

———. "Feminism, Marxism, Method, and the State." *Signs* 7.3 (1982): 515-44.

McLean, Robert C. "'Love by the Doctor's Direction': Disease and Death in *The Wings of the Dove.*" *Papers on Language and Literature* 8, supplement (1972): 128-48.

MacLelland, Bruce. *Prosperity through Thought and Force.* New York: Elizabeth Towne, 1907.

Mendelsohn, Robert S. *Mal(e)practice: How Doctors Manipulate Women.* Chicago: Contemporary Books, 1981.

Mercer, Caroline, and Sarah Wangensteen. "'Consumption, Heart-Disease, or Whatever': Chlorosis, a Heroine's Disease in *The Wings of the Dove.*" *Journal of the History of Medicine* 40.3 (1985): 259-85.

Michaels, Walter Benn. *The Gold Standard and the Logic of Naturalism: American Literature at the Turn of the Century.* Berkeley: University of California Press, 1987.

Michie, Helena. *The Flesh Made Word: Female Figures and Women's Bodies.* New York: Oxford University Press, 1987.

Milani, Laura. "Women in Waiting." *The New Physician.* 40 (March 1991): 21-25.

Miller, Nancy K., ed. *The Poetics of Gender.* New York: Columbia University Press, 1986.

Mitchell, Juliet. *Psychoanalysis and Feminism.* New York: Random House, 1975.

Mitchell, S. Weir. *A Comedy of Conscience.* New York: Century, 1903.

———. *Doctor and Patient.* Philadelphia: J. B. Lippincott, 1888.

Montrelay, Michèle. "Of Femininity." *M/F* 1 (1978): 83-101.

Moore, Rayburn S. "The Magazine and the Short Story in the Ante-Bellum Period." *South Atlantic Bulletin* 38 (1973): 44-51.

Morantz, Regina M. "The Perils of Feminist History." In *Women and Health in America,* edited by Judith Walzer Leavitt, 239-45. Madison: University of Wisconsin Press, 1984.

Morantz-Sanchez, Regina M. "So Honoured, So Loved?: The Decline of the Female Physician, 1900-1920." In *Send Us a Lady Physician: Women Doctors in America, 1835-1920,* edited by Ruth J. Abram. New York: W. W. Norton, 1985.

———. *Sympathy and Science: Women Physicians in American Medicine.* New York: Oxford University Press, 1985.

Mosher, Clelia. *Health and the Woman Movement.* 1915. Reprint. New York: The Woman's Press, 1918.

Myerson, Abraham. *The Nervous Housewife.* 1920. Reprint. Boston: Little, Brown, 1927.

Newton, Judith Lowder. *Women, Power, and Subversion: Social Strategies in British Fiction, 1778-1860.* Athens: University of Georgia Press, 1981.

Newton, Judith Lowder, and Deborah Rosenfelt, eds. *Feminist Criticism and Social Change.* New York: Methuen, 1985.

Nichter, Mark. "Negotiation of the Illness Experience: Ayurvedic Therapy and the Psychosocial Dimension of Illness." *Culture, Medicine, and Psychiatry* 5 (1981): 5-24.

Ortner, Sherry. "Is Female to Male as Nature Is to Culture?" In *Women, Culture, and Society,* edited by Michelle Zimbalist Rosaldo and Louise Lamphere, 67-88. Stanford: Stanford University Press, 1974.

Painter, Nell Irvin. *Standing at Armageddon: The United States, 1877-1919.* New York: W. W. Norton, 1987.

Papashvily, Helen W. *All the Happy Endings: A Study of the Domestic Novel in America, the Women Who Wrote It, the Women Who Read It, in the Nineteenth Century.* New York: Harper and Brothers, 1956.

Parker, Gail T. "Mary Baker Eddy and Sentimental Womanhood." *New England Quarterly* 43 (1970): 3-18.

———. *Mind Cure in New England: From the Civil War to World War I.* Hanover, N.H.: University Press of New England, 1973.

———, ed. *The Oven Birds: American Women on Womanhood, 1820-1920.* New York: Doubleday, 1972.

Person, Leland. *Aesthetic Headaches: Women and a Masculinist Poetics in Poe, Melville, and Hawthorne.* Athens: University of Georgia Press, 1988.

Phelps, Elizabeth Stuart. *Doctor Zay.* 1882. Reprint. New York: Feminist Press, 1987.

———. *Walled In.* New York: Harper and Brothers, 1907.

Plato. *The Phaedrus.* In *Euthyphro, Apology, Crito, Phaedo, Phaedrus,* translated by Harold N. Fowler. London: Loeb Library, 1971.

Poe, Edgar Allan. *The Complete Tales and Poems of Edgar Allan Poe.* Edited by Hervey Allen. New York: Modern Library, 1938.

———. *Essays and Reviews.* New York: Library of America, 1984.

———. Review of *The Biography . . . of Margaret Miller Davidson,* by Washington Irving. *Graham's Magazine* 19 (August 1841): 93-94.

Poirier, Suzanne. "The Weir Mitchell Rest Cure: Doctors and Patients." *Women's Studies* 10 (1983): 15-40.

Poovey, Mary. "Cultural Criticism: Past and Present." *College English* 52.6 (1990): 615-25.

———. *Uneven Developments: The Ideological Work of Gender in Mid-Victorian England.* Chicago: University of Chicago Press, 1988.

Price Herndl, Diane. "The Dilemmas of a Feminine Dialogic." In *Feminism and the Dialogic,* edited by Dale M. Bauer and Susan Jaret McKinstry, 7-24. Albany: State University of New York Press, 1991.

———. "'The Writing Cure': Charlotte Perkins Gilman, Anna O., and 'Hysterical Writing.'" *NWSA Journal* 1.1 (1988): 57-79.

Purvis, Andrew. "A Perilous Gap." *Time* 136 (1990): 66-67.

Rahv, Philip. "The Dark Lady of Salem." *Partisan Review* 8 (1941): 362-81.

Reed, James. "Doctors, Birth Control, and Social Values, 1830-1970." In *Women and Health in America,* edited by Judith Walzer Leavitt, 124-40. Madison: University of Wisconsin Press, 1984.

"Review of *Retribution.*" *American Whig Review* 10 (1849): 376-86.

Reynolds, David S. *Beneath the American Renaissance: The Subversive Imagination in the Age of Emerson and Melville.* New York: Alfred A. Knopf, 1988.

Riley, Glenda. *Inventing the American Woman: A Perspective on Women's History, 1865 to the Present.* Arlington Heights, Ill.: Harlan Davidson, 1986.

Romero, Lora. "Bio-Political Resistance in Domestic Ideology and *Uncle Tom's Cabin.*" *American Literary History* 1.4 (1989): 715-34.

Rosaldo, Michelle Zimbalist. "The Use and Abuse of Anthropology: Reflections on Feminism and Cross-Cultural Understanding." *Signs* 4.3 (1979): 497-513.

———. "Women, Culture, and Society: A Theoretical Overview." In *Women, Culture, and Society,* edited by Michelle Zimbalist Rosaldo and Louise Lamphere, 17-42. Stanford: Stanford University Press, 1974.

Rose, Jacqueline. *Sexuality in the Field of Vision.* London: Verso, 1986.

Rosenberg, Charles E. "Sexuality, Class, and Role in Nineteenth-Century America." *American Quarterly* 25.2 (1973): 131-53.

Rothstein, William. *American Physicians in the Nineteenth Century: From Sects to Science.* Baltimore: Johns Hopkins University Press, 1972.

Rowe, John Carlos. *The Theoretical Dimensions of Henry James.* Madison: University of Wisconsin Press, 1984.

Rowson, Susanna. *Charlotte Temple.* Edited by Ann Douglas. 1794. Reprint. New York: Penguin Books, 1991.

Rubin, Gayle. "The Traffic in Women." In *Toward an Anthropology of Women,* edited by Rayna Reiter, 157-210. New York: Monthly Review, 1975.

Salk, Hilary, et al. "The Politics of Women's Health." In Boston Women's Health Book Collective, *Our Bodies, Ourselves.* New York: Simon and Schuster, 1984.

Scarry, Elaine. *The Body in Pain.* New York: Oxford University Press, 1985.

———. Introduction to *Literature and the Body: Essays on Populations and Persons,* edited by Elaine Scarry, vii-xx. Selected Papers from the English Institute, 1986. Baltimore: Johns Hopkins University Press, 1988.

Schopp-Schilling, Beate. "'The Yellow Wallpaper': A Rediscovered 'Realistic' Story." *American Literary Realism* 8 (1975): 284-86.

Schriber, Mary. "Justice to Zenobia." *New England Quarterly* 55 (1982): 61-78.

Schweikart, Patrocinio, and Elizabeth Flynn. *Gender and Reading.* Baltimore: Johns Hopkins University Press, 1986.

Sedgwick, Eve Kosofsky. *Between Men: English Literature and Male Homosocial Desire.* New York: Columbia University Press, 1985.

Shorter, Edward. *A History of Women's Bodies.* New York: Basic Books, 1982.

Showalter, Elaine. *The Female Malady: Women, Madness, and English Culture, 1830-1980.* New York: Pantheon, 1985.

Smith, Barbara Herrnstein. *Contingencies of Value: Alternative Perspectives for Critical Theory.* Cambridge: Harvard University Press, 1988.

Smith, Henry Nash. "The Scribbling Women and the Cosmic Success Story." *Critical Inquiry* 1 (1974): 47-70.

Smith, Page. *Daughters of the Promised Land: Women in American History.* Boston: Little, Brown, 1970.

Smith-Rosenberg, Carroll. *Disorderly Conduct: Visions of Gender in Victorian America.* New York: Oxford University Press, 1985.

Smith-Rosenberg, Carroll, and Charles Rosenberg. "The Female Animal: Medical and Biological Views of Woman and Her Role in Nineteenth-Century America." In *Women and Health in America,* edited by Judith Walzer Leavitt, 12-27. Madison: University of Wisconsin Press, 1984.

Sontag, Susan. *Illness as Metaphor.* New York: Farrar, Straus, Giroux, 1978.

Southworth, E. D. E. N. *Retribution.* Chicago: M. A. Donahue and Company, 1849.

Spiller, Robert E., Willard Thorp, Thomas H. Johnson, and Henry Seidel Canby. *Literary History of the United States.* Vol. 1. New York: Macmillan, 1948.

Spillers, Hortense. "Changing the Letter: The Yokes, the Jokes of Discourse: Or, Mrs. Stowe, Mr. Reed." In *Slavery and the Literary Imagination,* edited by Deborah E. McDowell and Arnold Rampersad, 25-61. Baltimore: Johns Hopkins University Press, 1989.

Stage, Sarah. *Female Complaints: Lydia Pinkham and the Business of Women's Medicine.* New York: W. W. Norton, 1979.

Starr, Paul. *The Social Transformation of American Medicine.* New York: Basic Books, 1982.

Steele, Valerie. *Fashion and Eroticism: Ideals of Feminine Beauty from the Victorian Era to the Jazz Age.* New York: Oxford University Press, 1985.

Stein, Gertrude. *Three Lives.* 1909. Reprint. New York: Modern Library, 1933.

Stowe, Harriet Beecher. *Pink and White Tyranny: A Society Novel.* Boston: Roberts Brothers, 1871.

———. *Uncle Tom's Cabin; or, Life Among the Lowly.* Edited by Ann Douglas. 1852. Reprint. New York: Penguin American Library, 1981.

Stowe, Harriet Beecher, and Catharine Beecher. *The American Woman's Home: or, Principles of Domestic Science; Being a Guide to the Formation and Maintenance of Economical, Healthful, Beautiful, and Christian Homes.* New York: J. B. Ford and Company, 1869.

Strouse, Jean. *Alice James: A Biography.* Boston: Houghton Mifflin, 1980.

Suleiman, Susan, ed. *The Female Body in Western Culture.* Cambridge: Harvard University Press, 1985.

Tims, Margaret. *Mary Wollstonecraft: A Social Pioneer.* London: Millington, 1976.

Tompkins, Jane. "Highbrow-Lowbrow Revisited: The Revival of Mass-Culture Criticism." Paper presented at Modern Language Association Convention, San Francisco, 28 December 1987.

———. *Sensational Designs: The Cultural Work of American Fiction.* New York: Oxford University Press, 1985.

Treichler, Paula. "Escaping the Sentence: Diagnosis and Discourse in 'The Yellow Wallpaper.'" *Tulsa Studies in Women and Literature* 3.1-2 (1984): 61-77.

Turkle, Sherry. *Psychoanalytic Politics: Freud's French Revolution.* New York: Basic Books, 1978.

Uroff, M. D. "The Doctors in 'Rappaccini's Daughter.'" *Nineteenth-Century Fiction* 27 (1972): 61-70.

Veblen, Thorstein. *The Theory of the Leisure Class: An Economic Study of Institutions.* 1899. Reprint. New York: B. W. Huebsch, 1918.

Veeder, William. *Henry James: The Lessons of the Master—Popular Fiction and Personal Style in the Nineteenth Century.* Chicago: University of Chicago Press, 1975.

Verbrugge, Lois. "Gender and Health: An Update on Hypotheses and Evidence." *Journal of Health and Social Behavior* 26 (1985): 156-82.

Verbrugge, Martha. *Able-Bodied Womanhood: Personal Health and Social Change in Nineteenth-Century Boston.* New York: Oxford University Press, 1988.

Vernon, John. "Labor and Leisure: *The Wings of the Dove.*" in *Money and Fiction: Literary Realism in the Nineteenth and Early Twentieth Centuries.* Ithaca, N.Y.: Cornell University Press, 1984.

Wagenknecht, Edward. *Eve and Henry James: Portraits of Women and Girls in His Fiction.* Norman: University of Oklahoma Press, 1978.

Wagner, Vern. "Henry James: Money and Sex." *Sewanee Review* 93.2 (1985): 216-31.

Wakefield, Edward. "The National Disease of America." *McClure's Magazine* 2 (1893): 302-7.

Walsh, Mary Roth. *"Doctors Wanted: No Women Need Apply": Sexual Barriers in the Medical Profession, 1835-1975.* New Haven: Yale University Press, 1977.

Warhol, Robyn. *Gendered Interventions: Narrative Discourse in the Victorian Novel.* New Brunswick, N.J.: Rutgers University Press, 1989.

Wasserstrom, William. *Heiress of All the Ages: Sex and Sentiment in the Genteel Tradition.* Minneapolis: University of Minnesota Press, 1959.

Welter, Barbara. "The Cult of True Womanhood, 1820-1860." *American Quarterly* 18 (1966): 151-74.

———. *Dimity Convictions: The American Woman in the Nineteenth Century.* Athens: Ohio University Press, 1976.

White, Allon. *The Uses of Obscurity: The Fiction of Early Modernism.* London: Routledge and Kegan Paul, 1981.

White, Hayden. *Tropics of Discourse: Essays on Cultural Criticism.* Baltimore: Johns Hopkins University Press, 1978.

Williams, Stanley T. *The Life of Washington Irving.* Vol. 2. New York: Oxford University Press, 1935.

Wolp, A. M., and A. Kuhn. *Feminism and Materialism.* London: Routledge and Kegan Paul, 1978.

Woolf, Virginia. *Collected Essays.* Vol. 2. New York: Harcourt, Brace and World, 1966.

Woolson, Abba Goold. *Woman in American Society.* Boston: Roberts Brothers, 1873.

Yeazell, Ruth Bernard. Introduction to Alice James, *The Death and Letters of Alice James.* Berkeley: University of California Press, 1981.

Athena Vrettos (essay date 1995)

SOURCE: Vrettos, Athena. "Body Language and the Poetics of Illness." In *Somatic Fictions: Imagining Illness in Victorian Culture*, pp. 19-47. Stanford: Stanford University Press, 1995.

[*In the following essay, Vrettos explores the Victorian notion of gender identity based on "physical signs and medical symptoms" that denoted a connection between emotion and disease, especially in women.*]

If we trace the genesis of human character, by considering the conditions of existence through which the human race passed in early barbaric times and during
civilization, we shall see that the weaker sex has naturally acquired certain mental traits by its dealings with
the stronger. . . . The wives of merciless savages must,
other things equal, have prospered in proportion to
their powers of disguising their feelings. Women who
betrayed the state of antagonism produced in them by
ill-treatment, would be less likely to survive and leave
offspring than those who concealed their antagonism;
and hence, by inheritance and selection, a growth of
this trait proportionate to the requirement. In some
cases, again, the arts of persuasion enabled women to
protect themselves, and by implication their offspring;
where, in the absence of such arts, they would have
disappeared early, or would have reared fewer children.
One further ability may be named as likely to be cultivated and established—the ability to distinguish quickly
the passing feelings of those around. In barbarous times
a woman who could from a movement, tone of voice,
or expression of face, instantly detect in her savage
husband the passion that was rising, would be likely to
escape dangers run into by a woman less skilled in interpreting the natural language of feeling. Hence, from
the perpetual exercise of this power, and the survival of
those having most of it, we may infer its establishment
as a feminine faculty.

—Herbert Spencer, *The Study of Sociology*

Herbert Spencer's discussion of gender differences in
social and linguistic behavior is notable for its emphasis
on suppression, disguise, and the reading of bodily signs
as women's natural legacies from primitive human culture. To censor or transmute the expression of one's
own feelings and to decipher the subtle emotional gestures of others are, in Spencer's formulation, complementary feminine faculties. For Spencer, the human
body becomes both the source and the aim of women's
hermeneutic activity: it offers a "natural language of
feeling" that is both more primitive and more essential
to women's survival than spoken language. Because
they provided crucial adaptations to the conditions of
primitive human culture, these alternative semiotic systems helped to shape female identity and social roles in
the process of species survival, becoming, according to
Spencer's formula, part of the necessary biological programming of modern femininity.[1] As a result of this
programming, women would presumably be more adept
than men at disguising their feelings and would thus be
better adapted to interpreting indirect forms of communication. Spencer's social-Darwinian explanation of
women's linguistic and hermeneutic behaviors natural-
izes social practices while providing what is essentially
a unidirectional epistemology: What women must discover, decode, and be acutely sensitive to in men is precisely the emotional iterability (and readability) that
they must suppress in themselves. At the same time that
women must become good readers of men, they must
prevent themselves from being well-read. But the very
notion of women as unreadable made them subject to

increased scrutiny. Their strategies of emotional disguise produce Spencer's desire to interpret them. Furthermore, as strategies for survival, women's acts of
emotional and linguistic indirection constitute an aggressive mechanism of defense at the same time that
they suggest a severe degree of self-effacement. Spencer thus makes a virtue out of female necessity. In the
paradigm he constructs, women function as complacent
participants in Victorian ideology—in the inscription of
their own "meaning"—by encoding their own bodies,
and reading others, as texts.

Spencer's explanation of social and linguistic practices
demonstrates some common assumptions about gender
and body language that characterized Victorian culture.
Although there was no systematic psychological theory
that explored the relationship between emotional repression and somatic expression until Freud's early studies
of hysteria and his development of "the talking cure,"
there was, nevertheless, a widespread Victorian belief in
the expressive or communicative potential of the human—and particularly female—body. Like Sherlock
Holmes, many Victorians were deeply interested in
reading bodies as texts. They developed elaborate theories for decoding physical details, symptoms, and gestures—theories that assumed that people spoke through
their bodies and interpreted the bodies of others in particularly structured, usually gendered, ways.[2] This communicative potential is most explicitly, and extrava-
gantly, present in Victorian representations of illness.
What Spencer describes as women's special "aptitude
for guessing the state of mind through the external
signs" is, in effect, the basis for a feminine hermeneutics that Victorian fiction repeatedly manifests (343). In
this chapter I argue that the interpretation of both physical signs and medical symptoms as part of Spencer's
"natural language of feeling" was a crucial aspect of
how Victorians defined and understood the affective
structures of gender identity. In particular, I address
how literary and medical representations of illness contributed to a hermeneutics of bodily detail that assumed
a direct correspondence between emotion and symptom,
charting the physical consequences of feelings in order,
ultimately, to channel and control them. In this fashion,
we can see Spencer's account of women's behavioral
legacy as part of a larger cultural project that sought to
explain the relationship between language, gender, and
emotion. Spencer applauds the mystery of female emotion at the same time that he classifies it out of existence by turning it into a language that men can finally
"read" in the form of an evolutionary narrative.

It is not, of course, my intention to claim that Spencer's
account of women's discursive practices is linguisti-
cally or historically accurate, or that it describes the
nonverbal ways women communicated in the nineteenth
century.[3] Rather, my interest lies in the extent to which
Victorian culture *believed* that women communicated

and interpreted more somatically than men and how this belief shaped perceptions of social behavior and gender identity in the nineteenth century. Recently, feminist critics have tended to dismiss the terms in which nineteenth-century culture understood women's illnesses, particularly hysteria, by portraying them as monolithic assertions of medical and patriarchal power. This portrayal has resulted in interpretations of the female sufferer as either a transgressive feminist heroine who challenges cultural norms of behavior with her perplexing and metamorphic array of symptoms, or a passive victim of medical tyranny.[4] Neither of these perspectives provides a completely effective way of studying the competing and often contradictory cultural meanings of illness in the nineteenth century. Elaine Showalter, for example, dismisses as merely "traditional" Victorian theories of hysteria that explained it in terms of sexual repression: "It was much simpler to blame sexual frustration, to continue to see hysterical women as lovelorn Ophelias, than to investigate women's intellectual frustration, lack of mobility, or needs for autonomy and control" (*Female Malady,* 132). In rightly complicating the contributing factors of hysteria, Showalter ignores complex implications of apparently "simple" nineteenth-century explanations of female maladies. What exactly did it mean to see hysterical women as lovelorn Ophelias? What link between fiction, emotion, and medical symptom did this imply? How did this model shape the way early and mid-Victorian culture understood women's emotional lives, sexual needs, and discursive possibilities? Although nineteenth-century women's nervous illnesses undoubtedly arose from complex and imperfectly understood causes that contemporaries chose to ignore, we must nevertheless consider the terms through which Victorians understood such illnesses and explore their links to the formation of gender identities and ideologies.[5]

One of the central paradigms of nineteenth-century somatic ideology did, in fact, attempt to relate psychosomatic states to complex internal relations. In explaining early-nineteenth-century therapeutics, Charles Rosenberg has emphasized how a conceptualization of the human body as a system of dynamic exchange dominated both the medical and the popular imagination. This conceptualization was guided by two fundamental principles of bodily economy: First, "every part of the body was related inevitably and inextricably with every other. A distracted mind could curdle the stomach; a dyspeptic stomach could agitate the mind." Second, "the body was seen as a system of intake and outgo—a system which had, necessarily, to remain in balance if the individual were to remain healthy. . . . Equilibrium was synonymous with health, disequilibrium with illness" (40). As Rosenberg suggests, this way of viewing the relationship between mental and bodily functions was not limited to the field of medicine, but rather was part of a larger system of belief that shaped cultural behav-

ior and understanding (40). Although Rosenberg writes about the early nineteenth century, his explanation of both an internal paradigm of bodily economy and an external one that emphasized the body's "dynamic interactions with its environment" (40) form the basis for many later therapeutic suppositions. While diagnostic categories and therapeutic techniques underwent important transformations during the course of the century, medical and cultural beliefs about bodily economy, relationships of depletion and exchange maintained their importance (if not always in a consistent form) as conceptual frameworks. The discovery of the first law of thermodynamics (the conservation of energy) in the 1840's made economic theories of body and mind increasingly prominent after mid-century.[6] These accounts of mind/body economies help to explain the prevalent role "feelings" played in nineteenth-century discussions of illness. Insofar as physiological effects could be attributed to the emotional life of the subject, learning to read the physical signs of emotion formed a crucial medical and literary project.

If emotions could produce somatic effects, the heightened sensitivity of female emotions could magnify the production of physical symptoms. Physicians generally held that "the whole vasomotor system of the female was far more excitable than that of the male, marking her with a tendency to greater tension, irritability, and emotionalism. Laughing, crying, blushing and quickened heart beat were all marks of her peculiar mental state" (Haller and Haller, 73-74). Conditions including chronic headaches, brain fever, chlorosis, consumption, anorexia, hysteria, and eventually neurasthenia were all attributed (at least in part) to the emotional and mental state of the patient, and particularly the female patient, thereby reinforcing the idea that women's emotions were more somatic, and their diseases more complicated by emotions, than men's. Yet in attributing the heightened potential for female emotionalism to physiological causes, nineteenth-century physicians implied that excitability was a natural component of women's biological identity. If women were *naturally* prone to displays of emotion, there would seemingly be no need for the parental surveillance and medical interventions that doctors and advice manuals routinely recommended. While attempting to naturalize feminine affect, doctors defined this ostensibly normal condition as the source of women's dysfunctional behavior. By instructing mothers in the emotional meanings of their adolescent daughters' bodily symptoms and warning them to watch out for dangerous signs of ill health that could arise from various affective traumas, nineteenth-century advice literature participated in the pathologization of female emotion. It furthermore gave women an occupation suited to their hermeneutic proclivities, teaching them to become narcissistic watchdogs of their own symptoms while suggesting that they lacked (because of their constitutional susceptibility to heightened emotion) the capacity to solve the problems their own bodies "naturally" created.

The extent of this proliferation of causes and symptoms can be seen in the ever-widening inclusion of direct and indirect triggers of female maladies. Thus while women were both instructed and assumed to be privileged readers of the "natural language of feeling," their actual literary reading practices became the focus of medical scrutiny. This emphasis on the deleterious effects of reading dates back to eighteenth-century discussions of sensibility. As both Michel Foucault and John Mullan have indicated, eighteenth-century medical treatises frequently asserted that imaginary emotions and desires contracted through reading sentimental poetry and novels had the power to provoke nervous illness, particularly in susceptible young women.[7] Thomas Trotter's 1807 *View of the Nervous Temperament,* for example, warned that "the love-sick trash of most modern compositions" posed a threat to health. "To the female mind, in particular, as being endued with finer feeling, this species of literary poison has been often fatal; and some of the most unfortunate of the sex have imputed their ruin chiefly to reading novels" (88). As a result, many advice manuals cautioned mothers to censor their daughters' reading matter, particularly avoiding fictions that offered models of sentimental suffering. This form of emotional and literary censorship lasted well into the Victorian period, appropriated in the service of changing conceptions of illness and femininity during the course of the century. In 1808 Samuel Jennings listed "idleness" and "reading novels and romances" as two primary causes of female illness (18-19). Lydia Maria Child's 1831 *Mother's Book* stresses the "unhealthy influence" and "intellectual intemperance" of gothic and sentimental fiction, its tendency to produce "weakness and delirium" (93-94). An 1853 manual contends that young ladies' wounded affections form the "secret cause of much ill health, insanity, and even death" (Abell, 199). And a manual published as late as 1907 warns that "music, literature, and art, imaginative works of all sorts mix themselves up with sex feelings, so that the two help to form the emotional nature. . . . The falling in love and the disappointments connected therewith during early adolescence often lead to hysteria, to attacks of depression, and changes in character and conduct. In such cases there is usually hereditary nervousness or weakness of some sort" (Clouston, 51, 72). The significant differences between Jennings's and Child's advice and Clouston's are the latter's inclusion of heredity in his analysis of hysterical tendencies and his explicit emphasis on adolescent sexuality as the foundation of an emotional nature. These changes reflect the greater emphasis on hereditary causes of nervous illness in the latter decades of the nineteenth century and an increasing recognition of "sex feelings" in women's psychological and emotional development. Despite these important transformations in the conception of female

sexuality, however, there is a striking diachronic consistency in the anxiety about reading as an intensifying and destabilizing external influence on women's most private emotional lives. There is also a significant parallel between concern about female reading habits and concern about (primarily male) masturbation in Victorian advice manuals. Medical and social proscriptions against women's reading of sentimental, gothic, or sensational fiction constructed a female version of the dangers of "solitary practices." In both cases, the entrance of the imagination into unlicensed channels created a state of imbalance, potentially depleting nervous resources and thereby threatening physical health.

Ultimately, reading inculcated the very affective and responsive behaviors women would come to regard as the diagnosable (and natural) results of their disorders. Doctors reproduced this structure of assumptions in their own case studies, emphasizing the somatic effects of emotional fluctuation and interpreting women according to the literary conventions of the very sentimental fiction that supposedly contributed to their medical conditions. In an 1847 case study published in *The Lancet,* one doctor described the treatment of an unmarried, physically deformed woman who died after childbirth under medical care. Although the doctor suggested that her physical handicaps and small size added to the complications of her pregnancy, and he acknowledged that she suffered considerable pain both before and after the birth of her child by caesarean operation without anesthesia, he nevertheless attributed the cause of her death to her shame in being an unmarried mother (*The Lancet,* February 6, 1847, 139-40). In interpreting the deterioration of his patient's physical condition as an expression of her emotional trauma, the attending doctor assumed a direct correspondence and causal relationship between mind and body that outweighed the evidence of medical complications. In effect, he diagnosed the patient's illness according to the generic conventions of the sentimental novel in its portrayal of the fallen woman: the patient's dying body communicated, more than anything else, her state of emotional distress.

The role that literary conventions sometimes played in medical diagnoses was thus to explain the influence of the patient's emotional life on the progress of his (and more particularly her) condition. Emotional distress constituted a medical complication, and the doctor could recognize emotional distress by its similarity to fictional paradigms. This same interpretive correlation could, in turn, be applied to acts of emotional control. If distress could disrupt the healing process, the containment or rechanneling of distress could facilitate recovery. This correlation between emotional control and the recovery of health is perhaps most clearly enacted in the physician Samuel Warren's popularized descriptions of case studies published in *Blackwood's Edinburgh Magazine* in the 1830's. Warren describes the case of a well-bred young lady suffering from breast cancer, who is able to maintain a state of emotional stability and stoic resistance to pain throughout an operation to remove the tumor in her breast. Mrs. St.— spends the entire operation, performed before the discovery of anesthesia, with her eyes focused on a letter from her husband that she has requested the physician to hold before her. By channeling her emotions into their proper sphere, she is able to withstand the shock to her system. The sustaining (or anesthetizing) force of marital correspondence effectively contains the patient's dangerous emotional energies, thus preventing them from disrupting both operation and recovery. Only when the operation has been successfully completed and she has been conveyed upstairs to her own bed, does Mrs. St.— faint. Yet the focus of her affective containment is itself the most sentimental of objects. One could reasonably expect the love letter from an absent spouse to generate emotional excess rather than control. Warren's emphasis suggests that it is the letter's status as both a sentimental keepsake and a symbol of marital fidelity that makes it the proper container for a young wife's feelings. But rather than resolving the letter's contradictions, this alliance merely highlights the contested nature of sentimentality, sensibility, and affect in medical discussions of female nature. We find the cultural meaning of female sickness codified through a medical rhetoric that sought to diagnose and treat women's illnesses as products of their emotional instability or, conversely, to attribute the recovery of health to proper emotional balance, while still defining emotional fluctuation and excess as woman's most natural, biological inheritance. In stressing the links between emotionalism and illness, physicians implied that a woman's most natural channel for emotional communication was physiological, yet the translation of emotion into symptom constituted a source of dysfunctional health.

Ultimately, when doctors complained about women's tendency toward emotional excess and problematic reading habits, they identified the very qualities that made women ideal subjects, producing the need for medical advice and treatment. The embodied "nature" of female emotions created the very mystery that Victorian medicine sought to demystify and explain away. It is in this combined (and contradictory) attempt to naturalize, pathologize, and decode the semiotics of bodily communication that we can see Victorian anxieties about gender ideology at work. Women's symptoms took on multiple and coded meanings for Victorian medicine, providing the skilled diagnostician with a privileged access to the emotional life of the subject. Yet women's own presumed access to this inner life, through the intuitive reading of bodily signs, placed them in competition with the very practitioners who sought to "read" them. It is this hermeneutic paradox— that the most adept female interpreter of bodily signs might be the patient most in need of medical interpreta-

tion and intervention—that we find played out repeatedly in literary representations of female maladies. As nineteenth-century authors explored the conditions of women's discursive practices, they produced models for decoding the poetics of illness.

Doctors frequently exploited novels as both a contributing cause of female illness and a paradigm for interpreting the symptoms of emotional distress; but Victorian novels were no less absorbed by the links between fiction and illness, gender and emotion. Victorian authors cautioned about the somatic effects of emotional engagement while simultaneously seeking to produce sympathetic emotional responses in the reader. Harriet Martineau's novel *Deerbrook,* in its numerous portrayals of female illness, is a virtual handbook on the ways in which "looks and tones" may communicate "what words and acts had been forbidden to convey" (287). Functioning as a companion piece to her advice books, Martineau's novel provides an extended meditation on the medical consequences of women's disguised speech and emotions. The narrative voice laments at one point, "There are sad tales sung and told everywhere of brains crazed, and graves dug by hopeless love: and I fear that many more sink down into disease and death from this cause, than are at all suspected to be its victims" (163-64). According to Martineau's formula, illness or even death could constitute an elaborate form of body language that she instructs her readers to interpret. As I suggest in Chapter 3, the profusion of ailing heroines and sentimental deathbed scenes in Victorian fiction provided important training ground for both real and implied readers. Victorian writers routinely assumed the reader's fluency in the interpretation of body language; at the same time they provided lessons in somatic decoding for those less attuned to "the language of nature." Despite the overwhelmingly male control of the medical profession in the nineteenth century, expertise in reading the emotional language of the sickroom was constructed as a distinctly feminine (or potentially feminizing) practice.

As I have suggested, insofar as women's hermeneutic skills and their powers of emotional disguise were believed to be complementary attributes, women's intuitive relationship to body language took two forms: interpreting the physical symptoms of emotion and producing them. These twin gestures correspond, in turn, to the figures of nurse and patient in Victorian fiction. Representations of illness in nineteenth-century novels manifest many of the same contradictions about emotional iterability and readability that we find in the medical literature of the period. In particular, the figure of the nurse—as either an idealized enactment of feminine hermeneutics or a sensational spectacle of feminine emotion gone astray—highlights some of the tensions within Victorian culture over the proper interpretation of affect. Insofar as women's emotional lives were perceived as both somatically encoded and medically or intuitively legible, as mysterious texts that defied interpretation at the same time they demanded it, they could assume radically different ideological meanings and literary forms. The conflict between medical constructions of emotional susceptibility as a normal function of the female nervous system (and part of women's natural biological inheritance), and the pathologization of female emotional excess is perhaps most clearly enacted in Victorian fictions that highlight the interpretive (and in some cases narrative) skills of the nurse who makes the patient's body legible to the reader through a privileged access to unspoken feelings. In texts such as Alcott's *Hospital Sketches* and *Little Women*, Gaskell's *Cousin Phillis*, and Charlotte Brontë's *Shirley*, we find an emphasis on somatic communication that illuminates the network of cultural assumptions about gender, illness, and language that I have described.[8] Each highlights the failure of spoken language to provide adequate channels for the expression of intense feelings; each demonstrates a different way in which illness functions to communicate the inner life of the patient; and each posits the ailing body as simultaneously legible and illegible. Ultimately, these texts idealize the affective hermeneutics of nursing and the semiotics of emotional and somatic distress in ways that are later challenged by dangerous confrontations with affective excess in works such as Mrs. Henry Wood's *East Lynne* and Wilkie Collins's *Dead Secret*. Although a common cultural narrative about the "natural language of feeling" seems to emerge from these texts (and many others, such as Henry James's *Wings of the Dove*, which I take up in Chapter 3), the conflicting meanings ascribed to that narrative suggest that the relationship between gender, illness, and emotion was both formally and ideologically unstable.

EMOTIONAL VENTRILOQUISM

Alcott is perhaps the most explicit of the three writers in outlining the strengths of an intuitive feminine hermeneutics, seeing it as a necessary skill for nursing the sick and wounded. In her autobiographical *Hospital Sketches* (1863), recounting her experiences nursing Civil War soldiers, Alcott makes a claim for women's somatic literacy, describing the "sympathetic encouragement which women give, in look, touch, and tone more effectually than in words" (7). She demonstrates how this faculty can assist women in the field of nursing, recounting her own nonverbal communications with and interpretations of wounded soldiers. She describes staring at unconscious faces that "almost seemed to speak," claiming, "though they made no confidences in words, I read their lives" (44). In one detailed account of a soldier's death, Alcott interprets her patient's bodily movements as a language that provides access to his emotional experience:

> The strong body rebelled against death, and fought every inch of the way, forcing him to draw each breath with a spasm, and clench his hands with an imploring look, as if he asked, "How long must I endure this, and be still!" For hours he suffered dumbly, without a moment's respite, or a moment's murmuring; his limbs grew cold, his face damp, his lips white, and, again and again, he tore the covering off his breast, as if the lightest weight added to his agony; yet through it all, his eyes never lost their perfect serenity, and the man's soul seemed to sit therein, undaunted by the ills that vexed his flesh.
>
> (56)

Despite its grounding in the reality of a soldier's pain, the scene appears elaborately staged. The act of reading the patient's body involves Alcott's participation in a series of generic conventions that include the expansive physical gestures of melodrama (the "clenched hands," the "imploring look," the covering torn from his breast) and the pathos of sentimental fiction (the silent suffering and "perfect serenity" of the dying hero's soul). Alcott even provides hypothetical dialogue, substituting her own imaginative speech for the patient's silence. Ventriloquism becomes one of the defining gestures of *Hospital Sketches*, as Alcott describes her own "sympathizing murmur[s]" in response to the soldiers and her longing "to groan for them, when pride kept their white lips shut" (37). Alcott frames the scene in such a way that the reader is simultaneously encouraged to interpret the dying soldier's body and instructed in the hermeneutic conventions of nursing. These conventions are, Alcott stresses, quite different from those practiced by the doctor (and particularly the surgeon), whose sole concern is with interpreting the bodies of his patients *as* bodies.[9] She translates the efficiency of the surgeon's work into metaphors of domestic duty, describing how one surgeon who had served in the Crimea "seemed to regard a dilapidated body very much as I should have regarded a damaged garment; and, turning up his cuffs, whipped out a very unpleasant looking housewife, cutting, sawing, patching and piecing, with the enthusiasm of an accomplished surgical seamstress" (36). The surgeon's proper work is the patching of flesh, just as the housewife's is the patching of clothing, and "The more intricate the wound, the better he liked it" (36). Yet this relentless materialism leads Alcott to criticize the tendency of the medical profession to fragment body and soul, "regarding a man and his wound as separate institutions" (91). It is the nurse's job to reconstruct the patient's fragmented identity, reading his soul through his body and thus reaffirming their dynamic relationship. In observing some of the traumatic emotional effects of battle on Civil War soldiers—the same debilitating symptoms that first led Silas Weir Mitchell to develop his "rest cure"—Alcott finds that in some cases the patient's "mind had suffered more than his body" (45), thus necessitating the interpretive (and narrative) skills of a good nurse.[10]

Ultimately, nursing and femininity become interchangeable concepts in Alcott's *Sketches*. In learning to read the emotional language of the body, the nurse uses the skills of sympathy that are most closely associated with a distinctly feminine "nature." Yet the underlying gender ideology of this association involves a more complex definition of femininity than at first it seems, for as Alcott points out, not all women make good nurses; the more delicate ones' proper "sphere" is that of "a comfortable bandbox on a high shelf" (91). The femininity of the nurse is predicated first and foremost on her capacity for emotional bonding with the patient:

> You ask if nurses are obliged to witness amputations and such matters, as a part of their duty? I think not, unless they wish; for the patient is under the effects of ether, and needs no care but such as the surgeons can best give. Our work begins afterward, when the poor soul comes to himself, sick, faint, and wandering; full of strange pains and confused visions, of disagreeable sensations and sights. Then we must sooth and sustain, tend and watch; preaching and practicing patience, till sleep and time have restored courage and self-control.
>
> (90)

When Alcott is invited to attend a dissection she refuses, claiming, "my nerves belonged to the living, not to the dead, and I had better finish my education as a nurse before I began that of a surgeon" (91). Here Alcott implies that it is one's nervous system, rather than a strong stomach, medical expertise, or any other defining physical or intellectual qualities, that is most crucial for effective nursing practices. To participate in a dissection is to channel one's nervous energies away from an engagement with the living patient, and Alcott is vaguely disturbed by the transgression of the personal bond that dissection implies. She finds it "trying" to think of doctors cutting into "some person whom I had nursed and cared for," because to conceive of the body in such starkly material terms is to risk becoming like the doctor who "feared his profession blunted his sensibilities" (91).[11] Yet Alcott resists making a strictly biological distinction between the nurse's and doctor's roles, instead demonstrating a preference for the feminizing characteristics of intuition and empathy in both genders and professions. Thus she prefers the doctor "who suffered more in giving pain than did his patients in enduring it" to a more brutally efficient one who expected his patients to assist him in operations and who was capable of "whipping off legs like an animated guillotine" (92-93).[12] She admits, however, that this preference, and her "desire to insinuate a few of [the efficient doctor's] own disagreeable knives and scissors into him," amounts to little better than a "prejudice" (92). In *Sketches,* then, Alcott places the feminine interpretation of emotion at the center of the medical project at the same time that she constructs practical gender distinctions between doctors tending to bodies and nurses tending to souls. Alcott carves out a spiritual role for the nurse that asserts her unique capacity for reading silences and transforming them into narratives; she finds even (or perhaps especially) the unconscious body or the body convulsed with pain in pressing need of interpretation. Through these acts of emotional ventriloquism Alcott authorizes her own narrative voice, asserting her role as the chronicler of wounded bodies as they manifest wounded minds.

We can see the same emphasis on the translation of body into soul in Alcott's fictional work, particularly *Little Women* (1868), which in a limited way takes up the subject of nursing where *Hospital Sketches* leaves off. Here too Alcott poses the patient's emotional life as an interpretive problem that necessitates the skilled decoding of physical symptoms. Beth March's lingering illness confuses her sister Jo, who is more adept at reading literary texts than she is at reading bodies. Although Alcott was prone to interpret the embodied emotions of male invalids in the language of sentiment and melodrama, she parodies this formulaic mode of reading when Jo mistakes Beth's pallor for the conventional signs of unrequited love. Jo's first response is to try to write a new ending to Beth's story as she might for her own heroines, thereby transforming the deathbed drama into a narrative of miraculous recovery. But in this instance literature misleads Jo in reading bodily signs. When her efforts fail to produce the expected transformation, Jo slowly learns to interpret Beth's symptoms by intuition rather than generic literary design, as individual to Beth rather than conventional to heroines. Like Alcott's own response to nursing the wounded, Jo's response to Beth's illness teaches her to reaffirm the relationship between emotional and bodily experience. Jo's initiation into somatic interpretation is simultaneously an initiation into femininity. Outspoken and male-identified, Jo is forced to study the more nuanced gestures of Beth's life, gestures that draw on traditional codes of feminine domestic virtue. In this way, Jo becomes the end result of a dialectic in which linguistic and intuitive body hermeneutics coalesce; she becomes an "accurate" reader of somatic texts, as well as a producer of narratives about them.

If Jo's role in *Little Women* highlights the interpretation of body language, Beth's role explores its modes of production. In the textual economy of Alcott's novel, Beth's silences stand out from the surrounding narratives that her sisters construct. Beth's and Jo's sharply contrasting gender roles explore the conflict between feminine identity and linguistic authority. Whereas the strong, masculine Jo is the family "scribbler," making her way in the world through the art of storytelling, Beth is associated with the passive virtues of domesticity and silence. Beth is incapable of refiguring the world in fiction. Her only dream is "to stay at home safe with father and mother, and help take care of the family" (129). During a storytelling game at Laurie's picnic,

Beth "disappear[s] behind Jo" (118), leaving control of language to her more verbally dexterous sister. Whereas the other participants shape the interlocking stories to their own temperaments (Mr. Brooke fashions a tale of chivalrous knighthood; Meg a ghostly romance; Amy a fairy tale, and Jo a playful confusion of genres), Beth's life remains untransformed by linguistic play. In the world of *Little Women* progress to adulthood necessitates the power of self-transformation; even the selfish Amy learns to "mould her character as carefully as she moulds her little clay figures" (201). Beth never matures because she does not seek access to a self-authorizing discourse. Her inability to construct a narrative identity parallels her inability to leave the home, and invalidism becomes the logical extension of her domesticity. Beth tells Jo, "I never made any plans about what I'd do when I grew up; I never thought of being married as you all did. I couldn't seem to imagine myself anything but stupid little Beth, trotting about at home" (338-39). The fact that Beth's lingering death comes at the onset of adolescence allows her to retain her childhood identity amidst the changing structure of the March family. Volume 2 of *Little Women,* which Alcott titled *Good Wives,* charts the three sisters' assimilation into the adult world, their transformation from independent children into wives and mothers. Beth's role is excluded from the title, yet her disease provides a commentary on it, for as Nina Auerbach has pointed out, "Beth's lingering death symbolizes the marriages of the remaining sisters" ("Afterword," 466). Alcott envisions Beth's illness as a distinctly feminine form of communication and the logical consequence of a domestic ideal. In this way, *Little Women* provides a companion piece to *Hospital Sketches,* for in each the ailing body is both the source and the aim of narrative production and feminine hermeneutics; Alcott displays her literacy in both languages, using the genre of sentimental fiction and the nursing chronicle to reconnect material and spiritual definitions of the self.

ELOQUENT DECEPTIONS AND SOMATIC TRUTH

Alcott, like Showalter, critiques the conventional interpretation of female illness as a sign of unrequited love, suggesting a more complex reading of emotional causation and feminine speechlessness. Both Elizabeth Gaskell's novella *Cousin Phillis* (1865) and Charlotte Brontë's novel *Shirley* (1849) examine the somatic consequences of repressed desire and linguistic betrayal in their portrayals of illness. Each explores the psychological processes at work in the transformation of feelings into symptoms, and each charts the semiotic structures of women's body language in order to provide a commentary on acts of narrative production. Whereas Beth March's illness provides a substitute for the absence of a self-authorizing narrative, the illnesses of

Gaskell's and Brontë's heroines mark attempts to assert control over romantic narratives that have effectively eluded, betrayed, or erased their capacity for speech.

Gaskell's novella examines how illness functions as a response to the ambiguity of spoken and written language. In *Cousin Phillis,* the heroine's illness accentuates her inability to reconcile speech and action, identifying the indirect language of bodily symptom as the most powerful assertion of a material "truth." Questions of language—written, spoken, corporeal—and questions of interpretation—translation, multivalence, reader response—are at the center of Gaskell's story. In the course of the narrative we learn that the heroine, Phillis Holman, has been brought up by her father to believe in the unity of word and meaning and to treat her parents' speech with biblical reverence, "as if they had been St Peter and St Paul" (250). An Independent minister and a stern proponent of clear, straightforward words and deeds, Ebenezer Holman instructs his daughter in classical languages, teaching her a literal mode of translation. When the more worldly hero, Edward Holdsworth, enters the world of Hope Farm, he introduces Phillis to the possibility of double meanings, teasing her with "a style of half-joking talk that Phillis was not accustomed to" (259). Phillis's father believes Holdsworth's mode of speech to be a temptation akin to "dram-drinking" (266), because it manifests the storyteller's power to intoxicate his audience. In contrast, Holdsworth finds the minister's linguistic rigor to be a "very wholesome exercise, this trying to make one's words represent one's thoughts, instead of merely looking to their effect on others." Holdsworth attempts to curb his "random assertions and exaggerated expressions, such as one always uses" (264), but he is finally unable to embrace the family's moralistic fervor about language and complains, "Why make a bugbear of a word?" (265).

Holdsworth expresses his desire for Phillis indirectly, through marginalia in Phillis's Italian texts. Paul, Phillis's cousin and Gaskell's narrator, questions the propriety of Holdsworth's tactics, feeling that his friend's intrusion into Phillis's textual notes is "taking a liberty" (262) with her intellectual (and, implicitly, her sexual) privacy, transforming literary translation into a powerful medium for romantic expression.[13] Ultimately, Phillis and Edward's mediated dialogue is not congruent with the household's religious standards of linguistic honesty. Holdsworth's intrusion into female marginalia, like Lockwood's perusal of Cathy's diary in *Wuthering Heights,* generates sexually charged consequences. Phillis falls in love with Holdsworth before he has declared his intentions openly, and Holdsworth's subsequent transfer to work in Canada and marriage to a French-Canadian woman precipitate Phillis's case of brain fever.

Phillis's decline actually takes place in two stages that are shaped by Paul's attempts to read Phillis's bodily signs. Upon observing that Phillis has become pale, quiet, and listless in response to Holdsworth's departure, Paul tries to cure her by telling her that Holdsworth had spoken of his love for Phillis and his desire to marry her when he returned. Upon hearing that Holdsworth's spoken words, written messages, and physical gestures demonstrated a unity of emotional intentions, Phillis temporarily recovers and shows all the transformative physical signs of requited love. When Holdsworth then writes that he has met a woman who reminds him of Phillis, and later that he has married her (thereby suggesting the interchangeability, rather than uniqueness, of female identity), Phillis becomes ill with brain fever and almost dies. Here Paul's role as mediator parallels that of the textual marginalia. He is implicated in Holdsworth's betrayal of emotional truth by his own attempts at mediation; at the same time, Paul demonstrates his faith in these confidences as accurate reflections of Holdsworth's feelings and lasting expressions of his intentions. Paul subscribes, in effect, to the same interpretive values that Phillis and her family do, and is indirectly betrayed by this faith.

Gaskell is quite explicit about the relationship between textual ambiguity, emotional trauma, and the onset of illness. Because Phillis has no direct access to Holdsworth's emotional life, she has relied not only on Paul's testimony but also on the "language of nature" to provide a gloss on Holdsworth's marginalia. As her servant and nursemaid, Betty, notes, "there's eyes, and there's hands, as well as tongues" (298).[14] But in Holdsworth's case, neither physical signs nor marginal notations predict subsequent actions. Phillis's attempt to "read" Holdsworth according to an interpretive theory that would unify words and gestures as signs of an objective inner truth proves to be unreliable in a polyvalent world of human motives and interactions. Clinging to her faith in objective meaning, and seeking to repair the rift made by Holdsworth's indirect communications, Phillis responds to linguistic indeterminacy by offering her own body as the ultimate unified text. She thereby appropriates her father's biblical hermeneutics to the service of feminine somatic expression. As a gesture of protest, Phillis's wasted frame links emotions and actions; it proclaims her faith in a self unmediated by language. By asserting her insistently material presence (and her equally insistent refusal to translate emotions into speech), Phillis's symptoms force those around her to "read" her unspoken version of the romantic narrative as the true one.[15] Thus in becoming the author of her own illness, she simultaneously authorizes her own (silent) narrative, converting both the household and the extended community to an interpretive paradigm that places gestures above words. In the face of Phillis's illness the household is forced into a stance of mute sympathy that demands the careful reading of one another's facial expressions and bodily gestures. Paul describes how "in *these silent days* our very lives had been an

unspoken prayer. Now we met in the house-place, and *looked at each other* with strange recognition of the *thankfulness on all our faces.*" When he tries to speak, Reverend Holman's words come out only as sobs, and an aged farmhand declares, "I reckon we have blessed the Lord wi' all our souls, though *we've ne'er talked about it*; and maybe *He'll not need spoken words* this night" (315, emphases mine). The household becomes silent in response to Phillis's silence; they refuse to speak falsely in response to her refusal. Thus when asked by his fellow ministers to resign himself to giving his daughter up to God, the Reverend Holman declines to speak the words demanded of him, declaring, "What I do not feel I will not express; using words as if they were a charm" (313). Gaskell's narrative interrogates (and genders) the conditions of discursive authority, staging a confrontation between the desire for a unified, objective, and self-controlled meaning and the inevitable ambiguities, exaggerations, and falsehoods of the fictional project. In the disjunction between private (feminine, emotional, somatic) truth and public language, Gaskell identifies the ambiguity of her own project, an ambiguity that resonates in the unresolved ending of the story. The narrative ends soon after Phillis's recovery from brain fever, without her having regained either energy or good spirits. Phillis's final desire for a "change of thought and scene" as a way of going "back to the peace of the old days" (317) corresponds to the advice offered by many nineteenth-century health manuals but leaves the state of her health, like the narrative, unresolved. The very ability to write (rather than somatize) the narrative presupposes a relationship to language that the text identifies with the public realm of Holdsworth's verbal dexterity. As a narrator who is simultaneously complicitous in, confused by, and acutely attuned to his cousin's illness, Paul is poised between the position of a nurse who reads the patient's body and transforms it into narrative and the role of one who uses language for effect.[16] In the terms proposed by Gaskell's story, the literary text, unlike the heroine's body, is too implicated in the deceptions and mediations of fiction to control the production of meaning or claim the status of truth.[17]

MATERNAL NURSING AND THE DANGERS OF AFFECT

Charlotte Brontë's *Shirley* combines what I have identified as the affective hermeneutics of nursing with the construction of illness as an expression of the emotional life of the patient.[18] Like Alcott, Brontë instructs the reader in the accurate interpretation of bodily symptoms, and like Gaskell, she associates the somatic with both privacy and truth. But Brontë is more explicit than Gaskell in her critique of linguistic authority and social practice, employing illness to explore the ramifications of normative femininity on women's psychological development.

In many ways Caroline Helstone is one of Brontë's most conventional heroines; unlike the more passionately expressive Jane Eyre or the more independent and aggressive Shirley Keeldar, Caroline seems trapped in conduct book codes of proper feminine behavior. Even her illness serves as a proof of her femininity, as she responds to her lover's indifference through a process of self-starvation. Faced with the choice of whether "to pursue him, or to turn upon herself" (107), Caroline chooses a suitably maidenly decline. Brontë explicitly frames Caroline's dilemma as a linguistic one, observing, "A lover masculine so disappointed can speak . . . a lover feminine can say nothing. . . . Nature would brand such demonstration as a rebellion against her instincts, and would vindictively repay it afterwards by the thunderbolt of self-contempt smiting suddenly in secret" (105). This passage suggests that Caroline's illness arises out of a cultural demand for feminine quiescence. Brontë goes on to trace a tradition of silent, dying women through the Helstone family history; she describes Caroline's aunt, Mary Cave Helstone, as "a girl with the face of a Madonna; a girl of living marble; stillness personified" (52), whose "silent . . . lingering decline" (53) seems the natural consequence of her passive femininity. By associating her with both artistic stasis and silence, Brontë reveals Mary Cave's deadly acquiescence in her own objectification; Caroline stares at her aunt's framed portrait as she contemplates women's circumscribed lives. Like Mary Cave, Caroline is frequently described in metaphors of silence. Her beauty, according to the Reverend Hall, is of "a very quiet order" (271), and even Caroline's ladylike clothing conveys her restrained nature, for Caroline "never makes a bustle in moving" (157). Through these images Brontë explores Caroline's participation in cultural codes of genteel femininity that prohibit self-assertive behavior and speech; at the same time, Brontë exposes the fatal consequences of women's self-erasure.

Illness, then, becomes the direct result of Caroline's silence, forcing others to read her corporeal transformation and interpret its underlying message. The neighborhood watches and comments as Caroline grows paler, responding to her decline according to their own hermeneutic abilities. Her uncle, as baffled by Caroline's metamorphosis as by the death of his wife, complains, "These women are incomprehensible. . . . To-day you see them bouncing, buxom, red as cherries, and round as apples; to-morrow they exhibit themselves effete as dead weeds, blanched and broken down. And the reason of it all? that's the puzzle" (189). In posing the mutability of the female body as a "puzzle" to be solved, the Reverend Helstone articulates a sense of diagnostic confusion similar to what many nineteenth-century doctors felt when confronted with the mysterious correspondence between emotional fluctuations and somatic symptoms. It is, predictably, the female population of the neighborhood who are able to read this "natural language of feeling." Caroline perceives that "young ladies looked at her in a way she understood, and from which she shrank. Their eyes said they knew she had been 'disappointed,' as custom phrases it" (192).

The intended audience of Caroline's fading body is her lover, Robert Moore. When Caroline's illness is most eloquent, however, Robert's ability to read it remains in question. Preoccupied with questions of labor and management in the public sphere, Robert is unskilled in interpreting the nuances of feminine emotion and seemingly oblivious to the existence of Caroline's psychosomatic distress: "As he looked up, the light of the candles on the mantelpiece fell full on her face: all its paleness, all its change, all its forlorn meaning were clearly revealed. Robert had good eyes, and might have seen it, if he would: whether he did see it, nothing indicated" (252). As the reader becomes progressively attuned to the semiotics of Caroline's illness, Robert seems to become increasingly insensitive. When he begins to make love to the heiress Shirley Keeldar, Robert ignores the signs of Caroline's jealousy and despair. Each time Caroline watches Robert and Shirley together, her pallor and silence increase. Eventually she becomes, like Mary Cave, a symbol of walking death, haunting Robert as a ghost from the past rather than a living woman. Robert tells her:

> I walked into the cottage parlour. . . . There was no candle in the room . . . and broad moonbeams poured through the panes: there you were, Lina, at the casement, shrinking a little to one side in an attitude not unusual with you. You were dressed in white, as I have seen you dressed at an evening party. For half a second, your fresh, living face seemed turned towards me, looking at me. . . . Two steps forward broke the spell: the drapery of the dress changed outline; the tints of the complexion dissolved, and were formless: positively, as I reached the spot, there was nothing left but the sweep of a white muslin curtain.
>
> (255)

Robert's vision of the ghostly curtain parallels the progress of Caroline's disappearing body.[19] He watches as "the tints of the complexion dissolve" and become "formless," leaving only the clothing without the life. Brontë suggests that the real Caroline is dissolving herself in similarly haunting ways; like her habitual "shrinking . . . attitude," Caroline's shrinking body conveys her emotional trauma. Her illness simultaneously reveals the presence of a body beneath her ladylike clothing and causes its slow deterioration. Brontë implies that behind Robert's attempt to avoid recognizing his cousin's illness is buried the knowledge of his own participation in it. Though not yet dead, Caroline has already become a ghost in Robert's imagination, a manifestation of his own betrayal and guilt.

When Caroline's decline develops into a critical case of brain fever, Brontë indicates the serious consequences of Caroline's emotional constraint.[20] Not only a product of unrequited love, Caroline's disease also marks the conflict between realism and romanticism that divides the novel. Brontë implies that Caroline's despair arises from her continued feeling of displacement in the masculine world her uncle and Robert represent.[21] Torn between the romantic impulses of her nature and her lonely insignificance in the face of violent strikes and manufacturing crises, Caroline wearies of a life that has proved void of emotional fulfillment. Having tried "to see things as they were, and not to be romantic" (172), Caroline finds that the "real" world offers no place for her. She realizes, like Brontë, that "imagination" may be "a disease rather than a gift of the mind" (48), but finds she is unable to relinquish the imaginary romance that threatens her health.[22]

Brontë's interest in the emotional content of Caroline's illness is most explicit in the text's nursing scenes. Highlighting the connection between nursing a child and nursing a patient, Brontë makes nursing and maternity interchangeable occupations, revealing Caroline's nurse to be her long-absent mother.[23] This particular plot twist was reproduced in sentimental and sensational genres later in the century; as I suggest later, similar scenes occur in Mrs. Henry Wood's *East Lynne* and Wilkie Collins's *Dead Secret*; even *Bleak House* portrays a reunion between Esther and Lady Dedlock as Esther recovers from smallpox.[24] For Brontë, this mother-daughter reunion highlights the simultaneous recovery of health and identity, offering motherhood as the paradigmatic form of nursing that can provide privileged capacities for interpreting the external signs of internal emotions, thereby healing the patient. Finding that "she and her nurse coalesced in wondrous union" (424), Caroline experiences illness as a condition in which physical, rather than verbal, communication is paramount. When Mrs. Pryor finally reveals her "prior" relationship to her patient, Caroline exclaims, "But if you *are* my mother, the world is all changed to me. Surely I can live—I should like to recover—" (434). It is the nurse's (mother's) ability to read the emotional secrets and needs of her patient (daughter) that restores Caroline to health. In contrast, Caroline's uncle is only confused and alienated by the nuances of female illness and the mysteries of affect: "Let a woman ask me to give her an edible or a wearable . . . I can, at least, understand the demand: but when they pine for they know not what—sympathy—sentiment—some of these indefinite abstractions—I can't do it: I don't know it; I haven't got it" (440). Declaring himself master of the material world, Caroline's uncle relinquishes mental and emotional abstractions to the sphere of feminine knowledge. Brontë develops this correlation further when Mrs. Pryor declares her own property rights in the reproductive project: "Papa . . . gave you the oval of your face and the regularity of your lineaments: the outside *he* conferred; but the heart and the brain are *mine*: the germs are from *me*" (433). Reversing tradi-

tional accounts of reproduction, which saw the female as contributing matter for the development of the male "germ" or spirit, Caroline's mother stakes her unique claim to Caroline's internal organs of feeling and thought.

For Caroline, the effects of masculine denseness and duplicity are repaired by the union with maternal truth. Caroline's discovery of her origin symbolically reconnects signifier to signified through the unmediated communication between her own body and her mother's. The two women become virtually interchangeable during Caroline's illness: "And the child lulled the parent, as the parent had erst lulled the child" (436).[25] No longer entrapped in metaphors of silence, Caroline recovers both flesh and life:

> Long before the emaciated outlines of her aspect began to fill, or its departed colour to return, a more subtle change took place: all grew softer and warmer. Instead of a marble mask and glassy eye, Mrs. Pryor saw laid on the pillow a face pale and wasted enough, perhaps more haggard than the other appearance, but less awful; for it was a sick, living girl—not a mere white mould, or rigid piece of statuary.

(444)

Like Pygmalion's awakening statue, Caroline's body slowly comes to life. The references to a "marble mask," "glassy eye," "white mould," and "rigid piece of statuary" in this passage metaphorically recall Caroline's connection to the dead Mary Cave. But Brontë implies that Caroline has rejected her aunt's model of self-effacement and can now seek an identity and voice of her own. Once recovered, Caroline sheds her lassitude and begins to pursue her recalcitrant lover, arranging clandestine meetings and cheerfully braving freezing weather to visit him during his own recovery from a wound. Indeed, it is through Robert's own feminizing convalescence that the "romantic" half of the text emerges as the dominant genre; as Robert comes to terms with his own abstract feelings, the love story supersedes the narrative of labor unrest, educating the hero in the gestural nuances of emotional expression.

Brontë's idealized correlation between nursing, maternity, and the interpretation of emotion is challenged, however, in Victorian sensation novels such as *East Lynne* (1861) and *The Dead Secret* (1857), where the melodrama of maternal nursing produces its own pathologies. Both Wood and Collins construct the mother's act of nursing as dangerously overidentified with the child-patient; in these cases, interpretive capacities serve only to produce, rather than relieve, hysterical symptoms. Laurie Langbauer has noted the more general collapse between hysteria and maternity in *East Lynne,* arguing that the text not only makes hysteria natural to woman in the same ways that maternity is naturalized, but also makes maternity and hysteria virtually interchangeable conditions. Thus, rather than causing or curing hysteria, motherhood *is* a state of hysteria in Wood's text (Langbauer, 172). I would add that this collapse is most acute in the scenes of nursing precisely because of the interpretive engagement between illness and affect. When the heroine, Lady Isabel Vane, returns disguised as a governess and, ultimately, nurses one of her dying children, her nursing is, in effect, *too* sympathetic; she is *too* good at interpreting the emotional life of her patient because she is overinvolved in the illness of her child. As I argue in Chapter 3, this concern about excessive emotion in the sickroom marked a more widespread fear within the medical profession about the feminizing effects of medical sympathy. In Wood's novel, the nurse is endangered by her own hysterical maternity; Lady Isabel's agitation imperils her very access to the patient by threatening to expose her inappropriate identity. Alternately repressing her emotional and verbal outbursts and giving way to private expressions of emotional despair, Lady Isabel's fluctuating feelings are made acute in the face of her son's death, and they hasten her own death "from a broken heart."[26] In this way, Wood's likening of nursing to maternity becomes part of a cultural discourse about affective excess, which drew upon medical correlations between feminine excitability and somatic symptoms. Unable to restrain her emotions, the maternal nurse is condemned to die from them.

Like *East Lynne,* Wilkie Collins's *Dead Secret* pathologizes the threat of maternal overidentification, but Collins's spectacle of female emotion gone astray is even more acute than Wood's. In addition to endangering her own health, Collins's secretly maternal nurse endangers the health of her child. In *The Dead Secret* Sarah Leeson, a lady's maid turned housekeeper, is called in an emergency to nurse her own daughter, who was secretly given up at birth to be raised as the child of Sarah's former mistress. Upon meeting with her daughter, who is now recovering from the birth of her own child, Sarah, a.k.a. Mrs. Jazeph, suffers from a violent nervous agitation that leads the daughter to believe that her nurse is a madwoman. Collins transforms the idealized ministrations of the nurse into a disturbing parody of medical attendance:

> Mrs. Jazeph's touch, light and tender as it was, had such a strangely disconcerting effect on her, that she could not succeed, for the moment, in collecting her thoughts so as to reply, except in the briefest manner. The careful hands of the nurse lingered with a stealthy gentleness among the locks of her hair; the pale, wasted face of the new nurse approached, every now and then, more closely to her own than appeared at all needful. A vague sensation of uneasiness, which she could not trace to any particular part of her—which she could hardly say that she really felt, in a bodily sense, at all—seemed to be floating about her, to be hanging around and over her, like the air she breathed.

(115)

The smothering sense of discomfort and vaguely homophobic anxiety produced by the "stealthy gentleness" of Mrs. Jazeph's nursing technique collapses the very bodily distinctions that the daughter seeks to reassert when she attempts to identify a somatic source of her unease. Not only does the nurse intrude upon the patient's physical privacy, she also transmits her own emotional excitability in a process that reproduces the collapse of bodily boundaries between them. Mrs. Jazeph's nervous energy and anxiety extend into the very environment of the sickroom, and her patient breathes in air that is seemingly filled with the traces of her mother's emotional excess. The mother's hysterical symptoms thus reproduce the act of nursing as a disconcerting emotional spectacle, a nightmare of feminine affect. And in a further collapse of the boundaries between nurse and patient, Mrs. Jazeph refocuses attention from the interpretation of her patient's body to her own, commanding even the doctor's attention. He longingly speculates that the nurse "would be an interesting case to treat" (102). Eventually, Mrs. Jazeph's barely repressed emotional outbursts produce a state of screaming terror in her patient:

> The hot breath of the woman, as she spoke, beat on Rosamond's cheek, and seemed to fly in one fever-throb through every vein of her body. The nervous shock of that unutterable sensation burst the bonds of the terror that had hitherto held her motionless and speechless. She started up in bed with a scream, caught hold of the bell-rope, and pulled it violently.

(125)

Collins's portrayal of maternity as madness, and of the maternal nurse as catalyst for her patient's hysteria, challenges sentimental portrayals of mother-daughter relationships and empathetic ideals of nursing. Here we find the affective hermeneutics naturalized by Spencer, and celebrated, albeit in quite different ways, by Alcott, Gaskell, and Brontë, revealed as a form of emotional monstrosity that threatens both health and identity. Maternity and emotional excess are revealed as coterminous, the source rather than the cure of illness. The somatization of emotion becomes another proof of women's (and perhaps society's) dangerous permeability—between self and other, body and mind. Collins thus plays upon cultural apprehensions about feminine affect that lie beneath sentimental idealizations of motherhood, nursing, and even illness. He identifies the "natural language of feeling" as unsettling precisely because of its association with femininity, its tendency to excess, and its causal correlation with disease.

Ultimately, Wood's and Collins's hysterical maternal nurse is not so much a refutation of Brontë's and Alcott's idealized one as she is her dark twin; she extends the intuitive vision of nursing to its logical affective extreme. If the ideal nurse is empathically attuned to her patient's body, the hysterical nurse has crossed into a state of hermeneutic excess that threatens the boundaries of identity. In the sensational economy of female emotion, the nurse who is most adept at reading the signs of bodily distress, and therefore most feminine in her intuitive (and reproductive) bond with the patient, is threatened by her own capacity for illness. Her skill in reading the patient's feelings is inseparable from her own equally natural tendency to somatize emotional experience. In this way, the nurse's interpretive acumen enters the realm of pathology; she becomes, for Wood and Collins at least, a prime candidate for medical scrutiny and an emblem of feminine identity in its most problematically "natural" state of emotional extremes. To the extent that nurses function as narrators of their patients' stories, acting as ventriloquists for patients' emotions by translating the language of the suffering body into a more legible form, they become emblematic of the linguistic contradictions inherent in Victorian definitions of femininity. To interpret what someone else feels is to participate in an economy of feminine affect that is continually threatened by a potential loss of control. Medical definitions of emotional excess as both paradigmatically feminine and precipitously pathological sought, ultimately, to control that which was dangerously uncontrollable in the human psyche, first by displacing it onto a definition of femininity and then by subjecting it to classification as a form of body language with its own rules of grammar and codes of meaning. Yet in the often contradictory forms this language could take, in the competing "readings" and interlocking rhetorics of illness and affect, we can see that the cultural significance of female illness in nineteenth-century literature, medicine, and popular understanding, was considerably more complex than either a model of rebellion or a model of victimization can account for. To the extent that a common cultural narrative about the "natural language of feeling" emerges from these texts, it reveals both the symbolic importance and the ideological instability of body language as a category of meaning. On the one hand, illness becomes both a form and a substitute for language, a strategy of feminine communication that posits the material body as having a privileged access to "truth." On the other hand, the interpretation of illness mobilized conflicting theories of somatic legibility and illegibility, competing definitions of the normal and the pathological, and cultural apprehensions about emotional repression and emotional excess. In this way, the cultural significance of illness consistently exceeded the medical categorizations that attempted to control it, providing multiple strategies for reading the human body and its languages.

Notes

1. In his 1895 essay "The Psychology of Women," the American psychologist George T. W. Patrick extended Spencer's emphasis on linguistic indirection to claim the naturalness of feminine duplicity: "Deception and ruse in woman, far more than in man, have become a habit of thought and speech. A series of conditions, social, intellectual, and physiological, have forced this habit upon her as a means of self-defense" (217-18). See also Haller and Haller, 73-74. Another American, the physician and novelist Oliver Wendell Holmes, described women's capacity for unspoken communication in his 1867 novel about hysteria, *The Guardian Angel*. Holmes writes, "Talk without words is half their conversation, just as it is all the conversation of the lower animals. Only the dull senses of men are dead to it as to the music of the spheres" (9-10).

2. For example, see Henry Maudsley's discussion of reading human emotions through bodily signs in *The Physiology of Mind*, 379-89. Although I am primarily interested in how nineteenth-century culture understood the relationship between gender, language, and illness on its own (pre-Freudian) terms, there is a substantial amount of feminist scholarship, particularly in debates between feminist and psychoanalytic theorists, that has discussed the relationship between women and language through bodily symptoms. In particular, the interest in hysteria as a form of female communication through the body in the works of feminists such as Hélène Cixous, Catherine Clément, Luce Irigaray, Dianne Hunter, and Mary Jacobus (to name just a few) has provided models for reinterpreting psychoanalytic discourse, as well as literary and historical accounts of women's illnesses. Cixous writes, "Silence: silence is the mark of hysteria. The great hysterics have lost speech. . . . Their tongues are cut off and what talks isn't heard because it's the body that talks, and man doesn't hear the body" (49). While Cixous contends that women's—and particularly hysterics'—body language went unheard, I argue that Victorians were deeply interested in "hearing" the body, though only according to their own paradigms of somatic meaning.

3. There have been many recent studies of women's use of and relationship to language. Broadly defined, this issue has been at the center of feminist criticism, particularly in France. Toril Moi's *Sexual/Textual Politics* provides a useful discussion of Hélène Cixous's, Luce Irigaray's, and Julia Kristeva's theories. See also Margaret Homans's *Bearing the Word*; Deborah Cameron's *Feminist Critique of Language* and *Feminism and Linguistic Theory*; Jennifer Coates's *Women, Men, and Language*; Robin Lakoff's *Language and Woman's Place* and *Talking Power*.

4. These readings of the hysteric are not necessarily mutually exclusive. Cixous and Clément's interpretation of Dora and other hysterics in "the role of a resistant heroine: the one whom psychoanalytic treatment would never be able to *reduce*" (*Newly Born Woman,* 9) are perhaps the best (though certainly not the only) examples of this first model. Clément argues that we must look to figures defined as culturally "other"—in particular sorceresses and hysterics—for all that which society has suppressed. It is in studying these most transgressive, deviant, or delinquent figures that we may begin to find a new language of female sexuality, an *écriture féminine*. The hysteric, in particular, becomes a privileged figure of transgression for Cixous and Clément because, in Freudian terms, she relives the (collective) repressed past, "resum[ing] and assum[ing] the memories of the others" (5). Clément notes, however, the ambiguity of the hysteric's position, its essential conservatism, insofar as the hysteric ultimately ends up "inuring others to her symptoms." Ultimately, "the family closes around her again, whether she is curable or incurable" (5). Elaine Showalter's study of women and madness combines the first and second models, as does Diane Price Herndl's *Invalid Women.* Drawing on the work of Cixous, Clément, and Hunter, she identifies the madwoman and the female hysteric as rebellious heroines within her larger account of women's role as passive victim of a patriarchal and misogynist psychiatric history. Herndl, even more explicitly than Showalter, subscribes to both feminist models for interpreting women's illnesses, arguing that illness can be read as both a resistance to male medical authority and a product of it, a means of power and a form of victimization (5).

5. Although the feminist critics and theorists I have discussed focus primarily on hysteria, I have chosen in this chapter to discuss a number of conditions other than hysteria that were sometimes perceived as indirect forms of communication—anorexia, chlorosis, consumption, brain fever—and to examine their function in Victorian literature. In the following chapter I examine two Victorian fictions of hysteria that seek to reconnect women, and the disease that has been used most often to represent their silence, with the control of language and the act of narrative expression. For a reading of female suicide as a form of body language, see Margaret Higonnet's "Speaking Silences: Women's Suicide."

6. See, for example, the discussion of sexual difference and the applications of energy conservation in Cynthia Eagle Russett's *Sexual Science,* chapter 4.

7. See Foucault, *Madness and Civilization,* 219; Mullan, *Sentiment and Sociability,* 223-24. Connections between reading and illness are also the subject of Chapter 3, where I focus on audience responses to sentimental deathbed scenes.

8. In addition to the novels I analyze here, representations of illness in *Wuthering Heights, Scenes of Clerical Life, Uncle Tom's Cabin, Bleak House,* and *Diana of the Crossways,* as well as the nursing scenes in *Our Mutual Friend,* demonstrate many of the emphases I have discussed. I have chosen the texts I examine in this chapter because of the way they highlight the linguistic and interpretive implications of illness. In *The Madwoman in the Attic,* Sandra Gilbert and Susan Gubar read fictional illnesses as expressions of female "disease" with patriarchal power structures. Helena Michie has also discussed the communicative power of the heroine's body in *The Flesh Made Word.* Michie argues that both real women and fictional heroines used anorexia as a proof of virginity (16), denying their sexual "appetite" (13).

9. Alcott's division between the nurse's interpretation of spirit and the doctor's concern with flesh corresponds to what Martha Vicinus has identified as a specifically female vision of the nurse's role in medical care. In *Independent Women,* Vicinus argues that nursing ideology, at least in the early stages of the nursing reform movement, provided an alternative to the "narrow medical model of the doctors, who increasingly limited themselves to the care of bodies" (93). The nurse could potentially reform the moral and spiritual life of the patient, as well as tend to physical needs. This "unique mission," Vicinus claims, drew in part upon the ancient tradition of nursing as a religious vocation, but eventually "could not survive the growing power of the scientific approach" (93). While this idealistic "mission" may not have survived the professionalization of nursing and, as Vicinus makes clear, hardly corresponded to the actual expectations placed upon women who chose nursing as a career, it remained, nevertheless, an important component of Victorian ideals of the selfless nurse. Vicinus notes that "nurses captured the public imagination; they were surrogates for those who could not or would not give up their own lives for others. . . . Nurses were as close to saints as a Protestant country could have" (112).

10. For an excellent discussion of the relationship between shell shock and hysteria in World War I, see Showalter's *Female Malady,* chapter 7.

11. I take up this distinction between the proper role of feminine sympathy and the blunting of sensibilities in the medical profession in Chapter 3, where I outline the ways that women's association

with sympathy was used to prevent them from entering the field of medicine.

12. Alcott's assessment of surgical value is in conflict with the standard qualifications for a surgeon in this (and earlier) periods. Albert D. Hutter has noted that "the primary qualifications of a good surgeon were speed, nerve, manual dexterity, and great strength: surgeons who could hold down a patient with one hand while sawing off a limb with the other, requiring only one, or, at the most, two other assistants, were greatly admired" (167). See also M. Jeanne Peterson, *The Medical Profession in Mid-Victorian London.*

13. Paul's role as narrative interpreter of Phillis's emotional life and bodily symptoms marks his ambiguously "feminine" role in the text, which is partly a product of his youth. Gaskell repeatedly describes Paul in terms of his liminal manhood; apprenticed to an engineer and in his first stay away from home, Paul is only at the stage where he is "beginning to think of whiskers" (222).

14. Gaskell notes that Holdsworth's body has itself been made more acutely readable by a recent illness—a "low fever" that infected him while on a surveying job (255). Holdsworth declares to Paul, "Since my illness I am almost like a girl, and turn hot and cold with shyness, as they do, I fancy" (256).

15. Gaskell's account of this illness is structurally similar to the analysis of anorexia nervosa in contemporary family systems therapy. Self-starvation becomes the adolescent daughter's only means of control over dysfunctional family behaviors, bringing tensions within the family network to a somatic crisis that is nearly impossible to ignore. For a discussion of this process see Joan Jacobs Brumberg's *Fasting Girls: The History of Anorexia Nervosa.*

16. In Paul's case, as in Holdsworth's, the "effect" of language is to produce Phillis's illness.

17. It is interesting to note that while Spencer associated women's body language with layered, encoded, and indeterminate meaning—i.e., with a way of hiding the "truth" of their emotions—Gaskell associates it with univocality and the adherence to a materially grounded emotional "truth."

18. For other interpretations of illness in *Shirley,* see Sandra Gilbert and Susan Gubar, *The Madwoman in the Attic,* 372-98; Miriam Bailin, "'Varieties of Pain': The Victorian Sickroom and Brontë's *Shirley*"; and Linda Hunt, "Charlotte Brontë and the Suffering Sisterhood."

19. See Armstrong's discussion of how the domestic female body is expected to disappear "into the woodwork to watch over the household" (80).

20. Audrey C. Peterson's study of brain fever in nineteenth-century medicine and literature stresses the unusual combination of mental and emotional causes with severe physical effects. Possibly corresponding to modern conditions such as encephalitis or meningitis, brain fever was consistently linked to mental shock or strain in nineteenth-century medical textbooks, and its symptoms always included delirium. Fictional accounts of the disease, as Peterson has shown, go even further in assigning emotional causality, though less often fatality (448-49).

21. It is interesting to note that as an heiress in charge of a large family estate, Shirley is able to enter the masculine domains that are closed to Caroline. Throughout the novel Shirley jokes about her masculine characteristics and her androgynous name and behavior. Shirley's ability to cross gender boundaries indicates Brontë's interest in the way that distinctions of class often intersected with distinctions of gender.

22. Although Brontë's representation of Caroline's decline is the most extended exploration of illness in the novel, it is important to note that the four central characters in *Shirley*—Robert and Louis Moore, Shirley Keeldar, and Caroline—all become ill or wounded during the course of the narrative. For a discussion of Louis's illness and its parallel with Caroline's, see Margaret Smith's "Introduction" to the Oxford edition of *Shirley.* Smith argues that Louis's dependent position and unfulfilled love make him a "masculine version" of Caroline (xxi). Robert and Shirley, in contrast, are both wounded by external forces. The forms and causes of their illnesses thus correspond to their more active, masculine roles in the novel. For a discussion of Shirley's anxiety about hydrophobia and its parallels in *Jane Eyre,* see Gilbert and Gubar, *Madwoman in the Attic,* 392-93.

23. This idealized connection between nursing and motherhood became an important justification for the nursing profession later in the century. As Martha Vicinus has pointed out, late Victorian nursing journals emphasized "maternal instincts" as one of the most essential qualities for effective nursing. "Endless changes were rung on the metaphor of the nurturing, motherly nurse," influencing even Florence Nightingale's rhetoric, which had previously described nursing through military metaphors (*Independent Women,* 108). For another discussion of the rhetoric surrounding Nightingale's nursing career, see Mary Poovey's chapter in *Uneven Developments,* "A Housewifely Woman: The

Social Construction of Florence Nightingale." Poovey argues that these two narratives about the "patriotic service" of nursing, "a domestic narrative of maternal nurturing and self-sacrifice and a military narrative of individual assertion and will," actually converged. "The military narrative," Poovey claims, "was always at least compatible with—if not implicit in—the domestic narrative" (169).

24. Helena Michie has argued that Esther Summerson's illness helps her to construct a position of subjectivity in *Bleak House,* in part through the scarring of Esther's facial features from smallpox and the consequent distinction between her mother's face and her own. See "'Who Is This in Pain?' Scarring, Disfigurement, and Female Identity in *Bleak House* and *Our Mutual Friend.*"

25. Brontë's emphasis on the healing powers of maternity and the integration of maternal and romantic love has interesting parallels with a pattern of developmental figurations that Nancy Chodorow has proposed in *The Reproduction of Mothering.* Emphasizing the role of the pre-oedipal phase of development in the construction of female desire, Chodorow argues that "the mother remains a primary internal object to the girl" (198) and thus forms the basis of her later search for affection. "As a result of being parented by a woman, both sexes look for a return to this emotional and physical union" (199).

26. The attending physician suggests that William's death is from consumption, a hereditary predisposition to which, predictably, traces back to Lady Isabel's side of the family. Her own death combines the symptoms of hysteria, consumption, and emotional exhaustion.

Bibliography

Abell, Mrs. L. G. *Woman in Her Various Relations: Containing Practical Rules for American Females.* New York: R. T. Young, 1853.

Armstrong, Nancy. *Desire and Domestic Fiction: A Political History of the Novel.* New York: Oxford University Press, 1987.

Auerbach, Nina. "Afterword." In Louisa May Alcott, *Little Women.* New York: Bantam, 1983.

Brumberg, Joan Jacobs. *Fasting Girls: The History of Anorexia Nervosa.* New York: New American Library, 1988.

Cameron, Deborah, ed. *The Feminist Critique of Language: A Reader.* London: Routledge, 1990.

Chodorow, Nancy. *The Reproduction of Mothering: Psychoanalysis and the Sociology of Gender.* Berkeley: University of California Press, 1978.

Cixous, Hélène. "Castration or Decapitation?" Trans. Annette Kuhn. *Signs* 7, no. 1 (1981): 41-55.

Cixous, Hélène, and Catherine Clément. *The Newly Born Woman.* Trans. Betsy Wing. Minneapolis: University of Minnesota Press, 1986.

Clouston, Thomas Smith, M.D. *The Hygiene of Mind.* 4th ed. New York: E. P. Dutton, 1906.

Coates, Jennifer. *Women, Men, and Language: A Sociolinguistic Account of Sex Differences in Language.* London: Longman, 1986.

Foucault, Michel. *Madness and Civilization: A History of Insanity in the Age of Reason* [1961]. Trans. Richard Howard. New York: Random House, Vintage Books, 1988.

Gilbert, Sandra, and Susan Gubar. *The Madwoman in the Attic: The Woman Writer and the Nineteenth-Century Literary Imagination.* New Haven, Conn.: Yale University Press, 1979.

Haller, John S., and Robin Haller. *The Physician and Sexuality in Victorian America.* Urbana: University of Illinois Press, 1974.

Herndl, Diane Price. *Invalid Women: Figuring Feminine Illness in American Fiction and Culture, 1840-1940.* Chapel Hill: University of North Carolina Press, 1993.

Higonnet, Margaret. "Speaking Silences: Women's Suicide." In [Susan Rubin] Suleiman, ed., *The Female Body in Western Culture* [Cambridge, Mass.: Harvard University Press, 1986], 68-83.

Homans, Margaret. *Bearing the Word: Language and Female Experience in Nineteenth-Century Women's Writing.* Chicago: University of Chicago Press, 1986.

Hutter, Albert D. "Dismemberment and Articulation in *Our Mutual Friend.*" *Dickens Studies Annual: Essays on Victorian Fiction* II (1983): 135-75.

Lakoff, Robin. *Language and Woman's Place.* New York: Harper & Row, 1975.

Langbauer, Laurie. *Women and Romance: The Consolations of Gender in the English Novel.* Ithaca, N.Y.: Cornell University Press, 1990.

Maudsley, Henry. *The Physiology of Mind.* New York: D. Appleton, 1878.

Michie, Helena. *The Flesh Made Word: Female Figures and Women's Bodies.* New York: Oxford University Press, 1987.

———. "'Who Is This in Pain?' Scarring, Disfigurement, and Female Identity in *Bleak House* and *Our Mutual Friend.*" *Novel* 22 (Winter 1989): 199-212.

Moi, Toril. *Sexual/Textual Politics: Feminist Literary Theory.* London: Routledge, 1985.

Mullan, John. *Sentiment and Sociability: The Language of Feeling in the Eighteenth Century.* Oxford, Eng.: Clarendon Press, 1988.

Peterson, Audrey C. "Brain Fever in Nineteenth-Century Literature: Fact and Fiction." *Victorian Studies* 19 (June 1976): 445-64.

Peterson, M. Jeanne. *The Medical Profession in Mid-Victorian London.* Berkeley: University of California Press, 1978.

Poovey, Mary. *Uneven Developments: The Ideological Work of Gender in Mid-Victorian England.* Chicago: University of Chicago Press, 1988.

Rosenberg, Charles. "The Therapeutic Revolution: Medicine, Meaning, and Social Change in 19th-Century America." In [Judith Walzer] Leavitt and [Ronald L.] Numbers, eds., *Sickness and Health in America* [Madison: University of Wisconsin Press, 1985], 39-52.

Russett, Cynthia Eagle. *Sexual Science: The Victorian Construction of Womanhood.* Cambridge, Mass.: Harvard University Press, 1989.

Showalter, Elaine. *The Female Malady: Women, Madness, and English Culture, 1830-1980.* Harmondsworth, Eng.: Penguin, 1985.

Smith, Margaret. "Introduction." In Brontë, *Shirley* [(1849). Oxford, Eng.: Oxford University Press, 1981], vii-xxiii.

Spencer, Herbert. *The Study of Sociology.* New York: D. Appleton, 1896.

Vicinus, Martha. *Independent Women: Work and Community for Single Women, 1850-1920.* Chicago: University of Chicago Press, 1985.

Jason Daniel Tougaw (essay date 2006)

SOURCE: Tougaw, Jason Daniel. "Science and Sensibility: Invasions of Privacy in Breast Cancer Narratives." In *Strange Cases: The Medical Case History and the British Novel,* pp. 61-97. New York: Routledge, 2006.

[*In the following essay, Tougaw analyzes fictional and medical narratives of breast cancer to discern the ways in which these stories illuminate the most private aspects of women's lives and, arguably, the most authentic.*]

Early in *Belinda* (1801), Maria Edgeworth's naïve heroine is invited into the dressing closet of her guardian, Lady Delacour, a rakish woman who guards her social position through flamboyant displays of her own vanity. Lady Delacour, as if to show young Belinda Portman

what an education really means—outside the drawing room and beneath the face paint—leads her into a shadowy room, more carnival freak show than Lady's closet, where she reveals "a confusion of linen rags," vials that cast "a strong smell of medicines," and her own "death-like countenance" as she wipes the paint away (31). These, we soon learn, are the outward signs of a breast cancer slowly killing Lady Delacour. Belinda has been granted a viewing of what no one else has seen, save quack doctors and a maidservant. The remainder of the novel is a race, between Belinda's education and Lady Delacour's cancer. If the former can catch the latter, readers are led to feel, the cancer will be healed and Belinda will find the social niche a young woman with her sense deserves. One of the central questions of the novel is whether Lady Delacour should endure a mastectomy or not, and Edgeworth binds this question to one more familiar in novels of sensibility: what proportions of sensibility and reason make for good character? Edgeworth synthesizes medical debates about cancer raging in professional journals—What causes it? How should it be treated? What relations between mind and body does it imply? But she also demonstrates connections between these local questions and more general Enlightenment debates that troubled the culture at large—What is the role of the nerves in health and disease, on the one hand, and good character on the other? What is the ideal education for a woman? Is a person's class position inherited or earned? The closet is an inspired choice on Edgeworth's part. She invites readers to follow her heroine into a woman's most private milieu, and in the process we become privy to a view of the mysterious underbelly of a life, a view generally reserved for doctors and clergy.

A post-Richardsonian sentimental novel in the tradition of Frances Sheridan, Charlotte Lennox, Fanny Burney, William Godwin and Mary Wollstonecraft, *Belinda* invites readers—as one early nineteenth-century critic of Richardson's work phrased it—to "slip, invisible, into the domestic privacy of [its] characters" (qtd. in Watt 105). As we slip into Lady Delacour's closet and examine her disfigured breasts, we witness and sanction the diagnosis that leads to the narrative treatment (in both senses of the word) of her pathology. As Peter Brooks notes in *Body Work: Objects of Desire in Modern Narrative* [1993], individual novels represent fictionalized private lives, and to read them is to imagine violating the privacy of their characters (28). In *Belinda,* the mere presence of Dr. X—, a character based on physician and author John Moore, dramatizes the transformation of the private experience of characters into the very public experience of patients, or cases.[1] As a minor character remarks upon seeing him at a social gathering, "Dr X— the writer, do you mean, . . . then we'd better get out of his way as fast as we can, or he'll have some of us down in black and white, and curse me if I should choose to meet with myself in a book" (93).

This character wants to avoid becoming a case history, to retain authority over the privacy of his body. Medical authority, he recognizes, reduces human psyches and bodies to "black and white" text and exposes them to public scrutiny.

Virtually all realist fiction is involved with defining the terms and limits of privacy. The same is true for virtually every encounter between doctor and patient. In fiction dramatizing breast cancer and in actual medical cases on the same topic, the invasion of privacy is a prerequisite for producing knowledge about the disease and the patient out of the overdetermined details of her private life and the too often inscrutable symptoms she exhibits. In this respect, Brooks's argument about privacy and history of the novel applies also to the history of medicine:

> The history of the novel is a major episode in the long history of curiousity. The novel takes this curiosity into the sphere of private life, invading the domain it claims to speak of and for. And within private life, invading the domain it claims to speak of and for. And within private life, it finds that what is most private, most difficult to speak of, most a problem to represent, is the private body. The body cannot be left in a non-signifying somatic realm. It must mean. But it will do so only when made a part of a web of signifying practices.
>
> (53)

Breast cancer requires the public scrutiny of what was arguably the most private of eighteenth-century domains: a woman's body. For that reason, breast cancer is also a kind of limit-case for understanding the fine line between the public and the private. In the process of making sense of an inscrutable disease affecting the most symbolic portion of a woman's anatomy, breast cancer narratives record an increasing concern with the private self as authentic self, containing truths ordinarily concealed from public view but which emerge when the cancer compels the patient to let public in. Dr. X— is a fictional representative of the medical profession's overdetermined negotiations with "the private body." His presence in the novel calls attention to the overlapping concerns of fiction and medicine, two discourses motivated by shifting degrees of curiosity and moral responsibility to "slip into" private lives. Dr. X— is the hinge that unites Belinda's education plot and Lady Delacour's pathology plot. Able to penetrate the most mysterious circumstances and assemble solutions to seemingly unresolvable narrative problems, Dr. X— diagnoses each of Edgeworth's characters. He places their bodies within "a web of signifying practice," gives them meaning by invading their privacy. Dr. X—'s appearance pathologizes everybody, as the clinical gaze is apt to do, but Edgeworth is careful to depict him as a humane physician, a student of the mind as well as the body: "Accustomed to study human nature, Dr. X—

had acquired peculiar sagacity in judging of character" (125). As a scientist, he wields a pathologizing gaze; as a Humanist endowed with the gift of sensibility, he is careful, tactful, sympathetic. His knowledge augments Belinda's natural good sense, the final tool that allows her to educate those around her instead of falling victim to their cynical and sinister host of apparently infectious pathologies.

Another novel written by a woman during the second half of the eighteenth century, Frances Sheridan's *Memoirs of Miss Sidney Bidulph* (1761), dramatizes similar concerns about breast cancer and "the private body." Whereas Lady Delacour's breast cancer is a central concern in Edgeworth's novel, the breast disorder of a "pretty young gentlewoman" comprises just one episode in Sheridan's. Nevertheless, these two fictional depictions of suffering women are remarkably similar in their representation of the invasions of privacy that accompany medical intervention. While Sheridan and Edgeworth dramatized imagined invasions of privacy, Dr. X—'s real-life counterparts literally invaded the privacy of their patients in order to examine and treat their diseases. When these physicians and surgeons published the results of such invasions they exacerbated them. In order to diagnose and treat an illness, doctors make the body speak publicly, and when they document and publish such diagnoses and treatments, they give an even wider audience to that which is "most private, most difficult to speak of."

The private bodies represented in both novels and case histories are also suffering bodies. Writers of both genres capitalize on that suffering to justify the invasions of privacy they enact. During the period when both these novels were written, physicians published innumerable cases of breast disorders in medical journals, a remarkable number of which employ narrative techniques shared by sentimental novels, to chronicle and publicize the symptoms and treatments of actual women suffering from breast cancer and other breast disorders. One of these cases, that of a Mrs. Craib, was hotly debated by two of her surgeons, William Nisbet and Isaac Oliphant, in the pages of *London's Medical and Physical Journal* during 1800 and 1801. These two novels and this case history share a set of attributes common to both genres during the period: they rely on the shock of publicizing private bodily details for narrative impetus; they position themselves as socially vital documents, justifying the representation of socially taboo topics; they combine a clinical, pathologizing gaze with a rhetoric of sensibility in order to justify their violations of privacy and to limit the range of emotional responses they elicit; and they position their narratives as therapeutic documents, whose aim is to intervene in a pathological sequence of events and steer it toward a healthy (and moral) resolution. The narratives themselves are records, fictional or nonfictional, of the etiology and treatment of pathologies. As novelists like Sheridan and Edgeworth borrowed the concept of diagnosis to give meaning to the fictional suffering of their fictional characters, writers of case histories borrowed the novelistic conventions to temper their literal invasions of privacy. Reading these texts with the luxury of historical distance, medical theories and therapies seem very dated, and it is striking the degree to which treatment is shaped and constrained by anxieties about female sexuality *and* the period's narrative conventions. Physicians struggled to treat an illness whose origins and etiology eluded them and to find words commensurate with the suffering women's experience; novelists invited readers to imagine such suffering and to recognize signs of *their own* private selves in the fictional patients they represented.

In *Belinda,* for example, Lady Delacour's breast cancer compels her to allow physicians to violate the privacy and sanctity of her body throughout the novel. In desperation, she opens the doors of her dressing closet not just to Belinda, but also to a host of male medical practitioners and pathologizing gazes. Most of them lack sensibility, and their painful and violent treatments exacerbate her condition. Dr. X—'s medical intervention is perhaps no less traumatic or invasive, but his sensibility initiates a *therapeutic narrative,* resulting in Lady Delacour's recovery of physical health, mental stability, and moral sensibility. In sentimental realism, as in medical case histories, the narration of intimate bodily details is set in motion by a lapse or rupture in the health of its subjects.[2] Such lapses justify violations of privacy if they are therapeutic. Such violations are transformed from prurient representations of corporeal trauma into socially vital acts of heroism. With Lady Delacour, a range of complex and often inconsistent bodily, emotional, and intellectual maladies are "cured" in the process, ending with a moral reform that only the conventions of sentimental fiction could make convincing.

The most famous breast cancer narrative during the period—Fanny Burney's mastectomy letter (1811-12)—is telling for its eloquent use of the rhetorical conventions so many writers employed to make sense of such an overdetermined subject. Describing the letter, Julia Epstein writes in "Writing the Unspeakable: Fanny Burney's Mastectomy and the Fictive Body,"

> Narrating stories, for Burney, served two purposes. First, narration—writing the intimate and vulnerable self—represents an act of violence, a wrenching exposure that amounts to a self-inflicted incision, an aggressive attack on the writer's self. Second and concurrently, narration—exteriorizing the self's story—represents a therapeutic and healing process, a resolution and closure of wounds. In this sense, writing for Burney is like surgery: a deliberate infliction of pain in order to excise the pain, a violation of the body in order to cure the disease.
>
> (162)

Epstein describes Burney's letter as "part medico-surgical treatise and part sentimental fiction," noting that the act of narration requires authority generally reserved for the physician and denied the patient. Burney, she argues, takes on the roles of both narrator and narrative object in the letter and therefore produces a unique document in both literary and medical history. Burney's letter is unique for its representation of patient as author, but its blending of the conventions of sentimental fiction and medical discourse is typical of the period. Geoffrey Sill [*The Cure of the Passions and the English Novel* (2001)] points out that Epstein's feminist reading focuses on the invasive gaze of the seven surgeons who attended the surgery in black robes, without noting evidence in the letter—along with Burney's journals, her *Memoirs of Dr. Burney* (1832), and the breast wound suffered by the heroine of her subsequent novel, *The Wanderer, or Female Difficulties* (begun in the 1790s but not completed until after the mastectomy)—that Burney projected anxieties about what she considered her "writing mania" onto her breast (168-172). Epstein's social reading and Sill's psychological one, taken together, demonstrate the paradoxes that abounded when sickness compelled the peeling away of Enlightenment theory to reveal the mixed emotions of a private life. Burney, the brilliant novelist, shares with Lady Delacour, the young woman in Sheridan's *Sidney Bidulph,* and Mrs. Craib a sickness whose symbolism condenses personal, social, ideological, and scientific concerns. The bodies of these women become vehicles for competing, and often irreconcilable, anxieties and assumptions. Burney is both a woman helpless at the hands of patriarchal surgeons and self-willed celebrity authoress driven to cure her mania with the excision of her breast. The irony is that while all these women, real and fictional, become subjects in a medical debate about the efficacy of mastectomy, it is only Burney, the famous author, who submits to the knife.

If Burney's account is both sentimental fiction and medical treatise, this is possible because science and sensibility consistently operate as mutually reinforcing rhetorics in both published case histories and novels of the period—to justify the violence of exposing the vulnerable, often suffering, bodies and minds of characters and subjects. Novelists and physicians employed the language of sensibility to narrate health and disease because sensibility, combined with the clinical gaze of medicine, framed discussions of bodily violence and violation within a discourse of compassionate healing, offering a remedy for both symptoms of physical disease and the social discomfort that representing them elicits. The overdetermined social position of women's breasts, as Epstein writes, makes breast disorders ideal subjects for therapeutic narratives: "The breast emblematizes both privacy and sexuality, and breast cancer, by intruding on the radical privacy of the body and thus medicalizing sexuality, threatens and breaks down that emblematization" (155). The diseased breast of a Lady Delacour or a Mrs. Craib requires the intervention of a male physician or surgeon, and the narration of that intervention is itself a threat to a social order based on the sanctity of women's bodies. Narrative in medical case histories, to borrow Epstein's metaphor, is like surgery, "a deliberate infliction of pain in order to excise the pain, a violation of the body in order to cure the disease." Case histories borrow the rhetoric of sensibility from their fictional counterparts. At least since Richardson, writers of sentimental fiction had recognized that framing taboo, traumatic, or extremely private subject matter within discourses of sensibility eases the pain and justifies the violation of social taboos. Such novelists had already been incorporating diagnostic and therapeutic models for representing pathological characters. In both genres, the violence of narrating the traumatic experiences of human bodies in extraordinary detail was not justified by either the rhetoric of science or sensibility alone. A "scientific" profusion of details, linked through causal relations, creates a truth-effect and objectifies patients and characters; and sensibility frames the representation within codes of propriety and encourages readerly sympathy.

Eighteenth century novelists and writers of case histories are both very self-conscious of their readers' emotional responses to their violations of privacy. Laqueur argues that self-consciousness is the common denominator in "the new cluster of narratives" he calls the "Humanitarian Narrative." The "causal chain" of these narratives is structured around the suffering bodies of "ordinary" people. Breast cancer narratives fall squarely within Laqueur's model. Fiction or nonfiction, they employ sensibility as a discourse to represent women with breast cancer, linking patients, medical authorities, and readers in a network of contagion. Sensibility, as a discourse, unites consciousness and corporeality, and so corporeal disease and moral consciousness may contaminate each other. These links create a complex set of power relations, in which the consciousness of each player is judged as moral or immoral in relation to his or her display of sensibility. Simply stated: an overdose of sensibility leads one into danger and illness; too little sensibility breeds villainy and often illness; just the right dose of sensibility tempered with reason (in the form of education, religion, or science) is a recipe for both goodness and health.

In the sections that follow I will illustrate the use of mutually reinforcing rhetorics of science and sensibility as they manifest themselves in a case history and a novel in two extended readings, of competing versions of "The Case of Mrs. Craib" by two different surgeons and then of *Belinda*. The single "breast cancer" episode in Sheridan's novel outlines many of the salient details shared by all these texts. In both Sheridan's and Edgeworth's novels, the patient nearly submits to a mastec-

tomy but is rescued by a medical practitioner whose humanity and medical expertise are explicitly linked. The patient receives a new diagnosis and a cure without surgery. Both novels demonstrate their authors' familiarity with medical controversies about breast cancer, which focused on diagnosis and mastectomy.[3] In addition, the narrative techniques of both these fictional accounts of breast cancer are strikingly similar to their nonfictional counterparts in the medical journals. In both fiction and nonfiction, the woman with breast cancer becomes the subject of narrative suspense, with professionals vying for authority over her body. The suspense invites readers' involvement in the narrative and elicits sympathy for the suffering patient and her physicians.

Medicine's violation of otherwise rigidly enforced and gendered codes of privacy is consistently presented as a necessary precondition for the development of the therapeutic narrative. In Sheridan's novel, a suitor/physician examines the breast of a young woman he has been forbidden to marry. The physician's professional authority allows for the examination, and the language of sensibility allows for the representation of that examination. Nevertheless, the story is still a marriage plot, one in which the woman's ailing body places her in a vulnerable position from which only her male suitor's medical expertise can save her; the examination of her breasts, forbidden under ordinary circumstances, becomes a necessary violation of her privacy. In Dr. Oliphant's account, Mrs. Craib leaves her bed undressed, "in want of her stays," conjuring images of her exposed and diseased breasts, an act that occupies a crucial place in his narrative: it is the moment at which he loses hope for her recovery; the exposure of her breasts, he implies, made her vulnerable to a morbid turn in her illness. In both these scenes, the medical meanings of the woman's breasts are determined in relation to violation of social codes of privacy. The physician is a figure who may "violate" the privacy of the patient's body with impunity. Sensibility, as rhetoric, makes the representation of what he finds there publishable; at the same time, sensibility reinforces preexisting notions about the authority of the physician over his patient (and men over women), notions that link the disruptions of privacy that illness entails with the shortcomings, or even deviance, of the patients.

Illness, doctors, and medicine play a major role in nearly every turn of events in the virtuous Sidney Bidulph's rocky path to eventual marriage and happiness. In the "breast cancer" episode, the heroine (who spends much of the novel as Mrs. Arnold, having made an unfortunate "match" for the sake of propriety) narrates the event of an acquaintance's near-mastectomy. A "very pretty young gentlewoman" of the neighborhood, in love but forbidden to marry a young physician, Mr. Main, with a promising future, "had the misfortune to receive a hurt to her breast, by falling against the sharp corner of a desk from a stool, on which she had stood in order to reach down a book that was in a little case over it" (270). The blow "threw her into a fit of illness, which put a stop to all correspondence between her and her lover" (272). Neglect exacerbated the injury, and another surgeon was brought in: "By this bungler she was tortured for near three months; at the end of which time, through improper treatment, the malady was so far increased, that the operator declared the breast must be taken off, as the only possible means of saving her life" (272). An ordinary domestic act, reaching "down a book," sets a traumatic sequence of events in motion. In her progression from health to illness, she must forsake her identities as sister and lover and assume the role of the patient.

As Mrs. Arnold tells it, the day for the mastectomy approached, and the patient "conjured" her brother, "in the most earnest manner to permit Mr. Main to be present at the operation" (272). Mr. Main arrived at the scene "with an aching heart":

> He was introduced into her chamber, where he found the whole chirugical apparatus ready. The young woman herself was in her closet, but came out in a few minutes, with a countenance perfectly serene. She seated herself in an elbow chair, and desired she might speak a few words to her brother, before they proceeded to their work. Her brother was immediately called to her, when taking him by the hand, she requested him to sit down by her.
>
> (273)

Having successfully appealed to her brother's sensibility, the patient then declares that she had put off the operation so that it would occur after her twenty-first birthday, when she would become mistress of her own fortune, which she desires to be left to Mr. Main if she should die. Mrs. Arnold comments, "You imagine this had various effects on the different persons concerned. The brother, however displeased he might have been at this act of his sister's, had too much humanity to make any animadversion on it at the time" (273). His sister's illness, he recognizes, diminishes his authority over her body. Her brother having left the room, the surgeons begin the operation, Mr. Main "endeavouring to suppress his tears" (274). As the narrative continues, it becomes clear that this authority is now in the hands of a medical profession whose mastery of "cancer" is limited:

> Two maid servants stood on each side of her, and the surgeon drew near to do his painful work. He had uncovered her bosom, and taken off the dressings, when Mr Main, casting his eyes at her breast, begged he might have leave to examine it before they proceeded. The other surgeon, with some indignation, said, his doing so was only an unnecessary delay; and had already laid hold of his knife, when Mr Main having looked at it, said, he was of the opinion it might be saved, with-

out endangering the lady's life. The other, with a contemptuous smile, told him, he was sorry he thought him so ignorant of his profession, and without much ceremony putting him aside, was about to proceed to the operation; when Mr Main laying hold of him, said, that he never should do it in his presence; adding, with some warmth, that he would engage to make a perfect cure of it in a month, without pain or amputation.

> (274)

The image of the physician, scalpel in hand, suppressing his tears and contemplating his "painful work," is familiar within the confines of a sentimental novel. Aside from the fact that he is also suitor to the patient, such an image is entirely in keeping with public and professional representations of good doctors during the period. Precisely because of his sentimental relationship to the patient, Mr. Main is able to intervene and rediagnose her, probably saving her life and certainly saving her from unnecessary pain and suffering. His diagnosis is a product of his sensibility, tempered by a strong sense of reason and knowledge of current medical theory. As a result of Main's intervention the patient opts to forgo surgery and her body is allowed to heal itself. As she recovers, the first surgeon challenges Main to a duel, in which the latter is seriously wounded and confined to bed for five weeks, after which time the happy couple are united with their families' blessings.

The most striking element of this episode is that in the role of surgeon, a suitor examines the exposed breast of his lover, his professional identity taking precedence over his personal one. The scene also displays, in short hand, a major contention in medical theory of the period regarding mastectomies, which frequently resulted in death and whose benefits were regarded with suspicion by many physicians. The contention that arises is not only professional but personal as well; this is because medical practice always involves the "humanity" of the physicians. Medicine was in no respect regarded as an abstract or disinterested science by its practitioners. Throughout the chapter the violence of illness and medical treatments elicits both rational and emotional responses. A proper diagnosis and cure, Sheridan suggests, can only be effected when reason and sentiment are united. The physician is the hero of the scene, and his patient, though his beloved, is never named and remains the object of medical inquiry and economic and social exchange (between her brother and her suitor). Finally, the plot of forbidden love entangles questions about health, disease, sexuality, and agency. The patient's effort to delay surgery until she is mistress of her own body, mind, and fortune is a good indicator of just how far-reaching the inscrutable signs of breast cancer could become in the cultural imagination. To treat breast cancer was to engage, albeit indirectly, questions and assumptions well beyond the domain of medicine.

The combination of science and sensibility enables the representation of illness in the pursuit of bodily health *and* moral consciousness, resulting in narratives promising to influence readers to conduct their own delicate bodies with more rectitude than the subjects they read about and which, more often than not, resolve the threats to social order that had provided or at least magnified the narrative conflict in the first place. The two genres share this rhetorical strategy, but case histories differ from novels in that they are representations of actual events and people, whereas novels imaginatively reconstruct possible events and characters. In *Nobody's Story* [1995], Catherine Gallagher argues that "the novel was the first to articulate the idea of fiction for the culture as a whole" and that "readers identified with the characters in novels because of their fictiveness, not in spite of it" (xvi-xvii). According to Gallagher, novels elicit readerly identification because their protagonists are only imagined. Imaginary violations of bodily and domestic privacy in a novel elicit a range of strong emotional responses: fear, hope, disgust, compassion; the depiction of actual violations of privacy requires a narrative frame that will guarantee its author a similar emotional response. Fiction constructs imagined events and experiences, assembling details and arranging them as a series of causes and effects. Case histories reconstruct actual events and details, assembling details and re-arranging them so that their supposedly inherent cause-and-effect relationships become clear. In the process, the actual subjects, the *somebodies* of case histories, acquire the imaginative, sentimentalized characteristics of their fictional counterparts and elicit the emotional responses of readers whose "emotional dispositions," as Gallagher argues, were "created" at least in part through the reading of novels (4).

"FOR WANT OF HER STAYS": THE CASE OF MRS. CRAIB

By 1800 a growing network of journals reflected an increased organization of the medical profession.[4] Physicians and surgeons who published case histories in the professional journals at the end of the eighteenth century risked tainting their professional reputations as well as the public's perception of their treatments. To publish was to participate in medical debate, which called attention to the uncertainty behind medical theory and clinical practice.[5] In response, physicians often used the language of sensibility to humanize clinical medicine. The material in case histories is easily adapted to the demands of sentimental narration; case histories are, after all, stories about suffering bodies and mortality. In breast cancer cases, the woman's suffering body becomes the terrain for a medical discourse that reflects the profession's genuine struggle to solve the corporeal mysteries presented by the cancer as well as medical authors' anxious adaptation of narrative styles that could perform two very different functions. The cases had to demonstrate the physician's clinical acumen and display his position within current debates, while simulta-

neously justifying the publication of their patients' private bodily experiences.

Like the novelist, the physician requires a pathological sequence of events for his or her professional existence and must assume that certain narrative sequences are healthy while others are pathological. The story of Mrs. Craib's body has strayed out of sequence, become pathological. Dueling physicians Nisbet and Oliphant vie for the authority to reconstruct her narrative, searching for the causes of her current illness and attempting to intervene and reconnect the events of her story. Breast cancer was a largely unexplained ailment in 1800, yet both Nisbet and Oliphant interpret Mrs. Craib's body, produce diagnostic explanations, and use sensibility to establish rhetorical appeal for their particular reconstructions of the pathological sequence of events that they claim resulted in her disease. Throughout the development of two suspenseful accounts of the same case, Mrs. Craib's body becomes the object of intense clinical scrutiny—the morbid details of her condition supplying empirical data for her surgeons and the ground from which they elicit readers' sympathy.

The multiple publication of the case demonstrates each author's attempt to authorize narrative closure and therefore claim both narrative and medical truth. Nisbet (a member of the Royal College of Surgeons, Edinburgh) was first to publish an account of Mrs. Craib's case in 1800, followed by a refutation of his conclusions by attending surgeon Oliphant (a member of the Royal College of Surgeons, London). This pattern was then repeated, Nisbet publishing a rebuttal to Oliphant's refutation and Oliphant publishing yet another refutation. The case develops with each subsequent publication, demonstrating the extent to which physicians and surgeons who chose to publish case histories relied on narrative devices like suspense, characterization, and the language of sensibility. Claims to cures were especially contentious during the period. Physicians had developed an Enlightenment faith in the inherent curability of both physical and mental disorders, but they were cautious because the human body was still a largely unexplored field of scientific data.[6] In the case of Mrs. Craib, characterization and suspense produce egregious sentimentality for a clinical text aimed at a professional audience. This sentiment tempers the visceral quality of the clinical details and creates the impression of the author as a humane medical practitioner, whose relationship with his patient is both personal and professional, whose feeling for his patient forces him to confront and experience the patient's trauma along with her.

Mrs. Craib had been suffering from pain in her breast for two years. She consulted a total of six physicians and one friend with amateur medical knowledge. They all diagnosed cancer of the breast and prescribed a variety of treatments, including poultices, powders, leeches, and even the application of pigeon dung. Mrs. Craib finally consulted Oliphant, who concurred with the previous diagnoses but agreed to take the case, calling in Nisbet for a second opinion. In Oliphant's version of the case, Nisbet comes off like a quack, advertising his services and promising unrealistic cures; in Nisbet's version, Oliphant comes off like an outmoded medical traditionalist, still adhering to the vagaries of leeches, bleeding, and Hippocrates. In the cumulative narrative that emerges Mrs. Craib's suffering body becomes the field on which a battle of medical ideologies and personal disagreements takes place.

Nisbet's original version of the case, published in September of 1800, was titled "A Case of the Cure of Cancer of both Breasts, the One Ulcerated, the Other Schirrous." This was a typical title for a typical case of breast cancer for the period. Its claim of a cure was not unheard of, but it certainly defied the dominant approach to cancers.[7] Nisbet had made cancer a specialization, which put him in a complicated position in relation to his rapidly evolving profession. Many specialists in particular fields of medicine were quacks or charlatans who advertised their services with outlandish portfolios of supposedly incurable cases that they, with their new and often secret treatments, had miraculously cured. Nisbet advertised among physicians in London, not to the public, and he emphasized new, experimental methods of treatment—though he was vague about what comprised such treatment. His grandiose claim to have cured a seemingly hopeless case of breast cancer would plausibly have attracted both attention and suspicion from peers and the general public.

Nisbet's introduction, typical of the period's case histories, situates him within the profession:

> Having devoted my attention of late years to a particular line of medical practice, the subject of which has been deemed one of the chief opprobria of the profession; and from a conviction that this general opinion is by no means well founded, and that Cancer is equally curable as any other species of swelling or ulcer, it is incumbent on me, in entertaining such new sentiments, to support them by evidence of incontrovertible facts.—I shall therefore state the following case, one of the most melancholy that can occur, as an introduction to a number of others which shall be occasionally given to the public, through the medium of your useful Miscellany.
>
> (296)

Cancer was "one of the chief opprobria of the profession" because it remained incurable in an age of scientific medicine. (Physicians of the period, so optimistic that their still relatively new arsenal of experimental methods would sooner or later yield a cure, would probably be surprised that two-hundred years later, we still have no cure and that medical science still prescribes poisons to treat it.) Nisbet promised nothing less than a professional revolution with regard to his specialty. In this case he would use "evidence of incontrovertible facts" to influence his peers. However, even in this short introduction there is already an air of mystery and suspense surrounding the case, "the most melancholy that can occur." Nisbet deploys conventions of sentimental fiction rhetorically. He uses the language of sensibility to frame his narrative and provide links between details, links that become crucial for diagnosing the cause of a patient's complaint and theorizing about possible treatments. Inevitably, these links create suspense. They are presented as a sequence of events, one by one, leading the reader to guess or wonder what will happen next. Physicians tend to rely on the narrative desire their cases elicit in order to confirm their positions of authority. They provide information readers desire, the way any artful narrator does, establishing their own authority. At the same time, both physician and patient begin to develop as *characters,* as they would in a novel, with all the attendant moral and professional details that novelistic characterization involves. Science and sensibility converge throughout the diagnostic process, treatments and results creating more suspense, inviting readers to imagine Mrs. Craib's domestic life and to champion her surgeons' attempts to restore her health so that she can return to that life. Mrs. Craib becomes the object of readerly sympathy, to be pitied but not necessarily trusted with the health of her own body.

When Nisbet first introduces the patient, he conceals her identity with a pseudonym: "Mrs. G. the wife of Mr. G. a coal merchant in Tottenham Court Road, aged upwards of 40, about two years ago, felt a hardness and swelling of her left breast, with all the usual symptoms of schirrous or incipient cancer" (296). Nisbet's subsequent recitation of the names of physicians who have tried and failed to treat cancer—Mr. Ford, Mr. Cline, Sir James Earle, Mr. Budd, Mr. Cooper, Mr. Andrews, and Mr. Oliphant—characterizes him in opposition to his peers, who are well-meaning but lack vision. Nisbet imposes a cause-and-effect analysis on his "facts," thereby creating an engrossing narrative to make his medical case more convincing. Mrs. G. has had symptoms for two years and has consulted a number of physicians. According to the author, "Mr. Oliphant, of Percy-street; who, with a proper anxiety for his patient, and a zeal at the same time directed by humanity, which every practitioner of medicine should profess, soon after visiting her, and finding that tho' her complaints were palliated, no progress was made towards a cure, advised to call in Dr. Nisbet, whose attention, he understood, had been particularly devoted to this malady" (297). Those are the facts, but Nisbet's interpretation is suffused with the language of sensibility: the first two physicians were unable to offer any alleviation of her symptoms; under their care the symptoms were "aggravated," putting her in an "unhappy state." Because the patient was "anxious to obtain relief," she sought the advice of a third, who "humanely" declined to treat her but offered her a space in a hospital, which she declined. After at least five physicians had pronounced her case incurable, she was, in Nisbet's words, "deserted by the faculty," and so in desperation, "put herself in the hands of an ignorant empyric," under whom her illness made "horrid progress." Two more physicians pronounced Mrs. Craib's case incurable, and finally she found Mr. Oliphant, who called in Nisbet because of his "proper anxiety for his patient" and "zeal . . . directed by humanity" (296-297).

The language of sensibility enables Nisbet to use his diagnosis to set the stage for his own entrance as a sentimental hero. Nisbet, like most writers of the period's case histories, uses the convention of the "first visit" to initiate narrative development and to demonstrate his own professional acumen in contrast to the ignorance of the patient, family, friends, and other practitioners:

> On my first visit, I found the disease far advanced in its ultimate stage, a short description of which will be sufficient to convince every practitioner of its fatal and apparently speedy termination. An extensive foul spreading ulcer occupied the whole surface of the left breast with thick reverted edges covered with the particular sordes characterizing such sores, and occasionally pouring out quantities of blood from the eroded vessels. Besides the substance of the breast, itself totally diseased, the cuticular glands all round were hard and schirrous to a considerable extent. In the axilla, the glands were swelled to the size of a pigeon's egg, and the whole of that side as tight, contracted, and knotty, with clusters of swelled lymphatics in different parts of it. The patient could hardly use the left arm and was totally unable to lie on that side. An erysipelatous inflammation diffused itself for a considerable way beyond the actual limits of disease. On examining the right breast, I found a large schirrous formed in it, which had not yet arrived at an active state. The hectic fever was strongly formed, and the patient's health rapidly declining.
>
> Mr. Oliphant was of the opinion the disease was incurable, unless a complete sloughing of the whole breast took place; and I could not, in such a situation, flatter with strong hopes; determined, however, to follow the plan which I have generally found successful, I communicated my sentiments to him, who, with that liberality which every man of real science possesses, acquiesced, and gave every freedom in pursuing it.
>
> (297-298)

In this passage, the explicit details of Mrs. Craib's sores, bleeding, and swelled lymphatics subside into the rhetorics of sentimental fiction. First Nisbet uses a rhetorical ploy, claiming to have concurred with Oliphant in the opinion that the case was indeed incurable, but at the same time depicting himself as heroic innovator and Oliphant as a polite obstacle to a successful resolution of the case and the narrative. The therapeutic narra-

tive—or in Laqueur's words, "the humanitarian narrative"—promises that "ameliorative action is represented as possible, effective, and therefore morally imperative" because of its reliance on causality (178). The lack of action taken by other physicians and surgeons demonstrates their failure to live up to that moral imperative. Because Nisbet is willing to take this action, in a case "deserted by the Faculty" (even though by opposing the Royal College of Surgeons he risks his professional reputation) he becomes the moral hero.[8] The suspense that ensues centers around Nisbet's treatment, but Mrs. Craib's ailing body, its eruptions and swellings "beyond the actual limits of disease," is the precondition for his narrative. The horror of the scene elicits readerly sympathy, but in this case the sympathetic reaction is complicated by the knowledge of the professional dispute. Is Nisbet a hero willing to risk his professional reputation for the sake of his patient, or is he a quack willing to sacrifice her for the sake of publicity? Mrs. Craib is a sympathetic character, lacking the medical knowledge required to make decisions about her own treatment, but throughout both accounts of the case it is apparently her ignorance (in contrast to each physician's authority) that prevents her body from healing and ensures the development of the sentimental narrative.

In Nisbet's first account, events progress toward a happy resolution, Mrs. Craib's mortality held at bay for the time being. He describes the gentle healing of the "diseased parts," finally concluding: "The above facts will be sufficient to show, that the principle of cure is different from any that has yet been attempted; but at present I shall enter into no further detail of it than say, that it consists in no secret remedy or specific, but proceeds on the general principles which apply every form and stage of the malady" (298). On the surface Nisbet escorted his patient to a happy ending and reported it to his peers, but there are some important questions remaining: How did he effect this cure? The surgeon is never explicit about his method of treatment. What caused the illness? What cured it? The controversy that arose from the case further attests to the vagaries of cause-and-effect, which is, after all, an essential component of any plot. Nisbet avoids these crucial questions, opting instead to reassure readers by displaying Mrs. Craib's waning bodily eruptions. His references to the sore's healing, the fact that no "sloughing" was involved, and the breast's return to its "natural state," imbue the narrative with a sense of relief.

Both Nisbet and Oliphant are interested in the cause-and-effect relationships between the etiology of illness, method of treatment, and progress of symptoms, but their analyses of these relationships differ. Through debates about medical ethics and approaches, both surgeons attempt to humanize themselves and their profession, to represent the doctor-patient relationship as both a professional and a human one. Both surgeons are attempting to reconcile scientific methods with social expectations about their authority in the private realm of an ailing woman's body. In a sentimental novel, Mrs. Craib would be the heroine, but in a case history the physician becomes the hero. Oliphant's first response, published in November of 1800, attempts to clarify the case by providing a new narrative frame, one that traces the progress of the case by providing a longer and more detailed chronology of events. Like Nisbet, Oliphant begins with an account of the case that leads to his intervention in it:

> Mrs. Craib, of Tottenham-court-road, aged 46, has had three children, the last fifteen years ago; was never able to suckle with the left breast, but had no great inconvenience from this circumstance. The menses hitherto regular, till pleurisy seized her; otherwise she was extremely healthy, and constantly employed in an active life.
>
> Two years ago she got a violent bruise on the upper part of her left breast; the effects subsided as well as they usually do in common cases, only there was left some hardness with a little occasional pain.
>
> Six months after she received another bruise on the same part, and all the consequences of contusion, swelling, livid colour, and pain, were greater than in the former accident; and the remaining pain was more severe, and the hardness of greater extent. In the recent state, repeated application of leeches were ordered; and when the active condition of the disease was supposed to be removed, some saponanceous camphorated embrocation was applied.

(546-547)

Oliphant situates himself within a medical discourse that tended to look for causes outside the patient's body—an injury (as in both Sheridan's and Edgeworth's novels). Instead of seeing the body as an organic system capable of turning on itself, an event from outside was often cited as the cause of the body's morbid turn. At this early stage, details like Mrs. Craib's motherhood, the fact that she was never able to breast feed, that her menses were always regular, and that she had had pleurisy are all potentially relevant but are not necessarily related to the current progress of the disease. The profusion of domestic and corporeal details displays the thoroughness of Oliphant's examination, but it also reinforces the characterization of Mrs. Craib as a victim of her body and its surroundings, a misguided and helpless woman vulnerable to her own bouts of emotion.

With the application of remedies—leeches and a soapy camphor lotion—the progress of the narrative is under way. Medical intervention establishes a new set of cause-effect relationships, and the patient's own, pointedly non-medical view on her own case, provides the requisite complications to prolong the narrative, much the way the miscalculations of a novel's heroine would.

Oliphant recounts her medical history, without naming the physicians but describing previous treatments, including the application of pigeon dung and the painful application of "burnt allum" in an effort to "ripen for the knife" (547). These treatments, according to Oliphant, exacerbated her condition. It is only when Mrs. Craib finally puts herself in the hands of "an eminent and experienced surgeon" that she begins to make progress toward medical intervention that may do her some good, but the details Oliphant provides are second-hand; they occurred before he took the case. Like an omniscient narrator, though, he reports details that occurred in his absence with impunity, reconstructing the narrative of Mrs. Craib's pathology based "the marks of bad treatment" her body exhibits: depression, pain, oozing, irritation, discoloration, swelling, glandular inflammation, hardness. With the image of her ailing body established, Oliphant makes the point that she is otherwise "constitutionally unimpaired" (548). Mrs. Craib's constitution, he argues, is separable from her symptoms. The statement is unconvincing considering her depression and the severity of her illness, but it supports his point that her symptoms are the result of "irregular" treatments rather than endemic disease.

The corporeal details of this passage—shooting pains, oozing sanies, ulceration, yellow sloughing—set a dramatic scene for Oliphant's entrance as a figure whose intervention, complete with specific dates and technical descriptions of his treatments, is both humane and medically sound. Her symptoms are recognizable and so are his treatments: magnesia vitriolata, bleeding the ulcer with leeches, the application of a poultice. Under his more conservative care, "the choppings were much lessened, and she felt herself able to attend constantly to her shop, and had good nights rest. A favourable circumstance also was, that no bleeding attended this ulceration; as the whole breast, and its vessels, appeared enveloped in such disease, that I should have had little reason to expect their contracting to restraining hæmorrhage if it had occurred" (548-549). Oliphant is careful to show that his methods fall squarely within the most responsible medical practices of his time and that they temporarily restore the patient to ordinary life—to a healthy narrative of productivity and activity.

However, as he still believes the case incurable, Oliphant makes a decision to pursue a less traditional route in the hopes of providing relief for his patient. Nisbet enters, characterized by Oliphant as a surgeon whose methods fall outside the common methods of the time. Having advertised as a specialist in treating cancers, Nisbet promises new methods of treatment: nightly opium, vegetable alkali and sulpus, and an antinomial pill. Oliphant concedes, "wishing to wave delicacy for the possible benefit of my patient," but Mrs. Craib's condition worsens. Oliphant reports that "the breast had lessened in size in an equal proportion to the general waste of the body" and suggests that though convalescence in the country may be her only hope, her fatigue prevents her from traveling (549). In Oliphant's version, Nisbet becomes one more in a long line of attendants whose care exacerbates Mrs. Craib's symptoms. The steady stream of dates, new treatments, physical developments, and domestic details enhances the sentimental qualities of the case. Oliphant allows Nisbet to treat Mrs. Craib, "for the possible benefit of his patient" but is, four paragraphs later, "sorry that the plan had been pursued so long." Her condition is so morbid, he informs readers that "Mr Craib was obliged to part beds" (549). As the subject of his case history, Mrs. Craib has forfeited her bodily and domestic privacy.

Once again it is a miscalculation of Mrs. Craib's that gives rise to the next—and climactic—narrative development:

> On the 16th of August, in the evening, she got out of bed to have it put to rights; thinking she would shortly return to it, she did not put on her stays; and in this state remained longer up than she at first intended, or thought herself able.

> For want of her stays, as she thought, and in my opinion rightly, a pain seized her under the right breast, which she apprehended arose from flatulency, and drank some glasses of Madeira wine to dispel it; however, the pain increased, and I was called at five in the morning, when her pulse could be hardly felt; she was obliged to fit it up, was crying out continually with pain, at the same time pressing forcibly on her side for ease. . . . At this time the breast was not an object of attention, only the ordinary dressing and cleanliness were attended to; and when it again became necessary to be examined into, the ulcer was changed into a common sore, the breast shrunk, and considerably absorbed; and in a short time the whole was taken up as well as the swelling in the axilla, leaving for some little time after, a small discharge from the most deep-seated ulceration, which also, in defiance of stimulating application to keep up a discharge, closed.

> Ever since her breath has been short, and checked with cough, and glary expectoration; the pulse, which before, I believe, never exceeded 80, was now upwards of 130, creeping and indistinct. She appeared exsanguinated, and very feeble; an issue was made in the opposite arm, but with no marked advantage.

> (549-550)

The medical details of this incident are fairly straightforward. Mrs. Craib was "seized" with a pain under her right breast. The pain remained for several hours and was complicated by a cough. Oliphant treated these symptoms by bleeding her, applying oil to her ulcerated breast, and giving her an opiate for pain. Once again, the sequence of these events is sewn together by a host of non-medical details. The changing of her sheets, Mrs. Craib's leaving her bed without her stays, her crying out in pain and drinking Madeira wine to ease it,

and Oliphant's arrival at five A.M. are all relevant to the case at hand because medicine is not a science that can rely simply on the isolated functions of patients' bodies. Their lives impinge on their health. However, descriptions of the minutiae of Mrs. Craib's life create a sentimental scene of a suffering patient and her sympathetic doctor. "In want of her stays," her diseased breasts exposed, Mrs. Craib is alone, in the dark, able only to drink Madeira wine and cry out in pain, a portrait surely designed to elicit sympathy, but not confidence. The patient made the mistake of assuming the privacy of the healthy, walking around her home undressed; in her condition, Oliphant suggests, this mistake was fatal. She is "exsanguinated, feeble," her pulse faint. Mrs. Craib's poor judgment is the catalyst for the narrative climax, the patient's condition having taken a turn towards *denouement*—imminent death.

The next section of the account chronicles Mrs. Craib's gradual decline, directly attributed to the incident of her leaving her bed without her stays. On the second of October he treated her for shortness of breath and a "teasing cough"; on the twenty-first for a "swelling of the face," constipation, and "a scarcity of urine." On the twenty-fourth her urine and her pulse increased, her cough lessened, and "a little redness of health appeared again in the lips." This recovery of health enabled him to resume treatment of the breast, introducing a "seton" (or hole for draining), applying palliatives, and prescribing a pill of his own concoction. By the thirteenth of September her breath had improved, and all her chest complaints had disappeared by the eighteenth. After this, "The bleeding and relaxants employed, produced a quick absorption, and the general inflammation changed the ulceration to a common sore, which had such a tendency to heal, that it closed up in defiance of a stimulating ointment applied to keep it discharging" (551). Oliphant suggests that this happy if inconclusive turn of events is the result of his putting an end to Nisbet's treatments. Without them, the breast healed, leading Oliphant to conclude that the complaint was never cancer. In the process he has participated in the construction of a riveting narrative, in which two practitioners with different diagnoses of the same case vie for authority, using Mrs. Craib's body, her mortality, as their field of experimentation.

Nevertheless, Oliphant ends this version of the narrative with a strict disavowal of the narrative techniques he has employed to persuade readers that his diagnosis is the valid one: "I have confined myself to the statement of facts; and how far art had to do with the changes that took place, I leave the professional gentlemen to determine. What I now have to regret is that neither of them hold out hopes of remedy to suffering humanity afflicted with such a dreadful disease as cancer" (551-552). After concluding that the case was not cancer, Oliphant appended a footnote that quotes Hippocrates on the virtues of allowing the body to heal itself. What is clear is that even under the pretense of confining himself "to the statement of facts," Oliphant is relying on his readers to infer "how far art had to do with the changes that took place." He presents himself as an attentive and careful physician, cautious in his diagnoses. Still, his statement has the ring of the unreliable narrator, whose narrative is more than a simple analysis. It is a story, and he is the protagonist, one in search "of remedy to suffering humanity afflicted with such dreadful disease as cancer." In short, neither facts nor sensibility can stand alone in either account of this case; the two require each other. The dramatic narrative is fueled by each physician's attempt to prove both his professional authority and his ethical and humane conduct. With each subsequent version of the case, addressed to the editors of the journal and the public at large, the narrative takes on an almost epistolary quality, in which events are narrated from highly subjective points of view that make the truth almost impossible to locate.

The remainder of the debate consists of each physician's defense of his diagnosis, based on a re-framing of symptoms and developments within a cause-effect schema that lends itself to his own point of view. Nisbet defends his diagnosis, idiopathic cancer. Oliphant responds with yet another version of the events. What becomes clear is that no reader, no matter how knowledgeable about medical treatments or theories, could ever evaluate the merits of the case with any certainty. There are simply two different versions of the story. Oliphant's second rebuttal, though, is the last published version of the case and contains new information: Mrs. Craib has relapsed, a detail he uses to claim narrative closure. Oliphant is "wrong" with regard to diagnosis, as the relapse looks like cancer, but "right" with regard to result, death. The result, published in January of 1801, is a tragic one for any reader susceptible to the sentimental sway the narrative has developed through its several accounts:

> I am sorry my opinion has been realized. On the 1st of this month she sent for me, to shew me a few eruptions that had come out the preceding fortnight; and with considerable relief to her inside, she told me. When I saw her, I found there were innumerable affections of the miliary glands of the skin of both breasts, particularly under the absorbed one, extending a great way on the side under the arm. The last healed sore, where the absorbed one was, was re-opened; on several other parts of this surface considerable schirrous tubercles have arisen. The right breast, from being left with a small pendulous schirrus, sustained by the flaccid integuments; the skin has not contracted, which draws up the increased schirrus; and the whole threatens to become one mass of disease, of much more serious consideration to Mrs. Craib that any former state of her malady that I have witnessed: also her present weakness, indifferent appetite, bad digestion, a disposition to anasarca, and her pulse upwards of 112, have disabled

the constitution from sustaining such a grievous load for any great length of time.

(190-191)

Mrs. Craib's "grievous load" will kill her. This concluding statement carries a tremendous amount of sentimental weight. Despite the best efforts of her practitioners, Mrs. Craib had little hope of surviving. Current methods of treatment were simply insufficient to prolong her life.

In the process of seeking her cure she imbibed a host of prescriptions and submitted to the eyes and hands of at least nine men. Not only does she endure intense physical trauma and relinquish authority over her own body, but, unlike Fanny Burney or fictional counterparts like Lady Delacour, she does so futilely. Though represented as therapeutic, any individual case history is liable to end, not with a cure, but with death. Its value, as Oliphant suggests, lies in some future "remedy to suffering humanity." As the object of sympathy Mrs. Craib's body is manipulated for public observation, treated as a vessel of excessive sensibility. As empirical data, her case offers very little other than evidence of a professional squabble. Whereas the readers of *Sidney Bidulph* or *Belinda* are invited to "slip into" the private lives of imaginary characters, readers of Mrs. Craib's case are witness to a medical debate that centers around a patient's real-life suffering. A reader attentive to the ebb and flow of her case must also confront the idea that his or her own privacy is tenuous, dependent on the health of his or her body. Literary techniques help both surgeons to soften the effects of identification, disguising the patient as heroine, marking her with the trappings of characterization. This is not to say that such softening is the complete erasure of Mrs. Craib's corporeality, her actual existence. Instead, her embodiment in narrative creates a tension between two poles of interpretation. Readers are always aware that she existed, that she was sick, and that she died, but literary appeals to sensibility inevitably call attention to the fact that the case is a narrative, that to read about Mrs. Craib's suffering is very different from witnessing it. Her surgeons insulate us from the burden of witnessing it first-hand, inserting themselves between her and us, assuming the heroic position of the firsthand witness.

SLIPPING INTO LADY DELACOUR'S CLOSET: THE CASE OF *BELINDA*

The profusely detailed narration of Mrs. Craib's corporeal decline is more explicit than any bodily descriptions to be found in novels during the period. The authors of case histories, with the authority of science behind them, can represent with impunity subjects that are taboo in novels. A major problem faced by the realist novel is how to represent what was off limits in romance—primarily bodily functions and sexuality. In romance, heroes and heroines exist in foreign, enchanted places where bowel movements were unnecessary and copulation could be represented with an amorous trope. In realism, which focuses on the minutiae of life, the clinical, pathologizing gaze of medicine provides a model for representing the private experience of suffering. In fact, novels of the late-eighteenth century include a host of troubling, taboo subjects under the guise of medical discourse. In *Belinda,* narrative resolution relies on a careful balance between science and sensibility that delivers the principal characters from pathology to health and from depravity to virtue, a trajectory that involves the representation of breast cancer, cross-dressing, murder, infidelity, and gambling.

Like so many novels of sensibility, *Belinda* contains a variety of scenes and statements that mark its generic difference from Romance. Lady Delacour to Belinda: "My dear, you will be woefully disappointed, if in my story you expect any thing like a novel. I once heard a general say, that nothing was less like a review than a battle; and I can tell you that nothing is more unlike a novel than real life" (36). If Lady Delacour's story is not novelistic, then she is not a heroine (or anti-heroine). Instead, the novel continually pathologizes her, positioning her as patient, a narrative object to be studied but not necessarily admired—like Roxana and Pamela before her. Critics of *Belinda,* including Edgeworth herself, have continually complained that the novel's eponymous heroine is overshadowed by the more interesting Lady Delacour—in other words, that the *Bildungsroman* is overshadowed by the narrative of pathology.[9] The first two volumes of the novel are dominated by Lady Delacour, whose story is more complex and intriguing than Belinda's, but the relationship *between* these two characters—and these two plots—is the central concern of the novel. Lady Delacour's "history" is a warning to Belinda, whose actions, mostly displays of her sensibility, we see throughout the novel, but about whom there is very little narrative commentary or even description. Truly a heroine, Belinda is confronted with the sickly Lady Delacour, whose cancerous breast is presented as metonymic reminder of her more general "dissipation." Dr. X— is crucial to the eventual resolution of the plot, which centers on the relationship between Lady Delacour's disease and the naïve Belinda's vulnerability. At the novel's opening, Belinda's narrative has yet to take a pathological turn—and so, in fact, she has no narrative; her lack of pathology leaves her storyless. Edgeworth's solution is to surround her with pathological characters whose influence she must resist if she wants to retain her virtue, her sense, and her health. A model of Locke's *tabula rasa,* she is vulnerable to the inscriptions of the vice-ridden social realm into which she is thrust.

Under the gaze of Dr. X—, bodily health, good sense, and moral decorum are explicitly linked. Despite her

good sense, Belinda's lack of exposure to the depravity that lurks beneath the surface of drawing room niceties is dangerous. She does not know enough of treachery to fear it. The supporting characters all threaten her virtue in one way or another. In the end, having escaped all threats, Belinda marries Mr. Hervey, a reformed rake, and all is well. The narrative is universally therapeutic. It is preventive medicine in Belinda's case, staving off the contagious psychic and corporeal infections that threaten her, and curative for the supporting characters, whose moral, mental, and physical cures are enacted through the force of the good-natured Belinda's influence combined with Dr. X—'s clinical gaze. In opposition to Lady Delacour's depraved mind and ailing body, Belinda's intrinsic sense of reason and virtue corresponds to a healthy constitution, capable of sustaining the weaker characters who populate her story. Within a domestic setting, even a woman who manages to unite sense and feeling has limited power or influence. In fact, as Sill observes, "It is Belinda, not Dr. X—, who explains to Lady Delacour the deceptions that have been practiced on her, and who persuades her to give up her laudanum and her hallucinations" (189). As Sill points out, even Marriot, Lady Delacour's maid servant, "correctly declares that 'we may thank Miss Portman for this, for 'twas she who made everything right'" (189). However, for most of the novel Belinda's self-control and measured sensibility only give her the ability to regulate her *own* moral consciousness. She is still at the mercy of the dissolute figures around her. Their reformation requires the collaboration of Dr. X—, whose intervention amounts to a reversal of Locke's *tabula rasa,* the reinscription of Belinda's regulated consciousness onto Lady Delacour's dissolute and ailing body.

The narrative suggests that Lady Delacour's disreputable behavior is the cause of both her failing marriage and her failing health. Once a beauty, she has been desperate to hold onto her seductive charms. She has pursued every avenue for the preservation of youth available to her. In response, her body has rebelled; underneath her "paint," her skin is dry, cracked, hideous. Worse, a cancer is "eating" at her breast, consuming her body and her spirit. The hideous interior beneath Lady Delacour's charming veneer is only exposed when she enters the privacy of her closet. Consequently, it is only Marriot and before long, Belinda, who are privy to her secret—except for doctors. A male doctor has access to the privacy of her closet, a place no suitor, not even a husband, is allowed. (Recall the violation of Pamela's closet by Mr. B.) Worried about the society ties of more reputable scientific medical men, Lady Delacour opts for the underground, underhanded treatment of quacks, who prescribe medicines that exacerbate her condition. Her quest for health and secrecy is an impossible one, thrusting her into a world of toxic treatments and perilous experiments. To receive proper treatment, patients must enter the public sphere of medicine.

Belinda's initial glance into this world is also the reader's invitation to slip into Lady Delacour's closet and witness her private suffering. Lady Delacour faints during a masquerade she is hosting, requiring removal to her closet. Belinda's intrinsic moral consciousness moves her to Lady Delacour's aid. However, the scene she witnesses threatens to envelop her. Her new guardian is her role model; her surroundings are Belinda's surroundings:

> The room was rather dark, as there was no light in it, except what came from one candle, which Lady Delacour held in her hand, and which burned but dimly. Belinda, as she looked round, saw nothing but a confusion of linen rags—vials, some empty, some full—and she perceived that there was a strong smell of medicines.
>
> Lady Delacour, whose motions were all precipitate, like those of a person whose mind is in great agitation, looked from side to side of the room, without seeming to know what she was in search of. She then, with a species of fury, wiped the paint from her face, and returning to Belinda, held the candle so as to throw her cheeks hollow—not a trace of youth or beauty remained on her deathlike countenance, which formed a horrid contrast with her gay fantastic dress.
>
> (31)

The concealment of her illness has transformed Lady Delacour's dressing closet into an experimental medical chamber where quackery obfuscates reason. The milieu is obscure and terrifying, and in it Lady Delacour's infection festers. Both her mind and her body are sustained in a continuous state of dissolution. It is not until Belinda convinces her to open herself to the more public services of the highly reputable Dr. X— that Lady Delacour finds her cure. The novel is suffused with Enlightenment binary oppositions, between light and darkness, reason and madness, health and disease, publicity and privacy; and it hinges on the rational Dr. X—, who delivers the corporeal equivalent of the moral cure effected by Belinda's influence on Lady Delacour, putting her on the right side of such oppositions.

Edgeworth uses Belinda as a mediator between the reader and Lady Delacour. Having decided that Belinda is in fact the guileless creature she appears to be, the patient agrees to tell her "history"—a tale that links the causes of her moral dissipation and her cancer:

> 'Yes—I think—I may trust to you—for though a nice of Mrs. Stanhope's, I have seen this day, and have seen with surprise, symptoms of artless feeling about you. This was what tempted me to open my mind to you, when I found that I had lost the only friend—but I will

> think no more of that—if you have a heart, you must feel for me. Leave me now—tomorrow you shall hear my whole history—now I am quite exhausted—ring for Marriot.'
>
> (33)

Throughout the two-chapter narration that ensues, readers see Lady Delacour, along with Belinda, through two lenses. On the one hand we see her the way a the physician would, as a case in whose "history" we may find the source of her cure, and on the other hand we see her as a carrier of a potentially contagious infection. Each of Belinda's reactions is marked by fluctuating emotional responses. She is caught in a bind between clinical and emotional understandings of Lady Delacour's story. Unlike Dr. X—, Belinda lacks the rhetorical skill to reconcile the discourses of science and sensibility:

> Lady Delacour's history, and the manner in which it was related, excited in Belinda's mind astonishment—pity—admiration—and contempt. Astonishment at her inconsistency—pity for her misfortunes—and admiration of her talents—and contempt for her conduct. To these emotions succeeded the recollection of the promise which she had made, not to leave her in her last illness, at the mercy of an insolent attendant. This promise Belinda thought of with terrour—she dreaded the sight of sufferings, which she knew must end in death—she dreaded the sight of that affected gaiety, and of that real levity, which so ill became the condition of a dying woman. She trembled at the idea of being under the guidance of one, who was so little able to conduct herself; and she could not help blaming her aunt Stanhope severely, for placing her in such a perilous situation.
>
> (69)

As mediator, Belinda directs readers how to feel about Lady Delacour's illness. She feels pity, admiration, contempt, astonishment, terror; she dreads the sight of "sufferings" and "affected gaiety"; she trembles "at the idea of being under the guidance of one so little able to conduct herself"; with her newfound knowledge it becomes clear to both readers and heroine that her situation is perilous. Of Belinda's host of emotional responses to the scene of Lady Delacour's closet, pity and admiration stand out, ensuring her emotional involvement and cementing her a place in the narrative. She is the model of the sympathetic reader, whose compassion compels her to disregard the danger of contagion and commence treatment, or "ameliorative action," of Lady Delacour's case. But Belinda's sensibility also makes her vulnerable to the moral and physical contagion presented by the Lady Delacour's symbiotic diseases of mind and body.

Lady Delacour's history begins with a first love, Mr. Percival, who could not "endure her fault" (and whose eventual wife, the faultless Anne Percival, is the model of the sensible domestic woman). The history continues with her marriage to Lord Delacour and her discovery that they were well paired for mutual dissipation. They were both prone to excess and spending, and her strong will inspired in him a fear that he would appear to be dominated by her. She diagnoses his fault as "obstinacy," determining that it is not an "inveterate, incurable malady" and seeks to cure it with "poison of jealousy." Soon realizing her attempt to cure him is hopeless, she declares: "cases of obstinacy are always dangerous in proportion to the weakness of the patient" (38). Lady Delacour responds by affecting the appearance of a coquette, in attempt to subjugate her husband to her will. Instead, his jealousy becomes an "inveterate, incurable malady" itself. Like the treatment she later receives at the hands of her quack, the "poison of jealousy" not only exacerbates the original malady but also replaces it with one even more severe. To make matters worse Lord Delacour becomes a chronic drinker, and she gives birth to one still born child and experiences the death of another after three months of breast feeding, both tragedies attributed to her dissipation. (When a third child is born they send it to be "educated" by Lord Delacour's aunt.) As their marriage continues to deteriorate, Lady Delacour commences her association with Harriet Freke, whose cross-dressing, generally mannish behavior, delight in caprices, and total disregard for propriety leads Lady Delacour into an apparent (though not actual) affair with the foppish colonel Lawless, whom Lord Delacour avenges, killing him in a duel. Freke also goads Lady Delacour into a duel with their mutual enemy, a Mrs. Luttridge, which is avoided due to a sudden inflammation of her opponent's hand. They agree to fire their pistols into the air, but in Lady Delacour's words, "when I fired, it recoiled, and I received a blow on my breast, the consequences of which you have seen—or are to see. 'The pain was nothing at the moment compared with what I have since experienced'" (58).

Lady Delacour's mismanagement of her domestic relations leads to association with Harriet Freke and exacerbates the problems in her marriage, leading to the death of two children, the abandonment of a third, Lord Delacour's jealousy and alcoholism, and finally a "blow" that causes the cancer that presently afflicts her. The cause-and-effect relationships here are ludicrously overdetermined. Social behavior, moral sense, and physical health are categories so interrelated the narrative simply assumes their correspondence, suggesting that readers too would take their interpenetration for granted. A sound body requires a sound mind, and the relationship between the two is regulated by social decorum. Like Burney in her mastectomy letter, Lady Delacour, as narrator of these confessional chapters, assumes two positions: she is narrator and narrative object, possessing authority and eliciting sympathy. These chapters secure Belinda's identification with her guard-

ian, and while the tale terrifies Belinda, telling it offers Lady Delacour her only chance of moral reform and physical cure:

> "O!—I am, sometimes," resumed she, "as you see, in terrible pain. For two years after I gave myself that blow with the pistol I neglected the warning twinges that I felt from time to time—at last I was terrified. Marriot was the only person to whom I mentioned my fears, and she was profoundly ignorant. She flattered me with false hopes, till, alas! It was in vain to doubt the nature of my complaint. The she urged me to consult a physician—that I would not do—I could not—I never will consult a physician—I would not for the universe have my situation known. You stare—you cannot enter into my feelings. Why, my dear, if I lose admiration, what have I left? Would you have me live upon pity? Consider, what a dreadful thing it must be to me, who have no friends, no family, to be confined to a sick room—a sick bed—'tis what I must come to at last—but not yet—not yet—I have fortitude—I should despise myself if I had no species of merit—besides, it is still some occupation to me, to act my part in public—and bustle, noise, nonsense, if they do not amuse, or interest me, yet they stifle reflection—may you never know what it is to feel remorse! The idea of that poor wretch, Lawless, whom I actually murdered, as much as if I had shot him, haunts me whenever I am alone—it is now between eight and nine years since he died, and I have lived ever since in a constant course of dissipation—but it won't do. Conscience! Conscience will be heard. Since my health has been weakened, I believe I have acquired more conscience."

(64-65)

In fiction, the relationships between physical and moral pathology become explicit. Lady Delacour's dissipation, via the blow, causes her disease. As Belinda constructs Lady Delacour as pathological, the narrative constructs Belinda as susceptible to corruption because of her association with a dissipated woman. She is in danger of becoming infected through her identification with Lady Delacour; if her "goodness" is not sustained, the narrative threatens, Belinda will become her guardian. Through Lady Delacour, inconsistency and disease are posited as character flaws that reinforce each other. For Belinda, health relies on consistency of appearances, manners, and behavior—as they did for physicians whose practice, at the beginning of the nineteenth century, was based on study not only of the empirical sciences but also the Enlightenment philosophy that had become dominant over the course of the previous century.

In the end, Dr. X— steps in and rescues each woman from both moral and bodily disease. He diagnoses Lady Delacour's pathology and interprets the causal chain of events that led from her moral dissipation to her corporeal disease. Lady Delacour, it turns out, has never suffered from cancer. Her desire for secrecy and her facility with deception have made her easy prey for quacks whose "cures" do nothing but prolong her suffering, creating the appearance of a cancerous breast where in fact there is nothing but a wound that has not been left to heal. Lady Delacour, on the verge of a mastectomy, requires a re-education. In this fictional plot, healing and character reform can occur with a facility uncommon (but not unheard of) in case histories, whose outcomes are often grim. Nevertheless, the novel, like a case history, chronicles a sequence of events from illness to health, and the very public act of narrating her private experience of illness under the gaze of a physician is the catalyst for Lady Delacour's recovery.

Until Dr. X— steps in, Lady Delacour's "case" is in the wrong hands, preventing any cure. A famed medical author and practitioner, Dr. X— has a reputation for penetrating eyes. Clarence Hervey, in doubt whether to trust her apparent guilelessness, asks the physician to apply his penetrating gaze on her. The physician's response upon first glance is positive but tentative:

> to put you out of pain, I will tell you, that I approve of all I have seen of this young lady, but that it is absolutely out of my power, to form a decisive judgment of a woman's temper and character in the course of a single morning visit. Women, you know, as well as men, often speak with one species of enthusiasm, and act with another. I must see your Belinda act—I must study her, before I can give you my final judgment.
>
> (112)

His initial reaction is accurate, but Dr. X— is not hasty in his diagnoses. He must "study" his subjects before he can pass "final judgment." So, even as his gaze is primarily directed toward lady Delacour, when Dr. X— enters the narrative all the characters become "cases." Under his diagnostic gaze, recovery and reformation become possible; Belinda's healing influence can begin to take effect.

The diagnosis of lady Delacour, who refuses to see a reputable physician like Dr. X—, takes place at a party, where he observes:

> "These high spirits do not seem quite natural. The vivacity of youth and of health, miss Portman, always charms me; but this gayety of lady Delacour's does not appear to me that of a sound mind in a sound body . . . Lady Delacour," continued the doctor, "seems to be in a perpetual fever, either of mind or body—I cannot tell which—and as a professional man, I really have some curiosity to determine the question. If I could feel her pulse, I could instantly decide; but I have heard her say, that she has a horror of having her pulse felt—and a lady's horror is invincible—by reason—."
>
> (115)

Lady Delacour's command of her own body leaves her undiagnosable. Demanding privacy, she wields her authority as inhabitant of her own body boldly and will

not consent to an examination. Hervey, who has a penchant for drawing room intrigue, points out that if Dr. X— examines the shadow of her "ruff" closely, he will see, "distinctly," the pulse in her neck "vibrating" (115). However, if in this violation of lady Delacour's privacy Dr. X— does "instantly decide" what her malady is he does not mention it to the others. They (and we) are kept in suspense.

Dr. X—'s first observation comes early in the novel, as does his preliminary diagnosis, prompted by two intervening narrative events. Lady Delacour is injured in a carriage accident just as Dr. X— is called away to attend an associate who is seriously ill. His absence delays thorough examination of Lady Delacour and prolongs the narrative, much the way Nisbet's ineffective treatments did in Oliphant's account of Mrs. Craib. In the absence of effective treatment, Lady Delacour's health, like Mrs. Craib's, declines. After his departure, Belinda reads Dr. X—'s diagnosis, addressed to her in the form of a letter, and is left to her own devices to attempt a cure:

> Belinda, the moment the doctor was gone, shut herself up in her own room, to read the paper which he had given to her. Dr. X— first stated that he was by no means certain, that lady Delacour really had the complaint, which she so much dreaded; but it was impossible for him to decide without farther examination, to which her ladyship could not be prevailed upon to submit. Then he mentioned all that he thought would be most efficacious in mitigating the pain that lady Delacour might feel, and all that could be done, with the greatest probability of prolonging her life. And he concluded with the following words:
>
> "These are all temporizing expedients: according to the usual progress of the disease, Lady Delacour may live a year or perhaps two.
>
> "It is possible that her life might be saved by a *skilful* surgeon. By a few words that dropped from her ladyship last night, I apprehend that she has some thoughts of submitting to an operation; which will be attended with much pain and danger, even if she employ the most experienced surgeon in London; but if she put herself, in vain hope of secrecy, into ignorant hands, she will inevitably destroy herself."
>
> (136-137)

The caution against the surgical intervention of "ignorant hands" reflects the dominant medical attitude to breast cancer and mastectomy at the time when Edgeworth was writing, and it also becomes the core of the conflict between Belinda and Lady Delacour—the hinge that links the education and pathology plots—for the remainder of volume two of the novel:

> "I am resolved," said she, "to make one desperate effort for my life. New plans, new hopes of happiness, have opened to my imagination, and, with my hopes of being happy, my courage rises. I am determined to sub-

mit to the dreadful operation which alone can radically cure me—you understand me. But it must be kept a profound secret. I know of a person who could be got to perform this operation with the utmost secrecy."

"But surely," said Belinda, "safety must be your first object!"

"No; secrecy is my first object. Nay, do not reason with me; it is a subject on which I cannot, will not, reason."

(177)

Belinda urges lady Delacour not to submit to a secret operation, but lady Delacour insists, becoming increasingly paranoid. Thinking her life is nearing its end, she begins to study "methodistical" books that fill her mind with mystical, as opposed to rational, ideas.[10] At the same time she begins to suspect that Belinda is plotting to kill her and seduce lord Delacour so that she can literally become the new Lady Delacour. During one of her bouts of paranoia, she thinks to herself, "She has, in fact, become my banker; mistress of my house, my husband, and myself. Ten days I have been confined to my room. Truly, she has made a good use of her time; and I, fool that I am, have been thanking her for all her disinterested kindness!" (182). Lady Delacour begins to fear the literal enactment of the narrative threat to Belinda: that Lady Delacour's present is her future, that her dissipation is the heroine's inevitable fate, that the heroine, over time, will become a patient too.

As volume two hastens toward the dreaded operation, Belinda's sympathy and identification with Lady Delacour are already well secured, but they are imbued with a diagnostic horror. Having cast off her paranoia, Lady Delacour is convinced again of Belinda's constancy and once again recognizes in Belinda her one hope of moral reform: "'If I survive this business,' said she, 'it is my firm intention to appear in a new character, or rather to assert my real character. I will break through the spell of dissipation—I will at once cast off all acquaintance that are unworthy of me—I will, in one word, go with you, my dear Belinda! To Mr. Percival's'" (292). Mr. Percival's is the home of polite company, rational sensibility, and robust constitutions. Belinda is Lady Delacour's one hope of a re-introduction into that world, but at this point she is still too obstinate to see that she must submit both her mind and her body to Belinda's intrinsic good judgment. Secrecy, not safety, still guides her decisions. Secluding herself in a remote house, she waits for the date of her operation to arrive.

When the surgeon and Dr. X— arrive, Lady Delacour postpones the operation again, claiming she is convinced that she will die that night, operation or no operation: "'If I survive this night, manage me as you please. But I am the best judge of my own feelings. I shall die to night'" (305). Dr. X— sees through this story, but he doesn't know what the truth behind it is:

Dr. X— looked at her with a mixture of astonishment and compassion. Her pulse was high, she was extremely feverish, and he thought that the best thing which he could do was to stay with her till the next day, and to endeavour to divert her mind from this fancy, which he considered as an insane idea. He prevailed upon the surgeon to stay with her till the next morning; and he communicated his intentions to Belinda, who joined with him in doing all that was possible to entertain and interest Lady Delacour by conversation during the remainder of the day. She had sufficient penetration to perceive, that they gave not the least faith to her prognostics, and she never said one more word upon the subject; but appeared willing to be amused by their attempts to divert her, and resolute to support her courage till the last moment. She did not affect trifling gayety: on the contrary, there was in all she said more strength and less point than usual.

(305)

Dr. X—'s astonishment and compassion are the reactions of the student of human nature, which all along has been posited as an essential component of his medical acumen. Now, as he observes her symptoms, quick pulse and fever, he treats them with diversions, conversations, and amusements in an effort to observe the truth behind her story. As it turns out, Lady Delacour believes she has been experiencing nightly "visions" since her arrival in this house. Her vision turns out to be a spy, in the form of Harriet Freke, who is convinced Lady Delacour has secluded herself for a liaison with a lover. Unmasked, Harriet is forced to confess and Lady Delacour to see the folly of her mysticism. Dr. X—'s final examination is not represented, but his diagnosis is, to an audience of Marriot, Belinda, Lord Delacour, and Helena:

"There's no need of shrieks, or courage either, thank God!" said Marriot. "Dr. X— says so, and he is the best man in the world, and the cleverest. And I was right from the first; I said it was impossible that my lady should have such a shocking complaint as she thought she had. There's no such thing in the case, my lord! I said so always till I was persuaded out of my senses by that villainous quack, who contradicted me for his own molument. And Dr. X— says, if my lady will leave off the terrible quantities of laudanum she takes, he'll engage for her recovery." The surgeon and Dr. X— now explained to Lord Delacour, that the unprincipled wretch to whom her ladyship had applied for assistance had persuaded her that she had a cancer, though in fact her complaint arose merely from the bruise which she had received. He knew too well how to make a wound hideous and painful, and so continue her delusion for his own advantage. Dr. X— observed, that if lady Delacour would have permitted either the surgeon or him to have examined sooner in to the real state of the case, it would have saved herself infinite pain, and them all anxiety. Belinda at this moment felt too much to speak.

(313-314)

In the first edition of the novel (1801), the final diagnosis is reported only by Marriot. The addition of the more detailed, clinical explanation was added in the second edition (1802).[11] Its addition lends the cure more credence, balancing sentimentality with a causal explanation of Lady Delacour's condition. The narrative of her illness was the peculiar construction of the quack, whose medical expertise and lack of sensibility enabled him to construct a pathological sequence of bodily events where none previously existed. Now that she has been "examined," Lady Delacour's recovery promises to deliver her to safety and put an end to her narrative. Belinda, all along the passive sentimental heroine, feels "too much to speak."

But that is to forget that this novel contains a third book, one whose action takes place after Lady Delacour's recovery. This book contains the reformation of the principle characters, especially Hervey, whose ill-conceived seclusion of a young girl for education in the Rousseauian model—to make her a suitable wife—is exposed and eventually lamented. Mr. Vincent, the West Indian whom Belinda nearly marries, is exposed as a gambler, freeing Belinda for Hervey; Vincent also confesses and reforms. In every case, exposure is required for reformation to occur. The therapeutic narrative requires the publication of private details. Harriet Freke is the only exposed deviant who does not reform willingly, but having been caught in a mantrap when she was spying, her leg is injured and she laments that "she will never again appear to advantage in man's apparel." Though unreformed, she is cured of cross-dressing, her most deviant behavior.

With this series of reformations, the novel enacts Dr. X—'s theory of human nature, described by Hervey in a letter to Lady Delacour: "My friend Dr. X—. . . divides mankind into three classes. Those who learn from the experience of others. They are happy men. Those who learn from their own experience. They are wise men. And, lastly, those who learn neither from their own nor from other people's experience. They are fools. This class is by far the largest" (276).[12] By this account, Lady Delacour and Clarence Hervey have become wise; Belinda is ensured of happiness; and Harriet Freke is condemned to play the fool. Dr. Moore, Dr. X—'s real-life counterpart, was interested in the relationship between "Human Nature" and health and disease. In the moral philosophy that influenced the medicine of the period, human nature is a central concern, also described as "consciousness": "the state or faculty of being conscious, as a condition and concomitant of all thought, feeling, and volition" (OED 757). Edgeworth effectively dramatizes Locke's suggestion that the transfer of consciousness from "one thinking Substance to another" would transform "two thinking Substances" into "but one Person." This, of course, was the original danger for Belinda, the potential transfer of the consciousness

of a Lady Delacour or a Clarence Hervey onto her body; in the end, the reverse becomes the salvation for both Delacour and Hervey, and the transfer is effected by Dr. X—.

Edgeworth's Dr. X— suggests another way of seeing his real-life counterparts, Nisbet and Oliphant. These medical practitioners are caretakers of patients' bodies, but they tend to their patient's psychological condition, through their diagnoses and their appeals to readerly sympathy. Their excessive displays of their own sensibility portray them as suitable attendants, whose medical authority and moral consciousness may guide their patient from health to disease, whose intervention in pathological narratives set them on a healthy trajectory. The narratives are represented as therapeutic—as either curative or at least exemplary in their failure to cure. Either way, narrative becomes an example of what Laqueur calls "ameliorative action." A thorough reading of novels and case histories in relation to each other, however, produces a haunting image of the patient, whose agency is subjugated to that of medical practitioners. A doctor's ability to treat and an author's ability to write marks his or her participation in what Laqueur calls "the social action" that the observation of suffering demanded for any sensible observer. But Laqueur also argues that this social action "created a sense of property in the objects of compassion" and "appropriated them to the consciousness of the would-be benefactors" (179). The objectification of the patient in both novels and case histories takes place through the violations of privacy that illness compels. When the patient becomes the object of the medical gaze, she also becomes the object of moral regulation. Through the sensibility of her exposed body and the sensibility of her physician's attendance, her pathology becomes the primary marker of her selfhood.

Sentimental fiction and medical cases generally reinforced the physician's authority over the patient, with consequences ranging from the dismissal of the patient's agency as inconsequential to explicit associations between disease and either incompetence or deviance. When the somebodies of case histories are represented with the language and conventions of sentimental fictions, they resemble the nobodies of those fictions—stimulating readerly identification through acquiescence to the professional and narrative authority of the physician. In fiction, the clinical gaze of medicine pathologizes characters. The authors of both genres relied on the social importance of their writing to justify violations of bodily privacy, in the process presenting their narratives as therapeutic. The study of pathology, as "ameliorative action," supersedes privacy. In prefaces, sentimental novelists continually justify the representation of pathologies like this one on the basis of the social value of doing so. This is true also in case histories. Like sentimental novels, they must synthesize the violence and horror of diseased bodies, the representation of taboo or private experiences of bodies, and the linked Enlightenment discourses of scientific and social progress. "Unspeakable" bodily details become a necessary evil, a precondition of narration. Taboo subject matter and medical uncertainty become the hallmarks of a genre whose initial aim was to publicize success stories in the Enlightenment quest to know. Case histories *and* novels of the nineteenth century are consistently motivated by a tension between something like Belinda's education—a narrative of progress and illumination—and Lady Delacour's pathology—a narrative of suffering and doubt. Taboo and uncertainty become a motivating force in novels and case histories throughout the nineteenth century, and the narrative innovations, particularly with regard to voice and plot, of the century consistently negotiate unresolved tensions between progress and suffering on the one hand and illumination and doubt on the other—as we'll see in the next chapter, with Jane Austen's use of indirect discourse to control the intrusive voices of hypochondriac characters inexorably searching for medical sanctions for their dubious suffering.

When a case history ends in death, as Mrs. Craib's does, it demonstrates the limits of medical science. Physicians and surgeons of the period felt intensely the need to justify their actions in cases that eluded their expertise. Scenes of intense pain give them a dual motive: as sentimental hero and medical professional. Even if the patient dies, the case contributes to medical theory and sets a negative example for readers, who are always potential patients themselves. If we read as potential patients, we must reluctantly identify with the suffering of a Mrs. Craib. When we slip into her home and read about her relapse, imagining her undressed, sobbing and in pain, we are nevertheless *imagining* this scene. Reading a case history, like reading a novel, involves imaginative leaps to sustain identification between readers and the suffering subjects of narration. Mrs. Craib's surgeons have literally violated her privacy, but they ask readers only to imagine doing so. Mrs. Craib and Lady Delacour are not the same species of narrative subject, but they are both narrative subjects. As such, the identification they elicit from readers involves constant negotiations between science and sensibility, diagnosis and sympathy. In Edgeworth's novel, Belinda is in danger of being contaminated by her confrontation with Lady Delacour. She is a stand-in for readers. In fiction, the tables are easily turned: Belinda's goodness, with the help of Dr. X—'s medical expertise, infects Lady Delacour and makes for a tidy resolution. Mrs. Craib's case is a reminder that life is seldom as orderly as narrative, that even if a given reader is not at risk for breast cancer, s/he does have a body and is vulnerable to its mysteries.

Notes

1. In a sketch for an early draft of the novel, Edgeworth identifies Dr. Moore as the model for Dr. X— (originally "Dr. Sane"), which may account for his mysterious name:

   > Character of Doctor Sane, the physician who attends Lady Delacour in her illness; like Doctor Moore, if you can draw him like the ideas that may be found of Doctor Moore from his works; a benevolent man who knows human nature and what is called the world, perfectly: who has polite manners and talents for conversation in a high degree. He is interested for Belinda, a young girl who he thinks is in Lady Delacour's house on the verge of ruin and misery; make use of him to open her eyes to the real characters of all who frequent Lady Delacour's house. He warns her against Clarence Hervey. She is disposed to admire his dashing genius, but her eyes are opened to his real views, (which are not matrimonial) by the conversation she overhears at Ranelagh, and by the prudence and penetration of Doctor Sane, who makes him show off the worst parts of his character.

   (482)

   Dr. Moore was famous for writing a medical text for a popular audience, *Medical Sketches: In Two Parts* [1786], in which he covers such subjects as digestion, blood circulation, respiration, the nervous system, and fevers. He also published novelistic studies of "human nature," including *Edward: Various Views of Human Nature, Taken from Life and Manners, Chiefly in England* [1796] and *Sketches of Life, Characters, and Manners, in Various Countries; including the Memoirs of a French Lady of Quality* [1800]. In Moore's work, he consistently links morality, sensibility, consciousness, and corporeality, as components of the single system of his primary subject, "Humanity," maintaining that a balance between them is essential for good health *and* for sound medical practice. Though other aspects of Edgeworth's original draft were significantly altered from her original conception, it is safe to assume that Dr. Moore remains the model for Dr. X—.

2. As a rhetorical stance, sensibility is easily combined with medical discourse because it does not merely refer to affect but, in the words of Barker-Benfield, to a complex "psycho-perceptual" system that links corporeal and psychic phenomena as the central organizing system of human animation, or consciousness. Since Locke's theory of human consciousness as a *tabula rasa* (1690), impressionable and therefore changeable, and George Cheyne's influential treatise on nervous disorders, *The English Malady* (1733), sensibility, the system through which physical sensations are received and processed, had become widely em-

ployed as a gauge of human character. Empiricism linked the production of truth claims to detailed accounts of the material world, but those accounts represented a violation of social codes of privacy. Physicians and novelists alike needed a rhetorical strategy to justify those representations.

3. Physicians publishing on this topic during the period sometimes recommend partial or whole excision of the breast, but never without reservations and only when no other treatment is efficacious. See Rather, 26-41, for a discussion of the evolution of eighteenth-century cancer theory, most notably Hunter's theory of "coagulating lymph."

4. On the lack of information on the publication and distribution of these journals, see Lawrence, pages 271-276.

5. Debate was spirited among physicians and surgeons during the period, so the Nisbet-Oliphant exchange would not have been unheard of, but the lengths they pursue are excessive and somewhat atypical.

6. For a collection of essays on quacks versus "regular" practitioners, see *Medical Fringe and Medical Orthodoxy,* ed. Roy Porter. In his introduction, Porter makes the valuable observation that the relationship between a quack and a "regular" physician or surgeon is not simply one of opposition. The categories were more fluid and changeable in a period during which the institutionalization of medicine was still in its nascent stages.

7. There are two recurrent details in accounts of breast ailments during the period, the patient's nervous constitution and a past blow to the breast, often cited as the origin of the disease. Though neither of these details appears in every case, they appear consistently enough to constitute a major component of breast cancer diagnosis during the period. Physicians tended to see cancers as incurable maladies, which, in select cases, responded favorably to treatment or cured themselves over time.

8. By 1800 the Royal College of Surgeons and the Royal College of Physicians, complementary institutions, had acquired a high level of regulation and dominance within mainstream medicine, but that did not mean that patients did not regularly seek the advice of practitioners who had not had not earned membership in "The Faculty." The Royal College of Surgeons, Edinburgh, of which Nisbet was a member, was very well respected and included a number of reputable practitioners, including Alexander Monro. It isn't entirely clear, though, whether nationalism is part of the quarrel between Nisbet and Oliphant, though it is a very

strong possibility. See Christopher Lawrence for a discussion of medicine in Edinburgh, including a discussion of Alexander Monro; see also Susan Lawrence, 107, on the tensions between the Edinburgh and London colleges.

9. See Macfayden and Atkinson for discussions of the letter in which Edgeworth refers to "that stick or stone Belinda."

10. See Macfayden, pages 435-436, for an analysis of Lady Delacour's secret library of religious texts.

11. See notes to the Oxford World's Classic edition of *Belinda,* edited by Kathryn Kirkpatrick.

12. This theory reflects the ideas of Enlightenment philosophers regarding the subject. See Roy Porter, "Medical Science and Human Science," and Smith, "The Language of Human Nature," for discussions of the influence of natural philosophers (particularly Locke and Hume) upon eighteenth-century medicine.

Works Cited

Atkinson, Colin B. and Jo. "Maria Edgeworth and Women's Rights." *Eire-Ireland.* Winter 1984: 95-118.

Bynum, W. F., and Roy Porter, eds. *Medical Fringe and Medical Orthodoxy: 1750-1850.* London: Croom Helm, 1987.

Lawrence, Christopher. "Ornate Physicians and Learned Artisans: Edinburgh Medical Men, 1726-1776." *William Hunter and the Eighteenth-Century Medical World,* ed. W. F. Bynum and Roy Porter. Cambridge: Cambridge UP, 1985.

Lawrence, Susan. *Charitable Knowledge: Hospital Pupils and Practitioners in Eighteenth-Century London.* Cambridge: Cambridge UP, 1996.

Macfayden, Heather. "Lady Delacour's Library: Maria Edgeworth's Belinda and Fashionable Reading." *Nineteenth-Century Literature.* 48:4 (1994): 423-439.

Porter, Roy. "Medical Science and Human Science in the Enlightenment." *Inventing Human Science: Eighteenth-Century Domains.* Fox, Porter, and Robert Wokler, eds. Berkeley: University of California Press, 1995.

Rather, L. J. *The Genesis of Cancer: A Study in the History of Ideas.* Baltimore: Johns Hopkins UP, 1978.

Smith, Roger. "The Language of Human Nature." *Inventing Human Science: Eighteenth-Century Domains.* Fox, Porter, and Robert Wokler, eds. Berkeley: University of California Press, 1995.

THE "DOCTRESS"

Lilian R. Furst (essay date 1997)

SOURCE: Furst, Lilian R. "Halfway Up the Hill: Doctresses in Late Nineteenth-Century American Fiction." In *Women Healers and Physicians: Climbing a Long Hill,* edited by Lilian R. Furst, pp. 221-38. Lexington: University Press of Kentucky, 1997.

[*In the following essay, Furst discusses the proliferation of fictional heroines who were medical doctors in late nineteenth-century American novels and traces the phenomenon to women's efforts to break into the exclusively male medical profession.*]

Between 1881 and 1891 the figure of the "doctress," as she was then called, makes a prominent appearance in American fiction. During that decade five novels offer divergent portraits of this newcomer on the social scene. In chronological order they are *Dr. Breen's Practice* by William Dean Howells (1881), *Doctor Zay* by Elizabeth Stuart Phelps (1882), Sarah Orne Jewett's *A Country Doctor* (1884), *The Bostonians* by Henry James (1886), and Annie Nathan Meyer's *Helen Brent, M.D.* (1891). In four of the five novels the life, work, and status of the doctress is the main theme. Only in *The Bostonians* is the persona of the female physician, Dr. Mary Prance, not the central heroine. However, as the only fully independent professional woman she is an important character in a novel about the feminist movement.[1]

This spate of five novels in ten years suggests that the doctress had not only attained public visibility,[2] but had also captured the imagination. Certainly access to medical education for women had been a highly controversial issue in the United States after the middle of the century when they had begun to try to gain admission to regular medical schools. Women had always been informal healers within the kinship circle of family and neighbors. Many early housekeeping manuals, such as Mrs. E. Smith's *The Compleat Houswife* (1742) and the British Mrs. Beeton's *Book of Household Management* (1861) combined medical with food recipes. Self-help books, notably Dr. William Buchan's *Domestic Medicine; or a Treatise on the Prevention and Cure of Diseases by Regimen and Simple Medicines* (1772), John G. Gunn's *Domestic Medicine* (1830) and *The Maternal Physician* (1818) by "An American Matron," were all clearly addressed to female readers. Women also became active in the later nineteenth century in various sectarian health reform movements such as the then fashionable water cures and notably in the Physiological Societies, which taught the "laws of life" and especially hygiene to female audiences as an extension of domestic proficiency. But this casual exercise of para-

medical skills was superseded in the course of the nineteenth century by the gradual rise and increasingly powerful organization of medicine as a profession, and a decidedly *male* profession. Instruction by apprenticeship, such as Harriot and Sarah Hunter underwent in the early 1830s, gave way to training in medical schools, whose growth accelerated rapidly in the latter half of the century from 52 in 1850 to 75 in 1870, 100 in 1880, 133 in 1890, and 160 by 1900. The schools varied enormously in quality, so that serious efforts to improve medical education were initiated in 1870 by Harvard's President Eliot. The previous two-year program, consisting largely of theoretical, didactic lectures devoid of regular sequence, was expanded in 1871 into a three-year course in which anatomy, physiology, chemistry, and pathological anatomy, that is, the laboratory sciences, came to play an ever more important part. At about the same time hospitals moved from the periphery to the center of medical education and practice, changing from refuges for the homeless poor and insane into the physician's primary workshop. It was also in the 1870s and 1880s that medical men converged in agreement on the need for licensing and proper regulation of the profession. This stiffening and enforcement of the requirements is typified by the 1877 law in Illinois that empowered a state board of examiners to accept diplomas only from reputable schools.

The reform and institutionalization of medical education militated against women. As the historian Gerda Lerner has succinctly put it, "Women were the casualties of medical professionalization."[3] Whether such an oppression/victimization model is simplistic has been a matter of argument among historians, some of whom see women's attempts to enter into regular medicine as part of the larger nineteenth-century struggle for female self-determination. It was clearly a rebuff to such aims that women's repeated efforts to gain admission to medical schools met with scoffing rejection under a profusion of pretexts. Elizabeth Blackwell did achieve entrance to the medical school located in Geneva, New York in 1845 because students and faculty thought the application a joke and voted for it in jest; in 1849 she graduated at the top of her class. Another exceptional case is that of Marie Elizabeth Zakrzewska, who had been a brilliant midwife in Berlin and who graduated from the medical school in Cleveland in 1856. But by and large specious objections and excuses prevailed to exclude women from medical schools and hence from the profession. The very idea of a female doctor was considered to violate the norms of feminine behavior; women were regarded as unfit, physically and temperamentally, for the "blood and agony" of medical practice, which would compromise their innate delicacy; indeed, they were deemed constitutionally unfit for education after puberty, when all their energy should be directed to the development of the "pelvic power"[4] that would make them good mothers. That was the central argument of Dr. Edward H. Clarke in his 1873 treatise with the misleading title, *Sex in Education: A Fair Chance for Girls,* in which he asserted that intellectual activity during menstruation would surely lead to "neuralgia, uterine disease, hysteria, and other derangements of the nervous system."[5]

With the doors insolently slammed in their faces, the women began to organize their own medical colleges: the New England Female Medical College in 1848, the Women's Medical College of Pennsylvania in Philadelphia in 1850, the New York Women's Medical College (homeopathic) in 1863, the Homeopathic Medical College for Women in Cleveland in 1868, and, in the same year, the Women's Medical College of the New York Infirmary for Women and Children, the Woman's Hospital Medical College, in Chicago in 1870, and the New York Free Medical College for Women in 1871. None of these endeavors could have succeeded without the support and cooperation of some male physicians who were willing to act as instructors until the women themselves had acquired sufficient expertise and experience to teach their successors. Hands-on casework was also essential to medical training. As women were denied internships and residences, they founded first dispensaries and then hospitals for women and children, of which the earliest were the New York Infirmary for Women and Children, opened in 1857, and the New England Hospital for Women and Children in 1862. From these institutions the early pioneer women doctors were graduated, including three black women: Rebecca Lee in 1861, Rebecca Cole in 1867, and Sara McKinney Stewart in 1870. Some of the more affluent and ambitious went on to further training in those European universities that admitted women. Mary Putnam Jacobi, for instance, became the second woman to attain the M.D. in Paris in 1875. The University of Zurich, open to women since 1864, was another popular destination.[6] Back home, well prepared to practice, intending to serve women and children, the doctresses faced more difficulties in obtaining membership in the state medical associations. Such membership was not strictly a prerequisite for practice; nevertheless, it had important practical implications as a symbol of legitimate acceptance as well as for referrals, admission to hospital staffs, in other words, for full integration into the profession. Curiously evasive terms such as "inexpedient" and "inopportune" were advanced for a while as grounds for rejection; the qualifications necessary for admission were declared to apply to males only. But in 1877 the state societies of Kansas, Michigan, and Rhode Island did take women; others followed, with Massachusetts in 1884 among the last.

This necessarily brief overview of women's struggle to enter the medical profession in this country[7] is the context for the novels under discussion. It is no coincidence that doctresses feature in American fiction of the 1880s because by then they had begun to surface as a social phenomenon. They were by then, to adopt the metaphor in the title of this volume, half way up the hill. Nor is it coincidental that all the five novels are set in the Northeast—one in New York, and the other four in New England—for these were the prime centers of medical education for women, and had a far higher concentration of female physicians than anywhere else: in 1880 132 women were practicing in Boston alone, 14.9 percent of the city's medical force; by 1890 the figures had risen to 210 and 18.0 percent respectively (in the rest of the country the corresponding percentages are 2.8 for 1880, and 4.4 for 1890).[8] Clusters of women doctors were found elsewhere too: out west, where the pioneering spirit made the social climate less straitlaced, and in Washington, where some 90 women doctors formed part of a large and lively community of female professionals between 1870 and 1900, drawn to the capital by the postwar expansion of the federal government.[9]

The novels are interesting for the lively insight they give not only into the careers of the doctresses but also into the prevailing social attitudes toward them. A number of common preoccupations recur, although there are also considerable variations between them so that it is a spectrum of possibilities that emerges rather than a consensus. The novels portray doctresses at different stages in their careers: Nan Prince in *A Country Doctor* is just going through her apprenticeship and early training; Grace Breen is on the verge of starting to practice, while the other three are already well established. Atalanta Zay singlehandedly runs a large rural practice in Maine; Mary Prance engages in both clinical and research medicine in Boston, and *Helen Brent, M.D.* opens with the heroine's appointment to the presidency of a women's hospital and medical college after she has built a prodigious reputation.

A major source of diversity lies in the gendered perspective. Two of the works, *Dr. Breen's Practice* and *The Bostonians,* are authored by men, while the other three are by women. Here a clear dichotomy is apparent: the women are far more positive in their perception of the doctress, portraying independent, self-confident, successful practitioners. Elizabeth Phelps's *Dr. Zay* performs minor surgery with "a firm and fearless touch,"[10] goes out on night calls alone in her horse and buggy, is "sent for all over the county" (86), and earns $5,000 a year, though she could make much more if she did not treat the poor virtually for free. Helen Brent, described as "well known" and "popular,"[11] performs "difficult gynecological operations, the success of which had interested the entire medical profession—operations that required nerve, coolness, daring, skill, a steady hand, and a delicate one; and when they were over, she had never been known either to faint or to go into hysterics, as Dr. Manning had prophesied would be the conduct of the woman physician" (15). The young Nan Prince, too, in *A Country Doctor* shows a "a sort of self-dependence and . . . self-reliance"[12] together with an instinctive insight into people, and the "resource, bravery, and ability to think for one's self that make a physician worth anything" (184). In a revealing scene, during an outing with friends while she is still in medical school, she attends to a farmer who has dislocated his shoulder in a fall by taking off her boot and manipulating the joint back into position with a deft movement of her foot and arm (295).[13] By contrast, William Dean Howells's Dr. Grace Breen is an "inexperienced girl,"[14] timid, hesitant, in constant need of reassurance and approval from her mother, who undermines her as consistently as does the narrator (e.g., that "girl"). Self-deprecatory, lacking pride in achievement, in fact lacking in achievement, the pathetic Dr. Breen is the opposite to the commanding Dr. Zay and Helen Brent, who possess both dignity and panache. Midway between these extremes is James's Dr. Mary Prance, "a plain, spare young woman, with short hair and an eyeglass,"[15] an austere, dry, laconic observer of the feminist scene who pursues her studies far into the night, sharpening her instruments (probably for dissection) in a little physiological laboratory that she has set up in her back room (31). She is vehement in not wanting "the gentlemen doctors to get ahead of her" (37) nor in having anyone tell her "what a lady can do!" (38). At first the young Southern lawyer, Basil Ransom, sees her rather negatively, as a sexless creature who looks "like a boy, and not even like a good boy" (32), and is put off by "her flat, limited manner" (33). Gradually, however, he comes to appreciate that "this lady was tough and technical" (33), that she conducts business "with the greatest rapidity and accuracy" (331), that she is as successful as ambitious, has lucidity of mind to the point of "diabolical shrewdness" (319), and even a streak of humor.

Dr. Prance is always focalized through the eyes of Basil Ransom: "The little medical lady struck him as a perfect example of the 'Yankee female' . . . produced by the New England school system, the Puritan code, the ungenial climate, the absence of chivalry" (31). This and similar comments raise some vital issues of focalization: who is it that is seeing the doctress? what is the source of the information within the frame of the fiction? and what is the effect of the particular angle of vision? In *The Bostonians* the narrative disposition remains relatively simple, with a male figure acting as a surrogate for a male author, presenting an external image of the doctress (that is to say, we always see Dr. Prance through Basil's vision). At the opposite pole, the female author of *Helen Brent, M.D.* presents a kind of super-doctress, beautiful, strong, smiling, calm, always in control. In *Dr. Breen's Practice,* on the other hand, a male author takes a dualistic approach, both entering into Grace's thoughts and recording how others envisage her. A similar stance is adopted in *A Country Doc-*

tor, where Nan Prince is first filtered through the perceptions of her guardian and mentor, Dr. Leslie; later, as she matures into adolescence and early womanhood, her own reflections on her medical aspirations are added. The most complex crossgendering occurs in *Doctor Zay,* where the doctress in this novel by a woman is consistently focalized, as in *The Bostonians,* through the observations of a man, Waldo Yorke, who has become her patient as a result of a serious accident that befalls him while his is in Maine on business. So here a disabled, and, what is more, a decidedly lackadaisical male is viewing a strong, indeed imperious female. This reversal of the customary nineteenth-century role order accounts for much of the work's piquancy.

The situation in *Doctor Zay* builds to a climax as Waldo slowly comes to the alarming realization that his competent, gentle attendant is not a nurse, as he naturally supposes when he recovers consciousness. The technique of suspense is cleverly deployed; Waldo's hostess, herself a patient and admirer of Dr. Zay, deliberately conceals the physician's gender. This graphic scene is so typical of the surprised discomfort evoked by the doctresses that it is worth quoting in full:

> Only one person was in the room, a woman. He asked her for water. She brought it. She had a soft step. When he had satisfied his thirst, which he was allowed to do without protest, the woman gave him medicine. He recognized the familiar tumbler and teaspoon of his homeopathically educated infancy. He obeyed passively. The woman fed him with the medicine; she did not spill it, nor choke him; when she returned the teaspoon to the glass, he dimly saw the shape of her hand. He said,—
>
> "You are my nurse?"
>
> "I take care of you tonight, sir."
>
> "I thank you," said Yorke, with a faint touch of his Beacon-Street courtliness; and so fell away again.
>
> He moved once more at dawn. He was alarmingly feverish. . . . His agony had increased. He still moaned for water, and his mind reverted obstinately to its chief anxiety. He said,—
>
> "Where *is* that doctor? I am too sick a man to be neglected. I must see the doctor."
>
> "The doctor has been here," said the woman who was serving as nurse, "nearly all night."
>
> "Ah! I have been unconscious, I know."
>
> "Yes. But you have been cared for. I hope that you will be able to compose yourself. I trust you will feel no undue anxiety about your medical attendance. Everything shall be done, Mr. Yorke."
>
> "I like your voice," said the patient, with delicious frankness. "I haven't heard one like it since I left home. I wish I were at home! It is natural that I should feel some anxiety about this country physician. I want to know the worst. I shall feel better after I have seen him."

"Perhaps you may," replied the nurse, after a slight hesitation. "I will go and see about it. Sleep if you can. I shall be back directly."

This quieted him, and he slept once more. When he waked, it was broadening, brightening, beautiful day. The nurse was standing behind him at the head of the bed. She said:—

"The doctor is here, Mr. Yorke, and will speak with you in a moment. The bandage on your head is to be changed first."

"Oh, very well. That is right. I am glad you have come, sir." The patient sighed contentedly. He submitted to the painful operation without further comment or complaint. He felt how much he was hurt, and how utterly he was at the mercy of this unseen, unknown being, who stood in the mysterious dawn there, fighting for his fainting life.

He handled one gently enough; firmly, too,—not a tremor; it did seem a practiced touch.

The color slowly struck and traversed the young man's ghastly face.

"Is *this* the doctor?"

"Be calm, sir,—yes."

"Is *that* the doctor's hand I feel upon my head at this moment?"

"Be quiet, Mr. Yorke—it is."

"But this is a woman's hand!"

"I cannot help it, sir. I would if I could, just this minute, rather than to disappoint you so."

The startled color ebbed from the patient's face, dashing it white, leaving it gray. He looked very ill. He repeated faintly,—

"*A woman's hand!*"

"It is a good-sized hand, sir."

"I—Excuse me, madam."

"It is a strong hand, Mr. Yorke. It does not tremble. Do you see?"

"I see."

"It is not a rough hand, I hope. It will not inflict more pain than it must."

"I know."

"It will inflict all that it ought. It is not afraid. It has handled serious injuries before. Yours is not the first."

"*What shall I do?*" cried the sick man, with piteous bluntness.

"I wish we could have avoided this shock and worry," replied the physician. She still stood, unseen and unsummoned, at the head of his bed. "I beg that you will not disturb yourself. There is another doctor in the village. I can put you in his hands at once, if you desire. Your uneasiness is very natural. I will fasten this bandage first, if you please."

She finished her work in silence, with deft and gentle fingers.

"Come round here," said the patient feebly. "I want to look at you."

[*Dr. Zay,* 40-43]

This episode is a variant on the stock fairytale recognition scene, where the frog turns out to be a prince. Here things are more complicated: it is not merely that the prince (the doctor) turns out to be a frog (a woman), but that the entire system of social and moral values, on which the distinction between prince and frog rests, has to be thrown open to radical questioning. Yet even though Waldo's suspicious reluctance quickly yields to trust, he still feels the need to protect his mother in Boston from the knowledge that he is being cared for by a woman: "Write to my mother," he begs her, "Tell her not to worry. Don't say you are not a man" (48). Evidently he does not grasp the offensiveness of his request.

The motif of surprise at a woman practicing medicine recurs in one guise or another in all these novels, often linked to the underlying question of the propriety of such a career for a lady. The parameters of proper behavior for a lady were firmly drawn in the nineteenth century, and they excluded the active pursuit of a profession for pay outside the domestic sphere of the home. All the doctresses are transgressing a fundamental creed of the time; all are contrasted with what James calls "sweet *home-women*" (*The Bostonians,* 27; italics are author's). The foil to Dr. Zay is Mrs. Butterwell, with whom she lodges, and who represents the venerated ideal of the devoted housewife. Similarly, Helen Brent stands out against the socialites at New York tea parties, acknowledging that "her hopes, her aims, her theory of life were so irrevocably different from those of the women about her" (93). Yet these average, upper-class women are unmasked as hypocritical, shallow, and unscrupulous social climbers. Less pernicious but equally empty-headed is the circle of conventional women, friends of Nan's aunt, in *A Country Doctor.* They are deeply shaken by her nonchalant announcement that she is studying medicine. "What do you mean?" demands the aunt coldly before dismissing the idea as a "Nonsense, my dear" (249). Nan is reminded that it is "proper for young women to show an interest in domestic affairs" and that "a strong-minded woman is out of place" (279); she is further rebuked that for "a refined girl who has an honored and respected name to think of becoming a woman doctor" (281) is totally unnatural. While Nan is sufficiently resolute to brush these reproaches aside, Grace Breen is undone by the women's "distrust of a physician of their own sex" (*Dr. Breen's Practice,* 22). The young Mr. Libby's astonished question to Grace's sole patient, "You don't mean *that's* your doctor!" (17; italics are author's) is less hurtful to her than the rejection by other women. This is understandable in light of the pioneering women physicians' avowed aim, so eloquently articulated by the British Sophia Jex-Blake in her speech of 1869, "Medicine as a Profession for Women," that women should be trained "to attend medically to those of their own sex who need them," to give "sisterly help and counsel."[16]

The quality that redeems the doctresses from utter disgrace and that goes some way toward neutralizing their ambiguous social position is the acknowledgment that every one of them is a lady. Again, this is an absolutely crucial nineteenth-century concept that is categorically underscored in each novel. Even Dr. Prance in *The Bostonians,* despite her want of conventional femininity, is unequivocally seen to be a lady. Grace Breen has "a ladylike manner" (96), moderating her "business-like alertness" with "ladylike sweetness" (10). The adventurous Nan of *A Country Doctor* is, it is emphasized, by no means "mannish" (160); as "a young lady," she should, according to one of her elderly neighbors, "be made to look like the little lady she is" (129). That Dr. Zay "was unmistakably a lady" (17) is a real consolation for Waldo as he comes to terms with the revelation that his physician is female. It is reassuring to him that she has "the dress and carriage of a lady" (44). Her dress is given close attention: on calls she is unobtrusively modest in "blue, or black, or blue-black, or blue and black" (18) in winter, and cream or white in summer. But on social occasions, her colors are brilliant: a "parlor dress" of violet muslin with lace and satin ribbons at wrists and neck (155), or a ruby dress with a plush jacket and white lace. Likewise, Helen Brent, who wears a plain, stiff, black alpaca dress and large, wide, flat shoes in her professional guise, can, when she chooses, blossom into "a queenly lady" in a gown with a graceful train, a profusion of soft lace, and pretty kid slippers (175-76). She and Dr. Zay are idealized figures projected by a woman's imagination, able to combine "the decisive step" of "women of business" with "grace of movement and curves of femininity" (*Doctor Zay,* 97).

Just as being a lady makes social amends, so being useful acts as a moral justification. The urge to usefulness is potent in all the doctresses except the brisk Dr. Prance who, in her own words, doesn't "cultivate the sentimental" (33). Grace Breen, on the other hand, is obsessed by a Puritan sense of duty and a "severe morality" (39) that impels her to be "more useful to others" (12). Disappointed in love and rich enough not to have to work, she has chosen medicine "in the spirit in which other women enter convents, or go to heathen lands" (12). Perhaps she is the least successful of the doctresses precisely because her vocation is vaguely to be of service to womankind rather than specifically to study medicine, which she has found in part "almost insuperably repugnant" (12). Such hesitations are unknown to Nan,

who has the support of a powerful role model in Dr. Leslie as well as of a family tradition in her father, a surgeon who died young. Still, Nan too is motivated as much by her drive to be useful as by her innate attraction to medicine: "she was filled with energy and a great desire for usefulness" (159), excited by the "renown some women physicians had won, and the avenues of usefulness which lay open to her on every side" (193). Her final riposte to her aunt's objections is simply that to study medicine "is the best way I can see of making myself useful in the world" (283). Dr. Zay is like Nan in having had a doctor father, whom she loved to watch in his laboratory. Her inspiration to go into medicine derives from both a personal experience and a public need: she had seen how decisively her mother had been comforted by women doctors in Boston and in Paris, and while spending summers at Sherman near her hometown of Bangor she realizes "how terrible is the need of a woman by women in country towns" (175). Although she concedes that women doctors "pay a price for our privilege" (123), she is sustained by her awareness that "the women all depend on me" (138). Helen Brent also knows the price paid by doctresses, but even more she knows that "I have a mission, a duty to perform" (40). Hers is the most encompassing calling: her "chief aim is make all women find themselves" (104) for she is "determined to leave the world better" (31) than she found it.

What then happens to these doctresses in the course of the novels' action? Except for Dr. Prance, who is a minor, static character, all of them face the dilemma of marriage. In this way the plots tie in with one of the paramount objections to women doctors, namely the clash of professionalism and marriage.[17] To the nineteenth-century mentality there was no happy solution to this conflict: for a woman to remain a spinster was thought to be unsatisfying, but if she married and had a family, she would be unable to attend to her patients properly. Actually a fifth to a third of female physicians at that time did marry, often fellow doctors; some continued their practices, others chose not to do so. The entire range of possibilities is illustrated in these novels. Nan Prince turns down the rising young lawyer, George Gerry. Because she finds him attractive, she has her moments of hesitant indecision, particularly during a sleepless night when "her old ambitions were torn away from her one by one, and in their place came the hardly-desired satisfaction of love and marriage, and home-making and housekeeping, the dear, womanly, sheltered fashions of life" (307). But in the clear light of day she understands that to marry would be to lose "the true direction of my life" (326), and that her part is "to make many homes happy instead of one" (327). Marriage, she realizes, would limit her potential for usefulness. As a contributor to *Alpha,* a journal edited by the physician Caroline Winslow, wrote in 1886: "A woman who has before her the broad avenues of usefulness, who has ambition and energy to develop her powers, will not be satisfied to tie herself down in the soul-cramping marriage. . . . [woman's] highest duty to herself and humanity demands her full development as a *Woman,* not as a *Wife* or *Mother.*"[18]

Helen Brent makes the same choice, though not without some bitterness. She has been shabbily treated by her lawyer fiancé, Harold Skidmore, who breaks their engagement when she takes her medical degree and goes off to Germany. The prototype of the new liberated woman, she argues vehemently that women should no more be expected to give up their profession when they marry than men. Yet her life, full, rich, and busy as it is, is not complete. At the end of the novel, after Harold's wife has left him, he writes to Helen that "some day there will come knocking at your gates a broken Harold, as a suppliant" (196). The somewhat mawkish sentimentality implicit in this adumbration of a happy ending was no doubt pleasing to readers of that period, but it seems to contravene the astringent, stalwart independence basic to Helen's character and to her professional success.

Grace Breen's marriage is another matter, for her commitment to medicine never appears to be strong. Beset by self-doubts both about her competence and her suitability to the profession, she takes marriage as a way out, possibly also as a compensation for the early disappointment that led her into medicine. She turns down the proposal of the mature Dr. Mulbridge, who suggests that they be "physicians in partnership" (322) as well as husband and wife. Her refusal becomes less puzzling when the terms in which he addresses her are taken into consideration. She has, in his words, shown herself to be "faithful, docile, patient, intelligent beyond anything I have seen" (228); but, he assures her, "you could never succeed alone" (223). He is right about her intelligence, for she tells him bluntly that he is "a tyrant" who wants "a slave not a wife" (254). Meanwhile she has sought the advice of young Mr. Libby about Dr. Mulbridge's proposal, which gives her opportunity to declare to him: "don't you see that I love *you*?" (248; italics are author's). So Grace Breen-Libby moves to the factory town where her husband manages his father's mills and where she treats his workers' sick children. The male narrator makes the final comment that "the conditions under which she now exercises her skill certainly amount to begging the whole question of woman's fitness for the career she had chosen" (271).

There is no such begging of questions with Dr. Zay, who ends up marrying her patient, Waldo Yorke, on her own perfectionist terms, in the conviction that the marriage can be "*divinely* happy" (248; italics are author's). She sorely tests Waldo, treating his love "like a fit of measles" (248), and sending him back to his law office in Boston to apply himself more diligently to his work.

He returns after six months, the "new type of man" appropriate to the "new kind of woman," "a woman who diverged from her hereditary type" (244). She will, of course, maintain her practice, at once "a strong-minded doctor" and "a sweet woman" (254).

The endings of *Doctor Zay* and of *Helen Brent, M.D.* patently veer into the realm of romance, in a manner reminiscent of Jane Eyre's marriage to Mr. Rochester. All the novels have these romance elements, which nineteenth-century readers expected, indeed demanded. But on the whole the social context of the fictive doctresses climbing a long hill is predominantly realistic. The women conform to socio-historical demographic patterns by coming from financially comfortable middle-class settings, frequently from families progressive in outlook and with a medical tradition. Two of the five, Nan Prince and Atalanta Zay, are represented as orphans, freer from the directive constraints of blood relatives and with greater liberty to pursue their goal. Of Dr. Mary Prance's and Helen Brent's family circumstances nothing is known. However, the timorous Grace Breen, who has early lost her father, is very much under the control of a domineering and disapproving mother. All the doctresses portrayed in these novels receive an education in keeping with the options available at that period. Nan gets formal instruction in Boston after her apprenticeship with Dr. Leslie, and then goes to Zurich. Though offered an appointment at a city hospital, she prefers to go home to be a general practitioner, specializing in pediatrics, aspiring eventually to become her mentor's successor. Grace Breen, Helen Brent, and Atalanta Zay have all trained in New York; Dr. Zay has spent a further year in Zurich and Paris, while Helen Brent is the only woman whom Professor Schwetterberger has consented to instruct in Germany. In her speech on her accession to the presidency of the women's medical college she vows to provide women with "the very best training," upholding "the very highest scientific standards" (20). Significantly, three out of the five are devotees of homeopathy,[19] the gentler form of medicine, which uses minuscule doses of medication and was more favored by women physicians than the heroics of allopathy. They are also typical in envisaging themselves as ministering primarily to women and children; the bolder among them, Nan Prince and Dr. Zay, are not embarrassed by male patients either, whom they acquire either as a result of accidents requiring immediate attention or who are the elderly spouses of their female patients. But even Dr. Zay is forced to confess that she has never before treated a *young* man.

While the family background and medical training attributed to these doctresses is consonant with the possibilities open to women at that time, the information on their actual professional work is fairly scant. A surprising feature of all five novels is the far greater attention paid to the women's social dilemmas than to their medical activities. Nan in *A Country Doctor* accompanies Dr. Leslie on his rounds to patients, and on two occasions is able to give prompt and effective first aid. Dr. Prance in *The Bostonians* is seen attending to Miss Birdseye, taking her pulse and observing her with a cannily vigilant gaze as she approaches death. Despite her rejection of sentiment, "this competent little woman" shows a capacity for tact and compassion, addressing the old lady still "dryly" but also "gently" (328). On the other hand, when Grace Breen is faced with a critical medical situation, she reverts to the role of nurse, deferring to the superior judgment of Dr. Mulbridge, who is brought in to take charge of the case. her lack of assertiveness, admittedly the behavior expected of nineteenth-century women, contravenes the boldness characteristic of the pioneer female physicians. Helen Brent, by contrast, is said to perform the most daring surgeries and becomes a leader in her field, yet not once throughout the novel is she shown dealing with a patient. Readers have merely the narrator's hyperbolic reports of Helen's amazing feats—hardly convincing evidence. Only Dr. Zay interacts with a patient, Waldo Yorke, dressing his wound, dispensing medication, and supervising his convalescence with exemplary skill. But even here the emphasis is on the growth of the romantic relationship that develops out of their professional rapport. This greater concentration on the doctresses' social lives is in keeping with the conventions of the novel of manners, the genre to which all these works belong. In the fictional representations the tendency either to deflate or to inflate is very evident. Grace Breen is presented in a negative, reductive manner, while Helen Brent, Atalanta Zay, and Nan Prince are to varying degrees idealized. The historical inevitably yields at one point or another to the fictive.

These five American novels have a counterpart in five British fictions that appeared at roughly the same period: Charles Reade's *A Woman Hater* (1877), G. G. Alexander's *Dr. Victoria: A Picture from the Period* (1881), the anonymously published *Dr. Edith Romney* (1883), *Mona Maclean: Medical Student* by "Graham Travers," the pseudonym of Margaret Georgiana Todd, who was Sophia Jex-Blake's biographer, and Arthur Conan Doyle's short story, "The Doctors of Hoyland" from his collection, *Round the Red Lamp* (1894). As in the United States, the sudden popularity of women physicians as fictive heroines is a concomitant of the battles raging in Great Britain most acutely from the later 1860s through the 1870s.[20] The thematic parallels between the doctress fictions on the two sides of the Atlantic are quite striking as the same issues are aired: surprise at the very idea of a woman practicing medicine, and even more at her competence, composure, and erudition; doubts as to the propriety of such a course; the contrast with "sweet *home-women*;" justification through usefulness in the form of service to fellow women; the recognition of the women's essentially la-

dylike behavior as a conduit to social acceptability; and the culminating problem of marriage. The British fictions are also like the American ones in showing the doctresses at various stages in their careers, and in adopting a range of gendered perspectives. Although the British figures, too, are basically true to social history norms, the lengthy narratives have a rather more marked proclivity to the melodramatic than the American examples in their highly involved, at times frankly creaking plots and substantial romance elements. The signal exception is Conan Doyle's sparkling, ironic tale, whose outline is similar to that of *Dr. Zay*: the male patient, in this instance the town's doctor, in an accident sustains a compound fracture of a leg, which is expertly handled by the young woman; her follow-up visits lead to a proposal of marriage and partnership. But the end has a distinctive sting in the tail, for this doctress prefers to accept the opportunity she has just been offered to do research at the Physiological Laboratory in Paris. "There are many women with a capacity for marriage," she tells her suitor, "but few with a state for biology. I will remain true to my own line."[21]

After the early 1890s doctresses ceased to feature as a curiosity in literature. It would be nice to be able to conclude that this denoted their assimilation into the social landscape with the acceptance of medical practice as a normal role for women. This is not, however, what happened. Ironically, the percentage of women students in American medical schools dropped precipitously from a high of 18.22 percent in 1893-94 to a low of 4.6 percent in 1944.[22] This sharp decline was a direct consequence of the closure of the women's medical colleges or their absorption into coeducational schools between 1884 and 1903.[23] Only the Women's Medical College of Pennsylvania remained an exclusively female institution. The appearance of doctresses in American fictions between 1881 and 1891 is the literary inscription of a brief early window of opportunity for women physicians.

Notes

1. By contrast, the medical student, Ruth Bolton, in *The Gilded Age* (1873; Rpt. N.Y.: Trident Press, 1964) by Mark Twain with Charles Dudley Warner, is no more than a subsidiary figure. From a Quaker family in Philadelphia, Ruth rebels against the useless and dependent life that was the norm for women. She is a foil to the novel's heroine, Laura Hawkins, a socialite femme fatale in Washington. Ruth takes up medicine, against her mother's wishes, as "the only method of escape" from "the clutches of the old monotony" (179) of her dour, stiff home. Although medical study is draining for her, she shows "the utmost coolness," "skillful hands," and "a gentle firmness" (247) in tending a patient's wound. However, after nearly

dying of a fever contracted in the hospital, Ruth ends up by admitting her love for Philip Sterling. Her future is left open, but presumably it is marriage. *The Gilded Age* also makes mention of a successful female practitioner, Mrs. Dr. Longstreet, who "has a great income" (344). The novel is not included in my study because its primary focus is satire of social mores.

2. Nevertheless, William G. Rothstein's 362-page book, *American Physicians in the Nineteenth Century* (Baltimore and London: The Johns Hopkins Univ. Press, 1972) mentions the existence of women physicians only once, in a footnote (300) recording that in 1900 17 percent of students in homeopathic medical schools were female, as against 5 percent in regular medical schools.

3. "The Lady and the Mill Girl: Changes in the Status of Women in the Age of Jackson," *Midcontinent American Studies of Journal* 10 (spring 1969): 6.

4. James Compton Burnett, M.D. in 1895; rpt. in *Victorian Women,* eds. Erna Olafson Hellerstein, Leslie Parker Hume, and Karen M. Offen (Stanford: Stanford Univ. Press, 1981), 94.

5. Rpt. in *Women, the Family, and Freedom,* eds. Susan Groag Bell and Karen M. Offen (Stanford: Stanford Univ. Press, 1983), I:429. Clarke was a complicated figure whose position was paradoxical: he did support women physicians even while advocating that girls could not stand the strain of higher education after puberty.

6. See Paulette Meyer, "They Met in Zurich," this volume.

7. For a fine, detailed account see Regina M. Morantz-Sanchez, *Science and Sympathy* (New York: Oxford Univ. Press, 1985).

8. Mary Roth Walsh, *"Doctors Wanted: No Women Need Apply": Sexual Barriers in the Medical Profession, 1835-1975* (New Haven and London: Yale Univ. Press, 1977), 186.

9. See Gloria Moldow, *Women Doctors in Gilded Age Washington: Race, Gender and Professionalization* (Urbana and Chicago: Univ. of Illinois Press), 1987.

10. *Doctor Zay* (Boston: Houghton Mifflin, 1882), 47.

11. *Helen Brent, M.D.* (New York: Cassell, 1894), 14.

12. *A Country Doctor* (Boston: Houghton Mifflin, 1984), 137.

13. The young physician in Louisa May Alcott's *Jo's Boys* (1886) strongly echoes Nan, even in name. Like her, Alcott's character administers prompt and appropriate aid in an accident and, like her also, she remains "a busy, cheerful, independent spinster," dedicating "her life to her suffering sisters and their children" (*Jo's Boys* [New York: NAL, 1987], 277). Alcott's novel, directed at juvenile audiences, tends to simplify issues, and has therefore not been included.

14. *Dr. Breen's Practice* (Boston: Osgood, 1881), 76.

15. *The Bostonians* (New York: NAL, 1980), 23.

16. Sophia Jex-Blake, *Medical Women* (Edinburgh: Oliphant, Anderson, & Ferrier, and London: Hamilton Adams & Co., 1886; rpt. New York: Source Books, 1970), 44.

17. The marriage/profession problem is played out in *The Bostonians* in the central figure, Verena Tarrant, in the struggle between Basil Ransom and Olive Chancellor for her allegiance.

18. *Alpha* 8 (Dec. 1886) 13; italics are author's.

19. Homeopathy, brought to the United States from Germany in 1825, rapidly developed into a prosperous and progressive medical sect with an affluent, largely urban, upper- and middle-class clientele. Around the middle of the century several Institutes of Homeopathy were founded: the American Institute in 1841, the Medical College of Philadelphia in 1847, and similar institutions in Cleveland in 1850 and in Chicago and New York in 1860. By 1900 10,000 homeopaths were in practice, primarily in the northern states. Homeopathy reached its zenith in 1880 just as the doctresses were coming into prominence. Although the American Medical Association at first ostracized homeopaths as "irregulars" because of their exclusive dogma, the wealth and influence of the homeopathic clientele assured the group's success and longevity. But as late as 1878 the Fairfield County, Connecticut, Medical Society expelled a physician for consulting with his homeopathic wife. Through their support of homeopathy women were active in the first attack on the heroics (and brutalities) of conventional therapies. Cf. Rothstein, 152-74, 230-46, 299-300.

20. See Catriona Blake, *The Charge of the Parasols: Women's Entry to the Medical Profession* (London: The Women's Press, 1990), 207-10 for a chronological overview.

21. *Round the Red Lamp* (New York and London: Appleton, 1921), 294.

22. Walsh, 193 and 245.

23. Ibid., 180.

Kristine Swenson (essay date 2005)

SOURCE: Swenson, Kristine. "Sex and Fair Play: Establishing the Woman Doctor." In *Medical Women and Victorian Fiction*, pp. 85-118. Columbia: University of Missouri Press, 2005.

[*In the following essay, Swenson examines the debate over women in medicine in nineteenth-century Great Britain, particularly the question of whether practicing medicine would "unsex" a woman, by using women doctors who appeared in fiction as barometers of the argument.*]

When the young heroine of Radclyffe Hall's 1924 novel, *The Unlit Lamp,* announces to her father that she wishes to study medicine, he responds in a tirade:

> It's positively indecent—an unsexing, indecent profession for any woman, and any woman who takes it up is indecent and unsexed. . . . Not one penny will I spend on any education that is likely to unsex a daughter of mine. I'll have none of these new-fangled woman's rights ideas in my house. . . . A sawbones indeed! Do you think you're a boy? Have you gone stark, staring mad?[1]

Colonel Ogden's objections to women doctors typify those voiced throughout the Victorian period and down to his own; that medical study would unsex women was the trump card played by all opponents. However, the career's power—implicit in antifeminists' fierce resistance—made medical education particularly appealing to the most ambitious, intellectual, or feminist women. Despite unabated protests of their indecency, women doctors began to threaten the medical establishment in Britain as early as the 1860s.

The British medical-woman movement began in earnest in 1869 when Sophia Jex-Blake and four other women enrolled as medical students at the only British university that would take them—the University of Edinburgh. As the women were soon to learn, however, enrollment did not guarantee equal education or the right to graduate. The male medical establishment, represented by the Royal Colleges, fought the education, certification, and employment of women doctors at every step. As Sophia Jex-Blake remarked, the Medical Registration Act of 1858 effectively allowed protectionist British medical schools to keep women out of the established profession by denying registration to any doctor holding a foreign degree.[2] Even those men who supported medical women did so more in the spirit of fair play than from belief in woman's abilities. The medical establishment's most powerful weapon against this threat came from its own "scientific" findings that suggested that women were unsuited for the intellectual and physical work involved. Medical study and practice would harm women's health—particularly their reproductive health—and

unsex them. One male physician, writing in 1879, neatly summarized the arguments that filled the pages of the *Lancet* and other establishment publications:

> Many of the most estimable members of our profession perceive in the medical education and destination of women a horrible and vicious attempt deliberately to unsex themselves—in the acquisition of anatomical and physiological knowledge the gratification of a prurient and morbid curiosity and thirst after forbidden information—and in the performance of routine medical and surgical duties the assumption of offices which Nature intended entirely for the sterner sex.[3]

Such arguments demonstrate that, even as a fully certified physician, the Victorian medical woman could not completely dissociate herself from her cultural other, the prostitute. For instance, responding to calls for the repeal of the Contagious Diseases Acts, medical officials of the 1870s insisted that prostitutes were not the soiled doves that repealers painted them, but were unsexed and without womanly feeling. This charge carried particular physiological connotations that physicians, especially, would understand. The term *unsexed* was used in the medical community both to describe a woman who had undergone gynecological surgery such as a hysterectomy or ovariotomy and to describe women who suffered from gynecological diseases.[4] Eventually, as sexual identity became increasingly psychologized at the end of the century, sexologists applied this term to "sexual inverts" as well. At the same time, the broader moral connotations of the word entered general discourse, as implied by Colonel Ogden's rant against his daughter: knowledge of bodies and, presumably, sex would make women unwomanly. Thus, the same language used to define the prostitute and the lesbian as sexual deviants was applied to the women who threatened male medical hegemony. The conflation of these three figures—the prostitute, the lesbian, and the medical woman—goes far toward explaining the moral outrage of cultural conservatives such as Colonel Ogden over the medical-woman movement in Britain.

Two highly publicized events of Jex-Blake's Edinburgh campaign secured a great deal of public support for medical women in Britain and defined the battle along the lines of fair play and sex. In the class examinations of early 1870, Edith Pechey placed third in chemistry, entitling her to a prestigious Hope Scholarship. University officials, however, stripped Pechey of "the very name Hope Scholar" and gave the award to the next student in line who, as Jex-Blake remarked, "had the good fortune to be a man." This injustice, and the irony that the Hope Scholarship was founded from proceeds of lectures given to women years earlier, did not escape the women students or the press. Henry Kingsley's *Daily Review* ridiculed the university about this "very absurd matter": "If Miss Edith Pechey chooses to come in facile princeps at the head of the Chemistry class of her year, we . . . must have a bill for the protection of the superior sex." The *Spectator* termed the situation a "very odd and very gross injustice," and even the *British Medical Journal* admitted, "Whatever may be our views regarding the advisability of ladies studying medicine . . . the University has done no less an injustice to itself than to one of its most distinguished students." In the Hope Scholarship controversy, opponents of medical women within the university had violated Britons' sense of fair play and had engaged the interest of journalists and writers such as Charles Reade who were on the look-out for social causes to support.[5]

In November of the same year, the press reported the "Riot at Surgeons' Hall" in Edinburgh, when Jex-Blake and the other women students faced a mob of two hundred male students who were "howling" and singing "with more spirit than good taste" and barring their way to an anatomy lecture. Once the women pushed through to class, many of the mob crowded in, disrupting the lecture and unleashing there "Poor Mailie," the pet sheep of the college. Following this event, which received tacit support from several medical professors, the women were regularly harassed and pelted with mud and garbage on the streets of Edinburgh. Though a few papers carried articles defending the male students, most deplored the "unbecoming" and "undignified" behavior of the rioters.[6] As one of the women students explained in a letter to the *Scotsman*, the rioters had provided the medical-woman movement with a righteous cause:

> I began the study of medicine merely from personal motives; now I am also impelled by the desire to remove women from the care of such young ruffians. . . . I should be very sorry to see any poor girl under the care (!) of such men as those, for instance, who the other night followed me through the street, using medical terms to make the disgusting purport of their language more intelligible to me. When a man can put his scientific knowledge to such degraded use, it seems to me he cannot sink much lower.[7]

From this point, the interests of "unprotected servants and shop-girls" became central to arguments supporting women physicians.[8] That this rhetoric of protection against male sexuality resembles strongly the arguments surrounding the repeal of the Contagious Diseases Acts and the later purity campaigns is no accident.

The medical woman campaign did not occur in isolation, but was highly dependent upon (and contributed to) other movements and social forces that were occurring at the same time in Victorian Britain. For one, medical women derived strong support and basic strategies from other prominent feminists and, clearly, the campaign for medical women fits within the larger campaigns for increased education and employment opportunities for women. Women doctors and their supporters consciously built upon the work of Florence Nightingale and nursing reformers when constructing a public image for the female physician and arguing for society's need of her. The shift from nurses to women doctors parallels the shift within the women's movement from the separate-spheres feminism of the first-generation pioneers to the more directly competitive feminism represented by the suffragists and the "New Women." The nurse was merely an independent rather than a "New" woman because she endorsed "traditional sex, gender, and class distinctions"; she had been co-opted by orthodoxy to the degree that she now embodied the proper middle-class woman (albeit at work in the world) rather than a threat to domesticity. The figure of the woman doctor, who competed directly with male physicians, could not claim the nurse's subordinate and complementary role, and so became the new subversive/disruptive medical woman. At the same time, the woman doctor came to represent for many that side of late-nineteenth-and early-twentieth-century feminism which was highly separatist and critical of male sexuality, science, and politics.[9]

Nonmedical feminists lent greater support to the cause of medical education and employment than to that of nursing because physicians held more personal, professional, social, and economic power than nurses.[10] Pioneering woman doctor Elizabeth Garrett Anderson voiced an opinion about nursing that was typical of feminists and early women physicians. Though her family hoped that she might become a Nightingale-type "lady nurse," she rejected nursing because of its "sentimental, rather patronizing, approval" in the press and public opinion and its subordination to doctors. "I prefer," Garrett Anderson concluded succinctly, "to earn a thousand rather than twenty pounds a year." That the nurse—no matter how competent—was essentially subordinate to the will of her supervising physician, became crucial to feminist thinking with the advent of the "sexual science." Women doctors became "a source of scientific legitimacy" for suffragists who "sought a redefinition of sexual identity for women that would justify their political inclusion."[11] Unlike most other feminists, women doctors could make arguments about sex from within the medical profession and with the language and authority of science. Michel Foucault, among others, has credited nineteenth-century medicine with the power to shape definitions of sexuality and, thus, to order behavior. The particular province of nineteenth-century medicine was the "sexual physiology peculiar to women," and although men such as Havelock Ellis and Karl Pearson held sway on the topic, contributions by medical women are significant for their opposition to male medical opinion.[12] Women doctors lent their medical expertise to the cause of women's education—denying that intellectual work would damage a woman's health—and supported medically related feminist drives such as dress reform and physical exercise for girls. Finally, the fight for women doctors fed into and from late-century obsessions with male medical vice and sexual danger epitomized by the campaign to repeal the Contagious Diseases Acts. Occurring almost simultaneously, these two campaigns supported one another (often unintentionally) with their common concern over the Victorian sexual double-standard and the women exploited under it. Josephine Butler's volume of feminist essays, *Women's Work and Women's Culture* (1869), includes an important contribution by Sophia Jex-Blake, "Medicine as a Profession for Women." Though neither the repeal campaign nor the medical-woman movement was fully developed at this time, *Women's Work,* and specifically Jex-Blake's essay, establish the agenda and rhetorical strategies of both. Sounding much like Butler calling for women of all classes to band together against the immorality of the Contagious Diseases Acts and male doctors, Jex-Blake argues that "some of our saddest social problems" may be solved "when educated and pure-minded women are brought more constantly in contact with their sinning and suffering sisters, in other relations as well as those of missionary effort."[13]

Thus, the relative success of Victorian women who sought to practice medicine (as opposed to those who might have wished to practice law, to preach, or even to vote) resulted from a combination of professional and cultural conditions in late Victorian Britain, as well as the efforts of the pioneers themselves. While the medical community and most female medics were principally concerned with the question of integrating women into the profession, feminists and the general public were most interested in women doctors as New Women, and as protectors of other women against the sexual dangers of late-Victorian culture. These two interests were often opposed, since women doctors felt extreme pressure to conform to political and medical positions—on vivisection and the Contagious Diseases Acts, for instance—which were at odds with those of non-medical feminists. As contradictory as these two interests often seemed, however, they ultimately complemented each other in the public image which emerged of women doctors as appropriate practitioners for women and children.

The final three chapters of this project attempt to explicate and complicate our understanding of the conditions which created acceptance for the woman doctor in Victorian Britain and how, in turn, the woman doctor is emblematic of the "New" women of her period. Central to the creation of this image were contributions made by fiction: with the belief that fictional representations shape public thought and action, both advocates and opponents of women doctors employed fiction to support their positions. From Charles Reade's *A Woman-Hater* (1877) through Margaret Todd's *Mona Maclean, Medical Student* (1892) and Kipling's *The Naulahka*

(1891-1892), fiction assumed a self-consciously polemical attitude toward women and medicine. Regardless of their politics, however, nearly every piece of medical-woman fiction of the period covers similar ideological ground and consciously participates in a variety of debates related to the physical and sexual dangers of Victorian culture. My readings of these texts, however, will focus upon what I see to be the main work of fictional representations of the woman doctor: her undeniable status as a New Woman, and the tension that arises between that role and her equally undeniable status as a professional competitor with men. Medical-woman fiction tends to reduce the arguments for and against women doctors expressed by the medical establishment, the press, feminists, and the women medics themselves, to questions of sexuality and educational/professional fair play. Whether feminist or traditionalist in bent, medical-woman fiction portrays the female doctor as *the* exemplar of the New Woman, the representative of her sex most at home with the forces of modernity infiltrating Victorian culture. Indeed, with her initiation into a traditionally male profession and the "new religion" of science, the woman doctor holds a unique cultural position from which to explore the late-Victorian female condition.

Of the first women doctors in Britain, Sophia Jex-Blake is particularly important not only because of the material changes effected by her fight against the University of Edinburgh, but because through that fight she became "the pioneer woman doctor" in the public imagination.[14] The Jex-Blake with whom the public became familiar was less the measured, logical writer of "Medicine as a Profession for Women," than the "lion-hearted" heroine represented in press reports and later in Charles Reade's novelistic response to the Edinburgh campaign, *A Woman-Hater* (1877).

Inspired by what he had read of Jex-Blake and her medical education campaign, Charles Reade determined in 1876 to champion the cause of women doctors in a novel that would run in *Blackwood's Edinburgh Magazine*—"within the very gates, so to speak, of the enemy's citadel."[15] Like the male doctors and journalists who supported Jex-Blake's Edinburgh campaign, Reade seems to have been motivated primarily by his Victorian sense of fair play. His rather patronizing attitude toward Jex-Blake and her cause is perhaps best voiced by the woman-hater of his novel, Harrington Vizard, who champions the fictional woman doctor, Rhoda Gale:

> Really, when she told me that fable of learning maltreated, honorable ambition punished, justice baffled by trickery, and virtue vilified . . . I forgave the poor girl her petticoats—indeed I lost sight of them: she seemed to me a very brave little fellow, damnably ill used.
>
> (247)[16]

A Woman-Hater does consciously set out to redress the wrongs done to medical women and to popularize their cause; in this sense, it is very much a "novel with a purpose." But Reade did not write novels of unalloyed social commentary: "The reader of fiction is narrow and self-indulgent," he told a friend, "He will read no story the basis of which is not sexual." *A Woman-Hater,* then, embeds the plea for women doctors within a sensationalistic narrative of seduction and sex.[17]

Sex is as much the concern of Rhoda Gale as is medicine. And yet, though Reade's publisher feared that a woman doctor was too revolutionary for his magazine, she is not the romantic interest of the novel.[18] As the most distinctive if not the most important character of the novel, Dr. Rhoda Gale acts as a guardian of female purity against the licentiousness of male sexuality. The novel flirts with the fallen woman plot but, as Dr. Gale is first to discover, locates sexual danger instead in the figure of the male bigamist. After Reade's extraordinarily negative portrait of the nurse, Edith Archbold, in *Hard Cash,* the heroism of feminist Rhoda Gale is rather surprising. Critic Elton Smith casts Reade as an advocate of women, commenting that he "wrote not only a number of studies of women but at least one and possibly two works on feminism." It would be more accurate to say that although Reade wrote a number of studies of women, only one or two concerned themselves with feminism. Jex-Blake, who understood quite well that Rhoda Gale was at least a partial portrait of her, commented with characteristic spirit: "The sketch of Rhoda Gale is altogether kindly, and is drawn with a good deal of power; that it has at some points a touch of burlesque is certainly not due to any want of goodwill on the part of the author; for, to a woman's eye, this defect seems common to the great majority of Mr. Reade's female characters."[19] Rather than crediting Reade with a feminist awakening in *A Woman-Hater,* I would attribute this change in his portraits of medical women to the larger shift within Victorian culture away from an anxiety over female sexuality, which supported the Contagious Diseases Acts, to an anxiety over male sexuality, which was integral to the rhetoric which opposed them. Not only were reform-minded Victorians such as Reade more likely to sympathize with the prostitute (and the nurse) by the 1870s, some were coming to believe that women doctors, as morally female but professionally legitimate medical practitioners, could protect English womanhood from the sexual dangers that seemed to be multiplying in Victorian society. Finally, however, the novel's very form undermines its potential radicalism: although Reade made an apparently sincere attempt to campaign for women doctors, because he does so within a novel that maintains sensation-fiction conventions and traditional romance morality, the New Woman doctor is rendered a socially marginal and morally ambiguous figure.

Rhoda Gale is an Anglo-American physician whom the self-proclaimed woman-hater, Harrington Vizard, discovers starving in Leicester Square. Rhoda tells Vizard the story of her life—a modified version of Jex-Blake's medical education, including the siege of Edinburgh University and an eventual foreign medical degree.[20] Angered by the "trades-unionism" of the British medical profession, Vizard offers Rhoda the practice at Barfordshire, though it is technically illegal for her to practice in Britain with her foreign degree.

Vizard is guardian or protector of a cast of female characters whom Rhoda is now positioned to help him protect. This conventional story, crowded with types of women, affords the unconventional Rhoda Gale little room. Vizard explains the role he intends for Rhoda: "for her to play the woman would be an abominable breach of faith. We have got our gusher, likewise our flirt; and it was understood from the first that this was to be a new *dramatis persona* . . . the third grace, a virago; solidified vinegar" (290). Though Jex-Blake felt flattered by subsequent references to her as the "Happy Warrior," a "virago" who is not really a woman is hardly the most desirable female role in a Victorian marriage-plot romance. Nor is Rhoda allowed to be the sole or even the preferred "exceptional" female of the cast. Despite all of Rhoda's talents and misfortunes, Reade's narrator calls the opera singer, Ina Klosking, "the noblest figure in this story, and the most to be pitied" (304). Thus, though the narrator insists that Rhoda is not "a mere excrescence" (193), her structural position reflects her social status as an odd or superfluous woman.

What Rhoda's character does contribute to the novel is the social commentary for which the reform-minded Reade had become famous. Once she's placed in Barfordshire, Rhoda becomes a mouthpiece for sanitary and medical reform. Vizard calls her a "female detective" because she inspects the health conditions—the water, diet, and housing—of his tenants and then uses womanly persuasion to force him to make reforms (301). "For heaven's sake," Vizard tells her, "don't add woman's weakness to your artillery, or you will be irresistible; and I shall have to divide Vizard Court amongst the villagers. At present I get off cheap . . . only a granary—a well—and six cows" (339). The text makes clear that Rhoda is successful in this setting precisely because she is a woman exercising "domestic vigilance" and pleading in appropriate tones to the men in power: when local medical men tried to keep Rhoda from visiting the infirmary, "she went almost crying to Vizard" who "exploded with wrath" and threatened to withdraw his support of the hospital (526).

Again, Vizard's "manly" defense of his woman doctor mimics Reade's of Jex-Blake. Though more concerned with medicine's trades-unionism than with the rights of women, per se, Reade apparently felt an honest sympathy for the medical-woman movement after reading of the "battle of Edinburgh" in the press. He consulted Jex-Blake personally about the Cause and wove into Rhoda's lengthy story flattering biographical sketches of Elizabeth Blackwell, Elizabeth Garrett Anderson, Jex-Blake, and Mary Putnam Jacobi. The novel implies that women doctors have a special mission in Victorian society; unfortunately, it often portrays that mission as that of a glorified housewife or, at best, a nurse. Sounding much like Florence Nightingale, Rhoda asserts that "Medical women are wanted to moderate" male physicians' reliance upon drugs, and "to prevent disease by domestic vigilance" (336).

At the novel's close, the narrator does assign a "grander" role for women doctors. Medical study, he says, will give women "an honourable ambition, and an honourable pursuit . . . to elevate this whole sex, and its young children, male as well as female, and so will advance the civilization of the world" (533). Such statements hint at the coercive, class-biased nature of Reade's role for women doctors and the reformism that would, in coming decades, feed into a nationalist eugenics. If the poor are the beneficiaries of health reform, they are also its targets. Rhoda requests six milk cows of Vizard for the villagers of Islip whose boys have "no calves to their legs . . . a sure sign of a deteriorating species" since the "lower type of savage has next to no calf" (337). Commenting on the poor's resistance to "improvements," Rhoda tells Vizard: "with monarchical power we can trample on them for their good. . . . [A]s their superior in intelligence and power, you might do something to put down indecency, immorality, and disease" (334-35). Such sentiments, which were at the heart of late-century British and colonial public health efforts, imply that statist and secular reformism retained much of the moral charge of earlier evangelical movements. Doctors and scientists found no difficulty in translating the Christian reformers' equation of cleanliness and godliness into "scientific" language with terms such as *environment* and *degeneration*. And just as the nurse, with her traditional ties to Christian charity, was the fitting minister to the sick under evangelical reformism, the woman doctor better suited an era requiring scientific knowledge in its healthcare providers. In this respect, Rhoda Gale resembles many fictional and journalistic representations of Victorian women doctors whose "scientific" natures distinguished them from other emancipated women.[21]

Because she is tough and forthright, Rhoda Gale is trusted and obeyed—if not always liked—by the novel's well-meaning characters. Vizard admiringly names her "my virago" and appoints her "viceroy" of his estate in his absence. But between Rhoda and the duplicitous Ned Severne there springs up a mutual antipathy which reveals the potential danger of Rhoda's powerful nature. Severne, who can master any woman (and most men), fears Rhoda Gale:

> He had deluded . . . several ladies that were no fools; but here was one who staggered and puzzled him. Bright and keen as steel, quick and spirited, yet controlled by judgment, and always mistress of herself, she seemed to him a new species. The worst of it was, he felt himself in the power of this new woman, and indeed he saw no limit to the mischief she might possibly do him if she and Zoë compared notes.
>
> (279, emphasis added)

If the term *New Woman* was not coined officially until 1894, Reade anticipates its later usage with some precision here in his 1877 text.[22] Not only is Rhoda an unconventional woman, she is empowered rather than weakened by that unconventionality.

But despite the woman doctor's apparent superiority to all in the novel save Ina Klosking, the text reveals a distinct unease about Rhoda: ambiguity about the New Woman is expressed as moral and sexual ambiguity about Rhoda Gale. Severne, the dissolute womanizer, fears Rhoda because she combines the most potent traits of both sexes—quickness tempered by judgment, for instance—in a "new species" with "no limit" of agency. Reade is careful not to "unsex" his heroine entirely, compensating for her "masculine" traits with a feminine sensibility and an enthusiasm for beautiful landscapes (285). Even so, this androgynous doctor remains ambiguously strange and frightening. When Severne attempts to mollify Rhoda for instance, she retorts: "I'm not so very cruel; I'm only a little vindictive, and catlike. If people offend me, I like to play with them a bit, and amuse myself, and then kill them—kill them—kill them; that is all" (282). Spoken by a physician, such sentences are particularly disturbing; but they are also quite untrue since Rhoda saves Severne's life twice before he finally dies. On another occasion she confides to Vizard that had she lived when her ancestors emigrated "in search of liberty," she would have stayed in England and "killed a hundred tyrants. But I wouldn't have chopped their heads off. . . . I'd have poisoned 'em" (286). Here again, Rhoda appears more a power-hungry, man-hating sensation nurse than a levelheaded woman physician. But Rhoda's sensationalistic speeches are at odds with her sensible actions: far from poisoning anyone, Rhoda effects changes in the townspeople's diets and living conditions which stop their being poisoned. Caught between realism and romance, Reade creates in Rhoda a prototypical New Woman who nevertheless retains a strong measure of sensationalism and projects male ambivalence about emancipated women. Like Collins's Marian Halcombe, Rhoda Gale is intended as a progressive figure, but finally seems unsympathetically cobbled together out of ideological and gendered pieces, the effect of which is occasionally grotesque.

As part of her "ambiguity," Rhoda Gale exhibits the female homoeroticism that male writers such as Reade, Collins, and Dickens tended to incorporate into their representations of emancipated women.[23] In a twist upon the "sick-room romance," Rhoda Gale falls in love with her injured patient, Ina Klosking. Rhoda explains to Vizard that this is not an unusual occurrence for her and that she is "very unfortunate" in her "attachments": "If I fall in love with a woman, she is sure to hate me, or else die, or else fly away. I love this one to distraction, so she is sure to desert me" (415). Ina accepts Rhoda's affection to the point that the doctor "cooked for her, nursed her, lighted fires, aired her bed, and these two friends slept together in each other's arms" (475). Later, when Ina agrees to marry Vizard, Rhoda complains, "I must give up loving women. Besides, they throw me over the moment a man comes, if it happens to be the right one." (510).

Such language was not, in itself, uncommon among Victorian women, particularly among those who lived and worked with other women. Lesbian historiography has been particularly sensitive to the difficulties of interpreting the language of homoerotic friendships in order to determine sexual awareness.[24] Yet, whether or not Reade consciously intends to portray Rhoda as a lesbian is difficult to say. Though some critics simply assume Rhoda a lesbian, the text's uneasiness may not be directed at female homosexuality per se, but at displays of female sexuality more generally.[25] In this novel, for instance, the apparently heterosexual Zoë and Fanny make up after a quarrel in the following manner: "'Come, cuddle me quick!' Zoë was all round her neck in a moment, like a lace scarf, and there was violent kissing, with a tear or two. Then they put an arm around each other's waist, and went all about the premises intertwined like snakes" (59).

The question is further complicated by the unconventionality of Sophia Jex-Blake, Reade's principal model for Rhoda. Though the press made her "the" British medical woman of the period, Jex-Blake was unusual even among this group of exceptional women, and many, including Garrett Anderson and Jex-Blake's protégée Margaret Todd, feared that her reputation injured the medical-woman cause. Though "lion-hearted" and generous, Jex-Blake lacked "judgment" and good "temper" and rarely yielded in arguments—all of which made her friends as well as her enemies subject to passionate, sometimes public, tirades. Moreover, Jex-Blake did not cultivate a "feminine" appearance: she was large, demonstrative, and had, as one friend told her, "very peculiar, and . . . generally bad taste" in dress. "It is clear," writes Todd, "that there was about her a doggedness, a high-handedness, a disregard of tradition, an actual—if superficial—roughness, which are not common qualities among the highly-educated of either sex, and which were never admired in her own." A ca-

sual acquaintance with Jex-Blake, such as Reade had, would be enough to convince one that she lacked conventional femininity. Probably, latent prejudice against the possible sexual implications of "unfeminine" behavior underlies the unease of Reade's portrait; however, Jex-Blake's behavior would not necessarily imply to Reade or to most Victorians in 1877, that she was sexually attracted to women. At the same time, Jex-Blake was, without a doubt, a woman whose closest personal and professional relationships were with other women; she lived in intimate companionship with at least three over the course of her life, and commonly used language such as Rhoda Gale's to describe her emotional attachments. Reade, who "spent many mornings at [Jex-Blake's] house" studying her personal chronicle and "asking information about this happening and that," would have discerned this aspect of her life as he constructed his woman doctor. Whatever Jex-Blake's sexual orientation, and regardless of what Reade intended, the text does make female homoeroticism central to the character of the woman doctor. Within two decades of the novel's publication, the physically and emotionally hybridized "types" that Rhoda Gale and Jex-Blake represent would become pathologized by sexologists as congenital "inverts" or "lesbians." Though Rhoda's love for Ina Klosking almost surely did not signal a sexual attachment to most of the novel's *initial* audience (otherwise, it would not have passed the "Grundyish" Blackwood censors) it did establish the woman doctor as one who loved women more than men and who did not care to marry.[26]

On a more literal level, Rhoda's attachment to Ina, as well as to her "lesser" love, Zoë, establishes a protector's role for the woman doctor. Indeed, if Rhoda ultimately loses in love to the men of the novel, she supersedes them in their traditional role as guardians of women and female honor. Again, Rhoda's "androgynous" nature is largely responsible for her ability to play this role. It is precisely because she recognizes Zoë's attractions that she can also perceive Severne's dishonorable plans and act as his rival to spoil them. At one point, Rhoda has Severne follow her on her rounds to give Lord Uxmoor time to propose marriage to Zoë. Rhoda tells him, "Unless I see Zoë Vizard in danger, you have nothing to fear from me. But I love her, you understand" (357, 358).

In a parallel episode, when Severne throws Ina across a room and she lies "senseless, with the blood spurting in jets from her white temple," only Rhoda's "keen, but self-possessed" dressing of the wound keeps Ina from bleeding to death (365, 366). The contrast here between Rhoda and the manly Vizard is particularly (and, I think, unintentionally) comic. While the woman-hater sits on the floor and moans helplessly over his beloved's inert body, Rhoda performs a complicated operation, which the admiring narrator describes in tedious detail (366-

67). It is the woman doctor, then, who saves one heroine's life and the other's honor. This sort of skillful operation recurs in several other woman doctor fictions. As in *A Woman-Hater,* such an operation is evidence of "masculine" professional skill that renders the woman doctor sexually ambiguous.[27]

At the novel's close, Rhoda remains an "odd" woman—she has not been paired with a man. But her heroic services to Ina and Zoë render her no longer superfluous, for she has supplanted male characters in essential roles they were unable to fill. Nor, we are told, does Rhoda remain entirely socially marginal. The tenants of Barfordshire were at first skeptical of this anomalous woman, but now she visits the Taddington infirmary regularly and "[a] few mothers are coming to their senses, and sending for her to their unmarried daughters" (526). Ultimately, however, the novel's paternalism toward women doctors cannot be denied: Rhoda remains just what Vizard named her—"my virago"—dependent upon the goodwill and beneficence of a powerful man. In this sense, *A Woman-Hater* unintentionally recreates the position of early women physicians within their profession and their culture.

Charles Reade enticed John Blackwood into publishing *A Woman-Hater* by promising a story with a doctress, a character "entirely new in fiction, yet . . . of the day" who would "lead to profitable discussion." Reade's novel not only contributed to the immediate discussion surrounding women's admission to medical programs and practice in Britain, it began a literary fad. The woman doctor was a featured character in fiction of the 1880s and 1890s in both Britain and the U.S., after which she retains a distinctive if minor role or stock figure among women characters in fiction. Like much fiction written by and about women in the eighties and nineties, medical-woman fiction has been too easily lumped together as a "curiosity" with a single theme. Or, as Lilian Furst has done, critics treat the "best known" medical-woman novels by canonical American writers as interesting slices of life while deriding their British counterparts as overly melodramatic and romantic. Though Furst provides an instructive overview of "doctresses" in American fiction, she devotes a single paragraph to British "counterparts" of the same period, implying that while their concerns are the same they are inferior in literary quality: "the lengthy narratives have a rather more marked proclivity to the melodramatic than the American examples in their highly involved, at times frankly creaking plots and substantial romance elements."[28]

Though I don't disagree with Furst's assessments of individual works, I would like to recast her generalizations so as to place the British texts within their own cultural framework without segregating them too strictly from the American novels. The medical-woman movement, as I indicated earlier, was a self-consciously international campaign that shared rhetorical and narrative strategies across the Atlantic. Contemporary readers and reviewers of medical-woman fiction did not make clear national distinctions among the works but, rather, saw them as participating in a common discussion about the social and professional validity of this particular sort of New Woman. American editions of British texts and British of American were published both quickly and regularly. This meant that, for instance, *A Woman-Hater* was introduced to American readers in 1877 in the *Atlantic Monthly.* The editor of the *Atlantic,* W. D. Howells, and his acquaintance Elizabeth Stuart Phelps would both write their own woman doctor novels in the next few years. In their review essays of medical-woman fiction, both Jex-Blake and Hilda Gregg move easily between British and American novels, as if assuming a transatlantic readership and literary influence.[29] It is appropriate, then, to read the British woman doctor novels which followed the publication of *A Woman-Hater* in relation to those published in America. At the same time, though, the British variety does possess a distinct "flavor" which I would argue is a matter of cultural context rather than of intrinsic literary merit.

First, the educational and professional opportunities were greater for women in the U.S. When the London School of Medicine for Women opened its doors in 1874, seven comparable institutions were already operating in the eastern and midwestern U.S. By the time British women were admitted to medical examinations and degrees at the Irish College of Physicians and the Queen's University of Ireland in 1876 to all degrees at the University of London in 1878, over a hundred women were practicing medicine in the Boston area alone.[30] Though American medical professionalization at the end of the century increasingly ostracized women, British medicine was even more organized and centralized, which meant fewer opportunities to "break into" the existing system. And with a less dense and still expanding population, the U.S. simply had more room and greater need of women physicians. Rural and frontier America offered the work space for doctors that British women would have to find out in the empire. That American women doctors were, according to Alison Bashford, "much caricatured" in England as too radical and strident implies, too, that Americans were simply more advanced in their thinking about women practicing medicine.[31] All of these social factors influenced the differences between British and American medical-woman fiction.

In keeping with their relatively smoother integration into late-nineteenth-century culture, women doctors in American fiction tend to be both professionally and personally stable and fulfilled. The notable exception here is W. D. Howell's Grace Breen—*Dr. Breen's Practice* (1881)—who studies medicine "in the spirit in which other women enter convents, or go out to heathen lands" after an "unhappy love affair" when "she was not yet out of her teens" (11). Grace is "not fit to be a doctor," being at once "too nervous," and "too conscientious" (208). She is, a male rival tells her, "like the rest [of 'advanced' womanhood],—a thing of hysterical impulses, without conscience or reason!" (225). Grace's defeat by her male rival and ultimate marriage to a man who does not make her happy allows Howells to psychopathologize and belittle all advanced women. But Dr. Breen is more than adequately countered in American fiction by the noble and lovely female physicians in works by Elizabeth Stuart Phelps, Sarah Orne Jewett, Annie Nathan Meyer, and Louisa May Alcott.[32] And though *The Bostonians* could hardly be called a feminist novel, James's Dr. Prance is competent, stable, and successful. In fact, Jex-Blake asserts that with James's medical woman the reader feels for "almost the first time" in medical-woman fiction that she is "standing face to face with a real person" (267).

In contrast to these relatively positive American texts, the tone of British medical-woman fiction tends to be darker and more sensationalistic. British fiction containing women doctors—and even paid nurses—was much more often written by men who, even when supportive of the Cause, highlighted the ambiguities, oddities, or eccentricities of their characters. The British stories show greater concern with the public conflicts surrounding medical women—professional ethics or the struggle of education and passing examinations, for instance—as opposed to the conflicts of "the heart" that dominate the American texts. The British texts also concern themselves to a much greater degree with problems of sexuality as opposed to those of courtship and romance. For a variety of reasons, women doctors fostered more cultural anxiety in Britain than in the U.S. The British campaign for medical education and registration drew stronger resistance and its figureheads and supporters were proportionately more militant. Just as the sensationalism of the "Battle of Edinburgh" and its heroine, Sophia Jex-Blake, politicized Reade's novel, *A Woman-Hater*, with its sexually ambiguous and unconventional heroine, "queered" the subgenre of medical-woman fiction in Britain.

Much of the Victorian public derived its formative impressions of women doctors from the representations of Sophia Jex-Blake in the press and in *A Woman-Hater*. *The* woman doctor of Victorian culture, therefore, differed significantly from *the* nurse: she defied traditional gender roles and feminine behavior; she confronted and bested male competitors; she vigorously and tyrannically protected public health and especially the well-being of women; and if she was not unsexed, her sexuality was certainly ambiguous. Representations of women doctors after *A Woman-Hater* work from and often alter this rather uncomfortable model. Rhoda Gale

differs most obviously from most of the fictional women doctors who follow her by lacking beauty: "A tongue and a memory" are all that Rhoda needs. Her younger medical sisters, however, require more traditionally feminine aids. As the Victorian critic Hilda Gregg commented, "in view of the professional antagonism aroused by later [medical] heroines in the breasts of their male acquaintance, it is as well that the strength of their arguments should be reinforced by that of their personal charms."[33]

In fact, most medical-woman fiction after *A Woman-Hater* derives its principal conflict from this tension between professional antagonism and personal charm—or, as I put it earlier, fair play and sex. The woman doctor's role, in other words, shifts from the "virago" to the romantic heroine. This was perhaps inevitable considering, as Reade put it, the necessity of "sex" to book sales and the difficulty with which Reade integrated Doctress Gale into his romance plot. The romanticization of the woman doctor also fits Nancy Armstrong's claims that the nineteenth-century novel "turned political information into the discourse of sexuality" and with "strategies that distinguished private from social life . . . thus detached sexuality from political history."[34] Women doctors, then, become romantic heroines in fiction because of formal but also ideological imperatives. By subsuming the identity of the woman doctor within her professional role and then reducing that role to conflicts with potential suitors, these texts finally define her by her (defective) sexuality alone, rendering her less threatening professionally.

Whereas Reade accommodates the unconventional Rhoda Gale with some difficulty, these later writers show remarkable ingenuity in adapting romance fiction for beautiful women doctors. In fact, many of these plots resemble those surrounding romanticized nurses that have become commonplace in twentieth-century Western culture. The greatest difference is that women doctors are more committed to their profession and therefore relinquish it less willingly than nurses; as opposed to fictional nurses who happily marry and discard their work, the woman doctor must almost always either reject her suitor or have her career forcibly taken away.

George Gardiner Alexander's *Dr. Victoria* (1881) exemplifies both the tendency to write women doctors as sexually defective and the sensationalism that is more typical of British than American treatments of women doctors. Like Reade's *A Woman-Hater*, the novel borrows heavily from the conventions of sensation fiction, especially the effects of degenerate and excessive sexuality upon the innocent. Here, too, the woman doctor figures as the champion of victimized innocents—partly because of her inherent nobility but also because she is absolutely alienated from the normal womanhood of marriage and maternity. The beautiful and noble Victoria becomes an eye specialist in order to restore vision to her young cousin Madge. Madge's (and, thus, Victoria's) family is a eugenic nightmare of which she is the innocent victim. Her blindness results from a "curse in the blood," presumably venereal disease or the more nebulous moral and physical traits that predispose the family to the disease. Madge's father is described as profligate and dissolute. Having degenerated significantly since his youth, his face is now bloated and covered with boils, again perhaps visible signs of the syphilis pox. Nor is Madge's maternal line clean. Her mother deteriorates slowly throughout the first two volumes of the novel before she dies. Her disease is never specified, but Madge finds her repulsive to touch and is told by her uncle that the illness is, again, caused by "the curse": "She has caught it from him [her husband]—the curse. It is in his blood—the curse" (II.188). As his part in this curse, the uncle suffers from dementia and eventually dies by throwing himself in the river.

Dr. Victoria acts as the personal savior of this seemingly doomed girl, restoring her sight and eventually adopting her. In this act of charity, however, Victoria is motivated as much by a sense of affinity with Madge as she is by altruism. Though her branch of their family is not as excessively degenerate as Madge's, it nevertheless causes Victoria to become a doctor. Like Dickens's Esther Summerson, Victoria was born out of wedlock and compensates for the burden of her illegitimacy by good works and self-denial. Knowing of her illegitimacy, she rejects the marriage proposal of Sir Francis, an eligible and liberal M.P., and instead bestows upon him her look-alike (and legitimate) half-sister, Geraldine. Ironically, besides the question of her parentage, Geraldine is hardly Victoria's equal and must make herself worthy of Sir Francis by emulating Victoria. In this way, Victoria is typical of woman-doctor figures not only because she saves the victimized Madge but because she serves as a guide to proper womanhood for younger women such as Geraldine. Initially, Sir Francis can't love Geraldine, despite her Victorian beauty, because of her "mannish" and immodest manners: she smokes with men and loves hunting too enthusiastically. After several failed attempts to blatantly imitate Victoria, though, she finally gets it right and is awarded her place at his side.

The stain of her birth, her mother's untempered sexuality, ruins the possibility of conventional womanhood for Victoria. But that same stain also allows her to become a successful woman doctor. The text thus unites the fallen woman and the woman doctor by their irregular sexuality. Finally, by restoring her cousin's sight, Victoria makes amends for the "taint" within her family, and, like Rhoda Gale, establishes herself as a defender of women against the dangers of unbridled sexuality. Like Reade, Alexander is something of a champion of the

medical-woman movement: he acknowledges the prejudices against women doctors, but paints an optimistic picture of their ultimate acceptance once the public—especially women and young girls—realize the advantages of engaging a competent woman doctor.

Less optimistic and far less serious on this issue of women doctors was Wilkie Collins, whose short story, "Fie! Fie! the Fair Physician" (1882), associates women doctors and deviant sexuality not through melodrama or romance but burlesque comedy. The central conflict of this story involves a beautiful woman doctor named Sophia Pillico who, contrary to popular and medical expectations, is not in the least "unsexed." The lady doctor uses her charms to make regular patients of otherwise healthy men, and finally attempts to steal the fiancé of an innocent young woman named Salomé by telling him that he is not healthy enough to marry. Ideologically, "Fie! Fie!" moves in contrary directions. It reverses the stock literary convention of handsome male doctors who drum up business by flirting with—or otherwise "addicting"—their female patients; and Salomé's name, if nothing else, hints at the text's playfulness. Yet the story makes another point that was taken very seriously by opponents and supporters of medical women alike: women doctors must not practice on male patients. Though they privately recognized its hypocrisy, early women doctors publicly supported this marginalized professional role. In part, they did so to avoid conflict with jealous male medics and the public cries of "indecency." But women doctors also understood that their acceptance within Victorian culture depended upon arguments for same-sex medical care for women; they could not undercut their position by suggesting that a physician's sex did not matter. For this reason, even the most radically supportive statements for women doctors rarely suggested that they might practice on men.

An exception is *Doctor Zay* (1882), written by the American feminist Elizabeth Stuart Phelps. *Doctor Zay* was an important novel for establishing how the woman doctor could be portrayed as both heroic and womanly—for how, in other words, she might be accommodated by fictional Realism and what would eventually be called the New Woman Novel. It was also read as a rebuttal to Howells's *Dr. Breen's Practice*.[35] In Phelps's novel, Dr. Zaidee Atalanta Lloyd nurses/doctors Waldo Yorke back to life after the Bostonian lawyer drives into a river in the backwoods of Maine. In some senses, Zay is quite a conventional heroine of romance: beautiful, graceful and, above all, "womanly," she works from a sense of mission rather than ambition, channeling all her energies into the cause of doctoring poor women who need her. Yet, from the beginning of the novel, the gender roles of Zay and Yorke are reversed. Zay has an active and successful medical practice that takes her out at all hours; she is strong, independent, and competent. In contrast, Yorke lies on his invalid couch, dependent upon Zay for his well-being and awaiting her return. He spends much of his time speculating about her, allowing himself to fall in love with her, and so disturbing his "nerves."

The introspective Yorke is quite aware that his illness and his doctor have "unmanned" him: "I shall make rather a superior woman by the time I get well," he tells Zay (134). While he is in this "feminine" state, Zay feels no danger from him. But as he regains strength and health, she distances herself from him. As a physician, cognizant of Victorian theories of sexuality, she would have understood all too well that a real man would always conquer a woman and that, therefore, her heart and profession are in jeopardy. And, of course, Yorke does win her. Though she puts him off twice, his manly perseverance is finally stronger than her power to resist him. When her feminine nature predictably, inevitably, exhausts itself from overwork, Yorke is there to pick up the pieces. What is not predictable, however, is that Yorke's experience as a feminized invalid has transformed his masculinity. For instance, he insists that she continue her work: "It would make another woman of you. I want you just as you are" (246). When, in the midst of giving in to him, Zay criticizes Yorke's driving and pulls the reins from him, he replies easily, "I don't care who has the reins . . . as long as I have the driver!" (257). In this way, the New Womanly doctress not only cures but recreates her male patient. Under Zay's medical and moral guidance, Yorke emerges as a New Man sympathetic to feminist causes.

Phelps hangs her romance upon the story of Atalanta (Dr. Zay's middle name), who escapes marriage by outrunning her suitors, until she is finally tricked into slowing down by Hippomenes, who rolls three golden apples in her way. *Dr. Edith Romney* (1883), which provides an instructive British counterexample to the more optimistic *Doctor Zay*, also uses Greek myth to frame the woman doctor's romance. In this case, however, it is the Trojan War battle in which Achilles "tackled" Penthesilea, "that famous Amazon," and "slew her" (II.227, 229). Whereas Atalanta's conquering leads to marriage, Penthesilea's brings death and tragic love, for after Achilles "had given the mortal blow he took off her helmet and saw her face. . . . He fell in love—and so did she" (II.229). As this myth foretells, the battle between sex and fair play turns out rather differently for the English Dr. Romney than it did for the American Dr. Zay. Edith is set upon by the young and handsome Dr. Fane who first destroys her practice through slander and then falls in love with her. After she has succumbed to and recovered from brain-fever—brought on by Fane's destruction of her practice and good name—Edith, unbelievably, agrees to marry her rival. At the end of the novel, her professional status as well as her happiness are uncertain.

In that the main action of the novel depends upon a professional man first falling in love with and then winning a woman doctor, *Edith Romney* strongly resembles *Doctor Zay*. And the heroines themselves are remarkably similar: disarmingly beautiful and noble, each brings a keen intelligence and a strong yet "womanly" nature to her profession.[36] But, as I suggested above, the British version of this New Woman/New Man medical romance is much more social in orientation and less progressive politically. *Doctor Zay* is set in rural Maine, isolating Yorke and Zay from the influences of public opinion and allowing their romance to run its natural course. In contrast, *Dr. Edith Romney* has a huge cast of characters who populate the bustling and gossip-driven midlands town of Wanningster. Whereas Dr. Zay succeeds professionally because of her superior skill as a doctor, we're told that Edith Romney displaces the old-fashioned Dr. Fullagher in Wanningster simply because the town chases after "every new fashion—women's rights, aestheticism, cookery and ambulance classes" (I.12). Fullagher recruits the young and handsome Austin Fane to avenge the loss of his practice, which the new doctor manages to do within six months.

In keeping with the greater concern of British fiction for the public ramifications of women doctors, professional etiquette and loyalty are important themes in the novel. The public's taste for "fashion" over solid medical care encourages doctors to pander to patients' whims. In this way, blame for Fane's destruction of Edith's practice is shifted onto a fickle and ignorant public and then, even more pointedly, upon the working classes who remain immovably biased against women doctors. The cruel vengeance of the male doctors is displaced by the slanderous accusation of poisoning that an alcoholic, wife-beating grocer makes against Edith. These questions of professional etiquette and honor are woven into several parallel subplots that concern couples negotiating courtships and marriages, all of which contribute to the reduction of the professional plot to one of romance. For instance, before he falls in love with Edith, Fane engages himself to a young heiress named Violet. Whether he should break the engagement to marry Edith becomes a major moral dilemma at the end of the novel. At the same time, once Fane loves Edith—indeed, once he sees her—his professional concerns are set aside and he becomes her chivalrous defender. Edith's friend, Miss Jacques, informs her of her triumph over Fane's heart: "I want you to know that the man we thought your enemy, who derided you in the lump with strong-minded fanatics before he saw you, has made complete atonement. . . . [H]e loves you, in short. Why, my dear Edith, do you suppose his behaviour is to be set down to benevolent compassion? Do you suppose if you were plain and insignificant he would have taken your part so warmly? Never!" (III.141). In other words, Fane has not changed his mind about women doctors nor is he sorry for his unprofessional behavior toward a colleague. Edith has "triumphed" by her beauty, though she has not won a husband who will respect her choice of profession. When Edith tries to explain that they should not marry because her work as a physician "is part of me," Fane misunderstands her meaning: "I have never been influenced by your profession," he tells her, "I cannot say I have altered my former opinions . . . and sometimes I have blamed your calling as the cause of all the misery it has brought upon me . . . [but] I don't regard it as a part of you" (III.234-35).

The multiple marriage plots that parallel the central "medical" one underscore the degree to which this novel is "about" fair play in relations between the sexes. In every case in the novel, marriage brings both men and women into line with conventional gender roles. Perhaps the novel's most interesting character, for instance, is the "aesthetic" Mona Milward. Outspoken, angular, and modish before her marriage, she fills out to a matchmaking "lady" with lapdogs and brightly colored dresses once she's wed, even though her husband is clearly not her equal in spirit or intelligence. Indeed, much like *A Woman-Hater, Dr. Edith Romney* is full of types of women, all of whom are more or less domesticated or discredited by the novel's end. In this way, the novel tests and subdues advanced women with traditional gender roles as well as the facts of their biological natures. Edith Romney—all come to agree—is a paragon of female virtue, intelligence, and industriousness. Her male rivals learn that "she felt a true and honest conviction of her vocation" and that she was "well qualified . . . firm, gentle, sure and capable" in it (II.218, 273). Yet, she literally, physically, cannot bear the strain of "normal" male competition for patients. Her clergyman brother, Hugh, upbraids her for not taking the loss of her practice as a medical man would have: "All this hyper-sensitiveness, this prostration of spirit at your defeat, this unpractical putting off of a decision, prove the unfitness of your sex for the work you undertook" (III.71).

Thus, although the novel toys with and, at times, seems to advocate women's rights to education, employment, and self-determined happiness, its feminism is of a sad, masochistic sort. Oddly, Edith's illness itself provides her with an awakened feminist consciousness. She hadn't cared about women's issues before, largely because she'd been so successful with so little effort. She didn't share "strong-minded" and "odious" or "grim" views. But, ironically, after she's been beaten by Fane and has nearly died, she begins to understand the disadvantages that women face: "I see that our lot is a hard one—hard by nature, because we are physically weaker, and trebly hard on account of the burdens and restrictions put upon us by custom" (III.166). She complains that her lot had not been "fair": she wasn't allowed to compete as a professional; rather, she had been judged by her sex, ensuring that she would always lose (III.107).

Between the vacillation of an ignorant public and the self-justifying animosity of male physicians, the woman doctor has little chance of success. Though the novel repudiates the idea that doctoring is unsexing to women and that all women doctors are necessarily man-hating viragoes, it upholds the belief that woman's nature would not bear the physical or emotional strain of such a taxing profession for long. Edith learns of her true place in the world only through humiliation and defeat: "[The g]reater part . . . of the world declared women to be unfitted, physically and mentally [to practice medicine]; and Edith, in her new, unusual weakness, almost bowed to the hard sentence. . . . It seemed as if what she had already done had paralysed both brain and energies—surely this also was a sign that she had gone beyond her woman's strength" (II.284-85). All those around her seem to agree. Dr. Fullagher tells her that the "unnatural wish" to work in the professions is "taking away from us our ideal of womanhood, with all its grace and loveliness, and giving us in its place only a weaker man" (III.163). Even Miss Jacques, staunch supporter of Edith's work and women's rights, encourages Edith to marry Fane. Edith can continue to practice medicine—Fullagher has found her a job in an urban children's hospital—but it would mean the further loss of health, beauty, energy, and mental stability. Marriage to the chastened Fane seems the least self-destructive course open to Edith who, less than a year earlier, had been the model New Woman-independent, noble, strong, and healthy. Reviewing the novel, Sophia Jex-Blake agrees that Edith Romney is ill-fitted "for the ordinary buffets of life" as a physician but implies that this hardly reflects upon the question of actual medical women since "all the conditions pre-supposed [in the novel] are so utterly foreign to those of everyday life and experience, that, if they prevailed at all . . . it must have been upon another planet" (263).

Realistic or not, perhaps the most devastating effect of romanticizing the woman doctor was that by making her more "womanly" than Reade's prototype, Rhoda Gale, writers rendered her liable to collapse under the pressure of medical practice. Besides Edith Romney and Howells's Grace Breene, for instance, the heroine of Henry Curwen's *Dr. Hermione* (1890) possesses feminine "nerves" which cannot stand the strain of medical work. Despite an M.D. from Paris and a commitment to serve the poor of London, Hermione throws over her profession to marry a soldier of little worth. As a contemporary reviewer complained, "Tom has no good points beyond physical courage . . . yet Hermione loses all interest in life for his sake, and finally follows him out to Egypt, where she shows her fitness for her duties by going into hysterics when she sees him wounded."[37] Nurses and women doctors who fall into "hysterics" like this are favorite characters in antifeminist medical literature. By the end of the century "hysteria" had become medical and literary shorthand for the behavior of New Women who aspired to university educations, professional work, and the vote. Hysterics—as opposed to the more conventionally ladylike neuraesthenics—were described by physicians as women more rebellious than "normal" who "expressed 'unnatural' desires for privacy and independence," and showed other signs of "moral degeneration." Writers and critics helped to popularize the equation of "hysterical" with "feminist" and its application to women doctors. Elaine Showalter comments that Victorian and Edwardian physicians "perceived hysterical women as their powerful antagonists"; it is hardly surprising, then, that the medical establishment should reverse this formula and apply its label for female deviance to the upstart women in its own midst.[38]

Ironically, one of the most tolerant and good-natured portrayals of a Victorian woman doctor came from Arthur Conan Doyle, a trained and qualified physician, in his short story "The Doctors of Hoyland" (1894). Though Dr. Verrinder Smith is no great beauty, she is sufficiently attractive in mind and body to convert a vehement opponent of medical women, Dr. James Ripley, and to make him fall desperately in love with her, even after she has stolen most of his patients through her medical expertise. When Dr. Ripley proposes marital and professional partnership, Dr. Smith declines, responding: "I intend to devote my life entirely to science. There are many women with a capacity for marriage, but few with a taste for biology." Lilian Furst calls "The Doctors of Hoyland" the "most jovial" example of English woman doctor fiction; indeed, at first glance, it reads as a happy reversal of the competition and romance plots of *Dr. Edith Romney.*[39] In fact, though, this economical story is richer than that: it satirizes nearly every major woman doctor novel—English and American—to date, incorporating not only common themes such as romance and "fair play" between women doctors and skeptical men but quite distinctive plot elements as well. Verrinder Smith, with "plain, palish face" and her "pince-nez" (275) strongly resembles the androgynous Dr. Prance of *The Bostonians,* "a plain, spare young woman, with short hair and an eye-glass" (31). But whereas James's description of Mary Prance places her beyond the possibility of romance, Doyle's use of the androgynous woman doctor as love interest makes for unexpected comedy. If Verrinder Smith's personal charms are minimal, her professional credentials are "superb": she holds degrees from "Edinburgh, Paris, Berlin, and Vienna" and had been "awarded a gold medal and the Lee Hopkins scholarship for original research" (274). Clinically, she's innovative, calm, and skillful, performing operations that Dr. Ripley cannot.

The gendered traits which ensured that Edith Romney would fail in competition with her male rival are here reversed: "For all his knowledge" Ripley "lacked nerve as an operator, and usually sent his worst cases up to London. The lady, however, had no weakness of the sort, and took everything that came in her way" (278). Finally, like Waldo Yorke in *Doctor Zay,* this opponent of women doctors finds himself under one's care after breaking a leg in a carriage accident. Under the daily care and influence of Verrinder Smith for two months, Ripley discovers that "under all her learning and her firmness ran a sweet, womanly nature" (281). His invalidism feminizes Ripley, causing him to romanticize his doctor: "Her short presence during the long, weary day was like a flower in a sand waste. . . . [S]he had become the one woman" with her "dainty skill, her gentle touch, her sweet presence" (281). Quite unexpectedly, however, Dr. Smith does not melt as her predecessors had at the realization that a man loves her. Rather, she asks sarcastically if he proposes to marry her in order to "unite the practices" (since his is now lost) and announces her departure of the Paris Physiological Laboratory (282).

After so many examples in which women doctors sacrifice, compromise, or submit to marriage, Conan Doyle's story is amazingly refreshing. In her introduction to the story, however, Furst rightly asks whether "The Doctors of Hoyland" is really as "wrily comic" as it appears on "the surface" and whether the inversion of its fairytale plot might not "undermine its interest as a reflection of social reality."[40] I would suggest, first, that the story bears very little relation to social reality, nor was that Conan Doyle's intention. Rather, "Hoyland" is a conscious satire upon the literary conventions of woman doctor fiction which, as Jex-Blake points out, are often quite removed from the "real" lives of Victorian women doctors. Conan Doyle's satire is meant to emphasize that distance rather than, I think, to make any particular comment upon the value of women doctors or the medical-woman movement. And although the story does seem to sympathize with women doctors—at least in so far as it satirizes their opponents as "prigs and pedants" who don't know their own minds (281)—the comedy renders the "real" politics of the movement completely beside the point. However sympathetic, this story does little toward altering the stereotypes of women doctors that had grown up in Victorian culture.

Fiction perpetuated the stereotype of the New Woman doctor as unsexed or sexually abnormal long after she had won the rights to education and registered practice and even after the established profession had granted her a grudging acceptance. For instance, Elsa Nettles argues that Sophia Jex-Blake and, more broadly, the woman doctor is Virginia Woolf's "representative figure" of the professional woman who fights patriarchal oppression (242). For Woolf, as for Jex-Blake, this conflict is one of daughter against father, of the pioneering woman physician against a corrupt male medical establishment (242). Woolf's one fictional woman doctor, Peggy Pargiter from *The Years,* has inherited Victorian feminist politics and a social and professional system that remained prejudiced against women professionals as late as the Second World War.[41] My discussion of Jex-Blake and Reade's figuration of her in *A Woman-Hater* suggests that Peggy has *novelistic* ancestors as well. Like Rhoda Gale, Peggy is at once exceptional and odd, of central importance to the narrative and yet always occupying the marginal positions in the text. For instance, Peggy is a "brilliant" physician with a keen analytical skill, but this skill forces her to see too clearly the faults of humanity. "Pain must outbalance pleasure by two parts to one . . . in all social relations," she thinks (354). Medicine provides a professional outlet for Peggy and allows her to excel in ways that her Victorian aunts could not; yet Peggy feels ostracized from her family and the human community. She sees herself as "atrophied; withered; cold as steel" (361). Others mark her as not only marginal but, because of her profession, unsexed. Her Uncle Martin, for instance, assumes that because Peggy is a doctor and unmarried at thirty seven, she is a lesbian: "But you . . . your generation I mean—you miss a great deal . . . [l]oving only your own sex" (356).

Just as Charles Reade unwittingly aided adversaries of women doctors by figuring Rhoda Gale as a manly competitor of men and lover of women, later authors who supported the Cause often continued to focus on the woman doctor's odd physical appearance and aggressive, unwomanly behavior. This lingering, seemingly outdated, obsession with the woman doctor's lack of femininity is the logical result of the history of her representation in Victorian culture. Both advocates and opponents of women doctors at the height of the battle for medical education in the 1870s defined the woman doctor primarily in terms of her own sexuality and in relation to external sexual threat. While the medical establishment warned that medical knowledge of sex would unsex women, feminists argued that that same knowledge would give women doctors the power to prevent male doctors' "medical lust of indecently handling women."[42] That women doctors came to be defined by their (deviant) sexuality helps to explain the example from Radclyffe Hall's 1924 novel with which I began this piece. Colonel Ogden's animosity toward his daughter's desire to study medicine, in particular, rather than toward the abstract idea of a professional education for her, implies that medicine was thought worse than other careers open to women. In other words, British culture retained the impression of women doctors as indecent and unsexed long after the social conditions that had produced those characterizations had changed.

Notes

1. Radclyffe Hall, *The Unlit Lamp,* 110-11.

2. Sophia Jex-Blake, "Medical Education for Women," *Medical Women: A Thesis and a History,* 65.

3. Walter Rivington, *The Medical Profession,* 135-36.

4. For response of officials, see Frank Mort, *Dangerous Sexualities: Medico-Moral Politics in England since 1830,* 81-82. Regina Morantz-Sanchez, *Conduct Unbecoming a Woman: Medicine on Trial in Turn-of-the-Century Brooklyn,* 108, explains that the term *unsexed* was used by both conservatives and radicals within the medical profession to debate gynecological surgeries. Gynecological conservatives such as Elizabeth Blackwell (and the majority of women physicians, at least in the U.S.) argued that women were unsexed by the surgeries, whereas radicals, including Mary Dixon-Jones and Mary Putnam Jacobi, argued that these patients were, in fact, "unsexed by disease" and made "more perfect" by the surgery which allowed them to attend to their womanly duties (108).

5. Jex-Blake, "Medical Education for Women," 82; *Daily Review,* Apr. 1, 1870; quoted in Jex-Blake, *Medical Women,* appendix, 59; *Spectator,* Apr. 9, 1870; *British Medical Journal,* Apr. 16, 1870; both quoted in Jex-Blake, *Medical Women,* appendix, 60, 61.

6. *Courant,* Nov. 19, 1870; quoted in Margaret Todd, *The Life of Sophia Jex-Blake,* 291-92.

7. Mary Edith Pechey, letter to the *Scotsman,* July 13, 1871; quoted in Todd, *Life,* 318-19.

8. Alison Bashford notes, in fact, that "the issue of harassing male medical students" became "almost commonplace" as a justification for women's hospitals (staffed by women) in both Britain and Australia ("Separatist Health: Changing Meanings of Women's Hospitals in Australia and England, c. 1870-1920," 204.)

9. Josephine Butler, Harriet Martineau, Frances Power Cobbe, Millicent Garrett Fawcett, Barbara Bodichon, Bessie Rayner Parkes, Jessie Boucherett, and Emily Davies were among the prominent feminists who lent their support to the cause of women doctors. Ann L. Ardis, *New Women, New Novels: Feminism and Early Modernism,* 16.

10. Ray Strachey suggests, rightly I think, that feminists were reluctant to embrace nursing as the feminist profession because it was Florence Nightingale's particular cause. Not only must women such as Barbara Bodichon have thought that nurs-

ing needed no other advocate than her enormously popular and richly endowed cousin, but Nightingale's cool attitude toward the larger feminist movement after the Crimea undoubtedly affected the place of nursing within the woman's employment movement (*The Cause*, 98).

11. Jo Manton, *Elizabeth Garrett Anderson*, 77; Louisa Garrett Anderson, *Elizabeth Garrett Anderson*, 50; Kent, *Sex and Suffrage in Britain, 1860-1914*, 115.

12. Foucault, *History of Sexuality: Volume I, An Introduction*, 116. Elizabeth Blackwell asserted a theory of female sexuality which revised radically the medical orthodoxy of passionless women: "Physical sex is a larger factor in the life of the woman, married or unmarried, than in the life of the man. . . . Those who deny sexual feeling to women . . . quite lose sight of . . . [the] immense spiritual force of attraction which exists in so very large a proportion in their nature" (Blackwell, *The Human Element in Sex: being a medical enquiry into the relation of sexual physiology to Christian morality* [London: J. and A. Churchill, 1884], quoted in Mort, *Dangerous Sexualities*, 116.)

13. At the request of feminist educators, Elizabeth Garrett Anderson bravely responded to Dr. Henry Maudsley's scientist attack on women's education with her article, "Sex in Mind and Education: A Reply." EGA was responding to Maudsley's "Sex in Mind and Education." Jex-Blake, "Medicine as a Profession for Women," 44.

14. Manton, *Elizabeth Garrett Anderson*, 240.

15. Todd, *Life*, 435. In his article on the publication of the novel, David Finkelstein asserts that Reade wished to publish *A Woman-Hater* in the unsympathetic and conservative *Blackwood's* for less money than he could have earned elsewhere because it allowed him to "strike at the heart of the enemy" with his argument ("A Woman Hater and Women Healers: John Blackwood, Charles Reade, and the Victorian Women's Medical Movement," 338). Not incidentally, Finkelstein remarks, "There is nothing like public controversy to improve sale" (340).

16. Charles Reade, *A Woman-Hater.*

17. Reade's reading audience would have been, by all accounts, large. Critic Walter Phillips goes so far as to assert that after "the death of Thackeray and Dickens," Reade "divided with George Eliot the reputation of being the greatest living novelist" (*Dickens, Reade, and Collins, Sensation Novelists*, 20). Quotation in Wayne Burns, *Charles Reade: A Study in Victorian Authorship*, 284.

18. Finkelstein, "A Woman Hater and Women Healers," 340.

19. Smith, *Charles Reade*, 70. *The Bloomer* (1857), which Smith counts as a work on feminism, seems more interested in the possible titillations of dress reform and apparent transvestism of women in bloomers than in making any serious statement about feminism. Jex-Blake, "Medical Women in Fiction" 263.

20. In order to make Rhoda an M.D. at the time of writing *A Woman-Hater*, Reade models her degree upon that of Jex-Blake's friend Agnes M'Laren, who studied at Montpellier after the women reached a dead end at the University of Edinburgh. Jex-Blake received her M.D. from the Irish College of Physicians and the Queen's University of Ireland in 1877.

21. Henry James's *The Bostonians*, for example, shows unreserved asperity toward "hysterical, chattering" women's rights workers but portrays Dr. Mary J. Prance as "tough and technical," "impatient of the general question [of women], and bored with being reminded, even for the sake of her rights, that she was a woman—a detail she was in the habit of forgetting, having as many rights as she had time for" (112). It is interesting that in "Medical Women in Fiction" Jex-Blake comments that James's Dr. Prance has been "sketched with . . . a masterly hand" and that she "enable[s] medical readers to imagine more correctly even the standard of professional ability" of women physicians (268).

22. Ardis, *New Women, New Novels*, 10.

23. Collins's Marian Halcombe from *The Woman in White*, Reade's Edith Archbold from *Hard Cash*, and Dickens's Miss Wade from *Little Dorrit*, would be examples of such characters.

24. Martha Vicinus judges that "surely some were [sexually aware], while others were not," but that the "strong emphasis on the power of the emotions suggests an understanding of what we would now label as sexual desire" ("Distance and Desire: English Boarding School Friendships, 1870-1920," 213).

25. Wayne Burns says flatly that in order to please his publisher Reade revised his manuscript and "either glosses over or treats with apologetic discretion" Rhoda's "Lesbian attachments" (*Charles Reade*, 292). David Finkelstein refers matter-of-factly to Rhoda's "lesbian tendencies" ("A Woman Hater and Women Healers," 346). Elton Smith remarks, Reade's young women often "kiss [each other] with a violence only Reade seems to have noted and cringed at" (*Charles Reade*, 92).

26. "Lion-hearted" is a phrase Reade applied to her (as Rhoda Gale) in *A Woman-Hater*; Garrett

Anderson upbraided her for her "want of judgment" and "temper" in a personal letter (Todd, *Life,* 423). Todd, *Life,* 75, 104-5, 435. Freud, following the earlier work of sexologists, including Krafft-Ebing, Havelock Ellis, and Bloch, describes the female invert succinctly in his 1905 *Three Essays on the Theory of Sexuality*: "among [women] the active inverts exhibit masculine characteristics, both physical and mental, with peculiar frequency and look for femininity in their sexual objects" (245).

27. Regina Morantz-Sanchez notes that a woman doctor's ability to perform difficult surgical operations was an increasingly important status marker within the profession at the end of the nineteenth century (*Conduct Unbecoming a Woman*). Some women doctor fictions are Elizabeth Stuart Phelps, *Doctor Zay* (1882), Sarah Orne Jewett, *A Country Doctor* (1884), Arthur Conan Doyle, "The Doctors of Hoyland," *Dr. Edith Romney* (1883).

28. Reade quoted in Finkelstein, "A Woman Hater and Women Healers," 337; Lilian Furst, "Halfway up the Hill: Doctresses in Late Nineteenth-Century American Fiction," 235.

29. Review of *A Woman-Hater, Atlantic Monthly* 40 (1877): 507; Jex-Blake, "Medical Women in Fiction"; Hilda Gregg, "The Medical Woman in Fiction."

30. Furst, "Halfway," 223, 224.

31. Bashford, "Separatist Health," 201.

32. William D. Howells, *Dr. Breen's Practice. A Novel*; Elizabeth Stuart Phelps, *Doctor Zay* (1882), Sarah Orne Jewett, *A Country Doctor* (1884), Louisa May Alcott, *Jo's Boys* (1886), Annie Nathan Meyer, *Helen Brent, M.D.* (1891).

33. Gregg, "The Medical Woman in Fiction," 97-98.

34. Armstrong, *Desire and Domestic Fiction,* 21, 24.

35. Jex-Blake, "Medical Women in Fiction," 266.

36. This ideal of the womanly woman doctor, so unlike the popular image of Sophia Jex-Blake, is essentially that of Dr. Elizabeth Blackwell, the Anglo-American pioneer who argued that "womanliness" was essential to the medical-woman cause.

37. Gregg, "The Medical Woman in Fiction," 104.

38. Showalter, *The Female Malady,* 145, 134, 133.

39. Arthur Conan Doyle, "The Doctors of Hoyland," 238; Furst, "A Shocking Discovery! An Introduction to Arthur Conan Doyle's 'The Doctors of Hoyland,'" 268.

40. Furst, "Shocking Discovery!" 271, 272.

41. Elsa Nettles, "'Leaving the Private House': Women Doctors in Virginia Woolf's Life and Art," 251.

42. Josephine Butler, "A Few Words Addressed to True-Hearted Women," Mar. 18, 1872 (draft), Butler Collection, quoted in Kent, *Sex and Suffrage,* 122.

Bibliography

PRIMARY SOURCES

Alexander, G. G. *Dr. Victoria.* London, 1881.

Anonymous. *Dr. Edith Romney.* London, 1883.

"Appointments." *Magazine of London School of Medicine for Women and Royal Free Hospital* 3 (Oct. 1896) 246-47.

Armstrong-Hopkins, Salini. *"Within the Purdah." Also "In the Zenana Homes of Indian Princes"; and "Heroes and Heroines of Zion." Being the Personal Observations of a Medical Missionary in India.* New York: Eaton & Mains, 1898.

Arnold, Miss. "Our Medical Work in Furreedpore." *Our Indian Sisters: A Quarterly Magazine of the Ladies' Zenana Mission, in Connection with the Baptist Missionary Society* 142-43, no. 6 (Oct. 1886): 142. London: Elliot Stock.

Barraclough, George. "On Nursing as a Career for Ladies." *Fraser's Magazine* 99 (Apr. 1879): 468-70.

Bateman, Thomas. *A succinct account of the contagious fever of this country, exemplified in the epidemic now prevailing in London; with the appropriate method of treatment as practised in the House of recovery. To which are added observations on the nature and properties of contagion, tending to correct the popular notions on this subject, and pointing out the means of prevention.* London: Longman, 1818.

Blackwell, Elizabeth. *The Responsibility of Women Physicians in Relation to the Contagious Diseases Acts: Address Given to a Medical Meeting in London, April 27, 1897.* Privately printed, 1897.

Braddon, Mary E. *Lady Audley's Secret.* 1862. New York: Penguin Books, 1987.

Broughton, Rhoda. *Second Thoughts.* London, 1880.

Bushnan, J. S., M.D. "Private Asylums." *Daily News.* Reprinted in Charles Reade, *Hard Cash,* in *The Works of Charles Reade.* Boston: De Wolfe, Fiske, 1910.

Butler, Josephine, ed. *Woman's Work and Woman's Culture.* London, 1869.

Caird, Mona. *The Morality of Marriage and Other Essays on the Status and Destiny of Woman.* London: George Redway, 1897.

Chapman, Mrs. E. F. *Sketches of Some Distinguished Indian Women.* London, 1891.

Cobbe, Francis Power. "Workhouse Sketches." *History of Nursing Source Book.* New York: G. P. Putnam's Sons, 1957. 156-57.

Collins, Wilkie. *The New Magdalen.* London, 1873.

———. *The Woman in White.* 1860. New York: Penguin, 1985.

Conan Doyle, Arthur. "The Doctors of Hoyland." *Idler* 5: 227-38.

"The Countess of Dufferin's Fund: Fifty Years' Retrospect: India 1885-1935." Booklet, Wellcome Institute for the History of Medicine Library Archives (London). Box 16: Medical Women Overseas, C.146 (India).

Curwen, Henry. *Dr. Hermione.* Edinburgh: Blackwood & Sons, 1890.

Davies, Emily. "Medicine as a Profession for Women." In *Barbara Leigh Smith Bodichon and the Langham Place Group,* edited by Candida Ann Lacey, 410-14. London: Routledge & Kegan Paul, 1987.

Davis, Elizabeth. *The Autobiography of Elizabeth Davis.* Edited by Jane Williams (Ysgafell). Introduction by Deirdre Beddoe. Cardiff: Honno, 1987.

Dickens, Charles. "Bedside Experiments." *All the Year Round* 3 (Mar. 31, 1860): 537-42.

———. *Martin Chuzzlewit.* Oxford: Oxford University Press, 1984.

———. "The Nurse in Leading Strings." *Household Words* 17, no. 429 (June 12, 1858): 602-6.

Diver, Maud. *"The Englishwoman in India" and "Pioneer Women in India."* Edinburgh: Blackwood, 1909.

Ellis, Sarah. *Education of the Heart: Woman's Best Work.* London, 1869.

"An Episode of the War." *Harper's New Monthly Magazine* 10 (Dec. 1854): 508-11.

Gardiner, Mrs. "A Five Years' Retrospect of the National Association for Supplying Female Medical Aid to the Women of India." *Magazine of London School of Medicine for Women and Royal Free Hospital* 3 (Oct. 1896): 221-23.

Garrett Anderson, Elizabeth. "The History of a Movement." *Fortnightly Review* 59 (Jan.-June 1893): 404-17.

———. "Sex in Mind and Education: A Reply." *Fortnightly Review* 15 (May 1874): 582-94.

———. "Volunteer Hospital Nursing." *Macmillan's* 15 (1867): 494-99.

Gaskell, Elizabeth. *The Letters of Mrs. Gaskell.* Edited by J. A. V. Chapple and A. Pollard. Manchester: Manchester University Press, 1966.

———. *Ruth.* 1853. Oxford: Oxford University Press, 1991.

Green, Evelyn Everett. *Barbara's Brothers.* London: RTS, 1888.

Greg, W. R. "Prostitution." *Westminster Review* 23 (July 1850): 448-506.

Gregg, Hilda. "The Medical Woman in Fiction." *Blackwood's Edinburgh Magazine* 164 (July 1898): 94-109.

———. *Peace with Honour.* Edinburgh: Blackwood, 1897.

Griffen, G. Haxton, and Violet A. Penrose Coghill, eds. *Women Students' Medical Magazine* 1. Edinburgh: William Bryce, June 1902-1904.

Gull, Sir W. "On the Nursing Crisis at Guy's Hospital." *Nineteenth Century* 7 (May 1879): 884-91.

Hall, Radclyffe. *The Unlit Lamp.* 1924. New York: Dial Press, 1981.

Howells, William D. *Dr. Breen's Practice. A Novel.* 18th ed. Boston: Houghton, Mifflin, 1970.

James, Henry. *The Bostonians.* 1886. New York: Vintage Books, 1991.

James, P. D. *Shroud for a Nightingale.* New York: Warner, 1971.

Jewett, Sarah Orne. *A Country Doctor.* 1884. *Sarah Orne Jewett: Novels and Stories: Deephaven / A Country Doctor / The Country of the Pointed Firs / Dunnet Landing Stories / Selected Stories and Sketches.* New York: Library of America, 1994.

Jex-Blake, Sophia. *Medical Women: A Thesis and a History.* Edinburgh, 1886. New York: Source Books, 1970.

———. "Medical Women in Fiction." *Nineteenth Century* 33 (Feb. 1893): 261-72.

Kenealy, Arabella. *Dr. Janet of Harley Street.* London: Digby, Long, 1893.

———. *Feminism and Sex Extinction.* London: T. Fisher Unwin, 1920.

———. *The Human Gyroscope.* London: John Bale, Sons & Danielsson, 1934.

———. "The Talent of Motherhood." *National Review* 16 (1890): 446-549.

———. *The Whips of Time.* London: J. Long, 1908.

———. "Woman as Athlete." *Nineteenth Century* 45 (Apr. 1899): 636-45.

———. "Woman as Athlete: A Rejoinder." *Nineteenth Century* 45 (Jan./June 1899): 915-29.

Kingsley, Charles. *Two Years Ago.* 1857. London: Ward, Lock, 1901.

Lewes, George Henry. Review of "Ruth: A Novel." *Westminster Review* 59, no. 116 (Apr. 1853): 474-91.

Longfellow, Henry Wadsworth. "Santa Filomena." *Atlantic Monthly.* 1857.

Lonsdale, Margaret. "Doctors and Nurses." *Nineteenth Century* 7 (June 1880): 1105-8.

———. "The Present Crisis at Guy's Hospital." *Nineteenth Century* 7 (Apr. 1880): 677-84.

Maudsley, Henry. "Sex in Mind and Education." *Fortnightly Review* 15 (Apr. 1874): 466-83.

Meade, L. T. *The Doctor's Children.* Edinburgh: W & R Chambers, 1894.

———. *A Sister of the Red Cross: A Tale of South Africa.* London: Thomas Nelson & Sons, 1901.

Meade, L. T., and Clifford Halifax. "The Wrong Prescription." *Stories from the Diary of a Doctor.* 1895. New York: Arno Press, 1976.

Meyer, Annie Nathan. *Helen Brent, M.D.* New York: Cassell, 1891.

Nightingale, Florence. *Cassandra.* New York: Feminist Press, 1979.

———. *Ever Yours, Florence Nightingale: Selected Letters.* Edited by Martha Vicinus and Bea Nergaard. London: Virago Press, 1989.

———. *Notes on Nursing: What It Is and What It Is Not.* In *Selected Writings of Florence Nightingale,* edited by Lucy Ridgely Seymer, 123-220. New York: Macmillan, 1954.

———. "Nursing the Sick." In *Selected Writings of Florence Nightingale,* edited by Lucy Ridgely Seymer, 334-52. New York: Macmillan, 1954.

———. "On Trained Nursing for the Sick Poor." In *Selected Writings of Florence Nightingale,* edited by Lucy Ridgely Seymer, 310-18. New York: Macmillan, 1954.

———. *Subsidiary Notes as to the Introduction of Female Nursing into Military Hospitals.* In *Selected Writings of Florence Nightingale,* edited by Lucy Ridgely Seymer, 1-122. New York: Macmillan, 1954.

———. "Suggestions on the Subject of Providing, Training, and Organizing Nurses for the Sick Poor in Workhouse Infirmaries." In *Selected Writings of Florence Nightingale,* edited by Lucy Ridgely Seymer, 271-309. New York: Macmillan, 1954.

"The Nightingale's Song to the Sick Soldier." *Punch* 27 (1854): 184.

Osborne, Sidney Godolphin. "An Eye-Witness Account." In *Florence Nightingale: Saint, Reformer or Rebel?* edited by Raymond G. Herbert, 87-101. Malabar, FL: Robert E. Krieger Publishing, 1981.

———. *The Letters of S. G. O.* 2 vols. Edited by Arnold White. London: Griffith, Farran, Okeden & Welsh, n.d.

Our Indian Sisters: A Quarterly Magazine of the Ladies' Zenana Mission, in Connection with the Baptist Missionary Society no. 8 (Apr. 1887). London: Elliot Stock.

Perry, Anne. *A Dangerous Mourning.* New York: Ivy Books, 1990.

———. *A Sudden Fearful Death.* New York: Ivy Books, 1993.

Phelps, Elizabeth Stuart. *Doctor Zay.* 1882. New York: Feminist Press, 1987.

Ramabai, Pandita. *The High-Caste Hindu Woman.* Philadelphia: George Bell, 1887.

Reade, Charles. *The Bloomer.* London, 1857.

———. *Hard Cash.* 1863. In *The Works of Charles Reade.* New York: Peter Fenelon Collier, n.d.

———. *A Woman-Hater.* 1877. In *The Works of Charles Reade.* New York: Peter Fenelon Collier, n.d.

Review of *Dr. Janet of Harley Street.* By Arabella Kenealy. *Dial* (Nov. 1, 1894): 266.

Review of *Mona Maclean, Medical Student.* By Graham Travers (Margaret Todd). *Athenaeum* (Dec. 3, 1892): 774.

Rivington, Walter. *The Medical Profession.* 1st ed. London: Ballière, Tindall, 1879.

Satthianadhan, Krupabai. *Saguna: A Story of a Native Christian, 1887-1888.* Madras: Srinivasa, Varadachari, 1895.

Scharlieb, Dr. Mary. *Reminiscences.* London: Williams & Norgate, 1924.

Schreiner, Olive. *The Story of an African Farm.* 1883. London: Penguin, 1987.

Seacole, Mary Jane. *Wonderful Adventures of Mrs. Seacole in Many Lands.* 1857. New York: Oxford University Press, 1988.

Shore, A. and L. *War Lyrics.* London: Shoberl, 1855.

"Sister Joan." *The Wards of St. Margaret's.* In *Girls' Own Paper,* London, 1894.

Souvenir booklet from the 5th All India Obstetric and Gynaecological Congress, Bombay, Dec. 1947. Wellcome Library Archives, C.146 (INDIA), Box 16: Medical Women Overseas, SA/MWF: Medical Women's Federation; part c (historical).

Sprigge, S. Squire. "The Medicine of Dickens." *Cornhill Magazine* 35 (1877): 258-67.

Sturges, Octavius. "Doctors and Nurses." *Nineteenth Century* 7 (June 1879): 1089-96.

Swiney, Frances. "Alcohol." 1917. In *The Sexuality Debates,* edited by Sheila Jeffreys, 260-70. London: Routledge & Kegan Paul, 1987.

Todd, Margaret. "After Many Days." In *Fellow Travellers,* 1-54. Edinburgh: Blackwood & Sons, 1896.

———. *Mona Maclean, Medical Student.* Edinburgh: Blackwood & Sons, 1892.

———. "Some Thoughts on the Woman Question." *Blackwood's Edinburgh Magazine* 156 (Nov. 1894): 689-92.

Trollope, Anthony. *Orley Farm.* 1861-1862. London: Trollope Society, 1993.

Turner, Percival. *Guide to the Medical and Dental Professions, with a Chapter on Lady Doctors by Miss F. M. Strutt-Cavell.* London: Bailliere, Tindall, & Cox, 1895.

Ward, Mrs. Humphrey. *Marcella.* New York: Penguin, 1984.

Wesley, Elizabeth. *Nora Meade, MD.* New York: Bantam, 1957.

Woolf, Virginia. *A Room of One's Own.* New York: Harcourt Brace Jovanovich, 1989.

———. *The Years.* 1937. London: Hogarth Press, 1990.

SECONDARY SOURCES

Ackerknecht, Erwin H. "Anticontagionism between 1821-1867." *Bulletin of the History of Medicine* 22 (1948): 562-93.

Ackroyd, Peter. *Dickens.* New York: Harper Collins, 1990.

Alexander, Wendy. *First Ladies of Medicine: The Origins, Education and Destination of Early Women Graduates of Glasgow University.* Glasgow: Wellcome Unit for the History of Medicine, University of Glasgow, 1987.

Allen, Charles, ed. *Plain Tales from the Raj: Images of British India in the Twentieth Century.* New York: St. Martin's Press, 1976.

Altick, Richard. *Deadly Encounters: Two Victorian Sensations.* Philadelphia: University of Pennsylvania Press, 1986.

———. *Victorian Studies in Scarlet.* New York: Norton, 1970.

Amis, Kingsley. *Rudyard Kipling and His World.* London: Thames & Hudson, 1975.

Anderson, Louisa Garrett. *Elizabeth Garrett Anderson.* London: Faber, 1939.

Anderson, Olive. *A Liberal State at War.* London: Macmillan, 1967.

Ardis, Ann L. *New Women, New Novels: Feminism and Early Modernism.* New Brunswick: Rutgers University Press, 1990.

Armstrong, Nancy. *Desire and Domestic Fiction: A Political History of the Novel.* New York: Oxford University Press, 1987.

Auerbach, Nina. *Woman and the Demon: The Life of a Victorian Myth.* Cambridge: Harvard University Press, 1982.

Ballhatchet, Kenneth. *Race, Sex, and Class under the Raj.* London: Weidenfeld & Nicolson, 1980.

Baly, Monica E. "Florence Nightingale and the Establishment of the First School at St. Thomas's—Myth v. Reality." In *Florence Nightingale and Her Era: A Collection of New Scholarship,* edited by Vern Bullough, Bonnie Bullough, and Marietta P. Stanton, 3-22. New York: Garland Publishing, 1990.

Bashford, Alison. "Separatist Health: Changing Meanings of Women's Hospitals in Australia and England, c. 1870-1920." In *Women Healers and Physicians: Climbing a Long Hill,* edited by Lilian R. Furst, 198-220. Lexington: University Press of Kentucky, 1997.

Bennett, A. H. *English Medical Women: Glimpses of Their Work in Peace and War.* London: Pitman & Sons, 1915.

Blake, Catriona. *The Charge of the Parasols: Women's Entry to the Medical Profession.* London: Women's Press, 1990.

Boahen, A. Adu. *African Perspectives on Colonialism.* Baltimore: Johns Hopkins University Press, 1987.

Boone, Joseph. *Libidinal Currents: Sexuality and the Shaping of Modernism.* Chicago: University of Chicago Press, 1998.

Boyle, Thomas. *Black Swine in the Sewers of Hampstead: Beneath the Surface of Victorian Sensationalism.* New York: Viking Penguin, 1989.

Burns, Wayne. *Charles Reade: A Study in Victorian Authorship.* New York: Bookman Associates, 1961.

Burton, Antoinette M. "The White Woman's Burden: British Feminists and 'the Indian Woman,' 1865-1915." In *Western Women and Imperialism: Complicity and*

Resistance, edited by Nupur Chaudhuri and Margaret Strobel. Bloomington: Indiana University Press, 1993.

Butler, Judith. *Gender Trouble: Feminism and the Subversion of Identity.* New York: Routledge, 1990.

Caine, Barbara. *Victorian Feminists.* New York: Oxford University Press, 1992.

Callaway, Helen, and Dorothy O. Helly. "Crusader for Empire: Flora Shaw/Lady Lugard." In *Western Women and Imperialism: Complicity and Resistance,* edited by Nupur Chaudhuri and Margaret Strobel, 78-97. Bloomington: Indiana University Press, 1993.

Carpenter, Mick. "The Subordination of Nurses in Health Care." In *Gender, Work and Medicine: Women and the Medical Division of Labour,* edited by Elianne Riska and Katarina Wegar, 95-130. London: Sage, 1993.

Cartwright, F. F. *A Social History of Medicine.* London: Longman, 1977.

Chapple, J. A. V. *Science and Literature in the Nineteenth Century.* London: Macmillan, 1986.

Chauncey, George. *Gay New York: Gender, Urban Culture, and the Making of the Gay Male World, 1890-1940.* New York: Basic Books, 1994.

Chaudhuri, Nupur, and Margaret Strobel, eds. *Western Women and Imperialism: Complicity and Resistance.* Bloomington: Indiana University Press, 1993.

Colloms, Brenda. *Charles Kingsley: The Lion of Eversley.* London: Constable, 1975.

Cvetkovich, Ann. *Mixed Feelings: Feminism, Mass Culture, and Victorian Sensationalism.* New Brunswick: Rutgers University Press, 1992.

Davidoff, Leonore, and Catherine Hall. *Family Fortunes: Men and Women of the English Middle Class, 1780-1850.* Chicago: University of Chicago Press, 1987.

Davies, Celia. "A Constant Casualty: Nurse Education in Britain and the USA to 1939." In *Rewriting Nursing History,* edited by Celia Davies, 102-22. London: Croom Helm, 1980.

Dean, Mitchell, and Gail Bolton. "The Administration of Poverty and the Development of Nursing Practice in Nineteenth-century England." *Rewriting Nursing History,* edited by Celia Davies, 76-101. London: Croom Helm, 1980.

Dijkstra, Bram. *Evil Sisters: The Threat of Female Sexuality and the Cult of Manhood.* New York: Knopf, 1996.

Eby, Cecil Degrotte. *The Road to Armageddon: The Martial Spirit in English Popular Literature, 1870-1914.* Durham: Duke University Press, 1987.

Finkelstein, David. "A Woman Hater and Women Healers: John Blackwood, Charles Reade, and the Victorian Women's Medical Movement." *Victorian Periodicals Review* 28, no. 4 (Winter 1995): 330-52.

First, Ruth, and Ann Scott. *Olive Schreiner.* New Brunswick, NJ: Rutgers University Press, 1980.

Foucault, Michel. *The Birth of the Clinic: An Archaeology of Medical Perception.* New York: Random House, 1975.

———. *Discipline and Punish: The Birth of the Prison.* New York: Random House, 1979.

———. *History of Sexuality. Volume I: An Introduction.* New York: Vintage, 1990.

Freud, Sigmund. *Three Essays on the Theory of Sexuality.* In *The Freud Reader,* edited by Peter Gay. New York: W. W. Norton, 1989.

Froula, Christine. "The Daughter's Seduction: Sexual Violence and Literary History." *Signs* 11, no. 4 (Summer 1986): 621-44.

Furst, Lilian. "Halfway Up the Hill: Doctresses in Late Nineteenth-Century American Fiction." In *Women Healers and Physicians: Climbing a Long Hill,* 221-38. Lexington: University Press of Kentucky, 1997.

———. "A Shocking Discovery! An Introduction to Arthur Conan Doyle's 'The Doctors of Hoyland.'" In *Medical Progress and Social Reality: A Reader in Nineteenth-Century Medicine and Literature.* Albany: State University of New York Press, 2000.

Gamarnikow, Eva. "Sexual Division of Labour: The Case of Nursing." In *Feminism and Materialism: Women and Modes of Production,* edited by Annette Kuhn and AnnMarie Wolpe, 96-123. London: Routledge & Kegan Paul, 1978.

Gérin, Winifred. *Elizabeth Gaskell: A Biography.* Oxford: Clarendon Press, 1976.

Goldie, Sue M. *"I have done my duty": Florence Nightingale in the Crimean War, 1854-56.* Iowa City: University of Iowa Press, 1987.

Haldane, Elizabeth. *Mrs. Gaskell and Her Friends.* London: Hodder & Stoughton, 1931.

Hambly, Gavin R. G. "Muslims in English-Language Fiction." In *Asia in Western Fiction,* edited by Robin W. Winks and James R. Rush, 35-52. Manchester: Manchester University Press, 1990.

Heller, Tamar. *Dead Secrets: Wilkie Collins and the Female Gothic.* New Haven: Yale University Press, 1992.

Huxley, Elspeth. *Florence Nightingale.* New York: G. P. Putnam's Sons, 1975.

Hyam, Ronald. *Empire and Sexuality: The British Experience.* Manchester: Manchester University Press, 1990.

Jayawardena, Kumari. *The White Woman's Other Burden: Western Women and South Asia during British Rule.* London: Routledge, 1995.

Judd, Catherine. *Beside Seductions: Nursing and the Victorian Imagination, 1830-1880.* New York: St. Martin's, 1998.

Kabbani, Rana. *Europe's Myths of Orient: Devise and Rule.* London: Macmillan, 1986.

Kalikoff, Beth. *Murder and Moral Decay in Victorian Popular Literature.* Ann Arbor: UMI Research Press, 1986.

Kalisch, Philip, and Beatrice Kalisch. "'The Birth of Modern Nursing.' Florence Nightingale: Pioneer." In *Florence Nightingale: Saint, Reformer or Rebel?* edited by Raymond G. Herbert, 129-39. Malabar, FL: Robert E. Krieger Publishing, 1981.

———. *The Changing Image of the Nurse.* Menlo Park, CA: Addison-Wesley, 1987.

Katz, Wendy R. *Rider Haggard and the Fiction of Empire: A Critical Study of British Imperial Fiction.* Cambridge: Cambridge University Press, 1987.

Kent, Susan Kingsley. *Sex and Suffrage in Britain, 1860-1914.* Princeton: Princeton University Press, 1987.

Knapman, Claudia. *White Women in Fiji 1835-1930: The Ruin of Empire?* Sydney: Allen & Unwin, 1986.

Lansbury, Cora. *Elizabeth Gaskell: The Novel of Social Crisis.* New York: Barnes & Noble, 1975.

Ledger, Sally. *The New Woman: Fiction and Feminism at the Fin de Siècle.* Manchester: Manchester University Press, 1997.

Levy, Anita. *Other Women: The Writing of Class, Race, and Gender, 1832-1898.* Princeton: Princeton University Press, 1991.

Lind, Mary Ann. *The Compassionate Memsahibs: Welfare Activities of British Women in India, 1900-1947.* New York: Greenwood Press, 1988.

Loesburg, Jonathan. "The Ideology of Narrative Form in Sensation Fiction." *Representations* 13 (Winter 1986): 115-38.

Lokugé, Chandani. "The Cross-Cultural Experience of a Pioneer Indian Woman. Writer of English Fiction." *From Commonwealth to Post-Colonial.* Ed. Anna Rutherford. Sydney: Dangaroo Press, 1992. 102-16.

Macleod, Roy, and Milton Lewis. *Disease, Medicine, and Empire. Perspectives on Western Medicine and the Experience of European Expansion.* London: Routledge, 1988.

Maggs, Christopher. *The Origins of General Nursing.* London: Croom Helm, 1983.

Mangum, Teresa. *Married, Middlebrow, and Militant: Sarah Grand and the New Woman.* Ann Arbor: University of Michigan Press, 1998.

Manton, Jo. *Elizabeth Garrett Anderson.* New York: E. P. Dutton, 1965.

Martindale, Louisa. *The Woman Doctor and Her Future.* London: Mills & Boon, 1922.

Miller, D. A. *The Novel and the Police.* Berkeley: University of California Press, 1988.

Mills, Sara. *Discourses of Difference: An Analysis of Women's Travel Writing and Colonialism.* London: Routledge, 1991.

Mitchell, Sally. *The New Girl.* New York: Columbia University Press, 1995.

Monteiro, Lois A. "Nightingale and Her Correspondants: Portrait of the Era." In *Florence Nightingale and Her Era: A Collection of New Scholarship,* edited by Vern Bullough, Bonnie Bullough, and Marietta P. Stanton, 40-59. New York: Garland, 1990.

———. "On Separate Roads: Florence Nightingale and Elizabeth Blackwell." *Signs* 9 (Spring 1984): 520-605.

Morantz, Regina Markell. "Feminism, Professionalism, and Germs: The Thought of Mary Putnam Jacobi and Elizabeth Blackwell." *American Quarterly* 34 (1982): 459-78.

Morantz-Sanchez, Regina. *Conduct Unbecoming a Woman: Medicine on Trial in Turn-of-the-Century Brooklyn.* New York: Oxford University Press, 1999.

———. *Sympathy and Science: Women Physicians in American Medicine.* New York: Oxford University Press, 1985.

More, Ellen Singer. *Restoring the Balance: Women Physicians and the Profession of Medicine, 1850-1995.* Cambridge: Harvard University Press, 1999.

Morris, Timothy. "Professional Ethics and Professional Erotics in Elizabeth Stuart Phelps' *Doctor Zay.*" *Studies in American Fiction* 21, no. 2 (Autumn 1993): 141-52.

Mort, Frank. *Dangerous Sexualities: Medico-Moral Politics in England since 1830.* London: Routledge & Kegan Paul, 1987.

Murphy, Patricia. *Time Is of the Essence: Temporality, Gender, and the New Woman.* Albany: State University of New York Press, 2001.

Nadis, Mark. "Evolution of the Sahib." *Historian* 19, no. 4 (Aug. 1957).

Nestor, Pauline. *Female Friendships and Communities: Charlotte Brontë, George Eliot, Elizabeth Gaskell.* Oxford: Clarendon Press, 1985.

Nettles, Elsa. "'Leaving the Private House': Women Doctors in Virginia Woolf's Life and Art." In *Women Healers and Physicians: Climbing a Long Hill,* edited by Lilian Furst, 239-58. Lexington: University Press of Kentucky, 1997.

Nord, Deborah Epstein. *Walking the Victorian Streets: Women, Representation, and the City.* Ithaca: Cornell University Press, 1995.

Parry, Noel, and José Parry. *The Rise of the Medical Profession: A Study of Collective Social Mobility.* London: Croom Helm, 1976.

Pelling, Margaret. *Cholera, Fever and English Medicine, 1825-1865.* Oxford: Oxford University Press, 1978.

Peterson, M. Jeanne. "The Victorian Governess: Status Incongruence in Family and Society." In *Suffer and Be Still: Women in the Victorian Age,* edited by Martha Vicinus. Bloomington: Indiana University Press, 1972.

Phillips, Walter C. *Dickens, Reade, and Collins, Sensation Novelists.* New York: Columbia University Press, 1919.

Poovey, Mary. "Speaking of the Body: Mid-Victorian Constructions of Female Desire." In *Body/Politics. Women and the Discourses of Science,* edited by Mary Jacobus, Evelyn Fox Keller, and Sally Shuttleworth, 29-46. New York: Routledge 1990.

———. *Uneven Developments: The Ideological Work of Gender in Mid-Victorian England.* Chicago: University of Chicago Press, 1988.

Prochaska, F. K. *Women and Philanthropy in Nineteenth-Century England.* Oxford: Clarendon Press, 1980.

Pykett, Lyn. *The "Improper" Feminine: The Women's Sensation Novel and the New Woman Writing.* London: Routledge, 1992.

Rappaport, Erika Diane. *Shopping for Pleasure: Women in the Making of London's West End.* Princeton: Princeton University Press, 2000.

Rivington, Walter. *The Medical Profession.* 1st ed. London: Balliäre, Tindall, 1879.

Roberts, Shirley. *Sophia Jex-Blake: A Woman Pioneer in Nineteenth-Century Medical Reform.* London: Routledge, 1994.

Robinson, Ronald, and John Gallagher. *Africa and the Victorians. The Official Mind of Imperialism.* 2nd ed. London: Macmillan, 1981.

Rosenberg, Charles E. "The Cause of Cholera: Aspects of Etiological Thought in Nineteenth Century America." *Bulletin of the History of Medicine* 34 (1960): 331-54.

———. "Florence Nightingale on Contagion: The Hospital as Moral Universe." In *Healing and History: Essays for George Rosen,* edited by Charles E. Rosenberg, 116-36. New York: Dawson, Science History Publications, 1979.

Roy, Parama. *Indian Traffic: Identities in Question in Colonial and Post-colonial India.* Berkeley: University of California Press, 1998.

Rubenius, Anna. *The Woman Question in Mrs. Gaskell's Life and Works.* Uppsala: A.-B. Lundequistska Bokhandeln, 1950.

Said, Edward. *Culture and Imperialism.* New York: Knopf, 1993.

Schuyler, Constance B. Introduction to *Notes on Nursing,* by Florence Nightingale. Philadelphia: Lippincott, 1992. 3-17.

Sedgwick, Eve Kosofsky. *Between Men: English Literature and Male Homosocial Desire.* New York: Columbia University Press, 1985.

Shankar, D. A. "The Naulahka and Post-Kipling British Fiction on India." *Literary Criterion* (Mysore) 22, no. 4 (1987): 71-79.

Shanley, Mary Lyndon. *Feminism, Marriage, and the Law in Victorian England.* Princeton: Princeton University Press, 1989.

Showalter, Elaine. *The Female Malady: Women, Madness, and English Culture, 1830-1980.* New York: Penguin, 1985.

———. *A Literature of Their Own: British Women Novelists from Brontë to Lessing.* Princeton: Princeton University Press, 1977.

———. *Sexual Anarchy: Gender and Culture at the Fin de Siècle.* New York: Penguin, 1990.

Shryock, Richard H. *The History of Nursing: An Interpretation of the Social and Medical Factors Involved.* Philadelphia: W. B. Saunders, 1959.

Skilton, David. *The Early and Mid-Victorian Novel.* London: Routledge, 1993.

Slater, Michael. *Dickens and Women.* Stanford: Stanford University Press, 1983.

Smith, Elton E. *Charles Reade.* Boston: Twayne, 1976.

Smith, F. B. *Florence Nightingale: Reputation and Power.* London: Croom Helm, 1982.

———. *The People's Health, 1830-1910.* New York: Holmes & Meier, 1979.

Smith, Linda S. "Image Counts—Greeting Cards Mail It in When It Comes to Accurately Portraying Nurses." *Nursing Spectrum* (Oct. 1, 2003), [http://community.nursingspectrum.com/MagazineArticles/article.cfm?AID=10528].

Spear, Percival. *The Nabobs: A Study of the Social Life of the English in Eighteenth-Century India.* London: Oxford University Press, 1963.

Stevenson, Lionel. *The Pre-Raphaelite Poets.* New York: W. W. Norton, 1972.

Stoneman, Patsy. *Elizabeth Gaskell.* Brighton: Harvester Press, 1987.

Strachey, Lytton. *Eminent Victorians.* New York: HBJ, 1918.

Strachey, Ray. *The Cause: A Short History of the Women's Movement in Great Britain.* London: Virago Press, 1989.

Strobel, Margaret. *European Women and the Second British Empire.* Bloomington: Indiana University Press, 1991.

Summers, Anne. *Angels and Citizens: British Women as Military Nurses, 1854-1914.* London: Routledge & Kegan Paul, 1988.

———. "Pride and Prejudice: Ladies and Nurses in the Crimean War." *History Workshop Journal* 16 (Autumn 1983): 32-56.

Swenson, Kristine. "Evolution, Entropy, and the Construction of Empire in Kipling's *The Naulahka*." *Journal of Commonwealth and Postcolonial Studies* 8, no. 2 (Spring 2001): 45-58.

———. "Intimate Sympathy and Self-Effacement: Writing the Life of Sophia Jex-Blake." *A/B: Auto/Biography Studies* 14, no. 2 (Winter 1999): 222-40.

———. "The Menopausal Vampire: Arabella Kenealy and the Boundaries of True Womanhood." *Women's Writing,* vol. 10, no. 1 (2003): 27-46.

———. "Protection or Restriction? Women and Labor in Mary Barton." *Gaskell Society Journal* 7 (1993): 50-66.

———. "Teaching a 'highly exceptional' Text: Krupabai Satthianadhan's *Saguna* and Narratives of Empire." In *Teaching 18th and 19th Century British Women Writers,* edited by Jeanne Moskal and Shannon Wooden. New York: Peter Lang, 2004.

Thompson, Christine. "Disruptive Desire: Medical Careers for Victorian Women in Fact and Fiction." *Nineteenth-Century Contexts* 15, no. 2 (1991): 181-96.

Todd, Margaret. *The Life of Sophia Jex-Blake.* London: Macmillan, 1918.

Tompkins, Jane. *Sensational Designs: The Cultural Work of American Fiction, 1790-1860.* Oxford: Oxford University Press, 1985.

Vicinus, Martha. "Distance and Desire: English Boarding School Friendships, 1870-1920." In *Hidden from History: Reclaiming the Gay and Lesbian Past,* edited by Martin Bauml Duberman, Martha Vicinus, and George Chauncey, Jr., 211-29. New York: NAL Books, 1989.

———. *Independent Women: Work and Community for Single Women, 1850-1920.* Chicago: University of Chicago Press, 1985.

———. "What Makes a Heroine? Girls' Biographies of Florence Nightingale." In *Florence Nightingale and Her Era: A Collection of New Scholarship,* edited by Vern Bullough, Bonnie Bullough, and Marietta P. Stanton, 90-106. New York: Garland, 1990.

Vicinus, Martha, ed. *Suffer and Be Still: Women in the Victorian Age.* Bloomington: Indiana University Press, 1972.

Vicinus, Martha, and Bea Nergaard. Introduction to *Ever Yours, Florence Nightingale: Selected Letters.* Cambridge: Harvard University Press, 1990.

Walkowitz, Judith. *City of Dreadful Delight: Narratives of Sexual Danger in Late-Victorian London.* Chicago: University of Chicago Press, 1992.

———. *Prostitution and Victorian Society: Women, Class, and the State.* Cambridge: Cambridge University Press, 1980.

Webb, R. K. *Modern England.* 2nd ed. New York: Harper & Row, 1980.

Weeks, Jeffrey. *Sex, Politics, and Society: The Regulation of Sexuality since 1800.* London: Longman, 1981.

Welch, W. H. *Public Health in Theory and Practice.* New Haven: Yale University Press, 1925.

Witz, Anne. *Professions and Patriarchy.* London: Routledge, 1992.

Wohl, Anthony S. *Endangered Lives: Public Health in Victorian Britain.* London: J. M. Dent, 1983.

Woodham-Smith, Cecil. *Florence Nightingale: 1820-1910.* New York: McGraw-Hill, 1951.

MAJOR AUTHORS AND SIGNIFICANT WORKS

M. D. Uroff (essay date June 1972)

SOURCE: Uroff, M. D. "The Doctors in 'Rappaccini's Daughter.'" *Nineteenth-Century Fiction* 27, no. 1 (June 1972): 61-70.

[*In the following essay, Uroff regards Nathaniel Hawthorne's story "Rappaccini's Daughter" within the framework of a dispute between allopathic and homeopathic medicine, arguing that the story evidences Hawthorne's dislike of "unscientific" doctors.*]

Despite the diversity and wealth of critical commentary on "Rappaccini's Daughter," the earliest interpretation of the tale as a polemic against science has remained curiously unchallenged. While critics no longer view this theme as the central meaning of the story and while they identify the villain variously as Rappaccini, Baglioni, or Giovanni, their conclusions generally agree that Hawthorne had a contemptuous distrust of science which he personified in one scientific evildoer after another.[1] This view is supported by generalizations about the Romantic suspicion of science and Hawthorne's own horror at a mind cultivated at the expense of the heart. An examination of the three men who revolve around Beatrice Rappaccini suggests that these conclusions should be refined. In dramatizing the *libido sciendi* in these three men, Hawthorne expresses not so much his suspicion of science as his suspicion of an unscientific attitude toward medicine. In fact, Hawthorne's alleged antipathy toward science may be more accurately described as an antipathy toward doctors since most of the scientists in his tales actually work their experiments on human beings and conceive of their function, however perversely, as healing. And what Hawthorne finds most reprehensible in these doctors is not their cold objectivity about human nature nor their isolation from the world but the very opposite: their impassioned application of scientific principles and their unwillingness to remain isolated. In "Rappaccini's Daughter," Hawthorne does not display a distrust for scientists; rather he treats the vagaries of doctors. If "Rappaccini's Daughter" argues for any position concerning science, it argues for more objectivity, dispassionate research, and isolation. The doctors in Hawthorne's tale, like the doctors in mid-nineteenth-century America, are treacherously unscientific.

The frame of the tale is a medical dispute between Rappaccini and Baglioni which, although set in ancient and far-off Padua, actually raged in Hawthorne's own day in Massachusetts. It is the age-old debate between two medical philosophies about the nature of disease and forms of cures, specifically the allopathic approach of Baglioni and the homeopathic approach of Rappaccini. Obviously, this most complex tale is not simply an imaginative reconstruction of differences of medical opinion; but an examination of the medical issues will shed light on an aspect of the tale that has been generally obfuscated, and it will suggest a new interpretation of the characters' motives and actions.

The medical dispute between Rappaccini and Baglioni is an accurate portrayal of a dispute which divided the medical profession in the 1840's in Massachusetts. The orthodox practice of medicine in those days was allopathic. It regarded diseased states as either sthenic, due to inflammation, or asthenic, resulting from a weakening of stimuli. The treatment for the former disorder involved bleeding and purging and for the latter, stimu-

lants like opium. Heroic doses of medication were given, and, in the view of one commentator, the most remarkable aspect of this treatment was the capacity of patients to survive despite their medication.[2] This practice was obviously too uncertain to be scientific. Homeopathy, a rival theory of the nature of disease and the forms of cures, gained widespread support among Massachusetts doctors. Homeopathic doctors regarded disease not as a separate entity affecting a specific organ but as a derangement of the "immaterial vital principle" pervading and animating the body. This vital principle, homeopaths believed, had the capacity to expel morbid disturbances but its natural tendency to restoration was temporarily paralyzed by disease. To start the curative process, homeopathic practitioners afflicted the system with a more intense but similar disease whose presence spurred the vital principle to new efforts.[3] While this theory may appear no more scientific than that of allopathy, homeopathic practitioners in mid-nineteenth-century Massachusetts were in fact as scientific in their treatment as orthodox allopathic doctors. They were in general well educated, very observant about the effects of specific remedies, more anxious to reduce the uncertainty of medical treatment and to make the practice of medicine more exact and scientific. Also, their mild therapy and small doses of medication often proved more effective in combating disease than the heroic treatment of allopathic medicine.[4] Although homeopathic doctors were not quacks, their theories were soundly condemned by the medical profession. And the dispute between homeopathic and allopathic practitioners was made all the more vituperative by the fact that the medical profession in Massachusetts was in a state of flux over licensing practices, educational requirements and the large number of charlatans who dispensed cures.[5]

Hawthorne was certainly aware of homeopathy since he makes light of it in *The Blithedale Romance* where Miles Coverdale is treated by a homeopathic doctor who gave him "as much medicine, in the course of a fortnight's attendance, as would have laid on the point of a needle" and fed him on water-gruel so that he "speedily became a skeleton above ground."[6] Also Hawthorne's sister-in-law, Elizabeth Peabody, among other Transcendentalists, was a strong advocate of homeopathy.[7] From her, he must have heard, at least in general terms, of the bitter disagreements that homeopathy occasioned in the medical profession. In writing a tale of two rival doctors and setting it in ancient Padua, Hawthorne was not simply casting back in time a local and contemporary medical problem. Homeopathy is an ancient theory of medical treatment. Its basic position that the most effective medicines are those that induce symptoms similar to those of the disease has from the beginning rivaled the allopathic practice of medicine. By confronting the poisonous homeopathic therapy of Rappaccini with the violent allopathic treatment of Baglioni, Hawthorne does not take issue with either side in the medical debate; rather he dramatizes the perfidy of the medical profession.

Beatrice Rappaccini is the innocent victim of her father's experiments. She has grown up in the botanical garden where her father cultivates poisonous plants to use in his medical research. Her father's research is based on the theory, in the words of his professional rival, "that all medicinal virtues are comprised within those substances which we term vegetable poisons."[8] Rappaccini operates on the homeopathic principle of *similia similibus curantur,* and even his rival admits that he has worked marvelous cures on this basis. But the effect of these plants on his daughter has been disastrous. In the course of contact with these deadly flowers, her body has become permeated with poison. She is deadly. Her breath kills insects; her touch wilts flowers. But the plants have had a curious effect upon her spirit; deadly as she is, she appears "redundant with life, health, and energy" (133). This result too can be explained by homeopathic principles since the introduction of poison into a system should increase the intensity of the vital principle within her, and indeed Rappaccini's research has proved successful in this respect. Beatrice is vitalized by poison. The only cure for her poisonous body, from the homeopathic point of view, is contact with a more intense but similar disease. If like really cures like, then her father's researches must produce a more virulently poisonous plant to counteract the poisons she has already absorbed. But, we are told, Rappaccini has produced many new varieties of poisonous plants, and still Beatrice is not cured.

Then Giovanni appears. He seems to be just a homesick medical student, attracted by Beatrice's beauty. But, considering the facts that he is let into what is purported to be Rappaccini's inaccessible garden and that Rappaccini in passing him on the street appears to notice him, it is possible to assume that his chance appearance leads his neighbor, Rappaccini, to consider another means of curing Beatrice. In the tale it is Baglioni, Rappaccini's enemy, who suggests the possibility that Rappaccini intends to make Giovanni the subject of another experiment, and in my view it is the only insight Baglioni has. Intrigued by Beatrice's beauty and her apparently poisonous nature, Giovanni makes frequent but brief visitations to her father's garden. There, he not only becomes infatuated with Beatrice, he also by degrees becomes imbued with the same poison. Like Beatrice, his vital principle seems to be activated by contact with the poisonous plants as his cheeks take on "a hue of superabundant life" (168); but he too becomes deadly. If Rappaccini does intend to use Giovanni in his experiment and to extend his homeopathic principles to the art of matchmaking, his researches to this point have been successful. He has produced two equally poi-

sonous people. If like cures like, these two should be able to cure each other by bodily contact. And that, as we shall see, is exactly what Rappaccini has in mind.

In the controlled atmosphere of his laboratory-garden, Rappaccini operates safely; but the success of his experiment is threatened on two sides. First, by attempting to apply his theories to human beings and to work in the uncontrollable and unscientific area of the human heart, Rappaccini himself violates the first principle of scientific research. He must depend upon factors over which he has no control, and without control over his materials he can expect as a scientist no certain success. Also, as a theoretician, he should be objective, willing to accept any outcome of his research; but, as we have seen, he is actually trying to produce a certain result, and his interest in this particular experiment is far from dispassionate. But his experiment is open to another threat in the person of Baglioni who has taken a great interest in the events carried on in the garden. In fact, Rappaccini's laboratory is not so isolated as he had imagined. And it is the intervention of this outsider, Baglioni, that actually ruins the experiment.

Baglioni is another unscientific doctor whose desire to cure Beatrice is inextricably bound up with his desire to thwart Rappaccini. His interest in healing is subordinate to his professional jealousy. He offers to Giovanni his own cure for Beatrice, an antidote which "would have rendered the most virulent poisons of the Borgias innocuous" (165). As the allopathic doctors of Hawthorne's day, Baglioni is convinced that heroic doses of medication are the only cures; but, as a doctor, he should also know that any medicine that potent could have violent and disastrous results. And his antidote kills Beatrice. He vindicates himself in the end by calling out "in a tone of triumph mixed with horror," "'Rappaccini, Rappaccini! and is this the upshot of your experiment!'" (177). It is obviously the upshot of Baglioni's experiment since Rappaccini never had a chance to work his own cure. It is true that Rappaccini's poisonous flowers made Beatrice poisonous, but they did not kill her; for that, Baglioni is responsible.

In an earlier scene, Baglioni has described Rappaccini as "'a wonderful man indeed; a vile empiric, however, in his practice, and therefore not to be tolerated by those who respect the good old rules of the medical profession'" (166). Out of respect for these good old rules, Baglioni has killed Beatrice. There can be little question that these old rules are not good in this particular case. If Rappaccini is to be condemned on the grounds that he cares infinitely more for science than for mankind and would sacrifice human life for his experiments, as Baglioni contends, then on those same grounds, it is necessary also to condemn Baglioni who does in fact sacrifice human life to uphold the good old rules of medicine. We can only assume that he cares infinitely more for the medical profession than for human life. Baglioni is described as an "elderly personage, apparently of genial nature, and habits that might almost be called jovial" (136). But his geniality is apparent only in his social habits. Professionally motivated by jealousy and a fear of scientific experimentation, he exemplifies the conservatism and ignorance of the medical profession of mid-nineteenth-century America. It is with horror that he warns Giovanni that the young student is a subject of one of Rappaccini's experiments, as if experimentation could only be dangerous. Roy R. Male, Jr. has called Baglioni blasphemous in his materialistic skepticism.[9] But, it seems to me, that skepticism is exactly what Baglioni lacks; he is content with the good old rules.

In shifting the blame of earlier critics from Rappaccini to Baglioni, I do not mean to imply that Rappaccini is without flaws. Both as a doctor and a father, he is perverse. He has after all made his daughter poisonous. This development appears to be Hawthorne's imaginative elaboration of the medical possibilities of homeopathy. Homeopathic medicine should cure disease; it should make the patient immune from poisoning, not actually poisonous. In fact, Rappaccini has gone outside the bounds of homeopathy's purported method of following nature's own laws in the curative process by making his daughter unnatural. However, he has done so not out of moral perversion but from a desire to remove Beatrice from the "condition of a weak woman, exposed to all evil and capable of none" (177). In this sense, he is the most protective of fathers. He has not subordinated human values to scientific ones; instead he has tried to use his scientific experimentation toward the human end of safeguarding his daughter. And in this, he fails simply because he has set himself an impossible task. By trying to improve human nature and create a more perfect world, he abandons science and the safety of the laboratory and becomes vulnerable to all the flaws of human nature.

Rappaccini erred, as many fathers do, in imagining that he could protect his daughter from the world. And he erred even further in his preternatural fear that the world outside his isolated garden, the world of human relationships, would be so evil as to require such extreme protection. If Baglioni is unduly afraid of scientific advance, Rappaccini is too afraid of the world. Both fears stem from a conservative attitude; Baglioni fears the far-ranging activities of the mind, and Rappaccini is equally suspicious of the wanderings of the heart. However, Rappaccini does not discount the needs of the heart. He has made his daughter poisonous to protect her; but, from his homeopathic principles, he knows also that like cures like, that his daughter cannot be happily in love with flowers. She must have a human lover. But in introducing Giovanni to his daughter, Rappaccini commits the ancient error of fathers; he tries to live for his daughter, to give her the benefit of his experience and thus to keep her from making her own ex-

periments with human nature. His motives are explained in his penultimate speech:

> "My daughter," said Rappaccini, "thou art no longer lonely in the world. Pluck one of these precious gems from thy sister shrub and bid thy bridegroom wear it in his bosom. It will not harm him now. My science and the sympathy between thee and him have so wrought within his system that he now stands apart from common men, as thou dost, daughter of my pride and triumph, from ordinary women. Pass on, then, through the world, most dear to one another and dreadful to all besides!"
>
> (176)

When Beatrice recoils from these words, Rappaccini is dumbfounded and his threats darken:

> "What mean you, foolish girl? Dost thou deem it misery to be endowed with marvellous gifts against which no power nor strength could avail an enemy—misery, to be able to quell the mightiest with a breath—misery, to be as terrible as thou art beautiful? Wouldst thou, then, have preferred the condition of a weak woman, exposed to all evil and capable of none?"
>
> (176-77)

Here, Rappaccini seems to be speaking as an archfiend whose aim is to create evil. But, if we understand his position not only as a homeopath but as a rejected father, his words assume quite a different meaning. He is agonized not because his experiment has failed but because his beloved daughter has spurned it. She has preferred the experiment of her supposed suitor over her father's experiment, and all the collected wisdom of this devoted scientist-father cannot save her from the fate she willingly accepts.

And Beatrice's fate is unfortunately in the hands of yet another doctor or medical student. Giovanni is inadequate both as a scientist and as a lover, or perhaps it would be more accurate to say that he confuses his roles as scientist and lover with fatal results. As a lover, he has the passion of youth, "a quick fancy, and an ardent southern temperament, which rose every instant to a higher fever pitch" (145). Beatrice's beauty is "a madness to him" (145). But even during the first stages of his infatuation, he is sufficiently objective to realize that he has come "within the influence of an unintelligible power by the communication which he had opened with Beatrice" (144). And, as a scientist, this fact tortures him; "hope and dread kept a continual warfare in his breast" (145). He attempts to deal with his dilemma in a scientific manner by submitting all evidence to objective observation. When he first sees Beatrice at night in the garden he imagines that she and the poisonous flowers are "fraught with some strange peril" (135). But, the first thing that he does upon arising in the morning is to check his observations of the night, and, in the light of morning, he finds to his relief that the garden is "real and matter-of-fact" (135). Again, when Baglioni has given voice to certain suspicions in his own mind about Beatrice's poisonous nature, Giovanni decides to "institute some decisive test that should satisfy him, once and for all, whether there were those dreadful peculiarities in her physical nature which could not be supposed to exist without some corresponding monstrosity of soul" (167). Hawthorne comments that there "is something truer and more real than what we can see with the eyes and touch with the finger" (166), and Giovanni's flaw as a lover is in not founding his confidence on such evidence. Scientifically he is also on shaky ground since he assumes a correspondence between the physical and spiritual nature of Beatrice. Presumably science confines itself to physical nature, and empirical evidence is not sufficient to judge the monstrosity of the soul. The decisive test which he chooses to work on Beatrice ironically proves to him that he too is poisonous. He then goes to Beatrice and accuses her of filling his veins with poison. After he has vented his passion upon her and broken her heart, he relents and suggests that they both take Baglioni's antidote to cure themselves. Recognizing Giovanni for the cold lover and impassioned experimentalist he is, Beatrice says "with a peculiar emphasis, 'I will drink; but do thou await the result'" (175). And this final experiment proves the ruin of the scientist-lover.

Hawthorne's doctors are killers. Instead of healing, they poison, torment, and finally kill their patient. And they work neither from a dispassionate interest in scientific experimentation nor from a coldly objective view of human nature. Baglioni and Rappaccini are both motivated by an impassioned desire to prove their theory of medicine correct. They are not so much interested in experimentation as in producing definite medical results. Giovanni is an experimentalist, to be sure; but he knows little about medicine, nothing about research, and bases his own simple experiments on faulty assumptions. Finally, none of these three men is disinterested in Beatrice. Rappaccini loves her not only as his daughter but as his brightest student. Giovanni reacts to her with a mixture of love and horror. And Baglioni is suspicious of her vast knowledge of science and fears that she might be destined to fill the professor's chair he now holds. In this company, Beatrice is indeed "exposed to all evil."

Notes

1. This conclusion is expressed by Edward H. Rosenberry in "Hawthorne's Allegory of Science: 'Rappaccini's Daughter,'" *AL* [*American Literature*], 32 (1960), 39-46. However, other critics have made the same point. In the first symbolic readings of the tale, Richard Fogle and Hyatt H. Waggoner were anxious to subordinate the theme of Rappaccini to the theme of Beatrice, yet they agree that Rappaccini is the personification of the evil scientist. See Fogle, *Hawthorne's Fiction: The Light and the Dark* (Norman: Univ. of Oklahoma Press, 1952), pp. 91-103, and Waggoner, *Hawthorne* (Cambridge, Mass.: Harvard Univ. Press, 1955), pp. 101-16.

The identity of the villain has been the subject of several articles, but all agree that the villainy is somehow attributable to the fact that these men are scientists. For the role of Giovanni, See Frederick L. Gwynn, "Hawthorne's 'Rappaccini's Daughter,'" *NCF* [*Nineteenth-Century Fiction*], 7 (1952), 217-19, and Bernard McCabe, "Narrative Technique in 'Rappaccini's Daughter,'" *MLN* [*Modern Language Notes*], 74 (1959), 213-17. For Baglioni, see Arthur L. Scott, "The Case of the Fatal Antidote," *Arizona Quarterly,* 11 (Spring 1955), 38-43, and Sidney P. Moss, "A Reading of 'Rappaccini's Daughter,'" *SSF* [*Studies in Short Fiction*], 2 (1965), 145-56. The treachery is divided between Rappaccini and Baglioni by Chester E. Eisinger in "Hawthorne as Champion of the Middle Way," *NEQ* [*New England Quarterly*], 27 (1954), 27-52 and Roy R. Male, Jr., "The Dual Aspects of Evil in 'Rappaccini's Daughter,'" *PMLA,* 69 (1954), 99-109. Rappaccini and Giovanni, two scientists in conflict, are discussed by Sherwood R. Price, "The Heart, the Head and 'Rappaccini's Daughter,'" *NEQ,* 27 (1954), 399-403, and all three scientists are condemned by William Rossky in "Rappaccini's Garden or the Murder of Innocence," *ESQ* [*Emerson Society Quarterly*], No. 19 (1960), pp. 98-100.

Allegorical readings of the tale identify either Rappaccini or Baglioni as Satan and regard the Eden of the present world as a place of false values dominated by the false god of scientific materialism. See Oliver Evans, "Allegory and Incest in 'Rappaccini's Daughter,'" *NCF,* 19 (1964), 185-95, and Sheldon W. Liebman, "Hawthorne and Milton: The Second Fall in 'Rappaccini's Daughter,'" *NEQ,* 41 (1968), 521-35.

Freudian interpretations of the tale are also based on the theory that the scientist is evil. Charles Boewe argues that the evil in the garden is some kind of sexual irregularity, resulting from the immoral and scientific hybridization of plants ("Rappaccini's Garden," *AL,* 30 [1958], 37-49). Frederick C. Crews contends that Rappaccini has committed a kind of incest by polluting Beatrice with poison (*The Sins of the Fathers* [New York: Oxford Univ. Press, 1966], pp. 117-35).

Even general discussions of Hawthorne's themes emphasize the distrust he had for scientists. John F. Adams says that the garden in the tale is the evil product of Rappaccini's intellectual perversion ("Hawthorne's Symbolic Gardens," *TSLL* [*Texas Studies in Literature and Language*], 5

[1963], 242-54). Rudolph Von Abele calls Rappaccini an "analytic monster" (*The Death of the Artist* [The Hague: Martinus Nijhoff, 1955], p. 12).

Nina Baym demurs from the general view concerning Hawthorne's attitude toward science. She claims that he did not hate scientists; he rather treated them satirically. However, she exempts Rappaccini from this general view. Mrs. Baym sees Rappaccini as motivated not by love of science but by love of his daughter, and thus she regards him not as a cold experimentalist but as a man impassioned in his actions; however, her conclusion that science is not the issue in this tale is, in my view, unwarranted. See Baym's "The Head, the Heart, and the Unpardonable Sin," *NEQ*, 40 (1967), 31-47.

Hugh McPherson sees the tale as a struggle between Baglioni, whom he calls a demon, and Rappaccini, Hawthorne's supreme intellectual wizard, in which the immaculate Dark Lady Beatrice and the stupid sun hero, Giovanni, come to tragic ends. McPherson's mythological discussion of Hawthorne's character-types touches on several important issues; but its point is again that Hawthorne's scientists or moon wizards are inhuman. See *Hawthorne as Myth-Maker* (Toronto: Univ. of Toronto Press, 1969), pp. 231-34.

2. Joseph F. Kett, *The Formation of the American Medical Profession* (New Haven: Yale Univ. Press, 1968), p. 156.

3. Kett, p. 133.

4. Ibid., pp. 162-64.

5. Ibid., pp. 24-30.

6. *The Blithedale Romance, Works* (Columbus: Ohio State Univ. Press, Centenary ed., 1964), 3:41.

7. Kett, p. 154.

8. "Rappaccini's Daughter," *The Complete Writings of Nathaniel Hawthorne* (Boston: Riverside Press, 1900), 4:138. Citations in the text are to this edition.

9. Male, p. 101.

Lawrence Rothfield (essay date 1992)

SOURCE: Rothfield, Lawrence. "Disarticulating *Madame Bovary*: Flaubert and the Medicalization of the Real." In *Vital Signs: Medical Realism in Nineteenth-Century Fiction*, pp. 15-45. Princeton: Princeton University Press, 1992.

[*In the following essay, Rothfield interprets the failure of the attending doctors to treat Emma Bovary as a semiotic matter.*]

Over the past twenty-odd years, semiotics has established itself as a powerful, rigorous, and at times elegant technique for the close reading of literary texts. Until recently, however, literary semioticians tended to remain fixated on the text itself, squandering the promise of Barthes's early cultural criticism and leaving the issue of the relation between literature and society to either the liberal imagination or ideological criticism. In the last several years, however, context has reemerged as a respectable object for semiotic interrogation. Some Marxist academics have appropriated semiotic methods to forge a more formally sophisticated analysis of ideology; Fredric Jameson's *The Political Unconscious* [1980] offers the most interesting and successful example of this tendency. Concurrently, semioticians themselves have tried to come to grips with the social implications of texts by elaborating a concept of "intertextuality."

Michel Riffaterre's recent work illustrates this change in emphasis.[1] Following a line of investigation originally suggested by Jonathan Culler, Riffaterre argues that literary texts can best be understood as specific "actualizations" of cultural "presuppositions."[2] Culler's definition of *presupposition*—as "that which must be revealed by another, or by an effort of *dédoublement*: of thinking from the point of view of the other"—is heavily tinged with a Hegelianism that Riffaterre rejects, substituting the more Kantian (or Chomskian) formulation of presuppositions as simply "the implicit conditions of an explicit statement." The advantage of Riffaterre's redefinition is that it guides him to look for sets of conditions rather than for Culler's less easily delimited "point of view." In any given instance, the conditions governing statements will constitute a system, and it is this system of presuppositions that the Riffaterrean student of intertextuality hopes to be able to disengage from the literary text and locate in the sociolect.

In seeking to extend the semiotic project beyond the frontiers of the text itself into its context, Riffaterre is to be commended. But because his methodology for elucidating systems of statements within the sociolect remains rather undeveloped, he runs into major problems when he attempts to realize his theoretical claims in particular interpretations, most tellingly in the reading of *Madame Bovary* that he offers in support of his approach. The only prerequisite Riffaterre stipulates for declaring a set of statements to be a system of presuppositions is that they derive from a "matrix sentence" supplied by the dictionary or some other anonymous source. For *Madame Bovary*, the matrix sentence appears, according to Riffaterre, in the cliché—found in a popular dictionary of Flaubert's time in the entry "Adultery"—that "all evils stem from adultery." As a system, an "encoded ideology," adultery entails a number of subordinate consequences, all of which, as it happens, are played out in the course of Flaubert's narrative. Riffaterre concludes that the adultery system thus "entails the whole fictional text."

Apart from this highly dubious claim to account for *to-tal* textual production in terms of a single system, Riffaterre's approach leaves two questions unanswered. The first question is whether it is accurate to describe the literary performance that takes place in *Madame Bovary* as a straightforward actualization of the system of presuppositions about adultery. Of all writers, Flaubert is probably the most sensitive and resistant to the rehearsal of received ideas; when he does make use of such ideas, it is to struggle *against* their simplistic actualization. Flaubert's entire effort, in fact, seems to have been directed toward showing that literariness had nothing to do with a writer's overt subject, that even the most clichéd subject would do. And as Baudelaire points out in his review of *Madame Bovary*, "the tritest theme of all, worn out by repetition, by being played over and over like a tired barrel-organ," is adultery.[3] Flaubert's is a repetition with a difference, but that kind of artistic difference from ordinary actualization is only vaguely gestured toward by Riffaterre, who dismisses it as an *écart stylistique*.[4] Between dictionary and text, presupposition and actualization, Flaubert (and, one presumes, other artists as well) must be doing something extraordinary, and the nature of this deviation needs to be specified.

This leads us to the second question about Riffaterre's method: how does one find one's way from the text to the dictionary entry containing its most important presuppositions? Riffaterre looks up *adultery* because it seems to be the subject of the novel, but Baudelaire, in the review quoted earlier, argues explicitly that Flaubert is using not adultery but *hysteria* to "serve as the central subject, the true core" of his novel. Unfortunately, instead of going on to interpret *Madame Bovary* within the context of nineteenth-century France's presuppositions about hysteria, Baudelaire chooses to guard the artistic value of Flaubert's text from historical inspection by arguing that "the Academy of Medicine has not as yet been able to explain the mysterious condition of hysteria" (341). This was not quite true. Nineteenth-century medicine did have an explanation for hysteria, as for other diseases. That explanation, however, was not to be found in a general dictionary. The system of medical presuppositions about hysteria did not exist as an encoded ideology elaborated through a cliché (as in the instance of adultery), but as a subset of a coherent, intellectually formalized scientific discourse.

To grasp the presuppositions of hysteria thus would entail pursuing a discursive rather than a semiotic analysis. A good first move might be to look for an equivalent to the popular dictionary, a repository of medical knowledge. Even if one managed to find some such equivalent and describe the discourse on hysteria, however, one still would have to explain how medical presuppositions about hysteria inform and are actualized in *Madame Bovary*. And given the fact that discourse is so much more complex than Riffaterre's ideological codes, the relation between discourse and fiction is likely to be more complicated than one of simple actualization.

Luckily, these problems are not insuperable in the case of hysteria and *Madame Bovary*, for two reasons. First, a methodology for analyzing discourse already exists and has been used to describe in some detail the presuppositions of nineteenth-century clinical medicine.[5] Second, there was in fact a medical equivalent (at least in the nineteenth century) to the general dictionary—the *Dictionnaire des sciences médicales*. This dictionary provides an entry on hysteria. But it also contains the boiled-down entirety of medical discourse, for which it thus may stand. Flaubert uses the medical dictionary this synecdochal way in *Madame Bovary* to thematize the relation between medical discourse and his fictional universe—or, to use Riffaterre's terminology, between a presuppositional system and the text in which it is actualized. This thematization occurs in the midst of a typically exhaustive catalogue of the contents of Charles Bovary's study, when Flaubert pauses to note the characteristics of Bovary's dictionary: "Volumes of the 'Dictionary of Medical Science,' uncut, but the binding rather the worse for the successive sales through which they had gone, occupied almost alone the six shelves of a pinewood bookcase."[6] If Charles's dictionary may be taken as an icon of nineteenth-century medical discourse, this description exemplifies the strangely double status of that discourse in *Madame Bovary*. On one hand, the medical dictionary (and medical discourse) is shown both to exist and to enjoy cognitive authority; on the other hand, this source of cognitive power is never tapped by any of the central characters in the novel. Instead of being put into practical effect, the set of medical rules and commands symbolized by these volumes is treated only as an object of exchange, successively received and passed from hand to hand. Flaubert's description emphasizes the commodification of the dictionary ("successive sales"), the social indifference to its content ("uncut pages"), and its purely formal wear and tear ("suffering of its binding"), as if to underline the pathos of distance between discursive knowledge and *bêtise*.

All knowledge in Flaubert is like medical knowledge here, simultaneously present and inaccessible, ideas received yet uncomprehended. In *Madame Bovary*, however, the inaccessibility of *medical* knowledge in particular turns out to be crucial, a matter of life and death. When Charles discovers that Emma has taken poison, he turns to the medical dictionary for the first time since it was mentioned early in the novel. Faced with the task of discovering an antidote, "Charles tried to look up his medical dictionary, but could not read it; the lines were jumping before his eyes" (231). Canivet and Homais, Bovary's consultants on the case, are also unqualified to treat Emma properly—the former because his knowledge of internal medicine is scant and the latter because he is a quack. The lack of professional competence at this point is critical: Canivet's prescription of an emetic actually hastens Emma's death, as we learn from Dr. Larivière's "severe lecture" to the surgeon after the event.

Charles's dictionary, then, thematizes the determinate absence of medical knowledge in *Madame Bovary.* This knowledge—a system of presuppositions about illness and death—seems to be precisely what the novel excludes. But the strange and innovative fact about Flaubert's novel is that, if Baudelaire's insight is correct, Emma's life is shaped by medical discourse's assumptions about hysteria, even though her death is caused by the discourse's absence. But what are these assumptions? More generally, what is their systematic form, and how does this discursive formation differ from the *ideological* system of clichéd presuppositions that Riffaterre describes?

Taking the second question first, one broad difference between ideology and discourse is that while ideological presuppositions form a part of a widely shared everyday knowledge, discursive assumptions are esoteric. It is difficult to pin down the location of an ideology, which exists as what Terry Eagleton calls "a consensus of unconscious valuations";[7] discourse, on the other hand, tends to nest within an institutional framework that at once delimits and supports it. A discursive practice will be organized not only textually or lexically (in dictionaries, manuals, handbooks, and encyclopedias), but also technologically and politically. To grasp the extent to which discourse is actualized in a literary text, one must thus look for two kinds of presuppositions: those conceptual presuppositions that constitute the discourse proper, and those institutional presuppositions that attend the discourse.

In the case of medical discourse, a very specific institutional environment—a new intellectual and professional hierarchy, a new disposition of duties and status— emerges during the early years of the nineteenth century. One question then is how, and to what extent, these kinds of rearrangements affect Flaubert's imagination of the world of *Madame Bovary.* Although they may seem merely sociological, I shall try to show that the emerging institutional presuppositions do in fact structure *Madame Bovary* to a great degree, by providing a double template of relations upon which Flaubert elaborates. In the first instance, explicit relations between characters within the text are determined by the disciplinary and institutional constraints of the medical profession at this time. But institutional presuppositions also inform a more fundamental, tacit formal relation in Flaubert's work—that between knowledge and bêtise.

The Uses of Medical Bêtise

The inept Charles Bovary is probably the most egregious example in this novel (and perhaps in any novel) of a character both socially and intellectually determined by the medical institutions of the time. His peculiar mediocrity stems, in fact, from his position within a complex professional hierarchy. Despite his honorific title, Doctor Charles Bovary is not a full-fledged doctor, but an *officier de santé*—a category of medical practitioner created during the early years of the Napoleonic era under the direction of the Ideologue physician and philosopher Cabanis.[8] The revolutionary period was marked by a rapid growth in the number of poorly trained army surgeons (for obvious reasons) and the abolition of the older, theoretically oriented *Facultés.* The latter were replaced, by 1795, by new learned societies like the *Société d'émulation,* which counted Bichat, Cabanis, and Pinel among its members. Under the external pressure of public demands for commissions to screen out quack surgeons, and the internal pressure of a newly emerging institutional structure of medical authority, a general reorganization of the profession occurred. It followed a path leading to greater centralization and technocratic efficiency. Cabanis was in the forefront of this drive toward rationalization. He proposed that because medicine was an industry whose products' value could not be gauged by the public— "what price health?"—the government should ensure the value of treatment by controlling the producers but not the product. Under his plan, access to the profession was to be limited, and less qualified physicians were to be supervised by an elite group of clinicians belonging to the learned societies.

As a result of these reforms, the terms of medical authority shifted as it expanded its jurisdiction. The old and bitter conflict between Parisian Faculté doctors and practical surgeons (a rivalry epitomized in *Madame Bovary* by the old surgeon Canivet's bitter remark about "the fads from Paris" propagated by "these gentlemen from the capital!" [131]) gave way, in 1803, to a new consolidation in the division of duties between experienced clinicians (usually located in large cities) and trained officiers de santé. The latter were certified, as is Charles, by department juries on the basis of a shorter course of study, and were allowed to practice only "simple procedures" in specified and restricted areas of the country. In effect, this was the first nationalized health planning, the first attempt to ensure minimal standards of care through a whole society by the controlled deployment of medical technique. It marked the first penetration by a centrally controlled medical perspective into the areas of everyday life that novelists like Balzac, George Eliot, and Flaubert were attempting to penetrate and oversee as realists.

Charles Bovary is caught up genealogically in the transformation of the medical profession—his father served as an assistant-surgeon-major under Napoleon—so that Charles's choice of career (made by his mother, to be sure) is logical: he is following in his father's footsteps. But the intellectual landscape itself has changed, along with the change in title from surgeon to officer of health. Charles, unlike his father, cannot get by only on the strength of his "devil of an arm for pulling teeth," nor can he confidently espouse the brutal surgical egotism of Canivet, who rejects the advanced medical procedures of "strabismus, chloroform, lithotrity" without having the slightest understanding of them (44, 131).[9] Charles, as an officier de santé, must have the slightest understanding, but that is all. Permitted to treat only "primitive accidents" and "simple indispositions," but required to pass an examination in order to do even that, the officier de santé is a subordinate within the new medical institution.

Above all, he is an intellectual subordinate in the new diagnostic and therapeutic paradigm represented by the medical dictionary. His is an empirically oriented training, a closed circuit of perception and treatment; as Foucault points out, for the officier de santé it is "a question of knowing what to do after seeing; experience was integrated at the level of perception, memory, and repetition, that is, at the level of the example."[10] The words that stun Charles when he begins his studies—*physiology, pharmacy, botany, clinical medicine, therapeutics, hygiene, materia medica*—remain "names of whose etymologies he was ignorant, and that were to him as so many doors to sanctuaries filled with magnificent darkness" (6). Instead of entering into the sacred temple of medicine (whose "godlike" authority is Charles's old master, the clinician Larivière), Charles enters into the profane hovels of the peasantry: "He poked his arm into damp beds, received the tepid spurt of bloodletting in his face, listened to death-rattles, examined basins, turned over a good deal of dirty line."[11] The senses—sight, sound, touch, and smell—are at work here, but little else.

It should be clear from all this why it would be absurd to expect Charles to grasp the higher mysteries of medicine. His very mode of perception, one grounded in repetition yet linked to a knowledge that transcends such activity, goes with the job created by the medical profession. Charles's mediocrity, in other words, is not useless, but is exactly what is called for: his docile repetition—emblematized by Flaubert very early on in the book by the image of "a mill-horse, who goes round and round with his eyes bandaged, not knowing what work it is grinding out" (7)—*does perform work.* This fact tends to get obscured in deconstructive readings of Flaubert, like those of Tony Tanner and Eugenio Donato, which interpret the repetition and turning in the text as purely degenerative processes that reduce all difference to indifferentiation.[12] Charles's repetition is a regularized professional behavior that is useful both to the profession and to its clients, despite its often destructive and dehumanizing effect on the individual involved in it. He does succeed, for instance, in setting Farmer Rouault's leg, even though he is simply repeating by rote: on arriving at the farm, "Charles awoke with a start, suddenly remembered the broken leg, and tried to call to mind all the fractures he knew." Even his bedside manner is an imitation—"calling to mind the devices of his masters at the bedside of patients, he comforted the sufferer with all sorts of kindly remarks" (11)—and yet he gains Rouault as a patient for official medicine, a small victory for the profession.

The military connotations of the word *victory* are far from inappropriate here, for if Charles, as an officier de santé, is a subordinate within the medical hierarchy, he is by the same token a footsoldier in the campaign to extend medical authority throughout the provinces of France. By the time Charles enters the profession, medicine has reorganized itself internally and has received some official backing for its project of controlling the national health care market. But state support is not absolute, and, especially at the local level, the standard-bearers of official medicine during this period find themselves competing with several other authorities for legitimate control of many of the same aspects of human behavior. More traditionally sanctioned authorities—in particular religious healers and unaccredited folk doctors—as well as the more recently established legal functionaries, all claim some responsibility for the same deviants.[13] The story told by Emma's maid—about a fisherman's daughter whose "fog in the head" was treated by priest, doctor, and customs officer—shows the professional polyvalence of illness (especially mental illness) in the nineteenth century.

Given this crowded field, it is easy to understand why the medical profession during this period propagates a mythical history to support its own claims. In such accounts, as Matthew Ramsey points out, "the contest between the physicians and their rivals sometimes appears as the heroic phase of professionalization, pitting medical enlightenment against popular superstition."[14] For the officier de santé, however, this mythical clarity has little to do with reality at the local level, where lines are not so clearly drawn. To consolidate his own position in the community, a country doctor like Charles is forced to develop a series of alliances, accommodations, and defensive tactics.

In the priest, the country doctor is faced with a rival who, like Abbé Bournisien with Hyppolite in *Madame Bovary,* promises a cure in exchange for vows of prayer and pilgrimage. Having little hope of winning in head-on anticlerical attacks of the kind made by the pharmacist Homais, the country doctor tends instead to accommodate the priest, accepting the notion that, as Bournisien remarks to Emma when she seeks help,

Charles "is doctor of the body . . . and I of the soul" (80). The result is a therapeutic regime in which, as Jacques Donzelot has pointed out, priest and doctor "occupied two clearly separate registers"[15] while attending to the same problem of pathology, whether physical, sexual, or mental.[16]

With respect to the other two nonscientific authorities, legal and pseudo-medical, the officier de santé faces a more serious problem. The law, in the form of the medical police, is supposedly allied with him in a joint effort to crush illegal healers. In fact, this program for achieving a professional monopoly remains largely unrealized at the local level: folk healing and charlatanism do not constitute regular targets for the police, despite the official mandate. Thus, the officer of health often finds himself in a dangerous economic struggle for patients against an opponent who tends to operate underground. To make matters worse, there is not that much of a difference in the level of skills possessed by doctors like Charles and quacks like the chemist Homais, even though the officer of health's knowledge is sponsored by official medicine with its more advanced cognitive base. Minimally accredited practitioners and charlatans use many of the same basic therapeutic techniques.[17]

Homais's relation to Charles, of course, graphically illustrates this situation and its hazards for the officier de santé. The apothecary, we learn early in the novel, "had infringed the law of the nineteenth Ventôse, year xi, article 1 [Cabanis was one of the principal architects of this legislation] which forbade all persons not having a diploma to practice medicine" (61). Homais is summoned to Rouen, but instead of being incarcerated he is merely reprimanded. Although the apothecary fears the power of the law ("he saw the depths of dungeons, his family in tears, his shop sold, all the jars dispersed . . ."), Flaubert emphasizes the merely symbolic nature of medicine's legal power by focusing on the trappings of authority: the prosecutor receives Homais "in his private office . . . standing up, ermine on shoulder and cap on head." These signs are without content, however, a fact that Flaubert underlines by adding pointedly that "it was in the morning, before the court opened."

Unfortunately for Dr. Bovary, the apothecary is not deterred for long by the scare he has received. He adapts to the reality of his position and undertakes a guerrilla war against a series of officiers de santé who attempt to occupy his territory in the name of official medicine. In this he is remarkably successful: Charles's predecessor runs away, Charles himself is ruined, and, on the last page of the novel, Flaubert informs us that "since Bovary's death three doctors have succeeded one another in Yonville without any success, so effectively did Homais hasten to eradicate them" (255).

GETTING HYPEREXCITABLE: EMMA'S HYSTERIA IN MEDICAL CONTEXT

Because he looks directly to a general-knowledge dictionary for ideological presuppositions, Riffaterre remains blind to these kinds of sociological and institutional determinants of textual situations. His approach remains a quite elegant and rigorous one, thanks to its semiotic insistence that context is another kind of text and its demand that textual presuppositions be studied as linguistic entities locatable in anonymous social texts such as dictionaries. But, as the example of medicine shows, some kinds of presuppositions are embedded in discrete social and institutional procedures, disciplines, and hierarchies. To describe the presuppositions of a discourse, then, one must take account of the kinds of verbal entailments noted by Riffaterre, but one also must address assumptions about power that are irreducible to the sheerly lexical dimension of a dictionary.

But what if the dictionary is of a kind that encapsulates not generally held beliefs but the knowledge of a discipline or profession? What would one find if one followed Riffaterre's directions and Baudelaire's intuition, cut the pages of Charles's *Dictionnaire de Médecine* and turned to the entry on hysteria? One would find there a long article containing the following information:

> The circumstances that most predispose a patient to hysteria are . . . a nervous constitution, her female sex and her age, between twelve and twenty-five or thirty years of age. . . . A majority have from a young age shown a disposition toward convulsive ailments, a melancholic, angry, passionate, impatient character. . . . Exciting causes, more specifically, are morally powerful ailments [including] unrequited love, . . . acute disturbances of the soul, . . . a violent fit of jealousy, . . . powerful grief, . . . acute disappointment. . . . The nervous constitution and the unhealthy condition that precede and facilitate the development of attacks are caused by excessive masturbation.[18]

For a reader of Flaubert, the content of this entry is striking, for it describes Emma Bovary's condition quite accurately: her tendency to convulsive affections from an early age is shown by Flaubert in the flashback to her convent days, when "her nature, positive in the midst of its enthusiasms" (28), had led her to devotional excesses; every word used to define the "hysterical character" is also used at some point in the novel to refer to Emma; she falls into fits after she suffers various emotional shocks—for example, her violent chagrin at Rodolphe's letter or her dread of imminent bankruptcy after he turns down her request for money; and her nervous constitution, although not directly attributable to masturbation, is directly alluded to by herself, by Charles, and even by Larivière.

To point out that Emma acts like an hysteric, however, is to do no more than Baudelaire did one hundred years ago. One needs to clarify the extent of this analogy. Is

Flaubert borrowing only the overt representations or symptoms of hysteria, or is he also making use in some way of the logical and rhetorical presuppositions peculiar to clinical medicine? To answer this question requires taking a short detour to elucidate these presuppositions, with their complex interplay—evident in the entry just cited—among terms such as *predisposition, character, constitution,* and *exciting causes.*

The particular figure of hysteria, together with the conceptualization of disease in general, changes enormously between roughly 1780 and 1810, the period coinciding with the emergence of the twin disciplines of modern clinical medicine and morbid anatomy under Bichat's leadership. In the earlier eighteenth-century paradigm, medical classification tends to characterize disease according to two distinct systems of causation: one internal and animistic, relying on the notion of *temperament,* the other mechanistic and external, resting on the principle of *constitutional sympathy.* One can illustrate the concurrence of these two etiological factors by examining how hysteria is conceptualized before Bichat's time. Eighteenth-century nosographers, following the great English physician Sydenham's example, regard hysteria as an endogenous, essentially psychosomatic disease growing out of a mutually reinforcing imbalance between bodily fluids (or "vital spirits," in the Cartesian system) and the passions. This etiology, in turn, depends on the ancient medical concept of "temperament," which originally designates the particular mixture of humors in an individual, but that in the eighteenth century begins to refer to the relation between emotions and the body. As the historian Paul Hoffmann has pointed out, this reduction of hysteria to a problem of temperament condemns the female hysteric of the period to be "la prisonnière d'une sort de causalité réciproque, qui joue entre les esprits et l'esprit, entre la passion et le corps."[19]

During the same period, however, a second causal basis for hysteria is articulated by early, mechanistically oriented neurologists, who correlate the disease with a supposed qualitative effect on nervous fibers by climate, diet, and other so-called "non-naturals." Abrupt or capricious changes in the weather, the reasoning goes, communicate sympathetically with the body's fibers, gradually softening or moistening them until they completely dissolve and hysterical fits occur. Rameau's nephew repeatedly invokes this meteorological etiology, blaming the "maudites circonstances" of a "nature bévue" that "grimaced, then grimaced again and again," communicating its distortion to the nephew and leaving him as a "misshapen image" with unstrung fibers.[20] Philological evidence allows us to date this medical appropriation of climatic factors: the word *constitution,* originally used to describe the state of the atmosphere (*constitution atmosphérique*), comes at this time to stand for the observable and statistically tabulated rapport between environment and pathology.

Preclinical medicine thus understands disease as caused by the passions (through temperamental imbalance) as well as the environment (through constitutional sympathies). Not until after the emergence of pathological anatomy and clinical medicine in the early years of the nineteenth century, however, are the two causal networks linked. The key conceptual development for the emergence of clinical discourse is the elaboration of the concept of "sensitivity." Defined as the involuntary but active response by an organism to a positive stimulus, sensitivity becomes for nineteenth-century clinicians the sine qua non for gauging the condition of a living being. Bichat's contemporary, Cabanis, sums up the new centrality of this concept by paraphrasing Descartes: "Vivre, c'est sentir [To live is to feel]."[21]

When sensitivity becomes the primary property of living beings, the central terms of eighteenth-century pathology—*temperament* and *constitution*—are semantically transformed. Temperament, which previously signified a quantitative balance of fluids or spirits, is redefined as the spatial organization of sensitivity, the three-dimensional relationship between "centers" of sensitivity within the body. "The difference of temperaments," according to Cabanis, "depends upon the difference of centers of sensitivity, of relationships of strength, weakness or sympathetic communications among various organs."[22]

In medical discourse, the temperament thus comes to be the expression of "primitive functions" of sensitivity at work inside and between organs, in what Bichat calls the "organic life" of the individual. But sensitivity is not limited to the internal viscera, the organic life, alone; it is also affected by the relations established between a creature and its environment. This second set of relations constitutes what Bichat christens "animal life." Animal life differs from organic life in that its condition is open to some change under the control of the creature. Unlike organic life, which allocates its forces of sensitivity at birth, animal life has at its disposition a "somme déterminée de force," a vital force that can be channeled by the will or by external stimuli into the development of sensitivity in one organ or another.[23]

Finally, in Bichat's new framework, the term *constitution* ceases to refer to a sympathetic or qualitative similarity between the body's fibers and the external environment. Instead, an individual's constitution is to be understood as the total structure of sensitivities—a complex, constantly evolving web of "rapports" between the fixed temperament of the organic life and the variable pressures of the animal life. The web metaphor will be taken up self-consciously and in great detail by

George Eliot in *Middlemarch,* as we shall see, but a second metaphor growing out of this new conceptualization of the self-as-constitution is equally popular both in medicine and in nineteenth-century culture. In this other metaphor, the constitution represents the results of what might be thought of as an investment policy pursued by an individual using his or her vital force as a kind of capital. A wise (or lucky) investor, understanding that limited funds set limits to the possible development of organs, will prudently invest vital capital in those organs whose sensitivity needs strengthening if they are to perform the tasks imposed on them by the individual's situation. What this metaphor makes clear is that, from the medical point of view, there can be no such thing as a Renaissance man with a constitution for all seasons; on the contrary, specialization is quite literally a fact of life. Any organ's gain in power can only be achieved at the expense of another organ, a dilemma pointedly illustrated by Bichat's remark that "on châtre les hommes pour changer leur voix."[24]

As this specific example indicates, the investment capital of vital force easily can be, and to some degree is, identified with sexual force. The concrete form of sexual force (at least for men), seminal fluid, comes to stand for vital force just as money stands for capital. Of course, as Shakespeare's sonnet 129 shows, the belief that "Th' expense of spirit in a waste of shame / Is lust in action" had long been a popularly established notion. In nineteenth-century culture, however, a veritable obsession arises over the dangers of excessive sexual "spending," an obsession marked by the growth of a rhetoric of sexual economics that has been well documented by modern critics.[25] The nineteenth-century interest in this topic, I would argue, derives at least in part from the medical identification of the sexual with the vital, and the subsequent warnings to the public about the dangers of "les pertes seminales," the title of a popular book by the French physician Lallemand.[26] A strong constitution means a strong bodily economy, and requires the investment of vital force in organs, not its exhaustion in sexual expenditure.

Masturbation, which weakens the constitution by siphoning off necessary funds of energy, thus begins to be cited in treatises and medical dictionary entries as a predisposing factor for hysteria. To see how the conceptual field underlying hysteria has been altered with the effect of opening up a place for sexuality and masturbation, one need only compare the medical dictionary quoted above, which dates from 1820, with the following quotation from a medical textbook published in 1775: "The exacerbation of desires evidenced in masturbation, adultery, etc., which is one of the signs of hysteria, *is not a cause,* but is the effect of the repercussion of a disordered movement of the spirits upon the organs of generation" [my italics].[27] Only when all the terms used here have been replaced—*spirits* by *sensi-*

tivity, movement of spirits by *vital force, disordered movement* by what Pinel's successor Georget will call *hyperexcitability*[28]—will sexual activity cease to represent the *result* of a preexistent, direct sympathy between environmental and physical "disorder," and begin to appear as a contributing *cause* of hysteria.

By Freud's time, the sexual drive will have subsumed all other forms of vital force as a causal factor in hysteria, which itself will be reconceived as a phenomenon of the unconscious. Insofar as Freud's work accomplishes the transformation of the term vital force into sexuality, it is the culmination of a century-long tendency within the paradigm of pathological anatomy to equate the sexual with the vital: indeed, as early as 1853, four years before *Madame Bovary* is published, the English physician Robert Brudenell Carter already defines hysteria as a faulty "discharge" of "the sexual passion" in fits rather than in the service of reproduction.[29] Carter's work, however, is at the cutting edge of its time, and far from representative; for most clinicians, sexuality constituted only one among many causes of hysteria.

Pinpointing the status of sexuality in nineteenth-century medical explanations of hysteria, although interesting in itself (and even salutary, insofar as it historicizes what is all too often defined—especially in feminist criticism—as a sexual disease *tout court*), would be out of place here, however, if it did not help clarify how Flaubert imagines Emma Bovary's sexuality and its relationship to her illness. Masturbation cannot be represented in fiction during this period, but Flaubert seems to go further than he needs to in actively resisting any reduction of Emma's desire to sexual desire. Neither marriage nor adultery are seen by him as adequate outlets for what ails Emma—and this is not because she is sexually insatiable, but because it is her vital force, not her sexuality, that is constitutionally flawed. Ten years after Madame Bovary, her guttersnipe cousin, Zola's Thérèse Raquin, will suffer from a passion almost exclusively sexual, so much so that Henry James complains about Zola's tendency "to leave out the life of the soul, practically, and confine himself to the life of the instincts, the more immediate passions, such as can be easily and promptly sought in the fact."[30] For Flaubert, like Bichat and Cabanis, the two lives of the soul and the body—in medical parlance, the "moral" and the "physique," or the organic and animal lives—coexist in a tissue of rapports, irreducible to a sexual drive, which constitute the self.

Two important consequences follow from this tissular view of the embodied person, consequences evident both in nineteenth-century clinical medicine and in Flaubert's conception of character. First, one's constitution can no longer be attributed to the immediate, aleatory effects of external environmental causes (as in

Rameau's Nephew), nor can it yet be seen as an effect of the internal repression of sexuality. In Flaubert's late short story, "Saint Julien L'hospitalier," both these hypotheses about the cause of Julien's sickly constitution are explicitly advanced so as to be rejected: "Le mal de Julien," his doctors assert, "avait pour cause un vent funeste, ou un désir d'amour. Mais le jeune homme, à toutes les questions, sécouait la tête."[31] In *Madame Bovary,* similarly, the weather is a constant presence, but its moods never directly mirror the state of Emma's soul, as would be the case in a typical romantic novel.[32] For example, throughout the novel, wind blows—from the breath that raises the tissue paper covering an engraving in one of the earliest views of Emma, to the whirlwind that rises in Emma's soul as she feels herself approaching madness, to the gust that blows away a maiden's skirt in the blind tramp's final obscene song— yet Emma's psyche only registers an indirect effect at most. The fog in Emma's head, unlike the chaotic fibers in Rameau's nephew's brain, is not created by a single atmospheric imprinting.

Instead (and this is the second consequence of the new conception of the self in nineteenth-century medicine), the development or formation of a constitution must take place through a long, drawn-out, incremental process of stimulation from within and without. Stimuli or desires may act upon the embodied self, but they cannot act directly and cataclysmically. A kind of "interior distance" (to borrow a phrase from Georges Poulet) exists within everyone. This *medical* interiority, however, is not a pure, phenomenologically certain locus for the cogito, as Poulet would have it, but a highly organized and evolving system. Every impulse of vital force from the will or stimulus from the environment is disseminated through a network of various centers of sensibility and thus each stimulus can modify the whole only slightly.

In the case of hysteria, the constitution is thought to undergo four distinct steps in its slow process of pathological formation.[33] To grasp these four stages, one might think of them as material analogs to the four tropes of metaphor, metonymy, synecdoche, and irony, whose sequence Hayden White has proposed as providing a framework for the overall narrative movement of Flaubert's *L'Education sentimentale.*[34] In the first stage, a stimulus from passion or the environment is transmitted to the cerebral cortex, in a kind of metaphorical translation. Next, the force of sensation, having arrived in the brain, is relayed to the brain's different centers of sensibility, as significance would be relayed metonymically. Third, the organs of the brain in turn affect the whole range of bodily organs by means of what one important physician terms "interior sensibility," a radiating effect similar to what is said to occur semantically in synecdoche. Gradually, the various parts of the body accumulate sensitivity, until they are saturated, reaching

a state of "hyperexcitability" in which any stimulation whatsoever is intolerable. At this point, in the fourth and last stage of the development of an hysteric's constitution, the system of rapports connecting the nervous system has become a collection of "hyperexcitable" components, an ironic (but literal and material) dissociation of sensibility that predisposes the patient to suffer hysterical attacks at the slightest provocation.[35]

Emma's development follows these steps, and more generally, all Flaubert's characters exhibit complex constitutions. Flaubert, of course, does not use the medical terms I have been describing. Rather, he translates these terms into metaphysical and psychological ones more appropriate to the novel, while retaining clinical medicine's conceptual structure and emphasis on embodied sensation. For the physical constitution he substitutes memory; for the centers of sensibility or intellectual functions deployed through the body or brain, he substitutes the representations of which memory consists; and for vital force, he substitutes desire.

The Flaubertian self, in other words, is readable as a complex psychophysiological "constitution," a constantly evolving relation between present sensation and an always already existing set of memories. At moments when the interchange between sensation and memory becomes problematic—for example, during the transition between consciousness and sleep, or during a hallucination—the Flaubertian self can disintegrate into independent sets of memories (equivalent to the different functions into which the hysteric's constitution ironically breaks down during a fit). Dissociation, for Flaubert, is inherent in the human condition, not only a problem for sensitive types or women. It affects all his characters, even those as dull-witted and boringly masculine as Charles Bovary: "Charles from time to time opened his eyes but his mind grew weary, and sleep coming upon him, he soon fell into a doze wherein his recent sensations blending with memories, he became conscious of a double self, at once student and married man, lying in his bed as but now, and crossing the operation theatre as of old" (9).[36]

Whether overtly pathologized or not, then, the Flaubertian self is thus neither given nor unitary. And, as with a medical constitution, this self is capable of slow drifts into decomposition or transformation. As memory erodes or shifts, Flaubert's characters find themselves changing as well, sometimes even in spite of their efforts to avoid such a change. Charles, for example, finds that "while continually thinking of Emma, he was nevertheless forgetting her. He grew desperate as he felt this image fading from his memory in spite of all efforts to retain it" (252). Beyond and sometimes in spite of intention, memory (like the physical constitution) adjusts and reconstitutes itself.

Such are the vicissitudes of every embodied memory. For those who become ill, however, memory does not merely adjust, but develops in the same way that a patient's physical constitution does. In the case of hysteria, Emma does what Freud and Breuer will later say all hysterics do: she "suffers mainly from reminiscences."[37] Flaubert once described his own hysteria as "an illness of memory,"[38] and he anticipates Freud in psychologizing the disease. But Flaubert's presuppositions are Bichatian rather than Freudian, and Emma's illness follows a different course than does that of Dora. Emma's stages of consciousness correspond at a mental level to the four-stage series described above. These four steps occur again and again in a kind of cyclical spiral, each time preparing Emma's mental constitution for its recurrent disintegration in hysterical fits.

Because the first three steps toward constitutional hypersensitivity tend to resolve themselves in most instances without causing any dramatic breakdown of the self, these formative or "predisposing" steps are best observed in local instances such as paragraphs and brief episodes, rather than in the broad arc of narrative. A close reading of such passages—whose free indirect style takes us into Emma's consciousness—shows how the kind of language Flaubert uses to describe Emma's tug-of-war between sensations and memories contains the tropes one would expect for each stage of her developing hysteria. Like every medically defined person, Emma incorporates experience into memory by first metaphorically converting her sensation into feeling, then extending that feeling metonymically in imagination, and finally dissipating it in a plethora of representations stretching synecdochically through her memory as a whole.

Metaphors are sown most thickly in *Madame Bovary* where Emma's sensibility responds to an influx of sensations. The metaphors in this gorgeous paragraph, for example, seem intended to imitate Emma's consciousness during the first moments after sex:

> The shades of night were falling; the horizontal sun passing between the branches dazzled the eyes. Here and there around in the leaves or on the ground, trembled luminous patches, as if humming-birds flying about had scattered their feathers. Silence was everywhere; something sweet seemed to come forth from the trees. She felt her heartbeat return, and the blood coursing through her flesh like a river of milk. Then far away, beyond the wood, on the other hills, she heard a vague prolonged cry, a voice which lingered, and in silence she heard it mingling like music with the last pulsations of her throbbing nerves.
>
> (116)[39]

Within the space of three sentences, Flaubert packs three distinct metaphors, each addressing a different sense, as if to emphasize the dominance of sensation

within Emma's consciousness at this stage.[40] A similar transfusion of excitement, and one that is more clearly followed by a psychological retrenchment, occurs when Emma incorporates her experience at the Vaubyessard ball. In her first encounter with luxury, she is overwhelmed by the vivid sensations, which cancel (or at least obscure by their intensity) her previous memories: "In the splendor of the present hour her past life, so distinct until then, faded away completely, and she almost doubted having lived it. She was there; beyond the ball was only shadow overspreading all the rest."[41] On her return home, we later learn, "she devoutly put away in her drawers her beautiful dress, down to the satin shoes whose soles were yellowed with the slippery wax of the dancing floor. Her heart resembled them: in its contact with wealth, something had rubbed off on it that could not be removed." This simile signals the onset of an obsession: "The memory of this ball, then, became an occupation for Emma." In clinical terms, one would say that a sensation has made its way into Emma's cerebral centers of sensibility and has begun to work upon them.

Once Emma's sensation has been received, medical discourse teaches, its force need not remain bound to the representation that originally carried it. Like all direct impressions, Emma's images of the ball soon fade, as Charles's image of Emma fades: "Little by little the faces grew confused in her remembrance. She forgot the tune of the quadrilles [like the music that mingles with her nerves during her seduction by Rodolphe in the passage quoted earlier, this music has been absorbed into her nervous system]; she no longer saw the liveries and the guest-houses so distinctly; some of the details faded but the wistful feeling remained with her" (40). Emma's desire, like the power of sensibility or a vital force that can be aroused by a stimulus, then becomes capable of being redirected metonymically onto other memories, that is, other images. In this second phase, Emma seeks imaginary satisfaction for her own desires. Like her lover, Léon, who in her absence displaces his passion for her onto other objects, Emma applies this wistful feeling—the echo of her sensation, as it were—to substitute objects like the Vicomte's cigar box, whose odors and needlework reactivate sensation on an imaginary plane. This strategy of metonymic displacement of psychic force from physical to imaginary objects is effective, at least in the short run: "The memory of the Viscount always cropped up in everything she read. She made comparisons between him and the fictional characters in her books. But the circle of which he was the centre gradually widened round him, and the aureole that he bore, fading from his form and extending beyond his image, lit up her other dreams" (41).[42] Unfortunately, Emma's psychic energy has been invested in mere representations that in being extended synecdochically, always dissipate that energy: "At the end of some indefinite distance there was always a confused spot, into which her dream died." In the same way, the vital force of a future hysteric remains unfocused and simply fans out into the confusion of the body's or brain's organization, where it raises the general level of hyperexcitability. Prolonged imaginary investment leads, that is, to what Flaubert describes in Emma as "an expansion of selfishness, of nervous irritation," as her stock of energy is exhausted without return in the form of any new sensation: "Each morning, as she awoke, she hoped it would come that day; she listened to every sound, sprang up with a start, wondered that it did not come; then at sunset, always more saddened, she longed for the next day." As Emma's extreme responsiveness to the slightest sound shows, she has become saturated with hyperexcitability. Given her condition, Flaubert's next two sentences come as no surprise: "Spring came round. With the first warm weather, when the pear-trees began to blossom, she had fainting spells" (45).

What *is* surprising about Flaubert's description of Emma's breakdown is his insistence, at a moment of crisis for his heroine, on noting even the most minute specifications of the environmental conditions—"when the pear-trees began to blossom"—attending this event. The detail here could perhaps point to the pathos in Emma's situation: spring, which should bring love, instead yields only a nervous breakdown. But then why pear-trees, specifically? One answer commonly given is that the obsession with detail *qua* detail defines Flaubert's realism. As Jonathan Culler has argued, Flaubert's details, unlike those of his predecessor Balzac, do not lend themselves to symbolic recuperation, at least not in a fully satisfying way.[43] They supposedly work instead to produce what Barthes calls "l'effet de réel," a sense of sheer, unmotivated *thereness.* But if they are symbolically unrecuperated, Flaubert's descriptions remain, I would suggest, *discursively* recuperated, just as his characterizations are.[44] Flaubert's choice of descriptive techniques, in other words, is a second major consequence of his adopting a medical point of view. To see why this should be so, we need to note that Bichat's clinical notion of the self as a complex constitution implies that it will always be hard to determine which specific stimulus causes a predisposed constitution to go over the edge into actual breakdown. When all the centers of sensibility have become hyperexcitable, the "threshold of sensibility" drops so low that even sound or odor can trigger an attack. In such cases, as one prominent physician of the time cautions, it is often "impossible to find the immediate cause" of the breakdown.[45]

Because of this proliferation of possible exciting causes, the clinician must deepen his observation and analysis of the patient's environment to include the most trivial details if he wishes to fully understand how the disease progresses. This new epistemological imperative in medicine expresses itself in the emergence of the modern case study, which replaces the older, eighteenth-century record that correlated disease with statistical information about environmental conditions. In the case study, as opposed to the earlier mode of analysis, details provide the doctor with a web of possible connections, some spurious, some significant, that he must weave and unweave in order to make sense of the patient's illness.[46]

Merely accumulating details would be a waste of time, of course, if the physician had no epistemological guide to the pathways of illness within the body. Such a guide is provided by the new discipline of pathological anatomy, whose founder, Bichat, catalogues the various ways in which different "concatenations of phenomena" can lead to death, or more generally to the onset of an illness. In his masterpiece, *Recherches sur la vie et la mort* (a book with which Flaubert was familiar), Bichat illustrates the diagnostic implications of pathological anatomy with an example that is strikingly appropriate to *Madame Bovary*: "The simple action of a poisonous substance on the nerves of the lungs can have a very marked effect on the [physical] economy, and is even capable of disturbing its functions in a palpable way: somewhat like an odour, which striking simply upon the pituitary, acts sympathetically upon the heart, and determines the occurrence of a fit; just as the view of a hideous object produces the same effect."[47] A good doctor, Bichat concludes, must collect his details and observations carefully to have any chance of distinguishing between attacks caused physically by odor and those induced psychologically by the view of an object arousing strong emotions.

Madame Bovary teaches Bichat's lesson, using the exact same example. In the episode that culminates in Emma's hysterical fit, she receives a farewell letter from her lover, Rodolphe, hidden in a basket of fruit sent to the Bovarys as a going-away present. The shock of discovery about Rodolphe's infidelity raises Emma's sensitivity to its height, but she controls herself enough to come down to dinner. At the dinner table, however, Charles encourages her to taste the fruit, unaware of her hyperexcitability at the moment:

> "Smell them! Such perfume!" he insisted, moving it back and forth under her nose.

> "I am choking," she exclaimed, leaping up.

> By sheer willpower, she succeeded in forcing back the spasm.

> "It is nothing," she said, "it is nothing! Just nerves. Sit down and eat."

> For she dreaded most of all that he would question her, try to help and not leave her to herself.

> Charles, to obey her, sat down again, and he spat the stones of the apricots into his hands, afterwards putting them on his plate.

Suddenly a blue tilbury passed across the square at a
rapid trot. Emma uttered a cry and fell back rigid on
the floor.[48]

(150)

Like Bichat, Flaubert offers two alternative causes of
Emma's fit—either the odor of the fruit or the view of a
hideous object (the tilbury is Rodolphe's). Moreover,
Flaubert's laconic transcription of the events leading up
to Emma's syncope follows the epistemological rules of
a good case history: it does not attempt to judge causes
but only to describe as faithfully as possible the details,
both psychic and physical, that might be taken as causes
of Emma's attack. Although Flaubert weights the evidence in favor of a psychic causation by making the
physical apricots themselves into psychically "horrify-
ing objects" for Emma, who links them with the letter
she has just received, the novelist is careful to record
the temporal proximity linking the smell of fruit with
Emma's sensation of choking (a symptom that our
medical dictionary of the period tells us marks the preliminary stage of an hysterical paroxysm), so that we
are forced to consider the odor as data. Just as in the
passage quoted earlier—which associated the blossoming of pear-trees with Emma's fainting spells, but only
did so by contiguity, so here Flaubert registers the possible exciting causes, leaving to the reader the task of
determining which details are significant.

Flaubert, however, does more than simply observe with
what Freud would later formalize as *gleichschwebende
Aufmerksamkeit,* poised attention. He seems to go out
of his way to present Emma with possible exciting sensations, odors to sniff and fantasize upon, from "the
mystic languor that exhales from the perfume on the altar," to the Vicomte's cigar box, to the Oriental pastilles
she burns after she shuts herself up in her room. By
adopting a pathologist's attitude toward his heroine,
Flaubert ironically fulfills the wish expressed by Homais, who, upon learning that Emma had been smelling
apricots when she was stricken, remarks fatuously:
"Some people are so terribly sensitive to certain odours.
The subject would well repay study, in its pathological
no less than its physiological aspects."[49] As usual, Homais is pseudomedical, as well as behind the times, for
such studies were well under way by Flaubert's time, as
the quotation from Bichat shows. Doctors increasingly
sought not merely to observe symptoms and understand
the factors leading to the formation of a pathological
constitution, but also to manipulate the environment so
as to experimentally induce pathological effects on the
bodies of their patients. In this regard, Homais mentions a Pavlovian-like dog that "goes off into a fit if
anyone holds out a snuff-box to him," a susceptibility
that the dog's owner has "often demonstrated experimentally in the presence of friends." In the notes of one
of Charcot's students, an exact human counterpart to
this demonstration is recorded: "The subject exhibits

hysterical spasms; Charcot suspends an attack by placing first his hand, then the end of a baton, on the woman's ovaries. He withdraws the baton, and there is a
fresh attack, *which he accelerates by administering in-
halations of amyl nitrate.* The afflicted woman then
cries out for the sex-baton in words that are devoid of
any metaphor: 'G. is taken away and her delirium
continues.'"[50] Homais's overall response to Emma's seizure registers in parody the tactics of nineteenth-century
therapists. He recognizes that "it is quite possible that
the apricots caused the syncope," that odors act by stu-
pefying the senses, and that women's greater sensitivity
makes them more susceptible to "irregularities of the
nervous system." At the same time, he imitates Charcot,
trying to make Emma "come to" by using aromatic vinegar. Unfortunately, this smelling salt had been declared
totally ineffective in reviving patients in a treatise on
hysteria written in 1850. Homais's other suggestions for
treatment continue the medical charade. He recommends
the administration of sedatives, emollients, pacifiers,
and a strict diet. None of these therapeutic steps requires any special medical skill, and each has the added
advantage of requiring drugs sold at the chemist's own
shop. These treatments at least correspond to medically
approved efforts to suppress the somatic causes of hyperexcitability. But Homais's final suggestion is beyond
the competence of both the chemist and the officier de
santé:

> Then, don't you think we might attack the imagina-
> tion?
>
> —In what way? How? said Bovary.
>
> —Ah! That is the question! That is, indeed, the ques-
> tion! *"C'est là la question!"* as someone said in the
> newspaper the other day.
>
> But at this point Emma, waking up, shouted, "The let-
> ter! The letter!"
>
> They thought she was delirious; by midnight she *was*
> delirious; she was declared to have brain fever.[51]

Emma offers the clinically correct answer to Charles's
question about how to work on the imagination, but unfortunately neither Charles nor Homais know how to
read her delirium (Homais's reading, in fact, is limited
to the newspaper, while Charles, as we have seen, never
reads the medical dictionary). They see no clear connection between words and the imagination, and can
think of no way to prevent brain fever by manipulating
the representations available to the patient. Pre-Freudian
analysts of hysteria, on the other hand, *did* see a connection between reading and illness. Exposure to the
wrong kinds of representations, Georget warns, can increase the danger that dangerously heightened emotions
will be brought to bear on the constitutions of those
who, like young women, are already naturally weak:
"En résumé, une jeune femme de la bonne société, de
constitution nerveuse, n'accomplissant pas de travaux

manuels et menant une vie oisive entre les concerts et la lecture des romans, est le sujet idéal, prédisposé à l'hystérie."[52]

The moral therapy initiated by Pinel in France and by the Tuke brothers in England, although not firmly grounded theoretically in the conceptual field of official clinical medicine, did offer doctors specific ways of attacking the imagination by controlling access to the letter, and indeed to any stimulus whatsoever. Some of these techniques, in fact, find their way into Charles's medical dictionary, which counsels that

> To prevent the onset of hysteria, the following treatments are prescribed: exercise, manual labour, the study of natural science, continual occupation of the mind; in addition, one should avoid all occasions and anything that may be the cause of exalting the imagination, exciting the passions, and filling the head with illusions and chimaeras; one should also prevent dreams and of course the habit of masturbation.

Emma never undergoes such rehabilitation in any thorough way, and when she does go out for exercise—at Charles's suggestion, to improve her health!—she becomes involved in an affair with Rodolphe that exalts her imagination even further. Flaubert seems to imply that Emma's vexed relationship to her representations would not have been adequately dealt with by the moral treatment.[53] Far from undermining the connection between Flaubert's work and medical discourse, however, Flaubert's rejection of this method of treatment only confirms that his concept of hysteria involves a more complex, more *anatomical* notion of imagination and memory than that entertained by the moral managers and psychiatrists. His medical genealogy, that is to say, stems from Bichat and Cabanis rather than from Pinel.

THE AUTHOR AS CLINICIAN: SITUATING FLAUBERTIAN REALISM

Flaubert thus integrates medical presuppositions into his writing to an extraordinary degree and in extremely complex ways. He does not, however, "actualize" them in Riffaterre's sense. They do not provide a linear series of consequences forming the plot of *Madame Bovary* (as Riffaterre's presuppositions about adultery do). Rather, these medical presuppositions are taken up by Flaubert as directives about technique: in characterization, for instance, where Flaubert is guided by the medical presupposition that the individual develops as a complexly embodied constitution; or in description, where the novelist accepts the medical presupposition that alternative causes must be considered during diagnosis of hysterical attacks. More generally, *Madame Bovary* marks the emergence of a mode of writing in which the real has become medical, in which the relation between author and text is modeled on medical precepts, with the author viewing characters and situations as a doctor views patients and cases.

But stating things in this way raises further questions about the role and status of the author within the intertextual field of discourses. Why does Flaubert rely on medical discourse, rather than, say, legal, or religious, or military discourse? More specifically, why does he make Emma an hysteric? And why does he write about a situation in which that discourse is posed as unavailable, so that Emma is not treated effectively?

I will conclude by sketching out two broad answers to these questions. Both involve the internal hierarchy and social status of medicine discussed in the first half of the chapter. One answer is biographical, concerning Flaubert's personal encounter with hysteria and with the medical profession; the other is sociological, concerning the historical situation of the profession of literature within a society in which the profession of medicine also was evolving.

One fact about the concept of hysteria not yet mentioned is that in nineteenth-century medicine, hysteria and epilepsy are gender variants of the same basic disorder of the constitution. In fact, Flaubert himself suffered from a nervous condition that was diagnosed as "hystero-epilepsy." Determining what Flaubert's disease really was, an old and hoary issue in Flaubert criticism, is irrelevant here.[54] But it *is* relevant that Flaubert perceived his own illness in the terms provided by nineteenth-century clinical medicine, and in particular by his own father, Dr. Achille-Cléophas Flaubert, who studied under Bichat as well as under the great surgeon Dupuytren and who treated Flaubert.

That Flaubert understands his own form of hysteria in the clinical terms his father must have used is evident from his account of one seizure in a letter to Louise Colet:

> Each attack was like a hemorrhage of the nervous system. Seminal losses from the pictorial faculty of the brain, a hundred thousand images cavorting at once in a kind of fireworks. It was a snatching of the soul from the body, excruciating. (I am convinced I died several times.) But what constitutes the personality, the rational essence, was present throughout; had it not been, the suffering would have been nothing, for I would have been purely passive, whereas I was always conscious even when I could no longer speak.[55]

In another letter, Flaubert repeats the same image used here, describing how "sometimes, within the space of a single second, I have been aware of a thousand thoughts, images and associations of all kinds illuminating my brain like so many brilliant fireworks" (letter to Louise Colet, Tues., 6 July 1852). The grafting of medical or scientific terms ("seminal losses," "pictorial faculty of the brain") with psychic terms ("images," "soul," "rational essence") shows Flaubert's tendency to translate freely between medical and psychological codes.

Equally important, however, such passages provide direct evidence that Flaubert understands Emma by projecting his own experience onto her. The metaphor of fireworks, for example, turns up in his description of Emma's hallucination as well as of his own:

> She remained lost in stupor, and only conscious of herself through the beating of her arteries, that seemed to burst forth like a deafening music filling all the fields. The earth beneath her feet was more yielding than the sea, and the furrows seemed to her immense brown waves breaking into foam. All the memories and ideas that crowded her head seemed to explode at once like a thousand pieces of fireworks. She saw her father, Lheureux's closet, their room at home, another landscape. Madness was coming upon her.
>
> (228)[56]

Emma's dementia, one should note, involves an inverted, ironic return of the kind of metaphorizing that characterized her perception after intercourse with Rodolphe. Here, the music and her veins seem to explode from within, and the hyperconsciousness implied by the earlier metaphors gives way to its opposite, stupor. In the present context, however, what is most striking about this passage is that Emma's symptoms are an almost verbatim transcription of Flaubert's.[57]

Perhaps this symptomatic identification between novelist and character is what Flaubert had in mind when he remarked that "Madame Bovary, c'est moi." Certainly Flaubert was eminently qualified to portray Emma's fate from the point of view of a patient. Yet, at the same time, Flaubert also adopts the point of view of a doctor, with respect to his own illness and that of his characters, thinking in the terms and with the diagnostic presuppositions of a clinician.

Flaubert's peculiar experience of illness both as delirium and as knowledge deeply informs *Madame Bovary*. More generally, this same experience constitutes the phenomenological root of the bifurcated style that Albert Thibaudet, among others, sees as the essence of Flaubertian realism.[58] The novelist himself recognized that in the act of writing he became, in his own words, "literarily speaking, two distinct persons: one who is infatuated with bombast, lyricism, eagle flights, sonorities of phrase and lofty ideas; and another who digs and burrows into the truth as deeply as he can, who likes to treat a humble fact as respectfully as a big one, who would like to make you feel almost physically the things he reproduces." Traditionally, this passage has been adduced as evidence of Flaubert's vacillation between two styles, one romantic and the other analytic. Given what we now know about Flaubert, however, it may be more appropriate to speak not of romantic and analytic, but of hysterical and medical perspectives in tension. The hysterical aspect of Flaubert's prose appears in what he calls the "throbbing of sentences and the seething of

metaphors," stylistic events that, like the river of milk Emma feels in her veins, "flow from one another like a series of cascades, carrying the reader along." The medical side of Flaubert's style is evident from the anatomical and surgical implications of the second half of the quotation above, and can be supplemented by Flaubert's aspiration in another letter for "a style that would be precise as the language of the sciences . . . a style that would pierce your idea like a dagger."

Prescient in this as in so many other things, Sainte-Beuve was the first to recognize the predominance of the anatomical element in Flaubert's style, in the now-famous remark that "M. Flaubert wields the pen as others do the scalpel." The critic also recognized that to write in that way was "a sign of enormous power." We can now specify the nature of that medical power and the way in which it is exercised. It is the power to act upon, to control, and ultimately to constitute its intellectual object—the embodied self—without coming into direct contact with it or even being visible to it. Flaubert's ideal of stylistic power is exactly this kind of medical panopticism: "an author in his book must be like God in the universe, present everywhere and visible nowhere. Art being a second nature, the creator of that nature must behave similarly" (letter to Louise Colet, 9 Dec. 1852).

Certainly, as the plight of Charles Bovary's unread medical dictionary shows, the medical perspective of the author is visible nowhere in the world represented in *Madame Bovary*—or almost nowhere, for there is one competent medical figure who does appear at the end of the novel (although too late to redeem the world and save the doomed Emma with his healing power). That figure is Dr. Larivière, and as one might expect, there are many affinities between him and Flaubert. Larivière's relation to those outside the profession mirrors Flaubert's relation to the characters he portrays: both doctor and writer assume the status of deities. As Flaubert remarks about Larivière's arrival in town on the eve of Emma's death, "the apparition of a god would not have caused more commotion."

Larivière and Flaubert mirror each other in their personalities as well. The doctor is one of those

> who, cherishing their art with a fanatical love, exercised it with enthusiasm and wisdom. . . . Disdainful of honors, of titles, and of academies, hospitable, generous, fatherly to the poor, and practicing virtue without believing in it, he would almost have passed for a saint if the keenness of his intellect had not caused him to be feared as a demon. His glance, more penetrating than his scalpels, looked straight into your soul, and would detect [the French word is *désarticulait*, disarticulated in the anatomical sense] any lie, regardless how well hidden.
>
> (233-34)

Flaubert, similarly, is fanatical in his devotion to his art; he, too, disdains academies and honors, as is evident from his sarcastic award of the Cross of the Legion of Honor to Homais, as well as from comments in his correspondence (for example, "How honors swarm where there is no honor!" [letter to Louise Colet, 15 Jan. 1853]); he, too, feels that he acts charitably to the poor; he, too, is interested in burrowing and penetrating into the truth. And, like Larivière, who "belonged to that great school of surgeons created by Bichat," Flaubert claims to "feel at home only in analysis—in anatomy, if I may call it such" (letter to Louise Colet, 26 July 1852).

Both Emma and Dr. Larivière, hysteric and physician, thus are projections of Flaubert's own personality. In this sense, *Madame Bovary* might be described as a "disarticulated" autobiography. As Jean Starobinski argues, following Emile Benveniste, autobiography characteristically contains an inherent tension between historical and discursive subjects, between the self who lives and the self who makes sense in writing of that life. This structural tension between lived experience and (self-) knowledge, according to Starobinski, is usually mediated in narrative by some radical change in the life of the autobiographer, such change most often taking the form of a conversion into a new life.[59]

In *Madame Bovary*, however, the relevant tension arises between hysterical and discursive subjects, between lived-experience-as-illness and medical knowledge. Instead of finding resolution in a new life, the *bios* in a medically defined autobiography must by definition ultimately die. As Bichat's dictum puts it, life is that which resists death. Flaubert echoes this sentiment: "How annihilation stalks us! No sooner are we born than putrefaction sets in, and life is nothing but a long battle it wages against us, ever more triumphantly until the end—death—when its reign becomes absolute" (letter to Louise Colet, 31 March 1853; Steegmuller's translation). And the corollary of this premise, as Bichat points out, is that although the truth of life only becomes evident in death, when the anatomist disarticulates the body, illness is already a form of dissection. In this sense, Emma is dead even before the novel begins, and the novel itself is a patient anatomization.

This seems somewhat sadistic, and one may well wonder why, after all, Emma is denied medical treatment. Why, in other words, does Larivière come too late? For Jean-Paul Sartre, the reason is clear: Larivière's knowledge—and medical knowledge more generally—is foreign to Emma's existential pain, as it is to Flaubert's art. The doctor, according to Sartre, "*knows* the horror scientifically but does not *feel* it," because his medical knowledge is grounded in utilitarianism.[60] But this, I would suggest, is a philosopher's misreading (albeit a strong one), based on a distortion of actual medical knowledge into philosophical categories. Larivière represents not utilitarian but medical philosophy: Bichat is his mentor, not Bentham. Moreover, Larivière's professional *impassabilité*, imposed on him by the requirements of his clinical epistemology, does not destroy all feeling in him, as Sartre claims. The great physician's objective veneer cracks just enough at the sight of the horror to hint at a human interior: "this man, accustomed as he was to the sight of pain, could not keep back a tear that fell on his shirt front" (234).

This tear resembles those that Flaubert claimed to have himself shed over Emma while writing *Madame Bovary*, and marks another link between novelist and ideal doctor. But it also points toward a more complicated biographical connection between the two. For Larivière's tearfulness when faced with Emma may remind one that Flaubert's father wept over Gustave during the early days after his son's first "epileptic" attack. Several other characteristics link Achille-Cléophas with Larivière—both physicians served under Bichat, both wear cloaks that identify them as somewhat eccentric, both attempt to maintain a stern late-Enlightenment moral stance. These similarities have prompted several critics to argue that Larivière is a fictional depiction of Flaubert's father.[61] If Larivière represents Flaubert's *knowledge* confronting in Emma the novelist's *being*, Larivière as father figure must also be the focus of a second autobiographical problematic: the Oedipal tension between father and son.

Sartre's mammoth biography of Flaubert has dissected in great detail the intimate strains between Gustave and his father, stemming in large part from Achille-Cléophas's refusal to allow his younger son to follow in his footsteps and become a doctor. Flaubert's eventual breakdown, Sartre contends, was due to his medical disinheritance, and provided him with the freedom to write. Flaubert then used this freedom to gain his revenge against his father by portraying him—in what Sartre considers a less than flattering way—as Larivière in *Madame Bovary*. Seeing the filial tie as one of *ressentiment* depends upon accepting Sartre's claim that Larivière's portrait is laden with sarcasm. This claim, however, is based on an oversubtle reading of the textual evidence.[62] My less elegant but clearer reading interprets Larivière as positively representing Flaubert's father and the heritage of medical knowledge—but also recognizes that Larivière to some extent represents Flaubert himself. The son thus accedes to his father's place, in that he performs—as a writer—all the functions of a doctor.

In addition to its simplicity, this interpretation of the father: son relationship has another advantage over Sartre's: it accounts for not only two but three generations of medical genealogy in Flaubert's life as well as in his text. If the first medical generation is that of Bichat (recall Flaubert's description of Larivière as one of a "great line of surgeons that sprang from Bichat"), the second generation is that of Flaubert's father and Larivière, both of whom studied under Bichat. The third generation, then, belongs to Flaubert and . . . surprisingly enough, to Charles Bovary. No wonder Flaubert says that Larivière's kind of surgeon is now extinct. Neither Charles nor Flaubert is a successful physician. In this sense, Charles represents Flaubert's failed ambition to become a doctor—and indeed one can trace many of the signifiers of failure borne by Charles (stuttering, falling into stupors, and so on) back to Flaubert, the idiot of the family. At the same time, however, Charles's medical ineptitude makes it possible for Flaubert the writer to act as a doctor in monitoring the progress of Emma's illness. In the gap left by Charles's incompetence, the novelist can note Emma's symptoms, elicit her delirium, supervise her fantasies, and probe the constitution of her memory. Flaubert makes himself the true heir to Bichat's anatomical insights. By extending the anatomicoclinical concepts of constitution and diagnosis into the psychological domain, he secures his own position within the Bichatian genealogy.

Flaubert's choice of a novelistic situation in which medical knowledge is not available thus makes biographical sense as a response both to his personal experience of illness and to his family ties to medicine. The sociological issue, however, remains: given the literary strength of Flaubert's medical realism, what accounts for its authority? Why should the medical point of view become such an appropriate one, at this moment in history, for the task of representing reality?

The answer to this question has to do, I think, with the development of the professions—including the profession of letters and the profession of medicine—during the first half of the nineteenth century. This is an extraordinarily complicated event, to be examined in more detail in the following chapter, but the general results of the professionalization process can be summed up here. By the 1850s, literary and medical workers have reached the end of a period during which they sought professional status from the public. While the doctors by and large succeeded in gaining control over their market, the writers failed to control the vast new market for literature that opened up during the 1820s and 1830s. By the time Flaubert begins to write, it has become clear that instead of a unified reading public under the domination of men of letters, a stratified market has formed, with some writers knocking off what Sainte-Beuve disdainfully refers to as "industrial literature" intended for consumption by the newspaper-reading public, and a small elite group of novelists writing for Stendhal's "happy few."[63] The change can be indexed by the fact that Balzac is one of the first to write in the new large-circulation journals, and eagerly sets forth to conquer that market (although eventually he, too, turns against journalism with a vengeance, most

scathingly in his *Monograph on the Paris Press,* published in 1842), while Flaubert disdains and despises journalism.

In turning away from the mass reading public, Flaubert in effect accepts literature's marginal status as a profession. Unlike Balzac, he makes no ideological appeals to his readers—he does not loudly proclaim, as Balzac does, that he is a "doctor of social medicine" ready to heal the wounds of postrevolutionary French society.[64] Instead, Flaubert focuses on technique. But with this new emphasis in realism on a medicalized style (rather than on the persona of the doctor), and more generally on the importance of technique, is not Flaubert now appealing to successful doctors, and indeed to the professional class as a whole, for whom technical skill rather than ideological purity or personal authority is fast becoming the relevant measure of value? Given that the professional class—which would include literary and medical men, as well as lawyers, engineers, and architects—is the rising class during this period, Flaubert's realism would seem to be very much of its time, marginal only in the sense that a professional elite is marginal.[65]

Reading Flaubert in this way, as affiliated with a rising professional class, becomes possible only if one extends Riffaterre's concept of intertextuality beyond what semiotics contemplates. The discursive intertextuality I have traced not only links literature and society together in a much finer historical weave than does Riffaterre's ideological intertextuality, but also permits one to begin to address the much-vexed question of the influence Flaubert's social context has on his textual production. Semioticians have tended to leave this question—framed for them as one about the ideological determinants of literary form—to the Marxists, who in Flaubert's case (as Sartre's endless project reminds us) have had enormous trouble tying the writer's forms to his class situation or conjuncture. The classic working-through of the "Flaubert problem" in Marxist criticism, of course, occurs in Georg Lukács's work. For Lukács, literary texts qualify as "realistic" only insofar as they accurately represent, through types, the inner dynamic of historical development: the coming-to-power of an emerging dominant class (or at least, of that emergent class's ideology). The only possible progressive class in the modern age, however, is the proletariat, a class hardly visible in Flaubert, much less blessed by him. If the proletariat fails to materialize historically in the failed revolutions of 1848, this merely excuses Flaubert from responsibility for what Lukács must nevertheless ultimately regard as artistic failure. Flaubert, in this view, is denied the very possibility for success by his social and historical belatedness.[66]

Archaeological analysis suggests that although Lukács's conclusions are false (and his own agonizing over Flaubert indicates that even Lukács was troubled by the evaluation he found himself forced to make), his aesthetic principle remains sound. In order to claim that Flaubert is a realist in Lukács's sense, one need only substitute discourse for ideology and loosen the definition of class a bit. Flaubert may not be representing the ideology of the proletariat, but he *is* projecting the discourse, and with it a certain ideology of an emerging dominant class, that of professionals.[67] The drama and the dynamic thus map themselves textually not so much in the clash of typical characters, but in the impersonal, authoritative exercise, the powerful demonstration, of Flaubert's narrative technique, his point of view, and his control of knowledge. It is this power, the power not so much of capital or of labor as of information, that one should recognize in Flaubert's medicalized realism.

Notes

1. "Flaubert's Presuppositions," *Diacritics* 11, no. 4 (Winter 1981): 2-11.

2. Jonathan Culler, "Presupposition and Intertextuality," *Modern Language Notes* 91, no. 6 (1976): 1380-96.

3. Charles Baudelaire, "*Madame Bovary*, by Gustave Flaubert," excerpted in the fine English translation of *Madame Bovary* by Paul de Man (New York: Norton, 1965), 339. All future translated quotations from *Madame Bovary* in this chapter are from the Norton edition. All other translations are my own, except where noted.

4. Cf. Michel Riffaterre, *La Production du texte* (Paris: Seuil, 1979).

5. Cf. Foucault, *L'Archaéologie du savoir* [Paris: Gallimard, 1969] for Foucault's most extensive theoretical discussion of the concept of "discourse"; for Foucault's analysis of nineteenth-century medical discourse, cf. *Naissance de la clinique* [Paris: Presses universitaires de France, 1963] and *Les machines à guérir* (Paris: Institut de l'Environment, 1976). I have also found the following works very useful for gaining an overview of the intellectual and institutional structure of nineteenth-century medicine: Ernest Ackerknecht, "Medical Education in Nineteenth-century France," *The Journal of Medical Education* 1 (1957): 15-18; Ackerknecht, *Medicine at the Paris Hospital, 1794-1848* (Baltimore, Md.: Johns Hopkins University Press, 1967); Larson, *The Rise of Professionalism* [Berkeley and Los Angeles: University of California Press, 1977], chap. 3; Peterson, *The Medical Profession in Mid-Victorian London* [Berkeley and Los Angeles: University of California Press, 1978]; Waddington, *The Medical Profession in the Industrial Revolution* [Dublin: Gill and Macmillan, 1984]; George Rosen, *Madness in Society* (London: Routledge

and Kegan Paul, 1969); Andrew Scull, ed., *Madhouses, Mad-Doctors, and Madmen* (Philadelphia: University of Pennsylvania Press, 1981); Ivan Illich, *Medical Nemesis* (London: Trinity Press, 1975). For a comparable account of the medical profession in its American context, see Paul Starr, *The Social Transformation of American Medicine* (New York: Basic Books, 1982).

6. "Les tomes du *Dictionnaire des sciences médicales,* non coupés, mais dont la brochure avait souffert dans toutes les ventes successives par où ils avaient passé, garnissaient presque à eux seuls les six rayons d'une bibliothèque en bois de sapin." *Madame Bovary* (Paris: Club de l'Honnête Homme, 1971), 77. All future quotations in French from *Madame Bovary* cited in the footnotes are to this edition.

7. Terry Eagleton, *Literary Theory: An Introduction* (Minneapolis: University of Minnesota Press, 1983), 15.

8. On Cabanis, see Martin S. Staum, *Cabanis* (Princeton, N.J.: Princeton University Press, 1980). On the institutional transformation of medicine in France during the Revolutionary period, see Foucault, *Naissance,* chaps. 2-5.

9. Canivet's surgical background is evident even in his name, which puns *canif,* or penknife.

10. Foucault, *Birth of the Clinic* [New York: Vintage, 1975], 81.

11.   Il . . . entrait son bras dans des lits humides, reçevait au visage le jet tiède des saignées, écoutait des râles, examinait des cuvettes, retroussait bien du linge sale.

                                 (100)

12. See Eugenio Donato, "Flaubert and the Question of History," *Modern Language Notes* 91, no. 5 (1970): 864-65; Tony Tanner, *Adultery in the Novel* (Baltimore, Md.: Johns Hopkins University Press, 1979), especially 301-3.

13. For accounts of this competition, see Matthew Ramsey, "Medical Power and Popular Medicine: Illegal Healers in Nineteenth-Century France," *Journal of Social History,* 10, no. 4 (1977): 560-77, and Jacques Donzelot, *The Policing of Families,* trans. Robert Hurley (New York: Pantheon Books, 1979), especially the section on "The Priest and the Doctor," 171-87. For a comparative account that includes information on the conflict in France between the Church and the medical profession during the 1840s, see Ramsey, "The Politics of Professional Monopoly in Nineteenth-Century Medicine: The French Model and Its Rivals," in Gerald Geison, ed., *Professions and the French State, 1700-1900* (Philadelphia: University of Pennsylvania Press, 1984), 225-305.

14. Ramsey, "Medical Power," 579.

15. Donzelot, *Policing of Families,* 171.

16. As Foucault has pointed out, this new arrangement of duties between doctor and priest was connected with a broader discursive development in which sex ceased to be an object of religious control and came to be conceptualized as an object of scientific knowledge. Hysteria obviously participates in this transformation. But what was involved was less a displacement of terms than a shift in epistemological authority. The old connotations of hysteria as demonic possession were subsumed by the medical perspective, adduced no longer as evidence of damnation but as symptoms of illness. A standard mid-nineteenth-century medical textbook, for example, claims that hysteria is characterized by "vociferation, singing, cursing, aimless wandering; occasionally by more formal delirium of a religious or demoniacal character; or there are attacks of all kinds of noisy and perverse, but still coherent actions" (Wilhelm Griesinger, *Mental Pathology and Therapeutics,* trans. C. L. Robertson et al. [London: New Sydenham Society, 1867], 179). For a detailed discussion of the changing religious and medical attitudes toward hysteria, see Ilza Veith, *Hysteria: The History of a Disease* (Chicago: University of Chicago Press, 1965).

17. Cf. Ramsey, "Medical Power," 570.

18. "Les circonstances qui prédisposent le plus à l'hystérie sont . . . une constitution nerveuse, le sexe feminin et l'âge de douze à vingt-cinq ou trente ans. . . . La plupart ont montré dès le bas âge des dispositions aux affections convulsives, un caractère mélancolique, colère, emporté, impatient. . . . Les causes excitants sont plus particulièrement des affections morales vives, . . . amour contrarié, . . . affections vives de l'âme, . . . un mouvement violent de jalousie, . . . chagrins violens, . . . contrariété vive. . . . La constitution nerveuse et l'état maladif qui précédent et facilitent le développement des attaques sont occasionés par les excès de la masturbation." *Dictionnaire de Médecine* (Paris: Béchet jeune, 1824), vol. 11, 532-33. It is interesting to note that Flaubert himself not only makes use of the medical dictionary, but also corrects it. Writing to Sainte-Beuve (23-24 December 1862), for example, he defends his description in *Salammbô* of bitches' milk as a remedy for leprosy, referring the critic (himself an ex-medical student!) to the *Dictionnaire des sciences médicales.* Flaubert then goes on to say that he has revised the article on leprosy, correcting some of the facts and adding others from his own first hand observation of the disease in Egypt. Cf. *Corréspondance,* in *Oeuvres Complètes* (Paris: Conard, 1933), vol. 5, 59.

19. "the prisoner of a sort of reciprocal causality that operates between the vital spirits and the mind, between passion and the body." Paul Hoffmann, *La femme dans la pensée des Lumières* (Paris: Editions Ophrys, n.d.), 179.

20. Denis Diderot, *Rameau's Nephew,* trans. Leonard Tancock (New York: Penguin, 1978), 114. On eighteenth-century neurological theories of hysteria, see Veith, *Hysteria,* and Hoffmann, *La femme*; John F. Sena, "The English Malady," Ph.D. diss., Princeton University, 1967. Two excellent collections of source material on early psychiatric theories of insanity are Richard Hunter and Ida Macalpine, eds., *300 Years of English Psychiatry, 1535-1860* (New York: Oxford University Press, 1963) and Vieda Skultans, *English Madness: Ideas on Insanity, 1580-1880* (Boston: Routledge and Kegan Paul, 1979). See also Foucault, *L'Histoire de la folie à l'âge classique* (Paris: Gallimard, 1972), especially 193-226.

21. P.-J.-G. Cabanis, *Rapports du physique et du moral de l'homme* (Paris, 1824), 27.

22. P.-J.-G. Cabanis, *Oeuvres philosophiques,* ed. Claude Lehec and Jean Cazeneuve (Paris, 1956), vol. 1, 364. See Staum, *Cabanis,* chaps. 7 and 8, for a detailed discussion of Cabanis's theories of sensitivity and temperament. For a discussion of how the concepts of sensibility and reflex become tied to a notion of normality in the biological sciences of this period, see Georges Canguilhem, *Le normal et le pathologique* (Paris: Presses universitaires de France, 1966).

23. M.-F. Xavier Bichat, *Recherches physiologiques sur la vie et la mort* (Paris: Chez Brosson, Gabon, et Cie, 1800), 162. For a broader view of the conceptual transformation initiated by Bichat, see Foucault, *Birth,* chap. 8; P. Lain Entralgo, "Sensualism and Vitalism in Bichat's 'Anatomie Générale,'" *Journal of the History of Medicine* 3, no. 1 (1948): 47-55; and François Jacob, *La Logique du vivant* (Paris: Gallimard, 1970), chap. 2.

24. "one castrates men to change their voices." Bichat, *Recherches,* 100.

25. See in particular Steven Marcus, *The Other Victorians* (New York: Basic Books, 1966). Stephen Heath has traced the development of sexual rhetoric into a modern discourse on sexuality in *The Sexual Fix* (London: Macmillan, 1983).

26. François Lallemand, *Des pertes séminales involontaires* (Paris: Béchet, 1836).

27. Raymond de Vieussens, *Histoire des maladies internes suivis de la névrographie* (Toulouse: J. J. Robert, 1775-1776), quoted in Hoffmann, *La femme,* 178.

28. On Georget, see Jean Marie Bruttin, *Différentes théories sur l'hystérie dans la première moitié du XIXᵉ siècle* (Zurich: Jenris, 1969).

29. See Robert Brudenell Garter, *On the Pathology and Treatment of Hysteria* (London: J. Churchill, 1853). On Carter's position in the history of hysteria, see Skultans, *English Madness,* 21-30.

30. Henry James, *The Art of Fiction* (New York: Oxford University Press, 1948), 74.

31. "Julien's illness . . . was caused by a deadly breeze or an unfulfilled desire. But the young man, in response to all questions, shook his head." Gustave Flaubert, *Trois Contes* (Paris: Garnier Flammarion, 1965), 102.

32. For a discussion of Flaubert's relation to older theories of the relation between weather and emotional flux, see Terry Castle, "The Female Thermometer," *Representations* 17 (Winter 1987): 18-19. Castle correctly points out that Flaubert is "self-conscious, even sly" in invoking these earlier theories, but he does not recognize that Flaubert rejects the etiology purveyed by those theories, or that Flaubert promotes a different view of what Castle calls "modern man's unstable inner weather."

33. See Bruttin, *Différentes théories sur l'hystérie,* for a more detailed summary of these four steps.

34. Cf. Hayden White, "The Problem of Style in Realistic Representation: Marx and Flaubert," in Berel Lang, ed., *The Concept of Style* (Philadelphia: University of Pennsylvania Press, 1979), 213-32. For White, however, the movement through the four tropal modes is unconnected with medical logic or discursive structure. Instead, White places it within an Hegelian schema of cognitive development. Flaubert's novel, in this view, provides a classical example of bildungsroman, depicting the four-stage process whereby the Spirit, or Desire, comes to (ironic) self-consciousness. But Flaubert's term for what happens is "l'éducation sentimentale," not "l'éducation de l'esprit," and the former term has a precise connotation, for Ideologues and clinicians, of "power of sensitivity" (*sentiment, sensitivité,* and *sensibilité* are roughly interchangable in Bichatian discourse). The education of Frédéric's sentiments, then, although occurring in four stages, results not in a German idealist *Bildung* of the *Geist* but in a medicalized formation of constitution.

35. Bruttin, *Différentes théories sur l'hystérie,* 31.

36. Charles, de temps à autre, ouvrait les yeux; puis, son esprit se fatiguant et le sommeil revenant de soi-même, bientôt il entrait dans une sorte d'assoupissement où, ses sensations récentes se confondant avec des souvenirs, lui-même se percevait double, à la fois étudiant et marié, couché dans son lit comme tout à l'heure, traversant une salle d'opérés comme autrefois.

(61)

37. Josef Breuer and Sigmund Freud, *Studies on Hysteria,* trans. and ed. James Strachey (New York: Basic Books, 1955), 7.

38. Flaubert to Hippolyte Taine, 1 December 1866. Cf. *Correspondance,* ed. Jean Bruneau (Paris: Gallimard, 1973-1980).

39. Les ombres du soir déscendaient; le soleil horizontal, passant entre les branches, lui éblouissait les yeux. Ça et là, tout autour d'elle, dans les feuilles ou par terre, des taches lumineuses tremblaient, comme si des colibris, en volant, eussent éparpillé leurs plumes. Le silence était partout; quelque chose de doux semblait sortir des arbres; elle sentait son coeur, dont les battements recommençient, et le sang circuler dans sa chair comme un fleuve de lait. Alors, elle entendit tout au loin, au delà du bois, sur les autres collines, un cri vague et prolongé, une voix qui se traînait, et elle l'écoutait silencieusement, se mêlant comme une musique aux dernières vibrations de ses nerfs émus.

(193)

40. In *Littérature et sensation* (Paris: Editions de Seuil, 1954), Jean-Pierre Richard gives a brilliant phenomenological reading of this and other passages dealing with Emma's perception. The difference between Richard's phenomenological approach and my archaeological one is actually a matter of degree rather than of substance: Richard seeks to imitate the lived experience of the characters within Flaubert's literary universe, while my concern is to show how that experience is made sense of by means of encoded presuppositions that function as a phenomenological a priori.

41. Aux fulgurations de l'heure présente, sa vie passée, si nette jusqu'alors, s'évanouissait tout entière, et elle doutait presque de l'avoir vécue. Elle était là; puis autour du bal, il n'y avait plus que de l'ombre, étalée sur tout le reste.

(94)

42. Le souvenir du vicomte revenait toujours dans ses lectures. Entre lui et les personnages inventés, elle établissait des rapprochements. Mais le cercle dont il était le centre peu à peu s'élargit autour de lui, et cette auréole qu'il avait, s'écartant de sa figure, s'étala plus au loin, pour illuminer d'autres rêves.

(99)

43. Cf. Jonathan Culler, *Flaubert: The Uses of Uncertainty* (Ithaca, N.Y.: Cornell University Press, 1974), 91-108.

44. For a similar effort to account for a seemingly meaningless detail (in fact, the precise detail chosen by Barthes), see Castle, "The Female Thermometer," 26.

45. Cf. Bruttin, *Différentes théories sur l'hystérie,* 18: "Le seuil de la sensibilité, de l'excitabilité du cerveau malade étant ainsi de plus en plus abaissé, les plus petites stimulations suffiront à déclencher la crise. Une douleur, une petite contrariété, voire même un son ou une odeur désagréables, déchargeront le cerveau malade; la réaction hystérique est devenue inadéquate, totalement disproportionée et, tres souvent, il devient impossible de trouver la cause immédiate de ces accès répétés."

46. The case study has yet to be adequately defined as a literary genre, as G. S. Rousseau has pointed out in "Literature and Medicine: The State of the Field," *Isis* 72, no. 263 (1981): 406-24. Those critics who have dealt with case studies (most notably Steven Marcus and Peter Brooks) have focused almost exclusively on Freud's case histories, rather than examining Freud's work as a transformation of an already existing genre. Cf. Steven Marcus, "Freud and Dora: Story, History, Case History," in *Representations* (New York: Random House, 1975), 247-309; Peter Brooks, "Fictions of the Wolf Man: Freud and Narrative Understanding," in *Reading for the Plot* (New York: Knopf, 1984), 264-85. Foucault provides a brilliant but elliptical discussion of the change in medical hermeneutics in *Birth,* chap. 6, and offers a discussion of the role of a doctor's subjectivity within the process of writing case studies in "The Life of Infamous Men," in Morris and Patton, *Michel Foucault* [Sydney: Feral, 1979], 76-91. Flaubert, of course, is not a physician but a literary artist, and the generic constraints of the realistic novel clearly are not identical with those of the case study. Nevertheless, in terms of the epistemological and hermeneutic imperatives that structure the two genres, a certain commonality does exist.

47. Bichat, *Recherches,* 218.

48. —Sens donc: quelle odeur! fît-il en la lui passant sous le nez à plusieurs reprises.

    —J'étouffe! s'écria-t-elle en se levant d'un bond.

    Mais, par un effort de volonté, ce spasme disparut; puis:

    —Ce n'est rien! dit-elle, ce n'est rien! c'est nerveux! Assieds-toi, mange!

    Car elle rédoutait qu'on ne fût à la questionner, à la soigner, qu'on ne la quittât plus.

    Charles, pour lui obéir, s'était rassis, et il crachait dans sa main les noyaux des abricots, qu'il déposait ensuite dans son assiette.

Tout à coup, un tilbury bleu passa au grand trot sur la place. Emma poussa un cri et tomba roide par terre, à la renverse.

(233)

49. Il y a des natures si impressionnables a l'encontre de certaines odeurs! et ce serait même une belle question à étudier, tant sous le rapport pathologique que sous le rapport physiologique.

(234)

50. Quoted in Foucault, *The History of Sexuality,* trans. Robert Hurley (New York: Pantheon, 1978), 56, n. 1.

51. Puis, ne pensez-vous pas qu'il faudrait peut-être frapper l'imagination?

    —En quoi? comment? dit Bovary.

    —Ah! c'est là la question! Telle est effectivement la question: "That is the question!" comme je lisais dernièrement dans le journal.

    Mais Emma, se réveillant, s'écria:

    —Et la lettre? et la lettre?

    On crût qu'elle avait le délire; elle l'eût à partir de minuit: une fièvre cérébrale s'était déclarée.

(235)

52. "In short, a young woman from a good social background, with a nervous constitution, not doing manual work and leading an idle life between attending concerts and reading novels, is the ideal subject predisposed to hysteria." Bruttin, *Différentes théories sur l'hystérie,* 17.

53. Girard, *Deceit, Desire, and the Novel* [Baltimore, Md.: Johns Hopkins University Press, 1965], 149.

54. For a summary of the various medical positions on this question, see Dr. Eduard Allain, *Le mal de Flaubert* (Paris: M. Lac, 1928). Cf. also René Dumesnil, *Flaubert et la médecine* (Geneva: Slatkine, 1969) and Maxime Du Camp's unreliable but still fascinating reminiscences, "La maladie de Flaubert," *La Chronique médicale* 3 (1896): 584-87.

55. Quoted in *The Letters of Gustave Flaubert, 1830-1857,* trans. and ed. Francis Steegmuller (Cambridge, Mass.: Belknap Press, 1980), 22. All further English quotations from Flaubert's correspondence are from this edition.

56. Elle resta perdue de stupeur, et n'ayant plus conscience d'elle-même que par le battement de ses artères, qu'elle croyait entendre s'échapper comme une assourdissante musique qui emplissait la campagne. Le sol sous ses pieds était plus mou qu'une onde, et les sillons lui parurent d'immenses vagues brunes, qui déferlaient. Tout ce qu'il y avait dans sa tête de réminiscences, d'idées, s'échappait à la fois, d'un seul

bond. comme les mille pièces d'un feu d'artifice. Elle vît son père, le cabinet de Lheureux, leur chambre là-bas, un autre paysage. La folie la prenait.

(326)

57. Both Eugene F. Gray, in "The Clinical View of Life: Gustave Flaubert's *Madame Bovary,*" in *Medicine and Literature,* ed. Edmund Pellegrino (New York: N. Watson, 1980), 60-84, and John C. Lapp, in "Art and Hallucination in Flaubert," *French Studies* 10, no. 4 (1956): 322-43, have discussed this passage and pointed out the similarity between Emma's hallucinations and those of Flaubert. Neither critic, however, has adequately described or explained the parallelism between Flaubert's description of his and Emma's experience and the medical description of the same kind of experience.

58. Thibaudet's comment about what he called Flaubert's "binocular vision" is developed at length by Barbara Smalley, who emphasizes Flaubert's "awareness of two worlds, the world of private experience and the world of scientific reality," as a fundamental characteristic of his realism. No stylistic analysis in itself, however, could grasp the constituting conditions of this double perspective. Cf. Smalley, *George Eliot and Flaubert* (Athens: Ohio University Press, 1974), and Thibaudet, *Gustave Flaubert* (Paris: Gallimard, 1935), 119.

59. Jean Starobinski, "The Style of Autobiography," in *Literary Style: A Symposium,* ed. Seymour Chatman (New York: Oxford University Press, 1971), 285-94. Benveniste's distinction is actually between "l'énonciation historique" and "discours," not between different subjects. See Emile Benveniste, *Problèmes de linguistique générale* (Paris: Gallimard, 1966), 242.

60. Jean-Paul Sartre, *The Family Idiot,* trans. Carol Cosman (Chicago: University of Chicago Press, 1981), vol. 1, 443.

61. This is Sartre's position, as well as that of Harry Levin in *The Gates of Horn* [New York: Oxford University Press, 1963], 219. The identification seems to have been made first by René Dumesnil in *Flaubert et la médecine.*

62. Sartre claims that Larivière's "calm consciousness of having great talent can only be the acceptance of mediocrity," and concludes that Flaubert is therefore opposing Larivière's/Achille-Cléophas's talent (read "mediocrity" by Sartre) to his own genius. But Sartre fails to point out that Flaubert nowhere opposes genius to talent and mediocrity. In fact, Flaubert often cited the following maxims of

La Bruyère and Buffon as guides: "Un esprit médiocre croit écrire divinement, un bon esprit croit écrire raisonnablement," and "Le génie n'est qu'une plus grande aptitude à la patience" ["A mediocre writer believes he writes divinely; a good writer believes he writes reasonably," and "Genius is merely a great aptitude for patience"] (Steegmuller, *Letters of Gustave Flaubert,* 66 and 182). I would argue that for Flaubert, in many ways an antiromantic, the alternative to mediocrity is not genius, but professional competence.

63. Cf. Charles Augustin Sainte-Beuve, "De la littérature industrielle," in *Portraits Contemporaine* (Paris: Didier, 1846), vol. 1, 495-557. On the development of the professional writer during the 1820s and 1830s, as well as on the general phenomenon of professionalization during that period, see chapter 3.

64. See Honoré de Balzac, *Oeuvres Complètes* (Paris: Bibliophiles de l'Originales, 1968), vol. 19, 546, for Balzac's discussion of the "moral malady" of society that he proposes to solve in his writing.

65. On the formation of a self-conscious professional class, see Harold Perkin, *The Origins of Modern English Society, 1770-1880* (London: Routledge and Kegan Paul, 1969), 321-25. Perkin develops this argument at much greater length in *The Rise of Professional Society* (London and New York: Routledge, 1989).

66. Cf. Lukács, *The Historical Novel* [Lincoln: University of Nebraska Press, 1983], 182.

67. On the arguments within Marxism about whether or not professionals should be considered a class, see Barbara Ehrenreich and John Ehrenreich, eds., *Between Labor and Capital: The Professional-Managerial Class* (Boston: South End Press, 1979); Dietrich Rueschemeyer, *Power and the Division of Labor* (Cambridge, Mass.: Polity Press, 1986), 104-41.

Lois Keith (essay date 2001)

SOURCE: Keith, Lois. "Too Good to Live: Deathbed Scenes in Charlotte Brontë's *Jane Eyre* and Louisa May Alcott's *Little Women.*" In *Take Up Thy Bed and Walk: Death, Disability and Cure in Classic Fiction for Girls,* pp. 33-68. London: Women's Press Ltd., 2001.

[*In the following essay,* Keith *examines the sicknesses and deaths of Helen in* Jane Eyre *and Beth in* Little Women *as largely biographical recollections of Brontë's and Alcott's sisters' deaths and the sociocultural milieu in which young girls' deaths were viewed as beatific.*]

I would gaze on Thee, on Thy patient face;
Make me like Thyself, patient, sweet at peace;

Make my days all love, and my nights all praise,
Till all days and nights and patient sufferings cease.

from, *A Sick Child's Meditation*
by Christina Rossetti, 1885

The deaths of Helen Burns in *Jane Eyre* and of Beth in *Little Women* may occupy just a small space in the novels, but the parting scenes and the ultimate departure of Helen and Beth are crucial to the development of the story. Essentially different to the strong and life-loving central characters, these saintly girls, passive and resigned, serve to provide alternatives against which Jane Eyre and Jo March shape themselves. Removed from everyday concerns, reconciled to a short life within a safe, known world, they provide a clear contrast to the difficult journeys that their 'sisters' will have to make. Beth and Helen do not fight against the restrictions or unfairness of their enclosed worlds but submit humbly to their lot, believing that it is God's will to remove them from a difficult, bittersweet existence. To young readers they seem to be saintly girls, far better than any real children, possibly too good to live. We cry over their deaths but, like Jane and Jo, are able to move on in sadness because like the other characters in the story, we believe that they have gone to a better place.

The juxtaposition of the strong, difficult, potentially rebellious heroine alongside the sweet, passive and forgiving invalid was a common feature of nineteenth-century literature. In *Jane Eyre,* Jane has Helen to teach her that revenge and rage can be self-destructive, and in *Little Women* Jo has Beth to teach her patience and self-restraint. At the beginning of these stories, Jane and Jo are flawed, difficult, interesting characters. Both suffer from an excess of passion and strong feelings about the injustices of the world, and both have lessons to learn. Helen and Beth, apart from minor faults of untidy drawers or dreaminess, do not have to learn how to 'be' in the world; they are already well on their way to the next one. Neither Helen nor Beth engage with life; they are willing to submit to their removal from this earth with very little fuss. Death allows them to abdicate responsibility for having to make difficult choices, and they leave their stronger sister or friend free to continue on her own difficult voyage through life. Both of these stories use the metaphor of John Bunyan's *Pilgrim's Progress*: the idea of embarking upon a hazardous journey, where obstacles will be placed in your path and difficult decisions have to be made but where, in the end, you will return to your rightful place as a changed person, better, wiser and with more humility. By contrast, Helen and Beth's journeys are heavenward.

The deathbed scene in books intended for children started off as a way of teaching a moral lesson to those who needed to be saved from damnation and hellfire. They began as soon as books for children began, and continued to be popular whilst childhood deaths were still common. In the seventeenth century, the Puritans saw children as young souls to be saved and therefore a good deal of literature was aimed at the idea of rescuing them. One of their leading writers was James Janeway who, in 1671, published the snappily titled, *A Token for Children, Being an Exact Account of the Conversion, Holy and Exemplary Lives, and Joyful Deaths of Several Young Children*. Its preface asks the child reader, 'Whither do you think those children go when they die, that will not do what they are bid, but play the Truant and lie and speak naughty words and break the Sabbath? Whither do such children go, do you think? Why I will tell you; they which lie must to their Father the Devil into everlasting burning.'[1] In order to avoid this terrible fate and find a way to heaven, the book exhorts children to be dutiful to their parents, diligent at their book, learn their scriptures and their catechisms and live holy lives.

By the middle of the nineteenth century the deathbed scene was still a prominent feature in literature but had become softened and more sentimental. Readers were more likely to see good Christian children ascending into heaven in a gentle state of grace than falling into a pit full of fire and brimstone.

Charlotte Yonge's pivotal *The Daisy Chain* takes its title from the confident belief that loved ones will meet again in heaven. At the start of the story, the sisters Ethel and Margaret are in the unusual position in a Victorian novel of having both their parents alive. However, this is not to last. By page 25, there has been a terrible accident. The carriage has overturned, Mother has died, Father has broken his arm and Margaret is alive but paralysed. The doctor is called and looks anxiously at her. 'The want of power over the limbs is more than mere shock and debility . . . I cannot tell yet as to the spine.'

Margaret and Ethel are very different kinds of girls. Ethel is a model for many a later character in the domestic novel. Physically she is neither pretty nor angelic looking and has many similarities to Jane Eyre. She is a 'thin, lank, angular, sallow girl, just fifteen, trembling from head to toe with restrained eagerness as she tried to curb her tone into the requisite civility.' She is untidy (the state of her work-basket!) and hasty. After Margaret's accident, Ethel battles with her new domestic responsibilities, almost causing her little brother to be burned to death whilst paying too much attention to her 'books and Greek'. Meanwhile Margaret, who has been lying in bed for three months, struggles to accept her new condition. She is 'trying to prepare herself to submit thankfully whether she might be bidden to resign herself to helplessness or to let her mind open once more to visions of joyous usefulness'. Concerned with her slow recovery, her father calls in another doctor. In a scene which was to be almost duplicated in *What Katy Did* (published 16 years later), her father Mr

May tells her that the doctor thinks she might get about again, though it may not be for a long time. The doctor says, 'he has known the use of the limbs return almost suddenly even after a year or two', and is able to give an account that convinces Mr May that his daughter Margaret will eventually be cured. She is now allowed to be lifted onto the sofa or carried downstairs. Whilst Ethel struggles against her nature which is to be 'wild and high flying', Margaret is for a while content with her lot. She understood that her period of disability and illness had taught her the lessons young women needed to learn and gains the invalid status of near saintliness. 'For herself Margaret was perfectly content and happy. She knew the temptations of her character had been to be ruler and manager of everything, and she saw that it had been well for her to be thus assigned the role of Mary instead of Martha.'

At the beginning of the story, Margaret was betrothed to Alan, who was away at sea, but she knew that the marriage would only be possible if she were to recover. However, the doctor's predictions have been over-optimistic and her health declines. It is now, of course, unthinkable that she might marry and when Alan dies on board his ship, she thinks: 'There had been so little promise of happiness from the first, that there was more peace in thinking of him as sinking into rest in Harry's arms than in returning to grieve over her decline.'

After seven years, she dies. When Ethel is summoned to Margaret's deathbed, she asks her father, 'Will there be no rally?' 'Probably not', he replies. 'The brain is generally reached at this stage . . . The thing was done seven years ago. There was a rally for a time when her spirit was strong; but suspense and sorrow accelerated what began from the injury to the spine.' Margaret's years of captivity have given her the status of the Angel in the House. Her selflessness has had an effect on everybody, and Charlotte Yonge sums up her life as only a Victorian novelist can:

> Over now! The twenty-five years of life, the seven years of captivity on her couch, the anxious headship of a motherless household, the hopeless betrothal, the long suspense, the efforts of resignation, the widowed affections, the slow decay, the tardy, painful death agony—all was over; nothing left save what they had rendered the undying spirit, the impress her example had left on those around her.

Margaret has gone to meet her Maker but she has died for a cause. And the cause was to teach the reader that it is one thing for a girl to think about being the kind of woman who can go boldly into the world, but it is a better thing to be the kind of woman who can suffer unselfishly, thinking only of the needs of others.

At the end of the book, Mr May is comforted by the thought that his daughter has gone to be reunited with her mother: 'It seemed as if it were a home-like, com-fortable thought to him, that her mother had one of her children with her. He called her the first link of his Daisy Chain drawn up out of sight.'

Sickness which led to death was presented in literature as largely clean and pure and the purpose of such illness was the calm, safe transition to a better place. Robert Louis Stevenson, a children's writer who had long periods of ill health as a child and whose own experience of sickness must have been far from gentle, nevertheless described invalidism as 'a gentle, merciful preparation for the long sleep as one by one our desires quietly leave us.'[2]

Most families in the nineteenth century would have had a child who did not survive into adulthood. Both Charlotte Brontë and Louisa May Alcott had experienced the death of at least one sister when they wrote their novels, and they drew heavily on their own experiences of suffering and death. In Charlotte's case two sisters died in childhood and her brother and other two sisters died as adults. Maria and Elizabeth Brontë died of neglected consumption a few months after their father sent for them to come home from The Clergy Daughters' School (on which Lowood is based), Maria in May 1825 and Elizabeth in June the same year. They were eleven and ten years old, and Charlotte was filled with rage and desolation. Lyndall Gordon describes Helen Burns as an 'exact model' of Maria Brontë who for Charlotte personified perfection. At the age of fifteen, Charlotte described Maria as 'a little mother among the rest, superhuman in goodness and cleverness'.[3] Charlotte was forced to watch Maria's repeated humiliation at the hands of a schoolmistress called Miss Andrews (the Miss Scatcherd of *Jane Eyre*). Although excelling at lessons and with a rare 'mind of grace', Maria was in constant trouble for untidiness, and her younger sisters Emily and Charlotte had to watch helpless when she was beaten with bunched twigs for having dirty nails, even though the frozen water made it impossible to wash. Charlotte shook with 'impotent anger' but Maria, like the fictional Helen, preached a creed of endurance. For her, the purpose of life was to look beyond life.

Louisa May Alcott's sister Elizabeth died in 1858 after a long and indefinite illness, ten years before *Little Women* was written, and another sister died in 1879. Louisa's remarks in her diary on the death of Lizzie indicate something of what she was trying to do in Beth's deathbed scene. In her search for a meaning to the horrible and painful death of her 23-year-old sister, who in life had always been so passive and undemanding, she wrote: 'So the first break comes, and I know what death means—a liberator for her, a teacher for us.'[4] The following year, alone in Boston hunting for employment, Louisa, lonely and depressed, saw the death of her sister as 'beautiful; so I cannot fear it, but find it friendly and wonderful'.[5]

The painful memories of these much-loved, gentle sisters, so different from both writers' own questioning and challenging natures, found their way into these novels. The extraordinarily mature words of the young Maria Brontë with her unquestioning faith in God could have been spoken at the deathbed of either Helen Burns or Beth March: 'God waits only the separation of spirit from flesh to crown us with a full reward. Why then should we ever sink overwhelmed with distress, when life is so soon over and death is so certain an entrance to happiness: to glory?'[6]

HELEN BURNS AND JANE EYRE

Jane Eyre was not written specifically for girls, but for those who read it for the first time when they were young, it was perhaps the scenes of her girlhood which continued to inhabit the imagination. For such readers, the special force of this book was not her adult years at Thornfield or the time she spent with St John, Mary and Diana Rivers, but the first nine chapters of the book which cover the first ten years of Jane's life. For young readers, it can be argued, the central emotional experience of this book does not lie in Jane's relationship with Rochester but in her mostly unhappy and lonely childhood. Central to this are her early years with her cruel and unloving Aunt Reed and appalling cousins at Gateshead, particularly the scene in the Red Room where she is imprisoned as if she is a criminal and terrified by the sight of what she believes to be the ghost of her dead uncle. As a glimmer of hope in these dark times, the reader is offered the rare kindness shown by the apothecary and the servant Bessie. Jane's time at Lowood School, where she suffers terrible indignities and injustice but experiences being loved and valued for her own qualities for the first time, has extraordinary resonance.

However, as Adrienne Rich notes, it is not these childhood scenes but the Thornfield episode which is often recalled or referred to as if it *were* the novel *Jane Eyre*.[7] In this truncated version the story begins where a young woman arrives as governess in a large country house, meets and falls in love with the master of the house, has her wedding day turned on its head by the discovery that the madwoman at the top of the house is in fact his wife, steals away, returns to find the house burned to the ground and the madwoman dead, and finally marries her lover now blinded and disabled by the fire.[8]

Jane Eyre, subtitled *An Autobiography,* is not an autobiographical novel in strict terms, but incorporates many elements of Charlotte Brontë's life. Charlotte was not an orphan like Jane and her home was with her father, brother and sisters. But The Clergy Daughter's School where she spent several years was much like the terrible Lowood. This school was designed for the daughters of poor clergymen who had to be prepared to earn

their own living, mostly as governesses. The school was situated in an unhealthy and damp place and the children were fed a poor, sometimes inedible diet of stale bread and burnt porridge from a dirty kitchen. Stories such as those of the big girls forming a tight ring around the fire on their return from their walks so that the younger ones received no warmth are based exactly on the experiences of Charlotte and her sisters. The school's founder, William Carus Wilson, had much in common with the insufferable Mr Brocklehurst of *Jane Eyre*. Both believed that children, especially poor children, were essentially wicked and full of pride and both wrote Puritan tracts which encouraged children to believe that hell and damnation were just a moment away.

When Jane first meets Brocklehurst in Aunt Reed's parlour he seems to resemble a tall black pillar with a grim face at the top like a carved mask. This first meeting quickly establishes the difference between the received religious views and Jane's unique, independent spirit, even when she is intimidated and trembling with fear. When Brocklehurst asks her where the wicked go after death, she readily gives him the orthodox answer and tells him that they go to hell:

'And what is hell? Can you tell me that?'

'A pit full of fire.'

'And should you like to fall into that pit, and to be burning there for ever?'

'No, sir.'

'What must you do to avoid it?'

Jane knows that her answer will be considered 'objectionable' but when she replies 'I must keep in good health and not die', it is clear that she is refusing to play the adult's hypocritical game. She knows that Brocklehurst's response will be that she is a wicked girl who must pray to God to change her heart of stone into a heart of flesh, but she instinctively rejects the injustice of the adults who use God's name to justify their own cruelty. Her spirit will not allow her to accept a God who is so intolerant of questioning.

Both Aunt Reed and Mr Brocklehurst are in perfect agreement that Jane, who has no independent financial means, must be kept humble. 'Humility is a Christian grace, and one peculiarly appropriate to the pupils of Lowood . . . I have studied how best to mortify in them the worldly sentiment of pride', says Mr Brocklehurst. But Jane cannot easily be made humble. She has too much of the fighter in her, too much energy and spirit.

In the mid-nineteenth century, to describe a woman as having 'self-esteem' was an insult; it was synonymous with being selfish and wilful. But Jane's moral sense tells her that the sins she is accused of—self-interest, pride and deceit (and the accusation of falsehood is the most unfair of all)—are only sins if you are poor and dependent. Wealthy children like her cousins John, Georgiana and Eliza can be as proud and cruel and tell as many lies as they want. The spirit of religion is evoked not to comfort or shelter but to remind her that she is an orphan, without parents or friends; homeless even when she is living in the house of relatives.

As Mr Brocklehurst leaves, he presents Jane with a thin pamphlet entitled 'The Child's Guide'. He tells her to 'read it with prayer, especially the part containing "an account of the awfully sudden death of Martha G-, a naughty child addicted to falsehood and deceit."'

It is Jane's rebellious rage that enables her to survive this injustice. Her sense of fairness will not allow her to repent for sins she has not committed. However terrified she is, she knows that she must speak and before she leaves Gateshead she tells her aunt:

> 'I am not deceitful: if I were, I should say I loved *you*; but I declare I do not love you: I dislike you the worst of anybody in the world except John Reed: and this book about the Liar, you may give it to your girl Georgiana, for it is she who tells lies, and not I.'

When asked to justify her daring in speaking out like this, Jane replies passionately:

> 'How dare I? Because it is the *truth*. You think I have no feelings and can live without one bit of love or kindness; but I cannot live so: and you have no pity. I shall remember to my dying day how you thrust me back—roughly and violently thrust me back—into the red-room, and locked me up there, to my dying day, though I was in agony.'

Jane is exhausted by this but sees it as her first victory. Her action is an affirmation of the life force within her and her refusal to stay silent is a refusal to descend into a state of nothingness. Others believe that her passionate nature will mean that God will punish her. The servant Abbott comments: 'He might strike her dead in the midst of her tantrums, and then where will she go?' But Jane instinctively disbelieves this. To be silent would, to her, be the equivalent of death. As Adrienne Rich observes, 'It is at this moment that the germ of the person we are finally to know as Jane Eyre is born: a person determined to live, and to choose her life with dignity, integrity and pride.'⁹

Jane's sense of elation is short-lived. A Victorian child could not quarrel with adults without afterwards feeling remorse. Like aromatic wine, it seemed on swallowing to be warm and racy but its aftertaste was metallic and corroding and gave Jane the sensation of being poisoned. It was in this mood, but also with expectation and hope, that Jane began the next part of her journey and the second phase of her childhood at Lowood Institution.

From the beginning, the reader understands that Helen Burns is ill. Jane's first awareness of her is not a sighting, but the sound of a 'hollow cough'; unmistakable to the reader as a symptom of tuberculosis.

In mid-nineteenth century literature, tuberculosis was a straightforward and silent visitor which almost always resulted in the death of its blameless victim. Helen's tuberculosis, the literary disease of the nineteenth century, is only referred to indirectly; we know only of the hollow cough, the pain in her chest of which she never complains, her pale face and thin cheeks. As Susan Sontag describes in *Illness as Metaphor* [1983], consumption was often viewed as a lyrical, romantic taker of young lives, although in reality death from tuberculosis was ugly and painful. Helen embodies all the melancholy characteristics of the consumptive in literature: she is sensitive, powerless, a being apart. Like her name, she 'burns' with passion and suffering, but her passion is not for life. Nearly a hundred years later, Freud would describe Helen's state of mind as a death wish. In *Beyond the Pleasure Principle* [1920] he described the death wish as not unnatural but as a deeply pleasurable way to become nothing. But of course, Helen does not believe that she will descend into nothingness. Not quite life-loving enough to survive this world, she looks happily towards the next.

Jane's first view of this as yet unnamed girl is of her sitting on a bench, reading a book. Jane catches the title, *Rasselas,* and its strangeness interests her. She is used to reading only childish books, and this is serious and substantial. She is immediately attracted to the scholarly, self-reliant Helen who answers her questions politely but prefers to read alone.

Later that day, Jane witnesses the first of the many injustices meted out to Helen by the sadistic teacher Miss Scatcherd. When Helen is dismissed from class in disgrace and sent to stand in the middle of the large schoolroom, Jane expects her to show signs of great distress and shame, but to her surprise she neither weeps nor blushes. She seems to Jane to 'be thinking of something beyond her punishment—beyond her situation; of something not found before her.' The following day, Jane witnesses again Miss Scatcherd's continual bullying of 'Burns'. Everything her friend does seems to irritate this teacher. Even when Helen gets all the answers right and Jane expects to hear praise, Miss Scatcherd cries out, 'You dirty, disagreeable girl! You have never cleaned your nails this morning!', and her passive and respectful response only causes further insults. 'Hardened girl!' exclaimed Miss Scatcherd; 'nothing can correct you of your slatternly habits: carry the rod away.'

Whereas Jane furiously searches for truth and fairness, Helen accepts the way others define her. Helen's response to Jane's cry that if she had been in her place, she would have snatched the rod from Miss Scatcherd's hand and broken it under her nose, is:

> 'Probably you would do nothing of the sort . . . It is far better to endure patiently a smart which nobody feels but yourself, than to commit a hasty action whose evil consequences will extend to all connected with you; and, besides, the Bible bids us return good for evil.'

When Jane questions her about her acceptance of Miss Scatcherd's cruelty, she replies that it is her own fault. Helen's form of Christianity is based on the idea of the sanctity of suffering and the total denial of the self. Jane cannot comprehend such passivity:

> 'When we are struck at without a reason, we should strike back again very hard: I am sure we should—so hard as to teach the person who struck us never to do it again.'

Three weeks after Jane's arrival at Lowood, Brocklehurst makes his first appearance. Denouncing Jane as an 'interloper and an alien', he places her on a stool so that they can see this 'liar' and instructs the girls not to speak to her for the remainder of the day. As Helen passes Jane, she lifts her eyes and an extraordinary sensation and light seem to pass from her into Jane, giving Jane the courage to master her rising hysteria and stay silent. 'It was as if a martyr, a hero had passed a slave or victim, and imparted strength in the transit.'

In a conversation which follows this incident, Jane tells Helen that she would rather die than live solitary and hated; to gain love from those she cared about, she would happily have a bone broken or a bull toss her. Helen's response is to try to calm Jane down:

> 'Hush, Jane! You think too much of the love of human beings; you are too impulsive, too vehement: the sovereign Hand that created your frame, and put life into it, has provided you with other resources than your feeble self, or than creatures feeble as you.'

Helen's role is to teach Jane restraint. Whilst Jane engages in a constant struggle with life, Helen finds it simpler to disengage herself from such concerns. She espouses a Christianity quite different to the hypocritical and harsh doctrine that Brocklehurst represents, and believes that life is too short to be spent in nursing animosity or in registering wrongs. When Jane recounts her ill-treatment by Aunt Reed and her cousins, Helen's advice is to try to forget the severity of her past treatment and to calm the passionate emotions which such injustices excite. Her spiritual beliefs allow her to rise above the brutalities of life. Her response to the cruelties of this world is to look towards the next: 'Revenge never worries my heart, degradation never too deeply disgusts me, injustice never crushes me too low; I live in calm, looking to the end.'

But Helen's life is not without its battles. Some months after Jane has joined Lowood, typhus begins to spread through the school, a result of its unhealthy location and the semi-starvation and neglected colds of the girls. Death becomes a frequent visitor and Jane, distracted by new interests, realises that she has not seen Helen for some weeks. Although she knows that Helen is suffering from consumption and not the typhus which is killing so many pupils, she does not understand the seriousness of this condition. One evening, seeing the doctor leave, she is struck by the knowledge that Helen is dying and that she must see her to give her 'one last kiss, exchange with her one last word'. Jane creeps into Miss Temple's room where Helen lies sleeping. She kisses her cold forehead and her cold, thin cheeks.

The following scene is moving in its simplicity. With the two nestling together in the cold bed, Helen has full confidence that she is about to enter a better world. She whispers calmly:

> 'I am very happy Jane and when you hear that I am dead, you must be sure and not grieve: there is nothing to grieve about. We must all die one day, and the illness removing me is not painful: it is gentle and gradual.'

Jane longs to understand and believe but her nature is not to accept the spiritual; she is too much in the real world. Earlier that day she has, for the first time, forced her mind to try to understand what she has been taught about heaven and hell, but when she tries to picture what this might be, she recoils in confusion. She can see only an 'unfathomed gulf' and her mind recoils from the thought of plunging into that chaos. For Jane, there is no simple or comforting vision of life after death and her mind can only comprehend 'the one point where it stood—the present; all the rest was formless cloud and vacant depth'. At Helen's bedside she is full of questions: 'Where are you going to Helen? Can you see? Do you know?' Helen is reassuringly certain of their joint future in heaven:

> 'I am sure there is a future state. I believe that God is good: I can resign my immortal part to Him without any misgiving. God is my father; God is my friend: I love him: I believe he loves me . . . You will come to the same region of happiness: be received by the same mighty Universal Parent, no doubt, dear Jane.'

Like this they fall asleep. Their last words are the simple words of friendship:

> 'Don't leave me Jane, I like to have you near me.'

> 'I'll stay with you, dear Helen: no-one shall take me away.'

> 'Are you warm, darling?'

> 'Yes.'

'Good-night, Jane.'

'Good-night, Helen.'

Helen's deathbed is symbolic of the loneliness of these two orphans: she dies, not in the bosom of her family, but with another child, the two of them wrapped around each other against the cold. What prevents this from being a typically mawkish and sentimental deathbed scene is not just its brevity but Jane's unconventional scepticism about the existence of God and heaven.[10] Jane cannot share Helen's view that by dying young she is 'escaping great suffering' or that death is 'so certain an entrance to happiness—to glory'. Where Helen sees simple answers, Jane sees only questions and uncertainties. For both writer and reader there is a subtle casting off here; Helen's death marks the start of an independent self for Jane. Instead of turning heavenward, she embraces life, although she is by no means certain what kind of life this will be.

Helen Burns' role in the novel is often seen as teaching Jane to curb the negative side of her passion and to show her that it is possible to see injustice without the anger and despair she has known as a child; beating on the red-room door or raging against those who inevitably have control over her. She learns from Helen and her teacher, Miss Temple, that she cannot go out into the world with so much anger because socially she will have to occupy a lowly position and some humility is essential to her survival. She learns to distinguish between intense feelings which can lead to greater fulfilment and those which can only lead to self-destruction. But Helen's most important role is not just to 'counsel the indignant Jane in the virtues of patience and long-suffering', but to show her what she does *not* want to be.[11] Helen embraces death; Jane chooses life. Whilst Helen's only triumph over the daily tyranny and injustice of those around her is her own death, Jane wants to triumph by having the freedom and choice to regulate her own life. Helen's crucial role is to show Jane what she cannot choose to be, does not want to be, because her nature will not allow her to. As Lyndall Gordon writes of the relationship between Charlotte Brontë and her sister Maria, 'Maria was absolute for death, and as such, a formidable model against whom Charlotte was to choose her alternative.'[12] The same is true for Helen and Jane. In life Helen abdicates responsibility for choices or decisions; her complete faith means that all is given over to God. Jane cannot help but think for herself. Her passionate desire for a more fulfilling life means that she has to look outwards to the world even though this involves taking great risks.

Jane Eyre, like most of the books which will be discussed here, is the story of a journey. Jane's progress, like that of Bunyan's hero, is full of pitfalls and difficult, painful choices, but she is clear about what she wants from life:

Fears, of sensations and excitements, awaited those who had the courage to go forth into its expanse, to seek real knowledge of life amidst its perils.

'Reader, I married him' is Jane's famous announcement at the end of her story and it seems pertinent to comment here on the connection between Rochester's new status as a disabled person and their reinstated love. Jane, having fallen in love with her employer, flees Thornfield on the day of her marriage when she finds herself about to commit bigamy. A year later, having found safety but not happiness with the Rivers family, she hears Rochester's disembodied voice summoning her back. She returns to Thornfield to find it destroyed by fire. Enquiring of an old servant, Jane is informed that Rochester is alive, 'but many think he had better be dead', a common enough perception of the value of the life of a disabled person. He has been injured 'bravely' saving the life of the wife he once locked in the attic and pretended did not exist, and now has a full compliment of impairments: 'He is now helpless indeed—blind and a cripple.'

Brontë exploits the common idea in religion and literature that faith and love have the power to make cripples walk and blind men see, and Jane undertakes to 'rehumanise' the 'Bluebeard' of her past.[13] With the help of her arm he is able to walk again; with her unqualified love, he regains his sight and is able to look into the large, black eyes of his own son, a mirror image of his own.

Jo March and Beth March

Unlike *Jane Eyre*, *Little Women* was a book specifically written for girls. For years Louisa and her father Bronson Alcott had discussed the need for plain stories for boys and girls about childish victories over selfishness, and her publishers too wanted a 'girl's story', this being a newly discovered type of popular fiction. She agreed that 'simple, lively books were much needed for girls' and within a year she had produced perhaps the best-loved girls' book ever written. By the time *Little Women* came out in 1868, Louisa May Alcott had already published many stories and books, some in her own name and others, mostly racy melodramas and adventures, written under a variety of pseudonyms. *Little Women*, her first major book for children, outstripped all expectations and the character of Jo, the most unconventional and interesting of the four March girls, became the model for many literary heroines. As John Rowe Townsend points out, 'the very name of Jo still seems to bear her imprint.'[14]

Louisa May Alcott herself had four sisters, a loving and capable mother and a father who, despite his failings, she adored and respected.[15] The stories of the March girls in *Little Women* are clearly based on Louisa's own life. In her journal she wrote: 'I plod away, though I don't enjoy this sort of thing. Never liked girls or knew many except my sisters; but our queer plays and experience may prove interesting, though I doubt it.'[16] Brigid Brophy describes Jo as 'one of the most blatantly autobiographical yet most fairly treated heroines in print.'[17]

Louisa's own family life was, however, much more troubled than the fictitiously perfect March family. In one of the many studies of Alcott's life, Martha Saxton notes:

> Louisa adopted toward her parents a tone of sentimental pity that gave everything a heartbreak flavor, but that didn't necessarily correspond to reality. She chose to see them as baffled children buffeted mercilessly by arbitrary winds. This is the tone familiar to readers of *Little Women,* and it derives from Louisa's need to find a sentimental, loving vocabulary for articulating the family events. Rage, anger, and disappointment were not allowed.[18]

For all its affection and sentimentality, *Little Women* does not escape the didactic tone of earlier writings such as those of Charlotte Yonge and Maria Edgeworth. Every 'adventure' has its clear lesson, every sister (except Beth) an undesirable trait to overcome. Amy has to learn to be less selfish and vain, Meg needs to curb her desire for finery and learn that money cannot buy love, 'womanly skills' or true happiness, and Jo has to learn to dampen her wild, boyish energy and fiery temper and become what her father calls at the end of the novel 'a strong, helpful tender-hearted woman'. The emotions the girls feel are strong but not passionate. The strongest are jealousy and anger but with effort they can be replaced by admiration and love. Self-denial is the order of the day, along with suffering and duty. Through these trials the four girls journey, often literally clutching their copies of John Bunyan's *Pilgrim's Progress,* hoping to reach Celestial City. As Reynolds and Humble point out: 'At one level each of Jo's sisters can be seen to represent one of the personality traits which needs to be overcome if the self is to learn to forget itself and become the intensely sympathetic, immensely charming and utterly unselfish, "Angel in the House".'[19]

Beth is set apart from the rest of her sisters by being entirely without ambition or self-interest. Like Helen Burns in *Jane Eyre,* Beth is presented to the reader as entirely blameless, a kind, saintly creature who never does anyone any harm. (Except the time she killed the poor canaries by forgetting to feed them, but her remorse was so great that we instantly forgave her.) Both struggle with ill health and have an unfailing belief that the next world will be a better place. Like Helen, illness visits Beth because she is not fully engaged with life. She too has an 'other-worldly' quality about her—a dreaminess which keeps her happily at home whilst others long to have adventures. Like Helen Burns, Beth is also part of the pilgrimage of another, stronger, lifeloving character—in this case her unconventional, clever, difficult, older sister Jo.

The presentation of Beth's illness, like that of Helen Burns, plays on the stereotypical idea that what ill or disabled people need most is the pity and kindness of others. But in order to deserve this treatment, they must not burden those around them with strong emotions such as rage or disappointment. Their illness is sanitised and clean, their suffering spiritual rather than physical. Above all, they must be self-effacing, leaving plenty of space for the non-disabled character to develop and learn.

Beth's first line in *Little Women* establishes her unselfish (some might say self-righteous) personality. Whilst her sisters irritably complain about their poverty and lack of Christmas presents, Beth, sitting 'contentedly from her corner', reminds them 'we've got father and mother and each other'. This corner is significant. Beth remains in her corner both literally and metaphorically until her death three-quarters of the way through the second part of *Little Women.*[20] She is always sighing there so that only 'the hearthbrush and kettle holder can hear her', but such behaviour is always presented as unselfish and gentle rather than manipulative. When the others go off to have adventures, fall in love and get into scrapes they will always return to find Beth sitting in her corner ready to dispense love and sympathy. She is the peacemaker, particularly for troubled, clever Jo who wants more from life than an intelligent, robust, nineteenth-century female without independent means could possibly hope to get.

Beth's father calls her 'Little Tranquillity', and the name suits her 'for she seems to live in a happy world of her own, only venturing out to meet the few whom she trusted and loved.' She is thirteen years old, a crucial transitional time for girls in fiction, but Beth is not destined for womanhood. She is 'a child still', playing with her dolls, 'her little world peopled with imaginary friends'.

Jo and Beth are cast as opposites but there is a strong bond between them. 'To Jo alone did the shy child tell her thoughts; and over her big harum-scarum sister, Beth unconsciously exercised more influence than any one in the family.' Physically Jo (like many a heroine to follow) is the archetypal tomboy: tall, thin and coltish with a surplus of energy and zest for life. Her eyes are grey and sharp, by turns fierce, funny, or thoughtful. Beth is the very picture of passive femininity: rosy, with smooth hair and a shy manner, timid voice and peaceful expression. Jo, who always wants to be somewhere else, longs 'to do something splendid . . . something heroic or wonderful, that won't be forgotten after

I'm dead', whereas Beth's most ambitious thought is 'to stay at home safe with father and mother, and help take care of the family'. In one of their many conversations where they play at being 'pilgrims', Beth declares her longing to enter the Celestial City of heaven where they will all go, by and by, if they are good enough. 'It seems so long to wait, so hard to do; I want to fly away at once, as those swallows fly, and go in at that splendid gate.'

Beth almost has her wish in the first volume of *Little Women*. Alcott takes Beth right to the point of death, but saves her at the last moment. The description of her near-death experience contains all the classic elements of such scenes: the family around the bedside, the midnight vigil, the promises to be better in the future, the doctor's presence, the sympathy of the natural elements—for example, a biting wind and falling snow—the fever that miraculously 'turns' in the early hours of the morning.

There are, of course, also some serious lessons to be learned from Beth's first battle with death, and Alcott does not leave the reader guessing what these might be. It happens when the 'Heart of the House', Marmee, has been called away to Washington to visit her husband, who is dangerously ill. Everything starts off well.

> For a week the amount of virtue in the old house would have supplied the neighbourhood. It was really amazing, for every one seemed in a heavenly frame of mind, and self-denial was all the fashion.

But after a week, Jo subsides on the sofa, reading and writing, Meg spends too much time in writing long letters or dreamily reading the dispatches from Washington, and Amy gets sick of the housework and goes back to her art. Only Beth continues with her duties. When she tries to persuade her sisters to come with her to visit the Hummels, a poor fatherless German family whom we met in the opening pages of the book, each sister has her own, selfish excuse. So Beth 'quietly put on her hood, filled her basket with odds and ends for the poor children, and went out into the chilly air, with a heavy head and a grieved look in her patient eyes.' She returns with the story of how the baby died in her lap before its mother returned home and with the first signs of scarlet fever. Jo is frightened and filled with remorse and in the absence of their mother, they send Amy to Aunt March's. Beth chooses Jo to stay and look after her and Jo devotes herself to her sister, day and night. Beth typically bears her illness with patience and without complaint, but soon the fever overtakes her and she cannot recognise the familiar faces around her. The 'shadow of death hovers over the once happy home'. Jo's lesson is to discover:

> the beauty and the sweetness of Beth's nature . . . and to acknowledge the worth of Beth's unselfish ambition, to live for others, and make home happy by the exercise of all those simple virtues which all may possess and which all should love and value more than talent, wealth or beauty.

On the snowy first night of December when the year is symbolically 'getting ready for its death', the doctor tells Hannah the servant and Jo that it would be best to send for Mrs March. Jo is terrified when she learns how near to death Beth is. With tears streaming down her face she tells Laurie, 'she doesn't look like my Beth and there's no-one to help us bear it; mother and father both gone, and God seems so far away I can't find Him.' And later, 'Beth is my conscience, and I *can't* give her up. I can't! I can't!' He comforts her as best he can and they briefly debate God's motives for death. Laurie says hopefully that 'I don't think she will die; she's so good, and we all love her so much, I don't believe that God will take her away yet.' But Jo feels, 'The good and dear people always do die.' Both prove to be right, but Laurie is right first.

In an exhausting scene, guaranteed to wring every bit of emotion from the reader, both Meg and Jo promise to be better if only Beth lives. The doctor has been in to say that 'some change for better or worse would probably take place around midnight'. The snow falls, the bitter wind rages and all night the sisters sit by her bedside waiting for some change and for the arrival of their mother. The alert reader will recognise that in literature whenever a doctor warns that there will be some change around midnight for better or worse, the patient is likely to survive. Death in literature is rarely allocated a specific time; it either happens much more slowly, with the character drifting away as in Beth's actual death in the next volume, or much more suddenly, as in Judy's death in *Seven Little Australians* (see Chapter 6). The hour of midnight has a symbolic value in deathbed scenes. It is the turning point between night and day and when the clock strikes twelve in the March household, everything is 'as still as death' and nothing but the wailing of the wind breaks the deep hush. Beth's face is thin and wan and a 'pale shadow seemed to fall upon the little bed'.

At past two in the morning, Jo, standing by the window, turns to see Meg with her face hidden in the bed and assumes that Beth has died. A great change seems to have taken place. 'The fever flush and the look of pain were gone, and the beloved little face looked so pale and peaceful in its utter repose, that Jo felt no desire to weep or to lament.' Jo kisses the damp forehead of her favourite sister and says goodbye. But sensible Hannah, startled out of her sleep, hurries to the bedside, feels her hands, listens to her lips and exclaims in servant's dialect much loved by writers of domestic dramas, 'The fever's turned; she's sleepin' nat'ral; her skin's damp and she breathes easy. Praise be given! Oh, my goodness me!'

So Beth lives, for the time being at least. 'Never had the sun risen so beautifully, and never had the world seemed so lovely, as it did to the heavy eyes of Meg and Jo.' Then mother comes home and everything is complete.

It is hard not to be moved to tears by Jo's response to Beth's near death and the family's joy at her recovery, but writer Brigid Brophy is having none of it. Infuriated by her own tears after watching a weepy Hollywood film version of *Little Women,* she wrote in an article called, 'A Masterpiece and Dreadful':

> With Beth, I admit, Alcott went altogether too far. Beth's patience, humility and gentle sunniness are a quite monstrous imposition on the rest of the family—especially when you consider at what close, even cramped quarters they live (two bedrooms to four girls); no-one in the household could escape the blight of feeling unworthy which was imposed by Beth . . . She brings Beth to the point of dying in *Little Women* then lets her recover; whereupon instead of washing her hands—as not ruthless enough to do it—of the whole situation, she whips the situation up again in *Good Wives* and this time does ('As Beth had hoped, "the tide went out easily"') kill her off.[21]

Christianity, as presented in children's literature in the mid- to late-nineteenth century, provided a comforting view of a sweet and beatific after-life. Characters like Beth were not wrested from life but drifted gently away. Death was a fairly clean and tidy business and this tradition, although largely gone from literature, lives on in Hollywood where in the romantic story the nastiest medical symptom any dying person is likely to have is a spot of blood, a croaking voice, a pale face or a fevered brow and where everyone who lives has some positive lesson to learn.

Beth's real death in the second volume does not involve another midnight vigil but is more of a slow, slipping away from life. From the beginning of this book, (*Good Wives*) the author makes it clear that Beth is unlikely to survive to the end:

> Beth has grown slender, pale and more quiet than ever; the beautiful, kind eyes are larger, and in them lie an expression that saddens one although it is not sad itself. It is the shadow of pain which touches the young face with such pathetic patience, but Beth seldom complains and always speaks hopefully of "being better soon".

Meg is now married and is poor but happy and Jo, still battling with 'unacceptable' traits (bad temper and ambition in particular), is trying, as Louisa did herself, to find success as a writer. When she wins her first writing competition, she uses the money to send Marmee and Beth to the seaside for a month—this, along with the mountains, being the perfect literary place for cure and renewal. But Beth is not destined for cure and although Marmee returns feeling 'ten years younger', Beth is not 'quite so plump and rosy as could be desired'.

Jo's hopes for wider, more interesting horizons are dashed when Aunt March chooses more easygoing Amy to accompany her to Europe. She feels she is being punished for her strong-willed, direct nature. She tries to devote herself to literature and to Beth, but both girls are troubled and Jo confesses to her mother that she feels restless and anxious. She goes to Boston for the winter to work for a friend of the family and to develop her writing. She also meets the man who will become her husband, the middle-aged, philosophically minded German professor Herr Bhaer. Her rejection of Laurie, the handsome, fun-loving boy next door, remains a bitter disappointment to generations of her readers. Louisa May Alcott famously remarked in her journals, 'Girls write to ask who the little women marry, as if that was the only end and aim of a woman's life. I WON'T marry Jo to Laurie to please anyone.' But this remark turns out to be rather hypocritical, considering the lessons she had in mind for Jo following Beth's death.

When Jo returns from her time away from home, she finds Beth much changed. Beth has never been fully part of this world but now her body reflects her more or less complete disengagement from life. Matter is being replaced by the spirit and the soul:

> A heavy weight fell on Jo's heart as she saw her sister's face. It was no paler and but little thinner than in the autumn. Yet there was a strange, transparent look about it, as if the mortal was being slowly refined away and the immortal shining through the frail flesh with an indescribably pathetic beauty.

Beth is suffering from a nameless wasting disease, popular with sentimental Victorians and convenient for the novelist as the symptoms can be vague and relatively clean, unlike real illness.[22] Her dying lasts for many months, and in a style very different from the unsentimental, doubting lines in which Brontë describes Helen's death, Alcott writes:

> Ah me! Such heavy days, such long, long nights, such aching hearts and imploring prayer, when those who loved her best were forced to see the thin hands stretched out to them beseechingly, to hear the bitter cry, Help me, help me! and to feel that there was no help.

The reader almost drowns in the extended metaphor which sees the dying Beth as a traveller waiting to be taken across the river: 'Those about her felt that she was ready, saw that the first pilgrim called was likewise the fittest, and waited with her on shore, trying to see the Shining Ones coming to receive her when she crossed the river.' Finally, in the dark hour before dawn and 'with no farewell but one loving look, one little sigh', Beth's light goes out. Her peaceful death means that family and reader alike can 'thank God that Beth was well at last'.

Less sickly-sweet is the description in the following chapters of Jo's bitter despair at her sister's death. Jo is the only character in the book who is allowed any complex or subtle emotions and with Beth gone, she does not know what to do with herself. Nothing remains for her but 'loneliness and grief'. Amy is in Europe, Meg married and Jo does not know what 'useful, happy work to do' to take Beth's place. These are difficulties not easily solved and Jo (like Alcott herself) struggles with two opposing forces: the pressure on her to become the 'Little Woman' of the household, loved and remembered for her uncomplaining duty to others, and her desire for a more challenging, creative life which would necessarily involve separation from home and family.

But Alcott, unlike Brontë, does not allow Beth's death to be used as the start of a difficult journey, along which path Jo could become her real self. Such breaking free of family and home, she makes clear, could only lead to a loveless life. Shortly before her death, Beth foretold this as a route to unhappiness and she made Jo promise to take her place and be everything to Father and Mother: 'You'll be happier in doing that than writing splendid books or seeing all the world; for love is the only thing we carry with us when we go, and it makes the end so easy to carry.'

It is as if Alcott were denying the validity of her own life as a writer; as if the only real existence for a woman was love and domestic duty. Martha Saxton describes this as 'behaving spitefully towards her literary self and her readers'.[23] It is fascinating that most readers, even those who read the book many times over, remember Jo as our rebellious but loving heroine who forged a new way forward for herself. In fact Jo stays at home from this point, the only sister still remaining there, and modelling herself a little upon Beth, Jo learns to develop 'good womanly impulses':

> Brooms and dishcloths never could be as distasteful as they once had been, for Beth had presided over them both; and something of her housewifely spirit seemed to linger round the little mop, and the old brush that was never thrown away.

Alcott even has Jo humming Beth's songs as she cleans, brushes and sews. The 'splendid thing' she once wanted to do is now transformed into making her home as happy for her parents as they had for her and her sisters, even though nothing 'could be harder for a restless, ambitious girl than to give up her own hopes, plans and desires, and cheerfully live for others'. She doesn't quite turn Jo into saintly Beth, and Jo still finds it hard to carry out these duties entirely cheerfully, but the most difficult and therefore interesting sides of her nature—the hot temper, the vitality, the creativity, her indomitable self—are crushed by Beth's death, never to return.

Alcott, who would have preferred Jo to remain single, bowed to public pressure and married her to safe, older, unsexy Prof. Bhaer. They settled in Aunt March's old house and set up a school for boys. No wonder the sequels devoted to Jo (*Jo's Boys* and *Little Men*) are dull in comparison.

There is not a lot to be said about these last two sequels, which seem to have been written to please a voracious public rather than out of real commitment. The first of them, *Little Men,* contains a couple of disabled characters, but they are not central to the stories and pity is the sole emotion the reader is asked to feel about these two boys. The first, Billy Ward, 'a promising child changed to feeble idiot', is used to reflect the views of Louisa's father, Bronson Alcott, on education. Billy's father pressed him too hard and when he recovered from a fever, 'Billy's mind was like a slate over which a sponge has passed leaving it blank'. Jo tries to teach him simple things in order to 'give back intelligence enough to make the boy less a burden and an affliction', but presumably without success as he is never mentioned again. The second boy, Dick Brown, is cast in the 'Tiny Tim' mould of the cheerful cripple whose crooked body is tolerated because he bears it so cheerfully. Meg's little boy even asks him if 'crooked backs made people more cheerful'. His body would normally be considered abhorrent both to himself and others, but the Bhaers being of a philanthropic Christian frame of mind, 'soon led him to believe that people also loved his soul, and did not mind his body except to pity and help him bear it'. As with Jamie in *Pollyanna Grows Up* (discussed in Chapter 5) people try to ignore Dick Bown's impairment because his 'straight soul shone through it so beautifully'. Both boys die 'off-stage', and at the beginning of the next book, *Jo's Boys,* we are told that however kind these enlightened people were to them, their lives were scarcely worth living: 'Poor little Dick was dead, so was Billy; and no-one could mourn for them, since life would never be happy, afflicted as they were in mind and body.'

The deaths of Helen Burns and Beth March mark a particular point in literature about girls. As the century developed, writers were less likely to use the death of saintly, mild-tempered characters in order to give light and shade to the dilemmas of the strong heroine, and the 'burden' of illness and disability was more likely to be located in the protagonist. Death became rarer in domestic dramas and it was possible to have whole books in which nobody died. When they did, it was likely to be almost incidental, without any prolonged deathbed scene or sad mourning as in the case of Dick and Billy in the books mentioned above and Katy Carr's Aunt Izzie in *What Katy Did.*

The curing of the 'ill' fictional heroine had little to do with the progress of medical science or lower mortality rates for children and more to do with a more flexible, open-minded approach to children and the need for a happy, more child-centred ending to stories.

In the books which followed *Jane Eyre, Little Women* and *Good Wives* illness and accident were used to provide a space in which change could take place and through which the writer could explore a wide range of possibilities. These included: changing views about what could and should be expected of children, differing expectations for boys and girls, absolute faith in God to decide what is best for you, often set against the importance of the fictional child's own engagement with life and belief in self, and the rapid economic and social changes of the time.

Louisa May Alcott dealt with some of these elements in her story *Jack and Jill,* one of the many books for children which she wrote after the *Little Women* stories, but it does not bear comparison to her classic work. She called these later books her 'moral pap', and this is a fair description of her contribution to the paralysis/cure genre of children's fiction.

Jack and Jill was published in 1880, the same year as *Heidi* and eight years after Susan Coolidge's *What Katy Did,* to which it bears a striking resemblance. It is a long and rather pious tale of golden boy Jack, wild, dark, gypsyish Jill, and their many friends. At the beginning of the story, head-strong Jill persuades Jack to go sledging with her, even though he knows it is dangerous. When he refuses to go, Jill tells him, 'I won't be told I don't "dare" by any boy in the world. If you are afraid, I'll go alone.' Alas, down the hill come Jack and Jill, and Jill suffers serious injury. The details are suitably vague, but it is clear the problem is in her spine. She 'can't stir one bit', her 'backbone is cracked' and 'sprained', and they 'fear she might be a cripple for life'.

Her paralysis enables the transition from wild girlhood (she is about 14 or 15 at the time of the accident) to passive womanhood. She learns to be,

> so patient, other people were ashamed to complain of their small worries; so cheerful that her own great one grew lighter; so industrious that she made both money and friends by pretty things she worked and sold to her many visitors. And best of all, so wise and sweet that she seemed to get good out of everything.

When Jill learns obedience, she is given a back brace and allowed to sit up. Alcott overworks what Ellen Moers calls the distinctly female metaphor of the bird locked in the cage symbolising the longing for liberty.[24] This 'liberation' happens where it almost always happens in literature—in the open air. Jill is taken to the seaside and the first steps of 'a gentler Jill' are towards the shore. Ten years later she marries Jack and together 'they voyage down an ever widening river to the sea'.

It is not known if Alcott had some acquaintance with the earlier *What Katy Did*; if not, the parallels between the two stories are remarkable. Both deal with head-strong girls at a crucial age, both break their spines as a result of doing something they have been warned not to do, and both emerge from their long period in bed only when they have learned to be less selfish and more womanly. But it is *What Katy Did* which carries on the best tradition of the family story and it is this book which has survived.

Notes

1. James Janeway, *A Token for Children,* T. Norris & A. Bettesworth, London, 1709, Preface, point 3.

2. Robert Louis Stevenson, 'Ordered South 1881', in D. J. Enright, *Faber Book of Frets and Fevers,* Faber and Faber, London, 1989, p331.

3. Lyndall Gordon, *Charlotte Brontë, A Passionate Life,* Vintage, London, 1995, p20.

4. Martha Saxton, *Louisa May Alcott, A Modern Biography,* The Noonday Press, Boston, 1995, p227.

5. Ibid.

6. Lyndall Gordon, *Charlotte Brontë, A Passionate Life,* p16.

7. Adrienne Rich, 'The Temptations of a Motherless Woman, 1973', in *On Lies, Secrets and Silence: Selected Prose 1966-1978,* W. W. Norton and Company Inc, New York, 1980.

8. This is also the way the film industry deals with this story. In the most recent film of *Jane Eyre* the red-room scene, crucial in any understanding of Jane's struggle to break free of the injustices and restrictions of her own girlhood, is relegated to the title sequence and entirely omitted from the main part of the film. Jane's girlhood takes up only ten minutes of a film which lasts an hour and three quarters, suggesting that its purpose is merely as introduction to the main story of thwarted love and ultimate reconciliation.

9. Adrienne Rich, 'The Temptations of a Motherless Woman, 1973', p93.

10. Susie Campbell, *Jane Eyre,* Penguin Critical Studies, Penguin Books, London, 1988, p23.

11. Terry Eagleton, *Myths of Power: A Marxist Study of the Brontës,* Macmillan, London, 1988, p15.

12. Lyndall Gordan, *Charlotte Brontë, A Passionate Life,* p19.

13. John Sutherland, *Can Jane Eyre Ever Be Happy? More Puzzles in Classic Fiction,* The World's Classics, Oxford University Press, Oxford, 1997.

14. John Rowe Townsend, *Written for Children,* Penguin Books, London, 1974, p79.

15. Bronson Alcott, an idealist and transcentalist philosopher, kept his family in debt and poverty for most of his life.

16. Quoted in Helen Jones, 'The Part Played by Boston Publishers of 1860-1900 in the Field of Children's Books', *Horn Blood Magazine,* June 1969, p331.

17. Brigid Brophy, 'A Masterpiece and Dreadful', in Virginia Haviland, *Children and Literature—Views and Reviews,* The Bodley Head, London, 1973, p69.

18. Martha Saxton, *Louisa May Alcott, A Modern Biography,* p196.

19. Kimberley Reynolds and Nicola Humble, *Victorian Heroines: Representations of Femininity in Mid-Nineteenth Century Literature and Art,* Harvester Wheatsheaf, 1993, p154.

20. *Little Women* was first published in two parts: the first in 1869 and the second a year later. In England this second part is known as *Good Wives* but for the purposes of this chapter, I have referred to the books as *Little Women* parts one and two.

21. Brigid Brophy, 'A Masterpiece and Dreadful', p69. Writer Elaine Showalter, speaking on the BBC Radio 4 arts programme *Front Row,* described her self-disgust at the way her emotions were manipulated in the 1999 film *Stepmum,* where the dying mother says her long goodbyes to each of her children, extracting a promise from them one by one. She didn't like the characters and felt the film was reactionary and sentimental, but it made her cry, it 'moved her' in some way she could not control. This is what Louisa May Alcott's deathbed scenes do to the reader, however often they read *Little Women.* At least Alcott's writing has the saving grace of being about girls for whom the reader genuinely cares. As Brophy says, 'We should recognise that though sentimentality mars art, craftmanship in sentimentality is to be legitimately enjoyed', p70.

22. It is interesting to compare this to the realistic set of symptoms of childhood illness described by Hippocrates a millennium or two earlier: 'In the different ages the following complaints occur: to little children and babies, apthae, vomiting, coughs, sleeplessness, terrors, inflammation of the navel, watery discharge from the ears. At the approach of dentition, irritation of the gums, fevers, convulsions, diarrhoea, especially when cutting the canine teeth, and in the case of very fat children and if the bowels are hard. Among those who are older occur affections of the tonsils, curvature at the vertebrae at the neck, asthma, stone, round worms, ascarides, warts, swelling by the ears, scrofula and tumours generally' (Hippocrates, *Aphorisms,* ?460-?377).

23. Martha Saxton, op. cit., p11.

24. Ellen Moers, *Literary Women,* The Women's Press, London, 1976, p250.

Anna Richards (essay date 2002)

SOURCE: Richards, Anna. "Suffering, Silence, and the Female Voice in German Fiction around 1800." *Women in German Yearbook* 18 (2002): 89-110.

[*In the following essay, Richards explores the portrayal of women's illness in nineteenth-century German novels, finding that most upheld the traditional patriarchal view of the sick woman and her ability to articulate herself.*]

To be silent, modern feminist criticism has taught us, is not necessarily to withhold communication. If, in the past, women have had their voices suppressed, ignored, or belittled, they have also chosen to say nothing as a means of expression or a strategy for resistance. Feminist literary critics have read the gaps and absences in texts by women or the reticence of their female characters as a protest against patriarchal language, as a sign of integrity, or as the expression of an "alternative" truth.[1] Such recognition of the potentially positive value of silence has been tempered, however, by timely reminders from critics such as Elaine Showalter and Susan Bordo of the patriarchal origin of its association with the female sex. Bordo asks us not to forget that, although it may express a protest, "*at the same time* . . . , muteness is the condition of the silent, uncomplaining woman—an ideal of patriarchal culture" (99). Showalter insists that, in the past, women "have been forced into silence" rather than choosing it freely, and that the blanks and holes in texts are therefore "not the spaces where female consciousness reveals itself, but the blinds of a 'prison-house of language'" (255-56).

Both collusion and resistance, a symptom of gender stereotyping and the expression of a female point of view in a patriarchal world: feminist theorists' evaluation of women's silence has much in common with recent debates about that other historical phenomenon often associated with the female sex, illness. The work of medical historians such as Esther Fischer-Homberger, Claudia Honegger, and Lorna Duffin has illuminated the ways in which patriarchal society, particularly from the late eighteenth century onwards, has "pathologized" the female sex. First, they argue, "healthy" female physiological processes and states, because different from male, have been judged deviant. Second, the restrictive conditions, both physical and psychological, imposed on women have promoted a higher incidence of actual illness among them. Just as they have reclaimed the silence imposed on women as an expression of protest, however, feminist critics have suggested that women's illness could also be a way to *resist* a traditionally female role, by allowing women to escape duties such as housework and childbirth, for example. Literary critics such as Birgit Wägenbaur and Lilo Weber have interpreted the representation of women's illness in the fiction of German authors, including Fanny Tarnow (1779-1862) and Theodor Fontane (1819-1898), in this way.

Female silence and female sickness are often found together in literary and medical texts. Ill women, that is, often stop speaking, and reticent women often become ill. Critical opinion on the link between the two, as on each separately, has been divided. On the one hand, Bordo suggests that the loss of voice that has often accompanied women's nervous diseases testifies to the female body's inscription with patriarchy's "ideological construction of femininity" (93). In *The Gendering of Melancholia* (1992), a psychoanalytical feminist study of literary representations of grief in the Renaissance period, Juliana Scheisari similarly interprets the fact that sickness lends eloquence to male characters, but typically silences female characters (15) as a symptomatic of patriarchy's privileging of male creativity and suppression of the female voice (7-8). Other feminist critics view the link more positively, however, arguing that silence and illness are often found together because women use physical symptoms to express that which lies outside the symbolic linguistic order. They have argued that Freud's often mute hysterical patients, for example, reject language in favor of a more authentic, corporeal means of communication.[2]

In this essay, I want to investigate the nature of the link between the silence, the self-expression, and the illness of female literary characters in five German novels from around 1800, by both male and female authors. What effect does illness have on the female voice, and vice versa? The feminist theories discussed above will be important in my analysis, but it will become clear that an examination of the literary texts in the light of medical and popular thinking on women of the time offers the most insight into the significance of the heroines' speaking or their silence. I therefore draw extensively on medical history, on medical works, and on popular writing on women from the period. In the main part of my essay, I deal with four texts that, although very different, all put forward a largely conventional view of women: Johann Martin Miller's *Siegwart: Eine Klostergeschichte* (*Siegwart: A Monastic Tale*, 1776), Friedrich Hölderlin's *Hyperion, oder der Eremit in*

Griechenland (*Hyperion, or the Hermit in Greece*, 1797-1799), and Johanna Schopenhauer's two novels *Gabriele* (1819-1820) and *Die Tante* (*The Aunt*, 1823). In conclusion, I analyze in greater depth a novel by an author whose portrayal of the relationship between female suffering and the female voice is more unusual: Therese Huber's *Luise: Ein Beitrag zur Geschichte der Konvenienz* (*Luise: A Contribution to the History of the Marriage of Convenience*, 1796).

These five novels were published during a period when gender roles were both the subject of intense discussion and more immutable than they had ever been. Between 1770 and 1830, hundreds of medical, philosophical, literary, anthropological, and "moral" works redefined the female sex as the direct opposite of, rather than the complement to, the male.[3] Women's physical role in reproduction was interpreted as purely receptive and taken as a model, not only for female physiology, but for female "nature" in general. It was widely accepted that, while men were active and rational, women were passive and guided by their emotions; that, while it was for men to act upon the world, women should remain in the domestic sphere. They were naturally imbued with the modesty, propriety, and selflessness that were essential to the wellbeing of the family and the nation in general, and their weaker bodies and minds and tendency to ill-health were the necessary concomitants of these qualities.

The vulnerable female body was considered particularly susceptible to nervous illnesses such as chlorosis (*Chlorose*), also known in German as *Bleichsucht*. This condition, which typically affected women around puberty, involved the extreme manifestation of characteristics that at this period were considered desirably feminine. If the ideal woman, for example, was fair-skinned and slim, the chlorotic was typically deathly pale and thin. In non-medical circles, it was often attributed to unhappiness in love and referred to as "love-fever" (*Liebesfieber*) or "virgin's disease" (*Jungfernsucht*); physicians and laypeople alike agreed that sufferers were possessed of an unusual degree of "womanly" sensitivity and emotionality. In her speaking habits, too, the chlorotic exaggerated the qualities valued in her sex: if women in general were encouraged to be reserved and modest, the chlorotic was frequently disinclined to express herself at all or was at least silent on the subject of her love. Medical writers of the period frequently remark on this symptom. Carl Gustav Carus (1789-1869), the famous scientist and physician from Dresden, writes in his *Lehrbuch der Gynäkologie* (*Textbook of Gynecology*, 1820) that chlorotics speak very little (1: 161), while the American physician William P. Dewees (1768-1841), whose work was translated into German, observes that they withdraw from social intercourse and are taciturn (361). In the discussion of chlorosis to be found in his popular moral-anthropological work *Betrachtungen über das weibliche Geschlecht und dessen Ausbildung in dem geselligen Leben* (*Observations on the Female Sex and its Education in Society,* 1802), Ernst Brandes (1758-1810) cites the lines from Shakespeare's *Twelfth Night* (1601)[4] in which Viola describes the fate of an imaginary lovelorn sister who, rather than speaking of her feelings, "lets concealment, like the worm in the bud / Feed on her damask cheek" and falls as a result into "a green and yellow melancholy" (Act 2, Scene 4). As does Viola, Brandes explains, those who suffer from chlorosis usually harbor a passion that they do not express (112).

Brandes need not have delved 200 years into the past nor into the literature of another country in order to find literary evidence for the reticence of the lovesick, wasting woman. German fiction around 1800 is littered with women suffering from a literary version of chlorosis, who either are untalkative in general, or, more commonly, refuse to speak of their love. In Hölderlin's famous novel *Hyperion,* the hero comments on the disinclination to speak of his beloved, the angelic Diotima: she is "the sweet, silent one who was so reluctant to speak" (65). Diotima fades away when he leaves her to go to battle. *Siegwart: Eine Klostergeschichte* by Johann Martin Miller (1750-1814) is a highly sentimental novel that is much less well-known than *Hyperion* today but was enormously popular in its time. It is the story of a sensitive young man who enters a monastery in the mistaken belief that Marianne, the object of his affections, is dead. Only some time later, when called upon to attend her on her deathbed, does he realize his error. He soon follows her into the grave. These two are not the only sentimental deaths in *Siegwart.* Earlier in the novel, the reader learns the fate of Sophie, a young friend of Siegwart's family, who is deeply in love with him. Aware that her affection is not returned, she determines to speak of it to no-one, enters a convent, loses her voice, becomes pale and thin, and poignantly wastes away.

The three-volume novel *Gabriele* by Johanna Schopenhauer (1766-1838) is often described by critics as an *Entsagungsroman* (novel of renunciation), because it portrays in idealized fashion the life of a beautiful, reserved young woman who repeatedly sacrifices her own desires to those of others. Gabriele marries against her will to please her father. She subsequently meets and falls in love with the young nobleman Hippolit, but conceals her feelings from him until she is on her deathbed. Schopenhauer's later novel *Die Tante* (*The Aunt*) has a happier ending: the father of the young heroine Viktorine finally permits his daughter to marry her beloved Raimund, even though Raimund is a member of a class he despises. But he only does so because Viktorine falls seriously ill after concealing her feelings for Raimund from those around her.

As Schiesari argues is typically the case in Renaissance literature, the association between illness and silence in German fiction around 1800 is not gender-neutral. Male characters are far less likely than female ones either to grow ill as a result of unhappiness or to be silenced by their suffering. Siegwart, the hero of Miller's novel, does, it is true, grow pale and thin and eventually even waste away when disappointed in love, but not before he has given full voice to his feelings and even found success as a travelling preacher. Schiesari concludes that the silence of the sickly heroine is an example of society's gender bias written into the text, an extreme manifestation of the voicelessness from which all women suffer under patriarchy. Can the same diagnosis be applied to the sickness and the silence of Diotima, Sophie, Gabriele, and Viktorine?

In *Hyperion,* Diotima's reticence is not directly related to her illness: it is neither a precipitating factor in, nor a result of, her decline. Diotima is from the first a "quiet being" (66); it is not until later, when Hyperion departs for battle, that she begins to waste away. Her disinclination to speak is not portrayed as the result of external pressure; rather, it is valued positively as a mark of integrity. As critics such as Thomas E. Ryan have argued, Hölderlin was skeptical of language's representational ability.[5] In this novel, he suggests that the most powerful emotions are inexpressible, and that silence is therefore the most authentic response to them. When Hyperion and Diotima first meet, for example, their connection with one another is so profound that it takes place on an extra-linguistic level, and they speak very little (63). Similarly, Hölderlin suggests that the power and beauty of Nature exceed words. Hyperion criticizes himself for attempting to convey through language his delight at the beauty of Diotima's island Kalaurea (60), and Diotima communes with her natural surroundings with sight and touch, "with eye and hand" (66) more than with words.

Diotima's reticence would seem to lend itself, then, to interpretation by the feminist critic as the active rejection of a language insufficient to express her view of the world and a superior means of communication, rather than the condition of the oppressed. But, in fact, her reticence and her physical wasting, although not in a causal relationship to one another, are both aspects of a conventional, restrictive image of femininity. Both are, first, symptoms of her extreme emotionality: she wastes away for love and cannot speak because she feels too deeply. Second, her silence is a sign that she is at one with Nature and her death is a complete return to the natural sphere. In this period, both these qualities were idealized and attributed to the female sex, and both worked against women's emancipation. While men, it was argued, were perfectible, women were complete in themselves and therefore had little need of education, which would merely disturb their natural "unity" and be incompatible with their "emotional" wisdom. Impressed by Diotima's wordlessness, Hyperion himself contrasts the wisdom that comes from learning with that which is natural and feminine, and associates the latter with silence: "What is the wisdom of a book compared with the wisdom of an angel?" he asks, adding immediately afterwards, "She always seemed to say so little, and said so much" (66). But although he admires and even tries to imitate Diotima's silence and her depth of feeling (e.g., 72), unlike her, he carries neither to a fatal conclusion. The silent, sensitive Diotima, who is described as "miraculously omniscient" (71), may represent Hölderlin's ideal for humanity in general, but she at the same time reinforces the period's ideal of passive femininity.

In *Gabriele,* Schopenhauer often uses adjectives such as "indescribable" (*unbeschreiblich*) and "inexpressible" (*unaussprechlich*). But, unlike Hölderlin, she is not thereby making a point about language's inability fully to express reality and thus motivating her heroine's refusal to speak. These adjectives, employed to excess and almost always in reference to her characters' emotional states—as for example in "an inexpressible longing" (7: 21), "an indescribable sadness" (7: 347), or the superlative "the most inexpressible sympathy" (8: 16)—function in this novel simply as conventional sentimental signifiers. When the heroine Gabriele refuses to speak about her feelings, this is, likewise, not a philosophical response to the inadequacy of language: she conceals her love for Hippolit because she is married to Moritz von Aarheim. In *Die Tante* and *Siegwart,* it is also made clear that the heroine declines to speak of a particular matter as a concession to external pressure or social convention. Viktorine has to endure "the heavy burden of enforced silence" (13: 120) because her father will not sanction her union with Raimund; Sophie does not speak of her feelings for Siegwart because they are not returned and it was unseemly for a woman to entertain unrequited love. Their silences, far from constituting a rejection of or a resistance to patriarchal influence, must be interpreted as a surrender to it.

It does not follow, however, that the portrayal of their silence must therefore serve an unemancipatory end. On the contrary, by portraying its link with their heroines' illnesses, Schopenhauer and Miller display an insight into the workings of repression that could problematize the equation of femininity and voicelessness Scheisari suggests is present in texts she examines. A closer look at medical thinking of the period will help to illustrate this point.

Brandes, who was not a physician, uses a literary source—Shakespeare—to illustrate a point about women's illness. But the medical writers of the early nineteenth century were becoming increasingly "scientific" in their approach, which meant that where, in the past, emotional and psychological explanations for disorders had been given, they were eager to find physiological ones. The spheres of medicine and literature, then, were growing further apart. As its popular name suggests, chlorosis or "lovesickness" had traditionally been understood by physicians to be the result of unrequited affection or some other overwhelming sadness, in particular one that remained unexpressed, since feelings that were not given voice were liable to "turn in" on the sufferer and "consume" (*verzehren*) the inner self. But by 1800, this explanation was losing ground. The German physician Johann Jörg (1779-1856) does suggest in his *Handbuch der Krankheiten des Weibes* (*Handbook of Woman's Diseases,* 1809) that "silent and suppressed troubles" (217) may be a factor in the onset of chlorosis, while others, such as Carus, allow that unhappy love or grief may sometimes play a role (162). In general, however, physicians around 1800 were focusing more on organic disturbances in the blood system or a build-up of energies in the reproductive organs as causative factors, and mentioning silence and grief merely as symptoms. Even Brandes, although he cites lines from Shakespeare that, in keeping with the old-fashioned understanding of lovesickness, seem to ascribe an instrumental role in its development to silence, himself suggests no such causal link. Instead, he sees a lack of sexual activity as the provoking factor (111-12).

Literary authors, on the other hand, tended to stick to conventional ideas about the origins of female wasting and thus, paradoxically, to approach more closely the "new" understanding of nervous illness propounded by Freud in the late nineteenth and early twentieth centuries. Early in his career, Freud, together with his colleague Josef Breuer, developed the theory that emotions, drives, or traumatic memories that were "repressed" sought expression in physical symptoms (see *Studies on Hysteria,* 1895). Later, in the essay entitled "Mourning and Melancholia" ("Trauer und Melancholie," 1917), he argued that the unsuccessful mourning of a lost object entailed the internalization of that object, which would then "consume" the ego of the mourner, a theory that clearly resembles the traditional notion of unhappy grieving explained above. Although there is no intimation in their fiction of an unconscious region to which feelings, memories, and losses are banned, as there is in Freud's work, Miller and Schopenhauer do suggest that the repression of an emotion through a failure to verbalize it, and the "turning in" of feelings of grief that should be directed outward, are not just the symptoms, but part of the etiology of chlorosis.

In *Siegwart,* the link between reticence and the onset of wasting is implied, rather than stated directly. Sophie's repeated, almost obsessive reference in her diary to her inability to speak of her feelings for the hero can leave the reader in little doubt that this silence has been at least a precipitating factor in her decline, although the connection is never named. "I cannot speak!" she insists twice; "I may not speak" (463-64); "I have long suffered and struggled, and not opened my mouth" (459). Schopenhauer makes the causative role of silence rather than, or in addition to, suffering in her heroines' illnesses more explicit. When Gabriele falls in love with Hippolit, she determines "completely to conceal her inner being" (9: 220). This, Schopenhauer writes, is no easy task. Gabriele's attempts to conceal "that which often filled her impassioned heart to bursting" (9: 222) have a direct negative impact on her health: "her physical strength succumbed to the immense strain" (9: 222). Most of Gabriele's friends lack insight into the cause of her decline, but when she is near death, her fatherly friend Ernesto "saw clearly in Gabriele's heart all the unexpressed pain, the burden of which had defeated it" (8: 240). In *Die Tante,* likewise, Schopenhauer attributes her heroine's illness in unequivocal terms to the pressure of keeping her feelings to herself: "Thus the violent forcing back of the feelings of sorrow and anxiety about her loved one, which dominated her completely, had alone brought her to the brink of the grave" (13: 120). Viktorine's governess, like the novel's narrator, demonstrates an awareness of the role of self-expression in the maintenance of good health: "If only she had confided in me," she sighs, "but instead she said nothing and wept, and wept and said nothing, and now she's lying there" (13: 17).

In light of the fact that the failure of these heroines to express themselves makes them ill and that silence is imposed on rather than freely chosen by them, it could be argued that Miller and Schopenhauer avoid the essentialist association of the female sex with silence. But their agenda in depicting the workings of repression is not, ultimately, an emancipatory one. The heroines' voicelessness may be the result of social convention or imposed by their parents, and may be unhealthy, but it is nevertheless not called into question. It is portrayed, rather, as part of their "natural" destiny as women, or as Frau von Willangen, Gabriele's trusted friend and a reliable moral authority, puts it, quoting from the same speech by Shakespeare's Viola to which Brandes refers: "Shakespeare's 'Smiling at grief' is more or less the lot and the virtue of the best of all our sex; we are born for it" (8: 22-23).

The illnesses that result from such "feminine" behavior are not a device to illustrate critically the detrimental nature of contingent dictates of femininity: on the contrary, they are aestheticized and, in the case of *Gabriele* at least, presented as inevitable. Schopenhauer may suggest that repression contributed to Gabriele's early decline, but she also indicates that it was fated to happen: her heroine was born with only a "weak spark of life" and always had "something ethereal" about her (7: 40). Both Gabriele and Miller's Sophie are reconciled

to, even look forward to death; neither suffers much pain; and Gabriele even grows more beautiful the more ill she becomes. When, in the later stages of their decline, both heroines lose their voices, the pathos of their decline is heightened. Like Schopenhauer's frequent use of adjectives such as "inexpressible," their loss of voice may also suggest that words are insufficient to express intense emotional states, but this, once again, is more a conventional sentimental trope used to point up the heroines' exemplary sensitivity than part of a sustained critique of the language system.

If neither Miller's, Schopenhauer's, nor Hölderlin's portrayal of female silence can be read as emancipatory, what are we to make of their representation of women's self-expression? Although Sophie, Gabriele, Viktorine, and Diotima all refuse to speak on certain occasions or of certain subjects, the argument that their authors do not intend this to represent a radical rejection of language is reinforced by the fact that each heroine, at other times, uses words to communicate at length and with conviction. Diotima expresses herself through song, while Sophie, Gabriele, and Viktorine all hold forth at some length to the loved ones attending them in their sickness. Viktorine also writes a lot in her grief (13: 31), although the reader does not learn what, or to whom, her text is addressed. Sophie writes fervently in her diary, while Diotima is a prolific letter-writer; in both cases, their words are addressed to and grieved over by their beloved ones.[6] Their illnesses, then, although generally caused by silence and/or causing a further loss of voice, at the same time provide them with an impetus for communication and an attentive audience for their words. Could the link between illness and the female voice in fiction around 1800, then, in fact be interpreted in a more positive light than has hitherto been suggested? Could the heroine's illness, for example, be read as conducive to linguistic creativity, as Schiesari argues regarding the melancholia of *male* characters in Renaissance literature? Once again, an examination of the medical context will shed light on the significance of the sickly heroines' behavior.

When, in Schopenhauer's *Die Tante,* Viktorine becomes ill because she is forbidden to voice her anxieties, her doctor recommends quiet and repose to conserve her energies in an early version of Weir S. Mitchell's infamous "rest cure," commonly prescribed for nervous women in Europe and North America in the second half of the nineteenth century. But Viktorine persuades Anna, the aunt of the novel's title, to listen to her confession of her love and her fears, and speedily recovers. This, the narrator explains, is not only because Anna is able to assure Viktorine that Raimund, her loved one, is not going to leave, as Viktorine has feared he would, but also because speaking allows her "to pour out all the feelings in her heart, which was overflowing with fear and love" (13: 120). In direct opposition to the course of action suggested by the physician, then, Anna effects an early talking cure, albeit of a much less sophisticated nature than that of Freud, whose hysterical patients brought a repressed emotion into consciousness as they brought it into words and thereby relieved symbolically related symptoms.

The fact that Viktorine recovers as a result of self-expression makes this novel an exception in its period, however. Certainly, in analogy with the traditional medical notion that fluids that have built up inappropriately inside the body can be relieved by a process such as blood-letting, the majority of wasting heroines around 1800 experience self-expression through speech and writing as a welcome relief. Gabriele, for example, is "delighted, gladdened" (9: 266) when she tells Hippolit she loves him, and Diotima, who is "full of sighs" when she begins a letter to Hyperion, is "pure joy" (123) by the time she has completed it. But in these and in most cases, the heroine's speaking or writing does not lead to her recovery; it does not, therefore, prevent her ultimate silencing through death. On the contrary, what she delivers is a "swansong"—an image employed both in *Gabriele* (9: 250) and *Hyperion* (158)[7]—only able to speak freely because her death is certain and the desires she expresses pose no threat. "Let me speak to you after death!" (459), insists Sophie in the diary that she addresses to Siegwart; and "My life was silent; my death is loquacious" (161), Diotima tells Hyperion. It is Gabriele, however, who formulates most clearly the relationship between the heroine's approaching death and her license to express herself, telling Hippolit, "She who is dying may confess that which it was her stern duty, while she lived, to bury deep in her heart in unutterable pain" (9: 265-66).

In fact, far from inducing recovery, the loquacity and/or prolificity that follows or accompanies the taciturnity of the late eighteenth- and early nineteenth-century wasting heroine is in most cases the literary manifestation of a pathological trait. Freud's hysterics may sometimes have suffered from a *loss* of voice, but in the medical textbooks of around 1800, hysteria was more commonly associated with verbosity. Like chlorosis, hysteria—a nervous condition to which medical historians and literary critics alike have devoted much attention in recent years[8]—was particularly prevalent among young, single women and was often attributed by the medical profession to sexual frustration. But if the chlorotic was characterized by introversion, withdrawal, and a disinclination to speak, the hysteric was typically extremely extroverted and eager to talk. Carus writes that she is given to excessive singing, speaking in verses, telling her doctor at length about her pains, and "exceptional talkativeness" in general (235). Jörg agrees that hysterics frequently become "very talkative," particularly when it comes to speaking of their suffering (265), and the French medical writer Pierre-Jean-Georges Cabanis

(1757-1808), whose *Rapports du physique et du moral de l'homme* (*Relations between the Physical and the Moral in Man,* 1802) was published in German in 1804, notes that when suffering from attacks of "vapors," women often acquire great eloquence (French edition 1: 322). It was not until Freud, however, that it occurred to the medical profession that the hysteric's words might be worth listening to. Carus argues that her complaints are simply an attempt to elicit admiration, and Jörg dismisses half of them as "imaginary" (265). Dewees entreats the physician to be patient when the hysteric speaks, but only because he will otherwise lose her confidence, not because she has anything important to say:

> One should never appear impatient when the patient tells us at great length the history of her pains and her torments, because there is nothing to be gained from attempting to induce her to brevity, but much to be lost if she believes that we are ignoring her complaints.

> (171-72)

If, as has been argued, the pathological and the "normal" feminine at this period existed next to one another on the same continuum, and if the chlorotic's aphasia stood in exaggerated fashion for women's voicelessness in society, then the excessive talking of the hysteric can be seen as a parody of the ordinary woman's supposed relationship to language. The ideal woman may have been modest and reserved, but it was widely accepted in medical and lay circles that women were naturally loquacious, because they lacked the self-control to select and restrict their words. Kant (1724-1804) speaks in his *Beobachtungen über das Gefühl des Schönen und Erhabenen* (*Observations on the Feeling of the Sublime and the Beautiful,* 1764) of their "cheerful talkativeness" and warns against telling them any secrets, since they do not have the power to keep them (855). The French physician Pierre Roussel (1742-1802), whose medico-philosophical work on the female sex of 1775 was translated into German as *Physiologie des weiblichen Geschlechts* (*Physiology of the Female Sex*) in 1786, argues that women naturally have "a greater facility of speech than men" (19). Jörg writes that women tend to "chattiness" and are often guilty of the "fault of gossiping," and provides a wholly unconvincing "scientific" explanation: their smaller lungs and narrower thoracic cavity mean that they cannot hold their breath for long periods of time, and they are thus also unable to "hold back" their words. The things said by "healthy" women, like those said by the hysteric, were considered unlikely to be of any value or to be structured properly. Jörg remarks that their lack of verbal control means that they will never be good orators (75-76).

Women's written use of language was viewed in the same light as their speech. It was maintained that they were incapable of producing great literary works, because they could exercise no shaping power over their writing, but only "pour out" their feelings directly onto paper. As Brandes puts it, "they have to pour out their sentiments at the moment they are actually experiencing them" (3: 8).[9] Men, it was generally accepted, could write in order to change the world or create an aesthetic object, but when women wrote, their motives were personal, emotional, and "unartistic." The majority of women writing around 1800 themselves accepted this view, at least outwardly. As Magdalene Heuser writes, prefaces to novels by women typically included disclaimers of any aesthetic value (56-57). Women writers also frequently insisted on the predominant role played by feeling rather than reason in the composition of their novels. Fanny Tarnow, for example, insists in a dedication entitled "Den mir Wohlwollenden" ("To Those Who Wish Me Well," 1830) that in her works she lays "no claim to literary talent," and asserts, "My feelings were my muse" (quoted in Wägenbaur 97). If, as Schiesari argues, the silencing of women in grief was a consequence of patriarchy's devaluation of woman as artist, so, in the late eighteenth and early nineteenth centuries, was the ascription to the female sex of particular volubility in speech and in writing.

But Schiesari's argument that, on the rare occasions when the female literary melancholic of the Renaissance does speak, her laments "typically come across as mere chatter and thus as less dignified than the ranting of a Hamletian nobleman" (55) does not apply to the novels discussed here. Unlike those female patients treated by physicians such as Carus and Dewees, the heroine of the late eighteenth- and early nineteenth-century German novel, whose chlorotic silences alternate with hysterical (or, in other words, typically womanly) periods of loquacity or prolific writing, is listened to. Indeed, the message of abiding, self-sacrificing love she proclaims, far from being mere "chatter," is held up as an ideal in the text, and her gradual wasting death is one of its most "dignified" aspects. Not even the hero, typically, can emulate her.[10]

But this is precisely the point: the heroine expresses herself in an overwhelmingly "feminine" manner, speaking at some length, and in sentimental, often extreme, terms of feelings that prove to be the death of her. Her words are presented as the spontaneous "outpourings" of her soul. The reader does not hear Viktorine's words to her aunt in Schopenhauer's *Die Tante,* but he/she knows that she speaks exclusively of her feelings for Raimund, and the verb *ausschütten* (to spill/pour out) is used to describe the manner in which they are delivered. Diotima's favorite medium is the "feminine" medium of song; when she writes to Hyperion, she does so in poetic style, telling of her feelings for him and for Nature, of her decline and approaching death. Like Diotima and like those hysterical women observed by Carus, Gabriele, as she approaches death, takes to sing-

ing, delivering "an irregular song, inspired by the enthusiasm of the moment" (9: 250), in which she communicates her hopes, longings, and expectations to her loved ones. Sophie's diary is a repetitive, seemingly unstructured piece of writing, littered with dashes, exclamations, "Ach"s and "O"s, examples of apostrophe and images, often drawn from nature, which she uses to describe her emotions (2: 458-74).

It is clear that, although the wasting heroines of the novels from around 1800 examined here are neither completely silenced nor ignored, they nevertheless reinforce predominant, restrictive models of femininity. Their speaking and writing, like their silence, are more pathological female symptom than healthy self-expression. Certain feminist critics have interpreted the non-rational, fluid style of sentimental writing as a rejection of the constraints of patriarchal order, as an early example, even, of *écriture féminine,*[11] but in the speaking and writing of the characters Sophie, Diotima, Viktorine, and Gabriele, it is hard to see anything but faithful adherence to patriarchy's rules for female self-expression. While they are pouring out their souls in a passive, unstructured manner and expiring their last, male characters are speaking in controlled ways conducive to their acting on the world.

One novel from this period offers a very different perspective on the role of self-expression in women's health, however. In *The Madwoman in the Attic* (1979), Sandra Gilbert and Susan Gubar argue that nineteenth-century British women novelists often express their discontent at their status in society through the depiction of minor, "mad" female characters such as Mr. Rochester's first wife in Charlotte Brontë's *Jane Eyre* (1847). In Therese Huber's (1764-1829) *Luise: Ein Beitrag zur Geschichte der Konvenienz* (1796), the "madwoman" is not relegated to an attic and a secondary role, as was the first Mrs. Rochester, but is given center stage and allowed to document in detail the wrongs that society has inflicted on her.[12] *Luise* tells the unhappy, at times brutal story of a young woman's engagement and disastrous marriage to a man chosen for her by her mother. The eponymous heroine develops hypochondria, a disease common in the eighteenth century, which was believed by many to be of nervous origin and which manifested itself in a variety of physical and psychological symptoms. Luise suffers most, however, not as a result of her illness, but because of the violent or sometimes even sadistic treatment she receives at the hands of her husband, her family, and their servants, often in the name of a cure. The novel relates how she is starved, force-fed, deprived of water, locked up in a succession of different rooms, beaten, and on one occasion, taken outside, stripped naked, tied up, whipped with a birch until her blood colors the bushes and briars around her, and taken for dead (108-10). This physical torment is accompanied by a wealth of emotional abuse. Luise tries continually, almost obsessively, to be a good wife, a good daughter, and, after she gives birth to a baby girl, a good mother, but her efforts are thwarted at every turn by her unfeeling family. As a married woman who is relatively poor, however, no other roles are open to her. From this summary, the novel would seem, as critic Lydia Schieth suggests, to be "explosive stuff" (190).

But the accusatory power of Luise's account is complicated by the novel's lengthy preface, in which a male editor gives an account of the genesis of the novel and advises the reader how to read it. Luise was lucky enough, he writes, to have "a physician very worthy of esteem" (iii), who was of the belief that the body cannot be cured unless the soul is as well. Like Viktorine's aunt in Schopenhauer's *Die Tante,* but unlike Viktorien's physician, Luise's physician appreciated the importance of giving verbal expression to emotion. He suggested that Luise write down the story of her suffering, in the hope that this would help her to come to terms with it:

> Because it was impossible for her imagination to part with the black images of her past, he thought they could at least be kept within bounds if she could exert her reason at the same time to form a real and coherent whole from her fickle ideas.
>
> (iv)

Unfortunately, the editor writes, the attempted cure was unsuccessful. Rather than helping Luise to gain control of her morbid imaginings, he explains, "this task on the contrary entrenched the thought and the expectation of death deeper in her heart" (v), for Luise lacked the "strength" to stop herself from dwelling on her pain (ix). Soon after composing her story, she died. He now offers it to the public to read, but recommends that they do so with a certain skepticism. Since Luise's reason was not sound when she wrote it, she was not the most competent judge of events (vii), and in any case, the most superficial understanding of psychology should be sufficient to encourage readers "to employ certain general cautionary rules when reading any biographies written by their own heroes" (xi). Had Luise's husband, for example, been in the habit of brooding over events, like his unhappy wife, then he would certainly have presented a different view of things. However, this is not, the editor insists, to suggest that the reader should withhold sympathy from the unfortunate protagonist. He writes that there can be no doubt that she has suffered greatly, even if her ascription of blame is misguided. The preface concludes with the suggestion—commonly found in prefaces to novels by women around 1800 (Heuser 57)—that the publication of the text is justified on didactic grounds. Luise's account may be biased and it may have failed in its therapeutic aim, but the editor hopes that it will encourage readers to evince more pity

for those who suffer a similar fate and perhaps even prevent arranged marriages from taking place in the future (xxiv).

How are we to interpret this preface? At first, it seems to offer a more progressive understanding of women's self-expression than is present in those works examined thus far. Luise's physician not only believes that a patient's putting her suffering into words can contribute to psychological recovery, he also contradicts the popular view that women are incapable of imposing structure on their speech or their writing. Far from simply recording her thoughts and memories on paper as they occur to her, Luise, he suggests, should as she writes employ that unfeminine faculty, her reason, to construct "a coherent whole." In this, it could be argued, his conception of the talking cure—or, in this case, the writing cure—is more emancipatory even than Freud's, for Freud's female hysterics were expected to deliver up their emotions and recollections in stream-of-consciousness, fluid, typically "feminine" style to an authority figure, the psychoanalyst, who himself undertook to fashion them into coherent narratives to be imposed on the patients (see Freud and Breur, *Studies on Hysteria*). But in this preface the fictional editor of *Luise* also informs the reader that this enlightened cure is unsuccessful and that Luise proves unable to ward off her obsessional thoughts. Luise, he suggests, is too psychologically weak to compose the balanced account her physician proposes. Moreover, he undermines her point of view by insisting that her presentation of events is one-sided. Like the words of Rosalie, Gabriele, Sophie, and Diotima, Luise's story, he proposes, is a feminine, subjective account, for all her physician's insistence that she exercise artistic control over it.

According to Schieth, the preface was composed by Huber's editor in order to temper the novel's incendiary potential. But other critics, such as Heuser, are surely right to see Huber as its author. Are we to assume, then, that Huber herself wanted to weaken the impact of her heroine's words? Like the physician Dewees, she seems to be recommending that the madwoman's point of view, although it deserves to be heard, should be given little credence. Heuser writes that Huber often composed long, explanatory prefaces when the content of a novel was particularly unusual or daring (Heuser 61). Did she hope by means of this preface to render her novel more acceptable to a conservative reading public?

By adding the preface, Huber may have facilitated the publication of her novel. But it does not ultimately muffle the heroine's voice or obscure the controversial nature of the work. The fictional editor attempts to undermine the validity of Luise's narrative through his reference to her unstable mental state and to the precarious nature of truth in autobiography, but the reader does not necessarily persist in reading it as a biased account. The editor has, after all, encouraged the reader to approach the text with understanding if he/she is a true "philanthropist" (*Menschenfreund* xi). In the course of reading the novel, as the reader's striving to "understand" Luise's point of view becomes an acceptance of it, his/her allegiance is transferred from editor to supposed author.

There are several reasons for this. The reader may have been warned to exercise caution when reading life-stories composed by their protagonists, but Luise employs the third rather than the first person to narrate her story, which lessens the awareness of its autobiographical nature, and therefore its supposed lack of objectivity. As Schieth comments, what the reader is in fact presented with is not the immediate first-person narrative ("distanzlose Ich-Erzählung") for which he/she has been prepared, but an objective third-person narrative (191). Given that it is nevertheless told from Luise's perspective, it is difficult to suspend belief in her version of events. She describes more than one occasion on which people around her insist that she is mentally unwell in order to discredit her words or her point of view and to advance their own interest. When, for example, her chambermaid hits her and Luise tells her husband, the chambermaid convinces him that Luise is suffering from delusions (92).[13] The reader is aware each time that Luise is in the right. The editor's bid to dictate the reader's response is mirrored, then, within the text, and its authority thereby called into question.

Furthermore, the novel, though free neither from stylistic inconsistencies,[14] nor from the occasional sentimental cliché,[15] differs from most of the fiction written by women around 1800 and from much of that written by men in its emphasis on the description of events rather than feelings, its attention to the more sordid aspects of life, and relatively controlled, succinct style: in other words, in its "realism." Karl Gutzkow identified this aspect of Huber's writing when he commented in 1836, "Frau Huber by no means belongs amongst the gossiping tea-drinking crowd of our weak-nerved lady authoresses, with her you have something solid, something real" (228). Unlike the verbal or written outpourings of the heroines discussed above, the impression created by *Luise* is not one of subjective feminine fluidity. It is not surprising that as her career progressed, Huber, unlike most of her peers, increasingly laid claim to aesthetic value in her fiction instead of propagating the myth of spontaneous, unartistic female authorship (see Heuser 62, 64).

But the question remains: why, if Luise manages not only to express herself, but to do so in a masculine, "objective" manner, does her health deteriorate even further? Given that she ends up dead, can it still be claimed that the novel makes an emancipatory point in its depiction of female self-expression? Is Huber not

thereby after all reinforcing the notion so dear to late eighteenth- and nineteenth-century physicians that intellectual activity in women, although not inconceivable, runs contrary to their physiological constitution?

Luise, as suggested above, portrays the practical aspects of and difficulties in women's lives. Luise is revealed in concrete ways to be the victim of patriarchal society. She receives little education, is denied autonomy over her own body and over her finances, and has her daughter taken from her by the courts. The ideology of this society is shown to determine not only external social structures but also the way individuals interact in their familial and personal relationships: her brothers and husband treat her as an inferior, while her mother consistently privileges her sons over her. The novel lays bare the disastrous effects of this kind of discrimination: Luise's husband spends all their money and takes a mistress, their marriage disintegrates, and her health is destroyed. That she dies despite undergoing the progressive cure prescribed by her physician is not intended to imply that writing is unhealthy for women: rather, it serves to underline the fact that such suffering as Luise experiences cannot be relieved merely by giving it expression. Neither, the novel makes clear, is it the eternal, "poetic" lot of womanhood. Rather, it is portrayed as preventable through social and political change.

Huber's view of the role of self-expression is indeed more radical, then, not only than that of her contemporaries, but also than that of Freud. Freud's hysterical patients were typically highly intelligent women to whose talents society granted no outlet, but rather than suggesting a change to the material conditions of their lives, Freud saw the simple opportunity to voice their repressed feelings as an adequate solution. Putting one's suffering into words can, of course, serve a political end, but only when it goes beyond the level of personal therapeutic process and finds an audience in whom it inspires the urge for action. This, and not the portrayal of a writing cure in action, is the real intention behind Huber's novel. When the reader is told in the preface, then, that the aim of the publication is to encourage readers to act differently, this should not, in fact, be read as the conventional, formulaic gesture of a woman writer around 1800 justifying her writing by asserting its morally edifying effect, but as a genuine assertion of the potentially radical power of women's self-expression.

Notes

Unless otherwise indicated, all translations from original German texts are mine.

1. See, for example, Stout; Fishkin and Hedges; Laurence.

2. See Cixous and Clément (95); Ellman (72); Weber (39-40).

3. See Honegger for a discussion of this development.

4. Date of first performance. *Twelfth Night* was first published in 1623.

5. In *Hölderlin's Silence,* Ryan writes of Hölderlin's "acute awareness of language's frequent inadequacy and superfluity" (148).

6. The most famous example of a prolific wasting woman is, of course, Richardson's *Clarissa* (1747-48). See Ellman's *The Hunger Artists* (1993) for a discussion of the links between Clarissa's writing and her starving and for a fascinating analysis of the connections—literary, psychoanalytical, and historical—between food refusal and writing in general. The French model for many nineteenth-century wasting heroines, Germaine de Staël's *Corinne* (*Corinne, ou l'Italie,* 1807), a poet whose voice fails her in her last hours, composes a moving poetic address as she is dying, which is recited by someone else.

7. The address composed by de Staël's Corinne is also described as her "swansong" ("chant du cygne," 581).

8. See, for example, Smith-Rosenberg; Showalter; Weber; Veith.

9. On women's inability to write works of genius, see also Jörg (75); Campe (I: 89); Mauvillon (Chapter 2).

10. As Walter Silz writes, "Diotima embodies the ideal toward which the whole book tends" (49).

11. See, for example, Jirku (55-88).

12. In an essay on Huber, Jeannine Blackwell entitles her section on *Luise* "The Madwoman in the Pantry" (1992).

13. See also 83, 118, 194-97.

14. For example, there are sometimes jarring switches from past to present tense (17, 19) and unnecessary repetition (14-15).

15. For example, "The still of the night, the magical moonlight that painted the shadow of the black cross along the green grass, or silhouetted on the white gravestones the quivering leaves of tall lime trees, the blossoming branches of which filled the air with the sweetest scent, the peace of Nature united with the silence of death, all moved Luise's sensitive heart" (32).

Works Cited

Blackwell, Jeannine. "Marriage by the Book: Matrimony, Divorce, and Single Life in Therese Huber's Life and Works." *In the Shadow of Olympus: German Women Writers around 1800.* Ed. Katherine R. Goodman and Edith Waldstein. Albany: State U of New York P, 1992. 137-56.

Bordo, Susan. "The Body and the Reproduction of Femininity." *Writing on the Body: Female Embodiment and Feminist Theory.* Ed. Katie Conboy, Nadia Medina, and Sarah Stanbury. New York: Columbia UP, 1997. 90-110.

Brandes, Ernst. *Betrachtungen über das weibliche Geschlecht und dessen Ausbildung in dem geselligen Leben.* 3 vols. Rev. ed. of *Über die Weiber.* 1787. Hannover: Gebrüder Hahn, 1802.

Brontë, Charlotte. *Jane Eyre: An Autobiography.* London: Smith, Elder, and Co., 1847.

Cabanis, Pierre-Jean-Georges. *Rapports du physique et du moral de l'homme* (1802) [Published in German as *Über die Verbindung des Physischen und Moralischen in dem Menschen.* Aus dem Französischen übersetzt und mit einer Abhandlung über die Grenzen der Physiologie und der Anthropologie versehen von Ludwig Heinrich Jakob. Halle, 1804], 2 vols. Paris: Béchet jeune, 1824.

Campe, Joachim Heinrich. *Väterlicher Rath für meine Tochter: Ein Gegenstück zum Theophron. Der erwachsenern [sic] weiblichen Jugend gewidmet.* 1789. Braunschweig: Schulbuchhandlung, 1809.

Carus, Carl Gustav. *Lehrbuch der Gynäkologie, oder systematische Darstellung der Lehren von Erkenntniß und Behandlung eigenthümlicher gesunder und krankhafter Zustände, sowohl der nicht schwangern, schwangern und gebärenden Frauen, als der Wöchnerinnen und neugebornen Kinder.* 2 vols. Leipzig: Fleischer, 1820.

Clément, Catherine, and Hélène Cixous. *The Newly Born Woman.* Trans. Betsy Wing. Minneapolis: U of Minnesota P, 1986.

Dewees, William P. *Die Krankheiten des Weibes.* First published in English as *A Treatise on the Diseases of Females.* 1824. Trans. Dr. A. Moser. Berlin: Rücker & Püchler, 1837.

Dixon, Laurinda S. *Perilous Chastity: Women and Illness in Pre-Enlightenment Art and Medicine.* Ithaca: Cornell UP, 1995.

Duden, Barbara. *The Woman Beneath the Skin: A Doctor's Patients in Eighteenth-Century Germany.* Trans. Thomas Dunlop. Cambridge: Harvard UP, 1991.

Duffin, Lorna. "The Conspicuous Consumptive: Woman as Invalid." *Nineteenth-Century Woman: Her Cultural and Physical World.* Ed. Sara Delamont and Lorna Duffin. London: Croom Helm, 1978. 26-56.

Ellman, Maud. *The Hunger Artists: Starving, Writing and Imprisonment.* London: Virago, 1993.

Fishkin, Shelley Fisher, and Elaine Hedges, eds. *Listening to Silences: New Essays in Feminist Criticism.* New York: Oxford UP, 1994.

Fischer-Homberger, Esther. *Krankheit Frau und andere Arbeiten zur Medizingeschichte der Frau.* Bern: Huber, 1979.

Freud, Sigmund, and Joseph Breuer. "Studies on Hysteria." *The Standard Edition of the Complete Psychological Works of Sigmund Freud.* Ed. James Strachey, in collaboration with Anna Freud. London: Vintage, 2001. Vol. 2.

Freud, Sigmund. "Mourning and Melancholia." 1917. Vol. 14: 237-58.

———. "Femininity." Vol. 22: 112-35.

Gilbert, Sandra M., and Susan Gubar. *The Madwoman in the Attic: The Woman Writer and the Nineteenth-Century Literary Imagination.* New Haven: Yale UP, 1979.

Gutzkow, Karl. *Beiträge zur Geschichte der neuesten Literatur.* 1836. Stuttgart: Balz, 1839.

Heuser, Magdalene. "'Ich wollte dieß und das von meinem Buche sagen, und gerieth in ein Vernünfteln': Poetologische Reflexionen in den Romanvorreden." *Untersuchungen zum Roman von Frauen um 1800.* Ed. Helga Gallas and Magdalene Heuser. Tübingen: Niemeyer, 1990. 52-65.

Hölderlin, Friedrich. *Hyperion, oder der Eremit in Griechenland.* 1797-1799. *Sämtliche Werke und Briefe in drei Bänden.* Ed. Jochen Schmidt. Frankfurt a.M.: Deutscher Klassiker Verlag, 1992-1994. Vol. 2.

Honegger, Claudia, *Die Ordnung der Geschlechter: Die Wissenschaften vom Menschen und das Weib 1750-1850.* Frankfurt a.M.: Campus, 1991.

Huber, Therese. *Luise: Ein Beitrag zur Geschichte der Konvenienz.* 1796. Hildesheim: Olms, 1991.

Jirku, Brigitte E. *"Wollen Sie mit Nichts . . . ihre Zeit versplittern?": Ich-Erzählerin und Erzählstruktur in von Frauen verfassten Romanen des achtzehnten Jahrhunderts.* Frankfurt a.M.: Peter Lang, 1994.

Jörg, Dr. Johann Christian Gottfried. *Handbuch der Krankheiten des Weibes, nebst eine Einleitung in die Physiologie und Psychologie des weiblichen Organismus.* 1809. 2nd. ed. Leipzig: Cnobloch, 1821.

Kant, Immanuel. "Beobachtungen über das Gefühl des Schönen und Erhabenen" (1764). *Werke in sechs Bänden.* Ed. Wilhelm Weischedel. Wiesbaden: Insel, 1960. 1: 821-84.

Laurence, Patricia. "Women's Silence as a Ritual of Truth: A Study of Literary Expressions in Austen, Brontë, and Woolf." Fishkin and Hedges. 156-67.

Mauvillon, Jakob. *Mann und Weib nach ihren gegenseitigen Verhältnissen geschildert: Ein Gegenstück zu der Schrift "Über die Weiber."* Leipzig: Dykische Buchhandlung, 1791.

Miller, Johann Martin. *Siegwart: Eine Klostergeschichte.* 1776. 3 vols. Leipzig: Weygandsche Buchhandlung, 1777.

Moreau de la Sarthe, Jacques-Louis. *Histoire Naturelle de la Femme, suivie d'un Traité d'hygiène appliqué à son régime physique et moral aux différents époques de sa vie.* 3 vols. [Published in German as *Naturgeschichte des Weibes.* Leipzig, 1810] Paris: L. Duprat, Letellier, et comp., 1803.

Richardson, Samuel. *Clarissa, or the History of a Young Lady.* 7 vols. London: Printed by S. Richardson, 1747-1748.

Roussel, Pierre. *Système Physique et Moral de la Femme ou Tableau Philosophique de la Constitution, de l'État organique du Tempérament, des Moeurs et des Fonctions propre au Sexe.* 1775 [Trans. into German as *Physiologie des weiblichen Geschlechts.* Berlin, 1786]. Paris: Crapart, Caille et Ravier, 1803.

Ryan, Thomas E. *Hölderlin's Silence.* New York: Peter Lang, 1988.

Schiesari, Juliana. *The Gendering of Melancholia: Feminism, Psychoanalysis, and the Symbolics of Loss in Renaissance Literature.* Ithaca: Cornell UP, 1992.

Schieth, Lydia. *Die Entwicklung des deutschen Frauenromans im ausgehenden achtzehnten Jahrhundert: Ein Beitrag zur Gattungsgeschichte.* Frankfurt a.M.: Peter Lang, 1987.

Schopenhauer, Johanna. *Gabriele.* 1819/1820. *Sämmtliche Schriften.* 24 vols in 12. Leipzig: Brockhaus, 1834. Vols. 7, 8, 9.

———. *Die Tante.* 1823. *Sämmtliche Schriften.* Vols. 13, 14.

Shakespeare, William. *Twelfth Night.* [1623]. Ed. Rex Gibson. Cambridge: Cambridge UP, 1993.

Showalter, Elaine. *The Female Malady: Women, Madness and English Culture 1830-1980.* London: Virago, 1987.

———. "Feminist Criticism in the Wilderness." *The New Feminist Criticism: Essays on Women, Literature and Theory.* Ed. Showalter. London: Virago, 1986, 243-70.

Silz, Walter. *Hölderlin's "Hyperion": A Critical Reading.* Philadelphia: U of Pennsylvania P, 1969.

Smith-Rosenberg, Carroll. "The Hysterical Woman: Sex Roles and Role Conflict in Nineteenth-Century America." *Disorderly Conduct: A Vision of Gender in Victorian America* [1985]. Oxford: Oxford UP, 1986. 197-216.

Staël, Germaine de. *Corinne ou l'Italie.* 1807. Paris: Gallimard, 1985.

Stout, Janis P. *Strategies of Reticence: Silence and Meaning in the Works of Jane Austen, Willa Cather, Katherine Anne Porter, and Joan Didion.* Charlottesville: UP of Virginia, 1990.

Tarnow, Fanny. *Novellen.* Leipzig: Carl Fock, 1830.

———. "Den mir Wohlwollenden" (dedication). *Auswahl aus Fanny Tarnows Schriften.* Leipzig: Focke, 1830. 1.

Veith, Ilza. *Hysteria: The History of a Disease.* Chicago: U of Chicago P, 1965.

Wägenbaur, Birgit. *Die Pathologie der Liebe: Literarische Weiblichkeitsentwürfe um 1800.* Berlin: Erich Schmidt, 1996.

Weber, Lilo. *"Fliegen und Zittern": Hysterie in Texten von Theodor Fontane, Hedwig Dohm, Gabriele Reuter und Minna Kautsky.* Bielefeld: Aisthesis, 1996.

FURTHER READING

Criticism

Archimedes, Sondra M. *Gendered Pathologies: The Female Body and Biomedical Discourse in the Nineteenth-Century English Novel.* New York: Routledge, 2005, 202 p.

  Discusses the implications of gendered medical language for nineteenth-century writers like Charles Dickens and Rider Haggard.

Browner, Stephanie P. "Gender, Medicine, and Literature in Postbellum Fiction." In *Profound Science and Elegant Literature: Imagining Doctors in Nineteenth-Century America,* pp. 135-81. Philadelphia: University of Pennsylvania Press, 2005.

  Examines the ways in which American fiction in the second half of the nineteenth century approached the issue of the changing nature of the practice of medicine, from a largely home-based, female-centered endeavor to one focused on degreed male professionalism.

Caldwell, Janis McLarren. "*Wuthering Heights* and Domestic Medicine: The Child's Body and the Book." In *Literature and Medicine in Nineteenth-Century Britain: From Mary Shelley to George Eliot,* pp. 68-96. Cambridge: Cambridge University Press, 2004.

  Reflects on Emily Brontë's personal aversion to doctors and her focus in *Wuthering Heights* on the health of children.

Christensen, Allan Conrad. "Mothers, Daughters, and Lovers." In *Nineteenth-Century Narratives of Contagion: 'Our Feverish Contact',* pp. 156-200. London: Routledge, 2005.

  Explores the disruption of the mother-daughter dyad by the intrusion of a male lover and the literary metaphor of love as a contagious illness.

Duffin, Lorna. "The Conspicuous Consumptive: Woman as an Invalid." In *The Nineteenth-Century Woman: Her Cultural and Physical World,* edited by Sara Delamont and Lorna Duffin, pp. 26-56. London: Croom Helm, 1978.

  Examines the ways in which science and medicine took on a moralistic directive to control the bodies and activities of women and cast them as passive sufferers.

Gilbert, Pamela K. *Disease, Desire, and the Body in Victorian Women's Popular Novels.* Cambridge: Cambridge University Press, 1997, 207 p.

  Examines the connection between love and illness in popular novels aimed at female readers.

Logan, Peter Melville. *Nerves and Narratives: A Cultural History of Hysteria in Nineteenth-Century British Prose.* Berkeley: University of California Press, 1997, 248 p.

  Provides an overview of the portrayal of hysteria in literature from the late eighteenth century through the Victorian period, including an examination of George Eliot's view of the nervous body in *Middlemarch.*

Mancall, James N. *'Thoughts Painfully Intense': Hawthorne and the Invalid Author.* New York: Routledge, 2002, 145 p.

  Explains Nathaniel Hawthorne's interest in the theory that literary pursuits, including both reading and writing literature, had detrimental effects on readers' and writers' health.

Martin, Philip W. "Secret Lives: *Sense and Sensibility, The Bride of Lammermoor, Wuthering Heights, Great Expectations.*" In *Mad Women in Romantic Writing,* pp. 92-123. Brighton, England: Harvester Press, 1987.

  Addresses parallels between women's madness and written language in several nineteenth-century novels.

Newberry, Frederick. "Male Doctors and Female Illness in American Women's Fiction, 1850-1900." In *Separate Spheres No More: Gender Convergence in American Literature, 1830-1930,* edited by Monika M. Elbert, pp. 143-57. Tuscaloosa: University of Alabama Press, 2000.

  Explores the ways in which women writers in nineteenth-century America addressed the problem of male primacy in the practice of medicine, to the detriment of women's physical and psychological health.

Showalter, Elaine. *The Female Malady: Women, Madness, and English Culture, 1830-1980*. New York: Pantheon, 1985, 308 p.

Examines the imposition of "psychiatric Darwinism" and medical "management" on women's mental health issues from the Victorian era to the later twentieth century.

Skinner, Carolyn. "'The Purity of Truth': Nineteenth-Century American Women Physicians Write about Delicate Topics." *Rhetoric Review* 26, no. 2 (2007): 103-19.

Analyzes the ways female physicians shaped the language they used in their medical writings on subjects like sexuality, hygiene, and anatomy to appeal to women readers without breaking social taboos.

Small, Helen. "Love-Mad Women and the Rhetoric of Gentlemanly Medicine." In *Love's Madness: Medicine, the Novel, and Female Insanity, 1800-1865*, pp. 33-71. Oxford: Clarendon Press, 1996.

Explores nineteenth-century literary narratives of women driven to insanity by unrequited love and the rhetoric of male-dominated medical writing on the subject.

Torgerson, Beth. *Reading the Brontë Body: Disease, Desire, and the Constraints of Culture*. London: Palgrave Macmillan, 2005, 180 p.

Examines the preoccupation with illness, disease, and madness in the writings of Anne, Charlotte, and Emily Brontë, noting the influence of the social and cultural environment in which they wrote on their interpretation of the wider implications of illness.

Wiltshire, John. "*Sanditon*: The Enjoyments of Invalidism." In *Jane Austen and the Body: 'The Picture of Health'*, pp. 197-221. Cambridge: Cambridge University Press, 1992.

Contrasts Austen's portrayal of hypochondria in her novel fragment *Sanditon* with that in *Persuasion*, basing much of the discussion on biographical evidence of Austen's own experience of illness.

Wood, Jane. "Nature's Invalids: The Medicalization of Womanhood." In *Passion and Pathology in Victorian Fiction*, pp. 8-58. Oxford: Oxford University Press, 2001.

Traces the medical profession's redefinition of womanhood and women's ailments along essentialist lines, particularly the purported link between domesticity and good health.

How to Use This Index

The main references

> **Calvino, Italo**
> 1923-1985 .... CLC **5, 8, 11, 22, 33, 39,**
> **73; SSC 3, 48**

list all author entries in the following Gale Literary Criticism series:

AAL = Asian American Literature
BG = The Beat Generation: A Gale Critical Companion
BLC = Black Literature Criticism
BLCS = Black Literature Criticism Supplement
CLC = Contemporary Literary Criticism
CLR = Children's Literature Review
CMLC = Classical and Medieval Literature Criticism
DC = Drama Criticism
FL = Feminism in Literature: A Gale Critical Companion
GL = Gothic Literature: A Gale Critical Companion
HLC = Hispanic Literature Criticism
HLCS = Hispanic Literature Criticism Supplement
HR = Harlem Renaissance: A Gale Critical Companion
LC = Literature Criticism from 1400 to 1800
NCLC = Nineteenth-Century Literature Criticism
NNAL = Native North American Literature
PC = Poetry Criticism
SSC = Short Story Criticism
TCLC = Twentieth-Century Literary Criticism
WLC = World Literature Criticism, 1500 to the Present
WLCS = World Literature Criticism Supplement

The cross-references

> See also CA 85-88, 116; CANR 23, 61;
> DAM NOV; DLB 196; EW 13; MTCW 1, 2;
> RGSF 2; RGWL 2; SFW 4; SSFS 12

list all author entries in the following Gale biographical and literary sources:

AAYA = Authors & Artists for Young Adults
AFAW = African American Writers
AFW = African Writers
AITN = Authors in the News
AMW = American Writers
AMWR = American Writers Retrospective Supplement
AMWS = American Writers Supplement
ANW = American Nature Writers
AW = Ancient Writers
BEST = Bestsellers
BPFB = Beacham's Encyclopedia of Popular Fiction: Biography and Resources
BRW = British Writers
BRWS = British Writers Supplement
BW = Black Writers
BYA = Beacham's Guide to Literature for Young Adults
CA = Contemporary Authors
CAAS = Contemporary Authors Autobiography Series
CABS = Contemporary Authors Bibliographical Series
CAD = Contemporary American Dramatists
CANR = Contemporary Authors New Revision Series
CAP = Contemporary Authors Permanent Series
CBD = Contemporary British Dramatists
CCA = Contemporary Canadian Authors
CD = Contemporary Dramatists
CDALB = Concise Dictionary of American Literary Biography

CDALBS = *Concise Dictionary of American Literary Biography Supplement*
CDBLB = *Concise Dictionary of British Literary Biography*
CMW = *St. James Guide to Crime & Mystery Writers*
CN = *Contemporary Novelists*
CP = *Contemporary Poets*
CPW = *Contemporary Popular Writers*
CSW = *Contemporary Southern Writers*
CWD = *Contemporary Women Dramatists*
CWP = *Contemporary Women Poets*
CWRI = *St. James Guide to Children's Writers*
CWW = *Contemporary World Writers*
DA = *DISCovering Authors*
DA3 = *DISCovering Authors 3.0*
DAB = *DISCovering Authors: British Edition*
DAC = *DISCovering Authors: Canadian Edition*
DAM = *DISCovering Authors: Modules*
    DRAM: *Dramatists Module;* **MST:** *Most-studied Authors Module;*
    MULT: *Multicultural Authors Module;* **NOV:** *Novelists Module;*
    POET: *Poets Module;* **POP:** *Popular Fiction and Genre Authors Module*
DFS = *Drama for Students*
DLB = *Dictionary of Literary Biography*
DLBD = *Dictionary of Literary Biography Documentary Series*
DLBY = *Dictionary of Literary Biography Yearbook*
DNFS = *Literature of Developing Nations for Students*
EFS = *Epics for Students*
EW = *European Writers*
EWL = *Encyclopedia of World Literature in the 20th Century*
EXPN = *Exploring Novels*
EXPP = *Exploring Poetry*
EXPS = *Exploring Short Stories*
FANT = *St. James Guide to Fantasy Writers*
FW = *Feminist Writers*
GFL = *Guide to French Literature,* Beginnings to 1789, 1798 to the Present
GLL = *Gay and Lesbian Literature*
HGG = *St. James Guide to Horror, Ghost & Gothic Writers*
HW = *Hispanic Writers*
IDFW = *International Dictionary of Films and Filmmakers: Writers and Production Artists*
IDTP = *International Dictionary of Theatre: Playwrights*
LAIT = *Literature and Its Times*
LAW = *Latin American Writers*
JRDA = *Junior DISCovering Authors*
MAICYA = *Major Authors and Illustrators for Children and Young Adults*
MAICYAS = *Major Authors and Illustrators for Children and Young Adults Supplement*
MAWW = *Modern American Women Writers*
MJW = *Modern Japanese Writers*
MTCW = *Major 20th-Century Writers*
NCFS = *Nonfiction Classics for Students*
NFS = *Novels for Students*
PAB = *Poets: American and British*
PFS = *Poetry for Students*
RGAL = *Reference Guide to American Literature*
RGEL = *Reference Guide to English Literature*
RGSF = *Reference Guide to Short Fiction*
RGWL = *Reference Guide to World Literature*
RHW = *Twentieth-Century Romance and Historical Writers*
SAAS = *Something about the Author Autobiography Series*
SATA = *Something about the Author*
SFW = *St. James Guide to Science Fiction Writers*
SSFS = *Short Stories for Students*
TCWW = *Twentieth-Century Western Writers*
WLIT = *World Literature and Its Times*
WP = *World Poets*
YABC = *Yesterday's Authors of Books for Children*
YAW = *St. James Guide to Young Adult Writers*

Literary Criticism Series
Cumulative Author Index

Ammianus Marcellinus c. 330-c. 395 .... **CMLC 60**
See also AW 2; DLB 211

Ammons, A.R. 1926-2001 .. **CLC 2, 3, 5, 8, 9, 25, 57, 108; PC 16**
See also AITN 1; AMWS 7; CA 9-12R; 193; CANR 6, 36, 51, 73, 107, 156; CP 1, 2, 3, 4, 5, 6, 7; CSW; DAM POET; DLB 5, 165, 342; EWL 3; MAL 5; MTCW 1, 2; PFS 19; RGAL 4; TCLE 1:1

Ammons, Archie Randolph
See Ammons, A.R.

Amo, Tauraatua i
See Adams, Henry (Brooks)

Amory, Thomas 1691(?)-1788 .... **LC 48**
See also DLB 39

Anand, Mulk Raj 1905-2004 ..... **CLC 23, 93, 237**
See also CA 65-68; 231; CANR 32, 64; CN 1, 2, 3, 4, 5, 6, 7; DAM NOV; DLB 323; EWL 3; MTCW 1, 2; MTFW 2005; RGSF 2

Anatol
See Schnitzler, Arthur

Anaximander c. 611B.C.-c. 546B.C. .... **CMLC 22**

Anaya, Rudolfo A. 1937- . **CLC 23, 148, 255; HLC 1**
See also AAYA 20; BYA 13; CA 45-48; CAAS 4; CANR 1, 32, 51, 124, 169; CLR 129; CN 4, 5, 6, 7; DAM MULT, NOV; DLB 82, 206, 278; HW 1; LAIT 4; LLW; MAL 5; MTCW 1, 2; MTFW 2005; NFS 12; RGAL 4; RGSF 2; TCWW 2; WLIT 1

Anaya, Rudolpho Alfonso
See Anaya, Rudolfo A.

Andersen, Hans Christian 1805-1875 ...... **NCLC 7, 79, 214; SSC 6, 56; WLC 1**
See also AAYA 57; CLR 6, 113; DA; DA3; DAB; DAC; DAM MST, POP; EW 6; MAICYA 1, 2; RGSF 2; RGWL 2, 3; SATA 100; TWA; WCH; YABC 1

Anderson, C. Farley
See Mencken, H. L.; Nathan, George Jean

Anderson, Jessica (Margaret) Queale 1916- .... **CLC 37**
See also CA 9-12R; CANR 4, 62; CN 4, 5, 6, 7; DLB 325

Anderson, Jon (Victor) 1940- .... **CLC 9**
See also CA 25-28R; CANR 20; CP 1, 3, 4, 5; DAM POET

Anderson, Lindsay (Gordon) 1923-1994 .... **CLC 20**
See also CA 125; 128; 146; CANR 77

Anderson, Maxwell 1888-1959 .... **TCLC 2, 144**
See also CA 105; 152; DAM DRAM; DFS 16, 20; DLB 7, 228; MAL 5; MTCW 2; MTFW 2005; RGAL 4

Anderson, Poul 1926-2001 .... **CLC 15**
See also AAYA 5, 34; BPFB 1; BYA 6, 8, 9; CA 1-4R, 181; 199; CAAE 181; CAAS 2; CANR 2, 15, 34, 64, 110; CLR 58; DLB 8; FANT; INT CANR-15; MTCW 1, 2; MTFW 2005; SATA 90; SATA-Brief 39; SATA-Essay 106; SCFW 1, 2; SFW 4; SUFW 1, 2

Anderson, R. W.
See Anderson, Robert

Anderson, Robert 1917-2009 .... **CLC 23**
See also AITN 1; CA 21-24R; 283; CANR 32; CD 6; DAM DRAM; DLB 7; LAIT 5

Anderson, Robert W.
See Anderson, Robert

Anderson, Robert Woodruff
See Anderson, Robert

Anderson, Roberta Joan
See Mitchell, Joni

Anderson, Sherwood 1876-1941 ... **SSC 1, 46, 91; TCLC 1, 10, 24, 123; WLC 1**
See also CA 30; AMW; AMWC 2; BPFB 1; CA 104; 121; CANR 61; CDALB 1917-1929; DA; DA3; DAB; DAC; DAM MST, NOV; DLB 4, 9, 86; DLBD 1; EWL 3; EXPS; GLL 2; MAL 5; MTCW 1, 2; MTFW 2005; NFS 2; RGAL 4; RGSF 2; SSFS 4, 10, 11; TUS

Anderson, Wes 1969- .... **CLC 227**
See also CA 214

Andier, Pierre
See Desnos, Robert

Andouard
See Giraudoux, Jean(-Hippolyte)

Andrade, Carlos Drummond de
See Drummond de Andrade, Carlos

Andrade, Mario de
See de Andrade, Mario

Andreae, Johann V(alentin) 1586-1654 .... **LC 32**
See also DLB 164

Andreas Capellanus fl. c. 1185- .... **CMLC 45**
See also DLB 208

Andreas-Salome, Lou 1861-1937 ... **TCLC 56**
See also CA 178; DLB 66

Andreev, Leonid
See Andreyev, Leonid

Andress, Lesley
See Sanders, Lawrence

Andrew, Joseph Maree
See Occomy, Marita (Odette) Bonner

Andrewes, Lancelot 1555-1626 .... **LC 5**
See also DLB 151, 172

Andrews, Cicily Fairfield
See West, Rebecca

Andrews, Elton V.
See Pohl, Frederik

Andrews, Peter
See Soderbergh, Steven

Andrews, Raymond 1934-1991 .... **BLC 2:1**
See also BW 2; CA 81-84; 136; CANR 15, 42

Andreyev, Leonid 1871-1919 ... **TCLC 3, 221**
See also CA 104; 185; DLB 295; EWL 3

Andreyev, Leonid Nikolaevich
See Andreyev, Leonid

Andrezel, Pierre
See Blixen, Karen

Andric, Ivo 1892-1975 .... **CLC 8; SSC 36; TCLC 135**
See also CA 81-84; 57-60; CANR 43, 60; CDWLB 4; DLB 147, 329; EW 11; EWL 3; MTCW 1; RGSF 2; RGWL 2, 3

Androvar
See Prado (Calvo), Pedro

Angela of Foligno 1248(?)-1309 .... **CMLC 76**

Angelique, Pierre
See Bataille, Georges

Angell, Judie
See Angell, Judie

Angell, Judie 1937- .... **CLC 30**
See also AAYA 11, 71; BYA 6; CA 77-80; CANR 49; CLR 33; JRDA; SATA 22, 78; WYA; YAW

Angell, Roger 1920- .... **CLC 26**
See also CA 57-60; CANR 13, 44, 70, 144; DLB 171, 185

Angelou, Maya 1928- ...... **BLC 1:1; CLC 12, 35, 64, 77, 155; PC 32; WLCS**
See also AAYA 7, 20; AMWS 4; BPFB 1; BW 2, 3; BYA 2; CA 65-68; CANR 19, 42, 65, 111, 133; CDALBS; CLR 53; CP 4, 5, 6, 7; CPW; CSW; CWP; DA; DA3; DAB; DAC; DAM MST, MULT, POET, POP; DLB 38; EWL 3; EXPN; EXPP; FL 1:5; LAIT 4; MAICYA 2; MAICYAS 1;

MAL 5; MBL; MTCW 1, 2; MTFW 2005; NCFS 2; NFS 2; PFS 2, 3; RGAL 4; SATA 49, 136; TCLE 1:1; WYA; YAW

Angouleme, Marguerite d'
See de Navarre, Marguerite

Anna Comnena 1083-1153 .... **CMLC 25**

Annensky, Innokentii Fedorovich
See Annensky, Innokenty (Fyodorovich)

Annensky, Innokenty (Fyodorovich) 1856-1909 .... **TCLC 14**
See also CA 110; 155; DLB 295; EWL 3

Annunzio, Gabriele d'
See D'Annunzio, Gabriele

Anodos
See Coleridge, Mary E(lizabeth)

Anon, Charles Robert
See Pessoa, Fernando

Anouilh, Jean 1910-1987 ..... **CLC 1, 3, 8, 13, 40, 50; DC 8, 21; TCLC 195**
See also AAYA 67; CA 17-20R; 123; CANR 32; DAM DRAM; DFS 9, 10, 19; DLB 321; EW 13; EWL 3; GFL 1789 to the Present; MTCW 1, 2; MTFW 2005; RGWL 2, 3; TWA

Ansa, Tina McElroy 1949- .... **BLC 2:1**
See also BW 2; CA 142; CANR 143; CSW

Anselm of Canterbury 1033(?)-1109 .... **CMLC 67**
See also DLB 115

Anthony, Florence
See Ai

Anthony, John
See Ciardi, John (Anthony)

Anthony, Peter
See Shaffer, Anthony; Shaffer, Peter

Anthony, Piers 1934- .... **CLC 35**
See also AAYA 11, 48; BYA 7; CA 200; CAAE 200; CANR 28, 56, 73, 102, 133; CLR 118; CPW; DAM POP; DLB 8; FANT; MAICYA 2; MAICYAS 1; MTCW 1, 2; MTFW 2005; SAAS 22; SATA 84, 129; SATA-Essay 129; SFW 4; SUFW 1, 2; YAW

Anthony, Susan B(rownell) 1820-1906 .... **TCLC 84**
See also CA 211; FW

Antiphon c. 480B.C.-c. 411B.C. .... **CMLC 55**

Antoine, Marc
See Proust, (Valentin-Louis-George-Eugene) Marcel

Antoninus, Brother
See Everson, William

Antonioni, Michelangelo 1912-2007 .... **CLC 20, 144, 259**
See also CA 73-76; 262; CANR 45, 77

Antschel, Paul 1920-1970 .... **CLC 10, 19, 53, 82; PC 10**
See also CA 85-88; CANR 33, 61; CDWLB 2; DLB 69; EWL 3; MTCW 1; PFS 21; RGHL; RGWL 2, 3

Anwar, Chairil 1922-1949 .... **TCLC 22**
See also CA 121; 219; EWL 3; RGWL 3

Anyidoho, Kofi 1947- .... **BLC 2:1**
See also BW 3; CA 178; CP 5, 6, 7; DLB 157; EWL 3

Anzaldua, Gloria (Evanjelina) 1942-2004 .... **CLC 200; HLCS 1**
See also CA 175; 227; CSW; CWP; DLB 122; FW; LLW; RGAL 4; SATA-Obit 154

Apess, William 1798-1839(?) .... **NCLC 73; NNAL**
See also DAM MULT; DLB 175, 243

Apollinaire, Guillaume 1880-1918 .... **PC 7; TCLC 3, 8, 51**
See also CA 104; 152; DAM POET; DLB 258, 321; EW 9; EWL 3; GFL 1789 to the Present; MTCW 2; PFS 24; RGWL 2, 3; TWA; WP

Apollonius of Rhodes
  See Apollonius Rhodius
Apollonius Rhodius c. 300B.C.-c.
  220B.C. .... **CMLC 28**
  See also AW 1; DLB 176; RGWL 2, 3
Appelfeld, Aharon 1932- ... **CLC 23, 47; SSC
  42**
  See also CA 112; 133; CANR 86, 160;
  CWW 2; DLB 299; EWL 3; RGHL;
  RGSF 2; WLIT 6
Appelfeld, Aron
  See Appelfeld, Aharon
Apple, Max (Isaac) 1941- .... **CLC 9, 33; SSC
  50**
  See also AMWS 17; CA 81-84; CANR 19,
  54; DLB 130
Appleman, Philip (Dean) 1926- .... **CLC 51**
  See also CA 13-16R; CAAS 18; CANR 6,
  29, 56
Appleton, Lawrence
  See Lovecraft, H. P.
Apteryx
  See Eliot, T(homas) S(tearns)
Apuleius, (Lucius Madaurensis) c. 125-c.
  164 .... **CMLC 1, 84**
  See also AW 2; CDWLB 1; DLB 211;
  RGWL 2, 3; SUFW; WLIT 8
Aquin, Hubert 1929-1977 .... **CLC 15**
  See also CA 105; DLB 53; EWL 3
Aquinas, Thomas 1224(?)-1274 .... **CMLC 33**
  See also DLB 115; EW 1; TWA
Aragon, Louis 1897-1982 .... **CLC 3, 22;
  TCLC 123**
  See also CA 69-72; 108; CANR 28, 71;
  DAM NOV, POET; DLB 72, 258; EW 11;
  EWL 3; GFL 1789 to the Present; GLL 2;
  LMFS 2; MTCW 1, 2; RGWL 2, 3
Arany, Janos 1817-1882 .... **NCLC 34**
Aranyos, Kakay 1847-1910
  See Mikszath, Kalman
Aratus of Soli c. 315B.C.-c.
  240B.C. .... **CMLC 64, 114**
  See also DLB 176
Arbuthnot, John 1667-1735 .... **LC 1**
  See also DLB 101
Archer, Herbert Winslow
  See Mencken, H. L.
Archer, Jeffrey 1940- .... **CLC 28**
  See also AAYA 16; BEST 89:3; BPFB 1;
  CA 77-80; CANR 22, 52, 95, 136; CPW;
  DA3; DAM POP; INT CANR-22; MTFW
  2005
Archer, Jeffrey Howard
  See Archer, Jeffrey
Archer, Jules 1915- .... **CLC 12**
  See also CA 9-12R; CANR 6, 69; SAAS 5;
  SATA 4, 85
Archer, Lee
  See Ellison, Harlan
Archilochus c. 7th cent. B.C.- .... **CMLC 44**
  See also DLB 176
Ard, William
  See Jakes, John
Arden, John 1930- .... **CLC 6, 13, 15**
  See also BRWS 2; CA 13-16R; CAAS 4;
  CANR 31, 65, 67, 124; CBD; CD 5, 6;
  DAM DRAM; DFS 9; DLB 13, 245;
  EWL 3; MTCW 1
Arenas, Reinaldo 1943-1990 .. **CLC 41; HLC
  1; TCLC 191**
  See also CA 124; 128; 133; CANR 73, 106;
  DAM MULT; DLB 145; EWL 3; GLL 2;
  HW 1; LAW; LAWS 1; MTCW 2; MTFW
  2005; RGSF 2; RGWL 3; WLIT 1
Arendt, Hannah 1906-1975 .... **CLC 66, 98;
  TCLC 193**
  See also CA 17-20R; 61-64; CANR 26, 60,
  172; DLB 242; MTCW 1, 2

Aretino, Pietro 1492-1556 .... **LC 12, 165**
  See also RGWL 2, 3
Arghezi, Tudor
  See Theodorescu, Ion N.
Arguedas, Jose Maria 1911-1969 .... **CLC 10,
  18; HLCS 1; TCLC 147**
  See also CA 89-92; CANR 73; DLB 113;
  EWL 3; HW 1; LAW; RGWL 2, 3; WLIT
  1
Argueta, Manlio 1936- .... **CLC 31**
  See also CA 131; CANR 73; CWW 2; DLB
  145; EWL 3; HW 1; RGWL 3
Arias, Ron 1941- .... **HLC 1**
  See also CA 131; CANR 81, 136; DAM
  MULT; DLB 82; HW 1, 2; MTCW 2;
  MTFW 2005
Ariosto, Lodovico
  See Ariosto, Ludovico
Ariosto, Ludovico 1474-1533 ... **LC 6, 87; PC
  42**
  See also EW 2; RGWL 2, 3; WLIT 7
Aristides
  See Epstein, Joseph
Aristophanes 450B.C.-385B.C. .... **CMLC 4,
  51; DC 2; WLCS**
  See also AW 1; CDWLB 1; DA; DA3;
  DAB; DAC; DAM DRAM, MST; DFS
  10; DLB 176; LMFS 1; RGWL 2, 3;
  TWA; WLIT 8
Aristotle 384B.C.-322B.C. .... **CMLC 31;
  WLCS**
  See also AW 1; CDWLB 1; DA; DA3;
  DAB; DAC; DAM MST; DLB 176;
  RGWL 2, 3; TWA; WLIT 8
Arlt, Roberto (Godofredo Christophersen)
  1900-1942 .... **HLC 1; TCLC 29**
  See also CA 123; 131; CANR 67; DAM
  MULT; DLB 305; EWL 3; HW 1, 2;
  IDTP; LAW
Armah, Ayi Kwei 1939- . **BLC 1:1, 2:1; CLC
  5, 33, 136**
  See also AFW; BRWS 10; BW 1; CA 61-
  64; CANR 21, 64; CDWLB 3; CN 1, 2,
  3, 4, 5, 6, 7; DAM MULT, POET; DLB
  117; EWL 3; MTCW 1; WLIT 2
Armatrading, Joan 1950- .... **CLC 17**
  See also CA 114; 186
Armin, Robert 1568(?)-1615(?) .... **LC 120**
Armitage, Frank
  See Carpenter, John (Howard)
Armstrong, Jeannette (C.) 1948- .... **NNAL**
  See also CA 149; CCA 1; CN 6, 7; DAC;
  DLB 334; SATA 102
Arnauld, Antoine 1612-1694 .... **LC 169**
  See also DLB 268
Arnette, Robert
  See Silverberg, Robert
**Arnim, Achim von (Ludwig Joachim von
  Arnim)** 1781-1831 .. **NCLC 5, 159; SSC
  29**
  See also DLB 90
Arnim, Bettina von 1785-1859 ...... **NCLC 38,
  123**
  See also DLB 90; RGWL 2, 3
Arnold, Matthew 1822-1888 ..... **NCLC 6, 29,
  89, 126, 218; PC 5, 94; WLC 1**
  See also BRW 5; CDBLB 1832-1890; DA;
  DAB; DAC; DAM MST, POET; DLB 32,
  57; EXPP; PAB; PFS 2; TEA; WP
Arnold, Thomas 1795-1842 .... **NCLC 18**
  See also DLB 55
Arnow, Harriette (Louisa) Simpson
  1908-1986 ...... **CLC 2, 7, 18; TCLC 196**
  See also BPFB 1; CA 9-12R; 118; CANR
  14; CN 2, 3, 4; DLB 6; FW; MTCW 1, 2;
  RHW; SATA 42; SATA-Obit 47
Arouet, Francois-Marie
  See Voltaire

Arp, Hans
  See Arp, Jean
Arp, Jean 1887-1966 .... **CLC 5; TCLC 115**
  See also CA 81-84; 25-28R; CANR 42, 77;
  EW 10
Arrabal
  See Arrabal, Fernando
Arrabal, Fernando 1932- .. **CLC 2, 9, 18, 58;
  DC 35**
  See also CA 9-12R; CANR 15; CWW 2;
  DLB 321; EWL 3; LMFS 2
Arrabal Teran, Fernando
  See Arrabal, Fernando
Arreola, Juan Jose 1918-2001 .... **CLC 147;
  HLC 1; SSC 38**
  See also CA 113; 131; 200; CANR 81;
  CWW 2; DAM MULT; DLB 113; DNFS
  2; EWL 3; HW 1, 2; LAW; RGSF 2
Arrian c. 89(?)-c. 155(?) .... **CMLC 43**
  See also DLB 176
Arrick, Fran
  See Angell, Judie
Arrley, Richmond
  See Delany, Samuel R., Jr.
Artaud, Antonin (Marie Joseph)
  1896-1948 .... **DC 14; TCLC 3, 36**
  See also CA 104; 149; DA3; DAM DRAM;
  DFS 22; DLB 258, 321; EW 11; EWL 3;
  GFL 1789 to the Present; MTCW 2;
  MTFW 2005; RGWL 2, 3
Arthur, Ruth M(abel) 1905-1979 ..... **CLC 12**
  See also CA 9-12R; 85-88; CANR 4; CWRI
  5; SATA 7, 26
Artsybashev, Mikhail (Petrovich)
  1878-1927 .... **TCLC 31**
  See also CA 170; DLB 295
Arundel, Honor (Morfydd)
  1919-1973 .... **CLC 17**
  See also CA 21-22; 41-44R; CAP 2; CLR
  35; CWRI 5; SATA 4; SATA-Obit 24
Arzner, Dorothy 1900-1979 .... **CLC 98**
Asch, Sholem 1880-1957 .... **TCLC 3**
  See also CA 105; DLB 333; EWL 3; GLL
  2; RGHL
Ascham, Roger 1516(?)-1568 .... **LC 101**
  See also DLB 236
Ash, Shalom
  See Asch, Sholem
Ashbery, John 1927- ... **CLC 2, 3, 4, 6, 9, 13,
  15, 25, 41, 77, 125, 221; PC 26**
  See also AMWS 3; CA 5-8R; CANR 9, 37,
  66, 102, 132, 170; CP 1, 2, 3, 4, 5, 6, 7;
  DA3; DAM POET; DLB 5, 165; DLBY
  1981; EWL 3; GLL 1; INT CANR-9;
  MAL 5; MTCW 1, 2; MTFW 2005; PAB;
  PFS 11, 28; RGAL 4; TCLE 1:1; WP
Ashbery, John Lawrence
  See Ashbery, John
Ashbridge, Elizabeth 1713-1755 .... **LC 147**
  See also DLB 200
Ashdown, Clifford
  See Freeman, R(ichard) Austin
Ashe, Gordon
  See Creasey, John
Ashton-Warner, Sylvia (Constance)
  1908-1984 .... **CLC 19**
  See also CA 69-72; 112; CANR 29; CN 1,
  2, 3; MTCW 1, 2
Asimov, Isaac 1920-1992 ..... **CLC 1, 3, 9, 19,
  26, 76, 92**
  See also AAYA 13; BEST 90:2; BPFB 1;
  BYA 4, 6, 7, 9; CA 1-4R; 137; CANR 2,
  19, 36, 60, 125; CLR 12, 79; CMW 4;
  CN 1, 2, 3, 4, 5; CPW; DA3; DAM POP;
  DLB 8; DLBY 1992; INT CANR-19;
  JRDA; LAIT 5; LMFS 2; MAICYA 1, 2;
  MAL 5; MTCW 1, 2; MTFW 2005; NFS
  29; RGAL 4; SATA 1, 26, 74; SCFW 1,
  2; SFW 4; SSFS 17; TUS; YAW

Bachmann, Ingeborg 1926-1973 ..... **CLC 69; TCLC 192**
See also CA 93-96; 45-48; CANR 69; DLB 85; EWL 3; RGHL; RGWL 2, 3

Bacon, Francis 1561-1626 ..... **LC 18, 32, 131**
See also BRW 1; CDBLB Before 1660; DLB 151, 236, 252; RGEL 2; TEA

Bacon, Roger 1214(?)-1294 ... **CMLC 14, 108**
See also DLB 115

Bacovia, G.
See Bacovia, George

Bacovia, George 1881-1957 .... **TCLC 24**
See Bacovia, George
See also CA 123; 189; CDWLB 4; DLB 220; EWL 3

Badanes, Jerome 1937-1995 .... **CLC 59**
See also CA 234

Bage, Robert 1728-1801 .... **NCLC 182**
See also DLB 39; RGEL 2

Bagehot, Walter 1826-1877 .... **NCLC 10**
See also DLB 55

Bagnold, Enid 1889-1981 .... **CLC 25**
See also AAYA 75; BYA 2; CA 5-8R; 103; CANR 5, 40; CBD; CN 2; CWD; CWRI 5; DAM DRAM; DLB 13, 160, 191, 245; FW; MAICYA 1, 2; RGEL 2; SATA 1, 25

Bagritsky, Eduard
See Dzyubin, Eduard Georgievich

Bagritsky, Edvard
See Dzyubin, Eduard Georgievich

Bagrjana, Elisaveta
See Belcheva, Elisaveta Lyubomirova

Bagryana, Elisaveta
See Belcheva, Elisaveta Lyubomirova

Bailey, Paul 1937- .... **CLC 45**
See also CA 21-24R; CANR 16, 62, 124; CN 1, 2, 3, 4, 5, 6, 7; DLB 14, 271; GLL 2

Baillie, Joanna 1762-1851 ...... **NCLC 71, 151**
See also DLB 93, 344; GL 2; RGEL 2

Bainbridge, Beryl 1934- ...... **CLC 4, 5, 8, 10, 14, 18, 22, 62, 130**
See also BRWS 6; CA 21-24R; CANR 24, 55, 75, 88, 128; CN 2, 3, 4, 5, 6, 7; DAM NOV; DLB 14, 231; EWL 3; MTCW 1, 2; MTFW 2005

Baker, Carlos (Heard) 1909-1987 .... **TCLC 119**
See also CA 5-8R; 122; CANR 3, 63; DLB 103

Baker, Elliott 1922-2007 .... **CLC 8**
See also CA 45-48; 257; CANR 2, 63; CN 1, 2, 3, 4, 5, 6, 7

Baker, Elliott Joseph
See Baker, Elliott

Baker, Jean H.
See Russell, George William

Baker, Nicholson 1957- .... **CLC 61, 165**
See also AMWS 13; CA 135; CANR 63, 120, 138, 190; CN 6; CPW; DA3; DAM POP; DLB 227; MTFW 2005

Baker, Ray Stannard 1870-1946 .... **TCLC 47**
See also CA 118; DLB 345

Baker, Russell 1925- .... **CLC 31**
See also BEST 89:4; CA 57-60; CANR 11, 41, 59, 137; MTCW 1, 2; MTFW 2005

Bakhtin, M.
See Bakhtin, Mikhail Mikhailovich

Bakhtin, M. M.
See Bakhtin, Mikhail Mikhailovich

Bakhtin, Mikhail
See Bakhtin, Mikhail Mikhailovich

Bakhtin, Mikhail Mikhailovich 1895-1975 .... **CLC 83; TCLC 160**
See also CA 128; 113; DLB 242; EWL 3

Bakshi, Ralph 1938(?)- .... **CLC 26**
See also CA 112; 138; IDFW 3

Bakunin, Mikhail (Alexandrovich) 1814-1876 .... **NCLC 25, 58**
See also DLB 277

Bal, Mieke (Maria Gertrudis) 1946- .... **CLC 252**
See also CA 156; CANR 99

Baldwin, James 1924-1987 ...... **BLC 1:1, 2:1; CLC 1, 2, 3, 4, 5, 8, 13, 15, 17, 42, 50, 67, 90, 127; DC 1; SSC 10, 33, 98; WLC 1**
See also AAYA 4, 34; AFAW 1, 2; AMWR 2; AMWS 1; BPFB 1; BW 1; CA 1-4R; 124; CABS 1; CAD; CANR 3, 24; CDALB 1941-1968; CN 1, 2, 3, 4; CPW; DA; DA3; DAB; DAC; DAM MST, MULT, NOV, POP; DFS 11, 15; DLB 2, 7, 33, 249, 278; DLBY 1987; EWL 3; EXPS; LAIT 5; MAL 5; MTCW 1, 2; MTFW 2005; NCFS 4; NFS 4; RGAL 4; RGSF 2; SATA 9; SATA-Obit 54; SSFS 2, 18; TUS

Baldwin, William c. 1515-1563 .... **LC 113**
See also DLB 132

Bale, John 1495-1563 .... **LC 62**
See also DLB 132; RGEL 2; TEA

Ball, Hugo 1886-1927 .... **TCLC 104**

Ballard, James G.
See Ballard, J.G.

Ballard, James Graham
See Ballard, J.G.

Ballard, J.G. 1930-2009 ..... **CLC 3, 6, 14, 36, 137; SSC 1, 53**
See also AAYA 3, 52; BRWS 5; CA 5-8R; 285; CANR 15, 39, 65, 107, 133; CN 1, 2, 3, 4, 5, 6, 7; DA3; DAM NOV, POP; DLB 14, 207, 261, 319; EWL 3; HGG; MTCW 1, 2; MTFW 2005; NFS 8; RGEL 2; RGSF 2; SATA 93; SATA-Obit 203; SCFW 1, 2; SFW 4

Ballard, Jim G.
See Ballard, J.G.

Balmont, Konstantin (Dmitriyevich) 1867-1943 .... **TCLC 11**
See also CA 109; 155; DLB 295; EWL 3

Baltausis, Vincas 1847-1910
See Mikszath, Kalman

Balzac, Guez de (?)-
See Balzac, Jean-Louis Guez de

Balzac, Honore de 1799-1850 ... **NCLC 5, 35, 53, 153; SSC 5, 59, 102; WLC 1**
See also DA; DA3; DAB; DAC; DAM MST, NOV; DLB 119; EW 5; GFL 1789 to the Present; LMFS 1; RGSF 2; RGWL 2, 3; SSFS 10; SUFW; TWA

Balzac, Jean-Louis Guez de 1597-1654 .... **LC 162**
See also DLB 268; GFL Beginnings to 1789

Bambara, Toni Cade 1939-1995 ..... **BLC 1:1, 2:1; CLC 19, 88; SSC 35, 107; TCLC 116; WLCS**
See also AAYA 5, 49; AFAW 2; AMWS 11; BW 2, 3; BYA 12, 14; CA 29-32R; 150; CANR 24, 49, 81; CDALBS; DA; DA3; DAC; DAM MST, MULT; DLB 38, 218; EXPS; MAL 5; MTCW 1, 2; MTFW 2005; RGAL 4; RGSF 2; SATA 112; SSFS 4, 7, 12, 21

Bamdad, A.
See Shamlu, Ahmad

Bamdad, Alef
See Shamlu, Ahmad

Banat, D. R.
See Bradbury, Ray

Bancroft, Laura
See Baum, L(yman) Frank

Banim, John 1798-1842 .... **NCLC 13**
See also DLB 116, 158, 159; RGEL 2

Banim, Michael 1796-1874 .... **NCLC 13**
See also DLB 158, 159

Banjo, The
See Paterson, A(ndrew) B(arton)

Banks, Iain 1954- .... **CLC 34**
See also BRWS 11; CA 123; 128; CANR 61, 106, 180; DLB 194, 261; EWL 3; HGG; INT CA-128; MTFW 2005; SFW 4

Banks, Iain M.
See Banks, Iain

Banks, Iain Menzies
See Banks, Iain

Banks, Lynne Reid
See Reid Banks, Lynne

Banks, Russell 1940- . **CLC 37, 72, 187; SSC 42**
See also AAYA 45; AMWS 5; CA 65-68; CAAS 15; CANR 19, 52, 73, 118; CN 4, 5, 6, 7; DLB 130, 278; EWL 3; MAL 5; MTCW 2; MTFW 2005; NFS 13

Banks, Russell Earl
See Banks, Russell

Banville, John 1945- .... **CLC 46, 118, 224**
See also CA 117; 128; CANR 104, 150, 176; CN 4, 5, 6, 7; DLB 14, 271, 326; INT CA-128

Banville, Theodore (Faullain) de 1832-1891 .... **NCLC 9**
See also DLB 217; GFL 1789 to the Present

Baraka, Amiri 1934- .. **BLC 1:1, 2:1; CLC 1, 2, 3, 5, 10, 14, 33, 115, 213; DC 6; PC 4; WLCS**
See also AAYA 63; AFAW 1, 2; AMWS 2; BW 2, 3; CA 21-24R; CABS 3; CAD; CANR 27, 38, 61, 133, 172; CD 3, 5, 6; CDALB 1941-1968; CN 1, 2; CP 1, 2, 3, 4, 5, 6, 7; CPW; DA; DA3; DAC; DAM MST, MULT, POET, POP; DFS 3, 11, 16; DLB 5, 7, 16, 38; DLBD 8; EWL 3; MAL 5; MTCW 1, 2; MTFW 2005; PFS 9; RGAL 4; TCLE 1:1; TUS; WP

Baratynsky, Evgenii Abramovich 1800-1844 .... **NCLC 103**
See also DLB 205

Barbauld, Anna Laetitia 1743-1825 .... **NCLC 50, 185**
See also DLB 107, 109, 142, 158, 336; RGEL 2

Barbellion, W. N. P.
See Cummings, Bruce F.

Barber, Benjamin R. 1939- .... **CLC 141**
See also CA 29-32R; CANR 12, 32, 64, 119

Barbera, Jack (Vincent) 1945- .... **CLC 44**
See also CA 110; CANR 45

Barbey d'Aurevilly, Jules-Amedee 1808-1889 .... **NCLC 1, 213; SSC 17**
See also DLB 119; GFL 1789 to the Present

Barbour, John c. 1316-1395 .... **CMLC 33**
See also DLB 146

Barbusse, Henri 1873-1935 .... **TCLC 5**
See also CA 105; 154; DLB 65; EWL 3; RGWL 2, 3

Barclay, Alexander c. 1475-1552 .... **LC 109**
See also DLB 132

Barclay, Bill
See Moorcock, Michael

Barclay, William Ewert
See Moorcock, Michael

Barea, Arturo 1897-1957 .... **TCLC 14**
See also CA 111; 201

Barfoot, Joan 1946- .... **CLC 18**
See also CA 105; CANR 141, 179

Barham, Richard Harris 1788-1845 .... **NCLC 77**
See also DLB 159

Baring, Maurice 1874-1945 .... **TCLC 8**
See also CA 105; 168; DLB 34; HGG

Baring-Gould, Sabine 1834-1924 ... **TCLC 88**
See also DLB 156, 190

Berrigan, Daniel 1921- .... **CLC 4**
　See also CA 33-36R; 187; CAAE 187;
　CAAS 1; CANR 11, 43, 78; CP 1, 2, 3, 4,
　5, 6, 7; DLB 5
Berrigan, Edmund Joseph Michael, Jr.
　1934-1983 .... **CLC 37**
　See also CA 61-64; 110; CANR 14, 102;
　CP 1, 2, 3; DLB 5, 169; WP
Berrigan, Ted
　See Berrigan, Edmund Joseph Michael, Jr.
Berry, Charles Edward Anderson
　1931- .... **CLC 17**
　See also CA 115
Berry, Chuck
　See Berry, Charles Edward Anderson
Berry, Jonas
　See Ashbery, John
Berry, Wendell 1934- ..... **CLC 4, 6, 8, 27, 46,**
　　279; PC 28
　See also AITN 1; AMWS 10; ANW; CA
　73-76; CANR 50, 73, 101, 132, 174; CP
　1, 2, 3, 4, 5, 6, 7; CSW; DAM POET;
　DLB 5, 6, 234, 275, 342; MTCW 2;
　MTFW 2005; PFS 30; TCLE 1:1
Berryman, John 1914-1972 ... **CLC 1, 2, 3, 4,**
　　6, 8, 10, 13, 25, 62; PC 64
　See also AMW; CA 13-16; 33-36R; CABS
　2; CANR 35; CAP 1; CDALB 1941-1968;
　CP 1; DAM POET; DLB 48; EWL 3;
　MAL 5; MTCW 1, 2; MTFW 2005; PAB;
　PFS 27; RGAL 4; WP
Bertolucci, Bernardo 1940- ...... **CLC 16, 157**
　See also CA 106; CANR 125
Berton, Pierre (Francis de Marigny)
　1920-2004 .... **CLC 104**
　See also CA 1-4R; 233; CANR 2, 56, 144;
　CPW; DLB 68; SATA 99; SATA-Obit 158
Bertrand, Aloysius 1807-1841 .... **NCLC 31**
　See also DLB 217
Bertrand, Louis oAloysiusc
　See Bertrand, Aloysius
Bertran de Born c. 1140-1215 .... **CMLC 5**
Besant, Annie (Wood) 1847-1933 ..... **TCLC 9**
　See also CA 105; 185
Bessie, Alvah 1904-1985 .... **CLC 23**
　See also CA 5-8R; 116; CANR 2, 80; DLB
　26
Bestuzhev, Aleksandr Aleksandrovich
　1797-1837 .... **NCLC 131**
　See also DLB 198
Bethlen, T.D.
　See Silverberg, Robert
Beti, Mongo
　See Biyidi, Alexandre
Betjeman, John 1906-1984 ...... **CLC 2, 6, 10,**
　　34, 43; PC 75
　See also BRW 7; CA 9-12R; 112; CANR
　33, 56; CDBLB 1945-1960; CP 1, 2, 3;
　DA3; DAB; DAM MST, POET; DLB 20;
　DLBY 1984; EWL 3; MTCW 1, 2
Bettelheim, Bruno 1903-1990 .... **CLC 79;**
　　TCLC 143
　See also CA 81-84; 131; CANR 23, 61;
　DA3; MTCW 1, 2; RGHL
Betti, Ugo 1892-1953 .... **TCLC 5**
　See also CA 104; 155; EWL 3; RGWL 2, 3
Betts, Doris (Waugh) 1932- ... **CLC 3, 6, 28,**
　　275; SSC 45
　See also CA 13-16R; CANR 9, 66, 77; CN
　6, 7; CSW; DLB 218; DLBY 1982; INT
　CANR-9; RGAL 4
Bevan, Alistair
　See Roberts, Keith (John Kingston)
Bey, Pilaff
　See Douglas, (George) Norman
Beyala, Calixthe 1961- .... **BLC 2:1**
　See also EWL 3

Beynon, John
　See Harris, John (Wyndham Parkes Lucas)
　Beynon
Bialik, Chaim Nachman
　1873-1934 .... **TCLC 25, 201**
　See also CA 170; EWL 3; WLIT 6
Bialik, Hayyim Nahman
　See Bialik, Chaim Nachman
Bickerstaff, Isaac
　See Swift, Jonathan
Bidart, Frank 1939- .... **CLC 33**
　See also AMWS 15; CA 140; CANR 106;
　CP 5, 6, 7; PFS 26
Bienek, Horst 1930- .... **CLC 7, 11**
　See also CA 73-76; DLB 75
Bierce, Ambrose (Gwinett)
　1842-1914(?) . **SSC 9, 72, 124; TCLC 1,**
　　7, 44; WLC 1
　See also AAYA 55; AMW; BYA 11; CA
　104; 139; CANR 78; CDALB 1865-1917;
　DA; DA3; DAC; DAM MST; DLB 11,
　12, 23, 71, 74, 186; EWL 3; EXPS; HGG;
　LAIT 2; MAL 5; RGAL 4; RGSF 2; SSFS
　9, 27; SUFW 1
Biggers, Earl Derr 1884-1933 .... **TCLC 65**
　See also CA 108; 153; DLB 306
Billiken, Bud
　See Motley, Willard (Francis)
Billings, Josh
　See Shaw, Henry Wheeler
Billington, (Lady) Rachel (Mary)
　1942- .... **CLC 43**
　See also AITN 2; CA 33-36R; CANR 44;
　CN 4, 5, 6, 7
Binchy, Maeve 1940- .... **CLC 153**
　See also BEST 90:1; BPFB 1; CA 127; 134;
　CANR 50, 96, 134; CN 5, 6, 7; CPW;
　DA3; DAM POP; DLB 319; INT CA-134;
　MTCW 2; MTFW 2005; RHW
Binyon, T(imothy) J(ohn)
　1936-2004 .... **CLC 34**
　See also CA 111; 232; CANR 28, 140
Bion 335B.C.-245B.C. .... **CMLC 39**
Bioy Casares, Adolfo 1914-1999 ... **CLC 4, 8,**
　　13, 88; HLC 1; SSC 17, 102
　See also CA 29-32R; 177; CANR 19, 43,
　66; CWW 2; DAM MULT; DLB 113;
　EWL 3; HW 1, 2; LAW; MTCW 1, 2;
　MTFW 2005; RGSF 2
Birch, Allison .... **CLC 65**
Bird, Cordwainer
　See Ellison, Harlan
Bird, Robert Montgomery
　1806-1854 .... **NCLC 1, 197**
　See also DLB 202; RGAL 4
Birdwell, Cleo
　See DeLillo, Don
Birkerts, Sven 1951- .... **CLC 116**
　See also CA 128; 133, 176; CAAE 176;
　CAAS 29; CANR 151; INT CA-133
Birney, (Alfred) Earle 1904-1995 .. **CLC 1, 4,**
　　6, 11; PC 52
　See also CA 1-4R; CANR 5, 20; CN 1, 2,
　3, 4; CP 1, 2, 3, 4, 5, 6; DAC; DAM MST,
　POET; DLB 88; MTCW 1; PFS 8; RGEL
　2
Biruni, al 973-1048(?) .... **CMLC 28**
Bishop, Elizabeth 1911-1979 ..... **CLC 1, 4, 9,**
　　13, 15, 32; PC 3, 34; TCLC 121
　See also AMWR 2; AMWS 1; CA 5-8R;
　89-92; CABS 2; CANR 26, 61, 108;
　CDALB 1968-1988; CP 1, 2, 3; DA;
　DA3; DAC; DAM MST, POET; DLB 5,
　169; EWL 3; GLL 2; MAL 5; MBL;
　MTCW 1, 2; PAB; PFS 6, 12, 27, 31;
　RGAL 4; SATA-Obit 24; TUS; WP
Bishop, George Archibald
　See Crowley, Edward Alexander

Bishop, John 1935- .... **CLC 10**
　See also CA 105
Bishop, John Peale 1892-1944 ..... **TCLC 103**
　See also CA 107; 155; DLB 4, 9, 45; MAL
　5; RGAL 4
Bissett, Bill 1939- .... **CLC 18; PC 14**
　See also CA 69-72; CAAS 19; CANR 15;
　CCA 1; CP 1, 2, 3, 4, 5, 6, 7; DLB 53;
　MTCW 1
Bissoondath, Neil 1955- .... **CLC 120**
　See also CA 136; CANR 123, 165; CN 6,
　7; DAC
Bissoondath, Neil Devindra
　See Bissoondath, Neil
Bitov, Andrei (Georgievich) 1937- ... **CLC 57**
　See also CA 142; DLB 302
Biyidi, Alexandre 1932- ... **BLC 1:1; CLC 27**
　See also AFW; BW 1, 3; CA 114; 124;
　CANR 81; DA3; DAM MULT; EWL 3;
　MTCW 1, 2
Bjarme, Brynjolf
　See Ibsen, Henrik (Johan)
Bjoernson, Bjoernstjerne (Martinius)
　1832-1910 .... **TCLC 7, 37**
　See also CA 104
Black, Benjamin
　See Banville, John
Black, Robert
　See Holdstock, Robert
Blackburn, Paul 1926-1971 .... **CLC 9, 43**
　See also BG 1:2; CA 81-84; 33-36R; CANR
　34; CP 1; DLB 16; DLBY 1981
Black Elk 1863-1950 .... **NNAL; TCLC 33**
　See also CA 144; DAM MULT; MTCW 2;
　MTFW 2005; WP
Black Hawk 1767-1838 .... **NNAL**
Black Hobart
　See Sanders, Ed
Blacklin, Malcolm
　See Chambers, Aidan
Blackmore, R(ichard) D(oddridge)
　1825-1900 .... **TCLC 27**
　See also CA 120; DLB 18; RGEL 2
Blackmur, R(ichard) P(almer)
　1904-1965 .... **CLC 2, 24**
　See also AMWS 2; CA 11-12; 25-28R;
　CANR 71; CAP 1; DLB 63; EWL 3;
　MAL 5
Black Tarantula
　See Acker, Kathy
Blackwood, Algernon 1869-1951 .... **SSC 107;**
　　TCLC 5
　See also AAYA 78; CA 105; 150; CANR
　169; DLB 153, 156, 178; HGG; SUFW 1
Blackwood, Algernon Henry
　See Blackwood, Algernon
Blackwood, Caroline (Maureen)
　1931-1996 .... **CLC 6, 9, 100**
　See also BRWS 9; CA 85-88; 151; CANR
　32, 61, 65; CN 3, 4, 5, 6; DLB 14, 207;
　HGG; MTCW 1
Blade, Alexander
　See Hamilton, Edmond; Silverberg, Robert
Blaga, Lucian 1895-1961 .... **CLC 75**
　See also CA 157; DLB 220; EWL 3
Blair, Eric 1903-1950 .... **SSC 68; TCLC 2, 6,**
　　15, 31, 51, 123, 128, 129; WLC 4
　See also BPFB 3; BRW 7; BYA 5; CA 104;
　132; CDBLB 1945-1960; CLR 68; DA;
　DA3; DAB; DAC; DAM MST, NOV;
　DLB 15, 98, 195, 255; EWL 3; EXPN;
　LAIT 4, 5; LATS 1:1; MTCW 1, 2;
　MTFW 2005; NFS 3, 7; RGEL 2; SATA
　29; SCFW 1, 2; SFW 4; SSFS 4; TEA;
　WLIT 4; YAW X
Blair, Eric Arthur
　See Blair, Eric
Blair, Hugh 1718-1800 .... **NCLC 75**

Author Index

Bryan, William Jennings
1860-1925 .... **TCLC 99**
See also DLB 303
Bryant, William Cullen 1794-1878 . **NCLC 6,
46; PC 20**
See also AMWS 1; CDALB 1640-1865;
DA; DAB; DAC; DAM MST, POET;
DLB 3, 43, 59, 189, 250; EXPP; PAB;
PFS 30; RGAL 4; TUS
Bryusov, Valery Yakovlevich
1873-1924 .... **TCLC 10**
See also CA 107; 155; EWL 3; SFW 4
Buchan, John 1875-1940 .... **TCLC 41**
See also CA 108; 145; CMW 4; DAB;
DAM POP; DLB 34, 70, 156; HGG;
MSW; MTCW 2; RGEL 2; RHW; YABC
2
Buchanan, George 1506-1582 .... **LC 4**
See also DLB 132
Buchanan, Robert 1841-1901 .... **TCLC 107**
See also CA 179; DLB 18, 35
Buchheim, Lothar-Guenther
1918-2007 .... **CLC 6**
See also CA 85-88; 257
Buchner, (Karl) Georg 1813-1837 ..... **DC 35;
NCLC 26, 146**
See also CDWLB 2; DLB 133; EW 6;
RGSF 2; RGWL 2, 3; TWA
Buchwald, Art 1925-2007 .... **CLC 33**
See also AITN 1; CA 5-8R; 256; CANR 21,
67, 107; MTCW 1, 2; SATA 10
Buchwald, Arthur
See Buchwald, Art
Buck, Pearl S(ydenstricker)
1892-1973 .... **CLC 7, 11, 18, 127**
See also AAYA 42; AITN 1; AMWS 2;
BPFB 1; CA 1-4R; 41-44R; CANR 1, 34;
CDALBS; CN 1; DA; DA3; DAB; DAC;
DAM MST, NOV; DLB 9, 102, 329; EWL
3; LAIT 3; MAL 5; MTCW 1, 2; MTFW
2005; NFS 25; RGAL 4; RHW; SATA 1,
25; TUS
Buckler, Ernest 1908-1984 .... **CLC 13**
See also CA 11-12; 114; CAP 1; CCA 1;
CN 1, 2, 3; DAC; DAM MST; DLB 68;
SATA 47
Buckley, Christopher 1952- .... **CLC 165**
See also CA 139; CANR 119, 180
Buckley, Christopher Taylor
See Buckley, Christopher
Buckley, Vincent (Thomas)
1925-1988 .... **CLC 57**
See also CA 101; CP 1, 2, 3, 4; DLB 289
Buckley, William F., Jr. 1925-2008 ... **CLC 7,
18, 37**
See also AITN 1; BPFB 1; CA 1-4R; 269;
CANR 1, 24, 53, 93, 133, 185; CMW 4;
CPW; DA3; DAM POP; DLB 137; DLBY
1980; INT CANR-24; MTCW 1, 2;
MTFW 2005; TUS
Buckley, William Frank
See Buckley, William F., Jr.
Buckley, William Frank, Jr.
See Buckley, William F., Jr.
Buechner, Frederick 1926- ..... **CLC 2, 4, 6, 9**
See also AMWS 12; BPFB 1; CA 13-16R;
CANR 11, 39, 64, 114, 138; CN 1, 2, 3,
4, 5, 6, 7; DAM NOV; DLBY 1980; INT
CANR-11; MAL 5; MTCW 1, 2; MTFW
2005; TCLE 1:1
Buell, John (Edward) 1927- .... **CLC 10**
See also CA 1-4R; CANR 71; DLB 53
Buero Vallejo, Antonio 1916-2000 ... **CLC 15,
46, 139, 226; DC 18**
See also CA 106; 189; CANR 24, 49, 75;
CWW 2; DFS 11; EWL 3; HW 1; MTCW
1, 2
Bufalino, Gesualdo 1920-1996 .... **CLC 74**
See also CA 209; CWW 2; DLB 196

Bugayev, Boris Nikolayevich
1880-1934 .... **PC 11; TCLC 7**
See also CA 104; 165; DLB 295; EW 9;
EWL 3; MTCW 2; MTFW 2005; RGWL
2, 3
Bukowski, Charles 1920-1994 ... **CLC 2, 5, 9,
41, 82, 108; PC 18; SSC 45**
See also CA 17-20R; 144; CANR 40, 62,
105, 180; CN 4, 5; CP 1, 2, 3, 4, 5; CPW;
DA3; DAM NOV, POET; DLB 5, 130,
169; EWL 3; MAL 5; MTCW 1, 2;
MTFW 2005; PFS 28
Bulgakov, Mikhail 1891-1940 .... **SSC 18;
TCLC 2, 16, 159**
See also AAYA 74; BPFB 1; CA 105; 152;
DAM DRAM, NOV; DLB 272; EWL 3;
MTCW 2; MTFW 2005; NFS 8; RGSF 2;
RGWL 2, 3; SFW 4; TWA
Bulgakov, Mikhail Afanasevich
See Bulgakov, Mikhail
Bulgya, Alexander Alexandrovich
1901-1956 .... **TCLC 53**
See also CA 117; 181; DLB 272; EWL 3
Bullins, Ed 1935- ...... **BLC 1:1; CLC 1, 5, 7;
DC 6**
See also BW 2, 3; CA 49-52; CAAS 16;
CAD; CANR 24, 46, 73, 134; CD 5, 6;
DAM DRAM, MULT; DLB 7, 38, 249;
EWL 3; MAL 5; MTCW 1, 2; MTFW
2005; RGAL 4
Bulosan, Carlos 1911-1956 .... **AAL**
See also CA 216; DLB 312; RGAL 4
**Bulwer-Lytton, Edward (George Earle
Lytton)** 1803-1873 .... **NCLC 1, 45**
See also DLB 21; RGEL 2; SFW 4; SUFW
1; TEA
Bunin, Ivan
See Bunin, Ivan Alexeyevich
Bunin, Ivan Alekseevich
See Bunin, Ivan Alexeyevich
Bunin, Ivan Alexeyevich 1870-1953 ... **SSC 5;
TCLC 6**
See also CA 104; DLB 317, 329; EWL 3;
RGSF 2; RGWL 2, 3; TWA
Bunting, Basil 1900-1985 ...... **CLC 10, 39, 47**
See also BRWS 7; CA 53-56; 115; CANR
7; CP 1, 2, 3, 4; DAM POET; DLB 20;
EWL 3; RGEL 2
Bunuel, Luis 1900-1983 ... **CLC 16, 80; HLC
1**
See also CA 101; 110; CANR 32, 77; DAM
MULT; HW 1
Bunyan, John 1628-1688 .. **LC 4, 69; WLC 1**
See also BRW 2; BYA 5; CDBLB 1660-
1789; CLR 124; DA; DAB; DAC; DAM
MST; DLB 39; RGEL 2; TEA; WCH;
WLIT 3
Buravsky, Alexandr .... **CLC 59**
Burchill, Julie 1959- .... **CLC 238**
See also CA 135; CANR 115, 116
Burckhardt, Jacob (Christoph)
1818-1897 .... **NCLC 49**
See also EW 6
Burford, Eleanor
See Hibbert, Eleanor Alice Burford
Burgess, Anthony 1917-1993 . **CLC 1, 2, 4, 5,
8, 10, 13, 15, 22, 40, 62, 81, 94**
See also AAYA 25; AITN 1; BRWS 1; CA
1-4R; 143; CANR 2, 46; CDBLB 1960 to
Present; CN 1, 2, 3, 4, 5; DA3; DAB;
DAC; DAM NOV; DLB 14, 194, 261;
DLBY 1998; EWL 3; MTCW 1, 2; MTFW
2005; NFS 15; RGEL 2; RHW; SFW 4;
TEA; YAW
Buridan, John c. 1295-c. 1358 ...... **CMLC 97**
Burke, Edmund 1729(?)-1797 .... **LC 7, 36,
146; WLC 1**
See also BRW 3; DA; DA3; DAB; DAC;
DAM MST; DLB 104, 252, 336; RGEL
2; TEA

Burke, Kenneth (Duva) 1897-1993 ... **CLC 2,
24**
See also AMW; CA 5-8R; 143; CANR 39,
74, 136; CN 1, 2; CP 1, 2, 3, 4, 5; DLB
45, 63; EWL 3; MAL 5; MTCW 1, 2;
MTFW 2005; RGAL 4
Burke, Leda
See Garnett, David
Burke, Ralph
See Silverberg, Robert
Burke, Thomas 1886-1945 .... **TCLC 63**
See also CA 113; 155; CMW 4; DLB 197
Burney, Fanny 1752-1840 .... **NCLC 12, 54,
107**
See also BRWS 3; DLB 39; FL 1:2; NFS
16; RGEL 2; TEA
Burney, Frances
See Burney, Fanny
Burns, Robert 1759-1796 ... **LC 3, 29, 40; PC
6; WLC 1**
See also AAYA 51; BRW 3; CDBLB 1789-
1832; DA; DA3; DAB; DAC; DAM MST,
POET; DLB 109; EXPP; PAB; RGEL 2;
TEA; WP
Burns, Tex
See L'Amour, Louis
Burnshaw, Stanley 1906-2005 ..... **CLC 3, 13,
44**
See also CA 9-12R; 243; CP 1, 2, 3, 4, 5, 6,
7; DLB 48; DLBY 1997
Burr, Anne 1937- .... **CLC 6**
See also CA 25-28R
Burroughs, Augusten 1965- .... **CLC 277**
See also AAYA 73; CA 214; CANR 168
Burroughs, Edgar Rice 1875-1950 . **TCLC 2,
32**
See also AAYA 11; BPFB 1; BYA 4, 9; CA
104; 132; CANR 131; DA3; DAM NOV;
DLB 8; FANT; MTCW 1, 2; MTFW
2005; RGAL 4; SATA 41; SCFW 1, 2;
SFW 4; TCWW 1, 2; TUS; YAW
Burroughs, William S. 1914-1997 . **CLC 1, 2,
5, 15, 22, 42, 75, 109; TCLC 121; WLC
1**
See also AAYA 60; AITN 2; AMWS 3; BG
1:2; BPFB 1; CA 9-12R; 160; CANR 20,
52, 104; CN 1, 2, 3, 4, 5, 6; CPW; DA;
DA3; DAB; DAC; DAM MST, NOV,
POP; DLB 2, 8, 16, 152, 237; DLBY
1981, 1997; EWL 3; GLL 1; HGG; LMFS
2; MAL 5; MTCW 1, 2; MTFW 2005;
RGAL 4; SFW 4
Burroughs, William Seward
See Burroughs, William S.
Burton, Sir Richard F(rancis)
1821-1890 .... **NCLC 42**
See also DLB 55, 166, 184; SSFS 21
Burton, Robert 1577-1640 .... **LC 74**
See also DLB 151; RGEL 2
Buruma, Ian 1951- .... **CLC 163**
See also CA 128; CANR 65, 141
Busch, Frederick 1941-2006 .. **CLC 7, 10, 18,
47, 166**
See also CA 33-36R; 248; CAAS 1; CANR
45, 73, 92, 157; CN 1, 2, 3, 4, 5, 6, 7;
DLB 6, 218
Busch, Frederick Matthew
See Busch, Frederick
Bush, Barney (Furman) 1946- .... **NNAL**
See also CA 145
Bush, Ronald 1946- .... **CLC 34**
See also CA 136
Busia, Abena, P. A. 1953- .... **BLC 2:1**
Bustos, F(rancisco)
See Borges, Jorge Luis
Bustos Domecq, H(onorio)
See Bioy Casares, Adolfo; Borges, Jorge
Luis

Campbell, Joseph 1904-1987 .... **CLC 69; TCLC 140**
See also AAYA 3, 66; BEST 89:2; CA 1-4R; 124; CANR 3, 28, 61, 107; DA3; MTCW 1, 2

Campbell, Maria 1940- .... **CLC 85; NNAL**
See also CA 102; CANR 54; CCA 1; DAC

Campbell, Ramsey 1946- ... **CLC 42; SSC 19**
See also AAYA 51; CA 57-60, 228; CAAE 228; CANR 7, 102, 171; DLB 261; HGG; INT CANR-7; SUFW 1, 2

Campbell, (Ignatius) Roy (Dunnachie)
1901-1957 .... **TCLC 5**
See also AFW; CA 104; 155; DLB 20, 225; EWL 3; MTCW 2; RGEL 2

Campbell, Thomas 1777-1844 .... **NCLC 19**
See also DLB 93, 144; RGEL 2

Campbell, Wilfred
See Campbell, William

Campbell, William 1858(?)-1918 ..... **TCLC 9**
See also CA 106; DLB 92

Campbell, William Edward March
1893-1954 .... **TCLC 96**
See also CA 108; 216; DLB 9, 86, 316; MAL 5

Campion, Jane 1954- .... **CLC 95, 229**
See also AAYA 33; CA 138; CANR 87

Campion, Thomas 1567-1620 . **LC 78; PC 87**
See also CDBLB Before 1660; DAM POET; DLB 58, 172; RGEL 2

Camus, Albert 1913-1960 ...... **CLC 1, 2, 4, 9, 11, 14, 32, 63, 69, 124; DC 2; SSC 9, 76; WLC 1**
See also AAYA 36; AFW; BPFB 1; CA 89-92; CANR 131; DA; DA3; DAB; DAC; DAM DRAM, MST, NOV; DLB 72, 321, 329; EW 13; EWL 3; EXPN; EXPS; GFL 1789 to the Present; LATS 1:2; LMFS 2; MTCW 1, 2; MTFW 2005; NFS 6, 16; RGHL; RGSF 2; RGWL 2, 3; SSFS 4; TWA

Canby, Vincent 1924-2000 .... **CLC 13**
See also CA 81-84; 191

Cancale
See Desnos, Robert

Canetti, Elias 1905-1994 .. **CLC 3, 14, 25, 75, 86; TCLC 157**
See also CA 21-24R; 146; CANR 23, 61, 79; CDWLB 2; CWW 2; DA3; DLB 85, 124, 329; EW 12; EWL 3; MTCW 1, 2; MTFW 2005; RGWL 2, 3; TWA

Canfield, Dorothea F.
See Fisher, Dorothy (Frances) Canfield

Canfield, Dorothea Frances
See Fisher, Dorothy (Frances) Canfield

Canfield, Dorothy
See Fisher, Dorothy (Frances) Canfield

Canin, Ethan 1960- .... **CLC 55; SSC 70**
See also CA 131; 135; CANR 193; DLB 335, 350; MAL 5

Cankar, Ivan 1876-1918 .... **TCLC 105**
See also CDWLB 4; DLB 147; EWL 3

Cannon, Curt
See Hunter, Evan

Cao, Lan 1961- .... **CLC 109**
See also CA 165

Cape, Judith
See Page, P(atricia) K(athleen)

Capek, Karel 1890-1938 .... **DC 1; SSC 36; TCLC 6, 37, 192; WLC 1**
See also CA 104; 140; CDWLB 4; DA; DA3; DAB; DAC; DAM DRAM, MST, NOV; DFS 7, 11; DLB 215; EW 10; EWL 3; MTCW 2; RGSF 2; RGWL 2, 3; SCFW 1, 2; SFW 4

Capella, Martianus fl. 4th cent. - .. **CMLC 84**

Capote, Truman 1924-1984 . **CLC 1, 3, 8, 13, 19, 34, 38, 58; SSC 2, 47, 93; TCLC 164; WLC 1**
See also AAYA 61; AMWS 3; BPFB 1; CA 5-8R; 113; CANR 18, 62; CDALB 1941-1968; CN 1, 2, 3; CPW; DA; DA3; DAB; DAC; DAM MST, NOV, POP; DLB 2, 185, 227; DLBY 1980, 1984; EWL 3; EXPS; GLL 1; LAIT 3; MAL 5; MTCW 1, 2; MTFW 2005; NCFS 2; RGAL 4; RGSF 2; SATA 91; SSFS 2; TUS

Capra, Frank 1897-1991 .... **CLC 16**
See also AAYA 52; CA 61-64; 135

Caputo, Philip 1941- .... **CLC 32**
See also AAYA 60; CA 73-76; CANR 40, 135; YAW

Caragiale, Ion Luca 1852-1912 ...... **TCLC 76**
See also CA 157

Card, Orson Scott 1951- ...... **CLC 44, 47, 50, 279**
See also AAYA 11, 42; BPFB 1; BYA 5, 8; CA 102; CANR 27, 47, 73, 102, 106, 133, 184; CLR 116; CPW; DA3; DAM POP; FANT; INT CANR-27; MTCW 1, 2; MTFW 2005; NFS 5; SATA 83, 127; SCFW 2; SFW 4; SUFW 2; YAW

Cardenal, Ernesto 1925- .... **CLC 31, 161; HLC 1; PC 22**
See also CA 49-52; CANR 2, 32, 66, 138; CWW 2; DAM MULT, POET; DLB 290; EWL 3; HW 1, 2; LAWS 1; MTCW 1, 2; MTFW 2005; RGWL 2, 3

Cardinal, Marie 1929-2001 .... **CLC 189**
See also CA 177; CWW 2; DLB 83; FW

Cardozo, Benjamin N(athan)
1870-1938 .... **TCLC 65**
See also CA 117; 164

Carducci, Giosue (Alessandro Giuseppe)
1835-1907 .... **PC 46; TCLC 32**
See also CA 163; DLB 329; EW 7; RGWL 2, 3

Carew, Thomas 1595(?)-1640 ..... **LC 13, 159; PC 29**
See also BRW 2; DLB 126; PAB; RGEL 2

Carey, Ernestine Gilbreth
1908-2006 .... **CLC 17**
See also CA 5-8R; 254; CANR 71; SATA 2; SATA-Obit 177

Carey, Peter 1943- .... **CLC 40, 55, 96, 183**
See also BRWS 12; CA 123; 127; CANR 53, 76, 117, 157, 185; CN 4, 5, 6, 7; DLB 289; 326; EWL 3; INT CA-127; MTCW 1, 2; MTFW 2005; RGSF 2; SATA 94

Carey, Peter Philip
See Carey, Peter

Carleton, William 1794-1869 ... **NCLC 3, 199**
See also DLB 159; RGEL 2; RGSF 2

Carlisle, Henry (Coffin) 1926- .... **CLC 33**
See also CA 13-16R; CANR 15, 85

Carlsen, Chris
See Holdstock, Robert

Carlson, Ron 1947- .... **CLC 54**
See also CA 105, 189; CAAE 189; CANR 27, 155; DLB 244

Carlson, Ronald F.
See Carlson, Ron

Carlyle, Jane Welsh 1801-1866 ... **NCLC 181**
See also DLB 55

Carlyle, Thomas 1795-1881 ..... **NCLC 22, 70**
See also BRW 4; CDBLB 1789-1832; DA; DAB; DAC; DAM MST; DLB 55, 144, 254, 338; RGEL 2; TEA

Carman, (William) Bliss 1861-1929 ... **PC 34; TCLC 7**
See also CA 104; 152; DAC; DLB 92; RGEL 2

Carnegie, Dale 1888-1955 .... **TCLC 53**
See also CA 218

Carossa, Hans 1878-1956 .... **TCLC 48**
See also CA 170; DLB 66; EWL 3

Carpenter, Don(ald Richard)
1931-1995 .... **CLC 41**
See also CA 45-48; 149; CANR 1, 71

Carpenter, Edward 1844-1929 .... **TCLC 88**
See also BRWS 13; CA 163; GLL 1

Carpenter, John (Howard) 1948- ... **CLC 161**
See also AAYA 2, 73; CA 134; SATA 58

Carpenter, Johnny
See Carpenter, John (Howard)

Carpentier (y Valmont), Alejo
1904-1980 . **CLC 8, 11, 38, 110; HLC 1; SSC 35; TCLC 201**
See also CA 65-68; 97-100; CANR 11, 70; CDWLB 3; DAM MULT; DLB 113; EWL 3; HW 1, 2; LAW; LMFS 2; RGSF 2; RGWL 2, 3; WLIT 1

Carr, Caleb 1955- .... **CLC 86**
See also CA 147; CANR 73, 134; DA3; DLB 350

Carr, Emily 1871-1945 .... **TCLC 32**
See also CA 159; DLB 68; FW; GLL 2

Carr, H. D.
See Crowley, Edward Alexander

Carr, John Dickson 1906-1977 .... **CLC 3**
See also CA 49-52; 69-72; CANR 3, 33, 60; CMW 4; DLB 306; MSW; MTCW 1, 2

Carr, Philippa
See Hibbert, Eleanor Alice Burford

Carr, Virginia Spencer 1929- .... **CLC 34**
See also CA 61-64; CANR 175; DLB 111

Carrere, Emmanuel 1957- .... **CLC 89**
See also CA 200

Carrier, Roch 1937- .... **CLC 13, 78**
See also CA 130; CANR 61, 152; CCA 1; DAC; DAM MST; DLB 53; SATA 105, 166

Carroll, James Dennis
See Carroll, Jim

Carroll, James P. 1943(?)- .... **CLC 38**
See also CA 81-84; CANR 73, 139; MTCW 2; MTFW 2005

Carroll, Jim 1951- .... **CLC 35, 143**
See also AAYA 17; CA 45-48; CANR 42, 115; NCFS 5

Carroll, Lewis 1832-1898 . **NCLC 2, 53, 139; PC 18, 74; WLC 1**
See also AAYA 39; BRW 5; BYA 5, 13; CD-BLB 1832-1890; CLR 18, 108; DA; DA3; DAB; DAC; DAM MST, NOV, POET; DLB 18, 163, 178; DLBY 1998; EXPN; EXPP; FANT; JRDA; LAIT 1; MAICYA 1, 2; NFS 27; PFS 11, 30; RGEL 2; SATA 100; SUFW 1; TEA; WCH; YABC 2

Carroll, Paul Vincent 1900-1968 ...... **CLC 10**
See also CA 9-12R; 25-28R; DLB 10; EWL 3; RGEL 2

Carruth, Hayden 1921-2008 .... **CLC 4, 7, 10, 18, 84; PC 10**
See also AMWS 16; CA 9-12R; 277; CANR 4, 38, 59, 110, 174; CP 1, 2, 3, 4, 5, 6, 7; DLB 5, 165; INT CANR-4; MTCW 1, 2; MTFW 2005; PFS 26; SATA 47; SATA-Obit 197

Carson, Anne 1950- .... **CLC 185; PC 64**
See also AMWS 12; CA 203; CP 7; DLB 193; PFS 18; TCLE 1:1

Carson, Ciaran 1948- .... **CLC 201**
See also BRWS 13; CA 112; 153; CANR 113, 189; CP 6, 7; PFS 26

Carson, Rachel
See Carson, Rachel Louise

Carson, Rachel Louise 1907-1964 .... **CLC 71**
See also AAYA 49; AMWS 9; ANW; CA 77-80; CANR 35; DA3; DAM POP; DLB 275; FW; LAIT 4; MAL 5; MTCW 1, 2; MTFW 2005; NCFS 1; SATA 23

Cartagena, Teresa de 1425(?)- .... **LC 155**
See also DLB 286
Carter, Angela 1940-1992 ...... **CLC 5, 41, 76; SSC 13, 85; TCLC 139**
See also BRWS 3; CA 53-56; 136; CANR 12, 36, 61, 106; CN 3, 4, 5; DA3; DLB 14, 207, 261, 319; EXPS; FANT; FW; GL 2; MTCW 1, 2; MTFW 2005; RGSF 2; SATA 66; SATA-Obit 70; SFW 4; SSFS 4, 12; SUFW 2; WLIT 4
Carter, Angela Olive
See Carter, Angela
Carter, Martin (Wylde) 1927- .... **BLC 2:1**
See also BW 2; CA 102; CANR 42; CD-WLB 3; CP 1, 2, 3, 4, 5, 6; DLB 117; EWL 3
Carter, Nick
See Smith, Martin Cruz
Carter, Nick
See Smith, Martin Cruz
Carver, Raymond 1938-1988 ..... **CLC 22, 36, 53, 55, 126; PC 54; SSC 8, 51, 104**
See also AAYA 44; AMWS 3; BPFB 1; CA 33-36R; 126; CANR 17, 34, 61, 103; CN 4; CPW; DA3; DAM NOV; DLB 130; DLBY 1984, 1988; EWL 3; MAL 5; MTCW 1, 2; MTFW 2005; PFS 17; RGAL 4; RGSF 2; SSFS 3, 6, 12, 13, 23; TCLE 1:1; TCWW 2; TUS
Cary, Elizabeth, Lady Falkland 1585-1639 .... **LC 30, 141**
Cary, (Arthur) Joyce (Lunel) 1888-1957 .... **TCLC 1, 29, 196**
See also BRW 7; CA 104; 164; CDBLB 1914-1945; DLB 15, 100; EWL 3; MTCW 2; RGEL 2; TEA
Casal, Julian del 1863-1893 .... **NCLC 131**
See also DLB 283; LAW
Casanova, Giacomo
See Casanova de Seingalt, Giovanni Jacopo
Casanova, Giovanni Giacomo
See Casanova de Seingalt, Giovanni Jacopo
Casanova de Seingalt, Giovanni Jacopo 1725-1798 .... **LC 13, 151**
See also WLIT 7
Casares, Adolfo Bioy
See Bioy Casares, Adolfo
Casas, Bartolome de las 1474-1566
See Las Casas, Bartolome de
Case, John
See Hougan, Carolyn
Casely-Hayford, J(oseph) E(phraim) 1866-1903 .... **BLC 1:1; TCLC 24**
See also BW 2; CA 123; 152; DAM MULT
Casey, John (Dudley) 1939- .... **CLC 59**
See also BEST 90:2; CA 69-72; CANR 23, 100
Casey, Michael 1947- .... **CLC 2**
See also CA 65-68; CANR 109; CP 2, 3; DLB 5
Casey, Patrick
See Thurman, Wallace (Henry)
Casey, Warren (Peter) 1935-1988 .... **CLC 12**
See also CA 101; 127; INT CA-101
Casona, Alejandro
See Alvarez, Alejandro Rodriguez
Cassavetes, John 1929-1989 .... **CLC 20**
See also CA 85-88; 127; CANR 82
Cassian, Nina 1924- .... **PC 17**
See also CWP; CWW 2
Cassill, R(onald) V(erlin) 1919-2002 .... **CLC 4, 23**
See also CA 9-12R; 208; CAAS 1; CANR 7, 45; CN 1, 2, 3, 4, 5, 6, 7; DLB 6, 218; DLBY 2002
Cassiodorus, Flavius Magnus c. 490(?)-c. 583(?) .... **CMLC 43**
Cassirer, Ernst 1874-1945 .... **TCLC 61**
See also CA 157

Cassity, (Allen) Turner 1929- .... **CLC 6, 42**
See also CA 17-20R; 223; CAAE 223; CAAS 8; CANR 11; CSW; DLB 105
Cassius Dio c. 155-c. 229 .... **CMLC 99**
See also DLB 176
Castaneda, Carlos (Cesar Aranha) 1931(?)-1998 .... **CLC 12, 119**
See also CA 25-28R; CANR 32, 66, 105; DNFS 1; HW 1; MTCW 1
Castedo, Elena 1937- .... **CLC 65**
See also CA 132
Castedo-Ellerman, Elena
See Castedo, Elena
Castellanos, Rosario 1925-1974 .... **CLC 66; HLC 1; SSC 39, 68**
See also CA 131; 53-56; CANR 58; CD-WLB 3; DAM MULT; DLB 113, 290; EWL 3; FW; HW 1; LAW; MTCW 2; MTFW 2005; RGSF 2; RGWL 2, 3
Castelvetro, Lodovico 1505-1571 .... **LC 12**
Castiglione, Baldassare 1478-1529 ..... **LC 12, 165**
See also EW 2; LMFS 1; RGWL 2, 3; WLIT 7
Castiglione, Baldesar
See Castiglione, Baldassare
Castillo, Ana 1953- .... **CLC 151, 279**
See also AAYA 42; CA 131; CANR 51, 86, 128, 172; CWP; DLB 122, 227; DNFS 2; FW; HW 1; LLW; PFS 21
Castillo, Ana Hernandez Del
See Castillo, Ana
Castle, Robert
See Hamilton, Edmond
Castro (Ruz), Fidel 1926(?)- .... **HLC 1**
See also CA 110; 129; CANR 81; DAM MULT; HW 2
Castro, Guillen de 1569-1631 .... **LC 19**
Castro, Rosalia de 1837-1885 ... **NCLC 3, 78; PC 41**
See also DAM MULT
Castro Alves, Antonio de 1847-1871 .... **NCLC 205**
See also DLB 307; LAW
Cather, Willa (Sibert) 1873-1947 . **SSC 2, 50, 114; TCLC 1, 11, 31, 99, 132, 152; WLC 1**
See also AAYA 24; AMW; AMWC 1; AMWR 1; BPFB 1; CA 104; 128; CDALB 1865-1917; CLR 98; DA; DA3; DAB; DAC; DAM MST, NOV; DLB 9, 54, 78, 256; DLBD 1; EWL 3; EXPN; EXPS; FL 1:5; LAIT 3; LATS 1:1; MAL 5; MBL; MTCW 1, 2; MTFW 2005; NFS 2, 19; RGAL 4; RGSF 2; RHW; SATA 30; SSFS 2, 7, 16, 27; TCWW 1, 2; TUS
Catherine II
See Catherine the Great
Catherine, Saint 1347-1380 ... **CMLC 27, 116**
Catherine the Great 1729-1796 .... **LC 69**
See also DLB 150
Cato, Marcus Porcius 234B.C.-149B.C. .... **CMLC 21**
See also DLB 211
Cato, Marcus Porcius, the Elder
See Cato, Marcus Porcius
Cato the Elder
See Cato, Marcus Porcius
Catton, (Charles) Bruce 1899-1978 . **CLC 35**
See also AITN 1; CA 5-8R; 81-84; CANR 7, 74; DLB 17; MTCW 2; MTFW 2005; SATA 2; SATA-Obit 24
Catullus c. 84B.C.-54B.C. .... **CMLC 18**
See also AW 2; CDWLB 1; DLB 211; RGWL 2, 3; WLIT 8
Cauldwell, Frank
See King, Francis (Henry)

Caunitz, William J. 1933-1996 .... **CLC 34**
See also BEST 89:3; CA 125; 130; 152; CANR 73; INT CA-130
Causley, Charles (Stanley) 1917-2003 .... **CLC 7**
See also CA 9-12R; 223; CANR 5, 35, 94; CLR 30; CP 1, 2, 3, 4, 5; CWRI 5; DLB 27; MTCW 1; SATA 3, 66; SATA-Obit 149
Caute, (John) David 1936- .... **CLC 29**
See also CA 1-4R; CAAS 4; CANR 1, 33, 64, 120; CBD; CD 5, 6; CN 1, 2, 3, 4, 5, 6, 7; DAM NOV; DLB 14, 231
Cavafy, C. P.
See Kavafis, Konstantinos Petrou
Cavafy, Constantine Peter
See Kavafis, Konstantinos Petrou
Cavalcanti, Guido c. 1250-c. 1300 .... **CMLC 54**
See also RGWL 2, 3; WLIT 7
Cavallo, Evelyn
See Spark, Muriel
Cavanna, Betty
See Harrison, Elizabeth (Allen) Cavanna
Cavanna, Elizabeth
See Harrison, Elizabeth (Allen) Cavanna
Cavanna, Elizabeth Allen
See Harrison, Elizabeth (Allen) Cavanna
Cavendish, Margaret Lucas 1623-1673 .... **LC 30, 132**
See also DLB 131, 252, 281; RGEL 2
Caxton, William 1421(?)-1491(?) .... **LC 17**
See also DLB 170
Cayer, D. M.
See Duffy, Maureen (Patricia)
Cayrol, Jean 1911-2005 .... **CLC 11**
See also CA 89-92; 236; DLB 83; EWL 3
Cela (y Trulock), Camilo Jose
See Cela, Camilo Jose
Cela, Camilo Jose 1916-2002 .... **CLC 4, 13, 59, 122; HLC 1; SSC 71**
See also BEST 90:2; CA 21-24R; 206; CAAS 10; CANR 21, 32, 76, 139; CWW 2; DAM MULT; DLB 322; DLBY 1989; EW 13; EWL 3; HW 1; MTCW 1, 2; MTFW 2005; RGSF 2; RGWL 2, 3
Celan, Paul
See Antschel, Paul
Celine, Louis-Ferdinand
See Destouches, Louis-Ferdinand
Cellini, Benvenuto 1500-1571 .... **LC 7**
See also WLIT 7
Cendrars, Blaise
See Sauser-Hall, Frederic
Centlivre, Susanna 1669(?)-1723 .... **DC 25; LC 65**
See also DLB 84; RGEL 2
Cernuda (y Bidon), Luis 1902-1963 .... **CLC 54; PC 62**
See also CA 131; 89-92; DAM POET; DLB 134; EWL 3; GLL 1; HW 1; RGWL 2, 3
Cervantes, Lorna Dee 1954- ..... **HLCS 1; PC 35**
See also CA 131; CANR 80; CP 7; CWP; DLB 82; EXPP; HW 1; LLW; PFS 30
Cervantes (Saavedra), Miguel de 1547-1616 .... **HLCS; LC 6, 23, 93; SSC 12, 108; WLC 1**
See also AAYA 56; BYA 1, 14; DA; DAB; DAC; DAM MST, NOV; EW 2; LAIT 1; LATS 1:1; LMFS 1; NFS 8; RGSF 2; RGWL 2, 3; TWA
Cesaire, Aime
See Cesaire, Aime

Chesnutt, Charles W(addell)
1858-1932 .... **BLC 1; SSC 7, 54; TCLC 5, 39**
See also AFAW 1, 2; AMWS 14; BW 1, 3; CA 106; 125; CANR 76; DAM MULT; DLB 12, 50, 78; EWL 3; MAL 5; MTCW 1, 2; MTFW 2005; RGAL 4; RGSF 2; SSFS 11, 26

Chester, Alfred 1929(?)-1971 .... **CLC 49**
See also CA 196; 33-36R; DLB 130; MAL 5

Chesterton, G(ilbert) K(eith)
1874-1936 . **PC 28; SSC 1, 46; TCLC 1, 6, 64**
See also AAYA 57; BRW 6; CA 104; 132; CANR 73, 131; CDBLB 1914-1945; CMW 4; DAM NOV, POET; DLB 10, 19, 34, 70, 98, 149, 178; EWL 3; FANT; MSW; MTCW 1, 2; MTFW 2005; RGEL 2; RGSF 2; SATA 27; SUFW 1

Chettle, Henry 1560-1607(?) .... **LC 112**
See also DLB 136; RGEL 2

Chiang, Pin-chin 1904-1986 .... **CLC 68**
See also CA 118; DLB 328; EWL 3; RGWL 3

Chiang Ping-chih
See Chiang, Pin-chin

Chief Joseph 1840-1904 .... **NNAL**
See also CA 152; DA3; DAM MULT

Chief Seattle 1786(?)-1866 .... **NNAL**
See also DA3; DAM MULT

Ch'ien, Chung-shu 1910-1998 .... **CLC 22**
See also CA 130; CANR 73; CWW 2; DLB 328; MTCW 1, 2

Chikamatsu Monzaemon 1653-1724 ... **LC 66**
See also RGWL 2, 3

Child, Francis James 1825-1896 . **NCLC 173**
See also DLB 1, 64, 235

Child, L. Maria
See Child, Lydia Maria

Child, Lydia Maria 1802-1880 .. **NCLC 6, 73**
See also DLB 1, 74, 243; RGAL 4; SATA 67

Child, Mrs.
See Child, Lydia Maria

Child, Philip 1898-1978 .... **CLC 19, 68**
See also CA 13-14; CAP 1; CP 1; DLB 68; RHW; SATA 47

Childers, (Robert) Erskine
1870-1922 .... **TCLC 65**
See also CA 113; 153; DLB 70

Childress, Alice 1920-1994 .... **BLC 1:1; CLC 12, 15, 86, 96; DC 4; TCLC 116**
See also AAYA 8; BW 2, 3; BYA 2; CA 45-48; 146; CAD; CANR 3, 27, 50, 74; CLR 14; CWD; DA3; DAM DRAM, MULT, NOV; DFS 2, 8, 14, 26; DLB 7, 38, 249; JRDA; LAIT 5; MAICYA 1, 2; MAICYAS 1; MAL 5; MTCW 1, 2; MTFW 2005; RGAL 4; SATA 7, 48, 81; TUS; WYA; YAW

Chin, Frank (Chew, Jr.) 1940- .... **AAL; CLC 135; DC 7**
See also CA 33-36R; CAD; CANR 71; CD 5, 6; DAM MULT; DLB 206, 312; LAIT 5; RGAL 4

Chin, Marilyn (Mei Ling) 1955- .... **PC 40**
See also CA 129; CANR 70, 113; CWP; DLB 312; PFS 28

Chislett, (Margaret) Anne 1943- ...... **CLC 34**
See also CA 151

Chitty, Thomas Willes 1926- .... **CLC 6, 11**
See also CA 5-8R; CN 1, 2, 3, 4, 5, 6; EWL 3

Chivers, Thomas Holley
1809-1858 .... **NCLC 49**
See also DLB 3, 248; RGAL 4

Chlamyda, Jehudil
See Peshkov, Alexei Maximovich

Ch'o, Chou
See Shu-Jen, Chou

Choi, Susan 1969- .... **CLC 119**
See also CA 223; CANR 188

Chomette, Rene Lucien 1898-1981 .. **CLC 20**
See also CA 103

Chomsky, Avram Noam
See Chomsky, Noam

Chomsky, Noam 1928- .... **CLC 132**
See also CA 17-20R; CANR 28, 62, 110, 132, 179; DA3; DLB 246; MTCW 1, 2; MTFW 2005

Chona, Maria 1845(?)-1936 .... **NNAL**
See also CA 144

Chopin, Kate
See Chopin, Katherine

Chopin, Katherine 1851-1904 .... **SSC 8, 68, 110; TCLC 127; WLCS**
See also AAYA 33; AMWR 2; BYA 11, 15; CA 104; 122; CDALB 1865-1917; DA3; DAB; DAC; DAM MST, NOV; DLB 12, 78; EXPN; EXPS; FL 1:3; FW; LAIT 3; MAL 5; MBL; NFS 3; RGAL 4; RGSF 2; SSFS 2, 13, 17, 26; TUS

Chretien de Troyes c. 12th cent. - . **CMLC 10**
See also DLB 208; EW 1; RGWL 2, 3; TWA

Christie
See Ichikawa, Kon

Christie, Agatha (Mary Clarissa)
1890-1976 .. **CLC 1, 6, 8, 12, 39, 48, 110**
See also AAYA 9; AITN 1, 2; BPFB 1; BRWS 2; CA 17-20R; 61-64; CANR 10, 37, 108; CBD; CDBLB 1914-1945; CMW 4; CN 1, 2; CPW; CWD; DA3; DAB; DAC; DAM NOV; DFS 2; DLB 13, 77, 245; MSW; MTCW 1, 2; MTFW 2005; NFS 8, 30; RGEL 2; RHW; SATA 36; TEA; YAW

Christie, Ann Philippa
See Pearce, Philippa

Christie, Philippa
See Pearce, Philippa

Christine de Pisan
See Christine de Pizan

Christine de Pizan 1365(?)-1431(?) ...... **LC 9, 130; PC 68**
See also DLB 208; FL 1:1; FW; RGWL 2, 3

Chuang-Tzu c. 369B.C.-c. 286B.C. .... **CMLC 57**

Chubb, Elmer
See Masters, Edgar Lee

Chulkov, Mikhail Dmitrievich
1743-1792 .... **LC 2**
See also DLB 150

Churchill, Caryl 1938- .... **CLC 31, 55, 157; DC 5**
See also BRWS 4; CA 102; CANR 22, 46, 108; CBD; CD 5, 6; CWD; DFS 25; DLB 13, 310; EWL 3; FW; MTCW 1; RGEL 2

Churchill, Charles 1731-1764 .... **LC 3**
See also DLB 109; RGEL 2

Churchill, Chick
See Churchill, Caryl

Churchill, Sir Winston (Leonard Spencer)
1874-1965 .... **TCLC 113**
See also BRW 6; CA 97-100; CDBLB 1890-1914; DA3; DLB 100, 329; DLBD 16; LAIT 4; MTCW 1, 2

Chute, Carolyn 1947- .... **CLC 39**
See also CA 123; CANR 135; CN 7; DLB 350

Ciardi, John (Anthony) 1916-1986 . **CLC 10, 40, 44, 129; PC 69**
See also CA 5-8R; 118; CAAS 2; CANR 5, 33; CLR 19; CP 1, 2, 3, 4; CWRI 5; DAM POET; DLB 5; DLBY 1986; INT

CANR-5; MAICYA 1, 2; MAL 5; MTCW 1, 2; MTFW 2005; RGAL 4; SAAS 26; SATA 1, 65; SATA-Obit 46

Cibber, Colley 1671-1757 .... **LC 66**
See also DLB 84; RGEL 2

Cicero, Marcus Tullius
106B.C.-43B.C. .... **CMLC 3, 81**
See also AW 1; CDWLB 1; DLB 211; RGWL 2, 3; WLIT 8

Cimino, Michael 1943- .... **CLC 16**
See also CA 105

Cioran, E(mil) M. 1911-1995 .... **CLC 64**
See also CA 25-28R; 149; CANR 91; DLB 220; EWL 3

Circus, Anthony
See Hoch, Edward D.

Cisneros, Sandra 1954- .... **CLC 69, 118, 193; HLC 1; PC 52; SSC 32, 72**
See also AAYA 9, 53; AMWS 7; CA 131; CANR 64, 118; CLR 123; CN 7; CWP; DA3; DAM MULT; DLB 122, 152; EWL 3; EXPN; FL 1:5; FW; HW 1, 2; LAIT 5; LATS 1:2; LLW; MAICYA 2; MAL 5; MTCW 2; MTFW 2005; NFS 2; PFS 19; RGAL 4; RGSF 2; SSFS 3, 13, 27; WLIT 1; YAW

Cixous, Helene 1937- .... **CLC 92, 253**
See also CA 126; CANR 55, 123; CWW 2; DLB 83, 242; EWL 3; FL 1:5; FW; GLL 2; MTCW 1, 2; MTFW 2005; TWA

Clair, Rene
See Chomette, Rene Lucien

Clampitt, Amy 1920-1994 .... **CLC 32; PC 19**
See also AMWS 9; CA 110; 146; CANR 29, 79; CP 4, 5; DLB 105; MAL 5; PFS 27

Clancy, Thomas L., Jr. 1947- ... **CLC 45, 112**
See also AAYA 9, 51; BEST 89:1, 90:1; BPFB 1; BYA 10, 11; CA 125; 131; CANR 62, 105, 132; CMW 4; CPW; DA3; DAM NOV, POP; DLB 227; INT CA-131; MTCW 1, 2; MTFW 2005

Clancy, Tom
See Clancy, Thomas L., Jr.

Clare, John 1793-1864 .. **NCLC 9, 86; PC 23**
See also BRWS 11; DAB; DAM POET; DLB 55, 96; RGEL 2

Clarin
See Alas (y Urena), Leopoldo (Enrique Garcia)

Clark, Al C.
See Goines, Donald

Clark, Brian (Robert)
See Clark, (Robert) Brian

Clark, (Robert) Brian 1932- .... **CLC 29**
See also CA 41-44R; CANR 67; CBD; CD 5, 6

Clark, Curt
See Westlake, Donald E.

Clark, Eleanor 1913-1996 .... **CLC 5, 19**
See also CA 9-12R; 151; CANR 41; CN 1, 2, 3, 4, 5, 6; DLB 6

Clark, J. P.
See Clark Bekederemo, J.P.

Clark, John Pepper
See Clark Bekederemo, J.P.
See also AFW; CD 5; CP 1, 2, 3, 4, 5, 6, 7; RGEL 2

Clark, Kenneth (Mackenzie)
1903-1983 .... **TCLC 147**
See also CA 93-96; 109; CANR 36; MTCW 1, 2; MTFW 2005

Clark, M. R.
See Clark, Mavis Thorpe

Clark, Mavis Thorpe 1909-1999 ...... **CLC 12**
See also CA 57-60; CANR 8, 37, 107; CLR 30; CWRI 5; MAICYA 1, 2; SAAS 5; SATA 8, 74

Collier, Jeremy 1650-1726 .... **LC 6, 157**
See also DLB 336

Collier, John 1901-1980 . **SSC 19; TCLC 127**
See also CA 65-68; 97-100; CANR 10; CN
1, 2; DLB 77, 255; FANT; SUFW 1

Collier, Mary 1690-1762 .... **LC 86**
See also DLB 95

Collingwood, R(obin) G(eorge)
1889(?)-1943 .... **TCLC 67**
See also CA 117; 155; DLB 262

Collins, Billy 1941- .... **PC 68**
See also AAYA 64; CA 151; CANR 92; CP
7; MTFW 2005; PFS 18

Collins, Hunt
See Hunter, Evan

Collins, Linda 1931- .... **CLC 44**
See also CA 125

Collins, Merle 1950- .... **BLC 2:1**
See also BW 3; CA 175; DLB 157

Collins, Tom
See Furphy, Joseph

Collins, (William) Wilkie
1824-1889 .... **NCLC 1, 18, 93; SSC 93**
See also BRWS 6; CDBLB 1832-1890;
CMW 4; DLB 18, 70, 159; GL 2; MSW;
RGEL 2; RGSF 2; SUFW 1; WLIT 4

Collins, William 1721-1759 ...... **LC 4, 40; PC
72**
See also BRW 3; DAM POET; DLB 109;
RGEL 2

Collodi, Carlo
See Lorenzini, Carlo

Colman, George
See Glassco, John

Colman, George, the Elder
1732-1794 .... **LC 98**
See also RGEL 2

Colonna, Vittoria 1492-1547 .... **LC 71**
See also RGWL 2, 3

Colt, Winchester Remington
See Hubbard, L. Ron

Colter, Cyrus J. 1910-2002 .... **CLC 58**
See also BW 1; CA 65-68; 205; CANR 10,
66; CN 2, 3, 4, 5, 6; DLB 33

Colton, James
See Hansen, Joseph

Colum, Padraic 1881-1972 .... **CLC 28**
See also BYA 4; CA 73-76; 33-36R; CANR
35; CLR 36; CP 1; CWRI 5; DLB 19;
MAICYA 1, 2; MTCW 1; RGEL 2; SATA
15; WCH

Colvin, James
See Moorcock, Michael

Colwin, Laurie (E.) 1944-1992 .... **CLC 5, 13,
23, 84**
See also CA 89-92; 139; CANR 20, 46;
DLB 218; DLBY 1980; MTCW 1

Comfort, Alex(ander) 1920-2000 .... **CLC 7**
See also CA 1-4R; 190; CANR 1, 45; CN
1, 2, 3, 4; CP 1, 2, 3, 4, 5, 6, 7; DAM
POP; MTCW 2

Comfort, Montgomery
See Campbell, Ramsey

Compton-Burnett, I(vy)
1892(?)-1969 .... **CLC 1, 3, 10, 15, 34;
TCLC 180**
See also BRW 7; CA 1-4R; 25-28R; CANR
4; DAM NOV; DLB 36; EWL 3; MTCW
1, 2; RGEL 2

Comstock, Anthony 1844-1915 ...... **TCLC 13**
See also CA 110; 169

Comte, Auguste 1798-1857 .... **NCLC 54**

Conan Doyle, Arthur
See Doyle, Sir Arthur Conan

Conde (Abellan), Carmen
1901-1996 .... **HLCS 1**
See also CA 177; CWW 2; DLB 108; EWL
3; HW 2

Conde, Maryse 1937- .... **BLC 2:1; BLCS;
CLC 52, 92, 247**
See also BW 2, 3; CA 110, 190; CAAE 190;
CANR 30, 53, 76, 171; CWW 2; DAM
MULT; EWL 3; MTCW 2; MTFW 2005

Condillac, Etienne Bonnot de
1714-1780 .... **LC 26**
See also DLB 313

Condon, Richard 1915-1996 ...... **CLC 4, 6, 8,
10, 45, 100**
See also BEST 90:3; BPFB 1; CA 1-4R;
151; CAAS 1; CANR 2, 23, 164; CMW
4; CN 1, 2, 3, 4, 5, 6; DAM NOV; INT
CANR-23; MAL 5; MTCW 1, 2

Condon, Richard Thomas
See Condon, Richard

Condorcet
See Condorcet, marquis de Marie-Jean-
Antoine-Nicolas Caritat

Condorcet, marquis de
Marie-Jean-Antoine-Nicolas Caritat
1743-1794 .... **LC 104**
See also DLB 313; GFL Beginnings to 1789

Confucius 551B.C.-479B.C. .... **CMLC 19, 65;
WLCS**
See also DA; DA3; DAB; DAC; DAM
MST

Congreve, William 1670-1729 ... **DC 2; LC 5,
21, 170; WLC 2**
See also BRW 2; CDBLB 1660-1789; DA;
DAB; DAC; DAM DRAM, MST, POET;
DFS 15; DLB 39, 84; RGEL 2; WLIT 3

Conley, Robert J. 1940- .... **NNAL**
See also CA 41-44R; CANR 15, 34, 45, 96,
186; DAM MULT; TCWW 2

Connell, Evan S., Jr. 1924- .... **CLC 4, 6, 45**
See also AAYA 7; AMWS 14; CA 1-4R;
CAAS 2; CANR 2, 39, 76, 97, 140; CN
1, 2, 3, 4, 5, 6; DAM NOV; DLB 2, 335;
DLBY 1981; MAL 5; MTCW 1, 2;
MTFW 2005

Connelly, Marc(us Cook) 1890-1980 . **CLC 7**
See also CA 85-88; 102; CAD; CANR 30;
DFS 12; DLB 7; DLBY 1980; MAL 5;
RGAL 4; SATA-Obit 25

Connolly, Paul
See Wicker, Tom

Connor, Ralph
See Gordon, Charles William

Conrad, Joseph 1857-1924 ..... **SSC 9, 67, 69,
71; TCLC 1, 6, 13, 25, 43, 57; WLC 2**
See also AAYA 26; BPFB 1; BRW 6;
BRWC 1; BRWR 2; BYA 2; CA 104; 131;
CANR 60; CDBLB 1890-1914; DA; DA3;
DAB; DAC; DAM MST, NOV; DLB 10,
34, 98, 156; EWL 3; EXPN; EXPS; LAIT
2; LATS 1:1; LMFS 1; MTCW 1, 2;
MTFW 2005; NFS 2, 16; RGEL 2; RGSF
2; SATA 27; SSFS 1, 12; TEA; WLIT 4

Conrad, Robert Arnold
See Hart, Moss

Conroy, Pat 1945- .... **CLC 30, 74**
See also AAYA 8, 52; AITN 1; BPFB 1;
CA 85-88; CANR 24, 53, 129; CN 7;
CPW; CSW; DA3; DAM NOV, POP;
DLB 6; LAIT 5; MAL 5; MTCW 1, 2;
MTFW 2005

Constant (de Rebecque), (Henri) Benjamin
1767-1830 .... **NCLC 6, 182**
See also DLB 119; EW 4; GFL 1789 to the
Present

Conway, Jill K. 1934- .... **CLC 152**
See also CA 130; CANR 94

Conway, Jill Kathryn Ker
See Conway, Jill K.

Conybeare, Charles Augustus
See Eliot, T(homas) S(tearns)

Cook, Michael 1933-1994 .... **CLC 58**
See also CA 93-96; CANR 68; DLB 53

Cook, Robin 1940- .... **CLC 14**
See also AAYA 32; BEST 90:2; BPFB 1;
CA 108; 111; CANR 41, 90, 109, 181;
CPW; DA3; DAM POP; HGG; INT CA-
111

Cook, Roy
See Silverberg, Robert

Cooke, Elizabeth 1948- .... **CLC 55**
See also CA 129

Cooke, John Esten 1830-1886 .... **NCLC 5**
See also DLB 3, 248; RGAL 4

Cooke, John Estes
See Baum, L(yman) Frank

Cooke, M. E.
See Creasey, John

Cooke, Margaret
See Creasey, John

Cooke, Rose Terry 1827-1892 ...... **NCLC 110**
See also DLB 12, 74

Cook-Lynn, Elizabeth 1930- .... **CLC 93;
NNAL**
See also CA 133; DAM MULT; DLB 175

Cooney, Ray .... **CLC 62**
See also CBD

Cooper, Anthony Ashley 1671-1713 .. **LC 107**
See also DLB 101, 336

Cooper, Dennis 1953- .... **CLC 203**
See also CA 133; CANR 72, 86; GLL 1;
HGG

Cooper, Douglas 1960- .... **CLC 86**

Cooper, Henry St. John
See Creasey, John

Cooper, J. California (?)- .... **CLC 56**
See also AAYA 12; BW 1; CA 125; CANR
55; DAM MULT; DLB 212

Cooper, James Fenimore
1789-1851 .... **NCLC 1, 27, 54, 203**
See also AAYA 22; AMW; BPFB 1;
CDALB 1640-1865; CLR 105; DA3;
DLB 3, 183, 250, 254; LAIT 2; NFS 25;
RGAL 4; SATA 19; TUS; WCH

Cooper, Susan Fenimore
1813-1894 .... **NCLC 129**
See also ANW; DLB 239, 254

Coover, Robert 1932- .. **CLC 3, 7, 15, 32, 46,
87, 161; SSC 15, 101**
See also AMWS 5; BPFB 1; CA 45-48;
CANR 3, 37, 58, 115; CN 1, 2, 3, 4, 5, 6,
7; DAM NOV; DLB 2, 227; DLBY 1981;
EWL 3; MAL 5; MTCW 1, 2; MTFW
2005; RGAL 4; RGSF 2

Copeland, Stewart (Armstrong)
1952- .... **CLC 26**

Copernicus, Nicolaus 1473-1543 .... **LC 45**

Coppard, A(lfred) E(dgar)
1878-1957 .... **SSC 21; TCLC 5**
See also BRWS 8; CA 114; 167; DLB 162;
EWL 3; HGG; RGEL 2; RGSF 2; SUFW
1; YABC 1

Coppee, Francois 1842-1908 .... **TCLC 25**
See also CA 170; DLB 217

Coppola, Francis Ford 1939- ... **CLC 16, 126**
See also AAYA 39; CA 77-80; CANR 40,
78; DLB 44

Copway, George 1818-1869 .... **NNAL**
See also DAM MULT; DLB 175, 183

Corbiere, Tristan 1845-1875 .... **NCLC 43**
See also DLB 217; GFL 1789 to the Present

Corcoran, Barbara (Asenath)
1911- .... **CLC 17**
See also AAYA 14; CA 21-24R, 191; CAAE
191; CAAS 2; CANR 11, 28, 48; CLR
50; DLB 52; JRDA; MAICYA 2; MAIC-
YAS 1; RHW; SAAS 20; SATA 3, 77;
SATA-Essay 125

Cordelier, Maurice
See Giraudoux, Jean(-Hippolyte)

Cordier, Gilbert
See Scherer, Jean-Marie Maurice

Crevecoeur, Michel Guillaume Jean de
1735-1813 .... NCLC 105
See also AMWS 1; ANW; DLB 37
Crevel, Rene 1900-1935 .... TCLC 112
See also GLL 2
Crews, Harry 1935- .... CLC 6, 23, 49, 277
See also AITN 1; AMWS 11; BPFB 1; CA
25-28R; CANR 20, 57; CN 3, 4, 5, 6, 7;
CSW; DA3; DLB 6, 143, 185; MTCW 1,
2; MTFW 2005; RGAL 4
Crichton, John Michael
See Crichton, Michael
Crichton, Michael 1942-2008 .. CLC 2, 6, 54,
90, 242
See also AAYA 10, 49; AITN 2; BPFB 1;
CA 25-28R; 279; CANR 13, 40, 54, 76,
127, 179; CMW 4; CN 2, 3, 6, 7; CPW;
DA3; DAM NOV, POP; DLB 292; DLBY
1981; INT CANR-13; JRDA; MTCW 1,
2; MTFW 2005; SATA 9, 88; SATA-Obit
199; SFW 4; YAW
Crispin, Edmund
See Montgomery, Bruce
Cristina of Sweden 1626-1689 .... LC 124
Cristofer, Michael 1945(?)- .... CLC 28
See also CA 110; 152; CAD; CANR 150;
CD 5, 6; DAM DRAM; DFS 15; DLB 7
Cristofer, Michael Ivan
See Cristofer, Michael
Criton
See Alain
Croce, Benedetto 1866-1952 .... TCLC 37
See also CA 120; 155; EW 8; EWL 3;
WLIT 7
Crockett, David 1786-1836 .... NCLC 8
See also DLB 3, 11, 183, 248
Crockett, Davy
See Crockett, David
Crofts, Freeman Wills 1879-1957 .. TCLC 55
See also CA 115; 195; CMW 4; DLB 77;
MSW
Croker, John Wilson 1780-1857 .... NCLC 10
See also DLB 110
Crommelynck, Fernand 1885-1970 .. CLC 75
See also CA 189; 89-92; EWL 3
Cromwell, Oliver 1599-1658 .... LC 43
Cronenberg, David 1943- .... CLC 143
See also CA 138; CCA 1
Cronin, A(rchibald) J(oseph)
1896-1981 .... CLC 32
See also BPFB 1; CA 1-4R; 102; CANR 5;
CN 2; DLB 191; SATA 47; SATA-Obit 25
Cross, Amanda
See Heilbrun, Carolyn G.
Crothers, Rachel 1878-1958 .... TCLC 19
See also CA 113; 194; CAD; CWD; DLB
7, 266; RGAL 4
Croves, Hal
See Traven, B.
Crow Dog, Mary (?)- .... CLC 93; NNAL
See also CA 154
Crowfield, Christopher
See Stowe, Harriet (Elizabeth) Beecher
Crowley, Aleister
See Crowley, Edward Alexander
Crowley, Edward Alexander
1875-1947 .... TCLC 7
See also CA 104; GLL 1; HGG
Crowley, John 1942- .... CLC 57
See also AAYA 57; BPFB 1; CA 61-64;
CANR 43, 98, 138, 177; DLBY 1982;
FANT; MTFW 2005; SATA 65, 140; SFW
4; SUFW 2
Crowne, John 1641-1712 .... LC 104
See also DLB 80; RGEL 2
Crud
See Crumb, R.

Crumarums
See Crumb, R.
Crumb, R. 1943- .... CLC 17
See also CA 106; CANR 107, 150
Crumb, Robert
See Crumb, R.
Crumbum
See Crumb, R.
Crumski
See Crumb, R.
Crum the Bum
See Crumb, R.
Crunk
See Crumb, R.
Crustt
See Crumb, R.
Crutchfield, Les
See Trumbo, Dalton
Cruz, Victor Hernandez 1949- ... HLC 1; PC
37
See also BW 2; CA 65-68, 271; CAAE 271;
CAAS 17; CANR 14, 32, 74, 132; CP 1,
2, 3, 4, 5, 6, 7; DAM MULT, POET; DLB
41; DNFS 1; EXPP; HW 1, 2; LLW;
MTCW 2; MTFW 2005; PFS 16; WP
Cryer, Gretchen (Kiger) 1935- .... CLC 21
See also CA 114; 123
Csath, Geza
See Brenner, Jozef
Cudlip, David R(ockwell) 1933- .... CLC 34
See also CA 177
Cullen, Countee 1903-1946 ..... BLC 1:1; HR
1:2; PC 20; TCLC 4, 37, 220; WLCS
See also AAYA 78; AFAW 2; AMWS 4; BW
1; CA 108; 124; CDALB 1917-1929; DA;
DA3; DAC; DAM MST, MULT, POET;
DLB 4, 48, 51; EWL 3; EXPP; LMFS 2;
MAL 5; MTCW 1, 2; MTFW 2005; PFS
3; RGAL 4; SATA 18; WP
Culleton, Beatrice 1949- .... NNAL
See also CA 120; CANR 83; DAC
Culver, Timothy J.
See Westlake, Donald E.
Culver, Timothy J.
See Westlake, Donald E.
Cum, R.
See Crumb, R.
Cumberland, Richard
1732-1811 .... NCLC 167
See also DLB 89; RGEL 2
Cummings, Bruce F. 1889-1919 ..... TCLC 24
See also CA 123
Cummings, Bruce Frederick
See Cummings, Bruce F.
Cummings, E(dward) E(stlin)
1894-1962 .. CLC 1, 3, 8, 12, 15, 68; PC
5; TCLC 137; WLC 2
See also AAYA 41; AMW; CA 73-76;
CANR 31; CDALB 1929-1941; DA;
DA3; DAB; DAC; DAM MST, POET;
DLB 4, 48; EWL 3; EXPP; MAL 5;
MTCW 1, 2; MTFW 2005; PAB; PFS 1,
3, 12, 13, 19, 30; RGAL 4; TUS; WP
Cummins, Maria Susanna
1827-1866 .... NCLC 139
See also DLB 42; YABC 1
Cunha, Euclides (Rodrigues Pimenta) da
1866-1909 .... TCLC 24
See also CA 123; 219; DLB 307; LAW;
WLIT 1
Cunningham, E. V.
See Fast, Howard
Cunningham, J. Morgan
See Westlake, Donald E.
Cunningham, J(ames) V(incent)
1911-1985 .... CLC 3, 31; PC 92
See also CA 1-4R; 115; CANR 1, 72; CP 1,
2, 3, 4; DLB 5

Cunningham, Julia (Woolfolk)
1916- .... CLC 12
See also CA 9-12R; CANR 4, 19, 36; CWRI
5; JRDA; MAICYA 1, 2; SAAS 2; SATA
1, 26, 132
Cunningham, Michael 1952- .... CLC 34, 243
See also AMWS 15; CA 136; CANR 96,
160; CN 7; DLB 292; GLL 2; MTFW
2005; NFS 23
Cunninghame Graham, R. B.
See Cunninghame Graham, Robert Bontine
Cunninghame Graham, Robert Bontine
1852-1936 .... TCLC 19
See also CA 119; 184; DLB 98, 135, 174;
RGEL 2; RGSF 2
Cunninghame Graham, Robert Gallnigad
Bontine
See Cunninghame Graham, Robert Bontine
Curnow, (Thomas) Allen (Monro)
1911-2001 .... PC 48
See also CA 69-72; 202; CANR 48, 99; CP
1, 2, 3, 4, 5, 6, 7; EWL 3; RGEL 2
Currie, Ellen 19(?)- .... CLC 44
Curtin, Philip
See Lowndes, Marie Adelaide (Belloc)
Curtin, Phillip
See Lowndes, Marie Adelaide (Belloc)
Curtis, Price
See Ellison, Harlan
Cusanus, Nicolaus 1401-1464
See Nicholas of Cusa
Cutrate, Joe
See Spiegelman, Art
Cynewulf c. 770- .... CMLC 23
See also DLB 146; RGEL 2
Cyrano de Bergerac, Savinien de
1619-1655 .... LC 65
See also DLB 268; GFL Beginnings to
1789; RGWL 2, 3
Cyril of Alexandria c. 375-c. 430 . CMLC 59
Czaczkes, Shmuel Yosef Halevi
See Agnon, S.Y.
Dabrowska, Maria (Szumska)
1889-1965 .... CLC 15
See also CA 106; CDWLB 4; DLB 215;
EWL 3
Dabydeen, David 1955- .... CLC 34
See also BW 1; CA 125; CANR 56, 92; CN
6, 7; CP 5, 6, 7; DLB 347
Dacey, Philip 1939- .... CLC 51
See also CA 37-40R, 231; CAAE 231;
CAAS 17; CANR 14, 32, 64; CP 4, 5, 6,
7; DLB 105
Dacre, Charlotte c. 1772-1825(?) . NCLC 151
Dafydd ap Gwilym c. 1320-c. 1380 ..... PC 56
Dagerman, Stig (Halvard)
1923-1954 .... TCLC 17
See also CA 117; 155; DLB 259; EWL 3
D'Aguiar, Fred 1960- ..... BLC 2:1; CLC 145
See also CA 148; CANR 83, 101; CN 7;
CP 5, 6, 7; DLB 157; EWL 3
Dahl, Roald 1916-1990 ...... CLC 1, 6, 18, 79;
TCLC 173
See also AAYA 15; BPFB 1; BRWS 4; BYA
5; CA 1-4R; 133; CANR 6, 32, 37, 62;
CLR 1, 7, 41, 111; CN 1, 2, 3, 4; CPW;
DA3; DAB; DAC; DAM MST, NOV,
POP; DLB 139, 255; HGG; JRDA; MAI-
CYA 1, 2; MTCW 1, 2; MTFW 2005;
RGSF 2; SATA 1, 26, 73; SATA-Obit 65;
SSFS 4; TEA; YAW
Dahlberg, Edward 1900-1977 . CLC 1, 7, 14;
TCLC 208
See also CA 9-12R; 69-72; CANR 31, 62;
CN 1, 2; DLB 48; MAL 5; MTCW 1;
RGAL 4
Daitch, Susan 1954- .... CLC 103
See also CA 161

d'Isly, Georges
See Simenon, Georges (Jacques Christian)
Disraeli, Benjamin 1804-1881 ... **NCLC 2, 39, 79**
See also BRW 4; DLB 21, 55; RGEL 2
D'Israeli, Isaac 1766-1848 .... **NCLC 217**
See also DLB 107
Ditcum, Steve
See Crumb, R.
Dixon, Paige
See Corcoran, Barbara (Asenath)
Dixon, Stephen 1936- .... **CLC 52; SSC 16**
See also AMWS 12; CA 89-92; CANR 17, 40, 54, 91, 175; CN 4, 5, 6, 7; DLB 130; MAL 5
Dixon, Thomas, Jr. 1864-1946 ..... **TCLC 163**
See also RHW
Djebar, Assia 1936- .... **BLC 2:1; CLC 182; SSC 114**
See also CA 188; CANR 169; DLB 346; EWL 3; RGWL 3; WLIT 2
Doak, Annie
See Dillard, Annie
Dobell, Sydney Thompson 1824-1874 .... **NCLC 43; PC 100**
See also DLB 32; RGEL 2
Doblin, Alfred
See Doeblin, Alfred
Dobroliubov, Nikolai Aleksandrovich
See Dobrolyubov, Nikolai Alexandrovich
Dobrolyubov, Nikolai Alexandrovich 1836-1861 .... **NCLC 5**
See also DLB 277
Dobson, Austin 1840-1921 .... **TCLC 79**
See also DLB 35, 144
Dobyns, Stephen 1941- .... **CLC 37, 233**
See also AMWS 13; CA 45-48; CANR 2, 18, 99; CMW 4; CP 4, 5, 6, 7; PFS 23
Doctorow, Cory 1971- .... **CLC 273**
See also CA 221
Doctorow, Edgar Laurence
See Doctorow, E.L.
Doctorow, E.L. 1931- . **CLC 6, 11, 15, 18, 37, 44, 65, 113, 214**
See also AAYA 22; AITN 2; AMWS 4; BEST 89:3; BPFB 1; CA 45-48; CANR 2, 33, 51, 76, 97, 133, 170; CDALB 1968-1988; CN 3, 4, 5, 6, 7; CPW; DA3; DAM NOV, POP; DLB 2, 28, 173; DLBY 1980; EWL 3; LAIT 3; MAL 5; MTCW 1, 2; MTFW 2005; NFS 6; RGAL 4; RGHL; RHW; SSFS 27; TCLE 1:1; TCWW 1, 2; TUS
Dodgson, Charles Lutwidge
See Carroll, Lewis
Dodsley, Robert 1703-1764 .... **LC 97**
See also DLB 95; RGEL 2
Dodson, Owen (Vincent) 1914-1983 .... **BLC 1:1; CLC 79**
See also BW 1; CA 65-68; 110; CANR 24; DAM MULT; DLB 76
Doeblin, Alfred 1878-1957 .... **TCLC 13**
See also CA 110; 141; CDWLB 2; DLB 66; EWL 3; RGWL 2, 3
Doerr, Harriet 1910-2002 .... **CLC 34**
See also CA 117; 122; 213; CANR 47; INT CA-122; LATS 1:2
Domecq, H(onorio) Bustos
See Bioy Casares, Adolfo; Borges, Jorge Luis
Domini, Rey
See Lorde, Audre
Dominic, R. B.
See Hennissart, Martha
Dominique
See Proust, (Valentin-Louis-George-Eugene) Marcel
Don, A
See Stephen, Sir Leslie

Donaldson, Stephen R. 1947- ... **CLC 46, 138**
See also AAYA 36; BPFB 1; CA 89-92; CANR 13, 55, 99; CPW; DAM POP; FANT; INT CANR-13; SATA 121; SFW 4; SUFW 1, 2
Donleavy, J(ames) P(atrick) 1926- .... **CLC 1, 4, 6, 10, 45**
See also AITN 2; BPFB 1; CA 9-12R; CANR 24, 49, 62, 80, 124; CBD; CD 5, 6; CN 1, 2, 3, 4, 5, 6, 7; DLB 6, 173; INT CANR-24; MAL 5; MTCW 1, 2; MTFW 2005; RGAL 4
Donnadieu, Marguerite
See Duras, Marguerite
Donne, John 1572-1631 ... **LC 10, 24, 91; PC 1, 43; WLC 2**
See also AAYA 67; BRW 1; BRWC 1; BRWR 2; CDBLB Before 1660; DA; DAB; DAC; DAM MST, POET; DLB 121, 151; EXPP; PAB; PFS 2, 11; RGEL 3; TEA; WLIT 3; WP
Donnell, David 1939(?)- .... **CLC 34**
See also CA 197
Donoghue, Denis 1928- .... **CLC 209**
See also CA 17-20R; CANR 16, 102
Donoghue, Emma 1969- .... **CLC 239**
See also CA 155; CANR 103, 152; DLB 267; GLL 2; SATA 101
Donoghue, P.S.
See Hunt, E. Howard
Donoso (Yanez), Jose 1924-1996 ... **CLC 4, 8, 11, 32, 99; HLC 1; SSC 34; TCLC 133**
See also CA 81-84; 155; CANR 32, 73; CDWLB 3; CWW 2; DAM MULT; DLB 113; EWL 3; HW 1, 2; LAW; LAWS 1; MTCW 1, 2; MTFW 2005; RGSF 2; WLIT 1
Donovan, John 1928-1992 .... **CLC 35**
See also AAYA 20; CA 97-100; 137; CLR 3; MAICYA 1, 2; SATA 72; SATA-Brief 29; YAW
Don Roberto
See Cunninghame Graham, Robert Bontine
Doolittle, Hilda 1886-1961 . **CLC 3, 8, 14, 31, 34, 73; PC 5; WLC 3**
See also AAYA 66; AMWS 1; CA 97-100; CANR 35, 131; DA; DAC; DAM MST, POET; DLB 4, 45; EWL 3; FL 1:5; FW; GLL 1; LMFS 2; MAL 5; MBL; MTCW 1, 2; MTFW 2005; PFS 6, 28; RGAL 4
Doppo
See Kunikida Doppo
Doppo, Kunikida
See Kunikida Doppo
Dorfman, Ariel 1942- .... **CLC 48, 77, 189; HLC 1**
See also CA 124; 130; CANR 67, 70, 135; CWW 2; DAM MULT; DFS 4; EWL 3; HW 1, 2; INT CA-130; WLIT 1
Dorn, Edward (Merton) 1929-1999 .... **CLC 10, 18**
See also CA 93-96; 187; CANR 42, 79; CP 1, 2, 3, 4, 5, 6, 7; DLB 5; INT CA-93-96; WP
Dor-Ner, Zvi .... **CLC 70**
Dorris, Michael 1945-1997 .... **CLC 109; NNAL**
See also AAYA 20; BEST 90:1; BYA 12; CA 102; 157; CANR 19, 46, 75; CLR 58; DA3; DAM MULT, NOV; DLB 175; LAIT 5; MTCW 2; MTFW 2005; NFS 3; RGAL 4; SATA 75; SATA-Obit 94; TCWW 2; YAW
Dorris, Michael A.
See Dorris, Michael
Dorsan, Luc
See Simenon, Georges (Jacques Christian)
Dorsange, Jean
See Simenon, Georges (Jacques Christian)

Dorset
See Sackville, Thomas
Dos Passos, John (Roderigo) 1896-1970 ... **CLC 1, 4, 8, 11, 15, 25, 34, 82; WLC 2**
See also AMW; BPFB 1; CA 1-4R; 29-32R; CANR 3; CDALB 1929-1941; DA; DA3; DAB; DAC; DAM MST, NOV; DLB 4, 9, 274, 316; DLBD 1, 15; DLBY 1996; EWL 3; MAL 5; MTCW 1, 2; MTFW 2005; NFS 14; RGAL 4; TUS
Dossage, Jean
See Simenon, Georges (Jacques Christian)
Dostoevsky, Fedor Mikhailovich 1821-1881 .. **NCLC 2, 7, 21, 33, 43, 119, 167, 202; SSC 2, 33, 44; WLC 2**
See also AAYA 40; DA; DA3; DAB; DAC; DAM MST, NOV; DLB 238; EW 7; EXPN; LATS 1:1; LMFS 1, 2; NFS 28; RGSF 2; RGWL 2, 3; SSFS 8; TWA
Dostoevsky, Fyodor
See Dostoevsky, Fedor Mikhailovich
Doty, Mark 1953(?)- .... **CLC 176; PC 53**
See also AMWS 11; CA 161, 183; CAAE 183; CANR 110, 173; CP 7; PFS 28
Doty, Mark A.
See Doty, Mark
Doty, Mark Alan
See Doty, Mark
Doty, M.R.
See Doty, Mark
Doughty, Charles M(ontagu) 1843-1926 .... **TCLC 27**
See also CA 115; 178; DLB 19, 57, 174
Douglas, Ellen 1921- .... **CLC 73**
See also CA 115; CANR 41, 83; CN 5, 6, 7; CSW; DLB 292
Douglas, Gavin 1475(?)-1522 .... **LC 20**
See also DLB 132; RGEL 2
Douglas, George
See Brown, George Douglas
Douglas, Keith (Castellain) 1920-1944 .... **TCLC 40**
See also BRW 7; CA 160; DLB 27; EWL 3; PAB; RGEL 2
Douglas, Leonard
See Bradbury, Ray
Douglas, Michael
See Crichton, Michael
Douglas, Michael
See Crichton, Michael
Douglas, (George) Norman 1868-1952 .... **TCLC 68**
See also BRW 6; CA 119; 157; DLB 34, 195; RGEL 2
Douglas, William
See Brown, George Douglas
Douglass, Frederick 1817(?)-1895 .. **BLC 1:1; NCLC 7, 55, 141; WLC 2**
See also AAYA 48; AFAW 1, 2; AMWC 1; AMWS 3; CDALB 1640-1865; DA; DA3; DAC; DAM MST, MULT; DLB 1, 43, 50, 79, 243; FW; LAIT 2; NCFS 2; RGAL 4; SATA 29
Dourado, (Waldomiro Freitas) Autran 1926- .... **CLC 23, 60**
See also CA 25-28R; 179; CANR 34, 81; DLB 145, 307; HW 2
Dourado, Waldomiro Freitas Autran
See Dourado, (Waldomiro Freitas) Autran
Dove, Rita 1952- . **BLC 2:1; BLCS; CLC 50, 81; PC 6**
See also AAYA 46; AMWS 4; BW 2; CA 109; CAAS 19; CANR 27, 42, 68, 76, 97, 132; CDALBS; CP 5, 6, 7; CSW; CWP; DA3; DAM MULT, POET; DLB 120; EWL 3; EXPP; MAL 5; MTCW 2; MTFW 2005; PFS 1, 15; RGAL 4

Fouque, Friedrich (Heinrich Karl) de la Motte 1777-1843 .... **NCLC 2**
See also DLB 90; RGWL 2, 3; SUFW 1

Fourier, Charles 1772-1837 .... **NCLC 51**

Fournier, Henri-Alban 1886-1914 ... **TCLC 6**
See also CA 104; 179; DLB 65; EWL 3; GFL 1789 to the Present; RGWL 2, 3

Fournier, Pierre 1916-1997 .... **CLC 11**
See also CA 89-92; CANR 16, 40; EWL 3; RGHL

Fowles, John 1926-2005 .... **CLC 1, 2, 3, 4, 6, 9, 10, 15, 33, 87; SSC 33**
See also BPFB 1; BRWS 1; CA 5-8R; 245; CANR 25, 71, 103; CDBLB 1960 to Present; CN 1, 2, 3, 4, 5, 6, 7; DA3; DAB; DAC; DAM MST; DLB 14, 139, 207; EWL 3; HGG; MTCW 1, 2; MTFW 2005; NFS 21; RGEL 2; RHW; SATA 22; SATA-Obit 171; TEA; WLIT 4

Fowles, John Robert
See Fowles, John

Fox, Paula 1923- .... **CLC 2, 8, 121**
See also AAYA 3, 37; BYA 3, 8; CA 73-76; CANR 20, 36, 62, 105; CLR 1, 44, 96; DLB 52; JRDA; MAICYA 1, 2; MTCW 1; NFS 12; SATA 17, 60, 120, 167; WYA; YAW

Fox, William Price, Jr.
See Fox, William Price

Fox, William Price 1926- .... **CLC 22**
See also CA 17-20R; CAAS 19; CANR 11, 142, 189; CSW; DLB 2; DLBY 1981

Foxe, John 1517(?)-1587 .... **LC 14, 166**
See also DLB 132

Frame, Janet 1924-2004 ...... **CLC 2, 3, 6, 22, 66, 96, 237; SSC 29, 127**
See also CA 1-4R; 224; CANR 2, 36, 76, 135; CN 1, 2, 3, 4, 5, 6, 7; CP 2, 3, 4; CWP; EWL 3; MTCW 1,2; RGEL 2; RGSF 2; SATA 119; TWA

France, Anatole
See Thibault, Jacques Anatole Francois

Francis, Claude .... **CLC 50**
See also CA 192

Francis, Dick 1920- .... **CLC 2, 22, 42, 102**
See also AAYA 5, 21; BEST 89:3; BPFB 1; CA 5-8R; CANR 9, 42, 68, 100, 141, 179; CDBLB 1960 to Present; CMW 4; CN 2, 3, 4, 5, 6; DA3; DAM POP; DLB 87; INT CANR-9; MSW; MTCW 1, 2; MTFW 2005

Francis, Paula Marie
See Allen, Paula Gunn

Francis, Richard Stanley
See Francis, Dick

Francis, Robert (Churchill) 1901-1987 .... **CLC 15; PC 34**
See also AMWS 9; CA 1-4R; 123; CANR 1; CP 1, 2, 3, 4; EXPP; PFS 12; TCLE 1:1

Francis, Lord Jeffrey
See Jeffrey, Francis

Franco, Veronica 1546-1591 .... **LC 171**
See also WLIT 7

Frank, Anne(lies Marie) 1929-1945 .... **TCLC 17; WLC 2**
See also AAYA 12; BYA 1; CA 113; 133; CANR 68; CLR 101; DA; DA3; DAB; DAC; DAM MST; LAIT 4; MAICYA 2; MAICYAS 1; MTCW 1, 2; MTFW 2005; NCFS 2; RGHL; SATA 87; SATA-Brief 42; WYA; YAW

Frank, Bruno 1887-1945 .... **TCLC 81**
See also CA 189; DLB 118; EWL 3

Frank, Elizabeth 1945- .... **CLC 39**
See also CA 121; 126; CANR 78, 150; INT CA-126

Frankl, Viktor E(mil) 1905-1997 ...... **CLC 93**
See also CA 65-68; 161; RGHL

Franklin, Benjamin
See Hasek, Jaroslav (Matej Frantisek)

Franklin, Benjamin 1706-1790 .. **LC 25, 134; WLCS**
See also AMW; CDALB 1640-1865; DA; DA3; DAB; DAC; DAM MST; DLB 24, 43, 73, 183; LAIT 1; RGAL 4; TUS

Franklin, Madeleine
See L'Engle, Madeleine

Franklin, Madeleine L'Engle
See L'Engle, Madeleine

Franklin, Madeleine L'Engle Camp
See L'Engle, Madeleine

Franklin, (Stella Maria Sarah) Miles (Lampe) 1879-1954 .... **TCLC 7**
See also CA 104; 164; DLB 230; FW; MTCW 2; RGEL 2; TWA

Franzen, Jonathan 1959- .... **CLC 202**
See also AAYA 65; CA 129; CANR 105, 166

Fraser, Antonia 1932- .... **CLC 32, 107**
See also AAYA 57; CA 85-88; CANR 44, 65, 119, 164; CMW; DLB 276; MTCW 1, 2; MTFW 2005; SATA-Brief 32

Fraser, George MacDonald 1925-2008 .... **CLC 7**
See also AAYA 48; CA 45-48; 180; 268; CAAE 180; CANR 2, 48, 74, 192; DLB 352; MTCW 2; RHW

Fraser, Sylvia 1935- .... **CLC 64**
See also CA 45-48; CANR 1, 16, 60; CCA 1

Frater Perdurabo
See Crowley, Edward Alexander

Frayn, Michael 1933- .... **CLC 3, 7, 31, 47, 176; DC 27**
See also AAYA 69; BRWC 2; BRWS 7; CA 5-8R; CANR 30, 69, 114, 133, 166; CBD; CD 5, 6; CN 1, 2, 3, 4, 5, 6, 7; DAM DRAM, NOV; DFS 22; DLB 13, 14, 194, 245; FANT; MTCW 1, 2; MTFW 2005; SFW 4

Fraze, Candida (Merrill) 1945- .... **CLC 50**
See also CA 126

Frazer, Andrew
See Marlowe, Stephen

Frazer, J(ames) G(eorge) 1854-1941 .... **TCLC 32**
See also BRWS 3; CA 118; NCFS 5

Frazer, Robert Caine
See Creasey, John

Frazer, Sir James George
See Frazer, J(ames) G(eorge)

Frazier, Charles 1950- .... **CLC 109, 224**
See also AAYA 34; CA 161; CANR 126, 170; CSW; DLB 292; MTFW 2005; NFS 25

Frazier, Charles R.
See Frazier, Charles

Frazier, Charles Robinson
See Frazier, Charles

Frazier, Ian 1951- .... **CLC 46**
See also CA 130; CANR 54, 93, 193

Frederic, Harold 1856-1898 ... **NCLC 10, 175**
See also AMW; DLB 12, 23; DLBD 13; MAL 5; NFS 22; RGAL 4

Frederick, John
See Faust, Frederick

Frederick the Great 1712-1786 .... **LC 14**

Fredro, Aleksander 1793-1876 .... **NCLC 8**

Freeling, Nicolas 1927-2003 .... **CLC 38**
See also CA 49-52; 218; CAAS 12; CANR 1, 17, 50, 84; CMW 4; CN 1, 2, 3, 4, 5, 6; DLB 87

Freeman, Douglas Southall 1886-1953 .... **TCLC 11**
See also CA 109; 195; DLB 17; DLBD 17

Freeman, Judith 1946- .... **CLC 55**
See also CA 148; CANR 120, 179; DLB 256

Freeman, Mary E(leanor) Wilkins 1852-1930 .... **SSC 1, 47, 113; TCLC 9**
See also CA 106; 177; DLB 12, 78, 221; EXPS; FW; HGG; MBL; RGAL 4; RGSF 2; SSFS 4, 8, 26; SUFW 1; TUS

Freeman, R(ichard) Austin 1862-1943 .... **TCLC 21**
See also CA 113; CANR 84; CMW 4; DLB 70

French, Albert 1943- .... **CLC 86**
See also BW 3; CA 167

French, Antonia
See Kureishi, Hanif

French, Marilyn 1929-2009 . **CLC 10, 18, 60, 177**
See also BPFB 1; CA 69-72; 286; CANR 3, 31, 134, 163; CN 5, 6, 7; CPW; DAM DRAM, NOV, POP; FL 1:5; FW; INT CANR-31; MTCW 1, 2; MTFW 2005

French, Paul
See Asimov, Isaac

Freneau, Philip Morin 1752-1832 .. **NCLC 1, 111**
See also AMWS 2; DLB 37, 43; RGAL 4

Freud, Sigmund 1856-1939 .... **TCLC 52**
See also CA 115; 133; CANR 69; DLB 296; EW 8; EWL 3; LATS 1:1; MTCW 1, 2; MTFW 2005; NCFS 3; TWA

Freytag, Gustav 1816-1895 .... **NCLC 109**
See also DLB 129

Friedan, Betty 1921-2006 .... **CLC 74**
See also CA 65-68; 248; CANR 18, 45, 74; DLB 246; FW; MTCW 1, 2; MTFW 2005; NCFS 5

Friedan, Betty Naomi
See Friedan, Betty

Friedlander, Saul 1932- .... **CLC 90**
See also CA 117; 130; CANR 72; RGHL

Friedman, B(ernard) H(arper) 1926- .... **CLC 7**
See also CA 1-4R; CANR 3, 48

Friedman, Bruce Jay 1930- ...... **CLC 3, 5, 56**
See also CA 9-12R; CAD; CANR 25, 52, 101; CD 5, 6; CN 1, 2, 3, 4, 5, 6, 7; DLB 2, 28, 244; INT CANR-25; MAL 5; SSFS 18

Friel, Brian 1929- .. **CLC 5, 42, 59, 115, 253; DC 8; SSC 76**
See also BRWS 5; CA 21-24R; CANR 33, 69, 131; CBD; CD 5, 6; DFS 11; DLB 13, 319; EWL 3; MTCW 1; RGEL 2; TEA

Friis-Baastad, Babbis Ellinor 1921-1970 .... **CLC 12**
See also CA 17-20R; 134; SATA 7

Frisch, Max 1911-1991 ...... **CLC 3, 9, 14, 18, 32, 44; TCLC 121**
See also CA 85-88; 134; CANR 32, 74; CD-WLB 2; DAM DRAM, NOV; DFS 25; DLB 69, 124; EW 13; EWL 3; MTCW 1, 2; MTFW 2005; RGHL; RGWL 2, 3

Fromentin, Eugene (Samuel Auguste) 1820-1876 .... **NCLC 10, 125**
See also DLB 123; GFL 1789 to the Present

Frost, Frederick
See Faust, Frederick

Frost, Robert 1874-1963 . **CLC 1, 3, 4, 9, 10, 13, 15, 26, 34, 44; PC 1, 39, 71; WLC 2**
See also AAYA 21; AMW; AMWR 1; CA 89-92; CANR 33; CDALB 1917-1929; CLR 67; DA; DA3; DAB; DAC; DAM MST, POET; DLB 54, 284, 342; DLBD 7; EWL 3; EXPP; MAL 5; MTCW 1, 2; MTFW 2005; PAB; PFS 1, 2, 3, 4, 5, 6, 7, 10, 13; RGAL 4; SATA 14; TUS; WP; WYA

Frost, Robert Lee
See Frost, Robert
Froude, James Anthony
1818-1894 .... **NCLC 43**
See also DLB 18, 57, 144
Froy, Herald
See Waterhouse, Keith (Spencer)
Fry, Christopher 1907-2005 .. **CLC 2, 10, 14;**
DC 36
See also BRWS 3; CA 17-20R; 240; CAAS
23; CANR 9, 30, 74, 132; CBD; CD 5, 6;
CP 1, 2, 3, 4, 5, 6, 7; DAM DRAM; DLB
13; EWL 3; MTCW 1, 2; MTFW 2005;
RGEL 2; SATA 66; TEA
Frye, (Herman) Northrop
1912-1991 .... **CLC 24, 70; TCLC 165**
See also CA 5-8R; 133; CANR 8, 37; DLB
67, 68, 246; EWL 3; MTCW 1, 2; MTFW
2005; RGAL 4; TWA
Fuchs, Daniel 1909-1993 .... **CLC 8, 22**
See also CA 81-84; 142; CAAS 5; CANR
40; CN 1, 2, 3, 4, 5; DLB 9, 26, 28;
DLBY 1993; MAL 5
Fuchs, Daniel 1934- .... **CLC 34**
See also CA 37-40R; CANR 14, 48
Fuentes, Carlos 1928- .. **CLC 3, 8, 10, 13, 22,**
41, 60, 113; HLC 1; SSC 24, 125; WLC
2
See also AAYA 4, 45; AITN 2; BPFB 1;
CA 69-72; CANR 10, 32, 68, 104, 138;
CDWLB 3; CWW 2; DA; DA3; DAB;
DAC; DAM MST, MULT, NOV; DLB
113; DNFS 2; EWL 3; HW 1, 2; LAIT 3;
LATS 1:2; LAW; LAWS 1; LMFS 2;
MTCW 1, 2; MTFW 2005; NFS 8; RGSF
2; RGWL 2, 3; TWA; WLIT 1
Fuentes, Gregorio Lopez y
See Lopez y Fuentes, Gregorio
Fuertes, Gloria 1918-1998 .... **PC 27**
See also CA 178, 180; DLB 108; HW 2;
SATA 115
Fugard, (Harold) Athol 1932- . **CLC 5, 9, 14,**
25, 40, 80, 211; DC 3
See also AAYA 17; AFW; CA 85-88; CANR
32, 54, 118; CD 5, 6; DAM DRAM; DFS
3, 6, 10, 24; DLB 225; DNFS 1, 2; EWL
3; LATS 1:2; MTCW 1; MTFW 2005;
RGEL 2; WLIT 2
Fugard, Sheila 1932- .... **CLC 48**
See also CA 125
Fujiwara no Teika 1162-1241 .... **CMLC 73**
See also DLB 203
Fukuyama, Francis 1952- .... **CLC 131**
See also CA 140; CANR 72, 125, 170
Fuller, Charles (H.), (Jr.) 1939- ..... **BLC 1:2;**
CLC 25; DC 1
See also BW 2; CA 108; 112; CAD; CANR
87; CD 5, 6; DAM DRAM, MULT; DFS
8; DLB 38, 266; EWL 3; INT CA-112;
MAL 5; MTCW 1
Fuller, Henry Blake 1857-1929 .... **TCLC 103**
See also CA 108; 177; DLB 12; RGAL 4
Fuller, John (Leopold) 1937- .... **CLC 62**
See also CA 21-24R; CANR 9, 44; CP 1, 2,
3, 4, 5, 6, 7; DLB 40
Fuller, Margaret
See Ossoli, Sarah Margaret
Fuller, Roy (Broadbent) 1912-1991 ... **CLC 4,**
28
See also BRWS 7; CA 5-8R; 135; CAAS
10; CANR 53, 83; CN 1, 2, 3, 4, 5; CP 1,
2, 3, 4, 5; CWRI 5; DLB 15, 20; EWL 3;
RGEL 2; SATA 87
Fuller, Sarah Margaret
See Ossoli, Sarah Margaret
Fuller, Thomas 1608-1661 .... **LC 111**
See also DLB 151

Fulton, Alice 1952- .... **CLC 52**
See also CA 116; CANR 57, 88; CP 5, 6, 7;
CWP; DLB 193; PFS 25
Furey, Michael
See Ward, Arthur Henry Sarsfield
Furphy, Joseph 1843-1912 .... **TCLC 25**
See also CA 163; DLB 230; EWL 3; RGEL
2
Furst, Alan 1941- .... **CLC 255**
See also CA 69-72; CANR 12, 34, 59, 102,
159, 193; DLB 350; DLBY 01
Fuson, Robert H(enderson) 1927- .... **CLC 70**
See also CA 89-92; CANR 103
Fussell, Paul 1924- .... **CLC 74**
See also BEST 90:1; CA 17-20R; CANR 8,
21, 35, 69, 135; INT CANR-21; MTCW
1, 2; MTFW 2005
Futabatei, Shimei 1864-1909 .... **TCLC 44**
See also CA 162; DLB 180; EWL 3; MJW
Futabatei Shimei
See Futabatei, Shimei
Futrelle, Jacques 1875-1912 .... **TCLC 19**
See also CA 113; 155; CMW 4
GAB
See Russell, George William
Gaberman, Judie Angell
See Angell, Judie
Gaboriau, Emile 1835-1873 .... **NCLC 14**
See also CMW 4; MSW
Gadda, Carlo Emilio 1893-1973 ...... **CLC 11;**
TCLC 144
See also CA 89-92; DLB 177; EWL 3;
WLIT 7
Gaddis, William 1922-1998 ... **CLC 1, 3, 6, 8,**
10, 19, 43, 86
See also AMWS 4; BPFB 1; CA 17-20R;
172; CANR 21, 48, 148; CN 1, 2, 3, 4, 5,
6; DLB 2, 278; EWL 3; MAL 5; MTCW
1, 2; MTFW 2005; RGAL 4
Gage, Walter
See Inge, William (Motter)
Gaiman, Neil 1960- .... **CLC 195**
See also AAYA 19, 42; CA 133; CANR 81,
129, 188; CLR 109; DLB 261; HGG;
MTFW 2005; SATA 85, 146, 197; SFW
4; SUFW 2
Gaiman, Neil Richard
See Gaiman, Neil
Gaines, Ernest J. 1933- ..... **BLC 1:2; CLC 3,**
11, 18, 86, 181; SSC 68
See also AAYA 18; AFAW 1, 2; AITN 1;
BPFB 2; BW 2, 3; BYA 6; CA 9-12R;
CANR 6, 24, 42, 75, 126; CDALB 1968-
1988; CLR 62; CN 1, 2, 3, 4, 5, 6, 7;
CSW; DA3; DAM MULT; DLB 2, 33,
152; DLBY 1980; EWL 3; EXPN; LAIT
5; LATS 1:2; MAL 5; MTCW 1, 2;
MTFW 2005; NFS 5, 7, 16; RGAL 4;
RGSF 2; RHW; SATA 86; SSFS 5; YAW
Gaitskill, Mary 1954- .... **CLC 69**
See also CA 128; CANR 61, 152; DLB 244;
TCLE 1:1
Gaitskill, Mary Lawrence
See Gaitskill, Mary
Gaius Suetonius Tranquillus
See Suetonius
Galdos, Benito Perez
See Perez Galdos, Benito
Gale, Zona 1874-1938 .... **DC 30; TCLC 7**
See also CA 105; 153; CANR 84; DAM
DRAM; DFS 17; DLB 9, 78, 228; RGAL
4
Galeano, Eduardo 1940- ... **CLC 72; HLCS 1**
See also CA 29-32R; CANR 13, 32, 100,
163; HW 1
Galeano, Eduardo Hughes
See Galeano, Eduardo
Galiano, Juan Valera y Alcala
See Valera y Alcala-Galiano, Juan

Galilei, Galileo 1564-1642 .... **LC 45**
Gallagher, Tess 1943- .... **CLC 18, 63; PC 9**
See also CA 106; CP 3, 4, 5, 6, 7; CWP;
DAM POET; DLB 120, 212, 244; PFS 16
Gallant, Mavis 1922- ..... **CLC 7, 18, 38, 172;**
SSC 5, 78
See also CA 69-72; CANR 29, 69, 117;
CCA 1; CN 1, 2, 3, 4, 5, 6, 7; DAC; DAM
MST; DLB 53; EWL 3; MTCW 1, 2;
MTFW 2005; RGEL 2; RGSF 2
Gallant, Roy A(rthur) 1924- .... **CLC 17**
See also CA 5-8R; CANR 4, 29, 54, 117;
CLR 30; MAICYA 1, 2; SATA 4, 68, 110
Gallico, Paul (William) 1897-1976 ..... **CLC 2**
See also AITN 1; CA 5-8R; 69-72; CANR
23; CN 1, 2; DLB 9, 171; FANT; MAI-
CYA 1, 2; SATA 13
Gallo, Max Louis 1932- .... **CLC 95**
See also CA 85-88
Gallois, Lucien
See Desnos, Robert
Gallup, Ralph
See Whitemore, Hugh (John)
Galsworthy, John 1867-1933 .... **SSC 22;**
TCLC 1, 45; WLC 2
See also BRW 6; CA 104; 141; CANR 75;
CDBLB 1890-1914; DA; DA3; DAB;
DAC; DAM DRAM, MST, NOV; DLB
10, 34, 98, 162, 330; DLBD 16; EWL 3;
MTCW 2; RGEL 2; SSFS 3; TEA
Galt, John 1779-1839 .... **NCLC 1, 110**
See also DLB 99, 116, 159; RGEL 2; RGSF
2
Galvin, James 1951- .... **CLC 38**
See also CA 108; CANR 26
Gamboa, Federico 1864-1939 .... **TCLC 36**
See also CA 167; HW 2; LAW
Gandhi, M. K.
See Gandhi, Mohandas Karamchand
Gandhi, Mahatma
See Gandhi, Mohandas Karamchand
Gandhi, Mohandas Karamchand
1869-1948 .... **TCLC 59**
See also CA 121; 132; DA3; DAM MULT;
DLB 323; MTCW 1, 2
Gann, Ernest Kellogg 1910-1991 ..... **CLC 23**
See also AITN 1; BPFB 2; CA 1-4R; 136;
CANR 1, 83; RHW
Gao Xingjian 1940-
See Xingjian, Gao
Garber, Eric 1943(?)- .... **CLC 38**
See also CA 144; CANR 89, 162; GLL 1
Garber, Esther
See Lee, Tanith
Garcia, Cristina 1958- .... **CLC 76**
See also AMWS 11; CA 141; CANR 73,
130, 172; CN 7; DLB 292; DNFS 1; EWL
3; HW 2; LLW; MTFW 2005
Garcia Lorca, Federico 1898-1936 ...... **DC 2;**
HLC 2; PC 3; TCLC 1, 7, 49, 181,
197; WLC 2
See also AAYA 46; CA 104; 131; CANR
81; DA; DA3; DAB; DAC; DAM DRAM,
MST, MULT, POET; DFS 4; DLB 108;
EW 11; EWL 3; HW 1, 2; LATS 1:2;
MTCW 1, 2; MTFW 2005; PFS 20, 31;
RGWL 2, 3; TWA; WP
Garcia Marquez, Gabriel 1928- .... **CLC 2, 3,**
8, 10, 15, 27, 47, 55, 68, 170, 254; HLC
1; SSC 8, 83; WLC 3
See also AAYA 3, 33; BEST 89:1, 90:4;
BPFB 2; BYA 12, 16; CA 33-36R; CANR
10, 28, 50, 75, 82, 128; CDWLB 3; CPW;
CWW 2; DA; DA3; DAB; DAC; DAM
MST, MULT, NOV, POP; DLB 113, 330;
DNFS 1, 2; EWL 3; EXPN; EXPS; HW
1, 2; LAIT 2; LATS 1:2; LAW; LAWS 1;

Glasgow, Ellen (Anderson Gholson)
1873-1945 .... **SSC 34; TCLC 2, 7**
See also AMW; CA 104; 164; DLB 9, 12;
MAL 5; MBL; MTCW 2; MTFW 2005;
RGAL 4; RHW; SSFS 9; TUS

Glaspell, Susan 1882(?)-1948 ..... **DC 10; SSC 41; TCLC 55, 175**
See also AMWS 3; CA 110; 154; DFS 8,
18, 24; DLB 7, 9, 78, 228; MBL; RGAL
4; SSFS 3; TCWW 2; TUS; YABC 2

Glassco, John 1909-1981 .... **CLC 9**
See also CA 13-16R; 102; CANR 15; CN
1, 2; CP 1, 2, 3; DLB 68

Glasscock, Amnesia
See Steinbeck, John (Ernst)

Glasser, Ronald J. 1940(?)- .... **CLC 37**
See also CA 209

Glassman, Joyce
See Johnson, Joyce

Gleick, James (W.) 1954- .... **CLC 147**
See also CA 131; 137; CANR 97; INT CA-137

Glendinning, Victoria 1937- .... **CLC 50**
See also CA 120; 127; CANR 59, 89, 166;
DLB 155

Glissant, Edouard (Mathieu)
1928- .... **CLC 10, 68**
See also CA 153; CANR 111; CWW 2;
DAM MULT; EWL 3; RGWL 3

Gloag, Julian 1930- .... **CLC 40**
See also AITN 1; CA 65-68; CANR 10, 70;
CN 1, 2, 3, 4, 5, 6

Glowacki, Aleksander
See Prus, Boleslaw

Gluck, Louise 1943- . **CLC 7, 22, 44, 81, 160, 280; PC 16**
See also AMWS 5; CA 33-36R; CANR 40,
69, 108, 133, 182; CP 1, 2, 3, 4, 5, 6, 7;
CWP; DA3; DAM POET; DLB 5; MAL
5; MTCW 2; MTFW 2005; PFS 5, 15;
RGAL 4; TCLE 1:1

Gluck, Louise Elisabeth
See Gluck, Louise

Glyn, Elinor 1864-1943 .... **TCLC 72**
See also DLB 153; RHW

Gobineau, Joseph-Arthur
1816-1882 .... **NCLC 17**
See also DLB 123; GFL 1789 to the Present

Godard, Jean-Luc 1930- .... **CLC 20**
See also CA 93-96

Godden, (Margaret) Rumer
1907-1998 .... **CLC 53**
See also AAYA 6; BPFB 2; BYA 2, 5; CA
5-8R; 172; CANR 4, 27, 36, 55, 80; CLR
20; CN 1, 2, 3, 4, 5, 6; CWRI 5; DLB
161; MAICYA 1, 2; RHW; SAAS 12;
SATA 3, 36; SATA-Obit 109; TEA

Godoy Alcayaga, Lucila 1899-1957 .. **HLC 2; PC 32; TCLC 2**
See also BW 2; CA 104; 131; CANR 81;
DAM MULT; DLB 283, 331; DNFS;
EWL 3; HW 1, 2; LAW; MTCW 1, 2;
MTFW 2005; RGWL 2, 3; WP

Godwin, Gail 1937- ...... **CLC 5, 8, 22, 31, 69, 125**
See also BPFB 2; CA 29-32R; CANR 15,
43, 69, 132; CN 1, 2, 3, 4, 5, 6; CPW; CSW;
DA3; DAM POP; DLB 6, 234, 350; INT
CANR-15; MAL 5; MTCW 1, 2; MTFW
2005

Godwin, Gail Kathleen
See Godwin, Gail

Godwin, William 1756-1836 .. **NCLC 14, 130**
See also CDBLB 1789-1832; CMW 4; DLB
39, 104, 142, 158, 163, 262, 336; GL 2;
HGG; RGEL 2

Goebbels, Josef
See Goebbels, (Paul) Joseph

Goebbels, (Paul) Joseph
1897-1945 .... **TCLC 68**
See also CA 115; 148

Goebbels, Joseph Paul
See Goebbels, (Paul) Joseph

Goethe, Johann Wolfgang von
1749-1832 . **DC 20; NCLC 4, 22, 34, 90, 154; PC 5; SSC 38; WLC 3**
See also CDWLB 2; DA; DA3; DAB;
DAC; DAM DRAM, MST, POET; DLB
94; EW 5; GL 2; LATS 1; LMFS 1:1;
RGWL 2, 3; TWA

Gogarty, Oliver St. John
1878-1957 .... **TCLC 15**
See also CA 109; 150; DLB 15, 19; RGEL
2

Gogol, Nikolai (Vasilyevich)
1809-1852 .... **DC 1; NCLC 5, 15, 31, 162; SSC 4, 29, 52; WLC 3**
See also DA; DAB; DAC; DAM DRAM,
MST; DFS 12; DLB 198; EW 6; EXPS;
RGSF 2; RGWL 2, 3; SSFS 7; TWA

Goines, Donald 1937(?)-1974 .... **BLC 1:2; CLC 80**
See also AITN 1; BW 1, 3; CA 124; 114;
CANR 82; CMW 4; DA3; DAM MULT,
POP; DLB 33

Gold, Herbert 1924- ... **CLC 4, 7, 14, 42, 152**
See also CA 9-12R; CANR 17, 45, 125,
194; CN 1, 2, 3, 4, 5, 6, 7; DLB 2; DLBY
1981; MAL 5

Goldbarth, Albert 1948- .... **CLC 5, 38**
See also AMWS 12; CA 53-56; CANR 6,
40; CP 3, 4, 5, 6, 7; DLB 120

Goldberg, Anatol 1910-1982 .... **CLC 34**
See also CA 131; 117

Goldemberg, Isaac 1945- .... **CLC 52**
See also CA 69-72; CAAS 12; CANR 11,
32; EWL 3; HW 1; WLIT 1

Golding, Arthur 1536-1606 .... **LC 101**
See also DLB 136

Golding, William 1911-1993 . **CLC 1, 2, 3, 8, 10, 17, 27, 58, 81; WLC 3**
See also AAYA 5, 44; BPFB 2; BRWR 1;
BRWS 1; BYA 2; CA 5-8R; 141; CANR
13, 33, 54; CD 5; CDBLB 1945-1960;
CLR 94, 130; CN 1, 2, 3, 4; DA; DA3;
DAB; DAC; DAM MST, NOV; DLB 15,
100, 255, 326, 330; EWL 3; EXPN; HGG;
LAIT 4; MTCW 1, 2; MTFW 2005; NFS
2; RGEL 2; RHW; SFW 4; TEA; WLIT
4; YAW

Golding, William Gerald
See Golding, William

Goldman, Emma 1869-1940 .... **TCLC 13**
See also CA 110; 150; DLB 221; FW;
RGAL 4; TUS

Goldman, Francisco 1954- .... **CLC 76**
See also CA 162; CANR 185

Goldman, William 1931- .... **CLC 1, 48**
See also BPFB 2; CA 9-12R; CANR 29,
69, 106; CN 1, 2, 3, 4, 5, 6, 7; DLB 44;
FANT; IDFW 3, 4

Goldman, William W.
See Goldman, William

Goldmann, Lucien 1913-1970 .... **CLC 24**
See also CA 25-28; CAP 2

Goldoni, Carlo 1707-1793 .... **LC 4, 152**
See also DAM DRAM; EW 4; RGWL 2, 3;
WLIT 7

Goldsberry, Steven 1949- .... **CLC 34**
See also CA 131

Goldsmith, Oliver 1730(?)-1774 .... **DC 8; LC 2, 48, 122; PC 77; WLC 3**
See also BRW 3; CDBLB 1660-1789; DA;
DAB; DAC; DAM DRAM, MST, NOV,
POET; DFS 1; DLB 39, 89, 104, 109, 142,
336; IDTP; RGEL 2; SATA 26; TEA;
WLIT 3

Goldsmith, Peter
See Priestley, J(ohn) B(oynton)

Goldstein, Rebecca 1950- .... **CLC 239**
See also CA 144; CANR 99, 165; TCLE
1:1

Goldstein, Rebecca Newberger
See Goldstein, Rebecca

Gombrowicz, Witold 1904-1969 .... **CLC 4, 7, 11, 49**
See also CA 19-20; 25-28R; CANR 105;
CAP 2; CDWLB 4; DAM DRAM; DLB
215; EW 12; EWL 3; RGWL 2, 3; TWA

Gomez de Avellaneda, Gertrudis
1814-1873 .... **NCLC 111**
See also LAW

Gomez de la Serna, Ramon
1888-1963 .... **CLC 9**
See also CA 153; 116; CANR 79; EWL 3;
HW 1, 2

Goncharov, Ivan Alexandrovich
1812-1891 .... **NCLC 1, 63**
See also DLB 238; EW 6; RGWL 2, 3

Goncourt, Edmond (Louis Antoine Huot) de
1822-1896 .... **NCLC 7**
See also DLB 123; EW 7; GFL 1789 to the
Present; RGWL 2, 3

Goncourt, Jules (Alfred Huot) de
1830-1870 .... **NCLC 7**
See also DLB 123; EW 7; GFL 1789 to the
Present; RGWL 2, 3

Gongora (y Argote), Luis de
1561-1627 .... **LC 72**
See also RGWL 2, 3

Gontier, Fernande 19(?)- .... **CLC 50**

Gonzalez Martinez, Enrique
See Gonzalez Martinez, Enrique

Gonzalez Martinez, Enrique
1871-1952 .... **TCLC 72**
See also CA 166; CANR 81; DLB 290;
EWL 3; HW 1, 2

Goodison, Lorna 1947- .... **BLC 2:2; PC 36**
See also CA 142; CANR 88, 189; CP 5, 6,
7; CWP; DLB 157; EWL 3; PFS 25

Goodman, Allegra 1967- .... **CLC 241**
See also CA 204; CANR 162; DLB 244,
350

Goodman, Paul 1911-1972 ..... **CLC 1, 2, 4, 7**
See also CA 19-20; 37-40R; CAD; CANR
34; CAP 2; CN 1; DLB 130, 246; MAL
5; MTCW 1; RGAL 4

Goodweather, Hartley
See King, Thomas

GoodWeather, Hartley
See King, Thomas

Googe, Barnabe 1540-1594 .... **LC 94**
See also DLB 132; RGEL 2

Gordimer, Nadine 1923- ...... **CLC 3, 5, 7, 10, 18, 33, 51, 70, 123, 160, 161, 263; SSC 17, 80; WLCS**
See also AAYA 39; AFW; BRWS 2; CA
5-8R; CANR 3, 28, 56, 88, 131; CN 1, 2,
3, 4, 5, 6, 7; DA; DA3; DAB; DAC; DAM
MST, NOV; DLB 225, 326, 330; EWL 3;
EXPS; INT CANR-28; LATS 1:2; MTCW
1, 2; MTFW 2005; NFS 4; RGEL 2;
RGSF 2; SSFS 2, 14, 19; TWA; WLIT 2;
YAW

Gordon, Adam Lindsay
1833-1870 .... **NCLC 21**
See also DLB 230

Gordon, Caroline 1895-1981 . **CLC 6, 13, 29, 83; SSC 15**
See also AMW; CA 11-12; 103; CANR 36;
CAP 1; CN 1, 2; DLB 4, 9, 102; DLBD
17; DLBY 1981; EWL 3; MAL 5; MTCW
1, 2; MTFW 2005; RGAL 4; RGSF 2

Gordon, Charles William
1860-1937 .... **TCLC 31**
See also CA 109; DLB 92; TCWW 1, 2

Haliburton, Thomas Chandler
1796-1865 .... **NCLC 15, 149**
See also DLB 11, 99; RGEL 2; RGSF 2

Hall, Donald 1928- ... **CLC 1, 13, 37, 59, 151,
240; PC 70**
See also AAYA 63; CA 5-8R; CAAS 7;
CANR 2, 44, 64, 106, 133; CP 1, 2, 3, 4,
5, 6, 7; DAM POET; DLB 5, 342; MAL
5; MTCW 2; MTFW 2005; RGAL 4;
SATA 23, 97

Hall, Donald Andrew, Jr.
See Hall, Donald

Hall, Frederic Sauser
See Sauser-Hall, Frederic

Hall, James
See Kuttner, Henry

Hall, James Norman 1887-1951 ..... **TCLC 23**
See also CA 123; 173; LAIT 1; RHW 1;
SATA 21

Hall, Joseph 1574-1656 .... **LC 91**
See also DLB 121, 151; RGEL 2

Hall, Marguerite Radclyffe
See Hall, Radclyffe

Hall, Radclyffe 1880-1943 ...... **TCLC 12, 215**
See also BRWS 6; CA 110; 150; CANR 83;
DLB 191; MTCW 2; MTFW 2005; RGEL
2; RHW

Hall, Rodney 1935- .... **CLC 51**
See also CA 109; CANR 69; CN 6, 7; CP
1, 2, 3, 4, 5, 6, 7; DLB 289

Hallam, Arthur Henry
1811-1833 .... **NCLC 110**
See also DLB 32

Halldor Laxness
See Gudjonsson, Halldor Kiljan

Halleck, Fitz-Greene 1790-1867 .... **NCLC 47**
See also DLB 3, 250; RGAL 4

Halliday, Michael
See Creasey, John

Halpern, Daniel 1945- .... **CLC 14**
See also CA 33-36R; CANR 93, 174; CP 3,
4, 5, 6, 7

Hamburger, Michael 1924-2007 ... **CLC 5, 14**
See also CA 5-8R, 196; 261; CAAE 196;
CAAS 4; CANR 2, 47; CP 1, 2, 3, 4, 5, 6,
7; DLB 27

Hamburger, Michael Peter Leopold
See Hamburger, Michael

Hamill, Pete 1935- .... **CLC 10, 261**
See also CA 25-28R; CANR 18, 71, 127,
180

Hamill, William Peter
See Hamill, Pete

Hamilton, Alexander 1712-1756 .... **LC 150**
See also DLB 31

Hamilton, Alexander
1755(?)-1804 .... **NCLC 49**
See also DLB 37

Hamilton, Clive
See Lewis, C.S.

Hamilton, Edmond 1904-1977 .... **CLC 1**
See also CA 1-4R; CANR 3, 84; DLB 8;
SATA 118; SFW 4

Hamilton, Elizabeth 1758-1816 ... **NCLC 153**
See also DLB 116, 158

Hamilton, Eugene (Jacob) Lee
See Lee-Hamilton, Eugene (Jacob)

Hamilton, Franklin
See Silverberg, Robert

Hamilton, Gail
See Corcoran, Barbara (Asenath)

Hamilton, (Robert) Ian 1938-2001 . **CLC 191**
See also CA 106; 203; CANR 41, 67; CP 1,
2, 3, 4, 5, 6, 7; DLB 40, 155

Hamilton, Jane 1957- .... **CLC 179**
See also CA 147; CANR 85, 128; CN 7;
DLB 350; MTFW 2005

Hamilton, Mollie
See Kaye, M.M.

Hamilton, (Anthony Walter) Patrick
1904-1962 .... **CLC 51**
See also CA 176; 113; DLB 10, 191

Hamilton, Virginia 1936-2002 .... **CLC 26**
See also AAYA 2, 21; BW 2, 3; BYA 1, 2,
8; CA 25-28R; 206; CANR 20, 37, 73,
126; CLR 1, 11, 40, 127; DAM MULT;
DLB 33, 52; DLBY 2001; INT CANR-
20; JRDA; LAIT 5; MAICYA 1, 2; MAI-
CYAS 1; MTCW 1, 2; MTFW 2005;
SATA 4, 56, 79, 123; SATA-Obit 132;
WYA; YAW

Hammett, (Samuel) Dashiell
1894-1961 .... **CLC 3, 5, 10, 19, 47; SSC
17; TCLC 187**
See also AAYA 59; AITN 1; AMWS 4;
BPFB 2; CA 81-84; CANR 42; CDALB
1929-1941; CMW 4; DA3; DLB 226, 280;
DLBD 6; DLBY 1996; EWL 3; LAIT 3;
MAL 5; MSW; MTCW 1, 2; MTFW
2005; NFS 21; RGAL 4; RGSF 2; TUS

Hammon, Jupiter 1720(?)-1800(?) . **BLC 1:2;
NCLC 5; PC 16**
See also DAM MULT, POET; DLB 31, 50

Hammond, Keith
See Kuttner, Henry

Hamner, Earl (Henry), Jr. 1923- ...... **CLC 12**
See also AITN 2; CA 73-76; DLB 6

Hampton, Christopher 1946- .... **CLC 4**
See also CA 25-28R; CD 5, 6; DLB 13;
MTCW 1

Hampton, Christopher James
See Hampton, Christopher

Hamsun, Knut
See Pedersen, Knut

Hamsund, Knut Pedersen
See Pedersen, Knut

Handke, Peter 1942- .... **CLC 5, 8, 10, 15, 38,
134; DC 17**
See also CA 77-80; CANR 33, 75, 104, 133,
180; CWW 2; DAM DRAM, NOV; DLB
85, 124; EWL 3; MTCW 1, 2; MTFW
2005; TWA

Handler, Chelsea 1976(?)- .... **CLC 269**
See also CA 243

Handy, W(illiam) C(hristopher)
1873-1958 .... **TCLC 97**
See also BW 3; CA 121; 167

Hanley, James 1901-1985 ..... **CLC 3, 5, 8, 13**
See also CA 73-76; 117; CANR 36; CBD;
CN 1, 2, 3; DLB 191; EWL 3; MTCW 1;
RGEL 2

Hannah, Barry 1942- .. **CLC 23, 38, 90, 270;
SSC 94**
See also BPFB 2; CA 108; 110; CANR 43,
68, 113; CN 4, 5, 6, 7; CSW; DLB 6, 234;
INT CA-110; MTCW 1; RGSF 2

Hannon, Ezra
See Hunter, Evan

Hanrahan, Barbara 1939-1991 .... **TCLC 219**
See also CA 121; 127; CN 4, 5; DLB 289

Hansberry, Lorraine (Vivian)
1930-1965 ... **BLC 1:2, 2:2; CLC 17, 62;
DC 2; TCLC 192**
See also AAYA 25; AFAW 1, 2; AMWS 4;
BW 1, 3; CA 109; 25-28R; CABS 3;
CAD; CANR 58; CDALB 1941-1968;
CWD; DA; DA3; DAB; DAC; DAM
DRAM, MST, MULT; DFS 2; DLB 7, 38;
EWL 3; FL 1:6; FW; LAIT 4; MAL 5;
MTCW 1, 2; MTFW 2005; RGAL 4; TUS

Hansen, Joseph 1923-2004 .... **CLC 38**
See also BPFB 2; CA 29-32R; 233; CAAS
17; CANR 16, 44, 66, 125; CMW 4; DLB
226; GLL 1; INT CANR-16

Hansen, Karen V. 1955- .... **CLC 65**
See also CA 149; CANR 102

Hansen, Martin A(lfred)
1909-1955 .... **TCLC 32**
See also CA 167; DLB 214; EWL 3

Hanson, Kenneth O(stlin) 1922- .... **CLC 13**
See also CA 53-56; CANR 7; CP 1, 2, 3, 4,
5

Hardwick, Elizabeth 1916-2007 .... **CLC 13**
See also AMWS 3; CA 5-8R; 267; CANR
3, 32, 70, 100, 139; CN 4, 5, 6; CSW;
DA3; DAM NOV; DLB 6; MBL; MTCW
1, 2; MTFW 2005; TCLE 1:1

Hardwick, Elizabeth Bruce
See Hardwick, Elizabeth

Hardwick, Elizabeth Bruce
See Hardwick, Elizabeth

Hardy, Thomas 1840-1928 . **PC 8, 92; SSC 2,
60, 113; TCLC 4, 10, 18, 32, 48, 53, 72,
143, 153; WLC 3**
See also AAYA 69; BRW 6; BRWC 1, 2;
BRWR 1; CA 104; 123; CDBLB 1890-
1914; DA; DA3; DAB; DAC; DAM MST,
NOV, POET; DLB 18, 19, 135, 284; EWL
3; EXPN; EXPP; LAIT 2; MTCW 1, 2;
MTFW 2005; NFS 3, 11, 15, 19, 30; PFS
3, 4, 18; RGEL 2; RGSF 2; TEA; WLIT
4

Hare, David 1947- . **CLC 29, 58, 136; DC 26**
See also BRWS 4; CA 97-100; CANR 39,
91; CBD; CD 5, 6; DFS 4, 7, 16; DLB
13, 310; MTCW 1; TEA

Harewood, John
See Van Druten, John (William)

Harford, Henry
See Hudson, W(illiam) H(enry)

Hargrave, Leonie
See Disch, Thomas M.

**Hariri, Al- al-Qasim ibn 'Ali Abu
Muhammad al-Basri**
See al-Hariri, al-Qasim ibn 'Ali Abu Mu-
hammad al-Basri

Harjo, Joy 1951- ..... **CLC 83; NNAL; PC 27**
See also AMWS 12; CA 114; CANR 35,
67, 91, 129; CP 6, 7; CWP; DAM MULT;
DLB 120, 175, 342; EWL 3; MTCW 2;
MTFW 2005; PFS 15; RGAL 4

Harlan, Louis R(udolph) 1922- .... **CLC 34**
See also CA 21-24R; CANR 25, 55, 80

Harling, Robert 1951(?)- .... **CLC 53**
See also CA 147

Harmon, William (Ruth) 1938- .... **CLC 38**
See also CA 33-36R; CANR 14, 32, 35;
SATA 65

Harper, F. E. W.
See Harper, Frances Ellen Watkins

Harper, Frances E. W.
See Harper, Frances Ellen Watkins

Harper, Frances E. Watkins
See Harper, Frances Ellen Watkins

Harper, Frances Ellen
See Harper, Frances Ellen Watkins

Harper, Frances Ellen Watkins
1825-1911 . **BLC 1:2; PC 21; TCLC 14,
217**
See also AFAW 1, 2; BW 1, 3; CA 111; 125;
CANR 79; DAM MULT, POET; DLB 50,
221; MBL; RGAL 4

Harper, Michael S(teven) 1938- ..... **BLC 2:2;
CLC 7, 22**
See also AFAW 2; BW 1; CA 33-36R; 224;
CAAE 224; CANR 24, 108; CP 2, 3, 4, 5,
6, 7; DLB 41; RGAL 4; TCLE 1:1

Harper, Mrs. F. E. W.
See Harper, Frances Ellen Watkins

Harpur, Charles 1813-1868 .... **NCLC 114**
See also DLB 230; RGEL 2

Harris, Christie
See Harris, Christie (Lucy) Irwin

Hazlitt, William 1778-1830 ...... **NCLC 29, 82**
See also BRW 4; DLB 110, 158; RGEL 2; TEA

Hazzard, Shirley 1931- .... **CLC 18, 218**
See also CA 9-12R; CANR 4, 70, 127; CN 1, 2, 3, 4, 5, 6, 7; DLB 289; DLBY 1982; MTCW 1

Head, Bessie 1937-1986 . **BLC 1:2, 2:2; CLC 25, 67; SSC 52**
See also AFW; BW 2, 3; CA 29-32R; 119; CANR 25, 82; CDWLB 3; CN 1, 2, 3, 4; DA3; DAM MULT; DLB 117, 225; EWL 3; EXPS; FL 1:6; FW; MTCW 1, 2; MTFW 2005; RGSF 2; SSFS 5, 13; WLIT 2; WWE 1

Headley, Elizabeth
See Harrison, Elizabeth (Allen) Cavanna

Headon, (Nicky) Topper 1956(?)- ..... **CLC 30**

Heaney, Seamus 1939- . **CLC 5, 7, 14, 25, 37, 74, 91, 171, 225; PC 18, 100; WLCS**
See also AAYA 61; BRWR 1; BRWS 2; CA 85-88; CANR 25, 48, 75, 91, 128, 184; CDBLB 1960 to Present; CP 1, 2, 3, 4, 5, 6, 7; DA3; DAB; DAM POET; DLB 40, 330; DLBY 1995; EWL 3; EXPP; MTCW 1, 2; MTFW 2005; PAB; PFS 2, 5, 8, 17, 30; RGEL 2; TEA; WLIT 4

Hearn, (Patricio) Lafcadio (Tessima Carlos) 1850-1904 .... **TCLC 9**
See also CA 105; 166; DLB 12, 78, 189; HGG; MAL 5; RGAL 4

Hearne, Samuel 1745-1792 .... **LC 95**
See also DLB 99

Hearne, Vicki 1946-2001 .... **CLC 56**
See also CA 139; 201

Hearon, Shelby 1931- .... **CLC 63**
See also AITN 2; AMWS 8; CA 25-28R; CAAS 11; CANR 18, 48, 103, 146; CSW

Heat-Moon, William Least
See Trogdon, William

Hebbel, Friedrich 1813-1863 . **DC 21; NCLC 43**
See also CDWLB 2; DAM DRAM; DLB 129; EW 6; RGWL 2, 3

Hebert, Anne 1916-2000 . **CLC 4, 13, 29, 246**
See also CA 85-88; 187; CANR 69, 126; CCA 1; CWP; CWW 2; DA3; DAC; DAM MST, POET; DLB 68; EWL 3; GFL 1789 to the Present; MTCW 1, 2; MTFW 2005; PFS 20

Hecht, Anthony (Evan) 1923-2004 .... **CLC 8, 13, 19; PC 70**
See also AMWS 10; CA 9-12R; 232; CANR 6, 108; CP 1, 2, 3, 4, 5, 6, 7; DAM POET; DLB 5, 169; EWL 3; PFS 6; WP

Hecht, Ben 1894-1964 ..... **CLC 8; TCLC 101**
See also CA 85-88; DFS 9; DLB 7, 9, 25, 26, 28, 86; FANT; IDFW 3, 4; RGAL 4

Hedayat, Sadeq 1903-1951 .... **TCLC 21**
See also CA 120; EWL 3; RGSF 2

Hegel, Georg Wilhelm Friedrich 1770-1831 .... **NCLC 46, 151**
See also DLB 90; TWA

Heidegger, Martin 1889-1976 .... **CLC 24**
See also CA 81-84; 65-68; CANR 34; DLB 296; MTCW 1, 2; MTFW 2005

Heidenstam, (Carl Gustaf) Verner von 1859-1940 .... **TCLC 5**
See also CA 104; DLB 330

Heidi Louise
See Erdrich, Louise

Heifner, Jack 1946- .... **CLC 11**
See also CA 105; CANR 47

Heijermans, Herman 1864-1924 .... **TCLC 24**
See also CA 123; EWL 3

Heilbrun, Carolyn G. 1926-2003 ..... **CLC 25, 173**
See also BPFB 1; CA 45-48; 220; CANR 1, 28, 58, 94; CMW; CPW; DLB 306; FW; MSW

Heilbrun, Carolyn Gold
See Heilbrun, Carolyn G.

Hein, Christoph 1944- .... **CLC 154**
See also CA 158; CANR 108; CDWLB 2; CWW 2; DLB 124

Heine, Heinrich 1797-1856 .... **NCLC 4, 54, 147; PC 25**
See also CDWLB 2; DLB 90; EW 5; RGWL 2, 3; TWA

Heinemann, Larry 1944- .... **CLC 50**
See also CA 110; CAAS 21; CANR 31, 81, 156; DLBD 9; INT CANR-31

Heinemann, Larry Curtiss
See Heinemann, Larry

Heiney, Donald (William) 1921-1993 . **CLC 9**
See also CA 1-4R; 142; CANR 3, 58; FANT

Heinlein, Robert A. 1907-1988 .. **CLC 1, 3, 8, 14, 26, 55; SSC 55**
See also AAYA 17; BPFB 2; BYA 4, 13; CA 1-4R; 125; CANR 1, 20, 53; CLR 75; CN 1, 2, 3, 4; CPW; DA3; DAM POP; DLB 8; EXPS; JRDA; LAIT 5; LMFS 2; MAICYA 1, 2; MTCW 1, 2; MTFW 2005; RGAL 4; SATA 9, 69; SATA-Obit 56; SCFW 1, 2; SFW 4; SSFS 7; YAW

Held, Peter
See Vance, Jack

Heldris of Cornwall fl. 13th cent.
- .... **CMLC 97**

Helforth, John
See Doolittle, Hilda

Heliodorus fl. 3rd cent. - .... **CMLC 52**
See also WLIT 8

Hellenhofferu, Vojtech Kapristian z
See Hasek, Jaroslav (Matej Frantisek)

Heller, Joseph 1923-1999 . **CLC 1, 3, 5, 8, 11, 36, 63; TCLC 131, 151; WLC 3**
See also AAYA 24; AITN 1; AMWS 4; BPFB 2; BYA 1; CA 5-8R; 187; CABS 1; CANR 8, 42, 66, 126; CN 1, 2, 3, 4, 5, 6; CPW; DA; DA3; DAB; DAC; DAM MST, NOV, POP; DLB 2, 28, 227; DLBY 1980, 2002; EWL 3; EXPN; INT CANR-8; LAIT 4; MAL 5; MTCW 1, 2; MTFW 2005; NFS 1; RGAL 4; TUS; YAW

Hellman, Lillian 1905-1984 . **CLC 2, 4, 8, 14, 18, 34, 44, 52; DC 1; TCLC 119**
See also AAYA 47; AITN 1, 2; AMWS 1; CA 13-16R; 112; CAD; CANR 33; CWD; DA3; DAM DRAM; DFS 1, 3, 14; DLB 7, 228; DLBY 1984; EWL 3; FL 1:6; FW; LAIT 3; MAL 5; MBL; MTCW 1, 2; MTFW 2005; RGAL 4; TUS

Helprin, Mark 1947- .... **CLC 7, 10, 22, 32**
See also CA 81-84; CANR 47, 64, 124; CDALBS; CN 7; CPW; DA3; DAM NOV, POP; DLB 335; DLBY 1985; FANT; MAL 5; MTCW 1, 2; MTFW 2005; SSFS 25; SUFW 2

Helvetius, Claude-Adrien 1715-1771 .. **LC 26**
See also DLB 313

Helyar, Jane Penelope Josephine 1933- .... **CLC 17**
See also CA 21-24R; CANR 10, 26; CWRI 5; SAAS 2; SATA 5; SATA-Essay 138

Hemans, Felicia 1793-1835 ...... **NCLC 29, 71**
See also DLB 96; RGEL 2

Hemingway, Ernest (Miller) 1899-1961 .... **CLC 1, 3, 6, 8, 10, 13, 19, 30, 34, 39, 41, 44, 50, 61, 80; SSC 1, 25, 36, 40, 63, 117; TCLC 115, 203; WLC 3**
See also AAYA 19; AMW; AMWC 1; AMWR 1; BPFB 2; BYA 2, 3, 13, 15; CA 77-80; CANR 34; CDALB 1917-1929;

DA; DA3; DAB; DAC; DAM MST, NOV; DLB 4, 9, 102, 210, 308, 316, 330; DLBD 1, 15, 16; DLBY 1981, 1987, 1996, 1998; EWL 3; EXPN; EXPS; LAIT 3, 4; LATS 1:1; MAL 5; MTCW 1, 2; MTFW 2005; NFS 1, 5, 6, 14; RGAL 4; RGSF 2; SSFS 17; TUS; WYA

Hempel, Amy 1951- .... **CLC 39**
See also CA 118; 137; CANR 70, 166; DA3; DLB 218; EXPS; MTCW 2; MTFW 2005; SSFS 2

Henderson, F. C.
See Mencken, H. L.

Henderson, Mary
See Mavor, Osborne Henry

Henderson, Sylvia
See Ashton-Warner, Sylvia (Constance)

Henderson, Zenna (Chlarson) 1917-1983 .... **SSC 29**
See also CA 1-4R; 133; CANR 1, 84; DLB 8; SATA 5; SFW 4

Henkin, Joshua 1964- .... **CLC 119**
See also CA 161; CANR 186; DLB 350

Henley, Beth .... **CLC 23, 255; DC 6, 14**
See Henley, Elizabeth Becker
See also CABS 3; CAD; CD 5, 6; CSW; CWD; DFS 2, 21, 26; DLBY 1986; FW

Henley, Elizabeth Becker 1952- ...... **CLC 23, 255; DC 6, 14**
See Henley, Beth
See also AAYA 70; CA 107; CABS 3; CAD; CANR 32, 73, 140; CD 5, 6; CSW; DA3; DAM DRAM, MST; DFS 2, 21; DLBY 1986; FW; MTCW 1, 2; MTFW 2005

Henley, William Ernest 1849-1903 .. **TCLC 8**
See also CA 105; 234; DLB 19; RGEL 2

Hennissart, Martha 1929- .... **CLC 2**
See also BPFB 2; CA 85-88; CANR 64; CMW 4; DLB 306

Henry VIII 1491-1547 .... **LC 10**
See also DLB 132

Henry, O. 1862-1910 . **SSC 5, 49, 117; TCLC 1, 19; WLC 3**
See also AAYA 41; AMWS 2; CA 104; 131; CDALB 1865-1917; DA; DA3; DAB; DAC; DAM MST; DLB 12, 78, 79; EXPS; MAL 5; MTCW 1, 2; MTFW 2005; RGAL 4; RGSF 2; SSFS 2, 18, 27; TCWW 1, 2; TUS; YABC 2

Henry, Oliver
See Henry, O.

Henry, Patrick 1736-1799 .... **LC 25**
See also LAIT 1

Henryson, Robert 1430(?)-1506(?) ..... **LC 20, 110; PC 65**
See also BRWS 7; DLB 146; RGEL 2

Henschke, Alfred
See Klabund

Henson, Lance 1944- .... **NNAL**
See also CA 146; DLB 175

Hentoff, Nat(han Irving) 1925- .... **CLC 26**
See also AAYA 4, 42; BYA 6; CA 1-4R; CAAS 6; CANR 5, 25, 77, 114; CLR 1, 52; DLB 345; INT CANR-25; JRDA; MAICYA 1, 2; SATA 42, 69, 133; SATA-Brief 27; WYA; YAW

Heppenstall, (John) Rayner 1911-1981 .... **CLC 10**
See also CA 1-4R; 103; CANR 29; CN 1, 2; CP 1, 2, 3; EWL 3

Heraclitus c. 540B.C.-c. 450B.C. ... **CMLC 22**
See also DLB 176

Herbert, Frank 1920-1986 ... **CLC 12, 23, 35, 44, 85**
See also AAYA 21; BPFB 2; BYA 4, 14; CA 53-56; 118; CANR 5, 43; CDALBS; CPW; DAM POP; DLB 8; INT CANR-5; LAIT 5; MTCW 1, 2; MTFW 2005; NFS 17; SATA 9, 37; SATA-Obit 47; SCFW 1, 2; SFW 4; YAW

Hueffer, Ford Madox
See Ford, Ford Madox
Hughart, Barry 1934- .... **CLC 39**
See also CA 137; FANT; SFW 4; SUFW 2
Hughes, Colin
See Creasey, John
Hughes, David (John) 1930-2005 ..... **CLC 48**
See also CA 116; 129; 238; CN 4, 5, 6, 7;
DLB 14
Hughes, Edward James
See Hughes, Ted
Hughes, (James Mercer) Langston
1902-1967 .. **BLC 1:2; CLC 1, 5, 10, 15,
35, 44, 108; DC 3; HR 1:2; PC 1, 53;
SSC 6, 90; WLC 3**
See also AAYA 12; AFAW 1, 2; AMWR 1;
AMWS 1; BW 1, 3; CA 1-4R; 25-28R;
CANR 1, 34, 82; CDALB 1929-1941;
CLR 17; DA; DA3; DAB; DAC; DAM
DRAM, MST, MULT, POET; DFS 6, 18;
DLB 4, 7, 48, 51, 86, 228, 315; EWL 3;
EXPP; EXPS; JRDA; LAIT 3; LMFS 2;
MAICYA 1, 2; MAL 5; MTCW 1, 2;
MTFW 2005; NFS 21; PAB; PFS 1, 3, 6,
10, 15, 30; RGAL 4; RGSF 2; SATA 4,
33; SSFS 4, 7; TUS; WCH; WP; YAW
Hughes, Richard (Arthur Warren)
1900-1976 .... **CLC 1, 11; TCLC 204**
See also CA 5-8R; 65-68; CANR 4; CN 1,
2; DAM NOV; DLB 15, 161; EWL 3;
MTCW 1; RGEL 2; SATA 8; SATA-Obit
25
Hughes, Ted 1930-1998 . **CLC 2, 4, 9, 14, 37,
119; PC 7, 89**
See also BRWC 2; BRWR 2; BRWS 1; CA
1-4R; 171; CANR 1, 33, 66, 108; CLR 3,
131; CP 1, 2, 3, 4, 5, 6; DA3; DAB; DAC;
DAM MST, POET; DLB 40, 161; EWL
3; EXPP; MAICYA 1, 2; MTCW 1, 2;
MTFW 2005; PAB; PFS 4, 19; RGEL 2;
SATA 49; SATA-Brief 27; SATA-Obit
107; TEA; YAW
Hughes, Thomas 1822-1896 .... **NCLC 207**
See also BYA 3; DLB 18, 163; LAIT 2;
RGEL 2; SATA 31
Hugo, Richard
See Huch, Ricarda (Octavia)
Hugo, Richard F(ranklin)
1923-1982 .... **CLC 6, 18, 32; PC 68**
See also AMWS 6; CA 49-52; 108; CANR
3; CP 1, 2, 3; DAM POET; DLB 5, 206;
EWL 3; MAL 5; PFS 17; RGAL 4
Hugo, Victor (Marie) 1802-1885 .... **NCLC 3,
10, 21, 161, 189; PC 17; WLC 3**
See also AAYA 28; DA; DA3; DAB; DAC;
DAM DRAM, MST, NOV, POET; DLB
119, 192, 217; EFS 2; EW 6; EXPN; GFL
1789 to the Present; LAIT 1, 2; NFS 5,
20; RGWL 2, 3; SATA 47; TWA
Huidobro, Vicente
See Huidobro Fernandez, Vicente Garcia
Huidobro Fernandez, Vicente Garcia
1893-1948 .... **TCLC 31**
See also CA 131; DLB 283; EWL 3; HW 1;
LAW
Hulme, Keri 1947- .... **CLC 39, 130**
See also CA 125; CANR 69; CN 4, 5, 6, 7;
CP 6, 7; CWP; DLB 326; EWL 3; FW;
INT CA-125; NFS 24
Hulme, T(homas) E(rnest)
1883-1917 .... **TCLC 21**
See also BRWS 6; CA 117; 203; DLB 19
Humboldt, Alexander von
1769-1859 .... **NCLC 170**
See also DLB 90
Humboldt, Wilhelm von
1767-1835 .... **NCLC 134**
See also DLB 90

Hume, David 1711-1776 .. **LC 7, 56, 156, 157**
See also BRWS 3; DLB 104, 252, 336;
LMFS 1; TEA
Humphrey, William 1924-1997 .... **CLC 45**
See also AMWS 9; CA 77-80; 160; CANR
68; CN 1, 2, 3, 4, 5, 6; CSW; DLB 6, 212,
234, 278; TCWW 1, 2
Humphreys, Emyr Owen 1919- .... **CLC 47**
See also CA 5-8R; CANR 3, 24; CN 1, 2,
3, 4, 5, 6, 7; DLB 15
Humphreys, Josephine 1945- ..... **CLC 34, 57**
See also CA 121; 127; CANR 97; CSW;
DLB 292; INT CA-127
Huneker, James Gibbons
1860-1921 .... **TCLC 65**
See also CA 193; DLB 71; RGAL 4
Hungerford, Hesba Fay
See Brinsmead, H(esba) F(ay)
Hungerford, Pixie
See Brinsmead, H(esba) F(ay)
Hunt, E. Howard 1918-2007 .... **CLC 3**
See also AITN 1; CA 45-48; 256; CANR 2,
47, 103, 160; CMW 4
Hunt, Everette Howard, Jr.
See Hunt, E. Howard
Hunt, Francesca
See Holland, Isabelle (Christian)
Hunt, Howard
See Hunt, E. Howard
Hunt, Kyle
See Creasey, John
Hunt, (James Henry) Leigh
1784-1859 .... **NCLC 1, 70; PC 73**
See also DAM POET; DLB 96, 110, 144;
RGEL 2; TEA
Hunt, Marsha 1946- .... **CLC 70**
See also BW 2, 3; CA 143; CANR 79
Hunt, Violet 1866(?)-1942 .... **TCLC 53**
See also CA 184; DLB 162, 197
Hunter, E. Waldo
See Sturgeon, Theodore (Hamilton)
Hunter, Evan 1926-2005 .... **CLC 11, 31**
See also AAYA 39; BPFB 2; CA 5-8R; 241;
CANR 5, 38, 62, 97, 149; CMW 4; CN 1,
2, 3, 4, 5, 6, 7; CPW; DAM POP; DLB
306; DLBY 1982; INT CANR-5; MSW;
MTCW 1; SATA 25; SATA-Obit 167;
SFW 4
Hunter, Kristin
See Lattany, Kristin Hunter
Hunter, Mary
See Austin, Mary (Hunter)
Hunter, Mollie 1922- .... **CLC 21**
See also AAYA 13, 71; BYA 6; CANR 37,
78; CLR 25; DLB 161; JRDA; MAICYA
1, 2; SAAS 7; SATA 2, 54, 106, 139;
SATA-Essay 139; WYA; YAW
Hunter, Robert (?)-1734 .... **LC 7**
Hurston, Zora Neale 1891-1960 ..... **BLC 1:2;
CLC 7, 30, 61; DC 12; HR 1:2; SSC 4,
80; TCLC 121, 131; WLCS**
See also AAYA 15, 71; AFAW 1, 2; AMWS
6; BW 1, 3; BYA 12; CA 85-88; CANR
61; CDALBS; DA; DA3; DAC; DAM
MST, MULT, NOV; DFS 6; DLB 51, 86;
EWL 3; EXPN; EXPS; FL 1:6; FW; LAIT
3; LATS 1:1; LMFS 2; MAL 5; MBL;
MTCW 1, 2; MTFW 2005; NFS 3; RGAL
4; RGSF 2; SSFS 1, 6, 11, 19, 21; TUS;
YAW
Husserl, E. G.
See Husserl, Edmund (Gustav Albrecht)
Husserl, Edmund (Gustav Albrecht)
1859-1938 .... **TCLC 100**
See also CA 116; 133; DLB 296
Huston, John (Marcellus)
1906-1987 .... **CLC 20**
See also CA 73-76; 123; CANR 34; DLB
26

Hustvedt, Siri 1955- .... **CLC 76**
See also CA 137; CANR 149, 191
Hutcheson, Francis 1694-1746 .... **LC 157**
See also DLB 252
Hutchinson, Lucy 1620-1675 .... **LC 149**
Hutten, Ulrich von 1488-1523 .... **LC 16**
See also DLB 179
Huxley, Aldous (Leonard)
1894-1963 .... **CLC 1, 3, 4, 5, 8, 11, 18,
35, 79; SSC 39; WLC 3**
See also AAYA 11; BPFB 2; BRW 7; CA
85-88; CANR 44, 99; CDBLB 1914-1945;
DA; DA3; DAB; DAC; DAM MST, NOV;
DLB 36, 100, 162, 195, 255; EWL 3;
EXPN; LAIT 5; LMFS 2; MTCW 1, 2;
MTFW 2005; NFS 6; RGEL 2; SATA 63;
SCFW 1, 2; SFW 4; TEA; YAW
Huxley, T(homas) H(enry)
1825-1895 .... **NCLC 67**
See also DLB 57; TEA
Huygens, Constantijn 1596-1687 .... **LC 114**
See also RGWL 2, 3
Huysmans, Joris-Karl 1848-1907 ... **TCLC 7,
69, 212**
See also CA 104; 165; DLB 123; EW 7;
GFL 1789 to the Present; LMFS 2; RGWL
2, 3
Hwang, David Henry 1957- .... **CLC 55, 196;
DC 4, 23**
See also CA 127; 132; CAD; CANR 76,
124; CD 5, 6; DA3; DAM DRAM; DFS
11, 18; DLB 212, 228, 312; INT CA-132;
MAL 5; MTCW 2; MTFW 2005; RGAL
4
Hyatt, Daniel
See James, Daniel (Lewis)
Hyde, Anthony 1946- .... **CLC 42**
See also CA 136; CCA 1
Hyde, Margaret O. 1917- .... **CLC 21**
See also CA 1-4R; CANR 1, 36, 137, 181;
CLR 23; JRDA; MAICYA 1, 2; SAAS 8;
SATA 1, 42, 76, 139
Hyde, Margaret Oldroyd
See Hyde, Margaret O.
Hynes, James 1956(?)- .... **CLC 65**
See also CA 164; CANR 105
Hypatia c. 370-415 .... **CMLC 35**
Ian, Janis 1951- .... **CLC 21**
See also CA 105; 187
Ibanez, Vicente Blasco
See Blasco Ibanez, Vicente
Ibarbourou, Juana de
1895(?)-1979 .... **HLCS 2**
See also DLB 290; HW 1; LAW
Ibarguengoitia, Jorge 1928-1983 ..... **CLC 37;
TCLC 148**
See also CA 124; 113; EWL 3; HW 1
Ibn Arabi 1165-1240 .... **CMLC 105**
Ibn Battuta, Abu Abdalla
1304-1368(?) .... **CMLC 57**
See also WLIT 2
Ibn Hazm 994-1064 .... **CMLC 64**
Ibn Zaydun 1003-1070 .... **CMLC 89**
Ibsen, Henrik (Johan) 1828-1906 .. **DC 2, 30;
TCLC 2, 8, 16, 37, 52; WLC 3**
See also AAYA 46; CA 104; 141; DA; DA3;
DAB; DAC; DAM DRAM, MST; DFS 1,
6, 8, 10, 11, 15, 16, 25; EW 7; LAIT 1;
LATS 1:1; MTFW 2005; RGWL 2, 3
Ibuse, Masuji 1898-1993 .... **CLC 22**
See also CA 127; 141; CWW 2; DLB 180;
EWL 3; MJW; RGWL 3
Ibuse Masuji
See Ibuse, Masuji
Ichikawa, Kon 1915-2008 .... **CLC 20**
See also CA 121; 269
Ichiyo, Higuchi 1872-1896 .... **NCLC 49**
See also MJW

DAM NOV, POP; DLB 278; DLBY 1983;
FANT; INT CANR-10; MTCW 1, 2;
MTFW 2005; RHW; SATA 62; SFW 4;
TCWW 1, 2

Jakes, John William
See Jakes, John

James I 1394-1437 .... **LC 20**
See also RGEL 2

James, Alice 1848-1892 .... **NCLC 206**
See also DLB 221

James, Andrew
See Kirkup, James

James, C(yril) L(ionel) R(obert)
1901-1989 .... **BLCS; CLC 33**
See also BW 2; CA 117; 125; 128; CANR
62; CN 1, 2, 3, 4; DLB 125; MTCW 1

James, Daniel (Lewis) 1911-1988 ..... **CLC 33**
See also CA 174; 125; DLB 122

James, Dynely
See Mayne, William (James Carter)

James, Henry Sr. 1811-1882 .... **NCLC 53**

James, Henry 1843-1916 .... **SSC 8, 32, 47,
108; TCLC 2, 11, 24, 40, 47, 64, 171;
WLC 3**
See also AMW; AMWC 1; AMWR 1; BPFB
2; BRW 6; CA 104; 132; CDALB 1865-
1917; DA; DA3; DAB; DAC; DAM MST,
NOV; DLB 12, 71, 74, 189; DLBD 13;
EWL 3; EXPS; GL 2; HGG; LAIT 2;
MAL 5; MTCW 1, 2; MTFW 2005; NFS
12, 16, 19; RGAL 4; RGEL 2; RGSF 2;
SSFS 9; SUFW 1; TUS

James, M. R.
See James, Montague (Rhodes)

James, Mary
See Meaker, Marijane

James, Montague (Rhodes)
1862-1936 .... **SSC 16, 93; TCLC 6**
See also CA 104; 203; DLB 156, 201;
HGG; RGEL 2; RGSF 2; SUFW 1

James, P. D.
See White, Phyllis Dorothy James

James, Philip
See Moorcock, Michael

James, Samuel
See Stephens, James

James, Seumas
See Stephens, James

James, Stephen
See Stephens, James

James, T.F.
See Fleming, Thomas

James, William 1842-1910 .... **TCLC 15, 32**
See also AMW; CA 109; 193; DLB 270,
284; MAL 5; NCFS 5; RGAL 4

Jameson, Anna 1794-1860 .... **NCLC 43**
See also DLB 99, 166

Jameson, Fredric 1934- .... **CLC 142**
See also CA 196; CANR 169; DLB 67;
LMFS 2

Jameson, Fredric R.
See Jameson, Fredric

James VI of Scotland 1566-1625 .... **LC 109**
See also DLB 151, 172

Jami, Nur al-Din 'Abd al-Rahman
1414-1492 .... **LC 9**

Jammes, Francis 1868-1938 .... **TCLC 75**
See also CA 198; EWL 3; GFL 1789 to the
Present

Jandl, Ernst 1925-2000 .... **CLC 34**
See also CA 200; EWL 3

Janowitz, Tama 1957- .... **CLC 43, 145**
See also CA 106; CANR 52, 89, 129; CN
5, 6, 7; CPW; DAM POP; DLB 292;
MTFW 2005

Jansson, Tove (Marika) 1914-2001 ... **SSC 96**
See also CA 17-20R; 196; CANR 38, 118;
CLR 2, 125; CWW 2; DLB 257; EWL 3;
MAICYA 1, 2; RGSF 2; SATA 3, 41

Japrisot, Sebastien 1931-
See Rossi, Jean-Baptiste

Jarrell, Randall 1914-1965 .... **CLC 1, 2, 6, 9,
13, 49; PC 41; TCLC 177**
See also AMW; BYA 5; CA 5-8R; 25-28R;
CABS 2; CANR 6, 34; CDALB 1941-
1968; CLR 6, 111; CWRI 5; DAM POET;
DLB 48, 52; EWL 3; EXPP; MAICYA 1,
2; MAL 5; MTCW 1, 2; PAB; PFS 2, 31;
RGAL 4; SATA 7

Jarry, Alfred 1873-1907 .... **SSC 20; TCLC 2,
14, 147**
See also CA 104; 153; DA3; DAM DRAM;
DFS 8; DLB 192, 258; EW 9; EWL 3;
GFL 1789 to the Present; RGWL 2, 3;
TWA

Jarvis, E.K.
See Ellison, Harlan; Silverberg, Robert

Jawien, Andrzej
See John Paul II, Pope

Jaynes, Roderick
See Coen, Ethan

Jeake, Samuel, Jr.
See Aiken, Conrad (Potter)

Jean-Louis
See Kerouac, Jack

Jean Paul 1763-1825 .... **NCLC 7**

Jefferies, (John) Richard
1848-1887 .... **NCLC 47**
See also DLB 98, 141; RGEL 2; SATA 16;
SFW 4

Jeffers, John Robinson
See Jeffers, Robinson

Jeffers, Robinson 1887-1962 .... **CLC 2, 3, 11,
15, 54; PC 17; WLC 3**
See also AMWS 2; CA 85-88; CANR 35;
CDALB 1917-1929; DA; DAC; DAM
MST, POET; DLB 45, 212, 342; EWL 3;
MAL 5; MTCW 1, 2; MTFW 2005; PAB;
PFS 3, 4; RGAL 4

Jefferson, Janet
See Mencken, H. L.

Jefferson, Thomas 1743-1826 . **NCLC 11, 103**
See also AAYA 54; ANW; CDALB 1640-
1865; DA3; DLB 31, 183; LAIT 1; RGAL
4

Jeffrey, Francis 1773-1850 .... **NCLC 33**
See also DLB 107

Jelakowitch, Ivan
See Heijermans, Herman

Jelinek, Elfriede 1946- .... **CLC 169**
See also AAYA 68; CA 154; CANR 169;
DLB 85, 330; FW

Jellicoe, (Patricia) Ann 1927- .... **CLC 27**
See also CA 85-88; CBD; CD 5, 6; CWD;
CWRI 5; DLB 13, 233; FW

Jelloun, Tahar ben
See Ben Jelloun, Tahar

Jemyma
See Holley, Marietta

Jen, Gish
See Jen, Lillian

Jen, Lillian 1955- .... **AAL; CLC 70, 198, 260**
See also AMWC 2; CA 135; CANR 89,
130; CN 7; DLB 312; NFS 30

Jenkins, (John) Robin 1912- .... **CLC 52**
See also CA 1-4R; CANR 1, 135; CN 1, 2,
3, 4, 5, 6, 7; DLB 14, 271

Jennings, Elizabeth (Joan)
1926-2001 .... **CLC 5, 14, 131**
See also BRWS 5; CA 61-64; 200; CAAS
5; CANR 8, 39, 66, 127; CP 1, 2, 3, 4, 5,
6, 7; CWP; DLB 27; EWL 3; MTCW 1;
SATA 66

Jennings, Waylon 1937-2002 .... **CLC 21**

Jensen, Johannes V(ilhelm)
1873-1950 .... **TCLC 41**
See also CA 170; DLB 214, 330; EWL 3;
RGWL 3

Jensen, Laura (Linnea) 1948- .... **CLC 37**
See also CA 103

Jerome, Saint 345-420 .... **CMLC 30**
See also RGWL 3

Jerome, Jerome K(lapka)
1859-1927 .... **TCLC 23**
See also CA 119; 177; DLB 10, 34, 135;
RGEL 2

Jerrold, Douglas William
1803-1857 .... **NCLC 2**
See also DLB 158, 159, 344; RGEL 2

Jewett, (Theodora) Sarah Orne
1849-1909 . **SSC 6, 44, 110; TCLC 1, 22**
See also AAYA 76; AMW; AMWC 2;
AMWR 2; CA 108; 127; CANR 71; DLB
12, 74, 221; EXPS; FL 1:3; FW; MAL 5;
MBL; NFS 15; RGAL 4; RGSF 2; SATA
15; SSFS 4

Jewsbury, Geraldine (Endsor)
1812-1880 .... **NCLC 22**
See also DLB 21

Jhabvala, Ruth Prawer 1927- . **CLC 4, 8, 29,
94, 138; SSC 91**
See also BRWS 5; CA 1-4R; CANR 2, 29,
51, 74, 91, 128; CN 1, 2, 3, 4, 5, 6, 7;
DAB; DAM NOV; DLB 139, 194, 323,
326; EWL 3; IDFW 3, 4; INT CANR-29;
MTCW 1, 2; MTFW 2005; RGSF 2;
RGWL 2; RHW; TEA

Jibran, Kahlil
See Gibran, Kahlil

Jibran, Khalil
See Gibran, Kahlil

Jiles, Paulette 1943- .... **CLC 13, 58**
See also CA 101; CANR 70, 124, 170; CP
5; CWP

Jimenez (Mantecon), Juan Ramon
1881-1958 .... **HLC 1; PC 7; TCLC 4,
183**
See also CA 104; 131; CANR 74; DAM
MULT, POET; DLB 134, 330; EW 9;
EWL 3; HW 1; MTCW 1, 2; MTFW
2005; RGWL 2, 3

Jimenez, Ramon
See Jimenez (Mantecon), Juan Ramon

Jimenez Mantecon, Juan
See Jimenez (Mantecon), Juan Ramon

Jin, Ba 1904-2005 .... **CLC 18**
See Cantu, Robert Clark
See also CA 244; CWW 2; DLB 328; EWL
3

Jin, Xuefei 1956- .... **CLC 109, 262**
See also CA 152; CANR 91, 130, 184; DLB
244, 292; MTFW 2005; NFS 25; SSFS 17

Jin Ha
See Jin, Xuefei

Jodelle, Etienne 1532-1573 .... **LC 119**
See also DLB 327; GFL Beginnings to 1789

Joel, Billy
See Joel, William Martin

Joel, William Martin 1949- .... **CLC 26**
See also CA 108

John, St.
See John of Damascus, St.

John of Damascus, St. c.
675-749 .... **CMLC 27, 95**

John of Salisbury c. 1115-1180 ..... **CMLC 63**

John of the Cross, St. 1542-1591 .... **LC 18,
146**
See also RGWL 2, 3

John Paul II, Pope 1920-2005 .... **CLC 128**
See also CA 106; 133; 238

Johnson, B(ryan) S(tanley William)
1933-1973 .... **CLC 6, 9**
See also CA 9-12R; 53-56; CANR 9; CN 1;
CP 1, 2; DLB 14, 40; EWL 3; RGEL 2

Johnson, Benjamin F., of Boone
See Riley, James Whitcomb

Author Index

Kherdian, David 1931- .... **CLC 6, 9**
See also AAYA 42; CA 21-24R, 192; CAAE 192; CAAS 2; CANR 39, 78; CLR 24; JRDA; LAIT 3; MAICYA 1, 2; SATA 16, 74; SATA-Essay 125

Khlebnikov, Velimir .... **TCLC 20**
See Khlebnikov, Viktor Vladimirovich
See also DLB 295; EW 10; EWL 3; RGWL 2, 3

Khlebnikov, Viktor Vladimirovich 1885-1922
See Khlebnikov, Velimir
See also CA 117; 217

Khodasevich, V.F.
See Khodasevich, Vladislav

Khodasevich, Vladislav
1886-1939 .... **TCLC 15**
See also CA 115; DLB 317; EWL 3

Khodasevich, Vladislav Felitsianovich
See Khodasevich, Vladislav

Kidd, Sue Monk 1948- .... **CLC 267**
See also AAYA 72; CA 202; MTFW 2005; NFS 27

Kielland, Alexander Lange
1849-1906 .... **TCLC 5**
See also CA 104

Kiely, Benedict 1919-2007 . **CLC 23, 43; SSC 58**
See also CA 1-4R; 257; CANR 2, 84; CN 1, 2, 3, 4, 5, 6, 7; DLB 15, 319; TCLE 1:1

Kienzle, William X. 1928-2001 .... **CLC 25**
See also CA 93-96; 203; CAAS 1; CANR 9, 31, 59, 111; CMW 4; DA3; DAM POP; INT CANR-31; MSW; MTCW 1, 2; MTFW 2005

Kierkegaard, Soren 1813-1855 ..... **NCLC 34, 78, 125**
See also DLB 300; EW 6; LMFS 2; RGWL 3; TWA

Kieslowski, Krzysztof 1941-1996 .... **CLC 120**
See also CA 147; 151

Killens, John Oliver 1916-1987 ...... **BLC 2:2; CLC 10**
See also BW 2; CA 77-80; 123; CAAS 2; CANR 26; CN 1, 2, 3, 4; DLB 33; EWL 3

Killigrew, Anne 1660-1685 .... **LC 4, 73**
See also DLB 131

Killigrew, Thomas 1612-1683 .... **LC 57**
See also DLB 58; RGEL 2

Kim
See Simenon, Georges (Jacques Christian)

Kincaid, Jamaica 1949- . **BLC 1:2, 2:2; CLC 43, 68, 137, 234; SSC 72**
See also AAYA 13, 56; AFAW 2; AMWS 7; BRWS 7; BW 2, 3; CA 125; CANR 47, 59, 95, 133; CDALBS; CDWLB 3; CLR 63; CN 4, 5, 6, 7; DA3; DAM MULT, NOV; DLB 157, 227; DNFS 1; EWL 3; EXPS; FW; LAIT 1:2; LMFS 2; MAL 5; MTCW 2; MTFW 2005; NCFS 1; NFS 3; SSFS 5, 7; TUS; WWE 1; YAW

King, Francis (Henry) 1923- ...... **CLC 8, 53, 145**
See also CA 1-4R; CANR 1, 33, 86; CN 1, 2, 3, 4, 5, 6, 7; DAM NOV; DLB 15, 139; MTCW 1

King, Kennedy
See Brown, George Douglas

King, Martin Luther, Jr.
1929-1968 ... **BLC 1:2; CLC 83; WLCS**
See also BW 2, 3; CA 25-28; CANR 27, 44; CAP 2; DA; DA3; DAB; DAC; DAM MST, MULT; LAIT 5; LATS 1:2; MTCW 1, 2; MTFW 2005; SATA 14

King, Stephen 1947- .... **CLC 12, 26, 37, 61, 113, 228, 244; SSC 17, 55**
See also AAYA 1, 17; AMWS 5; BEST 90:1; BPFB 2; CA 61-64; CANR 1, 30, 52, 76, 119, 134, 168; CLR 124; CN 7;

CPW; DA3; DAM NOV, POP; DLB 143, 350; DLBY 1980; HGG; JRDA; LAIT 5; MTCW 1, 2; MTFW 2005; RGAL 4; SATA 9, 55, 161; SUFW 1, 2; WYAS 1; YAW

King, Stephen Edwin
See King, Stephen

King, Steve
See King, Stephen

King, Thomas 1943- .... **CLC 89, 171, 276; NNAL**
See also CA 144; CANR 95, 175; CCA 1; CN 6, 7; DAC; DAM MULT; DLB 175, 334; SATA 96

King, Thomas Hunt
See King, Thomas

Kingman, Lee
See Natti, Lee

Kingsley, Charles 1819-1875 .... **NCLC 35**
See also CLR 77; DLB 21, 32, 163, 178, 190; FANT; MAICYA 2; MAICYAS 1; RGEL 2; WCH; YABC 2

Kingsley, Henry 1830-1876 .... **NCLC 107**
See also DLB 21, 230; RGEL 2

Kingsley, Sidney 1906-1995 .... **CLC 44**
See also CA 85-88; 147; CAD; DFS 14, 19; DLB 7; MAL 5; RGAL 4

Kingsolver, Barbara 1955- .... **CLC 55, 81, 130, 216, 269**
See also AAYA 15; AMWS 7; CA 129; 134; CANR 60, 96, 133, 179; CDALBS; CN 7; CPW; CSW; DA3; DAM POP; DLB 206; INT CA-134; LAIT 5; MTCW 2; MTFW 2005; NFS 5, 10, 12, 24; RGAL 4; TCLE 1:1

Kingston, Maxine Hong 1940- .... **AAL; CLC 12, 19, 58, 121, 271; WLCS**
See also AAYA 8, 55; AMWS 5; BPFB 2; CA 69-72; CANR 13, 38, 74, 87, 128; CDALBS; CN 6, 7; DA3; DAM MULT, NOV; DLB 173, 212, 312; DLBY 1980; EWL 3; FL 1:6; FW; INT CANR-13; LAIT 5; MAL 5; MBL; MTCW 1, 2; MTFW 2005; NFS 6; RGAL 4; SATA 53; SSFS 3; TCWW 2

Kingston, Maxine Ting Ting Hong
See Kingston, Maxine Hong

Kinnell, Galway 1927- ..... **CLC 1, 2, 3, 5, 13, 29, 129; PC 26**
See also AMWS 3; CA 9-12R; CANR 10, 34, 66, 116, 138, 175; CP 1, 2, 3, 4, 5, 6, 7; DLB 5, 342; DLBY 1987; EWL 3; INT CANR-34; MAL 5; MTCW 1, 2; MTFW 2005; PAB; PFS 9, 26; RGAL 4; TCLE 1:1; WP

Kinsella, Thomas 1928- .... **CLC 4, 19, 138, 274; PC 69**
See also BRWS 5; CA 17-20R; CANR 15, 122; CP 1, 2, 3, 4, 5, 6, 7; DLB 27; EWL 3; MTCW 1, 2; MTFW 2005; RGEL 2; TEA

Kinsella, W.P. 1935- .... **CLC 27, 43, 166**
See also AAYA 7, 60; BPFB 2; CA 97-100, 222; CAAE 222; CAAS 7; CANR 21, 35, 66, 75, 129; CN 4, 5, 6, 7; CPW; DAC; DAM NOV, POP; FANT; INT CANR-21; LAIT 5; MTCW 1, 2; MTFW 2005; NFS 15; RGSF 2

Kinsey, Alfred C(harles)
1894-1956 .... **TCLC 91**
See also CA 115; 170; MTCW 2

Kipling, (Joseph) Rudyard 1865-1936 . **PC 3, 91; SSC 5, 54, 110; TCLC 8, 17, 167; WLC 3**
See also AAYA 32; BRW 6; BRWC 1, 2; BYA 4; CA 105; 120; CANR 33; CDBLB 1890-1914; CLR 39, 65; CWRI 5; DA; DA3; DAB; DAC; DAM MST, POET; DLB 19, 34, 141, 156, 330; EWL 3; EXPS; FANT; LAIT 3; LMFS 1; MAI-

CYA 1, 2; MTCW 1, 2; MTFW 2005; NFS 21; PFS 22; RGEL 2; RGSF 2; SATA 100; SFW 4; SSFS 8, 21, 22; SUFW 1; TEA; WCH; WLIT 4; YABC 2

Kircher, Athanasius 1602-1680 .... **LC 121**
See also DLB 164

Kirk, Russell (Amos) 1918-1994 .. **TCLC 119**
See also AITN 1; CA 1-4R; 145; CAAS 9; CANR 1, 20, 60; HGG; INT CANR-20; MTCW 1, 2

Kirkham, Dinah
See Card, Orson Scott

Kirkland, Caroline M. 1801-1864 . **NCLC 85**
See also DLB 3, 73, 74, 250, 254; DLBD 13

Kirkup, James 1918-2009 .... **CLC 1**
See also CA 1-4R; CAAS 4; CANR 2; CP 1, 2, 3, 4, 5, 6, 7; DLB 27; SATA 12

Kirkwood, James 1930(?)-1989 .... **CLC 9**
See also AITN 2; CA 1-4R; 128; CANR 6, 40; GLL 2

Kirsch, Sarah 1935- .... **CLC 176**
See also CA 178; CWW 2; DLB 75; EWL 3

Kirshner, Sidney
See Kingsley, Sidney

Kis, Danilo 1935-1989 .... **CLC 57**
See also CA 109; 118; 129; CANR 61; CDWLB 4; DLB 181; EWL 3; MTCW 1; RGSF 2; RGWL 2, 3

Kissinger, Henry A(lfred) 1923- ..... **CLC 137**
See also CA 1-4R; CANR 2, 33, 66, 109; MTCW 1

Kittel, Frederick August
See Wilson, August

Kivi, Aleksis 1834-1872 .... **NCLC 30**

Kizer, Carolyn 1925- ..... **CLC 15, 39, 80; PC 66**
See also CA 65-68; CAAS 5; CANR 24, 70, 134; CP 1, 2, 3, 4, 5, 6, 7; CWP; DAM POET; DLB 5, 169; EWL 3; MAL 5; MTCW 2; MTFW 2005; PFS 18; TCLE 1:1

Klabund 1890-1928 .... **TCLC 44**
See also CA 162; DLB 66

Klappert, Peter 1942- .... **CLC 57**
See also CA 33-36R; CSW; DLB 5

Klausner, Amos
See Oz, Amos

Klein, A(braham) M(oses)
1909-1972 .... **CLC 19**
See also CA 101; 37-40R; CP 1; DAB; DAC; DAM MST; DLB 68; EWL 3; RGEL 2; RGHL

Klein, Joe
See Klein, Joseph

Klein, Joseph 1946- .... **CLC 154**
See also CA 85-88; CANR 55, 164

Klein, Norma 1938-1989 .... **CLC 30**
See also AAYA 2, 35; BPFB 2; BYA 6, 7, 8; CA 41-44R; 128; CANR 15, 37; CLR 2, 19; INT CANR-15; JRDA; MAICYA 1, 2; SAAS 1; SATA 7, 57; WYA; YAW

Klein, T.E.D. 1947- .... **CLC 34**
See also CA 119; CANR 44, 75, 167; HGG

Klein, Theodore Eibon Donald
See Klein, T.E.D.

Kleist, Heinrich von 1777-1811 .... **DC 29; NCLC 2, 37; SSC 22**
See also CDWLB 2; DAM DRAM; DLB 90; EW 5; RGSF 2; RGWL 2, 3

Klima, Ivan 1931- .... **CLC 56, 172**
See also CA 25-28R; CANR 17, 50, 91; CDWLB 4; CWW 2; DAM NOV; DLB 232; EWL 3; RGWL 3

Klimentev, Andrei Platonovich
See Klimentov, Andrei Platonovich

Krylov, Ivan Andreevich
1768(?)-1844 .... **NCLC 1**
See also DLB 150

Kubin, Alfred (Leopold Isidor)
1877-1959 .... **TCLC 23**
See also CA 112; 149; CANR 104; DLB 81

Kubrick, Stanley 1928-1999 .... **CLC 16;**
TCLC 112
See also AAYA 30; CA 81-84; 177; CANR
33; DLB 26

Kueng, Hans
See Kung, Hans

Kumin, Maxine 1925- .... **CLC 5, 13, 28, 164;**
PC 15
See also AITN 2; AMWS 4; ANW; CA
1-4R, 271; CAAE 271; CAAS 8; CANR
1, 21, 69, 115, 140; CP 2, 3, 4, 5, 6, 7;
CWP; DA3; DAM POET; DLB 5; EWL
3; EXPP; MTCW 1, 2; MTFW 2005;
PAB; PFS 18; SATA 12

Kundera, Milan 1929- . **CLC 4, 9, 19, 32, 68,**
115, 135, 234; SSC 24
See also AAYA 2, 62; BPFB 2; CA 85-88;
CANR 19, 52, 74, 144; CDWLB 4; CWW
2; DA3; DAM NOV; DLB 232; EW 13;
EWL 3; MTCW 1, 2; MTFW 2005; NFS
18, 27; RGSF 2; RGWL 3; SSFS 18

Kunene, Mazisi 1930-2006 .... **CLC 85**
See also BW 1, 3; CA 125; 252; CANR 81;
CP 1, 6, 7; DLB 117

Kunene, Mazisi Raymond
See Kunene, Mazisi

Kunene, Mazisi Raymond Fakazi Mngoni
See Kunene, Mazisi

Kung, Hans
See Kung, Hans

Kung, Hans 1928- .... **CLC 130**
See also CA 53-56; CANR 66, 134; MTCW
1, 2; MTFW 2005

Kunikida, Tetsuo
See Kunikida Doppo

Kunikida Doppo 1869(?)-1908 .... **TCLC 99**
See also DLB 180; EWL 3

Kunikida Tetsuo
See Kunikida Doppo

Kunitz, Stanley 1905-2006 ..... **CLC 6, 11, 14,**
148; PC 19
See also AMWS 3; CA 41-44R; 250; CANR
26, 57, 98; CP 1, 2, 3, 4, 5, 6, 7; DA3;
DLB 48; INT CANR-26; MAL 5; MTCW
1, 2; MTFW 2005; PFS 11; RGAL 4

Kunitz, Stanley Jasspon
See Kunitz, Stanley

Kunze, Reiner 1933- .... **CLC 10**
See also CA 93-96; CWW 2; DLB 75; EWL
3

Kuprin, Aleksander Ivanovich
1870-1938 .... **TCLC 5**
See also CA 104; 182; DLB 295; EWL 3

Kuprin, Aleksandr Ivanovich
See Kuprin, Aleksander Ivanovich

Kuprin, Alexandr Ivanovich
See Kuprin, Aleksander Ivanovich

Kureishi, Hanif 1954- .. **CLC 64, 135; DC 26**
See also BRWS 11; CA 139; CANR 113;
CBD; CD 5, 6; CN 6, 7; DLB 194, 245,
352; GLL 2; IDFW 4; WLIT 4; WWE 1

Kurosawa, Akira 1910-1998 ..... **CLC 16, 119**
See also AAYA 11, 64; CA 101; 170; CANR
46; DAM MULT

Kushner, Tony 1956- .... **CLC 81, 203; DC 10**
See also AAYA 61; AMWS 9; CA 144;
CAD; CANR 74, 130; CD 5, 6; DA3;
DAM DRAM; DFS 5; DLB 228; EWL 3;
GLL 1; LAIT 5; MAL 5; MTCW 2;
MTFW 2005; RGAL 4; RGHL; SATA 160

Kuttner, Henry 1915-1958 .... **TCLC 10**
See also CA 107; 157; DLB 8; FANT;
SCFW 1, 2; SFW 4

Kutty, Madhavi
See Das, Kamala

Kuzma, Greg 1944- .... **CLC 7**
See also CA 33-36R; CANR 70

Kuzmin, Mikhail (Alekseevich)
1872(?)-1936 .... **TCLC 40**
See also CA 170; DLB 295; EWL 3

Kyd, Thomas 1558-1594 .. **DC 3; LC 22, 125**
See also BRW 1; DAM DRAM; DFS 21;
DLB 62; IDTP; LMFS 1; RGEL 2; TEA;
WLIT 3

Kyprianos, Iossif
See Samarakis, Antonis

L. S.
See Stephen, Sir Leslie

Labe, Louise 1521-1566 .... **LC 120**
See also DLB 327

Labrunie, Gerard
See Nerval, Gerard de

La Bruyere, Jean de 1645-1696 .. **LC 17, 168**
See also DLB 268; EW 3; GFL Beginnings
to 1789

LaBute, Neil 1963- .... **CLC 225**
See also CA 240

Lacan, Jacques (Marie Emile)
1901-1981 .... **CLC 75**
See also CA 121; 104; DLB 296; EWL 3;
TWA

Laclos, Pierre-Ambroise Francois
1741-1803 .... **NCLC 4, 87**
See also DLB 313; EW 4; GFL Beginnings
to 1789; RGWL 2, 3

Lacolere, Francois
See Aragon, Louis

La Colere, Francois
See Aragon, Louis

La Deshabilleuse
See Simenon, Georges (Jacques Christian)

Lady Gregory
See Gregory, Lady Isabella Augusta (Persse)

Lady of Quality, A
See Bagnold, Enid

La Fayette, Marie-(Madelaine Pioche de la
Vergne) 1634-1693 .... **LC 2, 144**
See also DLB 268; GFL Beginnings to
1789; RGWL 2, 3

Lafayette, Marie-Madeleine
See La Fayette, Marie-(Madelaine Pioche
de la Vergne)

Lafayette, Rene
See Hubbard, L. Ron

La Flesche, Francis 1857(?)-1932 ...... **NNAL**
See also CA 144; CANR 83; DLB 175

La Fontaine, Jean de 1621-1695 .... **LC 50**
See also DLB 268; EW 3; GFL Beginnings
to 1789; MAICYA 1, 2; RGWL 2, 3;
SATA 18

LaForet, Carmen 1921-2004 .... **CLC 219**
See also CA 246; CWW 2; DLB 322; EWL
3

LaForet Diaz, Carmen
See LaForet, Carmen

Laforgue, Jules 1860-1887 . **NCLC 5, 53; PC**
14; SSC 20
See also DLB 217; EW 7; GFL 1789 to the
Present; RGWL 2, 3

Lagerkvist, Paer 1891-1974 ... **CLC 7, 10, 13,**
54; SSC 12; TCLC 144
See also CA 85-88; 49-52; DA3; DAM
DRAM, NOV; DLB 259, 331; EW 10;
EWL 3; MTCW 1, 2; MTFW 2005; RGSF
2; RGWL 2, 3; TWA

Lagerkvist, Paer Fabian
See Lagerkvist, Paer

Lagerkvist, Par
See Lagerkvist, Paer

Lagerloef, Selma
See Lagerlof, Selma

Lagerloef, Selma Ottiliana Lovisa
See Lagerlof, Selma

Lagerlof, Selma 1858-1940 .... **TCLC 4, 36**
See also CA 108; 188; CLR 7; DLB 259,
331; MTCW 2; RGWL 2, 3; SATA 15;
SSFS 18

Lagerlof, Selma Ottiliana Lovisa
See Lagerlof, Selma

La Guma, Alex 1925-1985 .. **BLCS; CLC 19;**
TCLC 140
See also AFW; BW 1, 3; CA 49-52; 118;
CANR 25, 81; CDWLB 3; CN 1, 2, 3;
CP 1; DAM NOV; DLB 117, 225; EWL
3; MTCW 1, 2; MTFW 2005; WLIT 2;
WWE 1

Lahiri, Jhumpa 1967- .... **SSC 96**
See also AAYA 56; CA 193; CANR 134,
184; DLB 323; MTFW 2005; SSFS 19,
27

Laidlaw, A. K.
See Grieve, C. M.

Lainez, Manuel Mujica
See Mujica Lainez, Manuel

Laing, R(onald) D(avid) 1927-1989 . **CLC 95**
See also CA 107; 129; CANR 34; MTCW 1

Laishley, Alex
See Booth, Martin

Lamartine, Alphonse (Marie Louis Prat) de
1790-1869 .... **NCLC 11, 190; PC 16**
See also DAM POET; DLB 217; GFL 1789
to the Present; RGWL 2, 3

Lamb, Charles 1775-1834 ..... **NCLC 10, 113;**
SSC 112; WLC 3
See also BRW 4; CDBLB 1789-1832; DA;
DAB; DAC; DAM MST; DLB 93, 107,
163; RGEL 2; SATA 17; TEA

Lamb, Lady Caroline 1785-1828 ... **NCLC 38**
See also DLB 116

Lamb, Mary Ann 1764-1847 ...... **NCLC 125;**
SSC 112
See also DLB 163; SATA 17

Lame Deer 1903(?)-1976 .... **NNAL**
See also CA 69-72

Lamming, George (William)
1927- . **BLC 1:2, 2:2; CLC 2, 4, 66, 144**
See also BW 2, 3; CA 85-88; CANR 26,
76; CDWLB 3; CN 1, 2, 3, 4, 5, 6, 7; CP
1; DAM MULT; DLB 125; EWL 3;
MTCW 1, 2; MTFW 2005; NFS 15;
RGEL 2

L'Amour, Louis 1908-1988 .... **CLC 25, 55**
See also AAYA 16; BEST 89:2;
BPFB 2; CA 1-4R; 125; CANR 3, 25, 40;
CPW; DA3; DAM NOV, POP; DLB 206;
DLBY 1980; MTCW 1, 2; MTFW 2005;
RGAL 4; TCWW 1, 2

Lampedusa, Giuseppe di
See Tomasi di Lampedusa, Giuseppe

Lampedusa, Giuseppe Tomasi di
See Tomasi di Lampedusa, Giuseppe

Lampman, Archibald 1861-1899 .. **NCLC 25,**
194
See also DLB 92; RGEL 2; TWA

Lancaster, Bruce 1896-1963 .... **CLC 36**
See also CA 9-10; CANR 70; CAP 1; SATA
9

Lanchester, John 1962- .... **CLC 99, 280**
See also CA 194; DLB 267

Landau, Mark Alexandrovich
See Aldanov, Mark (Alexandrovich)

Landau-Aldanov, Mark Alexandrovich
See Aldanov, Mark (Alexandrovich)

Landis, Jerry
See Simon, Paul

Landis, John 1950- .... **CLC 26**
See also CA 112; 122; CANR 128

Landolfi, Tommaso 1908-1979 .... **CLC 11, 49**
See also CA 127; 117; DLB 177; EWL 3

Mankiewicz, Herman (Jacob)
1897-1953 .... **TCLC 85**
See also CA 120; 169; DLB 26; IDFW 3, 4
Manley, (Mary) Delariviere
1672(?)-1724 .... **LC 1, 42**
See also DLB 39, 80; RGEL 2
Mann, Abel
See Creasey, John
Mann, Emily 1952- .... **DC 7**
See also CA 130; CAD; CANR 55; CD 5, 6; CWD; DLB 266
Mann, (Luiz) Heinrich 1871-1950 ... **TCLC 9**
See also CA 106; 164, 181; DLB 66, 118; EW 8; EWL 3; RGWL 2, 3
Mann, (Paul) Thomas 1875-1955 . **SSC 5, 80, 82; TCLC 2, 8, 14, 21, 35, 44, 60, 168; WLC 4**
See also BPFB 2; CA 104; 128; CANR 133; CDWLB 2; DA; DA3; DAB; DAC; DAM MST, NOV; DLB 66, 331; EW 9; EWL 3; GLL 1; LATS 1:1; LMFS 1; MTCW 1, 2; MTFW 2005; NFS 17; RGSF 2; RGWL 2, 3; SSFS 4, 9; TWA
Mannheim, Karl 1893-1947 .... **TCLC 65**
See also CA 204
Manning, David
See Faust, Frederick
Manning, Frederic 1882-1935 .... **TCLC 25**
See also CA 124; 216; DLB 260
Manning, Olivia 1915-1980 .... **CLC 5, 19**
See also CA 5-8R; 101; CANR 29; CN 1, 2; EWL 3; FW; MTCW 1; RGEL 2
Mannyng, Robert c. 1264-c. 1340 .... **CMLC 83**
See also DLB 146
Mano, D. Keith 1942- .... **CLC 2, 10**
See also CA 25-28R; CAAS 6; CANR 26, 57; DLB 6
Mansfield, Katherine
See Beauchamp, Kathleen Mansfield
Manso, Peter 1940- .... **CLC 39**
See also CA 29-32R; CANR 44, 156
Mantecon, Juan Jimenez
See Jimenez (Mantecon), Juan Ramon
Mantel, Hilary 1952- .... **CLC 144**
See also CA 125; CANR 54, 101, 161; CN 5, 6, 7; DLB 271; RHW
Mantel, Hilary Mary
See Mantel, Hilary
Manton, Peter
See Creasey, John
Man Without a Spleen, A
See Chekhov, Anton (Pavlovich)
Manzano, Juan Franciso
1797(?)-1854 .... **NCLC 155**
Manzoni, Alessandro 1785-1873 ... **NCLC 29, 98**
See also EW 5; RGWL 2, 3; TWA; WLIT 7
Map, Walter 1140-1209 .... **CMLC 32**
Mapu, Abraham (ben Jekutiel)
1808-1867 .... **NCLC 18**
Mara, Sally
See Queneau, Raymond
Maracle, Lee 1950- .... **NNAL**
See also CA 149
Marat, Jean Paul 1743-1793 .... **LC 10**
Marcel, Gabriel Honore 1889-1973 . **CLC 15**
See also CA 102; 45-48; EWL 3; MTCW 1, 2
March, William
See Campbell, William Edward March
Marchbanks, Samuel
See Davies, Robertson
Marchi, Giacomo
See Bassani, Giorgio
Marcus Aurelius
See Aurelius, Marcus

Marcuse, Herbert 1898-1979 .... **TCLC 207**
See also CA 188; 89-92; DLB 242
Marguerite
See de Navarre, Marguerite
Marguerite d'Angouleme
See de Navarre, Marguerite
Marguerite de Navarre
See de Navarre, Marguerite
Margulies, Donald 1954- .... **CLC 76**
See also AAYA 57; CA 200; CD 6; DFS 13; DLB 228
Marias, Javier 1951- .... **CLC 239**
See also CA 167; CANR 109, 139; DLB 322; HW 2; MTFW 2005
Marie de France c. 12th cent. - ...... **CMLC 8, 111; PC 22**
See also DLB 208; FW; RGWL 2, 3
Marie de l'Incarnation 1599-1672 ..... **LC 10, 168**
Marier, Captain Victor
See Griffith, D.W.
Mariner, Scott
See Pohl, Frederik
Marinetti, Filippo Tommaso
1876-1944 .... **TCLC 10**
See also CA 107; DLB 114, 264; EW 9; EWL 3; WLIT 7
Marivaux, Pierre Carlet de Chamblain de
1688-1763 .... **DC 7; LC 4, 123**
See also DLB 314; GFL Beginnings to 1789; RGWL 2, 3; TWA
Markandaya, Kamala
See Taylor, Kamala
Markfield, Wallace (Arthur)
1926-2002 .... **CLC 8**
See also CA 69-72; 208; CAAS 3; CN 1, 2, 3, 4, 5, 6, 7; DLB 2, 28; DLBY 2002
Markham, Edwin 1852-1940 .... **TCLC 47**
See also CA 160; DLB 54, 186; MAL 5; RGAL 4
Markham, Robert
See Amis, Kingsley
Marks, J.
See Highwater, Jamake (Mamake)
Marks-Highwater, J.
See Highwater, Jamake (Mamake)
Markson, David M. 1927- .... **CLC 67**
See also AMWS 17; CA 49-52; CANR 1, 91, 158; CN 5, 6
Markson, David Merrill
See Markson, David M.
Marlatt, Daphne (Buckle) 1942- .... **CLC 168**
See also CA 25-28R; CANR 17, 39; CN 6, 7; CP 4, 5, 6, 7; CWP; DLB 60; FW
Marley, Bob
See Marley, Robert Nesta
Marley, Robert Nesta 1945-1981 ...... **CLC 17**
See also CA 107; 103
Marlowe, Christopher 1564-1593 . **DC 1; LC 22, 47, 117; PC 57; WLC 4**
See also BRW 1; BRWR 1; CDBLB Before 1660; DA; DA3; DAB; DAC; DAM DRAM, MST; DFS 1, 5, 13, 21; DLB 62; EXPP; LMFS 1; PFS 22; RGEL 2; TEA; WLIT 3
Marlowe, Stephen 1928-2008 .... **CLC 70**
See also CA 13-16R; 269; CANR 6, 55; CMW 4; SFW 4
Marmion, Shakerley 1603-1639 .... **LC 89**
See also DLB 58; RGEL 2
Marmontel, Jean-Francois 1723-1799 .. **LC 2**
See also DLB 314
Maron, Monika 1941- .... **CLC 165**
See also CA 201
Marot, Clement c. 1496-1544 .... **LC 133**
See also DLB 327; GFL Beginnings to 1789

Marquand, John P(hillips)
1893-1960 .... **CLC 2, 10**
See also AMW; BPFB 2; CA 85-88; CANR 73; CMW 4; DLB 9, 102; EWL 3; MAL 5; MTCW 2; RGAL 4
Marques, Rene 1919-1979 .. **CLC 96; HLC 2**
See also CA 97-100; 85-88; CANR 78; DAM MULT; DLB 305; EWL 3; HW 1, 2; LAW; RGSF 2
Marquez, Gabriel Garcia
See Garcia Marquez, Gabriel
Marquis, Don(ald Robert Perry)
1878-1937 .... **TCLC 7**
See also CA 104; 166; DLB 11, 25; MAL 5; RGAL 4
Marquis de Sade
See Sade, Donatien Alphonse Francois
Marric, J. J.
See Creasey, John
Marryat, Frederick 1792-1848 .... **NCLC 3**
See also DLB 21, 163; RGEL 2; WCH
Marsden, James
See Creasey, John
Marsh, Edward 1872-1953 .... **TCLC 99**
Marsh, (Edith) Ngaio 1895-1982 .. **CLC 7, 53**
See also CA 9-12R; CANR 6, 58; CMW 4; CN 1, 2, 3; CPW; DAM POP; DLB 77; MSW; MTCW 1, 2; RGEL 2; TEA
Marshall, Alan
See Westlake, Donald E.
Marshall, Allen
See Westlake, Donald E.
Marshall, Garry 1934- .... **CLC 17**
See also AAYA 3; CA 111; SATA 60
Marshall, Paule 1929- ..... **BLC 1:3, 2:3; CLC 27, 72, 253; SSC 3**
See also AFAW 1, 2; AMWS 11; BPFB 2; BW 2, 3; CA 77-80; CANR 25, 73, 129; CN 1, 2, 3, 4, 5, 6, 7; DA3; DAM MULT; DLB 33, 157, 227; EWL 3; LATS 1:2; MAL 5; MTCW 1, 2; MTFW 2005; RGAL 4; SSFS 15
Marshallik
See Zangwill, Israel
Marsilius of Inghen c. 1340-1396 .... **CMLC 106**
Marsten, Richard
See Hunter, Evan
Marston, John 1576-1634 .... **LC 33, 172**
See also BRW 2; DAM DRAM; DLB 58, 172; RGEL 2
Martel, Yann 1963- .... **CLC 192**
See also AAYA 67; CA 146; CANR 114; DLB 326, 334; MTFW 2005; NFS 27
Martens, Adolphe-Adhemar
See Ghelderode, Michel de
Martha, Henry
See Harris, Mark
Marti, Jose 1853-1895 ..... **HLC 2; NCLC 63; PC 76**
See also DAM MULT; DLB 290; HW 2; LAW; RGWL 2, 3; WLIT 1
Martial c. 40-c. 104 .... **CMLC 35; PC 10**
See also AW 2; CDWLB 1; DLB 211; RGWL 2, 3
Martin, Ken
See Hubbard, L. Ron
Martin, Richard
See Creasey, John
Martin, Steve 1945- .... **CLC 30, 217**
See also AAYA 53; CA 97-100; CANR 30, 100, 140; DFS 19; MTCW 1; MTFW 2005
Martin, Valerie 1948- .... **CLC 89**
See also BEST 90:2; CA 85-88; CANR 49, 89, 165
Martin, Violet Florence 1862-1915 .. **SSC 56; TCLC 51**

Martin, Webber
See Silverberg, Robert
Martindale, Patrick Victor
See White, Patrick (Victor Martindale)
Martin du Gard, Roger
1881-1958 .... **TCLC 24**
See also CA 118; CANR 94; DLB 65, 331;
EWL 3; GFL 1789 to the Present; RGWL
2, 3
Martineau, Harriet 1802-1876 ...... **NCLC 26,**
137
See also DLB 21, 55, 159, 163, 166, 190;
FW; RGEL 2; YABC 2
Martines, Julia
See O'Faolain, Julia
Martinez, Enrique Gonzalez
See Gonzalez Martinez, Enrique
Martinez, Jacinto Benavente y
See Benavente (y Martinez), Jacinto
Martinez de la Rosa, Francisco de Paula
1787-1862 .... **NCLC 102**
See also TWA
Martinez Ruiz, Jose 1873-1967 .... **CLC 11**
See also CA 93-96; DLB 322; EW 3; EWL
3; HW 1
Martinez Sierra, Gregorio
See Martinez Sierra, Maria
Martinez Sierra, Gregorio
1881-1947 .... **TCLC 6**
See also CA 115; EWL 3
Martinez Sierra, Maria 1874-1974 .. **TCLC 6**
See also CA 250; 115; EWL 3
Martinsen, Martin
See Follett, Ken
Martinson, Harry (Edmund)
1904-1978 .... **CLC 14**
See also CA 77-80; CANR 34, 130; DLB
259, 331; EWL 3
Marti y Perez, Jose Julian
See Marti, Jose
Martyn, Edward 1859-1923 .... **TCLC 131**
See also CA 179; DLB 10; RGEL 2
Marut, Ret
See Traven, B.
Marut, Robert
See Traven, B.
Marvell, Andrew 1621-1678 .... **LC 4, 43; PC**
10, 86; WLC 4
See also BRW 2; BRWR 2; CDBLB 1660-
1789; DA; DAB; DAC; DAM MST,
POET; DLB 131; EXPP; PFS 5; RGEL 2;
TEA; WP
Marx, Karl (Heinrich)
1818-1883 .... **NCLC 17, 114**
See also DLB 129; LATS 1:1; TWA
Masaoka, Shiki -1902
See Masaoka, Tsunenori
Masaoka, Tsunenori 1867-1902 ..... **TCLC 18**
See also CA 117; 191; EWL 3; RGWL 3;
TWA
Masaoka Shiki
See Masaoka, Tsunenori
Masefield, John (Edward)
1878-1967 .... **CLC 11, 47; PC 78**
See also CA 19-20; 25-28R; CANR 33;
CAP 2; CDBLB 1890-1914; DAM POET;
DLB 10, 19, 153, 160; EWL 3; EXPP;
FANT; MTCW 1, 2; PFS 5; RGEL 2;
SATA 19
Maso, Carole 1955(?)- .... **CLC 44**
See also CA 170; CANR 148; CN 7; GLL
2; RGAL 4
Mason, Bobbie Ann 1940- ... **CLC 28, 43, 82,**
154; SSC 4, 101
See also AAYA 5, 42; AMWS 8; BPFB 2;
CA 53-56; CANR 11, 31, 58, 83, 125,
169; CDALBS; CN 5, 6, 7; CSW; DA3;
DLB 173; DLBY 1987; EWL 3; EXPS;

INT CANR-31; MAL 5; MTCW 1, 2;
MTFW 2005; NFS 4; RGAL 4; RGSF 2;
SSFS 3, 8, 20; TCLE 1:2; YAW
Mason, Ernst
See Pohl, Frederik
Mason, Hunni B.
See Sternheim, (William Adolf) Carl
Mason, Lee W.
See Malzberg, Barry N(athaniel)
Mason, Nick 1945- .... **CLC 35**
Mason, Tally
See Derleth, August (William)
Mass, Anna .... **CLC 59**
Mass, William
See Gibson, William
Massinger, Philip 1583-1640 .... **LC 70**
See also BRWS 11; DLB 58; RGEL 2
Master Lao
See Lao Tzu
Masters, Edgar Lee 1868-1950 ...... **PC 1, 36;**
TCLC 2, 25; WLCS
See also AMWS 1; CA 104; 133; CDALB
1865-1917; DA; DAC; DAM MST,
POET; DLB 54; EWL 3; EXPP; MAL 5;
MTCW 1, 2; MTFW 2005; RGAL 4;
TUS; WP
Masters, Hilary 1928- .... **CLC 48**
See also CA 25-28R; 217; CAAE 217;
CANR 13, 47, 97, 171; CN 6, 7; DLB
244
Masters, Hilary Thomas
See Masters, Hilary
Mastrosimone, William 1947- .... **CLC 36**
See also CA 186; CAD; CD 5, 6
Mathe, Albert
See Camus, Albert
Mather, Cotton 1663-1728 .... **LC 38**
See also AMWS 2; CDALB 1640-1865;
DLB 24, 30, 140; RGAL 4; TUS
Mather, Increase 1639-1723 .... **LC 38, 161**
See also DLB 24
Mathers, Marshall
See Eminem
Mathers, Marshall Bruce
See Eminem
Matheson, Richard 1926- .... **CLC 37, 267**
See also AAYA 31; CA 97-100; CANR 88,
99; DLB 8, 44; HGG; INT CA-97-100;
SCFW 1, 2; SFW 4; SUFW 2
Matheson, Richard Burton
See Matheson, Richard
Mathews, Harry 1930- .... **CLC 6, 52**
See also CA 21-24R; CAAS 6; CANR 18,
40, 98, 160; CN 5, 6, 7
Mathews, John Joseph 1894-1979 .. **CLC 84;**
NNAL
See also CA 19-20; 142; CANR 45; CAP 2;
DAM MULT; DLB 175; TCWW 1, 2
Mathias, Roland 1915-2007 .... **CLC 45**
See also CA 97-100; 263; CANR 19, 41;
CP 1, 2, 3, 4, 5, 6, 7; DLB 27
Mathias, Roland Glyn
See Mathias, Roland
Matsuo Basho 1644(?)-1694 ...... **LC 62; PC 3**
See also DAM POET; PFS 2, 7, 18; RGWL
2, 3; WP
Mattheson, Rodney
See Creasey, John
Matthew, James
See Barrie, J(ames) M(atthew)
Matthew of Vendome c. 1130-c.
1200 .... **CMLC 99**
See also DLB 208
Matthews, (James) Brander
1852-1929 .... **TCLC 95**
See also CA 181; DLB 71, 78; DLBD 13
Matthews, Greg 1949- .... **CLC 45**
See also CA 135

Matthews, William (Procter III)
1942-1997 .... **CLC 40**
See also AMWS 9; CA 29-32R; 162; CAAS
18; CANR 12, 57; CP 2, 3, 4, 5, 6; DLB
5
Matthias, John (Edward) 1941- .... **CLC 9**
See also CA 33-36R; CANR 56; CP 4, 5, 6,
7
Matthiessen, F(rancis) O(tto)
1902-1950 .... **TCLC 100**
See also CA 185; DLB 63; MAL 5
Matthiessen, Peter 1927- ... **CLC 5, 7, 11, 32,**
64, 245
See also AAYA 6, 40; AMWS 5; ANW;
BEST 90:4; BPFB 2; CA 9-12R; CANR
21, 50, 73, 100, 138; CN 1, 2, 3, 4, 5, 6,
7; DA3; DAM NOV; DLB 6, 173, 275;
MAL 5; MTCW 1, 2; MTFW 2005; SATA
27
Maturin, Charles Robert
1780(?)-1824 .... **NCLC 6, 169**
See also BRWS 8; DLB 178; GL 3; HGG;
LMFS 1; RGEL 2; SUFW
Matute (Ausejo), Ana Maria 1925- .. **CLC 11**
See also CA 89-92; CANR 129; CWW 2;
DLB 322; EWL 3; MTCW 1; RGSF 2
Maugham, W. S.
See Maugham, W(illiam) Somerset
Maugham, W(illiam) Somerset
1874-1965 .. **CLC 1, 11, 15, 67, 93; SSC**
8, 94; TCLC 208; WLC 4
See also AAYA 55; BPFB 2; BRW 6; CA
5-8R; 25-28R; CANR 40, 127; CDBLB
1914-1945; CMW 4; DA; DA3; DAB;
DAC; DAM DRAM, MST, NOV; DFS
22; DLB 10, 36, 77, 100, 162, 195; EWL
3; LAIT 3; MTCW 1, 2; MTFW 2005;
NFS 23; RGEL 2; RGSF 2; SATA 54;
SSFS 17
Maugham, William Somerset
See Maugham, W(illiam) Somerset
Maupassant, (Henri Rene Albert) Guy de
1850-1893 . **NCLC 1, 42, 83; SSC 1, 64;**
WLC 4
See also BYA 14; DA; DA3; DAB; DAC;
DAM MST; DLB 123; EW 7; EXPS; GFL
1789 to the Present; LAIT 2; LMFS 1;
RGSF 2; RGWL 2, 3; SSFS 4, 21; SUFW;
TWA
Maupin, Armistead 1944- .... **CLC 95**
See also CA 125; 130; CANR 58, 101, 183;
CPW; DA3; DAM POP; DLB 278; GLL
1; INT CA-130; MTCW 2; MTFW 2005
Maupin, Armistead Jones, Jr.
See Maupin, Armistead
Maurhut, Richard
See Traven, B.
Mauriac, Claude 1914-1996 .... **CLC 9**
See also CA 89-92; 152; CWW 2; DLB 83;
EWL 3; GFL 1789 to the Present
Mauriac, Francois (Charles)
1885-1970 .... **CLC 4, 9, 56; SSC 24**
See also CA 25-28; CAP 2; DLB 65, 331;
EW 10; EWL 3; GFL 1789 to the Present;
MTCW 1, 2; MTFW 2005; RGWL 2, 3;
TWA
Mavor, Osborne Henry 1888-1951 .. **TCLC 3**
See also CA 104; DLB 10; EWL 3
Maxwell, Glyn 1962- .... **CLC 238**
See also CA 154; CANR 88, 183; CP 6, 7;
PFS 23
Maxwell, William (Keepers, Jr.)
1908-2000 .... **CLC 19**
See also AMWS 8; CA 93-96; 189; CANR
54, 95; CN 1, 2, 3, 4, 5, 6, 7; DLB 218,
278; DLBY 1980; INT CA-93-96; MAL
5; SATA-Obit 128
May, Elaine 1932- .... **CLC 16**
See also CA 124; 142; CAD; CWD; DLB
44

Merrill, James Ingram
See Merrill, James
Merriman, Alex
See Silverberg, Robert
Merriman, Brian 1747-1805 .... **NCLC 70**
Merritt, E. B.
See Waddington, Miriam
Merton, Thomas (James)
1915-1968 . **CLC 1, 3, 11, 34, 83; PC 10**
See also AAYA 61; AMWS 8; CA 5-8R;
25-28R; CANR 22, 53, 111, 131; DA3;
DLB 48; DLBY 1981; MAL 5; MTCW 1,
2; MTFW 2005
Merwin, W.S. 1927- ..... **CLC 1, 2, 3, 5, 8, 13,
18, 45, 88; PC 45**
See also AMWS 3; CA 13-16R; CANR 15,
51, 112, 140; CP 1, 2, 3, 4, 5, 6, 7; DA3;
DAM POET; DLB 5, 169, 342; EWL 3;
INT CANR-15; MAL 5; MTCW 1, 2;
MTFW 2005; PAB; PFS 5, 15; RGAL 4
Metastasio, Pietro 1698-1782 .... **LC 115**
See also RGWL 2, 3
Metcalf, John 1938- .... **CLC 37; SSC 43**
See also CA 113; CN 4, 5, 6, 7; DLB 60;
RGSF 2; TWA
Metcalf, Suzanne
See Baum, L(yman) Frank
Mew, Charlotte (Mary) 1870-1928 .. **TCLC 8**
See also CA 105; 189; DLB 19, 135; RGEL
2
Mewshaw, Michael 1943- .... **CLC 9**
See also CA 53-56; CANR 7, 47, 147;
DLBY 1980
Meyer, Conrad Ferdinand
1825-1898 .... **NCLC 81; SSC 30**
See also DLB 129; EW; RGWL 2, 3
Meyer, Gustav 1868-1932 .... **TCLC 21**
See also CA 117; 190; DLB 81; EWL 3
Meyer, June
See Jordan, June
Meyer, Lynn
See Slavitt, David R.
Meyer, Stephenie 1973- .... **CLC 280**
See also AAYA 77; CA 253; CANR 192;
CLR 142; SATA 193
Meyer-Meyrink, Gustav
See Meyer, Gustav
Meyers, Jeffrey 1939- .... **CLC 39**
See also CA 73-76, 186; CAAE 186; CANR
54, 102, 159; DLB 111
**Meynell, Alice (Christina Gertrude
Thompson)** 1847-1922 .... **TCLC 6**
See also CA 104; 177; DLB 19, 98; RGEL
2
Meyrink, Gustav
See Meyer, Gustav
Mhlophe, Gcina 1960- .... **BLC 2:3**
Michaels, Leonard 1933-2003 ..... **CLC 6, 25;
SSC 16**
See also AMWS 16; CA 61-64; 216; CANR
21, 62, 119, 179; CN 3, 45, 6, 7; DLB
130; MTCW 1; TCLE 1:2
Michaux, Henri 1899-1984 .... **CLC 8, 19**
See also CA 85-88; 114; DLB 258; EWL 3;
GFL 1789 to the Present; RGWL 2, 3
Micheaux, Oscar (Devereaux)
1884-1951 .... **TCLC 76**
See also BW 3; CA 174; DLB 50; TCWW
2
Michelangelo 1475-1564 .... **LC 12**
See also AAYA 43
Michelet, Jules 1798-1874 ...... **NCLC 31, 218**
See also EW 5; GFL 1789 to the Present
Michels, Robert 1876-1936 .... **TCLC 88**
See also CA 212

Michener, James A. 1907(?)-1997 . **CLC 1, 5,
11, 29, 60, 109**
See also AAYA 27; AITN 1; BEST 90:1;
BPFB 2; CA 5-8R; 161; CANR 21, 45,
68; CN 1, 2, 3, 4, 5, 6; CPW; DA3; DAM
NOV, POP; DLB 6; MAL 5; MTCW 1, 2;
MTFW 2005; RHW; TCWW 1, 2
Mickiewicz, Adam 1798-1855 . **NCLC 3, 101;
PC 38**
See also EW 5; RGWL 2, 3
Middleton, (John) Christopher
1926- .... **CLC 13**
See also CA 13-16R; CANR 29, 54, 117;
CP 1, 2, 3, 4, 5, 6, 7; DLB 40
Middleton, Richard (Barham)
1882-1911 .... **TCLC 56**
See also CA 187; DLB 156; HGG
Middleton, Stanley 1919-2009 ...... **CLC 7, 38**
See also CA 25-28R; CAAS 23; CANR 21,
46, 81, 157; CN 1, 2, 3, 4, 5, 6, 7; DLB
14, 326
Middleton, Thomas 1580-1627 ...... **DC 5; LC
33, 123**
See also BRW 2; DAM DRAM, MST; DFS
18, 22; DLB 58; RGEL 2
Mieville, China 1972(?)- .... **CLC 235**
See also AAYA 52; CA 196; CANR 138;
MTFW 2005
Migueis, Jose Rodrigues 1901-1980 . **CLC 10**
See also DLB 287
Mihura, Miguel 1905-1977 .... **DC 34**
See also CA 214
Mikszath, Kalman 1847-1910 .... **TCLC 31**
See also CA 170
Miles, Jack .... **CLC 100**
See also CA 200
Miles, John Russiano
See Miles, Jack
Miles, Josephine (Louise)
1911-1985 .... **CLC 1, 2, 14, 34, 39**
See also CA 1-4R; 116; CANR 2, 55; CP 1,
2, 3, 4; DAM POET; DLB 48; MAL 5;
TCLE 1:2
Militant
See Sandburg, Carl (August)
Mill, Harriet (Hardy) Taylor
1807-1858 .... **NCLC 102**
See also FW
Mill, John Stuart 1806-1873 ... **NCLC 11, 58,
179**
See also CDBLB 1832-1890; DLB 55, 190,
262; FW 1; RGEL 2; TEA
Millar, Kenneth 1915-1983 .. **CLC 1, 2, 3, 14,
34, 41**
See also AMWS 4; BPFB 2; CA 9-12R;
110; CANR 16, 63, 107; CMW 4; CN 1,
2, 3; CPW; DA3; DAM POP; DLB 2,
226; DLBD 6; DLBY 1983; MAL 5;
MSW; MTCW 1, 2; MTFW 2005; RGAL
4
Millay, E. Vincent
See Millay, Edna St. Vincent
Millay, Edna St. Vincent 1892-1950 ..... **PC 6,
61; TCLC 4, 49, 169; WLCS**
See also AMW; CA 104; 130; CDALB
1917-1929; DA; DA3; DAB; DAC; DAM
MST, POET; DLB 45, 249; EWL 3;
EXPP; FL 1:6; GLL 1; MAL 5; MBL;
MTCW 1, 2; MTFW 2005; PAB; PFS 3,
17, 31; RGAL 4; TUS; WP
Miller, Arthur 1915-2005 ..... **CLC 1, 2, 6, 10,
15, 26, 47, 78, 179; DC 1, 31; WLC 4**
See also AAYA 15; AITN 1; AMW; AMWC
1; CA 1-4R; 236; CABS 3; CAD; CANR
2, 30, 54, 76, 132; CD 5, 6; CDALB
1941-1968; DA; DA3; DAB; DAC; DAM
DRAM, MST; DFS 1, 3, 8; DLB 7, 266;
EWL 3; LAIT 1, 4; LATS 1:2; MAL 5;
MTCW 1, 2; MTFW 2005; RGAL 4;
RGHL; TUS; WYAS 1

Miller, Frank 1957- .... **CLC 278**
See also AAYA 45; CA 224
Miller, Henry (Valentine)
1891-1980 .... **CLC 1, 2, 4, 9, 14, 43, 84;
TCLC 213; WLC 4**
See also AMW; BPFB 2; CA 9-12R; 97-
100; CANR 33, 64; CDALB 1929-1941;
CN 1, 2; DA; DA3; DAB; DAC; DAM
MST, NOV; DLB 4, 9; DLBY 1980; EWL
3; MAL 5; MTCW 1, 2; MTFW 2005;
RGAL 4; TUS
Miller, Hugh 1802-1856 .... **NCLC 143**
See also DLB 190
Miller, Jason 1939(?)-2001 .... **CLC 2**
See also AITN 1; CA 73-76; 197; CAD;
CANR 130; DFS 12; DLB 7
Miller, Sue 1943- .... **CLC 44**
See also AMWS 12; BEST 90:3; CA 139;
CANR 59, 91, 128, 194; DA3; DAM
POP; DLB 143
Miller, Walter M(ichael, Jr.)
1923-1996 .... **CLC 4, 30**
See also BPFB 2; CA 85-88; CANR 108;
DLB 8; SCFW 1, 2; SFW 4
Millett, Kate 1934- .... **CLC 67**
See also AITN 1; CA 73-76; CANR 32, 53,
76, 110; DA3; DLB 246; FW; GLL 1;
MTCW 1, 2; MTFW 2005
Millhauser, Steven 1943- ... **CLC 21, 54, 109;
SSC 57**
See also AAYA 76; CA 110; 111; CANR
63, 114, 133, 189; CN 6, 7; DA3; DLB 2,
350; FANT; INT CA-111; MAL 5; MTCW
2; MTFW 2005
Millhauser, Steven Lewis
See Millhauser, Steven
Millin, Sarah Gertrude 1889-1968 ... **CLC 49**
See also CA 102; 93-96; DLB 225; EWL 3
Milne, A. A. 1882-1956 .... **TCLC 6, 88**
See also BRWS 5; CA 104; 133; CLR 1,
26, 108; CMW 4; CWRI 5; DA3; DAB;
DAC; DAM MST; DLB 10, 77, 100, 160,
352; FANT; MAICYA 1, 2; MTCW 1, 2;
MTFW 2005; RGEL 2; SATA 100; WCH;
YABC 1
Milne, Alan Alexander
See Milne, A. A.
Milner, Ron(ald) 1938-2004 .. **BLC 1:3; CLC
56**
See also AITN 1; BW 1; CA 73-76; 230;
CAD; CANR 24, 81; CD 5, 6; DAM
MULT; DLB 38; MAL 5; MTCW 1
Milnes, Richard Monckton
1809-1885 .... **NCLC 61**
See also DLB 32, 184
Milosz, Czeslaw 1911-2004 .... **CLC 5, 11, 22,
31, 56, 82, 253; PC 8; WLCS**
See also AAYA 62; CA 81-84; 230; CANR
23, 51, 91, 126; CDWLB 4; CWW 2;
DA3; DAM MST, POET; DLB 215, 331;
EW 13; EWL 3; MTCW 1, 2; MTFW
2005; PFS 16, 29; RGHL; RGWL 2, 3
Milton, John 1608-1674 ..... **LC 9, 43, 92; PC
19, 29; WLC 4**
See also AAYA 65; BRW 2; BRWR 2; CD-
BLB 1660-1789; DA; DA3; DAB; DAC;
DAM MST, POET; DLB 131, 151, 281;
EFS 1; EXPP; LAIT 1; PAB; PFS 3, 17;
RGEL 2; TEA; WLIT 3; WP
Min, Anchee 1957- .... **CLC 86**
See also CA 146; CANR 94, 137; MTFW
2005
Minehaha, Cornelius
See Wedekind, Frank
Miner, Valerie 1947- .... **CLC 40**
See also CA 97-100; CANR 59, 177; FW;
GLL 2
Minimo, Duca
See D'Annunzio, Gabriele

Minot, Susan (Anderson) 1956- ...... **CLC 44, 159**
See also AMWS 6; CA 134; CANR 118; CN 6, 7

Minus, Ed 1938- .... **CLC 39**
See also CA 185

Mirabai 1498(?)-1550(?) .... **LC 143; PC 48**
See also PFS 24

Miranda, Javier
See Bioy Casares, Adolfo

Mirbeau, Octave 1848-1917 .... **TCLC 55**
See also CA 216; DLB 123, 192; GFL 1789 to the Present

Mirikitani, Janice 1942- .... **AAL**
See also CA 211; DLB 312; RGAL 4

Mirk, John (?)-c. 1414 .... **LC 105**
See also DLB 146

Miro (Ferrer), Gabriel (Francisco Victor) 1879-1930 .... **TCLC 5**
See also CA 104; 185; DLB 322; EWL 3

Misharin, Alexandr .... **CLC 59**

Mishima, Yukio
See Hiraoka, Kimitake

Mishima Yukio
See Hiraoka, Kimitake

Miss C. L. F.
See Grimke, Charlotte L. Forten

Mister X
See Hoch, Edward D.

Mistral, Frederic 1830-1914 .... **TCLC 51**
See also CA 122; 213; DLB 331; GFL 1789 to the Present

Mistral, Gabriela
See Godoy Alcayaga, Lucila

Mistry, Rohinton 1952- ... **CLC 71, 196, 281; SSC 73**
See also BRWS 10; CA 141; CANR 86, 114; CCA 1; CN 6, 7; DAC; DLB 334; SSFS 6

Mitchell, Clyde
See Ellison, Harlan; Silverberg, Robert

Mitchell, Emerson Blackhorse Barney 1945- .... **NNAL**
See also CA 45-48

Mitchell, James Leslie 1901-1935 .... **TCLC 4**
See also BRWS 14; CA 104; 188; DLB 15; RGEL 2

Mitchell, Joni 1943- .... **CLC 12**
See also CA 112; CCA 1

Mitchell, Joseph (Quincy) 1908-1996 .... **CLC 98**
See also CA 77-80; 152; CANR 69; CN 1, 2, 3, 4, 5, 6; CSW; DLB 185; DLBY 1996

Mitchell, Margaret (Munnerlyn) 1900-1949 .... **TCLC 11, 170**
See also AAYA 23; BPFB 2; BYA 1; CA 109; 125; CANR 55, 94; CDALBS; DA3; DAM NOV, POP; DLB 9; LAIT 2; MAL 5; MTCW 1, 2; MTFW 2005; NFS 9; RGAL 4; RHW; TUS; WYAS 1; YAW

Mitchell, Peggy
See Mitchell, Margaret (Munnerlyn)

Mitchell, S(ilas) Weir 1829-1914 .... **TCLC 36**
See also CA 165; DLB 202; RGAL 4

Mitchell, W(illiam) O(rmond) 1914-1998 .... **CLC 25**
See also CA 77-80; 165; CANR 15, 43; CN 1, 2, 3, 4, 5, 6; DAC; DAM MST; DLB 88; TCLE 1:2

Mitchell, William (Lendrum) 1879-1936 .... **TCLC 81**
See also CA 213

Mitford, Mary Russell 1787-1855 ... **NCLC 4**
See also DLB 110, 116; RGEL 2

Mitford, Nancy 1904-1973 .... **CLC 44**
See also BRWS 10; CA 9-12R; CN 1; DLB 191; RGEL 2

Miyamoto, (Chujo) Yuriko 1899-1951 .... **TCLC 37**
See also CA 170, 174; DLB 180

Miyamoto Yuriko
See Miyamoto, (Chujo) Yuriko

Miyazawa, Kenji 1896-1933 .... **TCLC 76**
See also CA 157; EWL 3; RGWL 3

Miyazawa Kenji
See Miyazawa, Kenji

Mizoguchi, Kenji 1898-1956 .... **TCLC 72**
See also CA 167

Mo, Timothy (Peter) 1950- ...... **CLC 46, 134**
See also CA 117; CANR 128; CN 5, 6, 7; DLB 194; MTCW 1; WLIT 4; WWE 1

Mo, Yan
See Yan, Mo

Moberg, Carl Arthur
See Moberg, Vilhelm

Moberg, Vilhelm 1898-1973 .... **TCLC 224**
See also CA 97-100; 45-48; CANR 135; DLB 259; EW 11; EWL 3

Modarressi, Taghi (M.) 1931-1997 ... **CLC 44**
See also CA 121; 134; INT CA-134

Modiano, Patrick (Jean) 1945- .... **CLC 18, 218**
See also CA 85-88; CANR 17, 40, 115; CWW 2; DLB 83, 299; EWL 3; RGHL

Mofolo, Thomas (Mokopu) 1875(?)-1948 .... **BLC 1:3; TCLC 22**
See also AFW; CA 121; 153; CANR 83; DAM MULT; DLB 225; EWL 3; MTCW 2; MTFW 2005; WLIT 2

Mohr, Nicholasa 1938- .... **CLC 12; HLC 2**
See also AAYA 8, 46; CA 49-52; CANR 1, 32, 64; CLR 22; DAM MULT; DLB 145; HW 1, 2; JRDA; LAIT 5; LLW; MAICYA 2; MAICYAS 1; RGAL 4; SAAS 8; SATA 8, 97; SATA-Essay 113; WYA; YAW

Moi, Toril 1953- .... **CLC 172**
See also CA 154; CANR 102; FW

Mojtabai, A(nn) G(race) 1938- ..... **CLC 5, 9, 15, 29**
See also CA 85-88; CANR 88

Moliere 1622-1673 ..... **DC 13; LC 10, 28, 64, 125, 127; WLC 4**
See also DA; DA3; DAB; DAC; DAM DRAM, MST; DFS 13, 18, 20; DLB 268; EW 3; GFL Beginnings to 1789; LATS 1:1; RGWL 2, 3; TWA

Molin, Charles
See Mayne, William (James Carter)

Molnar, Ferenc 1878-1952 .... **TCLC 20**
See also CA 109; 153; CANR 83; CDWLB 4; DAM DRAM; DLB 215; EWL 3; RGWL 2, 3

Momaday, N. Scott 1934- ...... **CLC 2, 19, 85, 95, 160; NNAL; PC 25; WLCS**
See also AAYA 11, 64; AMWS 4; ANW; BPFB 2; BYA 12; CA 25-28R; CANR 14, 34, 68, 134; CDALBS; CN 2, 3, 4, 5, 6, 7; CPW; DA; DA3; DAB; DAC; DAM MST, MULT, NOV, POP; DLB 143, 175, 256; EWL 3; EXPP; INT CANR-14; LAIT 4; LATS 1:2; MAL 5; MTCW 1, 2; MTFW 2005; NFS 10; PFS 2, 11; RGAL 4; SATA 48; SATA-Brief 30; TCWW 1, 2; WP; YAW

Momala, Ville i
See Moberg, Vilhelm

Monette, Paul 1945-1995 .... **CLC 82**
See also AMWS 10; CA 139; 147; CN 6; DLB 350; GLL 1

Monroe, Harriet 1860-1936 .... **TCLC 12**
See also CA 109; 204; DLB 54, 91

Monroe, Lyle
See Heinlein, Robert A.

Montagu, Elizabeth 1720-1800 .... **NCLC 7, 117**
See also FW

Montagu, Mary (Pierrepont) Wortley 1689-1762 .... **LC 9, 57; PC 16**
See also DLB 95, 101; FL 1:1; RGEL 2

Montagu, W. H.
See Coleridge, Samuel Taylor

Montague, John (Patrick) 1929- ..... **CLC 13, 46**
See also CA 9-12R; CANR 9, 69, 121; CP 1, 2, 3, 4, 5, 6, 7; DLB 40; EWL 3; MTCW 1; PFS 12; RGEL 2; TCLE 1:2

Montaigne, Michel (Eyquem) de 1533-1592 .... **LC 8, 105; WLC 4**
See also DA; DAB; DAC; DAM MST; DLB 327; EW 2; GFL Beginnings to 1789; LMFS 1; RGWL 2, 3; TWA

Montale, Eugenio 1896-1981 ... **CLC 7, 9, 18; PC 13**
See also CA 17-20R; 104; CANR 30; DLB 114, 331; EW 11; EWL 3; MTCW 1; PFS 22; RGWL 2, 3; TWA; WLIT 7

Montesquieu, Charles-Louis de Secondat 1689-1755 .... **LC 7, 69**
See also DLB 314; EW 3; GFL Beginnings to 1789; TWA

Montessori, Maria 1870-1952 ...... **TCLC 103**
See also CA 115; 147

Montgomery, Bruce 1921(?)-1978 .... **CLC 22**
See also CA 179; 104; CMW 4; DLB 87; MSW

Montgomery, L(ucy) M(aud) 1874-1942 .... **TCLC 51, 140**
See also AAYA 12; BYA 1; CA 108; 137; CLR 8, 91, 145; DA3; DAM MST; DLB 92; DLBD 14; JRDA; MAICYA 1, 2; MTCW 2; MTFW 2005; RGEL 2; SATA 100; TWA; WCH; WYA; YABC 1

Montgomery, Marion, Jr. 1925- .... **CLC 7**
See also AITN 1; CA 1-4R; CANR 3, 48, 162; CSW; DLB 6

Montgomery, Marion H. 1925-
See Montgomery, Marion, Jr.

Montgomery, Max
See Davenport, Guy (Mattison, Jr.)

Montgomery, Robert Bruce
See Montgomery, Bruce

Montherlant, Henry (Milon) de 1896-1972 .... **CLC 8, 19**
See also CA 85-88; 37-40R; DAM DRAM; DLB 72, 321; EW 11; EWL 3; GFL 1789 to the Present; MTCW 1

Monty Python
See Chapman, Graham; Cleese, John (Marwood); Gilliam, Terry; Idle, Eric; Jones, Terence Graham Parry; Palin, Michael

Moodie, Susanna (Strickland) 1803-1885 .... **NCLC 14, 113**
See also DLB 99

Moody, Hiram
See Moody, Rick

Moody, Hiram F. III
See Moody, Rick

Moody, Minerva
See Alcott, Louisa May

Moody, Rick 1961- .... **CLC 147**
See also CA 138; CANR 64, 112, 179; MTFW 2005

Moody, William Vaughan 1869-1910 .... **TCLC 105**
See also CA 110; 178; DLB 7, 54; MAL 5; RGAL 4

Mooney, Edward 1951- .... **CLC 25**
See also CA 130

Mooney, Ted
See Mooney, Edward

Moorcock, Michael 1939- ...... **CLC 5, 27, 58, 236**
See also AAYA 26; CA 45-48; CAAS 5; CANR 2, 17, 38, 64, 122; CN 5, 6, 7; DLB 14, 231, 261, 319; FANT; MTCW 1, 2; MTFW 2005; SATA 93, 166; SCFW 1, 2; SFW 4; SUFW 1, 2
Moorcock, Michael John
See Moorcock, Michael
Moorcock, Michael John
See Moorcock, Michael
Moore, Al
See Moore, Alan
Moore, Alan 1953- .... **CLC 230**
See also AAYA 51; CA 204; CANR 138, 184; DLB 261; MTFW 2005; SFW 4
Moore, Brian 1921-1999 ... **CLC 1, 3, 5, 7, 8, 19, 32, 90**
See also BRWS 9; CA 1-4R; 174; CANR 1, 25, 42, 63; CCA 1; CN 1, 2, 3, 4, 5, 6; DAB; DAC; DAM MST; DLB 251; EWL 3; FANT; MTCW 1, 2; MTFW 2005; RGEL 2
Moore, Edward
See Muir, Edwin
Moore, G. E. 1873-1958 .... **TCLC 89**
See also DLB 262
Moore, George Augustus 1852-1933 .... **SSC 19; TCLC 7**
See also BRW 6; CA 104; 177; DLB 10, 18, 57, 135; EWL 3; RGEL 2; RGSF 2
Moore, Lorrie
See Moore, Marie Lorena
Moore, Marianne (Craig) 1887-1972 .... **CLC 1, 2, 4, 8, 10, 13, 19, 47; PC 4, 49; WLCS**
See also AMW; CA 1-4R; 33-36R; CANR 3, 61; CDALB 1929-1941; CP 1; DA; DA3; DAB; DAC; DAM MST, POET; DLB 45; DLBD 7; EWL 3; EXPP; FL 1:6; MAL 5; MBL; MTCW 1, 2; MTFW 2005; PAB; PFS 14, 17; RGAL 4; SATA 20; TUS; WP
Moore, Marie Lorena 1957- ...... **CLC 39, 45, 68, 165**
See also AMWS 10; CA 116; CANR 39, 83, 139; CN 5, 6, 7; DLB 234; MTFW 2005; SSFS 19
Moore, Michael 1954- .... **CLC 218**
See also AAYA 53; CA 166; CANR 150
Moore, Thomas 1779-1852 .... **NCLC 6, 110**
See also DLB 96, 144; RGEL 2
Moorhouse, Frank 1938- .... **SSC 40**
See also CA 118; CANR 92; CN 3, 4, 5, 6, 7; DLB 289; RGSF 2
Mora, Pat 1942- .... **HLC 2**
See also AMWS 13; CA 129; CANR 57, 81, 112, 171; CLR 58; DAM MULT; DLB 209; HW 1, 2; LLW; MAICYA 2; MTFW 2005; SATA 92, 134, 186
Moraga, Cherrie 1952- ... **CLC 126, 250; DC 22**
See also CA 131; CANR 66, 154; DAM MULT; DLB 82, 249; FW; GLL 1; HW 1, 2; LLW
Moran, J.L.
See Whitaker, Rod
Morand, Paul 1888-1976 .... **CLC 41; SSC 22**
See also CA 184; 69-72; DLB 65; EWL 3
Morante, Elsa 1918-1985 .... **CLC 8, 47**
See also CA 85-88; 117; CANR 35; DLB 177; EWL 3; MTCW 1, 2; MTFW 2005; RGHL; RGWL 2, 3; WLIT 7
Moravia, Alberto
See Pincherle, Alberto
Morck, Paul
See Rolvaag, O.E.
More, Hannah 1745-1833 ...... **NCLC 27, 141**
See also DLB 107, 109, 116, 158; RGEL 2

More, Henry 1614-1687 .... **LC 9**
See also DLB 126, 252
More, Sir Thomas 1478(?)-1535 ... **LC 10, 32, 140**
See also BRWC 1; BRWS 7; DLB 136, 281; LMFS 1; NFS 29; RGEL 2; TEA
Moreas, Jean
See Papadiamantopoulos, Johannes
Moreton, Andrew Esq.
See Defoe, Daniel
Moreton, Lee
See Boucicault, Dion
Morgan, Berry 1919-2002 .... **CLC 6**
See also CA 49-52; 208; DLB 6
Morgan, Claire
See Highsmith, Patricia
Morgan, Edwin 1920- .... **CLC 31**
See also BRWS 9; CA 5-8R; CANR 3, 43, 90; CP 1, 2, 3, 4, 5, 6, 7; DLB 27
Morgan, Edwin George
See Morgan, Edwin
Morgan, (George) Frederick 1922-2004 .... **CLC 23**
See also CA 17-20R; 224; CANR 21, 144; CP 2, 3, 4, 5, 6, 7
Morgan, Harriet
See Mencken, H. L.
Morgan, Jane
See Cooper, James Fenimore
Morgan, Janet 1945- .... **CLC 39**
See also CA 65-68
Morgan, Lady 1776(?)-1859 .... **NCLC 29**
See also DLB 116, 158; RGEL 2
Morgan, Robin (Evonne) 1941- .... **CLC 2**
See also CA 69-72; CANR 29, 68; FW; GLL 2; MTCW 1; SATA 80
Morgan, Scott
See Kuttner, Henry
Morgan, Seth 1949(?)-1990 .... **CLC 65**
See also CA 185; 132
Morgenstern, Christian (Otto Josef Wolfgang) 1871-1914 .... **TCLC 8**
See also CA 105; 191; EWL 3
Morgenstern, S.
See Goldman, William
Mori, Rintaro
See Mori Ogai
Mori, Toshio 1910-1980 ... **AAL; SSC 83, 123**
See also CA 116; 244; DLB 312; RGSF 2
Moricz, Zsigmond 1879-1942 .... **TCLC 33**
See also CA 165; DLB 215; EWL 3
Morike, Eduard (Friedrich) 1804-1875 .... **NCLC 10, 201**
See also DLB 133; RGWL 2, 3
Morin, Jean-Paul
See Whitaker, Rod
Mori Ogai 1862-1922 .... **TCLC 14**
See also CA 110; 164; DLB 180; EWL 3; MJW; RGWL 3; TWA
Moritz, Karl Philipp 1756-1793 .... **LC 2, 162**
See also DLB 94
Morland, Peter Henry
See Faust, Frederick
Morley, Christopher (Darlington) 1890-1957 .... **TCLC 87**
See also CA 112; 213; DLB 9; MAL 5; RGAL 4
Morren, Theophil
See Hofmannsthal, Hugo von
Morris, Bill 1952- .... **CLC 76**
See also CA 225
Morris, Julian
See West, Morris L(anglo)
Morris, Steveland Judkins (?)-
See Wonder, Stevie

Morris, William 1834-1896 . **NCLC 4; PC 55**
See also BRW 5; CDBLB 1832-1890; DLB 18, 35, 57, 156, 178, 184; FANT; RGEL 2; SFW 4; SUFW
Morris, Wright (Marion) 1910-1998 . **CLC 1, 3, 7, 18, 37; TCLC 107**
See also AMW; CA 9-12R; 167; CANR 21, 81; CN 1, 2, 3, 4, 5, 6; DLB 2, 206, 218; DLBY 1981; EWL 3; MAL 5; MTCW 1, 2; MTFW 2005; RGAL 4; TCWW 1, 2
Morrison, Arthur 1863-1945 .... **SSC 40; TCLC 72**
See also CA 120; 157; CMW 4; DLB 70, 135, 197; RGEL 2
Morrison, Chloe Anthony Wofford
See Morrison, Toni
Morrison, James Douglas 1943-1971 .... **CLC 17**
See also CA 73-76; CANR 40
Morrison, Jim
See Morrison, James Douglas
Morrison, John Gordon 1904-1998 ... **SSC 93**
See also CA 103; CANR 92; DLB 260
Morrison, Toni 1931- . **BLC 1:3, 2:3; CLC 4, 10, 22, 55, 81, 87, 173, 194; SSC 126; WLC 4**
See also AAYA 1, 22, 61; AFAW 1, 2; AMWC 1; AMWS 3; BPFB 2; BW 2, 3; CA 29-32R; CANR 27, 42, 67, 113, 124; CDALB 1968-1988; CLR 99; CN 3, 4, 5, 6, 7; CPW; DA; DA3; DAB; DAC; DAM MST, MULT, NOV, POP; DLB 6, 33, 143, 331; DLBY 1981; EWL 3; EXPN; FL 1:6; FW; GL 3; LAIT 2, 4; LATS 1:2; LMFS 2; MAL 5; MBL; MTCW 1, 2; MTFW 2005; NFS 1, 6, 8, 14; RGAL 4; RHW; SATA 57, 144; SSFS 5; TCLE 1:2; TUS; YAW
Morrison, Van 1945- .... **CLC 21**
See also CA 116; 168
Morrissy, Mary 1957- .... **CLC 99**
See also CA 205; DLB 267
Mortimer, John 1923-2009 .... **CLC 28, 43**
See Morton, Kate
See also CA 13-16R; 282; CANR 21, 69, 109, 172; CBD; CD 5, 6; CDBLB 1960 to Present; CMW 4; CN 5, 6, 7; CPW; DA3; DAM DRAM, POP; DLB 13, 245, 271; INT CANR-21; MSW; MTCW 1, 2; MTFW 2005; RGEL 2
Mortimer, John C.
See Mortimer, John
Mortimer, John Clifford
See Mortimer, John
Mortimer, Penelope (Ruth) 1918-1999 .... **CLC 5**
See also CA 57-60; 187; CANR 45, 88; CN 1, 2, 3, 4, 5, 6
Mortimer, Sir John
See Mortimer, John
Morton, Anthony
See Creasey, John
Morton, Thomas 1579(?)-1647(?) .... **LC 72**
See also DLB 24; RGEL 2
Mosca, Gaetano 1858-1941 .... **TCLC 75**
Moses, Daniel David 1952- .... **NNAL**
See also CA 186; CANR 160; DLB 334
Mosher, Howard Frank 1943- .... **CLC 62**
See also CA 139; CANR 65, 115, 181
Mosley, Nicholas 1923- .... **CLC 43, 70**
See also CA 69-72; CANR 41, 60, 108, 158; CN 1, 2, 3, 4, 5, 6, 7; DLB 14, 207
Mosley, Walter 1952- ... **BLCS; CLC 97, 184, 278**
See also AAYA 57; AMWS 13; BPFB 2; BW 2; CA 142; CANR 57, 92, 136, 172; CMW 4; CN 7; CPW; DA3; DAM MULT, POP; DLB 306; MSW; MTCW 2; MTFW 2005

Moss, Howard 1922-1987 . **CLC 7, 14, 45, 50**
See also CA 1-4R; 123; CANR 1, 44; CP 1, 2, 3, 4; DAM POET; DLB 5

Mossgiel, Rab
See Burns, Robert

Motion, Andrew 1952- .... **CLC 47**
See also BRWS 7; CA 146; CANR 90, 142; CP 4, 5, 6, 7; DLB 40; MTFW 2005

Motion, Andrew Peter
See Motion, Andrew

Motley, Willard (Francis)
1909-1965 .... **CLC 18**
See also AMWS 17; BW 1; CA 117; 106; CANR 88; DLB 76, 143

Motoori, Norinaga 1730-1801 .... **NCLC 45**

Mott, Michael (Charles Alston)
1930- .... **CLC 15, 34**
See also CA 5-8R; CAAS 7; CANR 7, 29

Moulsworth, Martha 1577-1646 .... **LC 168**

Mountain Wolf Woman 1884-1960 . **CLC 92; NNAL**
See also CA 144; CANR 90

Moure, Erin 1955- .... **CLC 88**
See also CA 113; CP 5, 6, 7; CWP; DLB 60

Mourning Dove 1885(?)-1936 .... **NNAL**
See also CA 144; CANR 90; DAM MULT; DLB 175, 221

Mowat, Farley 1921- .... **CLC 26**
See also AAYA 1, 50; BYA 2; CA 1-4R; CANR 4, 24, 42, 68, 108; CLR 20; CPW; DAC; DAM MST; DLB 68; INT CANR-24; JRDA; MAICYA 1, 2; MTCW 1, 2; MTFW 2005; SATA 3, 55; YAW

Mowat, Farley McGill
See Mowat, Farley

Mowatt, Anna Cora 1819-1870 ..... **NCLC 74**
See also RGAL 4

Moye, Guan
See Yan, Mo

Mo Yen
See Yan, Mo

Moyers, Bill 1934- .... **CLC 74**
See also AITN 2; CA 61-64; CANR 31, 52, 148

Mphahlele, Es'kia 1919-2008 .... **BLC 1:3; CLC 25, 133, 280**
See also AFW; BW 2, 3; CA 81-84; 278; CANR 26, 76; CDWLB 3; CN 4, 5, 6; DA3; DAM MULT; DLB 125, 225; EWL 3; MTCW 2; MTFW 2005; RGSF 2; SATA 119; SATA-Obit 198; SSFS 11

Mphahlele, Ezekiel
See Mphahlele, Es'kia

Mphahlele, Zeke
See Mphahlele, Es'kia

Mqhayi, S(amuel) E(dward) K(rune Loliwe)
1875-1945 .... **BLC 1:3; TCLC 25**
See also CA 153; CANR 87; DAM MULT

Mrozek, Slawomir 1930- .... **CLC 3, 13**
See also CA 13-16R; CAAS 10; CANR 29; CDWLB 4; CWW 2; DLB 232; EWL 3; MTCW 1

Mrs. Belloc-Lowndes
See Lowndes, Marie Adelaide (Belloc)

Mrs. Fairstar
See Horne, Richard Henry Hengist

M'Taggart, John M'Taggart Ellis
See McTaggart, John McTaggart Ellis

Mtwa, Percy (?)- .... **CLC 47**
See also CD 6

Mueller, Lisel 1924- .... **CLC 13, 51; PC 33**
See also CA 93-96; CP 6, 7; DLB 105; PFS 9, 13

Muggeridge, Malcolm (Thomas)
1903-1990 .... **TCLC 120**
See also AITN 1; CA 101; CANR 33, 63; MTCW 1, 2

Muhammad 570-632 .... **WLCS**
See also DA; DAB; DAC; DAM MST; DLB 311

Muir, Edwin 1887-1959 . **PC 49; TCLC 2, 87**
See also BRWS 6; CA 104; 193; DLB 20, 100, 191; EWL 3; RGEL 2

Muir, John 1838-1914 .... **TCLC 28**
See also AMWS 9; ANW; CA 165; DLB 186, 275

Mujica Lainez, Manuel 1910-1984 ... **CLC 31**
See also CA 81-84; 112; CANR 32; EWL 3; HW 1

Mukherjee, Bharati 1940- ..... **AAL; CLC 53, 115, 235; SSC 38**
See also AAYA 46; BEST 89:2; CA 107, 232; CAAE 232; CANR 45, 72, 128; CN 5, 6, 7; DAM NOV; DLB 60, 218, 323; DNFS 1, 2; EWL 3; FW; MAL 5; MTCW 1, 2; MTFW 2005; RGAL 4; RGSF 2; SSFS 7, 24; TUS; WWE 1

Muldoon, Paul 1951- .... **CLC 32, 72, 166**
See also BRWS 4; CA 113; 129; CANR 52, 91; CP 2, 3, 4, 5, 6, 7; DAM POET; DLB 40; INT CA-129; PFS 7, 22; TCLE 1:2

Mulisch, Harry (Kurt Victor)
1927- .... **CLC 42, 270**
See also CA 9-12R; CANR 6, 26, 56, 110; CWW 2; DLB 299; EWL 3

Mull, Martin 1943- .... **CLC 17**
See also CA 105

Muller, Wilhelm .... **NCLC 73**

Mulock, Dinah Maria
See Craik, Dinah Maria (Mulock)

Multatuli 1820-1881 .... **NCLC 165**
See also RGWL 2, 3

Munday, Anthony 1560-1633 .... **LC 87**
See also DLB 62, 172; RGEL 2

Munford, Robert 1737(?)-1783 .... **LC 5**
See also DLB 31

Mungo, Raymond 1946- .... **CLC 72**
See also CA 49-52; CANR 2

Munro, Alice 1931- .... **CLC 6, 10, 19, 50, 95, 222; SSC 3, 95; WLCS**
See also AITN 2; BPFB 2; CA 33-36R; CANR 33, 53, 75, 114, 177; CCA 1; CN 1, 2, 3, 4, 5, 6, 7; DA3; DAC; DAM MST, NOV; DLB 53; EWL 3; MTCW 1, 2; MTFW 2005; NFS 27; RGEL 2; RGSF 2; SATA 29; SSFS 5, 13, 19; TCLE 1:2; WWE 1

Munro, H. H. 1870-1916 .... **SSC 12, 115; TCLC 3; WLC 5**
See also AAYA 56; BRWS 6; BYA 11; CA 104; 130; CANR 104; CDBLB 1890-1914; DA; DA3; DAB; DAC; DAM MST, NOV; DLB 34, 162; EXPS; LAIT 2; MTCW 1, 2; MTFW 2005; RGEL 2; SSFS 1, 15; SUFW

Munro, Hector H.
See Munro, H. H.

Munro, Hector Hugh
See Munro, H. H.

Murakami, Haruki 1949- .... **CLC 150, 274**
See also CA 165; CANR 102, 146; CWW 2; DLB 182; EWL 3; MJW; RGWL 3; SFW 4; SSFS 23

Murakami Haruki
See Murakami, Haruki

Murasaki, Lady
See Murasaki Shikibu

Murasaki Shikibu 978(?)-1026(?) .. **CMLC 1, 79**
See also EFS 2; LATS 1:1; RGWL 2, 3

Murdoch, Iris 1919-1999 .. **CLC 1, 2, 3, 4, 6, 8, 11, 15, 22, 31, 51; TCLC 171**
See also BRWS 1; CA 13-16R; 179; CANR 8, 43, 68, 103, 142; CBD; CDBLB 1960 to Present; CN 1, 2, 3, 4, 5, 6; CWD; DA3; DAB; DAC; DAM MST, NOV; DLB 14, 194, 233, 326; EWL 3; INT CANR-8; MTCW 1, 2; MTFW 2005; NFS 18; RGEL 2; TCLE 1:2; TEA; WLIT 4

Murfree, Mary Noailles 1850-1922 .. **SSC 22; TCLC 135**
See also CA 122; 176; DLB 12, 74; RGAL 4

Murglie
See Murnau, F.W.

Murnau, Friedrich Wilhelm
See Murnau, F.W.

Murnau, F.W. 1888-1931 .... **TCLC 53**
See also CA 112

Murphy, Richard 1927- .... **CLC 41**
See also BRWS 5; CA 29-32R; CP 1, 2, 3, 4, 5, 6, 7; DLB 40; EWL 3

Murphy, Sylvia 1937- .... **CLC 34**
See also CA 121

Murphy, Thomas (Bernard) 1935- ... **CLC 51**
See also CA 101; DLB 310

Murphy, Tom
See Murphy, Thomas (Bernard)

Murray, Albert 1916- .... **BLC 2:3; CLC 73**
See also BW 2; CA 49-52; CANR 26, 52, 78, 160; CN 7; CSW; DLB 38; MTFW 2005

Murray, Albert L.
See Murray, Albert

Murray, James Augustus Henry
1837-1915 .... **TCLC 117**

Murray, Judith Sargent
1751-1820 .... **NCLC 63**
See also DLB 37, 200

Murray, Les(lie Allan) 1938- .... **CLC 40**
See also BRWS 7; CA 21-24R; CANR 11, 27, 56, 103; CP 1, 2, 3, 4, 5, 6, 7; DAM POET; DLB 289; DLBY 2001; EWL 3; RGEL 2

Murry, J. Middleton
See Murry, John Middleton

Murry, John Middleton
1889-1957 .... **TCLC 16**
See also CA 118; 217; DLB 149

Musgrave, Susan 1951- .... **CLC 13, 54**
See also CA 69-72; CANR 45, 84, 181; CCA 1; CP 2, 3, 4, 5, 6, 7; CWP

Musil, Robert (Edler von)
1880-1942 ... **SSC 18; TCLC 12, 68, 213**
See also CA 109; CANR 55, 84; CDWLB 2; DLB 81, 124; EW 9; EWL 3; MTCW 2; RGSF 2; RGWL 2, 3

Muske, Carol
See Muske-Dukes, Carol

Muske, Carol Anne
See Muske-Dukes, Carol

Muske-Dukes, Carol 1945- .... **CLC 90**
See also CA 65-68, 203; CAAE 203; CANR 32, 70, 181; CWP; PFS 24

Muske-Dukes, Carol Ann
See Muske-Dukes, Carol

Muske-Dukes, Carol Anne
See Muske-Dukes, Carol

Musset, Alfred de 1810-1857 . **DC 27; NCLC 7, 150**
See also DLB 192, 217; EW 6; GFL 1789 to the Present; RGWL 2, 3; TWA

Musset, Louis Charles Alfred de
See Musset, Alfred de

Mussolini, Benito (Amilcare Andrea)
1883-1945 .... **TCLC 96**
See also CA 116

Mutanabbi, Al-
See al-Mutanabbi, Ahmad ibn al-Husayn Abu al-Tayyib al-Jufi al-Kindi

My Brother's Brother
See Chekhov, Anton (Pavlovich)

Myers, L(eopold) H(amilton)
1881-1944 .... **TCLC 59**
See also CA 157; DLB 15; EWL 3; RGEL 2

Myers, Walter Dean 1937- ...... **BLC 1:3, 2:3; CLC 35**
See also AAYA 4, 23; BW 2; BYA 6, 8, 11; CA 33-36R; CANR 20, 42, 67, 108, 184; CLR 4, 16, 35, 110; DAM MULT, NOV; DLB 33; INT CANR-20; JRDA; LAIT 5; MAICYA 1, 2; MAICYAS 1; MTCW 2; MTFW 2005; NFS 30; SAAS 2; SATA 41, 71, 109, 157, 193; SATA-Brief 27; WYA; YAW

Myers, Walter M.
See Myers, Walter Dean

Myles, Symon
See Follett, Ken

Nabokov, Vladimir (Vladimirovich)
1899-1977 .... **CLC 1, 2, 3, 6, 8, 11, 15, 23, 44, 46, 64; SSC 11, 86; TCLC 108, 189; WLC 4**
See also AAYA 45; AMW; AMWC 1; AMWR 1; BPFB 2; CA 5-8R; 69-72; CANR 20, 102; CDALB 1941-1968; CN 1, 2; CP 2; DA; DA3; DAB; DAC; DAM MST, NOV; DLB 2, 244, 278, 317; DLBD 3; DLBY 1980, 1991; EWL 3; EXPS; LATS 1:2; MAL 5; MTCW 1, 2; MTFW 2005; NCFS 4; NFS 9; RGAL 4; RGSF 2; SSFS 6, 15; TUS

Naevius c. 265B.C.-201B.C. .... **CMLC 37**
See also DLB 211

Nagai, Kafu 1879-1959 .... **TCLC 51**
See also CA 117; 276; DLB 180; EWL 3; MJW

Nagai, Sokichi
See Nagai, Kafu

Nagai Kafu
See Nagai, Kafu

na gCopaleen, Myles
See O Nuallain, Brian

na Gopaleen, Myles
See O Nuallain, Brian

Nagy, Laszlo 1925-1978 .... **CLC 7**
See also CA 129; 112

Naidu, Sarojini 1879-1949 .... **TCLC 80**
See also EWL 3; RGEL 2

Naipaul, Shiva 1945-1985 .... **CLC 32, 39; TCLC 153**
See also CA 110; 112; 116; CANR 33; CN 2, 3; DA3; DAM NOV; DLB 157; DLBY 1985; EWL 3; MTCW 1, 2; MTFW 2005

Naipaul, Shivadhar Srinivasa
See Naipaul, Shiva

Naipaul, V. S. 1932- . **CLC 4, 7, 9, 13, 18, 37, 105, 199; SSC 38, 121**
See also BPFB 2; BRWS 1; CA 1-4R; CANR 1, 33, 51, 91, 126, 191; CDBLB 1960 to Present; CDWLB 3; CN 1, 2, 3, 4, 5, 6, 7; DA3; DAB; DAC; DAM MST, NOV; DLB 125, 204, 207, 326, 331; DLBY 1985, 2001; EWL 3; LATS 1:2; MTCW 1, 2; MTFW 2005; RGEL 2; RGSF 2; TWA; WLIT 4; WWE 1

Naipaul, Vidiahar Surajprasad
See Naipaul, V. S.

Nakos, Lilika 1903(?)-1989 .... **CLC 29**

Napoleon
See Yamamoto, Hisaye

Narayan, R.K. 1906-2001 ...... **CLC 7, 28, 47, 121, 211; SSC 25**
See also BPFB 2; CA 81-84; 196; CANR 33, 61, 112; CN 1, 2, 3, 4, 5, 6, 7; DA3; DAM NOV; DLB 323; DNFS 1; EWL 3; MTCW 1, 2; MTFW 2005; RGEL 2; RGSF 2; SATA 62; SSFS 5; WWE 1

Nash, Frediric Ogden
See Nash, Ogden

Nash, Ogden 1902-1971 ...... **CLC 23; PC 21; TCLC 109**
See also CA 13-14; 29-32R; CANR 34, 61, 185; CAP 1; CP 1; DAM POET; DLB 11; MAICYA 1, 2; MAL 5; MTCW 1, 2; PFS 31; RGAL 4; SATA 2, 46; WP

Nashe, Thomas 1567-1601(?) . **LC 41, 89; PC 82**
See also DLB 167; RGEL 2

Nathan, Daniel
See Dannay, Frederic

Nathan, George Jean 1882-1958 .... **TCLC 18**
See also CA 114; 169; DLB 137; MAL 5

Natsume, Kinnosuke
See Natsume, Soseki

Natsume, Soseki 1867-1916 .... **TCLC 2, 10**
See also CA 104; 195; DLB 180; EWL 3; MJW; RGWL 2, 3; TWA

Natsume Soseki
See Natsume, Soseki

Natti, Lee 1919- .... **CLC 17**
See also CA 5-8R; CANR 2; CWRI 5; SAAS 3; SATA 1, 67

Natti, Mary Lee
See Natti, Lee

Navarre, Marguerite de
See de Navarre, Marguerite

Naylor, Gloria 1950- . **BLC 1:3; CLC 28, 52, 156, 261; WLCS**
See also AAYA 6, 39; AFAW 1, 2; AMWS 8; BW 2, 3; CA 107; CANR 27, 51, 74, 130; CN 4, 5, 6, 7; CPW; DA; DA3; DAC; DAM MST, MULT, NOV, POP; DLB 173; EWL 3; FW; MAL 5; MTCW 1, 2; MTFW 2005; NFS 4, 7; RGAL 4; TCLE 1:2; TUS

Neal, John 1793-1876 .... **NCLC 161**
See also DLB 1, 59, 243; FW; RGAL 4

Neff, Debra .... **CLC 59**

Neihardt, John Gneisenau
1881-1973 .... **CLC 32**
See also CA 13-14; CANR 65; CAP 1; DLB 9, 54, 256; LAIT 2; TCWW 1, 2

Nekrasov, Nikolai Alekseevich
1821-1878 .... **NCLC 11**
See also DLB 277

Nelligan, Emile 1879-1941 .... **TCLC 14**
See also CA 114; 204; DLB 92; EWL 3

Nelson, Alice Ruth Moore Dunbar
1875-1935 .... **HR 1:2**
See also BW 1, 3; CA 122; 124; CANR 82; DLB 50; FW; MTCW 1

Nelson, Willie 1933- .... **CLC 17**
See also CA 107; CANR 114, 178

Nemerov, Howard 1920-1991 .... **CLC 2, 6, 9, 36; PC 24; TCLC 124**
See also AMW; CA 1-4R; 134; CABS 2; CANR 1, 27, 53; CN 1, 2, 3; CP 1, 2, 3, 4, 5; DAM POET; DLB 5, 6; DLBY 1983; EWL 3; INT CANR-27; MAL 5; MTCW 1, 2; MTFW 2005; PFS 10, 14; RGAL 4

Nepos, Cornelius c. 99B.C.-c. 24B.C. .... **CMLC 89**
See also DLB 211

Neruda, Pablo 1904-1973 .. **CLC 1, 2, 5, 7, 9, 28, 62; HLC 2; PC 4, 64; WLC 4**
See also CA 19-20; 45-48; CANR 131; CAP 2; DA; DA3; DAB; DAC; DAM MST, MULT, POET; DLB 283, 331; DNFS 2; EWL 3; HW 1; LAW; MTCW 1, 2; MTFW 2005; PFS 11, 28; RGWL 2, 3; TWA; WLIT 1; WP

Nerval, Gerard de 1808-1855 ... **NCLC 1, 67; PC 13; SSC 18**
See also DLB 217; EW 6; GFL 1789 to the Present; RGSF 2; RGWL 2, 3

Nervo, (Jose) Amado (Ruiz de)
1870-1919 .... **HLCS 2; TCLC 11**
See also CA 109; 131; DLB 290; EWL 3; HW 1; LAW

Nesbit, Malcolm
See Chester, Alfred

Nessi, Pio Baroja y
See Baroja, Pio

Nestroy, Johann 1801-1862 .... **NCLC 42**
See also DLB 133; RGWL 2, 3

Netterville, Luke
See O'Grady, Standish (James)

Neufeld, John (Arthur) 1938- .... **CLC 17**
See also AAYA 11; CA 25-28R; CANR 11, 37, 56; CLR 52; MAICYA 1, 2; SAAS 3; SATA 6, 81, 131; SATA-Essay 131; YAW

Neumann, Alfred 1895-1952 .... **TCLC 100**
See also CA 183; DLB 56

Neumann, Ferenc
See Molnar, Ferenc

Neville, Emily Cheney 1919- .... **CLC 12**
See also BYA 2; CA 5-8R; CANR 3, 37, 85; JRDA; MAICYA 1, 2; SAAS 2; SATA 1; YAW

Newbound, Bernard Slade 1930- .... **CLC 11, 46**
See also CA 81-84; CAAS 9; CANR 49; CCA 1; CD 5, 6; DAM DRAM; DLB 53

Newby, P(ercy) H(oward)
1918-1997 .... **CLC 2, 13**
See also CA 5-8R; 161; CANR 32, 67; CN 1, 2, 3, 4, 5, 6; DAM NOV; DLB 15, 326; MTCW 1; RGEL 2

Newcastle
See Cavendish, Margaret Lucas

Newlove, Donald 1928- .... **CLC 6**
See also CA 29-32R; CANR 25

Newlove, John (Herbert) 1938- .... **CLC 14**
See also CA 21-24R; CANR 9, 25; CP 1, 2, 3, 4, 5, 6, 7

Newman, Charles 1938-2006 .... **CLC 2, 8**
See also CA 21-24R; 249; CANR 84; CN 3, 4, 5, 6

Newman, Charles Hamilton
See Newman, Charles

Newman, Edwin (Harold) 1919- ...... **CLC 14**
See also AITN 1; CA 69-72; CANR 5

Newman, John Henry 1801-1890 . **NCLC 38, 99**
See also BRWS 7; DLB 18, 32, 55; RGEL 2

Newton, (Sir) Isaac 1642-1727 ...... **LC 35, 53**
See also DLB 252

Newton, Suzanne 1936- .... **CLC 35**
See also BYA 7; CA 41-44R; CANR 14; JRDA; SATA 5, 77

New York Dept. of Ed. .... **CLC 70**

Nexo, Martin Andersen
1869-1954 .... **TCLC 43**
See also CA 202; DLB 214; EWL 3

Nezval, Vitezslav 1900-1958 .... **TCLC 44**
See also CA 123; CDWLB 4; DLB 215; EWL 3

Ng, Fae Myenne 1956- .... **CLC 81**
See also BYA 11; CA 146; CANR 191

Ngcobo, Lauretta 1931- .... **BLC 2:3**
See also CA 165

Ngema, Mbongeni 1955- .... **CLC 57**
See also BW 2; CA 143; CANR 84; CD 5, 6

Ngugi, James T.
See Ngugi wa Thiong'o

Ngugi, James Thiong'o
See Ngugi wa Thiong'o

O'Brien, Edna 1932- ..... **CLC 3, 5, 8, 13, 36, 65, 116, 237; SSC 10, 77**
See also BRWS 5; CA 1-4R; CANR 6, 41, 65, 102, 169; CDBLB 1960 to Present; CN 1, 2, 3, 4, 5, 6, 7; DA3; DAM NOV; DLB 14, 231, 319; EWL 3; FW; MTCW 1, 2; MTFW 2005; RGSF 2; WLIT 4

O'Brien, E.G.
See Clarke, Arthur C.

O'Brien, Fitz-James 1828-1862 ..... **NCLC 21**
See also DLB 74; RGAL 4; SUFW

O'Brien, Flann
See O Nuallain, Brian

O'Brien, Richard 1942- .... **CLC 17**
See also CA 124

O'Brien, Tim 1946- .... **CLC 7, 19, 40, 103, 211; SSC 74, 123**
See also AAYA 16; AMWS 5; CA 85-88; CANR 40, 58, 133; CDALBS; CN 5, 6, 7; CPW; DA3; DAM POP; DLB 152; DLBD 9; DLBY 1980; LATS 1:2; MAL 5; MTCW 2; MTFW 2005; RGAL 4; SSFS 5, 15; TCLE 1:2

Obstfelder, Sigbjoern 1866-1900 .... **TCLC 23**
See also CA 123

O'Casey, Brenda
See Haycraft, Anna

O'Casey, Sean 1880-1964 .... **CLC 1, 5, 9, 11, 15, 88; DC 12; WLCS**
See also BRW 7; CA 89-92; CANR 62; CBD; CDBLB 1914-1945; DA3; DAB; DAC; DAM DRAM, MST; DFS 19; DLB 10; EWL 3; MTCW 1, 2; MTFW 2005; RGEL 2; TEA; WLIT 4

O'Cathasaigh, Sean
See O'Casey, Sean

Occom, Samson 1723-1792 .... **LC 60; NNAL**
See also DLB 175

Occomy, Marita (Odette) Bonner 1899(?)-1971 ..... **HR 1:2; PC 72; TCLC 179**
See also BW 2; CA 142; DFS 13; DLB 51, 228

Ochs, Phil(ip David) 1940-1976 .... **CLC 17**
See also CA 185; 65-68

O'Connor, Edwin (Greene) 1918-1968 .... **CLC 14**
See also CA 93-96; 25-28R; MAL 5

O'Connor, (Mary) Flannery 1925-1964 .... **CLC 1, 2, 3, 6, 10, 13, 15, 21, 66, 104; SSC 1, 23, 61, 82, 111; TCLC 132; WLC 4**
See also AAYA 7; AMW; AMWR 2; BPFB 3; BYA 16; CA 1-4R; CANR 3, 41; CDALB 1941-1968; DA; DA3; DAB; DAC; DAM MST, NOV; DLB 2, 152; DLBD 12; DLBY 1980; EWL 3; EXPS; LAIT 5; MAL 5; MBL; MTCW 1, 2; MTFW 2005; NFS 3, 21; RGAL 4; RGSF 2; SSFS 2, 7, 10, 19; TUS

O'Connor, Frank 1903-1966
See O'Donovan, Michael Francis

O'Dell, Scott 1898-1989 .... **CLC 30**
See also AAYA 3, 44; BPFB 3; BYA 1, 2, 3, 5; CA 61-64; 129; CANR 12, 30, 112; CLR 1, 16, 126; DLB 52; JRDA; MAICYA 1, 2; SATA 12, 60, 134; WYA; YAW

Odets, Clifford 1906-1963 ..... **CLC 2, 28, 98; DC 6**
See also AMWS 2; CA 85-88; CAD; CANR 62; DAM DRAM; DFS 3, 17, 20; DLB 7, 26, 341; EWL 3; MAL 5; MTCW 1, 2; MTFW 2005; RGAL 4; TUS

O'Doherty, Brian 1928- .... **CLC 76**
See also CA 105; CANR 108

O'Donnell, K. M.
See Malzberg, Barry N(athaniel)

O'Donnell, Lawrence
See Kuttner, Henry

O'Donovan, Michael Francis 1903-1966 .... **CLC 14, 23; SSC 5, 109**
See also BRWS 14; CA 93-96; CANR 84; DLB 162; EWL 3; RGSF 2; SSFS 5

Oe, Kenzaburo 1935- .. **CLC 10, 36, 86, 187; SSC 20**
See also CA 97-100; CANR 36, 50, 74, 126; CWW 2; DA3; DAM NOV; DLB 182, 331; DLBY 1994; EWL 3; LATS 1:2; MJW; MTCW 1, 2; MTFW 2005; RGSF 2; RGWL 2, 3

Oe Kenzaburo
See Oe, Kenzaburo

O'Faolain, Julia 1932- .... **CLC 6, 19, 47, 108**
See also CA 81-84; CAAS 2; CANR 12, 61; CN 2, 3, 4, 5, 6, 7; DLB 14, 231, 319; FW; MTCW 1; RHW

O'Faolain, Sean 1900-1991 ...... **CLC 1, 7, 14, 32, 70; SSC 13; TCLC 143**
See also CA 61-64; 134; CANR 12, 66; CN 1, 2, 3, 4; DLB 15, 162; MTCW 1, 2; MTFW 2005; RGEL 2; RGSF 2

O'Flaherty, Liam 1896-1984 .... **CLC 5, 34; SSC 6, 116**
See also CA 101; 113; CANR 35; CN 1, 2, 3; DLB 36, 162; DLBY 1984; MTCW 1, 2; MTFW 2005; RGEL 2; RGSF 2; SSFS 5, 20

Ogai
See Mori Ogai

Ogilvy, Gavin
See Barrie, J(ames) M(atthew)

O'Grady, Standish (James) 1846-1928 .... **TCLC 5**
See also CA 104; 157

O'Grady, Timothy 1951- .... **CLC 59**
See also CA 138

O'Hara, Frank 1926-1966 .... **CLC 2, 5, 13, 78; PC 45**
See also CA 9-12R; 25-28R; CANR 33; DA3; DAM POET; DLB 5, 16, 193; EWL 3; MAL 5; MTCW 1, 2; MTFW 2005; PFS 8, 12; RGAL 4; WP

O'Hara, John (Henry) 1905-1970 . **CLC 1, 2, 3, 6, 11, 42; SSC 15**
See also AMW; BPFB 3; CA 5-8R; 25-28R; CANR 31, 60; CDALB 1929-1941; DAM NOV; DLB 9, 86, 324; DLBD 2; EWL 3; MAL 5; MTCW 1, 2; MTFW 2005; NFS 11; RGAL 4; RGSF 2

O'Hehir, Diana 1929- .... **CLC 41**
See also CA 245; CANR 177

O'Hehir, Diana F.
See O'Hehir, Diana

Ohiyesa
See Eastman, Charles A(lexander)

Okada, John 1923-1971 .... **AAL**
See also BYA 14; CA 212; DLB 312; NFS 25

Okigbo, Christopher 1930-1967 ..... **BLC 1:3; CLC 25, 84; PC 7; TCLC 171**
See also AFW; BW 1, 3; CA 77-80; CANR 74; CDWLB 3; DAM MULT, POET; DLB 125; EWL 3; MTCW 1, 2; MTFW 2005; RGEL 2

Okigbo, Christopher Ifenayichukwu
See Okigbo, Christopher

Okri, Ben 1959- .... **BLC 2:3; CLC 87, 223; SSC 127**
See also AFW; BRWS 5; BW 2, 3; CA 130; 138; CANR 65, 128; CN 5, 6, 7; DLB 157, 231, 319, 326; EWL 3; INT CA-138; MTCW 2; MTFW 2005; RGSF 2; SSFS 20; WLIT 2; WWE 1

Old Boy
See Hughes, Thomas

Olds, Sharon 1942- .. **CLC 32, 39, 85; PC 22**
See also AMWS 10; CA 101; CANR 18, 41, 66, 98, 135; CP 5, 6, 7; CPW; CWP; DAM POET; DLB 120; MAL 5; MTCW 2; MTFW 2005; PFS 17

Oldstyle, Jonathan
See Irving, Washington

Olesha, Iurii
See Olesha, Yuri (Karlovich)

Olesha, Iurii Karlovich
See Olesha, Yuri (Karlovich)

Olesha, Yuri (Karlovich) 1899-1960 . **CLC 8; SSC 69; TCLC 136**
See also CA 85-88; DLB 272; EW 11; EWL 3; RGWL 2, 3

Olesha, Yury Karlovich
See Olesha, Yuri (Karlovich)

Oliphant, Mrs.
See Oliphant, Margaret (Oliphant Wilson)

Oliphant, Laurence 1829(?)-1888 .. **NCLC 47**
See also DLB 18, 166

Oliphant, Margaret (Oliphant Wilson) 1828-1897 .... **NCLC 11, 61; SSC 25**
See also BRWS 10; DLB 18, 159, 190; HGG; RGEL 2; RGSF 2; SUFW

Oliver, Mary 1935- ... **CLC 19, 34, 98; PC 75**
See also AMWS 7; CA 21-24R; CANR 9, 43, 84, 92, 138; CP 4, 5, 6, 7; CWP; DLB 5, 193, 342; EWL 3; MTFW 2005; PFS 15, 31

Olivi, Peter 1248-1298 .... **CMLC 114**

Olivier, Laurence (Kerr) 1907-1989 . **CLC 20**
See also CA 111; 150; 129

O.L.S.
See Russell, George William

Olsen, Tillie 1912-2007 .... **CLC 4, 13, 114; SSC 11, 103**
See also AAYA 51; AMWS 13; BYA 11; CA 1-4R; 256; CANR 1, 43, 74, 132; CDALBS; CN 2, 3, 4, 5, 6, 7; DA; DA3; DAB; DAC; DAM MST; DLB 28, 206; DLBY 1980; EWL 3; EXPS; FW; MAL 5; MTCW 1, 2; MTFW 2005; RGAL 4; RGSF 2; SSFS 1; TCLE 1:2; TCWW 2; TUS

Olson, Charles (John) 1910-1970 .. **CLC 1, 2, 5, 6, 9, 11, 29; PC 19**
See also AMWS 2; CA 13-16; 25-28R; CABS 2; CANR 35, 61; CAP 1; CP 1; DAM POET; DLB 5, 16, 193; EWL 3; MAL 5; MTCW 1, 2; RGAL 4; WP

Olson, Merle Theodore
See Olson, Toby

Olson, Toby 1937- .... **CLC 28**
See also CA 65-68; CAAS 11; CANR 9, 31, 84, 175; CP 3, 4, 5, 6, 7

Olyesha, Yuri
See Olesha, Yuri (Karlovich)

Olympiodorus of Thebes c. 375-c. 430 .... **CMLC 59**

Omar Khayyam
See Khayyam, Omar

Ondaatje, Michael 1943- ..... **CLC 14, 29, 51, 76, 180, 258; PC 28**
See also AAYA 66; CA 77-80; CANR 42, 74, 109, 133, 172; CN 5, 6, 7; CP 1, 2, 3, 4, 5, 6, 7; DA3; DAB; DAC; DAM MST; DLB 60, 323, 326; EWL 3; LATS 1:2; LMFS 2; MTCW 2; MTFW 2005; NFS 23; PFS 8, 19; TCLE 1:2; TWA; WWE 1

Ondaatje, Philip Michael
See Ondaatje, Michael

Oneal, Elizabeth 1934- .... **CLC 30**
See also AAYA 5, 41; BYA 13; CA 106; CANR 28, 84; CLR 13; JRDA; MAICYA 1, 2; SATA 30, 82; WYA; YAW

Oneal, Zibby
See Oneal, Elizabeth

Paget, Violet 1856-1935 .. **SSC 33, 98; TCLC 5**
See also CA 104; 166; DLB 57, 153, 156, 174, 178; GLL 1; HGG; SUFW 1

Paget-Lowe, Henry
See Lovecraft, H. P.

Paglia, Camille 1947- .... **CLC 68**
See also CA 140; CANR 72, 139; CPW; FW; GLL 2; MTCW 2; MTFW 2005

Pagnol, Marcel (Paul)
1895-1974 .... **TCLC 208**
See also CA 128; 49-52; DLB 321; EWL 3; GFL 1789 to the Present; MTCW 1; RGWL 2, 3

Paige, Richard
See Koontz, Dean R.

Paine, Thomas 1737-1809 .... **NCLC 62**
See also AMWS 1; CDALB 1640-1865; DLB 31, 43, 73, 158; LAIT 1; RGAL 4; RGEL 2; TUS

Pakenham, Antonia
See Fraser, Antonia

Palamas, Costis
See Palamas, Kostes

Palamas, Kostes 1859-1943 .... **TCLC 5**
See also CA 105; 190; EWL 3; RGWL 2, 3

Palamas, Kostis
See Palamas, Kostes

Palazzeschi, Aldo 1885-1974 .... **CLC 11**
See also CA 89-92; 53-56; DLB 114, 264; EWL 3

Pales Matos, Luis 1898-1959 .... **HLCS 2**
See Pales Matos, Luis
See also DLB 290; HW 1; LAW

Paley, Grace 1922-2007 ... **CLC 4, 6, 37, 140, 272; SSC 8**
See also AMWS 6; CA 25-28R; 263; CANR 13, 46, 74, 118; CN 2, 3, 4, 5, 6, 7; CPW; DA3; DAM POP; DLB 28, 218; EWL 3; EXPS; FW; INT CANR-13; MAL 5; MBL; MTCW 1, 2; MTFW 2005; RGAL 4; RGSF 2; SSFS 3, 20, 27

Paley, Grace Goodside
See Paley, Grace

Palin, Michael 1943- .... **CLC 21**
See also CA 107; CANR 35, 109, 179; DLB 352; SATA 67

Palin, Michael Edward
See Palin, Michael

Palliser, Charles 1947- .... **CLC 65**
See also CA 136; CANR 76; CN 5, 6, 7

Palma, Ricardo 1833-1919 .... **TCLC 29**
See also CA 168; LAW

Pamuk, Orhan 1952- .... **CLC 185**
See also CA 142; CANR 75, 127, 172; CWW 2; NFS 27; WLIT 6

Pancake, Breece Dexter 1952-1979 . **CLC 29; SSC 61**
See also CA 123; 109; DLB 130

Pancake, Breece D'J
See Pancake, Breece Dexter

Panchenko, Nikolai .... **CLC 59**

Pankhurst, Emmeline (Goulden)
1858-1928 .... **TCLC 100**
See also CA 116; FW

Panko, Rudy
See Gogol, Nikolai (Vasilyevich)

Papadiamantis, Alexandros
1851-1911 .... **TCLC 29**
See also CA 168; EWL 3

Papadiamantopoulos, Johannes
1856-1910 .... **TCLC 18**
See also CA 117; 242; GFL 1789 to the Present

Papadiamantopoulos, Yannis
See Papadiamantopoulos, Johannes

Papini, Giovanni 1881-1956 .... **TCLC 22**
See also CA 121; 180; DLB 264

Paracelsus 1493-1541 .... **LC 14**
See also DLB 179

Parasol, Peter
See Stevens, Wallace

Pardo Bazan, Emilia 1851-1921 .... **SSC 30; TCLC 189**
See also EWL 3; FW; RGSF 2; RGWL 2, 3

Paredes, Americo 1915-1999 .... **PC 83**
See also CA 37-40R; 179; DLB 209; EXPP; HW 1

Pareto, Vilfredo 1848-1923 .... **TCLC 69**
See also CA 175

Paretsky, Sara 1947- .... **CLC 135**
See also AAYA 30; BEST 90:3; CA 125; 129; CANR 59, 95, 184; CMW 4; CPW; DA3; DAM POP; DLB 306; INT CA-129; MSW; RGAL 4

Paretsky, Sara N.
See Paretsky, Sara

Parfenie, Maria
See Codrescu, Andrei

Parini, Jay (Lee) 1948- .... **CLC 54, 133**
See also CA 97-100, 229; CAAE 229; CAAS 16; CANR 32, 87

Park, Jordan
See Kornbluth, C(yril) M.; Pohl, Frederik

Park, Robert E(zra) 1864-1944 ..... **TCLC 73**
See also CA 122; 165

Parker, Bert
See Ellison, Harlan

Parker, Dorothy (Rothschild)
1893-1967 . **CLC 15, 68; PC 28; SSC 2, 101; TCLC 143**
See also AMWS 9; CA 19-20; 25-28R; CAP 2; DA3; DAM POET; DLB 11, 45, 86; EXPP; FW; MAL 5; MBL; MTCW 1, 2; MTFW 2005; PFS 18; RGAL 4; RGSF 2; TUS

Parker, Robert B. 1932- .... **CLC 27**
See also AAYA 28; BEST 89:4; BPFB 3; CA 49-52; CANR 1, 26, 52, 89, 128, 165; CMW 4; CPW; DAM NOV, POP; DLB 306; INT CANR-26; MSW; MTCW 1; MTFW 2005

Parker, Robert Brown
See Parker, Robert B.

Parker, Theodore 1810-1860 .... **NCLC 186**
See also DLB 1, 235

Parkes, Lucas
See Harris, John (Wyndham Parkes Lucas) Beynon

Parkin, Frank 1940- .... **CLC 43**
See also CA 147

Parkman, Francis, Jr. 1823-1893 .. **NCLC 12**
See also AMWS 2; DLB 1, 30, 183, 186, 235; RGAL 4

Parks, Gordon 1912-2006 . **BLC 1:3; CLC 1, 16**
See also AAYA 36; AITN 2; BW 2, 3; CA 41-44R; 249; CANR 26, 66, 145; DA3; DAM MULT; DLB 33; MTCW 2; MTFW 2005; SATA 8, 108; SATA-Obit 175

Parks, Suzan-Lori 1964(?)- ..... **BLC 2:3; DC 23**
See also AAYA 55; CA 201; CAD; CD 5, 6; CWD; DFS 22; DLB 341; RGAL 4

Parks, Tim(othy Harold) 1954- ...... **CLC 147**
See also CA 126; 131; CANR 77, 144; CN 7; DLB 231; INT CA-131

Parmenides c. 515B.C.-c. 450B.C. .... **CMLC 22**
See also DLB 176

Parnell, Thomas 1679-1718 .... **LC 3**
See also DLB 95; RGEL 2

Parr, Catherine c. 1513(?)-1548 .... **LC 86**
See also DLB 136

Parra, Nicanor 1914- ... **CLC 2, 102; HLC 2; PC 39**
See also CA 85-88; CANR 32; CWW 2; DAM MULT; DLB 283; EWL 3; HW 1; LAW; MTCW 1

Parra Sanojo, Ana Teresa de la 1890-1936
See de la Parra, Teresa

Parrish, Mary Frances
See Fisher, M(ary) F(rances) K(ennedy)

Parshchikov, Aleksei 1954- .... **CLC 59**
See also DLB 285

Parshchikov, Aleksei Maksimovich
See Parshchikov, Aleksei

Parson, Professor
See Coleridge, Samuel Taylor

Parson Lot
See Kingsley, Charles

Parton, Sara Payson Willis
1811-1872 .... **NCLC 86**
See also DLB 43, 74, 239

Partridge, Anthony
See Oppenheim, E(dward) Phillips

Pascal, Blaise 1623-1662 .... **LC 35**
See also DLB 268; EW 3; GFL Beginnings to 1789; RGWL 2, 3; TWA

Pascoli, Giovanni 1855-1912 .... **TCLC 45**
See also CA 170; EW 7; EWL 3

Pasolini, Pier Paolo 1922-1975 .. **CLC 20, 37, 106; PC 17**
See also CA 93-96; 61-64; CANR 63; DLB 128, 177; EWL 3; MTCW 1; RGWL 2, 3

Pasquini
See Silone, Ignazio

Pastan, Linda (Olenik) 1932- .... **CLC 27**
See also CA 61-64; CANR 18, 40, 61, 113; CP 3, 4, 5, 6, 7; CSW; CWP; DAM POET; DLB 5; PFS 8, 25

Pasternak, Boris 1890-1960 ... **CLC 7, 10, 18, 63; PC 6; SSC 31; TCLC 188; WLC 4**
See also BPFB 3; CA 127; 116; DA; DA3; DAB; DAC; DAM MST, NOV, POET; DLB 302, 331; EW 10; MTCW 1, 2; MTFW 2005; NFS 26; RGSF 2; RGWL 2, 3; TWA; WP

Patchen, Kenneth 1911-1972 .... **CLC 1, 2, 18**
See also BG 1:3; CA 1-4R; 33-36R; CANR 3, 35; CN 1; CP 1; DAM POET; DLB 16, 48; EWL 3; MAL 5; MTCW 1; RGAL 4

Patchett, Ann 1963- .... **CLC 244**
See also AAYA 69; AMWS 12; CA 139; CANR 64, 110, 167; DLB 350; MTFW 2005; NFS 30

Pater, Walter (Horatio) 1839-1894 . **NCLC 7, 90, 159**
See also BRW 5; CDBLB 1832-1890; DLB 57, 156; RGEL 2; TEA

Paterson, A(ndrew) B(arton)
1864-1941 .... **TCLC 32**
See also CA 155; DLB 230; RGEL 2; SATA 97

Paterson, Banjo
See Paterson, A(ndrew) B(arton)

Paterson, Katherine 1932- .... **CLC 12, 30**
See also AAYA 1, 31; BYA 1, 2, 7; CA 21-24R; CANR 28, 59, 111, 173; CLR 7, 50, 127; CWRI 5; DLB 52; JRDA; LAIT 4; MAICYA 1, 2; MAICYAS 1; MTCW 1; SATA 13, 53, 92, 133; WYA; YAW

Paterson, Katherine Womeldorf
See Paterson, Katherine

Patmore, Coventry Kersey Dighton
1823-1896 .... **NCLC 9; PC 59**
See also DLB 35, 98; RGEL 2; TEA

Paton, Alan 1903-1988 ... **CLC 4, 10, 25, 55, 106; TCLC 165; WLC 4**
See also AAYA 26; AFW; BPFB 3; BRWS 2; BYA 1; CA 13-16; 125; CANR 22; CAP 1; CN 1, 2, 3, 4; DA; DA3; DAB; DAC; DAM MST, NOV; DLB 225;

Postman, Neil 1931(?)-2003 .... **CLC 244**
   See also CA 102; 221
Potok, Chaim 1929-2002 ... **CLC 2, 7, 14, 26, 112**
   See also AAYA 15, 50; AITN 1, 2; BPFB 3;
   BYA 1; CA 17-20R; 208; CANR 19, 35,
   64, 98; CLR 92; CN 4, 5, 6; DA3; DAM
   NOV; DLB 28, 152; EXPN; INT CANR-
   19; LAIT 4; MTCW 1, 2; MTFW 2005;
   NFS 4; RGHL; SATA 33, 106; SATA-Obit
   134; TUS; YAW
Potok, Herbert Harold -2002
   See Potok, Chaim
Potok, Herman Harold
   See Potok, Chaim
Potter, Dennis (Christopher George)
   1935-1994 .... **CLC 58, 86, 123**
   See also BRWS 10; CA 107; 145; CANR
   33, 61; CBD; DLB 233; MTCW 1
Pound, Ezra (Weston Loomis)
   1885-1972 .. **CLC 1, 2, 3, 4, 5, 7, 10, 13,
   18, 34, 48, 50, 112; PC 4, 95; WLC 5**
   See also AAYA 47; AMW; AMWR 1; CA
   5-8R; 37-40R; CANR 40; CDALB 1917-
   1929; CP 1; DA; DA3; DAB; DAC; DAM
   MST, POET; DLB 4, 45, 63; DLBD 15;
   EFS 2; EWL 3; EXPP; LMFS 2; MAL 5;
   MTCW 1, 2; MTFW 2005; PAB; PFS 2,
   8, 16; RGAL 4; TUS; WP
Povod, Reinaldo 1959-1994 .... **CLC 44**
   See also CA 136; 146; CANR 83
Powell, Adam Clayton, Jr.
   1908-1972 .... **BLC 1:3; CLC 89**
   See also BW 1, 3; CA 102; 33-36R; CANR
   86; DAM MULT; DLB 345
Powell, Anthony 1905-2000 ... **CLC 1, 3, 7, 9,
   10, 31**
   See also BRW 7; CA 1-4R; 189; CANR 1,
   32, 62, 107; CDBLB 1945-1960; CN 1, 2,
   3, 4, 5, 6; DLB 15; EWL 3; MTCW 1, 2;
   MTFW 2005; RGEL 2; TEA
Powell, Dawn 1896(?)-1965 .... **CLC 66**
   See also CA 5-8R; CANR 121; DLBY 1997
Powell, Padgett 1952- .... **CLC 34**
   See also CA 126; CANR 63, 101; CSW;
   DLB 234; DLBY 01; SSFS 25
Power, Susan 1961- .... **CLC 91**
   See also BYA 14; CA 160; CANR 135; NFS
   11
Powers, J(ames) F(arl) 1917-1999 ..... **CLC 1,
   4, 8, 57; SSC 4**
   See also CA 1-4R; 181; CANR 2, 61; CN
   1, 2, 3, 4, 5, 6; DLB 130; MTCW 1;
   RGAL 4; RGSF 2
Powers, John
   See Powers, John R.
Powers, John R. 1945- .... **CLC 66**
   See also CA 69-72
Powers, Richard 1957- .... **CLC 93**
   See also AMWS 9; BPFB 3; CA 148;
   CANR 80, 180; CN 6, 7; DLB 350;
   MTFW 2005; TCLE 1:2
Powers, Richard S.
   See Powers, Richard
Pownall, David 1938- .... **CLC 10**
   See also CA 89-92, 180; CAAS 18; CANR
   49, 101; CBD; CD 5, 6; CN 4, 5, 6, 7;
   DLB 14
Powys, John Cowper 1872-1963 ... **CLC 7, 9,
   15, 46, 125**
   See also CA 85-88; CANR 106; DLB 15,
   255; EWL 3; FANT; MTCW 1, 2; MTFW
   2005; RGEL 2; SUFW
Powys, T(heodore) F(rancis)
   1875-1953 .... **TCLC 9**
   See also BRWS 8; CA 106; 189; DLB 36,
   162; EWL 3; FANT; RGEL 2; SUFW
Pozzo, Modesta
   See Fonte, Moderata

Prado (Calvo), Pedro 1886-1952 ... **TCLC 75**
   See also CA 131; DLB 283; HW 1; LAW
Prager, Emily 1952- .... **CLC 56**
   See also CA 204
Pratchett, Terence David John
   See Pratchett, Terry
Pratchett, Terry 1948- .... **CLC 197**
   See also AAYA 19, 54; BPFB 3; CA 143;
   CANR 87, 126, 170; CLR 64; CN 6, 7;
   CPW; CWRI 5; FANT; MTFW 2005;
   SATA 82, 139, 185; SFW 4; SUFW 2
Pratolini, Vasco 1913-1991 .... **TCLC 124**
   See also CA 211; DLB 177; EWL 3; RGWL
   2, 3
Pratt, E(dwin) J(ohn) 1883(?)-1964 . **CLC 19**
   See also CA 141; 93-96; CANR 77; DAC;
   DAM POET; DLB 92; EWL 3; RGEL 2;
   TWA
Premacanda
   See Srivastava, Dhanpat Rai
Premchand
   See Srivastava, Dhanpat Rai
Prem Chand, Munshi
   See Srivastava, Dhanpat Rai
Premchand, Munshi
   See Srivastava, Dhanpat Rai
Prescott, William Hickling
   1796-1859 .... **NCLC 163**
   See also DLB 1, 30, 59, 235
Preseren, France 1800-1849 .... **NCLC 127**
   See also CDWLB 4; DLB 147
Preussler, Otfried 1923- .... **CLC 17**
   See also CA 77-80; SATA 24
Prevert, Jacques (Henri Marie)
   1900-1977 .... **CLC 15**
   See also CA 77-80; 69-72; CANR 29, 61;
   DLB 258; EWL 3; GFL 1789 to the
   Present; IDFW 3, 4; MTCW 1; RGWL 2,
   3; SATA-Obit 30
Prevost, (Antoine Francois)
   1697-1763 .... **LC 1**
   See also DLB 314; EW 4; GFL Beginnings
   to 1789; RGWL 2, 3
Price, Edward Reynolds
   See Price, Reynolds
Price, Reynolds 1933- .. **CLC 3, 6, 13, 43, 50,
   63, 212; SSC 22**
   See also AMWS 6; CA 1-4R; CANR 1, 37,
   57, 87, 128, 177; CN 1, 2, 3, 4, 5, 6, 7;
   CSW; DAM NOV; DLB 2, 218, 278;
   EWL 3; INT CANR-37; MAL 5; MTFW
   2005; NFS 18
Price, Richard 1949- .... **CLC 6, 12**
   See also CA 49-52; CANR 3, 147, 190; CN
   7; DLBY 1981
Prichard, Katharine Susannah
   1883-1969 .... **CLC 46**
   See also CA 11-12; CANR 33; CAP 1; DLB
   260; MTCW 1; RGEL 2; RGSF 2; SATA
   66
Priestley, J(ohn) B(oynton)
   1894-1984 .... **CLC 2, 5, 9, 34**
   See also BRW 7; CA 9-12R; 113; CANR
   33; CDBLB 1914-1945; CN 1, 2, 3; DA3;
   DAM DRAM, NOV; DLB 10, 34, 77,
   100, 139; DLBY 1984; EWL 3; MTCW
   1, 2; MTFW 2005; RGEL 2; SFW 4
Prince 1958- .... **CLC 35**
   See also CA 213
Prince, F(rank) T(empleton)
   1912-2003 .... **CLC 22**
   See also CA 101; 219; CANR 43, 79; CP 1,
   2, 3, 4, 5, 6, 7; DLB 20
Prince Kropotkin
   See Kropotkin, Peter
Prior, Matthew 1664-1721 .... **LC 4**
   See also DLB 95; RGEL 2
Prishvin, Mikhail 1873-1954 .... **TCLC 75**
   See also DLB 272; EWL 3 !**

Prishvin, Mikhail Mikhailovich
   See Prishvin, Mikhail
Pritchard, William H(arrison)
   1932- .... **CLC 34**
   See also CA 65-68; CANR 23, 95; DLB
   111
Pritchett, V(ictor) S(awdon)
   1900-1997 .. **CLC 5, 13, 15, 41; SSC 14,
   126**
   See also BPFB 3; BRWS 3; CA 61-64; 157;
   CANR 31, 63; CN 1, 2, 3, 4, 5, 6; DA3;
   DAM NOV; DLB 15, 139; EWL 3;
   MTCW 1, 2; MTFW 2005; RGEL 2;
   RGSF 2; TEA
Private 19022
   See Manning, Frederic
Probst, Mark 1925- .... **CLC 59**
   See also CA 130
Procaccino, Michael
   See Cristofer, Michael
Proclus c. 412-c. 485 .... **CMLC 81**
Prokosch, Frederic 1908-1989 ...... **CLC 4, 48**
   See also CA 73-76; 128; CANR 82; CN 1,
   2, 3, 4; CP 1, 2, 3, 4; DLB 48; MTCW 2
Propertius, Sextus c. 50B.C.-c.
   16B.C. .... **CMLC 32**
   See also AW 2; CDWLB 1; DLB 211;
   RGWL 2, 3; WLIT 8
Prophet, The
   See Dreiser, Theodore
Prose, Francine 1947- .... **CLC 45, 231**
   See also AMWS 16; CA 109; 112; CANR
   46, 95, 132, 175; DLB 234; MTFW 2005;
   SATA 101, 149, 198
Protagoras c. 490B.C.-420B.C. ...... **CMLC 85**
   See also DLB 176
Proudhon
   See Cunha, Euclides (Rodrigues Pimenta)
   da
Proulx, Annie
   See Proulx, E. Annie
Proulx, E. Annie 1935- ...... **CLC 81, 158, 250**
   See also AMWS 7; BPFB 3; CA 145;
   CANR 65, 110; CN 6, 7; CPW 1; DA3;
   DAM POP; DLB 335, 350; MAL 5;
   MTCW 2; MTFW 2005; SSFS 18, 23
Proulx, Edna Annie
   See Proulx, E. Annie
Proust, (Valentin-Louis-George-Eugene)
   Marcel 1871-1922 ...... **SSC 75; TCLC 7,
   13, 33, 220; WLC 5**
   See also AAYA 58; BPFB 3; CA 104; 120;
   CANR 110; DA; DA3; DAB; DAC; DAM
   MST, NOV; DLB 65; EW 8; EWL 3; GFL
   1789 to the Present; MTCW 1, 2; MTFW
   2005; RGWL 2, 3; TWA
Prowler, Harley
   See Masters, Edgar Lee
Prudentius, Aurelius Clemens 348-c.
   405 .... **CMLC 78**
   See also EW 1; RGWL 2, 3
Prudhomme, Rene Francois Armand
   See Sully Prudhomme, Rene-Francois-
   Armand
Prus, Boleslaw 1845-1912 .... **TCLC 48**
   See also RGWL 2, 3
Prynne, William 1600-1669 .... **LC 148**
Prynne, Xavier
   See Hardwick, Elizabeth
Pryor, Aaron Richard
   See Pryor, Richard
Pryor, Richard 1940-2005 .... **CLC 26**
   See also CA 122; 152; 246
Pryor, Richard Franklin Lenox Thomas
   See Pryor, Richard
Przybyszewski, Stanislaw
   1868-1927 .... **TCLC 36**
   See also CA 160; DLB 66; EWL 3

Raine, Craig 1944- .... **CLC 32, 103**
   See also BRWS 13; CA 108; CANR 29, 51,
   103, 171; CP 3, 4, 5, 6, 7; DLB 40; PFS 7
Raine, Craig Anthony
   See Raine, Craig
Raine, Kathleen (Jessie) 1908-2003 .. **CLC 7,
   45**
   See also CA 85-88; 218; CANR 46, 109;
   CP 1, 2, 3, 4, 5, 6, 7; DLB 20; EWL 3;
   MTCW 1; RGEL 2
Rainis, Janis 1865-1929 .... **TCLC 29**
   See also CA 170; CDWLB 4; DLB 220;
   EWL 3
Rakosi, Carl
   See Rawley, Callman
Ralegh, Sir Walter
   See Raleigh, Sir Walter
Raleigh, Richard
   See Lovecraft, H. P.
Raleigh, Sir Walter 1554(?)-1618 .... **LC 31,
   39; PC 31**
   See also BRW 1; CDBLB Before 1660;
   DLB 172; EXPP; PFS 14; RGEL 2; TEA;
   WP
Rallentando, H. P.
   See Sayers, Dorothy L(eigh)
Ramal, Walter
   See de la Mare, Walter (John)
Ramana Maharshi 1879-1950 .... **TCLC 84**
Ramoacn y Cajal, Santiago
   1852-1934 .... **TCLC 93**
Ramon, Juan
   See Jimenez (Mantecon), Juan Ramon
Ramos, Graciliano 1892-1953 .... **TCLC 32**
   See also CA 167; DLB 307; EWL 3; HW 2;
   LAW; WLIT 1
Rampersad, Arnold 1941- .... **CLC 44**
   See also BW 2, 3; CA 127; 133; CANR 81;
   DLB 111; INT CA-133
Rampling, Anne
   See Rice, Anne
Ramsay, Allan 1686(?)-1758 .... **LC 29**
   See also DLB 95; RGEL 2
Ramsay, Jay
   See Campbell, Ramsey
Ramuz, Charles-Ferdinand
   1878-1947 .... **TCLC 33**
   See also CA 165; EWL 3
Rand, Ayn 1905-1982 ...... **CLC 3, 30, 44, 79;
   SSC 116; WLC 5**
   See also AAYA 10; AMWS 4; BPFB 3;
   BYA 12; CA 13-16R; 105; CANR 27, 73;
   CDALBS; CN 1, 2, 3; CPW; DA; DA3;
   DAC; DAM MST, NOV, POP; DLB 227,
   279; MTCW 1, 2; MTFW 2005; NFS 10,
   16, 29; RGAL 4; SFW 4; TUS; YAW
Randall, Dudley (Felker)
   1914-2000 .... **BLC 1:3; CLC 1, 135; PC
   86**
   See also BW 1, 3; CA 25-28R; 189; CANR
   23, 82; CP 1, 2, 3, 4, 5; DAM MULT;
   DLB 41; PFS 5
Randall, Robert
   See Silverberg, Robert
Ranger, Ken
   See Creasey, John
Rank, Otto 1884-1939 .... **TCLC 115**
Rankin, Ian 1960- .... **CLC 257**
   See also BRWS 10; CA 148; CANR 81,
   137, 171; DLB 267; MTFW 2005
Rankin, Ian James
   See Rankin, Ian
Ransom, John Crowe 1888-1974 .. **CLC 2, 4,
   5, 11, 24; PC 61**
   See also AMW; CA 5-8R; 49-52; CANR 6,
   34; CDALBS; CP 1, 2; DA3; DAM POET;
   DLB 45, 63; EWL 3; EXPP; MAL 5;
   MTCW 1, 2; MTFW 2005; RGAL 4; TUS

Rao, Raja 1908-2006 . **CLC 25, 56, 255; SSC
   99**
   See also CA 73-76; 252; CANR 51; CN 1,
   2, 3, 4, 5, 6; DAM NOV; DLB 323; EWL
   3; MTCW 1, 2; MTFW 2005; RGEL 2;
   RGSF 2
Raphael, Frederic (Michael) 1931- ... **CLC 2,
   14**
   See also CA 1-4R; CANR 1, 86; CN 1, 2,
   3, 4, 5, 6, 7; DLB 14, 319; TCLE 1:2
Raphael, Lev 1954- .... **CLC 232**
   See also CA 134; CANR 72, 145; GLL 1
Ratcliffe, James P.
   See Mencken, H. L.
Rathbone, Julian 1935-2008 .... **CLC 41**
   See also CA 101; 269; CANR 34, 73, 152
Rathbone, Julian Christopher
   See Rathbone, Julian
Rattigan, Terence (Mervyn)
   1911-1977 .... **CLC 7; DC 18**
   See also BRWS 7; CA 85-88; 73-76; CBD;
   CDBLB 1945-1960; DAM DRAM; DFS
   8; DLB 13; IDFW 3, 4; MTCW 1, 2;
   MTFW 2005; RGEL 2
Ratushinskaya, Irina 1954- .... **CLC 54**
   See also CA 129; CANR 68; CWW 2
Raven, Simon (Arthur Noel)
   1927-2001 .... **CLC 14**
   See also CA 81-84; 197; CANR 86; CN 1,
   2, 3, 4, 5, 6; DLB 271
Ravenna, Michael
   See Welty, Eudora
Rawley, Callman 1903-2004 .... **CLC 47**
   See also CA 21-24R; 228; CAAS 5; CANR
   12, 32, 91; CP 1, 2, 3, 4, 5, 6, 7; DLB
   193
Rawlings, Marjorie Kinnan
   1896-1953 .... **TCLC 4**
   See also AAYA 20; AMWS 10; ANW;
   BPFB 3; BYA 3; CA 104; 137; CANR 74;
   CLR 63; DLB 9, 22, 102; DLBD 17;
   JRDA; MAICYA 1, 2; MAL 5; MTCW 2;
   MTFW 2005; RGAL 4; SATA 100; WCH;
   YABC 1; YAW
Ray, Satyajit 1921-1992 .... **CLC 16, 76**
   See also CA 114; 137; DAM MULT
Read, Herbert Edward 1893-1968 ..... **CLC 4**
   See also BRW 6; CA 85-88; 25-28R; DLB
   20, 149; EWL 3; PAB; RGEL 2
Read, Piers Paul 1941- .... **CLC 4, 10, 25**
   See also CA 21-24R; CANR 38, 86, 150;
   CN 2, 3, 4, 5, 6, 7; DLB 14; SATA 21
Reade, Charles 1814-1884 .... **NCLC 2, 74**
   See also DLB 21; RGEL 2
Reade, Hamish
   See Gray, Simon
Reading, Peter 1946- .... **CLC 47**
   See also BRWS 8; CA 103; CANR 46, 96;
   CP 5, 6, 7; DLB 40
Reaney, James 1926-2008 .... **CLC 13**
   See also CA 41-44R; CAAS 15; CANR 42;
   CD 5, 6; CP 1, 2, 3, 4, 5, 6, 7; DAC;
   DAM MST; DLB 68; RGEL 2; SATA 43
Reaney, James Crerar
   See Reaney, James
Rebreanu, Liviu 1885-1944 .... **TCLC 28**
   See also CA 165; DLB 220; EWL 3
Rechy, John 1934- ..... **CLC 1, 7, 14, 18, 107;
   HLC 2**
   See also CA 5-8R, 195; CAAE 195; CAAS
   4; CANR 6, 32, 64, 152, 188; CN 1, 2, 3,
   4, 5, 6, 7; DAM MULT; DLB 122, 278;
   DLBY 1982; HW 1, 2; INT CANR-6;
   LLW; MAL 5; RGAL 4
Rechy, John Francisco
   See Rechy, John
Redcam, Tom 1870-1933 .... **TCLC 25**
Reddin, Keith 1956- .... **CLC 67**
   See also CAD; CD 6

Redgrove, Peter (William)
   1932-2003 .... **CLC 6, 41**
   See also BRWS 6; CA 1-4R; 217; CANR 3,
   39, 77; CP 1, 2, 3, 4, 5, 6, 7; DLB 40;
   TCLE 1:2
Redmon, Anne
   See Nightingale, Anne Redmon
Reed, Eliot
   See Ambler, Eric
Reed, Ishmael 1938- . **BLC 1:3; CLC 2, 3, 5,
   6, 13, 32, 60, 174; PC 68**
   See also AFAW 1, 2; AMWS 10; BPFB 3;
   BW 2, 3; CA 21-24R; CANR 25, 48, 74,
   128; CN 1, 2, 3, 4, 5, 6, 7; CP 1, 2, 3, 4,
   5, 6, 7; CSW; DA3; DAM MULT; DLB
   2, 5, 33, 169, 227; DLBD 8; EWL 3;
   LMFS 2; MAL 5; MSW; MTCW 1, 2;
   MTFW 2005; PFS 6; RGAL 4; TCWW 2
Reed, John (Silas) 1887-1920 .... **TCLC 9**
   See also CA 106; 195; MAL 5; TUS
Reed, Lou
   See Firbank, Louis
Reese, Lizette Woodworth
   1856-1935 .... **PC 29; TCLC 181**
   See also CA 180; DLB 54
Reeve, Clara 1729-1807 .... **NCLC 19**
   See also DLB 39; RGEL 2
Reich, Wilhelm 1897-1957 .... **TCLC 57**
   See also CA 199
Reid, Christopher (John) 1949- .... **CLC 33**
   See also CA 140; CANR 89; CP 4, 5, 6, 7;
   DLB 40; EWL 3
Reid, Desmond
   See Moorcock, Michael
Reid Banks, Lynne 1929- .... **CLC 23**
   See also AAYA 6; BYA 7; CA 1-4R; CANR
   6, 22, 38, 87; CLR 24, 86; CN 4, 5, 6;
   JRDA; MAICYA 1, 2; SATA 22, 75, 111,
   165; YAW
Reilly, William K.
   See Creasey, John
Reiner, Max
   See Caldwell, (Janet Miriam) Taylor
   (Holland)
Reis, Ricardo
   See Pessoa, Fernando
Reizenstein, Elmer Leopold
   See Rice, Elmer (Leopold)
Remarque, Erich Maria 1898-1970 . **CLC 21**
   See also AAYA 27; BPFB 3; CA 77-80; 29-
   32R; CDWLB 2; DA; DA3; DAB; DAC;
   DAM MST, NOV; DLB 56; EWL 3;
   EXPN; LAIT 3; MTCW 1, 2; MTFW
   2005; NFS 4; RGHL; RGWL 2, 3
Remington, Frederic S(ackrider)
   1861-1909 .... **TCLC 89**
   See also CA 108; 169; DLB 12, 186, 188;
   SATA 41; TCWW 2
Remizov, A.
   See Remizov, Aleksei (Mikhailovich)
Remizov, A. M.
   See Remizov, Aleksei (Mikhailovich)
Remizov, Aleksei (Mikhailovich)
   1877-1957 .... **TCLC 27**
   See also CA 125; 133; DLB 295; EWL 3
Remizov, Alexey Mikhaylovich
   See Remizov, Aleksei (Mikhailovich)
Renan, Joseph Ernest 1823-1892 . **NCLC 26,
   145**
   See also GFL 1789 to the Present
Renard, Jules(-Pierre) 1864-1910 .. **TCLC 17**
   See also CA 117; 202; GFL 1789 to the
   Present
Renart, Jean fl. 13th cent. - .... **CMLC 83**
Renault, Mary
   See Challans, Mary
Rendell, Ruth
   See Rendell, Ruth

Ritsos, Yannis 1909-1990 .... **CLC 6, 13, 31**
See also CA 77-80; 133; CANR 39, 61; EW
12; EWL 3; MTCW 1; RGWL 2, 3
Ritter, Erika 1948(?)- .... **CLC 52**
See also CD 5, 6; CWD
Rivera, Jose Eustasio 1889-1928 ... **TCLC 35**
See also CA 162; EWL 3; HW 1, 2; LAW
Rivera, Tomas 1935-1984 .... **HLCS 2**
See also CA 49-52; CANR 32; DLB 82;
HW 1; LLW; RGAL 4; SSFS 15; TCWW
2; WLIT 1
Rivers, Conrad Kent 1933-1968 .... **CLC 1**
See also BW 1; CA 85-88; DLB 41
Rivers, Elfrida
See Bradley, Marion Zimmer
Riverside, John
See Heinlein, Robert A.
Rizal, Jose 1861-1896 .... **NCLC 27**
See also DLB 348
Roa Bastos, Augusto 1917-2005 ...... **CLC 45;
HLC 2**
See also CA 131; 238; CWW 2; DAM
MULT; DLB 113; EWL 3; HW 1; LAW;
RGSF 2; WLIT 1
Roa Bastos, Augusto Jose Antonio
See Roa Bastos, Augusto
Robbe-Grillet, Alain 1922-2008 ..... **CLC 1, 2,
4, 6, 8, 10, 14, 43, 128**
See also BPFB 3; CA 9-12R; 269; CANR
33, 65, 115; CWW 2; DLB 83; EW 13;
EWL 3; GFL 1789 to the Present; IDFW
3, 4; MTCW 1, 2; MTFW 2005; RGWL
2, 3; SSFS 15
Robbins, Harold 1916-1997 .... **CLC 5**
See also BPFB 3; CA 73-76; 162; CANR
26, 54, 112, 156; DA3; DAM NOV;
MTCW 1, 2
Robbins, Thomas Eugene 1936- . **CLC 9, 32,
64**
See also AAYA 32; AMWS 10; BEST 90:3;
BPFB 3; CA 81-84; CANR 29, 59, 95,
139; CN 3, 4, 5, 6, 7; CPW; CSW; DA3;
DAM NOV, POP; DLBY 1980; MTCW
1, 2; MTFW 2005
Robbins, Tom
See Robbins, Thomas Eugene
Robbins, Trina 1938- .... **CLC 21**
See also AAYA 61; CA 128; CANR 152
Robert de Boron fl. 12th cent. - .... **CMLC 94**
Roberts, Charles G(eorge) D(ouglas)
1860-1943 .... **SSC 91; TCLC 8**
See also CA 105; 188; CLR 33; CWRI 5;
DLB 92; RGEL 2; RGSF 2; SATA 88;
SATA-Brief 29
Roberts, Elizabeth Madox
1886-1941 .... **TCLC 68**
See also CA 111; 166; CLR 100; CWRI 5;
DLB 9, 54, 102; RGAL 4; RHW; SATA
33; SATA-Brief 27; TCWW 2; WCH
Roberts, Kate 1891-1985 .... **CLC 15**
See also CA 107; 116; DLB 319
Roberts, Keith (John Kingston)
1935-2000 .... **CLC 14**
See also BRWS 10; CA 25-28R; CANR 46;
DLB 261; SFW 4
Roberts, Kenneth (Lewis)
1885-1957 .... **TCLC 23**
See also CA 109; 199; DLB 9; MAL 5;
RGAL 4; RHW
Roberts, Michele 1949- .... **CLC 48, 178**
See also CA 115; CANR 58, 120, 164; CN
6, 7; DLB 231; FW
Roberts, Michele Brigitte
See Roberts, Michele
Robertson, Ellis
See Ellison, Harlan; Silverberg, Robert
Robertson, Thomas William
1829-1871 .... **NCLC 35**
See also DAM DRAM; DLB 344; RGEL 2

Robertson, Tom
See Robertson, Thomas William
Robeson, Kenneth
See Dent, Lester
Robinson, Edwin Arlington
1869-1935 .... **PC 1, 35; TCLC 5, 101**
See also AAYA 72; AMW; CA 104; 133;
CDALB 1865-1917; DA; DAC; DAM
MST, POET; DLB 54; EWL 3; EXPP;
MAL 5; MTCW 1, 2; MTFW 2005; PAB;
PFS 4; RGAL 4; WP
Robinson, Henry Crabb
1775-1867 .... **NCLC 15**
See also DLB 107
Robinson, Jill 1936- .... **CLC 10**
See also CA 102; CANR 120; INT CA-102
Robinson, Kim Stanley 1952- ... **CLC 34, 248**
See also AAYA 26; CA 126; CANR 113,
139, 173; CN 6, 7; MTFW 2005; SATA
109; SCFW 2; SFW 4
Robinson, Lloyd
See Silverberg, Robert
Robinson, Marilynne 1943- ..... **CLC 25, 180,
276**
See also AAYA 69; CA 116; CANR 80, 140,
192; CN 4, 5, 6, 7; DLB 206, 350; MTFW
2005; NFS 24
Robinson, Mary 1758-1800 .... **NCLC 142**
See also BRWS 13; DLB 158; FW
Robinson, Smokey
See Robinson, William, Jr.
Robinson, William, Jr. 1940- .... **CLC 21**
See also CA 116
Robison, Mary 1949- .... **CLC 42, 98**
See also CA 113; 116; CANR 87; CN 4, 5,
6, 7; DLB 130; INT CA-116; RGSF 2
Roches, Catherine des 1542-1587 ...... **LC 117**
See also DLB 327
Rochester
See Wilmot, John
Rod, Edouard 1857-1910 .... **TCLC 52**
Roddenberry, Eugene Wesley
1921-1991 .... **CLC 17**
See also AAYA 5; CA 110; 135; CANR 37;
SATA 45; SATA-Obit 69
Roddenberry, Gene
See Roddenberry, Eugene Wesley
Rodgers, Mary 1931- .... **CLC 12**
See also BYA 5; CA 49-52; CANR 8, 55,
90; CLR 20; CWRI 5; INT CANR-8;
JRDA; MAICYA 1, 2; SATA 8, 130
Rodgers, W(illiam) R(obert)
1909-1969 .... **CLC 7**
See also CA 85-88; DLB 20; RGEL 2
Rodman, Eric
See Silverberg, Robert
Rodman, Howard 1920(?)-1985 .... **CLC 65**
See also CA 118
Rodman, Maia
See Wojciechowska, Maia (Teresa)
Rodo, Jose Enrique 1871(?)-1917 .... **HLCS 2**
See also CA 178; EWL 3; HW 2; LAW
Rodolph, Utto
See Ouologuem, Yambo
Rodriguez, Claudio 1934-1999 .... **CLC 10**
See also CA 188; DLB 134
Rodriguez, Richard 1944- .... **CLC 155; HLC
2**
See also AMWS 14; CA 110; CANR 66,
116; DAM MULT; DLB 82, 256; HW 1,
2; LAIT 5; LLW; MTFW 2005; NCFS 3;
WLIT 1
Roethke, Theodore 1908-1963 ... **CLC 1, 3, 8,
11, 19, 46, 101; PC 15**
See also AMW; CA 81-84; CABS 2;
CDALB 1941-1968; DA3; DAM POET;
DLB 5, 206; EWL 3; EXPP; MAL 5;
MTCW 1, 2; PAB; PFS 3; RGAL 4; WP

Roethke, Theodore Huebner
See Roethke, Theodore
Rogers, Carl R(ansom)
1902-1987 .... **TCLC 125**
See also CA 1-4R; 121; CANR 1, 18;
MTCW 1
Rogers, Samuel 1763-1855 .... **NCLC 69**
See also DLB 93; RGEL 2
Rogers, Thomas 1927-2007 .... **CLC 57**
See also CA 89-92; 259; CANR 163; INT
CA-89-92
Rogers, Thomas Hunton
See Rogers, Thomas
Rogers, Will(iam Penn Adair)
1879-1935 .... **NNAL; TCLC 8, 71**
See also CA 105; 144; DA3; DAM MULT;
DLB 11; MTCW 2
Rogin, Gilbert 1929- .... **CLC 18**
See also CA 65-68; CANR 15
Rohan, Koda
See Koda Shigeyuki
Rohlfs, Anna Katharine Green
See Green, Anna Katharine
Rohmer, Eric
See Scherer, Jean-Marie Maurice
Rohmer, Sax
See Ward, Arthur Henry Sarsfield
Roiphe, Anne 1935- .... **CLC 3, 9**
See also CA 89-92; CANR 45, 73, 138, 170;
DLBY 1980; INT CA-89-92
Roiphe, Anne Richardson
See Roiphe, Anne
Rojas, Fernando de 1475-1541 ... **HLCS 1, 2;
LC 23, 169**
See also DLB 286; RGWL 2, 3
Rojas, Gonzalo 1917- .... **HLCS 2**
See also CA 178; HW 2; LAWS 1
Rolaag, Ole Edvart
See Rolvaag, O.E.
Roland (de la Platiere), Marie-Jeanne
1754-1793 .... **LC 98**
See also DLB 314
**Rolfe, Frederick (William Serafino Austin
Lewis Mary)** 1860-1913 .... **TCLC 12**
See also CA 107; 210; DLB 34, 156; GLL
1; RGEL 2
Rolland, Romain 1866-1944 .... **TCLC 23**
See also CA 118; 197; DLB 65, 284, 332;
EWL 3; GFL 1789 to the Present; RGWL
2, 3
Rolle, Richard c. 1300-c. 1349 ...... **CMLC 21**
See also DLB 146; LMFS 1; RGEL 2
Rolvaag, O.E.
See Rolvaag, O.E.
Rolvaag, O.E.
See Rolvaag, O.E.
Rolvaag, O.E. 1876-1931 .... **TCLC 17, 207**
See also AAYA 75; CA 117; 171; DLB 9,
212; MAL 5; NFS 5; RGAL 4; TCWW 1,
2
Romain Arnaud, Saint
See Aragon, Louis
Romains, Jules 1885-1972 .... **CLC 7**
See also CA 85-88; CANR 34; DLB 65,
321; EWL 3; GFL 1789 to the Present;
MTCW 1
Romero, Jose Ruben 1890-1952 .... **TCLC 14**
See also CA 114; 131; EWL 3; HW 1; LAW
Ronsard, Pierre de 1524-1585 . **LC 6, 54; PC
11**
See also DLB 327; EW 2; GFL Beginnings
to 1789; RGWL 2, 3; TWA
Rooke, Leon 1934- .... **CLC 25, 34**
See also CA 25-28R; CANR 23, 53; CCA
1; CPW; DAM POP
Roosevelt, Franklin Delano
1882-1945 .... **TCLC 93**
See also CA 116; 173; LAIT 3

Shanley, John Patrick 1950- .... **CLC 75**
  See also AAYA 74; AMWS 14; CA 128;
  133; CAD; CANR 83, 154; CD 5, 6; DFS
  23

Shapcott, Thomas W(illiam) 1935- .. **CLC 38**
  See also CA 69-72; CANR 49, 83, 103; CP
  1, 2, 3, 4, 5, 6, 7; DLB 289

Shapiro, Jane 1942- .... **CLC 76**
  See also CA 196

Shapiro, Karl 1913-2000 ... **CLC 4, 8, 15, 53;**
  PC 25
  See also AMWS 2; CA 1-4R; 188; CAAS
  6; CANR 1, 36, 66; CP 1, 2, 3, 4, 5, 6;
  DLB 48; EWL 3; EXPP; MAL 5; MTCW
  1, 2; MTFW 2005; PFS 3; RGAL 4

Sharp, William 1855-1905 .... **TCLC 39**
  See also CA 160; DLB 156; RGEL 2;
  SUFW

Sharpe, Thomas Ridley 1928- .... **CLC 36**
  See also CA 114; 122; CANR 85; CN 4, 5,
  6, 7; DLB 14, 231; INT CA-122

Sharpe, Tom
  See Sharpe, Thomas Ridley

Shatrov, Mikhail .... **CLC 59**

Shaw, Bernard
  See Shaw, George Bernard

Shaw, G. Bernard
  See Shaw, George Bernard

Shaw, George Bernard 1856-1950 ..... **DC 23;**
  TCLC 3, 9, 21, 45, 205; WLC 5
  See also AAYA 61; BRW 6; BRWC 1;
  BRWR 2; CA 104; 128; CDBLB 1914-
  1945; DA; DA3; DAB; DAC; DAM
  DRAM, MST; DFS 1, 3, 6, 11, 19, 22;
  DLB 10, 57, 190, 332; EWL 3; LAIT 3;
  LATS 1:1; MTCW 1, 2; MTFW 2005;
  RGEL 2; TEA; WLIT 4

Shaw, Henry Wheeler 1818-1885 .. **NCLC 15**
  See also DLB 11; RGAL 4

Shaw, Irwin 1913-1984 .... **CLC 7, 23, 34**
  See also AITN 1; BPFB 3; CA 13-16R; 112;
  CANR 21; CDALB 1941-1968; CN 1, 2,
  3; CPW; DAM DRAM, POP; DLB 6,
  102; DLBY 1984; MAL 5; MTCW 1, 21;
  MTFW 2005

Shaw, Robert (Archibald)
  1927-1978 .... **CLC 5**
  See also AITN 1; CA 1-4R; 81-84; CANR
  4; CN 1, 2; DLB 13, 14

Shaw, T. E.
  See Lawrence, T. E.

Shawn, Wallace 1943- .... **CLC 41**
  See also CA 112; CAD; CD 5, 6; DLB 266

Shaykh, al- Hanan
  See al-Shaykh, Hanan

Shchedrin, N.
  See Saltykov, Mikhail Evgrafovich

Shea, Lisa 1953- .... **CLC 86**
  See also CA 147

Sheed, Wilfrid 1930- .... **CLC 2, 4, 10, 53**
  See also CA 65-68; CANR 30, 66, 181; CN
  1, 2, 3, 4, 5, 6, 7; DLB 6; MAL 5; MTCW
  1, 2; MTFW 2005

Sheed, Wilfrid John Joseph
  See Sheed, Wilfrid

Sheehy, Gail 1937- .... **CLC 171**
  See also CA 49-52; CANR 1, 33, 55, 92;
  CPW; MTCW 1

Sheldon, Alice Hastings Bradley
  1915(?)-1987 .... **CLC 48, 50**
  See also CA 108; 122; CANR 34; DLB 8;
  INT CA-108; MTCW 1; SCFW 1, 2; SFW
  4

Sheldon, John
  See Bloch, Robert (Albert)

Sheldon, Raccoona
  See Sheldon, Alice Hastings Bradley

Shelley, Mary Wollstonecraft (Godwin)
  1797-1851 .... **NCLC 14, 59, 103, 170;**
  SSC 92; WLC 5
  See also AAYA 20; BPFB 3; BRW 3;
  BRWC 2; BRWS 3; BYA 5; CDBLB
  1789-1832; CLR 133; DA; DA3; DAB;
  DAC; DAM MST, NOV; DLB 110, 116,
  159, 178; EXPN; FL 1:3; GL 3; HGG;
  LAIT 1; LMFS 1, 2; NFS 1; RGEL 2;
  SATA 29; SCFW 1, 2; SFW 4; TEA;
  WLIT 3

Shelley, Percy Bysshe 1792-1822 .. **NCLC 18,**
  93, 143, 175; PC 14, 67; WLC 5
  See also AAYA 61; BRW 4; BRWR 1; CD-
  BLB 1789-1832; DA; DA3; DAB; DAC;
  DAM MST, POET; DLB 96, 110, 158;
  EXPP; LMFS 1; PAB; PFS 2, 27; RGEL
  2; TEA; WLIT 3; WP

Shepard, James R.
  See Shepard, Jim

Shepard, Jim 1956- .... **CLC 36**
  See also AAYA 73; CA 137; CANR 59, 104,
  160; SATA 90, 164

Shepard, Lucius 1947- .... **CLC 34**
  See also CA 128; 141; CANR 81, 124, 178;
  HGG; SCFW 2; SFW 4; SUFW 2

Shepard, Sam 1943- .... **CLC 4, 6, 17, 34, 41,**
  44, 169; DC 5
  See also AAYA 1, 58; AMWS 3; CA 69-72;
  CABS 3; CAD; CANR 22, 120, 140; CD
  5, 6; DA3; DAM DRAM; DFS 3, 6, 7,
  14; DLB 7, 212, 341; EWL 3; IDFW 3, 4;
  MAL 5; MTCW 1, 2; MTFW 2005;
  RGAL 4

Shepherd, Jean (Parker)
  1921-1999 .... **TCLC 177**
  See also AAYA 69; AITN 2; CA 77-80; 187

Shepherd, Michael
  See Ludlum, Robert

Sherburne, Zoa (Lillian Morin)
  1912-1995 .... **CLC 30**
  See also AAYA 13; CA 1-4R; 176; CANR
  3, 37; MAICYA 1, 2; SAAS 18; SATA 3;
  YAW

Sheridan, Frances 1724-1766 .... **LC 7**
  See also DLB 39, 84

Sheridan, Richard Brinsley
  1751-1816 . **DC 1; NCLC 5, 91; WLC 5**
  See also BRW 3; CDBLB 1660-1789; DA;
  DAB; DAC; DAM DRAM, MST; DFS
  15; DLB 89; WLIT 3

Sherman, Jonathan Marc 1968- .... **CLC 55**
  See also CA 230

Sherman, Martin 1941(?)- .... **CLC 19**
  See also CA 116; 123; CAD; CANR 86;
  CD 5, 6; DFS 20; DLB 228; GLL 1;
  IDTP; RGHL

Sherwin, Judith Johnson
  See Johnson, Judith

Sherwood, Frances 1940- .... **CLC 81**
  See also CA 146; 220; CAAE 220; CANR
  158

Sherwood, Robert E(mmet)
  1896-1955 .... **DC 36; TCLC 3**
  See also CA 104; 153; CANR 86; DAM
  DRAM; DFS 11, 15, 17; DLB 7, 26, 249;
  IDFW 3, 4; MAL 5; RGAL 4

Shestov, Lev 1866-1938 .... **TCLC 56**

Shevchenko, Taras 1814-1861 .... **NCLC 54**

Shiel, M. P. 1865-1947 .... **TCLC 8**
  See also CA 106; 160; DLB 153; HGG;
  MTCW 2; MTFW 2005; SCFW 1, 2;
  SFW 4; SUFW

Shiel, Matthew Phipps
  See Shiel, M. P.

Shields, Carol 1935-2003 . **CLC 91, 113, 193;**
  SSC 126
  See also AMWS 7; CA 81-84; 218; CANR
  51, 74, 98, 133; CCA 1; CN 6, 7; CPW;
  DA3; DAC; DLB 334, 350; MTCW 2;
  MTFW 2005; NFS 23

Shields, David 1956- .... **CLC 97**
  See also CA 124; CANR 48, 99, 112, 157

Shields, David Jonathan
  See Shields, David

Shiga, Naoya 1883-1971 .... **CLC 33; SSC 23;**
  TCLC 172
  See also CA 101; 33-36R; DLB 180; EWL
  3; MJW; RGWL 3

Shiga Naoya
  See Shiga, Naoya

Shilts, Randy 1951-1994 .... **CLC 85**
  See also AAYA 19; CA 115; 127; 144;
  CANR 45; DA3; GLL 1; INT CA-127;
  MTCW 2; MTFW 2005

Shimazaki, Haruki 1872-1943 .... **TCLC 5**
  See also CA 105; 134; CANR 84; DLB 180;
  EWL 3; MJW; RGWL 3

Shimazaki Toson
  See Shimazaki, Haruki

Shirley, James 1596-1666 .... **DC 25; LC 96**
  See also DLB 58; RGEL 2

Shirley Hastings, Selina
  See Hastings, Selina

Sholem Aleykhem
  See Rabinovitch, Sholem

Sholokhov, Mikhail (Aleksandrovich)
  1905-1984 .... **CLC 7, 15**
  See also CA 101; 112; DLB 272, 332; EWL
  3; MTCW 1, 2; MTFW 2005; RGWL 2,
  3; SATA-Obit 36

Sholom Aleichem 1859-1916
  See Rabinovitch, Sholem

Shone, Patric
  See Hanley, James

Showalter, Elaine 1941- .... **CLC 169**
  See also CA 57-60; CANR 58, 106; DLB
  67; FW; GLL 2

Shreve, Susan
  See Shreve, Susan Richards

Shreve, Susan Richards 1939- .... **CLC 23**
  See also CA 49-52; CAAS 5; CANR 5, 38,
  69, 100, 159; MAICYA 1, 2; SATA 46,
  95, 152; SATA-Brief 41

Shue, Larry 1946-1985 .... **CLC 52**
  See also CA 145; 117; DAM DRAM; DFS
  7

Shu-Jen, Chou 1881-1936 . **SSC 20; TCLC 3**
  See also CA 104; EWL 3

Shulman, Alix Kates 1932- .... **CLC 2, 10**
  See also CA 29-32R; CANR 43; FW; SATA
  7

Shuster, Joe 1914-1992 .... **CLC 21**
  See also AAYA 50

Shute, Nevil
  See Norway, Nevil Shute

Shuttle, Penelope (Diane) 1947- .... **CLC 7**
  See also CA 93-96; CANR 39, 84, 92, 108;
  CP 3, 4, 5, 6, 7; CWP; DLB 14, 40

Shvarts, Elena 1948- .... **PC 50**
  See also CA 147

Sidhwa, Bapsi 1939-
  See Sidhwa, Bapsy (N.)

Sidhwa, Bapsy (N.) 1938- .... **CLC 168**
  See also CA 108; CANR 25, 57; CN 6, 7;
  DLB 323; FW

Sidney, Mary 1561-1621 .... **LC 19, 39**
  See also DLB 167

Sidney, Sir Philip 1554-1586 .... **LC 19, 39,**
  131; PC 32
  See also BRW 1; BRWR 2; CDBLB Before
  1660; DA; DA3; DAB; DAC; DAM MST,
  POET; DLB 167; EXPP; PAB; PFS 30;
  RGEL 2; TEA; WP

Sidney Herbert, Mary
  See Sidney, Mary

Siegel, Jerome 1914-1996 .... **CLC 21**
  See also AAYA 50; CA 116; 169; 151

Sturgeon, Theodore (Hamilton)
1918-1985 .... **CLC 22, 39**
See also AAYA 51; BPFB 3; BYA 9, 10; CA 81-84; 116; CANR 32, 103; DLB 8; DLBY 1985; HGG; MTCW 1, 2; MTFW 2005; SCFW; SFW 4; SUFW

Sturges, Preston 1898-1959 .... **TCLC 48**
See also CA 114; 149; DLB 26

Styron, William 1925-2006 .. **CLC 1, 3, 5, 11, 15, 60, 232, 244; SSC 25**
See also AMW; AMWC 2; BEST 90:4; BPFB 3; CA 5-8R; 255; CANR 6, 33, 74, 126, 191; CDALB 1968-1988; CN 1, 2, 3, 4, 5, 6, 7; CPW; CSW; DA3; DAM NOV, POP; DLB 2, 143, 299; DLBY 1980; EWL 3; INT CANR-6; LAIT 2; MAL 5; MTCW 1, 2; MTFW 2005; NCFS 1; NFS 22; RGAL 4; RGHL; RHW; TUS

Styron, William C.
See Styron, William

Styron, William Clark
See Styron, William

Su, Chien 1884-1918 .... **TCLC 24**
See also CA 123; EWL 3

Suarez Lynch, B.
See Bioy Casares, Adolfo; Borges, Jorge Luis

Suassuna, Ariano Vilar 1927- .... **HLCS 1**
See also CA 178; DLB 307; HW 2; LAW

Suckert, Kurt Erich
See Malaparte, Curzio

Suckling, Sir John 1609-1642 . **LC 75; PC 30**
See also BRW 2; DAM POET; DLB 58, 126; EXPP; PAB; RGEL 2

Suckow, Ruth 1892-1960 .... **SSC 18**
See also CA 193; 113; DLB 9, 102; RGAL 4; TCWW 2

Sudermann, Hermann 1857-1928 .. **TCLC 15**
See also CA 107; 201; DLB 118

Sue, Eugene 1804-1857 .... **NCLC 1**
See also DLB 119

Sueskind, Patrick
See Suskind, Patrick

Suetonius c. 70-c. 130 .... **CMLC 60**
See also AW 2; DLB 211; RGWL 2, 3; WLIT 8

Su Hsuan-ying
See Su, Chien

Su Hsuean-ying
See Su, Chien

Sukenick, Ronald 1932-2004 ..... **CLC 3, 4, 6, 48**
See also CA 25-28R; 209; 229; CAAE 209; CAAS 8; CANR 32, 89; CN 3, 4, 5, 6, 7; DLB 173; DLBY 1981

Suknaski, Andrew 1942- .... **CLC 19**
See also CA 101; CP 3, 4, 5, 6, 7; DLB 53

Sullivan, Vernon
See Vian, Boris

Sully Prudhomme, Rene-Francois-Armand
1839-1907 .... **TCLC 31**
See also CA 170; DLB 332; GFL 1789 to the Present

Su Man-shu
See Su, Chien

Sumarokov, Aleksandr Petrovich
1717-1777 .... **LC 104**
See also DLB 150

Summerforest, Ivy B.
See Kirkup, James

Summers, Andrew James
See Summers, Andy

Summers, Andy 1942- .... **CLC 26**
See also CA 255

Summers, Hollis (Spurgeon, Jr.)
1916- .... **CLC 10**
See also CA 5-8R; CANR 3; CN 1, 2, 3; CP 1, 2, 3, 4; DLB 6; TCLE 1:2

Summers, (Alphonsus Joseph-Mary Augustus) Montague
1880-1948 .... **TCLC 16**
See also CA 118; 163

Sumner, Gordon Matthew
See Sting

Sun Tzu c. 400B.C.-c. 320B.C. ...... **CMLC 56**

Surdas c. 1478-c. 1583 .... **LC 163**
See also RGWL 2, 3

Surrey, Henry Howard 1517-1574 ... **LC 121; PC 59**
See also BRW 1; RGEL 2

Surtees, Robert Smith 1805-1864 .. **NCLC 14**
See also DLB 21; RGEL 2

Susann, Jacqueline 1921-1974 .... **CLC 3**
See also AITN 1; BPFB 3; CA 65-68; 53-56; MTCW 1, 2

Su Shi
See Su Shih

Su Shih 1036-1101 .... **CMLC 15**
See also RGWL 2, 3

Suskind, Patrick 1949- .... **CLC 44, 182**
See also BPFB 3; CA 145; CWW 2

Suso, Heinrich c. 1295-1366 .... **CMLC 87**

Sutcliff, Rosemary 1920-1992 .... **CLC 26**
See also AAYA 10; BYA 1, 4; CA 5-8R; 139; CANR 37; CLR 1, 37, 138; CPW; DAB; DAC; DAM MST, POP; JRDA; LATS 1:1; MAICYA 1, 2; MAICYAS 1; RHW; SATA 6, 44, 78; SATA-Obit 73; WYA; YAW

Sutherland, Efua (Theodora Morgue)
1924-1996 .... **BLC 2:3**
See also AFW; BW 1; CA 105; CWD; DLB 117; EWL 3; IDTP; SATA 25

Sutro, Alfred 1863-1933 .... **TCLC 6**
See also CA 105; 185; DLB 10; RGEL 2

Sutton, Henry
See Slavitt, David R.

Su Yuan-ying
See Su, Chien

Su Yuean-ying
See Su, Chien

Suzuki, D. T.
See Suzuki, Daisetz Teitaro

Suzuki, Daisetz T.
See Suzuki, Daisetz Teitaro

Suzuki, Daisetz Teitaro
1870-1966 .... **TCLC 109**
See also CA 121; 111; MTCW 1, 2; MTFW 2005

Suzuki, Teitaro
See Suzuki, Daisetz Teitaro

Svareff, Count Vladimir
See Crowley, Edward Alexander

Svevo, Italo
See Schmitz, Aron Hector

Swados, Elizabeth 1951- .... **CLC 12**
See also CA 97-100; CANR 49, 163; INT CA-97-100

Swados, Elizabeth A.
See Swados, Elizabeth

Swados, Harvey 1920-1972 .... **CLC 5**
See also CA 5-8R; 37-40R; CANR 6; CN 1; DLB 2, 335; MAL 5

Swados, Liz
See Swados, Elizabeth

Swan, Gladys 1934- .... **CLC 69**
See also CA 101; CANR 17, 39; TCLE 1:2

Swanson, Logan
See Matheson, Richard

Swarthout, Glendon (Fred)
1918-1992 .... **CLC 35**
See also AAYA 55; CA 1-4R; 139; CANR 1, 47; CN 1, 2, 3, 4, 5; LAIT 5; NFS 29; SATA 26; TCWW 1, 2; YAW

Swedenborg, Emanuel 1688-1772 ..... **LC 105**

Sweet, Sarah C.
See Jewett, (Theodora) Sarah Orne

Swenson, May 1919-1989 ...... **CLC 4, 14, 61, 106; PC 14**
See also AMWS 4; CA 5-8R; 130; CANR 36, 61, 131; CP 1, 2, 3, 4; DA; DAB; DAC; DAM MST, POET; DLB 5; EXPP; GLL 2; MAL 5; MTCW 1, 2; MTFW 2005; PFS 16, 30; SATA 15; WP

Swift, Augustus
See Lovecraft, H. P.

Swift, Graham 1949- .... **CLC 41, 88, 233**
See also BRWC 2; BRWS 5; CA 117; 122; CANR 46, 71, 128, 181; CN 4, 5, 6, 7; DLB 194, 326; MTCW 2; MTFW 2005; NFS 18; RGSF 2

Swift, Jonathan 1667-1745 ..... **LC 1, 42, 101; PC 9; WLC 6**
See also AAYA 41; BRW 3; BRWC 1; BRWR 1; BYA 5, 14; CDBLB 1660-1789; CLR 53; DA; DA3; DAB; DAC; DAM MST, NOV, POET; DLB 39, 95, 101; EXPN; LAIT 1; NFS 6; PFS 27; RGEL 2; SATA 19; TEA; WCH; WLIT 3

Swinburne, Algernon Charles
1837-1909 ... **PC 24; TCLC 8, 36; WLC 6**
See also BRW 5; CA 105; 140; CDBLB 1832-1890; DA; DA3; DAB; DAC; DAM MST, POET; DLB 35, 57; PAB; RGEL 2; TEA

Swinfen, Ann .... **CLC 34**
See also CA 202

Swinnerton, Frank (Arthur)
1884-1982 .... **CLC 31**
See also CA 202; 108; CN 1, 2, 3; DLB 34

Swinnerton, Frank Arthur
1884-1982 .... **CLC 31**
See also CA 108; DLB 34

Swithen, John
See King, Stephen

Sylvia
See Ashton-Warner, Sylvia (Constance)

Symmes, Robert Edward
See Duncan, Robert

Symonds, John Addington
1840-1893 .... **NCLC 34**
See also BRWS 14; DLB 57, 144

Symons, Arthur 1865-1945 .... **TCLC 11**
See also BRWS 14; CA 107; 189; DLB 19, 57, 149; RGEL 2

Symons, Julian (Gustave)
1912-1994 .... **CLC 2, 14, 32**
See also CA 49-52; 147; CAAS 3; CANR 3, 33, 59; CMW 4; CN 1, 2, 3, 4, 5; CP 1, 3, 4; DLB 87, 155; DLBY 1992; MSW; MTCW 1

Synge, (Edmund) J(ohn) M(illington)
1871-1909 .... **DC 2; TCLC 6, 37**
See also BRW 6; BRWR 1; CA 104; 141; CDBLB 1890-1914; DAM DRAM; DFS 18; DLB 10, 19; EWL 3; RGEL 2; TEA; WLIT 4

Syruc, J.
See Milosz, Czeslaw

Szirtes, George 1948- .... **CLC 46; PC 51**
See also CA 109; CANR 27, 61, 117; CP 4, 5, 6, 7

Szymborska, Wislawa 1923- ... **CLC 99, 190; PC 44**
See also AAYA 76; CA 154; CANR 91, 133, 181; CDWLB 4; CWP; CWW 2; DA3; DLB 232, 332; DLBY 1996; EWL 3; MTCW 2; MTFW 2005; PFS 15, 27, 31; RGHL; RGWL 3

T. O., Nik
See Annensky, Innokenty (Fyodorovich)

Tabori, George 1914-2007 .... **CLC 19**
See also CA 49-52; 262; CANR 4, 69; CBD; CD 5, 6; DLB 245; RGHL

Trevor, William 1928- ... **CLC 1, 2, 3, 4, 5, 6, 7; SSC 21, 58**
See also BRWS 4; CA 9-12R; CANR 4, 37, 55, 76, 102, 139; CBD; CD 5, 6; DAM NOV; DLB 14, 139; EWL 3; INT CANR-37; LATS 1:2; MTCW 1, 2; MTFW 2005; RGEL 2; RGSF 2; SSFS 10; TCLE 1:2; TEA

Trifonov, Iurii (Valentinovich)
See Trifonov, Yuri (Valentinovich)

Trifonov, Yuri (Valentinovich)
1925-1981 .... **CLC 45**
See also CA 126; 103; DLB 302; EWL 3; MTCW 1; RGWL 2, 3

Trifonov, Yury Valentinovich
See Trifonov, Yuri (Valentinovich)

Trilling, Diana (Rubin) 1905-1996 . **CLC 129**
See also CA 5-8R; 154; CANR 10, 46; INT CANR-10; MTCW 1, 2

Trilling, Lionel 1905-1975 ..... **CLC 9, 11, 24; SSC 75**
See also AMWS 3; CA 9-12R; 61-64; CANR 10, 105; CN 1, 2; DLB 28, 63; EWL 3; INT CANR-10; MAL 5; MTCW 1, 2; RGAL 4; TUS

Trimball, W. H.
See Mencken, H. L.

Tristan
See Gomez de la Serna, Ramon

Tristram
See Housman, A(lfred) E(dward)

Trogdon, William 1939- .... **CLC 29**
See also AAYA 9, 66; ANW; CA 115; 119; CANR 47, 89; CPW; INT CA-119

Trogdon, William Lewis
See Trogdon, William

Trollope, Anthony 1815-1882 .... **NCLC 6, 33, 101, 215; SSC 28; WLC 6**
See also BRW 5; CDBLB 1832-1890; DA; DA3; DAB; DAC; DAM MST, NOV; DLB 21, 57, 159; RGEL 2; RGSF 2; SATA 22

Trollope, Frances 1779-1863 .... **NCLC 30**
See also DLB 21, 166

Trollope, Joanna 1943- .... **CLC 186**
See also CA 101; CANR 58, 95, 149, 191; CN 7; CPW; DLB 207; RHW

Trotsky, Leon 1879-1940 .... **TCLC 22**
See also CA 118; 167

Trotter (Cockburn), Catharine
1679-1749 .... **LC 8, 165**
See also DLB 84, 252

Trotter, Wilfred 1872-1939 .... **TCLC 97**

Troupe, Quincy 1943- .... **BLC 2:3**
See also BW 2; CA 113; 124; CANR 43, 90, 126; DLB 41

Trout, Kilgore
See Farmer, Philip Jose

Trow, George William Swift
See Trow, George W.S.

Trow, George W.S. 1943-2006 .... **CLC 52**
See also CA 126; 255; CANR 91

Troyat, Henri 1911-2007 .... **CLC 23**
See also CA 45-48; 258; CANR 2, 33, 67, 117; GFL 1789 to the Present; MTCW 1

Trudeau, Garretson Beekman
See Trudeau, G.B.

Trudeau, Garry
See Trudeau, G.B.

Trudeau, Garry B.
See Trudeau, G.B.

Trudeau, G.B. 1948- .... **CLC 12**
See also AAYA 10, 60; AITN 2; CA 81-84; CANR 31; SATA 35, 168

Truffaut, Francois 1932-1984 ... **CLC 20, 101**
See also CA 81-84; 113; CANR 34

Trumbo, Dalton 1905-1976 .... **CLC 19**
See also CA 21-24R; 69-72; CANR 10; CN 1, 2; DLB 26; IDFW 3, 4; YAW

Trumbull, John 1750-1831 .... **NCLC 30**
See also DLB 31; RGAL 4

Trundlett, Helen B.
See Eliot, T(homas) S(tearns)

Truth, Sojourner 1797(?)-1883 ...... **NCLC 94**
See also DLB 239; FW; LAIT 2

Tryon, Thomas 1926-1991 .... **CLC 3, 11**
See also AITN 1; BPFB 3; CA 29-32R; 135; CANR 32, 77; CPW; DA3; DAM POP; HGG; MTCW 1

Tryon, Tom
See Tryon, Thomas

Ts'ao Hsueh-ch'in 1715(?)-1763 .... **LC 1**

Tsurayuki Ed. fl. 10th cent. - .... **PC 73**

Tsvetaeva (Efron), Marina (Ivanovna)
1892-1941 .... **PC 14; TCLC 7, 35**
See also CA 104; 128; CANR 73; DLB 295; EW 11; MTCW 1, 2; PFS 29; RGWL 2, 3

Tuck, Lily 1938- .... **CLC 70**
See also AAYA 74; CA 139; CANR 90, 192

Tuckerman, Frederick Goddard
1821-1873 .... **PC 85**
See also DLB 243; RGAL 4

Tu Fu 712-770 .... **PC 9**
See also DAM MULT; RGWL 2, 3; TWA; WP

Tulsidas, Gosvami 1532(?)-1623 .... **LC 158**
See also RGWL 2, 3

Tunis, John R(oberts) 1889-1975 ..... **CLC 12**
See also BYA 1; CA 61-64; CANR 62; DLB 22, 171; JRDA; MAICYA 1, 2; SATA 37; SATA-Brief 30; YAW

Tuohy, Frank
See Tuohy, John Francis

Tuohy, John Francis 1925- .... **CLC 37**
See also CA 5-8R; 178; CANR 3, 47; CN 1, 2, 3, 4, 5, 6, 7; DLB 14, 139

Turco, Lewis 1934- .... **CLC 11, 63**
See also CA 13-16R; CAAS 22; CANR 24, 51, 185; CP 1, 2, 3, 4, 5, 6, 7; DLBY 1984; TCLE 1:2

Turco, Lewis Putnam
See Turco, Lewis

Turgenev, Ivan (Sergeevich)
1818-1883 ..... **DC 7; NCLC 21, 37, 122; SSC 7, 57; WLC 6**
See also AAYA 58; DA; DAB; DAC; DAM MST, NOV; DFS 6; DLB 238, 284; EW 6; LATS 1:1; NFS 16; RGSF 2; RGWL 2, 3; TWA

Turgot, Anne-Robert-Jacques
1727-1781 .... **LC 26**
See also DLB 314

Turner, Frederick 1943- .... **CLC 48**
See also CA 73-76, 227; CAAE 227; CAAS 10; CANR 12, 30, 56; DLB 40, 282

Turton, James
See Crace, Jim

Tutu, Desmond M(pilo) 1931- .... **BLC 1:3; CLC 80**
See also BW 1, 3; CA 125; CANR 67, 81; DAM MULT

Tutuola, Amos 1920-1997 .... **BLC 1:3, 2:3; CLC 5, 14, 29; TCLC 188**
See also AAYA 76; AFW; BW 2, 3; CA 9-12R; 159; CANR 27, 66; CDWLB 3; CN 1, 2, 3, 4, 5, 6; DA3; DAM MULT; DLB 125; DNFS 2; EWL 3; MTCW 1, 2; MTFW 2005; RGEL 2; WLIT 2

Twain, Mark 1835-1910 ... **SSC 6, 26, 34, 87, 119; TCLC 6, 12, 19, 36, 48, 59, 161, 185; WLC 6**
See also AAYA 20; AMW; AMWC 1; BPFB 3; BYA 2, 3, 11, 14; CA 104; 135; CDALB 1865-1917; CLR 58, 60, 66; DA; DA3; DAB; DAC; DAM MST, NOV; DLB 12, 23, 64, 74, 186, 189, 11, 343; EXPN; EXPS; JRDA; LAIT 2; LMFS 1; MAICYA 1, 2; MAL 5; NCFS 4; NFS 1, 6;

RGAL 4; RGSF 2; SATA 100; SFW 4; SSFS 1, 7, 16, 21, 27; SUFW; TUS; WCH; WYA; YABC 2; YAW

Twohill, Maggie
See Angell, Judie

Tyler, Anne 1941- . **CLC 7, 11, 18, 28, 44, 59, 103, 205, 265**
See also AAYA 18, 60; AMWS 4; BEST 89:1; BPFB 3; BYA 12; CA 9-12R; CANR 11, 33, 53, 109, 132, 168; CDALBS; CN 1, 2, 3, 4, 5, 6, 7; CPW; CSW; DAM NOV, POP; DLB 6, 143; DLBY 1982; EWL 3; EXPN; LATS 1:2; MAL 5; MBL; MTCW 1, 2; MTFW 2005; NFS 2, 7, 10; RGAL 4; SATA 7, 90, 173; SSFS 17; TCLE 1:2; TUS; YAW

Tyler, Royall 1757-1826 .... **NCLC 3**
See also DLB 37; RGAL 4

Tynan, Katharine 1861-1931 ... **TCLC 3, 217**
See also CA 104; 167; DLB 153, 240; FW

Tyndale, William c. 1484-1536 .... **LC 103**
See also DLB 132

Tyutchev, Fyodor 1803-1873 .... **NCLC 34**

Tzara, Tristan 1896-1963 .... **CLC 47; PC 27; TCLC 168**
See also CA 153; 89-92; DAM POET; EWL 3; MTCW 2

Uc de Saint Circ c. 1190B.C.-13th cent.
B.C. .... **CMLC 102**

Uchida, Yoshiko 1921-1992 .... **AAL**
See also AAYA 16; BYA 2, 3; CA 13-16R; 139; CANR 6, 22, 47, 61; CDALBS; CLR 6, 56; CWRI 5; DLB 312; JRDA; MAICYA 1, 2; MTCW 1, 2; MTFW 2005; NFS 26; SAAS 1; SATA 1, 53; SATA-Obit 72

Udall, Nicholas 1504-1556 .... **LC 84**
See also DLB 62; RGEL 2

Ueda Akinari 1734-1809 .... **NCLC 131**

Uhry, Alfred 1936- .... **CLC 55; DC 28**
See also CA 127; 133; CAD; CANR 112; CD 5, 6; CSW; DA3; DAM DRAM, POP; DFS 11, 15; INT CA-133; MTFW 2005

Ulf, Haerved
See Strindberg, (Johan) August

Ulf, Harved
See Strindberg, (Johan) August

Ulibarri, Sabine R(eyes)
1919-2003 .... **CLC 83; HLCS 2**
See also CA 131; 214; CANR 81; DAM MULT; DLB 82; HW 1, 2; RGSF 2

Ulyanov, V. I.
See Lenin

Ulyanov, Vladimir Ilyich
See Lenin

Ulyanov-Lenin
See Lenin

Unamuno (y Jugo), Miguel de
1864-1936 .. **HLC 2; SSC 11, 69; TCLC 2, 9, 148**
See also CA 104; 131; CANR 81; DAM MULT, NOV; DLB 108, 322; EW 8; EWL 3; HW 1, 2; MTCW 1, 2; MTFW 2005; RGSF 2; RGWL 2, 3; SSFS 20; TWA

Uncle Shelby
See Silverstein, Shel

Undercliffe, Errol
See Campbell, Ramsey

Underwood, Miles
See Glassco, John

Undset, Sigrid 1882-1949 .... **TCLC 3, 197; WLC 6**
See also AAYA 77; CA 104; 129; DA; DA3; DAB; DAC; DAM MST, NOV; DLB 293, 332; EW 9; EWL 3; FW; MTCW 1, 2; MTFW 2005; RGWL 2, 3

Vassilikos, Vassilis 1933- .... **CLC 4, 8**
　　See also CA 81-84; CANR 75, 149; EWL 3
Vaughan, Henry 1621-1695 .... **LC 27; PC 81**
　　See also BRW 2; DLB 131; PAB; RGEL 2
Vaughn, Stephanie .... **CLC 62**
Vazov, Ivan (Minchov) 1850-1921 . **TCLC 25**
　　See also CA 121; 167; CDWLB 4; DLB
　　147
Veblen, Thorstein B(unde)
　　1857-1929 .... **TCLC 31**
　　See also AMWS 1; CA 115; 165; DLB 246;
　　MAL 5
Vega, Lope de 1562-1635 ... **HLCS 2; LC 23,
　　119**
　　See also EW 2; RGWL 2, 3
Veldeke, Heinrich von c. 1145-c.
　　1190 .... **CMLC 85**
Vendler, Helen 1933- .... **CLC 138**
　　See also CA 41-44R; CANR 25, 72, 136,
　　190; MTCW 1, 2; MTFW 2005
Vendler, Helen Hennessy
　　See Vendler, Helen
Venison, Alfred
　　See Pound, Ezra (Weston Loomis)
Ventsel, Elena Sergeevna
　　1907-2002 .... **CLC 59**
　　See also CA 154; CWW 2; DLB 302
Venttsel', Elena Sergeevna
　　See Ventsel, Elena Sergeevna
Verdi, Marie de
　　See Mencken, H. L.
Verdu, Matilde
　　See Cela, Camilo Jose
Verga, Giovanni (Carmelo)
　　1840-1922 .... **SSC 21, 87; TCLC 3**
　　See also CA 104; 123; CANR 101; EW 7;
　　EWL 3; RGSF 2; RGWL 2, 3; WLIT 7
Vergil 70B.C.-19B.C. .. **CMLC 9, 40, 101; PC
　　12; WLCS**
　　See also AW 2; CDWLB 1; DA; DA3;
　　DAB; DAC; DAM MST, POET; DLB
　　211; EFS 1; LAIT 1; LMFS 1; RGWL 2,
　　3; WLIT 8; WP
Vergil, Polydore c. 1470-1555 .... **LC 108**
　　See also DLB 132
Verhaeren, Emile (Adolphe Gustave)
　　1855-1916 .... **TCLC 12**
　　See also CA 109; EWL 3; GFL 1789 to the
　　Present
Verlaine, Paul (Marie) 1844-1896 .. **NCLC 2,
　　51; PC 2, 32**
　　See also DAM POET; DLB 217; EW 7;
　　GFL 1789 to the Present; LMFS 2; RGWL
　　2, 3; TWA
Verne, Jules (Gabriel) 1828-1905 ... **TCLC 6,
　　52**
　　See also AAYA 16; BYA 4; CA 110; 131;
　　CLR 88; DA3; DLB 123; GFL 1789 to
　　the Present; JRDA; LAIT 2; LMFS 2;
　　MAICYA 1, 2; MTFW 2005; NFS 30;
　　RGWL 2, 3; SATA 21; SCFW 1, 2; SFW
　　4; TWA; WCH
Verus, Marcus Annius
　　See Aurelius, Marcus
Very, Jones 1813-1880 .... **NCLC 9; PC 86**
　　See also DLB 1, 243; RGAL 4
Very, Rev. C.
　　See Crowley, Edward Alexander
Vesaas, Tarjei 1897-1970 .... **CLC 48**
　　See also CA 190; 29-32R; DLB 297; EW
　　11; EWL 3; RGWL 3
Vialis, Gaston
　　See Simenon, Georges (Jacques Christian)
Vian, Boris 1920-1959(?) .... **TCLC 9**
　　See also CA 106; 164; CANR 111; DLB
　　72, 321; EWL 3; GFL 1789 to the Present;
　　MTCW 2; RGWL 2, 3
Viator, Vacuus
　　See Hughes, Thomas

Viaud, Julien 1850-1923 .... **TCLC 11**
　　See also CA 107; DLB 123; GFL 1789 to
　　the Present
Viaud, Louis Marie Julien
　　See Viaud, Julien
Vicar, Henry
　　See Felsen, Henry Gregor
Vicente, Gil 1465-c. 1536 .... **LC 99**
　　See also DLB 318; IDTP; RGWL 2, 3
Vicker, Angus
　　See Felsen, Henry Gregor
Vico, Giambattista
　　See Vico, Giovanni Battista
Vico, Giovanni Battista 1668-1744 .... **LC 138**
　　See also EW 3; WLIT 7
Vidal, Eugene Luther Gore
　　See Vidal, Gore
Vidal, Gore 1925- ...... **CLC 2, 4, 6, 8, 10, 22,
　　33, 72, 142**
　　See also AAYA 64; AITN 1; AMWS 4;
　　BEST 90:2; BPFB 3; CA 5-8R; CAD;
　　CANR 13, 45, 65, 100, 132, 167; CD 5,
　　6; CDALBS; CN 1, 2, 3, 4, 5, 6, 7; CPW;
　　DA3; DAM NOV, POP; DFS 2; DLB 6,
　　152; EWL 3; GLL 1; INT CANR-13;
　　MAL 5; MTCW 1, 2; MTFW 2005;
　　RGAL 4; RHW; TUS
Viereck, Peter 1916-2006 .... **CLC 4; PC 27**
　　See also CA 1-4R; 250; CANR 1, 47; CP 1,
　　2, 3, 4, 5, 6, 7; DLB 5; MAL 5; PFS 9,
　　14
Viereck, Peter Robert Edwin
　　See Viereck, Peter
Vigny, Alfred (Victor) de
　　1797-1863 .... **NCLC 7, 102; PC 26**
　　See also DAM POET; DLB 119, 192, 217;
　　EW 5; GFL 1789 to the Present; RGWL
　　2, 3
Vilakazi, Benedict Wallet
　　1906-1947 .... **TCLC 37**
　　See also CA 168
Vile, Curt
　　See Moore, Alan
Villa, Jose Garcia 1914-1997 ... **AAL; PC 22;
　　TCLC 176**
　　See also CA 25-28R; CANR 12, 118; CP 1,
　　2, 3, 4; DLB 312; EWL 3; EXPP
Villard, Oswald Garrison
　　1872-1949 .... **TCLC 160**
　　See also CA 113; 162; DLB 25, 91
Villarreal, Jose Antonio 1924- .... **HLC 2**
　　See also CA 133; CANR 93; DAM MULT;
　　DLB 82; HW 1; LAIT 4; RGAL 4
Villaurrutia, Xavier 1903-1950 .... **TCLC 80**
　　See also CA 192; EWL 3; HW 1; LAW
Villaverde, Cirilo 1812-1894 .... **NCLC 121**
　　See also LAW
Villehardouin, Geoffroi de
　　1150(?)-1218(?) .... **CMLC 38**
Villiers, George 1628-1687 .... **LC 107**
　　See also DLB 80; RGEL 2
**Villiers de l'Isle Adam, Jean Marie Mathias
　　Philippe Auguste** 1838-1889 ... **NCLC 3;
　　SSC 14**
　　See also DLB 123, 192; GFL 1789 to the
　　Present; RGSF 2
Villon, Francois 1431-1463(?) .... **LC 62, 166;
　　PC 13**
　　See also DLB 208; EW 2; RGWL 2, 3;
　　TWA
Vine, Barbara
　　See Rendell, Ruth
Vinge, Joan (Carol) D(ennison)
　　1948- .... **CLC 30; SSC 24**
　　See also AAYA 32; BPFB 3; CA 93-96;
　　CANR 72; SATA 36, 113; SFW 4; YAW
Viola, Herman J(oseph) 1938- .... **CLC 70**
　　See also CA 61-64; CANR 8, 23, 48, 91;
　　SATA 126

Violis, G.
　　See Simenon, Georges (Jacques Christian)
Viramontes, Helena Maria 1954- .... **HLCS 2**
　　See also CA 159; CANR 182; DLB 122,
　　350; HW 2; LLW
Virgil
　　See Vergil
Visconti, Luchino 1906-1976 .... **CLC 16**
　　See also CA 81-84; 65-68; CANR 39
Vitry, Jacques de
　　See Jacques de Vitry
Vittorini, Elio 1908-1966 .... **CLC 6, 9, 14**
　　See also CA 133; 25-28R; DLB 264; EW
　　12; EWL 3; RGWL 2, 3
Vivekananda, Swami 1863-1902 .... **TCLC 88**
Vives, Juan Luis 1493-1540 .... **LC 170**
　　See also DLB 318
Vizenor, Gerald Robert 1934- .... **CLC 103,
　　263; NNAL**
　　See also CA 13-16R, 205; CAAE 205;
　　CAAS 22; CANR 5, 21, 44, 67; DAM
　　MULT; DLB 175, 227; MTCW 2; MTFW
　　2005; TCWW 2
Vizinczey, Stephen 1933- .... **CLC 40**
　　See also CA 128; CCA 1; INT CA-128
Vliet, R(ussell) G(ordon)
　　1929-1984 .... **CLC 22**
　　See also CA 37-40R; 112; CANR 18; CP 2,
　　3
Vogau, Boris Andreevich
　　See Vogau, Boris Andreyevich
Vogau, Boris Andreyevich
　　1894-1938 .... **SSC 48; TCLC 23**
　　See also CA 123; 218; DLB 272; EWL 3;
　　RGSF 2; RGWL 2, 3
Vogel, Paula A. 1951- .... **CLC 76; DC 19**
　　See also CA 108; CAD; CANR 119, 140;
　　CD 5, 6; CWD; DFS 14; DLB 341;
　　MTFW 2005; RGAL 4
Voigt, Cynthia 1942- .... **CLC 30**
　　See also AAYA 3, 30; BYA 1, 3, 6, 7, 8;
　　CA 106; CANR 18, 37, 40, 94, 145; CLR
　　13, 48, 141; INT CANR-18; JRDA; LAIT
　　5; MAICYA 1, 2; MAICYAS 1; MTFW
　　2005; SATA 48, 79, 116, 160; SATA-Brief
　　33; WYA; YAW
Voigt, Ellen Bryant 1943- .... **CLC 54**
　　See also CA 69-72; CANR 11, 29, 55, 115,
　　171; CP 5, 6, 7; CSW; CWP; DLB 120;
　　PFS 23
Voinovich, Vladimir 1932- .. **CLC 10, 49, 147**
　　See also CA 81-84; CAAS 12; CANR 33,
　　67, 150; CWW 2; DLB 302; MTCW 1
Voinovich, Vladimir Nikolaevich
　　See Voinovich, Vladimir
Vollmann, William T. 1959- ...... **CLC 89, 227**
　　See also AMWS 17; CA 134; CANR 67,
　　116, 185; CN 7; CPW; DA3; DAM NOV,
　　POP; DLB 350; MTCW 2; MTFW 2005
Voloshinov, V. N.
　　See Bakhtin, Mikhail Mikhailovich
Voltaire 1694-1778 .. **LC 14, 79, 110; SSC 12,
　　112; WLC 6**
　　See also BYA 13; DA; DA3; DAB; DAC;
　　DAM DRAM, MST; DLB 314; EW 4;
　　GFL Beginnings to 1789; LATS 1:1;
　　LMFS 1; NFS 7; RGWL 2, 3; TWA
von Aschendrof, Baron Ignatz
　　See Ford, Ford Madox
von Chamisso, Adelbert
　　See Chamisso, Adelbert von
von Daeniken, Erich 1935- .... **CLC 30**
　　See also AITN 1; CA 37-40R; CANR 17,
　　44
von Daniken, Erich
　　See von Daeniken, Erich

Whitaker, Rodney William
 See Whitaker, Rod
White, Babington
 See Braddon, Mary Elizabeth
White, E. B. 1899-1985 .... **CLC 10, 34, 39**
 See also AAYA 62; AITN 2; AMWS 1; CA
 13-16R; 116; CANR 16, 37; CDALBS;
 CLR 1, 21, 107; CPW; DA3; DAM POP;
 DLB 11, 22; EWL 3; FANT; MAICYA 1,
 2; MAL 5; MTCW 1, 2; MTFW 2005;
 NCFS 5; RGAL 4; SATA 2, 29, 100;
 SATA-Obit 44; TUS
White, Edmund 1940- .... **CLC 27, 110**
 See also AAYA 7; CA 45-48; CANR 3, 19,
 36, 62, 107, 133, 172; CN 5, 6, 7; DA3;
 DAM POP; DLB 227; MTCW 1, 2;
 MTFW 2005
White, Edmund Valentine III
 See White, Edmund
White, Elwyn Brooks
 See White, E. B.
White, Hayden V. 1928- .... **CLC 148**
 See also CA 128; CANR 135; DLB 246
White, Patrick (Victor Martindale)
 1912-1990 ...... **CLC 3, 4, 5, 7, 9, 18, 65,**
 69; SSC 39; TCLC 176
 See also BRWS 1; CA 81-84; 132; CANR
 43; CN 1, 2, 3, 4; DLB 260, 332; EWL 3;
 MTCW 1; RGEL 2; RGSF 2; RHW;
 TWA; WWE 1
White, Phyllis Dorothy James
 1920- .... **CLC 18, 46, 122, 226**
 See also BEST 90:2; BPFB 2; BRWS 4;
 CA 21-24R; CANR 17, 43, 65, 112; CD-
 BLB 1960 to Present; CMW 4; CN 4, 5,
 6; CPW; DA3; DAM POP; DLB 87, 276;
 DLBD 17; MSW; MTCW 1, 2; MTFW
 2005; TEA
White, T(erence) H(anbury)
 1906-1964 .... **CLC 30**
 See also AAYA 22; BPFB 3; BYA 4, 5; CA
 73-76; CANR 37; CLR 139; DLB 160;
 FANT; JRDA; LAIT 1; MAICYA 1, 2;
 NFS 30; RGEL 2; SATA 12; SUFW 1;
 YAW
White, Terence de Vere 1912-1994 ... **CLC 49**
 See also CA 49-52; 145; CANR 3
White, Walter
 See White, Walter F(rancis)
White, Walter F(rancis)
 1893-1955 ..... **BLC 1:3; HR 1:3; TCLC**
 15
 See also BW 1; CA 115; 124; DAM MULT;
 DLB 51
White, William Hale 1831-1913 ..... **TCLC 25**
 See also CA 121; 189; DLB 18; RGEL 2
Whitehead, Alfred North
 1861-1947 .... **TCLC 97**
 See also CA 117; 165; DLB 100, 262
Whitehead, Colson 1969- ...... **BLC 2:3; CLC**
 232
 See also CA 202; CANR 162
Whitehead, E(dward) A(nthony)
 1933- .... **CLC 5**
 See also CA 65-68; CANR 58, 118; CBD;
 CD 5, 6; DLB 310
Whitehead, Ted
 See Whitehead, E(dward) A(nthony)
Whiteman, Roberta J. Hill 1947- ...... **NNAL**
 See also CA 146
Whitemore, Hugh (John) 1936- .... **CLC 37**
 See also CA 132; CANR 77; CBD; CD 5,
 6; INT CA-132
Whitman, Sarah Helen (Power)
 1803-1878 .... **NCLC 19**
 See also DLB 1, 243

Whitman, Walt(er) 1819-1892 .. **NCLC 4, 31,**
 81, 205; PC 3, 91; WLC 6
 See also AAYA 42; AMW; AMWR 1;
 CDALB 1640-1865; DA; DA3; DAB;
 DAC; DAM MST, POET; DLB 3, 64,
 224, 250; EXPP; LAIT 2; LMFS 1; PAB;
 PFS 2, 3, 13, 22, 31; RGAL 4; SATA 20;
 TUS; WP; WYAS 1
Whitney, Isabella fl. 1565-fl. 1575 ..... **LC 130**
 See also DLB 136
Whitney, Phyllis A. 1903-2008 .... **CLC 42**
 See also AAYA 36; AITN 2; BEST 90:3;
 CA 1-4R; 269; CANR 3, 25, 38, 60; CLR
 59; CMW 4; CPW; DA3; DAM POP;
 JRDA; MAICYA 1, 2; MTCW 2; RHW;
 SATA 1, 30; SATA-Obit 189; YAW
Whitney, Phyllis Ayame
 See Whitney, Phyllis A.
Whitney, Phyllis Ayame
 See Whitney, Phyllis A.
Whittemore, (Edward) Reed, Jr.
 1919- .... **CLC 4**
 See also CA 9-12R, 219; CAAE 219; CAAS
 8; CANR 4, 119; CP 1, 2, 3, 4, 5, 6, 7;
 DLB 5; MAL 5
Whittier, John Greenleaf
 1807-1892 .... **NCLC 8, 59; PC 93**
 See also AMWS 1; DLB 1, 243; RGAL 4
Whittlebot, Hernia
 See Coward, Noel
Wicker, Thomas Grey
 See Wicker, Tom
Wicker, Tom 1926- .... **CLC 7**
 See also CA 65-68; CANR 21, 46, 141, 179
Wicomb, Zoe 1948- .... **BLC 2:3**
 See also CA 127; CANR 106, 167; DLB
 225
Wideman, John Edgar 1941- .. **BLC 1:3, 2:3;**
 CLC 5, 34, 36, 67, 122; SSC 62
 See also AFAW 1, 2; AMWS 10; BPFB 4;
 BW 2, 3; CA 85-88; CANR 14, 42, 67,
 109, 140, 187; CN 4, 5, 6, 7; DAM
 MULT; DLB 33, 143; MAL 5; MTCW 2;
 MTFW 2005; RGAL 4; RGSF 2; SSFS 6,
 12, 24; TCLE 1:2
Wiebe, Rudy 1934- . **CLC 6, 11, 14, 138, 263**
 See also CA 37-40R; CANR 42, 67, 123;
 CN 1, 2, 3, 4, 5, 6, 7; DAC; DAM MST;
 DLB 60; RHW; SATA 156
Wiebe, Rudy Henry
 See Wiebe, Rudy
Wieland, Christoph Martin
 1733-1813 .... **NCLC 17, 177**
 See also DLB 97; EW 4; LMFS 1; RGWL
 2, 3
Wiene, Robert 1881-1938 .... **TCLC 56**
Wieners, John 1934- .... **CLC 7**
 See also BG 1:3; CA 13-16R; CP 1, 2, 3, 4,
 5, 6, 7; DLB 16; WP
Wiesel, Elie 1928- ...... **CLC 3, 5, 11, 37, 165;**
 WLCS
 See also AAYA 7, 54; AITN 1; CA 5-8R;
 CAAS 4; CANR 8, 40, 65, 125; CDALBS;
 CWW 2; DA; DA3; DAB; DAC; DAM
 MST, NOV; DLB 83, 299; DLBY 1987;
 EWL 3; INT CANR-8; LAIT 4; MTCW
 1, 2; MTFW 2005; NCFS 4; NFS 4;
 RGHL; RGWL 3; SATA 56; YAW
Wiesel, Eliezer
 See Wiesel, Elie
Wiggins, Marianne 1947- .... **CLC 57**
 See also AAYA 70; BEST 89:3; CA 130;
 CANR 60, 139, 180; CN 7; DLB 335
Wigglesworth, Michael 1631-1705 .... **LC 106**
 See also DLB 24; RGAL 4
Wiggs, Susan .... **CLC 70**
 See also CA 201; CANR 173

Wight, James Alfred 1916-1995 .... **CLC 12**
 See also AAYA 1, 54; BPFB 2; CA 77-80;
 148; CANR 40; CLR 80; CPW; DAM
 POP; LAIT 3; MAICYA 2; MAICYAS 1;
 MTCW 2; SATA 86, 135; SATA-Brief 44;
 TEA; YAW
Wilbur, Richard 1921- .. **CLC 3, 6, 9, 14, 53,**
 110; PC 51
 See also AAYA 72; AMWS 3; CA 1-4R;
 CABS 2; CANR 2, 29, 76, 93, 139;
 CDALBS; CP 1, 2, 3, 4, 5, 6, 7; DA;
 DAB; DAC; DAM MST, POET; DLB 5,
 169; EWL 3; EXPP; INT CANR-29;
 MAL 5; MTCW 1, 2; MTFW 2005; PAB;
 PFS 11, 12, 16, 29; RGAL 4; SATA 9,
 108; WP
Wilbur, Richard Purdy
 See Wilbur, Richard
Wild, Peter 1940- .... **CLC 14**
 See also CA 37-40R; CP 1, 2, 3, 4, 5, 6, 7;
 DLB 5
Wilde, Oscar 1854(?)-1900 ... **DC 17; SSC 11,**
 77; TCLC 1, 8, 23, 41, 175; WLC 6
 See also AAYA 49; BRW 5; BRWC 1, 2;
 BRWR 2; BYA 15; CA 104; 119; CANR
 112; CDBLB 1890-1914; CLR 114; DA;
 DA3; DAB; DAC; DAM DRAM, MST,
 NOV; DFS 4, 8, 9, 21; DLB 10, 19, 34,
 57, 141, 156, 190, 344; EXPS; FANT; GL
 3; LATS 1:1; NFS 20; RGEL 2; RGSF 2;
 SATA 24; SSFS 7; SUFW; TEA; WCH;
 WLIT 4
Wilde, Oscar Fingal O'Flahertie Willis
 See Wilde, Oscar
Wilder, Billy
 See Wilder, Samuel
Wilder, Samuel 1906-2002 .... **CLC 20**
 See also AAYA 66; CA 89-92; 205; DLB
 26
Wilder, Stephen
 See Marlowe, Stephen
Wilder, Thornton (Niven)
 1897-1975 .. **CLC 1, 5, 6, 10, 15, 35, 82;**
 DC 1, 24; WLC 6
 See also AAYA 29; AITN 2; AMW; CA 13-
 16R; 61-64; CAD; CANR 40, 132;
 CDALBS; CN 1, 2; DA; DA3; DAB;
 DAC; DAM DRAM, MST, NOV; DFS 1,
 4, 16; DLB 4, 7, 9, 228; DLBY 1997;
 EWL 3; LAIT 3; MAL 5; MTCW 1, 2;
 MTFW 2005; NFS 24; RGAL 4; RHW;
 WYAS 1
Wilding, Michael 1942- ...... **CLC 73; SSC 50**
 See also CA 104; CANR 24, 49, 106; CN
 4, 5, 6, 7; DLB 325; RGSF 2
Wiley, Richard 1944- .... **CLC 44**
 See also CA 121; 129; CANR 71
Wilhelm, Kate
 See Wilhelm, Katie
Wilhelm, Katie 1928- .... **CLC 7**
 See also AAYA 20; BYA 16; CA 37-40R;
 CAAS 5; CANR 17, 36, 60, 94; DLB 8;
 INT CANR-17; MTCW 1; SCFW 2; SFW
 4
Wilhelm, Katie Gertrude
 See Wilhelm, Katie
Wilkins, Mary
 See Freeman, Mary E(leanor) Wilkins
Willard, Nancy 1936- .... **CLC 7, 37**
 See also BYA 5; CA 89-92; CANR 10, 39,
 68, 107, 152, 186; CLR 5; CP 2, 3, 4, 5;
 CWP; CWRI 5; DLB 5, 52; FANT; MAI-
 CYA 1, 2; MTCW 1; SATA 37, 71, 127,
 191; SATA-Brief 30; SUFW 2; TCLE 1:2
William of Malmesbury c. 1090B.C.-c.
 1140B.C. .... **CMLC 57**
William of Moerbeke c. 1215-c.
 1286 .... **CMLC 91**
William of Ockham 1290-1349 ..... **CMLC 32**

Williams, Ben Ames 1889-1953 ..... **TCLC 89**
See also CA 183; DLB 102

Williams, Charles
See Collier, James Lincoln

Williams, Charles (Walter Stansby)
1886-1945 .... **TCLC 1, 11**
See also BRWS 9; CA 104; 163; DLB 100,
153, 255; FANT; RGEL 2; SUFW 1

Williams, C.K. 1936- .... **CLC 33, 56, 148**
See also CA 37-40R; CAAS 26; CANR 57,
106; CP 1, 2, 3, 4, 5, 6, 7; DAM POET;
DLB 5; MAL 5

Williams, Ella Gwendolen Rees
See Rhys, Jean

Williams, (George) Emlyn
1905-1987 .... **CLC 15**
See also CA 104; 123; CANR 36; DAM
DRAM; DLB 10, 77; IDTP; MTCW 1

Williams, Hank 1923-1953 .... **TCLC 81**
See Williams, Hiram King
See also CA 188

Williams, Helen Maria
1761-1827 .... **NCLC 135**
See also DLB 158

Williams, Hiram King 1923-1953
See Williams, Hank

Williams, Hugo (Mordaunt) 1942- ... **CLC 42**
See also CA 17-20R; CANR 45, 119; CP 1,
2, 3, 4, 5, 6, 7; DLB 40

Williams, J. Walker
See Wodehouse, P(elham) G(renville)

Williams, John A(lfred) 1925- .... **BLC 1:3;**
CLC 5, 13
See also AFAW 2; BW 2, 3; CA 53-56, 195;
CAAE 195; CAAS 3; CANR 6, 26, 51,
118; CN 1, 2, 3, 4, 5, 6, 7; CSW; DAM
MULT; DLB 2, 33; EWL 3; INT CANR-6;
MAL 5; RGAL 4; SFW 4

Williams, Jonathan 1929-2008 .... **CLC 13**
See also CA 9-12R; 270; CAAS 12; CANR
8, 108; CP 1, 2, 3, 4, 5, 6; DLB 5

Williams, Jonathan Chamberlain
See Williams, Jonathan

Williams, Joy 1944- .... **CLC 31**
See also CA 41-44R; CANR 22, 48, 97,
168; DLB 335; SSFS 25

Williams, Norman 1952- .... **CLC 39**
See also CA 118

Williams, Roger 1603(?)-1683 .... **LC 129**
See also DLB 24

Williams, Sherley Anne
1944-1999 .... **BLC 1:3; CLC 89**
See also AFAW 2; BW 2, 3; CA 73-76; 185;
CANR 25, 82; DAM MULT, POET; DLB
41; INT CANR-25; SATA 78; SATA-Obit
116

Williams, Shirley
See Williams, Sherley Anne

Williams, Tennessee 1911-1983 . **CLC 1, 2, 5,**
7, 8, 11, 15, 19, 30, 39, 45, 71, 111; DC
4; SSC 81; WLC 6
See also AAYA 31; AITN 1, 2; AMW;
AMWC 1; CA 5-8R; 108; CABS 3; CAD;
CANR 31, 132, 174; CDALB 1941-1968;
CN 1, 2, 3; DA; DA3; DAB; DAC; DAM
DRAM, MST; DFS 17; DLB 7, 341;
DLBD 4; DLBY 1983; EWL 3; GLL 1;
LAIT 4; LATS 1:2; MAL 5; MTCW 1, 2;
MTFW 2005; RGAL 4; TUS

Williams, Thomas (Alonzo)
1926-1990 .... **CLC 14**
See also CA 1-4R; 132; CANR 2

Williams, Thomas Lanier
See Williams, Tennessee

Williams, William C.
See Williams, William Carlos

Williams, William Carlos
1883-1963 .... **CLC 1, 2, 5, 9, 13, 22, 42,**
67; PC 7; SSC 31; WLC 6
See also AAYA 46; AMW; AMWR 1; CA
89-92; CANR 34; CDALB 1917-1929;
DA; DA3; DAB; DAC; DAM MST,
POET; DLB 4, 16, 54, 86; EWL 3; EXPP;
MAL 5; MTCW 1, 2; MTFW 2005; NCFS
4; PAB; PFS 1, 6, 11; RGAL 4; RGSF 2;
SSFS 27; TUS; WP

Williamson, David (Keith) 1942- ..... **CLC 56**
See also CA 103; CANR 41; CD 5, 6; DLB
289

Williamson, Jack
See Williamson, John Stewart

Williamson, John Stewart
1908-2006 .... **CLC 29**
See also AAYA 76; CA 17-20R; 255; CAAS
8; CANR 23, 70, 153; DLB 8; SCFW 1,
2; SFW 4

Willie, Frederick
See Lovecraft, H. P.

Willingham, Calder (Baynard, Jr.)
1922-1995 .... **CLC 5, 51**
See also CA 5-8R; 147; CANR 3; CN 1, 2,
3, 4, 5; CSW; DLB 2, 44; IDFW 3, 4;
MTCW 1

Willis, Charles
See Clarke, Arthur C.

Willis, Nathaniel Parker
1806-1867 .... **NCLC 194**
See also DLB 3, 59, 73, 74, 183, 250;
DLBD 13; RGAL 4

Willy
See Colette, (Sidonie-Gabrielle)

Willy, Colette
See Colette, (Sidonie-Gabrielle)

Wilmot, John 1647-1680 .... **LC 75; PC 66**
See also BRW 2; DLB 131; PAB; RGEL 2

Wilson, A.N. 1950- .... **CLC 33**
See also BRWS 6; CA 112; 122; CANR
156; CN 4, 5, 6, 7; DLB 14, 155, 194;
MTCW 2

Wilson, Andrew Norman
See Wilson, A.N.

Wilson, Angus (Frank Johnstone)
1913-1991 . **CLC 2, 3, 5, 25, 34; SSC 21**
See also BRWS 1; CA 5-8R; 134; CANR
21; CN 1, 2, 3, 4; DLB 15, 139, 155;
EWL 3; MTCW 1, 2; MTFW 2005; RGEL
2; RGSF 2

Wilson, August 1945-2005 .... **BLC 1:3, 2:3;**
CLC 39, 50, 63, 118, 222; DC 2, 31;
WLCS
See also AAYA 16; AFAW 2; AMWS 8; BW
2, 3; CA 115; 122; 244; CAD; CANR 42,
54, 76, 128; CD 5, 6; DA; DA3; DAB;
DAC; DAM DRAM, MST, MULT; DFS
3, 7, 15, 17, 24; DLB 228; EWL 3; LAIT
4; LATS 1:2; MAL 5; MTCW 1, 2;
MTFW 2005; RGAL 4

Wilson, Brian 1942- .... **CLC 12**

Wilson, Colin (Henry) 1931- .... **CLC 3, 14**
See also CA 1-4R; CAAS 5; CANR 1, 22,
33, 77; CMW 4; CN 1, 2, 3, 4, 5, 6; DLB
14, 194; HGG; MTCW 1; SFW 4

Wilson, Dirk
See Pohl, Frederik

Wilson, Edmund 1895-1972 .. **CLC 1, 2, 3, 8,**
24
See also AMW; CA 1-4R; 37-40R; CANR
1, 46, 110; CN 1; DLB 63; EWL 3; MAL
5; MTCW 1, 2; MTFW 2005; RGAL 4;
TUS

Wilson, Ethel Davis (Bryant)
1888(?)-1980 .... **CLC 13**
See also CA 102; CN 1, 2; DAC; DAM
POET; DLB 68; MTCW 1; RGEL 2

Wilson, Harriet
See Wilson, Harriet E. Adams

Wilson, Harriet E.
See Wilson, Harriet E. Adams

Wilson, Harriet E. Adams
1827(?)-1863(?) ..... **BLC 1:3; NCLC 78,**
219
See also DAM MULT; DLB 50, 239, 243

Wilson, John 1785-1854 .... **NCLC 5**
See also DLB 110

Wilson, John (Anthony) Burgess
See Burgess, Anthony

Wilson, Katharina .... **CLC 65**

Wilson, Lanford 1937- .. **CLC 7, 14, 36, 197;**
DC 19
See also CA 17-20R; CABS 3; CAD; CANR
45, 96; CD 5, 6; DAM DRAM; DFS 4, 9,
12, 16, 20; DLB 7, 341; EWL 3; MAL 5;
TUS

Wilson, Robert M. 1941- .... **CLC 7, 9**
See also CA 49-52; CAD; CANR 2, 41; CD
5, 6; MTCW 1

Wilson, Robert McLiam 1964- .... **CLC 59**
See also CA 132; DLB 267

Wilson, Sloan 1920-2003 .... **CLC 32**
See also CA 1-4R; 216; CANR 1, 44; CN
1, 2, 3, 4, 5, 6

Wilson, Snoo 1948- .... **CLC 33**
See also CA 69-72; CBD; CD 5, 6

Wilson, William S(mith) 1932- .... **CLC 49**
See also CA 81-84

Wilson, (Thomas) Woodrow
1856-1924 .... **TCLC 79**
See also CA 166; DLB 47

Winchester, Simon 1944- .... **CLC 257**
See also AAYA 66; CA 107; CANR 90, 130,
194

Winchilsea, Anne (Kingsmill) Finch
1661-1720
See Finch, Anne
See also RGEL 2

Winckelmann, Johann Joachim
1717-1768 .... **LC 129**
See also DLB 97

Windham, Basil
See Wodehouse, P(elham) G(renville)

Wingrove, David 1954- .... **CLC 68**
See also CA 133; SFW 4

Winnemucca, Sarah 1844-1891 .... **NCLC 79;**
NNAL
See also DAM MULT; DLB 175; RGAL 4

Winstanley, Gerrard 1609-1676 .... **LC 52**

Wintergreen, Jane
See Duncan, Sara Jeannette

Winters, Arthur Yvor
See Winters, Yvor

Winters, Janet Lewis
See Lewis, Janet

Winters, Yvor 1900-1968 .. **CLC 4, 8, 32; PC**
82
See also AMWS 2; CA 11-12; 25-28R; CAP
1; DLB 48; EWL 3; MAL 5; MTCW 1;
RGAL 4

Winterson, Jeanette 1959- .... **CLC 64, 158**
See also BRWS 4; CA 136; CANR 58, 116,
181; CN 5, 6, 7; CPW; DA3; DAM POP;
DLB 207, 261; FANT; FW; GLL 1;
MTCW 2; MTFW 2005; RHW; SATA 190

Winthrop, John 1588-1649 .... **LC 31, 107**
See also DLB 24, 30

Winthrop, Theodore 1828-1861 ... **NCLC 210**
See also DLB 202

Winton, Tim 1960- .... **CLC 251; SSC 119**
See also AAYA 34; CA 152; CANR 118,
194; CN 6, 7; DLB 325; SATA 98

Wirth, Louis 1897-1952 .... **TCLC 92**
See also CA 210

Wiseman, Frederick 1930- .... **CLC 20**
See also CA 159**

Literary Criticism Series
Cumulative Topic Index

This index lists all topic entries in Gale's *Children's Literature Review* (CLR), *Classical and Medieval Literature Criticism* (CMLC), *Contemporary Literary Criticism* (CLC), *Drama Criticism* (DC), *Literature Criticism from 1400 to 1800* (LC), *Nineteenth-Century Literature Criticism* (NCLC), *Short Story Criticism* (SSC), and *Twentieth-Century Literary Criticism* (TCLC). The index also lists topic entries in the Gale Critical Companion Collection, which includes the following publications: *The Beat Generation* (BG), *Feminism in Literature* (FL), *Gothic Literature* (GL), and *Harlem Renaissance* (HR).

Topic Index

NCLC Cumulative Nationality Index

Nationality Index

463

ISBN-13: 978-1-4144-3854-2
ISBN-10: 1-4144-3854-0

90000

9 781414 438542